2002 UPDATE

INTERNATIONAL MARKETING

**Harcourt
College Publishers**

Where Learning Comes to Life

TECHNOLOGY

Technology is changing the learning experience, by increasing the power of your textbook and other learning materials; by allowing you to access more information, more quickly; and by bringing a wider array of choices in your course and content information sources.

Harcourt College Publishers has developed the most comprehensive Web sites, e-books, and electronic learning materials on the market to help you use technology to achieve your goals.

PARTNERS IN LEARNING

Harcourt partners with other companies to make technology work for you and to supply the learning resources you want and need. More importantly, Harcourt and its partners provide avenues to help you reduce your research time of numerous information sources.

Harcourt College Publishers and its partners offer increased opportunities to enhance your learning resources and address your learning style. With quick access to chapter-specific Web sites and e-books . . . from interactive study materials to quizzing, testing, and career advice . . . Harcourt and its partners bring learning to life.

Harcourt's partnership with Digital:Convergence™ brings :CRQ™ technology and the :CueCat™ reader to you and allows Harcourt to provide you with a complete and dynamic list of resources designed to help you achieve your learning goals. You can download the free :CRQ software from www.crq.com. Visit any of the 7,100 RadioShack stores nationwide to obtain a free :CueCat reader. Just swipe the cue with the :CueCat reader to view a list of Harcourt's partners and Harcourt's print and electronic learning solutions.

http://www.harcourtcollege.com/partners

2002 UPDATE

INTERNATIONAL MARKETING

MICHAEL R. CZINKOTA

Georgetown University

ILKKA A. RONKAINEN

Georgetown University

Harcourt College Publishers

Fort Worth   Philadelphia   San Diego   New York   Orlando   Austin   San Antonio
Toronto   Montreal   London   Sydney   Tokyo

Publisher	Michael P. Roche
Acquisitions Editor	Mark Orr
Market Strategist	Beverly Dunn
Developmental Editor	Kerri Jones
Project Manager	Andrea Archer

ISBN: 0-03-033096-3
Library of Congress Catalog Card Number: 2001091148

Address for Domestic Orders
Harcourt College Publishers, 6277 Sea Harbor Drive, Orlando, Florida 32887-6777
800-782-4479

Address for International Orders
International Customer Service
Harcourt College Publishers, 6277 Sea Harbor Drive, Orlando, Florida 32887-6777
407-345-3800
(fax) 407-345-4060
(e-mail) hbintl@harcourt.com

Address for Editorial Correspondence
Harcourt College Publishers, 301 Commerce Street, Suite 3700, Fort Worth, TX 76102

Web Site Address
http://www.harcourtcollege.com

Harcourt College Publishers will provide complimentary supplements or supplement packages to those adopters qualified under our adoption policy. Please contact your sales representative to learn how you qualify. If as an adopter or potential user you receive supplements you do not need, please return to your sales representative or send them to:
Attn: Returns Department, Troy Warehouse, 465 South Lincoln Drive, Troy, MO 63379.

Printed in the United States of America

1 2 3 4 5 6 7 8 9 0 048 9 8 7 6 5 4 3 2 1

Harcourt College Publishers

The Harcourt Series in Marketing

Assael
Marketing

Bateson and Hoffman
Managing Services Marketing: Text and Readings
Fourth Edition

Blackwell, Blackwell, and Talarzyk
Contemporary Cases in Consumer Behavior
Fourth Edition

Blackwell, Miniard, and Engel
Consumer Behavior
Ninth Edition

Boone and Kurtz
Contemporary Marketing
Tenth Edition

Boone and Kurtz
Contemporary Marketing
2002 Update

Churchill
Basic Marketing Research
Fourth Edition

Churchill
Marketing Research: Methodological Foundations
Eighth Edition

Clark and Allen
Marketing: Hits on the Web

Czinkota and Ronkainen
International Marketing
Sixth Edition

Czinkota and Ronkainen
International Marketing
2002 Update

Czinkota and Ronkainen
International Marketing Strategy: Environmental Assessment and Entry Strategies

Dickson
Marketing Management
Second Edition

Dunne and Lusch
Retailing
Fourth Edition

Ferrell, Hartline, Lucas, and Luck
Marketing Strategy
Second Edition

Futrell
Sales Management: Teamwork, Leadership, and Technology
Sixth Edition

Hoffman
Marketing: Best Practices

Hoffman and Bateson
Essentials of Services Marketing
Second Edition

Hutt and Speh
Business Marketing Management: A Strategic View of Industrial and Organizational Markets
Seventh Edition

Ingram, LaForge, Avila, Schwepker, and Williams
Professional Selling: A Trust-Based Approach

Ingram, LaForge, Avila, Schwepker, and Williams
Sales Management: Analysis and Decision Making
Fourth Edition

Ingram, LaForge, Avila, Schwepker, and Williams
Selling

Lindgren and Shimp
Marketing: An Interactive Learning System
Second Edition

Parente
Advertising Campaign Strategy: A Guide to Marketing Communication Plans
Second Edition

Reedy
Electronic Marketing

Rosenbloom
Marketing Channels: A Management View
Sixth Edition

Sandburg
Discovering Your Marketing Career
CD-ROM

Schaffer
The Marketing Game

Schnaars
MICROSIM

Sheth, Mittal, and Newman
Customer Behavior: Consumer Behavior and Beyond
Second Edition

Shimp
Advertising, Promotions, and Supplemental Aspects of Integrated Marketing Communications
Fifth Edition

Stauble
Marketing Strategy: A Global Perspective

Terpstra and Sarathy
International Marketing
Eighth Edition

Watson
Electronic Commerce

Weitz and Wensley
Readings in Strategic Marketing Analysis, Planning, and Implementation
Second Edition

Zikmund
Exploring Marketing Research
Seventh Edition

Zikmund
Essentials of Marketing Research

Harcourt Brace College Outline Series

Peterson
Principles of Marketing

Preface

PRACTICING INTERNATIONAL MARKETING and writing a text on the subject have some things in common: It is a lot of work, the competition is tough, and it's fun to succeed. It is therefore with great pleasure that we present the 2002 edition of *International Marketing* to you. In order to bring you the most current information, we have made significant revisions in this edition. Maps have been updated with current data, and boxes and vignettes have been revised. :Cues have been added that will directly link students to additional information on the Internet. Our goal continues to be excellence and relevance in content, combined with user-friendliness for both the student and the professor.

Here are the key reasons that make this book special:

- The text reflects both the theory and the application of international marketing. It offers research insights from around the globe and shows how corporate practices are adjusting to the marketplace realities of today.
- This text covers the full spectrum of international marketing, from start-up operations to the formation of virtual alliances. It offers a thorough discussion of the operations of multinational corporations, but also presents a specific focus on the activities of small- and medium-sized forms, which are increasingly major players in the international market and are to many students their employers.
- We examine international marketing from a truly global perspective rather than just from the U.S. point of view. By addressing, confronting, and analyzing the existence of different environments, expectations, and market conditions, we highlight the need for awareness, sensitivity, and adaptation.
- This text also addresses the growing interaction between government and business. It emphasizes how businesses work with governments and what role governmental considerations can play for the international marketer. This policy orientation greatly contributes to the managerial orientation of the book.
- This text fully integrates e-commerce and the technology and information revolution, and their impact on the international marketer. Going beyond mere insight, it also offers information access to the user by providing detailed listings of websites and other data sources.
- This textbook also fully incorporates the important societal dimensions of diversity, environmental concern, ethics, and economic transformation.
- The 2002 edition includes a dynamic new feature that directly links the user to additional relevant information on the Internet. Strategically placed :Cues enable students to instantly access complementary web pages that amplify and further illustrate the principles and concepts described in the text. How does it work? Just download the free :CRQ software for Windows or Macintosh from www.crq.com, plug in a :CueCat reader, and start swiping the :Cues. No more laborious typing of lengthy URLs! No more endless clicking to find nested information!

Organization

The text is designed primarily for the advanced undergraduate student with prior exposure to the marketing field. Because of its in-depth development of topical coverage, however, it also presents an excellent challenge for graduate instruction and executive education.

The text is divided into four parts. First, the basic concepts of international marketing are outlined, and the environmental forces that the international marketer has to consider are discussed. The second part focuses on the various activities necessary for international marketing planning and concentrates on the beginning of international marketing activities. Export and import operations are covered here, together with elements of the marketing mix that tend to be most important for firms at an initial level of international experience. The third part discusses strategy and marketing management issues most relevant to the expanded global operations of multinational corporations. The final part addresses transitions in international marketing, with a particular focus on countertrade, newly emerging markets, and the future of the field and the student.

Both the instructor and the student can work with this text in two ways. One alternative is to cover the material sequentially, progressing from the initial international effort to multinational activities. In this way, marketing dimensions such as distribution, promotion, and pricing are covered in the order in which they are most relevant for the particular level of expertise within the firm. Another approach is to use the text in a parallel manner, by pairing comparable chapters from Parts Two and Three. In this way, the primary emphasis can be placed on the functional approach to international marketing.

Key Features

The 2002 edition contains updates and revisions that follow the trend of the highly dynamic international marketplace. Some of the elements that make up this expansive arena are highlighted in the following paragraphs.

We offer a perspective on the shift from marketplace to market space, and the impact of this revolution on international marketers in terms of outreach, research, and competition. Several Internet technology sections are now part of our chapters and international marketplace vignettes, reflecting state-of-the-art corporate practices. We have also included links to the websites of companies in our vignettes as well as those of our data sources, when practical. Students can follow up by gathering information directly from the Internet using the new :Cue Cat technology that links them directly to the website. We also provide several new appendices which list web addresses for governments, international organizations, and monitors of international marketing issues.

Our focus on the physical environment and geography is strong. New maps provide context in terms of social and economic data. An appendix addresses directly the relationship between geography and international marketing. New text components, marketplaces, and several cases focus specifically on the environment and the opportunities, challenges, and ambiguities that it represents to international marketers. Several marketplaces and case studies are included to broaden the focus on the long neglected continent of Africa.

This 2002 edition is divided into four parts: The environment, beginning international marketing activities, advanced international marketing management, and marketing in transition. The separation of marketing in transition is designed to pay appropriate attention to emerging markets and changing marketing practices while casting a predictive look to future developments and their possible impact.

The six chapters of Part One reflect the drivers behind the globalization phenomenon in the cultural, economic, financial, political, and legal areas. Both the established markets in Europe and North America as well as the growth markets of Asia and Latin America are emphasized. We also address the response of international marketers to financial crises. Our strong policy orientation continues with an update of the role of international agreements and organizations, as well as their interaction with national and regional policies. The World Trade Organization (WTO), the IMF, and the World Bank are discussed, together with the controversies and public debate surrounding these institutions. The section on export controls reflects the realities of the end of the Cold War. Also covered are newly emerging areas of international policy conflict, such as dumping, country of origin rules, intellectual property rights, the Helms-Burton Act, and the important issues of ethics, bribery, and human rights. This section also includes a major expansion of export promotion policies reflecting the growing attention paid to such activities by nations around the world.

Beginning international marketing activities in Part Two are placed in the context of market expansion strategy and the evolutionary nature of the internationalization process. The role of research in this process is highlighted in the chapter on building the knowledge base necessary for initial and more involved marketing activities across borders. Also included is a section on websites and Internet information to facilitate direct student access to international data. The discussion of the export process is now followed immediately by a presentation of export intermediaries, licensing, and franchising—thus offering insight into the continuity of the internationalization patterns of firms. Particular attention also rests with the emergence of the International Distribution Life Cycle. There is also an increased reflection of marketing theory and practices as emanating from outside North America.

Advanced international marketing activities in Part Three are presented with a strong strategy orientation. The opening chapter is dedicated to the global strategic planning framework, which addresses market choice, competitive strategy, and international marketing segmentation. The foreign direct investment process is more clearly linked to globalization trends and now also covers such investments from the local employee perspective. The product chapter has a new section dealing with brand management and how marketers can build global, regional, and local brands. The services chapter reflects the shift from marketplace to market space and the resulting mobility of corporate activities. Also highlighted is the global imbalance of skilled labor in the information technology field. The logistics chapter has "supply chain management" in its title, reflecting issues such as efficient customer response, the close cooperation between customers and suppliers, and the emerging linkages between logistics and the environment. In the pricing chapter, major emphasis rests with the marketing strategy implications of the euro currency and the implications of greater pricing transparency due to the Internet. Promotional strategies include a discussion of global community relations and the need for corporate preparedness for global crises management. The chapter on organization and control has a section dealing with a firm's ability to leverage resources and strengths across borders and includes approaches such as the Intranet.

Part Four is dedicated to marketing in transition, focusing both on new uses of existing approaches and the development of new strategies. It reflects the latest thinking on the economic transformation of emerging markets. This part also presents the results of a special delphi study on the future of international marketing that was conducted by the authors with a global panel of experts.

Innovative Learning Tools

Contemporary Realism

Each chapter offers several current International Marketplace boxes. All of them are revised in this edition. They focus on real marketing situations and are intended to help students understand and absorb the presented materials. The instructor can highlight the boxes to exemplify theory or use them as mini-cases for class discussion. Whenever possible, links to Internet addresses are provided to the companies featured in these boxes, so that students can obtain the latest information.

Research Emphasis

A special effort has been made to provide current research information and data using publications from around the world. Chapter notes are augmented by lists of relevant recommended readings incorporating the latest research findings. In addition, a wide variety of sources and organizations that provide international information are listed in the text. These materials enable the instructor and the student to go beyond the text whenever time permits.

Internet Focus

All chapters make specific reference to how the Internet, electronic commerce, and the World Wide Web affect international marketing. We highlight how the way of reaching customers and suppliers has changed given the new technology. We also explain the enhanced ability of firms to position themselves internationally in competition with other larger players. We offer insights into the electronic marketing research process and present details of how companies cope with new market realities. Whenever appropriate, :cues are provided to direct students toward Internet resources which can be useful in updating information. Each chapter also provides several Internet questions in order to offer training opportunities that make use of the Internet.

Geography

In order to improve students' geographical literacy, the 2002 edition contains several full-color maps covering the social, economic, and political features of the world. Several chapters have maps particularly designed for this book, which integrate the materials discussed in the text and reflect a truly "global" perspective. These maps enable the instructor to visually demonstrate concepts such as political blocs and socioeconomic variables. An appendix, dealing specifically with the impact of geography on international marketing, has also been added to Chapter 1.

Cases

Following each of the four parts of the text are a variety of cases, most written especially for this book, that present students with real business situations. All cases address the activities of actual companies and cover a broad geographic spectrum, including such areas as the continent of Africa. In addition, a number of video cases further assists to enliven classroom activity. Challenging questions accompany each case, permitting in-depth discussion of the materials covered in the chapters.

Supplementary Materials

Instructor's Manual

The text is accompanied by an in-depth *Instructor's Manual,* devised to provide major assistance to the professor. The material in the manual includes the following:

Teaching Plans   Alternative teaching plans and syllabi are presented to accommodate the instructor's preferred course structure and varying time constraints. Time plans are developed for the course to be taught in a semester format, on a quarter basis, or as an executive seminar.

Discussion Guidelines For each chapter, specific teaching objectives and guidelines are developed to help stimulate classroom discussion.

End-of-Chapter Questions Each question is fully developed in the manual to accommodate different scenarios and experience horizons. Where appropriate, the relevant text section is referenced. In addition, each chapter has two Internet based questions in order to offer students the opportunity to explore the application of new technology to international marketing on their own.

Cases A detailed case-chapter matrix is supplied that delineates which cases are most appropriate for each area of the international marketing field. In addition, detailed case discussion alternatives are provided, outlining discussion strategies and solution alternatives.

Video and Film References An extensive listing of video and film materials available from educational institutions, companies, and government agencies is provided. Materials are briefly discussed, possible usage patterns are outlined, and ordering/availability information is supplied. In addition, each adopter of this text can receive the free video cases in international marketing, which contain news stories relevant to issues in international marketing.

Test Bank The manual includes a greatly expanded test bank, consisting of more than 1,000 short essay questions, true/false questions, and multiple-choice questions. This test bank is also computerized and available to adopters on PC computer diskettes.

Transparency Masters The manual contains a substantial number of transparency masters, including some materials from the text, but also drawing heavily on nontext materials such as advertisements, graphs, and figures, which can be used to further enliven classroom interaction and to develop particular topics in more depth.

Correlation Guide

The *Correlation Guide* provides assistance to those professors who have used *International Marketing, Sixth Edition* in the past. The materials in this manual include the significant changes that have taken place in the 2002 edition, linkages to new web sites, and notes for new case materials.

Lecture Software in Microsoft PowerPoint

Created by Charlie Cook, University of Western Alabama. An asset to any instructor, the lectures in PowerPoint provide outlines of chapters, graphics of illustrations from the text, and additional examples providing instructors with a number of learning opportunities for students.

Companion Web Site

International Marketing's companion Web site at **www.harcourtcollege.com** provides additional instructor and students resources. Harcourt College Publishers has collaborated with Eric Sandburg and Crystal Barkley Corporation to develop a site especially for business students. This site includes ancillary materials, a resource library of articles with applications to text lessons, student activities, and online quizzing.

Distance Learning

For professors interested in supplementing classroom presentations with online content or who are interested in setting up a distance learning course, Harcourt College

Publishers, along with WebCT and Blackboard, can provide you with the industry's leading online courses.

These platforms facilitate the creation of sophisticated Web-based educational environments by providing tools to help you manage course content, facilitate online classroom collaboration, and track your students' progress. You may also adopt the *Student's Guide to the World Wide Web and WebCT* (0-03-045503-0). This manual gives step-by-step instructions on using WebCT tools and features.

In conjunction with WebCT and Blackboard, Harcourt College Publishers also offers information on adopting a Harcourt online course, testing services, free access to blank WebCT and Blackboard templates, and customized course creation. For more information, please contact your local sales representative. To view a demo of any of our online courses, go to **webct.harcourtcollege.com.**

Personal Support

Most important, we personally stand behind our product and we will work hard to delight you. Should you have any questions or comments on this book, you can contact us, talk to us, and receive feedback from us.

Michael R. Czinkota
(202) 687-4204
Czinkotm@msb.edu

Ilkka A. Ronkainen
(202) 687-3788
Ronkaii@msb.edu

Acknowledgments

We are deeply grateful to the professors, students, and professionals using this book. Your interest demonstrates the need for more knowledge about international marketing. As our market, you are telling us that our product adds value to your lives. As a result, you add value to ours. Thank you!

We also thank the many reviewers for their constructive and imaginative comments and criticisms, which were instrumental in making this edition even better.

We remain indebted to the reviewers and survey respondents of this and earlier editions of this text:

Sanjeev Agarwal
Iowa State University
Lyn S. Amine
St. Louis University
Jessica M. Bailey
The American University
Warren Bilkey
University of Wisconsin
S. Tamer Cavusgil
Michigan State University
Shih-Fen Chen
Kansas State University
Alex Christofides
Ohio State University
John Dyer
University of Miami
Luiz Felipe
IBMEC Business School (Rio de Janeiro, Brazil)

John P. Fraderich
Southern Illinois University— Carbondale
Roberto Friedmann
University of Georgia
Shenzhao Fu
University of San Francisco
Jim Gentry
University of Nebraska
Donna Goehle
Michigan State University
Neelima Gogumala
Kansas State University
Paul Groke
Northern Illinois University
Andrew Gross
Cleveland State University
John Hadjimarcou
University of Texas at El Paso

Hari Hariharan
DePaul University

Braxton Hinchey
University of Lowell

Carol Howard
Oklahoma City University

G. Thomas M. Hult
Florida State University

Basil Janavaras
Mankato State University

Denise Johnson
University of Louisville

Sudhir Kale
Arizona State University

Hertha Krotkoff
Towson State University

Kathleen La Francis
Central Michigan University

Trina Larsen
Drexel University

Edmond Lausier
University of Southern California

Bertil Liander
University of Massachusetts

Mushtaq Luqmani
Western Michigan University

Isabel Maignan
Florida State University

James Maskulka
Lehigh University

James McCullouch
Washington State University

Fred Miller
Murray State University

Joseph Miller
Indiana University

Mark Mitchell
*University of South Carolina—
Spartanburg*

Henry Munn
California State University, Northridge

Jacob Naor
University of Maine, Orono

Urban Ozanne
Florida State University

Tony Peloso
*Queensland University of Technology
(Australia)*

Ilsa Penaloza
University of Connecticut

John Ryans
Kent State University

Matthew Sim
Temesek Business School (Singapore)

James Spiers
Arizona State University

Janda Swinder
Kansas State University

Ray Taylor
Villanova University

Tyzoon T. Tyebjee
Santa Clara University

Robert Underwood
*Virginia Polytechnic Institute and
State University*

Robert Weigand
University of Illinois at Chicago

John Wilkinson
University of South Australia

Nittaya Wongtada
Thunderbird

Van R. Wood
Texas Tech University

Many thanks to all the faculty members and students who have helped us sharpen our thinking by cheerfully providing challenging comments and questions. In particular, we thank Bernard LaLonde, The Ohio State University; Lyn Amine, St. Louis University; Tamer Cavusgil, Michigan State University; and James Wills, University of Hawaii.

Many colleagues, friends, and business associates graciously gave their time and knowledge to clarify concepts; provide us with ideas, comments, and suggestions; and deepen our understanding of issues. Without the direct links to business and policy that you have provided, this book could not offer its refreshing realism. In particular, we are grateful to Secretaries Malcolm Baldrige, C. William Verity, Clayton Yeutter, and William Brock for the opportunity to gain international business policy experience and to William Morris, Paul Freedenberg, and J. Michael Farrell for enabling its implementation. We also thank William Casselman of Stairs Dillenbeck Kelly Merle and Finley, Robert Conkling of Conkling Associates, Lew Cramer of Summit Ventures, Mark Dowd of IBM, David Danjczek of Western Atlas, and Veikko Jaaskelainen and Reijo Luostarinen of HSE.

Valuable research assistance was provided by Elena Pasik as well as Jesse Nelson, Kristen Mehlum and Bridget McConnell, all of Georgetown University. We appreciate all of your work!

A very special word of thanks to the people at Harcourt College Publishers. Mark Orr and Kerri Jones made the lengthy process of writing a text bearable with their enthusiasm, creativity, and constructive feedback.

Foremost, we are grateful to our families, who have truly participated in the writing of this book. Only the patience, understanding, and love of Ilona and Margaret Victoria Czinkota and Susan, Sanna, and Alex Ronkainen enabled us to have the energy, stamina, and inspiration to write this book.

Michael R. Czinkota
Ilkka A. Ronkainen
Washington, D.C.
May 2001

About the Authors

Michael R. Czinkota is on the faculty of marketing and international business of the Graduate School and the Robert Emmett McDonough School of Business at Georgetown University. He has held professorial appointments at universities in Asia, Australia, Europe, and the Americas.

Dr. Czinkota served in the U.S. government as Deputy Assistant Secretary of Commerce. He was responsible for macro trade analysis, support of international trade negotiations and retaliatory actions, and policy coordination for international finance, investment, and monetary affairs. He also served as head of the U.S. Delegation to the OECD Industry Committee in Paris and as senior trade advisor for Export Controls.

Dr. Czinkota's background includes eight years of private sector business experience as a partner in an export-import firm and in an advertising agency and seventeen years of research and teaching in the academic world. His research has been supported by the U.S. government, the National Science Foundation, the National Commission of Jobs and Small Business, the Organization of American States and the International Council of the American Management Association. He was listed as one of the three most published contributors to international business research in the *Journal of International Business Studies* and has written several books including *Best Practices in International Business* (Harcourt) and *Trends in International Business* (Blackwell). He is also the author of the *STAT-USA/Internet Companion to International Business,* an official publication of the U.S. Department of Commerce.

Dr. Czinkota serves on the Global Advisory Board of the American Marketing Association and on the Board of Governors of the Academy of Marketing Science. He is on the editorial boards of *Journal of Business Research, Journal of the Academy of Marketing Science, International Marketing Review,* and *Asian Journal of Marketing.* For his work in international business and trade policy, he was named a Distinguished Fellow of the Academy of Marketing Science and a Fellow of the Chartered Institute of Marketing in the United Kingdom. He has also been awarded honorary degrees from the Universidad Pontificia Madre y Maestra in the Dominican Republic and the Universidad del Pacifico in Lima, Peru.

Dr. Czinkota serves on several corporate boards and has worked with corporations such as AT&T, IBM, GE, Nestlé, and US WEST. He also serves as advisor to the United Nations' and World Trade Organization's Executive Forum on National Export Strategies.

Dr. Czinkota was born and raised in Germany and educated in Austria, Scotland, Spain, and the United States. He studied law and business administration at the University of Erlangen-Nürnberg and was awarded a two-year Fulbright Scholarship. He holds an MBA in international business and a Ph.D. in logistics from The Ohio State University.

Ilkka A. Ronkainen is a member of the faculty of marketing and international business at the School of Business at Georgetown University. From 1981 to 1986 he served as Associate Director and from 1986 to 1987 as Chairman of the National Center for Export-Import Studies. Currently, he directs Georgetown University's Hong Kong Program.

Dr. Ronkainen serves as docent of international marketing at the Helsinki School of Economics. He was visiting professor at HSE during the 1987–1988 and 1991–1992 academic years and continues to teach in its Executive MBA, International MBA, and International BBA programs.

Dr. Ronkainen holds a Ph.D. and a master's degree from the University of South Carolina as well as an M.S. (Economics) degree from the Helsinki School of Economics.

Dr. Ronkainen has published extensively in academic journals and the trade press. He is a coauthor of *International Business* and *The Global Marketing Imperative.* He serves on the review boards of the *Journal of Business Research, International Marketing Review,* and *Journal of Travel Research* and has reviewed for the *Journal of Advertising* and the *Journal of International Business Studies.* He served as the North American coordinator for the European Marketing Academy, 1984–1990. He was a member of the board of the Washington International Trade Association from 1981 to 1986 and started the association's newsletter, *Trade Trends.*

Dr. Ronkainen has served as a consultant to a wide range of U.S. and international institutions. He has worked with entities such as IBM, the Rand Organization, and the Organization of American States. He maintains close relations with a number of Finnish companies and their internationalization and educational efforts.

Brief Contents

PART FOUR   International Marketing Transitions

Detailed Contents

CHAPTER 3 The Cultural Environment 57

PART TWO   Beginning International Marketing Activities

CHAPTER 7   Building the Knowledge Base 224

PART THREE   Global Marketing Management

CHAPTER 14   Global Strategic Planning 464

CHAPTER 18   Global Pricing Strategies 562

CHAPTER 19   Logistics and Supply Chain Management 582

PART FOUR   International Marketing Transitions

Part One

Internation

The International Environment

P

art One introduces the international trade framework and environment. It highlights the need for international marketing activities and explains why the international market is an entirely new arena for a firm and its managers. The chapters devoted to macroenvironmental factors explain the many forces to which a firm is exposed. The marketer must adapt to these foreign environments and adeptly resolve conflicts between political, cultural, and legal forces in order to be successful.

The International Marketing Imperative

Chapter 1

THE INTERNATIONAL MARKETPLACE 1.1

The Janus Faces of Globalization

GLOBALIZATION SHOWS ITS TWO FACES as foreign investment brings new industries to some communities while others lose their industrial base when labor cost is lower elsewhere. Both can occur almost simultaneously in the same region.

In the United States, South Carolina provides a good example: In the early 1990s, German carmaker BMW announced a $640 million direct investment in a new automotive plant in Spartanburg, South Carolina. BMW had surveyed 250 locations in ten countries before settling on Spartanburg. An important factor in BMW's decision was the hard work of then South Carolina governor Carroll Campbell. He had visited BMW headquarters in Germany and offered to spend $36 million to secure a 900-acre plant site, to provide $41 million in property tax breaks, and to extend the Spartanburg airport's free-trade zone status to include the BMW plant site.

Another important factor that influenced BMW's decision to locate in South Carolina was the state's willingness to devote large training resources to BMW. South Carolina agreed to spend $3 million of its technical training budget on a BMW–specific program, and local business agreed to provide $3 million for additional training.

By 2000, BMW's Spartanburg investment totaled over $2 billion and provided 4,300 jobs. Other international firms had decided to locate in South Carolina, including BASF, Rieter, Marzoli International, and Michelin. By the year 2000, Spartanburg County was home to over 100 international firms and its per capita international investment was the highest in the United States.

However, the international prosperity of Spartanburg did not reach all of South Carolina. Iva, population 1,200, is 70 miles from the BMW facility. The old brick façade of Jackson Mills at the center of Iva is a testament to the days when the textile industry employed 1.3 million people throughout the region. The looms that produced the majority of America's cloth were the staple of many small southern towns.

Despite technological advancement and improved efficiency, mill operators found the cost of labor in the region had risen too high during the last two decades for them to compete internationally. Much of the textile industry relocated to Latin America and Asia where labor costs are significantly lower. Jackson Mills closed its doors in 1995. Iva now has high unemployment and has lost its key tax base.

The industrial changes in South Carolina are but one example of the Janus faces of globalization. South Carolina may have permanently lost the textile industry, but the prosperity of the industry is not lost to the world: it adds to the economy of its new home elsewhere in the world. The flip side of globalization is new investments, such as BMW, that offset the demise of an old industry.

SOURCES: Chris Burritt, "Hit Hard by Textile Losses, S.C. Lifted by BMW Plant," *Atlanta Journal-Constitution*, April 8, 2001; Michael R. Czinkota and Peter Fitzmaurice, "Attracting Foreign Direct Investment: German Luxury Cars in the USA," Case study, 1999 Annual Meeting, Academy of International Business, Charleston, South Carolina; Sue Anne Pressley, "With Textile Jobs' Departure Goes a Way of Life," *The Washington Post*, March 28, 1999.

Y OU ARE ABOUT TO BEGIN an exciting, important, and necessary task: the exploration of international marketing. International marketing is exciting because it combines the science and the art of business with many other disciplines. Economics, anthropology, cultural studies, geography, history, languages, jurisprudence, statistics, demographics, and many other fields combine to help you explore the global market. Different business environments will stimulate your intellectual curiosity, which will enable you to absorb and understand new phenomena. International marketing has been compared by many who have been active in the field to the task of mountain climbing: challenging, arduous, and exhilarating.

International marketing is important because the world has become globalized. Figure 1.1 shows one large corporation's perspective of its global business activities. International marketing takes place all around us every day, has a major effect on our lives, and offers new opportunities and challenges, as *The International Marketplace 1.1* shows. After reading through this book and observing international marketing phenomena, you will see what happens, understand what happens, and, at some time in the future, perhaps even make it happen. All of this is much better than to stand by and wonder what happened.

International marketing is necessary because, from a national standpoint, economic isolationism has become impossible. Failure to participate in the global marketplace assures a nation of declining economic capability and its citizens of a decrease in their standard of living. Successful international marketing, however, holds the promise of an improved quality of life, a better society, and, as some have stated, even a more peaceful world.

This chapter is designed to increase your awareness of what international marketing is all about. It describes the current levels of world trade activities, projects future developments, and discusses the resulting repercussion on countries, institutions, and individuals worldwide. Both the opportunities and the threats that spring from the global marketplace are highlighted, and the need for an international "marketing" approach on the part of individuals and institutions is emphasized.

This chapter ends with an explanation of the major organizational thrust of this book, which is a differentiation between the beginning internationalist and the multinational corporation. This theme ties the entire book together by taking into account the concerns, capabilities, and goals of firms that will differ widely based on their level of international expertise, resources, and involvement. The approach to international marketing taken here will therefore permit you to understand the entire range of international activities and allow you easily to transfer your acquired knowledge into practice.

What International Marketing Is

In brief, **international marketing** is the process of planning and conducting transactions across national borders to create exchanges that satisfy the objectives of individuals and organizations. International marketing has forms ranging from export-import trade to licensing, joint ventures, wholly owned subsidiaries, turnkey operations, and management contracts.

As this definition indicates, international marketing very much retains the basic marketing tenets of "satisfaction" and "exchange." International marketing is a tool used to obtain improvement of one's present position. The fact that a transaction takes place across national borders highlights the difference between domestic and international marketing. The international marketer is subject to a new set of macroenvironmental factors, to different constraints, and to quite frequent conflicts resulting from different laws, cultures, and societies. The basic principles of marketing still

FIGURE	1.1	A Global Perspective

You might think our global perspective is
an unusual response to local problems. But on a planet
as small as this one has become, there's simply
no room for borders. Between nations or even between ideas.

Difficulties may remain, but we're bringing the Socratic
method to pressing issues. Asking the right
questions and encouraging new thinking.

And coming up with the answers that you would
expect from a citizen of the world.

Marubeni
CORPORATION
C.P.O. BOX 595, TOKYO 100-91, JAPAN

http://202.245.142.66/home/english/index.html

apply, but their applications, complexity, and intensity may vary substantially. It is in the international marketing field where one can observe most closely the role of marketing as a key agent of societal change and as a key instrument for the development of societally responsive business strategy. When we look, for example, at the emerging market economies of Central Europe, we can see the many new challenges that international marketing is confronted with. How does the marketing concept fit into these societies? How can marketing contribute to economic development and the improvement of society? How should distribution systems be organized? How can we get the price mechanism to work? Similarly, in the international areas of social responsibility and ethics, the international marketer is faced with a multicultural environment with differing expectations and often inconsistent legal systems when it comes to monitoring environmental pollution, maintaining safe working conditions, copying technology or trademarks, or paying bribes.[1] These are just a few of the issues that the international marketer needs to address. The capability to master these challenges successfully affords a company the potential for new opportunities and high rewards.

The definition also focuses on international transactions. The use of the term recognizes that marketing internationally is an activity that needs to be pursued, often aggressively. Those who do not participate in the transactions are only exposed to international marketing and subject to its changing influences. The international marketer is part of the exchange, recognizes the changing nature of transactions, and adjusts to a constantly moving target subject to shifts in the business environment. This need for adjustment, for comprehending change, and, in spite of it all, for successfully carrying out transactions, highlights the fact that international marketing is as much art as science.

To achieve success in the art of international marketing, it is necessary to be firmly grounded in its scientific aspects. Only then will individual consumers, policymakers, and business executives be able to incorporate international marketing considerations into their thinking and planning. Only then will they be able to consider international issues and repercussions and make decisions based on the answers to such questions as these:

- How will my idea, good, or service fit into the international market?
- Should I obtain my supplies domestically or from abroad?
- What marketing adjustments are or will be necessary?
- What threats from global competition should I expect?
- How can I work with these threats to turn them into opportunities?
- What are my strategic global alternatives?

If all these issues are integrated into each decision made by individuals and by firms, international markets can become a source of growth, profit, needs satisfaction, and quality of life that would not have existed for them had they limited themselves to domestic activities. The purpose of this book is to aid in this decision process.

The Importance of World Trade

World trade has assumed an importance heretofore unknown to the global community. In past centuries, trade was conducted internationally but never before did it have the broad and simultaneous impact on nations, firms, and individuals that it has today. Within three decades, world trade has expanded from $200 billion to almost $7 trillion.[2] Such growth is unique, particularly since, as Figure 1.2 shows, trade growth on a global level has consistently outperformed the growth of domestic economies in the past few decades. As a result, many new countries and firms have found it highly desirable to become major participants in international marketing.

The Iron Curtain has disintegrated, offering a vast array of new marketing opportunities—albeit amid uncertainty. Firms invest on a global scale, with the result that entire industries shift their locations. International specialization and cross-sourcing has made production much more efficient. New technologies have changed the way we do business, allowing us to both supply and receive products from across the world by using the Internet. As a result, consumers, union leaders, policymakers, and sometimes even the firms themselves are finding it increasingly difficult to define where a particular product was made. New trading blocs are emerging with the European

[1] Robert W. Armstrong and Jill Sweeney, "Industrial Type, Culture, Mode of Entry, and Perceptions of International Marketing Ethics Problems: A Cross-Culture Comparison," *Journal of Business Ethics* 13, 10: 775–785.

[2] International Monetary Fund, Washington D.C., 2000. **www.imf.org**

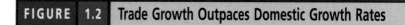

FIGURE   1.2   Trade Growth Outpaces Domestic Growth Rates

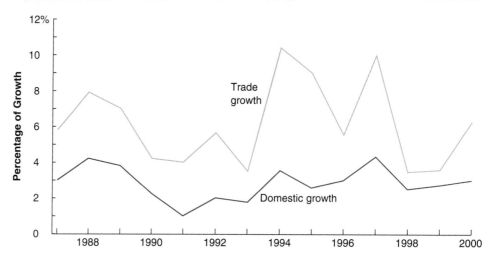

SOURCE: *International Financial Statistics Yearbook,* IMF, 2000.

Union in Europe, with NAFTA in North America, with Mercosur in Latin America and ASEAN in Asia.

Individuals and firms have come to recognize that they are competing not only domestically but also globally. World trade has given rise to global linkages of markets, technology, and living standards that were previously unknown and unanticipated. At the same time, it has deeply affected domestic policy-making and has often resulted in the emergence of totally new opportunities as well as threats to firms and individuals. *The International Marketplace 1.2* provides an example.

Global Linkages

World trade has forged a network of **global linkages** that bind us all—countries, institutions, and individuals—much more closely than ever before. These linkages were first widely recognized during the worldwide oil crisis of 1970, but they continue to increase. A drought in Brazil and its effects on coffee production are felt around the world. The sudden decline of the Mexican peso affected markets in the United States and reverberated throughout Poland, Hungary, and the Czech Republic. Iraq's invasion of Kuwait and the subsequent Persian Gulf War affected oil prices, stock markets, trade, and travel flows in all corners of the earth.

These linkages have also become more intense on an individual level. Communication has built new international bridges, be it through music or international programs transmitted by CNN. New products have attained international appeal and encouraged similar activities around the world—where many of us wear denim, dance the same dances, and eat pizzas and sushi.[3] Transportation linkages let individuals from different countries see and meet each other with unprecedented ease. Common cultural pressures result in similar social phenomena and behavior—for example, more dual-income families are emerging around the world, which leads to more frequent, and also more stressful, shopping.[4]

World trade is also bringing about a global reorientation of corporate processes, which opens up entirely new horizons. Never before has it been so easy to gather,

[3]Michael Marquardt and Angus Reynolds, *The Global Learning Organization* (Burr Ridge, IL: Irwin, 1994), vi.

[4]Eugene H. Fram and Riad Ajami, "Globalization of Markets and Shopping Stress: Cross-Country Comparisons," *Business Horizons* (January–February 1994): 17–23.

THE INTERNATIONAL MARKETPLACE 1.2

Cork versus Plastic

THE INTERNATIONALIZATION OF MARKETS has made industries and economies worldwide more subject to competition and change. The natural cork industry is one example. Portugal is home to the species of oak tree used to make bottling corks and has benefited from the worldwide commercial demand for this natural resource. It takes about forty years to produce a cork product from the time the trees are planted. Within the Alentejo region of Portugal, about 10 million corks are produced per day. However, the industry that has been a vital contributor to the Portuguese economy must now compete with an emerging technology. As the owner of farms containing over 1 million cork oak trees in Portugal, Pedro Cabral da Silveira finds his business facing new threats from emerging international competition.

In the suburbs of Seattle, Washington, Supreme Corq Inc. owner Dennis Burns has perfected the plastic cork. The synthetic corks can be sold at approximately the same price as natural corks. Additionally, plastic corks eliminate the chemical found in natural cork that causes an estimated one in twelve bottles of wine to spoil. According to Burns, plastic corks now seal "hundreds of millions of wine bottles" per year. The new plastic cork, with its ease of automated production and lack of reliance on a natural resource located in a specific geographic region, may revolutionize the corking industry and have a negative impact on the Portuguese economy.

The plastic cork has caused Mr. da Silveira and many of those reliant on sales of natural corks to combat the emergence of the synthetic corks. They have launched promotional campaigns aimed at communicating the possible negative consequences of shifting to plastic as well as the positive characteristics of natural corks. The Portuguese government and those in the natural cork industry have distributed studies that may indicate an increased health risk associated with plastic and argued that air pollution will increase if the industry adopts plastic as the material of choice. They have also opened natural cork plants that produce corks that do not contain the chemical that causes wine to spoil. Finally, to increase the awareness of the materials used in the end product, they have introduced a "cork mark" which will be used in the same manner as the cotton or cashmere trademarks in hopes of building a level of loyalty among consumers.

SOURCES: Reid, T.R., "Portugal Urges World to Put a Cork in It," *The Washington Post,* November 29, 1999, A1, A17. Rose, Anthony, "Food & Drink: Learn to Stop Worrying and Love the Screwcap," *The Independent* (London), June 19, 1999, 16.

www.supremecorq.com

manipulate, analyze, and disseminate information—but never before has the pressure been so great to do so. Ongoing global technological innovation in marketing has direct effects on the efficiency and effectiveness of all business activities. Products can be produced more quickly, obtained less expensively from sources around the world, distributed at lower cost, and customized to meet diverse clients' needs. As an example, only a decade ago, it would have been thought impossible for a firm to produce parts for a car in more than one country, assemble the car in yet another country, and sell it in still other nations. Today, such global investment strategies coupled with production and distribution sharing are becoming a matter of routine.

Advances in technology also allow firms to separate their activities by content and context. Firms can operate in a "market space" rather than a marketplace[5] by keeping the content while changing the context of a transaction. For example, a newspaper can

[5]John J. Sviokla and Jeffrey F. Rayport, "Mapping the Marketspace: Information Technology and the New Marketing Environment," *Harvard Business School Bulletin* 71 (June 1995): 49–51.

now be distributed globally on-line rather than house-to-house on paper, thereby allowing an unprecedented reach to new customer groups.

The level of global investment is at an unprecedented high. The shifts in financial flows have had major effects. They resulted in the buildup of international debt by governments, affected the international value of currencies, provided foreign capital for firms, and triggered major foreign direct-investment activities. For example, currently well over one-third of the workers in the U.S. chemical industry toil for foreign owners. Many of the office buildings Americans work in are owned by foreign landlords. The opening of plants increasingly takes the place of trade. All these developments make us more and more dependent on one another.

This interdependence, however, is not stable. On almost a daily basis, realignments taking place on both micro and macro levels make past trade orientations at least partially obsolete. For example, for the first 200 years of its history, the United States looked to Europe for markets and sources of supply. Today, U.S. two-way trade with Asia far outpaces U.S. trade with Europe.

Not only is the environment changing, but the pace of change grows faster. "A boy who saw the Wright brothers fly for a few seconds at Kitty Hawk in 1903 could have watched Apollo 11 land on the moon in 1969. The first electronic computer was built in 1946; today, the world rushes from the mechanical into the electronic age. The double helix was first unveiled in 1953; today, biotechnology threatens to remake mankind."[6]

These changes and the speed with which they come about significantly affect countries, corporations, and individuals. One change is the role participants play. For example, the United States accounted for nearly 25 percent of world merchandise exports in the 1950s, but by 1999, this share had declined to less than 13 percent. Also, the way countries participate in world trade is shifting. In the past two decades the role of primary commodities in international trade has dropped precipitously, while the importance of manufactured goods has increased. Even more dramatic has been the increase in the volume of services trade. In a few decades, international services went from being a nonmeasured activity to comprising a global volume of more than $1.3 trillion in 1999.[7] Figure 1.3 shows how substantial the growth rates for both merchandise and services trade have been.

Domestic Policy Repercussions

The effects of closer global linkages on the economics of countries have been dramatic. Policymakers have increasingly come to recognize that it is very difficult to isolate domestic economic activity from international market events. Decisions that once were clearly in the domestic purview have now become subject to revision by influences from abroad, and domestic policy measures are often canceled out or counteracted by the activities of global market forces.

A lowering of interest rates domestically may make consumers happy or may be politically wise, but it quickly becomes unsustainable if it results in a major outflow of funds to countries that offer higher interest rates. Agricultural and farm policies, which historically have been strictly domestic issues, are suddenly thrust into the international realm. Any policy consideration must now be seen in light of international repercussions due to influences from global trade and investment. The following examples highlight some of these influences in the United States:

- One of every three U.S. farm acres is producing for export.
- One of every six U.S. manufacturing jobs produces for export.
- One of every seven dollars of U.S. sales is to someone abroad.

[6]Arthur M. Schlesinger, Jr., *The Cycles of American History* (Boston: Houghton Mifflin, 1986), xi.

[7]The World Bank, *World Development Report 1999,* Washington, D.C., 2000, pp. 268–269.

FIGURE 1.3 The Changing Face of Exporting

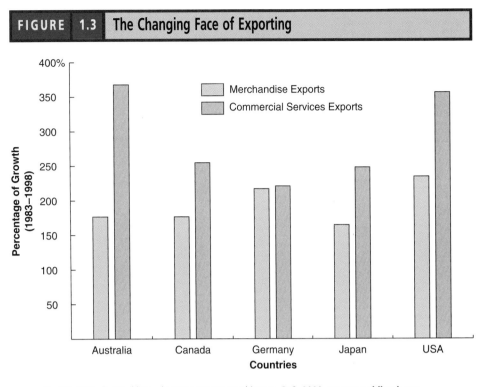

SOURCE: The World Bank, *World Development Report*, Washington, D.C. 2000. **www.worldbank.org**

- One of every three cars, nine of every ten television sets, two of every three suits, and every video recorder sold in the United States is imported.
- Travel and tourism is the number one source of U.S. foreign exchange.
- One of every four dollars of U.S. bonds and notes is issued to foreigners.[8]

To some extent, the economic world as we knew it has been turned upside down. For example, trade flows used to determine currency flows and therefore the level of the exchange rate. In the more recent past, **currency flows** took on a life of their own. Independent of trade, they set exchange rates, which is the value of currencies relative to each other. These **exchange rates** in turn have now begun to determine the level of trade. Governments that wish to counteract these developments with monetary policies find that currency flows outnumber trade flows by 100 to 1. Also, private-sector financial flows vastly outnumber the financial flows that can be marshaled by governments, even when acting in concert. Similarly, constant rapid technological change and vast advances in communication permit firms and countries to quickly emulate innovation and counteract carefully designed plans. As a result, governments are often powerless to implement effective policy measures, even when they know what to do.

Policymakers therefore find themselves with increasing responsibilities yet with fewer and less-effective tools to carry out these responsibilities. At the same time that more parts of a domestic economy are vulnerable to international shifts and changes, these parts are becoming less controllable. The global market imposes increasingly tight limits on national economic regulation and sovereignty.

To regain some of their power to influence events, policymakers have sought to restrict the impact of global trade and financial flows by erecting barriers, charging

[8]Raymond J. Waldmann, *Managed Trade: The Competition between Nations* (Cambridge, MA: Ballinger, 1986), 6; *Ward's Automotive Report*, January 9, 1989; John Naisbitt, *Global Paradox* (New York: Morrow and Co., 1994), 105; and Dan Glickman, U.S. Secretary of Agriculture, Speech to FarmAid 96, Columbia, SC, October 12, 1996.

THE INTERNATIONAL MARKETPLACE 1.3

Does International Marketing Create Peace?

ONE REALLY BIG SURPRISE of the postwar era has been that historic enemies, such as Germany and France, or Japan and the United States, have not had the remotest threat of war since 1945. Why should they? Anything Japan has that we want we can buy, and on very easy credit terms, so why fight for it? Why should the Japanese fight the United States and lose all those profitable markets? France and Germany, linked intimately through marketing and the European Union, are now each other's largest trading partners. Closed systems build huge armies and waste their resources on guns and troops; open countries spend their money on new machine tools to crank out Barbie dolls or some such trivia. Their bright young people figure out how to run the machines, not how to fire the latest missile. For some reason, they not only get rich fast but also lose interest in military adventures. Japan, that peculiar superpower without superguns, confounds everyone simply because no one has ever seen a major world power that got that way by selling you to death, not shooting you to death. In short, if you trade a lot with someone, why fight? The logical answer—you don't—is perhaps the best news mankind has had in millennia.

SOURCE: Adapted from Richard N. Farmer, "Would You Want Your Granddaughter to Marry a Taiwanese Marketing Man?" *Journal of Marketing* 51 (October 1987): 114–115.

tariffs, designing quotas, and implementing other import regulations. However, these measures too have been restrained by international agreements that regulate trade restrictions, particularly through the World Trade Organization (WTO)(**www.wto.org**). Global trade has therefore changed many previously held notions about nation-state sovereignty and extraterritoriality. The same interdependence that has made us more affluent has also left us more vulnerable. Because this vulnerability is spread out over all major trading nations, however, some have credited international marketing with being a pillar of international peace, as *The International Marketplace 1.3* shows. Clearly, closer economic relations can result in many positive effects. At the same time, however, interdependence brings with it risks, such as dislocations of people and economic resources and a decrease in a nation's capability to do things its own way. Given the ease—and sometimes the desirability—of blaming a foreign rather than a domestic culprit for economic failure, it may well also be a key task for the international marketer to stimulate societal thinking about the long-term benefits of interdependence.

Opportunities and Challenges in International Marketing

To prosper in a world of abrupt changes and discontinuities, of newly emerging forces and dangers, of unforeseen influences from abroad, firms need to prepare themselves and develop active responses. New strategies need to be envisioned, new plans need to be made, and the way of doing business needs to be changed. The way to obtain and retain leadership, economically, politically, or morally, is—as the examples of Rome, Constantinople, and London have amply demonstrated—not through passivity but rather through a continuous, alert adaptation to the changing world environment. To help a country remain a player in the world economy, governments, firms, and individuals need to respond aggressively with innovation, process improvements, and creativity.[9]

The growth of global business activities offers increased opportunities. International activities can be crucial to a firm's survival and growth. By transferring knowledge

[9]Peter R. Dickson and Michael R. Czinkota, "How the U.S. Can Be Number One Again: Resurrecting the Industrial Policy Debate," *The Columbia Journal of World Business* 31, 3 (Fall 1996): 76–87.

THE INTERNATIONAL MARKETPLACE 1.4

A Glimpse of the World in the New Century

ONE OF THE DRIVERS behind the move toward global marketing strategies has been the notion that consumer needs are becoming more alike. Yet drastic differences in the development of the various regions of the world remain and are bound to continue existing well into the new century.

Such differences warrant differentiation in both marketing and pricing strategies. Here are just a few examples of what a baby in the Western world and one in less developed countries may face upon birth in the new millennium.

THE WESTERN BABY:

In Switzerland she will live to the age of 82, while he will live to the age of 75.

In Netherlands there is a 1% risk he will not see his fifth birthday and a 9% risk of not seeing his sixtieth.

In the United States her family's income will likely exceed $21,541 per annum.

In Canada he will share 1 square mile with eight other people.

In Italy she will be living in a city, as 90% of the population does.

THE BABY OF THE LESS DEVELOPED WORLD:

In Sierra Leone she will live to the age of 39, while he will live to the age of 36.

In Niger he will run a 9% risk of not seeing his fifth birthday and a 36% risk of not seeing his fortieth.

In Uganda her family's annual income is likely to be about $602.

In China he will share 1 square mile with 327 other people.

In India she will be living in the rural area, as 72% of the population does.

SOURCE: UN Human Development Report, Population Reference Bureau, *World Almanac; The Washington Post,* July 31, 1999, A15.

around the globe, an international firm can build and strengthen its competitive position. Firms that heavily depend on long production runs can expand their activities far beyond their domestic markets and benefit from reaching many more customers. Market saturation can be avoided by lengthening or rejuvenating product life cycles in other countries. Production sites once were inflexible, but now plants can be shifted from one country to another and suppliers can be found on every continent. Cooperative agreements can be formed that enable all parties to bring their major strengths to the table and emerge with better products, services, and ideas than they could produce on their own. In addition, research has found that multinational corporations face a lower probability of insolvency and less average risk than do domestic companies.[10] At the same time, international marketing enables consumers all over the world to find greater varieties of products at lower prices and to improve their lifestyles and comfort.

International opportunities require careful exploration. What is needed is an awareness of global developments, an understanding of their meaning, and a development of capabilities to adjust to change. Firms must adapt to the international market if they are to be successful.

One key facet of the marketing concept is adaptation to the environment, particularly the market. Even though many executives understand the need for such an adaptation in their domestic market, they often believe that international customers are just like the ones the firm deals with at home. It is here that many firms commit grave mistakes which lead to inefficiency, lack of consumer acceptance, and sometimes even corporate failure. As *The International Marketplace 1.4* shows, conditions and constraints around the world can differ substantially, which in turn requires different market plans and approaches.

[10]Israel Shaked, "Are Multinational Corporations Safer?" *Journal of International Business Studies* 17 (Spring 1986): 100.

International Trade as a Percentage of Gross Domestic Product

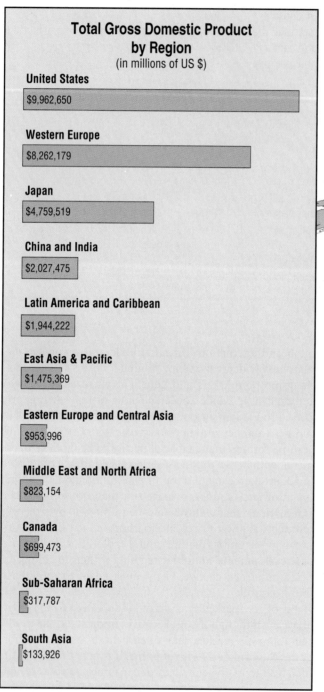

Total Gross Domestic Product by Region
(in millions of US $)

United States
$9,962,650

Western Europe
$8,262,179

Japan
$4,759,519

China and India
$2,027,475

Latin America and Caribbean
$1,944,222

East Asia & Pacific
$1,475,369

Eastern Europe and Central Asia
$953,996

Middle East and North Africa
$823,154

Canada
$699,473

Sub-Saharan Africa
$317,787

South Asia
$133,926

Source: *2001 World Development Indicators*, The World Bank.

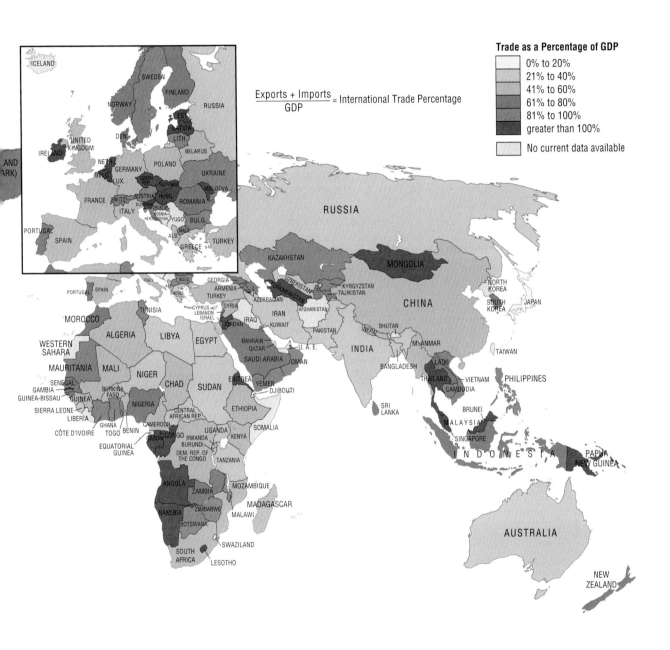

Trade as a Percentage of GDP

- 0% to 20%
- 21% to 40%
- 41% to 60%
- 61% to 80%
- 81% to 100%
- greater than 100%

No current data available

$$\frac{\text{Exports} + \text{Imports}}{\text{GDP}} = \text{International Trade Percentage}$$

Firms increasingly understand that many of the key difficulties encountered in doing business internationally are marketing problems. Judging by corporate needs, a background in international marketing is highly desirable for business students seeking employment, not only for today but also for long-term career plans.

Many firms do not participate in the global market. Often, managers believe that international marketing should only be carried out by large multinational corporations. It is true that there are some very large players from many countries active in the world market. But smaller firms are major players, too. For example, 50 percent of German exports are created by firms with 19 or fewer employees.[11] Increasingly we find smaller firms, particularly in the computer and telecommunications industries, that are born global, since they achieve a worldwide presence within a very short time.[12]

Those firms and industries that are not participating in the world market have to recognize that in today's trade environment, isolation has become impossible. Willing or unwilling, firms are becoming participants in global business affairs. Even if not by choice, most firms and individuals are affected directly or indirectly by economic and political developments that occur in the international marketplace. Those firms that refuse to participate are relegated to react to the global marketplace and therefore are unprepared for harsh competition from abroad.

Some industries have recognized the need for international adjustments. Farmers understand the need for high productivity in light of stiff international competition. Car producers, computer makers, and firms in other technologically advanced industries have learned to forge global relationships to stay in the race. Firms in the steel, textile, and leather sectors have shifted production, and perhaps even adjusted their core business, in response to overwhelming onslaughts from abroad. Other industries in some countries have been caught unaware and have been unable to adjust. The result is the extinction of firms or entire industries such as VCRs in the United States and coal mining and steel smelting in other countries.

The Goals of This Book

This book aims to make you a better, more successful participant in the international marketplace by providing information about what is going on in international markets and by helping you to translate knowledge into successful business transactions. By learning about both theory and practice, you can obtain a good conceptual understanding of the field of international marketing as well as become firmly grounded in the realities of the global marketplace. Therefore, this book approaches international marketing in the way the manager of a firm does, reflecting different levels of international involvement and the importance of business-government relations.

Firms differ widely in their international activities and needs, depending on their level of experience, resources, and capabilities. For the firm that is just beginning to enter the global market, the level of knowledge about international complexities is low, the demand on time is high, expectations about success are uncertain, and the international environment is often inflexible. Conversely, for a multinational firm that is globally oriented and employs thousands of people on each continent, much more leeway exists in terms of resource availability, experience, and information. In addition, the multinational firm has the option of responding creatively to the environment by shifting resources or even shaping the environment itself. For example, the heads of large corporations have access to government ministers to plead their case for a change in policy, an alternative that is rarely afforded to smaller firms.

[11]*Cognetics,* Cambridge, MA: 1993.

[12]Michael Kutschker, "Internationalisierung der Wirtschaft," *Perspektiven der Internationalen Wirtschaft,* Wiesbaden, Gabler GmbH, 1999: 22.

To become a large international corporation, however, a firm usually has to start out small. Similarly, to direct far-flung global operations, managers first have to learn the basics. The structure of this text reflects this reality by presenting initially a perspective of the business environment, which covers national marketing and policy issues and their cultural, economic, financial, political, and legal dimensions.

Subsequently, the book discusses in detail the beginning internationalization of the firm. The emphasis is on the needs of those who are starting out and the operational questions that are crucial to success. Some basic yet essential issues addressed are: What is the difference between domestic and international marketing? Does the applicability of marketing principles change when they are transferred to the global environment? How do marketers find out whether there is a market for a product abroad without spending a fortune in time and money on research? How can the firm promote its products in foreign markets? How do marketers find and evaluate a foreign distributor, and how do they make sure that their firm gets paid? How can marketers minimize government red tape yet take advantage of any governmental programs that are of use to them?

These questions are addressed both conceptually and empirically, with a strong focus on export and import operations. We will see how the international commitment is developed and strengthened within the firm.

Once these important dimensions have been covered, we make the transition to the multinational corporation. The focus is now on the transnational allocation of resources, the coordination of multinational marketing activities, and the attainment of global synergism. Finally, emerging issues of challenge to both policymakers and multinational firms, such as countertrade, marketing to economies in transition, and the future outlook of the global market, are discussed.

All the marketing issues are considered in relation to national policies so as to familiarize you with the divergent forces at play in the global market. Governments' increased awareness of and involvement with international marketing require managers to be aware of the role of governments and also to be able to work with them in order to attain marketing goals. Therefore, the continued references in the text to business-government interaction demonstrate a vital link in the development of international marketing strategy. In addition, we give full play to the increased ability of firms to communicate with a global market. Therefore, we develop and offer, for firms both small and large, our ideas and strategies for viable participation in electronic commerce.

We expect that this gradual approach to international marketing will permit you not only to master another academic subject, but also to become well versed in both the operational and the strategic aspects of the field. The result should be a better understanding of how the global market works and the capability to participate in the international marketing imperative.

SUMMARY

In the past three decades, world trade has expanded from $200 billion to almost $7 trillion. As a result, nations are much more affected by international business than in the past. Global linkages have made possible investment strategies and marketing alternatives that offer tremendous opportunities. Yet these changes and the speed of change also can represent threats to nations and firms.

On the policy front, decision makers have come to realize that it is very difficult to isolate domestic economic activity from international market events. Factors such as currency exchange rates, financial flows, and foreign economic actions increasingly render the policymaker powerless to implement a domestic agenda. International interdependence, which has contributed to greater affluence, has also increased our vulnerability.

Both firms and individuals are greatly affected by international trade. Whether willing or not, they are participating in global business affairs. Entire industries have been threatened in their survival as a result of international trade flows and have either adjusted to new market realities or left the market. Some individuals have lost their workplace and experienced reduced salaries. At the same time, global business changes have increased the opportunities available. Firms can now reach many more customers, product life cycles have been lengthened, sourcing policies have become variable, new jobs have been created, and consumers all over the world can find greater varieties of products at lower prices.

To benefit from the opportunities and deal with the adversities of international trade, business needs to adopt the international marketing concept. The new set of macroenvironmental factors has to be understood and responded to in order to let international markets become a source of growth, profit, and needs satisfaction.

QUESTIONS FOR DISCUSSION

1. Will expansion of world trade in the future be similar to that in the past?
2. Does increased world trade mean increased risk?
3. Is it beneficial for nations to become dependent on one another?
4. With foreign wages at one-tenth of U.S. wages, how can the United States compete?
5. Compare and contrast domestic and international marketing.
6. Why do more firms from other countries enter international markets than do U.S. firms?
7. Can you think of examples of international marketing contributing to world peace?
8. Describe some opportunities and challenges in international marketing created by new advances in information technology.
9. Using World Trade Organization data (**www.wto.org**), identify the following: a) the top ten exporting and importing countries in world merchandise trade and b) the top ten exporting and importing countries of commercial services.
10. Find the ten largest multinational corporations and briefly explain their key products. Hint: You may wish to use the websites of publications such as *Forbes, Fortune, Wirtschaftswoche*, etc.

Appendix A

Basics of Marketing

THIS APPENDIX PROVIDES a summary of the basic concepts in marketing for the reader who wishes to review them before applying them to international marketing.

The American Marketing Association defines *marketing* as "the process of planning and executing the conception, pricing, promotion, and distribution of ideas, goods, and services to create exchanges that satisfy individual and organizational goals."[1] The concepts of satisfaction and exchange are at the core of marketing. For an exchange to take place, two or more parties must come together in person, through the mail, or through technology, and they must communicate and deliver things of perceived value. Potential customers should be perceived as information seekers who evaluate marketers' efforts in terms of their own drives and needs. When the offering is consistent with their needs, they tend to choose the product; if it is not, they choose other alternatives. A key task of the marketer is to recognize the ever-changing nature of needs and wants. Increasingly, the goal of marketing has been expanded from sensing, serving, and satisfying individual customers to taking into consideration the long-term interests of society.

Marketing is not limited to business entities but involves governmental and nonbusiness units as well. Marketing techniques are applied not only to goods but also to ideas (for example, the "Made in the U.S.A." campaign) and to services (for example, international advertising agencies). The term *business marketing* is used for activities directed at other businesses, governmental entities, and various types of institutions. Business marketing accounts for well over 50 percent of all marketing activities.

Strategic Marketing

The marketing manager's task is to plan and execute programs that will ensure a long-term competitive advantage for the company. This task has two integral parts: (1) the determining of specific target markets, and (2) marketing management, which consists of manipulating marketing mix elements to best satisfy the needs of individual target markets.

Target Market Selection

Characteristics of intended target markets are of critical importance to the marketer. These characteristics can be summarized by eight Os: occupants, objects, occasions, objectives, outlets, organization, operations, and opposition.[2]

[1] Peter D. Bennett, ed., *Dictionary of Marketing Terms*, 2nd ed. (Chicago: American Marketing Association, 1995), 166.

[2] Philip Kotler presents the eight Os in the sixth edition of *Marketing Management: Analysis, Planning, and Control* (Englewood Cliffs, NJ: Prentice-Hall, 1988), 174–175.

Occupants are targets of the marketing effort. The marketer must determine which customers to approach and also define them along numerous dimensions, such as demographics (age, sex, and nationality, for example), geography (country or region), psychographics (attitudes, interests, and opinions), or product-related variables (usage rate and brand loyalty, for example). Included in this analysis must be the major influences on the occupants during their buying processes.

Objects are what is being bought at present to satisfy a particular need. Included in this concept are physical objects, services, ideas, organizations, places, and persons.

Occasions are moments when members of the target market buy the product or service. This characteristic is important to the marketer because a product's consumption may be tied to a particular time period—for example, imported beer and a festival.

Objectives are the motivations behind the purchase or adoption of the marketed concept. A computer manufacturer markets not hardware but solutions to problems. Additionally, many customers look for hidden value in the product they purchase, which may be expressed, for example, through national origin of the product or through brand name.

Outlets are places where customers expect to be able to procure a product or to be exposed to messages about it. Outlets include not only the entities themselves but also location within a particular place. Although aseptic packaging made it possible to shelve milk outside the refrigerated area in supermarkets, customers' acceptance of the arrangement was not automatic: the product was not where it was supposed to be. In the area of services, outlet involves (1) making a particular service available and communicating its availability, and (2) selecting the particular types of facilitators (such as brokers) who bring the parties together.

Organization describes how the buying or acceptance of a (new) idea takes place. Organization expands the analysis beyond the individual consumer to the decision-making unit (DMU). The DMU varies in terms of its size and its nature from relatively small and informal groups like a family to large groups (more than ten people) to formal buying committees. Compare, for example, the differences between a family buying a new home-entertainment center and the governing board at a university deciding which architectural firm to use. In either case, to develop proper products and services, the marketer should know as much as possible about the decision-making processes and the roles of various individuals.

Operations represents the behavior of the organization buying products and services. Increasingly, industrial organizations are concentrating their purchases with fewer suppliers and making longer-term commitments. Supermarkets may make available only the leading brands in a product category, thereby complicating the marketer's attempts to place new products in these outlets.

Opposition refers to the competition to be faced in the marketplace. The nature of competition will vary from direct product-type competition to competition from other products that satisfy the same need. For example, Prince tennis rackets face a threat not only from other racket manufacturers but also from any company that provides a product or service for leisure-time use. Competitive situations will vary from one market and from one segment to the next. Gillette is number one in the U.S. market for disposable razors, with Bic a distant runner-up; however, elsewhere, particularly in Europe, the roles are reversed. In the long term, threats may come from outside the industry in which the marketer operates. As an example, digital watches originated in the electronics industry rather than the watch industry.

Analyzing the eight Os, and keeping in mind other uncontrollable factors in the environment (cultural, political, legal, technological, societal, and economic), the marketer must select the markets to which efforts will be targeted. In the short term, the marketer has to adjust to these environmental forces; in the long term, they can be manipulated to some extent by judicious marketing activity. Consumerism, one of the major forces shaping marketing activities, is concerned with protecting the consumer whenever an exchange relationship exists with any type of organization. Manifestations of the impact of consumerism on marketing exist in labeling, product specifications, promotional campaigns, recycling expectations, and demands for environmentally friendly products.

Because every marketer operates in a corporate environment of scarcity and comparative strengths, the target market decision is a crucial one. In some cases, the marketer may select only one segment of the market (for example, motorcycles of +1,000 cc) or multiple segments (for example, all types of motorized two-wheeled vehicles), or the firm may opt for an undifferentiated product that is to be mass-marketed (for example, unbranded commodities or products that satisfy the same need worldwide, such as Coca-Cola).

Marketing Management

The marketing manager, having analyzed the characteristics of the target market(s), is in a position to specify the mix of marketing variables that will best serve each target market. The variables the marketing manager controls are known as the elements of the marketing mix, or the four Ps: product, price, place, and promotion.[3] Each consists of a submix of variables, and policy decisions must be made on each.

Product policy is concerned with all the elements that make up the good, service, or idea that is offered by the marketer. Included are all possible tangible characteristics (such as the core product and packaging) and intangible characteristics (such as branding and warranties). Many products are a combination of a concrete product and the accompanying service; for example, in buying an Otis elevator, the purchaser buys not only the product but an extensive service contract as well.

Pricing policy determines the cost of the product to the customer—a point somewhere between the floor created by the costs to the firm and the ceiling created by the strength of demand. An important consideration of pricing policy is pricing within the channel of distribution; margins to be made by the middlemen who assist in the marketing effort must be taken into account. Discounts to middlemen include functional, quantity, seasonal, and cash discounts, as well as promotional allowances. An important point to remember is that *price* is the only revenue-generating element of the marketing mix.

Distribution policy covers the *place* variable of the marketing mix and has two components: channel management and logistics management. Channel management is concerned with the entire process of setting up and operating the contractual organization, consisting of various types of middlemen (such as wholesalers, agents, retailers, and facilitators). Logistics management is focused on providing product availability at appropriate times and places in the marketing channel.[4] Place is the most long term of all the marketing mix elements; it is the most difficult to change in the short term.

Communications policy uses *promotion* tools to interact with customers, middlemen, and the public at large. The communications element consists of these tools: advertising, sales promotion, personal selling, and publicity. Because the purpose of all communications is to persuade, this is the most visible and sensitive of the marketing mix elements.

Blending the various elements into a coherent program requires trade-offs based on the type of product or service being offered (for example, detergents versus fighter aircraft), the stage of the product's life cycle (a new product versus one that is being revived), and resources available for the marketing effort (money and personnel), as well as the type of customer at whom the marketing efforts are directed.

[3]The four Ps were popularized by E. Jerome McCarthy. See E. Jerome McCarthy and William Perreault, *Basic Marketing: A Managerial Approach,* 9th ed. (Homewood, IL: Irwin, 1987).

[4]Bert Rosenbloom, *Marketing Channels: A Management View,* 5th ed. (Fort Worth, TX: The Dryden Press, 1995).

The Marketing Process

The actual process of marketing consists of four stages: analysis, planning, implementation, and control.

Analysis begins with collecting data on the eight Os and using various quantitative and qualitative techniques of marketing research. Data sources will vary from secondary to primary, internal to external (to the company), and informal to formal. The data are used to determine company opportunities by screening a plethora of environmental opportunities. The company opportunities must then be checked against the company's resources to judge their viability. The key criterion is competitive advantage.

Planning refers to the blueprint generated to react to and exploit the opportunities in the marketplace. The planning stage involves both long-term strategies and short-term tactics. A marketing plan developed for a particular market includes a situation analysis, objectives and goals to be met, strategies and tactics, and cost and profit estimates. Included in the activity is the formation of a new organizational structure or adjustments in the existing one to prepare for the execution of the plan.

Implementation is the actual carrying out of the planned activity. If the plans drawn reflect market conditions, and if they are based on realistic assessments of the company's fit into the market, the implementation process will be a success. Plans must take into account unforeseeable changes within the company and environmental forces and allow for corresponding changes to occur in implementing the plans.

For this reason, concurrently with implementation, *control* mechanisms must be put into effect. The marketplace is ever dynamic and requires the monitoring of environmental forces, competitors, channel participants, and customer receptiveness. Short-term control tools include annual plan control (such as comparing actual sales to quota), profitability control, and efficiency control. Long-term control is achieved through comprehensive or functional audits to make sure that marketing not only is doing things right but is doing the right things. The results of the control effort provide valuable input for subsequent planning efforts.

These marketing basics do not vary, regardless of the type of market one is planning to enter or to continue to operate within. They have been called the "technical universals" of marketing.[5] The different environments in which the marketing manager must operate will give varying emphases to the variables and will cause the values of the variables to change.

---

[5]Robert Bartels, "Are Domestic and International Marketing Dissimilar?" *Journal of Marketing* 36 (July 1968): 56–61.

Appendix B

Geographical Perspectives on International Marketing

THE GLOBALIZATION OF BUSINESS has made geography indispensable for the study of international marketing. Without significant attention to the study of geography, critical ideas and information about the world in which business occurs will be missing.

Just as the study of business has changed significantly in recent decades, so has the study of geography. Once considered by many to be simply a descriptive inventory that filled in blank spots on maps, geography has emerged as an analytical approach that uses scientific methods to answer important questions.

Geography focuses on answering "Where?" questions. Where are things located? What is their distribution across the surface of the earth? An old aphorism holds, "If you can map it, it's geography." That statement is true, because we use maps to gather, store, analyze, and present information that answers "Where?" questions. Identifying where things are located is only the first phase of geographic inquiry. Once locations have been determined, "Why?" and "How?" questions can be asked. Why are things located where they are? How do different things relate to one another at a specific place? How do different places relate to each other? How have geographic patterns and relationships changed over time? These are the questions that take geography beyond mere description and make it a powerful approach for analyzing and explaining geographical aspects of a wide range of different kinds of problems faced by those engaged in international marketing.

Geography answers questions related to the location of different kinds of economic activity and the transactions that flow across national boundaries. It provides insights into the natural and human factors that influence patterns of production and consumption in different parts of the world. It explains why patterns of trade and exchange evolve over time. And because a geographic perspective emphasizes the analysis of processes that result in different geographic patterns, it provides a means for assessing how patterns might change in the future.

Geography has a rich tradition. Classical Greeks, medieval Arabs, enlightened European explorers, and twentieth-century scholars in the United States and elsewhere have organized geographic knowledge in many different ways. In recent decades, however, geography has become more familiar and more relevant to many people because emphasis has been placed on five fundamental themes as ways to structure

NOTE: This appendix was contributed by Thomas J. Baerwald. Dr. Baerwald is deputy assistant director for the geosciences at the National Science Foundation in Arlington, Virginia. He is co-author of *Prentice-Hall World Geography*—a best-selling geography textbook.

SOURCES: Darrell Delamaide, *The New Superregions of Europe* (New York: Dutton, a division of Penguin Books, 1994); Joel Garreau, *The Nine Nations of North America* (New York: Houghton Mifflin Co., 1981).

geographic questions and to provide answers for those questions. Those themes are (1) location, (2) place, (3) interaction, (4) movement, and (5) region. The five themes are neither exclusive nor exhaustive. They complement other disciplinary approaches for organizing information, some of which are better suited to addressing specific kinds of questions. Other questions require insights related to two or more of the themes. Experience has shown, however, that the five themes provide a powerful means for introducing students to the geographic perspective. As a result, they provide the structure for this discussion.

Location

For decades, people engaged in real estate development have said that the value of a place is a product of three factors: location, location, and location. This statement also highlights the importance of location for international marketing. Learning the location and characteristics of other places has always been important to those interested in conducting business outside their local areas. The drive to learn about other kinds of places, and especially their resources and potential as markets, has stimulated geographic exploration throughout history. Explorations of the Mediterranean by the Phoenicians, Marco Polo's journey to China, and voyages undertaken by Christopher Columbus, Vasco da Gama, Henry Hudson, and James Cook not only improved general knowledge of the world but also expanded business opportunities.

Assessing the role of location requires more than simply determining specific locations where certain activities take place. Latitude and longitude often are used to fix the exact location of features on the earth's surface, but to simply describe a place's coordinates provides relatively little information about that place. Of much greater significance is its location relative to other features. The city of Singapore, for example, is between 1 and 2 degrees North latitude and is just west of 104 degrees East longitude. Its most pertinent locational characteristics, however, include its being at the southern tip of the Malay Peninsula near the eastern end of the Strait of Malacca, a critical shipping route connecting the Indian Ocean with the South China Sea. For nearly 150 years, this location made Singapore an important center for trade in the British Empire. After it attained independence in 1965, Singapore's leaders diversified its economy and complemented trade in its bustling port with numerous manufacturing plants that export products to nations around the world.

An understanding of the way location influences business therefore is critical for the international marketing executive. Without clear knowledge of an enterprise's location relative to its suppliers, to its market, and to its competitors, an executive operates like the captain of a fog-bound vessel that has lost all navigational instruments and is heading for dangerous shoals.

Place

In addition to its location, each place has a diverse set of characteristics. Although many of those characteristics are present in other places, the ensemble makes each place unique. The characteristics of places—both natural and human—profoundly influence the ways that business executives in different places participate in international economic transactions.

Natural Features

Many of the characteristics of a place relate to its natural attributes. **Geologic characteristics** can be especially important, as the presence of critical minerals or energy resources may make a place a world-renowned supplier of valuable products. Gold and diamonds help make South Africa's economy the most prosperous on that continent. Rich deposits of iron ore in southern parts of the Amazon Basin have made Brazil the world's leading exporter of that commodity, while Chile remains a preeminent exporter of copper. Coal deposits provided the foundation for massive industrial development in the eastern United States, in the Rhine River Basin of Europe, in western Russia, and in northeastern China. Because of abundant pools of petroleum beneath desert sands, standards of living in Saudi Arabia and nearby nations have risen rapidly to be among the highest in the world.

The geology of places also shapes its **terrain.** People traditionally have clustered in lower, flatter areas, because valleys and plains have permitted the agricultural development necessary to feed the local population and to generate surpluses that can be traded. Hilly and mountainous areas may support some people, but their population densities invariably are lower. Terrain also plays a critical role in focusing and inhibiting the movement of people and goods. Business leaders throughout the centuries have capitalized on this fact. Just as feudal masters sought control of mountain passes in order to collect tolls and other duties from traders who traversed an area, modern executives maintain stores and offer services near bridges and at other points where terrain focuses travel.

The terrain of a place is related to its **hydrology.** Rivers, lakes, and other bodies of water influence the kinds of economic activities that occur in a place. In general, abundant supplies of water boost economic development, because water is necessary for the sustenance of people and for both agricultural and industrial production. Locations like Los Angeles and Saudi Arabia have prospered despite having little local water, because other features offer advantages that more than exceed the additional costs incurred in delivering water supplies from elsewhere. While sufficient water must be available to meet local needs, overabundance of water may pose serious problems, such as in Bangladesh, where development has been inhibited by frequent flooding. The character of a place's water bodies also is important. Smooth-flowing streams and placid lakes can stimulate transportation within a place and connect it more easily with other places, while waterfalls and rapids can prevent navigation on streams. The rapid drop in elevation of such streams may boost their potential for hydroelectric power generation, however, thereby stimulating development of industries requiring considerable amounts of electricity. Large plants producing aluminum, for example, are found in the Tennessee and Columbia river valleys of the United States and in Quebec and British Columbia in Canada. These plants refine materials that originally were extracted elsewhere, especially bauxite and alumina from Caribbean nations like Jamaica and the Dominican Republic. Although the transport costs incurred in delivery of these materials to the plants is high, those costs are more than offset by the presence of abundant and inexpensive electricity.

Climate is another natural feature that has profound impact on economic activity within a place. Many activities are directly affected by climate. Locales blessed with pleasant climates, such as the Cote d'Azur of France, the Crimean Peninsula of Ukraine, Florida, and the "Gold Coast" of northeastern Australia, have become popular recreational havens, attracting tourists whose spending fuels the local economy. Agricultural production is also influenced by climate. The average daily and evening temperatures, the amount and timing of precipitation, the timing of frosts and freezing weather, and the variability of weather from one year to the next all influence the kinds of crops grown in an area. Plants producing bananas and sugar cane flourish in moist tropical areas, while cooler climates are more conducive for crops such as wheat and potatoes. Climate influences other industries as well. The aircraft manufacturing industry in the United States developed largely in warmer, drier areas, where conditions for test and delivery flights were more beneficial throughout the year. In a similar way, major rocket-launching facilities have been placed in locations where climatic conditions are most favorable. As a result, the primary launch site of the European Space Agency is not in Europe at all, but rather in the South American territory of

French Guiana. Climate also affects the length of the work day and the length of economic seasons. For example, in some regions of the world, the construction industry can build only during a few months of the year because permafrost makes construction prohibitively expensive the rest of the year.

Variations in **soils** have a profound impact on agricultural production. The world's great grain-exporting regions, including the central United States, the Prairie Provinces of Canada, the "Fertile Triangle" stretching from central Ukraine through southern Russia into northern Kazakhstan, and the Pampas of northern Argentina, all have been blessed with mineral-rich soils made even more fertile by humus from natural grasslands that once dominated the landscape. Soils are less fertile in much of the Amazon Basin of Brazil and in central Africa, where heavy rains leave few nutrients in upper layers of the soil. As a result, few commercial crops are grown.

The **interplay between climate and soils** is especially evident in the production of wines. Hundreds of varieties of grapes have been bred in order to take advantage of the different physical characteristics of various places. The wines fermented from these grapes are shipped around the world to consumers, who differentiate among various wines based not only on the grapes but also on the places where they were grown and the conditions during which they matured.

Human Features

The physical features of a place provide natural resources and influence the types of economic activities in which people engage, but its human characteristics also are critical. The **population** of a place is important because farm production may require intensive labor to be successful, as is true in rice-growing areas of eastern Asia. The skills and qualifications of the population also play a role in determining how a place fits into global economic affairs. Although blessed with few mineral resources and a terrain and climate that limit agricultural production, the Swiss have emphasized high levels of education and training in order to maintain a labor force that manufactures sophisticated products for export around the world. In recent decades, Japan and smaller nations such as South Korea and Taiwan have increased the productivity of their workers to become major industrial exporters.

As people live in a place, they modify it, creating a **built environment** that can be as important as or more important than the natural environment in economic terms. The most pronounced areas of human activity and their associated structures are in cities. In nations around the world, cities grew dramatically during the twentieth century. Much of the growth of cities has resulted from the migration of people from rural areas. This influx of new residents broadens the labor pool and creates vast new demand for goods and services. As urban populations have grown, residences and other facilities have replaced rural land uses. Executives seeking to conduct business in foreign cities need to be aware that the geographic patterns found in their home cities are not evident in many other nations. For example, in the United States, wealthier residents generally have moved out of cities, and as they established their residences, stores and services followed. Residential patterns in the major cities of Latin America and other developing nations tend to be reversed, with the wealthy remaining close to the city center while poorer residents are consigned to the outskirts of town. A store location strategy that is successful in the United States therefore may fail miserably if transferred directly to another nation without knowledge of the different geographic patterns of that nation's cities.

Interaction

The international marketing professional seeking to take advantage of opportunities present in different places learns not to view each place separately. The way a place functions depends not only on the presence and form of certain characteristics but also on interactions among those characteristics. Fortuitous combinations of features can spur a region's economic development. The presence of high-grade supplies of iron ore, coal, and limestone powered the growth of Germany's Ruhr Valley as one of Europe's foremost steel-producing regions, just as the proximity of the fertile Pampas and the deep channel of the Rio de la Plata combine to make Buenos Aires the leading economic center in southern South America.

Interactions among different features change over time within places, and as they do, so does that place's character and its economic activities. Human activities can have profound impacts on natural features. The courses of rivers and streams are changed as dams are erected and meanders are straightened. Soil fertility can be improved through fertilization. Vegetation is changed, with naturally growing plants replaced by crops and other varieties that require careful management.

Many human modifications have been successful. For centuries, the Dutch have constructed dikes and drainage systems, slowly creating polders—land that once was covered by the North Sea but that now is used for agricultural production. But other human activities have had disastrous impacts on natural features. A large area in Ukraine and Belarus was rendered uninhabitable by radioactive materials leaked from the Chernobyl reactor in 1986. In countless other places around the globe, improper disposal of wastes has seriously harmed land and water resources. In some places, damage can be repaired, as has happened in rivers and lakes of the United States following the passage of measures to curb water pollution in the last three decades, but in other locales, restoration may be impossible.

Growing concerns about environmental quality have led many people in more economically advanced nations to call for changes in economic systems that harm the natural environment. Concerted efforts are under way, for example, to halt destruction of forests in the Amazon Basin, thereby preserving the vast array of different plant and animal species in the region and saving vegetation that can help moderate the world's climate. Cooperative ventures have been established to promote selective harvesting of nuts, hardwoods, and other products taken from natural forests. Furthermore, an increasing number of restaurants and grocers are refusing to purchase beef raised on pastures that are established by clearing forests.

Like so many other geographical relationships, the nature of human-environmental interaction changes over time. With technological advances, people have been able to modify and adapt to natural features in increasingly sophisticated ways. The development of air conditioning has permitted people to function more effectively in torrid tropical environments, thereby enabling the populations of cities such as Houston, Rio de Janeiro, and Jakarta to multiply many times over in recent decades. Owners of winter resorts now can generate snow artificially to ensure favorable conditions for skiers. Advanced irrigation systems now permit crops to be grown in places such as the southwestern United States, northern Africa, and Israel. The use of new technologies may cause serious problems over the long run, however. Extensive irrigation in large parts of the U.S. Great Plains has seriously depleted groundwater supplies. In central Asia, the diversion of river water to irrigate cotton fields in Kazakhstan and Uzbekistan has reduced the size of the Aral Sea by more than one-half since 1960. In future years, business leaders may need to factor into their decisions the additional costs associated with the restoration of environmental quality after they have finished using a place's resources.

Movement

Whereas the theme of interaction encourages consideration of different characteristics within a place, movement provides a structure for considering how different places relate to each other. International marketing exists because movement permits the transportation of people and goods and communication of information and ideas among different places. No matter how much people in one place want something found elsewhere, they cannot have it unless transportation systems permit the good to be brought to them or allow them to move to the location of the good.

The location and character of transportation and communication systems long have had powerful influences on the economic standing of places. Especially significant have been places on which transportation routes have focused. Many ports have become prosperous cities because they channeled the movement of goods and people between ocean and inland waterways. New York became the largest city in North America because its harbor provided sheltered anchorage for ships crossing the Atlantic; the Hudson River provided access leading into the interior of the continent. In eastern Asia, Hong Kong grew under similar circumstances, as British traders used its splendid harbor as an exchange point for goods moving in and out of southern China.

Businesses also have succeeded at well-situated places along overland routes. The fabled oasis of Tombouctou has been an important trading center for centuries because it had one of the few dependable sources of water in the Sahara. Chicago's ascendancy as the premier city of the U.S. heartland came when its early leaders engineered its selection as the termination point for a dozen railroad lines converging from all directions. Not only did much of the rail traffic moving through the region have to pass through Chicago, but passengers and freight passing through the city had to be transferred from one line to another. This process generated numerous jobs and added considerably to the wealth of many businesses in the city.

In addition to the business associated directly with the movement of people and goods, other forms of economic activity have become concentrated at critical points in the transportation network. Places where transfers from one mode of transportation to another were required often were chosen as sites for manufacturing activities. Buffalo was the most active flour-milling center in the United States for much of the twentieth century because it was the point where Great Lakes freighters carrying wheat from the northern Great Plains and Canadian prairies were unloaded. Rather than simply transfer the wheat into rail cars for shipment to the large urban markets of the northeastern United States, millers transformed the wheat into flour in Buffalo, thereby reducing the additional handling of the commodity.

Global patterns of resource refining also demonstrate the wisdom of careful selection of sites with respect to transportation systems. Some of the world's largest oil refineries are located at places like Bahrain and Houston, where pipeliners bring oil to points where it is processed and loaded onto ships in the form of gasoline or other distillates for transport to other locales. Massive refinery complexes also have been built in the Tokyo and Nagoya areas of Japan and near Rotterdam in the Netherlands to process crude oil brought by giant tankers from the Middle East and other oil-exporting regions. For similar reasons, the largest new steel mills in the United States are near Baltimore and Philadelphia, where iron ore shipped from Canada and Brazil is processed. Some of the most active aluminum works in Europe are beside Norwegian fjords, where abundant local hydroelectric power is used to process imported alumina.

Favorable location along transportation lines is beneficial for a place. Conversely, an absence of good transportation severely limits the potential for firms to succeed in a specific place. Transportation patterns change over time, however, and so does their impact on places. Some places maintain themselves because their business leaders use their size and economic power to become critical nodes in newly evolving transportation networks. New York's experience provides a good example of this process. New York became the United States' foremost business center in the early nineteenth century because it was ideally situated for water transportation. As railroad networks evolved later in that century, they sought New York connections in order to serve its massive market. During the twentieth century, a complex web of roadways and major airports reinforced New York's supremacy in the eastern United States. In similar ways, London, Moscow, and Tokyo reasserted themselves as transportation hubs for their nations through successive advances in transport technology.

Failure to adapt to changing transportation patterns can have harmful impacts on a place. During the middle of the nineteenth century, business leaders in St. Louis discouraged railroad construction, seeking instead to maintain the supremacy of river transportation. Only after it became clear that railroads were the mode of preference did St. Louis officials seek to develop rail connections for the city, but by then it was too late; Chicago had ascended to a dominant position in the region. For about 30 years during the middle part of the twentieth century, airports at Gander (Newfoundland, Canada) and Shannon (Ireland) became important refueling points for transatlantic flights. The development of planes that could travel nonstop for much longer distances returned those places to sleepy oblivion.

Continuing advances in transportation technology have effectively "shrunk" the world. Just a few centuries ago, travel across an ocean took harrowing months. As late as 1873, readers marveled when Jules Verne wrote of a hectic journey around the world in 80 days. Today's travelers can fly around the globe in less than 80 hours, and the speed and dependability of modern modes of transport have transformed the ways in which business is conducted. Modern manufacturers have transformed the notion of relationships among suppliers, manufacturers, and markets. Automobile manufacturers, for example, once maintained large stockpiles of parts in assembly plants that were located near the parts plants or close to the places where the cars would be sold. Contemporary auto assembly plants now are built in places where labor costs and worker productivity are favorable and where governments have offered attractive inducements. They keep relatively few parts on hand, calling on suppliers for rapid delivery of parts as they are needed when orders for new cars are received. This "just-in-time" system of production leaves manufacturers subject to disruptions caused by work stoppages at supply plants and to weather-related delays in the transportation system, but losses associated with these infrequent events are more than offset by reduced operating costs under normal conditions.

The role of advanced technology and its effect on international marketing is even more apparent with respect to advances in communications systems. Sophisticated forms of telecommunication that began more than 150 years ago with the telegraph have advanced through the telephone to facsimile transmissions and electronic mail networks. As a result, distance has practically ceased to be a consideration with respect to the transmission of information. Whereas information once moved only as rapidly as the person carrying the paper on which the information was written, data and ideas now can be sent instantaneously almost anywhere in the world.

These communication advances have had a staggering impact on the way that international marketing is conducted. They have fostered the growth of multinational corporations, which operate in diverse sites around the globe while maintaining effective links with headquarters and regional control centers. International financial operations also have been transformed because of communication advances. Money and stock markets in New York, London, Tokyo, and secondary markets such as Los Angeles, Frankfurt, and Hong Kong now are connected by computer systems that process transactions around the clock. As much as any other factor, the increasingly mobile forms of money have enabled modern business executives to engage in activities around the world.

Region

In addition to considering places by themselves or how they relate to other places, regions provide alternative ways to organize groups of places in more meaningful ways. A region is a set of places that share certain characteristics. Many regions are defined by characteristics that all of the places in the group have in common. When economic characteristics are used, the delimited regions include places with similar kinds of economic activity. Agricultural regions include areas where certain farm products dominate. Corn is grown throughout the "Corn Belt" of the central United States, for example, although many farmers in the region also plant soybeans and many raise hogs. Regions where intensive industrial production is a prominent part of local economic activity include the manufacturing belts of the northeastern United States, southern Canada, northwestern Europe, and southern Japan.

Regions can also be defined by patterns of movement. Transportation or communication linkages among places may draw them together into configurations that differentiate them from other locales. Studies by economic geographers of the locational tendencies of modern high-technology industries have identified complex networks of firms that provide products and services to each other. Because of their linkages, these firms cluster together into well-defined regions. The "Silicon Valley" of northern California, the "Western Crescent" on the outskirts of London, and "Technopolis" of the Tokyo region all are distinguished as much by connections among firms as by the economic landscapes they have established.

Economic aspects of movement may help define functional regions by establishing areas where certain types of economic activity are more profitable than others. In the early nineteenth century, German landowner Johann Heinrich von Thünen demonstrated how different costs for transporting various agricultural goods to market helped to define regions where certain forms of farming would occur. Although theoretically simple, patterns predicted by von Thünen can still be found in the world today. Goods such as vegetables and dairy products that require more intensive production and are more expensive to ship are produced closer to markets, while less demanding goods and commodities that can be transported at lower costs come from more remote production areas. Advances in transportation have dramatically altered such regional patterns. Once, a New York City native enjoyed fresh vegetables and fruits only in the summer and early autumn when New Jersey, upstate New York, and New England producers brought their goods to market. Today, New Yorkers buy fresh produce year-round, with new shipments flown in daily from Florida, California, Chile, and even more remote locations during the colder months.

Governments have a strong impact on the conduct of business, and the formal borders of government jurisdictions often coincide with the functional boundaries of economic regions. The divisive character of these lines on the map has been altered in many parts of the world in recent decades. The formation of common markets and free trade areas in Western Europe and North America has dramatically changed the patterns and flows of economic activity, and similar kinds of formal restructuring of relationships among nations likely will continue into the next century. As a result, business analysts increasingly need to consider regions that cross international boundaries.

Some of the most innovative views of regional organization essentially have ignored existing national boundaries. In 1981, Joel Garreau published a book titled *The Nine Nations of North America,* which subdivided the continent into a set of regions based on economic activities and cultural outlooks. Seven of Garreau's nine regions include territory in at least two nations. In the Southwest, "Mexamerica" recognized the bicultural heritage of Anglo and Hispanic groups and the increasingly close economic ties across the U.S.-Mexican border that were spurred by the *maquiladora* and other export-oriented programs. The evolution of this region as a distinctive collection of places has been accelerated by the passage of the North American Free Trade Agreement (NAFTA). Another cross-national region identified by Garreau is "The Islands," a collection of nations in the Caribbean for which Miami has become the functional "capital." Many business leaders seeking to tap into this rapidly growing area have become knowledgeable of the laws and customs of those nations. They often have done so by employing émigrés from those nations who may now be U.S. citizens but whose primary language is not English and whose outlook on the region is multinational.

In a similar vein, Darrell Delamaide's 1994 book entitled *The New Superregions of Europe* divides the continent into ten regions based on economic, cultural, and social affinities that have evolved over centuries. His vision of Europe challenges regional structures that persist from earlier times. Seen by many as a single region known as Eastern Europe, the formerly communist nations west of what once was the Soviet Union are seen by Delamaide as being part of five different "superregions": "The Baltic League," a group of nations clustered around the Baltic Sea; "Mitteleuropa," the economic heartland of northern Europe; "The Slavic Federation," a region dominated by Russia with a common Slavic heritage; "The Danube Basin," a mélange of places along and near Europe's longest river; and "The Balkan Peninsula," a region characterized by political turmoil and less-advanced economies.

Delamaide's book has been as controversial as Garreau's was a decade earlier. In both cases, however, the value of the ideas they presented was measured not in terms of the "accuracy" of the regional structures they presented, but rather by their ability to lead more people to take a geographic perspective of the modern world and the way it functions. The regions defined by Garreau and Delamaide are not those described by traditional geographers, but they reflect the views of many business leaders who have learned to look across national boundaries in their search for opportunities. As marketing increasingly becomes international, the most successful entrepreneurs will be the ones who complement their business acumen with effective application of geographic information and principles.

For online activities, visit the following Web sites:

http://geography.state.gov/htmls/plugin.html
http://www.state.gov/www/regions/independent_states.html

Chapter 2

International Trade Institutions and U.S. Trade Policy

THE INTERNATIONAL MARKETPLACE 2.1

Who Should Regulate E-Commerce?

E-COMMERCE HAS INCREASING INFLUENCE on international trade systems. In the United States alone the value of business-to-business goods and services trade via the Internet is predicted to reach $183 billion in 2001, compared to only $8 billion in 1997.

Some governments in Europe and Asia believe that regulation and state control will aid in the development of the Internet. Such regulation, they claim, protects Internet consumers from fraud. This point of view is in contradiction to the United States' current policy that the e-commerce market should primarily police itself. U.S. Senator Joseph Lieberman and Representative Ellen Tauscher urged caution in regulating international e-commerce, saying "The Internet allows for buyers and sellers from different countries to meet and do business to an unprecedented degree, but because the technology is so new, the legal questions created by cross-border business-to-consumer transactions are very much undecided."

As countries begin to adopt an array of different rules and regulations, consistency needs to be established. To solve cross-border disputes in Europe the EU commission has proposed a system that favors the enforcement of the laws of the country in which the transaction originated. However, European businesses seem to disagree. In a strong statement regarding the potential to build wealth in a global e-commerce environment, Bertelsmann AG chairman Thomas Middelhoff said, "It can't happen if the digital realm is choked in an entanglement of local regulation."

While governments throughout the world support varying levels of regulation, an international group of executives has united to oppose Internet taxes and restrictions on data exports. This group, working together as the Global Business Dialogue on Electronic Commerce, has pushed for the adoption of a "seal of approval" for websites that protect consumer privacy. It has also advocated third-party arbitration in solving e-commerce disputes.

It seems clear that some supervision is needed to ensure fairness and privacy. What is unclear is who should conduct such supervision—domestic governments, international organizations such as the WTO, or a newly formed supranational group.

SOURCES: Andy Sullivan, "Hands Off e-Commerce, Democratic Lawmakers Say," *Reuters*, March 15, 2001; Victoria Shannon, "CEO's Lobby for E-Commerce; Technology Chiefs Call for Restraint in Regulation of Internet," *The Washington Post*, September 14, 1999, E3; Woranuj Maneerungsee, "E-Commerce—Electronic Trade to Be Encouraged," *The Bangkok Post*, October 20, 1999, News 1; Chris Philips, "A More Sensible Approach to Legislating for E-Commerce Security Is Emerging," *New Media Age*, July 8, 1999, New Media Vision 8.

T HE INTERNATIONAL ENVIRONMENT is changing rapidly. Firms, individuals, and policymakers are affected by these changes. As *The International Marketplace 2.1* shows, these changes offer new opportunities but also represent new challenges. Although major economic and security shifts will have a profound impact on the world, coping with them successfully through imagination, investment, and perseverance can produce a new, better world order and an improved quality of life.

This chapter begins by highlighting the importance of trade to humankind. Selected historical developments that were triggered or influenced by international trade are delineated. Subsequently, more recent trade developments are presented, together with the international institutions that have emerged to regulate and facilitate trade.

The chapter will analyze and discuss the position of the United States in the world trade environment and explain the impact of trade on the United States. Various efforts undertaken by governments to manage trade by restricting or promoting exports, imports, technology transfer, and investments will be described. Finally, the chapter will present a strategic outlook for future developments in trade relations.

The Historical Dimension

Many peoples throughout history have gained preeminence in the world through their trade activities. Among them were the Etruscans, Phoenicians, Egyptians, Chinese, Spaniards, and Portuguese. To underscore the role of trade, we will take a closer look at some selected examples.

One of the major world powers in ancient history was the Roman Empire. Its impact on thought, knowledge, and development can still be felt today. Even while expanding their territories through armed conflicts, the Romans placed primary emphasis on encouraging international business activities. The principal approaches used to implement this emphasis were the **Pax Romana,** or the Roman Peace, and the common coinage. The Pax Romana ensured that merchants were able to travel safely on roads that were built, maintained, and protected by the Roman legions and their affiliated troops. The common coinage, in turn, ensured that business transactions could be carried out easily throughout the empire. In addition, Rome developed a systematic law, central market locations through the founding of cities, and an excellent communication system that resembled an early version of the Pony Express; all of these measures contributed to the functioning of the international marketplace and to the reduction of business uncertainty. As a result, economic well-being within the empire rose sharply compared to the outside.

Soon, city-nations and tribes that were not part of the empire wanted to share in the benefits of belonging. They joined the empire as allies and agreed to pay tribute and taxes. Thus, the immense growth of the Roman Empire occurred through the linkages of business rather than through the marching of its legions and warfare. Of course, the Romans had to engage in substantial efforts to facilitate business in order to make it worthwhile for others to belong. For example, when pirates threatened the seaways, Rome, under Pompeius, sent out a large fleet to subdue them. The cost of international distribution, and therefore the cost of international marketing, was substantially reduced because fewer goods were lost to pirates. As a result, goods could be made available at lower prices, which, in turn, translated into larger demand.

The fact that international business was one of the primary factors holding the empire together can also be seen in its decay. When "barbaric" tribes overran the empire, it was not mainly through war and prolonged battles the Rome lost ground. The outside tribes were actually attacking an empire that was already substantially weakened, because it could no longer offer the benefits of affiliation. Former allies no longer saw any advantage in being associated with the Romans and willingly cooperated with the invaders, rather than face prolonged battles.

In a similar fashion, one could interpret the evolution of European feudalism to be a function of trade and marketing. Because farmers were frequently deprived of their harvests as a result of incursions by other (foreign) tribes, or even individuals, they decided to band together and provide for their own protection. By delivering a certain portion of their "earnings" to a protector, they could be assured of retaining most of their gains. Although this system initially worked quite well in reducing the cost of production and the cost of marketing, it did ultimately result in the emergence of the feudal system, which, perhaps, was not what the initiators had intended it to be.

Interestingly, the feudal system encouraged the development of a closed-state economy that was inwardly focused and ultimately conceived for self-sufficiency and security. However, medieval commerce still thrived and developed through export trade. In Italy, the Low Countries, and the German Hanse towns, the impetus for commerce was provided by East-West trade. Profits from the spice trade through the Middle East created the wealth of Venice and other Mediterranean ports. Europe also imported rice, oranges, dyes, cotton, and silk. Western European merchants in turn exported timber, arms, and woolen clothing in exchange for these luxury goods. A remaining legacy of this trade are the many English and French words of Arabic origin, such as divan, bazaar, artichoke, orange, jar, and tariff.[1]

The importance of trade has not always persisted, however. For example, in 1896, the Empress Dowager Tz'u-hsi, in order to finance the renovation of the summer palace, impounded government funds that had been designated for Chinese shipping and its navy. As a result, China's participation in world trade almost came to a halt. In the subsequent decades, China operated in almost total isolation, without any transfer of knowledge from the outside, without major inflow of goods, and without the innovation and productivity increases that result from exposure to international trade.

More recently, the effect of turning away from international trade was highlighted during the 1930s. The Smoot-Hawley Act raised duties to reduce the volume of imports into the United States, in the hopes that this would restore domestic employment. The result, however, was a raising of duties and other barriers to imports by most other trading nations as well. These measures were contributing factors in the subsequent worldwide depression and the collapse of the world financial system, which in turn set the scene for World War II.

International marketing and international trade have also long been seen as valuable tools for foreign policy purposes. The use of economic coercion—for example, by nations or groups of nations—can be traced back as far as the time of the Greek city-states and the Peloponnesian War or, in more recent times, to the Napoleonic wars. Combatants used blockades to achieve their goal of "bringing about commercial ruin and shortage of food by dislocating trade."[2] Similarly, during the Civil War in the United States, the North consistently pursued a strategy of denying international trade opportunities to the South and thus deprived it of export revenue needed to import necessary products. In the 1990s, the Iraqi invasion of Kuwait resulted in a trade embargo of Iraq by the United Nations, with the goal of reversing the aggression. Although such deprivations of trade do not often bring about policy change, they certainly have a profound impact on the standard of living of a nation's citizens.

[1]Henri Pirenne, *Economic and Social History of Medieval Europe* (New York: Harcourt, Brace, and World, 1933), 142–146.

[2]Margaret P. Doxey, *Economic Sanctions and International Enforcement* (New York: Oxford University Press, 1980), 10.

The Emergence of Global Division

After 1945, the world was sharply split ideologically into West and East, a division that had major implications for trade relations. The Soviet Union, as the leader of the Eastern bloc, developed the Council for Mutual Economic Assistance (CMEA or COMECON), which focused on developing strong linkages among the members of the Soviet bloc and discouraged relations with the West. The United States, in turn, was the leading proponent of creating a "Pax Americana" for the Western world, driven by the belief that international trade was a key to worldwide prosperity. Many months of international negotiations in London, Geneva, and Lake Success (New York) culminated on March 24, 1948, in Havana, Cuba, with the signing of the charter for an International Trade Organization (ITO).

This charter, a series of agreements between 53 countries, was designed to cover international commercial policies, domestic business practices, commodity agreements, employment and reconstruction, economic development and international investment, and a constitution for a new United Nations agency to administer the whole. In addition, a General Agreement on Tariffs and Trade was initiated, with the purpose of reducing tariffs among countries, and international institutions such as the World Bank and the International Monetary Fund were created.

Even though the International Trade Organization incorporated many farsighted notions, most nations refused to ratify it, fearing its power, its bureaucratic size, and its threat to national sovereignty. As a result, the most forward-looking approach to international trade never came about. However, other organizations conceived at the time are still in existence and have made major contributions toward improving international trade.

Transnational Institutions Affecting World Trade

World Trade Organization (WTO)[3]

The World Trade Organization has its origins in the General Agreement on Tariffs and Trade (GATT), to which it became the successor organization in January of 1995. In order to better understand the emergence of the WTO, a brief review of the GATT is appropriate. The GATT has been called "a remarkable success story of a postwar international organization that was never intended to become one."[4] It began in 1947 as a set of rules for nondiscrimination, transparent procedures, and settlement of disputes in international trade. One of the most important tools is the Most-Favored Nation (MFN) clause, which calls for each member country of the GATT to grant every other member country the most favorable treatment it accords to any other country with respect to imports and exports. In effect, MFN is the equal opportunity clause of international trade. Over time, the GATT evolved into an institution that sponsored successive rounds of international trade negotiations with a key focus on a reduction of prevailing high tariffs.

Early in its existence, the GATT achieved the liberalization of trade in 50,000 products, amounting to two-thirds of the value of the trade among its participants. In subsequent years, special GATT negotiations such as the Kennedy Round and the Tokyo Round further reduced trade barriers and developed improved dispute-settlement mechanisms, better provisions dealing with subsidies, and a more explicit definition of rules for import controls.

In spite of, or perhaps because of, these impressive gains, GATT became less effective over time. Duties had already been drastically reduced—for example, the average

[3]For more information about the World Trade Organization refer to the following web site: **http://www.wto.org.**

[4]Thomas R. Graham, "Global Trade: War and Peace," *Foreign Policy* (Spring 1983): 124–137.

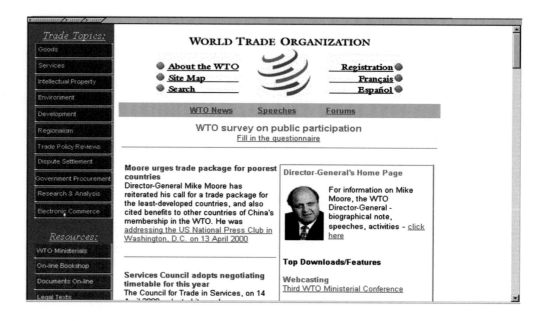

U.S. tariff rate fell from 26 percent in 1946 to 5 percent in 1987[5]—and further reductions were unlikely to have a major impact on world trade. Concurrently, many nations developed new tools for managing and distorting trade flows, nontariff tools that were not covered under GATT rules. Examples are "voluntary agreements" to restrain trade, bilateral or multilateral special trade agreements such as the multifiber accord that restricts trade in textiles and apparel, and other nontariff barriers. Also, GATT, which was founded by 24 like-minded governments, was designed to operate by consensus. With a membership of 110, this consensus rule often led to a stalemate of many GATT activities.

After many years of often contentious negotiations, the Uruguay Round accord was finally ratified in January of 1995. As part of this ratification, a new institution, the World Trade Organization, was created, which now is the umbrella organization responsible for overseeing the implementation of all the multilateral agreements negotiated in the Uruguay Round and those that will be negotiated in the future.[6] GATT has ceased to exist as a separate institution and has become part of WTO, which also is responsible for the General Agreement on Trade in Services (GATS), agreements on trade-related aspects of intellectual property rights (TRIPS), and trade-related investment measures (TRIMS), and administers a broad variety of international trade and investment accords.

The creation of the WTO has greatly broadened the scope of international trade agreements. Many of the areas left uncovered by the GATT such as services and agriculture are now addressed at least to some degree by international rules, speedier dispute settlement procedures have been developed, and the decision-making process has been streamlined. Even though the WTO will attempt to continue to make decisions based on consensus, provisions are now made for decisions to be made by majority vote if such consensus cannot be achieved.

The regime of the WTO has already made major contributions to improved trade and investment flows around the world. The results of the Uruguay Round alone are predicted to increase global exports by more than $755 billion by the year 2002.[7] The

<hr />

[5]Graham, "Global Trade," 127.

[6]*Business Guide to the Uruguay Round*, International Trade Centre and Commonwealth Secretariat, Geneva, 1995. **www.intracen.org**

[7]"Uruguay Round Results to Expand Trade by $755 Billion," *Focus: GATT Newsletter* (May 1994): 6.

THE INTERNATIONAL MARKETPLACE 2.2

The WTO: From Specialty Group to Public Forum

WORLD TRADE, ONCE RESERVED for the conversations of business leaders, trade lawyers, academics, and politicians, has become a topic of debate among the general public. While large corporations yearn for opportunities to expand into foreign markets, developing nations see trade as a way out of poverty, workers in industrial nations fear international labor competition, and social activists abhor environmentally unfriendly practices and questionable labor conditions. Caught in the middle, the WTO serves as the platform for international trade negotiation and policy.

For corporations, the opportunity to penetrate international markets with goods and services offers the hope of lucrative results. Whether this means that U.S. automobile companies compete in China or that Portuguese cork manufacturers sell their goods to France, companies long for the chance to reach international customers.

Developing countries see exports as a way out of poverty. In Thailand, shrimp fishermen can benefit greatly from open trade. However, with sanctions, their livelihood is jeopardized.

Manufacturing workers in many industrialized countries maintain that free global trade will lead to domestic unemployment and wage cuts as corporations open factories in less developed countries to hire cheaper labor. This threat of a shift to labor overseas has caused some workers to strongly oppose the international trade initiatives of the WTO.

Activists and environmentalists have displayed organized opposition to the WTO and free world trade due to practices they deem to be socially inappropriate. At the opening round of the WTO meetings in Seattle in December 1999, protesters were successful in sending the message that there is more at stake than just jobs.

International trade policy affects all aspects of people's lives, including health. WTO representatives met in 2001 with members of the World Health Organization, drug companies and other researchers and health experts to suggest approaches for drugs to be sold at affordable prices to those who need them in developing countries. Many major pharmaceutical groups provide HIV/AIDS medication to African countries below cost, but relief agencies say they could be doing more.

SOURCES: Doug Mellgren, "Affordable Medicine for Poor Sought," *Associated Press*, April 8, 2001; Neal Lipshultz, "Not Everyone Is on Board Economic Globalization Train," *The Star Tribune*, December 4, 1999, 1D; Steven Pearlstein, "Trade Theory Collides with Angry Reality," *The Washington Post*, December 3, 1999, A1; Peter M. Gerhart, "The WTO, Yes . . . ; Barter for Labor Rights, the Environment," *The Washington Post*, December 6, 1999, A27.

fact that so many new areas of the global economy are addressed by the WTO means that there will be ample room for additional negotiations. Many issues have been addressed in a very limited way, and a better understanding of these issues by countries as well as additional shifts in the composition of trade will require further refinement in the trading and investment rules. At the same time, however, a successful WTO may well infringe on the sovereignty of nations. For example, more streamlined dispute settlements will mean that decisions are made more quickly and that nations in violation of international trade rules will be confronted more often. Negative WTO decisions affecting large trading nations are likely to be received with resentment. In addition, some governments intend to broaden the mandate of the WTO to also deal with social causes and issues such as labor laws, competition, and emigration freedoms. Since many nations fear that social causes can be used to devise new rules of protectionism against their exports, the addition of such issues may become a key reason for divisiveness and dissent within the WTO.[8] In addition, outside groups such as nongovernmental organizations and special interest alliances believe that international trade and the WTO represent a threat to their causes. *The International Marketplace 2.2* explains how very different views about the WTO have emerged.

Unless trade advocates and the WTO are supported by their member governments and other outside stakeholders in trade issues, there is unlikely to be major progress on further liberalization of trade and investment. It will therefore be important to

[8]"Michael R. Czinkota, "The World Trade Organization—Perspectives and Prospects," *Journal of International Marketing* 3 (Number 1, 1995): 85–92.

have the WTO focus on its core mission, which is the facilitation of international trade and investment, while ensuring that an effective forum exists to afford a hearing and subsequent achievements for concerns surrounding the core.

International Monetary Fund (IMF)[9]

The International Monetary Fund (IMF), conceived in 1944 at Bretton Woods in New Hampshire, was designed to provide stability for the international monetary framework. It obtained funding from its members, who subscribed to a quota based on expected trade patterns and paid 25 percent of the quota in gold or dollars and the rest in their local currencies. These funds were to be used to provide countries with protection against temporary fluctuations in the value of their currency. Therefore, it was the original goal of the IMF to provide for fixed exchange rates between countries.

The perhaps not so unintended result of using the U.S. dollar as the main world currency was a glut of dollar supplies in the 1960s. This forced the United States to abandon the gold standard and devalue the dollar and resulted in flexible or floating exchange rates in 1971. However, even though this major change occurred, the IMF as an institution has clearly contributed toward providing international liquidity and to facilitating international trade.

Although the system has functioned well so far, it is currently under severe pressure. In the 1980s, some of this pressure was triggered by the substantial debts incurred by less-developed countries as a result of overextended development credits and changes in the cost of energy. In the 1990s, major additional pressure has resulted from the financial requirements of the former socialist countries, which search for funds to improve their economies. For example, on April 27, 1992, 12 former Soviet republics joined the IMF. In addition to the needs of these new members, major currency fluctuations among old customers have stretched the resources of the IMF to the limit. For example, the Mexican economic turmoil of 1995 required a $20 billion transfer from the IMF, and economic crises in Asia, Russia, and Brazil required further billions. As a result of all these global financial needs, the future role of the IMF may be very different. If the institution can mobilize its members to provide the financial means for an active role, its past accomplishments may pale in view of the new opportunities.

At the same time, however, the newness in orientation also will require a rethinking of the rules under which the IMF operates. For example, it is quite unclear whether stringent economic rules and performance measures are equally applicable to all countries seeking IMF assistance. New economic conditions that have not been experienced to date, such as the privatization of formerly centrally planned economies, may require different types of approaches. Also, perhaps the link between economic and political stability requires more and different considerations, therefore magnifying but also changing the mission of the IMF.

World Bank[10]

The World Bank, whose official name is the International Bank for Reconstruction and Development, has had similar success. It was initially formed in 1944 to aid countries suffering from the destruction of war. After completing this process most successfully, it has since taken on the task of aiding world development. With more and more new nations emerging from the colonial fold of the world powers of the early twentieth century, the bank has made major efforts to assist fledgling economies to participate in a modern economic trade framework. More recently, the bank has begun to participate actively with the IMF to resolve the debt problems of the

[9]For more information about the International Monetary Fund refer to the following web site: **http://www.imf.org**.

[10]For more information about the World Bank refer to the following web site: **http://www.worldbank.org**.

developing world and may also play a major role in bringing a market economy to the former members of the Eastern bloc.

A major debate, however, surrounds the effectiveness of the bank's expenditures. Particularly in the 1970s and 1980s, major funds were invested into infrastructure projects in developing countries, based on the expectation that such investment would rapidly propel the economies of these nations forward. However, in retrospect, it appears that many of these funds were squandered by corrupt regimes, and that many large projects have turned into white elephants—producing little in terms of economic progress. In addition, some projects have had major negative side effects for the recipient nations. For example, the highway through the rain forest in Brazil has mainly resulted in the migration of people to the area and an upsetting of a very fragile ecological balance. The World Bank is now trying to reorient its outlook, focusing more on institution building and the development of human capital through investments into education and health. A clearer differentiation of its role as an organization working on the micro level of the economy as opposed to the macro level of the IMF is also likely to redirect the work of the bank. *The International Marketplace 2.3* shows how the bank is involved in the issue of child labor. However, it has become clear that there is no single solution for bringing countries out of poverty.

Regional Institutions

The WTO, IMF, and World Bank operate on a global level. Regional changes have also taken place, based on the notion that trade between countries needs to be encouraged. Of particular importance was the formation of **economic blocs** that integrated the economic and political activities of nations.

The concept of regional integration was used more than 100 years ago when Germany developed the Zollverein. Its modern-day development began in 1952 with the establishment of the European Coal and Steel Community, which was designed to create a common market among six countries in coal, steel, and iron. Gradually, these nations developed a Customs Union and created common external tariffs. The ultimate goal envisioned was the completely free movement of capital, services, and people across national borders and the joint development of common international policies. Over time, the goals have been largely attained. The European Union (EU) now represents a formidable market size internally and market power externally, and the well-being of all EU members has increased substantially since the bloc's formation.

Similar market agreements have been formed by other groups of nations. Examples are the North American Free Trade Agreement (NAFTA), the Mercosur in Latin America, and the Gulf Cooperation Council (GCC). These unions were formed for different reasons and operate with different degrees of cohesiveness as appropriate for the specific environment. They focus on issues such as forming a customs union, a common market, an economic union, or a political union. Simultaneously with these economic bloc formations, the private sector has begun to develop international trade institutions of its own. Particularly when governments are not quick enough to address major issues of concern to global marketers, business has taken the lead by providing a forum for the discussion of such issues. One example is the Transatlantic Business Dialogue, which is a nongovernmental organization composed of business leaders from Europe and the United States. Recognizing the inefficiency of competing and often contradictory standards and lengthy testing procedures, this group is working to achieve mutual recognition agreements on an industry basis. Founded in November of 1995 in Seville, Spain, the executives of leading international firms that participate in this organization attempt to lead the way in simplifying global marketing. Currently, they search for ways to align international standards and regulations primarily in the pharmaceutical and telecommunication sectors, but are likely to expand their activities once progress is achieved.

THE INTERNATIONAL MARKETPLACE 2.3

A World Bank Perspective on Child Labor

IN DEVELOPING COUNTRIES about 250 million children between the ages of 5 and 14 work, at least 120 million of them full time. In Asia 61 percent of all children work full time; in Africa, 32 percent; and in Latin America, 7 percent. Around 70 percent of all child laborers are unpaid family workers. Fewer than 5 percent are employed in export-related production. The vast majority of children working in rural areas are engaged in agricultural activities, while urban children tend to work in services and manufacturing.

Official statistics suggest that more boys work than girls. Boys tend to work in more visible types of employment (in factories, for instance), while girls perform unpaid household tasks or work as domestics. When this difference is taken into account, boys and girls work in similar proportions. The intensity of work boys and girls perform may differ, however, with girls working longer hours, and girls in developing countries generally have lower school enrollment rates than boys.

Not all child labor is harmful. Working children who live in a stable environment with their parents or a guardian can benefit from informal education and job training. Many working children are also studying, and their wages help their siblings attend school. However, some working conditions are hazardous to the children's health, both physically and mentally.

The rate of children's participation in the labor force declines as a country's per capita GDP rises. While as many as half of all children in the poorest countries work, the numbers begin falling rapidly as per capita GDP reaches around $1,200.

The incidence of child labor also tends to decline as educational enrollment rises and school quality improves, although the cross-country variations in these relationships are large.

Policies that reduce child labor have strong support on purely economic grounds. When children are sent to work at very young ages for extended periods, they do not develop the skills necessary to earn higher wages later in life. Consequently, society loses needed human capital. As adults these individuals have low productivity levels that become a drag on economic growth.

Several approaches to reducing child labor have been suggested. They are not mutually exclusive and probably work best in combination.

- *Reducing poverty.* Poverty is a major cause of harmful child labor. In poor households, children's wages may be essential to the family's survival. Even though poverty reduction is a long-term process, programs that improve the earnings of the poor, address capital market constraints, and provide safety nets can help reduce child labor in the short term.
- *Educating children.* Increasing primary school enrollments tends to decrease child labor. Making it easier for children to attend school and work simultaneously may be the best approach in rural areas with the school year scheduled in order not to conflict with the peak agricultural season. Reducing the cost of education also gives households an incentive to send children to school

The activities of all these institutions demonstrate that the joining of forces internationally permits better, more successful international marketing activities, results in an improved standard of living, and provides an effective counterbalance to other large economic blocs. Just as in politics, trade has refuted the old postulate of "the strong is most powerful alone." Nations have come to recognize that trade activities are of substantial importance to their economic well-being. Over the long term, the export activities of a nation are the key to the inflow of imports and therefore to the provision of choice, competition, and new insights. In the medium and long run, the balance of payments has to be maintained. In the short run, "an external deficit can be financed by drawing down previously accumulated assets or by accumulating debts to other countries. In time, however, an adjustment process must set in to eliminate the deficit."[11]

The urgency of the adjustment will vary according to the country in question. Some countries find it very hard to obtain acceptance for an increasing number of IOUs. Others, like the United States, can run deficits of hundreds of billions of dollars and are still a preferred borrower because of political stability, perceived economic

[11]Mordechai E. Kreinin, *International Economics: A Policy Approach*, 5th ed. (New York: Harcourt Brace Jovanovich, 1987), 12.

rather than to work. Brazil's scholarships to poor families, granted on the condition that the children must not work, have helped prevent harmful child labor.

■ *Providing support services to working children.* These services can include meals, basic literacy classes, and night shelters. Since these programs usually concentrate on children working visibly on the street, their scope is somewhat limited.

■ *Raising public awareness.* This approach covers a wide spectrum: improving the general awareness of hazards to working children, raising parental awareness of the loss of human capital associated with child labor, and involving employers, unions, and civil society in efforts to reduce child labor.

■ *Enforcing legislation and regulations.* Most countries have laws and regulations governing child labor. Laws prohibiting child labor and enforcing school attendance are often difficult to enforce, however, and may push child workers into prostitution or crime-related activities if they reduce the income of poor families. The alternative is to focus legislation on the most intolerable forms of child labor. A new International Labour Organization (ILO) convention targeting the worst forms of child labor—including slavery, prostitution, forced labor, bonded labor, and illegal and hazardous work—was adopted in June 1999.

Many other proposals for reducing child labor—including trade sanctions, consumer boycotts, social clauses and certification, and labeling schemes—are fraught with problems. Exports produced in the formal sector are hit hardest by trade measures, and one effect can be to force workers (including child laborers) into the informal sector, where working conditions are typically worse. Trade sanctions, which may be little more than a cover for the introduction of protectionist measures, may be implemented in ways that have little to do with child labor. Finally, labeling schemes and social clauses are often impossible to monitor.

The World Bank has taken steps to reduce harmful child labor through its ongoing poverty reduction efforts and the child labor program established in May 1998. The program is the focal point for Bankwide child labor activities and supports initiatives such as child labor reduction evaluations. It draws upon the international experience of labor experts from academia, nongovernmental organizations, and other multilateral and bilateral organizations such as the United Nations Children's Fund (UNICEF) and the ILO.

At the World Bank's first international conference devoted to children's issues in April, 2000, Eduardo Doryan, vice-president of the World Bank's Human Development Network, called child labor a "burning stone in the hands of the international community."

"Two years ago the Bank did not explicitly address the issue of child labor. But now we have not only a framework. . . , we also have a Global Child Labor Program," said Doryan.

SOURCES: Fallon and Tzannatos 1998; Grootaert and Kanbur 1995; ILO 1993; World Bank, *World Development Report 1999/2000*, Washington, DC. **www.worldbank.com**

security, and the worldwide use of the U.S. dollar as a reserve and business reference currency. Such temporary advantages can change, of course. Before the rise of the dollar, the British pound was the reserve currency of choice for many years.

As a result of this understanding, much of the ideological trade separation of the world has been swept aside. Today, virtually all nations wish to take part in international trade and make efforts to participate in it as much as possible.

The Current U.S. International Trade Position

Over the years, the U.S. international trade position has eroded substantially when measured in terms of world market share. In the 1950s, U.S. exports composed 25 percent of total world exports. Since then, this share has declined precipitously. It is not that U.S. exports have actually dropped during that time. The history of the U.S. success in world market share began with the fact that the U.S. economy was not destroyed by the war. Because other countries had little to export and a great need for imports, the U.S. export position was powerful. Over time, however, as other trade partners entered the picture and aggressively obtained a larger world market share for

| FIGURE | 2.1 | Merchandise Exports and Imports as a Percentage of World Total |

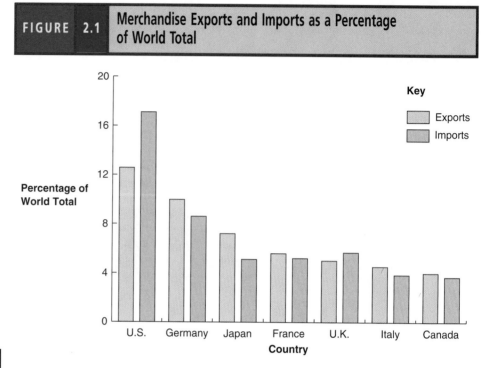

SOURCE: IMF, *International Financial Statistics,* Washington, DC, December 1999. **www.imf.org**

themselves, U.S. export growth was not able to keep pace with total world export growth. Figure 2.1 shows the world share of exports and imports of key trading countries. Notable is the degree to which U.S. imports exceed exports.

U.S. exports as a share of the GDP are about 11 percent. This level pales when compared with the international trade performance of other nations. Germany, for example, has consistently maintained an export share of over 20 percent of GDP. Japan, in turn, which is so often maligned as the export problem child in the international trade arena, now exports only about 10 percent of its GDP. Comparative developments of exports across countries in terms of percentage of GDP can be seen in Table 2.1.

| TABLE | 2.1 | Exports of Goods and Services as a Percentage of Gross Domestic Product |

PERIOD	UNITED STATES	FRANCE	GERMANY	ITALY	NETHER-LANDS	UNITED KINGDOM	JAPAN	CANADA
1985	7.3	23.9	32.5*	22.8	60.8	28.8	14.5	28.5
1987	7.8	19.7	29.0*	19.4	49.7	25.5	10.4	27.1
1989	9.4	21.7	31.5*	19.7	55.2	23.8	10.6	26.0
1991	10.2	21.5	26.3	18.5	54.0	23.2	10.2	25.4
1993	10.0	20.7	22.8	22.3	50.4	25.4	9.3	30.7
1995	11.3	22.5	24.5	27.0	53.1	28.4	9.4	38.2
1997	11.9	25.5	27.8	26.7	56.0	28.5	11.1	42.3
1999	11.0	21.1	28.3	24.8	53.2	25.4	10.2	42.6

*Data from West Germany

SOURCES: OECD, Quarterly National Accounts, No. 3, 1999, Paris. OECD, National Accounts, Vol. 2, 1998, Paris. **www.oecd.org**

Clearly, as an economy, the United States is not as internationally oriented as are many other nations. At the same time, the numbers themselves must be interpreted with caution, since they do not reflect the large size of the U.S. internal market. For example, if one considered the European Union as one market, the exclusion of intra-EU trade would drastically reduce the export percentage of GDP for the EU member nations.

The impact of international trade and marketing on individuals is highlighted when trade is scrutinized from a per-capita perspective. Table 2.2 presents this information on a comparative basis. Among the major industrialized nations, the United States has the lowest exports per capita, amounting to about one-third of Germany's figure and less than one-fifth of the per-person exports of the Netherlands. Even though imports per capita are also relatively low, they substantially exceed the level of export activity, thus producing major trade deficits for the United States.

A Diagnosis of the U.S. Trade Position

The developments just enumerated foster the question: Why did these shifts occur? We should not attribute changes in U.S. trade performance merely to temporary factors such as the value of the dollar, the subsidization of exports from abroad, or the price of oil. We need to search further to determine the root causes for the decline in U.S. international competitiveness.

Since World War II, it has been ingrained in the minds of American policymakers that the United States is the leading country in world power and world trade. Together with this opinion came the feeling that the United States should assist other countries with their trade performance because without American help, they would never be able to play a meaningful role in the world economy. At the same time, there was admiration for "Yankee ingenuity"—the idea that U.S. firms were the most aggressive in the world. Therefore, the U.S. private sector appeared not to need any help in its international trade efforts.

The result of this overall philosophy was a continuing effort to aid countries abroad in their economic development. At the same time, no particular attention was paid to U.S. domestic firms. This policy was well conceived and well intentioned and resulted in spectacular successes. Books written in the late 1940s describe the overwhelming economic power of the United States and the apparently impossible task of resurrecting foreign economies. Comparing those texts with the economic performance of countries such as Japan and Germany today demonstrates that the policies of helping to stimulate foreign economies were indeed crowned by success.

These policies were so successful that no one wished to tamper with them. The United States continued to encourage trade abroad and not to aid domestic firms

TABLE 2.2	Exports and Imports of Goods and Services per Capita for Selected Countries		
COUNTRY		EXPORTS PER CAPITA	IMPORTS PER CAPITA
United States		$ 3,442	$ 4,498
Canada		8,715	8,270
France		6,455	5,953
Germany		7,498	7,371
Netherlands		16,020	14,793
United Kingdom		6,226	6,750
Japan		3,791	3,362
Italy		4,265	3,629

SOURCE: WTO, *World Trade in 1999*, February 13, 2001, **www.wto.org;** CIA, *The World Factbook 2000*, February 13, 2001, **www.cia.gov.**

throughout the 1960s and the 1970s. Although the policies were well conceived, the environment to which they were applied was changing. In the 1950s and early 1960s, the United States successfully encouraged other nations again to become full partners in world trade. However, U.S. firms were placed at a distinct disadvantage when these policies continued for too long.

U.S. firms were assured that "because of its size and the diversity of its resources, the American economy can satisfy consumer wants and national needs with a minimum of reliance on foreign trade."[12] The availability of a large U.S. domestic market and the relative distance to foreign markets resulted in U.S. manufacturers simply not feeling a compelling need to seek business beyond national borders. Subsequently, the perception emerged within the private sector that exporting and international marketing were too risky, complicated, and not worth it.

This perception also resulted in increasing gaps in international marketing knowledge between managers in the United States and those abroad. Whereas business executives in most countries were forced, by the small size of their markets, to look very quickly to markets abroad and to learn about cultural sensitivity and market differences, most U.S. managers remained blissfully ignorant of the global economy. Similarly, U.S. education did not make knowledge about the global business environment, foreign languages, and cultures an area of major priority.

Given such lack of global interest, inadequacy of information, ignorance of where and how to market internationally, unfamiliarity with foreign market conditions, and complicated trade regulations, the private sector became fearful of conducting international business activities.

Lately, however, conditions have begun to change. Most institutions of higher learning have recognized the responsibilities and obligations that world leadership brings with it. Increasingly, universities and particularly business programs are emphasizing the international dimension, not only in theory but also in practice. Many schools are offering opportunities for study abroad, designing summer programs with global components, and expecting a global orientation from their students.

Managers have also grown more intense in their international commitment. Many newly founded firms are global from the very beginning, giving rise to the term "born global." Electronic commerce has made it more feasible to reach out to the global business community, whether the firm be large or small. The U.S. Department of State has begun to offer training in business-government relations to new ambassadors and now instructs them to pay close attention to the needs of the U.S. business community.

In effect, the attention paid to international markets as both an opportunity for finding customers and a source of supplies is growing rapidly. As a result, the need for international marketing expertise can be expected to rise substantially as well.

The Impact of Trade and Investment on the United States

The Effect of Trade

Exports are important in a macroeconomic sense, in terms of balancing the trade account. Exports are special because they can affect currency values and the fiscal and monetary policies of governments, shape public perception of competitiveness, and determine the level of imports a country can afford. The steady erosion of the U.S. share of total world exports that took place in the 1960s and 1970s has had more than purely optical repercussions. It has also resulted in a merchandise **trade deficit,** which since 1975 has been continuous. In 1987, the United States posted a then record trade deficit with imports of products exceeding exports by more than $171 billion. Due to increases in exports, the merchandise trade deficit declined in the following years, only

[12]Kreinin, *International Economics,* 6.

to climb again to record heights in 1999 by reaching $271 billion due to increased imports.[13] Such large trade deficits are unsustainable in the longer run.

These trade deficits have a major impact on the United States and its citizens. They indicate that a country, in its international activities, is consuming more than it is producing. One key way to reduce trade deficits is to increase exports. Such an approach is highly beneficial for various reasons.

One billion dollars worth of exports supports the creation, on average, of 15,500 jobs.[14] Increases in exports can become a major contributor to economic growth. This fact became particularly evident during the economic slowdown of the early 1990s, when export growth accounted for most of the domestic economic growth rate and produced most new employment.

Equally important, through exporting, firms can achieve **economies of scale.** By broadening its market reach and serving customers abroad, a firm can produce more and do so more efficiently. As a result, the firm may achieve lower costs and higher profits both at home and abroad. Through exporting, the firm also benefits from market diversification. It can take advantage of different growth rates in different markets and gain stability by not being overly dependent on any particular market. Exporting also lets the firm learn from the competition, makes it sensitive to different demand structures and cultural dimensions, and proves its ability to survive in a less-familiar environment in spite of higher transaction costs. All these lessons can make the firm a stronger competitor at home.[15]

On the import side, firms become exposed to new competition, which may offer new approaches, better processes, or better products and services. In order to maintain their market share, firms are forced to compete more effectively by improving their own products and activities. Consumers in turn receive more choices when it comes to their selection. The competitive pressures exerted by imports also work to keep quality high and prices low.

The Effect of International Investment

International marketing activities consist not only of trade but of a spectrum of involvement, much of which results in international direct investment activities. Such investment activities can be crucial to a firm's success in new and growing markets.

For decades, the United States was the leading foreign direct investor in the world. U.S. multinationals and subsidiaries sprouted everywhere. Of late, however, foreign firms increasingly invest in the United States. At the same time, investment continues to expand around the globe, following attractive factor conditions and entering new markets.

The extent of **foreign direct investment** in different U.S. industries is shown in Table 2.3. One in nine U.S. manufacturing employees works for a **foreign affiliate,** which is a U.S. firm of which foreign entities own at least 10 percent. However, the foreign ownership is not equally distributed across all industries. Foreign direct investment tends to be concentrated in specific sectors, where the foreign investors believe they are able to contribute the best and benefit the most from their investment. For example, in the U.S. chemical industry, more than one-third of all employees work for foreign owners, but this is the case for only 3 percent of employees in the retail industry. As a result of foreign investment, some individuals and policymakers may

[13]*Annual Summary for 1999*, Bureau of Economic Analysis, U.S. Department of Commerce, Washington, DC. **http://www.bea.doc.gov,** February 18, 2000.

[14]*U.S. Jobs Supported by Exports of Goods and Services*, U.S. Department of Commerce, Washington, DC, June 17, 1996, 3.

[15]Michael R. Czinkota, "A National Export Development Strategy for New and Growing Businesses," remarks delivered to the National Economic Council, Washington, DC, August 6, 1993.

| TABLE 2.3 | Employment by U.S. Affiliates of Foreign Corporations, 1997 | |

INDUSTRIES	EMPLOYEES (IN THOUSANDS)	AS PERCENTAGE OF U.S. INDUSTRY EMPLOYMENT
Chemicals and Allied Products	389	37.6
Electronic and Electric Equipment	369	21.2
Industrial Machinery and Equipment	261	12.0
Transportation Equipment	208	11.3
Primary + Fabricated Metal Products	219	10.0
Wholesale Trade	539	8.0
Retail Trade	689	3.0
Total Manufacturing	2,227	11.9

SOURCE: U.S. Bureau of Economic Analysis, *Survey of Current Business*, December 1999, Table 6.5 and Table 6.4C.
www.bea.doc.gov

grow concerned about dependency on foreign owners, even though firm proof for the validity of such concern has been difficult to establish.

Many of these investments are carried out by the largest trading partners of the United States. The United Kingdom leads all foreign countries in terms of the value of direct investment (it accounts for more than 18 percent of the total), but countries such as Japan, France, and Germany are large investors as well. Figure 2.2 shows how foreign direct investments by and into the United States are distributed.

To some extent, these foreign direct investments substitute for trade activities. As a result, firms operating only in the domestic market may be surprised by the onslaught of foreign competition and, unprepared to respond quickly, may lose their domestic market share. However, the substitution for trade is far from complete. In many instances, foreign affiliates themselves are major participants in trade. They may import raw materials or components and export some of their output.

| FIGURE 2.2 | International Investments in and by the United States |

U.S. Direct Investment Position Abroad, 1999
Host-Country Shares

Foreign Direct Investment Position in the United States, 1999
Parent-Country Shares

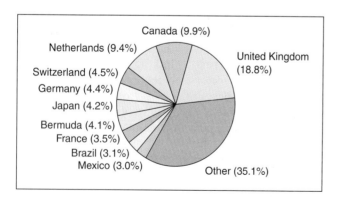

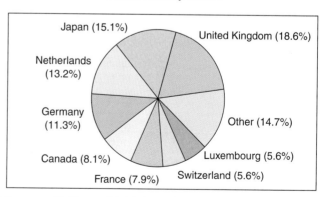

SOURCE: *Survey of Current Business*, Bureau of Economic Affairs, U.S. Department of Commerce, Washington, DC, July 2000, 59, 62.

www.bea.doc.gov

Even though the United States has an open investment policy that welcomes foreign corporations to U.S. shores, some degree of uneasiness exists about the rapid growth of such investment. Major foreign investments are reviewed by a specially created U.S. government interagency committee called the Committee for Foreign Investments in the United States (CFIUS). This committee primarily scrutinizes foreign investment activities from the standpoint of their impact on U.S. national security.

A general restriction of foreign investments might well be contrary to the general good of U.S. citizens. Domestic industries may be preserved, but only at great peril to the free flow of capital and at substantial cost to consumers. A restriction of investments may permit more domestic control over industries, yet it also denies access to foreign capital and often innovation. This in turn can result in a tightening up of credit markets, higher interest rates, and a decrease in willingness to adapt to changing world market conditions.

To avoid these negative repercussions, the United States as a nation and its citizens must encourage more involvement in the international market by U.S. firms. Greater participation in international trade can be achieved by exporting more and by investing, licensing, or franchising abroad. For all these activities, however, the key issue will be the maintenance of high levels of U.S. international competitiveness in order to retain and regain domestic and international market share.

Policy Responses to Trade Problems

The word *policy* implies that there is a coordinated set of continuous activities in the legislative and executive branches of government to attempt to deal with U.S. international trade. Unfortunately, such concerted efforts only rarely come about. Policy responses have consisted mainly of political ad hoc reactions, which over the years have changed from deep regret to protectionism. Whereas in the mid-1970s most lawmakers and administration officials simply regretted the lack of U.S. performance in international markets, more recently, industry pressures have forced increased action.

Restrictions of Imports

In light of persistent trade deficits, growing foreign direct investment, and the tendency by some firms and industries to seek legislative redress for failures in the marketplace, the U.S. Congress in the past two decades has increasingly been willing to provide the president with more powers to restrict trade. Many resolutions have also been passed and legislation enacted admonishing the president to pay closer attention to trade. However, most of these admonitions provided only for an increasing threat against foreign importers, not for better conditions for U.S. exporters. The power of the executive to improve international trade opportunities for U.S. firms through international negotiations and a relaxation of rules, regulations, and laws has become increasingly restricted over time.

A tendency has also existed to disregard the achievements of past international negotiations. For example, in Congress an amendment was attached to protectionistic legislation, stipulating that U.S. international trade legislation should not take effect if it is not in conformity with internationally negotiated rules. The amendment was voted down by an overwhelming majority, demonstrating a legislative lack of concern for such international trade agreements. There has also been a tendency to seek short-term political favors domestically in lieu of long-term international solutions. Trade legislation has become increasingly oriented to specific trading partners and specific industries. The United States often attempts to transfer its own trade laws abroad, in areas such as antitrust or export controls, resulting in bilateral conflicts. During international trade negotiations, U.S. expectations regarding production costs, social structure, and cultural patterns are often expected to be adopted in full abroad.

Yet, in spite of all these developments, the United States is still one of the strongest advocates of free trade, to which its large volume of imports and ongoing trade deficit attest. Although this advocacy is shared, at least officially, by nations around the world, governments have become very creative in designing and implementing trade barriers, examples of which are listed in Table 2.4.

One typical method consists of "voluntary" import restraints that are applied selectively against trading partners. Such measures have been used mainly in areas such as textiles, automobiles, and steel. Voluntary restrictions, which are, of course, implemented with the assistance of severe threats against trading partners, are intended to aid domestic industries to reorganize, restructure, and recapture their trade prominence of years past. They fail to take into account that foreign importers may not have caused the economic decline of the domestic industry.

The steel industry provides a good example. World steel production capacity and supply clearly exceed world demand. This is the result both of overly ambitious industrial development projects motivated by nationalistic aspirations and of technological innovation. However, a closer look at the steel industries of developed nations shows that demand for steel has also been reduced. In the automobile industry, for example, fewer automobiles are being produced, and they are being produced differently than ten years ago. Automobiles are more compact, lighter, and much more fuel efficient as a result of different consumer tastes and higher oil prices. The average automobile today weighs 700 pounds less than in the 1970s. Accordingly, less steel is needed for its production. In addition, many components formerly made of steel are now being replaced by components made from other materials such as plastic. Even

---

TABLE 2.4 Types of Trade Barriers

- Import policies (for example, tariffs and other import charges, quantitative restrictions, import licensing, customs barriers)
- Standards, testing, labeling and certification (including unnecessarily restrictive application of sanitary and phytosanitary standards and environmental measures, and refusal to accept U.S. manufacturers' self-certification of conformance to foreign product standards)
- Government procurement (for example, "buy national" policies and closed bidding)
- Export subsidies (for example, export financing on preferential terms and agricultural export subsidies that displace U.S. exports in third-country markets)
- Lack of intellectual property protection (for example, inadequate patent, copyright, and trademark regimes)
- Services barriers (for example, limits on the range of financial services offered by foreign financial institutions, regulation of international data flows, and restrictions on the use of foreign data processing)
- Investment barriers (for example, limitations on foreign equity participation and on access to foreign government-funded research and development (R&D) programs, local content and export performance requirements, and restrictions on transferring earnings and capital)
- Anticompetitive practices with trade effects tolerated by foreign governments (including anticompetitive activities of both state-owned and private firms that apply to services or to goods, and that restrict the sale of U.S. products to any firm, not just to foreign firms that perpetuate the practices)
- Trade restrictions affecting electronic commerce (for example, tariff and nontariff measures, burdensome and discriminatory regulations and standards, and discriminatory taxation)
- Other barriers (barriers that encompass more than one category, for example, bribery and corruption, or that affect a single sector)

SOURCE: Office of the United States Trade Representative, *2000 National Trade Estimate Report on Foreign Trade Barriers*, Washington, D.C., March 27, 2000.
For more information refer to **www.ustr.gov/reports/nte/2000/contents.html**

THE INTERNATIONAL MARKETPLACE 2.4

Toying with Tariffs

IS A HALLOWEEN COSTUME APPAREL or is it merely a toy? This seemingly irrelevant question has kept the court systems busy since a 1994 U.S. Customs ruling. The answer affects millions of dollars, worth of goods and will have a serious impact on the sourcing strategies of importers, manufacturers, and retailers of costumes.

In 1994, U.S. Customs declared that certain Halloween costumes could be classified, for import purposes, as "flimsy, non-durable and not a normal piece of apparel" and therefore as festive articles or toys. Thanks to this distinction between toys and apparel, importers could bring costumes into the United States without paying apparel tariffs, which can range up to 30%.

Rubie's Costume Co., of Queens, New York, has disputed the 1994 decision by taking on its competitor Franco American Novelty Co., of Glendale, New York, a Halloween costume importer. Rubie's has sued in the Court of International Trade, stating that costumes are apparel rather than toys. Rubie's president, Marc Beige, claims that imports of costumes have risen from approximately 10% to nearly 33% of the market in only a few years. If Rubie's wins, this could effectively kill off the import of Halloween costumes into the United States due to the tariff. The case could take 12 to 15 months to settle. Meanwhile, costumes continue to enter the United States without tariffs.

The importers argue that Rubie's is attempting to use trade barriers to gain a competitive advantage within the costume industry. Additionally, retail associations and textile manufacturers have opposed a tariff. They have stated that a tariff would not be in the best interest of the public and would negatively affect all holiday retailing.

SOURCES: Paula L. Green, "Which Is Witch? Costume Case Goes to Court," *The Journal of Commerce*, July 15, 1999, World Trade 4; Cindy Skrzycki, "A Customs Tariff on Halloween Costumes?," *The Washington Post*, March 6, 1998, G1, G4.

if imports of steel were to be excluded totally from the markets of industrialized nations, the steel industries could not regain the sales lost from a substantial change in the automotive industry.

If countries do not use the subtle mechanism of voluntary agreements, they often resort to old-fashioned tariffs. For example, Japanese heavy motorcycles imported into the United States were assessed a duty of 49.4 percent. This regulation kept the last U.S. producer of motorcycles, the Harley-Davidson Company, in business. Even though these tariffs have since been removed—and one year early at that—and the firm keeps on producing heavy motorcycles, one can rightfully question whether the cost imposed on U.S. consumers who preferred foreign products during the four years of tariff imposition was justified. Even though tariffs have been substantially reduced on average, their specific application can still have a major effect on trade flows. *The International Marketplace 2.4* demonstrates how a tariff classification can determine whether or not imports can compete.

A third major method by which trade has been restricted is through **nontariff barriers.** Typically, these barriers are much more subtle than tariffs. Compared with tariffs or even subsidies, which are visible and at least force products to compete for market acceptance on dimensions other than price, some nontariff barriers are much more difficult to detect, prove, and quantify. For example, these barriers may be government or private-sector "buy domestic" campaigns, which affect importers and sometimes even foreign direct investors. Other nontariff barriers consist of providing preferential treatment to domestic bidders over foreign bidders, using national standards that are not comparable to international standards, placing emphasis on design rather than performance, and providing for general difficulties in the market entry of foreign products. Most famous in this regard are probably the measures implemented by France. To stop or at least reduce the importation of foreign video recorders, France ruled in 1983 that all of them had to be sent through the customs station at

The Global Environment: A Source of Conflict Between Developed and Less-Developed Nations

DESERTIFICATION

High degree of desertification hazard

Moderate degree of desertification hazard

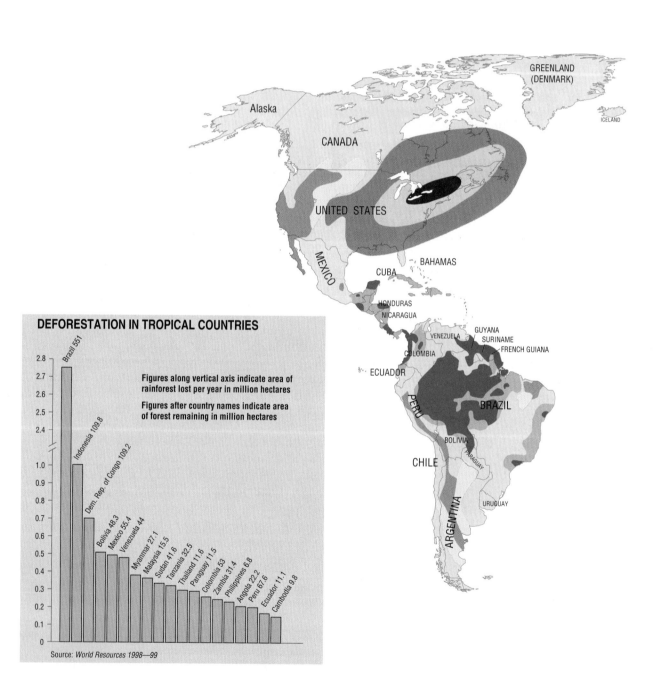

DEFORESTATION IN TROPICAL COUNTRIES

Figures along vertical axis indicate area of rainforest lost per year in million hectares

Figures after country names indicate area of forest remaining in million hectares

Source: *World Resources 1998—99*

RAINFOREST DESTRUCTION
Present distribution of forest area
Former extent of rainforest

ACID DEPOSITION
Estimated acidity of precipitation in the Northern Hemisphere
Slightly acid rain
Acid rain
Very acid rain

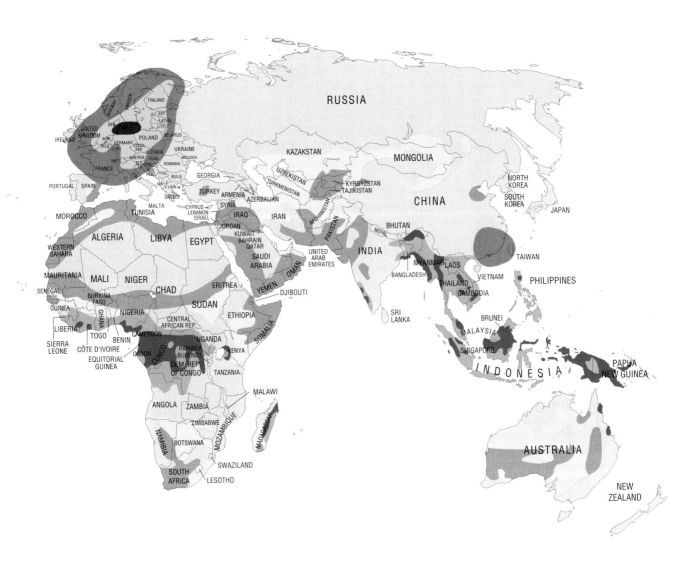

Sources: *Environment Atlas*

TABLE 2.5	Back-to-School Bill	

ITEM	FREE MARKET PRICE[a]	PRICE WITH CURRENT TRADE RESTRAINTS
1 boy's sweater	$20	$25
1 pair cotton blue jeans	$14.50	$18
1 book-bag knapsack	$12	$16
1 vinyl handbag	$10	$12
1 leather handbag	$40	$44
1 clock radio	$30	$32
1 Walkman-style radio	$18.70	$20
1 tuna sandwich	$ 1.80	$ 2
1 peanut butter sandwich	$ 1	$ 1.50
1 candy bar	$ 0.15	$ 0.30

[a]Prices calculated based on G. Hufbauer, Diane T. Berliner, and Kimberly Ann Elliott, *Trade Protection in the United States* (Washington, DC: Institute for International Economics, 1986), and 1986 tariff rates quoted by the U.S. International Trade Commission and the U.S. Commerce Department.

Poitiers. This customshouse is located in the middle of the country, was woefully understaffed, and was open only a few days each week. In addition, the few customs agents at Poitiers insisted on opening each package separately in order to inspect the merchandise. Within a few weeks, imports of video recorders in France came to a halt. The French government, however, was able to point to international agreements and to the fact that officially all measures were in full compliance with the law.

In the mid 1990s, the Clinton administration attempted a new approach to trade policy. Major efforts were made to introduce new import quotas abroad, this time not to keep foreign imports out but to increase U.S. exports. The focus of U.S.–Japanese trade negotiations rested on committing the Japanese government to agree to quantitative import goals for U.S. products. Basically, the idea was to ensure more U.S. exports to Japan, not through the negotiation of reduced import barriers, but through agreements that would guarantee specific market penetration outcomes for U.S. industries. While the Japanese government disagreed with the approach, it was widely hailed in the United States as a new strategy in trade policy. Yet at the same time, cautious voices argued that this approach encouraged government planning and control of the private economy, an approach that had proven unsuccessful with the demise of the centrally planned Soviet Union.[16]

The primary result of all of these trade restrictions is that many actions are taken that are contrary to what we know is good for the world and its citizens. Industries are preserved, but only at great peril to the world trade framework and at substantial cost to consumers. The direct costs of these actions are hidden and do not evoke much public complaint because they are spread out over a multitude of individuals. Yet, as Table 2.5 shows, these costs are real and burdensome and directly affect the standard of living of individuals and the competitiveness of firms. It has been estimated that each year the total cost to U.S. consumers alone due to import restraints amounts to $70 billion. For example, abolishing import barriers in the apparel industry would let U.S. consumers gain more than $21 billion. Consumer gains would be $3.2 billion for textiles, $1.3 billion for sugar, $1.2 billion for dairy products, and $54 million for

Countries are endowed with varying degrees of productive resources, and the production of goods is a function of the most intensive use of those resources. DeKalb Genetics Corporation, an international marketer of seed products, is the leading supplier of corn, grain sorghum, and sunflower seeds to Argentina, where the growing season is the opposite of the United States'.

[16]Michael R. Czinkota, "U.S. and Japan Must Find a New Common Ground," *The Asian Wall Street Journal Weekly*, February 28, 1994.

peanuts.[17] Even though each specific trade restriction may not be very significant in its impact on individuals, over time and across products these costs accumulate and prevent consumers from spending their hard-earned money on other products of their choice.

Export Promotion Efforts

Many countries provide export promotion assistance to their firms. Key reasons for such assistance are the national need to earn foreign currency, the encouragement of domestic employment, and the increase in domestic economic activity. Many forms of export promotion can also be seen as government distortion of trade since government support simply results in a subsidization of profitability or reduction of risk. Yet, there are instances where such intervention may be justified. Government support can be appropriate if it annuls unfair foreign practices, increases market transparency and therefore contributes to the better functioning of markets,[18] or helps overcome, in the interest of long-term national competitiveness, the short-term orientation of firms.[19]

U.S. policymakers have taken several steps to improve the international trade performance of U.S. firms. The Department of Commerce has added new information services that provide U.S. companies with an impressive array of data on foreign trade and marketing developments. The Commercial Service has been reformed and many new professionals were hired to provide an inward and outward link with U.S. businesses in terms of information flow and market assistance. In addition, new programs were implemented at the State Department and the Foreign Service Institute aimed at providing some training in international business to embassy staff serving abroad. A national export strategy has been formulated in order to coordinate the activities of diverse federal agencies. For the first time, the federal government has officially recognized that "American firms will simply not thrive at home unless they take full advantage of the tremendous opportunities abroad."[20] As a result of these efforts, a national network of export assistance centers has been created, capable of providing one-stop shops for exporters in search of export counseling and financial assistance. In addition, an official interagency advocacy network was created that helps U.S. companies win overseas contracts for large government purchases abroad. A variety of agencies have formed the Trade Promotion Coordination Committee in order to continue to improve services to U.S. exporters. A listing of these agencies together with their web sites is provided in the appendix to this chapter, so that readers can obtain the most up-to-date information about trade policy changes and export assistance.

In terms of comparative efforts, however, U.S. export promotion activities still lag far behind the support provided by other major industrial nations. Many countries also provide substantial levels of private-sector support, which exists to a much lesser degree in the United States. Even more importantly, of the total export promotion expenditures, the largest portion (almost 50 percent) continues to go to the agricultural sector, and relatively few funds are devoted to export counseling and market research.

A new focus has come about in the area of export financing. Policymakers have increasingly recognized that U.S. business may be placed at a disadvantage if it cannot

[17]Gary Clyde Hufbauer and Kimberly Ann Elliott, *Measuring the Costs of Protection in the United States* (Washington, DC: Institute for International Economics, 1994).

[18]*Die Aussenwirtschaftsförderung der wichtigsten Konkurrenzländer der Bundesrepublik Deutschland—Ein internationaler Vergleich* (The export promotion of the most important countries competing with the Federal Republic of Germany—An international comparison) (Berlin: Deutsches Institut für Wirtschaftsforschung, June 1991).

[19]Masaaki Kotabe and Michael R. Czinkota, "State Government Promotion of Manufacturing Exports: A Gap Analysis," *Journal of International Business Studies* (Winter 1992): 637–658.

[20]*National Export Strategy*, Fourth Annual Report to the United States Congress, Trade Promotion Coordinating Committee, Washington, DC, U.S. Government Printing Office, October 1996, 8.

meet the subsidized financing rates of foreign suppliers. The Export-Import Bank of the United States, charged with the new mission of aggressively meeting foreign export-financing conditions, has in recent years even resorted to offering **mixed aid credits.** These take the form of loans composed partially of commercial interest rates and partially of highly subsidized developmental aid interest rates. The bank has also launched a major effort to reach out to smaller-sized businesses and assist in their export success.

Tax legislation that inhibited the employment of Americans by U.S. firms abroad has also been altered to be more favorable to U.S. firms. In the past, U.S. nationals living abroad were, with some minor exclusion, fully subject to U.S. federal taxation. Because the cost of living abroad can often be quite high—rent for a small apartment can approach the range of $4,000-plus per month—this tax structure often imposed a significant burden on U.S. firms and citizens abroad. Therefore, companies frequently were not able to send U.S. employees abroad. However, as the result of a tax code revision that allows a substantial amount of income (up to $78,000 in 2001) to remain tax-free,[21] more Americans can now be posted abroad. In their work they may specify the use of U.S. products and thus enhance the competitive opportunities of U.S. firms.

One other export promotion development was the passage of the Export Trading Company Act of 1982. Intended to be the U.S. response to Japanese *sogoshoshas,* or international trading firms, this legislation permits firms to work together to form **export consortia.** The basic idea was to provide the foreign buyer with a one-stop shopping center in which a group of U.S. firms could offer a variety of complementary and competitive products. By exempting U.S. firms from current antitrust statutes, and by permitting banks to cooperate in the formation of these ventures through direct capital participation and the financing of trading activities, the government hoped that more firms could participate in the international marketplace. Although this legislation was originally hailed as a masterstroke and a key measure in turning around the decline in U.S. competitiveness abroad, it has not attracted a large number of successful firms. It appears that the legislation may not have provided sufficient incentive for banks, export service firms, or exporters to participate. Banks simply may find domestic profit margins to be more attractive and safe; export service firms may be too small; and exporters themselves may be too independent to participate in such consortia.

A Strategic Outlook

The U.S. national economy has become too intertwined with world trade to be considered independent from it. Critical in the years to come will be the development of a trade policy in a positive fashion rather than in a reactive way that aims only at reducing imports. Protectionistic legislation can be helpful if it is not enacted. Proposals in Congress can be quite useful as bargaining chips in international negotiations. However, if passed, signed into law, and implemented, protectionistic legislation can result in the destruction of the international trade framework.

The new century may also witness a new perspective on government-business relations. In previous decades, government and business stayed at arm's length, and it was seen as inappropriate to involve the government in private-sector activities. Now, however, closer government-business collaboration is seen as one key to enhanced competitiveness. More mutual listening to each other and joint consideration of the long-term domestic and international repercussions of policy actions and business strategy can indeed pay off. Perhaps it will make both business and government more responsive to each other's needs. At least it will reduce the failures that can result from a lack of collaboration and insufficient understanding of linkages, as described in *The International Marketplace 2.5.*

[21] *2000 U.S. Master Tax Guide,* Chicago, CCH Inc., 2000, 572.

THE INTERNATIONAL MARKETPLACE 2.5

A Marketing Approach to Trade

U.S. TRADE NEGOTIATIONS WITH JAPAN in the wood-products industry and subsequent results provide an excellent example of American industry's difficulties in understanding and responding to foreign demand. The U.S. General Accounting Office reports that for more than a decade, the United States has negotiated with the Japanese government to allow more U.S. solid wood products to enter the Japanese market, particularly in the construction field. High-level meetings, ongoing negotiations, government financial support, and industry demonstration projects were to achieve that goal.

After all of these efforts, much has been accomplished. Japanese building codes, which, due to fire-code provisions, had prohibited construction of multistory wooden buildings, were changed. Product certification was made less costly and less complicated. Certification authority, previously the exclusive purview of the Ministry of Construction, was delegated to foreign testing organizations such as the American Plywood Association in the United States. Japan's tariffs were lowered for processed solid wood products—for softwood plywood to 10 percent from 16 percent, for glue-laminated beams to 4 percent from 15 percent. To top it all off, the Foreign Agricultural Service spent close to $18 million to promote U.S. wood-product sales in Japan.

Considering these successes, one would expect U.S. leadership in the market for solid wood products in Japan and rapid employment growth back home. Instead, the market leadership belongs to Canada, and job increases in the United States have been marginal.

These are several reasons for this situation. First, Canadian firms were much quicker than U.S. companies to take advantage of the changes. Canadian firms obtained certification much faster and were more aggressive in their marketing. They understand the different specifications and grades of wood products used in Japan, they pay attention to product quality and appearance, and they demonstrate more commitment to market and after-sales service requirements such as the development of manuals in Japanese. By contrast, U.S. firms tend to provide their information in English, tend to be less reliable as long-range suppliers, show little interest in after-sales service, and do not meet Japanese quality and appearance standards.

Second, and of even greater importance, is the U.S. disregard of the Japanese market. American companies try to sell what they produce to the Japanese, rather than producing what the Japanese want to buy. The largest portion of Japan's market for solid wood products is in post and beam construction, not in timber frames. Only 7 percent of new wooden homes are built with U.S. two-by-four products. Most other wooden housing construction uses four-by-four posts and boards for framing and is based on a three-by-six-foot module that fits the standard-sized tatami mats that cover Japanese floors. In other words, U.S. companies have focused all of their energies on increasing their penetration of the smallest part of the market, and have done so with only limited success.

Third, those U.S. firms that do attempt to adjust their products to Japanese market requirements encounter major problems in financing the new equipment and longer export payment terms. They also run into human resource problems when trying to meet Japanese quality standards or searching for international business expertise.

What do U.S. companies need to do differently? As Washington becomes more involved in trade, it should do so in a market-oriented way. The key considerations of U.S. trade policy need to be:

- A focus on market opportunities that make a difference;
- Identification of the needs and desires of foreign customers;
- Industry commitment to government market-opening approaches; and
- A link between trade policy and domestic assistance to firms planning to go abroad.

Washington needs to explicitly recognize that the times when the United States opened foreign markets simply for the well-being of the world are over. Funds should only be expended if the market is large enough to warrant attention and government actions are fully supported and followed up by industry. American trade policy needs to be focused on those issues that make a meaningful difference in terms of jobs and economic activity. After all, that is what funds government operations, provides taxes, reduces adjustment expenditures, and pays for health care.

SOURCE: Michael Czinkota, "Washington Needs a Marketing Approach to Trade," *The Asian Wall Street Journal Weekly*, June 28, 1993, 12.

Very important is also the consideration of the **locus of control of trade policy.** A variety of regulatory agencies could become involved in administering U.S. trade policy. Although such agencies would be useful from the standpoint of addressing narrowly defined grievances, they carry the danger that commercial policy will be determined by a new chorus of discordant voices. This seems even more threatening when one considers that many regulatory agencies see themselves mainly responsible to Congress or to specific constituencies rather than to the administration. By shifting the power of setting trade policy from the administration to agencies or even to states, the term *new federalism* could be given a quite unexpected meaning and might cause progress at the international negotiation level to grind to a halt. No U.S. negotiator can expect to retain the goodwill of foreign counterparts if he or she cannot place on the table issues that can be negotiated without constantly having to check back with different authorities.

Trade policy can also take either a multilateral or a bilateral approach. In **a bilateral approach,** negotiations are carried out mainly between two nations, whereas in a **multilateral approach,** negotiations are carried out among a wide variety of nations. The approach can also be broad, covering a wide variety of products and services, or it can be narrow, focusing on specific sectoral problems.

As a quick and temporary measure, bilateral approaches and a **sectoral focus** seem quite appealing. Very specific problems can be discussed and can be resolved expediently. Yet, even though negotiators may be well intentioned, **sectoral negotiation** outcomes may, on occasion, produce some quite unexpected results. For example, when the United States negotiated a reduction of Japanese market barriers to citrus fruits and juice imports, the expectation was that mainly U.S. firms would benefit. Yet, in reality, it was Brazilian orange juice producers that were the primary beneficiaries. Their products were lower priced and most of them are owned by Japanese investors.

Bilateral approaches in turn may seem quite appealing, particularly in an era of new trading blocs in both Europe and the Western Hemisphere. The growth in bilateral legislation and the increasingly country-specific orientation of trade negotiators bear witness to the appeal. However, every time bilateral negotiations take place, their very nature excludes a multitude of other interested parties. To be successful, negotiations need to produce winners. If a constant set of winners and losers is produced, then negotiations have no chance for long-term success because no one wants to take the position of the loser. This points in the direction of multilateral negotiation approaches on a broad scale. Here concessions can be traded off, thus making it possible for all nations to emerge and declare themselves as winners. The difficulty lies in devising enough incentives to bring the appropriate and desirable partners to the bargaining table.

SUMMARY

International trade has often played a major role in world history. The rise and fall of the Roman Empire and the emergence of feudalism can be attributed to trade. Since 1945, the Western nations have made concerted efforts to improve the trade environment and expand trade activities. In order for them to do so, various multinational organizations, such as the WTO, the IMF, and the World Bank, were founded. In addition, several economic blocs like the EU, NAFTA, and Mercosur were formed. Many of these organizations have been very successful in their mission, yet new realities of the trade environment demand new types of action.

Over the years, the U.S. international trade position has eroded substantially, and the U.S. share of world exports has declined precipitously from 25 percent in the 1950s. This has occurred mainly because other countries have expanded their trade activities. U.S. firms have been too complacent and disinterested in foreign markets to keep up the pace.

However, a new interest in and commitment to international markets bodes well for growing U.S. international marketing activities.

Successful foreign competitiveness in international trade has resulted in major trade deficits for the United States. Since each billion dollars' worth of exports creates, directly and indirectly, more than 15,000 jobs, it is important for U.S. firms to concentrate on the opportunities the international market has to offer.

Some policymakers intend to enhance U.S. trade performance by threatening the world with increasing protectionism. The danger of such a policy lies in the fact that world trade would shrink and standards of living would decline. Protectionism cannot, in the long run, prevent adjustment or increase productivity and competitiveness. It is therefore important to improve the capability of firms to compete internationally and to provide an international trade framework that facilitates international marketing activities.

QUESTIONS FOR DISCUSSION

1. Why is international trade important to a nation?
2. Give examples of the effects of the "Pax Americana."
3. Discuss the role of "voluntary" import restraints in international marketing.
4. What is meant by multilateral negotiations?
5. How have consumer demands changed international trade?
6. Discuss the impact of import restrictions on consumers.
7. Does foreign direct investment have an effect on trade?
8. What is the major role played by the World Bank today? Check www.worldbank.org to report on key projects.
9. Determine the latest exports per capita for a country of your choice not listed in Table 2.2 (use data from www.imf.org and www.un.org).

RECOMMENDED READINGS

Bowen, Harry, and Abraham Hollander. *Applied International Trade Analysis*. Ann Arbor: University of Michigan Press, 1998.

Business Guide to the World Trading System, 2nd ed. Geneva: International Trade Centre UNCTAD/WTO, 1999.

Das, Bhagirath Lal. *An Introduction to the WTO Agreements*. New York: St. Martin's Press, 1998.

Delener, Nejdet. *Strategic Planning and Multinational Trading Blocs*. Westport, CT: Quorum, 1999.

Hufbauer, Gary Clyde, and Kimberly Ann Elliott. *Measuring the Costs of Protection in the United States*. Washington, DC: Institute for International Economics, 1994.

Jones, R. G. Barry. *Globalization and Interdependence in the International Political Economy: Rhetoric and Reality*. New York: Pinter Publishers, 1995.

McCue, Sarah S. *Trade Secrets: The Export Answer Book*, 3rd ed. Detroit, MI: Wayne State University Press, 2001.

Preeg, Ernest H. *From Here to Free Trade: Essays in Post–Uruguay Round Trade Strategy*. Chicago: University of Chicago Press, 1998.

Sazanami, Yoko, Shujiro Urata, Hiroki Kawai, and Gary Clyde Hufbauer. *Measuring the Cost of Protection in Japan*. Washington DC.: Institute for International Economics, 1995.

Sevilla, Christina R. *Explaining Patterns of GATT/WTO Trade Complaints*. Cambridge, MA: Harvard University, 1998.

Srinivasan, T. N. *Developing Countries and the Multilateral Trading System: From GATT to the Uruguay Round and the Future*. Boulder, CO: Westview Press, 1998.

Appendix A

Members of the U.S. Trade Promotion Coordination Committee (TPCC)

INFORMATION ON BOTH INDIVIDUAL TPCC agency programs and the National Export Strategy is available on the Internet. The TPCC's official repository of export promotion information is the National Trade Data Bank available from STAT-USA. Information about individual TPCC agency programs can be obtained by using the following Internet addresses:

- National Trade Data Bank (**http://www.stat-usa.gov**)
- Agency for International Development (**http://www.usaid.gov**)
- Council of Economic Advisers (**http://www.whitehouse.gov**)
- Department of Agriculture (**http://www.fas.usda.gov**)
- Department of Commerce (**http://www.ita.doc.gov**)
- Department of Defense (**http://www.dtic.dla.mil**)
- Department of Energy (**http://www.osti.gov**)
- Department of Interior (**http://www.doi.gov**)
- Department of Labor (**http://www.dol.gov**)
- Department of State (**http://www.state.gov**)
- Department of Transportation (**http://www.dot.gov**)
- Department of the Treasury (**http://www.ustreas.gov**)
- Environmental Protection Agency (**http://www.epa.gov**)
- Export-Import Bank of the United States (**http://www.exim.gov**)
- National Economic Council (**http://www.whitehouse.gov**)
- Office of the U.S. Trade Representative (**http://www.ustr.gov**)
- Office of Management and Budget (**http://www.whitehouse.gov/omb/circulars**)
- Overseas Private Investment Corporation (**http://www.opic.gov**)
- Small Business Administration (**http://www.sba.gov**)
- U.S. Information Agency (**www.usinfo.state.gov**)
- U.S. Trade and Development Agency (**http://www.tda.gov**)

SOURCE: *National Export Strategy*, Fourth Annual Report to the United States Congress, U.S. Government Printing Office, October 1996, 54.

Chapter 3

The Cultural Environment

Making Culture Work for Your Success

THOUSANDS OF EUROPEAN and U.S. companies have entered or expanded their operations in the fastest-growing region in the world, Asia. In the 1990s, the region outpaced the growth of the world's twenty-four leading industrial economies by more than six times. A total of 400 million Asian consumers have disposable incomes at least equal to the rich-world average.

Few have had as much experience—or success—as the 3M Company. The maker of everything from heart-lung machines to Scotch tape, the company's revenues for 1999 from international sales reached $8.181 billion (52% of total), a full third coming from the Asia-Pacific. At the root of the company's success are certain rules that allow it both to adjust to and exploit cultural differences.

- **Embrace local culture**—3M's new plant near Bangkok, Thailand, is one example of the way the company embraces local culture. A gleaming Buddhist shrine, wreathed in flowers, pays homage to the spirits Thais believe took care of the land prior to the plant's arrival. Showing sensitivity to local customs helps sales and builds employee morale, officials say. It helps the company understand the market and keeps it from inadvertently doing something to alienate people.
- **Employ locals to gain cultural knowledge**—The best way to understand a market is to have grown up in it. Of the 7,500 3M employees in Asia, fewer than ten are U.S. citizens. (As a matter of fact, of the 34,000 3M employees in companies outside the United States, fewer than 300 are expatriates not residing in their home countries.) The rest are locals who know the customs

and buying habits of their compatriots. 3M also makes grants of up to $50,000 available to its Asian employees to study product innovations, making them equals with their U.S. counterparts.

- **Build relationships**—3M executives started preparing for the Chinese market soon after President Nixon's historic visit in 1972. For ten years, company officials visited Beijing and invited Chinese leaders to 3M headquarters in St. Paul, Minnesota, building contacts and trust along the way. Such efforts paid off when, in 1984, the Chinese government made 3M the first wholly owned foreign venture on Chinese soil. 3Mers call the process FIDO ("first in defeats others"), which is a credo built on patience and long-term perspective.
- **Adapt products to local markets**—Examples of how 3M adapts its products read like insightful lessons on culture. In the early 1990s, sales of 3M's famous Scotchbrite cleaning pads were languishing. Company technicians interviewed maids and housewives to determine why. The answer: Filipinos traditionally scrub floors by pushing around a rough shell of coconut with their feet. 3M responded by making the pads brown and shaping them like a foot. In China, a big seller for 3M is a composite to fill tooth cavities. In the United States, dentists pack a soft material into the hole and blast it with a special beam of light, making it hard as enamel in five seconds. In the People's Republic, dentists cannot afford the light. The solution is an air-drying composite that does the same thing in two minutes: it takes a little longer but is far less expensive.

- **Help employees understand you**—At any given time, more than thirty Asian technicians are in the United States, where they learn the latest product advances while gaining new insight into how the company works. At the same time, they are able to contribute by infusing their insight into company plans and operations.
- **Coordinate by region**—When designers in Singapore discovered that consumers wanted to use 3M's Nomad household floor mats in their cars, they spread the word to their counterparts in Malaysia and Thailand. Today, the specially made car mats with easy-to-clean vinyl loops are big sellers across Southeast Asia. The company encourages its product managers from different Asian countries to hold regular meetings and

share insights and strategies. The goal of this cross-pollination is to come up with regional programs and "Asianize" a product more quickly. In addition, joint endeavors support the effort to build cross-border *esprit de corps*, especially when managers may have their own markets' interests primarily at heart.

SOURCES: "3M Operational Facts, Year-End 1999," available at www.mmm.com; Charlene Solomon, "Managing an Overseas Sales Force," *World Trade*, April 1999, S4–S6; John R. Engen, "Far Eastern Front," *World Trade*, December 1994, 20–24; "A Survey of Asia," *The Economist*, October 30, 1993.

http://www.mmm.com

T
HE EVER-INCREASING LEVEL of world trade, opening of markets, enhanced purchasing power of customers, and intensifying competition all have allowed and even forced marketers to expand their operations. The challenge for the marketing manager is to handle the differences in values and attitudes, and subsequent behavioral patterns that govern human interaction, on two levels: first, as they relate to customer behavior and, second, as they affect the implementation of marketing programs within individual markets and across markets.

For years, marketers have been heralding the arrival of the global customer, an individual or entity that would both think and purchase alike the world or region over.[1] These universal needs could then be translated into marketing programs that would exploit these similarities. However, if this approach were based on the premise of standardization, a critical and fatal mistake would be made. Overseas success is very much a function of cultural adaptability: patience, flexibility, and tolerance for others' beliefs.[2]

To take advantage of global markets or global segments, marketers are required to have or attain a thorough understanding of what drives customer behavior in different markets, and to detect the extent to which similarities exist or can be achieved through marketing efforts. After conducting market research throughout Europe, Whirlpool entered the fastest-growing microwave market with a product clearly targeted at the Euroconsumer but that offered various product features with different appeal in different countries.[3]

In expanding their presence, marketers will acquire not only new customers but new partners as well. These essential partners, whose efforts are necessary for market development and penetration, include agents, distributors, other facilitating agents

[1]Ernest Dichter, "The World Consumer," *Harvard Business Review* 40 (July–August 1962): 113–122; and Kenichi Ohmae, *Triad Power—The Coming Shape of Global Competition* (New York: The Free Press, 1985), 22–27.

[2]"Rule No. 1: Don't Diss the Locals," *Business Week*, May 15, 1995, 8.

[3]Warren Stugatch, "Make Way for the Euroconsumer," *World Trade*, February 1993, 46–50.

(such as advertising agencies and law firms), and, in many cases, the government. Expansion will also mean new employees or strategic alliance partners whose motivations will either make or break marketing programs. Thus understanding the hot buttons and turnoffs of these groups becomes critical.

In the past, marketing managers who did not want to worry about the cultural challenge could simply decide not to do so and concentrate on domestic markets. In today's business environment, a company has no choice but to face international competition. In this new environment, believing that concern about culture and its elements is a waste of time often proves to be disastrous. An understanding allows marketers to determine when adaptation may be necessary and when commonalities allow for regional or global approaches, as seen in *The International Marketplace 3.1*. Understanding culture is critical not only in terms of getting strategies right but also for ensuring that implementation by local operations is effective.

Cultural differences often are the subject of anecdotes, and business blunders may provide a good laugh. Cultural diversity must be recognized not simply as a fact of life but as a positive benefit; that is, differences may actually suggest better solutions to challenges shared across borders. Cultural competence must be recognized as a key management skill.[4] Adjustments will have to be made to accommodate the extraordinary variety in customer preferences and work practices by cultivating the ability to detect similarities and to allow for differences. Ideally, this means that successful ideas can be transferred across borders for efficiency and adapted to local conditions for effectiveness. For example, in one of his regular trips to company headquarters in Switzerland, the general manager of Nestlé Thailand was briefed on a promotion for a cold coffee concoction called Nescafé Shake. The Thai group swiftly adopted and adapted the idea. It designed plastic containers to mix the drink and invented a dance, the Shake, to popularize the product.[5] Cultural incompetence, however, can easily jeopardize millions of dollars in wasted negotiations, potential purchases, sales and contracts, and customer relations. Furthermore, the internal efficiency of a firm may be weakened if managers, employees, and intermediaries are not "on the same wavelength."

The intent of this chapter is first to analyze the concept of culture and its various elements and then to provide suggestions for meeting the cultural challenge.

Culture Defined

Culture gives an individual an anchoring point—an identity—as well as codes of conduct. Of the more than 160 definitions of culture analyzed by Alfred Kroeber and Clyde Kluckhohn, some conceive of culture as separating humans from nonhumans, some define it as communicable knowledge, and some see it as the sum of historical achievements produced by humanity's social life.[6] All the definitions have common elements: Culture is learned, shared, and transmitted from one generation to the next. Culture is primarily passed on by parents to their children but also by social organizations, special-interest groups, the government, the schools, and the church. Common ways of thinking and behaving that are developed are then reinforced through social pressure. Geert Hofstede calls this the "collective programming of the mind."[7] Culture is also multidimensional, consisting of a number of common elements that are

[4]Mary O'Hara-Devereaux and Robert Johansen, *Global Work: Bridging Distance, Culture, and Time* (San Francisco: Jossey-Bass Publishers, 1994), 11.

[5]Carla Rapoport, "Nestlé's Brand Building Machine," *Fortune*, September 19, 1994, 147–156.

[6]Alfred Kroeber and Clyde Kluckhohn, *Culture: A Critical Review of Concepts and Definitions* (New York: Random House, 1985), 11.

[7]Geert Hofstede, "National Cultures Revisited," *Asia-Pacific Journal of Management* 1 (September 1984): 22–24.

Religions of the World: A Part of Culture

Religious beliefs among 70% or more of the population

- Atheist
- Buddhism
- Confucian
- Christian, other
- Christian, Roman Catholic
- Hindu
- Indigenous
- Judaism
- Muslim
- Orthodox, no major sects

Source: *The World Factbook 2000*

interdependent. Changes occurring in one of the dimensions will affect the others as well.

For the purposes of this text, **culture** is defined as an integrated system of learned behavior patterns that are distinguishing characteristics of the members of any given society. It includes everything that a group thinks, says, does, and makes—its customs, language, material artifacts, and shared systems of attitudes and feelings.[8] The definition therefore encompasses a wide variety of elements, from the materialistic to the spiritual. Culture is inherently conservative, resisting change and fostering continuity. Every person is encultured into a particular culture, learning the "right way" of doing things. Problems may arise when a person encultured in one culture has to adjust to another one. The process of **acculturation**—adjusting and adapting to a specific culture other than one's own—is one of the keys to success in international operations.

Edward T. Hall, who has made some of the most valuable studies on the effects of culture on business, makes a distinction between high and low context cultures.[9] In **high context cultures,** such as Japan and Saudi Arabia, context is at least as important as what is actually said. The speaker and the listener rely on a common understanding of the context. In **low context cultures,** however, most of the information is contained explicitly in the words. North American cultures engage in low context communications. Unless we are aware of this basic difference, messages and intentions can easily be misunderstood. If performance appraisals of marketing personnel are to be centrally guided or conducted in a multinational corporation, those involved must be acutely aware of cultural nuances. One of the interesting differences is that the U.S. system emphasizes the individual's development, whereas the Japanese system focuses on the group within which the individual works. In the United States, criticism is more direct and recorded formally, whereas in Japan it is more subtle and verbal. What is not being said can carry more meaning than what is said.

Few cultures today are as homogeneous as those of Japan and Saudi Arabia. Elsewhere, intracultural differences based on nationality, religion, race, or geographic areas have resulted in the emergence of distinct subcultures. The international manager's task is to distinguish relevant cross-cultural and intracultural differences and then to isolate potential opportunities and problems. Good examples are the Hispanic subculture in the United States and the Flemish and the Walloons in Belgium. On the other hand, borrowing and interaction between national cultures may lead to narrowing gaps between cultures. Here the international business entity will act as a **change agent** by introducing new products or ideas and practices. Although this may consist of no more than shifting consumption from one product brand to another, it may lead to massive social change in the manner of consumption, the type of products consumed, and social organization. Consider, for example, that in the 1990s the international portion of McDonald's annual sales grew from 13 percent to 58 percent.[10] In markets such as Taiwan, one of the 119 countries on six continents entered, McDonald's and other fast food entities dramatically changed eating habits, especially of the younger generation.

The example of Kentucky Fried Chicken in India illustrates the difficulties marketers may have in entering culturally complex markets. Even though the company opened its outlets in two of India's most cosmopolitan cities (Bangalore and New Delhi), it found itself the target of protests by a wide range of opponents. KFC could have alleviated or eliminated some of the anti-Western passions by taking a series of preparatory steps. First, rather than opting for more direct control, KFC should have allied with local partners for advice and support. Second, KFC should have tried to appear more Indian rather than using high-profile advertising with Western ideas.

---

[8]Robert L. Kohls, *Survival Kit for Overseas Living* (Chicago: Intercultural Press, 1979), 3.

[9]Edward T. Hall, *Beyond Culture* (Garden City, NY: Anchor Press, 1976), 15.

[10]**http://www.mcdonalds.com**

Indians are quite ambivalent toward foreign culture, and ideas usable elsewhere do not work well in India. Finally, KFC should have planned for reaction by competition that came from small restaurants with political clout at the local level.[11]

In some cases, the international marketer may be accused of "cultural imperialism," especially if the changes brought about are dramatic or if culture-specific adaptations are not made in the marketing approach. Some countries, such as France, Canada, Brazil, and Indonesia, protect their "cultural industries" (e.g., music and movies) through restrictive rules and subsidies. The WTO agreement that will allow restrictions on exports of U.S. entertainment to Europe is justified by the Europeans as a cultural safety net intended to support a desire to preserve national and regional identities.[12] This is highlighted in *The International Marketplace 3.2.* In June 1998, Canada organized a meeting in Ottawa about U.S. cultural dominance. Nineteen countries attended, including Britain, Brazil, and Mexico; the United States was excluded. At issue were ways of exempting cultural goods from treaties lowering trade barriers, on the view that free trade threatened national cultures. The Ottawa meeting followed a similar gathering in Stockholm, sponsored by the United Nations, which resolved to press for special exemptions for cultural goods in the Multilateral Agreement on Investment.[13]

Even if a particular country is dominant in a cultural sector, such as the United States in movies and television programming, the commonly suggested solution of protectionism may not work. Although the European Union has a rule that 40 percent of the programming has to be domestic, anyone wanting a U.S. program can choose an appropriate channel or rent a video. Quotas will also result in behavior not intended by regulators. U.S. programming tends to be scheduled during prime time, while the 60 percent of domestic programming may wind up being shown during less attractive times. Furthermore, quotas may also lead to local productions designed to satisfy official mandates and capture subsidies that accompany them.

Popular culture is not only a U.S. bastion. In many areas, such as pop music and musicals, Europeans have had an equally dominant position worldwide. Furthermore, no market is only an exporter of culture. Given the ethnic diversity in the United States (as in many other country markets), programming from around the world is made readily available. Many of the greatest successes among cultural products in 1999–2000 in the United States were imports; e.g., in television programming, "Who Wants to Be a Millionaire?" is a British concept, as is the best-seller in children's literature, the Harry Potter series. In cartoons, Pokémon hails from Japan.

The Elements of Culture

The study of culture has led to generalizations that may apply to all cultures. Such characteristics are called **cultural universals,** which are manifestations of the total way of life of any group of people. These include such elements as bodily adornments, courtship, etiquette, family gestures, joking, mealtimes, music, personal names, status differentiation, and trade.[14] These activities occur across cultures, but their manifestation may be unique in a particular society, bringing about cultural diversity. Common denominators can indeed be found, but the ways in which they are actually accom-

[11]Marita von Oldenborgh, "What's Next for India?" *International Business*, January 1996, 44–47; and Ravi Vijh, "Think Global, Act Indian," *Export Today*, June 1996, 27–28.

[12]Michael T. Malloy, "America, Go Home," *The Wall Street Journal*, March 26, 1993, R7.

[13]"Culture Wars," *The Economist*, September 12, 1998, 97–99.

[14]George P. Mundak, "The Common Denominator of Cultures," in *The Science of Man in the World*, ed. Ralph Linton (New York: Columbia University Press, 1945), 123–142.

THE INTERNATIONAL MARKETPLACE 3.2

Culture Wars

FILMS MADE IN THE UNITED STATES have continued to sweep the globe. According to the list of the most successful movies of 1998 put together by *Variety* magazine, U.S. films took the top 39 places; Britain's *The Full Monty* came in at number 40. As a consequence, British movies' market share fell to 14 percent of the home market, while the respective figure for French films was 27 percent in France and 10 percent for German films in Germany. The European Union's trade deficit with the United States in films and television is annually between $5 and $6 billion.

A number of developments seem to conspire to favor U.S. films. Multiplex cinemas have spread throughout Europe, with attendance increasing dramatically. However, multiplexes tend to show more U.S. movies. Along with the multiplexes has come the return of the blockbuster, such as *Titanic* and *Star Wars: The Phantom Menace*. These movies are made with budgets beyond the Europeans' wildest dreams. At the same time, studios' spending on marketing has leaped. Marketing campaigns typically start six months before the release of a film, and spending has increased to an average of $3.2 million, doubling the average in the mid-1990s. Finally, U.S. studios are becoming increasingly dependent on overseas revenues and are, therefore, keen on investing more in developing those markets. In 1998, foreign revenues were almost level with the domestic ones; fifteen years earlier they had been only half as big.

The Europeans have found a powerful ally in Canada, which has long been concerned about being overly influenced by its closest neighbor. Of the films shown on Canadian screens, 96 percent are foreign, primarily from the United States.

A strong case for the dominance of the United States can be made. It does not make the most feature films, but its movies reach and are sought by every market in the world. Movies made in India and Hong Kong, although numerous, seldom travel outside their regions. However, many arguments can also be made that U.S. movies are not so dominant. The nature of U.S. films is increasingly not just "American." From its earliest days, Hollywood has been open to overseas talent and money. Some of its greatest figures—Chaplin and Hitchcock, for example—were imports. Today, two of the most powerful studios (Columbia Tristar and Fox) are owned by media conglomerates from abroad (Japan's Sony and Australia's News Corporation).

Several of Hollywood's most successful movies have drawn from international resources. *Three Men and a Baby* was a remake of a French comedy. *Total Recall* was made partly with French money, was directed by a Dutchman, and starred an Austrian. *The English Patient* was directed by a Briton, was shot in Italy, and starred French and British talent. The quest for new ideas and fresh talent has led studios to develop subsidiaries in Europe: Sony's Bridge in London, Miramax in Berlin, and Warner Brothers both in Berlin and Paris.

We could conclude that it is less a matter of Hollywood corrupting the world than of the world corrupting Hollywood. The more Hollywood becomes dependent on the world market, the more it produces generic blockbusters made to play from Pisa to Peoria to Penang. One could argue that since these films are more likely to be driven by special effects (that can be appreciated by people with minimal grasp of English) rather than by dialogue and plot, and to be about subjects that anyone can identify with, there is something inherently objectionable in them. The movie goer is the final arbiter.

SOURCES: "Think Globally, Script Locally," *Fortune*, November 9, 1999, 156–160; "European Film Industry: Worrying Statistics," *The Economist*, February 6, 1999, 40–41; "If in Doubt, Bash the French," *The Economist*, December 12, 1998, 70–73; "Culture Wars," *The Economist*, September 12, 1998, 97–99; and "Does Canadian Culture Need This Much Protection?" *Business Week*, June 8, 1998.

plished may vary dramatically.[15] Observation of the major ones summarized in Table 3.1 suggests that the elements are both material (such as tools) and abstract (such as attitudes). The sensitivity and adaptation to these elements by an international firm depends on the firm's level of involvement in the market—for example, licensing versus direct investment—and the product or service marketed. Naturally, some products and services or management practices require very little adjustment, whereas others have to be adapted dramatically.

[15]Philip R. Harris and Robert T. Moran, *Managing Cultural Differences* (Houston, TX: Gulf, 1987), 201.

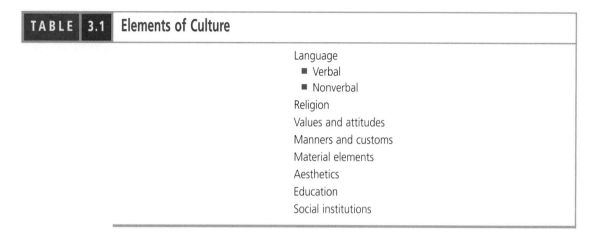

TABLE 3.1	Elements of Culture

Language
- Verbal
- Nonverbal

Religion

Values and attitudes

Manners and customs

Material elements

Aesthetics

Education

Social institutions

Language

Language has been described as the mirror of culture. Language itself is multidimensional by nature. This is true not only of the spoken word but also of what can be called the nonverbal language of international business. Messages are conveyed by the words used, by the way the words are spoken (for example, tone of voice), and by nonverbal means such as gestures, body position, and eye contact.

Very often, mastery of the language is required before a person is acculturated to a culture other than his or her own. Language mastery must go beyond technical competency, because every language has words and phrases that can be readily understood only in context. Such phrases are carriers of culture; they represent special ways a culture has developed to view some aspect of human existence.

Language capability serves four distinct roles in international marketing.[16] Language is important in information gathering and evaluation efforts. Rather than rely completely on the opinions of others, the manager is able to see and hear personally what is going on. People are far more comfortable speaking their own language, and this should be treated as an advantage. The best intelligence is gathered on a market by becoming part of the market rather than observing it from the outside. For example, local managers of a multinational corporation should be the firm's primary source of political information to assess potential risk. Second, language provides access to local society. Although English may be widely spoken, and may even be the official company language, speaking the local language may make a dramatic difference. For example, firms that translate promotional materials and information are seen as being serious about doing business in the country. Third, language capability is increasingly important in company communications, whether within the corporate family or with channel members. Imagine the difficulties encountered by a country manager who must communicate with employees through an interpreter. Finally, language provides more than the ability to communicate. It extends beyond mechanics to the interpretation of contexts.

The manager's command of the national language(s) in a market must be greater than simple word recognition. Consider, for example, how dramatically different English terms can be when used in Australia, the United Kingdom, or the United States. In negotiations, for U.S. delegates "tabling a proposal" means that they want to delay a decision, whereas their British counterparts understand the expression to mean that immediate action is to be taken. If the British promise something "by the end of the day," this does not mean within 24 hours, but rather when they have completed the job. Additionally, they may say that negotiations "bombed," meaning that

---

[16]David A. Ricks, *Big Business Blunders* (Homewood, IL: Irwin, 1983), 4.

they were a success; to a U.S. manager, this could convey exactly the opposite message. Similar challenges occur with other languages and markets. Swedish is spoken as a mother tongue by 8 percent of the population in Finland, where it has idioms that are not well understood by Swedes. Goodyear has identified five different terms for the word *tires* in the Spanish-speaking Americas: *cauchos* in Venezuela, *cubiertas* in Argentina, *gomas* in Puerto Rico, *neumaticos* in Chile, and *llantas* in most of the other countries in the region.[17]

Difficulties with language usually arise through carelessness, which is manifested in a number of translation blunders. The old saying "If you want to kill a message, translate it," is true. A classic example involves GM and its "Body by Fisher" theme; when translated into Flemish, this became "Corpse by Fisher." There is also the danger of sound-alikes. For example, Chanel No. 5 would have fared poorly in Japan had it been called Chanel No. 4, because the Japanese word for four (*shih*) also sounds like the word for death. This is the reason that IBM's series 44 computers had a different number classification in Japan than in any other market in which they were introduced. The danger of using a translingual homonym also exists; that is, an innocent English word may have strong aural resemblance to a word not used in polite company in another country. Examples in French-speaking areas include Pet milk products and a toothpaste called Cue. A French firm trying to sell pâté to a Baltimore importer experienced a problem with the brand name Tartex, which sounded like a shoe polish. Kellogg renamed Bran Buds in Sweden, where the brand name translated roughly to "burned farmer." In some cases, adjustments may not have to be dramatic to work. For example, elevator marketer Kone wanted to ensure the correct pronunciation of its name and added an accent *aigu* (Koné) to its name in French-speaking countries to avoid controversy.

An advertising campaign presented by Electrolux highlights the difficulties in transferring advertising campaigns between markets. Electrolux's theme in marketing its vacuum cleaners is interpreted literally in the United Kingdom, but in the United States, the slang implications would interfere with the intended message. In a Lucky Goldstar ad, adaptation into Arabic was carried out without considering that Arabic reads from right to left. As a result, the creative concept in this execution was destroyed.

Another consideration is the capability of language to convey different shades of meaning. As an example, a one-word equivalent to "aftertaste" does not exist in many languages and in others is far-fetched at best. To communicate the idea may require a lengthy translation of "the taste that remains in your mouth after you have finished eating or drinking." If a brand name or an advertising theme is to be extended, care has to be taken to make sure of a comfortable fit. Kellogg's Rice Krispies snap, crackle, and pop in most markets; the Japanese, who have trouble pronouncing these words, watch the characters "patchy, pitchy, putchy" in their commercials. To avoid market-by-market differences in the sound of dogs barking (i.e., "woof-woof" in Britain, "bau-bau" in Italy, "vov-vov" in Romania, or "wuff-wuff" in Austria), Pedigree dog food advertisements do not have dogs barking; the ads feature breeders talking about their dogs.[18]

The role of language extends beyond that of a communications medium. Linguistic diversity often is an indicator of other types of diversity. In Quebec, the French language has always been a major consideration of most francophone governments because it is one of the clear manifestations of the identity of the province that separates it from the English-speaking provinces. The Charter of the French Language states that the rights of the francophone collectivity are, among others, the right of

An ad campaign by Electrolux was effective in the United Kingdom but subject to misrepresentation in the United States.

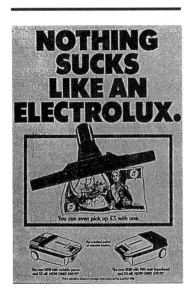

NOTHING SUCKS LIKE AN ELECTROLUX.

[17]David A. Hanni, John K. Ryans, and Ivan R. Vernon, "Coordinating International Advertising: The Goodyear Case Revisited for Latin America," *Journal of International Marketing* 3 (Number 2, 1995): 83–98.

[18]"For His Next Trick, He'll Help Trade Negotiators Communicate," *The Wall Street Journal*, December 1, 1992, B1.

consumers to be informed and served in French. The Bay, a major Quebec retailer, spends $8 million annually on its translation operations. It even changed its name to La Baie in appropriate areas. Similarly, in trying to battle English as the *lingua franca,* the French government has tried to ban the use of any foreign term or expression wherever an officially approved French equivalent exists (e.g., *mercatique,* not *un brainstorming*).[19] This applies also to Web sites that bear the ".fr" designation; they have to be in the French language.

Dealing with the language problem invariably requires the use of local assistance. A good local advertising agency and a good local market research firm can prevent many problems. When translation is required, as when communicating with suppliers or customers, care should be taken in selecting the translator. One of the simplest methods of control is **back-translation**—the translating of a foreign language version back to the original language by a different person than the one who made the first translation. This approach may help to detect only omissions and blunders, however. To assess the quality of the translation, a complete evaluation with testing of the message's impact is necessary.[20] In essence this means that international marketers should never translate words but emotion, which then, in turn, may well lead to the use of completely different words.

Language also has to be understood in its historic context. In Germany, Nokia launched an advertising campaign for the interchangable covers for its portable phones using the theme "*Jedem das Seine*" ("to each his own"). The campaign was withdrawn after the American Jewish Congress pointed out that the same slogan was found on the entry portal to Buchenwald, a Nazi-era concentration camp.[21]

Nonverbal Language

Managers must analyze and become familiar with the hidden language of foreign cultures.[22] Five key topics—time, space, material possessions, friendship patterns, and business agreements—offer a starting point from which managers can begin to acquire the understanding necessary to do business in foreign countries. In many parts of the world, time is flexible and not seen as a limited commodity; people come late to appointments or may not come at all. In Hong Kong, for example, it is futile to set exact meeting times, because getting from one place to another may take minutes or hours depending on the traffic. Showing indignation or impatience at such behavior would astonish an Arab, Latin American, or Asian.

In some countries, extended social acquaintance and the establishment of appropriate personal rapport are essential to conducting business. The feeling is that one should know one's business partner on a personal level before transactions can occur. Therefore, rushing straight to business will not be rewarded, because deals are made not only on the basis of the best product or price, but also on the entity or person deemed most trustworthy. Contracts may be bound on handshakes, not lengthy and complex agreements—a fact that makes some, especially Western, businesspeople uneasy.

Individuals vary in the amount of space they want separating them from others. Arabs and Latin Americans like to stand close to people they are talking with. If a U.S. executive, who may not be comfortable at such close range, backs away from an Arab, this might incorrectly be taken as a negative reaction. Also, Westerners are often taken

---

[19]"France: Mind Your Language," *The Economist,* March 23, 1996, 70–71.

[20]Margareta Bowen, "Business Translation," *Jerome Quarterly* 8 (August–September 1993): 5–9.

[21]"Nokia Veti Pois Mainoskampanjansa," *Uutislehti 100,* June 15, 1998, 5.

[22]Edward T. Hall, "The Silent Languge of Overseas Business," *Harvard Business Review* 38 (May–June 1960): 87–96.

aback by the more physical nature of affection between Slavs—for example, being kissed by a business partner, regardless of sex.

International body language must be included in the nonverbal language of international business. For example, a U.S. manager may, after successful completion of negotiations, impulsively give a finger-and-thumb OK sign. In southern France, the manager will have indicated that the sale is worthless, and in Japan that a little bribe has been asked for; the gesture is grossly insulting to Brazilians. An interesting exercise is to compare and contrast the conversation styles of different nationalities. Northern Europeans are quite reserved in using their hands and maintain a good amount of personal space, whereas Southern Europeans involve their bodies to a far greater degree in making a point.

Religion

In most cultures, people find in religion a reason for being and legitimacy in the belief that they are part of a larger context. To define religion requires the inclusion of the supernatural and the existence of a higher power. Religion defines the ideals for life, which in turn are reflected in the values and attitudes of societies and individuals. Such values and attitudes shape the behavior and practices of institutions and members of cultures.

Religion has an impact on international marketing that is seen in a culture's values and attitudes toward entrepreneurship, consumption, and social organization. The impact will vary depending on the strength of the dominant religious tenets. While religion's impact may be quite indirect in Protestant Northern Europe, its impact in countries where Islamic fundamentalism is on the rise (such as Algeria) may be profound.

Religion provides the basis for transcultural similarities under shared beliefs and behavior. The impact of these similarities will be assessed in terms of the dominant religions of the world: Christianity, Islam, Hinduism, Buddhism, and Confucianism. Other religions may have smaller numbers of followers, such as Judaism with 14 million followers around the world, but their impact is still significant due to the many centuries during which they have influenced world history. While some countries may officially have secularism, such as Marxism-Leninism, as a state belief (for example, China, Vietnam, and Cuba), traditional religious beliefs still remain a powerful force in shaping behavior. International marketing managers must be aware of the differences not only among the major religions but also within them. The impact of these divisions may range from hostility, as in Sri Lanka, to barely perceptible but long-standing suspicion, as in many European countries where Protestant and Catholic are the main divisions. With some religions, such as Hinduism, people may be divided into groups, which determines their status and to a large extent their ability to consume.

Christianity has the largest following among world religions, with more than 2 billion people.[23] While there are many significant groups within Christianity, the major ones are Catholicism and Protestantism. A prominent difference between the two of them is their attitude toward making money. While Catholicism has questioned it, the Protestant ethic has emphasized the importance of work and the accumulation of wealth for the glory of God. At the same time, frugality is stressed and the residual accumulation of wealth from hard work formed the basis for investment. It has been proposed that this is the basis for the development of capitalism in the Western world, and for the rise of predominantly Protestant countries to world economic leadership in the twentieth century.[24]

[23]*Statistical Abstract of the United States* (Washington, DC: U.S. Government Printing Office, 1999), 870.

[24]David McClelland, *The Achieving Society* (New York: Irvington, 1961), 90.

Major holidays are often tied to religion. Holidays will be observed differently from one culture to another, and the same holiday may have different connotations. Christian cultures observe Christmas and exchange gifts on either December 24 or 25, with the exception of the Dutch, who exchange gifts on St. Nicholas Day, December 6. Tandy Corporation, in its first year in the Netherlands, targeted its major Christmas promotion for the third week of December with less than satisfactory results. The international marketing manager must see to it that local holidays are taken into account in the scheduling of events ranging from fact-finding missions to marketing programs.

Islam, which reaches from the west coast of Africa to the Philippines and across a wide band that includes Tanzania, central Asia, western China, India, and Malaysia, has more than 1.2 billion followers.[25] Islam is also a significant minority religion in many parts of the world, including Europe. It plays a pervasive role in the life of its followers, referred to as Muslims, through the *shari'ah* (law of Islam). This is most obvious in the five stated daily periods of prayer, fasting during the holy month of Ramadan, and the pilgrimage to Mecca, Islam's holy city. While Islam is supportive of entrepreneurship, it nevertheless strongly discourages acts that may be interpreted as exploitation. Islam also lacks discrimination, except for those outside the religion. Some have argued that Islam's basic fatalism (that is, nothing happens without the will of Allah) and traditionalism have deterred economic development in countries observing the religion.

The role of women in business is tied to religion, especially in the Middle East, where women are not able to function as they would in the West. The effects of this are numerous; for example, a firm may be limited in its use of female managers or personnel in these areas, and women's role as consumers and influencers in the consumption process may be different. Except for food purchases, men make the final purchase decisions.[26] Access to women in Islamic countries may only be possible through the use of female sales personnel, direct marketing, and women's specialty shops.[27]

Religion affects the marketing of products and service delivery. When beef or poultry is exported to an Islamic country, the animal must be killed in the *halal* method and certified appropriately. Recognition of religious restrictions on products (for example, alcoholic beverages) can reveal opportunities, as evidenced by successful launches of several nonalcoholic beverages in the Middle East. Other restrictions may call for innovative solutions. A challenge for the Swedish firm that had the primary responsibility for building a traffic system to Mecca was that non-Muslims are not allowed access to the city. The solution was to use closed-circuit television to supervise the work. Given that Islam considers interest payments usury, bankers and Muslim scholars have worked to create interest-free banking products that rely on lease agreements, mutual funds, and other methods to avoid paying interest.[28]

Hinduism has 860 million followers, mainly in India, Nepal, Malaysia, Guyana, Suriname, and Sri Lanka. In addition to being a religion, it is also a way of life predicated on the caste, or class, to which one is born. While the caste system has produced social stability, its impact on business can be quite negative. For example, if one cannot rise above one's caste, individual effort is hampered. Problems in workforce integration and coordination may become quite severe. Furthermore, the drive for business success may not be forthcoming because of the fact that followers place value mostly on spiritual rather than materialistic achievement.

[25]*World Almanac and the Book of Facts* (Mahwah, NJ: Funk & Wagnalls, 1995), 734.

[26]Nora Fitzgerald, "Oceans Apart, but Closer than You Think," *World Trade*, February 1996, 58.

[27]Mushtaq Luqmami, Zahir A. Quraeshi, and Linda Delene, "Marketing in Islamic Countries: A Viewpoint," *MSU Business Topics* 23 (Summer 1980): 17–24.

[28]"Islamic Banking: Faith and Creativity," *The New York Times*, April 8, 1994, D1, D6.

The family is an important element in Hindu society, with extended families being the norm. The extended family structure will have an impact on the purchasing power and consumption of Hindu families. Market researchers, in particular, must take this into account in assessing market potential and consumption patterns.

Buddhism, which extends its influence throughout Asia from Sri Lanka to Japan, has 360 million followers. Although it is an offspring of Hinduism, it has no caste system. Life is seen as an existence of suffering, with achieving nirvana, a state marked by an absence of desire, as the solution to suffering. The emphasis in Buddhism is on spiritual achievement rather than worldly goods.

Confucianism has over 150 million followers throughout Asia, especially among the Chinese, and has been characterized as a code of conduct rather than a religion. However, its teachings that stress loyalty and relationships have been broadly adopted. Loyalty to central authority and placing the good of a group before that of the individual may explain the economic success of Japan, South Korea, Singapore, and the Republic of China. It also has led to cultural misunderstandings: In Western societies there has been a perception that the subordination of the individual to the common good has resulted in the sacrifice of human rights. The emphasis on relationships is very evident when developing business ties in Asia. The preparatory stage may take years before the needed level of understanding is reached and actual business transactions can take place.

Values and Attitudes

Values are shared beliefs or group norms that have been internalized by individuals.[29] Attitudes are evaluations of alternatives based on these values. The Japanese culture raises an almost invisible—yet often unscalable—wall against all *gaijin*, foreigners. Many middle-aged bureaucrats and company officials, for example, feel that buying foreign products is unpatriotic. The resistance therefore is not so much against foreign products as it is against those who produce and market them. As a result, foreign-based corporations have had difficulty in hiring university graduates or mid-career personnel because of bias against foreign employers. Dealing in China and with the Chinese, the international marketing manager will have to realize that marketing has more to do with cooperation than competition. The Chinese believe that one should build the relationship first and, if that is successful, transactions will follow. The relationship, or *guanxi*, is a set of exchanges of favors to establish trust.[30]

Even under these adverse conditions, the race can be run and won through tenacity, patience, and drive. As an example, Procter & Gamble has made impressive inroads with its products by adopting a long-term, Japanese-style view of profits. Since the mid-1970s, the company has gained some 20 percent of the detergent market and made Pampers a household word among Japanese mothers. The struggle toward such rewards can require foreign companies to take big losses for five years or more.

The more rooted values and attitudes are in central beliefs (such as religion), the more cautiously the international marketing manager has to move. Attitude toward change is basically positive in industrialized countries, whereas in more tradition-bound societies, change is viewed with great suspicion, especially when it comes from a foreign entity. These situations call for thorough research, most likely a localized approach, and a major commitment at the top level for a considerable period of time. For example, before launching Colac laxative in Japan, Richardson-Vicks studied the psychological dimensions of constipation. The reticent Japanese are willing to discuss such delicate subjects once they realize they are members of a group with a common

[29]James F. Engel, Roger D. Blackwell, and Paul W. Miniard, *Consumer Behavior* (Hinsdale, IL: Dryden, 1986), 223.

[30]Y.H. Wong and Ricky Yee-kwong, "Relationship Marketing in China: Guanxi, Favoritism and Adaptation," *Journal of Business Ethics* 22 (Number 2, 1999): 107–118; and Tim Ambler, "Reflections in China: Re-Orienting Images of Marketing," *Marketing Management* 4 (Number 1, 1995): 23–30.

problem, but not with Westerners present at the meetings. Research showed that the Japanese were dissatisfied with slow-acting herbal medicines but wary that a Western laxative might be too strong. Thus, Colac is presented as two little pink pills with natural qualities: "Three things to consider for stubborn constipation—salad, beauty exercise, and Colac before bedtime."

Cultural differences in themselves can be a selling point suggesting luxury, prestige, or status. Sometimes U.S. companies use domestic marketing approaches when selling abroad because they believe the American look will sell the product. In Japan, Borden sells Lady Borden ice cream and Borden cheese deliberately packaged and labeled in English, exactly as they are in the United States. Similarly, in France, General Foods sells a chewing gum called Hollywood with an accompanying Pepsi-generation type of ad campaign that pictures teenagers riding bicycles on the beach. The marketer has to be careful not to assume that success using the cultural extension in one market ensures success somewhere else; for example, the Disneyland concept worked well in Tokyo, but it had a tougher time in Paris. One of the main reasons was that while the Japanese are fond of U.S. pop culture, Europeans are quite content with their own cultural heritage.[31]

Occasionally, U.S. firms successfully use American themes abroad that would not succeed at home. In Japan, Levi Strauss promoted its popular jeans with a television campaign featuring James Dean and Marilyn Monroe, who represent the epitome of Japanese youths' fantasy of freedom from a staid, traditional society. The commercials helped to establish Levi's as *the* prestige jeans, and status-seeking Japanese youth willingly pay 40 percent more for them than for local brands. Their authentic Levi's, however, are designed and mostly made in Japan, where buyers like a tighter fit than do consumers in the United States. Similarly, many global brands, such as Nike and Reebok, are able to charge premium prices for their products due to their loyal following.[32] At the same time, in the U.S. market, many companies have been quite successful in emphasizing a foreign, imported image.

Manners and Customs

Changes occurring in manners and customs must be carefully monitored, especially in cases that seem to indicate narrowing of cultural differences between peoples. Phenomena such as McDonald's and Coke have met with success around the world, but this does not mean that the world is becoming Westernized. Modernization and Westernization are not at all the same, as can be seen in Saudi Arabia, for example.

Understanding manners and customs is especially important in negotiations, because interpretations based on one's own frame of reference may lead to a totally incorrect conclusion. To negotiate effectively abroad, one needs to read correctly all types of communication. U.S. executives often interpret inaction and silence as a negative sign, so Japanese executives tend to expect their U.S. counterparts to lower prices or sweeten the deal if they just say as little as possible. Even a simple agreement may take days to negotiate in the Middle East, because the Arab party may want to talk about unrelated issues or do something else for a while. The abrasive style of Russian negotiators, and their usual last-minute change requests, may cause astonishment and concern on the part of ill-prepared negotiators. And consider the reaction of a U.S. businessperson if a Finnish counterpart were to propose the continuing of negotiations in the sauna. Preparation is needed not only in the business sense but in a cultural sense as well. Some of the potential areas in which marketers may not be prepared include: (1) insufficient understanding of different ways of thinking; (2) insufficient attention

---

[31]Earl P. Spencer, "EuroDisney—What Happened?" *Journal of International Marketing* 3 (Number 3, 1995): 103–114.

[32]"Latest Nike Sneakers Fly off Tokyo Shelves Even at $1,300 a Pair," *The Washington Post*, November 7, 1996, A1, A10.

TABLE 3.2	When and What to Give as Gifts			
CHINA	INDIA	JAPAN	MEXICO	SAUDI ARABIA
Chinese New Year (January or February)	*Hindu Diwali festival* (October or November)	*Oseibo* (Jan. 1)	*Christmas/New Year*	*Id al-Fitr* (December or January)
✔ Modest gifts such as coffee table books, ties, pens	✔ Sweets, nuts, and fruit; elephant carvings; candleholders	✔ Scotch, brandy, Americana, round fruit such as melons	✔ Desk clocks, fine pens, gold lighters	✔ Fine compasses to determine direction for prayer, cashmere
✘ Clocks, anything from Taiwan	✘ Leather objects, snake images	✘ Gifts that come in sets of four or nine	✘ Sterling silver items, logo gifts, food baskets	✘ Pork and pigskin, liquor

✔ recommended

✘ to be avoided

SOURCE: Kate Murphy, "Gifts without Gaffes for Global Clients," *Business Week*, December 6, 1999, 153.

to the necessity of saving face; (3) insufficient knowledge and appreciation of the host country—history, culture, government, and image of foreigners; (4) insufficient recognition of the decision-making process and the role of personal relations and personalities; and (5) insufficient allocation of time for negotiations.[33]

One instance when preparation and sensitivity are called for is in the area of gift giving. Table 3.2 provides examples of what to give and when. Gifts are an important part of relationship management during visits and a way of recognizing partners during holidays. Care should be taken with the way the gift is wrapped; for example, it should be in appropriately colored paper. If delivered in person, the actual giving has to be executed correctly; in China, this is done by extending the gift to the recipient using both hands.[34]

Managers must be concerned with differences in the ways products are used. For example, General Foods' Tang is positioned as a breakfast drink in the United States; in France, where orange juice is not usually consumed at breakfast, Tang is positioned as a refreshment. The questions that the international manager must ask are, "What are we selling?" "What are the use benefits we should be providing?" and "Who or what are we competing against?" These questions are highlighted in *The International Marketplace 3.3*. Care should be taken not to assume cross-border similarities even if many of the indicators converge. For example, a jam producer noted that the Brazilian market seemed to hold significant potential because per capita jelly and jam consumption was one-tenth that of Argentina, clearly a difference not justified by obvious factors. However, Argentines consume jam at tea time, a custom that does not exist in Brazil. Furthermore, Argentina's climate and soil favor growing wheat, leading it to consume three times the amount of bread Brazil does.[35]

Many Western companies have stumbled in Japan because they did not learn enough about the distinctive habits of Japanese consumers. Purveyors of soup should know that the Japanese drink it mainly for breakfast. Johnson & Johnson had relatively little success selling baby powder in Japan until research was conducted on use conditions. In their small homes, mothers fear that powder will fly around and get into their spotlessly clean kitchens. The company now sells baby powder in flat boxes

[33]Sergey Frank, "Global Negotiations: Vive Les Differences!" *Sales & Marketing Management* 144 (May 1992): 64–69.

[34]See, for example, Terri Morrison, *Kiss, Bow, or Shake Hands: How to Do Business in Sixty Countries* (Holbrook, MA: Adams Media, 1994), or Roger Axtell, *Do's and Taboos around the World* (New York: John Wiley & Sons, 1993). For holiday observances, see **http://www.religioustolerance.org/main_day.htm#cal** and **http://www.yahoo.com/society_and_culture/holidays_and_observances**.

[35]James A. Gingrich, "Five Rules for Winning Emerging Market Consumers," *Strategy and Business* (second quarter, 1999): 68–76.

THE INTERNATIONAL MARKETPLACE 3.3

Soup: Now It's Mmmm-Mmmm-Global!

IN THE LATE 1990's, Campbell Soup aimed to generate half of its revenues outside the U.S. by the twenty-first century. An ambitious goal, its foreign sales were only a quarter of the total in 2000. Adding to the challenge is the fact that prepared food may be one of the toughest products to sell overseas. It is not as universal or as easily marketed as soap or soft drinks, given regional taste preferences. While an average Pole consumes five bowls of soup a week, 98 percent of Polish soups are homemade.

Campbell has managed to overcome some cultural obstacles in selected countries. In Poland, Campbell advertises to working Polish mothers looking for convenience. Says Lee Andrews, Campbell's new-product manager in Warsaw: "We can't shove a can in their faces and replace Mom."

However, in many regions, Campbell is trying to cook more like her. This means creating new products that appeal to distinctly regional tastes. The approach has been to use test kitchens and taste-testing with consumers. Results have included fiery cream of poblano soup in Mexico as well as watercress and duck-gizzard soup for China. Cream of pumpkin has become Australia's top-selling canned soup.

Asia has traditionally accounted for only 2 percent of Campbell's worldwide sales, but the region—China, in particular—is being targeted as the area with the strongest growth potential. In new markets, Campbell typically launches a basic meat or chicken broth, which consumers can doctor with meats, vegetables, and spices. Later, more sophisticated soups are brought on line. In China, the real competition comes from homemade soup, which accounts for over 99 percent of all consumption. With this in mind, Campbell's prices have been kept at an attractive level and the product promoted on convenience.

Local ingredients may count, but Campbell draws the line on some Asian favorites. Dog soup is out, as is shark's fin, since most species are endangered. For most other options, including snake, for example, the company keeps an open mind.

Campbell is also finding that ethnic foods are growing in popularity around the world. With its emphasis on vegetables, Asian cuisine benefits from a healthy image in Europe and North America. This means that some new products being presently developed for the Asian consumer may become global favorites in no time.

At the same time, the company has made a strategic shift, acknowledging that outside the U.S. cultural preferences for dry soups are well entrenched. While Campbell is succeeding in developing canned soups for local tastes, its acquisition of dry soup makers like the Anglo-Dutch Unilever will help it truly become a global soup company.

SOURCES: "Souping Up Campbell's," *Business Week*, November 3, 1997, 70–72; Linda Grant, "Stirring It Up at Campbell," *Fortune*, May 13, 1996, 80–86; "Ethnic Food Whets Appetites in Europe, Enticing Producers to Add Foreign Fare," *The Wall Street Journal*, November 1, 1993, B5A; "Hmmm, Could Use a Little More Snake," *Business Week*, March 15, 1993, 53; and "Canned and Delivered," *Business China*, November 16, 1992, 12; "Campbell Soup Creates a Stake in the European Market with Recent Aquisition," *The Philadelphia Inquirer*, January, 30, 2001, Harold Brubaker.

http://www.campbellsoup.com

with powder puffs so that mothers can apply it sparingly. Adults will not use it at all. They wash and rinse themselves before soaking in hot baths; powder would make them feel dirty again.

Usage differences have to be translated into product form and promotional decisions. Maxwell House coffee is a worldwide brand name. It is used to sell coffee in both ground and instant form in the United States. In the United Kingdom, Maxwell House is available only in instant form. In France and Germany, it is sold in freeze-dried form only, whereas in the Scandinavian countries, Maxwell House is positioned as the top-of-the-line entry. As a matter of fact, Maxwell House is called simply Maxwell in France and Japan because "House" is confusing to consumers in those countries. In one South American market, a shampoo maker was concerned about poor sales of the entire product class. Research uncovered the fact that many women wash their hair with bars of soap and use shampoo only as a brief rinse or topper.

Another classic case involves General Mills's Betty Crocker cake mix. The company designed a mix to be prepared in electric rice cookers. After the product's costly flop, the company found that the Japanese take pride in the purity of their rice, which they thought would be contaminated by cake flavors. General Mills's mistake was comparable to asking an English consumer to make coffee in his or her teapot.

Package sizes and labels must be adapted in many countries to suit the needs of the particular culture. In Mexico, for example, Campbell's sells soup in cans large enough to serve four or five because families are generally large. In Britain, where consumers are more accustomed to ready-to-serve soups, Campbell's prints "one can makes two" on its condensed soup labels to ensure that shoppers understand how to use it.

In the United States, men buy diamond engagement rings for their fiancées. This custom is not global, however. In Germany, for example, young women tend to buy diamond rings for themselves. This precludes the use of global advertising campaigns by a company such as De Beers.

Managers must be careful of myths and legends. One candy company was ready to launch a new peanut-packed chocolate bar in Japan, aimed at giving teenagers quick energy while they crammed for exams. The company then learned about a Japanese folk legend that eating chocolate with peanuts can cause nosebleed. The launch never took place. Approaches that might be rarely taken in the United States or Europe could be recommended in other regions; for example, Conrad Hotels (the international arm of Hilton) experienced low initial occupancy rates at its Hong Kong facility until the firm brought in a feng shui man. These traditional "consultants" are foretellers of future events and the unknown through occult means and are used extensively by Hong Kong businesses, especially for advising about where to locate offices and how to position office equipment.[36] In Conrad's case, the suggestion was to move a piece of sculpture outside of the hotel's lobby because one of the characters in the statue looked like it was trying to run out of the hotel.[37]

Meticulous research plays a major role in avoiding these types of problems. Concept tests determine the potential acceptance and proper understanding of a proposed new product. **Focus groups,** each consisting of eight to twelve consumers representative of the proposed target audience, can be interviewed and their responses used to check for disasters and to fine-tune research findings. The most sensitive types of products, such as consumer packaged goods, require consumer usage and attitude studies as well as retail distribution studies and audits to analyze the movement of the product to retailers and eventually to households. H.J. Heinz Co. uses focus groups to determine what consumers want in ketchup in the way of taste and image. U.S. consumers prefer a relatively sweet ketchup while Europeans go for a spicier variety. In Central

A consumer focus group in Mexico evaluates Campbell's soups, reviewing qualities such as packaging, preparation, appearance, and taste. The passage of NAFTA broadened market opportunities in Mexico, where nearly nine billion servings of soup are consumed each year. Marketing executives test reactions and assess whether products meet local needs.

[36]"Feng Shui Strikes Chord," available at **http://www.cnnfn.com/1999/09/11/life/q_fengshui/.**

[37]"Feng Shui Man Orders Sculpture out of the Hotel," *South China Morning Post,* July 27, 1992, 4.

74 Chapter 3 • THE CULTURAL ENVIRONMENT

Europe and Sweden, Heinz sells a hot ketchup in addition to the classic variety. In addition to changes in the product, the company may need to promote new usage situations. For example, in Greece this may mean running advertisements showing how ketchup can be poured on pasta, eggs, and cuts of meat. While some markets consider Heinz's U.S. origin a plus, there are others where it has to be played down. In Northern Europe, where ketchup is served as an accompaniment to traditional meatballs and fishballs, Heinz deliberately avoids reminding consumers of its heritage. The messages tend to be health related.[38]

The adjustment to cultural variables in the market place may have to be long term and accomplished through trial and error, as shown in the experience of U.S. retailers in Japan, highlighted in *The International Marketplace 3.4.*

Material Elements

Material culture results from technology and is directly related to the way a society organizes its economic activity. It is manifested in the availability and adequacy of the basic economic, social, financial, and marketing **infrastructures.** The basic economic infrastructure consists of transportation, energy, and communications systems. Social infrastructure refers to housing, health, and educational systems. Financial and marketing infrastructures provide the facilitating agencies for the international firm's operation in a given market in terms of, for example, banks and research firms. In some parts of the world, the international firm may have to be an integral partner in developing the various infrastructures before it can operate, whereas in others, it may greatly benefit from their high level of sophistication.

The level of material culture can be a segmentation variable if the degree of industrialization of the market is used as a basis. For companies selling industrial goods, such as General Electric, this can provide a convenient starting point. In developing countries, demand may be highest for basic energy-generating products. In fully developed markets, time-saving home appliances may be more in demand.

Technological advances have probably been the major cause of cultural change in many countries. For example, the increase in leisure time so characteristic in Western cultures has been a direct result of technological development. Workers in Germany are now pushing for a 35-hour work week. Increasingly consumers are seeking more diverse products–including convenience items–as a way of satisfying their demand for a higher quality of life and more leisure time. For example, a 1999 Gallup survey in China found that 44 percent of the respondents were saving to buy electronic items and appliances, second only to saving for a rainy day.[39] Marketers able to tailor and market their products to fit the new lifestyle especially in emerging markets stand to reap the benefits. For example, consumers around the world are showing greater acceptance of equipment for personal use, reflected in increased sales of mobile phones and small computers as well as increased Internet use. With technological advancement also comes **cultural convergence.** Black-and-white television sets extensively penetrated the U.S. market more than a decade before they reached similar levels in Europe and Japan. With color television, the lag was reduced to five years. With videocassette recorders, the difference was only three years, but this time the Europeans and the Japanese led the way while U.S. consumers concentrated on cable systems. With the compact disc, penetration rates were even after only one year. Today, with MTV available by satellite around the world, no lag exists at all.[40]

[38]"The New Life of O'Reilly," *Business Week,* June 13, 1994, 64–66; and "Heinz Aims to Export Taste for Ketchup," *The Wall Street Journal,* November 20, 1992, B1, B10.

[39]The results of the Gallup study are available in "What the Chinese Want," *Fortune,* October 11, 1999, 229–234; and at **http://www.fortune.com/fortune/china/chart.html.**

[40]Kenichi Ohmae, "Managing in a Borderless World," *Harvard Business Review* 67 (May–June 1989): 152–161.

THE INTERNATIONAL MARKETPLACE 3.4

U.S. Stores in Japan

OFFICE DEPOT AND OFFICEMAX entered the Japanese market to take advantage of the retail revolution that has been changing the landscape throughout the 1990s. The $13 billion stationery industry, for example, was archaic, and the 13,000 mostly small stationery stores usually charged full price. The two U.S. superstores had grand plans to open scores of office outlets, giants compared to their Japanese counterparts, filled with cut-price pens, notebooks, and fax machines. They joined the scores of other retailers such as J.C. Penney, Toys "R" Us, Gap, Spiegel, and Sports Authority to take advantage of recession-weary local consumers eager for lower-priced goods.

However, in most cases success has been elusive. Many retailers are scrambling to revise their strategies, while some are even scaling down or leaving the field altogether. In all cases, cultural differences played the major role. "Retailing is such a local business; one just cannot take the same formula and expect it to work in Japan," said one local marketing expert. Spiegel, after much prodding from Japanese staffers, is changing its strategy of selling the same products it sells in the United States to selling localized versions such as straight-leg pants and stretchy shirts to better fit the Japanese. Sports Authority reduced its stake in a joint venture from 51 percent to 8.4 percent, and its local partner is focused on opening smaller stores. J.C. Penney closed its five home-furnishings stores, mainly because many of its products have to be made differently for Japan.

Although both Office Depot and OfficeMax formed joint ventures with local partners to gauge the lay of the land, it was not enough. Japanese office products are so different from those in the United States (for example, looseleaf binders have two rings instead of three) that OfficeMax and Office Depot had to buy most of their supplies from local producers. Because they were selling the same product as their Japanese rivals, they had to compete on price, although the best sourcing deals were not necessarily available to them. In some cases, Japanese suppliers insisted on Home Depot going through intermediaries for the fear of annoying neighborhood stores.

The stores also turned out to be too different. Office Depot opened two U.S.-style stores in Tokyo and Hiroshima, with more than 20,000 square feet each, wide aisles, and signs in English. But with rents in Japan more than twice those in the United States and personnel costs sky-high, the stores were just too expensive to operate. Japanese customers were baffled by the English-language signs and the warehouse-like atmosphere. Indeed, when Office Depot later reduced the size of the Tokyo store by a third and crammed the merchandise closer together, sales remained at the same level as before.

Both Office Depot and OfficeMax changed their strategies to be competitive. Office Depot closed its large store in Hiroshima and is concentrating on Tokyo, where it opened up four mini-stores that are a fifth the size of U.S. stores. Similarly, OfficeMax, with its six large stores in Tokyo suburbs, also switched to the small-store format. In 2001, however, it ended its money-losing joint venture and began closing all Tokyo stores.

The Japanese market "has enormous risk and it has the potential of enormous payout," said Bruce Nelson, president of Office Depot's international division. "It will just be one of the best places we do business—or it will be one of the worst."

SOURCES: "U.S. Superstores Find Japanese Are a Hard Sell," *The Wall Street Journal*, February 14, 2000, B1, B4; and Denise Incandela, Kathleen McLaughlin, and Christiana Smith Shi, "Retailers to the World," *The McKinsey Quarterly* 35 (Number 3, 1999): 84–97; "Jusco to dissolve joint venture with OfficeMax," *Kyodo World News Service*, January 22, 2001.

Material culture–mainly the degree to which it exists and how much it is esteemed—will have an impact on marketing decisions. Many exporters do not understand the degree to which U.S. consumers are package-conscious; for example, cans must be shiny and beautiful. On the other hand, packaging problems may arise in other countries due to lack of certain materials, different specifications when the material is available, different line-fill machinery, and immense differences in quality and consistency of printing ink, especially in South America and the Third World. Even the ability of media to reach target audiences will be affected by ownership of radios, television sets, and personal computers.

Population Density and Growth

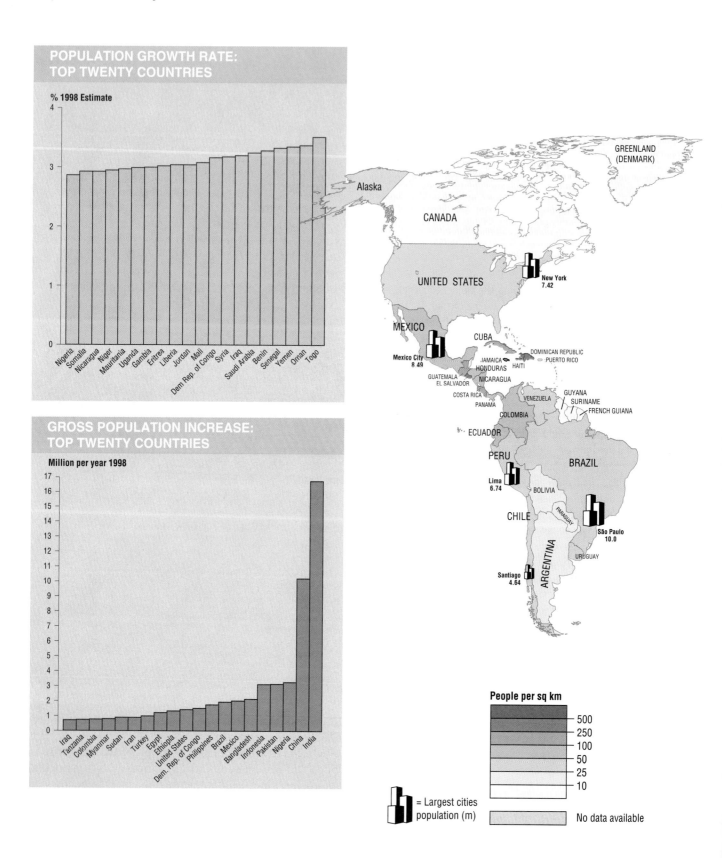

POPULATION GROWTH RATE: TOP TWENTY COUNTRIES

% 1998 Estimate

Nigeria, Somalia, Nicaragua, Niger, Mauritania, Uganda, Gambia, Eritrea, Liberia, Jordan, Mali, Dem Rep. of Congo, Syria, Iraq, Saudi Arabia, Benin, Senegal, Yemen, Oman, Togo

GROSS POPULATION INCREASE: TOP TWENTY COUNTRIES

Million per year 1998

Iraq, Tanzania, Colombia, Myanmar, Sudan, Iran, Turkey, Egypt, Ethiopia, United States, Dem. Rep. of Congo, Philippines, Brazil, Mexico, Bangladesh, Indonesia, Pakistan, Nigeria, China, India

People per sq km

500 / 250 / 100 / 50 / 25 / 10

= Largest cities population (m)

No data available

New York 7.42 · Mexico City 8.49 · Lima 6.74 · São Paulo 10.0 · Santiago 4.64

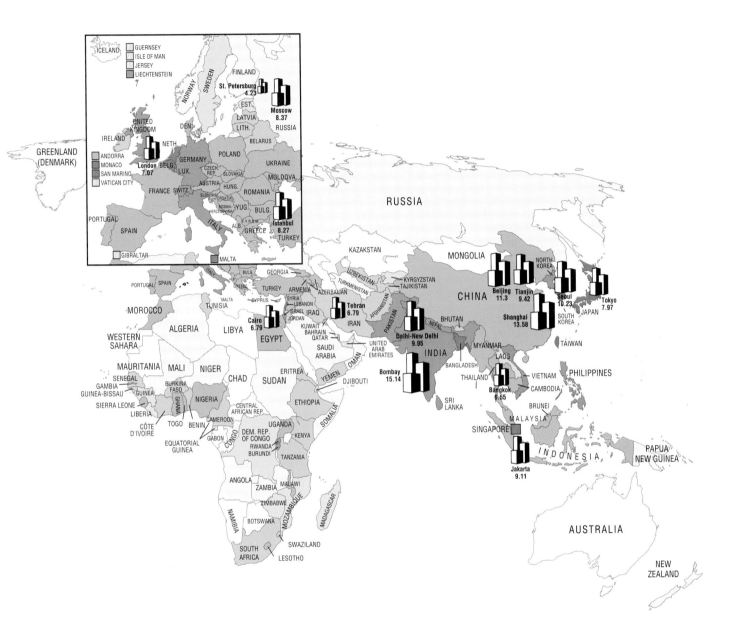

Sources: *The World Factbook, 1998—99; The World Almanac, 2000*

Aesthetics

Each culture makes a clear statement concerning good taste, as expressed in the arts and in the particular symbolism of colors, form, and music. What is and what is not acceptable may vary dramatically even in otherwise highly similar markets. Sex in advertising is an example. In an apparent attempt to preserve the purity of Japanese womanhood, Japanese advertisers frequently turn to blonde, blue-eyed foreign models to make the point. In introducing the shower soap Fa from the European market to the North American market, Henkel also extended its European advertising campaign to the new market. The main difference was to have the young woman in the waves don a bathing suit rather than be naked as in the German original.

Color is often used as a mechanism for brand identification, feature reinforcement, and differentiation. In international markets, colors have more symbolic value than in domestic markets. Black, for instance, is considered the color of mourning in the United States and Europe, whereas white has the same symbolic value in Japan and most of the Far East. A British bank interested in expanding its operations to Singapore wanted to use blue and green as its identification colors. A consulting firm was quick to tell the client that green is associated with death there. Although the bank insisted on its original choice of colors, the green was changed to an acceptable shade.[41] Similarly, music used in broadcast advertisements is often adjusted to reflect regional differences.

International firms have to take into consideration local tastes and concerns in designing their facilities. They may have a general policy of uniformity in building or office space design, but local tastes may often warrant modifications. Respecting local cultural traditions may also generate goodwill toward the international marketer. For example, McDonald's painstakingly renovated a seventeenth-century building for its third outlet in Moscow.

Education

Education, either formal or informal, plays a major role in the passing on and sharing of culture. Educational levels of a culture can be assessed using literacy rates and enrollment in secondary or higher education, information available from secondary data sources. International firms also need to know about the qualitative aspects of education, namely, varying emphases on particular skills, and the overall level of the education provided. Japan and the Republic of Korea, for example, emphasize the sciences, especially engineering, to a greater degree than do Western countries.

Educational levels will have an impact on various business functions. Training programs for a production facility will have to take the educational backgrounds of trainees into account. For example, a high level of illiteracy will suggest the use of visual aids rather than printed manuals. Local recruiting for sales jobs will be affected by the availability of suitably trained personnel. In some cases, international firms routinely send locally recruited personnel to headquarters for training.

The international marketing manager may also have to be prepared to fight obstacles in recruiting a suitable sales force or support personnel. For example, the Japanese culture places a premium on loyalty, and employees consider themselves to be members of the corporate family. If a foreign firm decides to leave Japan, employees may find themselves stranded midcareer, unable to find a place in the Japanese business system. University graduates are therefore reluctant to join all but the largest and most well known of foreign firms.[42]

[41]Joe Agnew, "Cultural Differences Probed to Create Product Identity," *Marketing News,* October 24, 1986, 22.

[42]Joseph A. McKinney, "Joint Ventures of United States Firms in Japan: A Survey," *Venture Japan* 1, no. 2 (1988): 14–19.

If technology is marketed, the level of sophistication of the product will depend on the educational level of future users. Product adaptation decisions are often influenced by the extent to which targeted customers are able to use the product or service properly.

Social Institutions

Social institutions affect the ways in which people relate to each other. The family unit, which in Western industrialized countries consists of parents and children, in a number of cultures is extended to include grandparents and other relatives. This will have an impact on consumption patterns and must be taken into account, for example, when conducting market research.

The concept of kinship, or blood relations between individuals, is defined in a very broad way in societies such as those in sub-Saharan Africa. Family relations and a strong obligation to family are important factors to be considered in human resource management in those regions. Understanding tribal politics in countries such as Nigeria may help the manager avoid unnecessary complications in executing business transactions.

The division of a particular population into classes is termed **social stratification.** Stratification ranges from the situation in Northern Europe, where most people are members of the middle class, to highly stratified societies such as India in which the higher strata control most of the buying power and decision-making positions.

An important part of the socialization process of consumers worldwide is **reference groups.** These groups provide the values and attitudes that become influential in shaping behavior. Primary reference groups include the family, coworkers, and other intimate groupings, whereas secondary groups are social organizations in which less-continuous interaction takes place, such as professional associations and trade organizations. Besides socialization, reference groups develop an individual's concept of self, which manifests itself, for example, through the use of products. Reference groups also provide a baseline for compliance with group norms through either conforming to or avoiding certain behaviors.

Social organization also determines the roles of managers and subordinates and the way they relate to one another. In some cultures, managers and subordinates are separated explicitly and implicitly by various boundaries ranging from social class differences to separate office facilities. In others, cooperation is elicited through equality. For example, Nissan USA has no reserved parking spaces and no private dining rooms, everyone wears the same type of white coveralls, and the president sits in the same room with a hundred other white-collar workers. The fitting of an organizational culture for internal marketing purposes to the larger context of a national culture has to be executed with care. Changes that are too dramatic may cause disruption of productivity or, at the minimum, suspicion.

While Western business practice has developed impersonal structures for channeling power and influence through reliance on laws and contracts, the Chinese emphasize getting on the good side of someone and storing up political capital with him or her. Things can get done without this capital, or *guanxi,* only if one invests enormous personal energy, is willing to offend even trusted associates, and is prepared to see it all melt away at a moment's notice.[43] For the Chinese, contracts form a useful agenda and a symbol of progress, but obligations come from relationships. McDonald's found this out in Beijing, where it was evicted from a central building after only two years

[43]Peter MacInnis, "Guanxi or Contract: A Way to Understand and Predict Conflict between Chinese and Western Senior Managers in China-Based Joint Ventures," in Daniel E. McCarthy and Stanley J. Hille, eds., *Multinational Business Management and Internationalization of Business Enterprises* (Nanjing, China: Nanjing University Press, 1993), 345–351.

despite having a twenty-year contract. The incomer had a strong *guanxi*, whereas McDonald's had not kept its relationships in good repair.[44]

Sources of Cultural Knowledge

The concept of cultural knowledge is broad and multifaceted. Cultural knowledge can be defined by the way it is acquired. Objective or factual information is obtained from others through communication, research, and education. **Experiential knowledge,** on the other hand, can be acquired only by being involved in a culture other than one's own.[45] A summary of the types of knowledge needed by the international manager is provided in Table 3.3. Both factual and experiential information can be general or country-specific. In fact, the more a manager becomes involved in the international arena, the more he or she is able to develop a meta-knowledge, that is, ground rules that apply to a great extent whether in Kuala Lumpur, Malaysia, or Asunción, Paraguay. Market-specific knowledge does not necessarily travel well; the general variables on which the information is based do.

In a survey on how to acquire international expertise, managers ranked eight factors in terms of their importance, as shown in Table 3.4. These managers emphasized the experiential acquisition of knowledge. Written materials were indicated to play an important but supplementary role, very often providing general or country-specific information before operational decisions must be made. Interestingly, many of today's international managers have precareer experience in government, the Peace Corps, the armed forces, or missionary service. Although the survey emphasized travel, a one-time trip to London with a stay at a large hotel and scheduled sight-seeing tours does not contribute to cultural knowledge in a significant way. Travel that involves meetings with company personnel, intermediaries, facilitating agents, customers, and government officials, on the other hand, does contribute.

However, from the corporate point of view, the development of a global capability requires experience acquisition in more involved ways. This translates into foreign assignments and networking across borders, for example through the use of multi-country, multicultural teams to develop strategies and programs. At Nestlé, for example, managers shuffle around a region (such as Asia or Latin America) at four- to

TABLE 3.3   Types of International Information

SOURCE OF INFORMATION	TYPE OF INFORMATION	
	GENERAL	COUNTRY-SPECIFIC
Objective	Examples: • Impact of GDP • Regional integration	Examples: • Tariff barriers • Government regulations
Experiential	Example: • Corporate adjustment to internationalization	Examples: • Product acceptance • Program appropriateness

[44]Tim Ambler, "Reflections in China: Re-Orienting Images of Marketing," *Marketing Management* 4 (Summer 1995): 23–30.

[45]James H. Sood and Patrick Adams, "Model of Management Learning Styles as a Predictor of Export Behavior and Performance," *Journal of Business Research* 12 (June 1984): 169–182.

| TABLE 3.4 | Managers' Ranking of Factors Involved in Acquiring International Expertise |

FACTOR	CONSIDERED CRITICAL	CONSIDERED IMPORTANT
1. Business travel	60.8%	92.0%
2. Assignments overseas	48.8	71.2
3. Reading/television	16.0	63.2
4. Training programs	6.4	28.8
5. Precareer activities	4.0	16.0
6. Graduate course	2.4	15.2
7. Nonbusiness travel	0.8	12.8
8. Undergraduate courses	0.8	12.0

SOURCE: Stephen J. Kobrin, *International Expertise in American Business* (New York: Institute of International Education, 1984), 38.

five-year intervals and may have tours at headquarters for two to three years between such assignments. This allows these managers to pick up ideas and tools to be used in markets where they have not been used or where they have not been necessary up to now. In Thailand, where supermarkets are revolutionizing consumer-goods marketing, techniques perfected elsewhere in the Nestlé system are being put to effective use. These experiences will then, in turn, be used to develop newly emerging markets in the same region, such as Vietnam.

Various sources and methods are available to the manager for extending his or her knowledge of specific cultures. Most of these sources deal with factual information that provides a necessary basis for market studies. Beyond the normal business literature and its anecdotal information, specific country studies are published by governments, private companies, and universities. The U.S. Department of Commerce's (**www.ita.doc.gov**) *Country Commercial Guides* cover 133 countries, while the Economist Intelligence Unit's (**www.eiu.com**) *Country Reports* cover 180 countries. *Culturegrams* (**www.culturegrams.com**) which detail the customs of peoples of 174 countries, are published by the Center for International and Area Studies at Brigham Young University. Many facilitating agencies—such as advertising agencies, banks, consulting firms, and transportation companies—provide background information on the markets they serve for their clients: Runzheimer International's (**www.runzheimer.com**) international reports on employee relocation and site selection for 44 countries and the Hong Kong and Shanghai Banking Corporation's (**www.hsbc.com**) *Business Profile Series* for 22 countries in the Asia-Pacific to *World Trade* magazine's (**www.worldtrademag.com**) "Put Your Best Foot Forward" series, which covers Europe, Asia, Mexico/Canada, and Russia.

Blunders that could have been avoided with factual information about a foreign market are generally inexcusable. A manager who travels to Taipei without first obtaining a visa and is therefore turned back has no one else to blame. Other oversights may lead to more costly mistakes. For example, Brazilians are several inches shorter than the average U.S. consumer, but this was not taken into account when Sears erected American-height shelves that block Brazilian shoppers' view of the rest of the store.

International business success requires not only comprehensive fact finding and preparation but also an ability to understand and fully appreciate the nuances of different cultural traits and patterns. Gaining this **interpretive knowledge** requires "getting one's feet wet" over a sufficient length of time.

Cultural Analysis

To try to understand and explain differences among cultures and subsequently in cross-cultural behavior, the marketer can develop checklists and models showing pertinent variables and their interaction. An example of such a model is provided in Figure 3.1. This model is based on the premise that all international business activity should be viewed as innovation and as producing change processes.[46] After all, exporters and multinational corporations introduce, from one country to other cultures, marketing practices as well as products and services, which are then perceived to be new and different. Although many question the usefulness of such models, they do bring together, into one presentation, all or most of the relevant variables that have an impact on how consumers in different cultures may perceive, evaluate, and adopt new behaviors. However, any manager using such a tool should periodically cross-check its results with reality and experience.

The key variable of the model is propensity to change, which is a function of three constructs: (1) cultural lifestyle of individuals in terms of how deeply held their traditional beliefs and attitudes are, and also which elements of culture are dominant; (2) change agents (such as multinational corporations and their practices) and strate-

---

FIGURE 3.1 A Model of Cross-Cultural Behavior

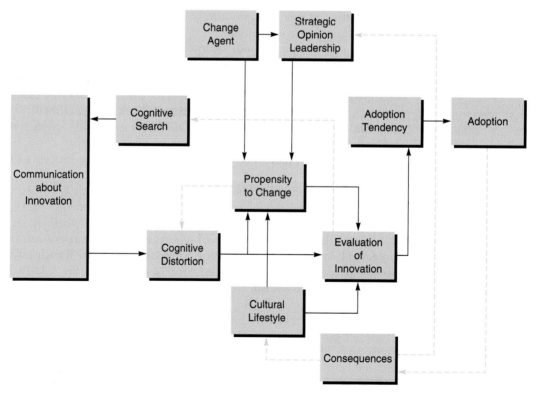

SOURCE: Adapted by permission of the publisher from "A Theory of Cross-Cultural Buying Behavior," by Jagdish N. Sheth and S. Prakash Sethi, in *Consumer and Industrial Buying Behavior*, eds. Arch G. Woodside, Jagdish N. Sheth, and Peter D. Bennett, 1977, 373. Copyright 1977 by Elsevier Science Publishing Co., Inc.

---

[46]Jagdish N. Sheth and S. Prakash Sethi, "A Theory of Cross-Cultural Buying Behavior," in *Consumer and Industrial Buying Behavior*, eds. Arch G. Woodside, Jagdish N. Sheth, and Peter D. Bennett (New York: Elsevier North-Holland, 1977), 369–386.

gic opinion leaders (for example, social elites); and (3) communication about the innovation from commercial sources, neutral sources (such as government), and social sources, such as friends and relatives.

It has been argued that differences in cultural lifestyle can be accounted for by four major dimensions of culture.[47] These dimensions consist of (1) individualism (e.g., "I" consciousness versus "we" consciousness), (2) power distance (e.g., level of equality in a society), (3) uncertainty avoidance (e.g., need for formal rules and regulations), and (4) masculinity (e.g., attitudes toward achievement, roles of men and women). Figure 3.2 presents a summary of twelve countries' positions along these dimensions. A fifth dimension has also been added to distinguish cultural differences: long-term versus short-term orientation.[48] All the high-scoring countries are Asian (e.g., China, Hong Kong, Taiwan, Japan, and South Korea), while most Western countries (such as the United States and Britain) have low scores. Some have argued that

| FIGURE | 3.2 | Culture Dimension Scores For Twelve Countries (0 = Low; 100 = High) |

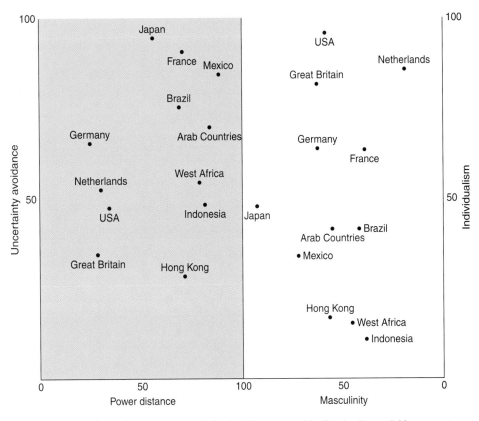

SOURCE: Data for the figure derived from Geert Hofstede, "Management Scientists Are Human," *Management Science* 40 (number 1, 1994): 4–13.

---

[47]Geert Hofstede, *Culture's Consequences: International Differences in Work-Related Values* (Beverly Hills, CA: Sage Publications, 1984).

[48]Geert Hofstede and Michael H. Bond, "The Confucius Connection: From Cultural Roots to Economic Growth," *Organizational Dynamics* 16 (Spring 1988): 4–21.

this cultural dimension may explain the Japanese marketing success based on market-share (rather than short-term profit) motivation in market development.

Knowledge of a target market's position on these dimensions will help the marketer design a strategy for optimal results. Marketers want to elicit a specific, common, and favorable response from their target markets. Geographic target markets can be segmented along cultural dimensions and subsequently marketing mixes can be developed to exploit the commonalities in these segments. Table 3.5 highlights an example of such cultural segmentation from the European market. Cluster 2, for example, displays the highest uncertainty avoidance and should therefore be targeted with risk-reducing marketing programs such as extended warranties and return privileges.[49] It is important to position the product as a continuous innovation that does not require radical changes in consumption patterns.[50]

Cultural analysis can also provide specific guidelines for marketing-mix development. Since the United States highly regards individualism, promotional appeals should be relevant to the individual. Also, in order to incorporate the lower power distance within the market, copy should be informal and friendly.[51] In opposite situations, marketing communications has to emphasize that the new product is socially accepted. However, if the product is imported, it can sometimes utilize global or foreign cultural positioning. For example, individualism is often used for imported products but almost never for domestic ones.[52] Similarly, channel choice is affected by cultural factors. Firms in societies emphasizing individualism are more likely to choose channel partners based on objective criteria, whereas firms at the opposite end would prefer to deal with other firms whose representatives they consider to be friends.[53] When negotiating in Germany, one can expect a counterpart who is thorough, systematic, very well prepared, but also rather dogmatic and therefore lacking in flexibility and compromise. Great emphasis is placed on efficiency. In Mexico, however, the counterpart may prefer to address problems on a personal and private basis rather than on a business level. This means more emphasis on socializing and conveying one's humanity, sincerity, loyalty, and friendship. Also, the differences in pace and business practices of the region have to be accepted. Boeing found in its annual study on world aviation safety that countries with both low individualism and substantial power distances had accident rates 2.6 times greater than at the other end of the scale. These findings will naturally have an impact on training and service operations of airlines.

Communication about the innovation takes place through the physical product itself (samples) or through a new policy in the company. If a new practice, such as quality circles or pan-regional planning, is in question, results may be communicated in reports or through word-of-mouth by the participating employees. Communication content depends on the following factors: the product's or policy's relative advantage over existing alternatives; compatibility with established behavioral patterns; complexity, or the degree to which the product or process is perceived as difficult to understand and use; trialability, or the degree to which it may be experimented with and not incur major risk; and observability, which is the extent to which the consequences of the innovation are visible.

[49]Sudhir H. Kale, "Grouping Euroconsumers: A Culture-Based Clustering Approach," *Journal of International Marketing* 3 (no. 3, 1995): 35–48.

[50]Jan-Benedict Steenkamp and Frenkel ter Hofstede, "A Cross-National Investigation into the Individual and National Cultural Antecedents of Consumer Innovativeness," *Journal of Marketing* 63 (April 1999): 55–69.

[51]Sudhir H. Kale, "Culture-Specific Marketing Communications: An Analytical Approach," *International Marketing Review* 8, no. 2 (1991): 18–30.

[52]Hong Cheng and John C. Schweitzer, "Cultural Values Reflected in Chinese and U.S. Television Commercials," *Journal of Advertising Research* 36 (May/June 1996): 27–45.

[53]Sudhir H. Kale, "Distribution Channel Relationships in Diverse Cultures," *International Marketing Review* 8, no. 3 (1991): 31–45.

TABLE 3.5	Culture-Based Segmentation

	SIZE (MILLION)	CULTURAL CHARACTERISTICS				ILLUSTRATIVE MARKETING IMPLICATIONS
		POWER DISTANCE	UNCERTAINTY AVOIDANCE	INDIVIDUALISM	MASCULINITY	
Cluster 1 Austria, Germany, Switzerland, Italy, Great Britain, Ireland	203	Small	Medium	Medium-High	High	Preference for "high-performance" products, use "successful-achiever" theme in advertising, desire for novelty, variety and pleasure, fairly risk-averse market.
Cluster 2 Belgium, France, Greece, Portugal, Spain, Turkey	182	Medium	Strong	Varied	Low-Medium	Appeal to consumer's status and power position, reduce perceived risk in product purchase and use, emphasize product functionality.
Cluster 3 Denmark, Sweden, Finland, Netherlands, Norway	37	Small	Low	High	Low	Relatively weak resistance to new products, strong consumer desire for novelty and variety, high consumer regard for "environmentally friendly" marketers and socially conscious firms.

SOURCE: Sudhir H. Kale, "Grouping Euroconsumers: A Culture-Based Clustering Approach," *Journal of International Marketing* 3 (no. 3, 1995): 42.

Before the product or policy is evaluated, information about it will be compared with existing beliefs about the circumstances surrounding the situation. Distortion will occur as a result of selective attention, exposure, and retention. As examples, anything foreign may be seen in a negative light, another multinational company's efforts may have failed, or the government may implicitly discourage the proposed activity. Additional information may then be sought from any of the input sources or from opinion leaders in the market.

Adoption tendency refers to the likelihood that the product or process will be accepted. Examples of this are advertising in the People's Republic of China and equity joint ventures with Western participants in Russia, both unheard of a few years ago. If an innovation clears the hurdles, it may be adopted and slowly diffused into the entire market. An international manager has two basic choices: adapt company offerings and methods to those in the market or try to change market conditions to fit company programs. In Japan, a number of Western companies have run into obstructions in the Japanese distribution system, where great value is placed on established relationships; everything is done on the basis of favoring the familiar and fearing the unfamiliar. In most cases, this problem is solved by joint venturing with a major Japanese entity that has established contacts. On occasion, when the company's approach is compatible with the central beliefs of a culture, the company may be able to change existing customs rather than adjust to them. Initially, Procter & Gamble's traditional hard-selling style in television commercials jolted most Japanese viewers accustomed to more subtle approaches. Now the ads are being imitated by Japanese competitors.

However, this should not be interpreted to mean that Japanese advertising will adapt necessarily to the influence of Western approaches. The emphasis in Japan is still on who speaks rather than on what is spoken. That is why, for example, Japan is a market where Procter & Gamble's company name is presented, as well as the brand name of the product, in the marketing communication for a brand rather than using only the product's brand name, which is customary in the U.S. and European markets.[54]

Although models like the one in Figure 3.2 may aid in strategy planning by making sure that all variables and their linkages are considered, any analysis is incomplete without the basic recognition of cultural differences. Adjusting to differences requires putting one's own cultural values aside. James E. Lee proposes that the natural **self-reference criterion**—the unconscious reference to one's own cultural values—is the root of most international business problems.[55] However, recognizing and admitting this are often quite difficult. The following analytical approach is recommended to reduce the influence of one's own cultural values:

1. Define the problem or goal in terms of domestic cultural traits, habits, or norms.
2. Define the problem or goal in terms of foreign cultural traits, habits, or norms. Make no value judgments.
3. Isolate the self-reference criterion influence in the problem and examine it carefully to see how it complicates the problem.
4. Redefine the problem without the self-reference criterion influence and solve for the optimal goal situation.

This approach can be applied to product introduction. If Kellogg Co. wants to introduce breakfast cereals into markets where breakfast is traditionally not eaten or where consumers drink very little milk, managers must consider very carefully how to instill this new habit. The traits, habits, and norms of breakfast are quite different in the United States, France, and Brazil, and they have to be outlined before the product can be introduced. In France, Kellogg's commercials are aimed as much at providing nutrition lessons as they are at promoting the product. In Brazil, the company advertised on a soap opera to gain entry into the market, because Brazilians often emulate the characters of these television shows.

Analytical procedures require constant monitoring of changes caused by outside events as well as the changes caused by the business entity itself. Controlling **ethnocentrism**—the belief that one's own culture is superior to others—can be achieved only by acknowledging it and properly adjusting to its possible effects in managerial decision making. The international manager needs to be prepared and able to put that preparedness to effective use.[56]

The Training Challenge

International managers face a dilemma in terms of international and intercultural competence. U.S. firms' lack of adequate foreign language and international business skills has resulted in lost contracts, weak negotiations, and ineffectual management. A UNESCO study of ten- and fourteen-year-old students in nine countries placed U.S. teens next to last in their comprehension of foreign cultures. Even when cultural awareness is high, there is room for improvement. For example, a survey of European executives found that a shortage of international managers was considered the single

[54]"Exploring Differences in Japan, U.S. Culture," *Advertising Age International*, September 18, 1995, I-8.

[55]James A. Lee, "Cultural Analysis in Overseas Operations," *Harvard Business Review* 44 (March–April 1966): 106–114.

[56]Peter D. Fitzpatrick and Alan S. Zimmerman, *Essentials of Export Marketing* (New York: American Management Organization, 1985), 16.

most important constraint on expansion abroad.[57] The increase in overall international activity of firms has increased the need for cultural sensitivity training at all levels of the organization. Today's training must take into consideration not only outsiders to the firm but interaction within the corporate family as well. However inconsequential the degree of interaction may seem, it can still cause problems if proper understanding is lacking. Consider, for example, the date 11/12/00 on a telex; a European will interpret this as the eleventh of December, but in the United States it is the twelfth of November.

Some companies try to avoid the training problem by hiring only nationals or well-traveled executives for their international operations. This makes sense for the management of overseas operations but will not solve the training need, especially if transfers to a culture unfamiliar to the manager are likely. International experience may not necessarily transfer from one market to another.

To foster cultural sensitivity and acceptance of new ways of doing things within the organization, management must institute internal education programs. These programs may include (1) culture-specific information (e.g., data covering other countries, such as videopacks and culturegrams), (2) cultural general information (e.g., values, practices, and assumptions of countries other than one's own), and (3) self-specific information (e.g., identifying one's own cultural paradigm, including values, assumptions, and perceptions about others).[58] One study found that Japanese assigned to the United States receive mainly language training as preparation for the task. In addition, many companies use mentoring whereby an individual is assigned to someone who is experienced and who will spend the required time squiring and explaining. Talks given by returnees and by visiting lecturers hired specifically for the task round out the formal part of training.[59]

The objective of formal training programs is to foster the four critical characteristics of preparedness, sensitivity, patience, and flexibility in managers and other personnel. These programs vary dramatically in terms of their rigor, involvement, and, of course, cost.[60] A summary of these programs is provided in Figure 3.3. In the 1990s, Korean firms embarked on a mission of *segyehwa*, or globalization, which meant preparing the managers and employees who will be in charge of implementing the program. At Kumho Group, the chairman required all airline and tire maker employees to spend an hour each morning studying a language or learning about foreign cultures. Cards taped up in bathrooms taught a new phrase in English or Japanese each day. Hyundai Motor Co. sent twenty-five managers in their thirties and forties to Cornell University for nearly a year to learn new disciplines and the less rigid U.S. management style.[61]

At Samsung, several special interest groups were formed to focus on issues such as Japanese society and business practices, the Chinese economy, changes in Europe, and the U.S. economy. In addition, groups also explored cutting-edge business issues, such as new technology and marketing strategies. And for the last few years, Samsung has been sending the brightest junior employees abroad for a year.[62]

[57]"Expansion Abroad: The New Direction for European Firms," *International Management* 41 (November 1986): 20–26.

[58]W. Chan Kim and R. A. Mauborgne, "Cross-Cultural Strategies," *Journal of Business Strategy* 7 (Spring 1987): 28–37.

[59]Mauricio Lorence, "Assignment USA: The Japanese Solution," *Sales & Marketing Management* 144 (October 1992): 60–66.

[60]Rosalie Tung, "Selection and Training of Personnel for Overseas Assignments," *Columbia Journal of World Business* 16 (Spring 1981): 68–78.

[61]"The Loneliness of the Hyundai Manager," *Business Week*, August 19, 1996, 12E4–6.

[62]"Special Interest Group Operations," available at **http://www.samsung.com**; and "Sensitivity Kick," *The Wall Street Journal*, December 30, 1996, 1, 4.

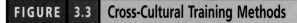

FIGURE 3.3 Cross-Cultural Training Methods

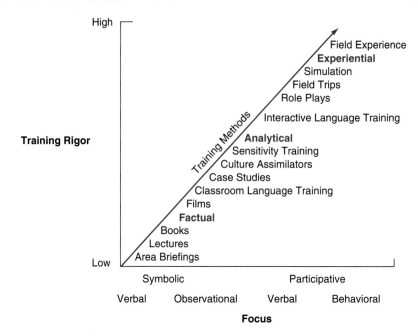

source: J. Stewart Black and Mark Mendenhall, "A Practical but Theory-Based Framework for Selecting Cross-Cultural Training Methods," in *International Human Resources Management*, eds. Mark Mendenhall and Gary Oddou (Boston: PWS-Kent, 1991), 188. © 1991 PWS-Kent.

Environmental briefings and cultural orientation programs are types of **area studies** programs. These programs provide factual preparation for a manager to operate in, or work with people from, a particular country. Area studies should be a basic prerequisite for other types of training programs. Alone, they serve little practical purpose because they do not really get the manager's feet wet. Other, more involved programs contribute the context in which to put facts so that they can be properly understood.

The **cultural assimilator** is a program in which trainees must respond to scenarios of specific situations in a particular country. These programs have been developed for the Arab countries, Iran, Thailand, Central America, and Greece.[63] The results of the trainees' assimilator experience are evaluated by a panel of judges. This type of program has been used in particular in cases of transfers abroad on short notice.

When more time is available, managers can be trained extensively in language. This may be required if an exotic language is involved. **Sensitivity training** focuses on enhancing a manager's flexibility in situations that are quite different from those at home. The approach is based on the assumption that understanding and accepting oneself is critical to understanding a person from another culture. While most of the methods discussed are best delivered in face-to-face settings, Web-based training is becoming more popular, as seen in *The International Marketplace 3.5.*

Finally, training may involve **field experience,** which exposes a manager to a different cultural environment for a limited amount of time. Although the expense of

[63]Harris and Moran, *Managing Cultural Differences*, 267–295.

THE INTERNATIONAL MARKETPLACE 3.5

On-Line Cultural Training

THE INTERNET CAN PLAY an important role in preparing marketing people for the international marketplace. While it cannot replace real-life interaction as an experiential tool, it does provide a number of benefits, including comparisons of behavior in different cultures, and can provide an opportunity to develop the skills needed to interact successfully with people from other cultures.

Companies typically rely on the following elements in designing Web-based training:

1. **Detailed Scenarios.** Much of the training material consists of a detailed, realistic story that is tied into elements of the learner's background; i.e., the session becomes more than a briefing. It becomes a narrated experience full of learning moments for participants. This is made possible by the ability of the Web to store and circulate a lot of information instantaneously around the world.

2. **Gradual Delivery.** The ability to control the flow of information to the participant supports the learning process in a number of ways. First, the participant is allowed to fit the training into his or her schedule. Secondly, the real-life flow of information is mimicked and a higher degree of realism is achieved.

3. **Support.** A set of detailed materials is provided to the participants twenty-four hours a day. At any hour and at any location, participants can check their perceptions against the materials, reinforce learning from a dimly recalled lesson, or seek feedback on an important point or issue.

4. **Relevant Exercises.** Participants can be provided topical exercises and activities, the level of which can be ad-

justed depending how the participated has invested into the training.

5. **On-Line Discussions.** Sessions can be simulcast to hundreds of participants around the world. The lack of face-to-face interaction can be remedied by having discussion groups where participants can share their experiences with each other. The pooled learning experience is stronger than the experience with one solitary participant.

The following case highlights some of the points made:

Joe Schmed is a marketing representative for a pharmaceutical company. His company has just undertaken a joint venture with a pan-Asian pharmaceutical company based in Kuala Lumpur. In order to develop a successful sales plan, over the next six months Joe will travel to Southeast Asia at least eight times. The first trip will be in two weeks. However, Joe lacks the time to take two full days out of his schedule for a traditional training program. Since his undergraduate major was in Asian studies, Joe feels that his cultural understanding is quite adequate. Nevertheless, he would like to brush up on some of his knowledge and gain a better understanding of Asian business. Logging on, he enters a training course, completing parts of it as he finds time—on airplanes and after work, for example.

SOURCE: Peter T. Burgi and Brant R. Dykehouse, "On-Line Cultural Training: The Next Phase," *International Insight*, Winter 2000, 7–10. See also **http://www.runzheimer.com.**

placing and maintaining an expatriate is high (and, therefore, the cost of failure is high), field experience is rarely used in training. One field experience technique that has been suggested when the training process needs to be rigorous is the host-family surrogate. This technique places a trainee (and possibly his or her family) in a domestically located family of the nationality to which they are assigned.[64]

Regardless of the degree of training, preparation, and positive personal characteristics, a manager will always remain foreign. A manager should never rely on his or her own judgment when local managers can be consulted. In many instances, a manager should have an interpreter present at negotiations, especially if the manager is not completely bilingual. Overconfidence in one's language capabilities can create problems.

[64]Simcha Ronen, "Training the International Assignee," in *Training and Career Development*, ed. I. Goldstein (San Francisco: Jossey-Bass, 1989), 426–440.

SUMMARY

Culture is one of the most challenging elements of the international marketplace. This system of learned behavior patterns characteristic of the members of a given society is constantly shaped by a set of dynamic variables: language, religion, values and attitudes, manners and customs, aesthetics, technology, education, and social institutions. An international manager, to cope with this system, needs both factual and interpretive knowledge of culture. To some extent, the factual can be learned; the interpretation comes only through experience.

The most complicated problems in dealing with the cultural environment stem from the fact that we cannot learn culture—we have to live it. Two schools of thought exist in the business world on how to deal with cultural diversity. One is that business is business the world around, following the model of Pepsi and McDonald's. In some cases, globalization is a fact of life; however, cultural differences are still far from converging.

The other school proposes that companies must tailor business approaches to individual cultures. Setting up policies and procedures in each country has been compared to an organ transplant; the critical question centers on acceptance or rejection. The major challenge to the international manager is to make sure that rejection is not a result of cultural myopia or even blindness.

The internationally successful companies all share an important quality: patience. They have not rushed into situations but rather built their operations carefully by following the most basic business principles. These principles are to know your adversary, know your audience, and know your customer.

QUESTIONS FOR DISCUSSION

1. Comment on the assumption, "If people are serious about doing business with you, they will speak English."
2. You are on your first business visit to Germany. You feel confident about your ability to speak the language (you studied German in school and have taken a refresher course), and you decide to use it. During introductions, you want to break the ice by asking *"Wie geht's?"* and insisting that everyone call you by your first name. Speculate as to the reaction.
3. What can a company do to culture-sensitize its staff?
4. What can be learned about a culture from reading and attending to factual materials? Given the tremendous increase in international marketing activities, where will companies in a relatively early stage of the internationalization process find the personnel to handle the new challenges?
5. Management at a U.S. company trying to market tomato paste in the Middle East did not know that, translated into Arabic, tomato paste is "tomato glue." How could they have known in time to avoid problems?
6. Give examples of how the self-reference criterion might be manifested.
7. Various companies, such as Windham International, are available to prepare and train international marketers for the cultural challenge. Using Windham's Web site (**www.windhamworld.com**), assess its role in helping the international marketer.
8. Compare and contrast an international marketer's home pages for presentation and content; for example, Coca-Cola (**www.coca-cola.com**) and its Japanese version (**www.cocacola.co.jp**). Are the differences cultural?

RECOMMENDED READINGS

Axtell, Roger E. *Do's and Taboos around the World.* New York: John Wiley & Sons, 1993.

Brislin, R. W., W. J. Lonner, and R. M. Thorndike, *Cross-Cultural Research Methods.* New York: Wiley, 1973.

Copeland, Lennie, and L. Griggs. *Going International: How to Make Friends and Deal Effectively in the Global Marketplace.* New York: Random House, 1990.

Hall, Edward T., and Mildred Reed Hall. *Understanding Cultural Differences.* Yarmouth, ME: Intercultural Press, 1990.

Hoecklin, Lisa. *Managing Cultural Differences.* Workingham, England: Addison-Wesley, 1995.

Hofstede, Geert. *Culture's Consequences.* London: Sage Publications, 1981.

Kenna, Peggy, and Sondra Lacy. *Business Japan: Understanding Japanese Business Culture.* Lincolnwood, IL: NTC, 1994.

Lewis, Richard D. *When Cultures Collide.* London: Nicholas Brealey Publishing, 1996.

Marx, Elizabeth. *Breaking through Culture Shock: What You Need to Succeed in International Business.* London: Nicholas Brealey Publishing, 1999.

O'Hara-Devereux, Mary, and Robert Johansen. *Global Work: Bridging Distance, Culture, and Time.* San Francisco: Jossey-Bass Publishers, 1994.

Parker, Barbara. *Globalization and Business Practice: Managing across Boundaries.* London: Sage Publications, 1999.

Terpstra, Vern, and K. David. *The Cultural Environment of International Business.* Cincinnati, OH: South-Western, 1991.

Trompenaars, Fons, and Charles Hampden-Turner. *Riding the Waves of Culture.* New York: Irwin, 1998.

Chapter 4

The Economic Environment

The Global Economy

THE GOOD NEWS is that the global economy is growing. The financial turbulence that struck Asia during the latter part of 1997 and continued to affect a number of countries in Latin America and Russia has abated more quickly than anticipated. Fast and far-reaching changes are everywhere—in international relations, domestic politics, economics, and business—unsettling policymakers, entrepreneurs, and employees in developed and developing countries alike.

A number of developing nations emerged as the engines of global growth in the 1990s. The International Monetary Fund forecast that the developing economies as a group would grow at about twice the rate of the industrialized countries in the mid-1990s. Latin America largely pulled free of the debt crisis that made the 1980s that region's "lost decade" and the effects of the Asian crisis. China's emergence has been declared as *the* economic event of this decade. There are ten particularly promising developing countries that are growing about twice as fast as the rest of the world. By the end of the century, South Korea, Greater China (including Hong Kong and Taiwan), Indonesia, India, South Africa, Turkey, Poland, Mexico, Brazil, and Argentina together accounted for about the same share of world imports as either Japan or the European Union.

If these forecasts were accurate, the industrialized countries and their marketers will benefit in a significant way. But, relative to the rest of the world, such changes will slowly diminish the industrialized countries' economic strength, which has underpinned their status and influence—despite their domination of certain key sectors such as computers, aircraft, and automobiles.

Economically, the world still stands to reap benefits from the end of the Cold War. The peaceful change in South Africa can open up new vistas of prosperity for that country and the continent as a whole. Developments in the Middle East have made it possible to think of economic cooperation in the region for the first time since World War II. The end of the Cold War may exacerbate rivalries between the established and developing countries; even old friends can fall out on trade issues when the common political enemy has disappeared.

The world is shrinking daily as the costs of computing power and telecommunications fall. The multimedia revolution could prove to be as significant in the development of mankind as the harnessing of steam and the development of the railways in the nineteenth century or the exploitation and spread of electric power in the early years of the twentieth century.

Globalization has been one of the most significant developments in the industrialized world in the last 20 years. Driven by the desire of companies to produce and sell goods and services in more markets, it has led to the spread of corporate operations across borders through international investment, trade, and collaboration for purposes such as product development, sourcing, and marketing. According to the *1999 World Investment Report*, 60,000 parent companies have over 500,000 affiliates in operation worldwide, making the total stock of foreign direct investment exceed $4 trillion. Despite the economic challenges of the period 1997–1999, FDI flows increased 39 percent during that time. In addition to the increased investment and employment

continued

around the world, the nature of foreign involvement is also changing. The Internet, for example, already allows professionals in India to do routine architectural or audit work for clients in Britain at a fraction of the cost of U.K.-based companies.

An A. T. Kearney study on globalization indicates that, overall, countries integrating rapidly with the world economy have fared better than those taking a slow and cautious approach. The nations quickest to globalize have enjoyed growth rates 30 to 50 percent higher over the past 20 years.

Added benefits for these nations have been notable improvements in political freedom and civil rights, growth in government spending for social programs, sustained improvements in life expectancy, and rising levels of funding for education.

SOURCES: Global Business Policy Council, *Globalization Ledger*, Washington, DC: A.T. Kearney, April 2000, Introduction; OECD, *OECD Annual Report 1999*, Paris, France, 1999, Introduction; United Nations, *World Investment Report 1999*, New York: United Nations, 1999, chapter 1.

THE ASSESSMENT OF A FOREIGN MARKET ENVIRONMENT should start with the evaluation of economic variables relating to the size and nature of the markets. Because of the large number of worthwhile alternatives, initial screening of markets should be done efficiently yet effectively enough, with a wide array of economic criteria, to establish a preliminary estimate of market potential. One of the most basic characterizations of the world economy is provided in Figure 4.1, which incorporates many of the economic variables pertinent to marketers.

The Group of Five—listed in Figure 4.1 as the United States, Britain, France, Germany, and Japan—consists of the major industrialized countries of the world. This

FIGURE 4.1   The Global Economy

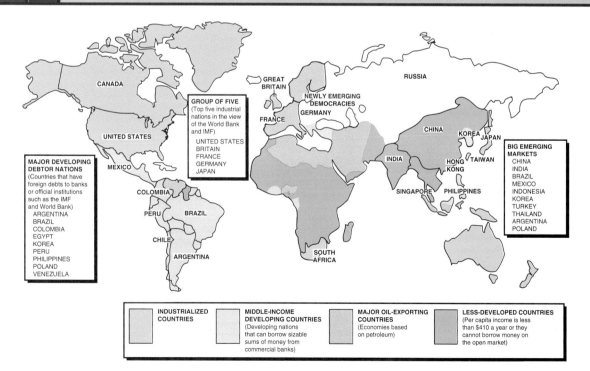

SOURCE: Adapted and updated from "The Global Economy," *The Washington Post*, January 19, 1986, H1. Reprinted with permission.

Economic Strength

Top World Economies (GDP in million dollars U.S.)

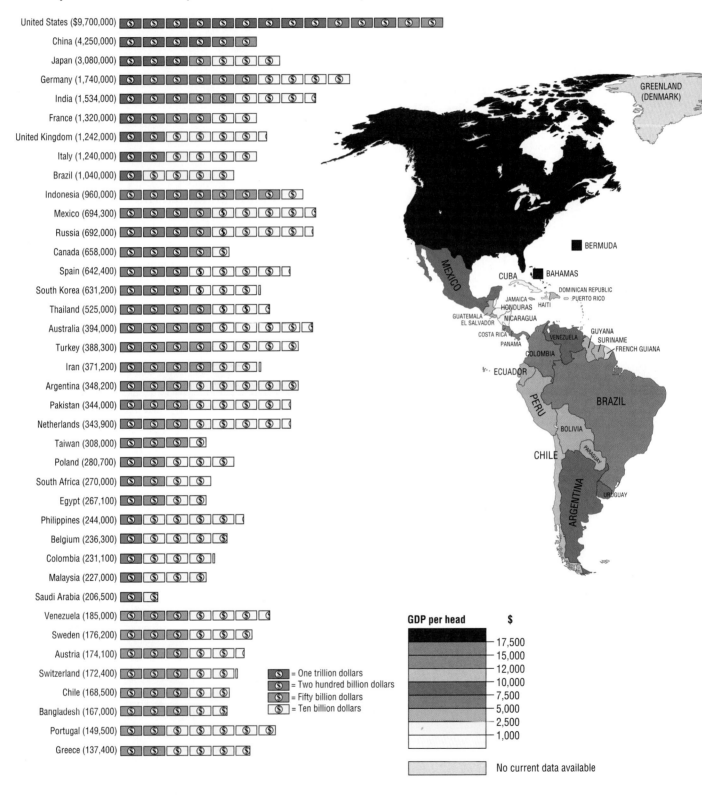

United States ($9,700,000)
China (4,250,000)
Japan (3,080,000)
Germany (1,740,000)
India (1,534,000)
France (1,320,000)
United Kingdom (1,242,000)
Italy (1,240,000)
Brazil (1,040,000)
Indonesia (960,000)
Mexico (694,300)
Russia (692,000)
Canada (658,000)
Spain (642,400)
South Korea (631,200)
Thailand (525,000)
Australia (394,000)
Turkey (388,300)
Iran (371,200)
Argentina (348,200)
Pakistan (344,000)
Netherlands (343,900)
Taiwan (308,000)
Poland (280,700)
South Africa (270,000)
Egypt (267,100)
Philippines (244,000)
Belgium (236,300)
Colombia (231,100)
Malaysia (227,000)
Saudi Arabia (206,500)
Venezuela (185,000)
Sweden (176,200)
Austria (174,100)
Switzerland (172,400)
Chile (168,500)
Bangladesh (167,000)
Portugal (149,500)
Greece (137,400)

$ = One trillion dollars
$ = Two hundred billion dollars
$ = Fifty billion dollars
$ = Ten billion dollars

GREENLAND (DENMARK)

BERMUDA
BAHAMAS
CUBA
DOMINICAN REPUBLIC
MEXICO   JAMAICA   PUERTO RICO
HAITI
HONDURAS
GUATEMALA   NICARAGUA
EL SALVADOR
COSTA RICA   VENEZUELA   GUYANA
PANAMA   SURINAME
COLOMBIA   FRENCH GUIANA
ECUADOR
PERU   BRAZIL
BOLIVIA
CHILE   PARAGUAY
ARGENTINA   URUGUAY

GDP per head $

— 17,500
— 15,000
— 12,000
— 10,000
— 7,500
— 5,000
— 2,500
— 1,000

No current data available

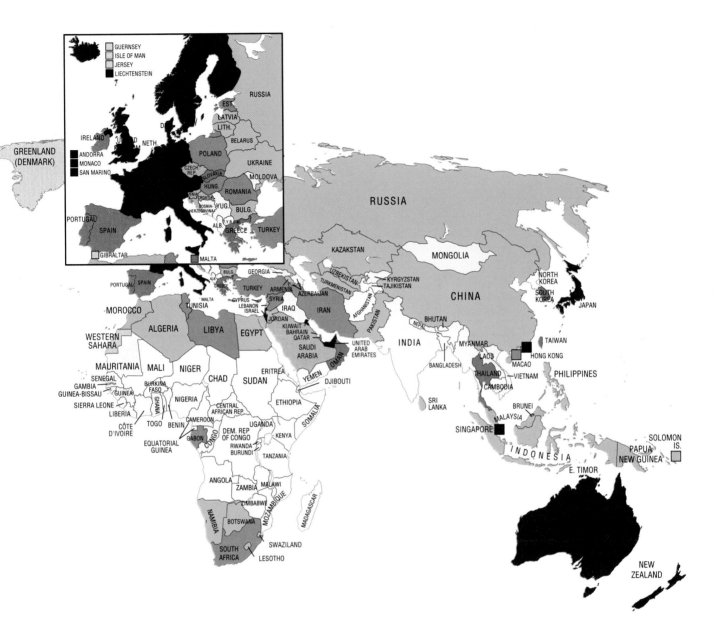

GUERNSEY
ISLE OF MAN
JERSEY
LIECHTENSTEIN

ANDORRA
MONACO
SAN MARINO

GREENLAND
(DENMARK)

IRELAND
UNITED
KINGDOM
NETH.
D

RUSSIA
EST.
LATVIA
LITH.
BELARUS
POLAND
UKRAINE
CZECH.
REP.
SLOVAKIA
MOLDOVA
HUNG.
SLOVENIA
CROATIA
ROMANIA
BOSNIA-
HERZEGOVINA
YUG.
BULG.
F.Y.R.O.M.
ALB.
GREECE
TURKEY

PORTUGAL
SPAIN
GIBRALTAR
MALTA

PORTUGAL   SPAIN
ALB.
GREECE
MALTA
BULG.
GEORGIA
UZBEKISTAN
KYRGYZSTAN
TAJIKISTAN
TURKMENISTAN
KAZAKSTAN
MONGOLIA
NORTH
KOREA
SOUTH
KOREA
JAPAN
TURKEY
ARMENIA
AZERBAIJAN
SYRIA
CYPRUS
LEBANON
ISRAEL
IRAQ
JORDAN
IRAN
AFGHANISTAN
PAKISTAN
CHINA
TAIWAN

MOROCCO
TUNISIA
MALTA
BHUTAN
NEPAL
INDIA
HONG KONG
MACAO

WESTERN
SAHARA
ALGERIA
LIBYA
EGYPT
SAUDI
ARABIA
KUWAIT
BAHRAIN
QATAR
UNITED
ARAB
EMIRATES
OMAN
YEMEN
MYANMAR
LAOS
VIETNAM
THAILAND
PHILIPPINES
BANGLADESH

MAURITANIA
MALI
NIGER
CHAD
SUDAN
ERITREA
DJIBOUTI
CAMBODIA
BRUNEI

SENEGAL
GAMBIA
GUINEA-BISSAU
GUINEA
BURKINA
FASO
NIGERIA
ETHIOPIA
SRI
LANKA
MALAYSIA
SINGAPORE

SIERRA LEONE
LIBERIA
GHANA
CENTRAL
AFRICAN REP.
SOMALIA
CÔTE
D'IVOIRE
TOGO
BENIN
CAMEROON
UGANDA
KENYA
INDONESIA
PAPUA
NEW GUINEA
SOLOMON
IS.

EQUATORIAL
GUINEA
GABON
CONGO
DEM. REP
OF CONGO
RWANDA
BURUNDI
TANZANIA
E. TIMOR

ANGOLA
ZAMBIA
MALAWI
MADAGASCAR

NAMIBIA
ZIMBABWE
MOZAMBIQUE
BOTSWANA

SOUTH
AFRICA
SWAZILAND
LESOTHO

NEW
ZEALAND

Source: The *World Factbook*, 1998–99

www.statusa.gov

C 62 00 00 00 00 00 11 52

group is sometimes expanded to the **Group of Seven** (by adding Italy and Canada) and to the **Group of Ten** (by adding Sweden, the Netherlands, and Belgium). It may also be expanded to encompass the members of the Organization for Economic Cooperation and Development, OECD (which consists of 29 countries: Western Europe, the United States, Australia, Canada, Czech Republic, Hungary, Japan, Mexico, New Zealand, South Korea, and Turkey).

Important among the middle-income developing countries are the newly industrialized countries (NICs), which include Singapore, Taiwan, Korea, Hong Kong, Brazil, and Mexico (some propose adding Malaysia and the Philippines to the list as well). Some of these NICs will earn a new acronym, RIC (rapidly industrializing countries). Over the past twenty years, Singapore has served as a hub, providing critical financial and managerial services to the Southeast Asian markets. Singapore has successfully attracted foreign investment, mostly regional corporate headquarters and knowledge-intensive industries, and has served as one of the main gateways for Asian trade. Its exports have reached well over 300 percent of GDP.[1] As seen in *The International Marketplace 4.1*, these countries are set to become the major markets of the future.

The major oil-exporting countries, in particular the eleven members of the Organization of Petroleum Exporting Countries (OPEC) and countries such as Russia, are dependent on the price of oil for their world market participation. A relatively high dollar price per barrel (as high as $34 in early 2000) works very much in these countries' favor.

Many of the less-developed countries will depend on the success of their industrialization efforts in the years to come, even in the case of resource-rich countries that may find commodity prices being driven down by humanmade substitutes. China, one of the major less-developed countries, became the second-largest exporter of textiles to the United States after it began increasing production in the 1980s. Despite an image of hopeless poverty, India has over 200 million middle-class consumers, more than Germany. A special group in this category consists of the countries saddled with a major debt burden, such as Egypt and Peru. The degree and form of their participation in the world market will largely depend on how the debt issue is solved with the governments of the major industrialized countries and the multilateral and commercial banks. In less-developed countries, debt problems and falling commodity prices make market development difficult. Africa, the poorest continent, owes the rest of the world $375 billion, an amount equal to three quarters of its GNP and nearly four times its annual exports. Another factor contributing to the challenging situation is that only 1 percent of the world's private investment goes to sub-Saharan Africa.[2]

In the former centrally planned economies, dramatic changes are under way. A hefty capital inflow will be key to modernizing both the newly emerging democracies of Central and Eastern Europe. They are crippled by $60 billion in foreign debt and decades of Communist misrule. Desperately needed will be Western technology, management, and marketing know-how to provide better jobs and put more locally made and imported consumer goods in the shops. Within the groups, prospects vary: The future for countries such as Hungary, the Baltics, the Czech Republic, and Poland looks far better than it does for Russia as they prepare to join the European Union.[3]

Classifications of markets will vary by originator and intended use. Marketers will combine economic variables to fit their planning purposes by using those that relate directly to the product and/or service the company markets, such as the market's ability to buy. For example, Table 4.1 provides a summary of an economic classification system for possible use by a marketer in power and electricity generation. This approach has countries divided into four basic categories, with the centrally planned

[1]Global Business Policy Council, *Globalization Ledger*, Washington, DC: A. T. Kearney, April 2000, 3.

[2]"African Debt, European Doubt," *Economist*, April 8, 2000, 46.

[3]"Who Will Join Europe's Club—and When?" *Economist*, April 8, 2000, 53–54.

TABLE 4.1 Economic Development Variable in Countries' Use of Electricity and Electrical Goods

Less developed: These countries have primarily agrarian and/or extractive economies. High birthrates, along with limited infrastructures, account for the low per capita income and usage of electricity. Electrification is limited to the main population centers. Generally, basic electrical equipment is imported.

Early developing: These countries have begun initial development of an infrastructure and have infant industries, especially mining and selected cottage manufactures. Target economic sectors may enjoy high growth rates even though per capita income and electricity consumption are still modest. Progressively more sophisticated electrical equipment is imported, frequently to achieve forward integration of extractive industries.

Semideveloped: These countries have started an accelerated expansion of infrastructure and wide industrial diversification. Thus, per capita income and electricity consumption are growing rapidly. Increased discretionary income and electrification allow greater ownership of autos and electrical appliances among the expanding middle class. Larger quantities of high-technology equipment are imported.

Developed: These countries enjoy well-developed infrastructures, high per capita income and electricity consumption, and large-scale industrial diversification. They are also characterized by low rates of population and economic growth, as well as shifts in emphasis from manufacturing to service industries—notably transportation, communication, and information systems.

Centrally planned: The separate listing for these countries does not imply that they represent either a higher or a lower stage of economic development. They could have been distributed among each of the above four categories.

SOURCE: Adapted from V. Yorio, *Adapting Products for Export* (New York: Conference Board, 1983), 11.

economies given separate consideration because of their unique characteristics of strict governmental control and centralized procurement. This format takes into account both general country considerations—such as population, GNP, geography, manufacturing as a percentage of national product, infrastructure, and per capita income—and narrower industry-specific considerations of interest to the company and its marketing efforts, such as extent of use of the product, total imports, and U.S. or EU share of these imports.

The discussion that follows is designed to summarize a set of criteria that helps identify foreign markets and screen the most opportune ones for future entry or change of entry mode. Discussed are variables on which information is readily available from secondary sources such as international organizations, individual governments, and private organizations or associations.

The Statistical Yearbook of the United Nations, World Bank publications, and individual countries' *Statistical Abstracts* provide the starting point for market investigations. The more developed the market, the more data are available. Data are available on past developments as well as on projections of broader categories such as population and income. *Business International*, for example, annually compiles market-size indicators for over 110 countries that account for more than 90 percent of the world's output in goods and services.

Market Characteristics

The main dimensions of a market can be captured by considering variables such as those relating to the population and its various characteristics, infrastructure, geographical features of the environment, and foreign involvement in the economy.

Population

The total world population exceeded six billion people in 1999. The number of people in a particular market provides one of the most basic indicators of market size and is, in itself, indicative of the potential demand for certain staple items that have universal appeal and are generally affordable. As indicated by the data in Figure 4.2, population is not evenly divided among the major regions of the world; Asia holds over half the world's population.

These population figures can be analyzed in terms of marketing implications by noting that countries belonging to the European Union (EU) constitute 79 percent of the Western European population, and with the expansion of the EU in 1995, the percentage rose to 85. The two largest entities in Asia, China and India, constitute nearly

| FIGURE | 4.2 | World Population: Present and the Shape of Things to Come |

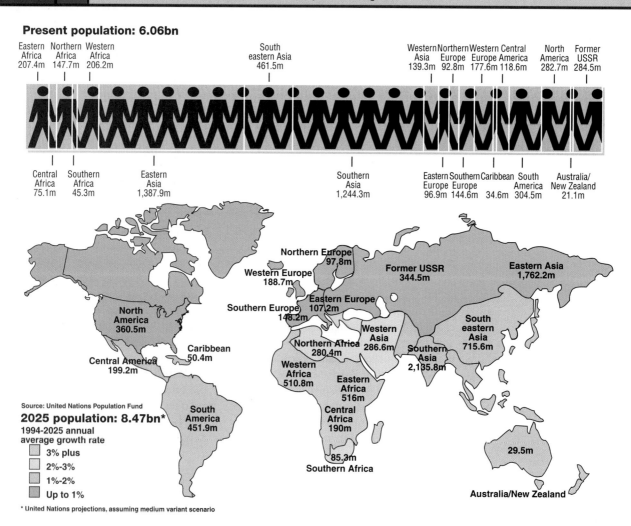

SOURCE: Thomas M. McDevitt, *World Population Profile: 1998* (Washington, DC: Government Printing Office, 1999), 1–2. See also **http://www.census.gov.**

70 percent of Asia's population. The greatest population densities are also to be found in Europe, providing the international marketer with a strategically located center of operation and ready access to the major markets of the world.

Population figures themselves must be broken down into meaningful categories in order for the marketer to take better advantage of them. Because market entry decisions may lie in the future, it is worthwhile to analyze population projections in the areas of interest and focus on their possible implications. Figure 4.2 includes United Nations projections that point to a population explosion, but mainly in the developing countries. Northern Europe will show nearly zero population growth for the next thirty years, whereas the population of Africa will triple. Even in the low- or zero-growth markets, the news is not necessarily bad for the international marketer. Those in the 25- to -45 age group, whose numbers are increasing, are among the most affluent consumers of all, having formed family units and started to consume household goods in large quantities as they reach the peak of their personal earnings potential. Early in this century, they are expected to start spending more on leisure goods and health care and related services.[4]

To influence population growth patterns, governments will have to undertake, with the help of private enterprise, quite different social marketing tasks. These will range from promoting and providing incentives for larger families (in Scandinavia, for example) to increased family planning efforts (in Thailand, for example). Regardless of the outcome of such government programs, current trends will further accelerate the division of world markets into the "haves" and the "have-nots." More adjustment capability will be required on the part of companies that want to market in the developing countries because of lower purchasing power of individuals and increasing government participation in the marketing of basic products.

Depending on the marketer's interest, population figures can be classified to show specific characteristics of their respective markets. Age distribution and life expectancy correlate heavily with the level of development of the market. Industrialized countries, with their increasing median age and a larger share of the population above 65, will open unique opportunities for international marketers with new products and services. A number of companies in the United States, for example, are marketing an adult diaper.

As the life expectancy in a market extends and new target markets become available, international marketers may be able to extend their products' life cycles by marketing them abroad. Interpretation of demographics will require some degree of experiential knowledge. As an example, which age categories of females should be included in an estimate of market potential for a new contraceptive? This would vary from the very early teens in the developing countries to higher age categories in developed countries, where the maturing process is later.

An important variable for the international marketer is the size of the household. A **household** describes all the persons, both related and unrelated, who occupy a housing unit.[5] Within the EU, the average household size has shrunk from 2.9 to 2.7 persons since 1977 and is expected to decline further.[6] One factor behind the overall growth in households, and the subsequent decline in the average size, has been the increase in the numbers of divorced and sole survivor households. One-person households are most common in Norway and Germany. This compares strikingly with countries such as Colombia, where the average household size is six. With economic development usually bringing about more, but smaller-sized, households, international marketers of food products, appliances, and household goods have to adjust to

---

[4]*Consumer Europe* (London: Euromonitor, 1988), 24; and Rahul Jacob. "The Big Rise,"*Fortune*, May 30, 1994, 74–90.

[5]Roger D. Blackwell, Paul W. Miniard, and James F. Engel, *Consumer Behavior* (Hinsdale, IL: Dryden, 1997), 311.

[6]*European Marketing Data and Statistics 1999* (London: Euromonitor, 1999), 395.

patterns of demand; for example, they may offer single-serving portions of frozen foods and smaller appliances.

The increased urbanization of many markets has distinctly changed consumption patterns. Urban populations as a percentage of the total will vary from a low of 6 percent in Burundi to a high of 97 percent in Belgium. The degree of urbanization often dictates the nature of the marketing task the company faces, not only in terms of distribution but also in terms of market potential and buying habits. Urban areas provide larger groups of consumers who may be more receptive to marketing efforts because of their exposure to other consumers (the demonstration effect) and to communication media. In markets where urbanization is recent and taking place rapidly, the marketer faces additional responsibility as a change agent, especially when incomes may be low and the conditions for the proper use of the products may not be adequate. This is especially true in countries where rapid industrialization is taking place, such as Greece, Spain, and Portugal.

When using international data sources, the international marketer must recognize that definitions of a construct may vary among the many secondary sources. The concept of **urbanization,** for example, has different meanings depending on where one operates. In the United States, an urban area is defined as a place of 2,500 or more inhabitants; in Sweden, it is a built-up area with at least 200 inhabitants with no more than 200 meters between houses; in Mauritius, it is a town with proclaimed legal limits. Comparability, therefore, is concerned with the ends and not the means (or the definition).

Income   Markets require not only people but also purchasing power, which is a function of income, prices, savings, and credit availability.

Apart from basic staple items, for which population figures provide an estimate, income is most indicative of the market potential for most consumer and industrial products and services. For the marketer to make use of information on gross national products of various nations, such as that summarized in Table 4.2, further knowledge is needed on distribution of income. Per capita GNP is often used as a primary indicator for evaluating purchasing power. This figure shows great variation between countries, as indicated by Luxembourg's $38,886 and Ethiopia's $103. The wide use of GNP figures can be explained by their easy availability, but they should nevertheless be used with caution. In industrialized countries, the richest 10 percent of the population consume 20 percent of all goods and services, whereas the respective figure for the developing countries may be as high as 50 percent.[7] In some markets, income distribution produces wide gaps between population groups. The more developed the economy, the more income distribution tends to converge toward the middle class.

The international marketer can use the following classification as a planning guide:

1. Very low family incomes. Subsistence economies tend to be characterized by rural populations in which consumption relies on personal output or barter. Some urban centers may provide markets. Example: Cameroon.
2. Very low, very high family incomes. Some countries exhibit strongly bimodal income distributions. The majority of the population may live barely above the subsistence level, but there is a strong market in urban centers and a growing middle class. The affluent are truly affluent and will consume accordingly. Examples: India, Mexico.
3. Low, medium, high family incomes. Industrialization produces an emerging middle class with increasing disposable income. The very low and very high income classes tend to remain for traditional reasons of social class barriers. Example: Portugal.

[7]The World Bank, *World Development Indicators* (Washington, DC, 2000), 85. See also **http://www.worldbank.org/data/wdi2000/**.

TABLE 4.2   Gross Domestic Product per Capita for Selected Countries, 1997

HIGHEST GDP PER HEAD (IN DOLLARS)

RANK	COUNTRY	GDP	RANK	COUNTRY	GDP
1	Luxembourg	38,886	18	Australia	22,000
2	Switzerland	35,996	19	Canada	21,000
3	Norway	35,028	20	Italy	20,200
4	Japan	33,277	21	Ireland	20,021
5	Denmark	31,985	22	UAE	17,200
6	Singapore	30,655	23	New Zealand	17,105
7	United States	30,276	24	Israel	16,907
8	Iceland	27,269	25	Kuwait	16,778
9	Sweden	26,718	26	Qatar	16,370
10	Hong Kong	26,701	27	Spain	13,541
11	Germany	25,840	28	Taiwan	13,000
12	Austria	25,485	29	Greece	11,400
13	France	24,338	30	South Korea	10,361
14	Belgium	23,822	31	Bahrain	9,835
15	Finland	23,632	32	Puerto Rico	9,378
16	Netherlands	23,276	33	Barbados	8,364
17	United Kingdom	22,229	34	Saudi Arabia	7,500

LOWEST GDP PER HEAD (IN DOLLARS)

RANK	COUNTRY	GDP	RANK	COUNTRY	GDP
1	Haiti	415	10	Tanzania	244
2	Kenya	357	11	Madagascar	218
3	Vietnam	348	12	Burkina Faso	198
4	Laos	337	13	Afghanistan	195
5	Uganda	336	14	Myanmar	190
6	Zambia	336	15	Nepal	190
7	Cambodia	303	16	Mozambique	106
8	Bangladesh	269	17	Sierra Leone	105
9	Malawi	262	18	Ethiopia	103

SOURCE: "Indicators of Market Size for 115 Countries," *Country Monitor,* December 15, 1999, 1–11.

4. Mostly medium family incomes. The advanced industrial nations tend to develop institutions and policies that reduce extremes in income distribution, resulting in a large and comfortable middle class able to purchase a wide array of both domestic and imported products and services. Example: Denmark.[8]

Although the national income figures provide a general indication of a market's potential, they suffer from various distortions. Figures available from secondary sources are often in U.S. dollars. The per capita income figures may not be a true reflection of purchasing power if the currencies involved are distorted in some way. For example, fluctuations in the value of the U.S. dollar may distort real-income and standard-of-living figures. The goods and services in different countries have to be valued consistently if the differences are to reflect real differences in the volumes of goods produced. The use of **purchasing power parities (PPP)** instead of exchange rates is intended to achieve this objective. PPPs show how many units of currency are needed in one country to buy the amount of goods and services that one unit of currency will buy in another country. Table 4.3 provides an example of such data.

[8]Philip Kotler, *Marketing Management* (Englewood Cliffs, NJ: Prentice-Hall, 1991), 405.

TABLE 4.3	Gross Domestic Product/Purchasing Power Parities							
	GROSS DOMESTIC PRODUCT (BILLIONS OF DOLLARS)				GROSS DOMESTIC PRODUCT PER CAPITA (DOLLARS)			
COUNTRY	1985	1990	1993	1997	1985	1990	1993	1997
United States	3,967.5	5,392.0	6,260	7,783	16,581	21,449	24,302	29,080
OECD Europe	3,980.2	5,871.0	6,889	8,408	9,857	14,070	15,646	18,698
Austria	81.2	128.0	153	225	10.748	16,620	19,128	22,010
Belgium	106.1	164.0	195	272	10,768	16,405	19,517	23,090
Denmark	62.8	86.0	100	184	12,279	16,765	19,335	23,450
Finland	56.1	82.0	79	127	11,447	16,453	15,530	19,660
France	646.6	984.0	1,079	1,542	11,720	17,431	18,709	22,210
Germany	738.7	1,157.0	1,503	2,321	12,105	18,291	18,510	21,170
Greece	59.7	75.0	91	122	6,010	7,349	8,797	12,540
Ireland	24.4	37.0	49	65	6,901	10,659	13,856	17,420
Italy	624.2	924.0	1,018	1,160	10,927	16,021	17,830	20,100
Netherlands	164.3	236.0	269	403	11,339	15,766	17,593	21,300
Portugal	53.2	82.0	118	110	5,516	8,389	11,953	14,180
Spain	292.5	459.0	521	570	7,597	11,792	13,311	15,690
Sweden	106.3	144.0	147	232	12,727	16,867	16,831	19,010
United Kingdom	624.0	903.0	985	1,231	11,020	15,720	17,036	20,710
Norway	58.0	68.0	84	159	13,963	15,921	19,476	24,260
Switzerland	94.3	143.0	161	305	14,440	20,997	23,195	26,580
Turkey	179.7	190.9	322	199	3,547	3,316	5,410	6,470
Australia	184.4	273.0	302	383	11,682	15,951	17,103	19,510
Canada	388.8	509.0	554	595	15,440	19,120	19,278	21,750
Japan	1,425.4	2,179.0	2,559	4,812	11,805	17,634	20,523	24,400
New Zealand	33.1	45.0	54	60	10,126	13,258	15,493	15,780

SOURCE: Adapted from Bureau of the Census, *Statistical Abstract of the United States*, 1999 (Washington, DC: Government Printing Office, 1999), tables 1362 and 1363. **www.statusa.gov**, August 17, 2000.

Second, using a monetary measure may not be a proper and all-inclusive measure of income. For example, in developing economies where most of the consumption is either self-produced or bartered, reliance on financial data alone would seriously understate the standard of living. Further, several of the service-related items (for example, protective services and travel), characteristic of the industrialized countries' national income figures, do not exist for markets at lower levels of development.

Moreover, the marketer will have to take into consideration variations in market potential in individual markets. Major urban centers in developing countries may have income levels comparable to those in more developed markets, while rural areas may not have incomes needed to buy imported goods.

The European outdoor market contrasts with the Asian electronics store, reflecting the consumer values.

In general, income figures are useful in the initial screening of markets. However, in product-specific cases, income may not play a major role, and startling scenarios may emerge. Some products, such as motorcycles and television sets in China, are in demand regardless of their high price in relation to wages because of their high prestige value. Some products are in demand because of their foreign origin. As an example, European luxury cars have lucrative markets in countries where per capita income figures may be low but there are wealthy consumers who are able and willing to buy them. For example, Mercedes Benz's target audience in India are families earning 1 million rupees (approximately $30,000). Earnings at that level are enough for a lifestyle to rival that of a U.S. or European family with an income three times higher due to much higher level of disposable income.[9] Further, the lack of income in a market may preclude the marketing of a standardized product but, at the same time, provide an opportunity for an adjusted product. A packaged goods company, confronted with considerable disparity in income levels within the same country, adapted a deodorant product to fit two separate target income groups—the regular product version in an aerosol can and the less expensive one in a plastic squeeze bottle. By substituting cheaper parts and materials, successful international marketers can make both consumer and industrial products more affordable in less affluent markets and therefore reach a wider target audience.

The impact of income changes on consumption patterns at present and in the future in China are described in *The International Marketplace 4.2.*

Consumption Patterns   Depending on the sophistication of a country's data collection systems, economic data on consumption patterns can be obtained and analyzed. The share of income spent on necessities will provide an indication of the market's development level as well as an approximation of how much money the consumer has left for other purchases. Engel's laws provide some generalizations about consumers' spending patterns and are useful generalizations when precise data are not available. They state that as a family's income increases, the percentage spent on food will decrease, the percentage spent on housing and household operations will be roughly constant, and the amount saved or spent on other purchases will increase. Private expenditure comparisons reveal that the percentage spent on food in 1997 varied from 10 percent in the United States to 49 percent in India (see Table 4.4).

In Western Europe, expenditures on clothing typically account for 5 to 9 percent of all spending, but in poorer countries the proportion may be lower. In some low-wage areas, a significant proportion of clothing is homemade or locally made at low cost, making comparisons not entirely accurate. Eastern European households spend an inordinate proportion of their incomes on foodstuffs but quite a low proportion on housing. The remaining, less absolutely central areas of consumption (household goods, leisure, and transportation) are most vulnerable to short-term cancellation or postponement and thus serve as indicators for the strength of confidence in the market in general.

Data on product saturation or diffusion—information on the percentage of households in a market that own a particular product—allow a further evaluation of market potential. Table 4.5 presents the percentage of households that own certain appliances and indicates that saturation levels in the markets for which the data exist are quite high. This does not necessarily indicate lack of market potential; replacement markets or the demand for auxiliary products may offer attractive opportunities to the international marketer. Low rates of diffusion should be approached cautiously, because they can signal a market opportunity or lack thereof resulting from low income levels, use of a substitute product, or lack of acceptance. As an example of lack

[9]"In India, Luxury Is Within Reach of Many," *The Wall Street Journal*, October 17, 1995, A17.

THE INTERNATIONAL MARKETPLACE 4.2

In Search of the New China

THE CHINESE MARKET has always been an elusive one, especially for Western marketers. Much of the challenge stems from the lack of reliable market and consumer data.

The Gallup Organization has helped to change all this. Every three years since 1994, the company has conducted wide-ranging surveys of Chinese citizens. In June 1999, a total of 4,000 randomly selected respondents were asked questions about what they own, what their dreams are, and how much money they make, revealing a snapshot of a megamarket undergoing major change. In August 1999, however, the Chinese government made future data collection difficult by sharply restricting foreign market research firms. The recent agreement between Chinese ccidnet.com, an online consultancy firm, and Gallup, may be one way for foreign surveyors to retain flexibility.

In any case, the most recent survey shows how China's rapid economic growth has affected individual families (e.g., appliance ownership) and how it continues to reshape Chinese life. The survey also reveals that urban China is profoundly different from rural China. An interesting example: while almost everyone in the ten big cities surveyed had seen a foreigner, more than half of rural Chinese have not.

The average national GDP per capita is $735 and varies anywhere from Guizhou's $280 (on a par with Bangladesh) to Sichuan's $525 (on a par with Pakistan) to Shanghai's $3,400 (on a par with South Africa). While the average rural citizen will spend only about $4 a month on goods other than food and less than a dollar on entertainment, the amount is $10 for both in the cities.

The differences between the old and the young are also striking. A third of Beijingers between 18 and 19 have used the Internet, four times the rate of those over 40. Nearly three-quarters of urban women under the age of 30 said they wore lipstick; of those over 60 almost none did.

The results presented in the charts below illustrate both the complexities and commonalities in Chinese society. For example, Chinese of all ages and in all parts of the country say things have improved for them in the past five years, and they are similarly confident that the improvement will continue.

SOURCES: "A Survey of China," *Economist*, April 8, 2000, 1–16; "In Search of the New China," *Fortune*, October 11, 1999, 230–232; "What the Chinese Want," *Fortune*, October 11, 1999, 233–237; "Sino-Foreign Consultancy Firms to Jointly Launch On-Line Survey," *Xinhua*, November 15, 2000.

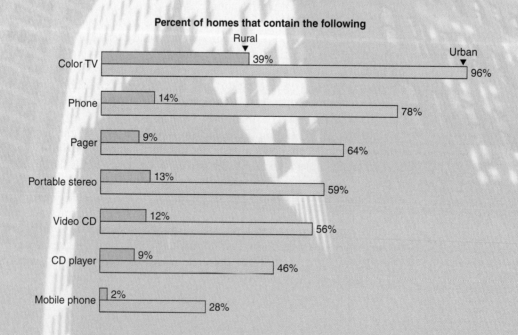

Percent of homes that contain the following

	Rural	Urban
Color TV	39%	96%
Phone	14%	78%
Pager	9%	64%
Portable stereo	13%	59%
Video CD	12%	56%
CD player	9%	46%
Mobile phone	2%	28%

Percent of people who have done the following

Rural ▼ — Urban ▼

	Rural	Urban
Eaten Western fast food	1%	49%
Attended Western movie	20%	48%
Bought Western music	6%	30%
Read Western book, magazine, or newspaper	6%	23%
Bought Western-brand clothing	2%	17%
Used computer	3%	39%
Heard of Internet	6%	44%
Ever used Internet	Less than 0.5%	8%
Heard of stocks	9%	42%
Owned stocks	1%	11%

Percent of people who, in the next two years, intend to purchase the following

'99 (% change from '97)

Color TV	30% (+9)
Life insurance	22% (+7)
Washing machine	22% (+6)
Refrigerator	21% (+5)
Video CD	19% (+11)
Motorcycle	16% (+7)
Property insurance	16% (+4)
Stereo/home theater	15% (+10)
Air conditioner	14% (+6)
Camera	14% (+3)
Pager	11% (+3)
Computer	10% (+5)
Microwave oven	10% (+6)
Mobile phone	10% (+7)
House	10% (+3)
Videogame	6% (+3)
Videocamera	6% (+3)

TABLE 4.4 Consumer Spending by Category, as Percent of Total, 1997

	FOOD, BEVERAGES, TOBACCO	CLOTHING, FOOTWEAR, TEXTILES	HOUSEHOLD FUELS	HOUSEHOLD GOODS & SERVICES	HOUSING	HEALTH	LEISURE AND EDUCATION	TRANSPORT AND COMMUNICATIONS
Argentina	30.3	11.3	4.3	7.7	11.2	7.7	8.3	12.5
Australia	23.9	5.0	2.1	11.2	13.4	5.1	10.9	13.9
Brazil	38.4	4.9	5.0	3.1	20.3	5.0	3.2	5.7
Canada	14.4	5.1	3.5	8.3	22.1	4.4	9.8	16.1
China	42.3	13.8	4.5	7.7	3.3	3.7	9.6	5.2
Colombia	32.0	13.7	1.9	4.6	6.6	4.1	7.2	20.6
Eastern Europe	41.2	7.0	7.8	4.3	7.0	4.0	7.7	10.5
European Union	17.6	6.3	3.7	7.9	19.2	5.5	9.1	16.2
India	49.4	9.0	3.5	2.0	4.8	1.9	3.2	20.1
Indonesia	44.6	4.6	2.9	9.2	14.1	1.6	1.2	3.5
Israel	20.7	5.6	4.3	9.5	19.5	10.6	9.0	18.5
Japan	15.9	4.8	6.1	4.1	23.7	11.7	11.0	11.1
Mexico	29.0	4.2	1.2	8.3	14.0	4.6	6.2	15.0
Nigeria	49.8	10.4	4.3	4.8	11.1	3.9	3.6	7.6
Singapore	16.7	5.2	5.1	8.3	13.6	4.9	10.0	13.5
South Korea	26.6	3.5	3.7	6.4	6.0	6.8	13.1	15.7
Thailand	25.2	10.5	1.6	8.9	4.9	6.5	12.2	11.0
United States	10.4	5.7	2.7	5.5	15.9	18.3	11.0	20.7

SOURCES: *International Marketing Data and Statistics* 1999 (London: Euromonitor, 1998), table 1103 and *European Marketing Data and Statistics*, 1999 (London, Euromonitor, 1999), table 1103.

TABLE 4.5 Percentage of Households Owning Selected Appliances, 1997

APPLIANCE	UNITED STATES	BELGIUM	DENMARK	FRANCE	GERMANY	ITALY	NETHERLANDS	SPAIN	SWEDEN	SWITZERLAND	UNITED KINGDOM
Car	100	78	49	78	87	74	72	61	74	46	68
CD player	62	27	79	23	44	13	82	9	72	42	57
Dishwasher	46	33	39	35	57	36	45	19	54	57	17
Freezer	60	47	92	47	71	47	67	34	96	65	91
Microwave oven	92	44	44	47	62	34	62	18	58	42	38
Mobile phone	21	10	28	10	10	20	15	11	36	15	15
Personal computer	44	37	48	32	48	20	47	10	37	46	27
Refrigerator	100	99	96	64	79	70	98	66	99	99	99
Telephone	94	94	91	96	98	96	93	92	95	98	94
Television (color)	98	98	96	96	97	94	97	87	97	96	98
Tumble dryer	22	37	36	24	35	17	48	15	33	31	30
Vacuum cleaner	96	95	96	96	100	85	94	68	95	96	93
VCR	80	64	79	59	81	60	74	58	74	68	82
Washing machine	82	98	74	98	98	96	94	93	74	73	92

n.a.—Not available.

*Data are for 1997.

SOURCES: *International Marketing Data and Statistics* 1999 (London: Euromonitor, 1998), table 1103; *Statistical Abstract of the United States 1999* (Washington, DC: U.S. Government Printing Office, 1999), table 1371; and *European Marketing Data and Statistics*, 1999 (London: Euromonitor, 1999), table 1608.

of acceptance, the time-saving feature of microwave ovens may not be as attractive in more tradition-bound societies as it is in the United States or the EU.

General consumption figures are valuable, but they must be viewed with caution because they may conceal critical product-form differences; for example, appliances in European households tend to be smaller than their U.S. counterparts. Information about existing product usage can nevertheless provide indirect help to international marketers. As an example, a large number of telephones, and their even distribution among the population or a target group, may allow market research via telephone interviewing.

A problem for marketers in general is **inflation;** varying inflation rates complicate this problem in international markets. Many of the industrialized countries, such as the United States, Germany and Japan, have recently been able to keep inflation rates at single-digit levels while some have suffered from chronic inflation (see Table 4.6). Inflation affects the ability of both industrial customers and consumers to buy and also introduces uncertainty into both the marketer's planning process and consumers' buying habits. In high-inflation markets, the marketer may have to make changes in the product (more economical without compromising quality), promotion (more rational), and distribution (more customer involvement) to meet customer needs and maintain demand. In response to rapidly escalating prices, a government will often invoke price controls. The setting of maximum prices for products may cause the international marketer to face unacceptable profit situations, future investments may not be made, and production may even have to be stopped.[10]

Another challenge for international marketers is the **debt problem.** Many of the developing countries are saddled with a collective debt of $1.2 trillion (see Figure 4.3). Debt crises crush nations' buying power and force imports down and exports up to meet interest payments. For example, during the Latin American debt crisis, the U.S. trade balance with Latin nations deteriorated from an annual surplus of $6 billion in 1980 to a deficit of $15 billion in 1990. To continue growing, many companies are looking at developing nations because of the potential they see 10 to 15 years ahead. U.S. companies typically face competition in these regions from entities that are often aided by their government's aid grants, as well as by Europeans that do business with the help of government export credits that have interest rates lower than those provided by U.S. entities. Access to these markets can be achieved by helping political leaders provide jobs and by increasing exports. Heinz, for example, operates in many developing countries through joint ventures in which Heinz holds 51 percent. To sell copiers and printers in Brazil, Xerox exports Brazilian steel to Europe and Brazilian venetian blinds to the United States, among other products worth $100 million annually.[11] Many industrialized countries, such as Japan, France, and the United States, are seeking ways to ease the burden facing debtor nations.[12]

Infrastructure

The availability and quality of an infrastructure is critically important in evaluating marketing operations abroad. Each international marketer will rely heavily on services provided by the local market for transportation, communication, and energy as well as on organizations participating in the facilitating functions of marketing: marketing communications, distributing, information, and financing. Indicators such as steel consumption, cement production, and electricity production relate to the overall industrialization of the market and can be used effectively by suppliers of industrial

---

[10]Victor H. Frank, Jr., "Living with Price Control Abroad," *Harvard Business Review* 62 (March–April 1984): 137–142.

[11]Louis Kraar, "How to Sell to Cashless Buyers," *Fortune*, November 7, 1988, 147–154.

[12]*World Development Report* (Washington, DC: World Bank, 1991), 124–127.

TABLE 4.6	Consumer Price Index					
COUNTRY	1994–1995	1995–1996	1996–1997	1997–1998	1998–1999	1999–2000
United States	2.8	1.3	1.2	0.9	1.3	1.5
Argentina	3.4	0.2	0.8	0.8	−0.8	0.6
Australia	4.6	2.7	1.7	1.6	1.8	3.8
Austria	2.3	1.7	1.2	0.8	0.7	0.9
Bangladesh	5.8	4.5	4.8	7.9	7.8	7.0
Belgium	1.5	1.8	1.5	0.9	1.1	1.2
Bolivia	10.2	12.4	4.7	6.5	—	—
Brazil	84.4	15.5	6.0	3.7	—	—
Canada	2.2	1.5	1.4	1.0	1.5	1.7
Chile	8.2	7.3	6.1	5.1	4.0	3.3
China	16.7	8.4	2.8	−1.0	−1.5	1.5
Colombia	21.0	20.8	18.5	18.7	11.7	10.7
Ecuador	22.9	24.4	30.6	36.1	55.1	36.2
Egypt	8.1	7.0	6.2	3.8	3.7	4.0
Finland	1.0	1.1	1.2	1.3	1.3	2.3
France	1.8	2.1	1.3	0.7	0.5	1.1
Germany	1.8	1.2	1.5	0.6	0.4	0.8
Ghana	59.5	45.6	28.8	19.3	10.0	6.4
Greece	9.3	7.9	5.4	4.5	2.3	2.2
Guatemala	8.4	11.0	7.1	7.5	6.5	6.0
India	10.2	9.0	7.2	13.0	6.5	7.2
Indonesia	9.4	7.9	6.6	60.0	22.7	5.7
Iran	49.6	23.1	17.3	22.0	15.0	10.0
Israel	10.0	11.3	9.1	5.4	5.5	4.6
Italy	5.2	3.9	1.7	1.7	1.5	1.6
Japan	−0.1	0.1	1.7	0.6	−0.4	−0.1
Malaysia	5.3	3.5	2.7	5.3	3.0	2.4
Mexico	35.0	34.4	20.6	16.7	17.1	11.1
Netherlands	1.9	2.1	2.2	2.0	2.3	2.1
Norway	2.5	1.3	2.6	2.3	2.3	2.3
Pakistan	12.3	10.3	12.5	7.8	6.1	6.5
Peru	11.1	11.5	8.5	7.3	4.4	5.3
Philippines	8.1	8.4	6.0	9.7	8.5	6.0
Portugal	4.1	3.1	2.2	2.8	2.3	2.2
Romania	32.2	38.8	154.8	59.1	40.4	16.8
South Africa	8.7	7.4	8.6	6.9	6.5	5.5
South Korea	4.7	4.9	4.4	7.5	0.1	2.8
Spain	4.5	3.6	1.9	1.8	2.1	2.1
Sweden	2.5	0.5	0.5	−0.1	0.2	1.0
Switzerland	1.8	0.8	0.5	0.1	0.8	1.0
Thailand	5.8	5.9	5.6	8.1	0.1	2.0
Turkey	91.6	82.3	85.7	84.6	60.4	38.2
United Kingdom	3.4	2.9	2.8	2.6	2.3	2.2
Venezuela	59.9	99.9	50.0	35.8	24.4	17.3

SOURCE: *International Financial Statistics* (Washington, DC: International Monetary Fund, monthly). See also **http://www.imf.org**

products and services. As an example, energy consumption per capita may serve as an indicator of market potential for electrical markets, provided evenness of distribution exists over the market. Yet the marketer must make sure that the energy is affordable and compatible (in terms of current and voltage) with the products to be marketed.

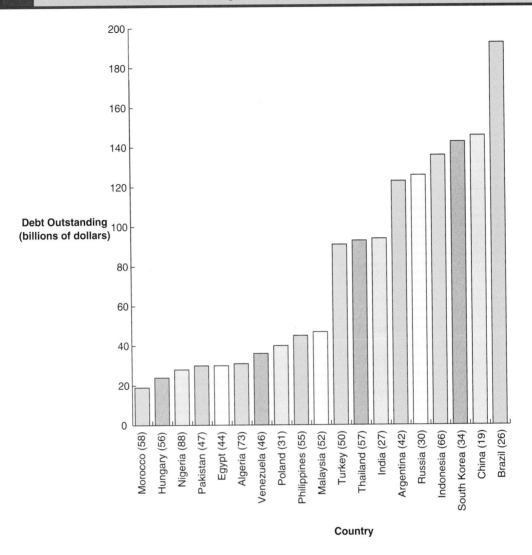

FIGURE 4.3 | **Nations in Debt: Debt Outstanding (Billions of Dollars)**

Numbers in parentheses indicate percentages of GDP.

SOURCE: *Global Development Finance 1999* (Washington, DC: World Bank, 1999), 102–109; see also **http://www.worldbank.org**.

The existence and expansion of basic infrastructure has contributed significantly to increased agricultural output in Asia and Latin America. The Philippines has allocated 5 percent of agricultural development funds to rural electrification programs. On a similar level, basic roads are essential to moving agricultural products. In many parts of Africa, farmers are more than a day's walk from the nearest road. As a result, measures to improve production without commensurate improvements in transportation and communications are of little use because the crops cannot reach the market. In addition, the lack of infrastructure cuts the farmers off from new technology, inputs, and ideas.

Transportation networks by land, rail, waterway, or air are essential for physical distribution. The major world land and ocean transportation flows are summarized in the following color map insert. An analysis of rail traffic by freight tons per kilome-

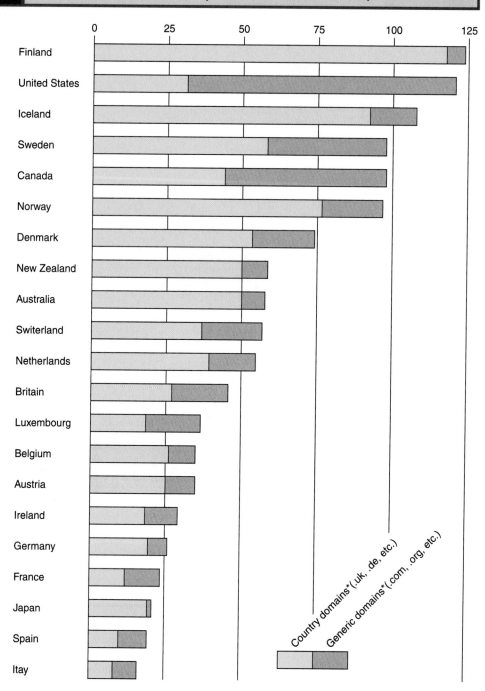

FIGURE 4.4 Network Effect (Internet Hosts per 1,000 Inhabitants in 1999)

SOURCE: "First America, Then the World," *Economist*, February 26, 2000, 49.

ter offers a possible way to begin an investigation of transportation capabilities; however, these figures may not always indicate the true state of the system. China's railway system carries five times as much freight as India's does, which is an amazing feat considering that only 20 percent of the network is doubletracked and that it is shared by an ever-growing amount of passenger traffic. In spite of the railway's greater use, the international marketer has to rely on other methods of distribution. The tremendous logistics challenge makes national distribution in China only a dream and slows down expansion from the major urban population centers of Guangzhou, Shanghai, and Beijing.[13] With the same type of caution, the number of passenger cars as well as buses and trucks can be used to analyze the state of road transportation and transportation networks.

Communication is as important as transportation. The ability of a firm to communicate with entities both outside and within the market can be estimated by using indicators of the communications infrastructure: telephones, computers, broadcast media, and print media in use. The countries of the former Eastern bloc possess some of the world's worst telephone systems. Western Europe has forty-nine main telephone lines per one hundred people, while Russia has twelve, Hungary has nine, and Poland has eight. Upgrading the telephone system will be expensive (estimated at $50 billion for Central Europe alone) but necessary for competing in the world market and attracting international investors. Official figures may not reveal the quality of the services provided and their possible reach. For example, the telephone system in Egypt, especially in Cairo, is notorious for its frequent breakdowns and lack of capacity. Wireless technology is poised to change the worldwide landscape in many ways. While the number of cellular phones in use in 2000 was estimated at 555 million, the estimated number for 2003 is set at over 900 million (with 150 million in use in North America, 285 million in Europe, 295 million in Asia, 128 million in Latin America, and 44 million in the Middle East and Africa).[14]

The diffusion of Internet technology into core business processes and into the lifestyles of consumers has been rapid, especially in industrialized countries. The number of Internet hosts (computers through which users connect to the network) has increased to 72.3 million by 2000, up from 9.4 million in 1993 and 43.2 million in 1999.[15] While the United States still has the majority of these, Northern Europe is also very active (see Figure 4.4). The total number of people using the Internet is difficult to estimate. One estimate in March 2000 placed the number at 304.36 million worldwide, with 136.86 million in North America, 83.35 million in Europe, 68.39 million in the Asia-Pacific, 10.74 million in Latin America, 2.58 million in Africa, and 1.90 million in the Middle East.[16] Given the changes expected in the first years of the twenty-first century, all the estimates indicating explosive growth may be low. The number of users will start evening out around the globe, with new technologies assisting. Computers priced at less than $500 will boost global computer ownership and subsequent online activity. Developments in television, cable, phone, and wireless technologies not only will make the market broader but will also allow for more services to be delivered more efficiently. For example, with the advent of third-generation mobile communications technology, systems will have 100-fold increase in data transfer, allowing the viewing of videos on mobile phones.[17] This will create an advantage for both European and Japanese players thanks to their lead over the United States in mobile telephony. Television will also become a mainstream Internet access method of the future. While the interactive TV market served only 3 million viewers in Europe and North America in 1999, the estimates are for 67 million subscribers by 2003.[18] The growth in international opportunities is leading to a

[13]Paul Cheng, "Gateway to China," presentation made to the 36th CIES Annual Executive Congress, Sydney, Australia, April 22–24, 1993.

[14]"Unplugging Data," *Advertising Age*, March 6, 2000, 50.

[15]*Internet Domain Survey, January 2000*, available at **http://www.isc.org**.

[16]*How Many Online?*, available at **http://www.nua.ie/surveys/how_many_online/index.html**.

[17]"The Mad Grab for Piece of Air," *Business Week*, April 17, 2000, 152–154; and "Hello, Internet," *Business Week*, May 3, 1999, 170–175.

[18]Jesse Berst, "It's Back: How Interactive TV Is Sneaking Back into Your Living Room," available at **http://www.zdnet.com/anchordesk/story/story_3368.html**.

THE INTERNATIONAL MARKETPLACE 4.3

Bringing the New Economy to New Markets

WITH THE U.S. MARKET crowded with competitors, Yahoo!, Excite, Lycos, and America Online are expanding their plans to establish brands in Asia, Europe, and Latin America before local competitors can create dominant positions of their own. With the non-U.S. share of users increasing, the fastest growth can be secured abroad.

One significant reason for the growth is falling costs. Internet users pay telephone charges on top of Internet access fees to use the Web, but more operators are offering free monthly access, and phone charges are dropping fast across the board.

Yahoo!, with the most worldwide customers, operates 24 overseas sites. Lycos' merger in 2000 with Terra Networks, S.A., boosted Terra Lycos' coverage to 140 sites in 41 countries. AOL, now serving 16 countries, gained access to a rich variety of content through its 2001 merger with media giant Time Warner, while Excite operates 9 international ventures. These sites offer native-language news, shopping links and other content tailored to the local population. Lycos's German site features tips on brewing beer at home, and Yahoo's Singapore site offers real-time information on haze and smog in Southeast Asia.

The top U.S. players face tough domestic competitors that often have a better sense of the local culture and Internet styles. In many countries, the dominant telephone companies offer portals, giving them a significant competitive advantage with customers who are automatically sent to their home pages when they log on. Germany's leading portal, T-Online, is run by Deutsche Telekom, while the leading portal, Wanadoo, is operated by France Telecom.

The danger for U.S. portals is that they might be viewed as "digital colonialists" trying to flex their muscles around the world. In Brazil, AOL was accused by its local competitor, Universo Online, of using a misleading slogan: "We're the biggest because we're the best." The operation has also been hurt because AOL's installation disks altered users' hard drives.

Market resistance may lead to a desire to form partnerships with local outfits that would also help in understanding the local culture. In Japan, Lycos teams up with Sumitomo, an ultra-traditional company with a 250-year history, while in Korea it teamed up with Mirae, a machinery and electronics company.

SOURCES: "For Internet Portals, the Next Battleground Is Overseas," *The Wall Street Journal*, March 23, 2000, B1, B4; and "Shopping around the Web," *Economist*, February 26, 2000, 5-54. Access international sites at

http://www.yahoo.com;

http://www.excite.com;

http://www.lycos.com;

http://www.aol.com.

rapid internationalization of Internet players, as shown in *The International Marketplace 4.3*.

The careful assessment of infrastructure spells out important marketing opportunities. While two billion people in Asia are without electricity and only 16 in 1,000 have access to a telephone, the Asian market is the most keenly watched by marketers. According to one estimate, between 1994 and 2000, Asian countries (excluding Japan) spent $1.5 trillion on power, transportation, telecommunications, water supplies, and sanitation.[19] China overtook the United States in pager use by late 1997 mainly because of the low cost of the needed infrastructure to support paging. The big winners will be companies like Motorola that are developing new products for this market such as pagers that play back voice mail. The booming middle class in cities such as Bangkok will ensure that cellular phone sales continue at record pace. With increasing affluence comes an increasing need for energy. General Electric estimates that China will place orders for 168,000 megawatts in additional power-generating capacity, and India more than 70,000 megawatts; the corresponding figure in the United States is 154,000.

Data on the availability of commercial (marketing-related) infrastructure are often not readily available. Data on which to base an assessment may be provided by gov-

[19]Rahul Jacob, "Asian Infrastructure: The Biggest Bet on Earth," *Fortune*, October 31, 1994, 139–150.

ernment sources, such as Overseas Business Reports; by trade associations, such as the Business Equipment Manufacturers' Association; and by trade publications, such as *Advertising Age*. The more extensive the firm's international involvement, the more it can rely on its already existing support network of banks, advertising agencies, and distributors to assess new markets.

Foreign Involvement in the Economy

For the international marketer interested in entering a foreign market, it is important to know the extent to which such entry is accepted by a country. An economy's overall acceptance of foreign involvement can be estimated by analyzing the degree of foreign direct investment by country and by industry in a given market as well as by the rules governing such investment.

A summary of the conditions for foreign direct investment in selected countries is provided in Figure 4.5 on page 116. Restrictions exist mainly by industry type, but also by origin of investor. Many nations have established investment-screening agencies to assess foreign direct investment proposals. For example, in the United States, major foreign direct investments must be reviewed by the Committee for Foreign Investments in the United States (CFIUS). Concerns have been raised mainly in terms of national security and origin of investors: in the 1970s, Arabs; in the late 1980s and early 1990s, the Japanese.

By 1999, the total number of **multinational corporations**—firms that own or control production or service facilities outside the country in which they are based—exceeded 59,900 with 508,000 affiliates around the world.[20] The global sales of foreign affiliates of the top multinationals are estimated to be $2.1 trillion. The largest 600 multinationals are estimated to generate between one-fifth and one-fourth of the value added in global production of goods and services. Cross-border business has been driven by three main factors: falling regulatory barriers to overseas investment, smaller costs in telecommunications and transportation, and freer domestic and international capital markets in which companies can be bought.[21] The estimated total world stock of direct investment abroad reached $4.1 trillion in 1998.[22]

The favored investment regions of U.S. companies are Europe and Canada; for Japanese companies, North America and Asia; and for German companies, Europe and North America. In general, direct investments are growing in the Far East (for example, Singapore and Malaysia), whereas certain regions are witnessing decline (for example, South Africa for political reasons). Driving this investment are need for efficiency and to participate directly in international markets that cannot adequately be reached through exports and imports alone. Investing companies come from an ever-increasing number of countries. In the 1970s, half of all multinational corporations were U.S. or British; today, just less than half are from the United States, Japan, Germany, and Switzerland (with Britain coming in seventh).

Impact of the Economic Environment on Social Development

Many of the characteristics discussed are important beyond numbers. Economic success comes with a price tag. All the social traumas that were once believed endemic only to the West are now hitting other parts of the world as well. Many countries, including the nations of Southeast Asia, were able to achieve double-digit growth for decades while paying scant attention to problems that are now demanding treatment:

[20]United Nations, *World Investment Report* (New York: United Nations, 1999), xvii.

[21]"A Survey of Multinationals," *Economist*, March 27, 1993.

[22]United Nations, *World Investment Report* (New York: United Nations, 1999), 9.

International Groupings

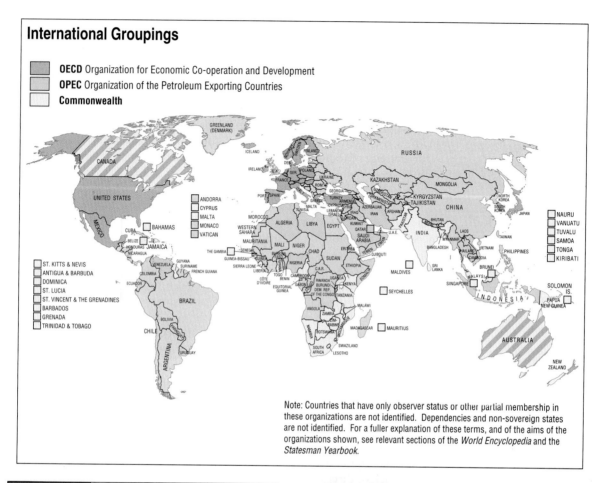

Note: Countries that have only observer status or other partial membership in these organizations are not identified. Dependencies and non-sovereign states are not identified. For a fuller explanation of these terms, and of the aims of the organizations shown, see relevant sections of the *World Encyclopedia* and the *Statesman Yearbook*.

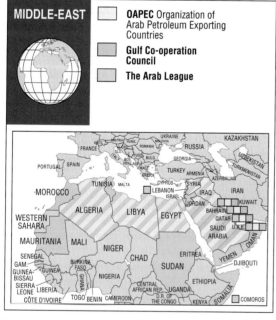

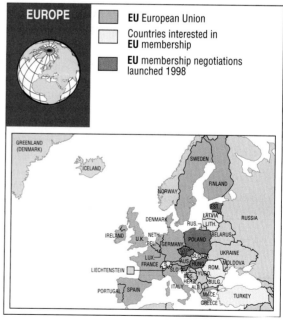

Sources: *Statesman Yearbook ; The European Union: A Guide for Americans*, 2000, www.eurounion.org/infores/euguide/euguide.html; "Afrabet Soup," *The Economist*, February 10, 2001, p. 77, www.economist.com

PACIFIC BASIN

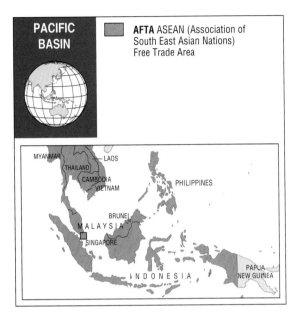

- **AFTA** ASEAN (Association of South East Asian Nations) Free Trade Area

AFRICA

- **OAU** *non*-members of the Organization for African Unity
- *Franc Zone** currency linked to the French Franc
- **SADC** Southern African Development Community
- **COMESA** Common Market for East and Southern Africa (formerly **PTA**)
- **ECOWAS** Economic Community of West African States

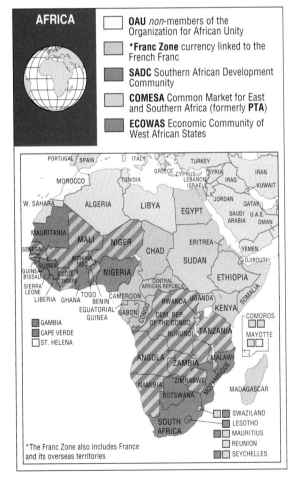

- GAMBIA
- CAPE VERDE
- ST. HELENA

*The Franc Zone also includes France and its overseas territories

AMERICAS

- **NAFTA** North American Free Trade Agreement
- **ANCOM** Andean Common Market
- **MERCOSUR** Southern Common Market
- **CARICOM** Caribbean Community and Common Market
- **CACM** Central American Common Market

- ST. KITTS & NEVIS
- ANTIGUA & BARBUDA
- MONTSERRAT
- DOMINICA
- ST. LUCIA
- ST. VINCENT & THE GRENADINES
- BARBADOS
- GRENADA
- TRINIDAD & TOBAGO

| FIGURE | 4.5 | A Sample of Regulations Governing Foreign Direct Investment |

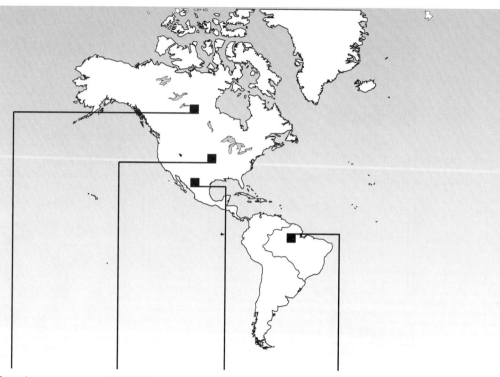

Canada
Canada took down its KEEP OUT sign with the Investment Canada Act of 1985. But the government is still reluctant to approve deals in film, publishing, and other areas that could compromise Canada's "cultural heritage or national identity."

United States
Come one, come all, unless you come from, Cuba, Iraq, Libya, North Korea, or Sudan. Buy anything, anywhere, but not more than 25 percent of a freshwater or coastal shipping enterprise, airline, or broadcast station. Expect heat from the government if you're eyeing a company that affects national security.

Mexico
The Law to Promote Mexican Investment and Regulate Foreign Investment is a bureaucratic migraine. Don't expect government clearance mañana. And save your breath if your business is oil, nuclear power, mining, electricity, railroads, or communications.

Brazil
Best bet: Buy some of Brazil's foreign debt and swap it for an equity stake in a local business. Like the rest of Latin America, Brazil is desperate to cut its debt burden.

infrastructure limits, labor shortages, demands for greater political freedom, environmental destruction, urban congestion, and even the spread of drug addiction.[23]

Because of the close relationship between economic and social development, many of the figures can be used as social indicators as well. Consider the following factors and their significance: share of urban population, life expectancy, number of physicians per capita, literacy rate, percentage of income received by the richest 5 percent of the population, and percentage of the population with access to electricity. In addition to these factors, several other variables can be used as cultural indicators: number of public libraries, registered borrowings, book titles published, and number of daily newspapers. The **Physical Quality of Life Index (PQLI)** is a composite measure of the level of welfare in a country. It has three components: life expectancy, infant mortality, and adult literacy rates.[24] The three components of the PQLI are among the

[23]Global Business Policy Council, *Globalization Ledger*, Washington, DC: A.T. Kearney, April 2000.

[24]Ben Crow and Alan Thomas, *Third World Atlas* (Milton Keynes, England: Open University Press, 1984), 85.

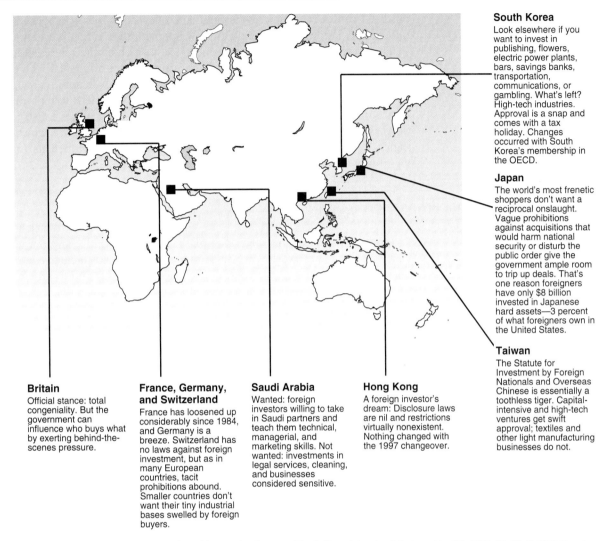

South Korea
Look elsewhere if you want to invest in publishing, flowers, electric power plants, bars, savings banks, transportation, communications, or gambling. What's left? High-tech industries. Approval is a snap and comes with a tax holiday. Changes occurred with South Korea's membership in the OECD.

Japan
The world's most frenetic shoppers don't want a reciprocal onslaught. Vague prohibitions against acquisitions that would harm national security or disturb the public order give the government ample room to trip up deals. That's one reason foreigners have only $8 billion invested in Japanese hard assets—3 percent of what foreigners own in the United States.

Taiwan
The Statute for Investment by Foreign Nationals and Overseas Chinese is essentially a toothless tiger. Capital-intensive and high-tech ventures get swift approval; textiles and other light manufacturing businesses do not.

Britain
Official stance: total congeniality. But the government can influence who buys what by exerting behind-the-scenes pressure.

France, Germany, and Switzerland
France has loosened up considerably since 1984, and Germany is a breeze. Switzerland has no laws against foreign investment, but as in many European countries, tacit prohibitions abound. Smaller countries don't want their tiny industrial bases swelled by foreign buyers.

Saudi Arabia
Wanted: foreign investors willing to take in Saudi partners and teach them technical, managerial, and marketing skills. Not wanted: investments in legal services, cleaning, and businesses considered sensitive.

Hong Kong
A foreign investor's dream: Disclosure laws are nil and restrictions virtually nonexistent. Nothing changed with the 1997 changeover.

few social indicators available to provide a comparison of progress through time in all of the countries of the world.

Differences in the degree of urbanization of target markets in lesser-developed countries influence international marketers' product strategies. If products are targeted only to urban areas, products need minimal adjustments, mainly to qualify them for market entry. However, when targeting national markets, firms may need to make extensive adaptations to match more closely the expectations and the more narrow consumption experiences of the rural population.[25]

In terms of infrastructure, improved access in rural areas brings with it an expansion of nonfarm enterprises such as shops, repair services, and grain mills. It also changes customs, attitudes, and values. As an example, a World Bank study on the impact of rural roads of Yucatán in Mexico found that roads offered an opportunity for

[25]John S. Hill and Richard R. Still, "Effects of Urbanization on Multinational Product Planning: Markets in Lesser-Developed Countries," *Columbia Journal of World Business* 19 (Summer 1984): 62–67.

enlarging women's role by introducing new ideas, education, medical care, and economic alternatives to maize cultivation.[26] In particular, women married later, had fewer children, and pursued more nondomestic activities. The same impact has been observed with increased access to radio and television. These changes can, if properly understood and utilized, offer major new opportunities to the international marketer.

The presence of multinational corporations, which by their very nature are change agents, will accelerate social change. If government control is weak, the multinational corporation bears the social responsibility for its actions. In some cases, governments restrict the freedom of multinational corporations if their actions may affect the environment. As an example, the Indonesian government places construction restrictions (such as building height) on hotels in Bali to avoid the overcrowding and ecological problems incurred in Hawaii when that state developed its tourism sector vigorously in the 1960s and 1970s.

Regional Economic Integration

Economic integration has been one of the main economic developments affecting world markets since World War II. Countries have wanted to engage in economic cooperation to use their respective resources more effectively and to provide larger markets for member-country producers. Some integration efforts have had quite ambitious goals, such as political integration; some have failed as the result of perceptions of unequal benefits from the arrangement or parting of ways politically. Figure 4.6, a summary of the major forms of economic cooperation in regional markets, shows the varying degrees of formality with which integration can take place. These economic integration efforts are dividing the world into trading blocs, as seen in *The International Marketplace 4.4.*

FIGURE 4.6   Forms of Economic Integration in Regional Markets

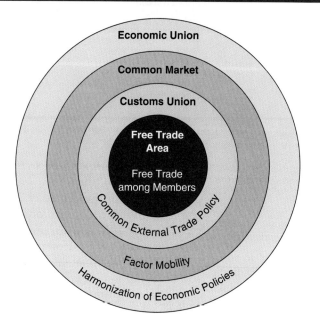

---

[26]The World Bank, *World Development Report 1982* (New York: Oxford University Press, 1982), 63.

THE INTERNATIONAL MARKETPLACE 4.4

The World of Trading Blocs

REGIONAL GROUPINGS based on economics became increasingly important in the 1990s. Thirty-two such groupings are estimated to be in existence: three in Europe, four in the Middle East, five in Asia, and ten each in Africa and the Americas. Trade within the three major blocs, the American, European, and Asian, has grown rapidly, while trading among these blocs or with outsiders is either declining or growing far more moderately.

Some of these groupings have the superstructure of nation-states (such as the European Union); some (such as the ASEAN Free Trade Area) are multinational agreements that are now more political than economic. Other arrangements are not trading blocs per se, but work to further them. The Free Trade Area of the Americas is a foreign policy initiative designed to further democracy in the region through incentives to capitalistic development and trade liberalization. The Andean Common Market and Mercosur intend to negotiate with the members of the North American Free Trade Agreement (NAFTA) to create a hemispheric market. In Asia, regional economic integration in Asia has been driven more by market forces than by treaties and by a need to maintain balance in negotiations with Europe and North America. The broader agreement of the Asia Pacific Economic Cooperation (APEC) brought together partners from multiple continents—AFTA members with economic powerhouses as China, Korea, Taiwan, and the United States.

Regional groupings are constantly being developed. In 1995 a new bloc was proposed between NAFTA and EU members. Called TAFTA (the Transatlantic Free Trade Area), this has not yet materialized. Since 1991, 12 former republics of the Soviet Union have tried to forge common economic policies, but to date only Belarus, Kazakhstan, Kyrgyzstan, Russia, and Tajikistan are signatories in the Customs Union.

Companies are facing ever-intensifying competition and trading difficulties for sales inside a bloc. In the long term, firms encounter pressure to globalize and source locally. Actions of these global companies may also allay fears that regional blocs are nothing but protectionism on a grander scale.

SOURCES: "World Trade Growth Slower in 1998 after Unusually Strong Growth in 1997," World Trade Organization press release, April 16, 1999, http:// www.wto.org; "American Politics, Global Trade," *Economist*, September 27, 1997, 23–26; Ilkka A. Ronkainen, "Trading Blocs: Opportunity or Demise for International Trade?;" *Multinational Business Review* 1 (Spring 1993): 1–9; Paivi Vihma, "Gatt Kittuu, Kauppablokit Nousevat," *Talouselama*, (Number 11, 1992), 42–43; and Joseph L. Brand, "The New World Order," *Vital Speeches of the Day* 58 (December): 155–160; "Blair Calls for Transatlantic Alliance," *Xinhua News Agency*, February 22, 2001; "Customs Union Brings Strong CIS Trade Growth," *ITAR-TASS*, December 7, 2000.

NAFTA
North American Free Trade Agreement

Canada, Mexico, United States
GNP: $8.8 trillion; 404 million people

FTAA
Free Trade Area of the Americas

EEA
European Economic Area

Total of 19 European nations

GNP: $9 trillion; 386 million people

EAEG
East Asian Economic Group

Add Hong Kong, Japan, South Korea, and Taiwan to AFTA
GNP: $5.2 trillion; 714 million people

AFTA ASEAN Free Trade Area

Brunei, Indonesia, Malaysia, Laos, Myanmar, Philippines, Singapore, Thailand, Vietnam

GNP: $546 billion; 512 million people

Levels of Economic Integration

Free Trade Area   The **free trade area** is the least restrictive and loosest form of economic integration among nations. In a free trade area, all barriers to trade among member countries are removed. Goods and services are freely traded among member countries. Each member country maintains its own trade barriers vis-à-vis nonmembers.

The European Free Trade Area (EFTA) was formed in 1960 with an agreement by eight European countries. Since that time, EFTA has lost much of its original significance due to its members joining the European Union (EU) (Denmark and the United Kingdom in 1973; Portugal in 1986; and Austria, Finland, and Sweden in 1995). All EFTA countries have cooperated with the EU through bilateral free trade agreements, and since 1994 through the European Economic Area (EEA) arrangement that allows for free movement of people, products, services, and capital within the combined area of the EU and EFTA. Of the EFTA countries, Iceland and Liechtenstein have decided not to apply for membership in the EU. Switzerland's decision to stay out of the EEA has stalled its negotiations with the EU. However, over a dozen nations, including Central European nations, are expected to join the EU eventually.

After three failed tries during this century, the United States and Canada signed a free trade agreement that went into effect in 1989. The agreement created a single, $5 trillion continental economy—one that is 10 percent bigger than the United States's own and 15 percent larger than the EU's.[27] The two countries already had sectoral free trade arrangements; for example, one for automotive products had existed for 23 years. Duties are eliminated in three stages over a ten-year period, with the sensitive sectors (such as textiles and steel) to be liberalized last. For both countries, the goal was to ensure enhanced global competitiveness, job creation, and enhanced growth. North American free trade expanded in 1994 by the inclusion of Mexico into the North American Free Trade Agreement (NAFTA). NAFTA will be discussed in detail later in the chapter.

Customs Union   The **customs union** is one step further along the spectrum of economic integration. As in the free trade area, members of the customs union dismantle barriers to trade in goods and services among members. In addition, however, the customs union establishes a common trade policy with respect to nonmembers. Typically, this takes the form of a common external tariff, whereby imports from nonmembers are subject to the same tariff when sold to any member country. The Benelux countries formed a customs union in 1921 that later became part of wider European economic integration.

Common Market   The **common market** amounts to a customs union covering the exchange of goods and services, the prohibition of duties in exports and imports between members, and the adoption of a common external tariff in respect to nonmembers. In addition, factors of production (labor, capital, and technology) are mobile among members. Restrictions on immigration and cross-border investment are abolished. The importance of **factor mobility** for economic growth cannot be overstated. When factors of production are mobile, then capital, labor, and technology may be employed in their most productive uses.

Despite the obvious benefits, members of a common market must be prepared to cooperate closely in monetary, fiscal, and employment policies. Furthermore, although a common market will enhance the productivity of members in the aggregate, it is by no means clear that individual member countries will always benefit. Because of these difficulties, the goals of common markets have proved to be elusive in many areas of the world, notably Central and South America and Asia. In the mid-1980s, the European Community (EC) embarked on an ambitious effort to remove the bar-

---

[27]"Summary of the U.S.-Canada Free Trade Agreement," *Export Today* 4 (November–December 1988): 57–61.

riers between the twelve member countries to free the movement of goods, services, capital, and people. The process was ratified by the passing of the **Single European Act** in 1987 with the target date of December 31, 1992, to complete the internal market. In December 1991, the EC agreed in Maastricht that the so-called 1992 process would be a step toward cooperation beyond the economic dimension. While many of the directives aimed at opening borders and markets were completed on schedule, some sectors, such as automobiles, will take longer to open up.[28]

Economic Union   The creation of a true **economic union** requires integration of economic policies in addition to the free movement of goods, services, and factors of production across borders. Under an economic union, members will harmonize monetary policies, taxation, and government spending. In addition, a common currency is to be used by members. This could be accomplished, de facto, by a system of fixed exchange rates. Clearly, the formation of an economic union requires members to surrender a large measure of their national sovereignty to supranational authorities in communitywide institutions such as the European Parliament. The final step would be a **political union** calling for political unification. The ratification of the Maastricht Treaty in late 1993 by all of the twelve member countries of the EC created the **European Union,** effective January 1, 1994. The treaty (jointly with the Treaty of Amsterdam in 1997) set the foundation for economic and monetary union (EMU) with the establishment of the euro (€) as a common currency by January 1, 1999. Twelve EU countries are currently part of "Euroland" (Austria, Belgium, Finland, France, Germany, Greece, Holland, Ireland, Italy, Luxembourg, Portugal, and Spain). In addition, moves would be made toward a political union with common foreign and security policy.[29]

European Integration

The most important implication of the freedom of movement for products, services, people, and capital within the EU and the EEA is the economic growth that is expected to result.[30] Several specific sources of increased growth have been identified. First, there will be gains from eliminating the transaction costs associated with border patrols, customs procedures, and so forth. Second, economic growth will be spurred by the economies of scale that will be achieved when production facilities become more concentrated. Third, there will be gains from more intense competition among European companies. Firms that were monopolists in one country will now be subject to competition from firms in other member countries. The introduction of

[28]Carla Rapoport, "Europe Looks Ahead to Hard Choices," *Fortune*, December 14, 1992, 144–149.

[29]"The Maths of Post-Maastricht Europe," *Economist*, October 16, 1993, 51–52.

[30]Rudiger Dornbusch, "Europe 1992: Macroeconomic Implications," *Brookings Papers on Economic Activity* 2 (1989): 341–362.

TABLE 4.7	**Proposed Company Responses to European Integration**	

COMPANY STATUS	CHALLENGES	RESPONSE
Established multinational market/multiple markets	Exploit opportunities from improved productivity	
	Meet challenge of competitors	Pan-European strategy
	Cater to customers/intermediaries doing same	
Firm with one European subsidiary	Competition	Expansion
	Loss of niche	Strategic alliances
		Rationalization
		Divestment
Exporter to Europe	Competition	European branch
	Access	Selective acquisition
		Strategic alliance
No interest	Competition at home	Entry
	Lost opportunity	

SOURCE: Developed from John F. Magee, "1992: Moves Americans Must Make," *Harvard Business Review* 67 (May–June 1989): 78–84.

the euro is expected to add to the efficiencies, especially in terms of consolidation of firms across industries and across countries. Furthermore, countries in Euroland will enjoy cheaper transaction costs and reduced currency risks, and consumers and businesses will enjoy price transparency and increased price-based competition. Marketer reactions to the euro will be discussed further in Chapter 18.

The enlargement of the EU has become one of the most debated issues. Thirteen countries, especially Central European nations, are eager to join. The earliest date for expansion has been pushed to 2003, with 2005–2006 more probable due to disagreements about agriculture and free movement of labor. The most likely to join at this stage are those in advanced negotiations with the EU (Cyprus, the Czech Republic, Estonia, Hungary, Poland, and Slovenia) and possibly those just starting (Latvia, Lithuania, Malta, and Slovakia).

The integration has important implications for firms within and outside Europe because it poses both threats and opportunities, benefits and costs. There will be substantial benefits for those firms already operating in Europe. These firms will gain because their operations in one country can now be freely expanded into others and their products may be freely sold across borders. In a borderless Europe, firms will have access to approximately 380 million consumers. Substantial economics of scale in production and marketing will also result. The extent of these economies of scale will depend on the ability of the marketers to find pan-regional segments or to homogenize tastes across borders through promotional activity.

For firms from nonmember countries, there are various possibilities depending on the firm's position within the market.[31] Table 4.7 provides four different scenarios with proposed courses of action. Well-established U.S.-based multinational marketers such as H.J. Heinz and Colgate-Palmolive will be able to take advantage of the new economies of scale. For example, 3M plants earlier turned out different versions of the company's products for various markets. Now, the 3M plant in Wales, for example, makes videotapes and videocassettes for all of Europe.[32] Colgate-Palmolive has to watch out for competitors, like Germany's Henkel, in the brutally competitive deter-

[31]John F. Magee, "1992: Moves Americans Must Make," *Harvard Business Review* 67 (May–June 1989): 72–84.

[32]Richard I. Kirkland, "Outsider's Guide to Europe in 1992," *Fortune*, October 24, 1988, 121–127.

gent market. At the same time, large-scale retailers, such as France's Carrefour and Germany's Aldi group, are undertaking their own efforts to exploit the situation with hypermarkets supplied by central warehouses with computerized inventories. Their procurement policies have to be met by companies like Heinz. Many multinationals are developing pan-European strategies to exploit the emerging situation; that is, they are standardizing their products and processes to the greatest extent possible without compromising local input and implementation.

A company with a foothold in only one European market is faced with the danger of competitors who can use the strength of multiple markets. Furthermore, the elimination of barriers may do away with the company's competitive advantage. For example, more than half of the forty-five major European food companies are in just one or two of the individual European markets and seriously lag behind broader-based U.S. and Swiss firms. Similarly, automakers PSA and Fiat are nowhere close to the cross-manufacturing presence of Ford and GM. The courses of action include expansion through acquisitions or mergers, formation of strategic alliances (for example, AT&T's joint venture with Spain's Telefonica to produce state-of-the-art microchips), rationalization by concentrating only on business segments in which the company can be a pan-European leader, and finally, divestment.

Exporters will need to worry about maintaining their competitive position and continued access to the market. Companies with a physical presence may be in a better position to assess and take advantage of the developments. Some firms, like Filament Fiber Technology Inc. of New Jersey, have established production units in Europe. Digital Microwave Corporation of California decided to defend its market share in Europe by joining two British communications companies and setting up a digital microwave radio and optical fiber plant in Scotland.[33] In some industries, marketers do not see a reason either to be in Europe at all or to change from exporting to more involved modes of entry. Machinery and machine tools, for example, are in great demand in Europe, and marketers in these companies say they have little reason to manufacture there.

The term **Fortress Europe** has been used to describe the fears of many especially U.S. firms about a unified Europe. The concern is that while Europe dismantles internal barriers, it will raise external ones, making access to the European market difficult for U.S. and other non-EU firms. In a move designed to protect European farmers, for example, the EU has occasionally banned the import of certain agricultural goods from the United States. The EU has also called on members to limit the number of American television programs broadcast in Europe. Finally, many U.S. firms are concerned about the relatively strict domestic content rules recently passed by the EU. These rules require certain products sold in Europe to be manufactured with European inputs. One effect of the perceived threat of Fortress Europe has been increased direct investment in Europe by U.S. firms. Fears that the EU will erect barriers to U.S. exports and fears of the domestic content rules governing many goods have led many U.S. firms to initiate or expand European direct investment.

North American Integration

Although the EU is undoubtedly the most successful and best-known integrative effort, North American integration efforts, although only a few years old, have gained momentum and attention. What started as a trading pact between two close and economically well-developed allies has already been expanded conceptually to include Mexico, and long-term plans call for further additions. However, North American integration is for purely economic reasons; there are no constituencies for political integration.

---

[33]"Should Small U.S. Exporters Take the Plunge?" *Business Week*, November 14, 1988, 64–68.

The ratification of NAFTA created the world's largest free market with 390 million consumers and a total output of $8.6 trillion, roughly the same size as the EEA.[34] The pact marked a bold departure: Never before have industrialized countries created such a massive free trade area with a developing-country neighbor.

Since Canada stands to gain very little from NAFTA (its trade with Mexico is 1 percent of its trade with the United States), much of the controversy has centered on the gains and losses for the United States and Mexico. Proponents argue that the agreement will give U.S. firms access to a huge pool of relatively low-cost Mexican labor at a time when demographic trends are resulting in labor shortages in many parts of the United States. At the same time, many new jobs are created in Mexico. The agreement will give firms in both countries access to millions of additional consumers, and the liberalized trade flows will result in higher economic growth in both countries. Overall, the corporate view toward NAFTA is overwhelmingly positive.

Opposition to NAFTA centers on issues relating to labor and the environment. Unions in particular worry about job loss to Mexico, given its lower wages and work standards; some estimate that six million U.S. workers would be vulnerable to migration of jobs. Similarly, any expansion of NAFTA is perceived as a threat. Distinctive features of NAFTA are the two side agreements that were worked out to correct perceived abuses in labor and the environment in Mexico. The North American Agreement on Labor Cooperation (NAALC) was set up to hear complaints about worker abuse, and the Commission on Environmental Compliance was established to act as a public advocate on the environment. These side agreements have had little impact, however, mainly because the mechanisms have almost no enforcement power.[35]

After a remarkable start in increased trade and investment, NAFTA suffered a serious setback due to a significant devaluation of the Mexican peso in 1995 and its negative impact on trade. Critics argue that too much was expected too fast of a country whose political system and economy were not ready for open markets. In response, advocates argue that there was nothing wrong with the Mexican real economy and that the peso crisis was a political one that would be overcome with time.

Trade between Canada, Mexico, and the United States has increased by 50 percent since NAFTA took effect, exceeding $560 billion in 1999.[36] Reforms have turned Mexico into an attractive market in its own right. Mexico's gross domestic product has been expanding by more than 3 percent every year since 1989, and exports to the United States have doubled since 1986 to $109 billion in 1999. By institutionalizing the nation's turn to open its markets, the free trade agreement will likely attract considerable new foreign investment. The United States has benefited from Mexico's success. U.S. exports to Mexico ($86.8 billion) surpass those to Japan at $57 billion. While the surplus of $1.3 billion in 1994 had turned to a deficit of $22.8 billion in 1999, these imports have helped Mexico's recovery and will, therefore, strengthen NAFTA in the long term. Furthermore, U.S. imports from Mexico have been shown to have much higher U.S. content than imports from other countries.[37]

Among the U.S. industries to benefit are computers, autos and auto parts, petrochemicals, and financial services. In 1990, Mexico opened its computer market by eliminating many burdensome licensing requirements and cutting the tariff from 50 to 20 percent. As a result, exports surged 23 percent in that year alone. IBM, which makes personal and mid-range computers in Mexico, anticipates sales growth to be about $1 billion from that country. In Mexico's growth toward a more advanced society, manufacturers of consumer goods will also stand to benefit. NAFTA has already had a major

[34]Raymond Ahearn, *Trade and the Americas* (Washington, DC: Congressional Research Service, 1997), 3–4.

[35]"NAFTA's Do-Gooder Side Deals Disappoint," *The Wall Street Journal*, October 15, 1997, A19.

[36]For annual trade information, see **http://www.census.gov/foreign-trade/**.

[37]"U.S. Trade with Mexico during the Third NAFTA Year," *International Economic Review* (Washington, DC: International Trade Commission, April 1997): 11.

impact on the emergence of new retail chains, many of which were developed to handle new products from abroad.[38] The top 20 exports and imports between Mexico and the United States are in virtually the same industries, indicating intra-industry specialization and building of economies of scale for global competitiveness.[39]

Free trade produces both winners and losers. Although opponents concede that the agreement is likely to spur economic growth, they point out that segments of the U.S. economy will be harmed by the agreement. It is likely that wages and employment for unskilled workers in the United States will decrease because of Mexico's low-cost labor pool. U.S. companies have been moving operations to Mexico since the 1960s. The door was opened when Mexico liberalized export restrictions to allow for more so-called **maquiladoras,** plants that make goods and parts or process food for export to the United States. The supply of labor in the maquiladoras is plentiful, the pay and benefits are low, and the work regulations are lax by U.S. standards. The average maquiladora wage is $1.73 per hour, compared with $2.17 an hour for Mexican manufacturers.[40] The maquiladora industry has grown remarkably within NAFTA, constituting nearly 40 percent of Mexico's manufactured exports.[41] The investment mix within the industry is changing, however, with the arrival of Asian consumer-electronics producers such as Sony and Samsung.[42]

A 1993 International Trade Commission assessment estimates that while NAFTA would create a net gain of 35,000 to 93,500 U.S. jobs, it would also cause U.S. companies to shed as many as 170,000 jobs.[43] Recent studies have declared the job gain or loss almost a washout. The good news is that free trade will create higher-skilled and better-paying jobs in the United States as a result of growth in exports. As a matter of fact, jobs in U.S. exporting firms tend to pay 10 to 15 percent more than the jobs they have replaced. Losers have been U.S. manufacturers of auto parts, furniture, and household glass; sugar, peanut, and citrus growers; and seafood and vegetable producers. The fact that job losses have been in more heavily unionized sectors has made these losses politically charged. In most cases, high Mexican shipping and inventory costs will continue to make it more efficient for many U.S. industries to serve their home market from U.S. plants.[44]

Countries dependent on trade with NAFTA countries are concerned that the agreement would divert trade and impose significant losses on their economies. Asia's continuing economic success depends largely on easy access to the North American markets, which account for more than 25 percent of annual export revenue for many Asian countries. Lower-cost producers in Asia are likely to lose some exports to the United States if they are subject to tariffs but Mexican firms are not and may, therefore, have to invest in NAFTA.[45] Similarly, many in the Caribbean and Central America fear that the apparel industries of these regions will be threatened as would much-needed investments.[46]

NAFTA may be the first step toward a hemispheric bloc, although nobody expects it to happen anytime soon. It took more than three years of tough bargaining to reach

[38]"Mexico Retail Feels NAFTA Pinch," *Advertising Age,* January 17, 1994, 1–4.

[39]Sidney Weintraub, *NAFTA at Three: A Progress Report* (Washington, DC: Center for Strategic and International Studies, 1997), 17–18.

[40]Jim Carlton, "The Lure of Cheap Labor," *The Wall Street Journal,* September 14, 1992, R16.

[41]"Mexico's NAFTA Trade Surge Led by Maquiladoras," *Crossborder Monitor,* July 23, 1997, 1–2.

[42]"Localizing Production," *Global Commerce,* August 20, 1997, 1.

[43]"A Noose around NAFTA," *Business Week,* February 22, 1993, 37.

[44]Ann Reilly Dowd, "Let's Just Say Yes to NAFTA," *Fortune,* November 29, 1993, 108–109.

[45]Andrew Stoeckel, David Pearce, and Gary Banks, *Western Trade Blocks* (Canberra, Australia: Centre for International Economics, 1990).

[46]Jose De Cordoba, "Alarm Bells in the Caribbean," *The Wall Street Journal,* September 24, 1992, R8.

an agreement between the United States and Canada—two countries with parallel economic, industrial, and social systems. The challenges of expanding free trade throughout Latin America will be significant. However, many of Latin America's groupings are making provisions to join in a hemispheric free trade area by 2005. Such a regime faces difficulties. As a first step, Chile was scheduled to join as a fourth member in 1997. However, the membership has not materialized due to U.S. political maneuvering, and Chile has since entered into bilateral trade agreements with both Canada and Mexico and joined Mercosur as an associate member. This has meant that U.S. marketers are reporting trade deals lost to Canadian competitors, who are free of Chile's 11 percent tariffs.[47] Overall, many U.S. marketers fear that Latin Americans will start moving closer to Europeans if free trade discussions are not seen to progress. For example, both Mercosur and Mexico have signed free-trade agreements with the EU.[48]

Other Economic Alliances

Perhaps the world's developing countries have the most to gain from successful integrative efforts. Because many of these countries are also quite small, economic growth is difficult to generate internally. Many of these countries have adopted policies of **import substitution** to foster economic growth. An import substitution policy involves developing industries to produce goods that were formerly imported. Many of these industries, however, can be efficient producers only with a higher level of production than can be consumed by the domestic economy. Their success, therefore, depends on accessible export markets made possible by integrative efforts.

Integration in Latin America   Before the signing of the U.S.-Canada Free Trade Agreement, all the major trading bloc activity had taken place elsewhere in the Americas. However, none of the activity in Latin America has been hemispheric; that is, Central America had its structures, the Caribbean nations had theirs, and South America had its own different forms. However, for political and economic reasons, these attempts have never reached set objectives. In a dramatic transformation, these nations sought free trade as a salvation from stagnation, inflation, and debt.[49] In response to these developments, Brazil, Argentina, Uruguay, and Paraguay set up a common market called Mercosur.[50] Bolivia, Colombia, Ecuador, Peru, and Venezuela have formed the Andean Common Market (ANCOM). Many Latin nations are realizing that if they do not unite, they will become increasingly marginal in the global market. In approaching the EU with a free trade agreement, Mercosur members want to diversify their trade relationships and reduce their dependence on U.S. trade.

The ultimate goal is a free trade zone from Point Barrow, Alaska, to Patagonia under a framework called the **Free Trade Area of the Americas (FTAA).** The argument is that free trade throughout the Americas would channel investment and technology to Latin nations and give U.S. firms a head start in those markets. Ministerials held since 1994 have established working groups to gather data and make recommendations in preparation for the FTAA negotiations and an agreement by 2005. Changes in corporate behavior have followed. Free market reforms and economic revival have had marketers ready to export and to invest in Latin America. For example, Brazil's opening of its computer market has resulted in Hewlett-Packard establishing a joint venture to produce PCs. In the past, Kodak dealt with Latin America through eleven

[47]"Latin America Fears Stagnation in Trade Talks with the United States," *The New York Times*, April 19, 1998, D1.

[48]"Mexico, EU Sign Free-Trade Agreement," *The Wall Street Journal*, March 24, 2000, A15.

[49]Thomas Kamm, "Latin Links," *The Wall Street Journal*, September 24, 1992, R6.

[50]Joachim Bamrud, "Mercosur: Uncertain Future," *World Trade*, April 1999, 26–28.

separate country organizations, but has since streamlined its operations to five "boundaryless" companies organized along product lines and taking advantage of trading openings, and has created centralized distribution, thereby making deliveries more efficient and decreasing inventory carrying costs.[51]

Integration in Asia   Development in Asia has been quite different from that in Europe and in the Americas. While European and North American arrangements have been driven by political will, market forces may force more formal integration on Asian politicians. The fact that regional integration is increasing around the world may drive Asian interest to it for pragmatic reasons. First, European and American markets are significant for the Asian producers, and some type of organization or bloc may be needed to maintain leverage and balance against the two other blocs. Second, given that much of the Asian trade growth is from intraregional trade, having common understandings and policies will become necessary. Future integration will most likely use the frame of the most established arrangement in the region, the Association of Southeast Asian Nations (ASEAN). Before late 1991, ASEAN had no real structures, and consensus was reached through informal consultations. In October 1991, ASEAN members announced the formation of a customs union called Asean Free Trade Area (AFTA). The Malaysians have pushed for the formation of the East Asia Economic Group (EAEG), which would add Hong Kong, Japan, South Korea, and Taiwan to the membership list. This proposal makes sense, because without Japan and the rapidly industrializing countries of the region such as South Korea and Taiwan, the effect of the arrangement would be nominal. Japan's reaction has been generally negative toward all types of regionalization efforts, mainly because it has the most to gain from free trade efforts. However, part of what has been driving regionalization has been Japan's reluctance to foster some of the elements that promote free trade, for example, reciprocity.[52] Should the other trading blocs turn against Japan, its only resort may be to work toward a more formal trade arrangement in the Asia-Pacific area.

Another formal proposal for cooperation would start building bridges between two emerging trade blocs. Some individuals have publicly called for a U.S.-Japan common market. Given the differences on all fronts between the two countries, the proposal may be quite unrealistic at this time. Negotiated trade liberalization will not open Japanese markets because of major institutional differences, as seen in many rounds of successful negotiations but totally unsatisfactory results. The only solution, especially for the U.S. government, is to forge better cooperation between the government and the private sector to improve competitiveness.[53]

In 1988, Australia proposed the Asia Pacific Economic Cooperation (APEC) as an annual forum to maintain a balance in negotiations. The proposal calls for ASEAN members to be joined by Australia, New Zealand, Japan, South Korea, Canada, Chile, Mexico, and the United States. Originally, the model for APEC was not the EU, with its Brussels bureaucracy, but the Organization for Economic Cooperation and Development (OECD), which is a center for research and high-level discussion. However, APEC has now established an ultimate goal of achieving free trade in the area among its 21 members by 2010.[54]

---

[51]"Regional Commonalities Help Global Ad Campaigns Succeed in Latin America," *Business International*, February 17, 1992, 47–52; and "Ripping Down the Walls across the Americas," *Business Week*, December 26, 1994, 78–80.

[52]Paul Krugman, "A Global Economy Is Not the Wave of the Future," *Financial Executive* 8 (March–April 1992): 10–13.

[53]Michael R. Czinkota and Masaaki Kotabe, "America's New World Trade Order," *Marketing Management* 1 (Summer 1992): 49–56.

[54]"Asia Free Trade Lags," *Export Today* (October 1999): 12.

Economic integration has also taken place on the Indian subcontinent. In 1985, seven nations of the region (India, Pakistan, Bangladesh, Sri Lanka, Nepal, Bhutan, and the Maldives) launched the South Asian Association for Regional Cooperation (SAARC). Cooperation has been limited to relatively noncontroversial areas, such as agriculture and regional development.

Integration in Africa and the Middle East

Africa's economic groupings range from currency unions among European nations and their former colonies to customs unions between neighboring states. In 1975, sixteen West African nations attempted to create a megamarket large enough to interest investors from the industrialized world and reduce hardship through economic integration. The objective of the Economic Community of West African States (ECOWAS) was to form a customs union and eventually a common market. Although many of its objectives have not been reached, its combined population of 160 million represents the largest economic entity in sub-Saharan Africa. Many of the other blocs, however, have not been successful due to small memberships and lack of economic infrastructure to produce goods to be traded within the blocs.

Countries in the Arab world have made some progress in economic integration. Economically speaking, the Gulf Corporation Council (GCC) is one of the most powerful of any trade groups. The per capita income of its six member states (Bahrain, Kuwait, Oman, Qatar, Saudi Arabia, and the United Arab Emirates) is well over $15,000. The GCC was formed in 1980 mainly as a defensive measure due to the perceived threat from the Iran-Iraq war. Its aim is to achieve free trade arrangements with the European nations.

A listing of the major regional trade agreements is provided in Table 4.8.

Economic Integration and the International Marketer

Regional economic integration creates opportunities and potential problems for the international marketer. It may have an impact on a company's entry mode by favoring direct investment because one of the basic rationales of integration is to generate favorable conditions for local production and intraregional trade. By design, larger markets are created with potentially more opportunity. Because of harmonization efforts, regulations may be standardized, thus positively affecting the international marketer.

The international marketer must, however, make integration assessments and decisions from four points of view.[55] The first task is to envision the outcome of the change. Change in the competitive landscape can be dramatic if scale opportunities can be exploited in relatively homogeneous demand conditions. This could be the case, for example, for industrial goods, consumer durables such as cameras and watches, and professional services. The international marketer will have to take into consideration varying degrees of change readiness within the markets themselves; that is, governments and other stakeholders, such as labor unions, may oppose the liberalization of competition in all market segments. For example, while plans have called for liberalization of competition in all market segments. For example, while plans have called for liberalization of air travel and automobile marketing in Europe, EU members have found loopholes to protect their own companies.

The international marketer will then have to develop a strategic response to the new environment to maintain a sustainable long-term competitive advantage. Those companies already present in an integrated market should fill in gaps in European product/market portfolios through acquisitions or alliances to create a balanced pan-regional company. Those with a weak presence, or none at all, may have to create al-

[55]Eric Friberg, Risto Perttunen, Christian Caspar, and Dan Pittard, "The Challenges of Europe 1992," *The McKinsey Quarterly* 21 (Number 2, 1988): 3–15.

TABLE 4.8	Major Regional Trade Agreements

AFTA	**ASEAN Free Trade Area**
	Brunei, Indonesia, Laos, Malaysia, Myanmar, Philippines, Singapore, Thailand, Vietnam
ANCOM	**Andean Common Market**
	Bolivia, Colombia, Ecuador, Peru, Venezuela
APEC	**Asia Pacific Economic Cooperation**
	Australia, Brunei, Canada, Chile, China, Hong Kong, Indonesia, Japan, Malaysia, Mexico, New Zealand, Papua New Guinea, Peru, Philippines, Russia, Singapore, South Korea, Taiwan, Thailand, Vietnam, United States
CACM	**Central American Common Market**
	Costa Rica, El Salvador, Guatemala, Honduras, Nicaragua
CARICOM	**Caribbean Community**
	Antigua and Barbuda, Bahamas, Barbados, Belize, Dominica, Grenada, Guyana, Jamaica, Montserrat, St. Kitts–Nevis, St. Lucia, St. Vincent and the Grenadines, Suriname, Trinidad-Tobago
ECOWAS	**Economic Community of West African States**
	Benin, Burkina Faso, Cape Verde, Gambia, Ghana, Guinea, Guinea-Bissau, Ivory Coast, Liberia, Mali, Mauritania, Niger, Nigeria, Senegal, Sierra Leone, Togo
EFTA	**European Free Trade Association**
	Iceland, Liechtenstein, Norway, Switzerland
EU	**European Union**
	Austria, Belgium, Denmark, Finland, France, Germany, Greece, Ireland, Italy, Luxembourg, Netherlands, Portugal, Spain, Sweden, United Kingdom
GCC	**Gulf Cooperation Council**
	Bahrain, Kuwait, Oman, Qatar, Saudi Arabia, United Arab Emirates
LAIA	**Latin American Integration Association**
	Argentina, Bolivia, Brazil, Chile, Colombia, Ecuador, Mexico, Paraguay, Peru, Uruguay, Venezuela
MERCOSUR	**Southern Common Market**
	Argentina, Brazil, Paraguay, Uruguay
NAFTA	**North American Free Trade Agreement**
	Canada, Mexico, United States
SAARC	**South Asian Association for Regional Cooperation**
	Bangladesh, Bhutan, India, Maldives, Nepal, Pakistan, Sri Lanka

For information, see **http://www.aseansec.org; http://www.apec.org; http://www.caricom.org; http://www.eurunion.org; http://www.mercosur.org; and http://www.nafta.org**.

liances with established firms[56] For example, to take advantage of the new situation in Europe, James River Corporation from the United States, Nokia from Finland, and Cragnotti & Partners from Italy launched a pan-European papermaking joint venture called Jamont. Before 1992, papermaking was highly fragmented in Europe, but the joint venture partners saw the chance to develop a regional manufacturing and marketing strategy. A total of thirteen companies in ten countries were acquired and production was consolidated. For example, before the new strategy, each individual company made colored napkins; now all of Jamont's products came from one plant in Finland.[57] One additional option for the international marketer is to leave the market altogether if it cannot remain competitive because of new competitive conditions or the level of investment needed. For example, Bank of America sold its operations

[56]John A. Quelch, Robert D. Buzzell, and Eric R. Salama, *The Marketing Challenge of 1992* (Reading, MA: Addison-Wesley, 1990), Chapter 13.

[57]"A Joint-Venture Papermaker Casts Net across Europe," *The Wall Street Journal*, December 7, 1992, B4.

THE INTERNATIONAL MARKETPLACE 4.5

Supporting Free Trade in Asia

GENERAL MOTORS—and all the major car makers—is driving into Asia. The world's largest industrial company has found challenges considerable despite the substantial market potential of a growing middle class. In addition to distribution challenges from aggressive competitors, the most daunting ones are free trade barriers. For example, in Indonesia, GM faces competition from a local model, the Timor, which costs substantially less due to government supports (that is, lower duties on imported components). Before President Suharto's resignation, the company was run by one of his sons.

To overcome distribution difficulties, GM invested $450 million in the mid-1990's in the Rayong Province manufacturing facility to build the specially designed Opel "Car for Asia" starting early this century. The Thai facility is the culmination of GM's buildup in Asia that started in 1990 with the establishment of a regional office in Hong Kong and representative offices in Bangkok, Jakarta, Kuala Lumpur, and Beijing. GM's Asia headquarters was moved from Detroit to Singapore. It established GM China in 1994 as a separate entity, and in Japan it bought a 37.5 percent equity stake in Isuzu and has been steadily increasing ownership in Suzuki to 20 percent by 2001. Due to the Asian economic crisis, GM scaled down the investment in Thailand and switched production from the Astra to a considerably cheaper model. GM has also recently shifted its strategy to the Suzuki YGM-I as its small car for Asia

To combat protectionism and further the cause of free trade, GM has developed a three-pronged strategy. The first approach focuses on executives working with government representatives from the United States, European Union, and Japan to dismantle what GM regards as the largest flaws. The company uses its clout as a major investor, but it can also call on support from industries that follow it into a new market, such as component manufacturers. On the second level, GM works within existing frameworks to balance the effects of nationalistic policies. In countries such as Indonesia and Malaysia, it develops company-specific plans to preserve avenues of sales even under challenging circumstances. Finally, GM is also pursuing its business strategy in Asia's free-trade areas. Since it will be a long time before barriers are taken down in the Asia Pacific Economic Cooperation Forum (APEC), its immediate focus is on the ASEAN Free Trade Area (AFTA). GM is hopeful that the automotive sector will be a beneficiary of tariff reductions—provided that member governments can be persuaded that such cuts are in their best interests.

SOURCES: "U.S. Automakers Demonstrate Commitment to Thailand," U.S.-ASEAN Business Council press release, May 12, 1999, available at **http://www.us-asean.org**; "GM Delays Plans to Open Big Thai Plant," *The Wall Street Journal*, January 6, 1998, A2; and "GM Presses for Free Trade in Asia," *Crossborder Monitor*, January 15, 1997, 1, 9; "GM Lifts Stake in Suzuki," *Waikato Times*, September 22, 2000; "Global Manufacturing: GM Gets Flexible in Thailand, *Wards Auto World*, September 1, 2000, Katherine Zachary.

in Italy to Deutsche Bank after it discovered the high cost of becoming a pan-European player.

Whatever changes are made, they will require company reorganization.[58] Structurally, authority will have to become more centralized to execute regional programs. In staffing, focus will have to be on individuals who understand the subtleties of consumer behavior across markets and are therefore able to evaluate the similarities and differences between cultures and markets. In developing systems for the planning and implementation of regional programs, adjustments have to be made to incorporate views throughout the organization. If, for example, decisions on regional advertising campaigns are made at headquarters without consultation with country operations, resentment from the local marketing staff could lead to less-than-optimal execution. Companies may even move corporate or divisional headquarters from the domestic market to be closer to the customer; for example, AT&T estimates that

[58]Gianluigi Guido, "Implementing a Pan-European Marketing Strategy," *Long Range Planning* 24 (Number 5, 1991): 23–33.

several of its units in the future may have their headquarters abroad, especially in Europe.

Finally, economic integration will create its own powers and procedures similar to those of the EU commission and its directives. The international marketer is not powerless to influence both of them; as a matter of fact, a passive approach may result in competitors gaining an advantage or it may put the company at a disadvantage. For example, it was very important for the U.S. pharmaceutical industry to obtain tight patent protection as part of the NAFTA agreement; therefore, substantial time and money were spent on lobbying both the executive and legislative branches of the U.S. government. Often, policymakers rely heavily on the knowledge and experience of the private sector to carry out its own work. Influencing change will therefore mean providing industry information, such as test results, to the policymakers. Many marketers consider lobbying a public relations activity and therefore go beyond the traditional approaches, as seen in *The International Marketplace 4.5*. Lobbying will usually have to take place at multiple levels simultaneously; within the EU, this means the European Commission in Brussels, the European Parliament in Strasbourg, or the national governments within the EU. Marketers with substantial resources have established their own lobbying offices in Brussels, while smaller companies get their voices heard through joint offices or their industry associations. In terms of lobbying, U.S. firms have an advantage because of their experience in their home market; however, for many European firms, lobbying is a new, yet necessary, skill to be acquired. At the same time, marketers operating in two or more major markets (such as the EU and North America) can work to produce more efficient trade through, for example, mutual recognition agreements (MRAs) on standards.[59]

SUMMARY

Economic variables relating to the various markets' characteristics—population, income, consumption patterns, infrastructure, geography, and attitudes toward foreign involvement in the economy—form a starting point for assessment of market potential for the international marketer. These data are readily available but should be used in conjunction with other, more interpretive data because the marketer's plans often require a long-term approach. Data on the economic environment produce a snapshot of the past; in some cases, old data are used to make decisions affecting operations two years in the future. Even if the data are recent, they cannot themselves indicate the growth and the intensity of development. Some economies remain stagnant, plagued by natural calamities, internal problems, and lack of export markets, whereas some witness booming economic development.

Economic data provide a baseline from which other more market/product–specific and even experiential data can be collected. Understanding the composition and interrelationships between economic indicators is essential for the assessment of the other environments and their joint impact on market potential. The international marketer needs to understand the impact of the economic environment on social development.

The emergence of economic integration in the world economy poses unique opportunities and challenges to the international marketer. Eliminating barriers between member markets and erecting new ones vis-à-vis nonmembers will call for adjustments in past strategies to fully exploit the new situations. In the late 1980s and early 1990s, economic integration increased substantially. The signing of the North American Free Trade Agreement produced the largest trading bloc in the world, whereas the Europeans are moving in their cooperation beyond the pure trade dimension.

[59]"TABD Uses Virtual Organization for Trade Lobbying," *Crossborder Monitor*, July 2, 1997, 1.

QUESTIONS FOR DISCUSSION

1. Place these markets in the framework that follows.

a. Indonesia	g. Turkey	m. Peru
b. Mozambique	h. Spain	n. Jamaica
c. India	i. Singapore	o. Poland
d. Bangladesh	j. Nigeria	p. United Kingdom
e. Niger	k. Algeria	q. Iraq
f. Brazil	l. Zambia	r. Saudi Arabia

	INCOME LEVEL		
	LOW	MIDDLE	HIGH
TRADE STRUCTURE			
Industrial			
Developing			
▪ Semi-Industrial			
▪ Oil-Exporting			
▪ Primary Producing			
▪ Populous South Asia			
▪ Least Developed			

2. Using available data, assess the market potential for (a) power generators and (b) consumer appliances in (1) the Philippines, (2) Jordan, and (3) Portugal.

3. From the international marketer's point of view, what are the opportunities and problems caused by increased urbanization in developing countries?

4. Comment on this statement: "A low per capita income will render the market useless."

5. What can a marketer do to advance regional economic integration?

6. Explain the difference between a free trade area and a common market. Speculate why negotiations were held for a North American Free Trade Agreement rather than for a North American Common Market.

7. Using the results of the Gallup Organization's survey findings in China in 1999 (**http://www.fortune.com/ fortune/china/gal.html**), suggest implications for the international marketer interested in entry or further market development.

8. Compare and contrast two different points of view on expanding NAFTA by accessing the web sites of America Leads on Trade, an industry coalition promoting increased access to world markets (**http:// www.fasttrack.org**), and the AFL–CIO, American Federation of Labor–Congress of Industrial Organizations (**http://www.aflcio.org**).

RECOMMENDED READINGS

The Arthur Andersen North American Business Sourcebook. Chicago: Triumph Books, 1994.

Business Guide to Mercosur. London: Economist Intelligence Unit, 1998.

Clement, Norris C., ed. *North American Economic Integration: Theory and Practice.* London: Edward Elgar Publications, 2000.

Current issues of *Country Monitor, Business Europe, Business East Europe, Business Asia, Business Latin America, Business China.*

International Marketing Data and Statistics 2000. London: Euromonitor, 1999.

Marber, Peter. *From Third World to World Class: The Future of Emerging Markets in the Global Economy.* New York: Perseus Books, 1998.

Ohmae, Kenichi. *The Borderless World: Power and Strategy in the Interlinked Economy.* New York: Harper Business, 1999.

Ryans, John K., and Pradeep A. Rau. *Marketing Strategies for the New Europe: A North American Perspective on 1992.* Chicago: American Marketing Association, 1990.

Sueo, Sekiguchi, and Noda Makito, eds. *Road to ASEAN-10: Japanese Perspectives on Economic Integration.* Tokyo: Japan Center for International Exchange, 2000.

U.S. Department of Commerce. "Annual Survey of Foreign Direct Investment Activity." Washington, DC: U.S. Government Printing Office, 1984.

Venables, Anthony, Richard E. Baldwin, and Daniel Cohen, eds. *Market Integration, Regionalism and the Global Economy.* Cambridge, England: Cambridge University Press, 1999.

The World in Figures. London: Economist Publications, 2000.

World Development Report 2000. New York: Oxford University Press, 2000.

Yearbook of International Trade Statistics. New York: United Nations, 2000.

The Financial Environment

Chapter 5

THE INTERNATIONAL MARKETPLACE 5.1

Easing the Credit Crunch

AFTER YEARS OF FEELING IGNORED by U.S. bankers, exporters and mid-size multinationals are being approached and actually getting their international trade transactions financed. "In the past, bankers never called us to pitch their trade finance services," says Anthony R. Williams of Acclaim Entertainment Inc., a video game program designer for Nintendo that generates 25 percent of its sales from abroad. "Now we get calls from a half-dozen bankers a month promising flexible, cut-rate funding." This turnaround is dramatic after the bankers' aversion to foreign-country risk following the 1980s' Third World sovereign-debt crisis. According to estimates by the Export-Import Bank of the United States (Ex-Im Bank), the federal credit agency that guarantees and insures loans made by commercial banks, only 25 commercial banks out of 11,328 (less than one-quarter of 1 percent) remained active providers of export loans to small and medium-sized exporters in the early 1990s. Ex-Im reports that in the last five years over 80 percent of its $65.5 billion in transactions have been for small businesses.

The banks' change of heart has been prompted by a growing demand for trade loans and services from globally minded firms. Aided by the weaker dollar, these firms are emphasizing international expansion as a survival technique.

For their part, U.S. banks are eager to finance international trade because they have been able to shore up their capital and show the healthiest balance sheets in years. The level of problem assets is down, and the vast majority of U.S. banks are now profitable. Banks have also been encouraged by the efforts of the Ex-Im Bank. Over the past few years, Ex-Im Bank has made trade financing more attractive. It has increased its guarantee on export loans to 100 percent and has developed

a program whereby banks can pool and scrutinize small trade loans and thus wipe the foreign-country risk off their books.

The banks expanding their scope range from small regionals to huge money-center institutions. For example, Silicon Valley Bank in San Jose finances fledgling technology exporters, while Capitol Bank in Los Angeles provides import and export financing to companies doing business in Taiwan or South Korea. Bank of America is expanding its product menu to meet its customers' global needs from pre-export financing to issuing import and export letters of credit to foreign exchange management to providing direct export loans backed by Ex-Im Bank. It plans to get involved in *forfait* financing, which involves the sale of discounted trade notes to institutions, international leasing, and local currency financing.

Non-U.S. banks are also further developing the beachhead they established during the years U.S. banks scaled down. Germany's Dresdner Bank Lateinamerika AG provides exporters to South America with working capital loans, based on receivables and inventory, and pre-export financing. In January 1995, Crédit Suisse set up a trade and export finance division at its New York office to focus on large corporations involved in capital equipment shipment and other big-ticket projects. It was a move to solidify service for companies such as Caterpillar and Deere who have long been the mainstays of U.S.business for Crédit Suisse and CS First Boston, its investment banking affiliate. Some have argued that "European banks are doing the large-project deals, while the nuts-and-bolts activities of export financing remain the domain of U.S. banks."

Interestingly, the U.S-based Bankers' Association for Foreign Trade, which has as one of its missions to "aid banks in adjusting to the globalization of markets and customers," boasts 115 banks as members, of which 70 are international members from Asia, Europe, and Latin America, as well as 46 domestic and global financial services companies.

http://www.exim.gov

http://www.credit-suisse.com

http://www.svb.com

SOURCES: Jim Freer, "The European Invasion," *World Trade,* September 1996, 48–52; *Federal Reserve Bulletin,* June 1996, 495–496; Lori Ioannou, "When the Banks Chase Foreign Trade," *International Business* (October 1993): 58–62; and Gary Hector, "Coping with the Credit Quake," *International Business* (August 1993): 25–26.

IN THE EXTREMELY COMPETITIVE INTERNATIONAL ENVIRONMENT, a marketing entity cannot always expect to sell in its own currency with cash in advance, especially when large or long-term contracts are sought. Most companies will be required to go beyond their own working capital and banking lines of credit and expose themselves to new types of risk. The marketer can be sure that if he or she does not finance customers' international trade, the company's competitors or the competitors' governments probably will. Therefore, establishing relationships with sources of financing and advice both in the private and public sectors is important, as seen in *The International Marketplace 5.1.*

This chapter will include a discussion of the financial concerns of the international marketer: How competitive is my total package? Am I going to be paid? What are the payment risks in executing the transaction? Who can I count on for support in securing a contract, getting paid, and avoiding financial risk?

Credit Policy

The international marketer cannot control the financial environment and thus needs to analyze it carefully and understand it in terms of the company's ability to operate within its demands. Effective financial arrangements can significantly support the marketing program if they are carefully formulated between the finance and marketing areas of the firm. Sales are often won or lost on the availability of favorable credit terms to the buyer. With large numbers of competent firms active in international markets, financing packages—often put together with the help of governments—have become more important. This is especially true in fields such as engineering and construction where superior technical capability and attractive cost may not be enough to secure a contract. Customers abroad may be prepared to accept higher prices if they can obtain attractive credit terms.[1]

The seller's primary concern is to be paid for the goods shipped. Before a particular order is received, the marketer has already formulated a policy on the acceptable degree of risk and preferable terms of international transactions. The extent of credit offered is determined by (1) firm-specific factors such as size, experience in international trade, and capacity for financing transactions; (2) market characteristics such as degree of economic development and availability of means of payment; and (3) factors relating to a particular transaction such as the amount of payment and the need for protection, terms offered by competitors, the relative strength and attractiveness

[1]Llewellyn Clague and Rena Grossfield, "Export Pricing in a Floating Rate World," *Columbia Journal of World Business* 9 (Winter 1974): 17–22; and Raj Aggarwal and Luc Soenen, "Managing Persistent Real Changes in Currency Values: The Role of Multinational Operating Strategies," *Columbia Journal of World Business* 24 (Fall 1989): 60–66.

of the trading partner, and the type of goods involved (for example, perishables or custom-made items). In some cases, the marketing and financial departments of the firm are at odds. Marketing may want to expand sales and move into new markets, whereas finance may want to minimize risks and, as a result, market selectively. Before finalizing any contract, the marketer must analyze the risks involved and decide how to manage them.[2]

The development of a credit policy requires teamwork between the company's marketing and finance departments and its commercial banks.[3] To get the best assistance, most companies need to access both regional banks, with which exporters maintain day-to-day relationships, and money-center banks, which typically provide more sophisticated and broader services than regional banks can (for two examples, see Figure 5.1). The larger banks provide a full range of finance, insurance, and advisory services. These are at the disposal of the exporter through the correspondent relationship that regional banks have with the large banks, although many large companies have direct relationships with money-center banks.

Both marketers and finance people need to properly understand the role of financing as a marketing tool. Export finance managers may not have time to listen to marketers and understand the kind of financing terms that are needed to make sales

| **FIGURE** | **5.1** | **Trade Financing Services** |

SOURCES: BankAmerica (**www.bankamerica.com**); Dresdner Bank (**www.dresdner-bank.com**).

[2]Neil Earle, "Financing the Deal," *World Trade,* July 1999, 44–48.

[3]Christine Topoulos, "The Link between Export Sales and Financing," *Export Today* 4 (November–December 1988): 37–40; and Daniel S. Levine, "What's a Nice Exporter Like You Doing in a Bank Like This?" *World Trade,* July 1996, 38–40.

or to work on the more complicated financing solutions needed. This can be overcome by helping marketing personnel better understand financing options and by allowing marketers to communicate their needs directly to the banks. Action to accomplish this may include regular roundtable discussions between marketers and bankers and trips abroad by teams of marketers and finance people working together to understand the sale and financing package from start to finish. The goal is to seek and provide the kind of financing that wins business.

The credit policy, once developed, should (1) help the exporter determine the extent of risk he or she is willing to absorb, (2) allow the exporter to explore new ways of financing exports, and (3) prepare the exporter for a changing environment. Each of these elements will be discussed.

Types of Financial Risk

Overseas political and commercial developments can destroy overnight even the most careful of credit judgments. In addition to macro-developments causing nonpayment, the buying entity may go out of business before paying the seller. The major types of financial risk are commercial risk, political risk, foreign exchange risk, and other risks such as those related to inflation.

The term **commercial risk** refers primarily to the insolvency of, or protracted payment default by, an overseas buyer. Commercial defaults, in turn, usually result from deterioration of conditions in the buyer's market, fluctuations in demand, unanticipated competition either domestically or internationally, or technological changes. The range of specific reasons may include:

1. Internal changes, such as the death or retirement of a key person. This is possible because many importing entities are dependent on the owner-operator.
2. The buyer's losing a key customer. This can occur when an importer buys raw materials or components to be used in production.
3. Unexpected difficulty experienced by the buyer in meeting operating expenses. As an example, the importer's final product may fall under price controls while input prices may not be controlled, especially in a high-inflation market.
4. Natural disasters, such as floods and industrial accidents. These can affect the ability of a buyer to operate in a market.
5. Slow payment by government buyers.

All these risks can emerge in the domestic environment as well, but the geographic and psychological distances to international markets make the risks more severe and more difficult to anticipate.

Noncommercial, or **political risk,** is completely beyond the control of either the buyer or the seller. For example, the foreign buyer may be willing to pay, but the government may use every trick in the book to delay payment as far into the future as possible. In addition to exchange transfer delay, which has the most direct impact on a transaction, other political risks include war, revolution, or similar hostilities; unforeseen withdrawal or nonrenewal of a license to export or import; requisition, expropriation, confiscation, or intervention in the buyer's business by a government authority; transport of insurance charges caused by interruption or diversion of shipments; and certain other government acts that may prevent or delay payment beyond the control of either the buyer or the seller.

The term **foreign exchange risk** refers to the effects of fluctuating exchange rates. The currency of quotation depends largely on the bargaining positions of the buyer and the seller as well as on accepted business practices in the industry. However, if the price quotation is not in the seller's currency, the seller firm must be prepared to protect itself against possible losses resulting from unfavorable changes in the value of the currency transaction.

Sources of Financing

Except in the case of larger companies that may have their own financing entities, most international marketers assist their customers abroad in securing appropriate financing. Export financing terms can significantly affect the final price paid by buyers. Consider, for example, two competitors for a $1 million sale. Exporter A offers an 8 percent interest rate over a ten-year payment period, while B offers 9 percent for the same term. Over the ten years, the difference in interest is $55,000. In some cases, buyers will award a contract to the provider of cheaper credit and overlook differences in quality and price.

Financing assistance is available from both the private and the public sectors. The international marketer should assess not only domestic programs but also those in other countries. For example, Japan and Taiwan have import financing programs that provide exporters added potential in penetrating these significant markets.

Commercial Banks

Commercial banks the world over provide trade financing depending on their relationship with the exporter, the nature of the transaction, the country of the borrower, and the availability of export insurance. This usually means that financing assistance is provided only to first-rate credit risks, leaving many U.S. exporters to report major problems in enlisting assistance from U.S. commercial banks. Furthermore, some U.S. banks do not see international trade finance as part of their core competence. Although the situation has improved (as seen in *The International Marketplace 5.1*), exporters still continue to complain about lack of export financing as it pertains to developing countries, financing high technology, or lending against foreign receivables. Many exporters complain that banks will not deal with them without a guarantee from the Ex-Im Bank or rock-solid collateral, such as property and/or equipment.

This pullback in the 1980s was driven by debt problems of less-developed countries and by major changes in the U.S. banking system, notably the erosion of "relationship" banking.[4] Many banks have seen profits from international trade transactions as too small, too risky, and too time-consuming. In addition, investor pressures have led banks to minimize foreign credit risks. Earlier, banks—in return for interest-free corporate deposits—provided companies with loans on preferential terms and low-cost access to bank services, such as trade finance. With changes in the U.S. financial services industry, such financial ties have broken. The result is that exporters have to look abroad for such financing and that some sales are lost to other countries because of the lack of financing.

However, as the share of international sales and reach of companies increases, banking relationships become all the more important, a fact that is also noted by banks themselves. Many banks offer enhanced services, such as electronic services, which help exporters monitor and expedite their international transactions to customers who do a certain amount of business with them. As with all suppliers, the more business done with a bank, the higher the level of service usually at a better price. As the relationship builds, the more comfortable bankers feel about the exporter's business and the more likely they will go out of their way to help, particularly with difficult transactions.

In addition to using the types of services a bank can provide as a criterion of choice, an exporter should assess the bank's overseas reach.[5] This is a combination of

---

[4]William F. Kolarik, "Financing American Exports: The Diminishing Role of U.S. Commercial Banks," in *Trade Finance,* ed. Michael R. Czinkota (Washington, DC: Government Printing Office, 1988), 76–85.

[5]Miles Maguire, "Reading Your Bank's Correspondence," *Export Today* 11 (November/December 1995): 27–31.

the bank's own network of facilities and correspondent relationships. While money-center banks can provide the greatest amount of coverage through their own offices and staff, they still use correspondents in regions outside the main banking or political centers of foreign markets. For example, Citibank has a worldwide correspondent network of 5,000 institutions in addition to its facilities in more than 100 countries.

Some banks have formed alliances to extend their reach to markets that their customers are going for. Wachovia, a super-regional bank from North Carolina, has developed relationships with global banks that have strong correspondent networks in place in emerging markets. Regional banks, such as Bank One, which have no intention of establishing branches abroad, rely only on strong alliances with foreign banks. Foreign banks can provide a competitive advantage to exporters because of their home country connections and their strong global networks. For example, Commerzbank, Germany's third largest bank, has branches in the Far East, Latin America, South America, and Eastern Europe to support its international trade financing activities in the NAFTA area.[6] Regardless of the arrangement, the bank's own branches or correspondents play an important role at all stages of the international transaction, from gathering market intelligence about potential new customers to actually processing payments. Additional services include reference checks on customers in their home markets and suggestions for possible candidates to serve as intermediaries.

Forfaiting and Factoring

A trade financing technique that was developed in Europe has only in the past decade become widely known in the United States. **Forfaiting** was first used by European commercial banks in financing trade to the Eastern European countries and has since spread to banks throughout the world. Forfaiting provides the exporter with cash at the time of the shipment. In a typical forfait deal, the importer pays the exporter with bills of exchange or promissory notes guaranteed by a leading bank in the importer's country. The exporter can sell them to a third party (for example, Citicorp) at a discount from their face value for immediate cash. The sale is without recourse to the exporter, and the buyer of the notes assumes all the risks. The discount rate takes into account the buyer's creditworthiness and country, the quality of the guaranteeing bank, and the interest cost over the term of the credit.[7]

The benefits to the exporter are the reduction of risk, simplicity of documentation (because the documents used are well known in the market), and 100 percent coverage, which official sources such as export-import banks do not provide. In addition, forfaiting does not involve either content or country restrictions, which many of the official trade financing sources may have.[8] The major complaints about forfaiting center on availability and cost. Forfaiting is not available where exporters need it most, that is, the high-risk countries. Furthermore, it is usually a little more expensive than public sources of trade insurance.

Certain companies, known as **factoring** houses, may purchase an exporter's receivables for a discounted price (2 to 4 percent less than face value). Factors do not only buy receivables but also provide the exporter with a complete financial package that combines credit protection, accounts-receivable bookkeeping, and collection services to take away many of the challenges that come with doing business overseas.[9]

[6]Miles Maguire, "Mergers and Money," *Export Today* (September 1995): 24–30.

[7]Louis G. Guadagnoli, *Practical Guide to Export Financing and Risk Management* (Arlington, VA: Government Information Services, 1989), III-33.

[8]"How U.S. Exporters Can Benefit from Forfait Financing," *Business International Money Report*, December 21, 1987, 418–420; and Lawrence W. Tuller, "Beyond the LC," *Export Today* (August 1996): 70–74.

[9]Daniel S. Levine, "Factoring Pays Off," *World Trade*, September 1998, 79–80.

Arrangements are typically with recourse, leaving the exporter ultimately liable for re-paying the factor in case of a default. Some factors accept export receivables without recourse but require a large discount.

The industry is dominated by a dozen major players, most of which are subsidiaries of major banks. Leaders include the CIT Group, 80 percent owned by Dai-Ichi Kangyo Bank of Japan and 20 percent owned by Chase Manhattan, and Bank of America Commercial Finance/Factoring, which has won the President's "E" Award for its excellence in export service.[10] However, with the increase in companies looking for factoring services, independent factors are also emerging. Factors can be found through the Commercial Finance Association or through marketing facilitators whose clients use factors.

Although the forfaiting and factoring methods appear similar, they differ in three significant ways: (1) factors usually want a large percentage of the exporter's business, while most forfaiters work on a one-shot basis; (2) forfaiters work with medium-term receivables (over 180 days to 5 years), while factors work with short-term receivables; and (3) factors usually do not have strong capabilities in the developing countries, but since forfaiters usually require a bank guarantee, most are willing to deal with receivables from these countries. Furthermore, forfaiters work with capital goods, factors typically with consumer goods.[11]

Official Trade Finance[12]

Official financing can take the form of either a loan or a guarantee, including credit insurance. In a loan, the government provides funds to finance the sale and charges interest on those funds at a stated fixed rate. The government lender accepts the risk of a possible default. In a guarantee, a private-sector lender provides the funds and sets the interest rate, with the government assuring that it will reimburse the lender if the loan is unpaid. The government is providing not funds but rather risk protection.[13] The programs provide assurance that the governmental agency will pay for a major portion of the loss should the foreign buyer default on payment. The advantages are significant: (1) protection in the riskiest part of an exporter's business (foreign sales receivables), (2) protection against political and commercial risks over which the exporter does not have control, (3) encouragement to exporters to make competitive offers by extending terms of payment, (4) broadening of potential markets by minimizing exporter risks, (5) the possibility of leveraging exporter accounts receivable, and (6) through the government guarantee, the opportunity for commercial banks to remain active in the international finance arena.[14]

Because credit has emerged as an increasingly important component in export selling, governments of most industrialized countries have established entities that insure credit risks for exports. Officially supported export credit agencies (ECAs) are organizations whose central purpose is to promote national trade objectives by providing financial support for national exports. ECAs benefit from varying degrees of explicit or implicit support from national governments. Some ECAs are divisions of government trade missions. Other ECAs operate as autonomous or even private

[10]Ray Pereira, "International Factoring," *World Trade*, December 1999, 68–69.

[11]Mary Ann Ring, "Innovative Export Financing," *Business America*, January 11, 1993, 12–14.

[12]The authors acknowledge the assistance of Robert J. Kaiser and Craig O'Connor of the Export-Import Bank of the United States and Louis G. Guadagnoli in the preparation of this section.

[13]Office of Trade Finance, "Survey of Finance Topics of Current Interest," in *Trade Finance*, ed. Michael R. Czinkota (Washington, DC: Government Printing Office, 1988), 34–43.

[14]"EXIM-Bank Program Summary," in *Export-Import Bank of the United States* (Washington, DC: EXIM Bank, 1985), 1; updated for 1999.

TABLE 5.1	Interest Rates for Officially Supported Export Credits

REPAYMENT TERMS[a]		
2 TO 5 YEARS	5 TO 8.5 YEARS	OVER 8.5 YEARS
6.92	6.97	7.17

[a]The minimum rates are reviewed each January and July. Rates quoted applied during December 15, 1999–January 14, 2000.

institutions, but most require a degree of recourse to national government support. The international union of export credit and investment insurers, or the "Berne Union," was established in 1934 by the leading trading nations for the purpose of establishing a voluntary international understanding on export insurance terms by recommending the length of periods for which credit can be extended. Recommended periods range from five years for heavy capital goods to eighteen months for consumer durable goods. The Organization for Economic Cooperation and Development (OECD) Agreement on Guidelines for Officially Supported Export Credits came into force in 1978 as a legally nonbinding agreement on the standardization of international financing.[15] Despite the agreement, some countries tend to circumvent the agreement by providing mixed credits—that is, a combination of commercial export financing funds and "soft" development aid funds. U.S. firms are estimated to lose from $400 million to $800 million yearly in export sales because of tied aid from other countries. International pressure has been directed at Japan, which typically reserves nearly half of its $11 billion in foreign aid for Japanese companies.[16]

The matrix of conditions in force in 1999 is summarized in Table 5.1. The Arrangement on Guidelines for Officially Supported Export Credits stipulates that minimum rates shall apply to official financing support for export credits. Rates are determined using OECD Commercial Interest Reference Rates, which vary according to the main invoicing currency.

The Export-Import Bank of the United States (Ex-Im Bank) was created in 1934 and established as an independent U.S. government agency in 1945. The purpose of the bank is "to aid in financing and facilitating exports." Since its inception, Ex-Im Bank has supported more than $300 billion in U.S. export sales, such as those described in *The International Marketplace 5.2.* In September 1992, Ex-Im Bank acquired its former insurance agent, the Foreign Credit Insurance Association (FCIA). The short-term insurance programs formerly offered by the FCIA are now offered as Ex-Im Bank insurance.

The data in Table 5.2 match products and services with the customary financing term and the appropriate Ex-Im Bank programs, although the applicability of a particular program depends on the details of the specific transaction. Ex-Im Bank financing, as with ECA financing overall, is most important for exporters seeking business in "emerging markets" where economic growth rates are high, where there is high demand for capital goods imports to fuel economic growth, and where capital markets have not yet fully developed to provide the necessary financing. Growth in the developing world is approximately double growth in the industrialized world, a trend that is likely to continue. Exports to the ten countries that the U.S. Department of Commerce has termed "Big Emerging Markets"—China, India, Indonesia, Brazil,

[15]Tuomas Larjavaara, *Export Credit Competition* (Helsinki, Finland: Helsinki School of Economics, 1988).

[16]"A Well-Hidden Pot of Gold," *Business International,* December 21, 1992, 2–3.

THE INTERNATIONAL MARKETPLACE 5.2

Inside the Export-Import Bank

A TOP PRIORITY FOR the Export-Import Bank of the United States ("Ex-Im Bank") is to increase its support for small-business, environmental, and underserved markets including women-owned, minority-owned, and rural business. The success of these exporters is driven in large part by their ability to offer financing to their international customers. Ex-Im Bank seeks to provide them with the financing solutions they need to do so. It is important to note that Ex-Im Bank has no minimum project size.

Wildflower International Ltd. is a small women-owned exporter of computer hardware and software based in Santa Fe, New Mexico. Wildflower International Ltd. has used Ex-Im Bank's insurance program to significantly expand its export sales to customers in Mexico, Israel, and Saudi Arabia by offering 90- and 180-day open account credit terms and insuring the repayment with Ex-Im Bank. Wildflower International Ltd., with Ex-Im Bank's insurance, is able to assign or "discount" these foreign receivables to its commercial bank and get paid immediately. The commercial bank receives an "enhanced assignment" from Ex-Im Bank, which states that by taking assignment of the Ex-Im Bank–insured receivables, the commercial bank will be covered against both exporter nonperformance and foreign buyer default. U.S. commercial banks that take Ex-Im Bank assignments typically charge interest rates ranging from 1.5%–2.5% over the London Interbank Offered Rate (LIBOR), which in December 1999 was about 6.00%. So ultimately the financing that is offered to the customer is in the range of 7.50%–9.00%. Compare these rates to those in Mexico and Brazil, where interest rates range from 30–0%.

Credit on open account insured by Ex-Im Bank is often the most attractive method of payment for foreign buyers, who prefer such credit to paying by cash in advance, local bank loans, or letter of credit (L/C), which typically has high bank fees and collateral charges. Foreign competition has long made offering open account credit standard practice. According to Wildflower owner Kimberly DeCastro, "Ex-Im Bank's Export Credit Insurance recently enabled us to win a $150,000 sale to a buyer in Israel. This represents our largest order ever. This sale would not have been possible without Ex-Im Bank."

In August 1998, Senstar Capital Corp. of Pittsburgh, Pennsylvania, used Ex-Im Bank's medium-term insurance to finance the purchase of $400,000 worth of waste-water treatment equipment for Ecopreneur SA of Buenos Aires, Argentina. Ex-Im Bank support was requested in this deal because U.S. banks are generally unable to provide medium-term financing to Argentina, while medium-term credits from Argentine banks are prohibitively expensive if available at all. This financing will enable Ecopreneur SA, an environmental engineering consulting company that represents six U.S. small-business water treatment suppliers, to build a private waste-water treatment facility in Buenos Aires Province. Ex-Im Bank's insurance enabled Senstar to offer the financing to Ecopreneur SA directly as part of a complete package of technology and financing. With Ex-Im Bank's insurance, Senstar provided four-year financing with a fixed interest rate of 7.5%. The exposure fee for this transaction was 3.61% for a four-year credit term (0.90% per year on a nominal basis), which was added to the financed portion. For Ecopreneur SA, the process was a "seamless" one in which it was required only to provide the necessary financial information for analysis by Ex-Im Bank, including three years of audited financial statements, a credit report, and a bank reference.

SOURCE: Courtesy of Craig O'Connor, Ex-Im Bank.

http://www.exim.gov

Mexico, Turkey, South Korea, Poland, Argentina, and Thailand—have grown nearly twice as fast as overall U.S. exports. Ex-Im Bank activity as a percentage of U.S. capital goods exports is quite significant in a number of these markets; e.g., 45 percent in India and 29 percent in Indonesia.

Pre-Export Support   One of the greatest impediments small businesses experience in attempting to fulfill export orders is a lack of adequate working capital to build the necessary inventory for the export order. Despite their creditworthiness, these exporters sometimes find their local bank is reluctant to make such financing available to them. In

TABLE 5.2	Selection Chart for Ex-Im Bank

EXPORTS	APPROPRIATE PROGRAMS
Pre-Export Any product or service when working capital is needed to fill an export order	Working capital loan guarantee
Short Term (up to 180 days) Consumables Small manufactured items Spare parts Raw materials Services less than one year	Export credit insurance
Short Term (up to 360 days) Consumer durables Bulk agricultural commodities	Export credit insurance
Medium Term (181 days to five years) Capital equipment Mining and refining equipment Construction equipment Agricultural equipment General aviation aircraft Planning/feasibility studies Breeding livestock	Export credit insurance Intermediary credit Financial guarantees
Long Term (five years and longer) Power plants LNG and gas-processing plants Other major projects	Direct loans Financial guarantees PEFCO

some cases, exporters have already reached the borrowing limits set by the banks, while others do not have the amount or type of collateral their banks require. In response to this need, Ex-Im Bank created a Working Capital Guarantee Program (WCG). It is the only pre-export program offered by Ex-Im Bank. All other Ex-Im Bank programs finance exports after shipment or performance.

Under this program, Ex-Im Bank guarantees the lender against default by the exporter. The guarantee is for 90 percent of the loan and interest up to 1 percent over the Treasury borrowing rate. The lender must retain 10 percent of the risk. Should the exporter default, only the commercial bank is covered. For example, if the foreign buyer of the U.S. goods defaults, only the exporter's outstanding loan to the commercial bank is covered under the WCG. For this reason, many exporters secure Ex-Im Bank insurance to protect themselves against failure of the foreign buyer to pay the obligation for either commercial or political reasons.

The WCG may be used for single sales or as a revolving facility. It may also be used for marketing and promotion purposes. However, most of the WCGs approved by Ex-Im Bank are for single-sale transactions. The exporter must put up collateral equal to 110 percent of the value of the loan. Ex-Im Bank takes a broad interpretation of acceptable collateral and will accept raw materials, fixed assets in certain cases, foreign receivables, or other collateral. Frequently, the personal guarantee of the exporting company's officers is also required. The exporter may approach Ex-Im Bank directly for a WCG or go through its bank.

Since 1995, Ex-Im Bank, in cooperation with the Small Business Administration (SBA), has been offering a "Harmonized" WCG. All transactions up to $833,000 are covered by SBA's 90 percent guarantee. Larger transactions than that are covered by the Ex-Im Bank's WCG.

Export Credit Insurance   The ability to offer financing or credit terms is often the most critical element in competing for, and winning, export sales. Increasingly, foreign buyers of goods and services expect U.S. suppliers to offer "open account" or unsecured credit terms rather than requiring letters of credit, which may be expensive, or cash in advance. In general, the more secure the payment terms are for the exporter, the less attractive the terms are for the foreign customer. Yet for a small or medium-sized exporter, extending credit terms to foreign customers may represent an unacceptable risk and may be an undue financial burden, especially when the exporter's bank is unwilling to accept foreign receivables as collateral for working lines of credit. Ex-Im Bank's Export Credit Insurance Program can meet the exporters' need to offer credit terms to foreign customers. Ex-Im Banks' insurance protects the exporter against political and commercial default by its foreign customers. The insurance provides the exporter with important advantages in competing for export business. First, the exporter can use extended credit terms as a "marketing tool" along with the technology and service. Secondly, the insurance provides the exporter with the ability to expand sales with existing customers and support prudent penetration of higher-risk foreign markets. Last but not least, the insurance gives the exporter and his or her bank greater flexibility in handling overseas accounts receiveable. Because Ex-Im Bank covers the risk of default, banks are willing to lend against or "discount" an exporter's foreign sales receivables.

Any entity—including the U.S. exporter, a U.S. or foreign bank, or the foreign buyer—may apply to Ex-Im Bank for a premium quote, at no cost, to determine the availability and cost of export credit insurance.[17] Ex-Im Bank offers eight standard policies, which fall into two basic categories; multibuyer and single-buyer types. These policies accommodate the special needs of various types of exporters and financing institutions, either of which can be an insured party. The insurance premiums charged are based on the buyer, the length of the repayment term, the country of importation, the experience of the insured, and the volume of business. The coverage offered under the policies may be comprehensive, meaning that both commercial and political risks of default are covered, or political only. A comprehensive policy is advisable because of the difficulty in predicting events. Also, devaluation is not covered as a political risk but, if it causes default, may be covered as a commercial risk. Ex-Im Bank does not offer commercial risk coverage alone. The policies have U.S. content requirements in order to fulfill the basic mission of supporting U.S. jobs. Products or services sold by small businesses with short-term repayment periods must have at least 50 percent U.S. content. Products or projects sold by large U.S. exporters must have at least 85 percent U.S. content. No value may be added after shipment from the United States.

Multibuyer Policies   These policies may cover short- or medium-term sales or a combination of both. They require that the insured pay premium on all, or a reasonable spread, of export credit sales. This requirement exists to prevent the insured from making an adverse selection of sales to be insured and increasing Ex-Im Bank's risk. Typically, it is used by an exporter for comprehensive coverage on worldwide short-term sales. Ex-Im Bank assigns an aggregate policy limit, which is the maximum dollar amount in claims that will be paid in a policy year. However, the insured must submit credit information to Ex-Im Bank and receive approval for each buyer whose receivables are to be insured. A discretionary credit limit may be granted to experienced insureds to relieve them from obtaining preapproval for sales under a certain dollar amount, provided they maintain a credit file on the buyer. A first-loss deductible for commercial

---

[17]John A. Hanson, "The Government Can Help," *Export Today* 4 (July–August 1988): 62–63.

TABLE 5.3	Example of Ex-Im Bank Insurance	
(1) Contract value		$100,000
(2) Cash payment (15%)		15,000
(3) Financial portion (85%)		85,000
(4) Exporter commercial retention (10% in line 3)		8,500
(5) Ex-Im Bank commercial risk coverage (90% of line 3)		76,500
(6) Ex-Im Bank political risks (100% of line 3)		85,000

SOURCE: Louis G. Guadagnoli.

risk claims is typical. The minimum premium is usually $500 per year paid up front, and the insured pays premiums monthly, based on shipments. A typical example is provided in Table 5.3.

Single-Buyer Policies   This type of policy allows exporters to select the sales they desire to insure. There is no first-loss deductible. It may cover single or repetitive sales to one buyer.

The many standard Ex-Im Bank policies include several designed specifically for financing institutions such as banks. These include the Bank Letter of Credit Policy, which covers the obligation of a foreign bank to remit funds to a bank that has confirmed a letter of credit opened by that foreign bank for the purchase of U.S. goods. Also, the Financial Institution Buyer Credit Policy covers the short-term credit obligations of a foreign buyer of U.S. goods to its funding bank, and the Bank Supplier Credit Policy covers the short-term financing provided to a U.S. exporter by its bank related to export credit sales. Other policies, such as the Trade-Association Policy and Umbrella Policy, allow organizations experienced in export trade and financing to act as intermediaries between Ex-Im Bank and potential insureds. The administrators of these policies are not insured but assist the exporter in obtaining insurance, maintaining documentation, and filing claims. Ex-Im Bank offers insurance for leases as well as sales. The Operating Lease Policy covers a specific number of lease payments plus the depreciated value of the equipment if expropriation occurs. No down payment is required for this medium-term coverage. The Financing Lease Policy covers the total of the lease payments, but a 15 percent cash payment is required.

A combination of short- and medium-term insurance is available, used mainly to protect U.S. exporters who offer floor plans to overseas dealers and distributors. This option offers protection on parts and accessories sales on terms up to 180 days and capital equipment inventory financing for up to 270 days that can be converted to a medium-term receivable of up to three years.

To insure against risks from the date of signing the sales contract instead of from the date of shipment, Ex-Im Bank offers comprehensive preshipment coverage. This coverage is necessary when goods are specially manufactured or require a long factory lead time. Nonacceptance coverage against the arbitrary refusal of the buyer to accept products that conform to the contract of sale may be offered at no extra cost in addition to the normal coverage except when greater-than-normal risk exists, such as with perishable items. In addition, Ex-Im Bank will insure political risks for goods on consignment where payment is made to the exporter only after the goods have been sold. Should an exporter consummate a sale requiring payment in foreign currency rather than U.S. dollars, Ex-Im Bank will cover such transactions under all policies; however, coverage is limited to "freely transferable" currencies, and no exchange or transfer risk is insurable under this endorsement.

To encourage U.S. firms to expand their foreign business during a period when there is a strong overseas demand for services, Ex-Im Bank developed services coverage. Industries benefiting from this include management consultants, engineering service firms, transportation companies, architecture and design firms, and other firms offering the service of U.S.-based personnel to foreign buyers with repayment being made in U.S. dollars in the United States. The New-to-Export Policy is for companies without exporting experience or those that have had limited export sales in the past. The policy gives added commercial risk protection of 95 percent to further cushion any potential losses. These criteria have to be met by the applying company: average annual export credit sales of less than $2 million during the preceding two years, and prior direct coverage under any Ex-Im Bank insurance program.

The exporter who insures foreign accounts receivable is often able to obtain financing from banks and other lending institutions with Ex-Im Bank coverage. As a result, the exporter can extend credit on more favorable terms to overseas customers without tying up resources required for internal operations.

Claims may be submitted immediately upon default, or there may be a waiting period of up to eight months, depending on the provisions of the policy and the cause of the default. At the time of the claim, the exporter must submit certain documents, such as copies of bills of lading, the debt instrument, evidence of attempts to collect, and evidence of compliance with any special conditions imposed by Ex-Im Bank. The exporter must therefore retain all documents until the claim has been paid.

Guarantees

Ex-Im Bank guarantees to provide repayment protection for private sector loans to creditworthy buyers of U.S. goods and services exports. Guarantees are backed in full by the U.S. government. Both medium- and long-term guarantees are available.

Medium-Term Guarantees   These are available for export transactions usually up to $10 million, with a maximum repayment term not to exceed seven years. Most typically, they are used by commercial banks that do not want exposure in a certain country or that have reached their internal "exposure limit" in a given country. The Ex-Im Bank guarantee overcomes these limitations. The medium-term guarantee provides the lender 100 percent political and commercial risk protection. Under this guarantee, the foreign buyer is required to make a 15 percent cash down payment, so the guarantee covers the "financed portion" of 85 percent.

Ex-Im Bank's fee schedule is determined by country risk and the repayment terms of the transaction. Rates vary from the highest-rated "A" country to the lowest-rated "E" country. By having a rate schedule based on perceived risk assumption, Ex-Im Bank is able to remain open for business longer in more countries because it is compensated for the risk it is being asked to take.

Long-Term Guarantees   These are used for transactions in excess of $10 million and repayment periods of eight or more years. The commercial and political risk cover is 100 percent. The fee structure is the same as under medium-term guarantees. One major difference is that loans made under the long-term guarantee may be denominated in foreign currencies acceptable to Ex-Im Bank. This enables foreign buyers with access to foreign currency earnings to use this currency to repay loans. A good example of this would be a foreign airline with earnings, through its flight routes, in Japanese yen. The airline wishes to buy U.S.-made airplanes but wants to borrow in yen and use its yen earnings to service the debt. An Ex-Im Bank long-term guarantee could be utilized for such a transaction.

Ex-Im Bank, by statute, does not compete with commercial banks. It complements and supplements commercial bank support for exports by assuming risks unacceptable to the banks. As is well known, commercial banks will only rarely provide fixed interest rate loans for any type of commercial transaction. Yet today, in the highly competitive international marketplace, many foreign buyers can demand financial support as a precondition to their purchase of goods from abroad. These foreign buyers may require fixed-rate financing as a condition of their purchase.

A commercial bank extending a medium-term loan under the Ex-Im Bank guarantee may liquidate the transaction at any time by selling it to the Private Export

TABLE	5.4	Typical Financing Plan for a Turnkey Project

COSTS (IN MILLIONS)		FINANCING PLAN (IN MILLIONS)	
Hardware	$10.0	Ex-Im Bank credit/guarantee	$ 8.5
Infrastructure	5.0	U.S. banks—U.S. costs	1.5
Interest during construction	2.0	U.S. banks—infrastructure	5.0
Working capital requirements	2.0	Sponsor's equity	4.0
Total	$19.0	Total	$19.0

SOURCE: Louis G. Guadagnoli.

Funding Corporation (PEFCO). This arrangement replaces a facility previously offered by the Ex-Im Bank wherein a commercial bank could borrow from the Ex-Im Bank at a discount and lend onward to the foreign buyer at a higher, fixed rate.

For fixed-rate loans in excess of $10 million and repayment periods of eight years or longer, Ex-Im Bank may act as a lender directly to the foreign buyer. This is so because most commercial banks simply do not extend loans beyond seven-year repayment terms. Often, too, these transactions are large ones, in excess of $100 million, and commercial banks do not want such large exposure for long periods of time in one country or in that industrial sector. Such major projects, or large product purchases, are often let through international bids, and competition is keen to secure these major orders. Without Ex-Im Bank participation, U.S. exporters would be unable to compete successfully. Under OECD regulations, a 15 percent cash down payment by the foreign buyer is required. Thus, the "financed portion" is 85 percent of the export value. Ex-Im Bank has eased its U.S. content requirements somewhat and is now prepared to finance up to a maximum of 15 percent foreign content in the export order. The rest of the export must be U.S.-produced goods and services. If the foreign content exceeds 15 percent of the shipment, then that foreign content will be excluded entirely from Ex-Im Bank support. Payment terms are normally determined by studying cash flow projections from the proposed project or the useful life of the product. In any case, repayment rarely exceeds a ten-year term. Normally, if a project is involved, repayment begins six months after the project commences commercial operations. For a product, such as a commercial jet aircraft, repayment begins six months after the plane goes into service.

An example of typical financing for a turnkey project is provided in Table 5.4. Ex-Im Bank funds or guarantees 85 percent of U.S. costs at a fixed rate, with the rate varying by country classification. The bank financing for infrastructure is a separate transaction. To be involved, Ex-Im Bank and commercial banks must be satisfied that the project is technically and financially feasible. For this they require extensive information, including a feasibility study. The balance of the financing requirements usually comes out of the project owner's resources.

Under its charter, Ex-Im Bank must have "reasonable assurance of repayment." Therefore, a careful analysis of the foreign buyer's creditworthiness and the project's viability is conducted. If necessary, government guarantees of the loan repayment, representing the full faith and credit of the host country of the foreign buyer, may be required. In other cases, guarantees of a commercial bank in the host country may also be satisfactory and necessary.

Annual competitiveness reports have assessed U.S. exporter ratings of official export credit facilities. Since the 1980s, Ex-Im Bank programs have been rated "basically competitive" or "uncompetitive." Where absolute improvement has been realized, other nations have matched these efforts.[18]

[18]Alfred C. Holden, "U.S. Official Export-Finance Support: Can American Exporters Expect a Competitive Ex-Im Bank to Emerge?" *Columbia Journal of World Business* 24 (Fall 1989): 33–46.

The export-import credit agencies of other countries should also be monitored to assess the structures, terms, and rates of import financing programs for U.S. goods and services. Included could be such entities as the Export-Import Bank of Japan, the State Export-Import Bank of Ukraine, or the Export Development Corporation of Canada.[19]

Other Public-Sector Financing Sources   The Overseas Private Investment Corporation (OPIC) is a federal agency that offers investment guarantees comparable to those offered by Ex-Im Bank to U.S. manufacturers that wish to establish plants in less-developed countries, either by themselves or as a joint venture with local capital. OPIC finances and/or insures only foreign direct investment through (1) direct loans from $2 million to $10 million per project with terms of 5 to 15 years, (2) loan guarantees to U.S. institutional lenders of $10 million to $100 million, and (3) political risk insurance against currency inconvertibility, expropriation, or takeover, and physical damage resulting from political strife.[20] The importance of this activity is increasing rapidly because foreign direct investment enables firms to remain competitive in the world marketplace. It is difficult to maintain viable market share without presence as a producer, making trade more dependent on investment with time.[21] Since its inception in 1971, OPIC has supported investments amounting to $121 billion, generated $58 billion in exports, and helped create 237,000 U.S. jobs. Currently, its programs are available in 140 countries worldwide.

The Agency for International Development (AID) administers most of the foreign economic assistance programs for the U.S. government. Because many AID agreements require that commodities be purchased from the United States, exporters should use this support mechanism. AID estimates that 70 percent of all U.S. aid comes back in purchases of goods and services from U.S. companies. In the long term, the agency's objective is to increase potential for increased exports by follow-up sales and by creating potential in the market for other purchases.[22] As a sister agency to AID, the U.S. Trade Development Program (TDP) uses foreign assistance funds to increase U.S. exports by financing the planning of projects and dispersing grants for feasibility studies of development projects.

In addition to these U.S. entities, the international marketer will find it worthwhile to monitor the activities of multilateral development banks such as the World Bank Group, regional development banks (such as the Inter-American Development Bank and the Asian Development Bank), and many national development banks as well as the United Nations. These banks specialize in financing investment activities and can provide valuable leads for future business activity, as seen in *The International Marketplace 5.3.* In 1999, the United Nations purchased $3 billion in goods and services, with about 12 percent of the budget for procurement going to U.S. companies.[23]

The World Bank Group has, since its inception, provided more than $313 billion in financing for more than 5,800 projects. In 1999, loans totaled $29.0 billion for more than 250 new operations. Projects cover a wide spectrum, including agriculture, industry, transportation, telecommunications, population planning, and—unique to one year—the Y2K problem. Loans are at variable rates, based on the cost of borrowing, and for 15- to 20-year terms. All loans must be guaranteed by the government of

[19]Martin R. Brill, "The East Asian Edge," *Export Today* 4 (July–August 1988): 50–53.

[20]*Program Handbook,* Overseas Private Investment Corporation, December 1995. Also available from **http://www.opic.gov**.

[21]Peter Drucker, "From World Trade to World Investment," *The Wall Street Journal,* May 26, 1987, 33.

[22]"Foreign Assistance Funds: Marketing U.S. Exports through Economic Development," *Export Today* 4 (March–April 1988): 6–9.

[23]David DeVoss, "The $3 Billion Question," *World Trade,* September 1998, 34–39.

THE INTERNATIONAL MARKETPLACE 5.3

Going for the Government Contracts

"THERE ARE MAJOR PUBLIC-SECTOR opportunities abroad," says Larry Mandell, senior vice president of the Keith Companies, a Costa Mesa, California–based group of environmental service companies. One of the major recent contracts received by the Keith Companies was for $1 million from the United States Agency for International Development (AID) to clean mud and ash off Mount Pinatubo. Also completed was a $50,000 feasibility study for the Inter-American Development Bank in Costa Rica.

The Keith Companies is just one of many businesses benefiting from a new flow of funds being committed by multilateral banks to projects around the world. From 1990 to 1995, the World Bank Group and the African, Asian, European, and Inter-American Development Banks committed nearly $200 billion in projects for agriculture, energy, industry and finance, transportation, and education. By the year 2000, they had committed $410 billion to developing countries in these sectors. With such large amounts at stake, some international marketing managers believe that these funds are out of reach, too big, bureaucratic, or difficult to obtain. While some funds are subject to competitive international bidding, others, at the lower end of the scale, are accessible and available via different methods of procurement, including direct negotiation.

Government-funded counseling and information services for foreign trade make finding and securing multilateral bank contracts easier. For example, AID's goals are to counsel small to mid-size companies on doing business with developing countries. The United Nations publishes *Development Business* twice a month, which offers information about projects to be launched in Africa, Asia, Latin America, and Eastern Europe. For example, Igloo Corp. sells annually $200,000 worth of picnic coolers to the United Nations Children's Fund for the transportation of temperature-sensitive vaccines in tropical climates.

The regional multilateral development banks offer a range of different information outlets. The Inter-American Development Bank publishes *IDB Projects* ten times a year. This report, which lists the opportunities coming down the pipeline

and contracts recently awarded, is available on its web site along with a wealth of other online information (**www.iadb.org**). The Asian Development Bank's project information guide is available on-line at **www.adb.org**, while the European Bank of Reconstruction and Development **www.ebrd.com** offers information on procurement opportunities on its web site. This means that information on the global procurement market comes directly from the financial sources, enabling subscribers to monitor any development projects in the pipeline as well as bidding processes and contract awards.

Once a marketer has identified contracts on which to bid, Mandell advises not to pursue all available ones. "You must determine whether this is the market you want to be in. Select projects you are qualified for, and then team up with other companies." He recommends becoming involved with a project even before it is up for consideration by a multilateral bank. "Build relationships at the banks, make contacts in trade and commerce, and learn as much about specific countries as possible. Right now, Keith Companies is going after a $100-million contract in Brazil."

SOURCES: David DeVoss, "The $3 Billion Question," *World Trade*, September 1998, 34–39; Adrienne Fox, "Global Capitalists," *International Business* (March 1996): 50–54; Adrian Feuchtwanger, "The Search for Eldorado," *World Trade*, November 1993, 116–118; and Nicholas H. Ludlow, "Tapping Development Bank Lines of Credit," *Export Today* 9 (October 1993): 26–30.

http://www.worldbank.org

http://www.iadb.org

http://www.adb.org

http://www.un.org

http://www.ebrd.com

the borrowing country.[24] To get business from World Bank projects, international marketers have to closely monitor the entire process—from the identification of the project to the approval of the loan.

In April 1988, an affiliate of the World Bank began operation. The Multilateral Investment Guaranty Agency (MIGA) encourages the flow of financial resources to its developing member countries. To accomplish this, MIGA is authorized to issue guar-

[24]Carol Stitt, "The World Bank and Project Finance," *Export Today* 5 (February 1989): 50–54.

antees against noncommercial risks in host countries, so that investors may assess the benefits of projects on economic and financial grounds rather than political risk. In 1999, MIGA facilitated investments worth $5.2 billion in 40 projects.

Private-Sector Export Credit Insurance

The Private Export Funding Corporation (PEFCO) is a private corporation founded in 1970 for the purpose of making fixed-rate U.S. dollar loans to foreign importers to finance purchases of goods and services of U.S. manufacture or origin. PEFCO's stockholders consist of 55 commercial banks, including most of the major U.S. banks involved in export financing, investment banking firms, and manufacturing firms (Boeing, Cessna, Combustion Engineering, General American Transportation, General Electric, McDonnell Douglas Finance, and United Technologies). The Ex-Im Bank and PEFCO maintain an agreement whereby Ex-Im Bank guarantees the principal and interest on debt obligations that are issued by foreign purchasers of U.S. products and services by PEFCO. PEFCO thereby acquires a portfolio of Ex-Im Bank–guaranteed paper that can be used as the basis for raising funds in the private market. Because all of its loans are guaranteed, PEFCO itself does not evaluate credit risks, appraise economic conditions in foreign countries, or review other factors that might affect the collectibility of its loans.

The role of private export credit insurers has increased in the past few years.[25] For example, American International Underwriters, a division of American International Group, offers coverage of commercial credit and political risks similar to that offered by Ex-Im Bank. Other firms that offer limited forms of commercial and political risk coverage include Citicorp International Trade and American Credit Indemnity. Private underwriters offer political risk coverage for confiscation, expropriation, and nationalization risks—coverage that is similar to the programs provided by OPIC.

Proponents of the private insurers cite their faster processing time, lower rates because of selectivity, absence of U.S.-origin requirement, and ability to do business in countries embargoed by the U.S. government. The drawbacks, however, are that they require a minimal but substantial amount of business to be covered, they cater mainly to the large multinational corporations and are not as interested in smaller firms, and, the most important caveat, their insurance may not be as acceptable to commercial banks that will be providing the financing.

Financial Risk Management

After financial risks have been assessed, the international marketer needs to decide whether to do business in the particular environment. If the decision is to do so, risk needs to be minimized through actions by either the company itself or support systems. The decision must be an informed one, based on detailed and up-to-date information in international credit and country conditions. In many respects, the assessment of a buyer's creditworthiness requires the same attention to credit checking and financial analysis as for domestic buyers; however, the assessment of a foreign private buyer is complicated by some of the following factors:

1. Credit reports may not be reliable.
2. Audited reports may not be available.
3. Financial reports may have been prepared according to a different format.
4. Many governments require that assets be annually reevaluated upward, which can distort results.

---

[25]H. Allan Legge, Jr., "Private-Sector Export Insurance: Taking Care of Business," *Export Today* 4 (September–October 1988): 74–75.

FIGURE	5.2	Providers of International Credit Information

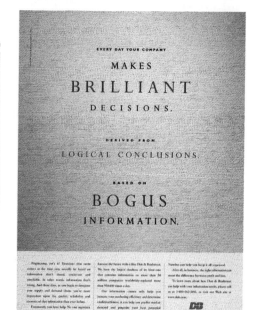

SOURCES: The Commercial Service Dun & Bradstreet
(http://www.dnb.com)

5. Statements are in local currency.
6. The buyer may have the financial resources in local currency but may be precluded from converting to dollars because of exchange controls and other government actions.

More than one credit report should be obtained (from sources such as the two in Figure 5.2), and it should be determined how each credit agency obtains its reports. They may use the same correspondent agency, in which case it does the exporter no good to obtain the same information from two sources and to pay for it twice. Table 5.5 provides a summary of the major sources of credit information. Where private-sector companies (such as Dun & Bradstreet or Veritas) are able to provide the needed credit information, the services of the U.S. Department of Commerce's International Company Profiles are not available. However, currently 50 countries are still served by the ICP. Local credit reporting agencies, such as Profancresa in Mexico, may also provide regional services (in this case, throughout Latin America). With the growth of e-commerce, a company may want to demonstrate its creditworthiness to customers and suppliers in a rapid and secure fashion. The Coface Group (of which Veritas is the information arm in the Americas) introduced the "@rating" system, available on the World Wide Web and designed to assess a company's performance in paying its commercial obligations.[26]

Beyond protecting oneself by establishing creditworthiness, an exporter can match payment terms to the customer. In the short term, an exporter may require payment

[26]http://www.cofacerating.com

| TABLE 5.5 | **Sources of International Credit Information** |

SOURCE	RESPONSE TIME	COST	COMMENTS
1. Dun & Bradstreet **www.dnb.com**	Same day to 40 days, depending on location	$100 to $375. Varies by geographic region	Standard in the Indus-try. Data are often sketchy, since subjects are reticent to respond to a credit inquiry.
2. @rating **www.cofacerating.com**	Instantaneous; on-line	Free	Launched late 1999; wishes to become a standard reference for e-commerce; supported by the EU Commission.
3. International Company Profiles **www.ita.doc.gov**	Variable; if known name, quick; otherwise, lengthy delays; 3–4 weeks	$100	If prominent name, comprehensive. Tendency to be out of date.
4. Local Credit Agency Report	Long, start from scratch	$100 to $200	Quality varies. International market perspective lacking.
5. Bank Reports	Slow	None	Limited in scope.
6. FCIB-NACM Corporation **www.fcibnacm.com**	Same day to 3 weeks	$66 to $310; members get 5% discount; membership $840	Network of 15 agencies worldwide.

SOURCE: Interviews with company and organization personnel, December 1999.

terms that guarantee payment. In the long term, the best approach is to establish a re-lationship of mutual trust, which will ensure payment even if complications arise dur-ing a transaction.[27] Payment terms need to be stated clearly and followed up effec-tively. If prompt payment is not stressed and enforced, some customers will assume they can procrastinate, as we see in *The International Marketplace 5.4.*

Should a default situation occur in spite of the preparatory measures discussed above, the exporter's first recourse is the customer. Communication with the cus-tomer may reveal a misunderstanding or error regarding the shipment. If the cus-tomer has financial or other concerns or objections, rescheduling the payment terms may be considered. Third-party intervention through a collection agency may be needed if the customer disputes the charges. For example, the Total Credit Management Group, a cooperative of leading credit and collection companies in 46 countries, can be employed. Only when further amicable demands are unwarranted should an at-torney be used.[28]

In many cases, financing requirements may go beyond export credits, and financial risk management gains added dimensions. In a hotly contested bid for its first two communications satellites, Brazil managed to bargain the price down to $150 million. In addition, it pressured the two consortia competing for the business, one French and one Canadian, to promise to buy shoes, coffee, and iron ore as partial payment. **Countertrade** provisions are making their way into many financing arrangements, es-pecially when developing countries or centrally planned economies are involved.

[27]Michael S. Tomczyk, "How Do You Collect When Foreign Customers Don't Pay?" *Export Today* 9 (November–December 1993): 33–35.

[28]James Welsh, "Covering Your Bets on Credit and Collections," *World Trade,* February 1999, 28–29; and Ron Stiegel and Mark Stoyas, "Foreign Collections," *Export Today* (April 1995): 44–46.

THE INTERNATIONAL MARKETPLACE 5.4

Now for the Hard Part: Getting Paid for Exports

SMALLER EXPORTERS OFTEN do not have the luxury that big corporations have to weigh risks of doing business abroad and to investigate the creditworthiness of foreign customers. The result may be a hard lesson about the global economy: Foreign sales do not help much when you cannot collect the bill.

More often than not, exporters will do less checking on an international account than they will on a domestic customer. For example, a U.S. fan blade manufacturer with less than $10 million in revenue was left with an overdue payment of $127,000 owed by an African customer. Before shipping the goods, the company had failed to call any of the customer's credit references. These turned out to be nonexistent—just like the company itself.

The simple guideline of selling only in countries where you are most likely to get paid may not be enough, given that collection periods for some of the more attractive markets may be long (as shown in the table below). However, in many cases, basic information about the economic and political conditions in markets may be enough to warrant caution. Old World Industries Inc., a mid-sized maker of antifreeze fluid and other automotive products, found that out after selling 500,000 gallons of antifreeze to a customer in a newly emerging market. After two years, Old World is still waiting to be paid in full, because the foreign bank it is dealing with has trouble obtaining U.S. dollars despite the country's strengthening foreign reserve position.

Your Check Is in the Mail

Length of time required for U.S. companies in different industries to collect on the average bill from concerns in selected foreign countries in the first half of 1999, as reported by the National Association of Credit Management (NACM):

COUNTRY	NUMBER OF DAYS
Kenya	96
Pakistan	80
Brazil	66–167
United Kingdom	65–71
Italy	64–93
Mexico	62–90
Argentina	60–117
Germany	47–78
Canada	43–66
Taiwan	34–69
Switzerland	34–54
Japan	33–74
Finland	32–55

SOURCES: Data updated by interview with FCIB, December 15, 1999; "Congratulations, Exporter! Now about Getting Paid . . ." *Business Week,* January 17,1994, 98; and "Small Firms Hit Foreign Obstacles in Billing Overseas," *The Wall Street Journal,* December 8,1992, B2.

Because of the prominent position of countertrade in international trade (according to some estimates up to 25 percent of the total), many firms not only have had to accept it but also have made major adjustments financially and organizationally to cope with it. Some U.S. construction companies are hoping to open new construction projects by devising ways to help debt-strapped developing countries with their financing problems. In Latin America, U.S. contractors, led by McDermott International, are already grossing $700 million a year in countertrade in such commodities as steel, fertilizer, and chemicals. McDermott also bought the international trading arm of Germany's Coutinho, Caro & Co. to help dispose of the items it takes in compensation for work performed abroad.[29]

A development related to the debt crisis is the emergence of debt/equity and debt/product swaps. Under a **debt/equity swap,** a firm wishing to invest in a country with debt problems arranges to swap the country's debt for an equity investment. For example, Chrysler purchased $110 million in Mexican debt for about 55 cents on the dollar. The debt was then converted into about $100 million in pesos and invested in

[29]"The Shrinking World of Engineering Contractors," *Business Week,* September 24, 1984, 84–90.

TABLE 5.6	Example of Foreign Exchange Impact

MONTHLY CONTRACT, £1,000
COST OF GOODS TO MARKETER, $1,600

DATE	EXCHANGE RATE	REVENUE	COST	NET INCOME
1/1	1£ = 1.65	$1,650	$1,600	$50
2/1	1£ = 1.60	1,600	1,600	0
4/1	1£ = 1.55	1,550	1,600	(50)

the Mexican subsidiary.[30] Since suitable investments may not be available, **debt/product swaps** may be used as another vehicle for managing debt. Peru has negotiated deals in which creditors have committed themselves to buying $3 worth of Peruvian products for every $1 of products paid by Peru against debt.[31]

Foreign Exchange Risk

When the international marketer is to receive payment in a currency other than that of his or her country, the risk exists of a decline (devaluation) in the foreign currency during the time between the signing of the contract and the receipt of the foreign currency. If the marketer takes no action to manage an exchange rate fluctuation, losses may be incurred. This is illustrated in Table 5.6, in which the British pound depreciates against the U.S. dollar. Protection against foreign exchange risk cannot be secured from the same sources as for commercial and political risk. It must emerge from sound management practices.

The Foreign Exchange Market

Foreign exchange traders, such as these at Republic National Bank of New York, can move millions of dollars, yen, or marks around the world with a few keystrokes on their networked computer terminals. In addition to technological advances in communications and data processing, the deregulation of international capital flows also contributes to faster, cheaper transactions in the currency markets.

The foreign exchange market is the market for currencies, that is, the physical and institutional structure through which the money of one country is exchanged for that of another country, the rate of exchange between currencies is determined, and foreign exchange transactions are physically completed.[32] The participants in this market include banks, governments, and speculators as well as individuals and firms conducting transactions.

The price of one currency in terms of another is called the **exchange rate.** Daily exchange rates such as those shown in Figure 5.3 are available from newspapers such as *The Wall Street Journal* and *Financial Times* and through on-line services such as Bloomberg. The marketer, however, has to contact a particular bank's foreign exchange trader for a firm quote. Both spot and forward transactions are made in the market. The market for buying and selling on the current day is the **spot market.** The market for closing contracts on subsequent periods of 30, 60, or 90 days is called the **forward market.** For example, for the rates quoted for June 29, 2000, the forward quote for Britain is less than spot, and the pound is said to be selling at a discount to the dollar. When the foreign currency is more expensive in the forward market than in the spot market, the foreign currency is said to be selling at a premium. Forward

[30]"Debt-Business Boom in Latin America," *Euromoney*, September 1987, 81.

[31]"Drexel's Milken Is Trying to Find a Lode in Latin Debt," *The Wall Street Journal*, September 14,1987, 6.

[32]David K. Eiteman, Arthur I. Stonehill, and Michael H. Moffett, *International Business Finance* (Reading, MA: Addison-Wesley, 1998), 81.

FIGURE	5.3	Foreign Exchange Rates

Thursday, June 29, 2000

EXCHANGE RATES

The New York foreign exchange mid-range rates below apply to trading among banks in amounts of $1 million and more, as quoted at 4 p.m. Eastern time by Reuters and other sources. Retail transactions provide fewer units of foreign currency per dollar. Rates for the 11 Euro currency countries are derived from the latest dollar-euro rate using the exchange ratios set 1/1/99.

Country	U.S. $ equiv. Thu	U.S. $ equiv. Wed	Currency per U.S. $ Thu	Currency per U.S. $ Wed
Argentina (Peso)	1.0002	1.0002	.9998	.9998
Australia (Dollar)	.6023	.6027	1.6604	1.6593
Austria (Schilling)	.06917	.06851	14.458	14.596
Bahrain (Dinar)	2.6525	2.6525	.3770	.3770
Belgium (Franc)	.0236	.0234	42.3850	42.7896
Brazil (Real)	.5523	.5495	1.8105	1.8200
Britain (Pound)	1.5187	1.5120	.6585	.6614
1-month forward	1.5196	1.5129	.6581	.6610
3-months forward	1.5213	1.5145	.6573	.6603
6-months forward	1.5244	1.5174	.6560	.6590
Canada (Dollar)	.6746	.6763	1.4823	1.4787
1-month forward	.6751	.6768	1.4812	1.4775
3-months forward	.6761	.6778	1.4790	1.4754
6-months forward	.6777	.6793	1.4755	1.4720
Chile (Peso)	.001857	.001862	538.55	537.05
China (Renminbi)	.1208	.1208	8.2780	8.2775
Colombia (Peso)	.0004664	.0004677	2144.00	2138.00
Czech. Rep. (Koruna)				
Commercial rate	.02670	.02637	37.460	37.922
Denmark (Krone)	.1276	.1264	7.8368	7.9113
Ecuador (Sucre)				
Floating rate	.00004000	.00004000	25000.00	25000.00
Finland (Markka)	.1601	.1586	6.2472	6.3068
France (Franc)	.1451	.1437	6.8921	6.9579
1-month forward	.1454	.1440	6.8790	6.9445
3-months forward	.1459	.1445	6.8532	6.9190
6-months forward	.1467	.1453	6.8171	6.8829
Germany (Mark)	.4866	.4820	2.0550	2.0746
1-month forward	.4875	.4830	2.0511	2.0706
3-months forward	.4894	.4847	2.0434	2.0630
6-months forward	.4920	.4873	2.0326	2.0523
Greece (Drachma)	.002826	.002798	353.88	357.35
Hong Kong (Dollar)	.1283	.1283	7.7953	7.7953
Hungary (Forint)	.003658	.003623	273.37	275.98
India (Rupee)	.02239	.02238	44.665	44.675
Indonesia (Rupiah)	.0001143	.0001152	8750.00	8682.50
Ireland (Punt)	1.2085	1.1970	.8275	.8354
Israel (Shekel)	.2446	.2443	4.0880	4.0925

Country	U.S. $ equiv. Thu	U.S. $ equiv. Wed	Currency per U.S. $ Thu	Currency per U.S. $ Wed
Italy (Lira)	.0004915	.0004869	2034.43	2053.85
Japan (Yen)	.009504	.009478	105.22	105.51
1-month forward	.009557	.009532	104.63	104.91
3-months forward	.009662	.009636	103.50	103.77
6-months forward	.009829	.009799	101.74	102.06
Jordan (Dinar)	1.4085	1.4065	.7100	.7110
Kuwait (Dinar)	3.2658	3.2648	.3062	.3063
Lebanon (Pound)	.0006634	.0006634	1507.50	1507.50
Malaysia (Ringgit)-b	.2632	.2632	3.8000	3.8000
1-month forward	.6130	.6096	1.6313	1.6404
3-months forward	.6165	.6130	1.6221	1.6313
6-months forward	.6215	.6180	1.6089	1.6180
Malta (Lira)	2.3267	2.3132	.4298	.4323
Mexico (Peso)				
Floating rate	.1011	.1003	9.8905	9.9725
Netherland (Guilder)	.4319	.4278	2.3154	2.3375
New Zealand (Dollar)	.4687	.4679	2.1336	2.1372
Norway (Krone)	.1165	.1153	8.5836	8.6710
Pakistan (Rupee)	.01913	.01914	52.275	52.250
Peru (new Sol)	.2876	.2868	3.4770	3.4873
Philippines (Peso)	.02315	.02320	43.200	43.100
Poland (Zloty)-d	.2279	.2271	4.3875	4.4025
Portugal (Escudo)	.004747	.004702	210.65	212.66
Russia (Ruble)-a	.03561	.03563	28.080	28.065
Saudi Arabia (Riyal)	.2666	.2666	3.7506	3.7506
Singapore (Dollar)	.5768	.5762	1.7338	1.7354
Slovak Rep. (Koruna)	.02213	.02191	45.180	45.643
South Africa (Rand)	.1466	.1468	6.8225	6.8100
South Korea (Won)	.0008971	.0008959	1114.75	1116.25
Spain (Peseta)	.005720	.005666	174.82	176.49
Sweden (Krona)	.1131	.1125	8.8448	8.8927
Switzerland (Franc)	.6112	.6078	1.6361	1.6453
Taiwan (Dollar)	.03252	.03253	30.755	30.745
Thailand (Baht)	.02554	.02555	39.155	39.145
Turkey (Lira)	.00000161	.00000161	620280.00	621900.00
United Arab (Dirham)	.2723	.2723	3.6729	3.6729
Uruguay (New Peso)				
Financial	.08258	.08254	12.110	12.115
Venezuela (Bolivar)	.001466	.001468	682.01	681.34
	—	—	—	
SDR	1.3365	1.3289	.7482	.7525
Euro	.9518	.9428	1.0506	1.0607

Special Drawing Rights (SDR) are based on exchange rates for the U.S., German, British, French , and Japanese currencies. Source: International Monetary Fund.

a-Russian Central Bank rate. Trading band lowered on 8/17/98. b-Government rate. d-Floating rate; trading band suspended on 4/11/00. Foreign exchange rates are available from Readers' Reference Service (413) 592-3600.

SOURCE: "Currency Trading," *The Wall Street Journal*, June 29, 2000, C21.

contracts for lesser-known currencies are not readily available, and for unstable currencies, they are quite expensive.

Forward contracts provide a form of protection, or **hedge**, against exchange risks. When a forward exchange contract is signed, the forward quote (such as the 90-day quote for Germany) is the rate that applies, although no payment is generally made until the settlement date of the contract. The user pays the price of forgoing possible gains in order to ensure protection against possible losses.

Foreign exchange quotations are given either directly or indirectly. The quote $.1451/FF is a direct quote for the French franc because it is the home currency price of one unit of a foreign currency. The indirect quote, the amount of foreign currency for one unit of the domestic currency, in this case is FF6.8921/$.

The rate of exchange between two countries is the result of supply and demand as well as governmental policy. Changes in the supply and demand conditions will have an impact on the value of the currency if the currency is in a *free float*. For example, an increase in a country's exports or its interest rates would increase demand for its currency and thus lead to an increase in its currency value. In some cases, governments will establish an exchange rate for their currency and absorb and counter market pressures (and thus accept foreign currency losses) up to a point before allowing the exchange rate to change. Some currencies move in and out of various types of pegged exchange rate relationships; for example, in 1998, a total of 21 currencies were tied to the U.S. dollar and 15 to the French franc. Occasionally, governments will coordinate their actions to rectify an imbalance in demand and supply conditions. In September 1985, for example, the United States, together with Great Britain, West Germany, Japan, and France, decided on a coordinated effort to bring the dollar down. Because market participants then expected the dollar to fall, they sold dollars, sparking a sharp decline in the value of the currency. A similar accord was reached in 1987 to stabilize the value of the dollar. The spot market exchange rate therefore reflects international trade flows, international capital flows, and governmental policy.

Forward markets exist for only a relatively small number of major currencies used in international transactions. The principal determinant for forward rates is the spot rate. Anything having an impact on the spot rate, such as balance-of-payments problems, will have the same impact on forward rates.

The Management of Foreign Exchange Risk

When an international marketer conducts transactions in foreign currencies, he or she runs the risk of suffering financial losses resulting from the change in the value of the currency used. Naturally, changes can also affect the marketer favorably. A firm is exposed to foreign exchange in three ways. **Transaction exposure** refers to the effect of outstanding contracts (for example, payables and receivables). Table 5.6 is an example of a loss to the U.S. exporter if it has chosen not to make any changes in policies or decided not to protect itself against such changes. If the contract had called for payment in U.S. dollars, however, the British buyer would have incurred the loss.

If the financial statements of the marketer are affected as a result of having to report consolidated worldwide results in home country currency, the firm has **translation exposure.** If the exporter in the example maintained a British bank account with a balance of £100,000, it would initially be worth $165,000 (1/1). Three months later, in its own books, the exporter would report the British bank balance to be worth $155,000. Translation exposure for a U.S. firm is a function of the rules issued by the Financial Accounting Standards Board (FASB), in particular FASB 52 ("Foreign Currency Translation"), issued in 1981.[33] If the long-term health of a business entity is affected by foreign exchange beyond transaction and translation exposure, the entity has **economic exposure.** Response to economic exposure involves the application of long-term strategy by all the functional units of the firm. Marketers can avoid unnecessary economic exposure by careful selection of target markets and prudent pricing and credit policies. Any firm with ongoing international marketing activities will have economic exposure.

Three types of devices to protect against currency-related risk have been proposed: (1) risk modifying, such as manipulating prices or incurring local debt (e.g., the firm borrows moneys in the market to which it exports its product; thus, if the foreign currency depreciates relative to domestic currency, the loss in the operating cash flows is buffered by the reduction in debt); (2) self-insuring, such as manipulating the leads and lags in terms of export and import payments in anticipation of either currency revaluations or devaluations; and (3) risk shifting, such as purchasing of options or futures.[34] With long-term shifts, marketers may have to shift their production bases and procurement sources as many Japanese companies have done in response to the strong yen. Some marketers have focused on products that are far less sensitive to pricing changes. In addition, marketers that may not be able to shift production overseas have increased their production efficiencies.[35]

---

[33]"Foreign Currency Translation," *FASB Statement No. 52* (December 1981), par. 15.

[34]Richard D. Robinson, *Internationalization of Business: An Introduction* (Hinsdale, IL: Dryden Press, 1984), 200–207.

[35]"The Cheap Buck Gives Japan a Yen for Asia," *Business Week*, May 23, 1994, 52.

Options and futures are a relatively new development in the foreign exchange markets (see Figure 5.4). An **option** gives the holder the right to buy or sell foreign currency at a prespecified price on or up to a prespecified date. The difference between the currency options market and the forward market is that the transaction in the options market gives the participant the *right* to buy or sell, whereas a transaction in the forward market entails a contractual *obligation* to buy or sell. Should the exporter not have that much currency when the contract comes due, it would have to go into the foreign exchange markets to buy the currency, potentially exposing itself to major losses if the currency had appreciated in the meanwhile. The greater flexibility of the options contract makes it more expensive relative to the forward contract. The currency **futures** market is conceptually similar to the forward market; that is, to buy futures on the pound implies an obligation to buy in the future at a prespecified price. However, the minimum transaction sizes are considerably smaller on the futures market. Forward quotes apply to transactions of $1 million or more, whereas on the futures market, transactions will typically be well below $100,000. This market, therefore, allows relatively small firms engaged in international trade to lock in exchange rates and lower their risk. Forward contracts, options, and futures are available from banks, the Chicago Mercantile Exchange, and the Philadelphia Stock Exchange.

FIGURE	5.4	An Example of a Currency Futures and Options Provider

SOURCE: Chase (**http://www.chase.com**)

Dealing with Financial Crises

A series of currency crises have shaken all emerging markets in the 1990s. The devaluation of the Mexican peso in 1994, the Asian crisis of July 1997, the Russian ruble collapse of August 1998, and the fall of the Brazilian real in January 1999 have all provided a spectrum of emerging market economic failures, each with its own complex causes and unknown outlooks.

Causes of the Crises   Both the Mexican and Thai cases of currency devaluation led to regional effects in which international investors saw Mexico and Thailand as only the first domino in a long series of failures to come. For example, the historically stable Korean won fell from Won 900/US$ to Won 1,100/US$ in one month. The reasons for the crises were largely in three areas allowing comparison: corporate socialism, corporate governance, and banking stability and management. In 1997, business liabilities exceeded the capacities of government to bail businesses out, and practices such as lifetime employment were no longer sustainable. Many firms in the Far East were often controlled by families or groups related to the governing party of the country. The interests of stockholders and creditors were secondary in an atmosphere of cronyism. With the speculative investments made by many banks failing, banks themselves had to close, severely hampering the ability of businesses to obtain the necessary capital financing needed for operations. The pivotal role of banking liquidity was the focus of the International Monetary Fund's bail-out efforts.

The Asian crisis had global impact. What started as a currency crisis quickly became a region-wide recession.[36] The slowed economies of the region caused major reductions in world demand for many products, especially commodities. World oil markets, copper markets, and agricultural products all saw severe price drops as demand kept falling. These changes were immediately noticeable in declined earnings and growth prospects for other emerging economies. The problems of Russia and Brazil were reflections of those declines.

Effects of the Crises   The collapse of the ruble in Russia and of Russia's access to international capital markets has brought into question the benefits of a free-market economy, long championed by the advocates of Western-style democracy. While Russia is the sixth-most populous nation, a nuclear power, and the holder of a permanent seat in the Security Council of the United Nations, its economic status is that of a developing country. There was a growing middle class, particularly in the largest cities. Some Russian businesses had revealed glimmerings of respect for shareholders, staff, and customers. Higher standards were encouraged by a growing international business presence. Many of these positive changes are being lost or are in jeopardy.

In Brazil, similar effects are being felt. A total of 30 million consumers have left the middle class. Many of the free-trade experiments within Mercosur are being reevaluated or endangered, especially by Brazilian moves in erecting tariff barriers. Many of the key sectors, such as automobiles, are hit by layoffs and suspended production.[37]

Consumer and Marketer Responses   Recessions have an impact on consumer spending. For example, the 30 million Brazilians who, as a result of the real crisis, were no longer able to consume in a middle-class tradition were also lost to many marketers, such as McDonald's. Rather than buying hamburgers, they would consume more traditional and therefore less expensive meals. Similarly, some consumption may turn not only toward local alternatives but even to generics. Especially hard hit may be big-ticket

[36]Pam Woodall, "Survey: East Asian Economies: Six Deadly Sins," *Economist*, March 7, 1998, S12–14.

[37]"Latin America and the Market," *Economist*, November 21, 1998, 23–25.

purchases, such as cars, furniture, and appliances, that may be put on long-term hold. Changes in consumption patterns during such hard times are summarized in Figure 5.5.

Marketers' responses to these circumstances have varied from abandoning markets to substantially increasing their efforts. While Daihatsu pulled out of Thailand, GM has decided to stay, with a change in the car model to be produced and reduced production volume. Returning to a market having once abandoned it may prove to be difficult. For example, distribution channels may be blocked by competition, or suspicion about the long-term commitment of a returnee may surface among local partners. Manipulating the marketing mix is also warranted. Imported products are going to be more expensive, sometimes many times what the local versions cost. Therefore, emphasizing the brand name, the country of origin, and other benefits may convince the consumer of a positive value-price relationship. If the perceived prices are too high, the product and/or its packaging may have to be changed by making the product smaller or the number of units in a pack fewer. For example, Unilever reduced the size of its ice cream packs, making them cheaper, and offers premiums in conjunction with the purchase of soap products (for example, buy three, get one free).[38]

While marketers from North America and Europe may be faced by these challenges, local companies may have an advantage, not only at home but in international markets as well. Their lower prices give them an opportunity to expand outside their home markets or aggressively pursue expansion in new markets. Similarly, companies with sourcing in markets hit by currency crises may be able to benefit from lower procurement costs.

FIGURE 5.5 Consumer Adjustment to Financial Hardship

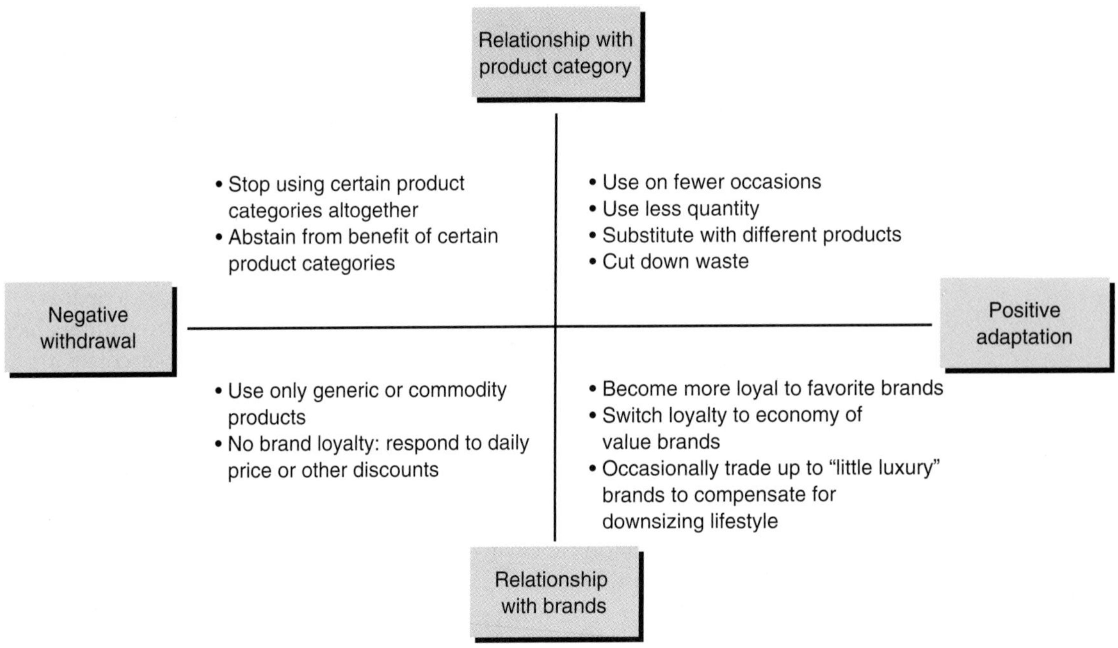

SOURCE: James Chadwick, "Communicating through Tough Times," *Economic Bulletin,* August 1998, 25–29, as referenced in Masaaki Kotabe and Kristiaan Helsen, *Global Marketing Management Update 2000* (New York: John Wiley, 2000), U10.

[38]"Asia's Sinking Middle Class," *Far Eastern Economic Review,* April 9, 1998, 12–13.

The most interesting approach in the face of challenges is to increase efforts in building market share. A number of U.S. companies in Mexico, such as Procter & Gamble, have decided to invest more due to decreasing competition (which resulted from some competitors leaving) and the increased buying power of their currencies. This strategy is naturally based on the premise that the market will rebound in the foreseeable future, thus rewarding investments made earlier.

SUMMARY

The financing terms of a transaction are an important marketing tool. The basics of an international marketer's credit policy involve two major concerns: (1) getting paid and (2) avoiding unnecessary risk in the process. This requires a good understanding, not only of the mechanisms of the foreign exchange market, but also of the various types of financial assistance available to the international marketer.

To help the international marketer deal with financial risk, both the government and the private sector have established various programs. Support systems exist as well to provide information on international credit and country conditions.

Foreign exchange risk is present any time the international marketer is to receive payment in a currency different from his or her own. The marketer can be protected through the purchase of forward contracts, for example. When financial crises emerge, the marketer will have to adjust strategies if the commitment is there to stay for a longer term in the market.

Use of the resources described in this chapter will allow the exporter to (1) offer competitive terms of payment to the buyer, (2) prudently penetrate foreign markets of higher risk, and (3) have greater financial liquidity and flexibility in administering the foreign receivables portfolio.

QUESTIONS FOR DISCUSSION

1. Discuss the various types of financial risk in terms of their impact on an international marketing entity.
2. Ex-Im Bank does not finance export sales, yet indirectly it is quite involved. How?
3. At times, subsidized export credit rates have been as low as half the rates at which national treasuries were borrowing. What is the rationale for this?
4. Suggest possible reasons Ex-Im Bank does not cover 100 percent of commercial risk.
5. What accounts for the fact that export finance managers and export marketing managers have traditionally not worked together as closely as possible?
6. Comment on this statement: "Many commercial banks today have only two objections to financing international trade: one, it is international; two, it involves trade."
7. What are the benefits of an on-line credit-information system such as @rating (www.cofacerating.com) for the customer and the supplier?
8. Assess the international trade financing commitment of different banks, using as examples Citibank (www.citibank.com), Bank One (www.bankone.com), and Silicon Valley Bank (www.svb.com).

RECOMMENDED READINGS

Chamber of Commerce of the United States. *Foreign Commerce Handbook.* Washington, DC: Chamber of Commerce, 1996.

Czinkota, Michael R., ed. *Trade Finance: Current Issues and Developments.* Washington, DC: Government Printing Office, 1988.

Exporter's Encyclopedia. 1998/99. New York: Dun and Bradstreet, 1999.

Foreign Credit Insurance Association. *Your Competitive Edge in Selling Overseas.* New York: FCIA, 1991.

Funabashi, Yoichi. *Managing the Dollar: From the Plaza to the Louvre.* Washington, DC: Institute for International Economics, 1989.

Guadagnoli, Louis G. *A Practical Guide to Export Financing and Risk Management.* Arlington, VA: Government Information Services, 1989.

Lanze, L. B. *Import/Export Can Make You Rich.* Englewood Cliffs, NJ: Prentice-Hall, 1988.

Shapiro, Alan C. *Multinational Financial Management.* New York: Wiley, 1999.

Wamsley, Julian. *The Foreign Exchange Handbook.* New York: Wiley, 1983.

Chapter 6

The International Political and Legal Environment

Is Your French Wine Really from Mexico?

To DECLARE A PRODUCT'S country of origin, importers in the United States must evaluate the import under two rulings. Firstly, they must adhere to the Gibson-Thomson ruling of 1940, which states that a product must be marked as originating in the country in which it has undergone a "substantial transformation." Thus, the labeling will communicate to consumers where the product was finished rather than where its materials originated. However, companies must also consider the rulings set forth in the North American Free Trade Agreement (NAFTA) of 1992. Under NAFTA rules, a product will be marked as originating from the country in which it was converted from one product classification to another. Thus, U.S. marketers must mark products coming from NAFTA and non-NAFTA countries differently.

While the "substantial transformation" ruling seems to make logical sense, it may yield misleading labeling. A "substantial transformation" may be different depending on who is making the judgment; that is, various members of the supply chain may disagree regarding the place of the product's transformation. For example, Florida orange juice, if blended with 1 percent Brazilian orange juice, must be labeled "Made in Brazil." Similarly, the U.S. company Bestfoods had to label its Skippy brand peanut butter "Made in Canada," even though it was made in Arkansas with ingredients that were 90 percent from the United States. In an appeal to the U.S. Court of International Trade, Bestfoods successfully argued that since no more than 7 percent of the value of the product was due to Canadian ingredients, Skippy warranted a "Made in the U.S.A." label, yet the rulings remain open to exploitation. Mexican wine blended with a small percentage of wine from France could be marketed as French wine.

SOURCES: Jack Lucentini, "A Sticky Case," July 17, 2000, *The Journal of Commerce* Web site, www.joc.com, accessed April 12, 2001; Neville, Peterson, Williams, "Country-of-Origin Rules Are Tangled," *The Journal of Commerce*, November 17, 1999, 10; Cam Simpson, "Made in Korea Fraud Snares Area Firm," *The Chicago Sun-Times*, October 30, 1999, NWS 1.

UCH AS MOST MANAGERS would like to ignore them, political and legal factors often play a critical role in international marketing activities. In addition, the interpretation and application of regulations can sometimes lead to conflicting and even misleading results, as *The International Marketplace 6.1* shows. Even the best business plans can go awry as a result of unexpected political or legal influences, and the failure to anticipate these factors can be the undoing of an otherwise successful business venture.

Of course, a single international political and legal environment does not exist. The business executive must be aware of political and legal factors on a variety of levels. For example, although it is useful to understand the complexities of the host country legal system, such knowledge does not protect against a home country–imposed export embargo.

The study of the international political and legal environment must therefore be broken down into several subsegments. Many researchers do this by separating the legal from the political. This separation—although perhaps analytically useful—is somewhat artificial because laws generally are the result of political decisions. Here no attempt will be made to separate legal and political factors, except when such a separation is essential.

Instead, this chapter will examine the political-legal environment from the manager's point of view. In making decisions about his or her firm's international marketing activities, the manager will need to concentrate on three areas: the political and legal circumstances of the home country; those of the host country; and the bilateral and multilateral agreements, treaties, and laws governing the relations between host and home countries.

Home Country Political and Legal Environment

No manager can afford to ignore the policies and regulations of the country from which he or she conducts international marketing transactions. Wherever a firm is located, it will be affected by government policies and the legal system.

Many of these laws and regulations may not be designed specifically to address international marketing issues, yet they can have a major impact on a firm's opportunities aboard. Minimum wage legislation, for example, affects the international competitiveness of a firm using production processes that are highly labor intensive. The cost of domestic safety regulations may significantly affect the pricing policies of firms in their international marketing efforts. For example, U.S. legislation that created the **Environmental Superfund** requires payment by chemical firms based on their production volume, regardless of whether the production is sold domestically or exported. As a result, these firms are at a disadvantage internationally when exporting their commodity-type products because they must compete against foreign firms that are not required to make such a payment in their home countries and therefore have a cost advantage.

Other legal and regulatory measures, however, are clearly aimed at international marketing activities. Some may be designed to help firms in their international efforts. The lack of enforcement of others may hurt the international marketer. For example, many firms are quite concerned about the lack of safeguards for **intellectual property rights** in China. Not only may counterfeiting result in inferior products and damage to the reputation of a company, but it also reduces the chances that an innovative firm can recoup its investment in research and development and spawn new products.

Violations of intellectual property rights can occur anywhere. As an example, in 1988, Anheuser-Busch agreed with Czechoslovak authorities to settle a trademark dispute with Budjovicky Budvar over the use of the name Budweiser. Anheuser-Busch agreed to give the Czech brewery a $15 million package, $10.3 million in brewing equipment and $4.7 million in cash, in return for which the two firms agreed to a division of the world into specified exclusive and shared markets. Chapter 9 will provide further in-depth discussions of intellectual property right problems and ways to protect a firm from infringement.

Another area in which governments may attempt to aid and protect the international marketing efforts of companies is **gray market** activities. Gray market goods are products that enter markets in ways not desired by their manufacturers. Companies may be hurt by their own products if they reach the consumer via uncontrolled distribution channels. Gray market activities will be discussed in detail later in the book.

Apart from specific areas that result in government involvement, the political environment in most countries tends to provide general support for the international marketing efforts of the country's firms. For example, a government may work to reduce trade barriers or to increase trade opportunities through bilateral and multilateral negotiations. Such actions will affect individual firms to the extent that they affect the international climate for free trade.

Often, however, governments also have specific rules and regulations restricting international marketing. Such regulations are frequently political in nature and are based on the fact that governments believe commerce to be only one objective among others, such as foreign policy and national security. Four main areas of governmental activities are of major concern to the international marketer here: embargoes or trade sanctions, export controls, import controls, and the regulation of international business behavior.

Embargoes and Sanctions

The terms **trade sanctions** and **embargoes** as used here refer to governmental actions that distort the free flow of trade in goods, services, or ideas for decidedly adversarial and political, rather than strictly economic, purposes. To understand them better, we need to examine the auspices and legal justifications under which they are imposed.

Trade sanctions have been used quite frequently and successfully in times of war or to address specific grievances. For example, in 1284, the Hansa, an association of north German merchants, felt that its members were suffering from several injustices by Norway. On learning that one of its ships had been attacked and pillaged by the Norwegians, the Hansa called an assembly of its members and resolved on an economic blockade of Norway. The export of grain, flour, vegetables, and beer was prohibited on pain of fines and confiscation of the goods. The blockade was a complete success. Deprived of grain from Germany, the Norwegians were unable to obtain it from England or elsewhere. As a contemporary chronicler reports: "Then there broke out a famine so great that they were forced to make atonement." Norway was forced to pay indemnities for the financial losses that had been caused and to grant the Hansa extensive trade privileges.[1]

The League of Nations set a precedent for the international legal justification of economic sanctions by subscribing to a covenant that provided for penalties or sanctions for breaching its provisions. The members of the League of Nations did not intend to use military or economic measures separately, but the success of the blockades of World War I fostered the opinion that "the economic weapon, conceived not as an instrument of war but as a means of peaceful pressure, is the greatest discovery and most precious possession of the League."[2] The basic idea was that economic sanctions could force countries to behave peacefully in the international community.

[1]Quoted in Philippe Dollinger, *The German Hansa* (Standford, CA: Stanford University Press, 1970), 49.

[2]Robin Renwick, *Economic Sanctions* (Cambridge, MA: Harvard University Press, 1981), 11.

THE INTERNATIONAL MARKETPLACE 6.2

Unilateral Sanctions: Who Really Loses?

THE U.S. DEPARTMENT of Commerce has predicted that the future of the U.S. economy is dependent upon strong exports. If the economy is so reliant on exports, why do politicians continue to lobby for unilateral trade sanctions against foreign governments? What price is the U.S. willing to pay in order to attempt to punish foreign governments for their participation in policies deemed to be inappropriate?

The United States is currently imposing economic trade sanctions on an estimated $800 billion worth of potential export markets for its businesses. The results of this huge barrier to trade translate into lost opportunities, lost U.S. economic growth, and lost jobs. Still, elected officials resort to such sanctions as a tool to wage formal protest against foreign countries.

The goals of unilateral trade sanctions are to show disapproval of another country's domestically unpopular policies, to have a negative impact on the economy of the foreign country, and ultimately to change the political policy that is being opposed. By placing sanctions on foreign countries, the United States is taking a worldwide political leadership stance against the country's policies.

As foreign countries are sanctioned from the import of U.S. goods and services, firms from other countries move in to supply them. Therefore, the net effect of a unilateral trade

sanction is merely to shift export sources away from the United States without putting a significant amount of additional economic pressure on the sanctioned foreign government.

Most successful trade sanctions have not been enforced unilaterally. To have a real economic impact on a government, a group of countries must jointly impose trade sanctions. It has been recommended by the State Department's Advisory Committee on International Economic Policy that the United States proceed cautiously when considering the implementation of unilateral trade sanctions. While sanctions can contribute to the achievement of political objectives, Congress should proceed on a case-by-case basis. Also, there should be an evaluation of the negative impact that sanctions will have on U.S. exports. The Bush administration may signal a change of economic climate. U.S. Trade Representative Robert Zoellick has opposed unilateral sanctions, urging options such as trade concessions or fines for governments who fail to meet international standards.

SOURCES: Richard Lawrence, "Zoellick Rising," March 16, 2001, *The Journal of Commerce* Web site, www.joc.com, accessed April 12, 2001; Greg Farmer, "Unilateral Sanctions: Who Really Loses?," *The Hill*, September 30, 1998, 20; Jesse Helms, "What Sanctions Epidemic?," *Foreign Affairs*, January/February 1999, 2–8.

The idea of the multilateral use of economic sanctions was again incorporated into international law under the charter of the United Nations, but greater emphasis was placed on the enforcement process. Once decided upon, sanctions are mandatory, even though each permanent member of the Security Council can veto efforts to impose sanctions. The charter also allows for sanctions as enforcement action by regional agencies such as the Organization of American States, the Arab League, and the Organization of African Unity, but only with the Security Council's authorization.

The apparent strength of the United Nations enforcement system was soon revealed to be flawed. Stalemates in the Security Council and vetoes by permanent members often led to a shift of emphasis to the General Assembly, where sanctions are not enforceable. Further, concepts such as "peace" and "breach of peace" are seldom perceived in the same way by all members, and thus no systematic sanctioning policy developed in the United Nations.[3]

Over the years, economic sanctions and embargoes have become an often-used foreign policy tool for many countries. Frequently, they have been imposed unilaterally in the hope of changing a country's government or at least changing its policies. Reasons for the impositions are varied, ranging from human rights to nuclear nonproliferation to antiterrorism. As *The International Marketplace 6.2* discusses, such unilateral imposition of sanctions, however, tends to have a major negative effect on

[3]Margaret P. Doxey, *Economic Sanctions and International Enforcement* (New York: Oxford University Press, 1980), 10.

the firms in the country that is exercising sanctions, mainly due to simple shifts in trade.

Another key problem with unilateral imposition of sanctions is that they typically do not produce the desired result. Sanctions may make the obtaining of goods more difficult or expensive for the sanctioned country, yet achievement of the purported objective almost never occurs. In order to work, sanctions need to be imposed multi-laterally. Only when virtually all nations in which a product is produced agree to deny it to a target can there be a true deprivation effect. Without such denial, sanctions do not have much bite. Yet to get all producing nations to agree can be quite difficult. Typically, individual countries have different relationships with the country subject to the sanctions due to geographic or historic reasons, and therefore cannot or do not want to terminate trade relations.

On rare occasions, however, global cooperation can be achieved. For example, when Iraq invaded Kuwait in August of 1990, virtually all members of the United Nations condemned this hostile action and joined a trade embargo against Iraq. Both major and minor Iraqi trading partners—including many Arab nations—honored the United Nations trade embargo and ceased trade with Iraq in the attempt to force it to withdraw its troops from Kuwait. Agreements were made to financially compensate those countries most adversely affected by the trade measures.

This close multinational collaboration has strengthened the sanctioning mecha-nism of the United Nations greatly. It may well be that sanctions will reemerge as a powerful and effective international political tool in the world. When we consider that sanctions may well be the middle ground between going to war or doing nothing, their effective functioning can represent a powerful arrow in the quiver of interna-tional policy measures. Economic sanctions can be used to extend political control over foreign companies operating abroad, with or without the support of their local government.[4]

One key concern with sanctions is the fact that governments often consider them as being free of cost. However, even though they may not affect the budget of gov-ernments, sanctions imposed by governments usually mean significant loss of busi-ness to firms. One estimate claims that the economic sanctions held in place by the United States annually costs the country some $20 billion in lost exports.[5]

Due to these costs, the issue of compensating the domestic firms and industries af-fected by these sanctions need to be raised. Yet, trying to impose sanctions slowly or making them less expensive to ease the burden on these firms undercuts their ulti-mate chance for success. The international marketing manager is often caught in this political web and loses business as a result. Frequently, firms try to anticipate sanc-tions based on their evaluations of the international political climate. Nevertheless, even when substantial precautions are taken, firms may still suffer substantial losses due to contract cancellations.

Export Controls

Many nations have **export control systems,** which are designed to deny or at least de-lay the acquisition of strategically important goods to adversaries. Most of these sys-tems make controls the exception, rather than the rule, with exports considered to be independent of foreign policy. The United States, however, differs substantially from this perspective in that exports are considered to be a privilege rather than a right, and exporting is seen as an extension of foreign policy.

[4]George E. Shambaugh, *States, Firms, and Power: Successful Sanctions in United States Foreign Policy* (Albany: State University of New York Press, 1999): 202.

[5]Gary Clyde Hufbauer, Jeffrey J. Schott, and Kimberly Elliott, *Economic Sanctions Reconsidered: History and Current Policy,* 3rd ed. (Washington, DC: Institute for International Economics, 2000).

THE INTERNATIONAL MARKETPLACE 6.3

National Security Stalls High-Tech Industry

WHAT DOES A U.S. COMPANY exporting sensitive technology to an unfriendly country have in common with one hiring a foreigner from that country to work on the technology? Both will face stiff penalties from the U.S. government if they fail to obtain an export license. While most export control rules govern the shipment of sensitive products to foreign countries, the regulation of "deemed exports" involves controlling the flow of technology to foreign individuals. U.S. companies must obtain a license before hiring a nonresident alien to work on a technology requiring license for export to his or her country. The wide reach of deemed export regulations could even extend to foreign students attending American universities or foreign professors participating in U.S. conferences. In effect, the United States treats foreign engineers or scientists as if they were foreign countries.

High-tech firms are seeking the abolition of the regulation, calling it "bureaucratic overkill" and a "leftover from the Cold War," which stalls the hiring of specialists who are in demand. A sympathetic Commerce Department official admitted, "These companies need those scientists to help maintain U.S. competitiveness." Despite the economic slowdown, the high-tech industry is trying to fill 425,000 jobs in 2001—a number expected to rise as the economy recovers." The companies argue that the technologies are adequately safeguarded without the deemed export regulations. They point out that exporters face separate regulations requiring them to act if they know an illegal transfer is about to occur, and

companies jealously guard their own technologies, signing nondisclosure agreements with employees.

The frustration of the companies is compounded by the fact that the deemed export rule became more stringent after 1994, when the industry itself asked for clarification of the rule. Before, firms only needed a license if they had knowledge of an "intent to export." Now, a license is required even if no export takes place. Industry advocates now seek at least a return to the pre-1994 form of the regulation, if not its outright elimination.

Even though many commentators heralded the end of the Cold War as an opportunity for U.S. policymakers to elevate economic competitiveness to the top of their priority list, the State Department, Congress, and the Pentagon often seem preoccupied with fears of China and other threats of nuclear proliferation. With an anti-China mood pervading the Capitol in the wake of the Los Alamos nuclear missile spying scandal, regulations are not likely to ease soon. In fact, the U.S. Senate Intelligence Committee report released in May 1999 criticized the Bush and Clinton administrations for lax security on technology exports. The high-pitched debate over military application of commercial technology exports continues, and the U.S. government continues to grapple with the conflict between its economic and security interests.

SOURCES: "Down but Not Out," *Chicago Tribune*, April 11, 2001; John Diamond, "Panel: Sales over Security Pushed," Associated Press, May 7, 1999; Michael S. Lelyveld, "'Deemed Export' Rule Deemed Nuisance," *The Journal of Commerce* (June 16, 1997): 1A, 5A.

The legal basis for export controls varies in nations. For example, in Germany armament exports are covered in the so-called War Weapons List, which is a part of the War Weapons Control Law. The exports of other goods are covered by the German Export List. **Dual-use items,** which are goods useful for both military and civilian purposes, are then controlled by the Joint List of the European Union.[6]

The U.S. export control system is based on the Export Administration Act, administered by the Department of Commerce, and the Munitions Control Act, administered by the Department of State. The Commerce Department focuses on exports in general, while the State Department covers products designed or modified for military use, even if such products have commercial applicability. The determinants for controls are national security, foreign policy, short supply, and nuclear nonproliferation.

U.S. laws control all exports of goods, services, and ideas. It is important to note here that an export of goods occurs whenever goods are physically transferred from

---

[6]Michael R. Czinkota and Erwin Dichtl, "Export Controls and Global Changes," *Der Markt* 37, 5 (1996) 148–155.

the United States. Services and ideas, however, are deemed exported whenever transferred to a foreign national, regardless of location. Permitting a foreign national from a controlled country to have access to a highly sensitive computer program in the United States is therefore deemed to be an export. *The International Marketplace 6.3* explains how the deemed export rule can affect firms.

In order for any export from the United States to take place, the exporter needs to obtain an export license. The administering government agencies have, in consultation with other government departments, drawn up a list of commodities whose export is considered particularly sensitive. In addition, a list of countries differentiates nations according to their political relationship with the United States. Finally, a list of individual firms that are considered to be unreliable trading partners because of past trade-diversion activities exists for each country.

After an export license application has been filed, government specialists match the commodity to be exported with the **critical commodities list,** a file containing information about products that are either particularly sensitive to national security or controlled for other purposes. The product is then matched with the country of destination and the recipient company. If no concerns regarding any of the three exist, an export license is issued. Control determinants and the steps in the decision process are summarized in Figure 6.1.

This process may sound overly cumbersome, but it does not apply in equal measure to all exports. Most international business activities can be carried out under NLR conditions, which stands for "no license required." NLR provides blanket permission to export. Products can be freely shipped to most trading partners provided that neither the end user nor the end use involved are considered sensitive. However, the process becomes more complicated and cumbersome when products incorporating high-level technologies and countries not friendly to the United States are involved. The exporter must then obtain an **export license,** which consists of written authorization to send a product abroad.

The international marketing repercussions of export controls are important. It is one thing to design an export control system that is effective and that restricts those international business activities subject to important national concerns. It is, however, quite another when controls lose their effectiveness and when one country's firms are placed at a competitive disadvantage with firms in other countries whose control systems are less extensive or even nonexistent.

FIGURE 6.1 The U.S. Export Control System

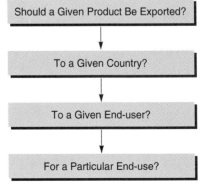

Determinants for Export Controls

- National Security
- Foreign Policy
- Short Supply
- Nuclear Nonproliferation

Decision Steps in the Export Licensing Process

Should a Given Product Be Exported?

↓

To a Given Country?

↓

To a Given End-user?

↓

For a Particular End-use?

A Changed Environment for Export Controls[7]

Six major changes have fundamentally altered the parameters of the traditional export control regime. The most important change has been the collapse of the Iron Curtain and the subsequent disappearance of the Soviet Union and the Eastern Bloc. As a result, both the focus and the principal objective of export controls have been altered. It makes little sense today to still speak of "Soviet adversaries," nor is the singular objective of maintaining the "strategic balance of power" still valid.

A second change derives directly from the first. Nowadays, the principal focus of export controls must rest on the Third World. Quite a number of countries from this region want chemical and nuclear weapons and the technology to make use of them. For example, a country such as Libya can do little with its poison gas shells without a suitable delivery system. As a result, export controls have moved from a "strategic balance" to a "tactical balance" approach. Nevertheless, even though the political hot spots addressed may be less broad in terms of their geographic expanse, the peril emanating from regional disintegration and local conflict may be just as dangerous to the world community as earlier strategic concerns with the Soviet Union.[8]

A third major change consists of the loosening of mutual bonds among allied nations. It used to be that the United States, Western Europe, and Japan, together with emerging industrialized nations, held a generally similar strategic outlook. This outlook was driven by the common desire to reduce, or at least contain, the influence of the Soviet Union. With the disappearance of the Soviet Union, however, individual national interests that had been subsumed by the overall strategic objective gained in importance. As a consequence, differences in perspectives, attitudes, and outlooks can now lead to ever-growing conflicts among the major players in the trade field.

Major change has also resulted from the increased **foreign availability** of high-technology products. In the past decade, the number of participants in the international trade field has grown rapidly. In earlier decades, industrializing countries mainly participated in world trade due to wage-based competition. Today, they are increasingly focused on technology-based competition. As a result, high-technology products are available worldwide from many sources. The broad availability makes any denial of such products more difficult to enforce. If a nation does control the exports of widely available products, it imposes a major competitive burden on its firms.

The speed of change and the rapid dissemination of information and innovation around the world also has shifted. For example, the current life cycle of computer chips is only 18 months. More than 70 percent of the data processing industry's sales resulted from the sale of devices that did not exist two years earlier.[9] This enormous technical progress is accompanied by a radical change in computer architecture. Instead of having to replace a personal computer or a workstation with a new computer, it is possible now to simply exchange microprocessors or motherboards with new, more efficient ones. Furthermore, today's machines can be connected to more than one microprocessor and users can customize and update configurations almost at will. Export controls that used to be based largely on capacity criteria have become almost irrelevant because they can no longer fulfill the function assigned to them. A user simply acquires additional chips, from whomever, and uses expansion slots to enhance the capacity of his or her computer.

Developing technology-based competition can be thwarted when the technology has global impact. Supporters of the technology protested in New Delhi when India was punished for its 1998 testing with diminished foreign aid after it conducted nuclear tests.

[7]This section has been adapted from Michael R. Czinkota and Erwin Dichtl, "Export Controls: Providing Security in a Volatile Environment," *The International Executive* 37 (Number 5, 1995): 485–497.

[8]Allan S. Krass, "The Second Nuclear Era: Nuclear Weapons in a Transformed World," in *World Security: Challenges for a New Century*, 2nd ed., M. Klare and D. Thomas, eds. (New York: St. Martin's Press, 1994), 85–105.

[9]Paul Freedenberg, testimony before the Subcommittee on International Finance and Monetary Policy of the Committee on Banking, Housing, and Urban Affairs, United States Senate, Washington, DC, February 3, 1994, 2.

The question arises as to how much of the latest technology is required for a country to engage in "dangerous" activity. For example, nuclear weapons and sophisticated delivery systems were developed by the United States and the Soviet Union long before supercomputers became available. Therefore, it is reasonable to assert that researchers in countries working with equipment that is less than state-of-the-art, or even obsolete, may well be able to achieve a threat capability that can result in major destruction and affect the world order.

From a control perspective, there is also the issue of equipment size. Due to their size, supercomputers and high-technology items used to be fairly difficult to hide and any movement of such products was easily detectable. Nowadays, state-of-the-art technology has been miniaturized. Much leading-edge technological equipment is so small that it can fit into a briefcase and most equipment is no larger than the luggage compartment of a car. Given these circumstances, it has become difficult, if not impossible, to closely supervise the transfer of such equipment.

Export Control Problems and Conflicts

There are four key export control problem areas for firms and policymakers. First is the continuing debate about what constitutes military-use products, civilian-use products, and dual-use products and the achievement of multilateral agreement on such classifications. Increasingly, goods are of a dual-use nature, meaning that they are commercial products which have potential military applications.[10] Examples are exported trucks that can be used to transport troops, or the exports of supplies to a pesticide factory that, some years later, is revealed to be a poison gas factory.[11] It is difficult enough to define weapons clearly. It is even more problematic to achieve consensus among nations regarding dual-use goods. For example, what about quite harmless screws if they are to be installed in rockets or telecommunications equipment used by the military? The problem becomes even greater with attempts to classify and list subcomponents and regulate their exportation. Individual country lists will lead to a distortion of competition if they deviate markedly from each other. The very task of drawing up any list is itself fraught with difficulty when it comes to components that are assembled. For example, the Patriot missile that was deployed in the Persian Gulf War consists only of simple parts whose individual export is permissible according to German law.

Even if governments were to agree on lists and continuously update them, the resulting control aspects would be difficult to implement. Controlling the transfer of components within and among companies across economic areas such as NAFTA or the European Union (EU) would significantly slow down business. Even more importantly, to subject only the export of physical goods to surveillance is insufficient. The transfer of knowledge and technology is of equal or greater importance. Weapons-relevant information easily can be exported via books, periodicals, and disks; therefore, their content also would have to be controlled. Foreigners would need to be prevented from gaining access to such sources during visits or from making use of data networks across borders. Attendance at conferences and symposia would have to be regulated, the flow of data across national borders would have to be controlled, and today's communication systems and highways such as the Internet would have to be scrutinized. These tasks would appear to be difficult if not impossible to perform.

Conflicts also result from the desire of nations to safeguard their own economic interests. Due to different industrial structures, these interests vary across nations. For example, Germany, with a strong world market position in machine tools, motors, and

---

[10]We are grateful to David Danjczek, vice president of Western Atlas Corporation, for his helpful comments.

[11]E. M. Hucko, *Aussenwirtschaftsrecht-Kriegswaffenkontrollrecht, Textsammlung mit Einführung*, 4th ed. (Köln, Germany: Bundesanzeiger, 1993).

chemical raw materials, will think differently about controls than a country such as the United States, which sees computers as an area of its competitive advantage. Adjustments in industrial structure add fuel to the fire. For example, as nations reduce their defense industries in size, many firms see exports as the road to survival. Yet, concerns about the export of military equipment and know-how lead to disagreements between and within nations.

These problems and conflicts seem to ensure that dissent and disagreement in the export control field are unlikely to decrease, but rather will multiply in the future. As long as key regulations are not harmonized internationally, firms will need to be highly sensitive to different and perhaps rapidly changing export control regimes.

Import Controls

Many nations exert substantial restraints on international marketers through import controls. This is particularly true of countries that suffer from major balance-of-trade deficits or major infrastructural problems. In these countries, either all imports or the imports of particular products are controlled through mechanisms such as tariffs, voluntary restraint agreements, or **quota systems** that result in quantitative import restraints. On occasion, countries cut off imports of certain products entirely in order to stimulate the development of a domestic industry.

For the international marketer, such restrictions may mean that the most efficient sources of supply are not available because government regulations restrict importation from those sources. The result is either second-best products or higher costs for restricted supplies. This in turn means that the customer receives inferior service and often has to pay significantly higher prices and that the firm is less competitive when trying to market its products internationally.

Policymakers are faced with several problems when trying to administer import controls. First, most of the time such controls exact a huge price from domestic consumers. Even though the wide distribution of the burden among many consumers may result in a less obvious burden, the social cost of these controls may be damaging to the economy and subject to severe attack by individuals. However, these attacks are counteracted by pressures from protected groups that benefit from import restrictions. For example, although citizens of the European Union may be forced—because of import controls—to pay an elevated price for all agricultural products they consume, agricultural producers in the region benefit from higher levels of income. Achieving a proper trade-off is often difficult, if not impossible, for the policymaker.

A second major problem resulting from import controls is the downstream change in import composition that results from these controls. For example, if the import of copper ore is restricted, either through voluntary restraints or through quotas, firms in copper-producing countries may opt to shift their production systems and produce copper wire instead, which they then export. As a result, initially narrowly defined protectionist measures may have to snowball in order to protect one downstream industry after another.

A final major problem that confronts the policymaker is that of efficiency. Import controls that are frequently designed to provide breathing room to a domestic industry either to grow or to recapture its competitive position often turn out not to work. Rather than improve the productivity of an industry, such controls provide it with a level of safety and a cushion of increased income yet let the drive for technological advancement fall behind. Alternatively, supply may respond to artificial stimulation and grow far beyond demand.

Regulation of International Business Behavior

Home countries may implement special laws and regulations to ensure that the international business behavior of their firms is conducted within the legal, moral, and ethical boundaries considered appropriate. The definition of appropriateness may vary from country to country and from government to government. Therefore, such regulations, their enforcement, and their impact on firms can differ substantially among nations.

Several major areas in which nations attempt to govern the international marketing activities of its firms are **boycotts,** whereby firms refuse to do business with someone, often for political reasons; antitrust measures, wherein firms are seen as restricting competition; and corruption, which occurs when firms obtain contracts with bribes rather than through performance. Arab nations, for example, have developed a blacklist of companies that deal with Israel. Even though enforcement of the blacklisting has decreased, some Arab customers still demand from their suppliers assurances that the source of the products purchased is not Israel and that the company does not do any business with Israel. The goal of these actions clearly is to impose a boycott on business with Israel. The U.S. government in turn, because of U.S. political ties to Israel, has adopted a variety of laws to prevent U.S. firms from complying with the Arab boycott. These laws include a provision to deny foreign income tax benefits to companies that comply with the boycott and also require notification of the U.S. government in case any boycott requests are received. U.S. firms that comply with the boycott are subject to heavy fines and denial of export privileges.

Boycott measures put firms in a difficult position. Caught in a web of governmental activity, they may be forced either to lose business or to pay fines. This is particularly the case if a firm's products are competitive yet not unique, so that the supplier can opt to purchase them elsewhere. Heightening of such conflict can sometimes force companies to withdraw operations entirely from a country.

The second area of regulatory activity affecting international marketing efforts of firms is **antitrust laws.** These can apply to the international operations of firms as well as to domestic business. In the European Union, for example, the commission watches closely when any firm buys an overseas company, engages in a joint venture with a foreign firm, or makes an agreement with a competing firm. The commission evaluates the effect these activities will have on competition and has the right to disapprove such transactions. However, given the increased globalization of national economies, some substantial rethinking is going on regarding the current approach to antitrust enforcement. One could question whether any country can still afford to define the competition only in a domestic sense or whether competition has to be seen on a worldwide scale. Similarly, one can wonder whether countries will accept the infringement on their sovereignty that results from the extraterritorial application of any nation's law abroad. There are precedents for making special allowances for international marketers with regard to antitrust laws. In the United States, for example, the Webb-Pomerene Act of 1918 excludes from antitrust prosecution those firms that are cooperating to develop foreign markets. This act was passed as part of an effort to aid U.S. export efforts in the face of strong foreign competition by oligopolies and monopolies. The exclusion of international marketing activity from antitrust regulation was further enhanced by the Export Trading Company Act of 1982, which does not expose cooperating firms to the threat of treble damages. It was specifically designed to assist small and medium-sized firms in their export efforts by permitting them to join forces in their international market development activities. Due to ongoing globalization of production, competition, and supply and demand, it would appear that over time the application of antitrust laws to international marketing activities will be revised to reflect global rather than national dimensions.

A third area in which some governments regulate international marketing actions concerns bribery and corruption. The United States has taken a lead on this issue. U.S. firms operating overseas are affected by U.S. laws against bribery and corruption. In many countries, payments or favors are a way of life, and "a greasing of the wheels" is expected in return for government services. In the past, many U.S. companies doing business internationally routinely paid bribes or did favors for foreign officials in order to gain contracts. In the 1970s, major national debts erupted over these business practices, led by arguments that U.S. firms should provide ethical and moral leadership, and that contracts won through bribes do not reflect competitive market activity. As a result, the Foreign Corrupt Practices Act was passed in 1977, making it a crime for U.S. firms to bribe a foreign official for business purposes.

A number of U.S. firms have complained about the act, arguing that it hinders their efforts to compete internationally against companies from countries that have no such antibribery laws. In-depth research supports this claim by indicating that in the years after the antibribery legislation was enacted, U.S. business activity in those countries in which government officials routinely received bribes declined significantly.[12] The problem is one of the ethics versus practical needs and also, to some extent, of the amounts involved. For example, it may be difficult to draw the line between providing a generous tip and paying a bribe in order to speed up a business transaction. Many business managers argue that the United States should not apply its moral principles to other societies and cultures in which bribery and corruption are endemic. If they are to compete internationally, these managers argue, they must be free to use the most common methods of competition in the host country. Particularly in industries that face limited or even shrinking markets, such stiff competition forces firms to find any edge possible to obtain a contract.

On the other hand, applying different standards to management and firms, depending on whether they do business abroad or domestically, is difficult to envision. Also, bribes may open the way for shoddy performance and loose moral standards among managers and employees and may result in a spreading of generally unethical business practices. Unrestricted bribery could result in a concentration on how best to bribe rather than on how best to produce and market products.

The international manager must carefully distinguish between reasonable ways of doing business internationally—including compliance with foreign expectations—and outright bribery and corruption. To assist the manager in this task, revisions were made in the 1988 Trade Act to clarify the applicability of the Foreign Corrupt Practices legislation. These revisions clarify when a manager is expected to know about violation of the act, and a distinction is drawn between the facilitation of routine governmental actions and governmental policy decisions. Routine actions concern issues such as obtaining permits and licenses, processing governmental papers such as visas and work orders, providing mail and phone service, and loading and unloading cargo. Policy decisions refer mainly to situations in which obtaining or retaining contracts is at stake. One researcher differentiates between **functional lubrication** and **individual greed.** With regard to functional lubrication, he reports the "express fee" charged in many countries, which has several characteristics: the amount is small, it is standardized, and it does not stay in the hands of the official who receives it but is passed on to others involved in the processing of the documents. The express service is available to anyone, with few exceptions. By contrast, in the process driven by "individual greed," the amount depends on the individual official and is for the official's own personal use.[13] Although the facilitation of routine actions is not prohibited, the illegal influencing of policy decisions can result in the imposition of severe fines and penalties.

Currently, the issue of global bribery has taken on new momentum. In 1995, the Organization of American States (OAS) (**www.oas.org**) officially condemned bribery. The Organization for Economic Cooperation and Development (OECD) (**www.oecd.org**) in 1999 agreed to change the bribery regulations among its member

---

[12]James R. Hines, Jr., *Forbidden Payment: Foreign Bribery and American Business after 1977*, working paper 5266 (Cambridge, MA: National Bureau of Economic Research, September 1995), 1.

[13]Magoroh Maruyama, "Bribing in Historical Context: The Case of Japan," *Human Systems Management* 15 (1996): 138–142.

countries not only to prohibit the tax deductibility of improper payments, but to prohibit such payments altogether. Similarly, the World Trade Organization has, for the first time, decided to consider placing bribery rules on its agenda.

A final, major issue that is critical for international marketers is that of general standards of behavior and ethics. Increasingly, public concerns are raised about such issues as global warming, pollution, and moral behavior. However, these issues are not of the same importance in every country. What may be frowned on or even illegal in one nation may be customary or at least acceptable in others. For example, cutting down the Brazilian rain forest may be acceptable to the government of Brazil, but scientists, concerned consumers, and environmentalists may object vehemently because of the effect of global warming and other climatic changes. The export of U.S. tobacco products may be legal but results in accusations of exporting death to developing nations. China may use prison labor in producing products for export, but U.S. law prohibits the importation of such products. Mexico may permit the use of low safety standards for workers, but the buyers of Mexican products may object to the resulting dangers. In the area of moral behavior, firms are increasingly not just subject to government rules, but are also held accountable by the public at large. For example, issues such as child labor, inappropriately low wages, or the running of sweat shops are raised by concerned individuals and communicated to customers. Firms can then be subject to public scorn, consumer boycotts, and investor scrutiny if their actions are seen as reprehensible and run the danger of losing much more money than they gained by engaging in such practices.

All of these issues pose difficult and complex problems, for they place managers in the position of having to choose between home country regulations and foreign business practices. This choice is made even more difficult because of diverging standards of behavior applied to businesses in different countries. The leaders of international firms must understand these conflicts and should assert leadership in implementing change. Not everything that is legally possible should be exploited for profit. Although companies need to return a profit on their investments, these issues must be seen in the context of time. By acting on existing, leading-edge knowledge and standards, firms will be able to benefit in the long term through consumer goodwill and the avoidance of later recriminations.

Host Country Political and Legal Environment

The host country environment, both political and legal, affects the international marketing operations of firms in a variety of ways. A good manager will understand the country in which the firm operates so that he or she is able to work within the existing parameters and can anticipate and plan for changes that may occur.

Political Action and Risk

Firms usually prefer to conduct business in a country with a stable and friendly government, but such governments are not always easy to find. Managers must therefore continually monitor the government, its policies, and its stability to determine the potential for political change that could adversely affect corporate operations.

There is **political risk** in every nation, but the range of risks varies widely from country to country. In general, political risk is lowest in countries that have a history of stability and consistency. Political risk tends to be highest in nations that do not have this sort of history. In a number of countries, however, consistency and stability that were apparent on the surface have been quickly swept away by major popular movements that drew on the bottled-up frustrations of the population. Three major types of political risk can be encountered: **ownership risk,** which exposes property and life; **operating risk,** which refers to interference with the ongoing operations of a

FIGURE	6.2	Exposure to Political Risk

Loss May Be the Result of:

Contingencies May Include:	The actions of legitimate government authorities	Events caused by factors outside the control of government
The involuntary loss of control over specific assets without adequate compensation	• Total or partial expropriation • Forced divestiture • Confiscation • Cancellation or unfair calling of performance bonds	• War • Revolution • Terrorism • Strikes • Extortion
A reduction in the value of a stream of benefits expected from the foreign-controlled affiliate	• Nonapplicability of "national treatment" • Restriction in access to financial, labor, or material markets • Controls on prices, outputs, or activities • Currency and remittance restrictions • Value-added and export performance requirements	• Nationalistic buyers or suppliers • Threats and disruption to operations by hostile groups • Externally induced financial constraints • Externally imposed limits on imports or exports

SOURCE: José de la Torre and David H. Neckar, "Forecasting Political Risks for International Operations," in H. Vernon-Wortzel and L. Wortzel, *Global Strategic Management: The Essentials.* 2nd ed. (New York: John Wiley and Sons, 1990), 195. Copyright © 1990 John Wiley and Sons. Reprinted by permission of John Wiley and Sons, Inc.

firm; and **transfer risk,** which is mainly encountered when attempts are made to shift funds between countries. Political risk can be the result of government action, but it can also be outside the control of government. The type of actions and their effects are classified in Figure 6.2.

A major political risk in many countries involves conflict and violent change. A manager will want to think twice before conducting business in a country in which the likelihood of such change is high. To begin with, if conflict breaks out, violence directed toward the firm's property and employees is a strong possibility. Guerrilla warfare, civil disturbances, and terrorism often take an anti-industry bent, making companies and their employees potential targets. For example, in the spring of 1991, Detlev Rohwedder, chairman of the German Treuhand (the institution in charge of privatizing the state-owned firms of the former East Germany), was assassinated at his home in Germany by the Red Army Faction because of his "representation of capitalism."

International terrorists have frequently targeted U.S. corporate facilities, operations, and personnel abroad for attack in order to strike a blow against the United States and capitalism. These firms are prominent symbols of the U.S. presence abroad, and by their nature they cannot have the elaborate security and restricted access of U.S. diplomatic offices and military bases. As a result, U.S. businesses are the primary target of terrorists worldwide and remain the most vulnerable targets in the future.[14]

---

[14]Michael G. Harvey, "A Survey of Corporate Programs for Managing Terrorist Threats," *Journal of International Business Studies* (Third Quarter 1993): 465–478.

Pakistan General Pervaiz Musharraf, left, pledged to return Pakistan to democracy after becoming the nation's leader following a coup d'etat.

These targets, however, may well be domestic rather than U.S. For example, when we see pictures of a burning McDonald's establishment, it is typically the domestic franchisee and the local employees and investors who are suffering the most. But then, destruction and terrorism are not known for their thoughtfulness and logic. The methods used by terrorists against business facilities include bombing, arson, hijacking, and sabotage. To obtain funds, the terrorists resort to kidnapping, armed robbery, and extortion.[15] The frequencies of such incidents around the world are shown in Figure 6.3.

In many countries, particularly in the developing world, coups d'état can result in drastic changes in government. The new government may attack foreign multinational corporations as remnants of the Western-dominated colonial past, as has happened in Cuba, Nicaragua, and Iran. Even if such changes do not represent an immediate physical threat to firms and their employees, they can have drastic effects. The past few decades have seen such coups in the countries of Ghana, Ethiopia, and Iraq, to name a few. These coups have seriously impeded the conduct of international marketing.

Less dramatic but still worrisome are changes in government policies that are caused not by changes in the government itself but by pressure from nationalist or religious factions or widespread anti-Western feeling. The aware manager will work to anticipate these changes and plan ways to cope with them.

| FIGURE | 6.3 | International Terrorist Incidents over Time, 1979–99 |

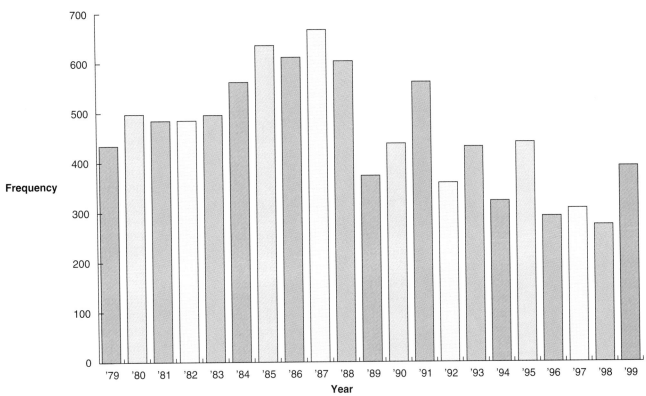

SOURCE: U.S. Department of State, *Patterns of Global Terrorism* (Washington, DC: U.S. Government Printing Office, 1999), Appendix C.
http://www.state.gov/www/global/terrorism

[15]Harvey J. Iglarsh, "Terrorism and Corporate Costs," *Terrorism* 10 (1987): 227–230.

What sort of changes in policy result from the various events described? The range of possible actions is broad. All of them can affect international marketing operations, but not all are equal in weight. Except for extreme cases, companies do not usually have to fear violence against employees, although violence against company property is quite common. Also common are changes in policy that take a strong nationalist and antiforeign investment stance. The most drastic steps resulting from such policy changes are usually confiscation and expropriation.

An important governmental action is **expropriation,** which is the seizure of foreign assets by a government with payment of compensation to the owners. Expropriation has appealed to some countries because it demonstrated nationalism and immediately transferred a certain amount of wealth and resources from foreign companies to the host country. It did have costs to the host country, however, to the extent that it made other firms more hesitant to invest in the country. Expropriation does provide compensation to the former owners. However, compensation negotiations are often protracted and result in settlements that are frequently unsatisfactory to the owners. For example, governments may offer compensation in the form of local, nontransferable currency or may base the compensation on the book value of the firm. Even though firms that are expropriated may deplore the low levels of payment obtained, they frequently accept them in the absence of better alternatives.

The use of expropriation as a policy tool has sharply decreased over time. Apparently, governments have come to recognize that the damage inflicted on themselves through expropriation exceeds the benefits.[16]

Confiscation is similar to expropriation in that it results in a transfer of ownership from the foreign firm to the host country. However, its effects are even harsher in that it does not involve compensation for the firm. Some industries are more vulnerable than others to confiscation and expropriation because of their importance to the host country economy and their lack of ability to shift operations. For this reason, sectors such as mining, energy, public utilities, and banking have been targets of such government actions.

Confiscation and expropriation constitute major political risks for foreign investors. Other government actions, however, are nearly as damaging. Many countries are turning from confiscation and expropriation to more subtle forms of control, such as **domestication.** The goal of domestication is the same, to gain control over foreign investment, but the method is different. Through domestication, the government demands partial transfer of ownership and management responsibility and imposes regulations to ensure that a large share of the product is locally produced and a larger share of the profit is retained in the country.

Domestication can have profound effects on the international marketer for a number of reasons. First, if a firm is forced to hire nationals as managers, poor cooperation and communication can result. If the domestication is imposed within a very short time span, corporate operations overseas may have to be headed by poorly trained and inexperienced local managers. Further, domestic content requirements may force a firm to purchase supplies and parts locally, which can result in increased costs, inefficiency, and lower-quality products, thus further damaging a firm's interest. Export requirements imposed on companies may also create havoc for the international distribution plan of a corporation and force it to change or even shut down operations in other countries. Finally, domestication will usually shield the industry within one country from foreign competition. As a result, inefficiencies will be allowed to grow due to a lack of market discipline. In the long run, this will affect the international competitiveness of an operation abroad and may become a major problem when, years later, the removal of domestication is considered by the government.

[16]Michael Minor, "LDCs, TNCs, and Expropriation in the 1980s," *CTC Reporter,* Spring 1988, 53.

Most businesses operating abroad face a number of other risks that are less dangerous, but probably more common, than the drastic ones already described. Host governments that face a shortage of foreign currency sometimes will impose controls on the movement of capital in and out of the country. Such controls may make it difficult for a firm to remove its profits or investments from the host country. Sometimes, **exchange controls** are also levied selectively against certain products or companies in an effort to reduce the importation of goods that are considered to be a luxury or unnecessary. Such regulations are often difficult to deal with because they may affect the importation of parts, components, or supplies that are vital for production operations. Restrictions on such imports may force a firm either to alter its production program or, worse yet, to shut down its entire plant. Prolonged negotiations with government officials may be necessary in order to reach a compromise agreement on what constitutes a "valid" expenditure of foreign currency resources. Because the goals of government officials and corporate managers may often be quite different, such compromises, even when they can be reached, may result in substantial damage to the international marketing operations of a firm.

Countries may also raise the tax rates applied to foreign investors in an effort to control the firms and their capital. On occasion, different or stricter applications of the host country's tax codes are implemented for foreign investors. The rationale for such measures is often the seeming underpayment of taxes by such investors, when comparing their payments to those of long-established domestic competitors. Overlooked is the fact that new investors in foreign lands tend to **"overinvest"** by initially buying more land, space, and equipment than is needed immediately and by spending heavily so that facilities are state-of-the-art. This desire to accommodate future growth and to be highly competitive in the early investment stages will, in turn, produce lower profits and lower tax payments. Yet over time, these investment activities should be very successful, competitive, and job-creating. Selective tax increases for foreign investors may result in much-needed revenue for the coffers of the host country, but they can severely damage the operations of the foreign investors. This damage, in turn, may result in decreased income for the host country in the long run.

The international marketing manager must also worry about **price controls.** In many countries, domestic political pressures can force governments to control the prices of imported products or services, particularly in sectors that are considered to be highly sensitive from a political perspective, such as food or health care. If a foreign firm is involved in these areas, it is a vulnerable target of price controls because the government can play on its people's nationalistic tendencies to enforce the controls. Particularly in countries that suffer from high inflation and frequent devaluations, the international marketer may be forced to choose between shutting down the operation or continuing production at a loss in the hope of recouping that loss once the government chooses to loosen or remove its price restrictions. How a firm can adjust to price controls is discussed in greater detail later in the book.

Managers face political and economic risk whenever they conduct business overseas, but there may be ways to lessen the risk. Obviously, if a new government that is dedicated to the removal of all foreign influences comes into power, a firm can do little. In less extreme cases, however, managers can take actions to reduce the risk if they understand the root causes of the host country policies. Most important is the accumulation and appreciation of factual information about a country's history, political background, and culture before making a long-term investment decision. Also, a high degree of sensitivity by a firm and its employees to country-specific approaches and concerns are important dimensions which help a firm to blend into the local landscape rather than standing out as a foreign object.

Adverse governmental actions are usually the result of a host country's nationalism, desire for independence, and opposition to colonial remnants. If a country's citizens feel exploited by foreign firms, government officials are more likely to take antiforeign action. To reduce the risk of government intervention, a firm needs to demonstrate that it is concerned with the host country's society and that it considers itself an integral part of the host country rather than simply an exploitative foreign corporation. Ways to do this include intensive local hiring and training practices, good pay, more charity, and more societally useful investment. In addition, a company can form joint ventures with local partners to demonstrate a willingness to share its benefits with nationals. Although such actions will not guarantee freedom from risk, they will certainly lessen the exposure.

Corporations can also protect against political risk by closely monitoring political developments. Increasingly, private-sector firms offer assistance in such monitoring activities, permitting the overseas corporation to discover potential trouble spots as early as possible and react quickly to prevent major losses. Firms can also take out insurance to cover losses due to political risk. Most industrialized countries offer insurance programs for their firms doing business abroad. In Germany, for example, Hermes Kreditanstalt provides exporters with insurance. In the United States, the Overseas Private Investment Corporation (OPIC) can cover three types of risk: currency inconvertibility insurance, which covers the inability to convert profits, debt service, and other remittances from local currency into U.S. dollars; expropriation insurance, which covers the loss of an investment due to expropriation, nationalization, or confiscation by a foreign government; and political violence insurance, which covers the loss of assets or income due to war, revolution, insurrection, or politically motivated civil strife, terrorism, and sabotage.[17] Rates vary by country and industry, but for $100 of coverage per year for a manufacturing project, the base rate is $0.30 for protection against inconvertibility, $0.60 to protect against expropriation, and $1.05 to protect against political violence.[18] Usually, insurance policies do not cover commercial risks and, in the event of a claim, cover only the actual loss—not lost profits. In the event of a major political upheaval, however, risk insurance can be critical to a firm's survival.

Clearly, the international marketer must consider the likelihood of negative political factors in making decisions on conducting business overseas. On the other hand, host country political and legal systems can have a positive impact on the conduct of international business. Many governments, for example, encourage foreign investments, especially if they believe that the investment will produce economic and political benefits domestically. Some governments have opened up their economy to foreign investors, placing only minimal constraints on them, in the hope that such policies will lead to rapid economic development. Others have provided for substantial subsidization of new investment activities in the hope that investments will generate additional employment. The international marketer, in his or her investment decision, can and should therefore also pay close attention to the extent and forms of incentives available from foreign governments. Although international marketing decisions should be driven by market forces, the basic economies of these decisions may change depending on incentives offered.

In this discussion of the political environment, laws have been mentioned only to the extent that they appear to be the direct result of political changes. However, each nation has laws regarding marketing, and the international manager must understand their effects on the firm's efforts.

Legal Differences and Restraints

Countries differ in their laws as well as in their use of these laws. For example, the United States has developed into an increasingly litigious society, in which institutions

[17]Overseas Private Investment Corporation (OPIC), Washington, DC, **http://www.opic.gov**, March 29, 2000.

[18]*Investment Insurance Handbook* (Washington DC: Overseas Private Investment Corporation, 1991).

and individuals are quick to take a case to court. As a result, court battles are often protracted and costly, and simply the threat of a court case can reduce marketing opportunities. In contrast, Japan's legal tradition tends to minimize the role of the law and of lawyers. Some possible reasons include the relatively small number of courts and attorneys, the delays, the costs and the uncertainties associated with litigation, the limited doctrines of plaintiffs' standing and rights to bring class action suits, the tendency of judges to encourage out-of-court settlements, and the easy availability of arbitration and mediation for dispute resolution.

Some estimates suggest that the number of lawyers in the United States is as much as 48 times higher than in Japan, based on the fact that Japan has only about 12,500 fully licensed lawyers. However, comparisons can be misleading because officially registered lawyers in Japan perform a small fraction of the duties performed by American lawyers. After accounting for the additional roles of American lawyers, the number of "lawyers" in Japan appears to be approximately one-fifth of those in the United States.[19]

Over the millennia of civilization, many different laws and legal systems emerged. King Hammurabi of Babylon codified a series of judges' decisions into a body of law. Hebrew law was the result of the dictates of God. Legal issues in many African tribes were settled through the verdicts of clansmen. A key legal perspective that survives today is that of **theocracy,** which has faith and belief as its key focus and is a mix of societal, legal, and spiritual guidelines. Examples are Hebrew law and Islamic law, or the *shari'ah*, which are the result of scripture, prophetic utterances and practices, and scholarly interpretations.[20]

While these legal systems are important to society locally, from an international business perspective the two major legal systems worldwide can be categorized into common law and code law. **Common law** is based on tradition and depends less on written statutes and codes than on precedent and custom. Common law originated in England and is the system of law found today in the United States.

On the other hand, **code law** is based on a comprehensive set of written statutes. Countries with code law try to spell out all possible legal rules explicitly. Code law is based on Roman law and is found in the majority of the nations of the world. In general, countries with the code law system have much more rigid laws than those with the common law system. In the latter, courts adopt precedents and customs to fit the cases, allowing the marketer a better idea of the basic judgment likely to be rendered in new situations.

Although wide in theory, the differences between code law and common law, and their impact on the international marketer, are not always as broad in practice. For example, many common law countries, including the United States, have adopted commercial codes to govern the conduct of business.

Host countries may adopt a number of laws that affect a company's ability to market. To begin with, there can be laws affecting the entry of goods, such as tariffs and quotas. Also in this category are **antidumping laws,** which prohibit below-cost sales of products, and laws that require export and import licensing. *The International Marketplace 6.4* explains with the example of the steel trade how these decisions can become highly politically charged, even though domestic laws would appear to settle such issues.

In addition, many countries have health and safety standards that may, by design or by accident, restrict the entry of foreign goods. Japan, for example, has particularly strict health standards that affect the import of pharmaceuticals. Rather than accepting test results from other nations, the Japanese government insists on conducting its own tests, which are time consuming and costly. It claims that these tests are

[19]Stuart M. Chemtob, Glen S. Fukushima, and Richard H. Wohl, *Practice by Foreign Lawyers in Japan* (Chicago: American Bar Association, 1989), 9.

[20]Surya Prakash Sinha, *What Is Law? The Differing Theories of Jurisprudence* (New York: Paragon House, 1989).

THE INTERNATIONAL MARKETPLACE 6.4

The Steel Dumping Controversy

U.S. STEEL COMPANIES feel threatened by foreign steel producers, who have allegedly been "dumping" steel in the United States by selling it at "prices unfairly below reasonable costs of production." However, low steel prices to manufacturers may lead to lower final product prices, thus helping consumers. For example, car prices may decline as the cost of steel declines.

The steel industry and steel unions have lobbied intensely to obtain new trade barriers for protection. However, by issuing trade quotas or tariffs, the United States might be cutting off foreign markets that have been experiencing severe difficulties themselves. In the case of steel, the government faced conflicting goals: either protect domestic steel makers or keep foreign countries' export income lines open.

The United States singled out Japan, Brazil, and Russia as countries that had been dumping steel in the United States. On hot-rolled steel from Japan and Brazil, the United States imposed provisional duties between 25 percent and 80 percent. Much to the dismay of U.S. steel workers, however, the government settled for an agreement on the vol-

untary curtailment of steel dumping by Russian companies, due to the severe economic problems within the Russian economy. Russia agreed to decrease steel exports to the United States by nearly 70 percent compared to 1998 levels. The agreement imposed a six-month moratorium that, in effect, reduced 1999 exports to 325,000 tons. However, it allowed annual increases which would allow exports to rise to 725,000 tons per year by 2003. The president of the U.S. Steel Group of USX Corp. stated, "The administration wants to mix their foreign policy and their trade policy and let all this fall on us. If we collectively as a country want to help Russia, that's fine. But don't put it all on the shoulders of our industry."

SOURCES: Robert Lyle, "Russia: Agreement Reduces Steel Exports to U.S.," February 23, 1999, www.rferl.org, accessed April 10, 2001; Paul Blustein, "Deal on Steel Imports Will Spare Moscow from U.S. Sanctions," *The Washington Post,* February 23, 1999, E02; Michael R. Czinkota, "The Specter of Government Intervention," *Japan Times,* October 1998, 21; William Roberts, "Bipartisan US Bill Scales Back WTO Steel Import Pact," *Journal of Commerce,* February 4, 1999, 3A.

necessary to take into account Japanese peculiarities. Yet some importers and their governments see these practices as thinly veiled protectionist barriers. As *The International Marketplace 6.5* shows, the role of culture is quite powerful when it comes to the implementation of laws.

A growing global controversy surrounds the use of genetic technology. Governments are increasingly devising new rules that affect trade in genetically modified products. For example, Australia introduced a mandatory standard for foods produced using biotechnology, which prohibits the sale of such products unless the food has been assessed by the Australia New Zealand Food Authority.

Other laws may be designed to protect domestic industries and reduce imports. For example Russia charges a 20 percent value-added tax on most imported goods; assesses high excise taxes on goods such as cigarettes, automobiles, and alcoholic beverages; and provides a burdensome import licensing regime for alcohol to depress Russian demand for imports.[21]

Very specific legislation may also exist to regulate where a firm can advertise or what constitutes deceptive advertising. Many countries prohibit specific claims by marketers comparing their product to that of the competition and restrict the use of promotional devices. Some countries regulate the names of companies or the foreign language content of a product's label. Even when no laws exist, the marketer may be hampered by regulations. For example, in many countries, governments require a firm to join the local chamber of commerce or become a member of the national trade association. These institutions in turn may have internal regulations that set standards for the conduct of business and may be seen as quite confining to the international marketer.

[21]*National Trade Estimate Report on Foreign Trade Barriers,* Washington, DC, Office of the United States Trade Representative, 1999, **http://www.ustr.gov.**

THE INTERNATIONAL MARKETPLACE 6.5

Two Air Disasters, Two Cultures, Two Remedies

WHEN TWO JUMBO JETS crashed ten days apart in Dallas and in the mountains near Tokyo, Americans and Japanese shared a common bond of shock and grief. Soon, however, all parties in Japan—from the airline to the employers of victims—moved to put the tragedy behind them. In the United States, legal tremors will be felt for years.

Lawyers hustled to the scene of the Delta Air Lines accident at the Dallas–Fort Worth airport and set up shop at an airport hotel. Proclaimed San Francisco attorney Melvin Belli, "I'm not an ambulance chaser—I get there before the ambulance." "We always file the first suit," bragged Richard Brown, a Melvin Belli associate who flew to Dallas "to get to the bottom of this and to make ourselves available." He added: "We never solicited anyone directly. We were called to Texas by California residents who lost their loved ones." Within 72 hours, the first suit against Delta was filed. Insurance adjusters working for Delta quickly went to work as well.

Seven thousand miles away, Japan Air Lines president Yasumoto Takagi humbly bowed to families of the 520 victims and apologized "from the bottom of our hearts." He vowed to resign once the investigation was complete. Next of kin soon received "condolence payments" and negotiated settlements with the airline. Traditionally few, if any, lawsuits are filed following such accidents.

Behind these differences lie standards of behavior and corporate responsibility that are worlds apart. "There is a general Japanese inclination to try to settle any disputes through negotiations between the parties before going to court," says Koichiro Fujikura, a Tokyo University law professor. Added Carl Green, a Washington, D.C., attorney and spe-

cialist on Japanese law: "There is an assumption of responsibility. In our adversarial society, we don't admit responsibility. It would be admitting liability."

After a JAL jet crashed into Tokyo Bay, killing twenty-four passengers, JAL president Takagi visited victims' families, offered gifts, and knelt before funeral altars. JAL offered families about $2,000 each in condolence payments, then negotiated settlements reported to be worth between $166,000 and $450,000, depending on the age and earning power of each victim. Only one family sued.

Japanese legal experts expected settlements to be as high as 500 million yen—about $2.1 million—apiece. Negotiations were prolonged. But with families believing that JAL was sincerely sorry, their feelings were soothed," according to attorney Takeshi Odagi. For the family that did file a lawsuit, it took until March 2000 for the High Court in London to rule that the two children of a Japanese businessman on board the plane were entitled to claim compensation.

Japan's legal system encourages these traditions. "Lawyers don't descend in droves on accident scenes because they barely have enough time to handle the suits they have," says John Haley, a law professor at the University of Washington who has studied and worked in Japan. "There are fewer judges per capita than there were in 1890," Haley added. Only 500 lawyers are admitted to the bar each year.

SOURCES: Clemens P. Work, Sarah Peterson, and Hidehiro Tanakadate, "Two Air Disasters, Two Cultures, Two Remedies," *U.S. News and World Report*, August 26, 1985, 25–26; "2 British Teenage Girls Declared Children of JAL Crash Victim," Kyodo News Service, March 13, 2000.

Finally, the enforcement of laws may have a different effect on national and on foreign marketers. For example, the simple requirement that an executive has to stay in a country until a business conflict is resolved may prove to be quite onerous to the international marketer.

The Influencing of Politics and Laws

To succeed in a market, the international marketer needs much more than business know-how. He or she must also deal with the intricacies of national politics and laws. Although a full understanding of another country's legal and political system will rarely be possible, the good manager will be aware of the importance of this system and will work with people who do understand how to operate within the system.

Many areas of politics and law are not immutable. Viewpoints can be modified or even reversed, and new laws can supersede old ones. Therefore, existing political and

| FIGURE | 6.4 | Advertising to Influence Public Policy |

ANOTHER VOICE JOINS THE CHORUS, FORMER UAW PRESIDENT LEONARD WOODCOCK SUPPORTS CHINA PNTR.

"Organized labor should support it. It's in both U.S. and Chinese interests."

Los Angeles Times March 9, 2000

"American labor has a tremendous interest in China's trading on fair terms with the U.S. The agreement we signed with China this past November marks the largest single step ever taken toward achieving that goal."

"Democracy, including rights for workers, is an evolutionary process. Isolation and containment will not promote improved rights for a people. Rather, working together and from within a society will, over time, promote improved conditions."

BRT THE BUSINESS ROUNDTABLE

To learn more visit www.gotrade.org
or call toll free 1-877-611-*TRADE*

SUPPORT PERMANENT NORMAL TRADE RELATIONS FOR CHINA.

legal restraints do not always need to be accepted. To achieve change, however, there must be some impetus for it, such as the clamors of a constituency. Otherwise, systemic inertia is likely to allow the status quo to prevail.

The international marketer has various options. One approach may be to simply ignore prevailing rules and expect to get away with it. Pursuing this option is a high-risk strategy because of the possibility of objection and even prosecution. A second, traditional option is to provide input to trade negotiators and expect any problem areas to be resolved in multilateral negotiations. The drawback to this option is, of course, the quite time-consuming process involved.

A third option involves the development of coalitions or constituencies that can motivate legislators and politicians to consider and ultimately implement change. This option can be pursued in various ways. One direction can be the recasting or redefinition of issues. Often, specific terminology leads to conditioned though inappropriate responses. For example, in the United States, the trade status accorded the People's Republic of China has been controversial for many years. The U.S. Congress had to decide annually whether to grant "Most Favored Nation" (MFN) status to China. The debate on this decision was always very contentious and acerbic and was often framed around the question why China deserved to be treated the "most favored way." Lost in the debate was the fact that the term "most favored" was simply taken from WTO terminology and indicated only that trade with China would be treated like that with any other country. Only in late 1999 was the terminology changed from MFN to NTR, or "normal trade relations." Even though there was still considerable debate regarding China, at least the controversy about special treatment had been avoided.[22]

Beyond terminology, marketers can also highlight the direct linkages and their cost and benefit to legislators and politicians. For example, the manager can explain the employment and economic effects of certain laws and regulations and demonstrate the benefits of change. The picture can be enlarged by including indirect linkages. For example, suppliers, customers, and distributors can be asked to participate in delineating to decision makers the benefit of change. Figure 6.4 gives an example of how a business group has gathered support for its effort to influence the U.S. Congress in favor of normal trade relations between the United States and China.

Developing such coalitions is not an easy task. Companies often seek assistance in effectively influencing the government decision-making process. Such assistance usually is particularly beneficial when narrow economic objectives or single-issue campaigns are needed. Typical providers of this assistance are lobbyists. Usually, these are well-connected individuals and firms that can provide access to policymakers and legislators.

Many countries and companies have been effective in their lobbying in the United States. Estimates of the number of U.S. lobbyists on behalf of foreign entities range into the thousands. As an example, Brazil has held on average nearly a dozen contracts per year with U.S. firms covering trade issues. Brazilian citrus exporters and computer manufacturers have hired U.S. legal and public relations firms to provide them with information on relevant U.S. legislative activity. The Banco do Brasil lobbied for the restructuring of Brazilian debt and favorable banking regulations. A key factor in successful lobbying, however, is the involvement of U.S. citizens and companies.

U.S. firms also have representation in Washington, D.C., as well as state capitals. Often, however, they are less adept at ensuring proper representation abroad. For example, a survey of U.S. international marketing executives found that knowledge and information about trade and government officials was ranked lowest among critical international business information needs. This low ranking appears to reflect the fact that many U.S. firms are far less successful in their interaction with

---

[22]Michael R. Czinkota, "The Policy Gap in International Marketing," *Journal of International Marketing*, 8 (Number 1, 2000): 99–111.

governments abroad and are far less intensive in their lobbying attempts than are foreign entities in the United States.[23]

Although representation of the firm's interests to government decision makers and legislators is entirely appropriate, the international marketer must also consider any potential side effects. Major questions can be raised if such representation becomes very strong. In such instances, short-term gains may be far outweighed by long-term negative repercussions if the international marketer is perceived as exerting too much political influence.

The International Environment

In addition to the politics and laws of both the home and the host countries, the international marketer must consider the overall international political and legal environment. Relations between countries can have a profound impact on firms trying to do business internationally.

International Politics

The effect of politics on international marketing is determined by both the bilateral political relations between home and host countries and the multilateral agreements governing the relations among groups of countries.

The government-to-government relationship can have a profound effect, particularly if it becomes hostile. Numerous examples exist of the linkage between international politics and international marketing. The premier example is perhaps U.S.-Iranian relations following the 1979 Iranian revolution. Although the internal political and legal changes in the aftermath of that revolution would certainly have affected international marketing in Iran, the deterioration in U.S.-Iranian political relations that resulted from the revolution had a significant impact. U.S. firms were injured not only by physical damage caused by the violence but also by the anti-American feelings of the Iranian people and their government. The clashes between the two governments completely destroyed any business relationships, regardless of corporate feelings or agreements on either side. It took more than twenty years to reopen governmental dialogue between the two countries.

A more recent example of government-to-government conflict was presented by the Helms-Burton Act. Passed in response to the shooting down of two unarmed small planes by the Cuban Air Force, this U.S. legislation granted individuals the right to sue, in U.S. courts, subsidiaries of those foreign firms that had invested in properties confiscated by the Cuban government in the 1960s. In addition, managers of these firms were to be denied entry into the United States. Many U.S. trading partners strongly disagreed with this legislation. In response, Canada proposed suing U.S. firms that had invested in properties taken from royalists in 1776, and the European Union threatened to permit European firms to countersue subsidiaries of U.S. firms in Europe and to deny entry permits to U.S. executives.

International political relations do not always have harmful effects on international marketers. If bilateral political relations between countries improve, business can benefit. A good example is the thawing of relations between the West and the countries of the former USSR. Political warming has opened up completely new frontiers for U.S. international marketers in Hungary, Poland, and Russia, just to name a few countries. Activities such as selling computers, which would have been considered treasonous only a few years ago, are now routine.

---

[23]Michael R. Czinkota, "International Information Needs for U.S. Competitiveness," *Business Horizons* 34 (November–December 1991): 86–91.

The good international marketer will be aware of political currents worldwide and will attempt to anticipate changes in the international political environment, good or bad, so that his or her firm can plan for them. Sometimes, however, management can only wait until the emotional fervor of conflict has subsided and hope that rational governmental negotiations will let cooler heads prevail.

International Law

International law plays an important role in the conduct of international business. Although no enforceable body of international law exists, certain treaties and agreements respected by a number of countries profoundly influence international business operations. As an example, the World Trade Organization (WTO) defines internationally acceptable economic practices for its member nations. Although it does not directly affect individual firms, it does influence them indirectly by providing a more stable and predictable international market environment.

A number of efforts have been made to simplify the legal aspects of business procedures. For example, firms wanting to patent their products in the past had to register them separately in each country in order to have protection. In response to the chaos and expense of such procedures, several multilateral simplification efforts have been undertaken. European countries have been at the forefront of such efforts with the European Patent Convention and the Community Patent Convention.

Similar efforts have been undertaken with regard to trademarks so that firms can benefit from various multilateral agreements. The two major international conventions on trademarks are the International Convention for the Protection of Industrial Property and the Madrid Arrangement for International Registration of Trademarks. Several regional conventions include the Inter-American Convention for Trademark Protection and a similar agreement in French West Africa.

In addition to multilateral agreements, firms are affected by bilateral treaties and conventions. The United States, for example, has signed bilateral treaties of friendship, commerce, and navigation (FCN) with a wide variety of countries. These agreements generally define the rights of U.S. firms doing business in the host country. They normally guarantee that the U.S. firms will be treated by the host country in the same manner in which domestic firms are treated. Although these treaties provide for some stability, they can be canceled when relationships worsen.

The international legal environment also affects the marketer to the extent that firms must concern themselves with jurisdictional disputes. Because no single body of international law exists, firms usually are restricted by both home and host country laws. If a conflict occurs between contracting parties in two different countries, a question arises concerning which country's laws will be followed. Sometimes the contract will contain a jurisdictional clause, which settles the matter. If not, the parties to the dispute can follow either the laws of the country in which the agreement was made or those of the country in which the contract will have to be fulfilled. Deciding on the laws to be followed and the location to settle the dispute are two different decisions. As a result, a dispute between a U.S. exporter and a French importer could be resolved in Paris with the resolution based on New York State law.

The parties to a business transaction can also choose either arbitration or litigation. Litigation is usually avoided for several reasons. It often involves extensive delays and is very costly. In addition, firms may fear discrimination in foreign countries. Companies therefore tend to prefer conciliation and arbitration because these processes result in much quicker decisions. Arbitration procedures are often spelled out in the original contract and usually provide for an intermediary who is judged to be impartial by both parties. Frequently, intermediaries will be representatives of chambers of commerce, trade associations, or third-country institutions. For example, the rules of the international chamber of commerce in Paris are frequently used for arbitration purposes.

SUMMARY

The political and legal environment in the home country, the environment in the host country, and the laws and agreements governing relationships among nations are all important to the international marketer. Compliance with them is mandatory in order to do business abroad successfully. Such laws can control exports and imports both directly and indirectly, and can also regulate the international business behavior of firms, particularly in the areas of boycotts, antitrust, corruption, and ethics.

To avoid the problems that can result from changes in the political and legal environment, the international marketer must anticipate changes and develop strategies for coping with them. Whenever possible, the manager must avoid being taken by surprise and thus not let events control business decisions.

On occasion, the international marketer may be caught between clashing home and host country laws. In such instances, the firm needs to conduct a dialogue with the governments in order to seek a compromise solution. Alternatively, managers can encourage their government to engage in government-to-government negotiations to settle the dispute. By demonstrating the business volume at stake and the employment that may be lost through such governmental disputes, government negotiators can often be motivated to press hard for a settlement of such intergovernmental difficulties. Finally, the firm can seek redress in court. Such international legal action, however, may be quite slow and, even if resulting in a favorable judgment for the firm, may not be adhered to by the government against which the judgment is rendered.

In the final analysis, a firm conducting business internationally is subject to the vagaries of political and legal changes and may lose business as a result. The best the manager can do is to be aware of political influences and laws and strive to adopt them as far as possible.

QUESTIONS FOR DISCUSSION

1. Discuss this statement: "High political risk requires companies to seek a quick payback on their investments. Striving for such a quick payback, however, exposes firms to charges of exploitation and results in increased political risk."

2. How appropriate is it for governments to help drum up business for their companies abroad? Should commerce not be completely separate from politics?

3. Discuss this statement: "The national security that our export control laws seek to protect may be threatened by the resulting lack of international competitiveness of U.S. firms."

4. After you hand your passport to the immigration officer in country X, he misplaces it. A small "donation" would certainly help him find it again. Should you give him money? Is this a business expense to be charged to your company? Should it be tax deductible?

5. Discuss the advantages and disadvantages of common versus code law for the international marketer.

6. The United States has been described as a "litigious" society. How does frequent litigation affect the international marketer, particularly in comparison with the situation in other countries?

7. What are your views on lobbying efforts by foreign firms?

8. Discuss how changes in technology have affected the effectiveness of U.S. export control policy.

9. Summarize the U.S. export licensing policy toward Cuba. (Go to **www.bxa.doc.gov**.)

10. What are the key components of the anti-corruption agreements passed by the European Union, the Organization of American States, and the United Nations? (Go to **www.oecd.org/daf/nocorruptionweb**.)

RECOMMENDED READINGS

Arend, Anthony Clark, *Legal Rules and International Society*. New York: Oxford University Press, 1999.

Export Administration Annual Report 1998 and *1999 Report on Foreign Policy Export Controls*. Washington DC: U.S. Department of Commerce, Bureau of Export Administration, 1999.

A Global Forum on Fighting Corruption. Washington DC: Bureau for International Narcotics and Law Enforcement Affairs, U.S. Department of State, September 1999.

Haass, Richard N., ed., *Economic Sanctions and American Diplomacy*. New York: Council on Foreign Relations Press, 1998.

Hufbauer, Gary C., Jeffrey J. Schott, and Kimberly Ann Elliott. *Economic Sanctions Reconsidered: History and Current Policy*, 3rd ed. Washington, DC: Institute for International Economics, 2000.

The OECD Guidelines for Multinational Enterprises. Paris: Organization for Economic Cooperation and Development, 2000.

Shambaugh, George E., *States, Firms, and Power: Successful Sanctions in United States Foreign Policy*. Albany: State University of New York Press, 1999.

Global Vendor Relations at Pier 1 Imports

Over 200,000 pieces of stainless steel flatware are just sitting in a Pier 1 Imports warehouse. Where did these come from? Most recently they were stocked in Pier 1 stores—that is until a couple of customers informed store managers that the stainless steel pieces rusted. The company response? After a very rapid testing process that confirmed the customers' observations, the offending product was pulled from all stores and sent to its "resting place"—all within a two-week period.

The people in merchandising at company headquarters in Fort Worth, Texas, and the local Pier 1 agent in China now have ascertained that while there are 47 different types of stainless steel, only one—referred to as 18-8—can be used to make serviceable flatware that won't rust. This newly recognized quality specification has been quickly communicated to all other company agents who purchase flatware, assuring that this product quality issue will not arise again.

It is John Baker's responsibility to oversee the network of corporate buyers and on-site agents who are directly responsible for finding, choosing, and assuring the quality of merchandise imported from around the world. Baker, the Senior Manager of Merchandise Compliance, accepted a position at Pier 1 Imports over twenty years ago after working for various department stores purchasing "tabletop" and kitchen wares. When he first came on board as a buyer, he spent nearly six months of the year on the road, working with the agent network and finding new vendors for Pier 1 merchandise. Today, Baker also handles the increasingly complex area of government regulations of merchandise.

Because such a high percentage of Pier 1 Imports' merchandise is imported (over 85 percent), it is especially critical that U.S. government regulations regarding various product categories be studied and communicated to the manufacturers in other countries. These government regulations form one of the two measures of quality as-surance for Pier 1 products. The second is that the products must conform to aesthetic standards that guarantee that the product fits the Pier 1 image and Pier 1 customer desires. It is in large part the buyer's expertise that assures that these standards are met.

What is the process for finding and selecting vendors in countries other than the United States? First of all, Pier 1 depends upon a well- and long-established network of agents in every country from which they import. In some lesser-developed regions, Pier 1 agents work with governments to help locate professional exporters. Some exporters are found at international trade fairs as well. The bulk of Pier 1 agents are native to the country in which they work, and some have been in place for as long as thirty years with their children now taking over the local positions.

The agents' jobs include finding local producers of handcrafted items that fit the Pier 1 customer needs. Buyers look for new sources of products at local craft fairs and even flea markets. Right now, for example, local agents in several countries are looking for sources of wooden furniture—primarily chests and tables—because Pier 1 would like to add to this in-store category. Based upon the location of raw materials, in this case in Italy, South America, Indonesia, and Thailand, agents are searching for just the right manufacturers to be brought to the buyers' attention.

Because it is the agents based within the various exporting countries who must enforce quality requirements, it is critical that John Baker and his colleagues carefully communicate both governmental and aesthetic product requirements to the agents. The agents can then "sit down at the table" with the manufacturers and work out the quality issues. If misunderstandings occur, Pier 1 is always ready to accept some of the responsibility because they view their manufacturers and agents as their partners in this business.

Because Pier 1 Imports has carefully carved out a unique niche in the specialty retail store industry, buyers are hard to hire from outside the company. As Baker noted, "The bulk of our staff has come out of our stores. It is easy for a buyer to move from Macy's to Hudson's—the products are the same as are most of the vendors. The Pier 1 buyer, however, must understand the Pier 1 store in order to be able to effectively and efficiently buy for it." These Pier 1 buyers, along with their agents on-site around the globe, serve as the company's primary link to product quality.

QUESTIONS FOR DISCUSSION

1. What are the implications for sales, customer satisfaction, and profits for companies like Pier 1 (**http://www. pier1.com**) when low-quality merchandise is not identified early in the purchasing process?

2. Do you think that Pier 1 might have avoided this problem if it had a very aggressive quality assurance program, i.e., ISO 9000, in place?

IKEA in the USA

IKEA, the world's largest home furnishings retail chain, was founded in Sweden in 1943 as a mail-order company and opened its first showroom ten years later. From its headquarters in Almhult, IKEA has since expanded to worldwide sales of $7 billion from 150 outlets in 28 countries (see Table 1). In fact, the second store that IKEA built was in Oslo, Norway. Today, IKEA operates large warehouse showrooms in Sweden, Norway, Denmark, Holland, France, Belgium, Germany, Switzerland, Austria, Canada, the United States, Saudi Arabia, and the United Kingdom. It has smaller stores in Kuwait, Australia, Hong Kong, Singapore, the Canary Islands, and Iceland. A store near Budapest, Hungary, opened in 1990, followed by outlets in Poland, the Czech Republic, and the United Arab Emirates in 1991 and Slovakia in 1992, followed by Taiwan in 1994, Finland and Malaysia in 1996, and mainland China in 1998. IKEA first appeared on the Internet in 1997 with the World

TABLE 1 · IKEA's International Expansion

YEAR	OUTLETS[a]	COUNTRIES[a]	COWORKERS[b]	CATALOG CIRCULATION[c]	TURNOVER IN SWEDISH CROWNS[d]
1954	1	1	15	285,000	3,000,000
1964	2	2	250	1,200,000	79,000,000
1974	10	5	1,500	13,000,000	616,000,000
1984	66	17	8,300	45,000,000	6,770,000,000
1988	75	19	13,400	50,535,000	14,500,000,000
1990	95	23	16,850	n.a.	19,400,000,000
1992	119	24	23,200	n.a.	24,275,000,000
1995	131	27	30,500	n.a.	38,557,000,000
1998	150	28	40,400	n.a.	56,645,000,000

[a]Stores/countries being opened by 1999.

[b]40,400 coworkers are equivalent to 30,500 full-time workers.

[c]17 languages, 28 editions; exact number no longer made available.

[d]Corresponding to net sales of the IKEA group of companies.

SOURCE: IKEA U.S., Inc.

SOURCES: This case, prepared by Ilkka A. Ronkainen, is based on "Furnishing the World," *Economist*, November 19, 1994, 79; Richard Norman and Rafael Ramirez, "From Value Chain to Value Constellation: Designing Interactive Strategy," *Harvard Business Review* 71 (July/August 1993): 65–77; "IKEA's No-Frills Strategy Extends to Management Style," *Business International*, May 18, 1992, 149–150; Bill Saporito, "IKEA's Got 'Em Lining Up," *Fortune*, March 11, 1991, 72; Rita Martenson, "Is Standardization of Marketing Feasible in Culture-Bound Industries? A European Case Study," *International Marketing Review* 4 (Autumn 1987): 7–17; Eleanor Johnson Tracy, "Shopping Swedish Style Comes to the U.S.," *Fortune*, January 27, 1986, 63–67; Mary Krienke, "IKEA—Simple Good Taste," *Stores*, April 1986, 58; Jennifer Lin, "IKEA's U.S. Translation," *Stores*, April 1986, 63; "Furniture Chain Has a Global View," *Advertising Age*, October 26, 1987, 58; Bill Kelley, "The New Wave from Europe," *Sales & Marketing Management*, November 1987, 46–48. Updated information available from **http://www.ikea.com**.

FIGURE 1 IKEA's Worldwide Sales Expressed as Percentages of Turnover by Market Unit

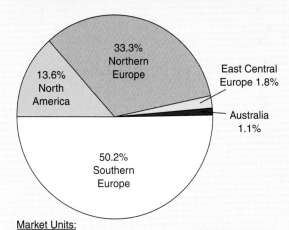

Market Units:
Southern Europe: Austria, France, Germany, Italy, Switzerland
Northern Europe: Belgium, Denmark, Finland, Holland,
                 Norway, Sweden, U.K.
North America: Canada, United States
East Central Europe: Czech Republic, Hungary, Poland,
                    Slovakia

Wide Living Room web site. The first store in Russia opened in March of 2000. The IKEA Group's new organization has three regions: Europe, North America, and Asia-Pacific.

The international expansion of IKEA has progressed in three phases, all of them continuing at the present time: Scandinavian expansion, begun in 1963; West European expansion, begun in 1973; and North American expansion, begun in 1976. Of the individual markets, Germany is the largest, accounting for 24.7 percent, followed by Sweden at 10.7 percent of company sales. The phases of expansion are detectable in the worldwide sales shares depicted in Figure 1. "We want to bring the IKEA concept to as many people as possible," IKEA officials have said. The company estimates that over 100 million people visit its showrooms annually.

The IKEA Concept

Ingvar Kamprad, the founder, formulated as IKEA's mission to "offer a wide variety of home furnishings of good design and function at prices so low that the majority of people can afford to buy them." The principal target market of IKEA, which is similar across countries and regions in which IKEA has a presence, is composed of people who are young, highly educated, liberal in their cultural values, white-collar workers, and not especially concerned with status symbols.

IKEA follows a standardized product strategy with a universally accepted assortment around the world. Today, IKEA carries an assortment of thousands of different home furnishings that range from plants to pots, sofas to soup spoons, and wine glasses to wallpaper. The smaller items are carried to complement the bigger ones. IKEA does not have its own manufacturing facilities but designs all of its furniture. The network of subcontracted manufacturers numbers nearly 2,330 in 64 different countries.

IKEA's strategy is based on cost leadership secured by contract manufacturers, many of whom are in low-labor-cost countries and close to raw materials, yet accessible to logistics links. High-volume production of standardized items allows for significant economies of scale. In exchange for long-term contracts, leased equipment, and technical support from IKEA, the suppliers manufacture exclusively at low prices for IKEA. IKEA's designers work with the suppliers to build savings-generating features into the production and products from the outset.

Manufacturers are responsible for shipping the components to large distribution centers, for example, to the central one in Almhult. These twelve distribution centers then supply the various stores, which are in effect mini-warehouses.

IKEA consumers have to become "prosumers"—half producers, half consumers—because most products have to be assembled. The final distribution is the customer's responsibility as well. Although IKEA expects its customers to be active participants in the buy-sell process, they are not rigid about it. There is a "moving boundary" between what consumers do for themselves and what IKEA employees will do for them. Consumers save the most by driving to the warehouses themselves, putting the boxes on the trolley, loading them into their cars, driving home, and assembling the furniture. Yet IKEA can arrange to provide these services at an extra charge. For example, IKEA cooperates with car rental companies to offer vans and small trucks at reasonable rates for customers needing delivery service. Additional economies are reaped from the size of the IKEA outlets; for example, the Philadelphia store is 169,000 square feet (15,700 square meters). IKEA stores include baby-sitting areas and cafeterias and are therefore intended to provide the value-seeking, car-borne consumer with a complete shopping destination. IKEA managers state that their competitors are not other furniture outlets but all attractions vying for the consumers' free time. By not selling through dealers, the company hears directly from its customers.

Management believes that its designer-to-user relationship affords an unusual degree of adaptive fit. IKEA has "forced both customers and suppliers to think about value in a new way in which customers are also suppliers

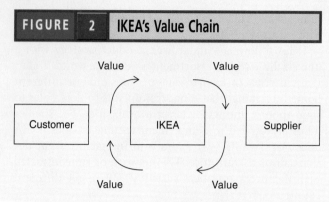

FIGURE 2   IKEA's Value Chain

SOURCE: Richard Norman and Rafael Ramirez, "From Value Chain to Value Constellation: Designing Interactive Strategy," *Harvard Business Review* 71 (July/August 1993): 72.

(of time, labor information, and transportation), suppliers are also customers (of IKEA's business and technical services), and IKEA itself is not so much a retailer as the central star in a constellation of services." Figure 2 provides a presentation of IKEA's value chain.

Although IKEA has concentrated on company-owned, larger-scale outlets, franchising has been used in areas in which the market is relatively small or where uncertainty may exist as to the response to the IKEA concept. These markets include Hong Kong and the United Arab Emirates. IKEA uses mail order in Europe and Canada but has resisted expansion into the United States, mainly because of capacity constraints.

IKEA offers prices that are 30 to 50 percent lower than fully assembled competing products. This is a result of large-quantity purchasing, low-cost logistics, store location in suburban areas, and the do-it-yourself approach to marketing. IKEA's prices do vary from market to market, largely because of fluctuations in exchange rates and differences in taxation regimes, but price positioning is kept as standardized as possible.

IKEA's promotion is centered on the catalog. The IKEA catalog is printed in seventeen languages and has a world-

wide circulation of well over 50 million copies. The catalogs are uniform in layout except for minor regional differences. The company's advertising goal is to generate word-of-mouth publicity through innovative approaches. The IKEA concept is summarized in Table 2.

IKEA in the Competitive Environment

IKEA's strategic positioning is unique. As Figure 3 illustrates, few furniture retailers anywhere have engaged in long-term planning or achieved scale economies in production. European furniture retailers, especially those in Sweden, Switzerland, Germany, and Austria, are much smaller than IKEA. Even when companies have joined forces as buying groups, their heterogeneous operations have made it difficult for them to achieve the same degree of coordination and concentration as IKEA. Because customers are usually content to wait for the delivery of furniture, retailers have not been forced to take purchasing risks.

The value-added dimension differentiates IKEA from its competition. IKEA offers limited customer assistance but creates opportunities for consumers to choose (for example, through informational signage), transport, and assemble units of furniture. The best summary of the competitive situation was provided by a manager at another firm: "We can't do what IKEA does, and IKEA doesn't want to do what we do."

IKEA in the United States

After careful study and assessment of its Canadian experience, IKEA decided to enter the U.S. market in 1985 by establishing outlets on the East Coast and, in 1990, one in Burbank, California. In 1999, a total of 15 stores (eight in the Northeast, five in California, one in Seattle, and

TABLE 2   The IKEA Concept

TARGET MARKET:	"Young people of all ages"
PRODUCT:	IKEA offers the same products worldwide. The number of active articles is 10,600. The countries of origin of these products are: Nordic countries (26 percent), Europe (50 percent), Far East (20 percent), and North America (4 percent). Most items have to be assembled by the customer. The furniture design is modern and light.
DISTRIBUTION:	IKEA has built its own distribution network. Outlets are outside the city limits of major metropolitan areas. Products are not delivered, but IKEA cooperates with car rental companies that offer small trucks. IKEA offers mail order in Europe and Canada.
PRICING:	The IKEA concept is based on low price. The firm tries to keep its price-image constant.
PROMOTION:	IKEA's promotional efforts are mainly through its catalogs. IKEA has developed a prototype communications model that must be followed by all stores. Its advertising is attention-getting and provocative. Media choices vary by market.

FIGURE	3	Competition in Furniture Retailing

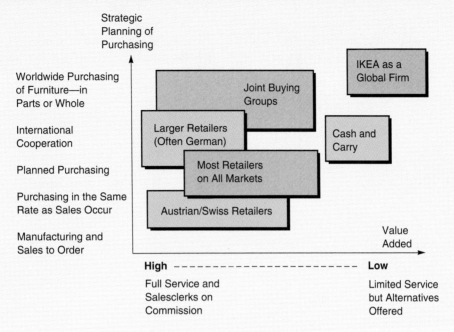

SOURCE: Rita Martenson, "Is Standardization of Marketing Feasible in Culture-Bound Industries? A European Case Study," *International Marketing Review* 4 (Autumn 1987): 14.

one in Texas) generated sales of over $400 million. The stores employ 2,300 workers. The overwhelming level of success in 1987 led the company to invest in a warehousing facility near Philadelphia that receives goods from Sweden as well as directly from suppliers around the world. Plans call for two to three additional stores annually over the next 25 years, concentrating on the northeastern United States and California.

Success today has not come without compromises. "If you are going to be the world's best furnishing company, you have to show you can succeed in America, because there is so much to learn here," said Goran Carstedt, head of North American operations. Whereas IKEA's universal approach had worked well in Europe, the U.S. market proved to be different. In some cases, European products conflicted with American tastes and preferences. For example, IKEA did not sell matching bedroom suites that consumers wanted. Kitchen cupboards were too narrow for the large dinner plates needed for pizza. Some Americans were buying IKEA's flower vases for glasses.

Adaptations were made. IKEA managers adjusted chest drawers to be an inch or two deeper because consumers wanted to store sweaters in them. Sales of chests increased immediately by 40 percent. In all, IKEA has redesigned

approximately a fifth of its product range in North America. Today, 45 percent of the furniture in the stores in North America is produced locally, up from 15 percent in the early 1990s. In addition to not having to pay expensive freight costs from Europe, this has also helped to cut stock-outs. And because Americans hate standing in lines, store layouts have been changed to accommodate new cash registers. IKEA offers a more generous return policy in North America than in Europe, as well as next-day delivery service.

In hindsight, IKEA executives are saying they "behaved like exporters, which meant not really being in the country. . . . It took us time to learn this." IKEA's adaptation has not meant destroying its original formula. Their approach is still to market the streamlined and contemporary Scandinavian style to North America by carrying a universally accepted product range but with a mind on product lines and features that appeal to local preferences. The North American experience has caused the company to start remixing its formula elsewhere as well. Indeed, now that Europeans are adopting some American furnishing concepts (such as sleeper sofas), IKEA is transferring some American concepts to other markets such as Europe.

QUESTIONS FOR DISCUSSION

1. What has allowed IKEA to be successful with a relatively standardized product and product line in a business with strong cultural influence? Did adaptations to this strategy in the North American market constitute a defeat to their approach?

2. Which features of the "young people of all ages" are universal and can be exploited by a global/regional strategy?

3. Is IKEA destined to succeed everywhere it cares to establish itself?

The World Car Market

Cars are as essential to people as the clothes they wear; after a home, a car is the second-largest purchase for many. The car provides more than just instant and convenient personal transportation: it can be a revered design or a sign of success. Developers estimate that 200 yards is the maximum distance an American is prepared to walk before getting into a car. When the Berlin Wall came down, one of the first exercises of a newfound freedom for the former East Germans was to exchange their Trabants and Wartburgs for Volkswagens and Opels.

Western Europe is the largest car market in the world (see Figure 1). But while the car markets of Western Europe, North America, and Japan account for 90 percent of the vehicles sold, these markets are quite saturated. Early in the twenty-first century, for example, there will probably be one car per person aged 20–64 in North America.

Two general approaches will become evident. First, car manufacturers need to sell fewer cars, but more profitably. Secondly, they need to look for new markets. In the coming decades market growth will come from Asia, Eastern and Central Europe, and Latin America. China and India will eventually provide millions of new drivers. These new realities will have a profound impact on the car market and its players in the future. For a long time, U.S. and European car makers neglected Asian markets, allowing them to become largely a Japanese preserve, but belatedly they are attempting to gain lost ground. General Motors is using its European Opel division to spearhead expansion into Asia. Assembly operations have started in Taiwan, Indonesia, and India. All leading producers are lining up to start or expand their operations in China.

In 1986, the Massachusetts Institute of Technology started a study that was published in a book, *The Machine that Changed the World*. The results showed that the Japanese took less time to make a car with fewer defects than the Americans or the Europeans. The main differences were due to the way factories were organized, as shown in Table 1. The higher productivity of the Japanese has given them an overwhelming advantage: though they have not used it to cut prices, it has given them more profit per car than competitors get. As earnings mount, they can spend more to develop better cars or build the sales networks they need to expand sales. For example, Japanese car companies cut prices by 1.1 percent in the 1997 model year, while Detroit hiked them up an average 2.8 percent.

Cars have also become a global business on the manufacturing front, as seen in Table 2. Japanese vehicle manufacturers have transferred more and more of their production abroad, first to North America, then Europe, and then to Southeast Asia. Economic pressures and the appreciation of the yen have accelerated the Japanese expansion overseas. For example, since the 1980s the Japanese have built in the United States an auto industry larger than that of the United Kingdom, Italy, or Spain (15 percent of U.S. car production is now coming from Japanese-owned plants). Japanese producers account for a quarter of U.K. car production. U.S. manufacturers have themselves restructured to remain competitive. Ford has undertaken a sweeping restructuring of its operations, hoping to run it as a single automotive company to reap benefits of scale and scope. The Europeans are following suit. The Volkswagen Group, Europe's biggest maker, is planning to reduce the number of platforms (from which all of its car ranges are derived) from a present sixteen to four to cut costs and to simplify global

SOURCES: This case was prepared by Ilkka A. Ronkainen. It is largely based on "The Endless Road," *Economist*, October 17, 1992, 1–8; "On Guard, Europe," *Business Week*, December 14, 1992, 54–55; Carla Rapoport, "Europe Takes On the Japanese," *Fortune*, January 11, 1993, 14–18; "Back to the Way We Were," *Economist*, November 6, 1993, 83–84; "World Car Industry," *Financial Times Survey*, October 4, 1994; "Asian Carmakers' European Plan," *Business Week*, November 7, 1994; Louis Kraar, "Korea's Automakers," *Fortune*, March 6, 1995, 152–164; and "Detroit Is Getting Sideswiped by the Yen," *Business Week*, November 11, 1996, 54.

FIGURE   1   World Car Sales by Region, 1992–2002 (in Millions of Cars)

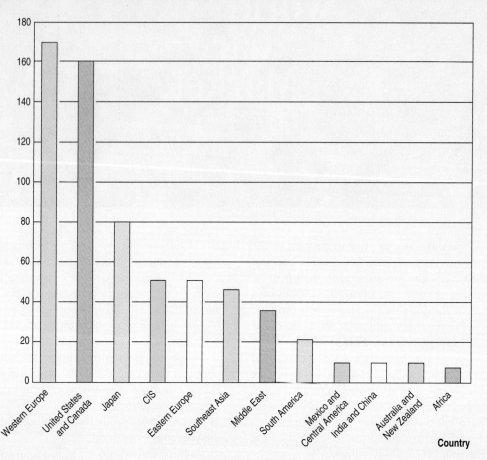

SOURCE: "The Car Industry: In Trouble Again," *Economist*, October 17, 1992, 4.

manufacturing activities. Daimler-Chrysler will launch a range of cars into new segments of the world market, including a four-wheel drive sports utility vehicle assembled in the United States. Inevitably the restructuring in the car industry will lead to new alliances and mergers, although the progress has not been smooth in the past for such endeavors.

 ## The European Car Market

The "1992" process was to have opened up the European car market to competition by December 31, 1992. However, largely due to the performance gap between the Europeans and the Japanese producers, the European Commission has pushed the dismantling of trade barriers to the end of 1999. This has taken the form of voluntary quotas, which for 1995 was 993,000 cars. The Europeans fear that while all the Japanese car makers to-

gether just barely equal the share of number two General Motors, things could change rapidly in a market where no one company has even a 20 percent market share (see Figure 2).

Japanese car manufacturers are also hindered in Europe due to exclusive dealerships; that is, dealers are not allowed to sell competing brands. Car manufacturers argue that such arrangements are critical in protecting the character, quality, and service of their cars. In practice, this means that outsiders would have to develop distribution systems from scratch. The European Commission has granted a block exemption for this practice from the antitrust provisions of the Treaty of Rome.

Behind the protectionism is that European car makers want to avoid the fate of their American counterparts a decade earlier, when Japanese market share jumped from 20 to 32 percent in the United States. By the end of the 1990s, the Japanese could be producing more than 1.5 million cars in Europe. Added to growing imports

TABLE	1	Differences in Car Manufacturing

	AVERAGE* FOR CAR PLANTS IN:		
	JAPAN	UNITED STATES	EUROPE
PERFORMANCE			
Productivity (hours per car)	16.8	25.1	36.2
Quality (defects per 100 cars)	60	82	97
LAYOUT			
Factory space (per sq ft per car per year)	5.7	7.8	7.8
Size of repair area (as % of assembly space)	4.1	12.9	14.4
Stocks**	0.2	2.9	2
EMPLOYEES			
Workforce in teams (%)	69.3	17.3	0.6
Suggestions (per employee per year)	61.6	0.4	0.4
Number of job classifications	12	67	15
Training of new workers (hours)	380	46	173
AUTOMATION (% OF PROCESS AUTOMATED)			
Welding	86	76	77
Painting	55	34	38
Assembly	2	1	3

*1989

**for eight sample parts

SOURCE: "The Secrets of the Production Line," *Economist*, October 17, 1992, 6.

TABLE	2	Leading World Passenger Automobile Producers (in Millions)

COUNTRY	1994	1995
Japan	7,801.3	7,613.1
United States	6,601.0	6,329.7
Germany	4,093.7	4,360.2
France	3,175.2	3,050.9
Spain	1,497.6	1,958.2
South Korea	1,453.6	1,892.5
Great Britain	1,466.8	1,532.1
Italy	1,111.0	1,422.4
Canada	1,215.8	1,348.3
Brazil	1,249.3	1,307.7
Belgium	798.9	1,189.7
Mexico	840.0	710.1

SOURCE: David J. Wallace, "Specialize or Perish," *World Trade*, October 1996, 30.

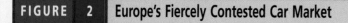

FIGURE   2   Europe's Fiercely Contested Car Market

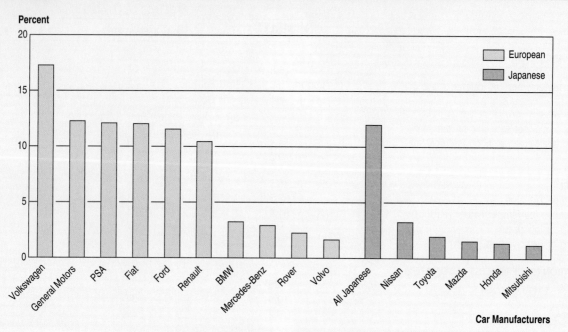

SOURCE: Carla Rapoport, "Europe Takes On the Japanese," *Fortune*, January 11, 1993, 14.

from Japan, Japanese market share could grow to 18 percent of the market from 12 percent in 1993. In addition, the Brussels-based European Automobile Association fears that 360,000 autos could be imported into the European Union by the year 2000—almost triple of 1993. These prospects have stirred both protectionist impulses, especially in France and Italy, and new competitiveness by the European producers.

Both in France and in Italy, the car industry is one of the national champions that have fared well in protected markets but are relative weaklings in the global marketplace. Italy's Fiat, for example, produces about 4 percent of the country's GNP, which makes it impossible for the government to let it go down. In France, Jacques Calvet, the chairman of PSA (producer of Peugeot and Citroën) has repeatedly called for prohibiting new Japanese transplant factories in Europe, strict quotas, and freezing Japanese market share within the European Union.

More alarming for the Europeans is their loss of share outside of Europe. France's Renault and PSA have completely written off the U.S. market, believing that they can prosper with a strong European base while holding off the Japanese. Even some of the European premium brands, such as Mercedes-Benz and Volvo, have been steadily losing share in the growing luxury segment of the U.S. market. Some have faith in their own markets. One auto executive forecast by saying: "The French are,

well, so French. I don't think foreign cars, especially Japanese cars will do well in France. Not in our lifetime."

Globalization and Realignment in the Auto Industry

Globalization has become a central reality for car makers and suppliers. Acquisition is now the name of the game for the biggest players in the industry, who wish to spread costs across increasingly global operations. In 1998, there were 320 mergers and acquisitions in the industry at a disclosed value of $30.4 billion, almost twice as many as in 1997. After Daimler-Benz and Chrysler merged in 1998, others followed suit. Ford bought Volvo and Land Rover, General Motors bought all of Saab and part of Subaru, and Volkswagen acquired Lamborghini, Rolls Royce, Bentley, and Bugatti. The Korean car makers are expected to be acquired by either U.S. or European players. Even well-established manufacturers, such as BMW, may not be safe—their smaller size may not allow them to survive in the competitive environment of the twenty-first century. While luxury cars are among the most profitable segments in the industry, dominant players acquire them to run as independent subsidiaries, while helping them procure parts as part of the larger entity.

QUESTIONS FOR DISCUSSION

1. What must the European car manufacturers do to face the global realities of their industry to survive and succeed? Would you agree with Paul Ingrassia and Joseph White, authors of *Comeback: The Fall and Rise of the American Automobile Industry*, who state that "while Detroit decried free trade as a threat to its existence, free trade is what saved Detroit by forcing it to improve"?

2. Two of the largest car manufacturers in Europe are General Motors and Ford. Neither has been targeted by European Commission moves, and they are not generally seen as a threat. Why?

3. What will the realignment of the auto industry mean to governments, car makers, and customers?

Hong Kong: The Market of the Future or No Future

The People's Republic of China (PRC) and Hong Kong are inextricably linked. Looking at the past, there are abundant reasons for the relationship to be one of pride and fear (see Table 1 for a time line). In fact, many will argue that Beijing never recognized Hong Kong's separation from the mainland after the Opium War in 1842. As a result of long-standing economic and cultural relationships—primarily between southern China and Hong Kong —some considered the reunification of July 1, 1997, mainly a symbolic flag-raising ceremony. What that symbolism meant is debated. "Hong Kong took over China, not the other way around," says a representative of the Hong Kong Trade Development Council, while an American businessman well entrenched in China and its system warns: "Hong Kong may be the scapegoat for what Chinese leaders perceive as Western injustice."

Although recent Eastern European history offers numerous examples of command economies giving way to market-oriented systems, it is difficult to predict what will happen in the long term when a command economy—the PRC—takes over an unbridled bastion of capitalism—Hong Kong. "There are bound to be, on both sides, uncertainties, and there are bound to be suspicions," said Sir David Wilson, governor of Hong Kong from 1987 to 1992. "This whole process is something which is unprecedented in terms of world history. There are no international historical blueprints to go by. We have to find our own way." However, by the third anniversary of the reunification, the consensus is that very little has changed.

The 1984 Sino-British Joint Declaration and Basic Law that returned Hong Kong to Chinese sovereignty in 1997 makes it a Special Administrative Region (SAR) of China for at least fifty years, presumably enough time for the two political and economic systems to mesh. China has also pledged that Hong Kong would be run largely by its own people under the concept of "one country, two systems." This means continuing the system of an elected government, rule of law, independent courts, and wide personal freedoms. The SAR will be run by a chief executive selected among longtime Chinese residents of Hong Kong. Hong Kong will remain a free port and separate customs territory and will be able to decide on and conduct its own economic policies. This will be evident in practice through Hong Kong keeping its own currency and retaining its separate membership in the World Trade Organization (WTO).

Hong Kong as a Business Center

Hong Kong is the world's tenth largest trading nation and the third largest financial center. In an area of just over 400 square miles, it has a population of 6.2 million. Its per capita income is over $25,300, second in Asia after Japan. It's the world's largest free port and top-ranking manufacturer and exporter of textiles, clothing, and toys. No other business center in the Asia-Pacific is as friendly to business, offering free trade, free enterprise, a well-educated work force, a policy of "positive nonintervention" in trade matters, and low taxes. Hong Kong has been ranked by the Heritage Foundation as the freest economy in the world consistently throughout the 1990s. For a summary of Hong Kong economic facts, see Table 2.

SOURCES: This case study was written by Ilkka A. Ronkainen and funded in part by a grant from the Business and International Education Program of the U.S. Department of Education. The assistance of the U.S. Consulate in Hong Kong, Inchcape Pacific, the Customs and Excise Department of the Hong Kong Government, the Hong Kong Trade Development Council, and the Hong Kong Economic and Trade Office in Washington, D.C., is also appreciated. For additional information, see http://www.info.gov.hk.

TABLE 1	**Hong Kong and China: A Time Line**

214 B.C. *China Takes Hong Kong* China colonized Hong Kong under emperor Qin Shi Huangdi—the powerful ruler in the north credited with first uniting the kingdom. However, Hong Kong remained a backwater.

1842 *The Opium War* China ceded Hong Kong island to the British under the Treaty of Nanjing. Subsequent treaties gave Britain permanent use of Kowloon Peninsula in 1860 and a ninety-nine-year lease of the New Territories starting in 1898. Chinese consider this period one of national shame and weakness.

THE 1900s *Hong Kong Emerges as a Port* Hong Kong's role as a transit port to China grew, as did its population, swelled by refugees fleeing civil war and the Japanese invasion of the mainland. Hong Kong boomed in the post–World War II era, and a class of Chinese business leaders emerged.

1949 *Communism Sweeps the Mainland* The Communist victory on the mainland resulted in an exodus to Hong Kong of many of China's capitalists, landowners, and entrepreneurs. Later, China's failed economic policies cause more people to cross the border.

1978 *China Opens Up, Hong Kong Cashes In* Economic reforms by Deng Xiaoping included special economic zones, one of which is across the border from Hong Kong, and businesses from the territory were the first to invest there. While benefiting from the transit trade, Hong Kong started changing into a financial center.

1984 *The Sino-British Joint Declaration* The agreement between China and Britain provided for the return of Chinese rule under a "one country–two systems" scheme. Hong Kong is to pay no taxes to Beijing and will remain a free port and financial center, with laws left unchanged for fifty years.

1989 *Tiananmen* Beijing's military crushed pro-democracy protests and cast a dark shadow across Hong Kong's return to China.

1990 *The Basic Law* The National People's Congress—China's lawmaking body—passed the Basic Law for Hong Kong, which is to become the constitution after the changeover. A broad article on treason could undermine other promises made in the document.

1992 *Face-Off with Beijing* Electoral reforms made by Governor Chris Patten turned relations with Beijing sour, complicating projects such as the new airport at Chek Lap Kok.

1993 *A Key Arrest* Beijing arrested Hong Kong–based journalist Xi Yang while he was reporting in the mainland and sentenced him to twelve years for subversion. This sent chills through the press in Hong Kong.

1995 *Democrats Win Elections* Under the new election scheme, Democrats won 16 of the 20 directly elected seats in the 60-member Legislative Council. Beijing swore to disband the council in 1997.

1996 *The Shadow Government* Beijing's response to the election was to form the Preparatory Committee—a group of 150 handpicked mainland officials and Hong Kong residents. Working parallel with the Legislative Council, it selected a 400-strong body of Hong Kong people who, in turn, chose the post-1997 chief executive to replace the governor of Hong Kong, shipping tycoon Tung Chee Hwa.

1997 *The Handover* On midnight July 1, a joint ceremony in the new convention center marked the "dignified departure" of the British. A provisional legislature, chosen by the Preparatory Committee, took the place of the Legislative Council. Tung Chee Hwa becomes first chief executive.

1998 *Hong Kong Elections* The first major test of Beijing's hands-off promise occurred when Hong Kong residents went to the polls for the first time in the postcolonial era.

1999 *Portugal Returns Macao* Macao returned to China December 31, 1999. Beijing is trying hard, alternating with carrot and stick, to forge a reunification agreement with Taiwan.

SOURCE: "Coming Full Circle," *MSNBC*, October 21, 1996.

For more information refer to **http://www.scmp.com**.

The economy as a whole is externally oriented and its growth and well-being depend mainly on its trade performance. Apart from trade in goods, trade in services also contributes significantly to Hong Kong's growth. Given its strategic location and well-established infrastructure and business contacts, Hong Kong has developed into a center for trade, finance, communications, and business services for the entire Asia-Pacific region.

The Hong Kong government plays no favorites, putting foreign policy and locally owned companies on the same footing. While there are no special incentives offered to overseas business to relocate, formalities to setting up a business are kept to as few as possible. There are no regulations concerning the minimum capital requirement of a company, or any regulations concerning the relative degree of local/overseas participation in the ownership of

TABLE	2	Hong Kong Essential Facts

POPULATION	6.2 million
GDP PER CAPITA	$25,300
FOREIGN EXCHANGE RESERVES	$57 billion
TOTAL EXPORTS	$173.4 billion
DOMESTIC EXPORTS	$29.5 billion
RE-EXPORTS	$143.9 billion
IMPORTS	$193.3 billion
U.S. EXPORTS TO HONG KONG	$11.6 billion
U.S. IMPORTS FROM HONG KONG	$35.2 billion
PRINCIPAL U.S. EXPORTS	Electrical machinery, resins and plastic materials, transport equipment, office machines, tobacco manufactures
PRINCIPAL U.S. IMPORTS	Garments, electronics, office machines, photographic apparatus, electrical machinery
U.S. INVESTMENT IN HONG KONG	$13 billion
U.S. EXPATRIATES IN HONG KONG	23,500
U.S. FIRMS WITH OFFICES/ PLANTS IN HONG KONG	900
CHINESE INVESTMENT IN HONG KONG	$25 billion
HONG KONG INVESTMENT IN CHINA	$133 billion

the company. The Hong Kong government assists in finding suitable local partners for joint ventures. Likewise, there are no regulations concerning the relative proportion of local to overseas staff that may be employed. Typically, however, the high cost of living (i.e., mainly housing) discourages companies from using a large number of expatriates. There are no restrictions on foreign exchange or on transferring capital or profits in or out of the colony.

The Economic Interdependence of Hong Kong and China

Existing Hong Kong–PRC economic ties will set the pattern for future developments. The PRC is currently Hong Kong's largest trading partner and its main source of investment capital. Hong Kong has evolved as the "International Division of China Inc."—both in managing China's exports and importing foreign goods for re-export to China. Approximately 70 percent of China's annual exports to the United States pass through Hong Kong in the form of re-exports. Hong Kong's established

business and social connections with both China and the rest of the world, excellent telecommunications and transportation facilities, and financial sophistication make it uniquely suited to its role as facilitator. An important part of this facilitation is to serve as an intermediary in trade between China and Taiwan.

Since the PRC implemented an "open door" policy in the 1980s, Hong Kong's and outsiders' economic importance to China has increased. There are now 84,000 foreign-funded enterprises in China, most of them in the south. These enterprises are estimated to account for 25 percent of all of China's foreign trade. The economic development of southern China—especially the Pearl River Delta in Guangdong Province and the coastal economic zones—has been the catalyst for China's economy to grow by almost 10 percent a year since 1978.

Guangdong Province itself has for the last ten years averaged real annual growth of a stunning 15 percent. Although the province has less than half a percent of China's land and a mere 16 million of its 1.2 billion people, it accounts for 5 percent of total industrial output and 10 percent of exports. Per capita income in Guangdong Province is roughly $600, double that of China as a whole. The star of the province is Shenzhen, a city across the border from Hong Kong, set up as a special economic zone by Beijing in 1979. Shenzhen residents enjoy rapidly increasing per capita incomes of $800, which is expected to increase to $2,800 by the year 2000. Figure 1 provides a summary of the major business centers of the Pearl River Delta.

During its thirty-year-old drive to attract foreign direct investment, estimated total realized investment reached $220 billion. About 60 percent is estimated to have come from or through Hong Kong. A full 80 percent of Hong Kong manufacturers have set up labor-intensive production facilities across the border. Hong Kong companies operating in Southern China now employ about four million people—more than ten times the number of manufacturing sector workers in Hong Kong itself. More than 60,000 Hong Kong managers, professionals, technicians, and supervisors are currently working in China. In addition, 20 percent of Hong Kong's currency circulation takes place in Guangdong Province.

At the same time, China is increasing its stake in Hong Kong. China is the biggest investor ($25 billion) in the economy, ahead of the United States and Japan, with major investments in the aviation sector (e.g., a majority ownership in Cathay Pacific), telecommunications, and property. As a matter of fact, it is estimated that PRC buyers controlled 20 percent of the Hong Kong property market by the time the takeover occured. The Bank of China, which is the second largest banking group (after Hong Kong Bank) in Hong Kong, currently issues Hong Kong's currency notes, fully backed by foreign exchange deposits with the Hong Kong government.

FIGURE	1	The Fastest-Growing Economy on Earth

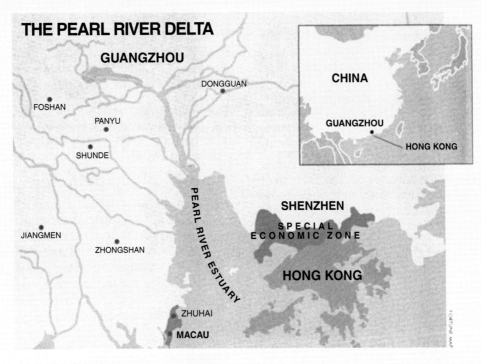

China's Economic and Consumer Boom

Economic growth in China has been rapid: GNP growth has been over 10 percent consistently in the 1990s. China's exports totaled $183 billion, imports $140 billion, resulting in a trade surplus of $43 billion in 1998.

Despite the austerity measures introduced in the summer of 1993 to cool down the economy, strong growth is still continuing. This growth is bringing affluence to many parts of China, not just the major cities, such as Guangzhou, Shanghai, and Beijing. Examples of the changes this growth is bringing include:

- Retail sales in China surged 10 percent in the early 1990s to approximately $200 billion. By the year 2000, annual retail sales are projected to have reached $600 billion.
- Department stores display a wide variety of consumer goods and are overflowing with eager consumers. Traffic through some of China's department stores is well over 100,000 people per day.
- For a working couple in Guangdong Province, monthly household income may be 1,200 yuan ($210). Although Ferrero Rochet chocolates sell for 68 yuan, and a pack of Brand's Essence of Chicken

is priced at 100 yuan, they sell very well to a broad range of customers.

While incomes in China are low by Western standards and by those in the developed economies of the Asia-Pacific, the proportion of disposable income is high as are savings. Living expenses take only 5 percent or less of family income in China, while the comparable figure in Hong Kong is 40 percent. There is tremendous pent-up demand for consumer goods among the population, who have had nothing to spend their money on for many years. Private savings are high even by Asian standards and amount to one-third of an average worker's annual income.

Chinese consumers are quality conscious. Joint-venture products (such as Head & Shoulders, Tang, and Pepsi-Cola) are perceived as quality items and often command double or triple the price of goods produced solely by Chinese companies.

In developing a strategy for China, companies such as Inchcape Pacific (which acts as a marketer and distributor for many companies including Cadbury's, SmithKline-Beecham, and Kellogg's) consider approaching China as one big market a mistake. Inchape's priority markets are Southern China (Pearl River Delta), Eastern China (Shanghai, Nanjing, and Hangzhou), and North China (Beijing, Tianjin, and Dalian). The rationale is that each is a very separate and different market from the others in terms of people, culture, dialect, way of life, climate, and diet. Most importantly, each is a huge consumer market in its own right. The sheer size and the logistics problems make national distribution in China an impossibility.

Taking advantage of this opportunity requires flexibility. Changes in the regulatory environment create both opportunities and challenges. Contacts have to be cultivated beyond the central government in Beijing. Provincial and municipal authorities enjoy autonomy and influence and tend to be quite entrepreneurial. The municipal government usually supports or has very close links with a few companies in its area. A potential entrant needs to develop good relations with these officials and the business leaders in the local companies.

Hong Kong–U.S. Business Links

The overall key to Asia is access—access to markets and market information. For many U.S. companies, Hong Kong's strategic location, developed infrastructure, and commercial expertise provide the best bang for the buck in Asia. Markets in Asia, China in particular, lack a solid legal framework for business and rely more on personal relationships. Leading overseas Chinese entrepreneurs can be invaluable facilitators because they operate through a network of personal contacts. Procter & Gamble, for example, got into the Chinese market in 1988 by forming an alliance with Hong Kong businessman Li Ka-shing.

More than 900 U.S. companies have operations in Hong Kong at present, more than double the number of five years earlier. Virtually every Fortune 500 company that does business in the Asia-Pacific region maintains a presence in Hong Kong, usually a regional headquarters. A good example of this is Polaroid Far East Limited. A wholly owned subsidiary of Polaroid Corporation, Polaroid Far East Limited's Hong Kong office is headquarters for a region that covers South Korea, Singapore, Malaysia, Taiwan, China, Indonesia, Thailand, and India. The Hong Kong office, which opened in 1971 and now has sixty-nine employees, controls finance, sales and marketing, and personnel.

Hong Kong is a major market for U.S.-made goods in its own right. As a matter of fact, Hong Kong imports more U.S. goods per capita than any country in the world—four times the level of Japan, five times that of Europe. Some of the major categories of traded goods can be found in Table 2.

Hong Kong also represents a convenient stepping-stone to China. Polaroid recently announced a manufacturing joint venture in Shanghai to produce consumer cameras for export. In addition to manufacturing cameras, Polaroid hopes to develop the Chinese domestic market for document photography. Hong Kong's role is to provide training for the new operation in China as well as sales and marketing support. C. C. Chan, sales and marketing manager for the Polaroid Far East China Trade Department, thinks most people in the PRC are still unfamiliar with free market Western-style business. "Hong Kong brings China closer to the world," says Chan.

Some of the other firms in the market are:

- Campbell's Soup, which opened a $500,000 R&D center to spearhead its thrust into the Asia-Pacific. The new center will be developing a wide range of canned products for the Chinese palate. The operation is also intended as a springboard into China.
- Motorola, the world's fourth largest semiconductor manufacturer, opened a multimillion-dollar state-of-the-art chip-manufacturing plant in Hong Kong. The plant will supply the entire Pacific Rim, which is a $14 billion market for semi-conductors.
- Waste Management International has a 70 percent stake in a consortium that won a multimillion-dollar contract to build and operate Asia's first chemical waste treatment facility in Hong Kong.

The Other Side of the Coin: Macro and Micro Challenges

Hong Kong's economy suffered badly as a result of the June 4, 1989, crackdown on student dissidents on Tiananmen Square. "The events reminded people of the uncertainty, risk, and lack of predictability in dealing with Beijing," says Robert Dorsee, vice president and managing director of Tyco (Hong Kong) Ltd., a division of American-owned Tyco Toys Inc.

The concerns grew as the changeover on July 1, 1997, got closer. In October 1992, the present governor of Hong Kong, Chris Patten, put forth proposals that would further democratic reform in Hong Kong by allowing more participation by the Hong Kong Chinese in the selection of members of the local legislature (the Legislative Council). The Chinese government objected ferociously on the grounds that major changes were a violation of the Joint Declaration, and that the proposed reforms were in breach of the Basic Law. Rhetoric from Beijing went as far as to suggest that the treaty with Britain be "scattered to the wind," and even that China might grab control over the colony even before 1997. Although discussions were held to resolve the disagreement, the confidence of people both in Hong Kong and those interested in investing there was shaken. For example, the Hong Kong Electronics Association, whose members do most of their manufacturing in the crown colony, sponsored trips to the Philippines, Malaysia, and Thailand to study the climate for new investments in those Asian nations. One of their concerns was that export control rules

TABLE 3	Hong Kong's Possible Roles (before and after 1997)

- Hong Kong will continue developing its entrepôt role—as the international marketing arm of China.
- Hong Kong is not just the world's gateway to China, it is also China's springboard to the world.
- Hong Kong has the knowledge and experience of international business; through Hong Kong, China can better understand how international business operates and what the expectations are.
- Hong Kong will continue acting as a broker for international firms looking to set up in China, often in three-way joint ventures.
- Hong Kong will continue to provide a secure base for capital.
- Hong Kong could also develop as China's own "Silicon Valley," providing R&D for China's expanding industrial sector. In the information arena, it can become the "cyberport" of Asia. It can also train mainland staff in Hong Kong or provide on-the-job training in China.
- Hong Kong's role as the link between Taiwan and China will also continue in the foreseeable future.

SOURCE: Adapted from Stephen Clark, "Hong Kong's Role in the Development of Greater China," presentation given July 30, 1993, Chinese University of Hong Kong.

would cut their access to Western technology once China took over. China's rough tactics also endangered its already shaky most-favored-nation (MFN) status with the United States, and the discussion of moving to "permanent and normal trading relations."

The latter concern points out the fact that the greatest threat to Hong Kong may not come from China but from the United States. China's trade surplus with the United States reached $56.9 billion in 1999 (up from $24.9 billion in 1993), a major irritant in the countries' trade relations. In October 1992, the two governments reached an agreement on market access (so-called 301 investigation), under which China pledged to liberalize its foreign trade regime. About 75 percent of the nontariff barriers were eliminated by 1994, the rest by 1997. Tariffs would also be reduced. The agreement did not, however, clear the way for China to join the WTO, as differences of opinion still remain between China and the United States, as well as the EU.

If China loses its MFN status with the United States because of its human rights record or concerns over protectionism, military goods exports, and intellectual property, Hong Kong will suffer the most. This is why a special Hong Kong Business Mission has lobbied in Washington for the renewal of China's MFN status every time it has been up. U.S. exports would also suffer as China would undoubtedly retaliate with higher tariffs. When China lost its bid to host the 2000 Olympic Games,

U.S. exporters worried about negative trade measures as a response to the opposition to the bid by the U.S. Congress. Similarly, when the Chinese embassy in Belgrade was accidentally bombed in 1999, many worried about the long-term effects on U.S.–China trade.

In the long term, many hope that the statement by Lu Ping, director of China's Hong Kong and Macau Affairs office, holds true in the positive sense: "Hong Kong is bound up with its Motherland. It will serve as a bridge, channel, and window between China and the rest of the world, and play its unique and positive role in China's development in the next century."

Whatever happens, Hong Kong is a Special Administrative Region of the People's Republic of China. Beijing will determine whether Hong Kong remains and grows as an open international business hub. It is already the unofficial commercial capital of the Overseas Chinese. For U.S. firms, Hong Kong will be the place to find appropriate partners and connections to enter the Chinese market. In many ways, Hong Kong's roles are, and continue to be, critical, as seen in the summary provided in Table 3.

However, if Beijing reneges on its guarantee that Hong Kong can retain its position as China's capitalist gateway to the world, not only will Hong Kong become a backwater for global business, but China itself will be hurt in terms of attracting foreign direct investment and its most-favored-nation status with the United States.

QUESTIONS FOR DISCUSSION

1. Would you agree or disagree with the following statement from the U.S. Information Agency in Hong Kong: "The reality, beyond the newspaper headlines, is that China is not going to kill the golden goose."
2. What are Hong Kong's benefits for a Western company that would make a move to the Philippines or Thailand undesirable or difficult?
3. Provide a possible strategy for a U.S. company operating in Hong Kong to leverage against political risk.
4. What are the benefits of using Hong Kong as a base for entering and marketing in the Chinese market?

REFERENCES

Auerbach, Stuart. "Toy-Making Losing in China Some Appeal." *The Washington Post*, December 2, 1989, D11–13.

The Basic Law of the Hong Kong Special Administrative Region of the People's Republic of China. Hong Kong: The Consultative Committee for the Basic Law of the Hong Kong Special Administrative Region of the People's Republic of China, April 1990.

"Campbell Soup Targets Asia with New R&D Center." *Business International*, January 27, 1992.

Cheng, Paul M. F. "Gateway to Greater China." Sydney, Australia: Presentation made to the 36th CIES Annual Executive Congress, April 22–24, 1993.

"China at a Boiling Point." *The Economist*, July 10, 1993, 15.

Conley, Kirsta. "Hong Kong: Business Center of the Future." *Export Today* 7 (February 1991): 20–22.

Country Report: China, Mongolia, second quarter. The Economist Intelligence Unit, 1993.

Establishing an Office in Hong Kong. 6th ed. Hong Kong: The American Chamber of Commerce in Hong Kong, 1989.

Johnson, W. Todd. "Hong Kong Exporter's Gateway to China." *Export Today* 7 (June 1991): 18–22.

Joint Declaration of the Government of the United Kingdom of Great Britain and Northern Ireland and the Government of the People's Republic of China on the Question of Hong Kong. Hong Kong: Hong Kong Government Information Services, December 1984.

Kraar, Louis. "Asia 2000." *Fortune*, October 5, 1992, 111–142.

———. "Storm over Hong Kong." *Fortune*, March 8, 1993, 98–105.

———. "Strategies that Win in Asia." *Fortune*, Fall 1991, 49–56.

Mutch, Andrew J. "Hong Kong: Tapping into the Dynamic Dragon." *Export Today* 9 (January/February 1993): 30–34.

Setting Up Business in Hong Kong. Hong Kong: Hong Kong General Chamber of Commerce, 1990.

Worthy, Ford S. "Where Capitalism Thrives in China." *Fortune*, March 9, 1992, 71–75.

U.S. Tobacco Exports: A New Perspective

Tobacco and its related products have traditionally played an important role in the U.S. economy. In 1997, tobacco represented the fifth largest cash crop in the United States. Twenty-three U.S. states and Puerto Rico grow tobacco, 21 states manufacture tobacco products, 33 states export tobacco, and all 50 states are engaged in the marketing of tobacco products.

In 1964, the *Surgeon General's Report* documented the adverse health effects of smoking. Since then, many medical experts have repeatedly warned the public that smoking causes lung cancer, low birth weights, and other health problems. As a result of increased awareness of the consequences of smoking, U.S. cigarette consumption, as well as other forms of tobacco use, have been gradually decreasing. Although health considerations played an important role in discouraging smoking, other factors such as higher cigarette prices, steeper federal and local taxes, and governmental restrictions on smoking in public places also contributed to this decline. Since reaching a peak in 1981, total domestic cigarette consumption declined by nearly 22 percent, and per capita consumption by nearly 31 percent. However, in 1995, there were still about 50 million cigarette consumers in the United States who bought over 485 billion pieces of cigarettes for $45 billion.

 ## The Importance of Tobacco for the U.S. Economy

Taxes on tobacco products contribute significantly to government income and help reduce the budget deficit. As the number of smokers has declined, the government has raised the cigarette tax in order to preserve the level of tax revenues from smoking. The cigarette tax was raised from 8 cents per pack of 20 cigarettes in the period between 1951 and 1982 to 16 cents from 1983 to 1990, 20 cents from 1991 to 1992 and, finally, 24 cents per pack as of January 1993. In 1995, the tobacco production and related industries contributed over $35 billion to government revenues in excise, sales, personal income, and corporate taxes. Out of this amount, nearly $6 billion (25 percent of total federal excise taxes) was generated by the federal excise tax on tobacco and $9 billion by state and local excise taxes. This means that about 31 percent of the retail price of tobacco products in the United States ends up in the treasuries of the federal and local governments (see Figure 1).

According to a study by the Tobacco Merchants Association, the tobacco industry, including growers, manufacturers, distributors, and core suppliers, employed over 690,000 people in 1996. In addition, 2.4 million jobs were generated as a result of the tobacco industry's expenditures such as promotion and transportation.

 ## The Importance of Tobacco Exports

In the face of their diminishing domestic market, U.S. tobacco companies are vigorously promoting cigarette exports. Developing countries are the home to most of the world's smokers and are therefore the number one target for cigarette exports (see Table 1). The international cigarette market is dominated by U.S. brands (see Table 2). However, U.S. companies would be able to sell even more

SOURCES: This study was prepared by Michael R. Czinkota and Veronika Cveckova, using the following background material: Foreign Agricultural Service statistics; "World Cigarette Situation" by the FAS; "Tobacco Industry Profile 1995" by the Tobacco Institute; Glenn Frankel, "U.S. Aided Cigarette Firms in Conquests Across Aisa," *The Washington Post*, November 17, 1996; Saundra Torry and John Schwartz, "Contrite Tobacco Executives Admit Health Risks before Congress," *The Washington Post*, January 30, 1998, A14; Chip Jones, "Cigarette Farmers to Buy Less Leaf," *Richmond Times-Dispatch*, December 3, 1997, A1; and John M. Broder, "Cigarette Makers Reach $368 Billion Accord," *New York Times*, June 21, 1997.

FIGURE 1   Federal Excise and Sales Tax Collections on Domestic Tobacco Sales (in Millions of Dollars)

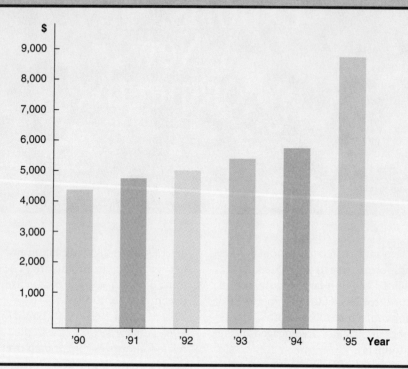

TABLE 1   Estimated Number of Smokers (in Millions of Persons)

	MEN	WOMEN
DEVELOPED COUNTRIES	200	100
DEVELOPING COUNTRIES	700	100

cigarettes in developing countries if their products were free of import restrictions.

In 1996, the U.S. tobacco industry produced 754 billion pieces of cigarettes. In the same year cigarette exports totaled about 241 billion pieces. The exports of tobacco and tobacco manufactures resulted in a $5.3 billion surplus in the 1996 trade balance for this group of products, about one-fourth of the surplus in all agricultural

TABLE 2   Leading International Brands Sold outside the North American Market (Manufactured in the U.S. and Other Countries)

BRAND	PRODUCER
Marlboro	Philip Morris
Mild Seven	Japan Tobacco
Winston	R.J. Reynolds
L&M	Philip Morris
Camel	R.J. Reynolds
Benson & Hedges	PM/BAT/AB
Gaulloise	Gaulloise
Bond Street	Philip Morris
SE555	British American Tobacco
Philip Morris	Philip Morris

FIGURE	2	U.S. Trade in Tobacco and Tobacco Manufactures (SITC Product Group No. 12) (in Millions of Dollars)

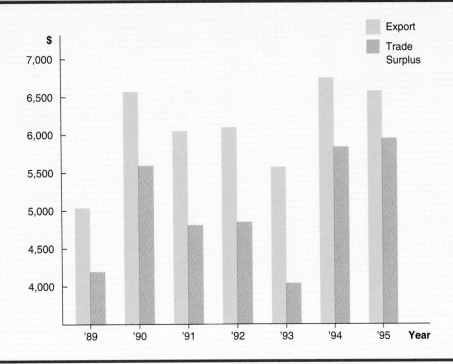

products (see Figure 2). U.S. firms exported cigarettes to 113 countries. The leading destinations for these exports were Belgium-Luxembourg (from there, cigarettes are distributed to individual EU countries), Japan, Saudi Arabia, Lebanon, and Singapore.

 ## U.S. Trade Policy

Tobacco-related revenue is an important source of income for the governments of many countries. As a result, many nations have traditionally blocked the import of cigarettes by imposing high import tariffs, discriminatory taxes, and restrictive marketing and distribution practices. Japan, China, South Korea, and Thailand even set up state monopolies to produce cigarettes. Throughout the 1980s, the Asian tigers were running huge trade surpluses with the United States. When the U.S. annual trade deficit reached a record high of $123 billion in 1984, the Reagan administration turned to the Office of the U.S. Trade Representative (USTR), a federal agency under the Executive Office of the president. Section 301 of the 1974 Trade Act empowered the USTR to investigate unfair trading practices by foreign countries toward U.S. exporters and required that the U.S. government impose sanctions if the foreign government found at fault in its trade policy toward U.S. firms does not make changes within one year.

As U.S. tobacco products were among the most restricted goods, the USTR soon turned its attention to this case of foreign trade discrimination. The scrutiny was aided by the fact that Japan, South Korea, and Thailand were signatories to the General Agreement on Tariffs and Trade (GATT), and Taiwan was interested in joining as well. By their discriminatory policies toward U.S. cigarette imports, these countries violated the free trade principles they had agreed to respect under the GATT. In September 1985, the White House filed a complaint with the USTR under Section 301 against Japanese restrictions on the sale of cigarettes. After a long series of negotiations and mounting pressure from the U.S. government, in September 1986, Japan gave in and allowed imports of U.S. cigarettes. Almost immediately, cigarettes rose from the fortieth to the second most-advertised product on Tokyo television. Imported brands currently control 21 percent of the Japanese market with $7 billion in annual sales.

In January 1988, the U.S. tobacco industry filed a 301 complaint with the USTR against South Korea. The USTR's efforts were supported by members of Congress from tobacco states. In July 1987, even before the USTR initiated its investigation, senators Dole (Kansas), Helms (North Carolina), Gore (Tennessee), and others wrote to the president of South Korea and demanded that U.S. companies be allowed to import and advertise tobacco products. The pressure on the South Korean government was intensified by a strong lobby in Seoul paid for by R.J. Reynolds and Philip Morris. In May 1988, Seoul agreed to the import of U.S. cigarettes and lifted its ban on cigarette advertising. Within one year, U.S. companies acquired more than 6 percent of the South Korean cigarette market. Taiwan was a similar story. Foreign brands went from 1 percent of the market to 20 percent within two years of the country's opening to cigarette imports in 1986. Thailand liberalized the market for imported cigarettes in August 1991. As a result, imports of foreign brands doubled in 1992 and rose again by 43 percent in 1993.

China is the world's largest cigarette producer with 1.7 trillion pieces produced in 1994. There are 350 million smokers in China today who consume 30 percent of the annual world cigarette production, which was 5.49 trillion pieces in 1994. China is also one of only a few countries where cigarette consumption is on the rise. All Chinese cigarettes are produced by a state monopoly. Because the Chinese government is eager to acquire advanced technology and marketing know-how from the West, it offered limited partnerships to a few foreign cigarette producers, including R.J. Reynolds and Philip Morris. Taxes from cigarette sales raise 12 percent of the Chinese government's annual revenue. As a consequence, the government wants to continue to protect its state monopoly from foreign competition. In 1992, the USTR negotiated an agreement under which China promised to eliminate tariffs and other trade barriers on U.S. cigarette imports within two years. However, the Chinese government has not enforced the agreement. In light of the current hostility on the part of the Clinton administration toward cigarette consumption, the U.S. tobacco industry has not asked the USTR to intervene against China's continuing restrictions on cigarette imports.

With the opening of the markets of the former Soviet Union and Eastern Europe at the beginning of the 1990s, U.S. tobacco manufacturers found new opportunities for expansion. With 60 percent of their populations smoking, Hungary, Poland, Bulgaria, the former Yugoslav republics, the Czech Republic, and Slovakia are among the top ten nations in per capita cigarette consumption. Armenia, Georgia, Azerbaijan, Russia, Ukraine, and Moldova rank among the top 20. Unlike in Asia in the 1980s, U.S. companies are welcomed here as contributors of new technology and scarce investment funds. As part of the privatization process in the formerly communist countries, U.S. cigarette producers were able to buy previously state-owned cigarette factories and are quickly gaining ground in these new markets. Some analysts project that over the next decade, Western tobacco manufacturers will gain control over the entire East European cigarette market, which will more than make up for the revenues lost at home.

In addition to these market developments, the conclusion of the Uruguay Round in 1992 and the founding of the World Trade Organization (WTO) brought a number of positive developments for the U.S. tobacco export industry: the European Union agreed to cut export subsidies and reduce tariffs on both unmanufactured and manufactured tobacco, Japan promised to maintain zero duty on cigarettes and to lower duty on cigars, and New Zealand reduced its tariff on cigarettes.

Government Support of the Tobacco Industry

The U.S. Department of Agriculture (USDA) administers laws to stabilize tobacco production and prices. According to the Tobacco Institute, without this regulation, more tobacco would be produced and prices would be lower. In 1994, the Commodity Credit Corporation, an agency established in 1933 to administer commodity stabilization programs for the USDA, made new loans to tobacco farmers of $351 million. These loans are to be repaid with interest as collateral tobacco is sold. The only direct cost incurred to the taxpayers is the administrative cost of this program.

Until the late 1980s, the U.S. government was in strong support of the tobacco industry. It funded three export promotion programs: the Foreign Market Development Program (also known as the Cooperator Program), the Targeted Export Assistance Program, and the Export Credit Guarantee Programs. The most important of these were the Export Credit Guarantee Programs administered by the Commodity Credit Corporation (CCC) of the Department of Agriculture. Under these programs, the CCC underwrote credit extended by the private banking sector in the United States to approved foreign banks, to pay for tobacco and other agricultural products sold by U.S. firms to foreign buyers. Between October 1985 and September 1989, sixty-six companies received guarantees of credits under these programs for the sale of 127 million pounds of tobacco with a market value of $214 million. The Targeted Export Assistance Program's purpose was to counteract the adverse effects of subsidies, import quotas, or other unfair trade practices on U.S. agricultural products. Under this program, Tobacco Associates, a private organization entrusted to carry out this endeavor, received $5 million in funding in 1990 to provide certain countries with the technical know-how, training, and equipment to manufacture cigarettes that use U.S. tobacco. In addition, Tobacco Associates received funds from the USDA to promote market development activities for U.S. tobacco products.

Currently, the U.S. government no longer funds export promotion programs related to tobacco and tobacco manufactures. All government programs that used to help the U.S. tobacco industry to enter foreign markets have been eliminated since 1990, under the Bush and Clinton administrations. For example, although the CCC still funds agricultural exports in general, it no longer assists in the exports of tobacco.

 ## Conflicting Objectives

The past involvement of the U.S. government in furthering the export of tobacco has generated controversy within the United States. The U.S. government, spearheaded by the Department of Health and Human Services, has been actively discouraging smoking on the domestic scene. In addition, the United States is a strong supporter of the worldwide antismoking movement. The Department of Health and Human Services serves as a collaborating headquarters for the United Nations World Health Organization and maintains close relationships with other health organizations around the world in sharing information on the detrimental health effects of smoking.

During congressional hearings in April 1994, top executives from R.J. Reynolds, Philip Morris, and U.S. Tobacco stated under oath their belief that nicotine was not addictive. In contrast, in 1996, the Food & Drug Administration concluded that nicotine was addictive and should be classified as a drug. In August 1996, President Clinton announced that the FDA will begin regulating cigarette and smokeless tobacco advertising and sales in the United States. During the same speech he said: "Cigarette smoking is the most significant public health problem facing our people. More Americans die every year from smoking-related diseases than from AIDS, car accidents, murders, suicides, and fires combined. The human cost doesn't begin to calculate the economic cost."

In 1998, the turnaround in the U.S. debate over domestic tobacco policy was evident in the conciliatory testimony of tobacco industry officials admitting before Congress that smoking is hazardous and addictive. Their statements followed four years in which attorneys general and private lawyers in 41 states mounted lawsuits against the industry, and tobacco industry executives agreed to pay $368.5 billion in a legislative proposal to settle the major lawsuits. If Congress approves the proposal, the industry would also agree to restrict marketing, do away with advertising figures like Joe Camel and the Marlboro man, pay fines if youth smoking did not fall to specific levels, and submit to FDA jurisdiction.

Although the Clinton administration has been the most antismoking administration in U.S. history, the government has not initiated any concrete steps to reduce U.S. tobacco exports and U.S. investment in cigarette production abroad. This is partly due to the fact that many in government believe that U.S. tobacco products are merely capturing an existing market share now or previously controlled by state monopolies. In contrast to this claim, the National Bureau of Economic Research estimated that U.S. entry in the 1980s into countries previously closed to cigarette imports pushed up the average per capita cigarette consumption by almost 10 percent in the targeted countries. This occurred due to increased advertising and price competition caused by the entry of U.S. products.

This situation reflects a conflict between morality and economics. Projections show that the declining U.S. cigarette consumption can be easily replaced by foreign markets over the next decade. Thus, by pursuing an antismoking policy only at home, the U.S. government is not risking too much. On the contrary, a smaller number of U.S. smokers will significantly reduce the U.S. health system's expenditures on the treatment of smoking-related illnesses. However, the U.S. policy of permissiveness toward cigarette exports is at odds with government's involvement in the worldwide campaign to reduce smoking for health reasons. Conflicting opinions can be heard from different representatives of the government. While Representative Henry A. Waxman of California and former U.S. Surgeon General C. Everett Koop continue to be staunch supporters of the antismoking campaign and principal opponents of U.S. tobacco exports, Representative Thomas J. Bliley of Virginia and Senator Jesse Helms of North Carolina continue to fight against government regulation of tobacco sales and are key supporters of tobacco exports. The dividing force is economics: North Carolina is the number one tobacco-growing state with annual cash receipts from tobacco crops of $1.05 billion, and Virginia is the sixth largest tobacco grower with $187 million in receipts in 1997.

QUESTIONS FOR DISCUSSION

1. Should U.S. exports of tobacco products be permitted in light of the domestic campaign against smoking?
2. Should the U.S. government be involved in tearing down foreign trade barriers to U.S. tobacco? Should the personal preference of the president affect U.S. trade policy?
3. Should export promotion support be provided to U.S. tobacco producers? What about such support for the export of U.S. beef, which may cause obesity abroad?

4. To what degree should ethics influence government policy or corporate decision making in the case of tobacco exports?

The Once and Future Ivory Trade

 ## Introduction

International trade in endangered species products is valued at an estimated $10–15 billion annually. Much of this trade, including the sale of rhinoceros, panda, turtle, and tiger products, is either partially or completely outlawed under the United Nations Convention on International Trade in Endangered Species (CITES), a U.N. organization established in 1973. Perhaps the most controversial animal covered by the treaty is the African elephant. In response to a halving of the African elephant population between the late 1970s and the mid-1980s, CITES imposed an unconditional ban on the international trade in African elephant products, most notably ivory, in 1989.

Backed strongly by the United States, Europe, and certain nations of central and eastern Africa, the ban has come under growing scrutiny as its opponents argue that certain African countries with stable or growing elephant populations should be afforded the opportunity to profit from existing ivory stockpiles. Without applying a tangible value to the African elephant, through means such as ivory sales, opponents of the ban believe that the endangered animal's preservation will fall victim to neglect. Conversely, supporters of the ban believe that any liberalization of the current rules will send the message that protection of the African elephant is no longer important. This will lead to a reintroduction of the worst aspects of the international ivory trade, they argue, including uncontrollable poaching and smuggling.

The debate culminated in June 1997 at a worldwide CITES conference in Harare, Zimbabwe. After a week's worth of testimony and cajoling from both sides, Botswana, Namibia, and Zimbabwe, home to over a quarter of all African elephants and among the most successful countries at protecting their elephant populations, were granted the right to sell 120 tons of stockpiled ivory to Japan under strict guidelines. While the debate over the ban was anything but congenial in the months prior to the CITES meeting, this decision to allow a brief resumption of the sale of ivory after nearly a decade, supported by over 75 percent of CITES member countries, raised the debate to a new level. Opponents of the ban have new hope that deserving African countries may once again be able to profit from one of their most unique natural resources. Conversely, ban supporters fear that subsequent exceptions will be granted by CITES and the world will once again witness a vast shrinkage of the African elephant population.

 ## Building Up to a Ban

The African elephant's misfortune is its tusks. Asian elephants have small tusks and have been trained by humans for over 4,000 years. The African elephant, however, has remained a creature of the wild. Its primary commercial worth for centuries, therefore, has been its ivory tusks. In 1930 there were between five and ten million elephants roaming the African plains and jungles. By

SOURCES: This case was written by Peter Fitzmaurice, under the supervision of Professor Michael R. Czinkota. Sources include: "Africans Reach Accord on Ivory Trade," *The Washington Post*, April 18, 2000, A21; Lynne Duke, "Limited Trade in Ivory Approved," *The Washington Post*, June 20, 1997, A16; Guy Gugliotta, "Hunting the Elephant in AID's Budget," *The Washington Post*, February 18, 1997, A11; Kevin A. Hill, "Conflicts over Development and Environmental Values: The International Ivory Trade in Zimbabwe's Historical Context, " **www.kevin-hill.com**; Michael Satchell, "Save the Elephant: Start Shooting Them," *U.S. News & World Report* (November 25, 1996): 51; Ken Wells, "The Hot New Slogan in Africa Game Circles Is 'Use It Or Lose It,'" *The Wall Street Journal*, January 7, 1997, A1; "Saving the Elephant: Nature's Great Masterpiece," *Economist*, July 1, 1989, 15, "Tiger Economics," *Far Eastern Economic Review* (August 1993): 19.

the time the first true census was conducted in 1979, there were only 1.2 million remaining. The fundamental problem is that elephants need a lot of room to live, and in this respect, humans have become their direct competitors. The tropical and subtropical realms where the African elephants dwell are precisely where human populations have been exploding the fastest, quadrupling in number since the turn of the century and claiming more and more elephant range for cropland, pastureland, and timber.

As economic and political instability became more the rule than the exception, in many African countries during the 1960s and 1970s the illegal killing of elephants grew. Traditionally, elephants in Africa have always been hunted for meat and to eliminate problem animals. But increasingly killings were for hard cash from ivory. Tusks became an underground currency, like drugs, spreading webs of corruption from remote villages to urban centers throughout the world. The 1970s saw the price of ivory skyrocket. Suddenly, to a herder or subsistence farmer, this was no longer an animal but a walking fortune, worth more than a dozen years of honest toil. To currency-strapped governments and revolutionaries alike, ivory was a way to pay for more firearms and supplies. In the 1980s, Africa had nearly ten times the weapons than a decade earlier, which encouraged more poaching. Ivory was running above a hundred dollars per pound, and everyone from poorly paid park rangers to high-ranking wildlife ministers had joined the poaching network.[1]

Total exports of unworked ivory from Africa rose from between 200 and 400 tons per year in the 1950s to around 1,000 tons in 1980, increasing by about 10 percent per year. Throughout the 1980s, annual export levels ranged between 700 and 1,000 tons (see Table 1). Such steady export levels hide the true impact on the African elephant population. By 1987, most mature bull elephants had been shot, leaving only the smaller tusks of elephant cows and calves to be traded. For this reason, one ton of traded ivory by the late 1980s represented approximately 113 dead elephants, up from an average of 54 in 1979.

At the beginning of the 1980s, there existed an estimated 1.2 million elephants in Africa, including 376,000 in Zaire and 204,000 in Tanzania (see Figure 1). As poaching accelerated over the next several years, the elephant population dropped to approximately 600,000 by 1988, with Zaire's total falling to 103,000 and Tanzania's to 75,000. To better control the declining populations, an ivory quota system was established in 1986 under the authority of CITES. Under the system, all ivory exports were to be authorized by CITES. During the system's first

TABLE 1   Who Exports Ivory

	TONS CUMULATIVE	
	EXPORTS 1986	EXPORTS 1979–87
Burundi	90	488
Botswana	0	58
Chad	0	111
Cent. Af. Rep.	19	1,136
Congo	17	917
Cameroon	1	28
Kenya	2	131
Namibia	1	37
Somalia	61	105
South Africa	41	329
Sudan	78	1,452
Tanzania	70	653
Uganda	36	424
Zaire	23	640
Zambia	10	149
Zimbabwe	8	94
Total (incl. other countries)	663	6,828

SOURCES: "Saving the Elephant: Nature's Great Masterpiece," *Economist* (July 1, 1989):17; Wildlife Trade Monitoring Unit, London Environmental Economics Centre.

year of operation, a global quota of 108,000 tusks was set. Though estimates can be extremely difficult to gauge, experts determined that this figure, which was thought by some conservationists to be ten times too high, was easily exceeded thanks to smugglers not interested in the paperwork of securing an authorization and unhindered by poaching laws that were not enforced.

As elephant populations continued to fall over the next two years, CITES convened in Switzerland in October 1989 under tremendous pressure to impose a full global ban on ivory and other elephant products. When the votes of the more than 100 CITES member countries were counted, supporters of the ban had won a very emotional and significant victory. However, one-third of the African countries most affected by the measure had voted against the ban. The agreement regulates only international ivory sales, and permits member countries to opt out of any commitment without sanction. Several southern African countries have done just that, continuing to permit big-game hunting under strict rules. However, with most nations adhering closely to the ban, the legal ivory trade has been decimated and the value of this natural resource for range countries has been vastly diminished.

Several southern African countries, including those recently permitted to sell stockpiled ivory, proposed at the

[1] This brief account of the African elephant's changing circumstances is excerpted from Douglas H. Chadwick, "Out of Time, Out of Space: Elephants," *National Geographic* (May 1991).

| FIGURE | 1 | Elephant Population by Selected Country |

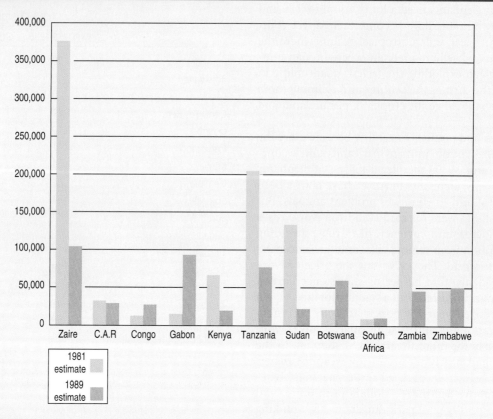

SOURCE: "Saving the Elephant: Nature's Great Masterpiece," *Economist* (July 1, 1989): 16.

1989 convention an exception to the ban for countries that had developed sustainable culling programs. The proposal was shelved, largely as a result of opposition from Western conservationists and east African countries, such as Kenya and Tanzania, which were experiencing rapidly declining elephant populations. In the aftermath of the 1989 meeting, a war of words between the two factions "escalated to proportions rarely seen at scientific or diplomatic conferences," according to one participant. CITES convened again in 1992, with similar calls for a loosening of the ban, and similar rejection by most countries outside southern Africa. It wasn't until 1997 that the majority of CITES member countries agreed that an exception to the ban was justified. This change in stance was largely affected by a growing belief, particularly among African wildlife and government officials, that a recommercialization of the ivory trade would enable nations to benefit economically from the elephant, creating a practical incentive to protect the species, something missing under the current ban.

A Market Approach to Preservation

Supporters of the ban argue that a legalized ivory trade would once again facilitate a thriving illegal parallel market. Only by making all ivory trade illegal will it become easier to police poaching, a major culprit of the African elephant's rapid population decline. But critics argue that a complete ban is simply inappropriate for saving the elephant. A much more probable effect of the ban, they say, will be an ever-rising price for ivory. Many who previously bought ivory legally would now buy the smuggled product. If the legal supply is choked off, but poaching continues, as it undoubtedly will, the increased demand for smuggled tusks will raise the black market value. This, in turn, will raise the profitability of poaching, and increase the risks poachers will be willing to take. The ban, they conclude, will only drive the ivory trade underground, making it as hard to police as cocaine smuggling from the forests of Latin America.

Critics of the ban propose an alternative approach to preserving the elephant. Summed up in the title of a front page January 1997 *Wall Street Journal* article on the subject, "use it or lose it" has become the rallying cry for supporters of legalized trade for ivory and other endangered species products. The argument goes as follows: Few of the species that humans find useful have become endangered so long as their commercialization was possible. When the Europeans came to North America there were no chickens, but millions of passenger pigeons. Today this type of pigeon is extinct, while millions of chickens are harvested each day. The reason is clear, say some: the demand for chickens ensures that there is a healthy profit in breeding them. Likewise, there is no danger that humans will soon run out of cows, sheep, ducks, or goats. Markets are irresistible forces, it is argued, and demand creates supply. Vast smuggling networks exist because of a growing demand that the market is prohibited from meeting. Today's problem, trade-ban critics argue, is that growing restrictions on the trade in ivory and other such products threaten to remove the profit from legitimate traders and increase the price and incentives for poachers who ignore the law.

Unable to utilize the tremendous value in elephants, few "locals" will bother with serious preservation efforts. "Unless we can make wildlife conservation profitable for all peoples, we cannot save our elephants for the future," according to Richard Leakey, a noted anthropologist and director of wildlife management for Kenya. Some have proposed an international regulatory system, or "Ivory Exchange," which would create an enforceable producers' cartel enabling open but limited trade in ivory. Either way, a legal ivory trade will recognize the economic value of the elephant, therefore creating a stake in its survival for those living among the animal and best able to promote its preservation. Coupled with this type of regulated trade should be the strong enforcement of poaching laws, an absolutely vital aspect of preservation. This combination of legal trade and strict enforcement of poaching laws is the environment within which the elephant has the best chances for long-term survival, critics of the ban contend.

Zimbabwe, Botswana, Namibia, and South Africa are in the forefront of efforts to implement such an approach. They argue that they have established very successful conservation programs, and should be permitted to profit from their elephants. If impoverished communities are prevented from profiting, "(the elephant) becomes a nuisance, people grow to detest it and feel that they have no stake in its survival," says Peter Kunjeku, director of the Wildlife Society of Zimbabwe. Support for a lifting of the ban is not a stance "against the traditional elephant in the traditional national park," says Kay Muir, a University of Zimbabwe economist and game specialist. Rather, it is a recognition that as rising human populations make new public parks impossible and put pressures on existing ones, animals and their protectors will increasingly have to assume the "true costs of paying their way." Gilbert Grosvenor, Chairman of the National Geographic Society, proclaimed a year after the ban went into effect that "all agree that elephants must earn their keep . . . the day of the free-roaming elephant is over."

Preservation Success Stories

Unless African countries properly manage their elephant stocks and enforce anti-poaching laws, nothing other countries may do will have much of an effect on the elephant's survival, say critics of the ban. In many countries, game scouts are vastly underpaid, poorly equipped, and unmotivated to do their job. Some scouts even choose to join the other side. The elephant's rate of decline, however, has never been consistent across Africa. Some range countries, particularly those in the south, have adeptly managed their elephant populations before and since the 1989 ban, and now actually contend with oftentimes problematic surpluses. South Africa's world famous Kruger National Park has recently begun the first-ever elephant contraceptive program to control the park's burgeoning pachyderm population. The park removes an average of 600 elephants per year, primarily through culling, but more recently through relocation, in order to keep the population at its carrying capacity of 7,500 elephants. Left to its own devices, the park's elephant population could double in 15 years.

Botswana's elephant population is increasing by 5 percent per year, and is now estimated at 80,000, up from 20,000 in 1980 and 58,000 in 1989. "That's elephants, not chickens," says Ketumile Masire, Botswana's president. "Many are starving and in some areas are destroying their own habitat. We fear they will do irreparable harm to the ecosystem. We would like to reduce our herds and market the ivory," he said. Zimbabwe, with 70,000 elephants, has over twice its carrying capacity. "It's not as if we're against preserving the elephant or that we're ungrateful for the help of the West," says Jon Hutton, director of Africa Resources Trust. He says, however, that Western conservationists need to take into account countries like Zimbabwe "that have a good track record of looking after their elephants."

These countries argue, by way of example, that there are successful models of government preservation programs that do not require the assistance (or hindrance, many would argue) of a trade ban. They point to Kenya, which arguably has the most at stake in the elephant's survival due to its huge safari industry, as an example of a failing approach to elephant protection. Kenya criminalized poaching in 1976, and has since seen over half of its elephant population killed off.

Profit Equals Protection

One vastly misunderstood aspect of the elephant issue is the utter antipathy that exists between the animal and African farmers and villagers. To put it in the words of Tony Prior, U.S. Agency for International Development's (AID) natural resources policy advisor for Africa, "elephants take up a lot of ecological space." An elephant can consume as much as 900 pounds of leaves and branches in a day and can be quite partial to maize fields. The overall effect is that elephants can decimate healthy vegetation and leave barren otherwise valuable land. In Zimbabwe, an average of ten farmers per year are trampled to death trying to defend their crops. One Zimbabwe elephant expert recently developed a mortarlike device that launches canisters of pepper spray at approaching elephants. "Elephants are the darlings of the Western world, but they are enemy number one in Kenya," says David Western, head of the Kenya Wildlife Service. "The African farmer's enmity toward elephants is as visceral as Western mawkishness is passionate," he says. Close to 400 Kenyans have been killed by wildlife, primarily elephants, since 1990. "You really have to pity these farmers," says Dourga Albert, a wildlife official in Cameroon. "See them weep after elephants have raided their crops. It's like a plague had befallen them." The typical result in villages throughout Africa is that the marauding invaders are killed, either by locals or, with the locals' gracious approval, poachers.

This condition, however, is changing in many areas of southern Africa. Damaged land and crop losses are not only being tolerated, but villages are doing their best to guard against poachers. This surprising change in behavior is due to the proliferation of government programs that dispense licenses to villages, enabling locals, or paying hunters, to cull an allotted number of elephants each year. One such program in Zimbabwe is known as CAMPFIRE (Communal Areas Management Program for Indigenous Resources). Begun the year the ivory ban came into effect, the program operates on the belief that if big game animals are to survive—both in and out of preserves—people who share the land must benefit. Participants of CAMPFIRE, usually individual villages, are able to sell permits under strict control to big-game trophy hunters, or cull the elephants themselves for hides, tusks, and meat. A single elephant can net a local community $20,000–$50,000. CAMPFIRE earns about $2.5 million a year from sport hunting, which is dispersed among 600,000 people living on communal lands. In one Zimbabwe village, residents received an annual payment of $25 apiece, significant when it is considered that the average Zimbabwean earns approximately $100–$150 per year. Revenues from the program have financed two grinding mills, a water line, and a small school for the village.

As for poaching, CAMPFIRE's spokesman Tawona Tavengwa says that it has dropped sharply in participating areas since the program began. "Local people now have an interest in preserving their wildlife." In many cases it has prompted local villages that had turned some of their own lands into economically doubtful cattle farms, to convert them back into game lands. "If you are taking lands that are marginally productive and putting them to a productive use, and game benefits, that's a plus," he says.

CAMPFIRE depends upon a $28 million multiyear AID grant for its operation. "This is a resource management project, not a wildlife project," according to Tony Prior, AID's overseer for the program. AID believes it is demonstrating to Zimbabweans that a properly managed environment is a renewable and lucrative resource. However, the Humane Society of the United States thinks the program is just an excuse to let Zimbabweans profit from the killing of endangered elephants. Prior says the goal of CAMPFIRE is to get people to see wildlife and the environment as income sources. "We want to make maintaining the wildlife population a matter of self-interest," Prior says. In response to the Humane Society and other conservation groups that have hurled accusations of mismanagement and corruption at CAMPFIRE, Prior responds by saying environmental projects take time to mature and AID is attempting "to put in place the conditions for long-term change." Elephant hunting is not the problem, he concludes, not with the threat of "30,000 elephants dying from drought."

Irrespective of the controversy, locals are grateful for the opportunity to share in the profit from their own resources. The program has brought the Zimbabwe village of Mahenya full circle. Villagers once hated nearby Gonarezhou Park because they were forced off the land thirty years ago to create the preserve and were forbidden to hunt the animals that had sustained them for centuries. "Now we use the skills and knowledge of our elders to conserve wildlife as they once did," says one villager. "Once again animals are a part of our livelihood." CAMPFIRE, emulated in other southern African countries, was expected to be funded into the new century, despite a fight by some members of Congress to abolish the program.

Eco-Imperialism?

After all the arguing and exchanging of information and statistics, those calling for a legalization of the ivory trade simply feel they should not have to obtain the approval of other countries in order to harvest their own natural resources. A University of Zimbabwe game economist states that Westerners, in not viewing the elephant firsthand, have no idea of the "lost opportunity costs" to vil-

...ften asked to forgo development of their ...s and accept crop losses, damaged housing, and sometimes loss of life for the sake of the elephant. "Would citizens of industrialized countries choose the survival of the whale, panda or bear . . . at the expense of their lives, the education of their children, or their pensions?" she asks. "I doubt it. Yet they ask Africans to give up very substantial needs in order to ensure that wildlife prospers." A Zimbabwe newspaper, referring to the controversy, denounced "well-fed and prosperous Europeans and North Americans, wearing leather shoes and tucking into high-priced meat dishes, telling African peasants that basically they are only on earth as picturesque extras in a huge zoo."

Much of the debate boils down to differences in culture and values. Opponents of the ivory trade fear that the doctrine of "consumptive use," taken to extremes, is ultimately harmful because it reduces the value of all animals to mere economics. "I don't like the idea of turning everything into a cow," says Josh Ginsberg of the Wildlife Conservation Society. Teresa Telecky, a top zoologist with the Humane Society, believes "it's insane to try to assign an economic value to every animal on Earth." In Africa, however, those who have managed to nurture their elephant populations see no reason why they should not be able to profit as a result. CITES Deputy Secretary-General Jacques Berney neatly phrased the distinction: "On the one side you have those who believe in . . . utilization of wildlife as an economic resource; on the other you have those who believe purely in protection . . . who would still like to ban the ivory trade tomorrow even if there were three million elephants in Africa instead of 650,000."

The Future

So how has the ivory ban worked? It's difficult to tell. Statistics on elephant populations are extremely difficult to collect—the animal does not stay in one place, or one country for that matter, very long. Additionally, some of the largest populations reside in very dense jungle. Many experts, agree, however, that the rapid slaughter of elephants in the 1980s has been largely reduced in the 1990s—though hardly ended. Two hundred tuskless elephant carcasses were found in Congo in late 1996. A Korean national arriving home from Gabon that same year was caught transporting over 100 kilograms of ivory and ivory products in a washing machine and sofa. More recently, in June 1997 Taiwanese officials seized 130 kilograms of ivory and ivory products, as well as two 300-kilogram ivory sculptures, from members of a South African–Taiwan smuggling ring.

A 1995 study on the effectiveness of the ban concluded that "the answer to this question (of effectiveness) remains . . . inconclusive." In assuming the ban has brought about a significant drop in poaching, critics characterize such an outcome as only temporary. Poaching or no poaching, the African elephant population is likely to continue to decline due to the encroachment of humans upon elephant habitat.

Supporters of the ban can rest assured that even a partial return to a normalized ivory trade is years away. In April 2000, African nations agreed to delay ivory sales for at least two years, to give them time to see if elephant poaching is a real threat or if it is safe to resume trade in tusks. The compromise was reached shortly before CITES was to debate controversial proposals to reopen the trade in ivory immediately. The implications of the CITES decision, however, are unmistakable; as African countries continue to exert pressure and make their case to the international community, and as elephant populations continue to rise in those nations with successful preservation programs, additional exceptions are likely to be granted and the current ban will come under increased scrutiny.

QUESTIONS FOR DISCUSSION

1. Critique the following argument: "Successful protection of the African elephant (or any other endangered species) requires a profit incentive."

2. If the United States and other nations are going to refuse ivory imports, should they compensate impoverished exporting nations by opening markets wider for other products?

3. Should elephant range countries direct their economic potential and limited resources toward more growth-related, higher-skilled industries?

4. Assess the implications of the 1997 CITES decision to permit limited ivory exports as it relates to trade in other types of endangered wildlife.

One Afternoon at the United States International Trade Commission

Chairwoman Stern: We turn now to investigation TA-201-55 regarding nonrubber footwear. Staff has assembled. Are there any questions? Vice Chairman Liebeler has a question. Please proceed.

Vice Chairman Liebeler: My questions are for the Office of Economics, Mr. Benedick. Do foreign countries have a comparative advantage in producing footwear?

Mr. Benedick: Yes, foreign producers generally have a comparative advantage vis-à-vis the domestic producers in producing footwear. Footwear production generally involves labor-intensive processes which favor the low-wage countries such as Taiwan, Korea, and Brazil, which are the three largest foreign suppliers by volume. For instance, the hourly rate for foreign footwear workers in these countries ranges from about one-twelfth to one-fourth of the rate for U.S. footwear workers.

Vice Chairman Liebeler: Is it likely that this comparative advantage will shift in favor of the domestic industries over the next several years?

Mr. Benedick: It is not very likely. There seems to be little evidence that supports this. The domestic industry's generally poor productivity performance over the last several years, which includes the period 1977 to 1981, roughly corresponding to the period of OMAs (Orderly Marketing Arrangements) for Taiwan and Korea, suggests that U.S. producers must significantly increase their modernization efforts to reduce the competitive advantage of the imported footwear.

Vice Chairman Liebeler: Have you calculated the benefits and costs of import relief using various assumptions about the responsiveness of supply and demand to changes in price?

Mr. Benedick: Yes. On the benefit side, we estimated benefits of import restrictions to U.S. producers, which included both increased domestic production and higher domestic prices. We also estimated the terms of trade benefits resulting from import restrictions. These latter benefits result from an appreciation of the U.S. dollar as a result of the import restrictions.

On the cost side, we estimated cost to consumers of the increase in average prices on total footwear purchases under the import restrictions and the consumer costs associated with the drop in total consumption due to the higher prices.

Vice Chairman Liebeler: In your work, did you take into account any retaliation by our trading partners?

Mr. Benedick: No.

Vice Chairman Liebeler: What was the 1984 level of imports?

Mr. Benedick: In 1984, imports of nonrubber footwear were approximately 726 million pairs.

Vice Chairman Liebeler: If a six-hundred-million-pair quota were imposed, what would the effect on price of domestic and foreign shoes be, and what would the market share of imports be?

Mr. Benedick: At your request, the Office of Economics estimated the effects of the six-hundred-million-pair quota. We estimate that prices of domestic footwear would increase by about 11 percent and prices of imported footwear would increase by about 19 percent.

The import share, however, would drop to about 59 percent of the market in the first year of the quota.

Vice Chairman Liebeler: What would aggregate cost to consumers be of that kind of quota?

Mr. Benedick: Total consumer cost would approach $1.3 billion in each year of such a quota.

Vice Chairman Liebeler: What would be the benefit to the domestic industry of this quota?

Mr. Benedick: Domestic footwear production would increase from about 299 million pairs for 1984 to about 367 million pairs, or by about 23 percent. Domestic sales would increase from about $3.8 billion to about $5.2 billion, an increase of about 37 percent.

SOURCE: Excerpts from the *Official Transcript Proceedings before the U.S. International Trade Commission*, meeting of the commission, June 12, 1985, Washington, DC.

Vice Chairman Liebeler: How many jobs would be saved?

Mr. Benedick: As a result of this quota, domestic employment would rise by about 26,000 workers over the 1984 level.

Vice Chairman Liebeler: What is the average paid to those workers?

Mr. Benedick: Based on questionnaire responses, each worker would earn approximately $11,900 per year in wages and another $2,100 in fringe benefits, for a total of about $14,000 per year

Vice Chairman Liebeler: So what then would be the cost to consumers of each of these $14,000-a-year jobs?

Mr. Benedick: It would cost consumers approximately $49,800 annually for each of these jobs.

Vice Chairman Liebeler: Thank you very much, Mr. Benedick.

Commissioner Eckes: I have a question for the General Counsel's Representative. I heard an interesting phrase a few moments ago, "comparative advantage." I don't recall seeing that phrase in Section 201. Could you tell me whether it is there and whether it is defined?

Ms. Jacobs: It is not.

Chairwoman Stern: I would like to ask about cost/benefit analysis. Perhaps the General Counsel's Office again might be the best place to direct this question. It is my understanding that the purpose of Section 201 is to determine whether a domestic industry is being injured, the requisite level for requisite reasons, imports being at least as important a cause of the serious injury as any other cause, and then to recommend a remedy which we are given kind of a short menu to select from to remedy the industry's serious injury.

Are we to take into account the impact on the consumer?

Are we to do a cost/benefit analysis when coming up with the remedy which best relieves the domestic industry's serious injury?

Ms. Jacobs: As the law currently stands, it is the responsibility of the commission to determine that relief which is a duty or import restriction which is necessary to prevent or remedy the injury that the commission has determined to exist. The president is to weigh such considerations as consumer impact, etc. The commission is not necessarily responsible for doing that. Of course, the commission may want to realize that, knowing the president is going to consider those factors, they might want to also consider them, but in fact, that is not the responsibility of the commission. It is the responsibility of the commission only to determine that relief which is necessary to remedy the injury they have found.

Chairwoman Stern: I can understand our reporting to the president other materials which aren't part of our consideration but nevertheless necessary for the president in his consideration, but having that information

and providing it to the president is different from its being part of the commission's consideration in its recommendations.

Ms. Jacobs: That's right. Your roles are quite different in that respect.

Vice Chairman Liebeler: Nations will and should specialize in production of those commodities in which they have a comparative advantage. Fortunately, our country has a large capital stock which tends to provide labor with many productive employments. Our comparative advantage is in the production of goods that use a high ratio of capital to labor. Shoes, however, are produced with a low ratio of capital to labor.

Therefore, American footwear cannot be produced as cheaply as foreign footwear. The availability of inexpensive imports permits consumers to purchase less expensive shoes and it allows the valuable capital and labor used in this footwear industry to shift to more productive pursuits.

This situation is not unique to the footwear industry. The classic example is agriculture, where the share of the labor force engaged in farming declined from 50 percent to 3 percent over the last 100 years. This shift did not produce a 47 percent unemployment rate. It freed that labor to produce cars, housing, and computers.

The decline of the American footwear industry is part of this dynamic process. This process is sometimes very painful. Congress, by only providing for temporary relief, has recognized that our continued prosperity depends on our willingness to accept such adjustments.

The industry has sought this so-called temporary import relief before. The ITC has conducted approximately 170 investigations relating to this industry. This is the fourth footwear case under Section 201, and so far the industry has gotten relief twice. The 1975 petition resulted in adjustment assistance. The 1976 case resulted in orderly marketing agreements with Taiwan and Korea.

In spite of the efforts of the domestic industry to suppress imports, the industry has been shrinking. Between 1981 and 1984, 207 plants closed; 94 of these closings occurred just last year. The closing of unprofitable plants is a necessary adjustment. Import relief at this stage will retard this process and encourage entry into a dying industry.

Because there is no temporary trade restriction that would facilitate the industry's adjustment to foreign competition, I cannot recommend any import barrier.

Chairwoman Stern: The intent of the General Import Relief law is to allow a seriously injured industry to adjust to global competition. The commission must devise a remedy which corresponds to the industry and the market forces it must face.

No other manufacturing sector of our economy faces stiffer competition from abroad than the U.S. shoe industry. Imports have captured three-fourths of our market. No relief program can change the basic conditions of competition that this industry must ultimately face on its own. The best that we as a commission can do—and under Section 201 that the president can do—is to give the industry a short, predictable period of relief to allow both large and small firms to adjust, coexist, and hopefully prosper.

I am proposing to the president an overall quota on imports of 474 million pairs of shoes in the first year. Shoes with a customs value below $2.50 would not be subject to this quota. The relief would extend for a full five years.

Commissioner Lodwick: Section 201 is designed to afford the domestic industry a temporary respite in order to assist it making an orderly adjustment to import competition. The fact that the law limits import relief to an initial period of up to five years, to be phased down after three years to the extent feasible, indicates that Congress did not intend domestic producers to find permanent shelter from import competition under the statute.

Accordingly, I intend to recommend to the president a five-year quota plan which affords the domestic nonrubber footwear industry ample opportunity to implement feasible adjustment plans which will facilitate, as the case may be, either the orderly transfer of resources to alternative uses or adjustments to new conditions of competition.

Commissioner Rohr: In making my recommendation, I emphasize the two responsibilities which are placed on the commission by statute. First, it must provide a remedy which it believes will effectively remedy the injury which is found to exist.

Secondly, Congress has stated that we, as commissioners, should attempt, to the extent possible, to develop a remedy that can be recommended to the president by a majority of the commission. I have taken seriously my obligation to attempt to fashion a remedy with which at least a majority of my colleagues can agree. Such remedy is a compromise.

I am concurring in the remedy proposal which is being presented today by a majority of the commission. This majority recommendation provides for an overall limit on imports of 474 million pairs; an exclusion from such limitation of shoes entering the United States with a value of less than $2.50 per pair; a growth in such limitation over a five-year period of 0 percent, 3 percent, and 9 percent; and the sale of import licenses through an auctioning system.

Commissioner Eckes: It is my understanding that a majority of the commission has agreed on these points. I subscribe to that and will provide a complete description of my views in my report to the president.

QUESTIONS FOR DISCUSSION

1. What are your views of the ITC recommendation?
2. Should the principle of comparative advantage always dictate trade flows?
3. Why are the consumer costs of quotas so often neglected?
4. Discuss alternative solutions to the job displacement problem.
5. How would you structure a "temporary relief program"?

Part
Two

International

Beginning International Marketing Activities

Part Two focuses on the company that is considering whether to fill an unsolicited export order, on the manager who wants to find out how the current product line can be marketed abroad, and on the firm searching for ways to expand its currently limited international activities. It concentrates on low-cost, low-risk international expansion, which permits a firm to enter the global market without an extraordinary commitment of human and financial resources. The reader will share the concerns of small and medium-sized firms—those that need international marketing assistance most and that supply the largest employment opportunities—before progressing to the advanced international marketing activities described in Part Three.

Chapter 7

Building the Knowledge Base

E VEN THOUGH MOST managers recognize the need for domestic marketing research, the single most important cause for failure in the international marketplace is insufficient preparation and information. Major mistakes often occur because the firm and its managers do not have an adequate understanding of the business environment. Hindsight, however, does not lead to an automatic increase in international marketing research. Many firms either do not believe that international market research is worthwhile or face manpower and resource bottlenecks that impede such research. The increase in international marketing practice is also not reflected in the orientation of the articles published in key research journals.[1] Yet building a good knowledge base is a key condition for subsequent marketing success. To do so, one needs to accumulate data and information through research. Two basic forms of research are available to the firm: primary research, where data are collected for specific research purposes, and secondary research, where data that have already been collected are used. This chapter will first outline secondary research issues, focusing primarily on ways to obtain basic information quickly, ensuring that the information is reasonably accurate, and doing so with limited corporate resources. Later, primary research and its ways of answering more in-depth questions for the firm are covered, together with the development of a decision-support system.

Defining the Issue

The American Marketing Association (AMA) defines **marketing research** as "the function that links the consumer, customer, and public to the marketer through information—information used to identify and define marketing opportunities and problems; generate, refine, and evaluate marketing actions; monitor marketing performance; and improve understanding of marketing as a process. Marketing research specifies the information required to address these issues, designs the method for collecting information, manages and implements the data collection process, analyzes the results, and communicates the findings and their implications."[2]

This very broad statement highlights the fact that research is the link between marketer and market, without which marketing cannot function. It also emphasizes the fact that marketing actions need to be monitored and outlines the key steps of the research process.

A more recent definition states that marketing research is the "systematic and objective identification, collection, analysis and dissemination for the purpose of improving decision making related to the identification and solution of problems and opportunities in marketing."[3] This statement is more specific to research activities for several reasons: It highlights the need for systematic work, indicating that research should be the result of planned and organized activity rather than coincidence. It stresses the need for objectivity and information, reducing the roles of bias, emotions, and subjective judgment. Finally, it addresses the need for the information to relate to specific problems. Marketing research cannot take place in a void; rather, it must have a business purpose.

---

[1]Naresh K. Malhotra, Mark Peterson, and Susan Bardi Kleiser, "Marketing Research: A State-of-the-Art Review and Directions for the Twenty-First Century," *Journal of the Academy of Marketing Science* 27 (Number 2, 1999): 160–183.

[2]"New Marketing Research Definition Approved," *Marketing News* 21 (January 2, 1987): 1, 14.

[3]Naresh K. Malhotra, *Marketing Research: An Applied Orientation,* 3rd ed. (Upper Saddle River, NJ: Prentice-Hall, 1999.)

International marketing research must also be linked to the decision-making process within the firm. The recognition that a situation requires action is the factor that initiates the decision-making process. The problem must then be defined. Often, symptoms are mistaken for causes; as a result, action determined by symptoms may be oriented in the wrong direction.

International and Domestic Research

The tools and techniques of international marketing research are said by some to be exactly the same as those of domestic marketing research, and only the environment differs. However, the environment is precisely what determines how well the tools, techniques, and concepts apply to the international market. Although the objectives of marketing research may be the same, the execution of international research may differ substantially from the process of domestic research. As a result, entirely new tools and techniques may need to be developed. The four primary differences are new parameters, new environments, an increase in the number of factors involved, and a broader definition of competition.

New Parameters

In crossing national borders, a firm encounters parameters not found in domestic marketing. Examples include duties, foreign currencies and changes in their value, different modes of transportation, international documentation, and port facilities. A firm that has done business only domestically will have had little or no prior experience with these requirements and conditions. Information about each of them must be obtained in order for management to make appropriate business decisions. New parameters also emerge because of differing modes of operating internationally. For example, a firm can export, it can license its products, it can engage in a joint venture, or it can carry out foreign direct investment.

New Environments

When deciding to go international in its marketing activities, a firm exposes itself to an unfamiliar environment. Many of the assumptions on which the firm was founded and on which its domestic activities were based may not hold true internationally. Firms need to learn about the culture of the host country, understand its political system, determine its stability, and appreciate the differences in societal structures and language. In addition, they must fully comprehend pertinent legal issues in the host country to avoid operating contrary to local legislation. They should also incorporate the technological level of the society in the marketing plan and understand the economic environment. In short, all the assumptions formulated over the years in the domestic market must be reevaluated. This crucial point has often been neglected, because most managers were born into the environment of their domestic operations and have subconsciously learned to understand the constraints and opportunities of their business activities. The process is analogous to learning one's native language. Being born to a language makes speaking it seem easy. Only in attempting to learn a foreign language do we begin to appreciate the complex structure of languages, the need for rules, and the existence of different patterns.

Number of Factors Involved

Going international often means entering into more than one market. As a result, the number of changing dimensions increases geometrically. Even if every dimension is understood, management must also appreciate the interaction between them. Because

of the sheer number of factors, coordination of the interaction becomes increasingly difficult. The international marketing research process can help management with this undertaking.

Broader Definition of Competition

By entering the international market, the firm exposes itself to a much greater variety of competition than existed in the domestic market. For example, fishery products compete not only with other fishery products but also with meat or even vegetarian substitutes. Similarly, firms that offer labor-saving devices in the domestic market-place may suddenly face competition from cheap manual labor. As a result, the firm must determine the breadth of the competition, track the competitive activities, and finally, evaluate the actual and potential impact on its own operations.

Recognizing the Need For Research

To serve a market efficiently, firms must learn what customers want, why they want it, and how they go about filling their needs. To enter a market without conducting marketing research places firms, their assets, and their entire operation at risk. Even though most firms recognize the need for domestic marketing research, this need is not fully understood for international marketing activities. Often, decisions concerning entry and expansion in overseas markets and the selecting and appointing of distributors are made after a cursory subjective assessment of the situation. The research done is less rigorous, less formal, and less quantitative than for domestic marketing activities. Many business executives appear to view foreign market research as relatively unimportant.

A major reason that firms are reluctant to engage in international marketing activities is the lack of sensitivity to differences in consumer tastes and preferences. Managers often tend to assume that their methods are both best and acceptable to all others. This is fortunately not true. What a boring place the world would be if it were!

A second reason is a limited appreciation for the different marketing environments abroad. Often, firms are not prepared to accept that distribution systems, industrial applications and uses, the availability of media, or advertising regulations may be entirely different from those in the home market. Barely aware of the differences, many firms are unwilling to spend money to find out about them.

A third reason is the lack of familiarity with national and international data sources and the inability to use them if obtained. As a result, the cost of conducting international marketing research is seen as prohibitively high, and therefore not a worthwhile investment relative to the benefits to be gained.[4] However, the Internet makes international marketing research much easier and much less expensive, as *The International Marketplace 7.1* has shown. Therefore, growing access to the Internet around the world will make research more accessible as well.

Finally, firms often build up their international marketing activities gradually, frequently on the basis of unsolicited orders. Over time, actual business experience in a country or with a specific firms may be used as a substitute for organized research.[5]

Yet, international marketing research is important. It permits management to identify and develop strategies for internationalization. This task includes the identification, evaluation, and comparison of potential foreign market opportunities and subsequent market selection. Second, research is necessary for the development of a marketing plan. The requirements for successful market entry and market penetration need to be determined. Subsequently, the research should define the appropriate marketing mix for each international market and should maintain continuous feedback in order to fine-tune the various marketing elements. Finally, research can provide management with foreign market intelligence to help it anticipate events, take appropriate action, and prepare for global changes.

The Benefits of Research

To carry out international research, firms require resources in terms of both time and money. For the typical smaller firm, those two types of resources are its most precious and scarce commodities. To make a justifiable case for allocating resources to international marketing research, management must understand what that value of research will be. This is even more important for international market research than for domestic market research because the cost tends to be higher. The value of research in making a particular decision may be determined by applying the following equation:

$$V(dr) - V(d) > C(r)$$

where

$V(dr)$ is the value of the decision with the benefit of research;

---

[4]C. Samuel Craig and Susan P. Douglas, *International Marketing Research,* 2nd ed. (New York: John Wiley & Sons, 1999).

[5]S. Tamer Cavusgil, "International Marketing Research: Insights into Company Practices," in *Research in Marketing,* vol. 7, ed. Jagdish N. Sheth (Greenwich, CT: JAI Press, 1984), 261–288.

$V(d)$ is the value of the decision without the benefit of research;
and
$C(r)$ is the cost of research.

Obviously, the value of the decision with the benefit of research should be greater than the value of the decision without research, and the value increase should exceed the cost of the research. Otherwise, international marketing research would be a waste of resources. It may be difficult to quantify the individual values because often the risks and benefits are not easy to ascertain. Yet, the use of decision theory permits a comparison of alternative research strategies.[6]

Determining Research Objectives

Research objectives will vary from firm to firm because of the views of management, the corporate mission, and the marketing situation. In addition, as discussed earlier, the information needs of firms are closely linked with the level of existing international expertise.

Going International: Exporting

The most frequent objective of international market research is that of **foreign-market opportunity analysis.** When a firm launches its international activities, information is needed to provide basic guidelines. The aim is not to conduct a painstaking and detailed analysis of the world on a market-by-market basis but instead to utilize a broad-brush approach. Accomplished quickly at low cost, this can narrow down the possibilities for international marketing activities.

Such an approach should begin with a cursory analysis of general market variables such as total and per capita GNP, mortality rates, and population figures. Although these factors in themselves will not provide detailed market information, they will enable the researcher to determine whether the corporation's objectives might be met in those markets. For example, expensive labor-saving consumer products may not be successful in the People's Republic of China because their price may be a significant proportion of the annual salary of the customer, and the perceived benefit to the customer may be only minimal. Such cursory evaluation will help reduce the number of markets to be considered to a more manageable number—for example, from 200 to 25.

Next, the researcher will require information about each individual market for a preliminary evaluation. This information typically identifies the fastest-growing markets, the largest markets for a particular product, market trends, and market restrictions. Although precise and detailed information for each product probably cannot be obtained, it is available for general product categories.

Governmental restrictions on markets must be considered as well. As an example, we can determine that Iraq represents a fast-growing market for computer hardware and software. However, an inspection of export licensing regulations may reveal that computer trade with Iraq is prohibited. Again, this overview will be cursory but will serve to evaluate markets quickly and reduce the number of markets subject to closer investigation.

At this stage, the researcher must select appropriate markets. The emphasis will shift to focus on market opportunities for a specific product or brand, including existing, latent, and incipient markets. Even though the aggregate industry data have already been obtained, general information is insufficient to make company-specific de-

---

[6]For an excellent exposition on measuring the value of research, see Gilbert A. Churchill, *Marketing Research: Methodological Foundations*, 7th ed. (Fort Worth, TX: The Dryden Press, 1999).

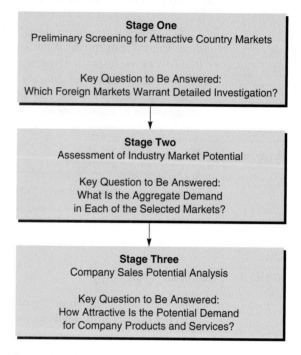

SOURCE: S. Tamer Cavusgil, "Guidelines for Export Market Research," *Business Horizons* 28 (November–December 1985): 29. Copyright 1985 by the Foundation for the School of Business at Indiana University. Reprinted by permission.

cisions. For example, the market demand for medical equipment should not be confused with the potential demand for a specific brand.[7] In addition, the research should identify demand-and-supply patterns and evaluate any regulations and standards. Finally, a competitive assessment needs to be made that matches markets with corporate strengths and provides an analysis of the best market potential for specific products. Figure 7.1 offers a summary of the various stages in the determination of market potential.

Going International: Importing

When importing, firms shift their major focus from supplying to sourcing. Management must identify markets that produce desired supplies or materials or that have the potential to do so. Foreign firms must be evaluated in terms of their capabilities and competitive standing.

The importer needs to know, for example, about the reliability of a foreign supplier, the consistency of its product or service quality, and the length of delivery time. Information obtained through the subsidiary office of a bank or through one's embassy can be very helpful. Information from business rating services and recommendations from current customers are also very useful in evaluating the potential business partner.

In addition, government rules must be scrutinized as to whether exportation is possible. For example, India may set limits on the cobra handbags it allows to be

---

[7]S. Tamer Cavusgil, "Guidelines for Export Market Research," *Business Horizons* 28 (November–December 1985): 27–33.

exported, and laws protecting the cultural heritage may prevent the exportation of pre-Columbian artifacts from Latin American countries. The international manager must also analyze domestic restrictions and legislation that may prohibit the importation of certain goods into the home country. Even though a market may exist in the United States for foreign umbrella handles, for example, quotas may restrict their importation in order to protect domestic industries. Similarly, even though domestic demand may exist for ivory, its importation may be illegal because of worldwide legislation enacted to protect wildlife.

Market Expansion

Research objectives may include obtaining detailed information for penetrating a market, for designing and fine-tuning the marketing mix, or for monitoring the political climate of a country so that the firm can expand its operation successfully. The better defined the research objective is, the better the researcher will be able to determine the information requirements and thus conserve time and financial resources of the firm.

Determining Secondary Information Requirements

Using the research objective as a guide, the researcher will be able to pinpoint the type of information needed. For example, if only general initial market information is required, perhaps macro data such as world population statistics will be sufficient. If research is to identify market restraints, then perhaps information is required about international accords and negotiations in the WTO. Alternatively, broad product category, production, and trade figures may be desired in order to pinpoint general market activities. For the fine-tuning of a marketing mix, very specific detailed product data may be necessary. Typically, management is likely to need both macro and micro data. Table 7.1 provides a listing of the type of information that, according to U.S. executives, is most crucial in international marketing.

TABLE 7.1 Most Critical International Information for U.S. Firms

Government Data
- Tariff information
- U.S. export/import data
- Nontariff measures
- Foreign export/import data
- Data on government trade policy

Corporate Data
- Local laws and regulations
- Size of market
- Local standards and specifications
- Distribution system
- Competitive activity

SOURCE: Michael R. Czinkota, "International Information Needs for U.S. Competitiveness," in *International Marketing Strategy*, eds. M. R. Czinkota and I. Ronkainen (Fort Worth, TX: The Dryden Press, 1994), 235–244.

THE INTERNATIONAL MARKETPLACE 7.2

Electronic Information Sources on the EU

WITH THE EXPANDING ECONOMIC and political union occurring within Europe, official information resources are becoming more centralized. A short sampling of government sources of information helpful to international managers targeting the EU are reviewed below.

EUROPA

Located at **www.europa.eu.int** is the main server that provides access to bibliographic, legal, and statistical databases offered by the European Commission. Many databases are available on Europa including IDEA, SCADPlus, CELEX, and ECLAS. IDEA is an electronic directory of the various European Union institutions. Searches can be conducted in three ways: by organization (directorate or service), by individual names, or by hierarchical ranking. A printed version of the directory is also available in 11 languages. SCADPlus is a bibliographic database with references to official legislative documents and publications, as well as secondary periodical literature on the EU. CELEX is a comprehensive information source on European Community law, offering coverage of acts, treaties, legislation, and resolutions. ECLAS is an on-line catalog of the Central Library of the Commission.

EUROSTAT

The Statistical Office of the European Communities (EUROSTAT), which is located at **www.europa.eu.int/en/comm/eurostat**, offers a wide selection of electronic information as well as software for graphics using COMEXT, along with map and graphic capabilities.

EUROPARL

EUROPARL is the documentary database of the European Parliament, Its files cover the status of legislation in progress; citations for sessions documents, debates, resolutions, and opinions; bibliographic references to studies done by Parliament; and a catalog of the Parliament's library. Please note, this is a restricted database, but **www.europarl.eu.int** offers free and timely information regarding the European Parliament.

SOURCE: On-line information about the European Union accessed at **www.europa.eu.int**, May 30, 2001.

Sources of Data

Secondary data for international marketing research purposes are available from a wide variety of sources. The major ones are briefly reviewed here. In addition, Appendix A to this chapter lists more than 100 publications and organizations that monitor international issues.

Governments   Of all data sources, governments typically have the greatest variety of data available. Typically, the information provided by governments addresses either macro or micro issues, or it offers specific data services. Macro information includes population trends, general trade flows between countries, and world agricultural production. Micro information includes materials on specific industries in a country, their growth prospects, and their foreign trade activities. Specific data services might provide custom-tailored information responding to the detailed needs of a firm. Alternatively, some data services may concentrate on a specific geographic region. More information about selected government publications and research services is presented in Appendix A to this chapter. *The International Marketplace 7.2* explains some of the information services offered by the European Union.

Most countries have a wide array of national and international trade data available. Increasingly these data are available on the Internet, which makes them much more current than ever before. Closer collaboration between governmental statistical agencies also makes the data more accurate and reliable, since it is now much easier to compare data such as bilateral exports and imports to each other. These information sources are often available at embassies and consulates, whose mission includes the enhancement of trade activities. The commercial counselor or commercial attaché can provide the information available from these sources.

International Organizations

International organizations often provide useful data for the researcher. The *Statistical Yearbook* produced by the United Nations contains international trade data on products and provides information on exports and imports by country. The *World Atlas* published by the World Bank provides useful general data on population, growth trends, and GNP figures. The World Trade Organization (WTO) and the Organization for Economic Cooperation and Development (OECD) also publish quarterly and annual trade data on their member countries. Finally, organizations such as the International Monetary Fund (IMF) and the World Bank publish occasional staff papers that evaluate region- or country-specific issues in depth.

Service Organizations

A wide variety of service organizations that may provide information include banks, accounting firms, freight forwarders, airlines, and **international trade consultants.** Frequently, they are able to provide data on business practices, legislative or regulatory requirements, and political stability as well as basic trade data. However, although some of this information is available without charge, its basic intent is to serve as an "appetizer." Much of the initial information is quite general in nature; more detailed answers often require an appropriate fee.

Trade Associations

Associations such as world trade clubs and domestic and international chambers of commerce (for example, the American Chamber of Commerce abroad) can provide valuable information about local markets. Often, files are maintained on international trade issues and trends affecting international marketers. Useful information can also be obtained from industry associations. These groups, formed to represent entire industry segments, often collect from their members a wide variety of data that are then published in an aggregate form. The information provided is often quite general in nature because of the wide variety of clientele served. However, it can provide valuable initial insights into international markets, since it permits a benchmarking effort, through which the international marketer can establish how it is faring when compared to its competition. For example, an industry summary that indicates firm average exports to be 10 percent of sales, and export sales growth to take place mainly in Asia, allows a better evaluation of a specific firm's performance by the international marketer.

Directories and Newsletters

Many industry directories are available on local, national, and international levels. These directories primarily serve to identify firms and to provide very general background information such as the name of the chief executive officer, the location, the address and telephone number, and some information about a firm's products. The quality of a directory depends, of course, on the quality of input and the frequency of updates. Some of the directories are becoming increasingly sophisticated and can provide quite detailed information to the researcher.

Many newsletters are devoted to specific international issues such as international trade finance, international contracting, bartering, countertrade, international payment flows, and customs news. Published by banks or accounting firms in order to keep their clientele current on international developments, newsletters usually cater to narrow audiences but can provide important information to the firm interested in a specific area.

Electronic Information Services

When information is needed, managers often cannot spend a lot of time, energy, or money finding, sifting through, and categorizing it. Consider laboring through every copy of a trade publication to find out the latest news on how environmental concerns are affecting marketing decisions in Mexico. With electronic information services, search results can be obtained within minutes. International on-line computer database services, numbering in the thousands, can be purchased to supply information external to the firm, such as exchange rates, international news, and import restrictions. Most database hosts do not charge any sign-up fee and request payment only for actual use. The selection of initial database hosts depends on the choice of relevant databases, taking into account their product and market limitations, language used, and geographical location.

A large number of databases and search engines provide information about products and markets. Many of the main news agencies through on-line databases provide information about events that affect certain markets. Some databases cover extensive lists of companies in given countries and the products they buy and sell. A large number of databases exist that cover various categories of trade statistics. The main economic indicators of the UN, IMF, OECD, and EU are available on-line. Standards institutes in most of the G7 nations provide on-line access to their databases of technical standards and trade regulations on specific products.

Compact Disk/Read-Only Memory (CD-ROM) technology allows for massive amounts of information (the equivalent of 300 books of 1,000 pages each, or 1,500 floppy disks) to be stored on a single 12-centimeter plastic disk. The technology increasingly is used for storing and distributing large volumes of information, such as statistical databases. Typically, the user pays no user fees but instead invests in a CD-ROM "reader" and purchases the actual CDs. Figure 7.2 provides an example.

A CD-ROM service widely used in the United States is the National Trade Data Bank (NTDB), a monthly product issued by the U.S. Department of Commerce. The NTDB includes more than 170,000 documents, including full-text market research reports, domestic and foreign economic data, import and export statistics, trade information and country studies, all compiled from 26 government agencies. The NTDB can also provide profiles of screened businesses that are interested in importing U.S. products.

Using data services for research means that researchers do not have to leave their offices, going from library to library to locate the facts they need. Many on-line services have late-breaking information available within twenty-four hours to the user. These techniques of research are cost-effective as well. Stocking a company's library with all the books needed to have the same amount of data that is available on-line or with CD-ROM would be too expensive and space-consuming. In spite of the ease of access of data on the Internet, search engines cover only a portion of international publications. Also, they are heavily biased toward English-language publications. As a result, sole reliance on electronic information may cause the researcher to lose out on valuable input.[8] Electronic databases should therefore be seen as only one important dimension of research scrutiny.

Other Firms

Often, other firms can provide useful information for international marketing purposes. Firms appear to be more open about their international than about their domestic marketing activities. On some occasions, valuable information can also be obtained from foreign firms and distributors.

[8]Michael R. Czinkota, "International Information Cross-Fertilization in Marketing: An Empirical Assessment," *European Journal of Marketing*, 34, 2000.

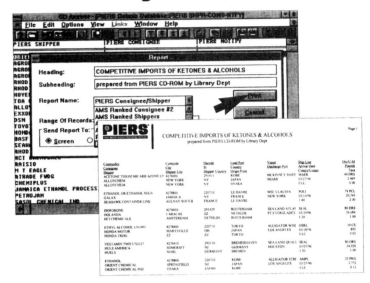

Get the import/export information you need. How you want it. When you want it.

Introducing PIERS' new report writing feature on CD-ROM

There's no better way to get import and export information than PIERS data on CD-ROM, now with enhanced report writing capabilities.

Our new report writing feature makes it easy to produce graphs, rankings and summaries, as well as detailed displays. Simply choose from a variety of customized reports that collate and present the data you want into easy-to-analyze information.

PIERS data on CD-ROM

makes it easier than ever before to keep tabs on the world market. Discover the names of your foreign competitors, as well as how much and how often they export. Or keep track of what and how much your domestic customers import from overseas and whether your "authorized" distributors are selling outside their territories.

In today's global economy, PIERS import/export data can be an invaluable marketing tool. No other source is as detailed, reliable or timely – because PIERS import/export information is gathered from the bills of lading for every ship calling on U.S. ports. And with PIERS' new report writing feature on CD-ROM, you'll find this vital data is more useful and revealing than ever! Call today for more information about PIERS data on CD-ROM.

PIERS®
PORT IMPORT/EXPORT REPORTING SERVICE
BUILDING A WORLD OF INFORMATION

PIERS is a division of The Journal of Commerce and a member of The Economist Group.
Two World Trade Center, Suite 2750, New York, NY 10048 800-952-3839 212-837-7051 Fax 212-837-7070
425 California Street, Suite 2450, San Francisco, CA 94104 800-824-7537 415-982-7642 Fax 415-788-6505
http://www.piers.com

SOURCE: http://www.piers.com

Evaluating Data

Before obtaining secondary data, the researcher needs to evaluate their appropriateness for the task at hand. As the first step of such an evaluation, the quality of the data source needs to be considered with a primary focus on the purpose and method of the original data collection. Next, the quality of the actual data needs to be assessed, which should include a determination of data accuracy, reliability, and recency. Obviously, outdated data may mislead rather than improve the decision-making process. In addition, the compatibility and comparability of the data need to be considered. Since they were collected with another purpose in mind, we need to determine whether the data can help with the issue of concern to the firm. In international research it is also important to ensure that data categories are comparable to each other, in order to avoid misleading conclusions. For example, the term *middle class* is likely to have very different implications for income and consumption patterns in different parts of the world.

Analyzing and Interpreting Secondary Data

After the data have been obtained, the researcher must use his or her research creativity to make good use of them. This often requires the combination and cross tabulation of various sets of data or the use of proxy information in order to arrive at conclusions that address the research objectives. For example, the market penetration of television sets may be used as a **proxy variable** for the potential market demand for video recorders. Similarly, in an industrial setting, information about plans for new port facilities may be useful in determining future containerization requirements. Also, the level of computerization of a society may indicate the future need for software.

The researcher must go beyond the scope of the data and use creative inferences to arrive at knowledge useful to the firm. However, such creativity brings risks. Once the interpretation and analysis have taken place, a consistency check must be conducted. The researcher should always cross-check the results with other possible sources of information or with experts.

In addition, the researcher should take another look at the research methods employed and, based on their usefulness, determine any necessary modifications for future projects. This will make possible the continuous improvement of international market research activities and enables the corporation to learn from experience.

Data Privacy

The attitude of society toward obtaining and using both secondary and primary data must be taken into account. Many societies are increasingly sensitive to the issue of data privacy, and the concern has grown exponentially as a result of e-business. Readily accessible databases may contain information valuable to marketers, but they may also be considered privileged by individuals who have provided the data.

In 1998, the European Union passed a directive that introduces high standards of data privacy to ensure the free flow of data throughout the 15 member states. More importantly, the directive also requires member states to block transmission of data to non-EU countries if these countries do not have domestic legislation that provides for a level of protection judged as adequate by the European Union. These laws will restrict access to lifestyle information and its use for segmentation purposes. It will be particularly difficult for direct marketers to obtain international access to voter rolls, birth records, or mortgage information.[9]

---

[9]Charles A. Prescott, "The New International Marketing Challenge: Privacy," *Target Marketing* 22 (Number 4, 1999): 28.

THE INTERNATIONAL MARKETPLACE 7.3

Privacy Can Be Contentious

THE WEB HAS EVOLVED into a marketplace and has transformed privacy from a right to a commodity. Sociologists call corporate data tracking "dataveillance," and it goes beyond the Web. When you surf the Net, buy through the mail, take a vacation, or use a credit card, you leave a data trail. The ultimate use of all this information is a new corporate strategy called "relationship marketing" in which companies seek to bond with consumers for life through an increasingly differentiated array of transactions. The rationale is an attempt to minimize uncertainty, but each of these strategies also shrinks the terrain of freedom and increases the need for privacy.

The legacy of data surveillance makes Europeans sensitive to spy commerce, which is why the EU's regulations deem consumer information private. U.S. courts and legislatures, on the other hand, regard such data as public property. In the United States, 85 percent of web sites collect some personal information from visitors, but only 14 percent post privacy policies. In the European Union, regulations guarantee citizens absolute control over data concerning them. If a company wants personal information, it must get the person's permission and explain what it will be used for. It must also promise not to use it for anything else without the citizen's consent. Yet a study by Consumer International challenges the effectiveness of European regulations. A survey of 750 commercial sites in Europe and the U.S. revealed that only 9 percent of European sites requested permission to sell customer information, compared with 50 percent in the U.S.

One part of the law is particularly stringent. Article 29 demands that foreign governments provide data protections every bit as rigorous as Europe's under a similar regulatory structure. Those failing to comply will find their data flows with Europe outlawed.

In Europe, web site owners are not able to use data tags known as "cookies" to track consumers' preferences and movements without their permission. Web merchants use these data tags to solve the problem of customer authentication. They want to know whether you are who you say you are, and the Internet's anonymity makes that difficult. The Pentium III chip was intended as one possible solution. In its initial version, each chip had a unique ID number that could be read remotely by a web server. The machine, if not the actual user, could then be associated with click-streams and other identifiable information. Click-stream monitoring, a page-by-page tracking of people as they wander through the Web, reveals your interests and tastes. Privacy advocates promptly launched a boycott of the chip, which caused Intel to beat a partial retreat by disabling the ID feature. The Pentium 4 processor, released in November 2000, does not feature click-stream monitoring capabilities.

SOURCES: Joris Evers, "U.S. Beats Europe in On-Line Privacy Protection," January 21, 2001, **www.infoworld.com**, accessed April 16, 2001; Peter McGrath, "Knowing You All Too Well," *Newsweek*, March 29, 1999, 62–64; Stephen Baker, Marsha Johnston, and William Echikson, "Europe's Privacy Cops," *Business Week*, November 2, 1998, 49–51; and Mark Boal, "Spy Commerce," *The Village Voice*, December 15, 1998, 72–78.

Other parts of the world are even more strict. For example, a violation of Hong Kong's data protection principles can earn the violator jail time.[10] *The International Marketplace 7.3* illustrates how contentious privacy issues can become.

In order to settle conflicts between divergent government policies, companies are increasingly likely to adapt global privacy rules for managing information on-line and to get certified by watchdog groups, which tell users when a site adheres to specific privacy guidelines.[11] Overall, the international marketer must pay careful attention to the privacy laws and expectations in different nations and to possible consumer reactions to the use of data in the marketing effort.

The Primary Research Process

Primary research is conducted to fill specific information needs. The research may not actually be conducted by the firm with the need, but the work must be carried out for

[10]Denny Hatch, "Marketing Abroad: Play by Their Rules," *Business and Management Practices* 20 (Number 2, 1997): 38–40.

[11]Elizabeth De Bony, "EU, U.S. Plug Away at Data Privacy Accord," *Industry Standard* (December 10, 1998): 45–46.

a specific research purpose. Primary research therefore goes beyond the activities of secondary data collection, which often cannot supply answers to the specific questions posed. Conducting primary research internationally can be complex due to different environments, attitudes, and market conditions. Yet, it is precisely because of these differences that such research is necessary.

Primary research is essential for the formulation of strategic marketing plans. One particular area of research interest is international market segmentation. Historically, firms segmented international markets based on macro variables such as income per capita or consumer spending on certain product categories. Increasingly, however, firms recognize that segmentation variables, such as lifestyles, attitudes, or personality, can play a major role in identifying similar consumer groups in different countries, which can then be targeted across borders. One such group could consist, for example, of educationally elite readers who read *Scientific American, Time, Newsweek, The Financial Times,* and *The Economist.* Members in this group are likely to have more in common with each other than with their fellow citizens.[12] Alternatively, in marketing to women, it is important to understand the degree to which they have entered the workforce in a country, what their life cycle stage is, and how women in different economic segments make or influence purchase decisions.[13] In order to identify these groups and to devise ways of meeting their needs, primary international market research is indispensable.

Determining Information Requirements

Specific research questions must be formulated to determine precisely the information that is sought. The following are examples of such marketing questions:

- What is the market potential for our furniture in Indonesia?
- How much does the typical Nigerian consumer spend on soft drinks?
- What will happen to demand in Brazil if we raise our product price along monthly inflation levels?
- What effect will a new type of packaging have on our "green" consumers in Germany, France, and England?

Only when information requirements are determined as precisely as possible will the researcher be able to develop a research program that will deliver a useful product.

Industrial versus Consumer Research

The researcher must decide whether to conduct research with consumers or with industrial users. This decision will in part determine the size of the universe and respondent accessibility. For example, consumers are usually a very large group and can be reached through interviews at home or through intercept techniques. On the other hand, the total population of industrial users may be smaller and more difficult to reach. Further, cooperation by respondents may be quite different, ranging from very helpful to very limited. In the industrial setting, differentiating between users and decision makers may be much more important because their personality, their outlook, and their evaluative criteria may differ widely.

---

[12]Salah S. Hassan and A. Coskun Samli, "The New Frontiers of Intermarket Segmentation," in *Global Marketing: Perspectives and Cases*, eds. Salah S. Hassan and Roger D. Blackwell (Fort Worth, TX: The Dryden Press, 1994), 76–100.

[13]Rena Bartos, "Marketing to Women around the World," in *Global Marketing: Perspectives and Cases*, 1994, 119–146.

Determining Research Administration

The major issues in determining who will do the research are whether to use a centralized, coordinated, or decentralized approach and whether to engage an outside research service.

Degree of Research Centralization   The level of control that corporation headquarters exercises over international marketing research activities is a function of the overall organizational structure of the firm and the nature and importance of the decision to be made. The three major approaches to international research organization are the centralized, coordinated, and decentralized approaches.

The centralized approach clearly affords the most control to headquarters. All **research specifications** such as focus, thrust, and design are directed by the home office and are forwarded to the local country operations for implementation. The subsequent analysis of gathered information again takes place at headquarters. Such an approach can be quite valuable when international marketing research is intended to influence corporate policies and strategy. It also ensures that all international market studies remain comparable to one another. On the other hand, some risks exist. For example, headquarters management may not be sufficiently familiar with the local market situation to be able to adapt the research appropriately. Also, headquarters cultural bias may influence the research activities. Finally, headquarters staff may be too small or insufficiently skilled to provide proper guidance for multiple international marketing research studies.

A coordinated research approach uses an intermediary such as an outside research agency to bring headquarters and country operations together. This approach provides for more interaction and review of the international marketing research plan by both headquarters and the local operations and ensures more responsiveness to both strategic and local concerns. If the intermediary used is of high quality, the research capabilities of a corporation can be greatly enhanced through a coordinated approach.

The decentralized approach requires corporate headquarters to establish the broad thrust of research activities and to then delegate the further design and implementation to the local countries. The entire research is then carried out locally under the supervision of the local country operation, and only a final report is provided to headquarters. This approach has particular value when international markets differ significantly, because it permits detailed adaptation to local circumstances. However, implementing research activities on a country-by-country basis may cause unnecessary duplication, lack of knowledge transference, and lack of comparable results.

Local country operations may not be aware of research carried out by corporate units in other countries and may reinvent the wheel. This problem can be avoided if a proper intracorporate flow of information exists so that local units can check whether similar information has already been collected elsewhere within the firm. Corporate units that operate in markets similar to one another can then benefit from the exchange of research findings.

Local units may also develop their own research thrusts, tools, and analyses. A researcher in one country may, for example, develop a creative way of dealing with a nonresponse problem. This new technique could be valuable to company researchers who face similar difficulties in other countries. However, for the technique to become widely known, systems must be in place to circulate information to the firm as a whole.

Finally, if left to their own devices, researchers will develop different ways of collecting and tabulating data. As a result, findings in different markets may not be comparable, and potentially valuable information about major changes and trends may be lost to the corporation.

International marketing research activities will always be carried out subject to the organizational structure of a firm. Ideally, a middle ground between centralization and decentralization will be found, one that permits local flexibility together with an ongoing exchange of information within the corporation. As the extent of a firm's international activities grows, the exchange of information becomes particularly important, because global rather than local optimization is the major goal of the multinational corporation.

Outside Research Services   One major factor in deciding whether or not to use outside research services is, of course, the size of the international operations of a firm. No matter how large a firm is, however, it is unlikely to possess specialized expertise in international marketing research for every single market it currently serves or is planning to serve. Rather than overstretch the capabilities of its staff or assert a degree of expertise that does not exist, a corporation may wish to delegate the research task to outside groups. This is particularly the case when corporate headquarters have little or no familiarity with the local research environment. Figure 7.3 provides an example of such a situation. The use of outside research agencies may be especially appropriate for large-scale international marketing research or when highly specialized research skills are required. Increasingly, marketing research agencies operate worldwide, in order to accommodate the research needs of their clients. Table 7.2 provides information about the top 25 global research organizations and their international activities.

The selection process for outside research providers should emphasize the quality of information rather than the cost. Low price is no substitute for lack in data pertinence or accuracy.

Before a decision is made, the capabilities of an outside organization should be carefully evaluated and compared with the capabilities available in-house and from competing firms. Although general technical capabilities are important, the prime selection criterion should be previous research experience in a particular country and a particular industry. Some experience is transferable from one industry or country to another; however, the more the corporation's research needs overlap an agency's past research accomplishment, the more likely it is that the research task will be carried out satisfactorily. Although the research may be more difficult to administer, multinational corporations should consider subcontracting each major international marketing research task to specialists, even if research within one country is carried out by various international marketing research agencies as a result. To have experts working on a problem is usually more efficient than to conserve corporate resources by centralizing all research activities with one service provider, who is only marginally familiar with key aspects of the research. However, if different firms carry out the research, it becomes very important to ensure that data are comparable. Otherwise, the international firm will not be able to transfer lessons learned from one market to another.

Determining the Research Technique

Selection of the research technique depends on a variety of factors. First, the objectivity of the data sought must be determined. Standardized techniques are more useful in the collection of objective data than of subjective data. **Unstructured data** will require more open-ended questions and more time than structured data. Since the willingness and ability of respondents to spend the time and provide a free-form response are heavily influenced by factors such as culture and education, the prevailing conditions in the country and segments to be studied need to be understood in making these decisions. Whether the data are to be collected in the real world or in a controlled environment also must be decided. Finally, a decision needs to be made as to whether the research is to collect historical facts or gather information about future developments. This is particularly important for consumer research because firms frequently desire to determine consumers' future intentions to purchase a certain product.

Cultural and individual preferences, which vary significantly among nations, play a major role in determining research techniques. U.S. managers frequently prefer to

THE INTERVIEWING IS EASY...
IF THIS MAN DOESN'T SHOOT YOU FIRST

TASK :

Interview Afghans who fled across the border into Pakistan to see if they're listening to the BBC. Problem: you have to get past the local warlords who control the area.

Hand this problem to any old research company claiming to do international research, and you're in trouble. The BBC turned to Research International.

KNOWING WHAT WORKS

In today's competitive world, companies are increasingly looking toward off-shore markets. And that means good information is essential, even in developed markets.

But international research isn't just a case of taking what you do here and transplanting it there.

A national probability sample in Brazil will have you climbing a palm tree. "I will buy" on a scale in Japan doesn't mean the same thing in Spain. In tax-shy Italy, quota sampling on the basis of income won't get you very far!

GLOBAL PERSPECTIVE
+ LOCAL INSIGHT

We have Research International offices on the ground in 38 of the world's most important markets, from France to Argentina, the USA to Russia, London to Singapore. All our companies are leaders in their markets.

Our professional staff know their markets because they live there—not through visits or by reading the statistics.

We have conducted more than 4,000 international projects. In the last two years alone, we've worked in over 100 countries.

We know what works. And what doesn't. We know what research should cost. We know how to insure comparable high quality standards worldwide.

RESEARCH INTERNATIONAL
IN NORTH AMERICA

You may be surprised to know that Research International has 6 companies and 9 offices in this region. Whether it's large scale survey work, product testing, customer satisfaction research, qualitative or observational research, we can help.

We can put together an unrivaled team drawing on Research International resources in place in New York, Boston, San Francisco, Chicago, Toronto, Mexico City and in San Juan.

COMMITMENT TO
INNOVATION WORLDWIDE

Being on the ground all around the world also means that we have access to the best brains and the best thinking around the globe. Which means that we can offer our clients innovative, powerful techniques regardless of place of origin.

Our commitment to R. & D. runs very deep. Each year, we spend more of our own money on basic research than most of our competitors bring to the bottom line.

FREE OFFER

We've prepared a paper to help avoid some of the traps. Called "8 Common Pitfalls of International Research," it's free to marketers. Simply fax Daphne Chandler at— 212-889-0487.

For specific help right now—call Daphne at 212-679-2500.

RESEARCH INTERNATIONAL

SOURCE: http://www.research-int.com

TABLE 7.2 Top 25 Global Research Organizations

RANK	ORGANIZATION	HEADQUARTERS	PARENT COUNTRY	NO. OF COUNTRIES WITH SUBSIDIARIES/ BRANCH OFFICES[1]	FULL-TIME EMPLOYEES	TOTAL RESEARCH REVENUES[2] (MILLIONS)	PERCENT OF TOTAL REVENUES OUTSIDE HOME COUNTRY
1	ACNielsen Corp.	Stamford, Conn.	U.S.	80	21,000	$1,525.4	68.1%
2	IMS Health Inc.	Westport, N.Y.	U.S.	74	9,000	1,275.7	60.7
3	The Kantar Group Ltd.	London	U.K.	57	4,800	773.5	74.8
4	Taylor Nelson Sofres plc	London	U.K.	41	6,000	601.3	72.3
5	Information Resources Inc.	Chicago	U.S.	17	4,400	546.3	23.7
6	NFO Worldwide Inc.	Greenwich, Conn.	U.S.	38	3,300	457.2	61.3
7	Nielsen Media Research	New York	Netherlands	2	2,800	453.3	2.6
8	GfK Group AG	Nürnberg	Germany	34	3,676	414.0	55.6
9	United Information Group Ltd.	London	U.K.	6	1,467	246.3	63.0
10	Ipsos Group S.A.	Paris	France	20	1,681	245.8	71.3
11	Westat Inc.	Rockville, Md.	U.S.	1	1,347	242.0	—
12	The Arbitron Co.	New York	U.S.	2	587	215.4	3.7
13	Maritz Marketing Research Inc.	St.Louis, Mo.	U.S.	3	673	174.3	31.0
14	Market Facts Inc.	Arlington Heights,Ill.	U.K.	2	1,000	160.0	15.1
15	Video Research Ltd.	Tokyo	Japan	2	346[3]	153.4[3]	—
16	The NPD Group Inc.	Port Washington, N.Y.	U.S.	13	950	143.4	18.4
17	Marketing Intelligence Corp.	Tokyo	Japan	2	385[3]	110.3[3]	1.4[3]
18	Opinion Research Corp. International	Princeton, N.J.	U.S.	8	1,630	109.4	36.0
	Opinion Research Corp.	*Princeton, N.J.*	*U.S.*	6	1,148	56.7	34.9
	Macro International Inc.	*Calverton, Mo.*	*U.S.*	3	482	52.7	37.2
19	J.D. Power and Associates	Agoura Hills, Calif.	U.S.	5	500	75.4	12.5
20	Roper Starch Worldwide Inc.	Harrison, N.Y.	U.S.	3	761	65.7	13.2
21	Dentsu Research Inc.	Tokyo	Japan	1	118	59.4	0.3
22	Sample Institut GmbH & Co. KG	Mölln	Germany	7	350	58.5	54.8
23	Abt Associates Inc.	Cambridge, Mass.	U.S.	3	1,000[4]	50.8	15.0
24	Sifo Research & Consulting	Stockholm	Sweden	3	395	49.7	21.1
25	IBOPE Group	Rio de Janeiro	Brazil	7	1,416	49.4	29.7
	Total				69,582	$8,255.9	49.1%

[1]Includes countries which have subsidiaries with an equity interest or branch offices or both.

[2]Total revenues that include nonresearch activities for some companies are significantly higher. This information is given in the individual company profits.

[3]For fiscal year ending March 31.

[4]Total company.

SOURCE: *Marketing News*, August 14, 2000.

gather large quantities of data through surveys, which provide numbers that can be manipulated statistically and directly compared to other sets of data. In some other countries managers appear to prefer the "soft" approach. For example, much of Japanese-style market research relies heavily on two kinds of information: **soft data** obtained from visits to dealers and other channel members and **hard data** about shipments, inventory levels, and retail sales.

Once the structure of the type of data sought has been determined, a choice must be made among the types of research instruments available. Each provides a different depth of information and has its unique strengths and weaknesses.

Interviews   Interviews with knowledgeable persons can be of great value to a corporation desiring international marketing information. Because bias from the individual may be part of the findings, the intent should be to obtain in-depth information rather than a wide variety of data. Particularly when specific answers are sought to very narrow questions, interviews can be most useful.

Focus Groups   Focus groups are a useful research tool resulting in interactive interviews. A group of knowledgeable persons is gathered for a limited period of time (two to four hours). Usually, the ideal size for a focus group is seven to ten participants. A specific topic is introduced and thoroughly discussed by all group members. Because of the interaction, hidden issues are sometimes raised that would not have been addressed in an individual interview. The skill of the group leader in stimulating discussion is crucial to the success of a focus group. Discussions are often recorded on tape and subsequently analyzed in detail. Focus groups, like in-depth interviews, do not provide statistically significant information; however, they can be helpful in providing information about perceptions, emotions, and other nonovert factors. In addition, once individuals are gathered, focus groups are highly efficient in terms of rapidly accumulating a substantial amount of information. With the advances occurring in the communications field, focus groups can also be carried out internationally, with interaction between groups.

When conducting international research via focus groups, the researcher must be aware of the importance of culture in the discussion process. Not all societies encourage frank and open exchange and disagreement among individuals. Status consciousness may result in situations in which the opinion of one is reflected by all other participants. Disagreement may be seen as impolite, or certain topics may be taboo.

Observation   Observation techniques require the researcher to play the role of a nonparticipating observer of activity and behavior. Observation can be personal or impersonal—for example, mechanical. Observation can be obtrusive or inobtrusive, depending on whether the subject is aware or unaware of being observed. In international marketing research, observation can be extremely useful in shedding light on practices not previously encountered or understood. This aspect is particularly valuable for the researcher who is totally unfamiliar with a market or market situation and can be quickly achieved through, for example, participation in a trade mission. Observation can also help in understanding phenomena that would have been difficult to assess with other techniques. For example, Toyota sent a group of its engineers and designers to southern California to unobtrusively observe how women get into and operate their cars. They found that women with long fingernails have trouble opening the door and operating various knobs on the dashboard. Based on their observations, Toyota engineers and designers were able to observe the women's plight and redraw some of the automobile exterior and interior designs.[14]

---

[14]Michael R. Czinkota and Masaaki Kotabe, "Product Development the Japanese Way," in *Trends in International Business: Critical Perspectives*, eds. M. Czinkota and M. Kotabe (Oxford, England: Blackwell Publishers, 1998), 153–158.

Conducting observations can also have its pitfalls. For example, people may react differently to the discovery that their behavior has been observed. The degree to which the observer has to be familiarized or introduced to other participants may vary. The complexity of the task may differ due to the use of multiple languages. To conduct in-store research in Europe, for example, store checks, photo audits of shelves, and store interviews must be scheduled well in advance and need to be preceded by a full round of introductions of the researchers to store management and personnel. In some countries, such as Belgium, a researcher must remember that four different languages are spoken and their use may change from store to store.

The research instruments discussed so far—interviews, focus groups, and observation—are useful primarily for gathering **qualitative information**. The intent is not to amass data, or to search for statistical significance, but rather to obtain a better understanding of given situations, behavioral patterns, or underlying dimensions. The researcher using these instruments must be cautioned that even frequent repetition of the measurements will not lead to a statistically valid result. However, statistical validity often is not the major focus of corporate international marketing research. Rather, it is the better understanding, description, and prediction of events that have an impact on marketing decision making. When **quantitative data** are desired, surveys are appropriate research instruments.

Surveys

Survey research is useful in providing the opportunity to quantify concepts. In the social sciences, it is generally accepted that "the cross-cultural survey is scientifically the most powerful method of hypothesis testing."[15] Surveys are usually conducted via questionnaires that are administered personally, by mail, or by telephone. Use of the survey technique presupposes that the population under study is able to comprehend and respond to the questions posed. Also, particularly in the case of mail and telephone surveys, a major precondition is the feasibility of using the postal system or the widespread availability of telephones. In many countries, only limited records are available about dwellings, their location, and their occupants. In Venezuela, for example, most houses are not numbered but rather are given individual names like "Casa Rosa" or "El Retiro." In some countries, street maps are not even available. As a result, it becomes virtually impossible to reach respondents by mail.

In other countries, obtaining a correct address may be easy, but the postal system may not function well. The Italian postal service, for example, repeatedly has suffered from scandals that exposed such practices as selling undelivered mail to paper mills for recycling.

Telephone surveys may also be inappropriate if telephone ownership is rare. In such instances, any information obtained would be highly biased even if the researcher randomizes the calls. In some instances, telephone networks and systems may also prevent the researcher from conducting surveys. Frequent line congestion or a lack of telephone directories are examples. There are also great variations between countries or regions of countries in terms of unlisted telephone numbers. For example, authors of comparative research have reported that only 2.1 percent of households with telephones in Kobe, Japan, have unlisted numbers, while the figure for Seattle's King County is estimated to be approximately 20 percent.[16]

Surveys can be hampered by social and cultural constraints. Recipients of letters may be illiterate or may be reluctant to respond in writing. In some nations, entire population segments—for example, women—may be totally inaccessible to interviewers. One must also assess the purpose of the survey in the context of the popula-

[15]Lothar G. Winter and Charles R. Prohaska, "Methodological Problems in the Comparative Analysis of International Marketing Systems," *Journal of the Academy of Marketing Science* 11 (Fall 1983): 421.

[16]Raymond A. Jussaume, Jr., and Yoshiharu Yamada, "A Comparison of the Viability of Mail Surveys in Japan and the United States," *Public Opinion Quarterly* 54 (1990): 219–228.

tion surveyed. It has been argued, for example, that one should not rely on consumer surveys for new product development information. Key reasons are the absence of responsibility—the consumer is sincere when spending but not when talking; conservative attitudes—ordinary consumers are conservative and tend to react negatively to a new product; vanity—it is human nature to exaggerate and put on a good appearance; and insufficient information—the research results depend on the product characteristics information that is given to survey participants and that may be incomplete or unabsorbed.[17]

In spite of all these difficulties, however, the survey technique remains a useful one because it allows the researcher to rapidly accumulate a large quantity of data amenable to statistical analysis. Even though quite difficult, **international comparative research** has been carried out very successfully between nations, particularly if the environments studied are sufficiently similar so that the impact of uncontrollable macrovariables is limited. However, even in environments that are quite dissimilar, in-depth comparative research can be carried out.[18] Doing so may require a country-by-country adjustment of details while preserving the similarity of research thrust. For example, researchers have reported good results in mail surveys conducted simultaneously in Japan and the United States after adjusting the size of the return envelope, outgoing envelope, address style, signature, and cover letter to meet specific societal expectations.[19] With constantly expanding technological capabilities, international marketers will be able to use the survey technique more frequently in the future. Figure 7.4 provides an overview of the extent of the technology available to help the international research process.

Designing the Survey Questionnaire

International marketing surveys are usually conducted with questionnaires. These questionnaires should contain questions that are clear and easy to comprehend by the respondents, as well as easy for the data collector to administer. Much attention must therefore be paid to question format, content, and wording.

Question Format   Questions can be structured or unstructured. Unstructured or open-ended questions permit the capture of more in-depth information, but they also increase the potential for interviewer bias. Even at the cost of potential bias, however, "the use of open-ended questions appears quite useful in cross-cultural surveys, because they may help identify the frame of reference of the respondents, or may even be designed to permit the respondent to set his own frame of reference."[20]

Another question format decision is the choice between direct and indirect questions. Societies have different degrees of sensitivity to certain questions. Questions related to the income or age of a respondent may be accepted differently in different countries. Also, the social desirability of answers may vary. In some cultures, questions about employees, performance, standards, and financing are asked directly of a respondent, while in others, particularly in Asia or the Middle East, these questions are thought to be rude and insulting.[21] As a result, the researcher must be sure that the

---

[17]R. Nishikawa, "New Product Planning at Hitachi," *Long Range Planning* 22 (1989): 20–24.

[18]For an excellent example, see Alan Dubinsky, Marvin Jolson, Masaaki Kotabe, and Chae Lim, "A Cross-National Investigation of Industrial Salespeople's Ethical Perceptions," *Journal of International Business Studies* 22 (1991): 651–670.

[19]Jussaume and Yamada, 222.

[20]Sydney Verba, "Cross-National Survey Research: The Problem of Credibility," in *Comparative Methods in Sociology: Essays on Trends and Applications*, ed. I. Vallier (Berkeley: University of California Press, 1971), 322–323.

[21]Camille P. Schuster and Michael J. Copeland, "Global Business Exchanges: Similarities and Differences around the World," *Journal of International Marketing* (Number 2, 1999): 63–80.

Main telephone lines per 1000 inhabitants

- 0 to 50
- 50 to 150
- 150 to 250
- 250 to 350
- Over 350

Source: The *World Bank Atlas*, 2000

questions are culturally acceptable. This may mean that questions that can be asked directly in some cultures will have to be asked indirectly in others. For example, rather than ask "How old are you?" one could ask "In what year were you born?"

The researcher must also be sure to adapt the complexity of the question to the level of understanding of the respondent. For example, a multipoint scaling method, which may be effectively used in a developed country to discover the attitudes and attributes of company executives, may be a very poor instrument if used among rural entrepreneurs. It has been found that demonstration aids are useful in surveys among poorly educated respondents.[22]

The question format should also ensure data equivalence in international marketing research. This requires categories used in questionnaires to be comparatively structured. In a developed country, for example, a white-collar worker may be part of the middle class, whereas in a less-developed country, the same person would be part of the upper class. Before using categories in a questionnaire, the researcher must therefore determine their appropriateness in different environments. This is particularly important for questions that attempt to collect attitudinal, psychographic, or lifestyle data, since cultural variations are most pronounced in these areas.

Question Content   Major consideration must be given to the ability and willingness of respondents to supply the answers. The knowledge and information available to respondents may vary substantially because of different educational levels and may affect their ability to answer questions. Further, societal demands and restrictions may influence the willingness of respondents to answer certain questions. For various reasons, respondents may also be motivated to supply incorrect answers. For example, in countries where the tax collection system is consistently eluded by taxpayers, questions regarding level of income may deliberately be answered inaccurately. Distrust in the researcher, and the fear that research results may be passed on to the government, may also lead individuals to consistently understate their assets. Because of government restrictions in Brazil, for example, individuals will rarely admit to owning an imported car. Nevertheless, when we observe the streets of Rio de Janeiro, a substantial number of foreign cars are seen. The international market researcher is unlikely to change the societal context of a country. The objective of the content planning process should therefore be to adapt the questions to societal constraints.

Question Wording   The impact of language and culture is of particular importance when wording questions. The goal for the international marketing researcher should be to ensure that the potential for misunderstandings and misinterpretations of spoken or written words is minimized. Both language and cultural differences make this issue an extremely sensitive one in the international marketing research process. As a result, attention must be paid to the translation equivalence of verbal and nonverbal questions that can change in the course of translation. One of this book's authors, for example, used the term *group discussion* in a questionnaire for Russian executives, only to learn that the translated meaning of the term was "political indoctrination session."[23]

The key is to keep questions clear by using simple rather than complex words, by avoiding ambiguous words and questions, by omitting leading questions, and by asking questions in specific terms, thus avoiding generalizations and estimates.[24] To reduce problems of question wording, it is helpful to use a **translation-retranslation**

---

[22]Kavil Ramachandran, "Data Collection for Management Research in Developing Countries," in *The Management Research Handbook*, eds. N. Craig Smith and Paul Dainty (London: Routledge, 1991), 304.

[23]Michael R. Czinkota, "Russia's Transition to a Market Economy: Learning about Business," *Journal of International Marketing* 5 (Number 4, 1997): 73–93.

[24]Gilbert A. Churchill, Jr., *Marketing Research: Methodological Foundations*, 7th ed. (Fort Worth, TX: The Dryden Press, 1999).

approach. The researcher formulates the questions, has them translated into the language of the country under investigation, and subsequently has a second translator return the foreign text to the researcher's native language. Through the use of this method, the researcher can hope to detect possible blunders. An additional safeguard is the use of alternative wording. Here the researcher uses questions that address the same issue but are worded differently and that resurface at various points in the questionnaire in order to check for consistency in question interpretation by the respondents.

In spite of superb research planning, a poorly designed instrument will yield poor results. No matter how comfortable and experienced the researcher is in international research activities, an instrument should always be pretested. Ideally, such a pretest is carried out with a subset of the population under study. At least a pretest with knowledgeable experts and individuals should be conducted. Even though a pretest may mean time delays and additional cost, the risks of poor research are simply too great for this process to be omitted.

Developing the Sampling Plan

To obtain representative results, the researcher must reach representative members of the population under study. Many methods that have been developed in industrialized countries for this purpose are useless abroad. For example, address directories may simply not be available. Multiple families may live in one dwelling. Differences between population groups living, for example, in highlands and lowlands may make it imperative to differentiate these segments. Lack of basic demographic information may prevent the design of a sampling frame.

The international marketing researcher must keep in mind the complexities of the market under study and prepare his or her sampling plan accordingly. Often, samples need to be stratified to reflect different population groups, and innovative sampling methods need to be devised in order to assure representative responses. *The International Marketplace 7.4* provides an example of the creativity required.

Data Collection

The international marketing researcher must check the quality of the data collection process. In some cultures, questionnaire administration is seen as useless by the local population. Instruments are administered primarily to humor the researcher. In such cases, interviewer cheating may be quite frequent. Spot checks on the administration procedures are vital to ensure reasonable data quality. A **realism check** of data should also be used. For example, if marketing research in Italy reports that very little spaghetti is consumed, the researcher should perhaps consider whether individuals responded to their use of purchased spaghetti rather than homemade spaghetti. The collected data should therefore be compared with secondary information and with analogous information from a similar market in order to obtain a preliminary understanding of data quality.

Analyzing and Interpreting Primary Data

Interpretation and analysis of accumulated information are required to answer the research questions that were posed initially. The researcher should, of course, use the best tools available and appropriate for analysis. The fact that a market may be in a less developed country does not preclude the subjecting of good data to good analysis. On the other hand, international researchers should be cautioned against using overly sophisticated tools for unsophisticated data. Even the best of tools will not improve data quality. The quality of data must be matched with the quality of the research tools to achieve appropriately sophisticated analysis and yet not overstate the value of the data.

THE INTERNATIONAL MARKETPLACE 7.4

Creative Primary Research

WHEN U.S. ENTREPRENEUR Peter Johns went to Mexico to do business, he couldn't buy what he needed most: information. So he dug it up himself. Johns wanted to distribute mail-order catalogs for upscale U.S. companies to consumers in Mexico. He thought that a large market was there just waiting to be tapped. However, when he tried to test his theory against hard data, he ran into a big blank.

Johns, who has spent thirty years in international marketing, couldn't find a useful marketing study for Mexico City. Government census reports weren't much help because they stop breaking down income levels at about $35,000, and they give ranges, rather than precise numbers, on family size.

So Johns embarked on some primary research. He went into the affluent neighborhoods and found just what he had suspected: satellite dishes, imported sports cars, and women carrying Louis Vuitton handbags. He reached his own conclusions about the target market for his catalogs. "There is no question there is a sense of consumer deprivation in the luxury market of Mexico City," says Johns.

After deciding to pursue his new enterprise, Johns reached another obstacle. His new enterprise, Choices Unlimited, had gotten rights from about 20 U.S. companies to distribute their catalogs in Mexico City. Now he needed mailing lists—and he couldn't find them. Owner of mailing lists do not like to sell them because buyers tend to recycle the lists without authorization. Some of those that are available are expensive and may not include information like zip codes—important barometers of household wealth.

Johns asked his local investors for membership lists of the city's exclusive golf clubs. He also obtained directories of the parents of students at some of the city's exclusive private schools. Johns received these lists for free."That's called grass-roots marketing intelligence," says Johns.

SOURCE: Dianna Soils, "Grass-Roots Marketing Yields Clients in Mexico City," *The Wall Street Journal*, October 24, 1991, B2.

Presenting Research Results

The primary focus in the presentation of research results must be communication. In multinational marketing research, communication must take place not only with management at headquarters but also with managers in the local operations. Otherwise, little or no transference of research results will occur, and the synergistic benefits of a multinational operation are lost. To minimize time devoted to the reading of reports, the researcher must present results clearly and concisely. In the worldwide operations of a firm, particularly in the communication efforts, lengthy data and analytical demonstrations should be avoided. The availability of data and the techniques used should be mentioned, however, so that subsidiary operations can receive the information on request.

The researcher should also demonstrate in the presentation how research results relate to the original research objective and fit with overall corporate strategy. At least schematically, possibilities for analogous application should be highlighted. These possibilities should then also be communicated to local subsidiaries, perhaps through a short monthly newsletter. A newsletter format, ideally distributed through an intranet, can be used regardless of whether the research process is centralized, coordinated, or decentralized. The only difference will be the person or group providing the input for the newsletter. It is important to maintain such communication in order for the entire organization to learn and to improve its international marketing research capabilities.

Follow-Up and Review

Although the research process may be considered to be at an end here, from a managerial perspective, one more stage is important. Now that the research has been carried out, appropriate managerial decisions must be made based on the research, and the organization must absorb the research. For example, if it has been found that a product needs to have certain attributes to sell well in Latin America, the manager must determine whether the product development area is aware of this finding and the degree to which the knowledge is now incorporated into new product projects. Without such follow-up, the role of research tends to become a mere "staff" function, increasingly isolated from corporate "line" activity and lacking major impact on corporate activity. If that is the case, research will diminish and even be disregarded—resulting in an organization at risk.

The International Information System

Many organizations have data needs going beyond specific international marketing research projects. Most of the time, daily decisions must be made, and there is neither time nor money for special research. An information system already in place is needed to provide the decision maker with basic data for most ongoing decisions. Information and data management for the international market are more complex than for the domestic market because of separation in time and space as well as wide differences in cultural and technological environments.[25] Yet these same factors highlight the increased need for an information system that assists in the decision-making process. Corporations have responded by developing marketing decision support systems. Defined as "an integrated system of data, statistical analysis, modeling, and display formats using computer hardware and software technology," such a system serves as a mechanism to coordinate the flow of information to corporate managers for decision-making purposes.[26]

To be useful to the decision maker, the system needs various attributes. First, the information must be *relevant*. The data gathered must have meaning for the manager's decision-making process. Only rarely can corporations afford to spend large amounts of money on information that is simply "nice to know." Second, the information must be *timely*. It is of little benefit to the manager if decision information help that is needed today does not become available until a month from now. To be of use to the international decision maker, the system must therefore feed from a variety of international sources and be updated frequently. For multinational corporations, this means a real-time linkage between international subsidiaries and a broad-based ongoing data input operation.

Third, information must be *flexible*—that is, it must be available in the forms needed by management. A marketing decision support system must therefore permit manipulation of the format and combining of the data. Therefore, great effort must be expended to make diverse international data compatible with and comparable to each other. Fourth, information contained in the system must be *accurate*. This attribute is particularly relevant in the international field because information quickly becomes outdated as a result of major changes. Obviously, a system is of no value if it provides incorrect information that leads to poor decisions. Fifth, the system's information bank must be reasonably *exhaustive*. Because of the interrelationship between variables, factors that may influence a particular decision must be appropriately represented in the information system. This means that the marketing decision support system must be based on a broad variety of factors. Finally, to be useful to managers, the system must be *convenient*, both to use and to access. Systems that are

[25]Sayeste Daser, "International Marketing Information Systems: A Neglected Prerequisite for Foreign Market Planning," in *International Marketing Management*, ed. E. Kaynak (New York: Praeger Publishers, 1984), 139–154.

[26]Thomas C. Kinnear and James R. Taylor, *Marketing Research: An Applied Approach*, 5th ed. (New York: McGraw-Hill, 1996).

cumbersome and time-consuming to reach and to use will not be used enough to justify corporate expenditures to build and maintain them.

More international information systems are being developed successfully due to progress in computer technology in both hardware and software, increased familiarity with technology, and the necessity of dealing with increasing shifts in market conditions. To build an information system, corporations use the internal data that are available from divisions such as accounting and finance and also from their subsidiaries. In addition, many organizations put mechanisms in place to enrich the basic data flow. Three such tools are environmental scanning, Delphi studies, and scenario building.

Environmental Scanning

Any changes in the business environment, whether domestic or foreign, may have serious repercussions on the marketing activities of the firm. Corporations therefore should understand the necessity for tracking new developments and obtaining continuous updates. To carry out this task, some large multinational organizations have formed environmental scanning groups.

Environmental scanning activities are useful to continuously receive information on political, social, and economic affairs internationally; on changes of attitudes held by public institutions and private citizens; and on possible upcoming alterations in international markets.

The precision required for environmental scanning varies with its purpose. Whether the information is to be used for mind stretching or for budgeting, for example, must be taken into account when constructing the framework and variables that will enter the scanning process. The more immediate and precise the exercise is to be in its application within the corporation, the greater the need for detailed information. At the same time, such heightened precision may lessen the utility of environmental scanning for the strategic corporate purpose, which is more long-term in its orientation.

Environmental scanning can be performed in various ways. One method consists of obtaining factual input regarding many variables. For example, the U.S. Census Bureau collects, evaluates, and adjusts a wide variety of demographic, social, and economic characteristics of foreign countries. Estimates for all countries of the world are developed, particularly on economic variables, such as labor force statistics, GDP, and income statistics, but also on health and nutrition variables. Similar factual information can be obtained from international organizations such as the World Bank or the United Nations.

Frequently, corporations believe that such factual data alone are insufficient for their information needs. Particularly for forecasting future developments, other methods are used to capture underlying dimensions of social change. One significant method is **content analysis**. This technique investigates the content of communication in a society and entails literally counting the number of times preselected words, themes, symbols, or pictures appear in a given medium. It can be used productively in international marketing to monitor the social, economic, cultural, and technological environment in which the marketing organization is operating.

Corporations can use content analysis to pinpoint upcoming changes in their line of business, and new opportunities, by attempting to identify trendsetting events. For example, the Alaska oil spill by the tanker *Exxon Valdez* resulted in entirely new international concern about environmental protection and safety, reaching far beyond the incident itself.

Environmental scanning is conducted by a variety of groups within and outside the corporation. Frequently, small corporate staffs are created at headquarters to coordinate the information flow. In addition, subsidiary staff can be used to provide occasional intelligence reports. Groups of volunteers are also formed to gather and analyze information worldwide and feed individual analyses back to corporate headquarters, where they can be used to form the "big picture."

Although environmental scanning is perceived by many corporations as quite valuable for the corporate planning process, there are dissenting voices. For example, it has been noted by researchers "that in those constructs and frameworks where the environment has been given primary consideration, there has been a tendency for the approach to become so global that studies tend to become shallow and diffuse, or impractical if pursued insufficient depth."[27] This presents one of the major continuous challenges faced by corporations in their international environmental scanning. There is a trade-off between the breadth and the depth of information. The continuous evolution of data processing capabilities may reduce the scope of the problem. Yet the cost of data acquisition and the issue of actual data use will continue to be major restraints on the development of environmental scanning systems.

Finally, it should be kept in mind that internationally there may be a fine line between tracking and obtaining information, and misappropriating corporate secrets. With growing frequency, governments and firms claim that their trade secrets are being obtained and abused by foreign competitors. The perceived threat from economic espionage has led to legislation[28] and accusations of government spying networks trying to undermine the commercial interests of companies.[29] Information gatherers must be sensitive to these issues in order to avoid conflict or controversy.

Delphi Studies

To enrich the information obtained from factual data, corporations resort to the use of creative and highly qualitative data-gathering methods. Delphi studies are one such method. These studies are particularly useful in the international marketing environment because they are "a means for aggregating the judgments of a number of . . . experts . . . who cannot come together physically."[30] This type of research approach clearly aims at qualitative rather than quantitative measures by aggregating the information of a group of experts. It seeks to obtain answers from those who know instead of seeking the average responses of many with only limited knowledge.

Typically, Delphi studies are carried out with groups of about thirty well-chosen participants who possess particular in-depth expertise in an area of concern, such as future developments in the international trade environment. These participants are asked via mail to identify the major issues in the area of concern. They are also requested to rank their statements according to importance and explain the rationale behind the order. Next, the aggregated information is returned to all participants, who are encouraged to state clearly their agreements or disagreements with the various rank orders and comments. Statements can be challenged, and in another round, participants can respond to the challenges. After several rounds of challenge and response, a reasonably coherent consensus is developed.

The Delphi technique is particularly valuable because it uses the mail or facsimile method of communication to bridge large distances and therefore makes individuals quite accessible at a reasonable cost. It does not suffer from the drawback of ordinary mail investigations: lack of interaction among the participants. One drawback of the technique is that it requires several steps, and therefore months may elapse before the information is obtained. Even though the increasing availability of electronic mail may hasten the process, the researcher must be cautious to factor in the different penetration and acceptance levels of such technology. One should not let the research

---

[27]Winter and Prohaska, "Methodological Problems," 429.

[28]Barry R. Shapiro, "Economic Espionage," *Marketing Management* (Spring 1998): 56–58.

[29]Peter Clarke, "The Echelon Questions," *Electronic Engineering Times* (March 6, 2000): 36.

[30]Andre L. Delbecq, Andrew H. Van de Ven, and David H. Gustafson, *Group Techniques for Program Planning* (Glenview, IL: Scott, Foresman, 1975), 83.

process be driven by technology to the exclusion of valuable key informants who utilize less sophisticated methods of communication.

Also, substantial effort must be expended in selecting the appropriate participants and in motivating them to participate in this exercise with enthusiasm and continuity. When obtained on a regular basis, Delphi information can provide crucial augmentation to the factual data available for the marketing information system. For example, a large portion of the last chapter of this book was written based on an extensive Delphi study carried out by the authors. Since the study focused on the future of international marketing, and since we wanted to obtain interactive input from around the world, the Delphi method was one of the few possible research alternatives, and it produced insightful results.

Scenario Building

Some companies use **scenario analysis** to look at different configurations of key variables in the international market. For example, economic growth rates, import penetration, population growth, and political stability can be varied. By projecting such variations for medium- to long-term periods, companies can envision completely new environmental conditions. These conditions are then analyzed for their potential domestic and international impact on corporate strategy.

Of major importance in scenario building is the identification of crucial trend variables and the degree of their variation. Frequently, key experts are used to gain information about potential variations and the viability of certain scenarios.

A wide variety of scenarios must be built to expose corporate executives to multiple potential occurrences. Ideally, even far-fetched variables deserve some consideration, if only to build worst-case scenarios. A scenario for Union Carbide Corporation, for example, could have included the possibility of an environmental disaster such as occurred in Bhopal. Similarly, oil companies need to work with scenarios that factor in dramatic shifts in the supply situation, precipitated by, for example, regional conflict in the Middle East, and that consider major alterations in the demand picture, due to, say, technological developments or government policies.

Scenario builders also need to recognize the nonlinearity of factors. To simply extrapolate from currently existing situations is insufficient. Frequently, extraneous factors may enter the picture with a significant impact. Finally, in scenario building, the possibility of joint occurrences must be recognized because changes may not come about in an isolated fashion but may be spread over wide regions. An example of a joint occurrence is the indebtedness of developing nations. Although the inability of any one country to pay its debts would not present a major problem for the international banking community, large and simultaneous indebtedness may well pose a problem of major severity. Similarly, given large technological advances, the possibility of "wholesale" obsolescence of current technology must also be considered. For example, quantum leaps in computer development and new generations of computers may render obsolete the technological investment of a corporation or even a country.

For scenarios to be useful, management must analyze and respond to them by formulating contingency plans. Such planning will broaden horizons and may prepare management for unexpected situations. Familiarization in turn can result in shorter response times to actual occurrences by honing response capability. The difficulty, of course, is to devise scenarios that are unusual enough to trigger new thinking yet sufficiently realistic to be taken seriously by management.[31]

The development of an international information system is of major importance to the multinational corporation. It aids the ongoing decision process and becomes a vital corporate tool in carrying out the strategic planning task. Only by observing

---

[31]David Rutenberg, "Playful Plans," Queen's University working paper, 1991.

global trends and changes will the firm be able to maintain and increase its international competitive position. Many of the data available are quantitative in nature, but attention must also be paid to qualitative dimensions. Quantitative analysis will continue to improve, as the ability to collect, store, analyze, and retrieve data increases through the use of high-speed computers. Nevertheless, qualitative analysis should remain a major component of corporate research and strategic planning.

SUMMARY

Constraints of time, resources, and expertise are the major inhibitors of international marketing research. Nevertheless, firms need to carry out planned and organized research in order to explore global market alternatives successfully. Such research needs to be closely linked to the decision-making process.

International market research differs from domestic research in that the environment, which determines how well tools, techniques, and concepts apply, is different abroad. In addition, the manager needs to deal with new parameters, such as duties, exchange rates, and international documentation, a greater number of interacting factors, and a much broader definition of the concept of competition.

Given the scarcity of resources, companies beginning their international effort often need to use data that have already been collected, that is, secondary data. Such data are available from governments, international organizations, directories, trade associations, or on-line databases.

To respond to specific information requirements, firms frequently need primary research. The researcher needs to select an appropriate research technique to collect the information needed. Sensitivity to different international environments and cultures will guide the researcher in deciding whether to use interviews, focus groups, observation, surveys, or experimentation as data collection techniques. The same sensitivity applies to the design of the research instrument, where issues such as question format, content, and wording are decided. Also, the sampling plan needs to be appropriate for the local environment in order to ensure representative and useful responses.

Once the data have been collected, care must be taken to use analytical tools appropriate for the quality of data collected so that management is not misled about the sophistication of the research. Finally, the research results must be presented in a concise and useful form so that management can benefit in its decision making, and implementation of the research needs to be tracked.

To provide ongoing information to management, an international information support system is useful. Such a system will provide for the systematic and continuous gathering, analysis, and reporting of data for decision-making purposes. It uses a firm's internal information and gathers data via environmental scanning, Delphi studies, or scenario building, thus enabling management to prepare for the future and hone its decision-making skills.

QUESTIONS FOR DISCUSSION

1. Discuss the possible shortcomings of secondary data.
2. Why should a firm collect primary data in its international marketing research?
3. Discuss the trade-offs between centralized and decentralized international marketing research.
4. How is international market research affected by differences in language?

5. Compare the use of telephone surveys in the United States and in Egypt.

6. What are some of the crucial variables you would track in an international information system?

7. How has the information technology revolution affected international marketing research?

8. What were the industries and countries against which the United States filed antidumping actions last year? (Check **www.usitc.gov.**)

9. Where would it be most difficult to conduct business due to a high degree of corruption? (Check **www.transparency. de.**)

RECOMMENDED READINGS

Churchill, Gilbert A. *Marketing Research: Methodological Foundations*, 7th ed. Fort Worth, TX: The Dryden Press, 1999.

Craig, Samuel C., and Susan P. Douglas: *International Marketing Research: Concepts and Methods*, 2nd ed., New York: John Wiley & Sons, 1999.

Delphos, William A. *Inside Washington: Government Resources for International Business.* Washington, DC: Venture Publishing, 1995.

Directory of Online Databases. Santa Monica, CA: Cuadra Associates, published annually.

Directory of Websites for Exporters. METCO Information Services Online, **http://bitd.metco. net**, 2000.

Export Programs Guide. Trade Information Center, U.S. Department of Commerce, Washington, DC, 2000.

Predicasts Services. Cleveland, OH, published monthly.

European Union

EUROPA
The umbrella server for all institutions
www.europa.eu.int

ISPO (Information Society Project Office)
Information on telecommunications and information market developments
www.ispo.cec.be

I'M-EUROPE
Information on telematics, telecommunications, copyright, IMPACT program for the information market

CORDIS
Information on EU research programs
www.cordis.lu

EUROPARL
Information on the European Parliament's activities
www.europarl.eu.int

Delegation of the European Commission to the US Press releases, EURECOM: Economic and Financial News,

EU-US relations, information on EU policies and Delegation programs
www.eurunion.org

Citizens Europe
Covers rights of citizens of EU member states
citizens.eu.int

EUDOR (European Union Document Repository)
Bibliographic database
www.eudor.com

Euro
The Single Currency
euro.eu.int

European Agency for the Evaluation of Medicinal Products
Information on drug approval procedures and documents of the Committee for Proprietary Medicinal Products and the Committee for Veterinary Medicinal Products
www.eudra.org/emea.html

European Centre for the Development of Vocational Training
Under construction with information on the Centre and contact information
www.cedefop.gr

European Environment Agency
Information on the mission, products and services, and organizations and staff of the EEA
www.eea.dk

European Investment Bank
Press releases and information on borrowing and loan operations, staff, and publications
www.eib.org

European Monetary Institute
Related Treaty provisions setting up the Institute, rules of procedure, function and staff, list of publications
europa.eu.int/emi/emi.html

European Training Foundation
Information on vocational education and training programs in Central and Eastern Europe and Central Asia

Office for Harmonization in the Internal Market
Guidelines, application forms and other information to registering an EU trademark
europa.eu.int/agencies/ohim/ohim.htm

Council of the European Union
Information and news from the Council with sections covering Common Foreign and Security

Policy (CFSP) And Justice and
Home Affairs
Under Construction
ue.eu.int

Court of Justice
Overview, press releases, publications, and full-text
proceedings of the court
europa.eu.int/cj/en/index.htm

Court of Auditors
Information notes, annual reports,
and other publications
www.eca.eu.int

European Community Information
Service
200 Rue de la Loi
1049 Brussels, Belgium
and
2100 M Street NW, 7th Floor
Washington, DC 20037

European Bank for Reconstruction
and Development
One Exchange Square
London EC2A 2EH
United Kingdom
www.ebrd.com

European Union
200 Rue de la Loi
1049 Brussels, Belgium
and
2100 M Street NW 7th Floor
Washington, DC 20037
www.eurunion.org

United Nations

www.un.org

Conference of Trade and
Development
Palais des Nations
1211 Geneva 10
Switzerland
www.unicc.unctad.org

Department of Economic and Social
Affairs
I United Nations Plaza
New York, NY 10017
www.un.org/ecosocdev/

Industrial Development
Organization
1660 L Street NW
Washington, DC 20036
and
Post Office Box 300
Vienna International Center
A-1400 Vienna,
Austria
www.unido.org

International Trade Centre
UNCTAD/WTO
54–56 Rue de Mountbrillant
CH-1202 Geneva
Switzerland
www.intracen.org

UN Publications
Room 1194
1 United Nations Plaza
New York, NY 10017
www.un.org/pubs/

Statistical Yearbook
1 United Nations Plaza
New York, NY 10017
www.un.org/pubs/

Yearbook of International Trade
Statistics
United Nations Publishing Division
1 United Nations Plaza
Room DC2-0853
New York, NY 10017
www.un.org/pubs/

U.S. Government

Agency for International
Development
Office of Business Relations
Washington, DC 20523
www.info.usaid.gov

Customs Service
1301 Constitution Avenue NW
Washington, DC 20229
www.customs.ustreas.gov

Department of Agriculture
12th Street and Jefferson Drive SW
Washington, DC 20250
www.usda.gov

Department of Commerce
Herbert C. Hoover Building
14th Street and Constitution
Avenue NW
Washington, DC 20230
www.doc.gov

Department of State
2201 C Street NW
Washington, DC 20520
www.state.gov

Department of the Treasury
15th Street and Pennsylvania
Avenue NW
Washington, DC 20220
www.ustreas.gov

Federal Trade Commission
6th Street and Pennsylvania
Avenue NW
Washington, DC 20580
www.ftc.gov

International Trade Commission
500 E Street NW
Washington, DC 20436
www.usitc.gov

Small Business Administration
409 Third Street SW
Washington, DC 20416
www.sbaonline.sba.gov

U.S. Trade and Development Agency
1621 North Kent Street
Rosslyn, VA 22209
www.tda.gov

World Trade Centers Association
1 World Trade Center, Suite 7701
New York, NY 10048
www.wtca.org

Council of Economic Advisers—
**www.whitehouse.gov/gov/wh/
eop/cea**
Department of Defense—
www.dod.gov
Department of Energy—
www.osti.gov
Department of Interior—
www.doi.gov
Department of Labor—
www.dol.gov
Department of Transportation—

www.dot.gov
Environmental Protection Agency—
www.epa.gov
National Trade Data Bank—
www.stat-usa.gov
National Economic Council—
**www.whitehouse.gov/gov/wh/eo
p/nec**
Office of the U.S. Trade
Representative—**www.ustr.gov**
Office of Management and Budget—
**www.whitehouse.gov/gov/wh/eo
p/omb**
Overseas Private Investment
Corporation—**www.opic.gov**

Selected Organizations

American Bankers Association
1120 Connecticut Avenue NW
Washington, DC 20036
www.aba.com

American Bar Association
750 N. Lake Shore Drive
Chicago, IL 60611
and
1800 M Street NW
Washington, DC 20036
www.abanet.org/intlaw/home.html

American Management Association
440 First Street NW
Washington, DC 20001
www.amanet.org

American Marketing Association
311 S. Wacker Drive, Suite 5800
Chicago, IL 60606
www.ama.org

American Petroleum Institute
1220 L Street NW
Washington, DC 20005
www.api.org

Asia-Pacific Economic Cooperation
Secretariat
438 Alexandra Road
#41-00, Alexandra Road
Singapore 119958
www.apecsec.org.sg

Asian Development Bank

2330 Roxas Boulevard
Pasay City, Philippines
www.asiandevbank.org

Association of South East
Asian Nations (ASEAN)
Publication Office
c/o The ASEAN Secretariat
70A, Jalan Sisingamangaraja
Jakarta 11210
Indonesia
www.asean.or.id

Canadian Market Data
www.strategis.ic.gc.ca

Chamber of Commerce of the
United States
1615 H Street NW
Washington, DC 20062
www.uschamber.org

Commission of the European
Communities to the United States
2100 M Street NW
Suite 707
Washington, DC 20037
www.eurunion.org

Conference Board
845 Third Avenue
New York, NY 10022
and
1755 Massachusetts Avenue
NW Suite 312
Washington, DC 20036
www.conference-board.org

Deutsche Bundesbank
Wilhelm-Epstein-Str. 14
P.O.B. 10 06 02
D-60006 Frankfurt am Main
www.bundesbank.de

Electronic Industries Association
2001 Pennsylvania Avenue NW
Washington, DC 20004
www.eia.org

Export-Import Bank of the United
States
811 Vermont Avenue NW
Washington, DC 20571
www.exim.gov

Federal Reserve Bank of New York

33 Liberty Street
New York, NY 10045
www.ny.frb.org

FIBER
Foundation for International
Business Education and Research
1101 30th Street NW, Suite 200
Washington, DC 20007
www.fiberus.org

Inter-American Development Bank
1300 New York Avenue NW
Washington, DC 20577
www.iadb.org

International Bank for
Reconstruction and Development
(World Bank)
1818 H Street NW
Washington, DC 20433
www.worldbank.org

International Monetary Fund
700 19th Street NW
Washington, DC 20431
www.imf.org

International Telecommunication
Union
Place des Nations
Ch-1211 Geneva 20
Switzerland
www.itu.int

Michigan State University
Center for International Business
Education and Research
www.ciber.bus.msu.edu/busres

Marketing Research Society
111 E. Wacker Drive, Suite 600
Chicago, IL 60601

National Association of
Manufacturers
1331 Pennsylvania Avenue
Suite 1500
Washington, DC 20004
www.nam.org

National Federation of Independent
Business
600 Maryland Avenue SW
Suite 700

Washington, DC 20024
www.nfib.org

Organization for Economic
    Cooperation and Development
2 rue Andre Pascal
75775 Paris Cedex Ko, France
and
2001 L Street NW, Suite 700
Washington, DC 20036
www.oecd.org

Organization of American States
17th and Constitution Avenue NW
Washington, DC 20006
www.oas.org

Society for International
    Development
1401 New York Avenue NW
Suite 1100
Washington, DC 20005
www.aed.org

Transparency International
Otto-Suhr-Allee 97-99
D-10585 Berlin
Germany
www.transparency.de

Indexes to Literature

Business Periodical Index
H.W. Wilson Co.
950 University Avenue
Bronx, NY 10452

New York Times Index
University Microfilms International
300 N. Zeeb Road
Ann Arbor, MI 48106
www.nytimes.com

Public Affairs Information
    Service Bulletin
11 W. 40th Street
New York, NY 10018

Reader's Guide to Periodical
    Literature
H.W. Wilson Co.
950 University Avenue
Bronx, NY 10452
www.tulane.edu/~horn/rdg.html

Wall Street Journal Index
University Microfilms International
300 N. Zeeb Road
Ann Arbor, MI 48106
www.wsj.com

Directories

American Register of Exporters and
    Importers
38 Park Row
New York, NY 10038

Arabian Year Book
Dar Al-Seuassam Est. Box
42480
Shuwahk, Kuwait

Directories of American Firms
    Operating in Foreign Countries
World Trade Academy Press
Uniworld Business Publications Inc.
50 E. 42nd Street
New York, NY 10017

The Directory of International
    Sources of Business Information
Pitman
128 Long Acre
London WC2E 9AN, England

Encyclopedia of Associations
Gale Research Co.
Book Tower
Detroit, MI 48226

Polk's World Bank Directory
R.C. Polk & Co.
2001 Elm Hill Pike
P.O. Box 1340
Nashville, TN 37202

Verified Directory of Manufacturer's
    Representatives
MacRae's Blue Book Inc.
817 Broadway
New York, NY 10003

World Guide to Trade Associations
K.G. Saur & Co.
175 Fifth Avenue
New York, NY 10010

Encyclopedias, Handbooks, and Miscellaneous

A Basic Guide to Exporting
U.S. Government Printing Office
Superintendent of Documents
Washington, DC 20402

Doing Business In . . . Series
Price Waterhouse
1251 Avenue of the Americas
New York, NY 10020

Economic Survey of Europe
United Nations Publishing Division
1 United Nations Plaza
Room DC2-0853
New York, NY 10017

Economic Survey of Latin America
United Nations Publishing Division
I United Nations Plaza
Room DC2-0853
New York, NY 10017

Encyclopedia Americana,
    International Edition
Grolier Inc.
Danbury, CT 06816

Encyclopedia of Business
    Information Sources
Gale Research Co.
Book Tower
Detroit, MI 48226

Europa Year Book
Europa Publications Ltd.
18 Bedford Square
London WCIB 3JN, England

Export Administration Regulations
U.S. Government Printing Office
Superintendent of Documents
Washington, DC 20402

Exporters' Encyclopedia—World
    Marketing Guide
Dun's Marketing Services
49 Old Bloomfield Rd.
Mountain Lake, NJ 07046

Export-Import Bank of the United
    States Annual Report
U.S. Government Printing Office

Superintendent of Documents
Washington, DC 20402

Exporting for the Small Business
U.S. Government Printing Office
Superintendent of Documents
Washington, DC 20402

Exporting to the United States
U.S. Government Printing Office
Superintendent of Documents
Washington, DC 20402

Export Shipping Manual
U.S. Government Printing Office
Superintendent of Documents
Washington, DC 20402

Foreign Business Practices: Materials
  on Practical Aspects of Exporting,
  International Licensing, and
  Investing
U.S. Government Printing Office
Superintendent of Documents
Washington, DC 20402

A Guide to Financing Exports
U.S. Government Printing Office
Superintendent of Documents
Washington, DC 20402

Handbook of Marketing Research
McGraw-Hill Book Co.
1221 Avenue of the Americas
New York, NY 10020

Periodic Reports, Newspapers, Magazines

Advertising Age
Crain Communications Inc.
740 N. Rush Street
Chicago, IL 60611
www.adage.com

Advertising World
Directories International Inc.
150 Fifth Avenue, Suite 610
New York, NY 10011

Arab Report and Record
84 Chancery Lane
London WC2A 1DL, England

Barron's
University Microfilms International
300 N. Zeeb Road
Ann Arbor, MI 48106
www.barrons.com

Business America
U.S. Department of Commerce
14th Street and Constitution
  Avenue NW
Washington, DC 20230
www.doc.gov

Business International
Business International Corp.
One Dag Hammarskjold Plaza
New York, NY 10017

Business Week
McGraw-Hill Publications Co.
1221 Avenue of the Americas
New York, NY 10020
www.businessweek.com

Commodity Trade Statistics
United Nations Publications
1 United Nations Plaza
Room DC2-0853
New York, NY 10017

Conference Board Record
Conference Board Inc.
845 Third Avenue
New York, NY 10022

Customs Bulletin
U.S. Customs Service
1301 Constitution Avenue NW
Washington, DC 20229

Dun's Business Month
Goldhirsh Group
38 Commercial Wharf
Boston, MA 02109

The Economist
Economist Newspaper Ltd.
25 St. James Street
London SWIA 1HG, England
www.economist.com

Europe Magazine
2100 M Street NW Suite 707
Washington, DC 20037

The Financial Times
Bracken House
10 Cannon Street
London EC4P 4BY, England
www.ft-se.co.uk

Forbes
Forbes, Inc.
60 Fifth Avenue
New York, NY 10011
www.forbes.com

Fortune
Time, Inc.
Time & Life Building
1271 Avenue of the Americas
New York, NY 10020
www.pathfinder.com/fortune

Global Trade
North American Publishing Co.
401 N. Broad Street
Philadelphia, PA 19108

Industrial Marketing
Crain Communications, Inc.
740 N. Rush Street
Chicago, IL 60611

International Financial Statistics
International Monetary Fund
Publications Unit
700 19th Street NW
Washington, DC 20431
www.imf.org

Investor's Daily
Box 25970
Los Angeles, CA 90025
Journal of Commerce
110 Wall Street
New York, NY 10005

Journal of Commerce
100 Wall Street
New York, NY 10005
www.joc.com

Sales and Marketing Management
Bill Communications Inc.
633 Third Avenue
New York, NY 10017

Wall Street Journal
Dow Jones & Company
200 Liberty Street

New York, NY 10281
www.wsj.com

World Agriculture Situation
U.S. Department of Agriculture
Economics Management Staff
www.econ.ag.gov

Pergamon Press Inc.
Journals Division
Maxwell House
Fairview Park
Elmsford, NY 10523

*World Trade Center Association
(WTCA) Directory*
World Trade Centers Association
1 World Trade Center
New York, NY 10048

*International Encyclopedia of the
Social Sciences*
Macmillan and the Free Press
866 Third Avenue
New York, NY 10022

*Marketing and Communications
Media Dictionary*
Media Horizons Inc.
50 W. 25th Street
New York, NY 10010
www.horizons-media.com

Market Share Reports
U.S. Government Printing Office
Superintendent of Documents
Washington, DC 20402
www.access.gpo.gov

*Media Guide International:
Business/Professional Publications*
Directories International Inc.
150 Fifth Avenue, Suite 610
New York, NY 10011

Overseas Business Reports
U.S Government Printing Office
Superintendent of Documents
Washington, DC 20402
www.access.gpo.gov

Trade Finance
U.S. Department of Commerce
International Trade Administration

Washington, DC 20230
www.doc.gov

*World Economic Conditions in
Relation to Agricultural Trade*
U.S. Government Printing Office
Superintendent of Documents
Washington, DC 20402
www.access.gpo.gov

Selected Trade Databases

News agencies
Comline-Japan Newswire
Dow Jones News
Nikkei Shimbun News
Database Omninews
Lexis-Nexis
Reuters Monitor
UPI

Trade Publication References with Bibliographic Keywords

Agris
Biocommerce Abstracts & Directory
Findex
Frost (short) Sullivan Market
Research Reports
Marketing Surveys Index
McCarthy Press Cuttings Service
Paperchern
PTS F & S Indexes
Trade and Industry Index

Trade Publication References with Summaries

ABI/Inform
Arab Information Bank
Asia-Pacific
BFAI
Biobusiness
CAB Abstracts
Chemical Business Newbase
Chemical Industry Notes
Caffeeline
Delphes
InfoSouth Latin American
Information System
Management Contents
NTIS Bibliographic Data Base
Paperchem

PIRA Abstract
PSTA
PTS Marketing & Advertising
Reference Service
PTS PromtRapra Abstracts
Textline
Trade & Industry ASAP
World Textiles

Full Text of Trade Publications

Datamonitor Market Reports
Dow Jones News
Euromonitor Market Direction
Federal News Service
Financial Times Business Report
File
Financial Times Fulltext
Globefish
ICC Key Notes Market Research
Investext
McCarthy Press Cuttings Service
PTS Promt
Textline
Trade & Industry ASAP

Statistics

Agrostat (diskette only)
ARI Network/CNS
Arab Information Bank
Comext/Eurostat
Comtrade
FAKT-German Statistics
Globefish
IMF Data
OECD Data
Piers Imports
PTS Forecasts
PTS Time Series
Reuters Monitor
Trade Statistics
Tradstat World Trade Statistics
TRAINS(CD-ROM being developed)
US I/E Maritime Bills of Lading
US Imports for Consumption
World Bank Statistics

Price Information

ARI Network/CNS
Chemical Business Newsbase
COLEACP
Commodity Options

Commodities 2000
Market News Service of ITC
Nikkei Shimbun News Database
Reuters Monitor
UPI
US Wholesale Prices

Company Registers

ABC Europe Production Europe
Biocommerce Abstracts & Directory
CD-Export (CD-ROM only)
Company Intelligence
D&B Duns Market Identifiers
(U.S.A.)
D&B European Marketing File
D&B Eastern Europe
Dun's Electronic Business
    Directory
Firmexport/Firmimport
Hoppenstedt Austria
Hoppenstedt Germany
Hoppenstedt Benelux
Huco-Hungarian Companies
ICC Directory of Companies
Kompass Asia/Pacific
Kompass Europe (EKOD)
Mexican Exporters/Importers

Piers Imports
Polu-Polish Companies
SDOE
Thomas Register
TRAINS(CD-ROM being devel-
    oped)
UK Importers
UK Importers (DECTA)
US Directory of Importers
US I/E Maritime Bills of Lading
World Trade Center Network

Trade Opportunities, Tenders

Business
Federal News Service
Huntech-Hungarian Technique
Scan-a-Bid
Tenders Electronic Daily
World Trade Center Network

Tariffs and Trade Regulations

Celex
ECLAS
Justis Eastern Europe (CD_ROM
    only)

Scad
Spearhead
Spicer's Centre for Europe
TRAINS(CD-ROM being devel-
    oped)
US Code of Federal Regulations
US Federal Register
US Harmonized Tariff Schedule

Standards

BSI Standardline
Noriane/Perinorm
NTIS Bibliographic Data Base
Standards Infodisk ILI (CD-ROM
    only)

Shipping Information

Piers Imports
Tradstat World Trade Statistics
US I/E Maritime Bills of Lading

Others

Fairbase
Ibiscus

Appendix B

Description of Selected U.S. Government Publications and Services

Macro Data

The majority of the data listed here are most easily available at **www.stat-usa.org**.

World Population is issued by the U.S. Bureau of the Census. Information is provided about total population, fertility, mortality, urban population, growth rate, and life expectancy. Also published are detailed demographic profiles, including an analysis of the labor force structure of individual countries.

Foreign Trade Highlights are annual reports published by the Department of Commerce. They provide basic data on U.S. merchandise trade with major trading partners and regions. They also contain brief analyses of recent U.S. trade developments.

Foreign Trade Report FT410 provides a monthly statistical record of shipments of all merchandise from the United States to foreign countries, including both the quantity and dollar value of exports to each country. It also contains cumulative export statistics from the first of the calendar year.

World Agriculture, a publication of the U.S. Department of Agriculture, provides production information, data, and analyses by country along with a review of recent economic conditions and changes in agricultural and trade policies. Frequent supplements provide an outlook of anticipated developments for the coming year.

Country Information

National Trade Data Bank, a key product of the U.S. Department of Commerce, provides monthly CD-ROM disks that contain overseas market research, trade statistics, contact information, and other reports that may assist U.S. exporters in their international marketing efforts.

Country Marketing Plan reports on commercial activities and climate in a country and is prepared by the Foreign Commercial Service staffs abroad. It also contains an action plan for the coming year, including a list of trade events and research to be conducted.

Industry SubSector Analyses are market research reports on specific product categories, for example, electromedical equipment in one country, ranging from five to twenty pages.

Overseas Business Reports (OBR) present economic and commercial profiles on specific countries and provide background statistics. Selected information on the direction and the volume and nature of U.S. foreign trade is also provided.

Background Notes, prepared by the Department of State, present a survey of a country's people, geography, economy, government, and foreign policy. The reports also include important national economic and trade information.

263

Foreign Economic Trends presents recent business and economic developments and the latest economic indicators of more than 100 countries.

Product Information

Export Statistics Profiles analyze exports for a single industry, product by product, country by country, over a five-year period. Data are rank-ordered by dollar value for quick identification of the leading products and industries. Tables show the sales of each product to each country as well as competitive information, growth, and future trends. Each profile also contains a narrative analysis that highlights the industry's prospects, performance, and leading products.

U.S. Industrial Outlook, an annual publication of the U.S. Department of Commerce, provides an overview of the domestic and international performance of all major U.S. industries, complete with employment and shipment information and a forecast of future developments.

Export Information System Data Reports, available from the U.S. Small Business Administration, provide small businesses with a list of the twenty-five largest importing markets for their products and the ten best markets for U.S. exporters of the products. Trends within those markets and the major sources of foreign competition are also discussed.

Services

Agent Distributor Service (ADS): The Commercial Service (CS) provides a customized search for interested and qualified foreign representatives for a firm's product.

Aglink: Collaborative effort between the Foreign Agricultural Service and the Small Business Administration to match foreign buyers with U.S. agribusiness firms.

Catalog Exhibitions: The Department of Commerce organizes displays of product literature and videotape presentations overseas.

Customized Market Analysis: The CS provides a custom foreign market survey on a product's overall marketability, names of competitors, comparative prices, and customary business practices.

Economic Bulletin Board: The Department of Commerce provides access to the latest economic data releases, including trade opportunities, for on-line users.

Foreign Agricultural Service: Employees of the U.S. Department of Agriculture, stationed both abroad and in the United States, with the mission to facilitate agricultural exports from the United States. Provides counseling, research, general market information, and market introduction services.

Foreign Buyer Program: The CS brings foreign buyers to U.S. trade shows for industries with high export potential.

Going Global: A computerized, on-line information system that lists market opportunities, information on foreign countries, and export intermediaries. Primarily focused on agricultural firms.

International Company Profiles: The CS publishes background research conducted by CS officers abroad on potential trading partners, such as agents, distributors, and licensees.

Matchmaker Events: The Department of Commerce introduces U.S. companies to new markets through short visits abroad to match the U.S. firm with a representative or prospective partner.

Seminar Missions: The Department of Commerce sponsors technical seminars abroad designed to promote sales of sophisticated products and technology.

Trade Missions: Groups of U.S. business executives, led by Commerce Department staff, meet with potential foreign buyers, agents, and distributors.

Trade Opportunity Program: The CS daily collection of trade opportunities worldwide is published and electronically distributed to subscribers.

Chapter 8

The Export Process

Exporting On-Line

SMALL AND MEDIUM-SIZED business owners can now sell their products and source components anywhere in the world with just a few keystrokes on their personal computers. This is possible through an on-line system called Unibex ("the Universal Business Exchange"), launched by a group including AT&T, Dun & Bradstreet, General Electric, Microsoft, and the U.S. Chamber of Commerce.

The Unibex software allows companies to anonymously sign on and submit requests for goods or services using an array of categories, including location, product type, payment, and shipping terms. Customers then receive bids from businesses hoping to land contracts. Once a bid is chosen, the identities of the businesses are disclosed and negotiations may begin. Unibex allows users to attach documents, such as confidentiality agreements, contracts, and purchase orders. The participation of Dun & Bradstreet permits users to check each others' company profiles by tapping into D&B's vast international database of company information and references. In April 2001, Unibex partnered with Ozro, an online supply-chain specialist, to provide its customers with one-stop shopping for E-Commerce, including Ozro's patented negotiation engine, contract management capabilities, and materials procurement technology. The Unibex system can also do a basic translation of terms of a deal from English into Spanish, French, or any of ten other languages. After a deal is completed, Unibex allows users to locate freight forwarders, bankers, accountants, or customs brokers.

The system is meant to benefit smaller companies. Its launch coincides with a small business trend toward increasing exports and rapid integration of computers and technology. "Thanks to Unibex, the benefits of electronic commerce and a global reach are no longer the monopoly of big business," says Mark Van Fleet, the U.S. Chamber of Commerce's Unibex manager. Bruce Valley, president of Globalnet, Inc., a transportation equipment supplier, was involved in Unibex test simulations and is very enthusiastic: "It has the potential of allowing me to be a General Electric or a Boeing on my computer screen here in my eleven-person business." The Unibex service is a good, quick way to engage in true electronic commerce without the baggage of Internet security concerns. While potential users can learn about and subscribe to the service through the Internet, actual business negotiations are conducted on a more private and secure electronic mail network. Additionally, users avoid the relatively high cost of commercial on-line services. The system has several thousand users in approximately twenty-five countries. An estimated 1.5 million users are expected to sign on within five years.

SOURCES: **www.unibex.com**, accessed April 16, 2001; Jared Sandberg, "On-Line Service to Assist Global Trade," *The Wall Street Journal*, September 26, 1995, 30; James Worsham, "A Global Reach for Small Firms," *Nation's Business*, October 1995, 40; interview with U.S. Chamber of Commerce officials, November 1996.

http://www.unibex.com

P ARTICIPATION IN THE INTERNATIONAL MARKETPLACE is increasingly within the grasp of firms both large and small, as *The International Marketplace 8.1* shows. Doing so can be very rewarding and may turn out to be the key to prosperity for both corporations and employees. Research has found that firms that export grow faster, are more productive, and, equally important, have employees who tend to earn more.[1] But most firms cannot simply jump into international marketing and expect to be successful. New activities in an unfamiliar environment also increase a firm's risk. Therefore, companies must prepare their activities and adjust to the needs and opportunities of international markets in order to become long-term participants.

Because most firms start their international involvement with exporting, and most exporters are small and medium-sized firms, this chapter will discuss the export process by addressing the activities that take place within the firm preparing to enter the international marketplace. It will focus on the basic stimuli for exporting and will discuss the change agents, both internal and external, that activate these stimuli. In addition, the concerns and preoccupations of firms as they begin their international marketing operations will be discussed. Finally, a model of the export development process and strategic issues within the firm will be presented.

Managers must understand what "sells" to owners and decision makers in the firm so that they can aid in the move toward internationalization. Current and prospective employees must be able to assess the strategic direction of the firm. An awareness of the inherent attributes that make firms international can aid students in selecting the best environment in which to become active in international marketing.

Motivations to Internationalize

Many researchers have worked on determining the reasons why firms go international. A key factor is apparently the type and quality of management. Some researchers have shown that dynamic management is important when firms take their first international steps.[2] Over the long term, management commitment and management's perceptions and attitudes are also good predictors of export success.[3] Also, managers of exporting firms typically show a higher level of formal education and foreign language fluency than do managers of nonexporting firms.[4] Similarly, firms have been segmented into active and passive or aggressive and nonaggressive, with aggressive firms typically found to be more long-term oriented and active in a larger number of markets.[5]

All of the differentiations point toward a conclusion that the international marketing behavior of firms is related to managerial aspirations, capabilities, and the level of commitment and planning that management is willing to devote to the

[1]David Richardson and Karin Rindal, *Why Exports Matter: More!* (Washington, DC: Institute for International Economics and The Manufacturing Institute, February 1996), 9.

[2]Warren J. Bilkey and George Tesar, "The Export Behavior of Smaller Sized Wisconsin Manufacturing Firms," *Journal of International Business Studies* 8 (Spring/Summer 1977): 93–98.

[3]Nils-Erik Aaby and Stanley F. Slater, "Management Influences on Export Performance: A Review of the Empirical Literature, 1978–1988," *International Marketing Review* 6 (1989): 7–26.

[4]F. N. Burton and B. B. Schlegelmilch, "Profile Analyses of Non-Exporters versus Exporters Grouped by Export Involvement," *Management International Review* 27 (First Quarter, 1987): 38–49.

[5]Angela de Rocha, Carl H. Christensen, and Carlos Eduardo da Cunha, "Aggressive and Passive Exporters: A Study in the Brazilian Furniture Industry," *International Marketing Review* 7 (1990): 6–15.

international marketing effort. Simply put, the companies that grow internationally are willing to dedicate organizational resources to the management of foreign business.[6] To a large extent, this conclusion has been formulated by reverse deduction: The managers of firms that are unsuccessful or inactive in the international marketplace usually exhibit a lack of determination to or preparation for international marketing. Because international markets cannot be penetrated overnight—but rather require a vast amount of market-development activity, market research, and sensitivity to foreign market factors—the issue of managerial commitment is a crucial one. This commitment must be able to endure stagnation and sometimes even setbacks and failure. To obtain such a commitment, it is important to involve all levels of management early on in the export planning process and to impress on all players that the effort will only succeed with a commitment that is companywide.[7] Planning and execution of an export venture must be incorporated into the firm's strategic management process. A firm that sets no strategic goals for its export venture is less likely to make the venture a long-term success.[8]

In addition to the broad commitment, it is also important to establish a specific export structure in which someone has the responsibility for exporting. Without some specified responsibility center, the focus that is necessary for success is lost. Just one person assigned part-time to international marketing activities can begin exploring and entering international markets, but it is crucial to assign the export responsibility to a specific person.

In most business activities, one factor alone rarely accounts for any given action. Usually a mixture of factors results in firms taking steps in a given direction. This is true of internationalization; motivation consists of a variety of factors both pushing and pulling firms along the international path.[9] Table 8.1 provides an overview of the

TABLE 8.1	Major Internationalization Motivations of Small and Medium-Sized Firms

PROACTIVE
- Profit advantage
- Unique products
- Technological advantage
- Exclusive information
- Managerial urge
- Tax benefit
- Economies of scale

REACTIVE
- Competitive pressures
- Overproduction
- Declining domestic sales
- Excess capacity
- Saturated domestic markets
- Proximity to customers and ports

[6]Daniele Dalli, "The Organization of Exporting Activities: Relationships Between Internal and External Arrangements," *Journal of Business Research* 34 (1995): 107–115.

[7]S. Tamer Cavusgil, "Preparing for Export Marketing," *International Trade Forum* 2 (1993): 16–30.

[8]S. Tamer Cavusgil and Shaoming Zou, "Marketing Strategy–Performance Relationship: An Investigation of the Empirical Link in Export Marketing Ventures," *Journal of Marketing* 58 (Number 1, 1994): 1–21.

[9]S. Tamer Cavusgil, "Global Dimensions of Marketing," in *Marketing*, eds. Patrick E. Murphy and Ben M. Enis (Glenview, IL: Scott, Foresman, 1985), 577–599.

major motivations to internationalize. They are differentiated into proactive motivations. Proactive motivations represent stimuli to attempt strategic change. Reactive motivations influence firms that are responsive to environmental changes and adjust to them by changing their activities over time. In other words, proactive firms go international because they want to, while reactive ones go international because they have to.

Proactive Motivations

The most stimulating proactive motivation to become involved in international marketing is the profit advantage. Management may perceive international sales as a potential source of higher profit margins or of more added-on profits. Of course, the perceived profitability, when planning to enter into international markets, is often quite different from profitability actually attained. Research has indicated that the initial profitability of international start-up operations may be quite low,[10] mainly due to relatively high start-up costs.[11] The gap between perception and reality may be particularly large when the firm has not previously engaged in international market activities. Despite thorough planning, imponderable influences often shift the profit picture substantially. For example, a sudden shift in exchange rates may drastically alter profit forecasts even though they were based on careful market evaluation.

A second major stimulus results either from unique products or from a technological advantage. A firm may produce goods or services that are not widely available from international competitors or may have made technological advances in a specialized field. Again, real and perceived advantages should be differentiated. Many firms believe that theirs are unique products or services, even though this may not be the case in the international market. If products or technology are unique, however, they can certainly provide a competitive edge and result in major business success abroad. The intensity of marketing's interaction with the research and development function, as well as the level of investment into R & D, have been shown to have a major effect on the success of exported products.[12]

One issue to consider is how long such a technological or product advantage will continue. Historically, a firm with a competitive edge could count on being the sole supplier to international markets for years to come. This type of advantage, however, has shrunk dramatically because of competing technologies and a frequent lack of intellectual property rights protection.

Exclusive market information is another proactive stimulus. This includes knowledge about foreign customers, marketplaces, or market situations that is not widely shared by other firms. Such special knowledge may result from particular insights based on a firm's international research, special contacts a firm may have, or simply being in the right place at the right time (for example, recognizing a good business situation during a vacation trip). Although exclusivity can serve well as an initial stimulus for international marketing activities, it will rarely provide prolonged motivation because competitors—at least in the medium run—can be expected to catch up with the information advantage of the firm, particularly in light of the growing ease of global information access.

Managerial urge is a motivation that reflects the desire, drive, and enthusiasm of management toward international marketing activities. This enthusiasm can exist simply because managers like to be part of a firm that operates internationally. (It sounds impressive.) Further, it can often provide a good reason for international

---

[10]Masaaki Kotabe and Michael R. Czinkota, "State Government Promotion of Manufacturing Exports: A Gap Analysis," *Journal of International Business Studies* (Winter 1992): 637–658.

[11]*U.S. Manufacturers in the Global Marketplace* (New York: The Conference Board, 1994), 10.

[12]Tiger Li, "The Impact of the Marketing-R&D Interface on New Product Export Performance: A Contingency Analysis," *Journal of International Marketing* 7 (Number 1, 1999): 10–33.

THE INTERNATIONAL MARKETPLACE 8.2

The Personal Touch in Exporting

For SMALL BUSINESSES, SIZE can be an unexpected strength in tackling overseas markets. Export giants once seemed to have all the right advantages to enter new markets: well-established distribution systems and plenty of money, personnel, and political clout. But small companies have a personal touch, putting foreign clients in direct contact with the chief executive seeking a sale. They also have the ability to fly in under the radar without getting noticed and to make a quiet splash.

Several small companies in the midwestern state of Indiana are proving that the growth of U.S. exports doesn't just come from household names like Motorola or General Electric, but rather from companies like Red Spot Paint & Varnish Co., which sells paint and other coatings to auto makers. International sales used to be so rare for that company that its president would handle them on Saturday mornings, but now four full-time employees cover exports, which compose 20 percent of the company's annual sales of $90 million. On its overseas journey, Red Spot learned some basic lessons about selling abroad, according to their director of international sales. The major one: Personal contact works best. One Argentinean customer was impressed enough by the hospitality Red Spot offered on his visit to offer a $100,000 contract—an insignificant amount in the eyes of Red Spot's competitors.

Gaining a client base abroad has certainly been hard work for the small company; it courted a German auto parts maker for seven years before winning its business. But now that account is giving Red Spot additional business in Germany and Mexico. Red Spot also maintains that its research and development for new products will give it a further edge in international competition.

Other Indiana companies seeking to enter the global market have found help from their state government. The Indiana Department of Commerce has thirteen offices around the world that provide specialists for consultation in business and export development, financing assistance to Indiana exporters, trade show assistance, and help on reducing operating costs. Indiana state commerce officials also meet with local businesses to discuss practical issues of foreign business trips ranging from how to catch a cab in Mexico City to which gastrointestinal medicine works best.

As more small businesses realize the gains to be found in fast-moving international markets, their overall exports will continue to rise. They will be banking on the increased global appetite for international goods.

SOURCE: "Our History," Red Spot Paint & Varnish Company web site, **www.redspot.com**, accessed April 16, 2001; "Indiana Overseas Offices" and "International Trade Incentives," Indiana Department of Commerce web site, **www.state.in.us/doc**, accessed April 16, 2001; and Robert L. Rose and Carl Quintanilla, "Tiptoeing Abroad: More Small U.S. Firms Take Up Exporting, with Much Success," *The Wall Street Journal*, December 20, 1996: A1, A8.

travel—for example, to call on a major customer in the Bahamas during a cold winter month. Often, however, the managerial urge to internationalize is simply the reflection of general entrepreneurial motivation—of a desire for continuous growth and market expansion.[13] *The International Marketplace 8.2* provides an example of a firm that has been able to combine a passion for exporting with a personal touch.

Tax benefits have historically also played a major motivating role. Many countries offer tax concessions to their firms in order to encourage export activities. In the United States, a tax mechanism called the **Foreign Sales Corporation (FSC)** provides exporting firms with certain tax deferrals, thus making international marketing activities potentially more profitable. However, the rules of the World Trade Organization prohibit the subsidy of exports by all but the poorest countries. For example, the FCS mechanism of the United States was found to be in violation of WTO regulations, and the United States was advised to terminate such benefits in 2001. It can therefore be expected that tax benefits will play a decreasing role in future motivations to export.

A final major proactive motivation is economies of scale. Becoming a participant in international marketing activities may enable the firm to increase its output and

[13]Yoo S. Yang, Robert P. Leone, and Dana L. Alden, "A Market Expansion Ability Approach to Identify Potential Exporters," *Journal of Marketing* 56 (January 1992): 84–96.

therefore slide down more rapidly on the learning curve. Ever since the Boston Consulting Group showed that a doubling of output can reduce production costs up to 30 percent, this effect has been very much sought. Increased production for the international market can therefore also help in reducing the cost of production for domestic sales and make the firm more competitive domestically as well.[14] This effect often results in the seeking of market share as a primary objective of firms. At an initial level of internationalization this may mean an increased search for export markets; later on, it can result in the opening of foreign subsidiaries and foreign production facilities. These latter effects are discussed in Chapter 14 of this book.

Reactive Motivations

A second type of motivation, primarily characterized as reactive, influences firms to respond to changes and pressures in the business environment rather than attempt to blaze trails.

A prime form of such motivation is the reaction to competitive pressures. A firm may fear losing domestic market share to competing firms that have benefited from the effect of the economies of scale gained by international marketing activities. Further, it may fear losing foreign markets permanently to domestic competitors that decide to focus on these markets. Observing that domestic competitors are beginning to internationalize, and knowing that market share is most easily retained by the firm that obtains it initially, firms frequently enter the international market head over heels. Quick entry may result in similarly quick withdrawal once the firm recognizes that its preparation has been insufficient.

Similarly, overproduction can serve as a major reactive motivation. Historically, during downturns in the domestic business cycle, markets abroad were initially unaffected because of time lags. They provided an ideal outlet for inventories that were significantly above desired levels. Frequently, however, international market expansion motivated by overproduction did not represent full commitment by management, but rather **safety-valve activity** designed for short-term activities only. Rather than develop an international marketing perspective by adjusting the marketing mix to needs abroad, firms using this strategy typically stimulate export sales with short-term price cuts.[15] As soon as the domestic market demand returns to previous levels, international marketing activities are curtailed or even terminated. Firms that have used such a strategy once may encounter difficulties when trying to employ it again because many foreign customers are not interested in temporary or sporadic business relationships. This reaction from abroad, together with the lessons learned about the danger of large inventories—and the fact that the major industrial economies appear to be increasingly synchronized, may well lead to a decrease in the importance of this motivation over time.

Stable or declining domestic sales, whether measured in sales volume or market share, have a similar motivating effect. Products marketed by the firm domestically may be at the declining stage of the product life cycle. Instead of attempting a push-back of the life cycle process domestically, or in addition to such an effort, firms may opt to prolong the product life cycle by expanding the market. In the past, such efforts often met with success because customers in many countries only gradually reached a level of need and sophistication already attained by customers in industrialized nations. Increasingly, however, if lag times exist at all in foreign markets, they

---

[14]Michael L. Ursic and Michael R. Czinkota, "An Experience Curve Explanation of Export Expansion," in *International Marketing Strategy: Environmental Assessment and Entry Strategies* (Fort Worth, TX: The Dryden Press, 1994), 133–141.

[15]C. P. Rao, M. Krishna Erramilli, and Gopala K. Ganesh, "Impact of Domestic Recession on Export Marketing Behaviour," *International Marketing Review* 7 (1990): 54–65.

are quite short. Nevertheless, this motivation is still a valid one, particularly in the context of developing nations, which often still have very good use for products for which the demand in the industrialized world is already on the decline. This holds particularly true for high-technology products that are outdated by the latest innovations. Such "just-dated" technology can be highly useful in countries that, due to their level of economic development, can still achieve vast progress in the manufacturing or services sectors.

Excess capacity can also be a powerful motivation. If equipment for production is not fully utilized, firms may see expansion into the international market as an ideal possibility for achieving broader distribution of fixed costs. Alternatively, if all fixed costs are assigned to domestic production, the firm can penetrate international markets with a pricing scheme that focuses mainly on variable costs. Although such a strategy may be useful in the short term, it may result in the offering of products abroad at a cost lower than at home, which in turn may trigger dumping charges. In the long run, fixed costs have to be recovered to ensure replacement of production equipment that growing international marketing activities may overtax. Market penetration strategy based on variable cost alone is therefore not feasible over the long term.

The reactive motivation of a saturated domestic market is similar in results to that of declining domestic sales. Again, firms in this situation can use the international market to prolong the life cycle of their product and of their organization.

A final major reactive motivation is proximity to customers and ports. Physical closeness to the international market can often play a major role in the export activities of a firm. For example, Canadian firms established near the U.S. border may not even perceive of their market activities in the United States as international marketing. Rather, they are simply an extension of domestic activities, without any particular attention being paid to the fact that some of the products go abroad. Except for some firms close to the Canadian or Mexican border, however, this factor is much less prevalent in North America than in many other countries. Unlike European firms, most American firms are situated far away from foreign countries. Consider the radius of domestic activity of many U.S. firms, which may be 200 miles. When applying such a radius to a European scenario, most European firms automatically become international marketers simply because their neighbors are so close. As an example, a European company operating in the heart of Belgium need go only 50 miles to be in multiple foreign markets.

In this context, the concept of psychic or **psychological distance** needs to be understood. Geographic closeness to foreign markets may not necessarily translate into real or perceived closeness to the foreign customer. Sometimes cultural variables, legal factors, and other societal norms make a foreign market that is geographically close seem psychologically distant. For example, research has shown that U.S. firms perceive Canada to be much closer psychologically than Mexico. Even England, mainly because of the similarity in language, is perceived by many U.S. firms to be much closer than Mexico or other Latin American countries, despite the geographic distances. However, in light of the reduction of trade barriers as a result of the North American Free Trade Agreement (NAFTA), and a growing proportion of the U.S. population with Hispanic background, this long-standing perception may well change rapidly.

It is important to remember two major issues in the context of psychological distance. First off, some of the distance seen by firms is based on perception rather than reality. For example, German firms may view the Austrian market simply as an extension of their home market due to so many superficial similarities, just as many U.S. firms may see the United Kingdom as psychologically very close due to the similarity in language. However, the attitudes and values of managers and customers may vary substantially between markets. Too much of a focus on the similarities may let the firm lose sight of the differences. Many Canadian firms have incurred high costs in learning this lesson when entering the United States.[16] At the same time, the fact is that closer psychological proximity does make it easier for firms to enter markets. Therefore, for firms new to international marketing it may be advantageous to begin this new activity by entering the psychologically closer markets first in order to gather experience before venturing into markets that are farther away.[17]

An overall contemplation of these motivations should also consider the following factors. First, firms that are most successful in exporting are motivated by proactive—that is, firm-internal—factors. Second, the motivations of firms do not seem to shift dramatically over the short term but are rather stable. For the student who seeks involvement in international markets and searches for firms most likely to provide good opportunities, an important consideration should be whether a firm is proactive or reactive.

The proactive firm is also more likely to be service-oriented than are reactive firms. Further, it is frequently more marketing- and strategy-oriented than reactive firms, which have as their major concern operational issues. The clearest differentiation between the two types of firms can probably be made after the fact by determining how they initially entered international markets. Proactive firms are more likely to solicit their first international marketing order, whereas reactive firms frequently begin international marketing activities after receiving an unsolicited order from abroad.

All these considerations lead to the questions of how the activities of firms can be changed and, ideally, how the student and future employee can be part of this change.

Change Agents

For change to take place, someone or something within the firm must initiate it and shepherd it through to implementation. This intervening individual or variable is here called a **change agent.** Change agents in the internationalization process are shown in Table 8.2.

TABLE 8.2 Change Agents in the Internationalization Process

FIRM INTERNAL
- Enlightened management
- New management
- Significant Internal event

FIRM EXTERNAL
- Demand
- Other firms
- Distributors
- Banks
- Chambers of commerce
- Export agents
- Governmental activities

[16]Shawna O'Grady and Henry W. Lane, "The Psychic Distance Paradox," *Journal of International Business Studies* 27 (Number 2, 1996): 309–333.

[17]Aviv Shoham and Gerald S. Albaum, "Reducing the Impact of Barriers to Exporting: A Managerial Perspective," *Journal of International Marketing* 3 (Number 4, 1995): 85–105.

Internal Change Agents

A primary change agent internal to the firm is enlightened management. Such enlightenment can occur when the current management of a firm discovers and understands the value of international markets and decides to pursue international marketing opportunities. Trigger factors frequently are foreign travel, during which new business opportunities are discovered, or information is received that leads management to believe that such opportunities exist. Managers who have lived abroad, have learned foreign languages, or are particularly interested in foreign cultures are likely, sooner rather than later, to investigate whether international marketing opportunities would be appropriate for their firm. Key managerial characteristics that have been shown to affect firms' export involvement are shown in Table 8.3.

A second set of major internal change agents consists of new management or new employees. Often, managers enter a firm having already had some international marketing experience in previous positions and try to use this experience to further the business activities of their new firm. Also, in developing their goals in the new job, managers frequently consider an entirely new set of options for growth and expansion, one of which may be international marketing activities. *The International Marketplace 8.3* shows how a firm can start its initial international involvement through serendipity, and later on expand into full-fledged export activity due to expertise from a new employee.

A significant internal event can be another major change agent. A new employee who firmly delives that the firm should undertake international marketing may find ways to motivate management. The development of a new product useful abroad can serve as such an event, as can the receipt of new information about current product uses. As an example, a manufacturer of hospital beds learned that beds it was selling domestically were being resold in a foreign country. Further, the beds it sold for $600 each were resold overseas for approximately $1,300. This new piece of information served to trigger a strong interest on the part of the company's management in entering international markets.

In small and medium-sized firms (firms with fewer than 250 employees) the initial decision to export is usually made by the president, with substantial input provided by the marketing department. The carrying out of the decision—that is, the initiation of actual international marketing activities and the implementation of these activities—is then primarily the responsibility of marketing personnel. Only in the final decision stage of evaluating international marketing activities does the major emphasis rest again with the president of the firm. In order to influence a firm internally, it therefore appears that the major emphasis should be placed first on convincing the president to enter the international marketplace and then on convincing the marketing department that international marketing is an important activity. Conversely, the marketing department is a good place to be if one wants to become active in international business.

TABLE 8.3	**Key Managerial Characteristics Affecting Export Involvement**
	Education
	International exposure
	Expertise
	International orientation
	Commitment

SOURCE: Michael R. Czinkota, "A National Export Assistance Policy for New and Growing Businesses," in *Trends in International Business: Critical Perspectives*, M. Czinkota and M. Kotabe, eds. (Oxford, England: Blackwell Publishers, 1998): 69–77.

THE INTERNATIONAL MARKETPLACE 8.3

An Accidental Exporter

MAYNARD SAUDER, president and CEO of ready-to-assemble furniture maker Sauder Woodworking Company of Archbold, Ohio, thought for the longest while that exporting was not for him. The do-it-yourself household furnishings market in the United States had been gathering steam in the late 1980s. Sauder Woodworking was a supplier to national general merchandisers such as Wal-Mart, Kmart, Sears, and JCPenney. It was supplying retailers with products in the $19 to $399 range and had just reached a sales volume of $200 million. Annual growth was humming at 12 to 15 percent. Exports at this time were negligible and occurred almost by accident. For instance, the firm started to sell products in the Caribbean because a salesman vacationed there.

How times have changed. Today, Sauder Woodworking does business in more than 70 countries worldwide, shipping over $525 million in goods annually. Domestic volume has gone flat, while international accounts have posted an average annual increase of 30 percent. It wasn't until Jerry Paterson, a former export manager for Owens-Corning Fiberglass Corp., caught Sauder's attention that the company became serious about exporting. "I questioned our ability to compete in foreign markets," Sauder says today. "I wasn't sure we could make it on price, and then I wondered if customers outside the U.S. would accept our designs." But the cost-benefit analysis, plus Paterson's presence, made it worth a try. "If Jerry Paterson can bring our export sales up to two million dollars a year, it will more than pay his expenses," Sauder recalls. "It took us three to four years to reach a critical mass in exporting, but I knew after a year or so that we were going to give our program full support, and that we were in it for the long pull, not casually and not lukewarm."

Paterson quickly went to work, and allayed Sauder's initial fears about jumping into exporting. Soon he realized that the company's proximity to particleboard suppliers in central Ohio would help keep prices competitive worldwide. Concerns over decor preferences also evaporated. "Our styles and colors have proved very acceptable, especially in France, where our penetration has been remarkable. But we're doing very well in Turkey too." Add to this a positive outlook for sales in India and plans to ship to China via Hong Kong.

"We proved in a very short time that we can compete anywhere in the world," Sauder says. Many U.S. exporters are discovering that American labor can compete with workers anywhere in the world, thanks to increased efficiency and the higher quality of the finished product. "[Our made-in-the-U.S.A. products] are a great sales booster for us the world over."

SOURCE: Daniel McConville, "An Accidental Exporter Turns Serious," *World Trade*, March 1996, 28; Sauder Company web site, **www.sauder.com**, accessed April 16, 2001.

External Change Agents

The primary outside influence on a firm's decision to become international is foreign demand. Expressions of such demand through, for example, inquiries from abroad have a powerful effect on initial interest in entering the international marketplace. Unsolicited orders from abroad are the one major factor that encourages firms to begin exporting—even though firms increasingly have come to recognize that they must take the initiative in getting started in exporting.[18]

Another major outside influence is the statements and actions of other firms in the same industry. Information that an executive in a competing firm considers international markets to be valuable and worthwhile to develop easily captures the attention of management. Such statements not only have source credibility but also are viewed with a certain amount of fear because a successful competitor may eventually infringe on the firm's business. Formal and informal meetings among managers from

---

[18]Anthony C. Koh and Robert A. Robicheaux, "Variation in Export Performance Due to Differences in Export Marketing Strategy: Implications for Industrial Marketers," *Journal of Business Research* 17 (November 1988): 249–258.

different firms at trade association meetings, conventions, or business roundtables therefore often serve as a major change agent.

A third, quite influential, change agent consists of distributors. Often, distributors of firms are engaged, through some of their other business activities, in international marketing. To increase their international distribution volume, they encourage purely domestic firms also to participate in the international market. This is true not only for exports but also for imports. For example, a major customer of a manufacturing firm may find that materials available from abroad, if used in the domestic production process, would make the product available at lower cost. In such instances, the customer may approach the supplier and strongly encourage foreign sourcing. Many firms, although they may not like the suggestion, are flexible when they face the potential loss of a major account.

Banks and other service firms, such as accountants, can serve as major change agents by alerting domestic clients to international opportunities. Although these service providers historically follow their major multinational clients abroad, increasingly they are establishing a foreign presence. They frequently work with domestic clients on expanding their market reach in the hope that their services will be used for any international transactions that result.

Chambers of commerce and other business associations that interact with firms locally can frequently heighten international marketing interests. In most instances, these organizations function only as secondary intermediaries, because true change is brought about by the presence and encouragement of other managers.

Export agents are experienced in bringing about an international marketing orientation through two major kinds of activities. Some agents actively seek new international business activities. They visit firms and encourage them to penetrate international markets. More details on agents and their activities will be presented in Chapter 9, where export intermediaries are discussed.

Governmental efforts on the national or local level can also serve as a major change agent. In light of the contributions exports make to growth, employment, and tax revenue, governments increasingly are becoming active in encouraging and supporting exports. As was explained in Chapter 2, export promotion has become an integral part of most nations' trade policies. *The International Marketplace 8.4* explains how Ghana goes about helping firms to export.

In the United States, the Department of Commerce is particularly involved in encouraging exports. Its district offices are charged with increasing the international marketing activities of U.S. firms. Frequently, district officers, with the help of voluntary groups such as district export councils, visit firms and attempt to analyze their international marketing opportunities. Such activities raise questions about market and product specialization. Rarely will Department of Commerce employees have expertise in all areas. However, they can draw on the vast resources of the department to provide more information to an interested firm. For a firm new to exporting, Department of Commerce activities can be quite useful, particularly when searching for information services and buyer contacts.[19] As firms acquire more expertise in international marketing, the assistance may decline in value.

Increasingly, other governmental entities are also actively encouraging firms to participate in the international market. This takes place primarily on the state and local level. Many states have formed economic development agencies that assist companies by providing information, displaying products abroad, and sometimes even helping

[19]Jennifer Bremer, *Report Card on Trade: Evaluating Support Services for American Exporters*, International Business Education Center and the Kenan Institute for Private Enterprise, University of North Carolina–Chapel Hill, February 1995, 1–3.

THE INTERNATIONAL MARKETPLACE 8.4

The Ghana Export School

FOR DEVELOPING NATIONS, exporting is often a key element in the process of serious economic reform. One case in point is the West African nation of Ghana.

In an effort to diversify and promote exports, Ghana implemented a series of policy and institutional reforms. To expand the country's exports, a number of government goals were formulated: the need for increased knowledge of export opportunities, greater familiarity with export techniques, and a heightened export consciousness among current and potential export enterprises.

To meet these goals, a well-organized program of foreign trade training was called for, which could best be provided by a special school created for that purpose. A national survey showed that several existing training institutions were providing some programs in trade-related topics, but very few offered practical export marketing courses on a regular basis for business executives and trade promotion officials. Therefore, the Ghana Export Promotion Council established the Ghana Export School (GES) with the following objectives:

- Generate export consciousness in the business sector, which had traditionally been import-oriented;
- Create an awareness of the importance of exports in official circles to obtain positive responses from the government;
- Provide the business community with the necessary techniques for developing and managing export business efficiency;
- Spread the results of such training throughout the export community to as many companies as possible; and
- Provide a forum for discussing, evaluating, and finding solutions to export development problems in the country.

The Ghana Export School is a particularly innovative experiment, as it has no campus, training facilities, or faculty of its own. It draws its speakers and course developers from

business and government, uses the facilities of existing training institutions, and develops its own training materials based on local experience. By cooperating closely with the business sector and established training institutions, the school is able to provide a wide range of practical seminars and workshops in the foreign trade sector. It does so with minimum investment, tailored to the needs of the export community.

The GES offers approximately 30 training events annually. They cover a broad spectrum of subjects dealing with both techniques and products, reflecting exporters' training needs as well as the country's efforts to diversify its export product mix. The school holds workshops on mushroom production for export, packaging and labeling, the role of banks in export, export marketing for women entrepreneurs, and export production management for village enterprises.

The school has already trained nearly 1,600 government officials, export executives, and future exporters. It is expected that approximately 1,000 persons will be trained annually in the next several years. Besides serving as a means to upgrade export skills, the training programs have increased export consciousness in the country and have improved export performance. Through the training, exporters have been able to improve the quality and presentation of their products, which has resulted in a significant drop in the number of export goods rejected by both the Standards Institute in Ghana and importers in foreign markets.

Both the concept and the role of the Ghana Export School have been firmly accepted by the export community, academia, and trade-supporting institutions. A significant and sustainable contribution to the development of human resources in the foreign trade sector of Ghana has been achieved.

SOURCE: Claude Cellich and Kwesi Ahwoi, "The Ghana Export School: Success with Minimum Investment," *International Trade Forum* (January–March 1992): 20–27; Ghana Export Promotion Council web site, **www.exportghana.org**, accessed April 16, 2001.

with financing. Trade missions and similar activities are also being carried out by some of the larger cities. Although it is difficult to measure the effects of these efforts,[20] it appears that due to their closeness to firms, such state and local government authorities can become a major factor in influencing firms to go international.

[20]Thomas Singer and Michael R. Czinkota, "Factors Associated with Effective Use of Export Assistance," *Journal of International Marketing* 2 (Number 1, 1994): 53–71.

Internationalization Stages

For many firms, internationalization is a gradual process. Particularly in a market as large as the United States, firms are rarely formed expressly to engage in international marketing activities. In small markets, however, firms may very well be **born global,** founded for the explicit purpose of marketing abroad because of the recognized importance of international marketing and because the domestic economy may be too small to support their activities. Research conducted in Israel, for example, has shown that such **innate,** or start-up, **exporters** may have a distinct role to play in an economy's international trade involvement.[21]

In addition, firms with a strong e-commerce focus may also be gaining rapid global exposure due to the ease of outreach and access. Such rapid exposure, however, should not be confused with internationalization, since it may often take a substantial amount of time to translate exposure into international business activities.

In most instances today, firms begin their operations in the domestic market. From their home location, they gradually expand, and, over time, some of them become interested in the international market. The development of this interest typically appears to proceed in several stages. In each one of these stages, firms are measurably different in their capabilities, problems, and needs.[22] In looking at the internationalization process, one finds that initially the vast majority of firms are not at all interested in the international marketplace. Frequently, management will not even fill an unsolicited export order if one is received. Should unsolicited orders or other international market stimuli continue over time, however, a firm may gradually become **a partially interested exporter.** Management will then fill unsolicited export orders.

Prime candidates among firms to make this transition from uninterested to partially interested are those companies that have a track record of domestic market expansion.[23] In the next stage, the firm gradually begins to explore international markets, and management is willing to consider the feasibility of exporting. After this **exploratory** stage, the firm becomes an **experimental exporter,** usually to psychologically close countries. However, management is still far from being committed to international marketing activities.

At the next stage, the firm evaluates the impact that exporting has had on its general activities. Here, of course, the possibility exists that a firm will be disappointed with its international market performance and will withdraw from these activities. On the other hand, frequently, it will continue to exist as an experienced small exporter. The final stage of this process is that of **export adaptation.** Here a firm is an experienced exporter to a particular country and adjusts its activities to changing exchange rates, tariffs, and other variables. Management is ready to explore the feasibility of exporting to additional countries that are psychologically farther away. Frequently, this level of adaptation is reached once export transactions comprise 15 percent of sales volume. Just as parking ticket income, originally seen as unexpected revenue, gradually became incorporated into city budgets, the income from export marketing may become incorporated into the budget and plans of the firm. In these instances, the firm can be considered a strategic participant in the international market.

The population of exporting firms within these stages does not remain stable. Researchers of U.S. firms have found that in any given year, 15 percent of exporters

---

[21]Joseph Ganitsky, "Strategies for Innate and Adoptive Exporters: Lessons from Israel's Case," *International Marketing Review* 6 (1989): 50–65.

[22]Masaaki Kotabe and Michael R. Czinkota, "State Government Promotion of Manufacturing Exports: A Gap Analysis," *Journal of International Business Studies* (Winter 1992): 637–658.

[23]Yoo S. Yang, Robert P. Leone, and Dana L. Alden, "A Market Expansion Ability Approach to Identify Potential Exporters," *Journal of Marketing* 56 (January 1992): 84–96.

will stop exporting by the next year, while 10 percent of non-exporters will enter the foreign market. The most critical junctures for the firm are the points at which it begins or ceases exporting.[24]

Internationalization Concerns

As can be expected, firms that enter the international marketplace are faced with a host of new problems.

Firms at an export awareness stage—partially interested in the international market—are primarily concerned with operational matters such as information flow and the mechanics of carrying out international business transactions. They understand that a totally new body of knowledge and expertise is needed and try to acquire it. Companies that have already had some exposure to international markets begin to think about tactical marketing issues such as communication and sales effort. Finally, firms that have reached the export adaptation phase are mainly strategy- and service-oriented, which is to say that they worry about longer-range issues such as service delivery and regulatory changes. Utilizing the traditional marketing concept, one can therefore recognize that increased sophistication in international markets translates into increased application of marketing knowledge on the part of firms. The more they become active in international markets, the more firms recognize that a marketing orientation internationally is just as essential as it is in the domestic market.

Linking the various decision components and characteristics discussed so far facilitates an understanding of the process that a firm must undergo in its internationalization efforts. Figure 8.1 presents a model of the internationalization process, with a

---

FIGURE 8.1   A Model of the Export Development Process

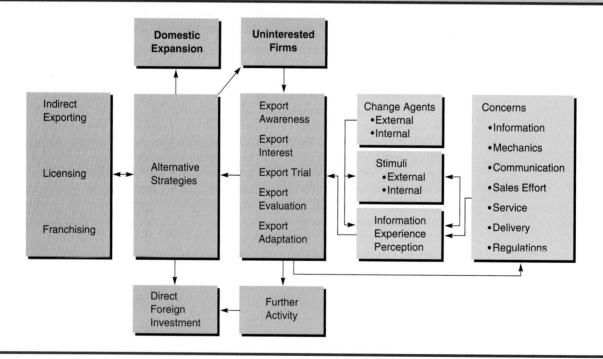

---

[24]Andrew B. Bernard and J. Bradford Jensen, *Exceptional Exporter Performance: Cause Effect or Both*, Census Research Data Center, Pittsburgh, Carnegie Mellon University, 1997.

particular focus on exporting. The model demonstrates the interaction between components and shows how a firm gradually grows into becoming a full participant in the global arena. With the help of this model, both management and the prospective employee can determine the firm's stage in the export development process and the changes needed to attain continued progress. To highlight the key implications of the different internationalization stages, the following profiles of companies delineate some of the more outstanding characteristics of firms in each one of these stages. A deeper insight into the international level of the firm permits a better understanding of what needs to be done to propel the firm forward in its internationalization. In addition, current or future employees can also use the internationalization process in order to position themselves best for employment or advancement in the firm.

Stage 1: The Completely Uninterested Firm

Profile Most firms at this stage have an annual sales volume of less than $5 million and fewer than 100 employees. The main decision maker is the president. The firm does not export and does not plan to do so in the future. Management is not exploring the possibility of exporting nor will unsolicited export orders be filled. Management tends to believe that exports will not contribute to the firm's profits or growth.

Help Needed Raise awareness level of exporting.

Implementation Strategies Increase communication that expounds the value of exporting on an unsolicited basis. Through trade associations and miniconferences, communicate the tangible benefits of exporting. Use successful small exporters from a peer or reference group as role models, asking them to provide testimonials and case studies to firms not interested in exporting. Increase information dissemination showing the size and profitability of foreign markets. Increase international education in schools to foster awareness of the international marketplace. Expose management to export activity figures by industry, export profitability statistics, and data about the impact of specific export activities on the balance of trade.

Stage 2: The Partially Interested Firm

Profile Most of these firms have an annual sales volume below $5 million and fewer than 100 employees. The current average annual export volume is below $200,000, which is sold to fewer than ten customers. One-quarter of the firms have actively sought their first export order. Almost half of the firms started exporting to a psychologically close country, to which they currently ship half of their exports. The president of the firm has the most input in the export decision; the marketing manager is a close second. Management knows that the firm has exportable products and tries to fill export orders. Management tends to believe that exporting may be a desirable activity and undertakes some exploration of export possibilities. Management is uncertain whether the firm will export more in the future and whether exports will contribute to the firm's growth and profits. The main motivations for exporting are a unique product and profit advantage.

Areas that the firm tends to see as being to some degree a problem in the export effort are financing, information on business practices, communication, the providing of technical advice, and sales effort. Firms believe that outsiders can be of substantial help to their export effort by assisting with obtaining financial information, financing, documentation handling, communication, and funds transfer.

Help Needed Raise awareness levels of export benefits. Assist with information about the mechanics of exporting.

Implementation Strategies   Use case studies to demonstrate the benefits that can be derived from exporting. Increase communications to make firms more aware of existing services. Provide these services in an accurate and timely fashion. Respond to export financing requests from such firms through more active small-volume export financing by government agencies or by establishing a facility that provides occasional exporters with small-sized credits (below $100,000) in a rapid fashion. Train employees to handle routine documentation problems and to have a general knowledge of the mechanics of the international transfer of funds. Institute a centralized task force that provides firms with rapid answers to nonroutine questions. Encourage universities to include commercial aspects in their foreign-language courses. Create university language banks that, for a small fee, aid firms in translating foreign documents.

Stage 3: The Exploring Firm

Profile   Most firms in this stage have an annual sales volume below $10 million and fewer than 100 employees. These firms export about $500,000 worth of merchandise to fewer than 20 customers. More than one-third of the firms have actively sought the first export order, which mainly originated from a psychologically close country that also absorbs currently about one-third of their exports.

In management, the president is the major export decision maker. The desirability of exporting is well known, as is the fact that the firm has exportable products. The firm is planning on exporting and is actively exploring export possibilities. The potential contribution of exporting to the firm's growth and profits is acknowledged, but past export profits have not met expectations. Having a unique product and obtaining a profit advantage are principal motivating factors for exporting. Important problems are encountered in the areas of communication, sales effort, marketing information gathering, information on business practices, and obtaining financial information.

Outside assistance is seen as valuable in the areas of obtaining financial information, information on business practices, marketing information gathering, documentation handling, and communication.

Help Needed   Make exporting more profitable. Provide general information and practical assistance.

Implementation Strategies   Entering into risk-and profit-sharing agreements with a government agency for a specified amount of initial exports could be considered. Books, CD-ROMs, and online bulletin boards containing current general market data and their wide distribution can help satisfy the general information needs. Cooperation with universities, as mentioned for Stage 2, would also help, particularly in learning how to obtain and use information about international markets.

Stage 4: Experimental Exporter

Profile   Most firms in this category have an annual sales volume of less than $5 million and have fewer than 100 employees. Average exports are about $750,000 and are shipped to about ten customers. One-third of the firms actively sought their first export order, which came mostly from a psychologically close country, where also one-third of the current exports go.

The president is the major decision maker. Exporting is seen favorably, but little active exploration of export possibilities takes place. Principal motivating factors for exporting are a unique product, technological advantage, and profit advantage.

Important exporting problems are seen in the areas of sales effort, obtaining financial information, physical product adaptation, marketing information gathering, and information on business practices.

Outside assistance is seen as somewhat helpful in the areas of marketing information gathering, information on business practices, handling documentation, obtaining financial information, and communication.

Help Needed Encourage the active exploration of exporting. Provide general assistance and help with product adaptation.

Implementation Strategies Provide management with foreign purchasing requests for products manufactured by these firms. Increase participation of these firms in exhibitions and fairs abroad. Search for contacts for these firms and carry out initial contacts for them. By functioning as an intermediary placing export orders with firms, an institution could clearly demonstrate the benefits of exporting without forcing firms to partake in the initial risk. Apart from the general assistance, increased information on foreign product standards should be communicated to these firms. Tax legislation that would permit increased deductions for costs incurred in product adaptations would help to keep firms internationally competitive.

Stage 5: The Experienced Small Exporter

Profile Average annual sales volume is below $10 million. Most firms employ fewer than 100 people. The export volume is slightly below $1.5 million and is shipped to an average of 40 customers. Four of ten firms actively sought their first export order. One-third of the firms started their exporting to a psychologically close country, to which they currently ship one-fourth of their exports.

The president is the major decision maker, with strong input from the marketing manager. Exporting is seen in a very favorable light. Only the past profitability of export activities is called into question. Profit advantage, a unique product, managerial urge, and a technological advantage are the main factors motivating exporting. Problems encountered in exporting are important in the areas of communication, sales effort, marketing information gathering, obtaining financial information, and handling documentation. Outside assistance is seen as somewhat helpful in the areas of gathering information on business practices, marketing information gathering, obtaining financial information, communication, and financing.

Help Needed Make exporting more profitable. Provide general assistance. Help with financing.

Implementation Strategies Financial assistance is now needed in greater size and for longer time periods than for firms in lower stages. Rapid responses to financing requests are not that important here. An increase in the cooperation between government and the banking sector will help satisfy this need. Training seminars on export financing would be of value to firms in this stage. Request for financial information need to be addressed rapidly and accurately.

Stage 6: The Experienced Larger Exporter

Profile Most firms have an average annual sales volume below $50 million and employ between 100 and 250 persons. Average annual export volume is about $6 million, shipped to about 140 customers. About one-half of the firms actively sought their first export order. One-fifth of the firms began their export activities with a psychologically close country, to which they now ship only a small portion of their exports.

The president and the marketing manager are the main export decision makers in the firm. Exporting is seen in a very favorable light, with the firm planning to be continuously active in the future. Main motivating factors for exporting are profit advantage, technological advantage, competitive pressures, tax benefits, a unique product, and managerial urge. Important problems are encountered in the areas of communication, sales effort, marketing information gathering, the providing of repair service, and information on business practices. Outside assistance is seen as possibly helpful in the areas of marketing information gathering, information on business practices, obtaining financial information, financing, and funds transfer.

Help Needed   Facilitate customer service.

Implementation Strategies   To facilitate customer service abroad, companies should be encouraged to train foreign personnel, enabling them to provide such services abroad. These training costs, together with other internationalization expenditures such as the translation of manuals, should be seen as customer service investments crucial for long-term success abroad. The further granting of assistance to such firms should be reconsidered because they are already satisfied with the profitability of the exporting efforts and sufficiently committed to the continuation of their international activities even without public-sector support.

Corporate Strategy and Exporting

As a firm moves through the internationalization stages, unusual things can happen to both risk and profit. In light of the gradual development of expertise, the many concerns about engaging in a new activity, and a firm's uncertainty with the new environment it is about to enter, management's perception of risk exposure grows. Domestically, the firm has gradually learned about the market and therefore managed to decrease its risk. In the course of new international expansion, the firm now encounters new and unfamiliar factors, exposing it to increased risk. At the same time, because of the investment needs required by a serious export effort, immediate profit performance may slip. In the longer term, increasing familiarity with international markets and the benefits of serving diversified markets will decrease the firm's risk below the previous "domestic only" level and increase profitability as well. For the most part, the more advanced and experienced the firm, the lower the perception of the costs and risks of exporting and the higher the perceived benefits.[25] In the short term, however, managers may face an unusual, and perhaps unacceptable, situation: rising risk accompanied by decreasing profitability. In light of this reality, which is depicted in Figure 8.2, many executives are tempted to either not initiate export activities or discontinue them.[26]

Understanding the internationalization stages together with the behavior of risk and profitability can help management overcome the seemingly prohibitive cost of going international by understanding that the negative developments are only short-term. Yet, export success does require the firm to be a risk taker, and firms must realize that satisfactory export performance will take time.[27] This satisfactory performance can be achieved in three ways: export effectiveness, efficiency, and competitive strength. Effectiveness is characterized by the acquisition of market share abroad and by increased sales. Efficiency is manifested later by rising profitability. Competitive strength refers then to the firm's position compared to other firms in the industry, and is, due

[25]Jonathan L. Calof and Wilma Viviers, "Internationalization Behavior of Small- and Medium-Sized South African Enterprises," *Journal of Small Business Management* 33 (Number 4, 1995): 71–79.

[26]Michael R. Czinkota, "A National Export Development Policy for New and Growing Businesses," in *Trends in International Business: Critical Perspectives*, M. Czinkota and M. Kotabe, eds. (Oxford, England: Blackwell Publishers, 1998), 69–97.

[27]Van Miller, Tom Becker, and Charles Crespy, "Contrasting Export Strategies: A Discriminant Analysis Study of Excellent Exporters," *The International Trade Journal* 7 (Number 3, 1993): 321–340.

FIGURE	8.2	Profit and Risk During Export Initiation

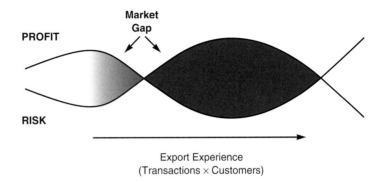

SOURCE: Michael R. Czinkota, "A National Export Development Policy for New and Growing Businesses," in *Trends in International Business: Critical Perspectives*, M. Czinkota and M. Kotabe, eds. (Oxford, England: Blackwell Publishers, 1998), 69–77.

to the benefits of international market experience, likely to grow. The international marketer must appreciate the time and performance dimensions associated with going abroad in order to overcome short-term setbacks for the sake of long-term success.

SUMMARY

Firms do not become experienced exporters overnight but rather progress gradually through an export development process. This process is the result of different motivations to internationalize, varying managerial and corporate characteristics of the firm, the influence of change agents, and the capability of the firm to overcome internationalization barriers.

The motivations can be either proactive or reactive. Proactive motivations are initiated by the firm's management and can consist of a perceived profit advantage, technological advantage, product advantage, exclusive market information, or managerial urge. Reactive motivations are the responses of management to environmental changes and pressures. Typical are competitive pressures, overproduction, declining domestic sales, or excess capacity. Firms that are primarily stimulated by proactive motivations are more likely to enter international markets aggressively and successfully.

An international orientation can also be brought about by change agents both external and internal to the firm. Typically, these are individuals and institutions that, due to their activities or goals, highlight the benefits of international activities. They can be managers who have traveled abroad or have carried out successful international marketing ventures, foreign distributors who have inquired about the possibility of representing a firm, or organizations such as banks, government agencies, or trading consortia.

Over time, firms will progress through stages of international expertise and activity. In each one of these stages, firms are likely to have a distinct level of interest in the international market and require different types of information and help. Their outlook toward international markets is likely to progress gradually from purely operational concerns to a strategic international orientation. Only at that level will the firm have become a truly international marketer.

In spite of temporary unfavorable conditions for risk and profit, management must understand that export activities only develop gradually through the internationalization stages, and that satisfactory export performance consists of the three dimensions of growing sales and market share, higher profitability, and an improved competitive position.

QUESTIONS FOR DISCUSSION

1. How might advances in information technology encourage a potential exporter to pursue international sales?

2. Discuss the difference between a proactive and a reactive firm, focusing your discussion on the international market.

3. How have the benefits that accrue to firms from unique products or technological advantages changed over time?

4. Explain the benefits that international sales can have for domestic market activities.

5. Discuss the benefits and the drawbacks of treating international market activities as a safety valve mechanism.

6. What is meant by the concept of "psychological, or psychic, distance"?

7. Give some of the reasons why distributors would want to help a firm gain a stronger foothold in the international market.

8. How do the concerns of firms change as the firms progress in their internationalization efforts?

9. What programs does the Ex-Im bank (**www.exim.gov**) offer that specifically benefit small businesses trying to export? What benefits can be derived from each?

10. Carefully examine the Overseas Private Investment Corporation web site (**www.opic.gov**). Describe the type of country-specific information an exporter can gather using this web site.

RECOMMENDED READINGS

Czinkota, Michael R., and Ilkka A. Ronkainen. *International Marketing Strategy: Environmental Assessment and Entry Strategies*. Fort Worth, TX: The Dryden Press, 1994.

Joyner, Nelson T. *How to Build an Export Business*, 2nd ed. Reston, VA: Federation of International Trade Associations, 2000.

McCue, Sarah. *Trade Secrets: The Export Answer Book*. Detroit: Michigan Small Business Development Center, Wayne State University, 1998.

Metropolitan Area Exports: An Export Performance Report on Over 250 U.S. Cities. Washington, DC: U.S. Department of Commerce, 1996.

Nelson, Carl A. *Exporting: A Manager's Guide to the World Market*. Cincinnati, OH: International Thomson Business Press, 1999.

Noonan, Chris. *CIM Handbook of Export Marketing*. Boston: Butterworth-Heinemann, 2000.

Richardson, David J., and Karin Rindal. *Why Exports Matter: More!* Washington, DC: Institute for International Economics and The Manufacturing Institute, 1996.

Root, Franklin R. *Entry Strategies for International Markets: Revised and Expanded*. San Francisco: Jossey-Bass Publishers, 1999.

Seyoum, Belay. *Export-Import Theory, Practices, and Procedures*. New York: International Business Publishers, 2000.

Woznick, Alexandra, and Edward G. Hinkelman. *A Basic Guide to Exporting*, 3rd ed. Novato, CA: World Trade Press, 2000.

Export Intermediaries, Licensing, and Franchising

Chapter 9

THE INTERNATIONAL MARKETPLACE 9.1

Sogoshosha: Surviving in Changing Times

MITSUBISHI, ONE OF Japan's largest sogoshosha or trading companies, has annual revenues in excess of $127 million. In serving its 45,000 customers, Mitsubishi's 7,211 employees plus 1,533 overseas local staff move as many as 100,000 products, from kernels of corn to huge power generators, around the world. Among the dozens of properties it owns outright are cattle feedlots and coal mines in Australia, pulp mills and iron ore mines in Canada, copper mines in Chile, a resort in Hawaii, and liquefied gas fields off the coast of Brunei.

Ironically enough, Mitsubishi is scraping by on a meager profit margin of approximately 0.04 percent. The other sogoshosha suffer similarly—even at their best in the 1960s and 1970s, these trading companies had profit margins of no more than 3 percent. Now rising costs threaten to swallow earnings altogether. The core business that built the companies, hauling raw materials into Japan and speeding finished goods out into the world, has been declining for more than a decade. Experts believe that many Japanese manufacturers who once depended on the sogoshosha no longer need a trading company. They now make their own arrangements with shippers, dealers, and advertising agencies.

Luckily for Mitsubishi, a portion of its import business is protected from erosion because it has bought all or a slice of many supply sources. Take the corn trade it runs between the United States and Japan. It owns three grain elevators in central Nebraska where it stores the corn it buys locally. Back home, Mitsubishi owns Japan's largest livestock operation, so it feeds some of that American corn to its own chickens and pigs. A number of those chickens, in turn, end up on the ta-

bles of Japan's 1,050 Kentucky Fried Chicken restaurants, of which Mitsubishi is a proprietor.

Mitsubishi's greatest strength for the long haul, however, is its ability to continually attract top talent. The company ranks among the most desired employers among Japanese university students. So Mitsubishi can dispatch some of the brightest and the best of Japan's graduates to its 108 overseas offices, which comprise one of the world's great information-gathering networks. (During the Gulf War, Mitsubishi's expatriates in the Middle East sent the home office more political and economic intelligence than foreign service officers provided the Japanese government.) How and where should this and other trading companies focus their talent as they struggle for a new role? The prevailing wisdom as to the "where" is simple—fast-growing Southeast Asia, China, and India. "As Japanese companies increase their direct investment in the region, they're going to travel in caravans," says Victor Fung, head of one of the largest Overseas China trading companies in Hong Kong. "And they're going to need someone to show them the way. That should make this a golden age for traders."

SOURCES: Mitsubishi web site, accessed April 17, 2001; Lee Smith, "Does the World's Biggest Company Have a Future?" *Fortune*, August 7, 1995, 124.

http://www.Mitsubishi.co.jp

285

Q UITE FREQUENTLY, FIRMS recognize the value of marketing internationally, but either they lack sufficient capital or human resources for exporting or they consider such a strategy to be inappropriate. This chapter suggests alternatives for participation in the international marketplace. The chapter then focuses on licensing and franchising. It describes how these arrangements function, the opportunities they provide, and their drawbacks. Initially, the use of market intermediaries is explained. These include export management companies, Webb-Pomerene associations, and export trading companies.

Export Intermediaries

Firms that do not care to export can still participate in international marketing by making use of international market intermediaries. One obvious possibility is the selling of merchandise to a domestic firm that in turn sells it abroad. For example, many products are sold to multinational corporations that use them as input for their foreign sales. Similarly, products sold to the U.S. Department of Defense may ultimately be shipped to military outposts abroad. Alternatively, an exporter may buy products domestically to round out an international product line or a buyer from abroad may purchase goods during a visit.

Frequently firms also enter the international market with the help of market intermediaries who specialize in bringing firms or their goods and services to the global market. *The International Marketplace 9.1* provides an example of one such intermediary. These intermediaries can be crucial to success in international marketing because their special expertise can help overcome knowledge and performance gaps of firms. Often, they have detailed information about the competitive conditions in certain markets or they have personal contacts with potential buyers abroad. They can also assist by evaluating credit risk, calling on customers abroad in person, and handling the physical delivery of the product to the buyer.[1] Here we will consider three such intermediaries: export management companies, Webb-Pomerene associations, and export trading companies.

Export Management Companies

Export management companies (EMCs) are domestic firms that specialize in performing international marketing services as commission representatives or as distributors for several other firms. Most EMCs are quite small. They were frequently formed by one or two major principals with experience in international marketing or in a particular geographic area. Their expertise enables them to offer specialized services to domestic corporations.

EMCs have two primary forms of operation. They either take title to goods and operate internationally on their own account, or they perform services as agents. In the first instance, the EMC offers a conventional export channel in that it does not have any form of geographic exclusivity, and tends to negotiate price with suppliers on every transaction. As an agent, an EMC is likely to have either an informal or a formal contractual relationship, which specifies exclusivity agreements and, often, sales quotas. In addition, price arrangements and promotional support payments are

---

[1]Richard M. Castaldi, Alex F. DeNoble, and Jeffrey Kantor, "The Intermediary Service Requirements of Canadian and American Exports," *International Marketing Review* 9 (Number 2, 1992): 21–40.

agreed on, which simplifies ongoing transactions.[2] Because EMCs often serve a variety of clients, their mode of operation may vary from client to client and from transaction to transaction—that is, an EMC may act as an agent for one client, whereas for another client, or even for the same one on a different occasion, it may operate as a distributor.

The EMC as an Agent

When serving as an agent, the EMC is primarily in charge of developing foreign marketing and sales strategies and establishing contacts abroad. Because the EMC does not share in the profits from a sale, it depends heavily on a high sales volume, on which it charges commission. It may therefore be tempted to take on as many products and as many clients as possible in order to obtain a high turnover. The risk in this is that the EMC will spread itself too thin and cannot adequately represent all the clients and products it carries. This risk is particularly great for small EMCs.

In addition to its international activities, this type of EMC must concentrate a substantial amount of effort on the development of domestic clients. These clients often are exactly the firms that are unwilling to commit major resources to international marketing efforts. They must be convinced that it is worthwhile to consider international marketing.

EMCs that have specific expertise in selecting markets because of language capabilities, previous exposure, or specialized contacts appear to be the ones most successful and useful in aiding client firms in their export marketing efforts. For example, they can cooperate with firms that are already successful in international marketing but have been unable to penetrate a specific region. By sticking to their expertise and representing only a limited number of clients, such agent services can be quite valuable.

The EMC as a Distributor

When operating as a distributor, the EMC purchases products from the domestic firm, takes the title, and assumes the trading risk. Selling in its own name offers the opportunity to reap greater profits than does acting as an agent. The potential for greater profitability is appropriate because the EMC has drastically reduced the risk for the domestic firm while increasing its own risk. The burden of the merchandise acquired provides a major motivation to complete an international sale successfully. The domestic firm selling to the EMC is in the comfortable position of having sold its merchandise and received its money without having to deal with the complexities of the international market. On the other hand, the firm is unlikely to gather much international marketing expertise and therefore relegates itself to some extent to remaining a purely domestic firm.

Compensation of EMCs

The mechanism of an EMC may be very useful to the domestic firm if such activities produce additional sales abroad that otherwise would not have occurred. However, certain services must be performed that demand resources for which someone must pay. As an example, to develop foreign markets, market development expenses must be incurred. At the very least, product availability must be communicated, goods must be shown abroad, visits must be arranged, or contacts must be established in order to enter the market. Even though it may often not be discussed, the funding for these activities must be found.

One possibility is a fee charged to the manufacturer by the EMC for market development, sometimes in the form of a retainer and often on an annual basis. These retainers vary and are dependent on the number of products represented and the difficulty of foreign market entry. Frequently, manufacturers are also expected to pay all or part of the direct expenses associated with foreign market penetration. Some of

[2]Daniel C. Bello and Nicholas C. Williamson, "Contractual Arrangement and Marketing Practices in the Indirect Export Channel," *Journal of International Business Studies* 16 (Summer 1985): 65–82.

these expenses may involve the production and translation of promotional brochures. Others may concern the rental of space at foreign trade shows, the provision of product samples, or trade advertising.

Alternatively, the EMC may set the price for the product. Because it will take on many of the marketing activities for the manufacturer, the EMC wants the price discounted for these activities. Therefore, sales to EMCs may occur only at a reduced price.

In one way or another, the firm that uses an EMC must pay the EMC for the international marketing effort. This compensation can be in the form of fees and/or cost-sharing or in terms of lower prices and resulting higher profits for the EMC. Otherwise, despite promises, the EMC may simply add the firm and product in name only to its product offering and do nothing to achieve international market penetration. Manufacturers need to be aware of this cost and the fact that EMCs do not offer a free ride. Depending on the complexity of a product and the necessity to carry out developmental research, promotion, and service, manufacturers must be prepared to part with some portion of the potential international profitability to compensate the EMC for its efforts.

Power Conflicts between EMCs and Clients

The EMC in turn faces the continuous problem of retaining a client once foreign market entry is achieved. Many firms use an EMC's services mainly to test international markets, with the clear desire to become a direct exporter once successful operations have been established. Of course, this is particularly true if foreign demand turns out to be strong and profit levels are high. As a result there is a conflict between the EMC and its clients, with one side wanting to retain market power by not sharing too much international market information, and the other side wanting to obtain that power, which often results in short-term relationships and a lack of cooperation. Because international market development is based on long-term efforts, however, this conflict frequently precipitates unsuccessful international marketing efforts.

For the concept of an export management company to work, both parties must fully recognize the delegation of responsibilities; the costs associated with these activities; and the need for information sharing, cooperation, and mutual reliance. On the manufacturer's side, use of an EMC should be viewed as a domestic channel commitment. This requires a thorough investigation of the intermediary and the advisability of relying on its efforts, a willingness to cooperate on a prolonged basis, and a willingness to reward it properly for these efforts. If the intermediary is chosen with proper care, the use of EMCs can be a very effective strategy for entering foreign markets.[3] The EMC in turn must adopt a flexible approach to managing the export relationship. As access to the Internet is making customers increasingly sophisticated, export management companies must ensure that they continue to deliver true value added. They must acquire, develop, and deploy resources such as new knowledge about foreign markets or about export processes, in order to lower their client firm's export-related transaction costs and therefore remain useful intermediaries.[4] By doing so, the EMC can clearly let the client know that the cost is worth the service.

Webb-Pomerene Associations

One form of export intermediary particular to the United States is the Webb-Pomerene association. Legislation enacted in 1918 permitted firms to cooperate in terms of sales

---

[3]Robert W. Haigh, "Thinking of Exporting? Export Management Companies Could Be the Answer," *Columbia Journal of World Business* 29 (Number 4, Winter 1994): 66–81.

[4]Mike W. Peng and Anne Y. Ilinitch, "Export Intermediary Firms: A Note on Export Development Research," *Journal of International Business Studies* 3 (1998): 609–620.

allocation, financing, and pricing information regarding their international sales contrary to antitrust legislation. The associations must take care not to engage in activities that would reduce competition within the United States. To penetrate international markets more successfully, however, they can use mechanisms such as market allocation, quota fixing, and selection of exclusive distributors or brokers.

In spite of this early effort to encourage joint activities by firms in the international market, the effectiveness of Webb-Pomerene associations has not been substantial. At their peak from 1930 to 1934, fifty Webb-Pomerene associations accounted for about 12 percent of U.S. exports. By 2000, only 12 associations were active and accounted for less than 1 percent of U.S. exports.[5] In addition, it appears that most of the members are not the small and medium-sized firms that the act was initially intended to assist but rather are the dominant representatives in their respective industries.

The limited success of this particular intermediary has mainly been ascribed to the fact that the antitrust exemption granted was not sufficiently ironclad. Further, specialized export firms are thought to have more to offer a domestic firm than does an association, which may be particularly true if an association is dominated by one or two major competitors in an industry. This makes joining the association undesirable for smaller firms in that industry. Finally, it appears that with the creation of new U.S. antitrust exemption vehicles such as export trading companies, many Webb-Pomerene associations have reregistered with the government under the new mechanisms.

Trading Companies

A third major facilitating intermediary is the trading company. The concept was originated by the European trading houses such as the Fuggers and was soon formalized by the monarchs. Hoping to expand their imperial powers and wealth, kings chartered traders to form corporate bodies that enjoyed exclusive trading rights and protection by the naval forces in exchange for tax payments. Examples of such early trading companies are the East India Company of the Netherlands (Oost-Indische Compagnie), formed in 1602, followed shortly by the British East India Company and the French East India Company (La Compagnie des Indes).[6] Today, the most famous trading companies are the sogoshosha of Japan. Names like Sumitomo, Mitsubishi, Mitsui, and C. Itoh have become household words around the world. These general trading companies play a unique role in world commerce by importing, exporting, countertrading, investing, and manufacturing. Because of their vast size, they can benefit from economies of scale and perform their operations at very low profit margins.

Four major reasons have been given for the success of the Japanese sogoshosha. First, by concentrating on obtaining and disseminating information about market opportunities and by investing huge funds in the development of information systems, these firms now have the mechanisms and organizations in place to gather, evaluate, and translate market information into business opportunities. Second, economies of scale permit them to take advantage of their vast transaction volume to obtain preferential treatment by, for example, negotiating transportation rates or even opening up new transportation routes. Third, these firms serve large internal markets, not only in Japan but also around the world, and can benefit from opportunities for barter trade. Finally, sogoshosha have access to vast quantities of capital, both within Japan and in the international capital markets. They can therefore carry out many transactions that are larger and riskier than is palatable or feasible for other firms.[7] In the

[5]James F. Mongoven, Federal Trade Commission, Washington, DC, April 6, 2000.

[6]Dong-Sung Cho, *The General Trading Company: Concept and Strategy* (Lexington, MA: Lexington Books, 1987), 2.

[7]Yoshi Tsurumi, *Sogoshosha: Engines of Export-Based Growth* (Montreal, Quebec: Institute for Research on Public Policy, 1980).

1990s, as more Japanese firms set up their own global networks, the share of Japan's trade handled by the sogoshosha declined. However, these giants continued to succeed by shifting their strategy to expand their domestic activities in Japan, entering more newly developing markets, increasing their trading activities between countries, and forming joint ventures with non-Japanese firms. Mitsui, for example, has more than 100 affiliated companies involved in joint ventures with local business groups in Thailand alone.[8]

For many decades, the emergence of trading companies was commonly believed to be a Japan-specific phenomenon. Particularly, Japanese cultural factors were cited as the reason why such intermediaries could operate successfully only from that country. In 1975, however, trading companies were established by government declaration in Korea. The intent was to continue Korea's export-led growth in a more efficient fashion. With the new legislation, the Korean government tied access to financing and government contracts to the formation of trading companies. By 1981, the major trading companies of Korea (such as Hyundai, Samsung, and Daewoo) were handling 43 percent of Korea's total exports.[9] They were therefore considered to be a major success. Similarly, the Brazilian government stimulated the creation of trading companies by offering preferential financing arrangements. Within a short time, these Brazilian firms dramatically increased their activities and accounted for almost 20 percent of total Brazilian exports.[10] Also, the government of Turkey devised special incentives to develop export trading firms, which resulted within a few years in such trading companies accounting for 46 percent of Turkey's exports.[11]

Export trading company (ETC) legislation designed to improve the export performance of small and medium-sized firms has also been implemented in the United States. Bank participation in trading companies was permitted and the antitrust threat to joint export efforts was reduced through precertification of planned activities by the U.S. Department of Commerce. Businesses were encouraged to join together to export, or offer export services, by passage of the Export Trading Company Act.

Permitting banks to participate in ETCs was intended to allow ETCs better access to capital and therefore to more trading transactions and easier receipt of title to goods. The relaxation of antitrust provisions in turn was to enable firms to form joint ventures more easily. The cost of developing and penetrating international markets would then be shared, with the proportional share being, for many small and medium-sized firms, much easier to bear. As an example, in case a warehouse is needed to secure foreign-market penetration, one firm alone does not have to bear all the costs. A consortium of firms can jointly rent a foreign warehouse. Similarly, each firm need not station a service technician abroad at substantial cost. Joint funding of a service center by several firms makes the cost less prohibitive for each one. The trading company concept also offers a one-stop shopping center for both the firm and its foreign customers. The firm can be assured that all international functions will be performed efficiently by the trading company, and at the same time, the foreign customer will have to deal with fewer individual firms.

The legislation permits a wide variety of possible structures for an ETC. General trading companies handle many commodities, perform import and export services, countertrade, and work closely with foreign distributors. Regional trading companies handle commodities produced in only one region, specializing in products in which

[8]Louise de Rosario, "Leaky Umbrellas," *Far Eastern Economic Review* 11 (February 1993): 48.

[9]Chang-Kyun Shin, "Korean General Trading Companies: A Study of Their Development and Strategies," doctoral dissertation, George Washington University, Washington, DC, 1984, 236.

[10]Umberto Costa Pinto, "Trading Companies: The Brazilian Experience," in *U.S. Latin American Trade Relations*, ed. M. Czinkota (New York: Praeger Publishers, 1983), 251.

[11]I. Atilla Dicle and Ulku Dicle, "Effects of Government Export Policies on Turkish Export Trading Companies," *International Marketing Review* 9 (Number 3, 1992): 62–76.

this region possesses a comparative advantage. Product-oriented trading companies concentrate on a limited number of products and offer their market penetration services only for these products. Trading companies may also be geographically oriented, targeting one particular foreign region, or can be focused on certain types of projects, such as turnkey operations and joint ventures with foreign investors. Finally, trading companies may develop an industry-oriented focus, handling only goods of specific industry groups, such as metals, chemicals, or pharmaceuticals.[12]

Independent of its form of operation, an ETC can deliver a wide variety of services. It can be active chiefly as an agent, or it can purchase products or act as a distributor abroad. It can provide information on distribution costs and even handle domestic and international distribution and transportation. This can range from identifying distribution costs to booking space on ocean or air carriers and handling shipping contracts.

Although ETCs seem to offer major benefits to many U.S. firms wishing to penetrate international markets, they have not been used very extensively. By 2000 only 178 individual ETCs had been certified by the U.S. Department of Commerce. Yet these certificates covered more than 5,000 firms, mainly because various trade associations had applied for certification for all of their members.[13] Perhaps the greatest potential of ETCs lies with trade associations. However, it may also be a worthwhile concept to consider by firms and banks.

Banks need to evaluate whether the mentalities of bankers and traders can be made compatible. Traders, for example, are known for seizing an opportunity whereas bankers often appear to move more slowly. A key challenge will be to find ways to successfully blend business entrepreneurship with banking regulations.

Banks also need to understand the benefits they can derive from working with small or medium-sized exporters. The first impression may be that an ETC offers only added risk and cost. Yet involvement with an ETC may provide the bank with a broader client base, profitable use of its extensive international information system and network of corresponding institutions, and a stepping stone toward the internationalization of its own banking services. However, many banks are hesitant to increase the volume of their international activities. This hesitation has been reinforced by the attitudes of shareholders. Research has shown that past announcements of ETC formation by U.S. banks caused significant negative stock price reactions. Apparently, the market believed that U.S. banks' involvement in ETCs would not be value-enhancing.[14] In the long run, however, an improved understanding of the type and profitability of transactions and the increasing pressure of a highly competitive deregulated home market may well lead again to more international involvement by U.S. banks.

Firms participating in trading companies by joining or forming them should be aware of the difference between product- and market-driven ETCs. Firms may have a strong tendency to use their trading company primarily to dispose of their merchandise. International sales, however, depend primarily on the demand and the market. An ETC must therefore accomplish a balance between the demands of the market and the supply of the members in order to be successful.

The trading company itself must solicit continuous feedback on foreign market demands and changes in these demands so that its members will be able to maintain a winning international product and service mix. Substantial attention must be paid to

---

[12] *The Export Trading Company Act of 1982* (Washington, DC: Chamber of Commerce of the United States, 1983), 4.

[13] Vanessa Bachman, Office of Export Trading Companies, U.S. Department of Commerce, Washington, DC, March 27, 2000.

[14] Lawrence Kryzanowski and Nancy D. Ursel, "Market Reaction to the Formation of Export Trading Companies by American Banks," *Journal of International Business Studies* (Second Quarter 1993): 373–381.

FIGURE	9.1	Service Requirements for American Export Trading Companies

Products Exported

Suppliers Represented	Undifferentiated	Differentiated
Low Export Volume	Requires a Less-Than-Average Capability in Promotion, Market Contact, and Consolidation	Requires an Above-Average Capability in Promotion but an Average Capability in Market Contact and Consolidation
High Export Volume	Requires a Less-Than-Average Capability in Promotion but an Average Capability in Market Contact and Consolidation	Requires an Above-Average Capability in Promotion, Market Contact, and Consolidation

SOURCE: Reprinted from Daniel C. Bello and Nicholas C. Williamson. "The American Export Trading Company: Designing a New International Marketing Institution," *Journal of Marketing* 49 (Fall 1985): 67, published by the American Marketing Association.

gathering information on the needs and wants of foreign customers and disseminating this information to the participating U.S. firms. Otherwise, lack of responsiveness to foreign market demands will result in a decline of the ETC's effectiveness.[15] The ETC also should determine the activities on which to concentrate, basing this determination on the types of suppliers represented and the types of products exported. Figure 9.1 provides one possible differentiation for such service requirements based on the type of product exported and the type of suppliers represented.

Depending on whether products are differentiated or undifferentiated, such as commodities, the ETC should place varying degrees of emphasis on developing its capability for international promotion. At the same time, undifferentiated products require greater price competitiveness, which may be precisely the chief advantage offered by an ETC as a result of economies of scale. For differentiated products, an ETC may be able to place emphasis on promotion and have greater flexibility in price determination.

The future success of U.S. export trading companies is still uncertain. The concepts of synergism and cooperation certainly make sense in terms of enhancing the international competitiveness of firms. Yet the focus of ETCs should perhaps not be pure exporting. Importing and countertrading may also generate substantial activity and profit. By carrying out a wide variety of export transactions, ETCs can obtain international market knowledge. This management and consulting expertise may in itself become a salable service.

Licensing and Franchising

Licensing and franchising are alternatives open to and used by all types of firms, large and small. They offer flexibility in the international market approach, reflecting the needs of the firm and the circumstances in the market. A small firm, for example, may

[15]Michael R. Czinkota, "The Business Response to the Export Trading Company Act of 1982," *Columbia Journal of World Business* 19 (Fall 1984): 111.

choose to use licensing to benefit from a foreign business concept or to expand without much capital investment. A multinational corporation may use the same strategy to rapidly enter foreign markets in order to take advantage of new conditions and foreclose some opportunities to its competition. It is important to recognize licensing and franchising as additional opportunities for market expansion. These options can be used both in lieu of or in addition to the export strategy discussed previously. Another set of options—consisting of foreign direct investment, joint ventures, and management contracts—will be addressed later in the book.

Licensing

Under a licensing agreement, one firm, the licensor, permits another to use its intellectual property in exchange for compensation designated as a royalty. The recipient firm is the licensee. The property might include patents, trademarks, copyrights, technology, technical know-how, or specific marketing skills. For example, a firm that has developed new packaging for liquids can permit other firms abroad to use the same process. Licensing therefore amounts to exporting and importing intangibles. As *The International Marketplace 9.2* shows, licensing has great potential that may increase for a long time to come.

Assessment of Licensing

Licensing has intuitive appeal to many potential international marketers. As an entry strategy, it may require neither capital investment nor knowledge and marketing strength in foreign markets. By earning royalty income, it provides an opportunity to obtain an additional return on research and development investments already incurred. After initial costs, the licensor can reap benefits until the end of the contract period. Licensing reduces risk of exposure to government intervention in that the licensee is typically a local company that can provide leverage against government action. Licensing will help to avoid host country regulations that are focused on equity ventures. Licensing may also serve as a stage in the internationalization of the firm by providing a means by which foreign markets can be tested without major involvement of capital or management time. Similarly, licensing can be used as a strategy to preempt a market before the entry of competition, especially if the licensor's resources permit full-scale involvement only in selected markets. A final reason that licensing activities are increasing is the gradual implementation of intellectual property rights protection. In many countries pirated technology, processes, and products are still abundant. However, progress by the World Trade Organization (WTO) has improved the protection of intellectual property and the enforcement of such protection by governments. With greater protection of their proprietary knowledge, companies are more willing to transfer such knowledge internationally.[16] In instances of high levels of piracy, a licensing agreement with a strong foreign partner may also add value because now the partner becomes a local force with a distinct interest in rooting out unlicensed activities.

Licensing has nevertheless come under criticism from supranational organizations, such as the United Nations Conference on Trade and Development (UNCTAD). It has been alleged that licensing provides a mechanism by which older technology is capitalized on by industrialized-country multinational corporations (MNCs). Licensees may often want labor-intensive techniques or machinery, however. Guinness Brewery, for example, in order to produce Guinness Stout in Nigeria, imported

---

[16]Farok J. Contractor and Sumit K. Kundu, "Franchising versus Company-Run Operations: Modal Choice in the Global Hotel Sector," *Journal of International Marketing* 6 (Number 2, 1998): 28–53.

THE INTERNATIONAL MARKETPLACE 9.2

Success in China Licensing

*P*LAYBOY MAGAZINE may be banned in China, but Playboy clothes are more than welcomed. That paradox amuses John Chan, founder and chairman of Chaifa Holdings Company, which holds the exclusive license to sell Playboy-branded garments and accessories on the mainland. Mr. Chan has managed to make the Playboy rabbit silhouette one of the most popular emblems on shirts, sweaters, shoes, leather belts, key chains, and neckties sold in China.

Chaifa's number of outlets selling Playboy goods has mushroomed from a handful to 500. "What Chaifa has done in four years might take a more experienced, better-connected retailer 10 to 20 years to do," says one industry analyst. In contrast to the company's impressive sales and profit growth, the China operations of some larger Hong Kong garment retailers have rung up losses over the past several years.

Mr. Chan founded Chaifa, which means "going to be rich" in Chinese, in 1986. Unlike most Hong Kong retailers, Chaifa concentrates on mainland China. The Playboy outlets sell only garments and accessories made by Chaifa's factory in Shantou, China. This way, capital outlay and business risks are minimized and the headache of managing hundreds of stores with thousands of employees is avoided. Chaifa pays Playboy Enterprises, Inc., U.S. owner of the trademark, royalties based on sales.

To find suitable dealers, Mr. Chan visits duty-free shops, department stores, and other retailers all over the country. "It was hard work at first, getting a cold shoulder here and there. But without contacts, that was the only way," he says. He recalls those early years when he traveled with only a briefcase stocked with goods to show potential retailers. These days, Mr. Chan advertises for prospective dealers in mainland newspapers and trade magazines. He visits all potential business partners and often helps them search for retail space.

Mr. Chan, often dressed in business suits, socks, and shoes emblazoned with the Playboy logo, attributes his company's success to choosing mid-priced brand-name products that he knows will appeal to Chinese consumers. "Many Chinese still prefer buying Western brand-name products to generic goods because of the cachet," Mr. Chan says. "And I go for mid-price goods because to make money, one has to sell to China's growing middle class, not the few elites," he adds.

Chaifa spends an average 3 to 4 percent of sales on advertising and promotion through the media, fashion shows, exhibitions, and trade events all across China. Since most Chinese have never seen *Playboy* magazine, the company tries to project a healthy, youthful image for the name. "I always explain that Playboy is a lifestyle, a culture, not sex," Mr. Chan says. Chaifa also promotes Garfield the cat, as a children's buddy, and Arnold Palmer, as a model of success for mature men. "I intend to make Playboy, Garfield, and Arnold Palmer household names in China," explains Mr. Chan.

SOURCE: Chaifa Holdings Company web site, **www.chaifa.com.hk**, accessed April 17, 2001; Lotte Chow, "Chinese Consumers Embrace Market for Attire Emblazoned by Playboy," *The Wall Street Journal*, August 25, 1995, A5E.

http://www.chaifa.com.hk

licensed equipment that had been used in Ireland at the turn of the century. Even though this equipment was obsolete by Western standards, it had additional economic life in Nigeria because it presented a good fit with Nigeria's needs.

Licensing offers a foreign entity the opportunity for immediate market entry with a proven concept. It therefore reduces the risk of R&D failures, the cost of designing around the licensor's patents, or the fear of patent infringement litigation. Furthermore, most licensing agreements provide for ongoing cooperation and support, thus enabling the licensee to benefit from new developments.

Licensing may enable the international marketer to enter a foreign market that is closed to either imports or direct foreign investments. In addition, licensing arrangements may enable the licensor to negotiate parallel contracts that are not related directly to the agreement but provide for foreign purchases of materials and components. The licensor can thereby expand participation in the particular market.

Licensing is not without disadvantages. To a large degree, it may leave the international marketing functions to the licensee. As a result, the licensor may not gain sufficient international marketing expertise to ready itself for subsequent world market penetration. Moreover, the initial toehold in the foreign market may not be a foot in the door. Depending on the licensing arrangement, quite the opposite may take place. In exchange for the royalty, the licensor may create its own competitor not only in the markets for which the agreement was made but also in third markets. As a result, some companies are hesitant to enter into many licensing agreements. For example, Japanese firms are delighted to sell goods to China but are unwilling to license the Chinese to produce the goods themselves. They fear that because of the low wage structure in China, such licenses could create a powerful future competitor in markets presently held by Japan.

Licensing agreements typically have time limits. Although terms may be extended one time after the start-up period, additional extensions are not readily permitted by a number of foreign governments. If the licensee ties in with the licensor's global marketing network, quality control in terms of both production and marketing effort can become a concern.

Principal Issues in Negotiating Licensing Agreements

The key issues in negotiating licensing agreements include the scope of the rights conveyed, compensation, licensee compliance, dispute resolution, and the term and termination of the agreement.[17] The more clearly these are spelled out, the more trouble-free the association between the two parties can be.

The rights conveyed are product and/or patent rights. Defining their scope involves specifying the technology, know-how, or show-how to be included, the format, and guarantees. An example of format specification is an agreement on whether manuals will be translated into the licensee's language.

Compensation issues may be heavily disputed and argued. The costs the licensor wants to cover are (1) **transfer costs,** which are all variable costs incurred in transferring technology to a licensee and all ongoing costs of maintaining the agreement, (2) **R&D costs** incurred in researching and developing the licensed technology, and (3) **opportunity costs** incurred in the foreclosure of other sources of profit, such as exports or direct investment. To cover these costs, the licensor wants a share of the profits generated from the use of the license.

Licensees usually do not want to include allowances for opportunity costs, and they often argue that R&D costs have already been covered by the licensor through the profit from previous sales. In theory, royalties can be seen as profit sharing; in practice, royalties are a function of both the licensor's minimum necessary return and the cost of the licensee's next-best alternative. In the past, U.S. marketers have been able to obtain licensing returns above their transfer costs as a result of the unique features of their technology and intellectual property, but changes in the marketplace may result in a different future.[18] These changes include maturing technologies, intensifying competition among suppliers, growing sophistication among licensees, and greater involvement by governments in arranging for the licensing agreements.

The methods of compensating the licensor can take the form of running royalties, such as 5 percent of the licensee sales, and/or up-front payments, service fees, and disclosure fees (for proprietary data). Sometimes, government regulations pose an

[17]Martin F. Connor, "International Technology Licensing," Seminars in International Trade, National Center for Export-Import Studies, Washington, DC.

[18]Franklin R. Root and Farok J. Contractor, "Negotiating Compensation in International Licensing Agreements," *Sloan Management Review* 22 (Summer 1981): 23–32.

obstacle to the collection of royalties or know-how payments. In such instances, the know-how transferred can be capitalized as part of a cooperative venture, where a specific value is attributed to the information. Payments are then received as profits or dividends.

Licensee compliance on a number of dimensions must be stipulated in the agreement: (1) export control regulations; (2) confidentiality of the intellectual property and technology provided; and (3) record keeping and provisions for licensor audits, which are done periodically, usually a minimum of once a year.

Dispute resolution discussions center on the choice of law for contract interpretation and the choice of forum. Typically, the parties involved choose a third country's law to govern the agreement. Great care should be taken to determine the laws of the particular third country with respect to licensing. Swedish law, which is often used, stipulates on certain issues that the law of the licensee's country govern. When the parties cannot agree on an applicable legal system, an arbitration clause is warranted. This should be spelled out by using, for example, the International Chamber of Commerce model clause: "All disputes arising in connection with the present contract shall be finally settled under the Rules of Conciliation and Arbitration of the International Chamber of Commerce by one or more arbitrators appointed in accordance with the said rules." Also needed is a statement regarding the arbitrators' authority.[19]

Finally, the term, termination, and survival of rights must be specified. Government regulations in the licensee's market will have to be studied, and if the conditions are not favorable (for example, in terms of the maximum allowable duration), a waiver should be applied for.

Trademark Licensing

For companies that can trade on their names and characters, **trademark licensing** has become a substantial source of worldwide revenue. The names or logos of designers, literary characters, sports teams, and movie stars appear on clothing, games, foods and beverages, gifts and novelties, toys, and home furnishings. British designer Laura Ashley started the first major furniture program, licensing her name to Henredon Furniture Industries. Coca-Cola licensed its name to Murjani to be used on blue jeans, sweatshirts, and windbreakers. The licensors are likely to make millions of dollars with little effort, whereas the licensees can produce a branded product that consumers will recognize immediately. Licensing costs in such instances are typically an average fee of 5 percent of the wholesale price.

Both licensor and licensee may run into difficulty if the trademark is used for a product too far removed from the original success or if the licensed product casts a shadow on the reputation of the licensor. In licensing a trademark, consumer perceptions have to be researched to make sure the brand's positioning will not change. As an example, when Löwenbräu was exported to the United States, it was the number-one imported beer sold in the market. However, when the product name was licensed to Miller Brewing Company for domestic production, the beer's positioning (and subsequently its target audience) changed drastically in the minds of the consumers, resulting in a major decline in sales.

Franchising

Franchising is a form of licensing in which a parent company (the franchiser) grants another, independent entity (the franchisee) the right to do business in a prescribed manner. This right can take the form of selling the franchiser's products or using its

[19]William W. Park, "Arbitration of International Contract Disputes," *Business Lawyer* 39 (August 1984): 83–99.

THE INTERNATIONAL MARKETPLACE 9.3

Food Franchisers Continue the International Voyage

SOME OF THE MOST profitable and best-known international franchises are U.S. restaurants like McDonald's and Pizza Hut. For a U.S. tourist they serve as a friendly reminder of home, while for the local consumer such a restaurant can serve as a mini excursion to the United States. The global demand for fast food does not seem to be dwindling. As a result an increasing number of U.S. restaurants are beginning to make their way abroad. One of the most recent entries is a Maryville, Tennessee–based chain by the name of Ruby Tuesday.

Ruby Tuesday began its international venture in 1997, when two top executives, Tom Johnson and John Brisco, were lured away from T.G.I. Friday's to spearhead the international expansion of the chain. In just two years, the international division of Ruby Tuesday has managed to open eight locations; its goal is to open 100 restaurants in 18 countries within the next several years. Johnson and Brisco spend a great deal of their time on the road, visiting various locations around the world. "There will be 200 days a year that we'll be out of the country," says Brisco. "One year it was more than 300. We go out for two and a half to three weeks at a time."

The menus around the world basically look the same, but adjustments for local taste have been made. Ruby Tuesday staples like hamburgers, ribs, fajitas, and salads remain intact but in India, for instance, vegetables or chicken are used in the fajitas rather than beef. In Chile, the salads contain a lot more pasta and have a mayonnaise base, while in Kuwait pork and alcohol are excluded from the menu.

The most recent restaurant to open is in Iceland, where fresh fish is served. A future target is Asia, which is the next trip on the agenda of Johnson and Brisco. By all accounts the chain's global outlook seems bright. Many customers have come to describe the dining experience as a "two-hour vacation to America."

SOURCES: Stan Delozier, "Ruby Tuesday Going Worldwide; Menus Look Similar around the World, But There Are Adjustments," *Knoxville News-Sentinel*, September 28, 1999, C5; Associated Press, "Maryville-Based Ruby Tuesday Takes American Cuisine around the World," *Chattanooga Times*, September 29, 1999, C2; Ruby Tuesday web site, **www.ruby-tuesday.com**, accessed April 17, 2001.

name, production and marketing techniques, or general business approach.[20] Usually, franchising involves a combination of these elements. The major forms of franchising are manufacturer-retailer systems (such as car dealerships), manufacturer-wholesaler systems (such as soft drink companies), and service firm–retailer systems (such as lodging services and fast-food outlets). One can differentiate between product/trade franchising, where the major emphasis rests on the product or commodity to be sold, and business format franchising, where the focus is on ways of doing business. Even though many franchising firms are large, as *The International Marketplace 9.3* shows, franchising can be a useful international market expansion method for any business operation with international appeal.

Franchising origins are in Bavaria, but it has been adopted by various types of businesses in many countries. Its U.S. market penetration has resulted in 1999 total franchising sales for goods and services of more than $800 billion, accounting for about 40 percent of all retail sales. Concurrent with this domestic growth, franchising has also grown internationally. Of the nearly 2,900 franchise systems in the United States, more than 20 percent have units in other countries,[21] which often make significant contributions to corporate income. For example, McDonald's generates 45 percent

[20]Donald W. Hackett, "The International Expansion of U.S. Franchise Systems," in *Multinational Product Management*, eds. Warren J. Keegan and Charles S. Mayer (Chicago: American Marketing Association, 1979), 61–81.

[21]Leonard N. Swartz, "International Trends in Retailing: Franchising Successfully Circles the Globe," Arthur Andersen, December 1999, **http://www.accenture.com**.

FIGURE	9.2	A Sign of Change

and Coca-Cola 80 percent of income from international operations.[22] Figure 9.2 shows an example of a U.S. fast-food franchise that has successfully entered the Hungarian market. Non-U.S. franchisers are penetrating international markets as well and are doing so more aggressively. For example, 24 percent of British franchisers and 30 percent of French franchisers are active outside their home countries.[23] Very successful international franchising examples include Holiday Rent-a-Car of Canada and Descamps, a French firm selling linens and tablecloths.

The typical reasons for the international expansion of franchise systems are market potential, financial gain, and saturated domestic markets. U.S. franchisers

[22]Andrew E. Serwer, "McDonald's Conquers the World," *Fortune*, October 17, 1994, 103–116.

[23]Josh Martin, "Profitable Supply Chain Supporting Franchises," *Journal of Commerce*, Global Commerce Section (March 11, 1998): 1C.

expanded dramatically in Europe in the mid-1980s, taking advantage of the strong U.S. dollar. The initial impetus for ComputerLand's expansion into the Asia/Pacific region was "Asian entrepreneurs coming knocking on our door asking for franchises."[24] In some cases, international expansion is a reaction to a competitor's entry into foreign markets. In the 1980s, McDonald Corporation's biggest push was into France because France was the only major European country where McDonald's lagged behind Burger King.[25]

From a franchisee's perspective, the franchise is beneficial because it reduces risk by implementing a proven concept. In Malaysia, for example, the success rate in the franchise business is 90 percent, compared to the 80 percent failure rate of all new businesses.[26]

Franchising agreements are usually also beneficial from a governmental perspective. From a source-country view, franchising does not replace exports or export jobs. From a recipient-country view, franchising requires little outflow of foreign exchange, and the bulk of the profit generated remains within the country.[27]

With all its benefits, franchising also encounters some problems. One key issue is that companies first need to find out what their special capabilities are. This requires that there be an identification and codification of knowledge assets in firms—that "they know what they have."[28] After such an investigation, companies can then launch an aggressive program to share knowledge. For example, Dow Chemical, after a knowledge audit, was able to sign licensing agreements that are said to yield an estimated $100 million.[29]

A second concern is the need for a great degree of standardization. Without such standardization, many of the benefits of the transferred know-how are lost. Typically, such standardization will include the use of a common business name, similar layout, and similar production or service processes. Apart from leading to efficient operations, all of these factors will also contribute to a high degree of international recognizability. At the same time, however, standarization does not mean 100 percent uniformity. Adjustments may be necessary in the final end product so that local market conditions can be taken into account. For example, fast-food outlets in Europe often need to serve beer and wine to be attractive to the local clientele. In order to enter the Indian market, McDonald's has developed nonbeef burgers. Domino's Pizza in Japan serves seafood and eggplant pizza.[30] Key to success is the development of a franchising program that maintains a high degree of recognizability and efficiency benefits while being responsive to local cultural preferences.

Another key issue is the protection of the total business system that a franchise offers. Whereas it is possible to protect a name, the type of product or service and the general style of operation can be readily copied abroad.[31] As a result, franchise operations may meet competition head on shortly after their introduction.

[24]ComputerLand Debugs Its Franchising Program for Asia/Pacific Region," *Business International*, September 13, 1985, 294–295.

[25]"U.S. Fast-Food Giants Moving In on France," *Advertising Age*, October 22, 1984, 54.

[26]Leonard N. Swartz, "International Trends in Retailing," Arthur Andersen, December 1999.

[27]Nizamettin Aydin and Madhav Kacker, "International Outlook of U.S.-Based Franchisers," *International Marketing Review* 7 (1990): 43–53.

[28]Farok J. Contractor, "Economic and Environmental Reasons for the Continuing Growth in Alliances and Interfirm Cooperation," presented at the International Research Symposium, Temple University, Philadelphia, PA, April 7–8, 2000.

[29]T. Davenport, D. De Long, and M. Beers, "Successful Knowledge Management Projects," *Sloan Management Review* 39 (Number 2, 1998): 43–57.

[30]Katherine Zapf, "Home Alone? Call the Pizza Lifeline," *City Life News Tokyo*, October 1993, 6.

[31]Lawrence S. Welch, "Diffusion of Franchise System Use in International Operations," *International Marketing Review* 6 (1989): 7–19.

TABLE 9.1	The Most Important Impediments to International Franchising

Locating good and reliable franchisees overseas
Knowing how to franchise overseas
Protection of industrial property and trademarks in foreign countries
Obtaining information on market prospects overseas
Familliarity with business practices overseas
Foreign government regulations on business operations
Foreign regulations or limitations on royalty fees
Negotiation with foreign franchisees
Foreign regulations or limitations on entry of franchise business
Collection and transfer of franchise fee
Quality or quantity of product or service
Providing technical support overseas
Pricing franchise for a foreign market
Advertising franchise overseas
Sourcing and availability of raw materials, equipment, and other products
Shipping and distribution of raw materials required to operate a foreign franchise
Financing franchise operations overseas
Shipping and handling of equipment needed to operate a foreign franchise

SOURCE: Ben L. Kedia, David J. Ackerman, and Robert T. Justis, "Changing Barriers to the Internationalization of Franchising Operations: Perceptions of Domestic and International Franchisors," *The International Executive,* 37 (Number 4, July/August 1995): 329–348.

Government intervention can also represent major problems. For example, government restrictions on the type of services to be offered or on royalty remissions can prevent franchising arrangements or lead to a separation between a company and its franchisees.

Selection and training of franchisees present another key concern. McDonald's lag behind Burger King in France was a result of the company's suing to revoke the license of its largest franchise for failure to operate fourteen stores according to McDonald's standards. Many franchise systems have run into difficulty by expanding too quickly and granting franchises to unqualified entities. Although the local franchisee knows the market best, the franchiser still needs to understand the market for product adaptation purposes and operational details. The franchiser should be the conductor of a coordinated effort by the individual franchisees—for example, in terms of sharing ideas and engaging in joint marketing efforts, such as cooperative advertising. However, even here difficulties can emerge consisting mostly of complications in selecting appropriate advertising media, effective copy testing, effective translation of the franchiser's message, and the use of appropriate sales promotion tools. Table 9.1 summarizes research findings regarding the challenges faced in international franchising.

To encourage better-organized and more successful growth, many companies turn to the **master franchising system,** wherein foreign partners are selected and awarded the rights to a large territory in which they in turn can subfranchise. As a result, the franchiser gains market expertise and an effective screening mechanism for new franchises, without incurring costly mistakes. However, in order to preserve control, many companies also prefer to own their outlets abroad.[32]

[32]Faye S. McIntyre and Sandra M. Huszagh, "Internationalization of Franchise Systems," *Journal of International Marketing* 3 (Number 4, 1995): 39–56.

Franchising is often thought of as a strategy to be used for foreign market entry only by large firms. Yet franchising is also a viable alternative for small firms if the firm can offer a special business concept. Automation Papers Company, a New Jersey–based supplier of high-technology paper products, opted for franchising to gain exclusive representation by a highly motivated sales force in its target markets. The franchisees receive rights to the Automation Papers trademarks, intensive training for local staff members, and the benefit of the franchiser's experience, credit lines, and advertising budget.

SUMMARY

In addition to direct exporting, other possibilities for international market entry or expansion are the use of export intermediaries, licensing, or franchising.

Firms with products that do not lend themselves to exporting may use intermediaries to enter international markets. Typical intermediaries are EMCs, Webb-Pomerene associations, and trading companies. For international market entry mechanisms to be successful, various international marketing functions need to be performed. Export intermediaries can take on these functions. For them to do so viably, however, a proper form of compensation must exist. The major disadvantage to using such intermediaries is that they may take on more clients or more diverse functions than they are staffed to perform.

Alternatively, firms may consider to expand internationally via licensing and franchising. The basic advantage of licensing is that it requires relatively less capital investment or knowledge of foreign markets than most other forms of international involvement. The major disadvantage is that licensing agreements typically have time limits, often prescribed by foreign governments, and may even result in creating a competitor. The principal issues in negotiating licensing agreements are the scope of the rights conveyed, compensation, license compliance, dispute resolution, and the term and termination of the agreement. Franchising is a form of licensing. Since 1970, the expansion of global franchisers into foreign markets has been dramatic. The reasons for this international expansion are typically market potential, financial gain, and saturated domestic markets. Franchisers must strike a balance between the need to adapt to local environments and the need to standardize to maintain international recognizability.

QUESTIONS FOR DISCUSSION

1. What is the purpose of export intermediaries?
2. How can an export intermediary avoid circumvention by a client or customer?
3. Is there a need for export trading companies?
4. Why is it useful to have antitrust exemption for an export trading company?
5. How can the discrepancy between product-driven and market-driven orientations within export trading companies be resolved?
6. Why would a trade association want to form an ETC?
7. Will the greater availability of international information terminate the usefulness of trading companies?

8. Comment on this statement: "Licensing is really not a form of international involvement because it requires no substantial additional effort on the part of the licensor."
9. Assume that the government of Thailand wants to start producing F-20 Tigershark fighter aircraft under license from Northrop. What types of concerns will enter into the negotiations?
10. Suggest reasons for the explosive international expansion of U.S.-based franchise systems.
11. What benefits could a potential franchiser receive from joining the International Franchise Association (**www.franchise.org**)?

12. Imagine you are an investor trying to enter the Asian market and you have decided to use a sogoshosha as a means of entry. Go to the web site of Sumitomo Corporation (**www.sumitomocorp.co.jp/products/indpark-e/index.html**) and see what information you can gather about the country of your choice.

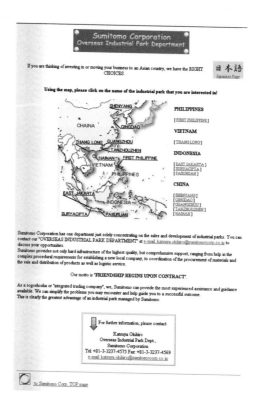

RECOMMENDED READINGS

Alon, Ilan. *The Internationalization of U.S. Franchising Systems.* New York: Garland Publishing, 2000.

Jones, Geoffrey (ed.). *The Multinational Traders.* New York: Routledge, 1999.

Mendelsohn, Martin. *The Guide to Franchising*, 6th ed. New York: Cassell Academic, 2000.

Peng, Mike W. *Behind the Success and Failure of U.S. Export Intermediaries: Transactions, Agents and Resources.* Westport, CT: Quorum Books, 1998.

Perry, Anne C. *The Evolution of U.S. Trade Intermediaries: The Changing International Environment.* Westport, CT: Quorum Books, 1992.

Product
Adaptation

Product
Adaptation

THE INTERNATIONAL MARKETPLACE 10.1

Europeanizing Products

MURRAY, Inc. has had to change the way it has made lawn mowers for decades. Its riding and walking models are now quieter because of new noise standards imposed by the European Union (EU). "We had to slow down the fan blade to cut noise,"says Ray Elmy, vice president for design engineering. "However, it will not exhaust and bag grass as well, and our costs have increased."In spite of increased production costs, the company made the changes because a significant portion of its $1 billion in sales comes from European customers.

Murray's changes are not unique. For regulated products, that is, products covered by directive, the EU has developed single sets of requirements that must be met in order to sell products in the 15 member countries of the EU. With the European Economic Area (EEA) agreement in force January 1, 1994, the number of countries affected increased to 18. Many different categories of products are regulated—toys, construction products, pressure vessels, gas appliances, medical devices, telecommunications terminal equipment, and machinery, among others. Overall, approximately half the annual $150 billion of U.S. goods exported to the EU falls within the regulated product category. The harmonization of technical standards focuses essentially on health and safety aspects of products, with minimum levels being established. Compliance with the standards means that goods may circulate freely throughout the EEA and bear the "CE"safety mark, if needed.

For unregulated products, that is, those not covered by Europewide directives, such as paper and furniture, mutual recognition of national standards applies. This means that a U.S. exporter can certify to U.S. standards, and if these standards are accepted by at least one member country, they will be accepted throughout the EEA. For example, a French charter airline was refused certification for a new model Boeing 737 because no French standard for the model existed. The airline registered the aircraft in Ireland, and because the Irish Department of Transport had accepted U.S. requirements as an Irish standard, the airliner was then able to operate throughout Europe, including France.

A word of caution is in order. The "CE"mark is a minimal requirement and not the only one the exporter may be asked to meet. The "Geprüfte Sicherheit"(GS) mark has never been officially mandatory for goods sold in Germany, although in many cases an insurance company may require its client to buy only products that have this mark. German consumers also look for this mark in much the same way as U.S. consumers look for the "*Good Housekeeping* Seal of Approval." Products without the GS mark can certainly be placed in the market but they might not be bought.

Although U.S. firms need to comply with European standards, it is more challenging to participate in their development. However, many U.S. firms have their personnel participate in international standardization programs. For example, executives from Bison Gear & Engineering take part in the Transatlantic Business Dialog, a government-industry effort to harmonize product standards. Furthermore, Mutual Recognition Agreements (MRAs) reached in 1998 allow for product assessments such as testing, inspecting, and certifying, to be performed in the United States to EU standards and regulations, and vice versa. Thus, companies will be able to gain access to markets without regulatory delays.

Overall, the standards do come with these significant benefits:

- Companies that had to make as many as 18 versions of their products for Europe because of differing national standards now are able to produce just one.
- Marketing should prove more efficient. Approval in one country will serve as an EEA passport permitting the sale throughout the market.
- U.S. manufacturers may be forced to improve the quality of all of their products, a benefit to U.S. customers and U.S. competitiveness. To ensure that EU standards are not violated inadvertently through sloppy manufacturing, some product rules require adoption of an overall quality system approved by the International Organization for Standardization (ISO).

SOURCES: "The Secret of U.S. Exports: Great Products,"*Fortune*, January 10, 2000, 154(A-J); Erika Morphy, "CE-ing, and Believing,"*Export Today* 14 (March 1998): 52–57; "U.S./Mutual Recognition Agreements," *USIS Washington Files*, June 23, 1997; Walter Poggi, "Trans-Atlantic Recognition,"*Export Today* 12 (March 1996): 61; Paul Jensen, "Europe: The Uncommon Market," *Export Today* 10 (June 1994): 20–27; Erika Morphy, "American Labs and Foreign Approvals," *Export Today* 10 (June 1994): 29–32; Stephen C. Messner, "Adapting Products to Western Europe," *Export Today* 10 (March/April 1994): 16–18; Phillippe Bruno, "EC Product Standards Will Be Headache Relief,"*Export Today* 9 (June 1993): 33–36; and Patrick Oster, "Europe's Standards Blitz Has Firms Scrambling,"*The Washington Post*, October 18, 1992, H1–H4.

http://www.eurunion.org/websites

BECAUSE MEETING AND SATISFYING customer needs and expectations is the key to successful marketing, research findings on market traits and potential should be used to determine the optimal degree of customization needed in products and product lines relative to incremental cost of the effort. Even if today's emerging market trends allow this assessment to take place regionally or even globally, as seen in *The International Marketplace 10.1*, both regulations and customer behavior differences require that they and the severity of their impact be taken into consideration. Adapting to new markets should be seen not only in the context of one market but also as to how these changes can contribute to operations elsewhere. A new feature for a product or a new line item may have applicability on a broader scale.

Take the Boeing 737, for example. Due to saturated markets and competitive pressures, Boeing started to look for new markets in the Middle East, Africa, and Latin America for the 737 rather than kill the program altogether. To adjust to the idiosyncrasies of these markets, such as softer and shorter runways, the company redesigned the wings to allow for shorter landings and added thrust to the engines for quicker takeoffs. To make sure that the planes would not bounce even if piloted by less experienced captains, Boeing redesigned the landing gear and installed low-pressure tires to ensure that the plane would stick to the ground after initial touchdown. In addition to becoming a success in the intended markets, the new product features met with approval around the world and made the Boeing 737 the best-selling commercial jet in history.[1]

This chapter is concerned with how the international marketer should adjust the firm's product offering to the marketplace, and it discusses the influence of an array of both external and internal variables. The challenge of intellectual property violation will be focused on as a specialty topic. International marketers must be ready to defend themselves against theft of their ideas and innovations.

---

[1]Andrew Kupfer, "How to Be a Global Manager," *Fortune*, March 14, 1988, 24–27.

Product Variables

The core of a firm's international operations is a product or service. This product or service can be defined as the complex combination of tangible and intangible elements that distinguishes it from the other entities in the marketplace, as shown in Figure 10.1. The firm's success depends on how good its product or service is and on how well the firm is able to differentiate the product from the offerings of competitors. Products can be differentiated by their composition, by their country of origin, by their tangible features such as packaging or quality, or by their augmented features such as warranty. Further, the positioning of the product in consumers' minds (for example, Volvo's reputation for safety) will add to its perceived value. The **core product**—for example, the ROM BIOS component of a personal computer or the recipe for a soup—may indeed be the same as or highly similar to those of competitors, leaving the marketer with the other tangible and **augmented features** of the product with which to achieve differentiation. Winnebago Industries, a leading exporter of motor homes, is finding increased interest in Europe for its "American-styled" recreation vehicles, or RVs, that offer more features and options than those made available by local competitors, such as automatic transmission and air conditioning. The only significant modifications made today are the conversion of the electrical system and installation of European-made kitchen appliances familiar to the customer. Furthermore, European buyers are assured that they will receive the same quality of product and service as customers in the United States.[2]

To the potential buyer, a product is a complete cluster of value satisfactions. A customer attaches value to a product in proportion to its perceived ability to help solve problems or meet needs. This will go beyond the technical capabilities of the product

FIGURE 10.1   **Elements of a Product**

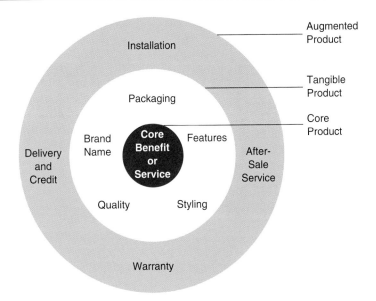

SOURCE: Adapted from Philip Kotler, *Marketing Management,* 10th ed., 2000, 395. Reprinted by permission of Prentice-Hall, Inc., Englewood Cliffs, New Jersey.

---

[2]"Winnebago Goes Camping in Germany," *Export Today* 10 (June 1994): 22.

to include intangible benefits sought. In Latin America, for example, great value is placed on products made in the United States. If packaging is localized, then the product may no longer have the "*Hecho in E.E.U.U.*" appeal that motivates customers to choose the product over others, especially over local competitors. Within international markets, these psychological expectations may vary dramatically from one market to another without having a serious effect on the core product, yet warranting a careful assessment of the appropriate product elements.

Standardization versus Adaptation

The first question, after the internationalization decision has been made, concerns the product modifications that are needed or warranted. A firm has four basic alternatives in approaching international markets: (1) selling the product as is in the international marketplace, (2) modifying products for different countries and/or regions, (3) designing new products for foreign markets, and (4) incorporating all the differences into one product design and introducing a global product. Different approaches for implementing these alternatives exist. For example, a firm may identify only target markets where products can be marketed with little or no modification. A large consumer products marketer may have in its product line for any given markets global products, regional products, and purely local products. Some of these products developed for one market may later be introduced elsewhere, including the global marketer's "home" market. The Dockers line of casual wear originated at Levi Strauss's Argentine unit and was applied to loosely cut pants by Levi's Japanese subsidiary. The company's U.S. operation later adopted both, and the line now generates over $500 million in North American sales.[3] Occasionally, the international marketplace may want something that the domestic market discards. By exporting chicken cuts that are unpopular (e.g., dark meat) or would be hauled off to landfills (such as chicken feet), U.S. poultry producers earn well over $1 billion annually from Russian and Chinese markets.[4]

The overall advantages and drawbacks of standardization versus adaptation are summarized in Table 10.1. The benefits of standardization—that is, selling the same product worldwide—are cost savings in production and marketing. In addition to

TABLE 10.1 Standardization versus Adaptation

Factors Encouraging Standardization
- Economies of scale in production
- Economies in product R&D
- Economies in marketing
- "Shrinking" of the world marketplace/economic integration
- Global competitions

Factors Encouraging Adaptation
- Differing use conditions
- Government and regulatory influences
- Differing consumer behavior patterns
- Local competition
- True to the marketing concept

[3]"For Levi's, a Flattering Fit Overseas," *Business Week*, November 5, 1990, 76–77.

[4]Stephanie Nall, "American Exports Chicken Out," *World Trade*, September 1998, 44–45.

FIGURE 10.2 Strategic Adaptation to Foreign Markets

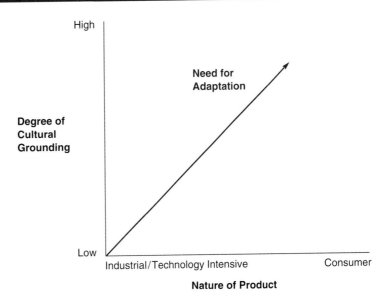

SOURCES: Adapted from W. Chan Kim and R. A. Mauborgne, "Cross-Cultural Strategies," *Journal of Business Strategy* 7 (Spring 1987): 31; and John A. Quelch and Edward J. Hoff, "Customizing Global Marketing," *Harvard Business Review* 64 (May–June 1986): 92–101.

these economies of scale, many point to economic integration as a driving force in making markets more unified. As a response to integration efforts around the world, especially in Europe, many international marketers are indeed standardizing many of their marketing approaches, such as branding and packaging, across markets. Similarly, having to face the same competitors in the major markets of the world will add to the pressure of having a worldwide approach to international marketing. However, in most cases, demand and usage conditions vary sufficiently to require some changes in the product or service itself.

Coca-Cola, Levi's jeans, and Colgate toothpaste have been cited as evidence that universal product and marketing strategy can work.[5] Yet the argument that the world is becoming more homogenized may actually be true for only a limited number of products that have universal brand recognition and minimal product knowledge requirements for use.[6] Although product standardization is generally increasing, there are still substantial differences in company practices, depending on the products marketed and where they are marketed.[7] As shown in Figure 10.2, industrial products such as steel, chemicals, and agricultural equipment tend to be less culturally grounded and warrant less adjustment than consumer goods. Similarly, marketers in technology-intensive industries such as scientific instruments or medical equipment find universal acceptability for their products.[8]

[5]W. Chan Kim and R. A. Mauborgne, "Cross-Cultural Strategies," *Journal of Business Strategy* 7 (Spring 1987): 28–36.

[6]"Marketers Turn Sour on Global Sales Pitch Harvard Guru Makes," *The Wall Street Journal*, May 12, 1988, 1, 13.

[7]J.J. Boddewyn, Robin Soehl, and Jacques Picard, "Standardization in International Marketing: Is Ted Levitt in Fact Right?" *Business Horizons* 29 (November–December 1986): 69–75.

[8]S. Tamer Cavusgil and Shaoming Zou, "Marketing Strategy–Performance Relationship: An Investigation of the Empirical Link in Export Market Ventures," *Journal of Marketing* 58 (January 1994): 1–21.

Adaptation needs in the industrial sector may exist even though they may not be overt. As an example, capacity performance is seen from different perspectives in different countries. Typically, the performance specifications of a German product are quite precise; for example, if a German product is said to have a lifting capacity of 1,000 kilograms, it will perform precisely up to that level. The U.S. counterpart, however, is likely to maintain a safety factor of 1.5 or even 2.0, resulting in a substantially higher payload capacity. Buyers of Japanese machine tools have also found that these tools will perform at the specified level, not beyond them, as would their U.S.-made counterparts.

Consumer goods generally require product adaptation because of their higher degree of cultural grounding. The amount of change introduced in consumer goods depends not only on cultural differences but also on economic conditions in the target market. Low incomes may cause pressure to simplify the product to make it affordable in the market.

Beyond the dichotomy of standardization and adaptation exist other approaches. The international marketer may design and introduce new products for foreign markets in addition to the firm's relatively standardized "flagship" products and brands. Some of these products developed specifically for foreign clients may later be introduced elsewhere, including in the domestic market.

Even companies that are noted for following the same methods worldwide have made numerous changes in their product offering. Some products, like Coca-Cola Company's Hi-C Soy Milk in Hong Kong, may be restricted to markets for which they were specifically developed. Although Colgate toothpaste is available worldwide, the company also markets some products locally, such as a spicy toothpaste formulated especially for the Middle East. McDonald's serves abroad the same menu of hamburgers, soft drinks, and other foods that it does in the United States, and the restaurants look the same. But McDonald's has also tried to tailor its product to local styles; for example, in Japan, the chain's trademark character, known as Ronald McDonald in the United States, is called Donald McDonald because it is easier to pronounce that way. Menu adjustments include beer in Germany and wine in France, mutton burgers in India, and rye-bread burgers in Finland.

Increasingly, companies are attempting to develop global products by incorporating differences regionally or worldwide into one basic design. This is not pure standardization, however. To develop a standard in the United States, for example, and use it as a model for other markets is dramatically different from obtaining inputs from the intended markets and using the data to create a standard. What is important is that adaptability is built into the product around a standardized core. For example, IBM makes more than 20 different keyboards for its relatively standardized personal computers to adjust to language differences in Europe alone. The international marketer attempts to exploit the common denominators, but local needs are considered from product development to the eventual marketing of the product. Car manufacturers like Ford and Nissan may develop basic models for regional, or even global, use, but they allow for substantial discretion in adjusting the models to local preferences.

Factors Affecting Adaptation

In deciding the form in which the product is to be marketed abroad, the firm should consider three sets of factors: (1) the market(s) that have been targeted, (2) the product and its characteristics, and (3) company characteristics, such as resources and policy. In a survey of firms with products or services in the international marketplace, 40 percent said that the adaptation issue comes up frequently, whereas another 40 percent reported that the issue arises sometimes.[9] For most firms, the key question linked

[9]V. Yorio, *Adapting Products for Export* (New York: Conference Board, 1983), 1.

to adaptation is whether the effort is worth the cost involved—in adjusting production runs, stock control, or servicing, for example—and the investigative research involved in determining, for example, features that would be most appealing. For six out of ten firms surveyed, the expense of modifying products was moderate. This may mean, however, that the expense is moderate when modifications are considered and acted on, whereas modifications are considered but rejected when the projected cost is substantial.

A detailed examination of 174 consumer-packaged goods destined for the developing countries has shown that, on average, 4.1 changes per product were made in terms of brand name, packaging, measurement units, labeling, constituents, product features, and usage instructions.[10] Only one of ten products was transferred without modification.

There is no panacea for resolving questions of adaptation. Many firms are formulating decision-support systems to aid in product adaptation, and some consider every situation independently. Figure 10.3 provides a summary of the factors that determine the need for either **mandatory** or **discretionary product adaptation.** All products have to conform to the prevailing environmental conditions, over which the marketer has no control. These relate to legal, economic, and climatic conditions in the market. Further adaptation decisions are made to enhance the exporter's competitiveness in the marketplace. This is achieved by matching competitive offers, catering to customer preferences, and meeting demands of local distribution systems.

FIGURE 10.3 | Factors Affecting Product-Adaptation Decisions

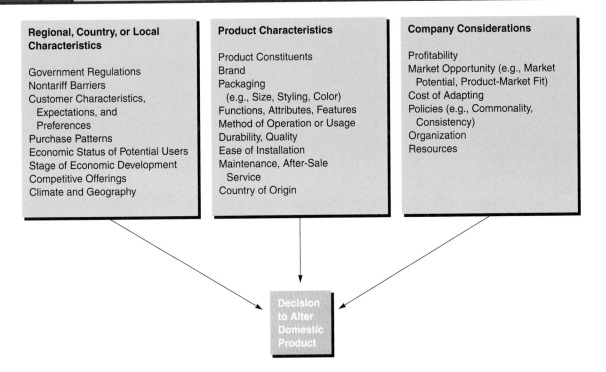

SOURCE: Adapted from V. Yorio, *Adapting Products for Export* (New York: Conference Board, 1983), 7. Reprinted with permission.

---

[10]John S. Hill and Richard R. Still, "Adapting Products to LDC Tastes," *Harvard Business Review* 62 (March–April 1984): 92–101.

The Market Environment

Government Regulations

Government regulations often present the most stringent requirements. Some of the requirements may serve no purpose other than political (such as protection of domestic industry or response to political pressures). Because of the sovereignty of nations, individual firms need to comply but can influence the situation by lobbying, directly or through their industry associations, for the issue to be raised during trade negotiations. Government regulations may be spelled out, but firms need to be ever vigilant in terms of changes and exceptions.

Sweden was the first country in the world to enact legislation against most aerosol sprays on the grounds that they may harm the atmosphere. The ban, which went into effect January 1, 1979, covers thousands of hair sprays, deodorants, air fresheners, insecticides, paints, waxes, and assorted sprays that use Freon gases as propellants. It does not apply to certain medical sprays, especially those used by people who suffer from asthma. The Swedish government, which has one of the world's most active environmental protection departments, was the first to take seriously warnings by scientists that continued release of these chemicals could eventually degrade the earth's ozone layer. As a matter of fact, certain markets, such as Sweden and California, often serve as precursors of changes to come in broader markets and should, therefore, be monitored by marketers.

Although economic integration usually reduces discriminatory governmental regulation (as seen in The International Marketplace 10.1), some national environmental restrictions may stay in place. For example, a ruling by the European Court of Justice let stand Danish laws that require returnable containers for all beer and soft drinks. These laws seriously restrict foreign brewers, whose businesses are not on a scale large enough to justify the logistics system necessary to handle returnables.[11]

Government regulations are probably the single most important factor contributing to product adaptation and, because of bureaucratic red tape, often the most cumbersome and frustrating factor to deal with. In some cases, government regulations have been passed and are enforced to protect local industry from competition from abroad. In early 2000, the EU decided to limit the use of older commercial aircraft that have "hush kit" mufflers on their engines to cut down airplane noise. U.S. marketers saw a two-dimensional threat in this new regulation: what the EU was really trying to do was keep out U.S. goods (hush kits are typically U.S. made) and, in forcing airlines to buy new aircraft, to direct them to buy European Airbus rather than U.S. Boeing planes.[12]

Nontariff Barriers

Nontariff barriers include product standards, testing or approval procedures, subsidies for local products, and bureaucratic red tape. The nontariff barriers affecting product adjustments usually concern elements outside the core product. For example, France requires the use of the French language in any offer, presentation, or advertisement whether written or spoken, in instructions for use, and in specification or guarantee terms for goods or services, as well as for invoices and receipts.

Because nontariff barriers are usually in place to keep foreign products out and/or to protect domestic producers, getting around them may be the toughest single problem for the international marketer. The cost of compliance with government regula-

[11]Eric C. Friberg, "1992: Moves Europeans Are Making," *Harvard Business Review* 67 (May–June 1989): 85–89.

[12]"U.S. and EU at Odds over Jet Noise," *The Washington Post*, January 19, 2000, E1, E10.

tions is high. The U.S. Department of Commerce estimates that a typical machine manufacturer can expect to spend between $50,000 and $100,000 a year on complying with foreign standards. For certain exports to the European Union, that figure can reach as high as $200,000.[13] As an example, Mack International has to pay $10,000 to $25,000 for a typical European engine certification. Brake system changes to conform with other countries' regulations run from $1,500 to $2,500 per vehicle. Wheel equipment changes will cost up to $1,000 per vehicle. Even with these outlays and the subsequent higher price, the company is still able to compete successfully in the international marketplace.

Small companies with limited resources may simply give up in the face of seemingly arbitrary harassment. For example, product testing and certification requirements have made the entry of many foreign companies into Japanese markets quite difficult, if not impossible.[14] Japan requires testing of all pharmaceutical products in Japanese laboratories, maintaining that these tests are needed because the Japanese may be physiologically different from Americans or Swiss. Similarly, foreign ski products were kept out because Japanese snow was somehow unique. Many exporters, rather than try to move mountains of red tape, have found ways to accommodate Japanese regulations. U.S. cookie marketers, for example, create separate product batches to meet Japanese requirements and avoid problems with the Japanese Health and Welfare Agency.

With a substantial decrease in tariff barriers, nontariff forms of protectionism have increased. On volume alone, agriculture dominates the list. The United States and the EU have fought over beef produced with the aid of hormones. Although it was declared safe for consumption by U.N. health authorities, the Europeans have banned the importation of such beef and demand appropriate labeling as a precondition for market entry. In a similar debate, an international trade agreement was reached in 2000 that requires the labeling of genetically modified food in the world market. This will mean that U.S. farmers have to separate the increasingly controversial foods from the overall supply.[15]

One way to keep a particular product or producer out of a market is to insist on particular standards. Since the EU chose ISO 9000 as a basis to harmonize varying technical norms of its member states, some of its trading partners have accused it of erecting a new trade barrier against outsiders.[16] ISO 9000, created by the International Organization for Standardization (ISO), is a set of technical standards designed to offer a uniform way of determining whether manufacturing plants and service organizations implement and document sound quality procedures. The ISO itself does not administer or regulate these standards; that job is left to the 143 countries that have voluntarily adopted them. The feeling that ISO registration is a trade barrier comes from the Europeans' earlier start and subsequent control of the program. Of the 272,000 registrations made by 1999, Europe accounts for 166,000, while North American companies have reached 33,500.[17] Growth has been dramatic in the United States, from about 500 companies in 1992 to nearly 30,000 at present. Studies show that over half the U.S. companies with ISO 9000 registration have fewer than 500 employees, and one-quarter have fewer than 150. There is no legal requirement to adopt the standards; however, many agree that these guidelines are already determining what may be sold to and within the EU and increasingly around the world. This is

[13]Erika Morphy, "Cutting the Cost of Compliance," *Export Today* 12 (January 1996): 14–18.

[14]Vernon R. Alden, "Who Says You Can't Crack Japanese Markets?" *Harvard Business Review* 64 (January–February 1986): 52–56.

[15]"A Conventional Argument," *The Economist*, January 29, 2000, 95.

[16]Davis Goodman, "Thinking Export? Think ISO 9000," *World Trade*, August 1998, 48–49.

[17]*ISO Survey 1999*, available at **www.iso.ch**.

especially true for products for which there are safety or liability issues, or that require exact measurements or calibration, such as medical or exercise equipment.

The International Organization for Standardization also issued the first standards on environmental management, the ISO 14000 series in 1996. The standards, which basically require that a firm design an environmental management system, do provide benefits for the adopters such as substantial efficiencies in pollution control (e.g., packaging) and a better public image.[18] However, these standards can also serve as a nontariff barrier if advanced nations impose their own requirements and systems on developing countries that often lack the knowledge and resources to meet such conditions. The adoption rate has remained relatively low, at 7,887 in 1999, with Europe accounting for 54 percent and North America for 5.5 percent of the total.

Customer Characteristics, Expectations, and Preferences

The characteristics and behavior of intended customer groups are as important as governmental influences on the product adaptation decision. Even when the benefits sought are quite similar, the physical characteristics of customers may dictate product adaptation. Quaker Oats' extension of the Snapple soft drink product to Japan suffered from lack of fit on three dimensions: the glass bottles the drink comes in are almost twice the size that Japanese customers are used to; the product itself was too sweet for the palate; and the Japanese did not feel comfortable with the sediment that characteristically collects at the bottom of the bottle.[19] GE Medical Systems has designed a product specifically for Japan in addition to computerized tomography scanners produced for the U.S. market. The unit is smaller because Japanese hospitals are smaller than most U.S. facilities but also because of the smaller size of Japanese patients.[20]

Product decisions of consumer-product marketers are especially affected by local behavior, tastes, attitudes, and traditions—all reflecting the marketer's need to gain customers' approval. This group of variables is critical in that it is the most difficult to quantify but is nevertheless essential in making a go/no-go decision. The reason most Europeans who wear western boots buy those made in Spain may be that U.S. footwear manufacturers are unaware of style conscious Europeans' preference for pointed toes and narrow heels. They view U.S.-made boots as "practical, but not interesting." Similarly, the U.S. Mint has been unable to penetrate the Asian market with its gold coins, which are 22 carat (.916 pure) because customers there value pure gold (i.e., 24 carat, .999 pure).

Three groups of factors determine cultural and psychological specificity in relation to products and services: consumption patterns, psychosocial characteristics, and general cultural criterial. The types of questions asked in Table 10.2 should be answered and systematically recorded for every product under consideration. Use of the list of questions will guide the international marketer through the analysis, ensuring that all the necessary points are dealt with before a decision is made.

Because Brazilians are rarely breakfast eaters, Dunkin' Donuts is marketing doughnuts in Brazil as snacks and desserts and for parties. To further appeal to Brazilians, the company makes doughnuts with local fruit fillings like papaya and guava. Campbell Soup Company failed in Brazil with its offerings of vegetable and beef combinations, mainly because Brazilians prefer the dehydrated products of competitors such as Knorr and Maggi; Brazilians could use these products as soup starter but still add their own flair and ingredients. The only way of solving this problem is through proper cus-

---

[18]Enrique Sierra, "The New ISO 14000 Series: What Exporters Should Know," *Trade Forum* (Number 3, 1996): 16–31.

[19]Kirk Loncar, "Look Before You Leap," *World Trade*, June 1997, 92–93.

[20]Kate Betrand, "Marketing to the Land of the Rising Yen," *Business Marketing* 12 (October 1986): 77–86.

| **TABLE 10.2** | **Cultural and Psychological Factors Affecting Product Adaptation** |

I. Consumption patterns
  A. Pattern of Purchase
    1. Is the product or service purchased by relatively the same consumer income group from one country to another?
    2. Do the same family members motivate the purchase in all target countries?
    3. Do the same family members dictate brand choice in all target countries?
    4. Do most consumers expect a product to have the same appearance?
    5. Is the purchase rate the same regardless of the country?
    6. Are most of the purchases made at the same kind of retail outlet?
    7. Do most consumers spend the same amount of time making the purchase?
  B. Pattern of Usage
    1. Do most consumers use the product or service for the same purpose or purposes?
    2. Is the product or service used in different amounts from one target area or country to another?
    3. Is the method of preparation the same in all target countries?
    4. Is the product or service used along with other products or services?

II. Psychosocial Characteristics
  A. Attitudes Toward the Product or Service
    1. Are the basic psychological, social, and economic factors motivating the purchase and use of the product the same for all target countries?
    2. Are the advantages and disadvantages of the product or service in the minds of consumers basically the same from one country to another?
    3. Does the symbolic content of the product or service differ from one country to another?
    4. Is the psychic cost of purchasing or using the product or service the same, whatever the country?
    5. Does the appeal of the product or service for a cosmopolitan market differ from one market to another?
  B. Attitudes Toward the Brand
    1. Is the brand name equally known and accepted in all target countries?
    2. Are customer attitudes toward the package basically the same?
    3. Are customer attitudes toward pricing basically the same?
    4. Is brand loyalty the same throughout target countries for the product or service under consideration?

III. Cultural Criteria
    1. Does society restrict the purchase and/or use of the product or service to a particular group?
    2. Is there a stigma attached to the product or service?
    3. Does the usage of the product or service interfere with tradition in one or more of the targeted markets?

SOURCE: Adapted from Steuart Henderson Britt, "Standardizing Marketing for the International Market," *Columbia Journal of World Business* 9 (Winter 1974): 32–40. Copyright © 1974 Columbia Journal of World Business. Reprinted with permission.

tomer testing, which can be formidably expensive for a company interested only in exports.

Often, no concrete product changes are needed, only a change in the product's **positioning.** Positioning refers to consumers' perception of a brand as compared with that of competitors' brands, that is, the mental image that a brand, or the company as a whole, evokes. For example, Gillette has a consistent image worldwide as a masculine, hardware, sports-oriented company. A brand's positioning, however, may have to change to reflect the differing lifestyles of the targeted market. Coca-Cola Company took a risk in marketing Diet Coke in Japan, because trying to sell a diet drink is difficult in a nation where "diet" is a dirty word and the population is not overweight by Western standards. The problem was addressed by changing the name of the drink to Coke Light and subtly shifting the promotion theme from "weight loss" to "figure maintenance." Japanese women do not like to admit that they are dieting by drinking something clearly labeled diet (see Figure 10.4).

| FIGURE | 10.4 | Diet Coke Marketed as Coke Light in Japan |

Health and beauty-care products often rely on careful positioning to attain a competitive advantage. Timotei shampoo, which is Unilever's brand leader in that category, has a natural-looking image with a focus on mildness and purity. Because people around the world have different hair, Timotei's formula varies, but it always has the same image. The selling of "lifestyle" brands is common for consumer goods for which differentiation may be more difficult. Lifestyles may be more difficult for competitors to copy, but they are also more susceptible to changes in fashion.[21]

The influence of culture is especially of concern where society may restrict the purchase of the product, or when the product or one of its features may be subject to a

---

[21]"Better to Be on the Inside Looking Out," *Economist*, December 24, 1988, 96–98.

stigma. Uncle Ben's, Australia's foremost producer of pet foods, produces pork-free pet products for Muslim markets. A symbol in packaging may seem fully appropriate in one culture yet be an insult elsewhere. Dogs, for example, were alleged to have eaten one of Mohammed's regiments and therefore are considered signs of bad luck and uncleanliness in parts of North Africa. A U.S. cologne manufacturer discovered this after launching a product featuring a man and his dog in a rural setting.

Another primary cultural consideration is the perception of numbers. In the West, 7 is considered lucky, whereas 13 is regarded as the opposite. In Japan, however, the ideogram for the number 4 can also be read as "death." Therefore, consumer goods shipped to Japan in packages of four have experienced limited sales. On the other hand, 3 and 5 are considered luckier numbers.[22]

Even the export of TV culture, which is considered by many as a local product, can succeed abroad if concepts are adjusted to reflect local values, as seen in *The International Marketplace 10.2*.

Economic Development

Management must take into account the present stage of economic development of the overseas market. As a country's economy advances, buyers are in a better position to buy and to demand more sophisticated products and product versions. With broad country considerations in mind, the firm can determine potentials for selling certain kinds of products and services. This means managing affordability in a way that makes the marketer's products accessible. For example, C&A, an apparel retailer from Holland, has been able to build a successful business in Latin American countries because it offers reasonable-quality goods at various price points—the best $10, $20, $30 dresses on the market. In Brazil, two-thirds of its sales are to families with incomes below $8,000 per year.[23] In some cases, the situation in a developing market may require **backward innovation;** that is, the market may require a drastically simplified version of the firm's product due to lack of purchasing power or usage conditions.

Economic conditions will affect packaging in terms of size and units sold in a package. In developing markets, products such as cigarettes and razor blades are often sold by the piece so that consumers with limited incomes can afford them. Soft drink companies have introduced four-can packs in Europe, where cans are sold singly even in large stores. On the other hand, products oriented to families, such as food products, appear in larger sizes in developing markets. Pillsbury packages its products in six- and eight-serving sizes for developing countries, whereas the most popular size in the North American market is for two.

Economic conditions may change rapidly, thus warranting change in the product or the product line. During the Asian currency crisis, McDonald's replaced french fries with rice in its Indonesian restaurants due to cost considerations. With the collapse of the local rupiah, potatoes, the only ingredient McDonald's imports to Indonesia, quintupled in price. In addition, a new rice and egg dish was introduced to maintain as many customers as possible despite the economic hardship.[24]

Competitive Offerings

Monitoring competitors' product features, as well as determining what has to be done to meet and beat them, is critical. Competitive offerings may provide a baseline

---

[22]Nancy Hollander, "Judging a Book by Its Cover," *Export Today* 4 (July–August 1988): 47–49.

[23]James A. Gingrich, "Five Rules for Winning Emerging Market Consumers," *Strategy and Business* (Second Quarter, 1999): 35–42.

[24]"Holding the Fries—At the Border," *Business Week*, December 14, 1998, 8.

THE INTERNATIONAL MARKETPLACE 10.2

The Muppets Hit Ulitsa Sezam, Zhima Jie, Shara'a Simsim, and Rechov Sumsum

A SEVEN-FOOT-TALL CREATURE covered in blue feathers, with a stupendous orange nose and a sweet disposition, was introduced to Russian families in October 1996. He introduced himself as Zeliboda and gave his address as Ulitsa Sezam.

Six years in the making, the Russian version of *Sesame Street* is 70 percent locally produced, with other segments dubbed from the Sesame Street International Library. The set is a Russian courtyard—part village, part city —but distinctly more rural than the U.S. counterpart, and a place where boys and girls live and learn their ABCs (i.e., Cyrillic) with a handful of adults and Muppets. The writers and producers were determined to create a community that drew on the best of Russian tradition. The courtyard is meant to be safe and fun, where neighbor helps neighbor in a gentle spirit of cohesion. For example, a central figure in the courtyard is caretaker Aunt Dasha, a quintessential Russian character who lives in a traditional cottage and spouts folklore and homespun wisdom.

Zeliboda was created from the house spirits that inhabit Russian folklore. His Muppet cohorts, conceived in Russia and produced in the United States by Jim Henson Productions, are shocking-pink, bubbly Busya and bright orange Kubik. Bert and Ernie are also staples, but in their dubbed personas they are known as Vlas and Yenik.

The Russians' initial reaction to the show's concept was that it was yet another attempt to introduce U.S. approaches into Russia. However, after they saw different versions of *Sesame Street* made for Latin American countries and Northern Europe, the Russians realized that the Children's Television Workshop was very sensitive to the cultures of targeted countries. Among the challenges in creating the show was to marry the funny, goofy, and slapstickish flavor of the U.S. show with the tradition of Russian comedy writers, which focuses more on irony and wordplay.

To achieve the objectives, brainstorming between the U.S. writers and the Russians included writing workshops and improvisation sessions to hash out ideas. At one point, as the discussion focused on how to make the courtyard set fun but realistic, a Russian writer suggested that a rusting car be parked in the courtyard. The Americans pointed out that a rusting car could be hazardous for the kids on the set. The idea was dropped. To make sure that the show would get the laughs intended while still bearing the educational content, video segments were tested in classrooms of Russian preschoolers.

By 2000, Muppets were being seen in 140 countries, including 19 co-productions reflecting local languages, customs, and educational needs. Co-productions, such as the Russian one, have all sought to produce a formula that suits the special characteristics of the children in that country. In China, new characters were added for local color (such as Little Berry, "Xiao Mei," and a blustering vegetarian Puff Pig, "Hu Hu Zhu"). The creators of the joint Israeli-Palestinian production hope that the exploits of Dafi, a purple Israeli Muppet, and Haneen, an orange Palestinian one, will help teach mutual respect and understanding by exposing children to each other's culture and languages and breaking down stereotypes.

SOURCES: "Hope Lives on New Israeli-Palestinian 'Sesame Street,'" *CNN Interactive*, March 26, 1998; "Chinese Children to Come and Play on Sesame Street," *CNN Interactive*, November 7, 1997; "Moscow Moppets Meet the Muppets," *The Washington Post*, October 23, 1996, A1, 28.

http://www.ctw.org

Dafi, left, an Israeli Muppet, and Haneen, a Palestinian Muppet, co-star in the Mideast version of *Sesame Street*.

against which the firm's resources can be measured—for example, what it takes to reach a critical market share in a given competitive situation. An analysis of competitors' offerings may reveal holes in the market or suggest avoiding certain market segments. American Hospital Supply, a Chicago-based producer of medical equipment, adjusts its product in a preemptive way by making products that are hard to duplicate. As a result, the firm achieved increases of about 40 percent per year in sales and earnings in Japan over a ten-year period. The products are so specialized that it would be hard for Japanese firms to duplicate them on a mass production basis.

In many markets, the international marketer is competing with local manufacturers and must overcome traditional purchasing relationships and the certainty they provide. BNN, a marketer of highly interactive data-processing equipment and support services, is facing, with its $30 million in export sales, giants such as Siemens and Philips, BBN must prove not only that its products are competitive in price and quality but also that the company will honor its commitments and provide any necessary after-sales service. However, by concentrating on one area alone and targeting carefully, BBN can invest far more resources and stay ahead of its competition.[25]

Climate and Geography

Climate and geography will usually have an effect on the total product offering: the core product; tangible elements, mainly packaging; and the augmented features. Some products, by design, are vulnerable to the elements. Marketing of chocolate products is challenging in hot climates, which may restrict companies' options. Cadbury Schweppes has its own display cases in shops, while Toblerone has confined its distribution to air-conditioned outlets. Nestlé's solution was to produce a slightly different Kit Kat chocolate wafer for Asia with reduced fat content to raise the candy's melting point. The international marketer must consider two sometimes contradictory aspects of packaging for the international market. On the one hand, the product itself has to be protected against longer transit times and possibly for longer shelf life; on the other hand, care has to be taken that no nonallowed preservatives are used. One firm experienced this problem when it tried to sell Colombian guava paste in the United States. Because the packaging could not withstand the longer distribution channels and the longer time required for distribution, the product arrived in stores in poor condition and was promptly taken off the shelves. If a product is exposed to a lot of sunshine and heat as a result of being sold on street corners, as may be the case in developing countries, marketers are advised to use special varnishing or to gloss the product wrappers. Without this, the coloring may fade and make the product unattractive to the customer.

Product Characteristics

Product characteristics are the inherent features of the product offering, whether actual or perceived. The inherent characteristics of products and the benefits they provide to consumers in the various markets make certain products good candidates for standardization, others not. Consumer nondurables, such as food products, generally show the highest amount of sensitivity toward differences in national tastes and habits. Consumer durables, such as cameras and home electronics, are subject to far more homogeneous demand and more predictable adjustment (for example, adjustment to a different technical system in television sets and videotape recorders).

[25]"Divide and Conquer," *Export Today* 5 (February 1989): 10.

Industrial products tend to be more shielded from cultural influences. However, substantial modifications may sometimes be required—in the telecommunications industry, for example—as a result of government regulations and restraints.

Product Constituents

The international marketer must make sure products do not contain ingredients that might be in violation of legal requirements or religious or social customs. As an example, DEP Corporation, a Los Angeles manufacturer with $19 million annual sales of hair and skin products, takes particular pains to make sure that no Japan-bound products contain formaldehyde—an ingredient commonly used in the United States but illegal in Japan. To ensure the purity of the Japanese batches, the company repeatedly cleans and sterilizes the chemical vats, checks all ingredients for traces of formaldehyde, and checks the finished product before shipment. When religion or custom determines consumption, ingredients may have to be replaced in order for the product to be acceptable. In Islamic countries, for example, animal fats have to be replaced by ingredients such as vegetable shortening. In deference to Hindu and Muslim beliefs, McDonald's "Maharaja Mac" is made with mutton in India.

Branding

Brand names convey the image of the product or service. The term **brand** refers to a name, term, symbol, sign, or design used by a firm to differentiate its offerings from those of its competitors. Brands are one of the most easily standardized items in the product offering; they may allow further standardization of other marketing elements such as promotional items. The brand name is the vocalizable part of the brand, the brand mark the nonvocalizable part (for example, Camel's "camel"). The brand mark may become invaluable when the product itself cannot be promoted but the symbol can be used. As an example, Marlboro cannot be advertised in most European countries because of legal restrictions on cigarette advertising; however, Philip Morris features advertisements showing only the Marlboro cowboy, who is known throughout the world. Unfortunately, most brands do not have such recognition. The term *trademark* refers to the legally protected part of the brand, indicated by the symbol ®. Increasingly, international markets have found their trademarks violated by counterfeiters who are illegally using or abusing the brand name of the marketer.

The international marketer has a number of options in choosing a branding strategy. The marketer may choose to be a contract manufacturer to a distributor (the generics approach) or to establish national, regional, or worldwide brands. The international diffusion of U.S. brands, for example, is quite limited. Except for certain **global brands,** the majority of U.S. brands achieve roughly four-fifths of their sales in the domestic market.[26] The use of standardization in branding is strongest in culturally similar markets; for example, for U.S. marketers this means Canada and the United Kingdom. Standardization of product and brand do not necessarily move hand in hand; a regional brand may well have local features, or a highly standardized product may have local brand names.[27]

The establishment of worldwide brands is difficult; how can a consumer marketer establish world brands when it sells 800 products in more than 200 countries, most of them under different names? This is Gillette's situation. A typical example is Silkience hair conditioner, which is sold as Soyance in France, Sientel in Italy, and Silkience in Germany. Gillette has announced, however, a massive standardization

[26]Barry N. Rosen, J. J. Boddewyn, and Ernst A. Louis, "U.S. Brands Abroad: An Empirical Study of Global Branding," *International Marketing Review* 6 (Spring 1989): 7–19.

[27]Boddewyn, Soehl, and Picard, "Standardization in International Marketing," 69–75.

program of brand names, packaging, and advertising.[28] Standardizing names to reap promotional benefits can be difficult, because a particular name may already be established in each market and the action raises objections from local managers.

The psychological power of brands is enormous. Surveys about U.S. consumer goods have shown the number-one brand in a product category to be earning a 20 percent return, the number-two brand around 5 percent, and the rest losing money.[29] Brand loyalty translates into profits despite the fact that favored brands may not be superior by any tangible measure. New brands may be very difficult and expensive to build, and as a result, the company may seek a tie-in with something that the customer feels positively toward. For instance, a small Hong Kong–based company markets a product line called American No. 1 because the market prefers U.S. products.

Brand names often do not travel well. Semantic variations can hinder a firm's product overseas. Even the company name or the trade name should be checked out. For instance, Mirabell, the manufacturer of the genuine Mozart Kugel (a chocolate ball of marzipan and nougat), initially translated the name of its products as "Mozart balls" but has since changed the name to the "Mozart round."[30] Most problems associated with brands are not as severe but require attention nevertheless. To avoid problems with brand names in foreign markets, NameLab, a California-based laboratory for name development and testing, suggests these approaches:

1. Translation. Little Pen Inc. would become La Petite Plume, S.A., for example.
2. Transliteration. This requires the testing of an existing brand name for connotative meaning in the language of the intended market. Flic Pen Corporation, for example, would be perceived in France as a manufacturer of writing instruments for the police because the slang term *flic* connotes something between "cop" and "pig." In other instances, positive connotations are sought, as shown in *The International Marketplace 10.3.*
3. Transparency. This can be used to develop a new, essentially meaningless brand name to minimize trademark complexities, transliteration problems, and translation complexities. (Sony is an example.)
4. Transculture. This means using a foreign-language name for a brand.[31] Vodkas, regardless of where they originate, should have Russian-sounding names or at least Russian lettering, whereas perfumes should sound French.

Brands are powerful marketing tools; for example, the chemicals and natural ingredients in any popular perfume retailing for $140 an ounce may be worth less than $3.

In some markets, brand name changes are required by the government. In Korea, unnecessary foreign words are barred from use; for example, Sprite has been renamed Kin. The same situation has emerged in Mexico, where local branding is primarily used to control foreign companies in terms of the marketing leverage they would have with a universal brand.

Packaging

Packaging serves three major functions: protection, promotion, and user convenience. The major consideration for the international marketer is making sure the product reaches the ultimate user in the form intended. Packaging will vary as a function of

[28]Dean M. Peebles, "Don't Write Off Global Advertising: A Commentary," *International Marketing Review* 6 (Spring 1989): 73–78.

[29]"The Year of the Brand," *Economist*, December 24, 1988, 95–96.

[30]"Mozart's Genius Extends to Selling Lederhosen in Japan," *The Wall Street Journal Europe*, January 6, 1992, Section 1.1.

[31]NameLab, Inc. (**http://www.namelab.com**).

THE INTERNATIONAL MARKETPLACE 10.3

When There Is More to a Name

IN EUROPE AND THE Americas, brand names such as Coca-Cola and Sharp have no meaning in themselves, and few are even aware of the origins of the name. But to Chinese-speaking consumers, brand names include an additional dimen-

(Tasty and happy)

(Hundred happy things)

(Treasure of sound)

sion: meaning. Coca-Cola means "tasty and happy" and Sharp stands for "treasure of sound."

Chinese and Western consumers share similar standards when it comes to evaluating brand names. Both appreciate a brand name that is catchy, memorable, and distinct, and says something indicative of the product. But, because of cultural and linguistic factors, Chinese consumers expect more in terms of how the names are spelled, written and styled and whether they are considered lucky. When PepsiCo Inc. introduced Cheetos in the Chinese market, it did so under a Chinese name that translates as "Many Surprises"; in Chinese *qi duo*—roughly pronounced "chee-do."

A name is like a work of art, and the art of writing (*shu fa*—calligraphy) has had a long tradition all over Asia. A name has to look good and be rendered in appealing writing thereby functioning like a logo or trademark. Companies will consequently have to take into account this dimension of Chinese and Chinese-based languages such as Korean, Japanese, and Vietnamese when they create corporate and brand names and the related communications strategies.

SOURCES: Eugene Sivadas, "Watching Chinese Marketing, Consumer Behavior," *Marketing News*, July 20, 1998, 10; "The Puff, the Magic, the Dragon," *The Washington Post*, September 2, 1994, B1, B3; "Big Names Draw Fine Line on Logo Imagery," *South China Morning Post*, July 7, 1994, 3.

---

transportation mode, transit conditions, and length of time in transit. Because of the longer time that products spend in channels of distribution, firms in the international marketplace, especaially those exporting food products, have had to use more expensive packaging materials and/or more expensive transportation modes. The solution of food processors has been to utilize airtight, reclosable containers that reject moisture and other contaminants.

Pilferage is a problem in a number of markets and has forced companies to use only shipping codes on outside packaging.[32] With larger shipments, containerization has helped alleviate the theft problem. An exporter should anticipate inadequate, careless, or primitive loading methods. The labels and loading instructions should be not only in English but also in the market's language as well as in symbols.

The promotional aspect of packaging relates mostly to labeling. The major adjustments concern bilingual legal requirements, as in the case of Canada (French and English), Belgium (French and Flemish), and Finland (Finnish and Swedish). Even

---

[32]Barry M. Tarnef, "How to Protect Your Goods in Transit without Going Along for a Ride," *Export Today* 9 (May 1993): 55–57.

when the same language is spoken across markets, nuances will exist requiring labeling adaptation. Ace Hardware's Paint Division had to be careful in translating the world "plaster" into Spanish. In Venezuela, *friso* is used, while Mexicans use *yeso*. In the end, *yeso* was used for the paint labels, because the word was understood in all of Latin America.[33] Governmental requirements include more informative labeling on products. Inadequate identification, failure to use the needed languages, or inadequate or incorrect descriptions printed on the labels may cause problems. If in doubt, a company should study foreign competitors' labels.

Package aesthetics must be a consideration in terms of the promotional role of packaging. This mainly involves the prudent choice of colors and package shapes. African nations, for example, often prefer bold colors, but flag colors may be alternately preferred or disallowed. Red is associated with death or witchcraft in some countries. Color in packaging may be faddish. White is losing popularity in industrialized countries because name brands do not want to be confused with generic products, usually packaged in white. Black, on the other hand, is increasingly popular and is now used to suggest quality, excellence, and "class." Package shapes can be selected for promotional as well as handling and storage reasons, but marketers should also recognize reuse and waste as considerations.

Package size varies according to purchasing patterns and market conditions. For instance, a six-pack format for soft drinks may not be feasible in certain markets because of the lack of refrigeration capacity in households. Quite often, overseas consumers with modest or low discretionary purchasing power buy smaller sizes or even single units in order to stretch a limited budget. As a result, the smaller size or unit may sell for more per gram or ounce than the U.S. economy size, which has caused concern among supranational organizations and consumer groups monitoring the marketing activities of foreign firms.

Marketers are wise to monitor packaging technolgy developments in the world marketplace. A major innovation was in aseptic containers for fruit drinks and milk. Tetra Pak International, the $6.5-billion Swedish company, converted 40 percent of milk sales in Western Europe to its aseptic packaging system, which keeps perishables fresh for five months without refrigeration. The company claimed 5 percent of the fruit juice packaging market and 20 percent of the fruit drink market in the United States. Today, it markets its technologies in over 160 countries.[34]

Finally, the consumer mandate for marketers to make products more environmentally friendly also affects the packaging dimension, as can be seen in *The International Marketplace 10.4.*

Appearance

Adaptations in product styling, color, size, and other appearance features are more common in consumer marketing than in industrial marketing. Color plays an important role in the way consumers perceive a product, and marketers must be aware of the signal being sent by the product's color.[35] Color can be used for brand identification—for example, the yellow of Hertz, red of Avis, and green of National. It can be used for feature reinforcement; for example, Honda adopted the color black to give its motorcycles a Darth Vader look, whereas Rolls Royce uses a dazzling silver paint that denotes luxury. Colors communicate in a subtle way in developed societies; they have direct meaning in more traditional societies. For instance, in the late 1950s, when Pepsi Cola changed the color of its coolers and vending machines from deep regal blue

[33]Jesse Wilson, "Are Your Spanish Translations Culturally Correct?" *Export Today* 10 (May 1994): 68–69.

[34]**www.tetrapak.com**

[35]Laurence Jacobs, Charles Keown, Reginald Worthley, and Kyung-II Ghymn, "Cross-Cultural Colour Comparisons: Global Marketers Beware," *International Marketing Review* 8 (1991): 21–30.

THE INTERNATIONAL MARKETPLACE 10.4

Thinking Green in Packaging

IN 1994, THE EUROPEAN UNION (EU) launched a two-pronged attack on packaging waste. It wanted both to sharply decrease the amount of packaging waste that is generated and to increase the level of recycling of necessary packaging. To accomplish these objectives, two key targets were established. First, by 1998, 60 percent of packaging waste by weight had to be recoverable for recycling or other uses and by 2003, the percentage has to reach 90. The second target requires that no more that 10 percent by weight of the waste remains to be disposed of (e.g., in landfills).

Each EU country is free to determine how to achive these targets and how to finance the waste recovery infrastructure. Most countries place the bulk of the burden on those manufacturing, using, or selling packaging. Marketers are encouraged to adopt the four Rs: redesign, reduce, reuse, recycle.

As the issue's leader, Germany requires producers, importers, distributors, wholesalers, and retailers to take packaging from their customers for use or recycling independently of the public waste disposal system. All packaging introduced on German territory must be reusable or recyclable, and packaging must be kept to the minimum needed for proper protection and marketing of the product. Transportation packaging (e.g., crates or sacks) must be taken back through the chain of distribution all the way to the economic operator that first introduced it in the German market.

Germany's consumer goods marketers, retailers, and the packaging industry banded together to form Duales System Deutschland to collect, sort, and recycle empty packaging throughout the country. The 600 member companies, and 18,000 licensees, display green dot emblems on their products, which signal consumers to return the used packaging to the system's collection containers. By 2001, the green dot was used in 11 countries.

These criteria directly affect U.S. and other exporters seeking European market, since products failing to meet requirements may be denied entry. Because similar frameworks do not exist elsewhere, exporters cannot rely on their domestic standards but should find distributors with experience in waste management requirements. Distribution agreements must specify which party bears the cost of packaging compliance and/or participation in a private waste management system, as well as the cost of the Green Dot licensing fees. Recently, the EU Commission ruled that Dudles System Deutschland could no longer charge companies for using the Green Dot if they arranged their own recycling.

While the system is a burden, it offers some benefits. Cutting down on packaging can save on materials and shipping costs. Kodak, for example, keeps the packaging when it sells its high-volume copiers, and turns it into another packaging product. With its film products, it uses the Green Dot system.

SOURCES: Barry Lynn, "Germany the Packaging Environment," *Export Today* 11 (July 1995): 58–64; Stephen C. Messner, "Adapting Products to Western Europe," *Export Today* 10 (March–April 1994): 16–18; and Phillippe Bruno and Bernd Graf, "The New EC Environmental Framework for Packaging,"*Export Today* 9 (March 1993): 17–23; "UPDATE 2–EU Bars Charge for 'Geen Dot' Trademark," *Reuters*, April 20, 2001, David Lawsky.

http://www.gruener-punkt.de/en

to light ice blue, the result was catastrophic in Southeast Asia. Pepsi had a dominant market share, which it lost to Coca-Cola because light blue is associated with death and mourning in that part of the world. AVG Inc., a California-based provider of technology for theme-park rides, had to change the proposed colors of a ride it designed for a park outside Beijing because the client felt they conveyed the wrong attitude for the ride. Instead the client wanted the colors to be "happy" ones.[36] The only way companies can protect themselves against incidents of this kind is through thorough on-site testing, or, as in AVG's case, on-site production.

[36]"Riding the Theme Park Wave," *World Trade*, October 1999, 86.

Method of Operation or Usage

The product as it is offered in the domestic market may not be operable in the foreign market. One of the major differences faced by appliance manufacturers is electrical power systems. In some cases, variations may exist within a country, such as Brazil. An exporter can learn about these differences through local government representatives or various trade publications such as the U.S. Department of Commerce publication *Electric Current Abroad.* However, exporters should determine for themselves the adjustments that are required by observing competitive products or having their product tested by a local entity.

Many complicating factors may be eliminated in the future through standardization efforts by international organizations and by the conversion of most countries to the metric system. Some companies have adjusted their products to operate in different systems, for example, VCR equipment that will record and play back on different color systems.

The most blatant blunders in international marketing are usually the result of exporters' failure to adjust their products to local systems. But different operating systems and environments can also provide opportunities. When Canada adopted the metric system in 1977–1978, many U.S. companies were affected. Perfect Measuring Tape Company in Toledo, for example, had to convert to metric if it wanted to continue selling disposable paper measuring tape to textile firms in Canada. Once the conversion was made, the company found an entire world of untapped markets. It was soon shipping nearly 30 percent of its tape to overseas markets as disparate as Australia and Zimbabwe.[37] Products that rely heavily on the written or spoken language have to be adapted for better penetration of the market. For example, SPSS, Inc., the marketer of statistical software, localizes both DOS and Windows for German, English, Kanji, and Spanish. Producing software in the local language has also proven to be a weapon in the fight against software piracy.

An exporter may also have to adapt the product to different uses for different cultures. MicroTouch Systems, which produces touch-activated computer screens for video poker machines and ATMs, makes a series of adjustments in this regard. Ticket vending machines for the French subway need to be waterproof, since they are hosed down. Similarly, for the Australian market, video poker screens are built to take a beating because gamblers there take losing more personally than anywhere else.[38]

The international marketer should be open to ideas for new uses for the product being offered. New uses may substantially expand the market potential of the product. For example, Turbo Tek, Inc., which produces a hose attachment for washing cars, has found that foreign customers have expanded the product's functions. In Japan, Turbo-Wash is used for cleaning bamboo, and the Dutch use it to wash windows, plants, and the sidings of their houses.[39]

Quality

Many Western exporters must emphasize quality in their strategies because they cannot compete on price alone. Many new exporters compete on value in the particular segments in which they have chosen to compete. In some cases, producers of cheaper Asian products have forced international marketers to reexamine their strategies, allowing them to win contracts on the basis of technical advantage. To maintain a position of product superiority, exporting firms must invest in research and development for new products as well as manufacturing methods. For example, Sargent and Burton, a small Australian producer of high-technology racing boats, invested in

[37]"Made in the U.S.A.," *Business Week,* February 29, 1988, 60–66.

[38]Carla Kruytbosch, "The Minds behind the Winners," *International Business,* January 1994, 56–70.

[39]"Awash in Export Sales," *Export Today* 5 (February 1989): 11.

CAD/CAM technology to develop state-of-the-art racing boats that have proven successful in international competition against sophisticated overseas entries.[40]

An important aspect of improving quality is an emphasis on design. Some countries, such as Singapore and Taiwan, provide financial assistance to help companies improve product design. Cash grants help defer design costs, and publicity-oriented programs increase overall design consciousness.[41]

Increasingly, many exporters realize that they have to meet ISO 9000 standards to compete for business abroad and to win contracts from multinational corporations. Foreign buyers, especially in Europe, are requiring compliance with international ISO 9000 quality standards. For example, German electronics giant Siemens requires ISO compliance in 50 percent of its supply contracts and is encouraging other suppliers to conform. This has helped eliminate the need to test parts, which saves time and money. DuPont began its ISO drive after losing a big European order for polyester films to an ISO-certified British firm.[42]

Many exporters may overlook the importance of product quality especially when entering a developing market. While Fedder, the largest U.S. manufacturer of room air conditioners, had planned to market its most up-to-date air conditioners in China, it quickly discovered that even that was not going to be enough. The reason was that many Chinese buyers want a more sophisticated product than the standard unit sold in the United States. In China, it is a major purchase, and therefore often a status symbol. The Chinese also want special features such as remote control and an automatic air-sweeping mechanism.[43]

Service

When a product sold overseas requires repairs, parts, or service, the problem of obtaining, training, and holding a sophisticated engineering or repair staff is not easy. If the product breaks down, and the repair arrangements are not up to standard, the image of the product will suffer. In some cases, products abroad may not even be used for their intended purpose and may thus require modifications not only in product configuration but also in service frequency. For instance, snow plows exported from the United States are used to remove sand from driveways in Saudi Arabia. Closely related to servicing is the issue of product warranties. Warranties not only are instructions to customers about what to do if the product fails within a specified period of time but also are effective promotional tools.

Country-of-Origin Effects

The country of origin of a product, typically communicated by the phrase "Made in (country)," has a considerable influence on the quality perceptions of a product. The manufacture of products in certain countries is affected by a built-in positive or negative sterotype of product quality. One study of machine tool buyers found that the United States and Germany were rated higher than Japan, with Brazil being rated below all three.[44] These types of findings indicate that steps must be taken by the international marketer to overcome, or at least neutralize, biases. This issue may be espe-

[40]Ian Wilkinson and Nigel Barrett, "In Search of Excellence in Exports: An Analysis of the 1986 Australian Export Award Winners," paper given at the Australian Export Award presentations, Sydney, November 28, 1986.

[41]John S. Blyth, "Other Countries Lead U.S. in Supporting Design Efforts," *Marketing News*, February 13, 1989, 14–15.

[42]"Want EC Business? You Have Two Choices," *Business Week*, October 19, 1992, 58–59.

[43]"Keeping Cool in China," *The Economist*, April 6, 1996, 73–74.

[44]Phillip D. White and Edward W. Cundiff, "Assessing the Quality of Industrial Products," *Journal of Marketing* 42 (January 1978): 80–86.

cially important to developing countries, which need to increase exports, and for importers, who source products from countries different from those where they are sold.[45] In some markets, however, there may be a tendency to reject domestic goods and embrace imports of all kinds.

Some products have fared well in the international marketplace despite negative country-of-origin perceptions. For example, Belarus tractors (manufactured both in Belarus and Russia) have fared well in Europe and the United States not only because of their reasonable price tag but also because of their ruggedness. Only the lack of an effective network has hindered the company's ability to penetrate Western markets to a greater degree.[46]

Country-of-origin effects lessen as customers become more informed. Also, as more countries develop the necessary bases to manufacture products, the origin of the products becomes less important. This can already be seen with so-called hybrid products (for example, a U.S. multinational company manufacturing the product in Malaysia). The argument has been made that with the advent of more economic integration, national borders become less important.[47]

Company Considerations

Before launching a product in the international marketplace, the marketer needs to consider organizational capabilities as well as the nature of the product and the level of adaptation needed to accommodate various market-related differences between domestic and international markets.

The issue of product adaptation most often climaxes in the question "Is it worth it?" The answer depends on the firm's ability to control costs, correctly estimate market potential, and finally, secure profitability, especially in the long term. However, the question that used to be posed as "Can we afford to do it?" should now be "Can we afford not to do it?"

The decision to adapt should be preceded by a thorough analysis of the market. Formal market research with primary data collection and/or testing is warranted. From the financial standpoint, some firms have specific return-on-investment levels to be satisfied before adaptation (for instance, 25 percent), whereas some let the requirement vary as a function of the market considered and also the time in the market—that is, profitability may be initially compromised for proper market entry.

Most companies aim for consistency in their marketing efforts. This translates into the requirement that all products fit in terms of quality, price, and user perceptions. An example of where consistency may be difficult to control is in the area of warranties. Warranties can be uniform only if the use conditions do not vary drastically and if the company is able to deliver equally on its promise anywhere it has a presence.

A critical element of the adaptation decision has to be human resources, that is, individuals to make the appropriate decisions. Individuals are needed who are willing to make risky decisions and who know about existing market conditions. A characteristic of the U.S. export boom in the late 1980s was that foreigners and recent immigrants were often the first to see overseas opportunities. Foreign-born managers may look for goods that many U.S. executives overlook or consider too difficult for the international marketplace.[48]

[45]Warren J. Bilkey and Erik Nes, "Country-of-Origin Effects on Product Evaluations," *Journal of International Business Studies* 13 (Spring–Summer 1982): 88–99.

[46]Johny K. Johansson, Ilkka A. Ronkainen, and Michael R. Czinkota, "Negative Country-of-Origin Effects: The Case of the New Russia," *Journal of International Business Studies* 25 (First Quarter, 1994): 1–21.

[47]Johny K. Johansson, "Determinants and Effects of the Use of 'Made in' Labels," *International Marketing Review* 6 (1989): 47–58.

[48]"The Little Guys Are Making It Big Overseas," *Business Week*, February 27, 1989, 94–96.

Product Counterfeiting

Counterfeit goods are any goods bearing an unauthorized representation of a trademark, patented invention, or copyrighted work that is legally protected in the country where it is marketed. The International Trade Commission estimated that U.S. companies lose a total of $60 billion every year because of product counterfeiting and other infringement of intellectual property. Hardest hit are the most innovative, fastest-growing industries, such as computer software, pharmaceuticals, and entertainment.[49] In 1999, the software, publishing and distribution industries lost more than $11 billion due to software theft.[50] Worldwide, more than 38 percent of all software is illegally copied, with the percentage rising to over 90 percent in countries such as Vietnam.

The practice of product counterfeiting has spread to high-technology products and services from the traditionally counterfeited products: high-visibility, strong-brand-name consumer goods. In addition, previously the only concern was whether a company's product was being counterfeited; now, companies have to worry about whether the raw materials and components purchased for production are themselves real.[51] The European Union estimates that trade in counterfeit goods now accounts for 2 percent of total world trade. The International Chamber of Commerce estimates the figure at close to 5 percent. In general, countries with lower per capita incomes, higher levels of corruption in government, and lower levels of involvement in the international trade community tend to have higher levels of intellectual property violation.[52]

Counterfeiting problems occur in three ways and, depending on the origin of the products and where they are marketed, require different courses of action. Approximately 75 percent of counterfeit goods are estimated to be manufactured outside the United States, and 25 percent are either made in this country or imported and then labeled here. Problems originating in the United States can be resolved through infringement actions brought up in federal courts. Counterfeit products that originate overseas and that are marketed in the United States should be stopped by the customs barrier. Enforcement has been problematic because of the lack of adequate personnel and the increasingly high-tech character of the products. When an infringement occurs overseas, action can be brought under the laws of the country in which it occurs. The sources of the largest number of counterfeit goods are China, Brazil, Taiwan, Korea, and India, which are a problem to the legitimate owners of intellectual property on two accounts: the size of these countries' own markets and their capability to export. For example, Nintendo estimated its losses to video-game piracy at $725 million in 1998, with the origin of the counterfeits mainly China and Taiwan.[53] Countries in Central America and the Middle East are typically not sources but rather markets for counterfeit goods. Counterfeiting is a pervasive problem in terms not only of geographic reach but of the ability of the counterfeiters to deliver products, and the market's willingness to buy them, as shown in *The International Marketplace 10.5.*

[49]Faye Rice, "How Copycats Steal Billions," *Fortune*, April 22, 1991, 157 164.

[50]**www.bsa.org**

[51]Ilkka A. Ronkainen, "Imitation as the Worst Kind of Flattery: Product Counterfeiting," *Trade Analyst* 2 (July–August 1986): 2.

[52]Ilkka A. Ronkainen and Jose-Luis Guerrero-Cusumano, "Correlates of Intellectual Property Violation," paper presented at the annual meeting of the Academy of International Business, November 20–23, 1999.

[53]"In Pursuit of Pokémon Pirates," *The Wall Street Journal*, November 8, 1999, B1, B4.

THE INTERNATIONAL MARKETPLACE 10.5

The Phantom Pirates

VIDEO PIRATES MOVED faster than a speeding pod racer to release the latest *Star Wars* episode *The Phantom Menace* in Southeast Asia. The first copies appeared in Malaysia only two days later after the U.S. opening, with videodisc copies also reaching other parts of Asia, Europe, South Africa, and Latin America. "This shows how amazingly efficient this industry has become," said Michael Ellis, the Asia anti-piracy chief of the Motion Picture Association. "They have gotten it down to a sophisticated science."

With advances in technology and continued demand for U.S. films abroad, pirate-video making has become big business. In 1998, officials seized 42 million copies, up nearly tenfold from the year before. The Motion Picture Association of America estimates that worldwide piracy costs Hollywood $2.5 billion annually. Asia remains by far the biggest producer and consumer of pirate versions.

The three main types of copies of *The Phantom Menace* in Asia each have their own distinctive marks and character, depending on how and when they were filmed. The "Z" Species, named for the computer-generated letter that dances across the screen's edge, was filmed in a crowded theater and is marked by a loud scream of "Yeah, wooo!" throughout the opening sequence, and frequent applause for Yoda. "The Shakes" features shaky camera work, with audience members getting up to go to the bathroom during the important Darth Maul scene. The "Flying Horse" version

is also called "AB" for the blinking letters on the screen and a flying horse on the package cover. It features audience noise and frequent flash bulbs from viewers taking pictures.

It is unclear how the smugglers got the disks to market so quickly. Most of the copies sold in Asia appear to have come from the three master versions, which had been shipped via air courier to Malaysia and Hong Kong, where they were transferred to VCD-production lines in Malaysia. New technologies have facilitated the process as well. Whereas a pirated VCR tape has to be recorded in real time, taking up to two hours for each copy, a videocassette can be stamped out in three seconds and quite inexpensively. Consumers can buy a VCD player for under $100, and movies are typically less than $5.

Officials suspect that most of the copies were produced in Malaysia. With its lax law enforcement, low labor costs, and central location in Asia, Malaysia has become the new hub of the pirate CD industry. Whereas Hong Kong and Macau used to be the capital for this activity, crackdowns have chased the industry away. Malaysian officials have been repeatedly told of the violations, but little action has been taken. Experts say most of the factories producing the films are legitimate CD makers that produce pirate products on the side.

SOURCE: "Video Pirates Rush Out 'Phantom Menace,'" *The Wall Street Journal*, May 28, 1999, B1, B4; **www.mpaa.org**.

The first task in fighting intellectual property violation is to use patent application or registration of trademarks or mask works (for semiconductors). The rights granted by a patent, trademark, copyright, or mask work registration in the United States confer no protection in a foreign country. There is no such thing as an international patent, trademark, or copyright. Although there is no shortcut to worldwide protection, some advantages exist under treaties or other international agreements. These treaties, under the World Intellectual Property Organization (WIPO), include the Paris Convention for the Protection of Industrial Property, the Patent Cooperation

Treaty, the Berne Convention for the Protection of Literary and Artistic Works, and the Universal Copyright Convention, as well as regional patent and trademark offices such as the European Patent Office. Applicants are typically granted international protection throughout the member countries of these organizations.[54]

After securing valuable intellectual property rights, the international marketer must act to enforce, and have enforced, these rights. Four types of action against counterfeiting are legislative action, bilateral and multilateral negotiations, joint private sector action, and measures taken by individual companies.

In the legislative arena, the Omnibus Tariff and Trade Act of 1984 amended Section 301 of the Trade Act of 1974 to clarify that the violation of intellectual property rights is an unreasonable practice within the statute. The act also introduced a major carrot-and-stick policy: The adequacy of protection of intellectual property rights of U.S. manufacturers is a factor that will be considered in the designation of **Generalized System of Preferences (GSP)** benefits to countries. The United States has denied selected countries duty-free treatment on goods because of lax enforcement of intellectual property laws.

The Trademark Counterfeiting Act of 1984 made trading in goods and services using a counterfeit trademark a criminal rather than a civil offense, establishing stiff penalties for the practice. The Semiconductor Chip Protection Act of 1984 clarified the status and protection afforded to semiconductor masks, which determine the capabilities of the chip. Protection will be available to foreign-designed masks in the United States only if the home country of the manufacturer also maintains a viable system of mask protection. The Intellectual Property Rights Improvement Act requires the U.S. Trade Representative to set country-specific negotiating objectives for reciprocity and consideration of retaliatory options to assure intellectual property protection. The United States imposed punitive tariffs on $39 million of Brazilian imports to retaliate against Brazil's refusal to protect U.S. pharmaceutical patents.

The U.S. government is seeking to limit counterfeiting practices through bilateral and multilateral negotiations as well as education. A joint International Trade Administration and Patent and Trademark Office action seeks to assess the adequacy of foreign countries' intellectual property laws and practices, to offer educational programs and technical assistance to countries wishing to establish adequate systems of intellectual property protection, to offer educational services to the industry, and to review the adequacy of U.S. legislation in the area. Major legislative changes have occurred in the past few years in, for example, Taiwan and Singapore, where penalties for violations have been toughened. The WTO agreement includes new rules on intellectual property protection, under the Trade-Related Aspects of Intellectual Property Rights (TRIPS) agreement. Under them, trade-related intellectual property will enjoy 20 years of protection. More than 100 countries have indicated they will amend their laws and improve enforcement. Violators of intellectual property will face retaliation not only in this sector, but in others as well.[55] Similarly, the NAFTA agreement provides extensive patent and copyright protection.

A number of private-sector joint efforts have emerged in the battle against counterfeit goods. In 1978, the International Anti-Counterfeiting Coalition was founded to lobby for stronger legal sanctions worldwide. The coalition consists of 375 members. The International Chamber of Commerce established the Counterfeit Intelligence and Investigating Bureau in London, which acts as a clearinghouse capable of synthesizing global data on counterfeiting.

In today's environment, companies are taking more aggressive steps to protect themselves. The victimized companies are losing not only sales but also goodwill in the longer term if customers believe they have the real product rather than a copy of

---

[54]An Introductory Guide for U.S. Businesses on Protecting Intellectual Property Abroad," *Business America*, July 1, 1991, 2–7.

[55]"Intellectual Property . . . Is Theft," *Economist*, January 22, 1993, 72–73.

inferior quality. In addition to the normal measures of registering trademarks and copyrights, companies are taking steps in product development to prevent knockoffs of trademarked goods. For example, new authentication materials in labeling are extremely difficult to duplicate. Some companies, such as Disney, have tried to legitimize offenders by converting them into authorized licenses. These local companies would then be a part of the fight against counterfeiters, because their profits would be the most affected by fakes.

Many companies maintain close contact with the government and the various agencies charged with helping them. Computer makers, for example, loan testing equipment to customs officers at all major U.S. ports, and company attorneys regularly conduct seminars on how to detect pirated software and hardware. Other companies retain outside investigators to monitor the market and stage raids with the help of law enforcement officers. For example, when executives at WD-40 Co., the maker of an all-purpose lubricant, realized a counterfeit version of their product was being sold in China, they launched an investigation and then approached local authorities about the problem. Offending retailers were promptly raided and, in turn, led police to the counterfeiter.[56]

The issue of intellectual property protection will become more important for the United States and the EU in future years. It is a different problem from what it was a decade ago, when the principal victims were manufacturers of designer items. Today, the protection of intellectual property is crucial in high technology, one of the strongest areas of U.S. competitiveness in the world marketplace. The ease with which technology can be transferred and the lack of adequate protection of the developers' rights in certain markets make this a serious problem.[57]

SUMMARY

The international marketer must pay careful attention to variables that may call for an adaptation in the product offering. The target market will influence the adaptation decision through factors such as government regulation and customer preferences and expectations. The product itself may not be in a form ready for international market entry in terms of its brand name, its packaging, or its appearance. Some marketers make a conscious decision to offer only standardized products; some adjust their offerings by market.

Like the soft drink and packaged-goods marketers that have led the way, the newest marketers of world brands are producing not necessarily identical products, but recognizable products. As an example, the success of McDonald's in the world marketplace has been based on variation, not on offering the same product worldwide. Had it not been for the variations, McDonald's would have limited its appeal unnecessarily.

Firms entering or participating in the international marketplace will certainly find it difficult to cope with the conflicting needs of the domestic and international markets. They will be certain to ask whether adjustments in their product offerings, if the marketplace requires them, are worthwhile. There are, unfortunately, no magic formulas for addressing the problem of product adaptation. The answer seems to lie in adopting formal procedures to assess products in terms of the markets' and the company's own needs.

The theft of intellectual property—ideas and innovations protected by copyrights, patents, and trademarks—is a critical problem for many industries and countries. Governments have long argued about intellectual property protection, but the lack of results in some parts of the world has forced companies themselves to take action on this front.

[56]"Lubricating a Crackdown," *Export Today* (June 1999): 29.

[57]Michael G. Harvey and Ilkka A. Ronkainen, "International Counterfeiters: Marketing Success without the Cost and the Risk," *Columbia Journal of World Business* 20 (Fall 1985): 37–45.

QUESTIONS FOR DISCUSSION

1. Comment on the statement "It is our policy not to adapt products for export."
2. What are the major problems facing companies, especially smaller ones, in resolving product adaptation issues?
3. How do governments affect product design decisions of firms?
4. Are standards like those promoted by the International Organization for Standardization (see **www.iso.ch**) a hindrance or an opportunity for exporters?
5. Is any product ever the same everywhere it is sold?
6. How can marketers satisfy the 4 Rs of environmentally correct practice? See, for example, the approaches proposed by the Duales System Deuschland (**www.gruener-punkt.de/e/**).
7. Propose ways in which intellectual property piracy could be stopped permanently.
8. The software industry is the hardest hit by piracy. Using the web site of the Business Software Alliance (**www.bsa.org**), assess how this problem is being tackled.

RECOMMENDED READINGS

The Economist Intelligence Unit. *151 Checklists for Global Management.* New York: The Economist Intelligence Unit, 1993.

Keegan, Warren J., and Charles S. Mayer. *Multinational Product Management,* Chicago: American Marketing Association, 1977.

Levitt, Theodore. *The Marketing Imagination.* New York: Free Press, 1986.

Lorenz, C. *The Design Dimension: Product Strategy and the Challenge of Global Markets.* New York: Basil Blackwell, 1996.

Papadopoulos, Nicolas, and Louise A. Heslop. *Product-Country Images.* Binghamton, NY: International Business Press, 1993.

Renner, Sandra L., and W. Gary Winget. *Fast-Track Exporting.* New York: AMACOM, 1991.

Rodkin, Henry. *The Ultimate Overseas Business Guide for Growing Companies.* Homewood, IL: Dow Jones–Irwin, 1990.

Urban, Glen L, and John Hauser. *Design and Marketing of New Products.* Englewood Cliffs, NJ: Prentice-Hall, 1993.

Webber, Robert. *The Marketer's Guide to Selling Products Abroad.* Westport, CT: Quorum Books, 1989.

Chapter 11

Export Pricing Strategies

Adjusting to the Currency Squeeze

THE SURGING DOLLAR, up 50 percent or more against Asian currencies and 20 percent against European ones in the latter part of the 1990s, has had many U.S. exporters worried. Small exporters, especially those with ties to big-ticket infrastructure projects, have seen their customer base dry up in Korea, Malaysia, and Thailand and across the Pacific Rim. Their products have gotten too pricey compared with those of overseas rivals. But rather than complain about their fate, these marketers have adapted their operations by taking a number of steps to ensure long-term success.

Chicago's Aerotek International, which makes hydraulic hose repair systems used in industrial construction and mining, cut 50 of its Asian distributors and then set up a company in Singapore to market its product directly. Besides showing long-term commitment to the market place, the direct approach allows Aerotek to weed out financially weakened customers and avoid possibly unstable intermediaries. Besides developing their own distribution networks, many U.S. exporters are also insisting on bank-backed agreements to reduce losses on receivables. In effect, they are abandoning open-account financing in which a business relies on its customers to pay up in good faith.

Smaller exporters are also redirecting or shifting their emphases from Asia to healthier markets in Europe as well as Central and South America. However, while they can reduce their presence in Asia, U.S. exporters cannot avoid competing with Asian rivals and their heavily discounted prices. In Latin America, U.S. toolmakers have countered 15 to 20 percent price cuts on Korean and Japanese products with more value-added services and the "made-in-the USA" image.

Protected at least partly from the dollar swings are U.S.

exporters that occupy niche and specialty markets. Semiconductor producers enjoyed growth averaging 15 percent during this time. Farm equipment maker John Deere's exports rose 30 percent thanks to strong agricultural economies in Europe, Australia, and South Africa. Diebold, a maker of automatic teller machines, stepped up shipments to Latin America and Asia by 40 percent.

The strong dollar not only is a challenge but may also open strategic opportunities as well. U.S. marketers have expanded the assembly work they do in Asia to take advantage of the more economical factors of production there and the lower costs for raw materials ranging from oil to resin. Some exporters engage in strategies that eliminate the effects of currency swings. For example, Vermeer Manufacturing, which makes industrial and agricultural equipment, invoices its dealers abroad in the local currency and then uses the proceeds to pay for supplies and services bought locally. Billing in dollars may be perceived as a method of eliminating currency risk, but it also means that someone else, a competitor, is taking advantage of that currency movement and offering a lower-priced product.

SOURCES: "Competitive Exports, Sky-High Imports," *Financial Mail*, October 2, 1998, 19; "Turning Small into a Big Advantage," *Business Week*, July 13, 1998, 42–44; Erika Morphy, "Dollar Daze," *Export Today*, September 1998, 27–33; and "How Sweet It Is for Europe's Exporters," *Business Week*, May 5, 1997, 52–53.

http://www.deere.com;
http://www.diebold.com;
http://www.vermeer.com.

T HIS CHAPTER WILL FOCUS on the pricing decision from the exporter's point of view: the setting of export price, terms of sale, and terms of payment. The setting of export prices is complicated by factors such as increased distance from the markets, currency fluctuations, governmental policies such as duties, and typically longer and different types of channels of distribution. In spite of new factors influencing the pricing decision, the objective remains the same: to create demand for the marketer's offerings and to do so profitably in the long term. Two special considerations in export pricing—leasing and dumping—are discussed at the end of this chapter. Foreign market pricing (by subsidiaries) and intracompany transfer pricing, that is, pricing for transactions between corporate entities, will be discussed in Chapter 18.

Price Dynamics

Price is the only element of the marketing mix that is revenue generating; all the others are costs. It should therefore be used as an active instrument of strategy in the major areas of marketing decision making, as seen in *The International Marketplace 11.1*. Price serves as a means of communication with the buyer by providing a basis for judging the attractiveness of the offer. It is a major competitive tool in meeting and beating close rivals and substitutes. Competition will often force prices down, whereas intracompany financial considerations have an opposite effect. Prices, along with costs, will determine the long-term viability of the enterprise.

Price should not be determined in isolation from the other marketing mix elements. It may be used effectively in positioning the product in the marketplace—for example, JLG, the world leader in self-propelled aerial work platforms used at construction sites, is able to charge premium prices because its products are powered by non-polluting hydrogen fuel cells.[1] The feasibility range for price setting established by demand, competition, costs, and legal considerations may be narrow or wide in a given situation (for example, the pricing of a commodity versus an innovation). Regardless of how narrow the gap allowed by these factors, however, pricing should never be considered a static element. The marketer's ultimate goal is to make the customer as inelastic as possible; i.e., the customer should prefer the marketer's offer even at a price premium.

A summary of international pricing situations is provided as a matrix in Figure 11.1. Pricing challenges—such as pricing for a new market entry, changing price either as an attack strategy or in response to competitive changes, and multiple-product coordination in cases of related demand—are technically the same as problems encountered in domestic markets. The scope of these pricing situations will vary according to the degree of foreign involvement and the type of market encountered.

In first-time pricing, the general alternatives are (1) skimming, (2) following the market price, and (3) penetration pricing. The objective of **skimming** is to achieve the highest possible contribution in a short time period. For an exporter to use this approach, the product has to be unique, and some segments of the market must be willing to pay the high price. As more segments are targeted and more of the product is made available, the price is gradually lowered. The success of skimming depends on the ability and speed of competitive reaction.

If similar products already exist in the target market, **market pricing** can be used. The final customer price is determined based on competitive prices, and then both production and marketing must be adjusted to the price. This approach requires the exporter to have a thorough knowledge of product costs, as well as confidence that

---

[1]"The Secret of U.S. Exports: Great Products," *Fortune*, January 10, 2000, 154A–J.

| FIGURE 11.1 | **International Pricing Situations** |

Pricing Situation	International Involvement		
	Exporting	Foreign-Market Pricing	Intracompany Pricing
First-Time Pricing			
Changing Pricing			
Multiple-Product Pricing			

SOURCE: Adapted from Helmut Becker, "Pricing: An International Marketing Challenge," in *International Marketing Strategy*, eds. Hans Thorelli and Helmut Becker (New York: Pergamon Press, 1980), 207. Adapted with permission.

the product life cycle is long enough to warrant entry into the market. It is a reactive approach and may lead to problems if sales volumes never rise to sufficient levels to produce a satisfactory return. Although firms typically use pricing as a differentiation tool, the international marketing manager may have no choice but to accept the prevailing world market price.

When **penetration pricing** is used, the product is offered at a low price intended to generate volume sales and achieve high market share, which would compensate for a lower per-unit return. One company found, for example, that a 20 percent reduction in average pricing roughly doubled the demand for its product.[2] This approach typically requires mass markets, price-sensitive customers, and decreasing production and marketing costs as sales volumes increase. The basic assumption of penetration pricing is that the lower price will increase sales, which may not always be the case. This approach can also be used to discourage other marketers from entering the market.

Price changes are called for when a new product is launched, when a change occurs in overall market conditions (such as a change in the value of the billing currency), or when there is a change in the exporter's internal situation, such as costs of production. An exporter may elect not to change price even though the result may be lower profitability. However, if a decision is made to change prices, related changes must also be considered. For example, if an increase in price is required, it may at least initially be accompanied by increased promotional efforts. Price changes usually follow changes in the product's stage in the life cycle. As the product matures, more pressure will be put on the price to keep the product competitive despite increased competition and less possibility of differentiation.

With multiple-product pricing, the various items in the line may be differentiated by pricing them appropriately to indicate, for example, an economy version, a standard version, and the top-of-the-line version. One of the products in the line may be priced to protect against competitors or to gain market share from existing competitors. The other items in the line are then expected to make up for the lost contribution of such a "fighting brand."

Although foreign market pricing and intracompany pricing are discussed later in conjunction with multinational pricing challenges, they do have an impact on the exporter as well. For example, distributors in a particular market may want to keep their

[2]James A. Gingrich, "Five Rules for Winning Emerging Market Consumers," *Strategy & Business* (Second Quarter 1999), 35–46.

profit margins up. This means that the exporter will have to lower prices to the distributor and take less profit to ensure sales and to remain competitive, or, if the market conditions warrant it, to move into more direct distribution.[3] Similarly, the exporter, in providing products to its own sales offices abroad, may have to adjust its transfer prices according to foreign exchange fluctuations.

The Setting of Export Prices

The setting of export price is influenced by both internal and external factors, as well as their interaction. Internal factors include the company's philosophy, goals, and objectives; the costs of developing, producing, and marketing the export product; and the nature of the exporter's product and industry. External factors relate to international markets in general or to a specific target market in particular and include such factors as customer, regulatory, competitive, and financial (mainly foreign exchange) characteristics. The interaction of these elements causes pricing opportunities and constraints in different markets. For example, company management may have decided to challenge its main foreign competitor in the competitor's home market. Regulation in that market requires expensive product adaptation, the cost of which has to be absorbed now for the product to remain competitive.

In setting the export price, a company can use a process such as the one summarized in Figure 11.2. As in all marketing decisions, the intended target market will establish the basic premise for pricing. Factors to be considered include the importance of price in customer decision making (in particular, the ability to pay), the strength of perceived price-quality relationships, and potential reactions to marketing-mix manipulation by marketers. For example, an exporter extending a first-world product to an emerging market may find its potential unnecessarily limited and thus opt for a new version of a product that costs a fraction of the original version. Customers' demands will also have to be considered in terms of support required by the intermedi-

FIGURE 11.2 Stages in Setting of Prices

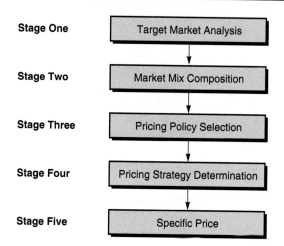

SOURCE: Reprinted by permission of Harvard Business Review. An excerpt from Alfred R. Oxenfeldt, "Multistage Approach to Pricing," *Harvard Business Review* 38 (July–August 1960): 126. Copyright © by the President and Fellows of Harvard College; all rights reserved.

[3]"Sizing Up the Customers' Needs," *Export Today* 5 (February 1989): 32–35.

ary. The marketing mix must be planned to match the characteristics of the target market. Pricing will be a major factor in determining the desired brand image as well as the distribution channels to be used and the level of promotional support required.

Pricing policies follow from the overall objectives of the firm for a particular target market and involve general principles or rules that a firm follows in making pricing decisions. Policies include profit maximization, market share, survival, percentage return on investment, and various competitive policies such as copying competitors' prices, following a particular competitor's prices, or pricing so as to discourage competitors from entering the market.[4] For example, an exporter entering a new market may allow wholesalers and retailers above-normal profit margins to encourage maximum sales volume, geographic distribution, and loyalty. Loctite Corporation, in marketing adhesives for industrial uses, requires a highly technical selling effort from distributors and uses higher-than-average compensation packages to secure their services. These types of demands are common especially in the early stages of the export effort and may have to be satisfied to gain market penetration. They should be phased out later on, however, with sales volume increases making up for the difference.[5]

Export Pricing Strategy

Three general price-setting strategies in international marketing are a standard worldwide price; dual pricing, which differentiates between domestic and export prices; and market-differentiated pricing.[6] The first two methods are cost-oriented pricing methods that are relatively simple to establish and easy to understand. The third strategy is based on demand orientation and may thus be more consistent with the marketing concept. However, even the third approach has to acknowledge costs in the long term.

The **standard worldwide price** may be the same price regardless of the buyer (if foreign product or foreign marketing costs are negligible) or may be based on average unit costs of fixed, variable, and export-related costs.

In **dual pricing**, domestic and export prices are differentiated, and two approaches to pricing products for export are available: the **cost-plus method** and the **marginal cost method**. The cost-plus strategy is the true cost, fully allocating domestic and foreign costs to the product. Although this type of pricing ensures margins, the final price may be so high that the firm's competitiveness is compromised. This may cause some exporters to consider a flexible cost-plus strategy, which allows for variations in special circumstances.[7] Discounts may be granted, depending on the customer, the size of the order, or the intensity of competition. Changes in prices may also be put into effect to counter exchange rate fluctuations. Despite these allowances, profit is still a driving motive, and pricing is more static as an element of the marketing mix.

The marginal cost method considers the direct costs of producing and selling products for export as the floor beneath which prices cannot be set. Fixed costs for plants, R&D, and domestic overhead as well as domestic marketing costs are disregarded. An exporter can thus lower export prices to be competitive in markets that otherwise might have been beyond access. On certain occasions, especially if the exporter is large, this may open a company to dumping charges, because determination of dumping may be based on average total costs, which are typically considerably higher. A

[4]Donald V. Harper and Jack L. Caldwell, "Pricing," in *Marketing Manager's Handbook*, eds. Steuart Henderson Britt and Norman Guess (Chicago: Dartnell, 1983), 723–736.

[5]John A. Boyd, "How One Company Solved Its Export Pricing Problems," *Small Business Forum*, Fall 1995, 28–38.

[6]Richard D. Robinson, *Internationalization of Business: An Introduction* (Hinsdale, IL: The Dryden Press, 1984), 49–54.

[7]S. Tamer Cavusgil, "Unraveling the Mystique of Export Pricing," *Business Horizons* 31 (May–June 1988): 54–63.

TABLE 11.1 Export Pricing Alternatives

PRODUCTION COSTS	STANDARD	COST PLUS	MARGINAL COST
Materials	2.00	2.00	2.00
Fixed costs	1.00	1.00	0.00
Additional foreign product costs	0.00	0.10	0.10
Production overhead	0.50	0.50	0.00
Total production costs	3.50	3.60	2.10
U.S. marketing costs	1.50	0.00	0.00
General and administrative	0.75	0.75	0.00
Foreign marketing	0.00	1.00	1.00
Other foreign costs	0.00	1.25	1.25
Subtotal	5.75	6.60	4.35
Profit margin (25%)	1.44	1.65	1.09
Selling price	7.19	8.25	5.44

SOURCES: Adapted from Lee Oster, "Accounting for Exporters," *Export Today* 7 (January 1991): 28–33.

comparison of the cost-oriented methods is provided in Table 11.1. Notice how the rigid cost-plus strategy produces the highest selling price by full-cost allocation.

Market-differentiated pricing calls for export pricing according to the dynamic conditions of the marketplace. For these firms, the marginal cost strategy provides a basis, and prices may change frequently due to changes in competition, exchange rate changes, or other environmental changes. The need for information and controls becomes crucial if this pricing alternative is to be attempted.

The way some exporters meet these challenges is highlighted in *The International Marketplace 11.2*.

Export-Related Costs

In preparing a quotation, the exporter must be careful to take into account and, if possible, include unique export-related costs. These are in addition to the normal costs shared with the domestic side. They include the following:

1. The cost of modifying the product for foreign markets
2. Operational costs of the export operation: personnel, market research, additional shipping and insurance costs, communications costs with foreign customers, and overseas promotional costs
3. Costs incurred in entering the foreign markets: tariffs and taxes; risks associated with a buyer in a different market (mainly commercial credit risks and political risks); and risks from dealing in other than the exporter's domestic currency—that is, foreign exchange risk

The combined effect of both clear-cut and hidden costs results in export prices that far exceed domestic prices. The cause is termed **price escalation**. In the case of Geochron, the marketer of world time indicators, the multi-layered distribution system with its excessive markups makes the price of a $1,300 clock exceed $3,800 in Japan.[8]

---

[8]"Keeping Time with the Global Market," *World Trade*, December 1999, 82–83.

THE INTERNATIONAL MARKETPLACE 11.2

The Exporter's Pricing Dilemma

SETTING THE RIGHT PRICE for a product can be the key to success or failure in the international marketplace. The complexity of export pricing as well as the importance placed on export operations cause companies to take different approaches to export pricing.

Dairy Equipment Co. produces milk machines, bulk coolers, and other high-quality equipment for the dairy industry. Although the company has exported continuously over the past decade, export earnings have been negligible. Gross profit has remained the company's primary export goal, but the rigid cost-plus strategy has not proved to be effective. The company has always sought equal profitability from foreign sales; however, fierce competition in some markets has forced it to consider lower profit margins. The company's export pricing policy remains a static element of the marketing mix.

Baughman, a division of Fuqua industries, manufactures steel grain storage silos and related equipment. The company has traditionally exported approximately 30 percent of its sales. Baughman's products are of high quality, and pricing has not often been an active element of the marketing mix. The firm's export sales terms consist of an irrevocable confirmed letter of credit in U.S. dollars with no provisions for fluctuating exchange rates. Export and domestic prices are identical before exporting costs are added. However, Baughman will make concessions to this policy to secure strategically important sales.

Ray-O-Vac, a producer of batteries and other consumer goods, has been exporting successfully since the 1950s. Exports account for 20 percent of total business, and major markets include Europe, the Far East, and Japan. These markets are entered through wholly owned subsidiaries that are treated as cost or profit centers depending on market circumstances. Competitive pressures demand flexible pricing, and discounts are often granted to gain market share. Branch managers may adjust prices on a day-to-day basis to counter exchange rate fluctuations. Export pricing is a very active ingredient in the firm's marketing mix.

While many, especially new, exporters calculate their export price by the cost-plus method to counter the uncertainties of international business, market forces and internal goal setting may force them to reconsider their strategy.

SOURCES: "The Architecture of International Business," *World Trade*, February 1999, 34–40; "Price, Quotations, and Terms of Sale Are Key to Successful Exporting," *Business America*, October 4, 1993, 12–15; S. Tamer Cavusgil, "Unraveling the Mystique of Export Pricing," *Business Horizons* 31 (May–June 1988): 54–63.

http://www.rayovac.com

Four different export scenarios are compared with a typical domestic situation in Table 11.2. The first case is relatively simple, adding only the CIF (cost, insurance, freight) and tariff charges. The second adds a foreign importer and thus lengthens the foreign part of the distribution channel. In the third case, a **value-added tax (VAT)** is included in the calculations. This is imposed on the full export selling price, which represents the "value added" to or introduced into the country from abroad. In Italy, for example, where most food items are taxed at 2 percent, processed meat is taxed at 18 percent because the government wants to use the VAT to help reduce its trade deficit. The fourth case simulates a situation typically found in less-developed countries where distribution channels are longer. Lengthy channels can easily double the landed (CIF) price.

Complicating price escalation in today's environment may be the fact that price increases are of different sizes across markets. If customers are willing to shop around before purchasing, the problem of price differentials will make distributors unhappy and could result in a particular market's being abandoned altogether.

TABLE 11.2 Export Price Escalation

INTERNATIONAL MARKETING CHANNEL ELEMENTS AND COST FACTORS	DOMESTIC WHOLESALE-RETAIL CHANNEL	EXPORT MARKET CASES			
		CASE 1 SAME AS DOMESTIC WITH DIRECT WHOLESALE IMPORT CIF/TARIFF	CASE 2 SAME AS 1 WITH FOREIGN IMPORTER ADDED TO CHANNEL	CASE 3 SAME AS 2 WITH VAT ADDED	CASE 4 SAME AS 3 WITH LOCAL FOREIGN JOBBER ADDED TO CHANNEL
Manufacturer's net price	6.00	6.00	6.00	6.00	6.00
+ Insurance and shipping cost (CIF)	—	2.50	2.50	2.50	2.50
= Landed cost (CIF value)	—	8.50	8.50	8.50	8.50
+ Tariff (20% on CIF value)	—	1.70	1.70	1.70	1.70
= Importer's cost (CIF value + tariff)	—	10.20	10.20	10.20	10.20
+ Importer's margin (25% on cost)	—	—	2.55	2.55	2.55
+ VAT (16% on full cost plus margin)	—	—	—	2.04	2.04
= Wholesaler's cost (= importer's price)	6.00	10.20	12.75	14.79	14.79
+ Wholesaler's margin ($33\frac{1}{3}$% on cost)	2.00	3.40	4.25	4.93	4.93
+ VAT (16% on margin)	—	—	—	.79	.79
= Local foreign jobber's cost (= wholesale price)	—	—	—	—	20.51
+ Jobber's margin ($33\frac{1}{3}$% on cost)	—	—	—	—	6.84
+ VAT (16% on margin)	—	—	—	—	1.09
= Retailer's cost (= wholesale or jobber price)	8.00	13.60	17.00	20.51	28.44
+ Retailer's margin (50% on cost)	4.00	6.80	8.50	10.26	14.22
+ VAT (16% on margin)	—	—	—	1.64	2.28
= Retail price (what consumer pays)	12.00	20.40	25.50	32.41	44.94
Percentage price escalation over domestic		70%	113%	170%	275%
Percentage price escalation over Case 1			25%	59%	120%
Percentage price escalation over Case 2				27%	76%
Percentage price escalation over Case 3					39%

SOURCE: Helmut Becker, "Pricing: An International Marketing Challenge," in *International Marketing Strategy*, eds. Hans Thorelli and Helmut Becker (New York: Pergamon Press, 1980), 215. Reprinted with permission.

Price escalation can be overcome through creative strategies, depending on what the demand elasticities in the market are. Typical methods, such as the following, focus on cost cutting:

1. Reorganize the channel of distribution. The example in Figure 11.3, based on import channels for spaghetti and macaroni in Japan, shows how the flow of merchandise through the various wholesaling levels has been reduced to only an internal wholesale distribution center, resulting in savings of 25 percent and increasing the overall potential for imports. Shortening of channels may, however, bring about other costs such as demands for better discounts if a new intermediary takes the role of multiple previous ones.

2. Adapt the product. The product itself can be reformulated by including less expensive ingredients or unbundling costly features, which can be made optional. Remaining features, such as packaging, can also be made less expensive. If price escalation causes price differentials between markets, the product can be altered to avoid cross-border price shopping by customers. For example, Geochron alters its clocks' appearance from one region to another.

FIGURE 11.3 | **Distribution Adjustment to Decrease Price Escalation**

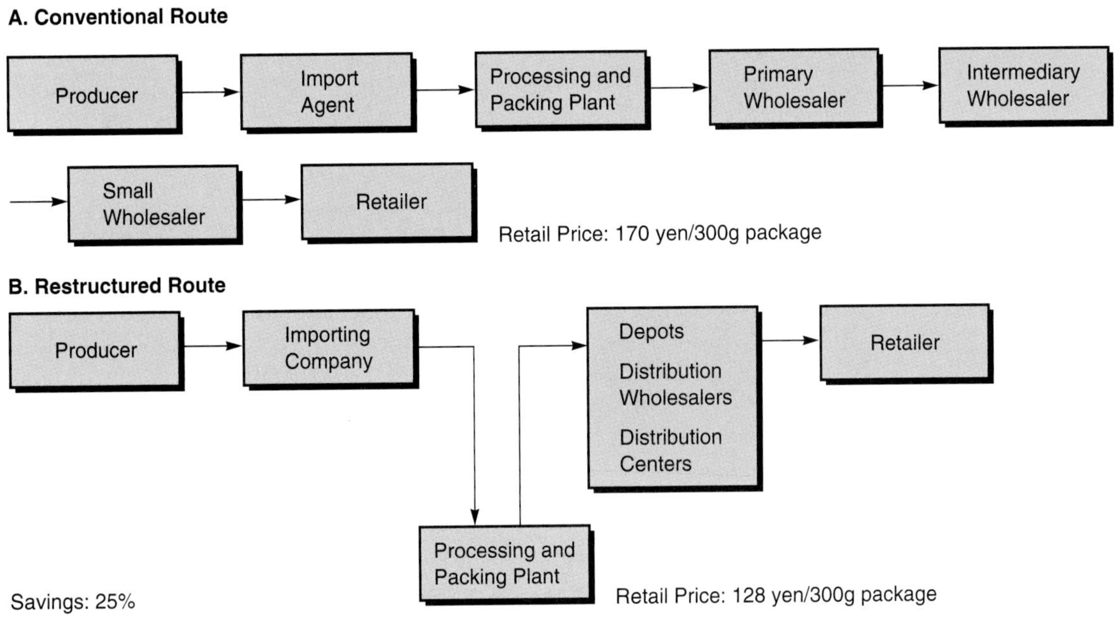

A. Conventional Route

Producer → Import Agent → Processing and Packing Plant → Primary Wholesaler → Intermediary Wholesaler

→ Small Wholesaler → Retailer

Retail Price: 170 yen/300g package

B. Restructured Route

Producer → Importing Company → Depots / Distribution Wholesalers / Distribution Centers → Retailer

Processing and Packing Plant

Savings: 25%   Retail Price: 128 yen/300g package

SOURCE: Michael R. Czinkota, "Distribution of Consumer Products in Japan: An Overview," *International Marketing Review* 2 (Autumn 1985): 39–51.

3. Use new or more economical tariff or tax classifications. In many cases, products may qualify for entry under different categories that have different charges levied against them. The marketer may have to engage in a lobbying effort to get changes made in existing systems, but the results may be considerable savings. For example, when the U.S. Customs Service ruled that multi-purpose vehicles were light trucks and, therefore, subject to 25 percent tariffs (and not the 2.5 percent levied on passenger cars), Britain's Land Rover had to argue that its $56,000 luxury vehicle, the Range Rover, was not a truck. When the United States introduced a luxury tax (10 percent of the part of a car's price that exceeded $33,000), Land Rover worked closely with the U.S. Internal Revenue Service to establish that its vehicles were trucks (since trucks were free of such tax). Before it got its way, however, it had to make slight adjustments in the vehicle, since the IRS defines a minimum weight for trucks at 6,000 lbs. Land Rover's following year model weighed in at 6,019 lbs.[9]

4. Assemble or produce overseas. In the longer term, the exporter may resort to overseas sourcing or eventually production. Through foreign sourcing, the exporter may accrue an additional benefit to lower cost: **duty drawbacks.** An exporter may be refunded up to 99 percent of duties paid on imported goods when they are exported or incorporated in articles that are subsequently exported within five years of the importation.[10] Levi Strauss, for example, imports zippers from China that are sewn into the company's jackets and jeans in the United States. The amount that Levi's reclaims can be significant, because the duty on zippers can climb to 30 percent of the product's value.[11]

[9]"What's in a Name," *Economist*, February 2, 1991, 60.

[10]Al D'Amico, "Duty Drawback: An Overlooked Customs Refund Program," *Export Today* 9 (May 1993): 46–48. See also **http://www.customs.treas.gov**.

[11]Michael D. White, "Money-Back Guarantees," *World Trade*, September 1999, 74–77.

If the marketer is able to convey a premium image, it may then be able to pass the increased amounts to the final price.

Appropriate export pricing requires the establishment of accounting procedures to assess export performance. Without such a process, hidden costs may bring surprises. For example, negotiations in the Middle Eastern countries or Russia may last three times longer than the average domestic negotiations, dramatically increasing the costs of doing business abroad. Furthermore, without accurate information, a company cannot combat phenomena such as price escalation.

Terms of Sale

The responsibilities of the buyer and the seller should be spelled out as they relate to what is and what is not included in the price quotation and when ownership of goods passes from seller to buyer. **Incoterms** are the internationally accepted standard definitions for terms of sale set by the International Chamber of Commerce (ICC) since 1936.[12] The Incoterms 2000 went into effect on January 1, 2000, with significant revisions to better reflect changing transportation technologies and the increased use of electronic communications.[13] Although the same terms may be used in domestic transactions, they gain new meaning in the international arena. The terms are grouped into four categories, starting with the term whereby the seller makes the goods available to the buyer only at the seller's own premises (the "E"-terms), followed by the group whereby the seller is called upon to deliver the goods to a carrier appointed by the buyer (the "F"-terms). Next are the "C"-terms, whereby the seller has to contract for carriage but without assuming the risk of loss or damage to the goods or additional costs after the dispatch, and finally the "D"-terms, whereby the seller has to bear all costs and risks to bring the goods to the destination determined by the buyer. The most common of the Incoterms used in international marketing are summarized in Figure 11.4.

Prices quoted **ex-works (EXW)** apply only at the point of origin, and the seller agrees to place the goods at the disposal of the buyer at the specified place on the date or within the fixed period. All other charges are for the account of the buyer.

One of the new Incoterms is **free carrier (FCA)**, which replaced a variety of FOB terms for all modes of transportation except vessel. FCA (named inland point) applies only at a designated inland shipping point. The seller is responsible for loading goods into the means of transportation; the buyer is responsible for all subsequent expenses. If a port of exportation is named, the costs of transporting the goods to the named port are included in the price.

Free alongside ship (FAS) at a named U.S. port of export means that the exporter quotes a price for the goods, including charges for delivery of the goods alongside a vessel at the port. The seller handles the cost of unloading and wharfage; loading, ocean transportation, and insurance are left to the buyer.

Free on board (FOB) applies only to vessel shipments. The seller quotes a price covering all expenses up to, and including, delivery of goods on an overseas vessel provided by or for the buyer.

Under **cost and freight (CFR)** to a named overseas port of import, the seller quotes a price for the goods, including the cost of transportation to the named port of debarkation. The cost of insurance and the choice of insurer are left to the buyer.

With **cost, insurance, and freight (CIF)** to a named overseas port of import, the seller quotes a price including insurance, all transportation, and miscellaneous charges

---

[12]*International Trade Procedures* (Philadelphia: CoreStates Bank, 1995), 49.

[13]International Chambers of Commerce, *Incoterms 2000* (Paris: ICC Publishing, 2000).

FIGURE 11.4 **Selected Trade Terms**

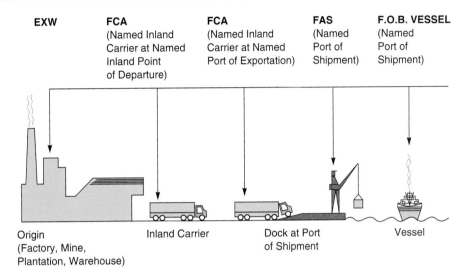

EXW

FCA
(Named Inland
Carrier at Named
Inland Point
of Departure)

FCA
(Named Inland
Carrier at Named
Port of Exportation)

FAS
(Named
Port of
Shipment)

F.O.B. VESSEL
(Named
Port of
Shipment)

Origin
(Factory, Mine,
Plantation, Warehouse)

Inland Carrier

Dock at Port
of Shipment

Vessel

Country of Origin

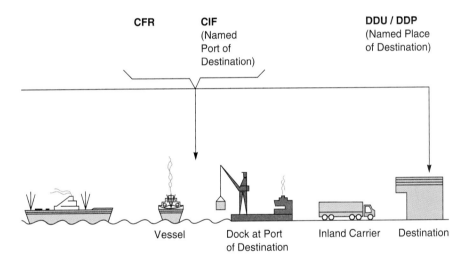

CFR

CIF
(Named
Port of
Destination)

DDU / DDP
(Named Place
of Destination)

Vessel

Dock at Port
of Destination

Inland Carrier

Destination

Country of Destination

to the point of debarkation from the vessel. If other than waterway transport is used, the terms are **CPT** (carriage paid to) or **CIP** (carriage and insurance paid to).

With **delivered duty paid (DDP)**, the seller delivers the goods, with import duties paid, including inland transportation from import point to the buyer's premises. With **delivered duty unpaid (DDU)**, only the destination customs duty and taxes are paid by the consignee. Ex-works signifies the maximum obligation for the buyer; delivered duty paid puts the maximum burden on the seller.

Careful determination and clear understanding of terms used, and their acceptance by the parties involved, are vital if subsequent misunderstandings and disputes are to be avoided not only between the parties but also within the marketer's own organization.[14]

---

[14]Kevin Maloney, "Incoterms: Clarity at the Profit Margin," *Export Today* 6 (November–December 1990): 45–46.

These terms are also powerful competitive tools. The exporter should therefore learn what importers usually prefer in the particular market and what the specific transaction may require. An inexperienced importer may be discouraged from further action by a quote such as ex-plant Jessup, Maryland, whereas CIF Helsinki will enable the Finnish importer to handle the remaining costs because they are incurred in a familiar environment.

Increasingly, exporters are quoting more inclusive terms. The benefits of taking charge of the transportation on either a CIF or DDP basis include the following: (1) exporters can offer foreign buyers an easy-to-understand "delivered cost" for the deal; (2) by getting discounts on volume purchases for transportation services, exporters cut shipping costs and can offer lower overall prices to prospective buyers; (3) control of product quality and service is extended to transport, enabling the exporter to ensure that goods arrive to the buyer in good condition; and (4) administrative procedures are cut for both the exporter and the buyer.[15] These benefits are highlighted in *The International Marketplace 11.3*.

When taking control of transportation costs, however, the exporter must know well in advance what impact the additional costs will have on the bottom line. If the approach is implemented incorrectly, exporters can be faced with volatile shipping rates, unexpected import duties, and restive customers. Most exporters do not want to go beyond the CIF quotation because of uncontrollables and unknowns in the destination country. Whatever terms are chosen, the program should be agreed to by the exporter and the buyer(s) rather than imposed solely by the exporter.

Freight forwarders are useful in determining costs, preparing quotations, and making sure that unexpected changes do not cause the exporter to lose money. Freight forwarders are useful to the exporter not only as facilitators and advisors but also in keeping down some of the export-related costs. Rates for freight and insurance provided to freight forwarders may be far more economical than to an individual exporter because of large-volume purchases, especially if export sales are infrequent. Some freight forwarders can also provide additional value-added services, such as taking care of the marketer's duty-drawback receivables.

Terms of Payment

Export credit and terms add another dimension to the profitability of an export transaction. The exporter has in all likelihood already formulated a credit policy that determines the degree of risk the firm is willing to assume and the preferred selling terms. The main objective is to meet the importer's requirements without jeopardizing the firm's financial goals. The exporter will be concerned over being paid for the goods shipped and will therefore consider the following factors in negotiating terms of payment: (1) the amount of payment and the need for protection, (2) terms offered by competitors, (3) practices in the industry, (4) capacity for financing international transactions, and (5) relative strength of the parties involved.[16] If the exporter is well established in the market with a unique product and accompanying service, price and terms of trade can be set to fit the exporter's desires. If, on the other hand, the exporter is breaking into a new market or if competitive pressures call for action, pricing and selling terms should be used as major competitive tools. Both parties have their own concerns and sensitivities; therefore, this very basic issue should be put on the negotiating table at the very beginning of the relationship.

---

[15]"How Exporters Efficiently Penetrate Foreign Markets," *International Business*, December 1993, 48.

[16]"Getting Paid: Or What's a Transaction For?" *World Trade*, September 1999, 42–52; and Chase Manhattan Bank, *Dynamics of Trade Finance* (New York: Chase Manhattan Bank, 1984): 10–11.

THE INTERNATIONAL MARKETPLACE 11.3

Penetrating Foreign Markets by Controlling Export Transport

COMPANIES THAT ONCE SOUGHT short-term customers to smooth out recessions are searching for every means to get an edge over rivals in foreign markets. To achieve that, they are increasingly concerned about controlling quality and costs at every step, including the transportation process.

International transport costs are far higher than domestic shipping expenses. International ocean transport typically accounts for 4 to 20 percent of the product's delivered cost but can reach as high as 50 percent for commodity items. That makes transport a factor in situations where a single price disadvantage can cause a sale to be lost to a competitor.

Still, most U.S. companies continue to abdicate responsibility for export shipping—either because they lack sophistication or simply because they do not want to be bothered. Increasingly, however, companies like Deere & Co. are paying for, controlling, and often insuring transport from their factories either to foreign ports or to the purchasing companies' doorsteps.

Deere exports premium-quality farm and lawn equipment worldwide. For years, it has insisted on overseeing transportation because it boosts sales, cuts costs, and ensures quality. "We have a long-term relationship with our dealers. It is in our best interest to do the transport job," says Ann Salaber, an order control manager in the export order department.

One goal of Deere's approach to transportation is to ensure that equipment is delivered to customers in good condition—a factor that Deere considers central to its image as a quality producer. The goal is to avoid cases like the one in which an inexperienced customer insisted on shipping a tractor himself. The tractor was unwittingly put on a ship's deck during a long, stormy sea voyage and arrived in terrible shape.

The process also helps when Deere tractor windows are inadvertently broken during the transport. Because Deere closely monitors the tractors, it can quickly install new windows at the port and avoid the huge cost of flying replacements to a customer as far away as Argentina.

Cost is an important consideration as well. Depending on where a $150,000 combine is shipped, transport costs can range between $7,500 and $30,000, or between 5 and 20 percent of delivered cost. Deere's ability to buy steamship space in volume enables it to reduce transport costs by 10 percent. That in turn enables it to cut the combine's delivered cost by between $750 and $3,000. "That adds up," says Salaber. Because of those savings, "you do not have to discount so much, and Deere gets more profit."

SOURCES: "How Badly Will the Dollar Whack the U.S.?" *Business Week*, May 5, 1997; and Gregory L. Miles, "Exporter's New Bully Stick," *International Business*, December 1993, 46–49.

http://www.deere.com

The basic methods of payment for exports vary in terms of their attractiveness to the buyer and the seller, from cash in advance to open account or consignment selling. Neither of the extremes will be feasible for longer-term relationships, but they do have their use in certain situations. For example, in the 1999–2000 period very few companies were exporting into Russia except on a cash-in-advance basis, due to the country's financial turmoil. A marketer may use multiple methods of payment with the same buyer. For example, in a distributor relationship, the distributor may purchase samples on open account, but orders have to be paid for with a letter of credit. These methods are depicted in the risk triangle presented in Figure 11.5.

The most favorable term to the exporter is **cash in advance** because it relieves the exporter of all risk and allows for immediate use of the money. It is not widely used, however, except for smaller, first-time transactions or situations in which the exporter has reason to doubt the importer's ability to pay. Cash-in-advance terms are also found when orders are for custom-made products, because the risk to the exporter is beyond that of a normal transaction. In some instances, the importer may not be able to buy on a cash-in-advance basis because of insufficient funds or government restrictions.

FIGURE	11.5	Risk Triangle

BUYER'S PERSPECTIVE   SELLER'S PERSPECTIVE

Most Advantageous   High Risk/ High Trust

Consignment

Open Account

Documents against Acceptance

Documents against Payment

Letter of Credit

Confirmed Letter of Credit

Cash in Advance

Least Advantageous   Low Risk / Low Trust

SOURCE: Adapted from Chase Manhattan Bank, *Dynamics of Trade Finance* (New York: Chase Manhattan Bank, 1984), 5.

A **letter of credit** is an instrument issued by a bank at the request of a buyer. The bank promises to pay a specified amount of money on presentation of documents stipulated in the letter of credit, usually the bill of lading, consular invoice, and a description of the goods.[17] Letters of credit are one of the most frequently used methods of payment in international transactions. Figure 11.6 summarizes the process of obtaining a letter of credit and the relationship between the parties involved.

Letters of credit can be classified among three dimensions:

1. Irrevocable versus revocable. An irrevocable letter of credit can neither be canceled nor modified without the consent of the beneficiary (exporter), thus guaranteeing payment. According to the new rules drawn by the International Chamber of Commerce, effective January 1, 1994, all letters of credit are considered irrevocable unless otherwise stated.[18]
2. Confirmed versus unconfirmed. In the case of a U.S. exporter, a U.S. bank might confirm the letter of credit and thus assume the risk, including the transaction (exchange) risk. The single best method of payment for the exporter in most cases is a confirmed, irrevocable letter of credit. Banks may also assume an advisory role but not assume the risk; the underlying assumption is that the bank and its correspondent(s) are better able to judge the credibility of the bank issuing the letter of credit than is the exporter.
3. Revolving versus nonrevolving. Most letters of credit are nonrevolving, that is, they are valid for the one transaction only. In case of established relationships, a revolving letter of credit may be issued.

Figure 11.7 provides an example of a letter of credit.

[17]David K. Eiteman, Arthur I. Stonehill, and Michael H. Moffett, *Multinational Business Finance* (Reading, MA: Addison-Wesley, 1997), 480–508.

[18]International Chamber of Commerce, *Uniform Customs and Practice for Documentary Credit/1993 Revision* (New York: ICC Publishing Corp., 1993).

FIGURE 11.6 Letter of Credit: Process and Parties

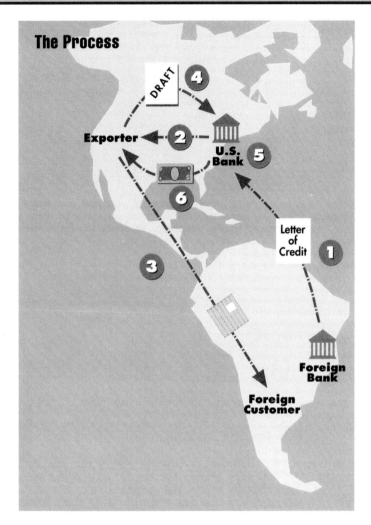

SOURCE: Faren L. Foster and Lynn S. Hutchins, "Six Steps to Quicker Collection of Export Letters of Credit," *Export Today* 9 (November–December 1993): 26–30. Reprinted with permission from *Export Today* magazine.

The letter of credit provides advantages to both the exporter and the importer, which explains its wide use. The approach substitutes the credit of the bank for the credit of the buyer and is as good as the issuing bank's access to dollars. In custom-made orders, an irrevocable letter of credit may help the exporter secure pre-export financing. The importer will not need to pay until the documents have arrived and been accepted by the bank, thus giving an additional float. The major caveat is that the exporter has to comply with all the terms of the letter of credit.[19] For example, if the documents state that shipment is made in crates measuring 4 × 4 × 4 and the goods are shipped in crates measuring 4 × 3 × 4, the bank will not honor the letter of credit. If there are changes, the letter of credit can be amended to ensure payment. Importers have occasionally been accused of creating discrepancies to slow down the payment process or to drive down the agreed-upon price.[20] In some cases, the

[19]Vincent M. Maulella, "Payment Pitfalls for the Unwary," *World Trade*, April 1999, 76–79.

[20]Erika Morphy, "Form vs. Format," *Export Today* (August 1999), 47–52.

FIGURE 11.7 Letter of Credit

First Union National Bank
International Division

IRREVOCABLE LETTER OF CREDIT
DECEMBER 05, 20____

SAMPLE COPY

ABC EXPORTERS, LTD.
9876 FIRST STREET
ANYWHERE, JAPAN

LETTER OF CREDIT NO.
L000000

WE HEREBY OPEN OUR IRREVOCABLE LETTER OF CREDIT IN YOUR FAVOR, FOR THE ACCOUNT
OF XYZ IMPORTERS, INC 1234 MAIN STREET, ANYWHERE, U.S.A. 54321 IN THE
AGGREGATE AMOUNT OF: USD100,000.00 (UNITED STATES DOLLARS ONE HUNDRED THOUSAND
AND 00/100) AVAILABLE WITH ANY BANK BY NEGOTIATION OF YOUR DRAFTS AT 90 DAYS
OF BILL OF LADING DATE ON FIRST UNION NATIONAL BANK WHEN ACCOMPANIED BY THE
FOLLOWING DOCUMENTS:

1. COMMERCIAL INVOICE IN TRIPLICATE
2. CERTIFICATE OF ORIGIN
3. PACKING LIST IN DUPLICATE
4. FULL SET CLEAN "ON BOARD" OCEAN BILL OF LADING ISSUED TO ORDER OF FIRST
   UNION NATIONAL BANK MARKED NOTIFY XYZ IMPORTERS, INC AND MARKED FREIGHT
   "COLLECT"

COVERING MERCHANDISE AS PER P.O. NUMBER 10205 DATED NOVEMBER 25, 20____

PARTIAL SHIPMENTS ALLOWED / TRANSHIPMENTS PROHIBITED

SHIPMENT FROM: FOB ANY JAPANESE PORT   FOR TRANSPORTATION TO: USA PORT
LATEST SHIPMENT DATE: JANUARY 15, 20 ____
EXPIRY DATE: JANUARY 31, 20____

SPECIAL CONDITIONS:
1. IF DOCUMENTS PRESENTED DO NOT COMPLY WITH THE TERMS AND CONDITIONS OF THIS
CREDIT, A DISCREPANCY FEE FOR EACH SET OF DOCUMENTS WILL BE DEDUCTED FROM ANY
REMITTANCE MADE TO THE BENEFICIARY UNDER THE CREDIT.
2. DOCUMENTS MUST BE PRESENTED FOR NEGOTIATION WITHIN 15 DAYS OF SHIPMENT
DATE, BUT WITHIN THE VALIDITY OF THE CREDIT.
3. DRAFT(S) DRAWN UNDER THIS CREDIT MUST STATE ON THEIR FACE "DRAWN UNDER
FIRST UNION NATIONAL BANK IRREVOCABLE LETTER CREDIT NUMBER L000000 DATED
DECEMBER 05, 20____" AND DATED SAME DATE AS ON BOARD DATE OF BILL OF LADING.

WE HEREBY ENGAGE WITH DRAWERS, ENDORSERS, AND BONA FIDE HOLDERS OF DRAFTS
DRAWN UNDER AND IN COMPLIANCE WITH THE TERMS AND CONDITIONS OF THIS CREDIT,
THAT THE SAME SHALL BE HONORED ON DUE PRESENTATION AND DELIVERY OF DOCUMENTS
TO THE DRAWEE. THE AMOUNT OF ANY DRAFT(S) DRAWN UNDER THIS CREDIT MUST,
CONCURRENTLY WITH NEGOTIATION, BE ENDORSED BY THE NEGOTIATING BANK ON THE
REVERSE HEREOF.

UNLESS EXPRESSLY STATED HEREIN, THIS CREDIT IS SUBJECT TO UNIFORM CUSTOMS AND
PRACTICES FOR DOCUMENTARY CREDITS PUBLICATION NO. 500.

DIRECT ALL INQUIRIES TO FIRST UNION NATIONAL BANK, INTERNATIONAL DIVISION,
301 SOUTH TRYON STREET/T-7, CHARLOTTE, NC 28288-0742.

SINCERELY,   **SAMPLE COPY**

AUTHORIZED SIGNATURE
FIRST UNION NATIONAL BANK
CHARLOTTE, NORTH CAROLINA

 www.firstunion.com

exporter must watch out for fraudulent letters of credit, especially in the case of less-developed countries. For example, exporters are advised to ship to Nigeria only on the basis of an irrevocable letter of credit, confirmed by their bank, even after the credentials of the Nigerian contact have been established.[21] With the increasing amount of e-commerce, things will have to change. Solutions include on-line issuance and status reporting on letters of credit, creating a worldwide network of electronic trade hubs, and offering a smart card that will allow participating companies to transact financial business on-line.[22]

The letter of credit is a promise to pay but not a means of payment. Actual payment is accomplished by means of a **draft,** which is similar to a personal check. Like a check, it is an order by one party to pay another. Most drafts are documentary, which means that the buyer must obtain possession of various shipping documents before obtaining possession of the goods involved in the transaction. Clean drafts—orders to pay without any other documents—are mainly used by multinational corporations in their dealings with their own subsidiaries and in well-established business relationships.

In **documentary collection** situations, the seller ships the goods, and the shipping documents and the draft demanding payment are presented to the importer through banks acting as the seller's agent. The draft, also known as the bill of exchange, may be either a sight draft or a time draft (see Figure 11.8). A sight draft documents against payment and is payable on presentation to the drawee, that is, the party to whom the draft is addressed. A time draft documents against acceptance and allows for a delay of 30, 60, 90, 120, or 180 days. When a time draft is drawn on and accepted by a bank, it becomes a **banker's acceptance,** which is sold in the short-term money market. Time drafts drawn on and accepted by a business firm become trader's acceptances, which are normally not marketable. A draft is presented to the drawee, who accepts it by writing or stamping a notice of acceptance on it. With both sight and time drafts, the buyer can effectively extend the period of credit by avoiding receipt of the goods. A date draft requires payment on a specified date, regardless of the date on which the goods and the draft are accepted by the buyer.

To illustrate, an exporter may have a time draft accepted by Citibank for $1 million to be paid in 90 days. Like many exporters who extend credit for competitive reasons, the firm may have immediate need for the funds. It could contact an acceptance dealer and sell the acceptance at a discount, with the rate depending on the market rate of interest. If the annual interest rate was 12 percent, for example, the acceptance could be sold for $970,873 ($1 million divided by 1.03). Interest rates for banker's acceptances of various maturities are listed daily in the *The Wall Street Journal.*

Even if the draft is not sold in the secondary market, the exporter may convert it into cash by **discounting**. To discount the draft simply means that the draft is sold to a bank at a discount from face value. If the discounting is with recourse, the exporter is liable for the payment to the bank if the importer defaults. If the discounting is without recourse, the exporter will not be liable even if the importer does not pay the bank. Discounting without recourse is known as factoring or, in the case of higher credit risk and longer-term receivables, forfaiting.

The normal manner of doing business in the domestic market is **open account** (open terms). The exporter selling on open account removes both real and psychological barriers to importing. However, no written evidence of the debt exists, and the exporter has to put full faith in the references contacted. Worst of all, there is no guarantee of payment. If the debt turns bad, the problems of overseas litigation are considerable. Bad debts are normally easier to avoid than to rectify. In less-developed

[21]"Fraudulent Business Activity Is Growing in Nigeria, and Efforts Are Often Made to Involve Foreign Firms," *Business America,* January 1992, 21–22.

[22]Miles Maguire, "Beyond the LC?" *Export Today,* June 1998, 32–37.

FIGURE 11.8 Documentary Collection

(1) U.S. $ _500,000.00_	(2) _Anywhere, Japan_	(3) _December 17, 20 00_

AT _____Sight_____(4)_____ DAYS AFTER _____(5)_____

(6)
PAY TO THE ORDER OF _____ABC Exporters, Ltd._____

Five Hundred Thousand and 00/100 U.S. (7) ------------------------ DOLLARS

VALUE RECEIVED AND CHARGE THE SAME TO THE ACCOUNT OF:
(9)   (8) _"Drawn under First Union National Bank_
TO: _First Union National Bank_   _Irrevocable L/C No. L000000 dated_
    Charlotte, N.C.   _December 4, 2000"_

                                            (10)   _ABC Exporters, Ltd._

                                                   (12)
NO. _____(11) ABC35_   _____
                                                   (AUTHORIZES SIGNATURE)

SAMPLE COPY

(1) U.S. $ _100,000.00_	(2) _Anywhere, Japan_	(3) _December 17, 2000_

AT _90 Days of B/L Date_(4)_____ DAYS AFTER _____(5)_____

(6)
PAY TO THE ORDER OF _____ABC Exporters, Ltd._____

One Hundred Thousand and 00/100 U.S. (7) ----------------------- DOLLARS

VALUE RECEIVED AND CHARGE THE SAME TO THE ACCOUNT OF:
(9)   (8) _"Drawn under First Union National Bank_
TO: _First Union National Bank_   _Irrevocable L/C No. L000000 dated_
    Charlotte, N.C.   _December 5, 2000"_

                                            (10)   _ABC Exporters, Ltd._

                                                   (12)
NO. _____(11) ABC18_   _____
                                                   (AUTHORIZES SIGNATURE)

SAMPLE COPY

countries, importers will usually need proof of debt in the application to the central bank for hard currency, which will not allow them to deal on an open-account basis. Again, open account is used by multinationals in their internal transactions and when there is implicit trust among the partners.

The most favorable term to the importer is **consignment selling,** which allows the importer to defer payment until the goods are actually sold. This approach places all the burden on the exporter, and its use should be carefully weighed against the objectives of the transaction. If the exporter wants entry into a specific market through specific intermediaries, consignment selling may be the only method of gaining acceptance by intermediaries. The arrangement will require clear understanding as to the parties' responsibilities—for example, which party is responsible for insurance until the goods have actually been sold. If the goods are not sold, returning them will be costly and time-consuming; for example, there is getting through customs or paying, avoiding paying, or trying to get refunds on duties. Due to its burdensome characteristics, consignment is not widely used.

Adjusting to Foreign Currency Fluctuations

Another important matter to be resolved in payment for exports is the currency in which to invoice. Unless currencies are closely linked, for example, between the twelve countries of Euroland, exchange rate movements may harm one or the other of the parties. If the price is quoted in the exporter's currency, the exporter will get exactly the price it wants but may lose some sales as a result. The currency chosen will depend on the parties themselves and the particular transaction. If the exporter needs the sale, the invoice may be in the importer's currency, and the exchange risk will be the burden of the exporter. Some exporters, if they are unable to secure payment in their own currency, try to minimize the risk by negotiating shorter terms of payment, such as ten or fifteen days. Exchange risks may be a result of an appreciating or depreciating currency or result from a revaluation or devaluation of a currency by a central bank. Assume that a U.S. importer bought $250,000 or DM500,000 worth of goods from a German company, which agreed to accept U.S. dollars for payment in 90 days. At the time of the quotation, the exchange rate for $1 was DM2.00, whereas at the time of payment, it had changed to DM1.90. This means that the German exporter, instead of receiving DM500,000, winds up with DM475,000.

When invoicing in foreign currencies, an exporter cannot insulate itself from the problems of currency movements, but it can at least know how much it will eventually receive by using the mechanism of the **forward exchange market**. In essence, the exporter gets a bank to agree to a rate at which it will buy the foreign currency the exporter will receive when the importer makes payment. The rate is expressed as either a premium or a discount on the current spot rate. The risk still remains if the exchange rate does not move as anticipated, and the exporter may be worse off than if it had not bought forward.

U.S. exporters have faced both high and low values of the dollar with respect to other currencies in the past ten years: low values in the early to mid-1990s and high values in the late 1990s. When the exporter's domestic currency is weak, strategies should include stressing the price advantage to customers and expanding the scale and scope of the export operation. Sourcing can be shifted to domestic markets and the export price can be subjected to full-costing. However, under the opposite scenario, the exporter needs to engage in non-price competition, minimizing the price dimension as much as possible. Costs should be reduced by every means, including enhancing productivity. At this time, the exporter should prioritize efforts to markets that show the greatest returns. Alternatives available to marketers under differing currency conditions are summarized in Table 11.3.

TABLE 11.3 Exporter Strategies under Varying Currency Conditions

WEAK	STRONG
1. Stress price benefits	**1.** Non-price competition
2. Expand product line	**2.** Improve productivity/cost reduction
3. Shift sourcing to domestic market	**3.** Sourcing overseas
4. Exploit all possible export opportunities	**4.** Prioritize exports
5. Cash-for-goods trade	**5.** Countertrade with weak currency countries
6. Full-costing	**6.** Marginal-cost pricing
7. Speed repatriation	**7.** Slow collections
8. Minimize expenditure in local currency	**8.** Buy needed services abroad

SOURCE: Adapted from S. Tamer Cavusgil, "Unraveling the Mystique of Export Pricing," *Business Horizons* 31 (May–June 1988): 54–63.

Whatever the currency movements are, the marketer needs to decide how to adjust pricing to international customers in view of either a more favorable or an unfavorable domestic currency rate. A U.S. exporter, during a strong dollar, has three alternatives. First, making no change in the dollar price would result in a less favorable price in foreign currencies and, most likely, lower sales, especially if no corrective marketing steps are taken. Second, the export price could be decreased in conjunction with increases in the value of the dollar to maintain stable export prices in foreign currencies. This first alternative is an example of **pass-through,** while the second alternative features the **absorption** approach; i.e., the increase in the price is absorbed into the margin of the product, possibly even resulting in a loss. For pass-through to work, customers have to have a high level of preference for the exporter's product. In some cases, exporters may have no choice but to pass most of the increase to the customer due to the cost structure of the firm. Exporters using the absorption approach have as their goal long-term market-share maintenance especially in a highly competitive environment.

The third alternative is to pass through only a share of the increase, maintaining sales if possible while at the same time preserving profitability. On the average, exporters to the United States absorbed about half the decline in the trading value of the dollar during the mid- to late 1980s. If prices had fully reflected the currency adjustment, they would have risen 34 percent; instead they rose only about 19 percent.[23]

The strategic response depends on market conditions and may result in different strategies for each market or product. Destination-specific adjustment of mark-ups in response to exchange-rate changes have been referred to as **pricing-to-market.**[24] For example, a mark-up change will be more substantial in a price-sensitive market and/or product category. In addition, the exporter needs to consider the reactions of local competitors, who may either keep their prices stable (hoping that price increases in imports will improve their position) or increase their prices along with those of imports in search of more profits. U.S. automakers were criticized for raising their domestic prices at a time when Japanese imports were forced up by the higher value of the yen during the mid-1990s. Instead of trying to capture more market share, the automakers went for more profits.[25] If the exporter faces a favorable domestic currency rate, pass-through means providing international customers with a more favorable price, while absorption means that the exporter keeps the export price stable and pockets a higher level of profits.

Some exporters prefer price stability to the greatest possible degree and allow mark-ups to vary in maintaining stable local currency prices. Harley-Davidson, for example, maintains its price to distributors as long as the spot exchange rate does not move more than plus or minus 5 percent from the rate in effect when the quote was made. If the movement is an additional 5 percentage points in either direction, Harley and its distributors will share the costs or benefits. Beyond that the price will have to be renegotiated to bring it more in line with current exchange rates and the economic and competitive realities of the market.[26] During times of exchange-rate gains, rather than lower the price, some exporters use other support tools (such as training and trade deals) with their distributors or customers, on the premise that increasing prices after a future currency swing in the opposite direction may be difficult.

[23]"How Dollar Weakness Affects Pricing Policies of U.S. and Non-U.S. Firms," *Business International*, December 7, 1988, 387.

[24]Paul R. Krugman, "Pricing-to-Market When the Exchange Rate Changes," in S. W. Arndt and J. D. Robinson, eds., *Real-Financial Linkages among Open Economies* (Cambridge, MA: MIT Press, 1987), 49–70.

[25]"Did U.S. Car Makers Err by Raising Prices When the Yen Rose?" *The Wall Street Journal*, April 18, 1988, A1, A14.

[26]Michael H. Moffett, "Harley-Davidson: Hedging Hogs," in Michael R. Czinkota, Ilkka A. Ronkainen, and Michael H. Moffett, *International Business* (Fort Worth, TX: The Dryden Press, 2000): 802–805.

| **TABLE 11.4** | Absorption vs. Pass-Through: Japanese and German Automarketer Behavior |

MODEL	REAL DOLLAR APPRECIATION	REAL RETAIL PRICE CHANGE IN US MARKET
Honda Civic 2-Dr. Sedan	39%	−7%
Nissan 200 SX 2-Dr.	39	−10
Toyota Cressida 4-Dr.	39	6
BMW 320i 2-Dr. Sedan	42	−8
BMW 733i 4-Dr. Sedan	42	−17
Mercedes 300 TD Sta. Wgn.	42	−39

SOURCE: Jospeh A. Gagnon and Michael M. Knetter, "Markup Adjustment and Exchange Rate Fluctuations: Evidence from Panel Data on Automobile Exports," *Journal of International Money and Finance* 14 (Number 2, 1995): 289–310.

According to a study on exporter responses to foreign-exchange rate changes over a period of 1973 and 1997, Japanese exporters have the highest tendency to dampen the effects of exchange-rate fluctuations in foreign-currency export prices in both directions by adjusting their home-currency prices.[27] Furthermore, Japanese exporters put a larger emphasis on stabilizing the foreign currency prices of their exports during a weak yen than when the yen is strong. German exporters display completely the opposite behavior. The data in Table 11.4 for German and Japanese auto exports support these findings for the period in the early 1990s, when the dollar appreciated against the German mark and the Japanese yen.

Beyond **price manipulation**, other adjustment strategies exist. They include the following:

1. Market re-focus. If lower values of the target market currencies make exporting more difficult by, for example, making collections times longer, marketers may start looking at other markets for growth. For example, U.S. construction industry sales to Mexico grew nearly by 150 percent in 1998 after markets in Thailand and Indonesia dried up.[28] In some cases, the emphasis may switch to the domestic market, where market share gain at the expense of imports may be the most efficient way to grow. Currency appreciation does not always lead to a dire situation for the exporter. Domestic competitors may depend very heavily on imported components and may not able to take advantage of the currency-related price pressure on the exporter. The manufacturing sectors of Indonesia, Malaysia, Philippines, and Thailand use over 30 percent imported parts and raw materials in the production process.[29]

2. Streamlined operations. The marketer may start using more aggressive methods of collection, insisting on letters of credit and insurance to guarantee payments. Some have tightened control of their distribution networks by cutting layers or taking over the responsibility from independent intermediaries. On the product side, marketers may focus on offerings that are less sensitive to exchange-rate changes. Streamlined operations may also include shifting procurement to more economical locations.

3. Shift in production. Especially when currency shifts are seen as long-term, marketers will increase direct investment. With the high value of the yen in the early 1990s, Japanese companies shifted production bases to lower-cost locations or

---

[27]Saied Mahdavi, "Do German, Japanese, and U.S. Export Prices Asymmetrically Respond to Exchange Rate Changes?" *Contemporary Economic Policy* 18 (January 2000): 70–81.

[28]"Turning Small into a Big Advantage," *Business Week*, July 13, 1998, 42–44.

[29]"Competitive Exports, Sky High Imports," *Financial Mail*, October 2, 1998, 19.

closer to final customers. Matsushita Electric, for example, moved a substantial share of its production to Southeast Asian countries, while earthmoving-equipment maker Komatsu launched a $1 billion joint venture with Texas-based Dresser Industries to build equipment in the United States.[30]

In some cases, even adverse developments in the currency market have not had an effect on international markets or marketers. During the currency crisis in Asia, U.S. oil toolmakers and oil-field service companies were never hurt by the high value of the dollar because their expertise was in demand. Similarly, many U.S. firms such as IBM did not suffer because their exported products are both built and sold in other countries. In some cases, imported goods may be in demand because no domestic production exists, which is the case in the United States with consumer goods such as electronics and cameras.

Price Negotiations

The final export price is negotiated in person or electronically. Since pricing is the most sensitive issue in business negotiations, the exporter should be ready to discuss price as part of a comprehensive package and should avoid price concessions early on in the negotiations.[31]

An importer may reject an exporter's price at the outset in the hopes of gaining an upper hand or obtaining concessions later on. These concessions include discounts, an improved product, better terms of sales/payment, and other possibly costly demands. The exporter should prepare for this by obtaining relevant information on the target market and the customer, as well as by developing counterproposals for possible objections. For example, if the importer states that better offers are available, the exporter should ask for more details on such offers and try to convince the buyer that the exporter's total package is indeed superior. In the rare case that the importer accepts the initial bid without comment, the exporter should make sure the extended bid was correct by checking the price calculations and the Incoterm used. Furthermore, competitive prices should be revisited to ascertain that the price reflects market conditions accurately.

During the actual negotiations, pricing decisions should be postponed until all of the major substantive issues have been agreed upon. Since quality and reliability of delivery are the critical dimensions of supplier choice (in addition to price), especially when long-term export contracts are in question, the exporter may want to reduce pressure on price by emphasizing these two areas and how they fit with the buyer's needs.

Leasing

Organizational customers frequently prefer to lease major equipment, making it a $183 billion industry. About 30 percent of all capital goods (50 percent of commercial aircraft) are leased in the United States, with eight out of ten companies involved in leasing.[32] Although a major force in the United States, Japan, and Germany, leasing has grown significantly elsewhere as well; for example, one of the major international trade activities of Russia, in addition to shipping and oil, is equipment leasing.

[30]"The Cheap Buck Gives Japan a Yen for Asia," *Business Week*, May 23, 1994, 52.

[31]Claude Cellich, "Negotiating Strategies: The Question of Price," *International Trade Forum* 5 (April–June 1991): 10–13.

[32]Equipment Leasing Association, **http://www.elaonline.com**.

The Russians view leasing not only as a potential source of hard currency but also as a way of attracting customers who would be reluctant to buy an unfamiliar product.

Trade liberalization around the world is expected to benefit lessors both through expected growth in target economies and through the eradication of country laws and regulations hampering outside lessors. For example, the NAFTA agreement and the pent-up demand for machinery, aircraft, and heavy equipment for road building provide a promising opportunity for U.S. leasing companies in Mexico.[33]

For the marketing manager who sells products such as printing presses, computers, forklift trucks, and machine tools, leasing may allow penetration of markets that otherwise might not exist for the firm's products if the firm had to sell them outright. Balance-of-payment problems have forced some countries to prohibit the purchase and importation of equipment into their markets; an exception has been made if the import is to be leased.[34] In developing countries, the fact that leased products are serviced by the lessor may be a major benefit because of the shortage of trained personnel and scarcity of spare parts. At present, leasing finances over $40 billion in new vehicles and equipment each year in developing countries. The main benefit for the lessor is that total net income, after charging off pertinent repair and maintenance expenses, is often higher than it would be if the unit was sold.

In today's competitive business climate, traditional financial considerations are often only part of the asset-financing formula. Many leasing companies have become more than a source of capital, developing new value-added services that have taken them from asset financiers to asset managers or forming relationships with others who can provide these services. In some cases, lessors have even evolved into partners in business activities. El Camino Resources International, which has leased assets of $836 million (half of it outside the United States), targets high-growth, technology-dependent companies such as Internet providers and software developers for their hardware, software, and technical services needs, including e-commerce as well as Internet and intranet development.[35]

Dumping

Inexpensive imports often trigger accusations of dumping—that is, selling goods overseas for less than in the exporter's home market or at a price below the cost of production, or both. Charges of dumping range from those of Florida tomato growers, who said that Mexican vegetables were being dumped across the border, to those of the Canadian Anti-Dumping Tribunal, which ruled that U.S. firms were dumping radioactive diagnostic reagents in Canada. Such disputes have become quite common, especially in highly competitive industries such as computer chips, ball bearings, and steel. For example, 12 U.S. steel makers and the steelworkers' union asked the U.S. government to investigate its complaint that Japan, Russia, and Brazil have dumped hot-rolled carbon steel on the U.S. market at unfair prices, tripling their sales in the last three years. The petition sought tariffs ranging from 28 to 199 percent to offset unfair margins.[36] Similarly, the European Union was asked to investigate dumping of made fibers by Asian producers, which grew 56 percent in 1998 alone to account for 12 percent of the market. The concern by the European fiber industry was that Asian

[33]Elnora M. Uzzelle, "American Equipment Leasing Companies Should Consider the International Arena," *Business America*, June 28, 1993, 11–12.

[34]David A. Ricks and Saeed Samiee, "Leasing: It May Be Right Abroad Even When It Is Not at Home," *Journal of International Business Studies* 5 (Fall 1974): 87–90.

[35]**http://www.elcamino.com**

[36]"U.S. Steel Files Trade Cases against Three Nations," *Metal Center News* 38 (November 1998): 90–91.

producers were selling their product in the European market below cost of production, simply to generate cash flow for their beleaguered domestic operations.[37]

Dumping ranges from predatory dumping to unintentional dumping. **Predatory dumping** refers to a tactic whereby a foreign firm intentionally sells at a loss in another country in order to increase its market share at the expense of domestic producers, which amounts to an international price war. **Unintentional dumping** is the result of time lags between the dates of sales transaction, shipment, and arrival. Prices, including exchange rates, can change in such a way that the final sales price turns out to be below the cost of production or below the price prevailing in the exporter's home market. It has been argued that current dumping laws, especially in the United States, do not take into adequate account such developments as floating exchange rates, which make dumping appear to be more widespread.[38]

In the United States, domestic producers may petition the government to impose antidumping duties on imports alleged to be dumped (see *The International Marketplace 11.4*). The duty is imposed if the International Trade Administration within the Department of Commerce determines that sales have occurred at less than fair market value and if the U.S. International Trade Commission finds that domestic industry is being, or is threatened with being, materially injured by the imports. The remedy is an **antidumping duty** equal to the dumping margin. International agreements and U.S. law provide for **countervailing duties**, which may be imposed on imports that are found to be subsidized by foreign governments and which are designed to offset the advantages imports would otherwise receive from the subsidy. The prevalence of anti-dumping actions has increased sharply in the 1990s. In 1990, the United States had 193 anti-dumping orders in place, with other members of the WTO having 212. By 1998, the U.S. number was 294, while other countries had registered a total of 538.[39]

Governmental action against dumping and subsidized exports violating WTO may result in hurting the very industries seeking relief. Action against Russian or Brazilian steel, for example, could result in retaliatory measures against U.S. steelmakers, who themselves export billions of dollars' worth of steel products. European governments have also threatened to retaliate against U.S. exports of other products.

In some cases, dumping suits have strong competitive motivations, for example, to discourage an aggressive competitor by accusing it of selling at unfair prices. Antidumping and unfair subsidy suits have led in some cases to formal agreements on voluntary restraints, whereby foreign producers agree that they will supply only a certain percentage of the U.S. market. One such arrangement is the semiconductor trade agreements signed by the United States and Japan in 1986, 1991, and 1996. The agreements required the Japanese to stop selling computer chips below cost and to try to increase sales of foreign-made computer chips in Japan.[40]

To minimize the risk of being accused of dumping (as well to be protected from dumping), the marketer can focus on value-added products and increase differentiation by including services in the product offering. If the company operates in areas made sensitive by virtue of the industry (such as electronics) or by the fact that local competition is economically vulnerable yet powerful with respect to the government, it may seek to collaborate with local companies in gaining market access, for example.[41]

[37]"EU Charges Asian Fiber Dumping," *Textile World*, May 1999, 134.

[38]Paul Magnusson, "Bring Anti Dumping Laws Up to Date," *Business Week*, July 19, 1999, 45.

[39]Thomas Klitgaard and Karen Schiele, "Free Trade versus Fair Trade: The Dumping Issue," *Current Issues in Economics and Finance* 4 (August 1998): 1–6.

[40]Edward L. Hudgins, "U.S.–Japan Semiconductor Agreement," *Regulation* 19 (Number 3, 1996): 11–15 and "Chip Pact Falls Short of Goals," *New York Times*, August 2, 1988, D1.

[41]Delener Nejdet, "An Ethical and Legal Synthesis of Dumping: Growing Concerns in International Marketing," *Journal of Business Ethics* 17 (November 1998): 1747–1753.

THE INTERNATIONAL MARKETPLACE 11.4

Dumping in the United States

U.S. LAW PROHIBITS DUMPING, but the federal government has been cautious in enforcing the law, especially in the case of allies. In the 1970s, Timken had to sue the U.S. government to force it to carry out its own dumping order against Japanese tapered roller bearings. Zenith labored for a decade to get U.S. dumping duties assessed against Japanese TV manufacturers, and then the governments of the two countries negotiated the penalty down to 10 cents on the dollar. Three times Hitachi was charged with dumping different types of semiconductors. But by the time the cases were resolved, Hitachi was dumping a whole new generation of chips. As a result, the Japanese doubled their U.S. market share from 12 percent to 24 percent.

Timken, Smith Corona, Zenith, and the semiconductor industry claim that the way the United States calculates dumping margins—the difference between the home market price and the import price as a percentage of import price—makes it harder to prove dumping in the United States than in Europe. This is especially true when transactions include so-called related parties, such as manufacturers and their in-house distributors. In such cases, the United States, unlike most of its competitors, includes profits in its import price estimate (making the price higher) and excludes indirect selling costs in its calculation of the home market price (making that price lower). As a result, dumping margins can be lower in the United States than in Europe.

Importers counter that these companies are trying to use the dumping laws as protection against foreign competition. In October 1991, the U.S. Department of Commerce, after complaints from the U.S. paper industry, determined that Belgian, British, Finnish, French, and German producers had dumped lightweight coated magazine paper in the United States. The European companies vehemently denied any intentional dumping and referred to the substantial fluctuations in the value of the dollar as the main reason for lower prices. In December, the International Trade Commission exonerated the companies from having injured U.S. industry. Despite the favorable ruling, the Europeans had already suffered injury themselves. Sales had, in some companies' cases, dropped by half (due to U.S. customers' fears of price hikes caused by duties); furthermore, they had to pay substantial legal costs incurred during the defense.

While some prefer doing away with antidumping laws entirely, based on the premise that no customer was ever hurt by lowest possible prices, a better solution is to streamline dumping laws. For example, in cases where foreign price-fixing cartels are involved in strategic and capital-intensive industries such as steel and semiconductors, the barrier for proving dumping should be lowered and the process made swifter. Some argue that antitrust legislation should cover threats to domestic industries by the actions of foreign rivals.

SOURCES: Paul Magnusson, "Bring Antidumping Laws Up to Date," *Business Week*, July 19, 1999, 45; "Hintojen Lasku Lamautti Kaupan, Dumpingin Jalkeen," *Kauppalehti*, January 15, 1992, 4; and Ann Reilly Dowd, "What to Do about Trade Policy," *Fortune*, May 8, 1989, 106–112.

www.ita.doc.gov

SUMMARY

The status of price has changed to that of a dynamic element of the marketing mix. This has resulted from both internal and external pressures on business firms. Management must analyze the interactive effect that pricing has on the other elements of the mix and how pricing can assist in meeting the overall goals of the marketing strategy.

The process of setting an export price must start with the determination of an appropriate cost baseline and should include variables such as export-related costs to avoid compromising the desired profit margin. The quotation needs to spell out the respective responsibilities of the buyer and the seller in getting the goods to the intended destination. The terms of sale indicate these responsibilities but may also be used as a competitive tool. The terms of payment have to be clarified to ensure that the exporter will indeed get paid for the products and services rendered. Facilitating agents such as freight forwarders and banks are often used to absorb some of the risk and uncertainty in preparing price quotations and establishing terms of payment.

Exporters also need to be ready to defend their pricing practices. Competitors may petition their own government to investigate the exporter's pricing to determine the degree to which it reflects costs and prices prevailing in the exporter's domestic market.

QUESTIONS FOR DISCUSSION

1. Propose scenarios in which export prices are higher/lower than domestic prices.
2. What are the implications of price escalation?
3. Discuss the use of the currency of quotation as a competitive tool.
4. Argue for the use of more inclusive shipping terms from the marketing point of view.
5. Suggest different importer reactions to a price offer and how you, as an exporter, could respond to them.
6. Who is harmed and who is helped by dumping?
7. Banks have come up with ways of using the Internet for functions beyond the initiation of a transaction. Imperial

Bank (**www.imperialbank.com/intlbank/swiftrade**) has introduced a new program called SWIFTrade that allows for on-line issuance and status reporting on letters of credit. What are the benefits for the exporter using this service?
8. The International Trade Administration monitors cases filed against U.S. exporters on charges of dumping, to assist them in the investigations and their subsequent defense. Using their data on such cases (**www.ita.doc.gov/import_admin/records/**), focus on a few countries (e.g., EU, Canada, South Africa, Japan) and assess what industries seem to come under the most scrutiny.

RECOMMENDED READINGS

Contino, Richard M. and Tony Valmis, eds. *Handbook of Equipment Leasing: A Deal Maker's Guide.* New York: AMACOM, 1996.

Hinkelman, Edward G. and Molly Thurmond. *A Short Course in International Payments.* New York: World Trade Press, 1998.

Jackson, John H. and Edwin A. Vermulst, eds. *Antidumping Law and Practice.* Ann Arbor, MI: University of Michigan Press, 1989.

Johnson, Thomas E. *Export/Import Procedures and Documentation.* New York: AMACOM, 1997.

Palmer, Howard. *International Trade Finance and Pre-Export Finance.* London: Euromoney Publications, 1999.

Ramberg, Jan. *ICC Guide to Incoterms.* Paris: ICC Publishing, Inc., 2000.

U.S. Department of Commerce. *A Basic Guide to Exporting.* New York: World Trade Press, 2000.

U.S. Department of Treasury. *A Basic Guide to Importing.* Lincolnwood, IL: NTC Business Books, 1995.

Venedikian, Harry M. and Gerald A. Warfield. *Export-Import Financing.* New York: John Wiley & Co., 1996.

International Communications

THE INTERNATIONAL MARKETPLACE 12.1

Making Deals in Any Language

Effective communication as a cornerstone of marketing becomes even more important in the international arena. Whether it is a question of generating promotional campaigns or negotiating to set up a marketing system, the international marketer needs to understand what pleases or displeases the target audience or counterpart.

One interaction occurred between representatives of Atacs Products, Inc.—a Seattle-based supplier of aircraft repair systems—and Aviation Transactions Conseils, which stocks those supplies, in Juilly, France, during the Goodwill Games International Trade Exhibition in Seattle.

Terry Cooney, Atacs's sales manager, discovered a mutual interest during a chance meeting with ATC's Pierre-Jean Back, president, and Patrick Naumann, sales manager. Cooney then arranged a more formal meeting, and they reconvened with Andrew Thibault, an interpreter.

Cooney began his presentation—speaking slowly and clearly, but without condescension—on technical fronts. During the product demonstration for a heat-sensitive device, Cooney took care to speak in terms of ambient temperature in Bordeaux instead of just saying "72 degrees." And Naumann understood English well enough to laugh at Cooney's references to misuse of the product causing "permanently curly hair." Throughout the presentation, Thibault softly translated, primarily for Back's benefit. Occasionally, the demonstration slowed if either had a question. After the demonstration, Cooney explained Atacs's stance on foreign distributors. "If you start losing business," he joked, "I'm in the Irish mafia."

He mentioned several sales techniques, whom to contact, and the latitude of offers ATC would be able to make to customers. Naumann and Back conferred in French, and then Thibault presented Back's objection: What would prevent Atacs from ending its agreement once ATC had nurtured the territory?

Cooney said he didn't "know how to overcome" that objection. Then, force of personality began to transcend language. "I am soon to be the biggest (expletive) you ever met," Cooney said, "but I'm honest. I don't even cheat in tennis against my sons."

Cooney closed with two more appeals, posed vehemently yet calmly. One mentioned the amount of dollars it could cost ATC not to accept the arrangement. The other: "If you place an order, you still have 90 days for payment, unless the dollar drops against the franc. Then we'll give you 120 days." They all laughed at that remark, but ATC's representatives still did not agree. Cooney said, "That's all I've got to say."

After the meeting, Back said in an interview, "I'm not suspicious of this gentleman, in particular, but it's the general manner of doing business in the American way. In general, when working with Americans, when things are going fine, there's no problem. But when the market starts to go down, Americans tend to bail out. Good business relationships take time to develop. . . . You know that relations are really good when there are problems with money and they'll still allow you to operate.

"However, I would not trust a large American company. There's such a turnover rate in employees that from one day to another it changes completely, so it's really hard to have continuous relations. The best prospects for American businesses to operate in France is with small businesses because there's a more personal relationship."

It would have been useful for Mr. Cooney to know about the French as negotiating partners. U.S.-centric references should be avoided, especially self-congratulatory ones, which are perceived as arrogant. Any notion of superiority or the attitude that "We are No. 1" can rub a French businessperson the wrong way. U.S. speakers often try to export baseball, football, or golf metaphors they use at home but that are mostly unknown abroad. However, if one is speaking in France or to the French, relating sports metaphors to World Cup soccer (and especially to the French success in 1998) is appropriate. Throughout the preliminary and middle stages of negotiating, the French manager will judge counterparts carefully on their intellectual skills and their ability to react quickly and with authority. As one French manager put it: "Sometimes I am more impressed by brilliant savvy than by a well-reasoned argument." Because the French education stresses mathematics and logic, doing business is a highly in-

tellectual process for French managers. One __ the style of French negotiators was the most aggre__ thirteen diverse cultural groups analyzed.

SOURCES: Sherrie Zhan, "Trade Shows Mean Big Business," World Trade, September 1999, 88; Dave Zielinski, "Going Global," Presentations 12 (October 1998): 40–48; John L. Graham, "Vis-à-Vis International Business Negotiations," in International Business Negotiations, Jean-Claude D. Usunier and Pervez N. Ghauri, end. (London: The Dryden Press, 1996), chapter 7; "Negotiating in Europe," Hemispheres, July 1994, 43–47; and David Jacobson, "Marketers Swap More than Goodwill at Trade Show," Business Marketing 75 (September 1990): 48–51.

http://www.atacs.com

EFFECTIVE COMMUNICATION IS PARTICULARLY IMPORTANT in international marketing because of the geographic and psychological distances that separate a firm from its intermediaries and customers. By definition, communication is a process of establishing a "commonness" of thought between a sender and a receiver.[1] This process extends beyond the conveying of ideas to include persuasion and thus enables the marketing process to function more effectively and efficiently. Ideally, marketing communication is a dialogue that allows organizations and consumers to achieve mutually satisfying exchange agreements. This definition emphasizes the two-way nature of the process, with listening and responsiveness as integral parts. The majority of communication is verbal, but nonverbal communication and the concept of silent languages must also be considered because they often create challenges for international marketers, as seen in The International Marketplace 12.1.

This chapter will include an overview of the principles of marketing communications in international markets. Because face-to-face, buyer-seller negotiations are possibly the most fundamental marketing process,[2] guidelines for international business negotiations are first discussed. Second, the chapter will focus on the management of the international communications mix from the exporter's point of view. Because the exporter's alternatives may be limited by the entry mode and by resources available, the tools and the challenges are quite different from those of the multinational entity. We discuss the promotional approaches used by global marketers in Chapter 20.

The Marketing Communications Process

As shown in the communications model presented in Figure 12.1, effective communications requires three elements—the sender, the message, and the receiver—connected by a message channel. The process may begin with an unsolicited inquiry from

[1]Wilbur Schramm and Donald F. Roberts, The Process and Effects of Mass Communications (Urbana: University of Illinois Press, 1971), 12–17.

[2]John L. Graham, Dong Ki Kim, Chi-Yuan Lin, and Michael Robinson, "Buyer-Seller Negotiations around the Pacific Rim: Differences in Fundamental Exchange Processes," Journal of Consumer Research 15 (June 1988): 48–54.

FIGURE 12.1 **The Marketing Communications Process**

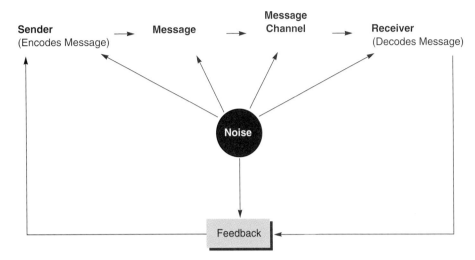

SOURCE: Terence A. Shimp, *Advertising, Promotion, and Supplemental Aspects of Integrated Marketing Communications* (Fort Worth, TX: The Dryden Press, 2000), 118.

a potential customer or as a planned effort by the marketer. Whatever the goal of the communications process, the sender needs to study receiver characteristics before encoding the message in order to achieve maximum impact. **Encoding** the message simply means converting it into symbolic form that is properly understood by the receiver. This is not a simple task, however. For example, if a Web site's order form asks only for typical U.S.-type address information, such as a zip code, and does not include anything for other countries, the would-be buyer abroad will interpret this as unwillingness to do business outside the United States. Similarly, if an export price is quoted on an ex-works basis (which includes only the cost of goods sold in the price), the buyer may not be interested in or be able to take responsibility for the logistics process and will go elsewhere.

The message channel is the path through which the message moves from sender (source) to receiver. This link that ties the receiver to the sender ranges from sound waves conveying the human voice in personal selling to transceivers or intermediaries such as print and broadcast media. Although technological advances (for example, fax, video conferencing, and the Internet) may have made buyer-seller negotiations more efficient, the fundamental process and its purpose have remained unchanged. Face-to-face contact is still necessary for two basic reasons. The first is the need for detailed discussion and explanation, and the second is the need to establish the rapport that forms the basis of lasting business relationships.

The message channel also exists in mass communications. Complications in international marketing may arise if a particular medium does not reach the targeted audience, which is currently the case for Internet communications, for example, due to varying on-line penetration rates around the world.[3] Other examples of complications are the banning of advertising for certain product categories, such as for cigarettes in most of Europe, and the fact that some marketing practices may not be allowed, such as direct selling in China.

Once a sender has placed a message into a channel or a set of channels and directed them to the intended destination, the completion of the process is dependent on the

[3]Joel Reedy, Shauna Schullo, and Kenneth Zimmerman, *Electronic Marketing* (Fort Worth, TX: The Dryden Press, 2000), chapter 17.

receiver's **decoding**—that is, transforming the message symbols back into thought. If there is an adequate amount of overlap between sender characteristics and needs reflected in the encoded message and receiver characteristics and needs reflected in the decoded message, the communications process has worked.

A message moving through a channel is subject to the influence of extraneous and distracting stimuli, which interfere with the intended accurate reception of the message. This interference is referred to as **noise.** In the international marketing context, noise might be a bad telephone connection, failure to express a quotation in the inquirer's system of currency and measurement, or lack of understanding of the recipient's environment, for example, having only an English-language web site. A U.S. company got a complaint from its Thai client complaining of an incomplete delivery: an order of 85,000 units was four short! When the U.S. company shipped in bulk, the number of units was estimated by weight. In Thailand, however, labor is cheap and materials expensive, allowing the client to hand count shipments. The solution was to provide a slight overage in each shipment without incurring a major expense but achieving customer satisfaction.[4] Similarly, a valid inquiry from overseas may not be considered seriously by an international marketer because of noise consisting of low-quality paper, grammatical errors, or a general appearance unlike domestic correspondence.

The international marketer should be most alert to cultural noise. The lack of language skills may hinder successful negotiations, whereas translation errors may render a promotional campaign or brochure useless. Similarly, nonverbal language and its improper interpretation may cause problems. For example, in the United States, lack of eye contact is a signal that something is wrong. This is not necessarily so in Japan, where the cultural style of communication involves markedly less eye contact.[5]

Regardless of whether the situation calls for interpersonal or mass communications, the collection and observation of feedback is necessary to analyze the success of the communications effort. The initial sender-receiver relationship is transposed, and interpretative skills similar to those needed in developing messages are needed. To make effective and efficient use of the communications requires considerable strategic planning. Examples of concrete ways in which feedback can be collected are inquiry cards or toll-free numbers distributed at trade shows to gather additional information. Similarly, the Internet allows marketers to track traffic flows and to install registration procedures that identify individuals and track their purchases over time.[6]

International Negotiations

When international marketing managers travel abroad to do business, they are frequently shocked to discover the extent to which the many variables of foreign behavior and custom complicate their efforts.[7] One of these differences is negotiation. The process of negotiation in most countries differs from that in the United States. This means that international marketing managers have to adjust their approaches to establishing rapport, information exchange, persuasion, and concession making if they are to be successful in dealing with their clients and partners, such as intermediaries.[8]

---

[4]"What's Working for Other American Companies," *International Sales & Marketing*, November 22, 1996, 5.

[5]John L. Graham, "A Hidden Cause of America's Trade Deficit with Japan," *Columbia Journal of World Business* 16 (Fall 1981): 5–15.

[6]John A. Quelch and Lisa R. Klein, "The Internet and International Marketing," *Sloan Management Review* 38 (Spring 1996): 60–75.

[7]Edward T. Hall, "The Silent Language of Overseas Business," *Harvard Business Review* 38 (May–June 1960): 87–96.

[8]John L. Graham, "Across the Negotiating Table from the Japanese," *International Marketing Review* 4 (Autumn 1986): 58–71.

The level of adjustment depends on the degree of cultural familiarity the parties have and their ability to use that familiarity effectively.[9] For example, in China, the ideal negotiator is someone who has an established relationship with the Chinese and is trusted by them. This is especially true in making the initial contact or stepping in if problems emerge. However, Chinese-Americans or overseas Chinese may be less effective in leading a negotiation. Where the Chinese are often willing to make an exception for visitors, they will expect ethnic Chinese to accept the Chinese way of doing things. The ideal team would, therefore, include a non-Chinese who understands the culture and an ethnic-Chinese individual. Together, the two can play "good guy–bad guy" roles and resist unreasonable demands.[10] If neither party is familiar with the counterpart's culture, outside facilitators should be employed.

Stages of the Negotiation Process

The process of international business negotiations can be divided into five stages: the offer, informal meetings, strategy formulation, negotiations, and implementation.[11] Which stage is emphasized and the length of the overall process will vary dramatically by culture. The negotiation process can be a short one, with the stages collapsing into one session, or a prolonged endeavor taking weeks. The differences between northern and southern Europe highlight this. Northern Europe, with its Protestant tradition and indoor culture, tends to emphasize the technical, the numerical, and the tested. Careful prenegotiations preparations are made. Southern Europe, with its Catholic background and open-air lifestyle, tends to favor personal networks, social contexts, and flair. Meetings in the South are often longer, but the total decision process may be faster.[12]

The offer stage allows the two parties to assess each other's needs and degree of commitment. The initiation of the process and its progress are determined to a great extent by background factors of the parties (such as objectives) and the overall atmosphere (for example, a spirit of cooperativeness). As an example, many European buyers may be skittish about dealing with a U.S. exporter, given the number of U.S. companies that "fold their tents and go away when an initial sale blitz fizzles" or when environmental factors turn sour.[13]

After the buyer has received the offer, the parties meet to discuss the terms and get acquainted. In many parts of the world (Asia, the Middle East, southern Europe, and Latin America), informal meetings may often make or break the deal. Foreign buyers may want to ascertain that they are doing business with someone who is sympathetic and whom they can trust. For example, U.S. exporters to Kuwait rank the strength of the business relationship ahead of price as the critical variable driving buying decisions.[14] In some cases, it may be necessary to utilize facilitators (such as consultants or agents) to establish the contact.

Both parties have to formulate strategies for formal negotiations. This means not only careful review and assessment of all the factors affecting the deal to be negotiated but also preparation for the actual give-and-take of the negotiations. For example, research studies have found that U.S. and Canadian English-speaking bargainers

---

[9]Stephen E. Weiss, "Negotiating with the Romans—Part I," *Sloan Management Review* 36 (Spring 1994): 85–99.

[10]Arnold Pachtman, "Getting to 'Hao!'" *International Business* (July/August 1998): 24–26.

[11]Pervez N. Ghauri, "Guidelines for International Business Negotiations," *International Marketing Review* 4 (Autumn 1986): 72–82.

[12]"Negotiating in Europe," *Hemispheres*, July 1994, 43–47.

[13]"Made in the U.S.A.," *Business Week*, February 29, 1988, 60–66.

[14]Virginia J. Rehberg, "Kuwait: Reality Sets In," *Export Today* 7 (December 1991): 56–58.

can be taken advantage of by competitive bargainers[15] and that they are more trusting than other cultural groups.[16] Thus, these managers should consciously and carefully consider competitive behaviors of clients and partners. Especially in the case of governmental buyers, it is imperative to realize that public-sector needs may not necessarily fit into a mold that the marketer would consider rational. Negotiators may not necessarily behave as expected; for example, the negotiating partner may adjust behavior to the visitor's culture.

The actual face-to-face negotiations and the approach used in them will depend on the cultural background and business traditions prevailing in different countries. The most commonly used are the competitive and collaborative approaches.[17] In a competitive strategy, the negotiator is concerned mainly about a favorable outcome at the expense of the other party, while in the collaborative approach focus is on mutual needs, especially in the long term. For example, an exporter accepting a proposal that goes beyond what can be realistically delivered (in the hopes of market entry or renegotiation later) will lose in the long term. To deliver on the contract, the exporter may be tempted to cut corners in product quality or delivery, eventually leading to conflict with the buyer.

The choice of location for the negotiations plays a role in the outcome as well. Many negotiators prefer a neutral site. This may not always work, for reasons of resources or parties' perceptions of the importance of the deal. The host does enjoy many advantages, such as lower psychological risk due to familiar surroundings. Guests may run the risk of cultural shock and being away from professional and personal support systems. These pressures are multiplied if the host chooses to manipulate the situation with delays or additional demands. Visiting teams are less likely to walk out; as a matter of fact, the pressure is on them to make concessions. However, despite the challenges of being a guest, the visitor has a chance to see firsthand the counterpart's facilities and resources, and to experience culture in that market. In addition, visiting a partner, present or potential, shows commitment to the effort.[18]

How to Negotiate in Other Countries[19]

A combination of attitudes, expectations, and habitual behavior influences negotiation style. Although some of the following recommendations may go against the approach used at home, they may allow the negotiator to adjust to the style of the host-country negotiators.

> **1.** *Team assistance.* Using specialists will strengthen the team substantially and allow for all points of view to be given proper attention. Further, observation of negotiations can be valuable training experience for less-experienced participants. Whereas Western teams may average two to four people, a Chinese negotiating team may consist of up to ten people.[20] A study on how U.S. pur-

[15]Nancy J. Adler, John L. Graham, and Theodore Schwarz Gehrke, "Business Negotiations in Canada, Mexico, and the United States," *Journal of Business Research* 15 (1987): 411–429.

[16]D.L. Harnett and L.L. Cummings, *Bargaining Behavior: An International Study* (Houston, TX: Dame Publications, 1980), 231.

[17]Claude Cellich, "Negotiations for Export Business: Elements for Success," *International Trade Forum* 9 (Number 4, 1995): 20–27.

[18]Jackie Mayfield, Milton Mayfield, Drew Martin, and Paul Herbig, "How Location Impacts International Business Negotiations," *Review of Business* 19 (Winter 1998): 21–24.

[19]Framework for this section adapted from John L. Graham and Roy A. Herberger, Jr., "Negotiators Abroad—Don't Shoot from the Hip," *Harvard Business Review* 61 (July–August 1983): 160–168.

[20]Sally Stewart and Charles F. Keown, "Talking with the Dragon: Negotiating in the People's Republic of China," *Columbia Journal of World Business* 24 (Fall 1989): 68–72.

chasing professionals conduct negotiations abroad revealed that while the vast majority believed a small team (two to five individuals) was ideal, they also said their teams were often outnumbered by their international counterparts.[21] Even if there are intra-group disagreements during the negotiations, it is critical to show one face to the counterparts and handle issues within the team privately, outside the formal negotiations.

2. *Traditions and customs.* For newcomers, status relations and business procedures must be carefully considered with the help of consultants or local representatives. For example, in highly structured societies, such as Korea, great respect is paid to age and position.[22] What seem like simple rituals can cause problems. No first encounter in Asia is complete without an exchange of business cards. Both hands should be used to present and receive cards, and respect should be shown by reading them carefully.[23] One side should be translated into the language of the host country.

3. *Language capability.* Ideally, the international marketing manager should be able to speak the customer's language, but that is not always possible. The use of interpreters allows for longer response time and a more careful articulation of arguments (see *The International Marketplace 12.2*). If English is being used, a native speaker should avoid both jargon and idiomatic expressions, avoid complex sentences, and speak slowly and enunciate clearly. An ideal interpreter is one who briefs the negotiator on cultural dimensions, such as body language, before any meetings. For example, sitting in what may be perceived as a comfortable position in North America or Europe may be seen by the Chinese as showing a lack of control of one's body and, therefore, of one's mind.

4. *Determination of authority limits.* Negotiators from North America and Europe are often expected to have full authority when they negotiate in the Far East, although their local counterparts seldom if ever do. Announcing that the negotiators do not have the final authority to conclude the contract may be perceived negatively; however, if it is used as a tactic to probe the motives of the buyer, it can be quite effective. It is important to verify who does have that authority and what challenges may be faced in getting that decision. In negotiating in Russia, for example, the international marketer will have to ascertain who actually has final decision-making authority—the central, provincial, or local government—especially if permits are needed.

5. *Patience.* In many countries, such as China, business negotiations may take three times the amount of time that they do in the United States and Europe. Showing impatience in countries such as Brazil or Thailand may prolong negotiations rather than speed them up. Also, U.S. executives tend to start relatively close to what they consider a fair price in their negotiations, whereas Chinese negotiators may start with "unreasonable" demands and a rigid posture.[24]

6. *Negotiation ethics.* Attitudes and values of foreign negotiators may be quite different from those that a U.S. marketing executive is accustomed to. Being tricky can be valued in some parts of the world, whereas it is frowned on elsewhere. For example, Western negotiators may be taken aback by last-minute changes or concession requests by Russian negotiators.[25]

[21]Hokey Min and William P. Galle, "International Negotiation Strategies of U.S. Purchasing Professionals," *International Journal of Purchasing and Materials Management* 29 (Summer 1993): 41–53.

[22]Frank L. Acuff, "Just Call Me Mr. Ishmael," *Export Today* 11 (July 1995): 14–15.

[23]Frederick H. Katayama, "How to Act Once You Get There," *Fortune*, Fall 1989, 87–88.

[24]Berry J. Kesselman and Bryan Batson, "China: Clause and Effect," *Export Today* 12 (June 1996): 18–26.

[25]Ilkka A. Ronkainen, "Project Exports and the CMEA," in *International Marketing Management*, ed. Erdener Kaynak (New York: Praeger, 1984), 305–317.

THE INTERNATIONAL MARKETPLACE 12.2

Interpreters as Part of the Marketing Team

AN INTERNATIONAL MARKETING EXECUTIVE on a business trip abroad faces a risk seldom encountered at home: losing something in the translation—literally. Whether to take along an interpreter or have company materials translated into a foreign language is an early, key decision. With today's new telecommunications technology and language services, interpreters can actually be physically quite a distance away from the negotiations site. To assume that English will be understood when speaking to businesses overseas, and then to discover that it is not, provides a rude shock.

Sarah Pilgrim, president of OmniLingua, Inc., has suggested: "You need to do some research and think about what you are doing. Are you going to sell your product? Or going for social reasons to develop contacts? Do the people you are meeting with speak English—and with what level of competency? If you are making initial contacts, trying to find out about the market potential, you may not want to spend the money for an interpreter or translation of your literature. But if you are trying to sell something in a foreign country, it is important to have literature in the language of the target country. Although an interpreter costs $150 to $300 a day, it is wise to take one to important negotiations. If you bring your own interpreter, you can be sure that person is on your side. The interpreter should be well briefed ahead of time so he or she is familar with the product and can act as a company representative." Bilingual speakers should really try to avoid being their own interpreters or to swap languages in mid-stream. It may be prudent, however, to deliver the first few minutes in the local language before switching to English, for example.

An experienced and qualified individual can act as a consultant to help you avoid cross-cultural *faux pas*, tell you when to talk and when to listen, and become an integral part of the informal channel (to pick up casual conversations

and communicate the nuances behind the official statements). An interpreter should be selected carefully by assessing past clients or samples of work. The head of Osaka's $47 billion international airport project still tells a story of a U.S. construction company president who became indignant when he discovered that the project head could not speak English. As a matter of fact, according to one expert, "If you are with a Japanese who speaks fluent English, you may be dealing with the wrong person."

These eight rules should be followed when using interpreters: (1) plan for more time in negotiation; (2) evaluate the interpreter's ability in terms of language skills, knowledge of technical terminology, and familiarity with appropriate dialects; (3) provide the interpreter with materials beforehand; (4) brief the interpreter on the purpose of the meeting; (5) avoid using slang; (6) ask questions that require short answers; (7) take breaks and, if negotiations are long, use multiple interpreters; and (8) make sure customs and traditions are followed (e.g., seating arrangements).

Some of the drawbacks of using interpreters are that (1) interpreters can slow down negotiations or inject their own point of view into the discussion; (2) they may diminish the spontaneity and negotiating strength of the presentation; (3) using an interpreter may offend a foreign business executive who thinks his or her English is good; and (4) interpreters are a risk in communicating confidential information.

SOURCES: Kathy Schmidt, "How to Speak So You're Open to Interpretation," *Presentations* 13 (December 1999): 126–127; Paul Jensen, "Interpretive Dances," *Export Today* 12 (November 1996): 66–67; John Frievalds, "Translators on Call," *Export Today* 12 (July 1996): 60–62; Grace Leonard, "Interpreting Your Translator," *Export Today* 12 (January 1996): 69; and "10 Rules for Using an Interpreter," *Export Today* 9 (June 1993): 18.

7. *Silence.* To negotiate effectively abroad, a marketer needs to read correctly all types of communication. U.S. businesspeople often interpret inaction and silence as a negative sign. As a result, Japanese executives tend to expect that they can get them to lower prices or sweeten the deal. Finns may sit through a meeting expressionless, hands folded and not moving much. There is nothing necessarily negative about this; they show respect to the speaker with their focused, dedicated listening.[26]

[26]Richard D. Lewis, *When Cultures Collide* (London: Nicholas Brealey Publishing, 1996), chapter 17.

8. *Persistence.* Insisting on answers and an outcome may be seen as a threat by negotiating partners abroad. In some markets, negotiations are seen as a means of establishing long-term commercial relations, not as an event with winners and losers. Confrontations are to be avoided because minds cannot be changed at the negotiation table; this has to be done informally. Face is an important concept throughout the Far East.

9. *Holistic view.* Concessions should be avoided until all issues have been discussed, so as to preclude the possibility of granting unnecessary benefits to the negotiation partners. Concessions traditionally come at the end of bargaining. This is especially true in terms of price negotiations. If price is agreed on too quickly, the counterpart may want to insist on too many inclusions for that price.

10. *The meaning of agreements.* What constitutes an agreement will vary from one market to another. In many parts of the world, legal contracts are still not needed; as a matter of fact, reference to legal counsel may indicate that the relationship is in trouble. For the Chinese, the written agreement exists mostly for the convenience of their Western partners and represents an agenda on which to base the development of the relationship.

When a verbal agreement is reached, it is critical that both parties leave with a clear understanding of what they have agreed to. This may entail only the relatively straightforward act of signing a distributor agreement, but in the case of large-scale projects, details must be explored and spelled out. In contracts that call for cooperative efforts, the responsibilities of each partner must be clearly specified. Otherwise, obligations that were anticipated to be the duty of one contracting party may result in costs to another. For example, foreign principal contractors may be held responsible for delays that have been caused by the inability of local subcontractors (whose use might be a requisite of the client) to deliver on schedule.

Marketing Communications Strategy

ABSOLUT MANUAL.

The international marketing manager has the responsibility of formulating a communications strategy for the promotion of the company and its products and services. The basic steps of such a strategy are outlined in Figure 12.2.

Few, if any, firms can afford expenditures for promotion that is done as "art for art's sake" or only because major competitors do it. The first step in developing communications strategy is therefore assessing what company or product characteristics and benefits should be communicated to the export market. This requires constant monitoring of the various environments and target audience characteristics. For example, Volvo has used safety and quality as its primary themes in its worldwide promotional campaigns since the 1950s. This approach has provided continuity, repetition, and uniformity in positioning Volvo in relation to its primary competitors: Mercedes Benz (prestige) and BMW (sportiness).

Absolut, which is owned by the Swedish government, in 1979 started exporting its vodka into the United States with 45,000 cases and an introductory promotion effort by its distributor, Carillon Importers, Ltd. At the time, import vodka sales were almost nonexistent and Absolut's brand name unknown. With a very small budget ($750,000) and the capability to do only print advertising, Carillon's agency TBWA set about to establish brand awareness. Since then the ads have featured a fullpage shot of the bottle and a two-word headline.[27] In twenty years, Absolut has grown to number ten in volume and number three in revenue in the U.S. spirits category. In addition to a strong marketing effort, Absolut benefited from changing U.S. drinking

---

[27]Richard W. Lewis, *The Absolut Vodka Advertising Story* (New York: Journey Editions, 1996).

| FIGURE 12.2 | **Steps in Formulating Marketing Communications Strategy** |

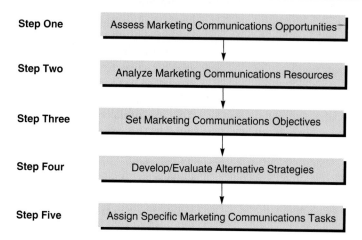

SOURCE: Framework adapted from Wayne DeLozier, *The Marketing Communication Process* (New York: McGraw-Hill, 1976), 272.

ABSOLUT WINOKUR.

habits.[28] Vodkas are now the largest category in the distilled spirits business, with Absolut ruling the high-class vodka crowd. Certain rules of thumb can be followed in evaluating resources to be allocated for export communications efforts. A sufficient commitment is necessary, which means a relatively large amount of money. The exporter has to operate in foreign markets according to the rules of the marketplace, which in the United States, for example, means high promotional costs—perhaps 30 percent of exports or even more during the early stage of entry. For example, Absolut's annual promotional budget is approximately $20 million, a significant amount when compared with retail sales of $260 million.[29]

Because of monetary constraints that most exporters face, promotional efforts should be concentrated on key markets. For example, European liquor marketers traditionally concentrate their promotional efforts on the United States, where volume consumption is greatest, and Great Britain, which is considered the world capital of the liquor trade. A specific objective might be to spend more than the closest competitors do in the U.S. market. In the United States, for example, this would require a new import brand, aimed at the lower-price segment, to spend at the minimum $10 million during the rollout year.[30] In some cases, an exporter will have to limit this to one country, even one area, at a time to achieve set goals with the available budget. International campaigns require patient investment; the market has to progress through awareness, knowledge, liking, preference, and favorable purchase intentions before payback begins. Payback periods of one or two years cannot be realistically expected. For many exporters, a critical factor is the support of the intermediary. Whether a distributor is willing to contribute a $3 million media budget or a few thousand dollars makes a big difference. In some cases, intermediaries take a leading role in the promotion of the product in a market. In the case of Absolut, for example, Carillon Importers has been credited with the creative advertising widely acknowl-

[28]"Neat Shot," *Marketing & Media Decisions* 24 (March 1989): 73–78.

[29]Ira Teinowitz, "Grand Met Thirsts or Absolut-Style Phenom," *Advertising Age*, January 10, 1994, 6.

[30]Gary Levin, "Russian Vodka Plans U.S. Rollout," *Advertising Age*, November 11, 1991, 4.

edged as a primary reason for the brand's success. In most cases, however, the exporter should retain some control of the campaign rather than allow intermediaries or sales offices a free hand in the various markets operated. Although markets may be dissimilar, common themes and common objectives need to be incorporated into the individual campaigns. For example, Duracell, the world leader in alkaline batteries, provides graphics—such as logos and photos—to country operations. Although many exporters do not exert pressure to conform, overseas distributors take advantage of annual meetings to discuss promotional practices with their head office counterparts.

Alternative strategies are needed to spell out how the firm's resources can be combined and adapted to market opportunities. The tools the international marketer has available to form a total communications program for use in the targeted markets are referred to as the **promotional mix.** They consist of the following:

1. Advertising: Any form of nonpersonal presentation of ideas, goods, or services by an identified sponsor, with predominant use made of *mass* communication, such as print, broadcast, or electronic media, or *direct* communication that is pinpointed at each business-to-business customer or ultimate consumer using computer technology and databases.
2. Personal selling: The process of assisting and persuading a prospect to buy a good or service or to act on an idea through use of person-to-person communication with intermediaries and/or final customers.
3. Publicity: Any form of nonpaid, commercially significant news or editorial comment about ideas, products, or institutions.
4. Sales promotion: Direct inducements that provide extra product value or incentive to the sales force, intermediaries, or ultimate consumers.
5. Sponsorship: The practice of promoting the interests of the company by associating it with a specific event (typically sports or culture) or a cause (typically a charity or a social interest).

In some cases, packaging serves a promotional role—for example, when it is distinctive and unique in its color or shape. The use of tools will vary by company and by situation. Although all Harley-Davidson motorcycles are on allocation in overseas markets, they are still promoted by advertising stressing postpurchase reinforcement. The company also sells "motor clothes," illustrated in catalogs. Copies are made for overseas dealers, who cannot afford to translate and reprint them, and they pass them on to their customers with notes that not all items are available or permissible in their markets.[31]

The choice of tools leads to either a push or a pull emphasis in marketing communications. **Push strategies** focus on the use of personal selling. Despite its higher cost per contact, personal selling is appropriate for the international marketing of industrial goods, which have shorter channels of distribution and smaller target populations than do consumer goods. Governmental clients are typically serviced through personal selling efforts. Some industries, such as pharmaceuticals, traditionally rely on personal selling to service the clientele.

On the other hand, **pull strategies** depend on mass communications tools, mainly advertising. Advertising is appropriate for consumer-oriented products with large target audiences and long channels of distribution. Of its promotional budget, Absolut spends 85 percent in print media in the United States, with the balance picked up by outdoor advertising, mainly billboards. The base of the advertising effort is formed by magazines such as *Sports Illustrated, Vanity Fair, Business Week, Rolling Stone, Esquire, Time,* and *Newsweek.*

No promotional tool should be used in isolation or without regard to the others; hence, we see a trend toward **integrated marketing communications.** An example of

---

[31]Mel Mandell, "Getting the Word Out," *World Trade,* November 1993, 30–34.

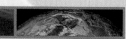

THE INTERNATIONAL MARKETPLACE 12.3

Integrated Marketing Communications to Create Awareness

BEFORE MERGING WITH SEAGATE in 1996 to form the world's largest independent storage device manufacturer, Conner Peripherals engaged in an integrated marketing communications program to create awareness among its target audience: OEMs (original equipment makers). Rather than creating disk-drive products and marketing them to computer makers, Conner focused its efforts on providing leading-edge products designed in close cooperation with the customers to fit into the products they were developing.

A critical dimension of this effort was to establish direct sales forces in each of the geographic target markets, such as Japan and China, to include customer liaisons, service technicians, quality assurance representatives, and administrators.

The marketing communications program included other elements as well. The company began advertising in Japan in mid-1990 with a spread designed specifically for that market.

Headlined "Unique ideas are often the most enduring," the first ad featured a photograph of handmade chopsticks with a Japanese maple leaf.

A similar ad ran in other regions, including China and Southeast Asia. But the art direction was quite different in the non-Japanese spreads.

"When we did it for Southeast Asia, we used a whole different kind of chopstick, a different kind of scene, different coloration, different everything, to reflect obvious differences in culture," says Charles Schoenhoeft, president of Conner's ad agency, Transphere International.

The image in the Southeast Asian and Japanese versions of Conner's "Unique ideas" ad differed in subtle but important ways. For example, the Southeast Asian execution pictured bone Chinese chopsticks on a black cloth; the Japanese version showed enameled Japanese (pointed) chopsticks on a marble slab to appeal to a different aesthetic.

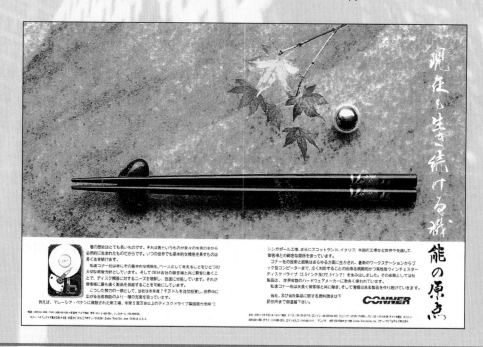

this is provided in *The International Marketplace 12.3*. Promotional tools should be coordinated according to target market and product characteristics, the size of the promotional budget, the type and length of international involvement, and control considerations. As an example, industrial purchasing decisions typically involve eight to eleven people. Because a salesperson may not reach all of them, the use of advertising may be necessary to influence the participants in the decision-making process.

Visual and text messages in those ads held a softer sell than Conner's ads for Western markets.

In Japan, Schoenhoeft explains: "Subtle messages often work better. In the States we tend to hit each other on the head with a two-by-four. In Japan it's not that way. They feel you're bragging and wonder what's wrong with your product."

The ads helped build awareness and preference for the drive maker among Japanese OEMs, according to Lynda Laszlo, manager of corporate communications with Conner.

The campaign ran in *Nikkei Business, Electronic Business Asia,* the Asian edition of *Electronic Design News,* and *Electronic World News,* a global publication with a total ad budget of $1.5 million to $2 million. Conner spent "more than 50%" of its Asian advertising budget to reach Japanese readers.

The company did not use direct mail or broadcast advertising but did supplement its print ads with trade shows, specifically Japan Data and Comdex. Conner had its own exhibit at Japan Data, a major electronics trade show held annually in Tokyo. Its participation at Comdex, the U.S. computer reseller exposition, was peripheral; Conner set up suites at the show, instead of an exhibit, and hosted special events such as press conferences and golf tournaments. Trade shows and special events typically had a 20 percent share of the overall communications budget.

SOURCE: Kate Bertrand, "Conner's Japanese Success Drive," *Business Marketing,* December 1991, 18–20. Ads courtesy of Transphere International.

http://www.seagate.com

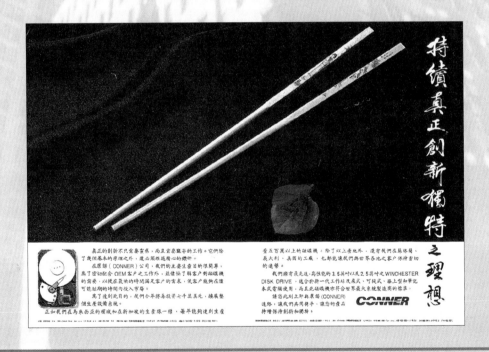

Finally, specific marketing communications tasks must be assigned, which may require deciding on a division of labor with foreign intermediaries or with other exporters for cooperative communications efforts.[32] For example, Koss, a Milwaukee-

---

[32]Dean M. Peebles and John K. Ryans, *Management of International Advertising: A Marketing Approach* (Boston: Allyn and Bacon, 1984), chapter 8.

based company that is one of the most recognized names in stereophones, concentrates on in-store display through a cooperative program with its distributors.[33] More money is thus made available for promotion, and its execution is carried out locally, with central control from Koss.

In cases where the locally based intermediaries are small and may not have the resources to engage in promotional efforts, the exporter may suggest dealer-participatory programs. In exchange for including the intermediaries' names in promotional material without any expense to them—for example, in announcing a sweepstakes—the exporter may request increased volume purchases from the intermediaries.

Communications Tools

The main communications tools used by exporters to communicate with the foreign marketplace from their domestic base are business and trade journals, directories, direct advertising, the Internet, trade fairs and missions, and personal selling. If the exporter's strategy calls for a major promotional effort in a market, it is advisable either to use a domestic agency with extensive operations in the intended market or to use a local agency and work closely with the company's local representatives in media and message choices.

Because the promoter-agency relationship is a close one, it may be helpful if the exporter's domestic agency has an affiliate in the target foreign market. The management function and coordination can be performed by the agency at home, while the affiliate can execute the program as it seems appropriate in that market. An exporter, if it has a sufficient budget, may ask its domestic agency to set up a branch overseas. Some exporters, especially those that have a more significant presence overseas, leave the choice of the agency to local managers. If a local agency is to be chosen, the exporter must make sure that coordination and cooperation between the agency and the exporter's domestic agency can be achieved. Whatever the approach used, the key criterion must be the competence of the people who will be in charge of the creation and implementation of the promotional programs.

Business/Trade Journals and Directories

Many varied business and trade publications, as well as directories, are available to the exporter. Some, such as *Business Week, Fortune, The Economist, The Wall Street Journal*, and *Financial Times*, are standard information sources worldwide. Extensions of these are their regional editions; for example, *The Asian Wall Street Journal* or *Business Week—Europe*. Trade publications can be classified as (1) horizontal, which cater to a particular job function cutting across industry lines, such as *Purchasing World* or *Industrial Distribution*, and (2) vertical, which deal with a specific industry, such as *Chemical Engineering* or *International Hospital Supplies*. These journals are global, regional, or country-specific in their approaches. Many U.S.-based publications are available in national language editions, with some offering regional buys for specific export markets—for example, the Spanish edition of *Feed Management*, titled *Alimentos Balanceados Para Animales*.

The exporter should also be aware of the potential of government-sponsored publications. For example, *Commercial News USA*, published by the U.S. Department of Commerce, is an effective medium for the marketer interested in making itself and its products known worldwide for a modest sum. For less than $500, an exporter can reach 137,000 potential buyers in 152 countries through the publication, distributed to recipients free of charge ten times a year.[34]

---

[33]"The Sound of America," *Export Today* 5 (February 1989): 33–34.

[34]http://www.cnewsusa.com

FIGURE 12.3 **Examples of International Trade Publications and Directories**

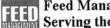

 Feed Management
Serving the United States & Canada

 Feed International
Serving Europe, Asia, Pacific, Middle
East & Africa

 Alimentos Balanceados Para Animales
Serving Latin America in Spanish

 Feed International China Edition
Serving the People's Republic of China in
Chinese

SOURCES: **http://www.wattmm.com;**
http://www.guiaexport.bellsouth.com.

Directories provide a similar tool for advertising efforts. Many markets feature exporter yellow pages, some of which offer on-line versions in addition to the traditional print ones. For example, **myEXPORTS.COM** (formerly the *U.S. Exporters' Yellow Pages*) offers U.S. firms a means to promote their businesses worldwide at no cost (if they just want to be listed), and at low cost for an advertisement or link to their e-mail or homepage. Some of the directories are country-specific. For example, BellSouth's *Guia Internacional* allows exporters to showcase their products to over 200,000 Latin American and Caribbean importers.[35] A number of on-line directories, such as *Internet International Business Exchange* (**www.imex.com**) provide the exporter the opportunity to have banner ads (i.e., ads placed on frequently visited Web sites) for $250 to $1,000 a month. Examples of international trade publications and directories are provided in Figure 12.3.

The two main concerns when selecting media are effectiveness in reaching the appropriate target audience(s) and efficiency in minimizing the cost of doing so, measured in terms of cost per thousand. If the exporter is in a position to define the target audience clearly (for example, in terms of demographics or product-related variables), the choice of media will be easier. In addition, consideration should be given to how well a given medium will work with the other tools the exporter wishes to employ. For example, advertisements in publications and directories may have the function of driving customers and prospects to the exporter's Web site.[36]

[35]http://guiaexport.bellsouth.com

[36]Sean Callahan, "McCann-Erickson Offers B-to-B Clients the World," *Business Marketing* (January 2000): 35.

In deciding which publications to use, the exporter must apply the general principles of marketing communications strategy. Coverage and circulation information is available from **Standard Rate & Data Service (www.srds.com)**. SRDS provides a complete list of international publications in the International Section of the *Business Publication*, and audit information similar to that on the U.S. market is provided for the United Kingdom, Italy, France, Austria, Switzerland, Germany, Mexico, and Canada. Outside these areas, the exporter has to rely on the assistance of publishers or local representatives. Actual choices are usually complicated by lack of sufficient funds and concern over the information gap. The simplest approach may be to use U.S. publishers, in which the exporter may have more confidence in terms of rates and circulation data. If a more localized approach is needed, a regional edition or national publication can be considered. Before advertising is placed in an unfamiliar journal, the marketer should analyze its content and overall quality of presentation.

Direct Marketing

The purpose of direct marketing is to establish a relationship with a customer in order to initiate immediate and measurable responses.[37] This is accomplished through direct-response advertising, telemarketing, and direct selling.

Direct mail is by far the dominant direct-response medium, but some advertising is also placed in mass media, such as television, magazines, and newspapers. Direct mail can be a highly personalized tool of communication if the target audience can be identified and defined narrowly. Ranging from notices to actual samples, it allows for flexibility in the amount of information conveyed and in its format. Direct mail is directly related in its effectiveness to the availability and quality of the mailing lists. Mailing lists may not be available around the world in the same degree that they are in, say, the United States. However, more and better lists are surfacing in Asia, Latin America, and the Middle East. In addition, reliable, economical, global postal service has become available.[38] Magnavox CATV, which markets cable television equipment, has boosted its international mailings to support its broad schedule of trade shows, many of which are in developing regions.

Even when mailing lists are available, they may not be as up-to-date or as precise as the international marketer would desire. In China, for example, lists are available to send literature directly to factories, ministries, professional societies, research institutes, and universities. However, such mailings can be extremely costly and produce few results. An effective and efficient direct-mail campaign requires extensive market-by-market planning of materials, format, and mode of mailing.

Catalogs are typically distributed to overseas customers through direct mail, although many catalogs have on-line versions as well. Their function is to make the exporter's name known, generate requests for further information, stimulate orders, and serve as a reminder between transactions. Catalogs are particularly useful if a firm's products are in a highly specialized field of technology and if only the most highly qualified specialists are to be contacted. In many markets, especially the developing ones, people may be starving for technology information and will share any mailings they receive. Due to this unsatisfied demand, a very small investment can reach many potential end users.

The growing mail-order segment is attracting an increasing number of foreign entrants to markets previously dominated by local firms. However, because consumers are wary of sending orders and money to an unknown company overseas, the key to market penetration is a local address. In Japan, L. L. Bean, the U.S. outdoor clothing merchandiser, works through McCann Direct, the specialized direct-marketing

---

[37]*Fact Book on Direct Response Marketing* (New York: Direct Marketing Association, Inc., 1982), xxiii.

[38]Hope Katz Gibbs, "Mediums for the Message," *Export Today* (June 1999): 22–27.

division of McCann-Erickson Hakuhodo Inc., Japan's largest foreign advertising agency. Bean places ads for its catalogs in Japanese media, orders for catalogs are sent to McCann Direct, and McCann Direct then forwards the addresses to Bean's headquarters in Maine, where all the orders for catalogs or goods are filled.[39] More and more catalogs of catalogs are published, which, in turn, contain information about foreign catalogs along with contact details.[40]

Traditional direct mail is undergoing major change. New types of mail services (e.g., the Mexican Post Office's Buzon Espresso) will enable companies to deal with their customers more efficiently when customers buy through catalogs or electronic means. New electronic media will assume an increasing share in the direct-response area. However, direct marketing will continue to grow as a function of its targetability, its measurability, and the responsiveness of consumers to direct marketing efforts.

In the past, U.S. marketers thought that country-specific offices were almost essential to bringing their companies closer to overseas customers. Now with functioning telecommunication systems and deregulation in the industry, **telemarketing** (including sales, customer service, and help-desk-related support) is flourishing throughout the world. A growing number of countries in Latin America, Asia, and Europe are experiencing growth in this area as consumers are becoming more accustomed to calling toll-free numbers and more willing to receive calls from marketers.

In Europe, companies using this service publicize their assigned local phone numbers on television or print ads, direct mailings, catalogs, or web sites, and then the calls are routed to a call center. The number and location of such call centers will depend on a variety of issues, such as what the distribution area of the product is, what the fulfillment logistics are, how important local presence is, and how important certain capabilities are, such as language and the ability to handle calls from various time zones.[41] Costa Rica is the choice for Central and Latin American call center opera-

[39]"Direct Marketers in Japan Find Receptive Consumers But Practical Problems," *Business International*, September 14, 1992, 291; and Deborah Begum, "U.S. Retailers Find Mail-Order Happiness in Japan," *World Trade*, May 1996, 22–25.

[40]Cynthia Myashita, "Cataloging Japan," *Export Today* 12 (March 1996): 16–18.

[41]Hope Katz Gibbs, "It's Your Call," *Export Today* (May 1997): 46–51.

tions, Australia for the Asia-Pacific, and Singapore for Asia itself, while Belgium, Holland, Ireland, and Portugal are leading locations in Europe.[42] If only one center is used in Europe, for example, access to a multilingual work force is a major factor in selecting the location. When a call comes in, the name of the country in which the call originates is displayed above the switchboard so that it can be taken by an operator who speaks the language(s) native to that country.[43]

Call center activity has developed more slowly in Asia than it has in North America and Europe, mostly because of infrastructural reasons and cultural resistance to the new form of communicating with business. However, new technologies are helping to overcome such resistance. **Database marketing** allows the creation of an individual relationship with each customer or prospect. For example, a call center operator will know a customer's background with the company or overall purchasing habits.[44] The development of the needed databases through direct mail or the Internet will advance the use of telemarketing.

Some exporters see the use of call centers as a preliminary step to entering an international market with a deeper presence such as a sales office.

Internet[45]

Having a web site is seen as necessary if for no other reason than image; lack of a Web presence may convey a negative image to the various constituents of the marketer. The web site should be linked to the overall marketing strategy and not just be there for appearance's sake. This means having a well-designed and well-marketed site.[46] Quality is especially critical if customers use the web site to find more information or clarification, as triggered by the exporter's other communications efforts, such as advertisements or telemarketing efforts.

Having a Web presence will support the exporter's marketing communications effort in a number of ways. First, it allows the company to increase its presence in the marketplace and to communicate its overall mission and information about its marketing mix. Second, the Internet will allow 24-hour access to customers and prospects. Providing important information during decision making can help the customer clarify the search. The potential interactivity of the web site (e.g., in providing tailor-made solutions to the customer's concerns) may provide a competitive advantage as the customer compares alternative sites. For example, the web site for apparel marketer Lands' End allows consumers to identify their body type and then mix and match clothing items that suit them.[47] Interactivity is also critical when the site is designed, in determining what features to include (e.g., should sites adjust to different dialects of a language in a region?).

Third, the Internet can improve customer service by allowing customers to serve themselves when and where they choose. This is an area where an exporter's Web presence can reduce overall communications costs in the most significant way. Naturally, the exporter must have the necessary capacity to serve all interested customers through

[42]Sam Bloomfield, "Reach Out and Touch Someone Far, Far Away," *World Trade*, April 1999, 80–84.

[43]Roger Hickey, "Toll-Free Europe: Continental Call Centers," *Export Today* (January 1995): 20–21.

[44]Rolf Rykken, "Call Waiting?" *Export Today* (November 1998): 55–57.

[45]For a discussion on marketing on the Internet, see Michael R. Czinkota, Peter R. Dickson, Patrick Dunne, Abbie Griffith, K. Douglas Hoffman, Michael D. Hutt, John H. Lindgren, Robert F. Lusch, Ilkka A. Ronkainen, Bert Rosenbloom, Jagdish N. Sheth, Terence A. Shimp, Judy A. Siguaw, Penny M. Simpson, Thomas W. Speh, and Joel E. Urbany, *Marketing: Best Practices* (Fort Worth, TX: The Dryden Press, 2000), chapter 15.

[46]Michael Borgeon, "Linking the Internet to Your Marketing Strategy," *International Trade Forum*, April 1999, 17–18.

[47]"International in Internet Closes U.S. Lead," *Marketing News*, February 14, 2000, 7.

the web site, especially if there is an increase in interest and demand. An important dimension of customer service is after-sales service to solve consumer problems and to facilitate the formation of consumer groups. A Web forum where customers can exchange news and views on product use will not facilitate product research, but it *will* build loyalty among consumers.

The fourth advantage is the ability of the exporter to gather information, which has its uses not only in research but also in database development for subsequent marketing efforts. While the data collected may be biased, they are also very inexpensive to collect. If it is used to better cater to existing customers, then data collected through Internet interaction are the best possible.

The fifth advantage of the Internet is the opportunity to actually close sales. This function is within the realm of e-commerce. It will require a significant commitment on part of the exporter in terms of investment in infrastructure, to deliver not only information but also the product to the customer. E-commerce is discussed in more detail in Chapter 13.

In addition to communications with customers, the Internet provides the possibility to communicate with internal constituents. Exporters may have part of their web sites set up with detailed product and price information that only their agents, representatives, or distributors have access to. Especially when changes are called for, this is an efficient way of communicating about them without having to mail or fax each and every overseas party.[48] Web sites can also be used in the recruitment of intermediaries and partners. P&D Creative, a manufacturer of environmentally safe cleaning products, uses its site (**www.pdcreative.pair.com**) to attract intermediaries. The company promotes its site in search engines and internationally oriented newsgroups and provides information of special interest to intermediaries.[49]

Internet strategy is not restricted to the exporter's own web site. The exporter needs to determine with which portals, such as AOL (**www.aol.com**) or Yahoo! (**www.yahoo.com**), or with what type of hyperlinks with related products or services, such as Internet International Business Exchange (**www.imex.com**) or China Webdirect (**www.cybridge.com**), to negotiate for banner advertising on those sites.

The challenges faced by exporters in Internet-based communications are related to the newness of the medium and the degree to which adjustments need to be made for each market served. A very large portion of the world population has yet to adopt the Internet, and its users have a distinct profile. In some cases this might match the exporter's intended target market (such as for on-line music); however, in many cases Internet diffusion has yet to reach the targeted customer.

While English-only web sites can deliver information and support to some international customers, having local-language sites and registering with local search engines demonstrate appropriate market and cultural sensitivity. The choice of languages will depend on the target audience. The most popular languages are French, Spanish, German, Japanese, and Chinese. For some, a dialect must be specified; for example, Spanish has three main variants: European, Mexican, and South American. The exporter needs also to determine which pages have to be modified. Pages that emphasize marketing, sales, and corporate identity are normally the ones chosen.[50]

While the exporter's local web sites may (and for global product or service offerings, should) be quite similar in terms of aesthetics, adjustments should also be made for such dimensions as depth of product line and level of market presence. Customers who are familiar with the Internet may access information about products and

---

[48]Carl R. Jacobsen, "How Connecticut Companies Use the Internet for Exporting," *Business America*, January 1998, 17.

[49]Nick Wreden, "Internet Opens Markets Abroad," *Information Week*, November 16, 1998, 46–48.

[50]Gerry Dempsey, "A Hands-On Guide for Multilingual Web Sites," *World Trade*, September 1999, 68–70.

Trade and Travel Networks

Civilization depends on trade for growth and travel makes this possible. Shipping is the most important method of world transport but economic progress and mobility are constantly being improved by the development of new routes and new methods of transport.

Road and Rail

Integrated road and rail networks are the basis of industrial society. Containerization and the extension of modern highway systems have increased flexibility and reduced the emphasis on railways transporting freight.

Roads

Bar length equals the total road network in log scale.
Number next to country name is the total road network in thousands of kilometers.

68 / 277	(24) USA 6366
49 / 23	(1) India 1604
16 / 115	(7) Brazil 1399
296 / 95	(34) Japan 1118
9 / 9	(1) China 890
9 / 367	(14) Canada 884
11 / 552	(9) Australia 817
146 / 149	(27) France 803
6 / 53	(11) Russia 620
172 / 78	(54) Germany 613
154 / 63	(40) UK 353
96 / 83	(10) Poland 299
98 / 51	(64) Italy 294
7 / 74	(20) Argentina 208

○ Number of vehicles per km of road

Density of population per length of road
(100km/1 million people)

■ High
■ Medium
□ Low

Road density
(km/100km²)

■ High
■ Medium
□ Low

Railways

8 3	UK 18
7 4	Italy 20
8 7	Poland 24
7 2	Japan 26
0.4 3	Brazil 31
6 6	France 34
2 12	Argentina 35
0.5 27	Australia 40
.3 5	Germany 41
0.5 1	China 50
2 1	India 61
7 28	Canada 68
0.5 6	Russia 86
3 14	USA 320

Density of population per
length of road
(100km/1 million people)

High
Medium
Low

Rail density
(km/100km²)

High
Medium
Low

Bar length equals the total road network in log scale.
Number next to country name is the total road network in thousands of kilometers.

Journey Time

The Suez Canal cuts 3600 nautical miles
off the London-Singapore route, while
the Concorde halves the London-New
York journey time.

Air and Sea Routes

A complex network of primary air routes
centered on the Northern Hemisphere provides
rapid transit across the world for mass travel,
mail, and urgent freight.

Ships also follow these principal routes,
plying the oceans between major ports and
transporting the commodities of world trade
in bulk.

Concorde	Propeller
3½ hours	12 hours

Jet	First Flight
7 hours	4½ days

Singapore ⟶ London ⟶ New York

Sail (via Cape)	Steam (via Cape)	Steam (via Suez)	Supertanker (via Cape)	Diesel (via Suez)
164 days	43 days	28 days	28 days	15 days

Source: Bartholomew.

services before purchasing them and may visit sites in several countries. Second-generation technology is increasing the interactivity of advertising on the Web. Given that individuals around the world have different information needs, varying levels of company and product familiarity, and different user capabilities, exporters can adjust their web sites' content and develop paths tailored to each group of customers or even to an individual customer.

Marketers using the Web as an advertising medium will have to be concerned about market-by-market differences in regulations. For example, Germany sued Benetton (**www.benetton.com**) for "exploiting feelings of pity" with one of its "United Colors of Benetton" campaigns.[51] Finally, on-line communications strategy should also include provisions for technological development. For example, a full-color site with lots of text will not be legible or attractive on the monochrome screens of smart phones using WAP (wireless application protocol) technology, already in use in Northern Europe.

Trade Shows and Missions

Marketing goods and services through trade shows is a European tradition that dates back to 1240 A.D. After sales force costs, trade shows are one of the most significant cost items in marketing budgets. Although they are usually associated with industrial firms, some consumer-products firms are represented as well. Typically, a trade show is an event at which manufacturers, distributors, and other vendors display their products or describe their services to current and prospective customers, suppliers, other business associates, and the press.[52] The International Automotive Services Industries Show and the International Coal Show, for example, run eight hours for three days, plus one or two preview days, and register 25,000 attendees. In the consumer goods area, expositions are the most common type of show. Tickets are usually sold; typical expositions include home/garden, boat, auto, stereo, and antiques. Although a typical trade show or typical participant does not exist, an estimated $73,000 is allocated for each show, and the median manufacturer or distributor attends nine or ten shows annually.

Whether an exporter should participate in a trade show depends largely on the type of business relationship it wants to develop with a particular country. More than 16,000 trade shows create an annual $50 billion in business worldwide.[53] A company looking only for one-time or short-term sales might find the expense prohibitive, but a firm looking for long-term involvement may find the investment worthwhile. Arguments in favor of participation include the following:

1. Some products, by their very nature, are difficult to market without providing the potential customer a chance to examine them or see them in action. Trade fairs provide an excellent opportunity to introduce, promote, and demonstrate new products.
2. An appearance at a show produces goodwill and allows for periodic cultivation of contacts. Beyond the impact of displaying specific products, many firms place strong emphasis on "waving the company flag" against competition.[54] This facet also includes morale boosting of the firm's sales personnel and distributors.

---

[51]Lewis Rose, "Before You Advertise on the Net—Check the International Marketing Laws," *Bank Marketing*, May 1996, 40–42.

[52]Thomas V. Bonoma, "Get More out of Your Trade Shows," *Harvard Business Review* 61 (January–February 1983): 137–145.

[53]Kathleen V. Schmidt, "Trading Plätze," *Marketing News*, July 19, 1999, 11.

[54]Richard Barovick, "Exporters Fit Trade Fairs into Larger Marketing Strategy," *Business America*, December 10, 1984, 3–5.

3. The opportunity to find an intermediary may be one of the best reasons to attend a trade show. A show is a cost-effective way to solicit and screen candidates to represent the firm, especially in a new market. Copylite Products of Ft. Lauderdale used the CeBIT computer-and-automation show in Hannover, Germany, to establish itself in Europe. The result was a distribution center in Rotterdam and six distributors covering eight countries. Its $40,000 investment in the trade show has reaped millions in new business.[55]

4. Attendance is one of the best ways to contact government officials and decision makers, especially in China. For example, participation in the Chinese Export Commodities Fair, which is held twice a year in Guangzhou, China, is "expected" by the host government.

5. Trade fairs provide an excellent chance for market research and collecting competitive intelligence. The exporter is able to view most rivals at the same time and to test comparative buyer reactions. Trade fairs provide one of the most inexpensive ways of obtaining evaluative data on the effectiveness of a promotional campaign.

6. Exporters are able to reach a sizable number of sales prospects in a brief time period at a reasonable cost per contact. More than 86 percent of all attendees represent buying influences (managers with direct responsibility for purchasing products and services). Of equal significance is the fact that trade show visitors are there because they have a specific interest in the exhibits.[56] Similarly, suppliers can be identified. One U.S. apparel manufacturer at the International Trade Fair for Clothing Machinery in Cologne in 1997 paid for its participation by finding a less expensive thread supplier.[57]

On the other hand, the following are among the reasons cited for nonparticipation in trade fairs:

1. High costs. These can be avoided by participating in events sponsored by the U.S. Department of Commerce or exhibiting at U.S. trade centers or export development offices. An exporter can also lower costs by sharing expenses with distributors or representatives. Further, the costs of closing a sale through trade shows are estimated to be much lower than for a sale closed through personal representation.

2. Difficulty in choosing the appropriate trade fairs for participation. This is a critical decision. Because of scarce resources, many firms rely on suggestions from their foreign distributors on which fairs to attend and what specifically to exhibit. Caterpillar, for example, usually allows its foreign dealers to make the selections for themselves. In markets where conditions are more restricted for exporters, such as China, Caterpillar in effect serves as the dealer and thus participates itself.

3. For larger exporters with multiple divisions, the problem of coordination. Several divisions may be required to participate in the same fair under the company banner. Similarly, coordination is required with distributors and agents if joint participation is desired, which requires joint planning.

Trade show participation is too expensive to be limited to the exhibit alone. A clear set of promotional objectives would include targeting accounts and attracting them to the show with preshow promotion using mailings, advertisements in the trade

[55]Richard B. Golik, "The Lure of Foreign Trade Shows," *International Business*, March 1996, 16–20.

[56]"Taking Advantage of Trade Fairs for Maximum Sales Impact," *Business International*, October 12, 1987, 321–323.

[57]"IMB '97 A Hit: Cologne Show Draws 30,000 Manufacturers from 100 Countries," *Apparel Industry Magazine*, August 1997, 16–26.

journals, or web site information. Contests and giveaways are effective in attracting participants to the company's exhibition area. Major customers and attractive prospects often attend, and they should be acknowledged, for example, by arranging for a hospitality suite.[58] Finally, a system is needed to evaluate post-show performance and to track qualified leads.

Exporters may participate in general or specialized trade shows. General trade fairs are held in Hannover, Germany (see *The International Marketplace 12.4*) and Milan, Italy. An example of a specialized one is Retail Solutions, a four-day trade show on store automation held in London. Participants planning to exhibit at large trade shows may elect to do so independently or as part of a national pavilion. For small and medium-sized companies the benefit of a group pavilion is in both cost and ease of the arrangements. These pavilions are often part of governmental export-promotion programs. Even foreign government assistance may be available; for example, the Japanese External Trade Organization (JETRO) helps non-Japanese companies participate in the country's two largest trade shows.

Other promotional events that the exporter can use are trade missions, seminar missions, solo exhibitions, video/catalog exhibitions, and virtual trade shows. **Trade missions** can be U.S. specialized trade missions or industry-organized, government-approved (IOGA) trade missions, both of which aim at expanding the sales of U.S. goods and services and the establishment of agencies and representation abroad. The U.S. Department of Commerce is actively involved in assistance of both types. **Seminar missions** are events in which eight to ten firms are invited to participate in a one- to four-day forum, during which the team members conduct generic discussions on technological issues—that is, follow a soft-sell approach. This is followed up by individual meetings with end users, government agencies, research institutions, and other potentially useful contacts. Individual firms may introduce themselves to certain markets by proposing a technical seminar there. Synopses of several alternative proposed lectures, together with company details and the qualifications of the speakers, must be forwarded to the proper body, which will circulate the proposals to interested bodies and coordinate all the arrangements. The major drawback is the time required to arrange for such a seminar, which may be as much as a year. **Solo exhibitions** are generally limited to one, or at the most, a few product themes and are held only when market conditions warrant them. **Video/catalog exhibitions** allow exporters to publicize their products at low cost. They consist of 20 to 35 product presentations on videotapes, each lasting five to ten minutes. They provide the advantage of actually showing the product in use to potential customers. **Virtual trade shows** enable exporters to promote their products and services over the Internet and to have electronic presence without actually attending a trade show. Trade leads and international sales interests are collected and forwarded by the sponsor to the companies for follow-up. The information stays on-line for 365 days for one flat fee. E-Expo USA (**www.e-expousa.doc.gov**), a pilot virtual trade show promoted by the U.S. Department of Commerce, attracted 376 companies to exhibit on the site in 1999.[59]

Personal Selling

Personal selling is the most effective of the promotional tools available to the marketer; however, its costs per contact are high. The average cost of sales calls may vary

---

[58]"Don't Just Exhibit—Do Something," *Business Marketing* 74 (May 1989): 78; Bob Lamons, "Involve Your Staff in Trade Shows for Better Results," *Marketing News*, March 1, 1999, 9–10.

[59]Rosalind McLymont, "Agency Fires Three-Stage Rocket into Cyberspace with Virtual Trade Shows," *Journal of Commerce*, October 14, 1999, 7A–8A.

TABLE 12.1	Levels of Exporter Involvement in International Sales		
TYPE OF INVOLVEMENT	TARGET OF SALES EFFORT	LEVEL OF EXPORTER INVOLVEMENT	ADVANTAGE/DISADVANTAGE
Indirect exports	Home-country-based intermediary	Low	+No major investment in international sales −Minor learning from/control of effort
Direct exports	Locally based intermediary	Medium	+Direct contact with local market −Possible gatekeeping by intermediary
Integrated exports	Customer	High	+Generation of market-specific assets −Cost/risk

SOURCE: Framework adapted from Reijo Luostarinen and Lawrence Welch, *International Operations of the Firm* (Helsinki, Finland: Helsinki School of Economics, 1990), chapter 1.

from $200 to $1,100, depending on the industry and the product or service. Personal selling allows for immediate feedback on customer reaction as well as information on markets.

The exporter's sales effort is determined by the degree of internationalization in its efforts, as shown in Table 12.1. As the degree of internationalization advances, so will the exporter's own role in carrying out or controlling the sales function.

Indirect Exports   When the exporter uses indirect exports to reach international markets, the export process is externalized; in other words, the intermediary, such as an EMC, will take care of the international sales effort. While there is no investment in international sales by the marketer, there is also no, or very little, learning about sales in the markets that buy the product. The sales effort is basically a domestic one directed at the local intermediary. This may change somewhat if the marketer becomes party to an ETC with other similar producers. Even in that case, the ETC will have its own sales force and exposure to the effort may be limited. Any learning that takes place is indirect; for example, the intermediary may advise the marketer of product adaptation requirements to enhance sales.

Direct Exports   At some stage, the exporter may find it necessary to establish direct contact with the target market(s), although the ultimate customer contact is still handled by locally based intermediaries, such as agents or distributors. Communication with intermediaries must ensure both that they are satisfied with the arrangement and that they are equipped to market and promote the exporter's product appropriately. Whatever the distribution arrangement, the exporter must provide basic selling aid communications, such as product specification and data literature, catalogs, the results of product testing, and demonstrated performance information—everything needed to present products to potential customers. In some cases, the exporter has to provide the intermediaries with incentives to engage in local advertising efforts. These may include special discounts, push money, or cooperative advertising. Cooperative advertising will give the exporter's product local flavor and increase the overall promotional budget for the product. However, the exporter needs to be concerned that the advertising is of sufficient quality and that the funds are spent as agreed.

THE INTERNATIONAL MARKETPLACE 12.4

At the Fair

THE HANNOVER INDUSTRIAL FAIR (Hannover Messe) is the Olympic Games of European industrial exposition. With more than 4,000,000 square feet of indoor exhibition space and 7,500 exhibitors, it is ten times as large as most trade shows anywhere in the world. It is also superbly organized, with its own train station, post office, 35 restaurants, and 600 permanent staff. In 2000, the show focused on factory automation as well as materials handling and logistics.

The sheer magnitude of the Hannover Fair and the technology displayed there are impressive but are not the most significant aspects of this event. Rather, it is the opportunity it presents for people from everywhere in the world to view the technology and learn an incredible amount about their industries.

Most important, it provides the opportunity to meet hundreds of people who can be invaluable future resources, if not necessarily a direct source of future business. More than 500,000 people attend the event, and though only 25 percent are from outside Germany, almost all are from businesses rather than members of the general public.

Of the 7,500 exhibitors from 70 countries in 2000, 65 percent were German. The balance were mostly European, with France, Italy, Switzerland, Spain, Great Britain, Denmark, and Netherlands accounting for an additional 25 percent. U.S. firms accounted for less than 3 percent of the exhibits, excluding European subsidiaries of large U.S. multinationals.

SOURCES: "The World Attends Hannover Fair 2000," *Modern Materials Handling*, November 1999, 16; "Hannover Wraps Up until 2000," *Control Engineering*, June 1999, 21–22; "Hannover's Trade Fair: The Week of the Widget," *The Washington Post*, April 29, 1996, A13; Valerio Giannini, "The Hannover Messe," *Export Today* 9 (July–August 1993): 29–32; advertisement from *The Economist*, March 13, 1996, 70.

http://www.messe.de

Three-way partnership: Mechanical Engineering, Electrical Engineering, Information Technology.

 20 – 25 March 2000

All the details: www.hannovermesse.de

Come to the HANNOVER FAIR and experience the true meaning of the word partnership. Six leading trade fairs with more than 7,500 exhibitors will show-case an unrivalled cross-section of industrial technology.

- Factory Automation
- CeMAT – Materials Handling and Logistics
- Energy
- Surface Treatment
- SubconTechnology
- Research and Technology

HANNOVER MESSE

For further information:
Deutsche Messe AG · Messegelände · D-30521 Hannover · Tel. +49-511/89-0 · Fax +49-511/89-326 26 · hannovermesse@messe.de

For the marketer-intermediary interaction to work, four general guidelines have to be satisfied.[60]

1. Know the sales scene. Often what works in the exporter's home market will not work somewhere else. This is true especially in terms of compensation schemes. In U.S. firms, incentives and commission play a significant role, while in most other markets salaries are the major share of compensation. The best way to approach this is to study the salary structures and incentive plans in other competitive organizations in the market in question.

2. Research the customer. Customer behavior will vary across markets, meaning the sales effort must adjust as well. ECA International, which sells marketing information worldwide based on a membership concept (companies purchase memberships to both participate in information gathering and receive appropriate data), found that its partners' sales forces could not sell the concept in Asia. Customers wanted instead to purchase information piece by piece. Only after research and modification of the sales effort was ECA able to sell the membership idea to customers.

3. Work with the culture. Realistic objectives have to be set for the sales people based on their cultural expectations. This is especially true in setting goals and establishing measures such as quotas. If either of these is set unrealistically, the result will be frustration for both parties. Cultural sensitivity also is required in situations where the exporter has to interact with the intermediary's sales force—in training situations, for example. In some cultures, such as those in Asia, the exporter is expected to act as a teacher and more or less dictate how things are done, while in some others, such as in Northern Europe, training sessions may be conducted in a seminar-like atmosphere of give and take.

4. Learn from your local representatives. If the sales force perceives a lack of fit between the marketer's product and the market, as well as inability to do anything about it, the result will be sub-optimal. A local sales force is an asset to the exporter, given its close contact with customers. Beyond daily feedback, the exporter is wise to undertake two additional approaches to exploit the experience of local salespeople. First, the exporter should have a program by which local salespeople can visit the exporter's operations and interact with the staff. If the exporter is active in multiple markets of the same region, it is advisable to develop ways to put salespeople in charge of the exporter's products in different markets to exchange ideas and best practice. Naturally, it is in the best interest of the exporter also to make regular periodic visits to markets entered.

An approach that requires more commitment from the exporter is to employ its own sales representatives, whose main function is to represent the firm abroad to existing and potential customers and to seek new leads. It is also important to sell with intermediaries, by supporting and augmenting their efforts. This type of presence is essential at some stage of the firm's international involvement. Other promotional tools can facilitate foreign market entry, but eventually some personal selling must take place. A cooperative effort with the intermediaries is important at this stage, in that some of them may be concerned about the motives of the exporter in the long term. For example, an intermediary may worry that once the exporter has learned enough about the market, it will no longer need the services of the intermediary. If these suspicions become prevalent, sales information may no longer flow to the exporter in the quantity and quality needed.

Integrated Exports   In the final stage of export-based internationalization, the exporter internalizes the effort through either a sales office in the target market or a direct contact

---

[60]Charlene Solomon, "Managing an Overseas Sales Force," *World Trade*, April 1999, S4–S6.

THE INTERNATIONAL MARKETPLACE 12.5

Automating the Sales Force

IN THE EARLY 1990s, Dataram Corp. saw its sales shriveling and its distributor-based sales struggling to meet the needs of a rapidly changing market. To survive, Dataram executives decided the company had to go directly to its worldwide customers. However, with only a few in-house sales representatives and inadequate mechanisms to track leads and service customers, the Princeton, New Jersey–based supplier of storage and memory products for high-end computers faced an uphill battle against formidable odds.

The most critical decision in Dataram's change of approach was to automate its sales force. The company's sales representatives and managers worldwide now are equipped with Dell notebook computers listing vital information about their clients and the company's products and services. The system is used to manage database marketing activity, such as lead generation and tracking, trade shows, telemarketing, advertising tracking, product support, and customer service. Management can also spot emerging trends, avert impending disasters, and forecast sales with the help of the system. "When a sales rep can answer a question in 15 minutes instead of three days, the company is perceived as a consultant as much as a vendor," say company officials. Recruiting salespeople may be easier when a company can offer state-of-the-art support. Futhermore, if turnover takes place, important customer information is not lost but preserved in the database.

Sales force automation, like anything else in marketing, is subject to the realities of the international environment: borders, time zones, languages, and cultures. Sales professionals may see their customer accounts as proprietary and are not willing to share the information in fear of losing their leverage. Furthermore, in markets where personal relationships drive sales practices, such as in Latin America, technological wizardry may be frowned upon. Representatives in every country may want to do things slightly differently, which means that a system that can be localized is needed. This localization may be as comprehensive as complete language translations or as minor as changing address fields in the database. Another issue to be considered is cost—hardware costs are higher in Europe, and telecommunications costs have to be factored in. Finally, with transoceanic support needs, the company may want to look for local support or invest in keeping desk personnel on board at off-hours.

A significant concern is the cost. A Latin American company may face a price tag of $2 million for a large company or $700,000 for a mid-sized or small firm. However, according to a recent study, automated companies have realized sales increases of 10 to 30 percent, and in some cases as much as 100 percent.

SOURCES: Kathleen V. Schmidt, "Why SFA Is a Tough Sell in Latin America," *Marketing News*, January 3, 2000; Steven Barth, "Building a Global Infrastructure," *World Trade*, April 1999, S8–S10; Eric J. Adams, "Sales Force Automation: The Second Time Around," *World Trade*, March 1996, 72–74; "Risky Business," *World Trade*, December 1995, 50–51; and "Power Tool," *World Trade*, November 1993, 42–44.

with the buyer from home base. This is part of the exporter's perceived need for increased **customer relationship management**, where the sales effort is linked to call-center technologies, customer-service departments, and the company's web site. This may include also automating the sales force as seen in *The International Marketplace 12.5*. The establishment of a sales office does not have to mean an end to the use of intermediaries; the exporter's salespeople may be dedicated to supporting intermediaries' sales efforts.

At this stage, expatriate sales personnel, especially those needed to manage the effort locally or regionally, may be used. The benefits of expatriates are their better understanding of the company and its products, and their ability to transfer best practice to the local operation. With expatriate management, the exporter can exercise a high amount of control over the sales function. Customers may also see the sales office and its expatriate staff as a long-term commitment to the market. The challenges lie mostly in the fit of the chosen individual to the new situation. The cost of having expatriate staff is considerable, approximately 2.5 times the cost at home, and the availability of suitable talent may be a problem, especially if the exporting organization is relatively small.[61]

The role of personal selling is greatest when the exporter sells directly to the end user or to governmental agencies, such as foreign trade organizations. Firms selling products with high price tags (such as Boeing commercial aircraft) or companies selling to monopsonies (such as Seagrams liquor to certain Northern European countries, where all liquor sales are through state-controlled outlets) must rely heavily on person-to-person communication, oral presentations, and direct-marketing efforts. Many of these firms can expand their business only if their markets are knowledgeable about what they do. This may require corporate advertising and publicity generation through extensive public relations efforts.

Whatever the sales task, effectiveness is determined by a number of interrelated factors. One of the keys to personal selling is the salesperson's ability to adapt to the customer and the selling situation.[62] This aspect of selling requires cultural knowledge and empathy; for example, in the Middle East, sales presentations may be broken up by long discussions of topics that have little or nothing to do with the transaction at hand. The characteristics of the buying task, whether routine or unique, have a bearing on the sales presentation. The exporter may be faced by a situation in which the idea of buying from a foreign entity is the biggest obstacle in terms of the risks perceived. If the exporter's product does not provide a clear-cut relative advantage over that of competitors, the analytical, interpersonal skills of the salesperson are needed to assist in the differentiation. A salesperson, regardless of the market, must have a thorough knowledge of the product or service. The more the salesperson is able to apply that knowledge to the particular situation, the more likely it is that he or she will obtain a positive result. The salesperson usually has front-line responsibility for the firm's customer relations, having to handle conflict situations such as the parent firm's bias for domestic markets and thus the possibility that shipments of goods to foreign clients receive low priority.

SUMMARY

Effective communication is essential in negotiating agreements. To maximize the outcome of negotiations with clients and partners from other cultural backgrounds, international marketers must show adjustment capability to different standards and behaviors. Success depends on being prepared and remaining flexible, whatever the negotiation style in the host country.

Effective and efficient communication is needed for the dual purpose of (1) informing prospective customers about the availability of products or services and (2) persuading customers to opt for the marketer's offering over those of competitors. Within the framework of the company's opportunities, resources, and objectives, decisions must be made about whether to direct communications to present customers, potential customers, the general public, or intermediaries. Decisions must be made on how to reach each of the intended target audiences without wasting valuable resources. A decision also has to be made about who will control the communications effort: the exporter, an agency, or local representatives. The U.S. Department of Commerce is the single best source of export promotion support, which is essential in alleviating the environmental threats perceived by many exporters.

[61]For a detailed discussion of the expatriate phenomenon, see Michael R. Czinkota, Ilkka A. Ronkainen, and Michael H. Moffett, *International Business: 2000 Update* (Fort Worth, TX: The Dryden Press, 2000), chapter 20.

[62]Alf H. Walle, "Conceptualizing Personal Selling for International Business: A Continuum of Exchange Perspective," *Journal of Personal Selling and Sales Management* 6 (November 1986): 9–17.

The exporting international marketer must also choose tools to use in the communications effort. Usually, two basic tools are used: (1) mass selling through business and trade journals, direct mail, the Internet, trade shows and missions, and (2) personal selling, which brings the international marketer face-to-face with the targeted customer.

QUESTIONS FOR DISCUSSION

1. What is potentially harmful in going out of one's way to make clients feel comfortable by playing down status distinctions such as titles?
2. Discuss this statement: "Lack of foreign-language skills puts U.S. negotiators at a disadvantage."
3. Compare and contrast the usefulness to a novice exporter of elements of the promotional mix.
4. Why do exporters usually choose U.S.-based services when placing advertisements to boost export sales specifically?
5. Some exporters report that they value above all the broad exposure afforded through exhibiting at a trade show, regardless of whether they are able to sell directly at the event. Comment on this philosophy.
6. What specific advice would you give to an exporter who has used domestic direct marketing extensively and wishes to continue the practice abroad?

7. Many traditionalists do not foresee that virtual trade shows will become a major threat to the actual shows themselves. Their view is that nothing can replace the actual seeing or touching of a product in person. Visit the E-Expo USA site (**www.e-expousa.doc.gov**) and develop arguments for and/or against this view.
8. The U.S. Exporters' Yellow Pages changed to www.myEXPORTS.COM in 2000. Will the fact that it is now an Internet-based service add to its ability to "offer U.S. firms a means to promote their businesses worldwide" and "attract appropriate foreign customers"? The service is available at **www.myEXPORTS.com**.

RECOMMENDED READINGS

Handbook of International Direct Marketing. London: Kogan Page Ltd., 1999.

Hendon, Donald W., Rebecca A. Hendon, and Paul Herbig. *Cross-Cultural Business Negotiations.* New York: Praeger, 1999.

Jagoe, John R. and Agnes Brown. *Export Sales and Marketing Manual.* Washington, D.C.: Export Institute, 1999.

Reedy, Joel, Shauna Schullo, and Kenneth Zimmerman. *Electronic Marketing.* Fort Worth, TX: The Dryden Press, 2000.

Schuster, Camille P. and Michael J. Copeland. *Global Business: Planning for Sales and Negotiations.* Fort Worth, TX: The Dryden Press, 1997.

Shimp, Terence A. *Advertising, Promotion, and Supplemental Aspects of Integrated Marketing Communications.* Fort Worth, TX: The Dryden Press, 2000.

Tussie, Diane, ed. *The Environment and International Trade Negotiations.* London: St. Martin's Press, 1999.

Zeff, Robbin Lee and Brad Aronson. *Advertising on the Internet.* New York: John Wiley & Sons, 1999.

Zimmerman, Jan and Jerry Yang. *Marketing on the Internet.* New York: Maximum Press, 1999.

Channels and Distribution Strategies

Different Ways of Getting the Job Done in Latin America

CHANGING MARKET CONDITIONS from the Rio Grande to Tierra del Fuego are making U.S., European, and Japanese companies reassess their distribution strategies in South and Central America. Regional trade pacts and free trade are enabling companies both to consider entry and to reformulate their strategies in the region. In the past, the infrastructure for effective and efficient distribution was largely missing. For example, in the past underdeveloped and monopolistic distributor networks saw as their primary job distributing sales literature and cutting through red tape and charging invariably high fees.

Times are changing for these intermediaries, however. The agent of that change is competition. Outside competition has forced distributors to add value to what they do, either by carrying inventory, providing specialized packaging, participating in the logistics infrastructure, handling shipments when they arrive, or otherwise serving the customers' needs. And if locals do not measure up, companies are willing to look for other solutions, such as using outside captive distribution systems or putting their people in place.

There are no standard answers as to distribution system design. In many cases, companies have found that a mix of techniques yields the best results and allows greater responsiveness to customer requests, as shown by the following three examples.

Motorola in Brazil Motorola's subsidiary combines in-house systems with an independent distributor network. It uses an in-house sales force to service large manufacturing clients and major end users of its line of imported and domestic semiconductors and portable radios, as well as cellular tele-

phones and pagers. Other customers are served through four large distribution firms. Subrepresentatives are contracted by distributors to provide coverage in areas where they do not have a direct presence. The company has determined that sales made via a distributor at this level are cheaper than direct sales. Distributors can offer fast delivery because in-house inventories are maintained.

ICI in Mexico ICI markets agrochemicals, explosives, paints, specialty chemicals, and dyes and chooses a distribution approach based on the size of sales and need for technical assistance. The company prefers to sell industrial products directly when possible due to the technical service they require. For example, the firm trains mining clients in explosives and provides on-site studies to determine appropriate blasting methods. The paint business in Mexico City is handled by in-house sales representatives that sell directly to retail stores. ICI products are oriented toward the high-quality, high-price market.

Management takes pains to ensure the quality of retail service, with sales representatives monitoring outlets. Even when independents handle products, the company's sales department continuously assesses the performance of the distribution chain.

Eveready in Argentina Battery makers sell a large share of their product through small retailers. In Argentina, which is one of the 160 countries in which Energizer and Eveready brands are available, kiosks are one of the most important outlets and product turnover is high. Eveready reaches thousands of kiosks by selling to some 600 independent distributors throughout the country. Distributors are attracted to the firm because of the high product turnover rate and its strong name recognition. Eveready reaches distributors through a national shipping company that carries products to remote markets.

SOURCES: Judi E. Loomis, "Shipping to Latin America," *World Trade,* November 1999, 62–68; Erika Morphy, "Pan-American Byways," *Export Today,* December 1996, 20–28; Joseph V. Barks, "Penetrating Latin America," *International Business,* February 1994, 76–80; "Choosing the Right System: Direct Sales vs. Independents," *Business International,* January 13, 1992, 12; and "Winning Approaches to Distribution in LA," *Business International,* January 13, 1992, 12–13.

http://www.mot.com

http://www.ici.com

http://www.eveready.com

CHANNELS OF DISTRIBUTION provide the essential linkages that connect producers and customers. The links are intracompany and extracompany entities that perform a number of functions. Optimal distribution systems are flexible and are able to adjust to market conditions, as seen in *The International Marketplace 13.1.* In general, companies use one or more of the following distribution systems: (1) the firm sells directly to customers through its own field sales force or through electronic commerce; (2) the company operates through independent **intermediaries,** usually at the local level; or (3) the business depends on an outside distribution system that may have regional or global coverage. For example, a number of Asian and European computer makers use the services of Merisel, Inc, a $5 billion technology products company based in California, to reach resellers throughout the North American market in addition to their own direct efforts.

A channel of distribution should be seen as more than a sequence of marketing institutions connecting producers and consumers; it should be a team working toward a common goal. In today's marketing environment, being close to customers, be they the final consumer or intermediary, and solving their problems is vital to bringing about success. When an office supplies superstore customer kicked off a joint venture in Australia, 3M dispatched two employees to its Australian subsidiary to educate that division on the special needs of a superstore.[1]

Since most marketers cannot or do not want to control the distribution function completely, structuring channel relationships becomes a crucial task. The importance of this task is further compounded by the fact that the channel decision is the most long-term of the marketing mix decisions in that, once established, it cannot easily be changed. In export marketing operations a new dimension is added to the task: the export channel decision in addition to making market-specific decisions. An experienced exporter may decide that control is of utmost importance and choose to perform tasks itself and incur the information collection and adaptation costs. An infrequent exporter, on the other hand, may be quite dependent on experienced intermediaries to get its product to markets. Whether export tasks are self-performed or assigned to export intermediaries, the distribution function should be planned so that the channel will function as one rather than as a collection of different or independent units. The decisions involved in the structuring and management of the export channel of distribution are discussed first. The chapter will end with a discussion of the steps needed in preparation for e-commerce. Logistics issues will be discussed in detail in Chapter 19.

[1]Rahul Jacob, "Why Some Customers Are More Equal Than Others," *Fortune,* September, 1994, 215–224.

Channel Structure

A generalization of channel configurations for consumer and industrial products as well as services is provided in Figure 13.1. Channels can vary from direct, producer-to-consumer types to elaborate, multilevel channels employing many types of intermediaries, each serving a particular purpose. For example, Amstrad, a British telecommunication and consumer-products manufacturer, sells its products in Spain in more than 4,200 retail outlets. To have this reach, it sells through four types of channels: (1) large accounts, such as the country's largest department stores, (2) buyer groups, consisting of national and regional associations of consumer electronics retailers, (3) independent appliance retailers and informatics stores, and (4) wholesalers, who reach accounts that the other channel types cannot reach.[2] It also makes its products available through on-line retailers such as Universal Direct.

Channel configurations for the same product will vary within industries, even within the same firm, because national markets quite often have their unique features. This may mean dramatic departures from accepted policy for a company. For example, to reach the British market, which is dominated by a few retailers such as J. Sainsbury, TESCO, and ASDA, marketers such as Heinz may have to become suppliers to these retailers' private-label programs in addition to making their own efforts.[3] A firm's international market experience will also cause variation in distribution patterns. AMPAK, a manufacturer of packaging machinery, uses locally based distributors in markets where it is well established. Others are entered indirectly by using domestically based intermediaries: either by using the services of trading companies or through selling to larger companies, which then market the products alongside their own.[4]

The connections made by marketing institutions are not solely for the physical movement of goods. They also serve as transactional title flows and informational communications flows. Rather than unidirectional, downward from the producer, the flows are usually multidirectional, both vertical and horizontal. As an example, the manufacturer relies heavily on the retailer population for data on possible changes in demand. Communications from retailers may be needed to coordinate a cooperative advertising campaign instituted by a manufacturer. The three flows—physical, transactional, and informational—do not necessarily take place simultaneously or occur at every level of the channel. Agent intermediaries, for example, act only to facilitate the information flow; they do not take title and often do not physically handle the goods. Similarly, electronic intermediaries, such as Amazon.com, have to rely on facilitating agents to perform the logistics function of their operation.

Because only a few products are sold directly to ultimate users, an international marketer has to decide on alternative ways to move products to chosen markets. The basic marketing functions of exchange, physical movement, and various facilitating activities must be performed, but the marketer may not be equipped to handle them. Intermediaries can therefore be used to gain quick, easy, and relatively low-cost entry to a targeted market.

[2]"How Amstrad Successfully Set Up a Distribution Channel in Spain," *Business International/Ideas in Action,* March 14, 1988, 4–6. See also **http://www.amstrad.com**.

[3]François Glémet and Rafel Mira, "The Brand Leader's Dilemma," *The McKinsey Quarterly,* 33 (Number 2, 1993): 3–15.

[4]"Exporting Pays Off," *Business America,* October 7, 1991, 9.

FIGURE 13.1 | **Channel Configurations**

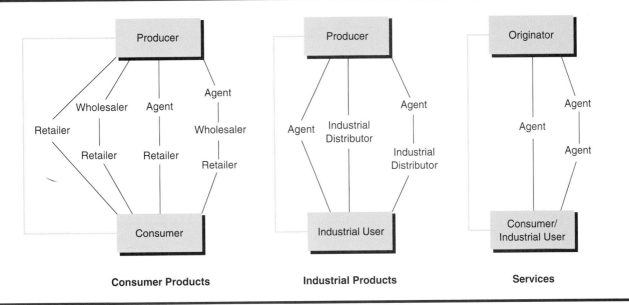

Consumer Products   **Industrial Products**   **Services**

Channel Design

The term *channel design* refers to the length and the width of the channel employed. Length is determined by the number of levels, or different types, of intermediaries. In the case of consumer products, the most traditional is the producer-wholesaler-retailer-customer configuration. Channel width is determined by the number of institutions of each type in the channel. An industrial goods marketer may grant exclusive distribution rights to a foreign entity, whereas a consumer goods marketer may want to use as many intermediaries as possible to ensure intensive distribution.

Channel design is determined by factors that can be summarized as the 11 Cs, listed in Table 13.1. These factors are integral to both the development of new marketing channels and the modification and management of existing ones. Their individual influences will vary from one market to another, and seldom, if ever, can one factor be considered without the interactive effects of the others. The marketer should use the 11 Cs checklist to determine the proper approach to reach intended target audiences before selecting channel members to fill the roles. The first three factors are givens, since the firm must adjust to the existing structures. The other eight are controllable to a certain extent by the international marketer.

Customer Characteristics

The demographic and psychographic characteristics of targeted customers will form the basis for channel design decisions. Answers to questions such as what customers need—as well as why, when, and how they buy—are used to determine ways in which the products should be made available to generate a competitive advantage. As an example, Anheuser-Busch entered Japan when Suntory, one of the country's largest liquor distillers, acquired the importing rights. Suntory's marketing plan stressed distribution of Budweiser in discos, pubs, and other night spots where Japan's affluent, well-traveled youth gather. Young people in Japan are influenced by U.S. culture and

TABLE 13.1	**Determinants of Channel Structure and Relationships**

EXTERNAL
Customer characteristics
Culture
Competition

INTERNAL
Company objectives
Character
Capital
Cost
Coverage
Control
Continuity
Communication

adapt themselves more readily to new products than do older Japanese. Taking advantage of this fact, Suntory concentrated its efforts on one generation, and on-premise sales led to major off-premise (retail outlet) sales as well.

In the early stages of product introduction, the international marketer may concentrate efforts on only the most attractive markets and later, having attained a foothold, expand distribution. When Kronenbourg, the best-selling beer in Europe, entered the U.S. market, distribution was initiated in New York City and then extended to the metropolitan area. The reason was the area's prominence in both domestic and imported beer consumption. The national rollout took place five years later. In the industrial sector, certain industries cluster geographically, allowing the international marketer to take a more direct approach.

Customer characteristics may cause the same product to be distributed through two different types of channels. Many industrial goods marketers' sales, such as those of Caterpillar, are handled by individual dealers, except when the customer might be the central government or one of its entities, in which case sales are direct from the company itself. Furthermore, primary target audiences may change from one market to another. For example, in Japan, McDonald's did not follow the U.S. pattern of locating restaurants in the suburbs. The masses of young pedestrians that flood Japanese cities were more promising than affluent but tradition-minded car owners in the suburbs.[5]

In business-to-business marketing, the adoption of e-commerce provides new opportunities for international marketers. New export markets can be accessed by expanding network and customer bases. Six sectors are forecast to leading the way in business-to-business online transactions by 2003: retail, motor vehicles, shipping, industrial equipment, technological products, and government.[6]

Culture

In planning a distribution system, the marketer must analyze existing channel structures, or what might be called **distribution culture.** As an example, the manner in which Japanese channels of distribution are structured and managed presents one of the major reasons for the apparent failure of foreign firms to establish major market

[5]Frederick H. Katayama, "Japan's Big Mac," *Fortune,* September 15, 1986, 114–120.

[6]The Boston Consulting Group, December 21, 1999; available at **http://www.bcg.com**

TABLE 13.2 Examples of Function Performance in the Channel System for the Japanese Cosmetics Industry

	CHANNEL MEMBER	
MANUFACTURER	INTERMEDIARY	RETAIL
Production	Order taking	Selling
Advertising	Inventory maintenance	Organizing consumers
National sales promotion	Space control at the retail level	In-store promotion
Dealer aids	Product assortment	
Education of dealers	Dispatching of sales support personnel	
Financing	Area marketing	
	Financing	

SOURCE: Michael R. Czinkota, "Distribution of Consumer Products in Japan: An Overview," *International Marketing Review* 2 (Autumn 1985): 39–51.

penetration in Japan.[7] In any case, and in every country, international marketers must study distribution systems in general and the types of linkages between channel members for their specific type of product. Usually, the international marketer has to adjust to existing structures to gain distribution. For example, in Finland, 92 percent of all distribution of nondurable consumer goods is through four wholesale chains. Without their support, no significant penetration of the market is possible.

In addition to structure, functions performed by the various types of intermediaries have to be outlined. Retailers in Japan demand more from manufacturers and wholesalers than do U.S. retailers; for example, they expect returns of merchandise to be fully accepted even if there is no reason other than lack of sales. Retailers also expect significant amounts of financing and frequent delivery of products. Retailers, on their part, offer substantial services to their clientele and take great pains to build close relationships with their customers. As can be seen in Table 13.2, which lists channel members in the Japanese cosmetics industry, functions are—and should be—clearly delineated. Manufacturers concentrate mainly on production and promotional activities; intermediaries work on logistics activities, financing, and communication with manufacturers and retailers; retailers focus on sales and promotional activities.

Changing existing distribution systems may be quite difficult. Porsche tried to change the way it sold automobiles in the United States from traditional independent franchised dealers to a "dealerless system." Whereas dealers buy cars for resale, Porsche would have instituted agents who would order cars as they sold them and work on an 8 percent commission rather than the normal 16 to 18 percent margin. After an uproar, Porsche abandoned the plan.[8] Toys 'Я' Us, which opened its first outlet in Japan in 1992, initially had a difficult time getting Japanese toy manufacturers to sell to it directly (as happens in the United States) rather than through multiple layers of distributors. Similarly, direct sales by marketers through the Internet are raising concerns among distributors who feel that they lose out on these opportunities. Regardless of whether these are completely new sales or come from customers who would have used traditional channels before, intermediaries should be compensated for these sales in some way, such as through e-credits on their next purchase from the marketer, to acknowledge their role in developing the local market.

Additionally, an analysis is needed of the relationships between channel members—for example, the extent of vertical integration. The linkage can be based on

[7]Michael R. Czinkota and Jon Woronoff, *Unlocking Japan's Market* (Rutland, VT: Tuttle Co., 1993).

[8]David B. Tinnin, "Porsche's Civil War with Its Dealers," *Fortune*, April 16, 1984, 63–68.

ownership, contract, or the use of expert or referent power by one of the channel members. The Japanese distribution system often financially links producers, importers, distributors, and retailers, either directly or through a bank or a trading company. Interdependence in a number of southern European markets is forged through family relationships or is understood as an obligation.

Foreign legislation affecting distributors and agents is an essential part of the distribution culture of a market. For example, legislation may require that foreign firms be represented only by firms that are 100 percent locally owned. In China, for example, foreign companies are barred from importing their own products, distributing them or providing after-sales service. These functions are to be performed by Chinese companies or Sino-foreign joint ventures. With China joining the WTO, however, these restrictions will all be phased out within three years. This means that General Motors China Group will regain control over its Opel Vectra. Up to now, Chinese companies have handled the importing, distributing and selling, and the cars have often passed through four different entities before customers see them. In the future, GM wants to build a consistent network of dealers and start providing financing, which also becomes allowed.[9]

While distribution decisions have been mostly tactical and made on a market-by-market basis, marketing managers have to be cognizant of globalization in the distribution function as well.[10] This is taking place in two significant ways. Distribution formats are crossing borders, especially to newly emerging markets. While supermarkets accounted only for 8 percent of consumer nondurable sales in urban areas in Thailand in 1990, the figure today approaches 45 percent.[11] Other such formats include department stores, minimarts, and supercenters. The second globalization trend is the globalization of intermediaries themselves either independently or through strategic alliances. Entities such as Toys 'Я' Us from the United States, Galeries Lafayette from France, Marks & Spencer from the United Kingdom, and Takashimaya and Isetan from Japan have expanded to both well developed and newly emerging markets. Within the European Union, a growing number of EU-based retailers are merging and establishing a presence in other EU markets. For example, the merger of France's Carrefour and Promodes in 1999 created the world's second largest retailer after Wal-Mart. The merger was partly in response to Wal-Mart's European expansion.[12] Some intermediaries are entering foreign markets by acquiring local entities (e.g., Germany's Tengelmann and Holland's Ahold acquiring the U.S. chains A&P and Giant, respectively) or forming alliances. For example, in Mexico, joint ventures between Wal-Mart and Cifra, Fleming Cos. and Gigante, and Price/Costco and Comercial Mexicana are changing the distribution landscape by concentrating retail power. Beyond opportunity for marketers for more and broader-based sales, these entities are applying the same type of margin pressure marketers find in more developed markets. In many cases, marketers are providing new technologies to these intermediaries and helping to train them with the hope of establishing solid relationships that will withstand competition, especially from local entities that typically start beefing up their own operations.[13] *The International Marketplace 13.2* highlights some of these approaches.

[9]"WTO May Help Foreign Firms Clear China's Distribution Hurdles," *The Wall Street Journal,* December 17, 1999, A12.

[10]Alan Treadgold, "The Developing Internationalisation of Retailing," *International Journal of Retailing* 18 (1990): 4–11.

[11]Carla Rapoport, "Nestle's Brand Building Machine," *Fortune,* September 19, 1994, 147–156.

[12]"European Retailing: French Fusion," *The Economist,* September 4, 1999, 68–69.

[13]"Teach Me Shopping," *The Economist,* December 18, 1993, 64–65.

THE INTERNATIONAL MARKETPLACE 13.2

Retailers to the World

RETAILING CROSSING BORDERS is difficult at best of times, and few players have been able to establish cross-border presence successfully. Nonetheless, rising incomes, improvements in infrastructure, and deregulation are enlarging consumer markets around the world and accelerating the convergence of consumer tastes. The Internet is making customers more accessible, while computers and videoconferencing are cutting the cost of doing business far from headquarters. Wal-Mart, based entirely in the United States until 1991, had more than 700 stores in Canada, South America, Europe, and Asia by the year 2000. Carrefour, which has been international since the 1970s, has built store networks on three continents. Ahold, in turn, has bought businesses in more than ten countries since 1995. To win in international retailing, most players will have to position themselves so that they can reinvent competitive advantage in each new market. This can be achieved in four possible ways:

Business Exporter These retailers will reconfigure their entire retailing approach across and within individual markets. IKEA, the Swedish furniture retailer, has mastered the management of relationships with both customers and suppliers. By teaching customers to assemble furniture, it has cut its manufacturing and distribution costs. By intensely communicating its fashion perspective, it has built up a following across widely different markets for a relatively consistent line of Scandinavian-inspired furniture, thus boosting volume, which again reduces costs. Its buying offices scan the globe for potential suppliers, and its staff coach them to raise productivity and achieve high quality standards. Other retailers such as Wal-Mart, Carrefour, and Makro are adopting this approach. The Dutch Makro is expanding its discounting approach by focusing on selling bulk to small shopkeepers.

Concept Exporter Benetton's strategy is to export a distinctive concept, but let someone else run it. Benetton's strength lies in its image, which it controls very closely. A vital ingredient in this is effective control of the franchise execution. The Body Shop is another company following this internationalization approach.

Skills Exporter Companies can export unique skills rather than entire business systems, as Price/Costco has done with Shinsegae in Korea. Shinsegae, which in itself is a large and diversified retail group, operates Seoul Price Club under a ten-year agreement. Price/Costco is contributing a number of important assets and skills to this arrangement, including its brand name, its operating approach, its merchandising systems, and its access to low-cost suppliers, through which 25 percent of the Seoul outlet's goods are imported. Shinsegae provides capital, sites, staff, and sourcing.

Superior Operator The retailer expands internationally on the strength of its operating capability. The German retailer Tengelmann's acquisition and turnaround of A&P in the United States is an example of this approach. After it acquired A&P, Tengelmann was able to restructure operations, launch new store formats, and buy new stores. Hard discounters such as Germany's Aldi (which focuses mostly on its private-label brands) have already secured sizable market share in Germany, Belgium, and Denmark, and are growing fast in countries such as France.

Difficulties will abound. Some may not be perceived as providing an advantage. For example, when Galeries Lafayette attempted to export a high-end Parisian fashion concept to the United States, it was not seen as exclusive enough in the highly competitive Manhattan market. In addition, governments may step up to support their small to medium-sized businesses that are threatened by large chains and large outlets such as hypermarkets.

SOURCES: Denise Incandela, Kathleen L. McLaughlin, and Christiana Smith Shi, "Retailers to the World," *The McKinsey Quarterly* 35 (Number 3, 1999): 84–97; Karen Barth, Nancy J. Karch, Kathleen McLaughlin, and Christiana Smith Shi, "Global Retailing: Tempting Trouble?" *The McKinsey Quarterly* 32 (Number 1, 1996): 116–125; Joy L. Jentes, "Walling Out Wal-Mart?" *Export Today* 12 (April 1996): 61–62; "Change at the Check-Out," *The Economist*, March 4, 1995, a survey of retailing; and Carla Rapoport, "Retailers Go Global," *Fortune*, February 20, 1995, 102–108.

Competition

Channels used by competitors may be the only product distribution system that is accepted by both the trade and consumers. In this case, the international marketer's task is to use the structure effectively and efficiently. One challenge, even for a sizable entity such as IBM, may be to create a distribution system as extensive as that of an established competitor. IBM can send a sales team out of its Tokyo office or one of its 50 branch offices to sell a system to a large buyer, such as a bank or industrial company. Hitachi, on the other hand, has 10,000 exclusive retail dealers and a sales force already selling motors and other machinery to hundreds of commercial customers. To emulate the distribution approach of this major competitor, IBM enlisted the help of more than 60 outside dealers, such as Nissan Motor outlets, to sell small computers to their customers.

The alternative is to use a distribution approach totally different from that of the competition and hope to develop a competitive advantage. A new approach will have to be carefully analyzed and tested against the cultural, political, and legal environments in which it is to be introduced. For example, Black Box, a Pittsburgh-based manufacturer of computer-communications equipment, found that its independent foreign distributors often pushed only the most profitable lines regardless of who made them. Black Box's solution was to form jointly owned sales companies.[14] In some cases, the international marketer cannot manipulate the distribution variable. For example, in Sweden and Finland, all alcoholic beverages must be distributed through state monopoly–owned outlets. In Japan, the Japan Tobacco & Salt Public Corporation is a state monopoly that controls all tobacco imports and charges a 20 percent fee for distribution.

In some cases, all feasible channels may be blocked by domestic competitors either through contractual agreements or through other means. U.S. suppliers of soda ash, which is used in glass, steel, and chemical products, have not been able to penetrate the Japanese market even though they offer a price advantage. The reason is the cartel-like condition developed by the Japan Soda Industry Association, which allegedly sets import levels, specifies which local trading company is to deal with each U.S. supplier, and buys the imports at lower U.S. prices for resale by its members at higher Japanese prices. Efforts by U.S. producers to distribute directly or through smaller, unaffiliated traders have faced strong resistance. The end users and traders fear alienating the domestic producers, on whom their business depends.

Company Objectives

A set of management considerations will have an effect on channel design. No channel of distribution can be properly selected unless it meets the requirements set by overall company objectives for market share and profitability. Sometimes management may simply want to use a particular channel of distribution, and there may be no sound business basis for the decision.

Channels of distribution will have to change as the operations of the company expand. For example, Xerox set a goal of having noncopier sales account for 50 percent of the company's worldwide business in the 1990s. Before this decision, copiers, accounting for 95 percent of sales, were sold mainly through the company's own direct sales force. In France, Xerox dramatically changed its distribution by setting up a chain of retail sales outlets, wholly owned and run by the company. To improve its coverage of rural areas and small towns, Xerox withdrew its direct sales force and replaced it with independent distributors, called **concessionaires,** who work on an exclusive basis.[15] One of the most expedient methods of market development is partnerships. However, many companies balk at this notion due to the perceived loss of control. As shown in the Starbucks example in Figure 13.2, partnerships can be undertaken if appropriate controls are in place to secure expansion with relatively little investment. If

[14]"Made in the U.S.A.," *Business Week,* February 29, 1988, 60–66.

[15]"Rank Xerox Reorganizes Distribution to Succeed in Europe," *Business International/Ideas in Action,* February 15, 1988, 2–5.

FIGURE 13.2 **Distribution Expansion Through Partnerships**

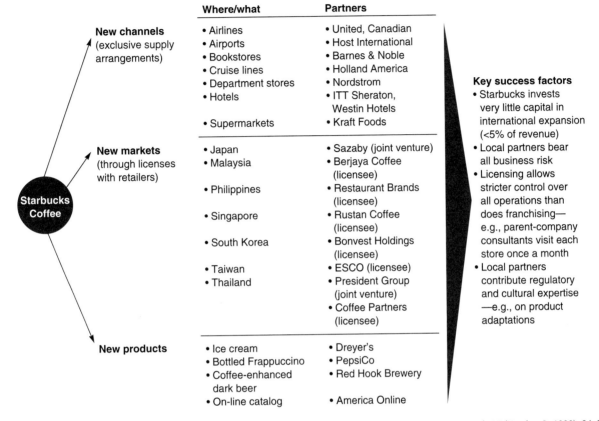

SOURCE: Denise Incandela, Kathleen L. McLaughlin, and Christiana Smith Shi, "Retailers to the World," *The McKinsey Quarterly* 35 (Number 3, 1999): 84–97. See also **http://www.starbucks.com**.

expansion is too rapid and the adjustments made to local market conditions too extensive, a major asset—standardization and economies of scale and scope—can be lost.

Character

The nature of the product, its character, will have an impact on the design of the channel. Generally, the more specialized, expensive, bulky, or perishable the product and the more after-sale service it may require, the more likely the channel is to be relatively short. Staple items, such as soap, tend to have longer channels.

The type of channel chosen must match the overall positioning of the product in the market. Changes in overall market conditions, such as currency fluctuations, may require changes in distribution as well. An increase in the value of the billing currency may cause a repositioning of the marketed product as a luxury item, necessitating an appropriate channel (such as an upper-grade department store) for its distribution.

Rules of thumb aside, particular products may be distributed in a number of ways even to the same target audience. Figure 13.3 shows the variety of distribution alternatives for soap in Japan. Case 1 presents the most frequently used channel. Product deliveries are made from the manufacturer to a wholesaler, who in turns delivers to a retailer. Payment flows go from the retailer to the wholesaler, who in turn pays the manufacturer. In Case 2, the larger wholesaler acts as an agent, receiving a 5 percent commission on the sale from the manufacturer. Case 3 is an example of the channel structures necessary to ensure the most intensive type of distribution.

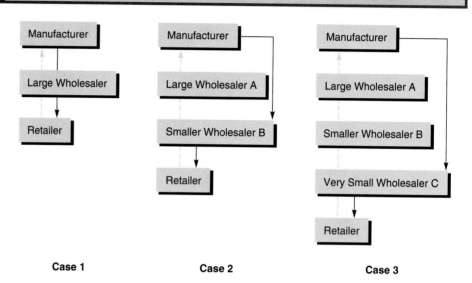

FIGURE 13.3 Variety of Distribution Alternatives: The Channels for Soap in Japan

SOURCE: Michael R. Czinkota, "Distribution of Consumer Products in Japan: An Overview," *International Marketing Review* 2 (Autumn 1985): 39–51.

Capital

The term *capital* is used to describe the financial requirements in setting up a channel system. The international marketer's financial strength will determine the type of channel and the basis on which channel relationships will be built. The stronger the marketer's finances, the more able the firm is to establish channels it either owns or controls. Intermediaries' requirements for beginning inventories, selling on a consignment basis, preferential loans, and need for training all will have an impact on the type of approach chosen by the international marketer. For example, an industrial goods manufacturer may find that potential distributors in a particular country lack the capability of servicing the product. The marketer then has two options: (1) set up an elaborate training program at headquarters or regionally or (2) institute company-owned service centers to help distributors. Either approach will require a significant investment.

Cost

Closely related to the capital dimension is cost—that is, the expenditure incurred in maintaining a channel once it is established. Costs will naturally vary over the life cycle of a relationship with a particular channel member as well as over the life cycle of the products marketed. An example of the costs involved is promotional money spent by a distributor for the marketer's product. A cooperative advertising deal between the international marketer and the intermediary would typically split the costs of the promotional campaign executed in the local market.

Costs will vary in terms of the relative power of the manufacturer vis-à-vis its intermediaries. The number of European retailers accounting for 75 percent of consumer sales has decreased from 132 in 1980 to 43 in 1999. This consolidation includes not only large retailers such as Ahold and Migros but also smaller retailers that have joined forces to form buying groups. One of the most significant is Expert Global (**www.expert.org**), which has a total of 6,400 participating retailers in 20 European, North American, and South American countries. The concentrated distribution systems being developed by these giants are eroding the marketing strength of manufac-

TABLE 13.3	Advantages of a Single Distributor

1. One corporate presence eliminates confusion among buyers and local officials.
2. The volume of business that results when exports are consolidated will attract a larger distributor. The larger distributor will have greater influence in its local business community.
3. Communication is less plagued by noise. This will have a positive effect in many areas, from daily information flows to supervising and training.
4. More effective coordination of the sales and promotional effort can be achieved.
5. Logistics flows are more economical.
6. A stronger presence can be maintained in smaller markets or markets in which resources may dictate a holding mode, until more effective penetration can be undertaken.
7. Distributor morale and the overall principal-intermediary relationship are better.

SOURCE: Business International Corporation, *201 Checklists: Decision Making in International Operations* (New York: Business International Corporation, 1980), 26–27.

turers, which lay in their networks of distribution depots that delivered direct to stores. Now, retailers want delivery to their central distribution centers. In addition, they are pushing stockholding costs to manufacturers by demanding more frequent deliveries, in smaller, mixed loads, with shorter delivery time.[16]

Costs may also be incurred in protecting the company's distributors against adverse market conditions. A number of U.S. manufacturers helped their distributors maintain competitive prices through subsidies when the exchange rate for the U.S. dollar caused pricing problems. Extra financing aid has been extended to distributors that have been hit with competitive adversity. Such support, although often high in monetary cost, will pay back manyfold through a faultless manufacturer-distributor relationship.

Coverage

The term *coverage* is used to describe both the number of areas in which the marketer's products are represented and the quality of that representation. Coverage is therefore two-dimensional in that horizontal and vertical coverage need to be considered in channel design. The number of areas to be covered depends on the dispersion of demand in the market and also on the time elapsed since the product's introduction to the market. Three different approaches are available:

1. Intensive coverage, which calls for distributing the product through the largest number of different types of intermediaries and the largest number of individual intermediaries of each type
2. Selective coverage, which entails choosing a number of intermediaries for each area to be penetrated
3. Exclusive coverage, which involves only one entity in a market

Generally, intensive and selective coverage call for longer channels using different types of intermediaries, usually wholesalers and agents. Exclusive distribution is conductive to more direct sales. For some products, such as ethnic products, markets are concentrated geographically and allow for more intensive distribution with a more direct channel. A company typically enters a market with one local distributor, but as volume expands, the distribution base often has to be adjusted. The advantages of a single distributor are listed in Table 13.3.

Expanding distribution too quickly may cause problems. Benetton, one of Italy's major exporters of clothing, had planned to have 1,000 stores in the United States by

[16]"How Dairy Crest Transformed Customer Service by Better Physical Distribution," *Business International/Ideas in Action,* April 11, 1988, 8–11.

1990. The plan was abandoned because of concerns about oversaturation of certain urban areas and overprojection of retail sales. Rather, more emphasis is being put on customer service, and the number of stores in major North American cities was 200 in 2000.[17] Similarly, expanding distribution from specialty outlets to mass distribution may have an impact on the product's image and the after-sales service associated with it. The impact on channel relations may be significant if existing dealers perceive loss of sales as a result of such a move. This may be remedied by keeping the product lines in mass-distribution outlets different or possibly developing a different brand for the new channels.

Control

The use of intermediaries will automatically lead to loss of some control over the marketing of the firm's products. The looser the relationship is between the marketer and intermediaries, the less control the marketer can exert. The longer the channel, the more difficult it becomes for the marketer to have a final say in pricing, promotion, and the types of outlets in which the product will be made available.

The decision to use intermediaries or to distribute via a company-owned, or integrated, distribution channel requires a major trade-off between the desire to control export efforts and the desire to minimize resource commitment costs.[18] In the initial stages of internationalization or specific market entry, an intermediary's specialized knowledge and working relationships are needed, but as exporters' experience base and sales in the market increase, many opt to establish their own sales offices.

The issue of control correlates heavily with the type of product or service being marketed. In the case of industrial and high-technology products, control will be easier to institute because intermediaries are dependent on the marketer for new products and service. Where the firm's marketing strategy calls for a high level of service, integrated channels are used to ensure that the service does get performed.[19]

The marketer's ability and willingness to exercise any type of power—whether reward, coercive, legitimate, referent, or expert—determines the extent of control. The exercise of control causes more incidents of conflict in channels of distribution than any other activity in the relationship. This points to the need for careful communication with foreign intermediaries about the marketer's intentions and also the need for certain control measures. These might include the marketer's need to be the sole source of advertising copy or to be in charge of all product-modification activities. Generally, the more control the marketer wishes to have, the more cost is involved in securing that control.

Continuity

Channel design decisions are the most long-term of the marketing mix decisions. Utmost care must therefore be taken in choosing the right type of channel, given the types of intermediaries available and any environmental threats that may affect the channel design. Occasionally, however, unpredictable events may occur. As an example, Cockspur, the largest distiller of rum in Barbados, negotiated an arrangement with one of the largest distributors in the United States. Almost immediately, the distributor was acquired by a company that thought liquor distribution did not fit its

[17]Curtis Pepper, "Fast Forward," *Business Month,* February 1989, 25–30.

[18]Erin Anderson and Hubert Gatignon, "Modes of Foreign Entry: A Transaction Cost Analysis and Propositions," *Journal of International Business Studies* 17 (Fall 1986): 1–26.

[19]Erin Anderson and Anne T. Coughlan, "International Market Entry and Expansion via Independent or Integrated Channels of Distribution," *Journal of Marketing* 51 (January 1987): 71–82.

mission and thus eliminated the products and reassigned the salespeople. Years later, Cockspur was still without substantial distribution in the United States.[20]

Nurturing continuity rests heavily on the marketer because foreign distributors may have a more short-term view of the relationship. For example, Japanese wholesalers believe that it is important for manufacturers to follow up initial success with continuous improvement of the product. If such improvements are not forthcoming, competitors are likely to enter the market with similar, lower-priced products, and the wholesalers of the imported product will turn to the Japanese suppliers.

The U.S. manufacturers of Odoreaters experienced such a development. After three years of costly market development efforts together with a Japanese wholesaler, the firm had reached a sales level of 3.8 million pairs. However, six months after product introduction, 12 comparable Japanese products had already been introduced. Because Odoreaters was not able to improve its product substantially over time, its wholesaler made an exclusive agreement with a competing firm—Scholl Inc.—and terminated the relationship with Odoreaters. Even though Odoreaters managed to find a new distributor, its sales dropped significantly.[21]

Continuity is also expressed through visible market commitment. Industries abroad may be quite conservative; distributors will not generally support an outsider until they are sure it is in the market to stay. Such commitments have included Kraft's listing on the Tokyo exchange[22] and some exporters' setting up wholly-owned sales subsidiaries from the start in Europe—and staffing them with locals to help communicate that the company is there for the long term.[23]

Communication

Communication provides the exchange of information that is essential to the functioning of the channel. Communication is an important consideration in channel design, and it gains more emphasis in international distribution because of various types of distances that may cause problems. In the buyer-seller relationships in industrial markets, the distance that is perceived to exist between a buyer and a seller has five aspects:

1. Social distance: the extent to which each of the two entities in a relationship is familiar with the other's ways of operating
2. Cultural distance: the degree to which the norms, values, or working methods between the two entities differ because of their separate national characteristics
3. Technological distance: the differences between the product or process technologies of the two entities
4. Time distance: the time that must elapse between establishing contact or placing an order and the actual transfer of the product or service involved.
5. Geographical distance: the physical distance between the locations of the two entities[24]

All these dimensions must be considered when determining whether to use intermediaries and, if they are to be used, what types to use.

---

[20]We are indebted to Dr. James H. Sood of the American University for this example.

[21]Michael R. Czinkota, "Distribution of Consumer Products in Japan: An Overview," *International Marketing Review* 2 (Autumn 1985): 39–51.

[22]"Opening of Japan's Food Market Spells Opportunity for Foreign Corporations," *Business International*, November 21, 1988, 366.

[23]Andrea Knox, "The European Minefield," *World Trade*, November 1999, 36–40.

[24]David Ford, "Buyer/Seller Relationships in International Industrial Markets," *Industrial Marketing Management* 13 (May 1984): 101–112.

Communication, if properly utilized, will assist the international marketer in conveying the firm's goals to the distributors, in solving conflict situations, and in marketing the product overall. Communication is a two-way process that does not permit the marketer to dictate to intermediaries. Cases are well known in which the marketer is not able to make the firm's marketing program functional. Prices may not be competitive; promotional materials may be obsolete or inaccurate and not well received overall.[25] Solving these problems is important to the welfare of both parties. However, the marketer's attempts to solve them may have met with resentment because of the way the distributor was approached.

Channels of distribution, because of their sequential positioning of the entities involved, are not conducive to noiseless communication. The marketer must design a channel and choose intermediaries that guarantee good information flow. Proper communication involves not only the passage of information between channel members but also a better understanding of each party's needs and goals. This can be achieved through personal visits, exchange of personnel, or distribution advisory councils. Consisting of members from all channel participants, advisory councils meet regularly to discuss opportunities and problems that may have arisen.

Selection of Intermediaries

Once the basic design of the channel has been determined, the international marketer must begin a search to fill the defined roles with the best-available candidates and must secure their cooperation.

Types of Intermediaries

Two basic decisions are involved in choosing the type of intermediaries to serve a particular market. First, the marketer must determine the type of relationship to have with intermediaries. The alternatives are distributorship and agency relationship. A **distributor** will purchase the product and will therefore exercise more independence than agencies. Distributors are typically organized along product lines and provide the international marketer with complete marketing services. **Agents** have less freedom of movement than distributors because they operate on a commission basis and do not usually physically handle the goods. This, in turn, allows the marketer control to make sure, for example, that the customer gets the most recent and appropriate product version. In addition to the business implications, the choice of type will have legal implications in terms of what the intermediary can commit its principal to and the ease of termination of the agreement.

Second, the international marketer must decide whether to utilize indirect exporting, direct exporting, or integrated distribution in penetrating a foreign market.[26] **Indirect exporting** requires dealing with another domestic firm that acts as a sales intermediary for the marketer, often taking over the international side of the marketer's operations. The benefits, especially in the short term, are that the exporter can use someone else's international channels without having to pay to set them up. But there may be long-term concerns in using this strategy if the marketer wants to actively and aggressively get into the markets itself. Indirect exporting is only practiced by firms very early on in their internationalization process. With **direct exporting,** the marketer takes direct responsibility for its products abroad by either selling directly to the

[25]Phillip J. Rosson, "Success Factors in Manufacturer–Overseas Distributor Relationships in International Marketing," in *International Marketing Management,* ed. Erdener Kaynak (New York: Praeger Publishing, 1984), 91–107.

[26]"Market Entry Strategy," *Business America,* March 25, 1991, 12–17; Frank Reynolds, "How to Capture the Flag," *Exporter* 3 (October 1991): 27–28.

| TABLE 13.4 | International Channel Intermediaries |

AGENTS

FOREIGN (DIRECT)	DOMESTIC (INDIRECT)
Brokers	Brokers
Manufacturer's representatives	Export agents
Factors	EMCs
Managing agents	Webb-Pomerene associations
Purchasing agents	Commission agents

DISTRIBUTORS

Distributors/dealers	Domestic wholesalers
Import jobbers	EMCs
Wholesalers/retailers	ETCs
	Complementary marketing

SOURCES: Peter B. Fitzpatrick and Alan S. Zimmerman, *Essentials of Export Marketing* (New York: American Management Association, 1985), 20; Bruce Seifert and John Ford, "Export Distribution Channels," *Columbia Journal of World Business* 24 (Summer 1989): 16.

foreign customer or finding a local representative to sell its products in the market. The third category of export marketing strategy, **integrated distribution,** requires the marketer to make an investment into the foreign market for the purpose of selling its products in that market or more broadly. This investment could be the opening, for example, of a German or EU sales office, a distribution hub, or even an assembly operation or manufacturing facility. Although the last set of strategies indicates longer-term commitment to a market, it is riskier than the first two because the marketer is making a major financial investment. For example, if the exporter moves from an agency agreement to a sales office, its costs for that market are now fixed costs (i.e., will be incurred even if no sales are made) from the previous variable costs. Setting up even a modest office may be expensive. For example, the monthly costs in 1996 of an office manager and secretary were $6,050 in the United States, $11,942 in Japan, $6,615 in Hong Kong, and $9,579 in Germany.[27] In addition, real estate costs can be substantial if the office is in a main business district.

The major types of intermediaries are summarized in Table 13.4. Care should be taken to understand conceptual differences that might exist from one market to another. For example, a **commissionario** may sell in his or her own name (as a distributor would) but for an undisclosed principal (an agency concept). Similarly, **a del credere agent** guarantees the solvency of the customer and may therefore be responsible to the supplier for payment by the customer.[28]

The respective strengths and weaknesses of various export intermediary types were discussed in Chapter 9.

Sources for Finding Intermediaries

Firms that have successful international distribution attest to the importance of finding top representatives. This undertaking should be held in the same regard as recruiting and hiring within the company because "an ineffective foreign distributor can

[27]"It Could Be Worse," *International Business,* April 1996, 8.

[28]Peter B. Fitzpatrick and Alan S. Zimmerman, *Essentials of Export Marketing* (New York: American Management Association, 1985), 43.

THE INTERNATIONAL MARKETPLACE 13.3

Putting the Best Boot Forward

IN THE EARLY 1980s, when most U.S. exporters were getting out of foreign markets, Timberland Shoes decided to find a new market for its line of rugged outdoor footgear. Initially, the firm had no idea it could be successful in international sales. "A tremendous amount of our decision was really luck. We were discovered by people in Europe who saw an opportunity for us to export at a time we did not believe we could. The good news is that once we realized there was an opportunity, we went after it," says the company's president.

Timberland's first choice—Italy—surprised many in the industry. Home to many of the world's best-known and high-priced brands of leather footwear, Italy had earned the reputation as the most sophisticated market in Europe. Today, Italy is one of the most profitable of Timberland's more than 50 export markets. The success gave Timberland the confidence to make exporting a major profit center for the company: International revenues accounted for over 29 percent of total sales in 1998, and the company now operates subsidiaries in Chile, France, Germany, Italy, Spain, and the United Kingdom.

To find new markets, Timberland takes a somewhat unconventional approach. Instead of scouting for markets where management thinks it can get a foothold, the company responds especially to those distributors who approach it. "We have talented distributors who understand the market better than we ever could." Timberland looks at the line of footwear the distributor carries and how it is marketed. If the line is high quality and the distributor has a good success rate, then Timberland will go into the market.

Timberland also maintains close relationships with each distributor. Every year the company conducts two sales meetings in the United States and abroad for its foreign distributors. And despite a preference for coordinating international sales efforts from the United States, Timberland sends top officers from the company on periodic visits to each local market.

SOURCES: Sherrie E. Zhan, "Booting Up in Santiago," *World Trade,* July 1999, 30–34; and "Sizing Up the Customers' Needs," *Export Today* 5 (February 1989): 32–33.

http://www.timberland.com

set you back years; it is almost better to have no distributor than a bad one in a major market."[29]

The approach can be either passive or active. Foreign operations for a number of smaller firms start through an unsolicited order; the same can happen with foreign distribution. Distributors, wherever they are, are always on the lookout for product representation that can be profitable and status enhancing, as seen in *The International Marketplace 13.3.* The initial contact may result from an advertisement or from a trade show the marketer has participated in.

The marketer's best interest lies in taking an active role. The marketer should not simply use the first intermediary to show an interest in the firm. The choice should be a result of a careful planning process. The exporter should start by gaining an understanding of market conditions in order to define what is expected of an intermediary and what the exporter can offer in the relationship. At the same time, procedures need to be set for intermediary identification and evaluation.[30] The exporter does not have to do all of this independently; both governmental and private agencies can assist the marketer in locating intermediary candidates.

Governmental Agencies The U.S. Department of Commerce has various services that can assist firms in identifying suitable representatives abroad. Some have been designed specifically for that purpose. A firm can subscribe to the department's Trade Opportunities

[29]"How to Evaluate Foreign Distributors: A *BI* Checklist," *Business International,* May 10, 1985, 145–149.

[30]"Five Steps to Finding the Right Business Partners Abroad," *World Trade,* March 1999, 86–87.

Program (TOP), which matches product interests of over 70,000 foreign buyers with those indicated by the U.S. subscribers. The Country Directories of International Contacts (CDIC) provides the names and contact information for directories of importers, agents, trade associations, and government agencies on a country-by-country basis.[31] The government also provides a mechanism by which the marketer can indicate its interest in international markets. *The U.S. Exporters Yellow Pages* is a free directory that includes information and display advertisements on more than 17,000 U.S. companies interested in exporting. *Commercial News USA* is a catalog-magazine featuring advertisements by U.S. producers distributed worldwide 12 times each year.

Two services are specifically designed for locating foreign representatives. The Agent/Distributor Service (ADS) locates foreign firms that are interested in export proposals submitted by U.S. firms and determines their willingness to correspond with the U.S. firm. Both U.S. and foreign commercial service posts abroad supply information on up to six representatives who meet these requirements. The International Company Profile (ICP) is a valuable service, especially when the screening of potential candidates takes place in markets where reliable data are not readily available. ICPs provide a trade profile of specific foreign firms. They also provide a general narrative report on the reliability of the foreign firm. All of the services are available for relatively small fees; for example, the cost for an ADS application is $250 per country.[32] An example of an ICP is provided in Figure 13.4. Furthermore, individual state agencies provide similar services. These are all available on an on-line basis.

Private Sources   The easiest approach for the firm seeking intermediaries is to consult trade directories. Country and regional business directories such as Kompass (Europe), Bottin International (worldwide), Nordisk Handelskalendar (Northern Europe), and the Japan Trade Directory are good places to start. Company lists by country and line of business can be ordered from Dun & Bradstreet, Reuben H. Donnelly, Kelly's Directory, and Johnston Publishing. Telephone directories, especially the yellow page sections or editions, can provide distributor lists. The Jaeger and Waldmann International Telex Directory can also be consulted. Although not detailed, these listings will give addresses and an indication of the products sold.

The firm can solicit the support of some of its facilitating agencies, such as banks, advertising agencies, shipping lines, and airlines. All these have substantial international information networks and can put them to work for their clients. The services available will vary by agency, depending on the size of its foreign operations. Some of the major U.S. flagship carriers—for example, Northwest Airlines—have special staffs for this purpose within their cargo operations. Banks usually have the most extensive networks through their affiliates and correspondent banks.

The marketer can take an even more direct approach by buying space to solicit representation. Advertisements typically indicate the type of support the marketer will be able to give to its distributor. An example of an advertisement for intermediaries placed in a trade medium is provided in Figure 13.5. For example, Medtech International, an exporter of surgical gloves, advertises for intermediaries in magazines such as *International Hospital Supplies*. Trade fairs are an important forum to meet potential distributors and to get data on intermediaries in the industry. Increasingly, marketers are using their web sites to attract international distributors and agents. For example, P&D Creative, Inc. uses its web page to solicit distribution for its line of environmentally safe cleaning products. It promotes its site in search engines and internationally oriented newsgroups and provides pricing and product

[31]Both TOP and CDIC are available on the National Trade Data Bank at **http://www.stat-usa.gov**.

[32]U.S. Department of Commerce, *2000 Export Programs Guide* (Washington, DC: Department of Commerce, 1999). Also available through **http://www.ita.doc.gov/tic**.

FIGURE 13.4 Sample Report from the International Company Profile

I. FOREIGN COMPANY CONTACT and SIZE INFORMATION:

China Power
Rm. 2301, Saxson Road
Beijing 1000301, China
Mr. Sam, President
Tel: 86-10-6606-3072
Fax: 86-10-6606-3071
1992
Sales: RMB 100,000,000
Employees: 80 including 15 at the headquarters

II. BACKGROUND AND PRODUCT INFORMATION:

Operation
The firm is mainly engaged in selling industrial automation products. It is also engaged in contracting factory automation system projects which consist of system design, programming, installation, and presales service. The firm started to provide services for machine tools refitting in the United States in 1996.

Company background/history:
The firm is wholly foreign owned enterprise registered in June of 1992 with the Municipal Administration for Industry & Commerce. The registered capital was USD 1,250,000. The firm is a subsidiary of Can International Ltd., who owns 100% of the firm.

Business size: small
Major Subsidiaries:
Name: China Power
Add: Rm. 22, Saxson Road, Beijing
Tel: 86-10-6606-3072
Ownership: 80% owned by the firm

Parent Company:
Name: ABZ Ltd., Hong Kong
Line of Business: Investment

Public Record:
According to management, an introduction to the firm and its products was included in editions of the following publications: The People's Daily Overseas Edition, the Science & Technology Daily, the Industrial & Commercial Times, the Worker's Daily, and the Computer World.

Location:
A site visit was made on September 19, 1996. The firm is located in a prime commercial area. It rents office space of 130 square meters at the address shown above. It occupies one floor in a ten-story building, the condition of which is good.

Key Company Officials:
Mr. Sam, President, born on October 24, 1958, is a graduate of Oxford University in 1982. He is now active in the firm's day to day operation in charge of the overall management. Prior to joining the firm, he was employed by the Ministry of Communications from 1982–1989 and China Harbor Engineering Co. 1989–1992.

Mr. Taylor, Vice President, was born in 1948. He joined the firm in 1995 and is currently active in the day to day operations responsible for marketing and sales. Prior to joining the firm, he was employed as Chief Representative from 1984–1995 by CROWE, a foreign plastic company merged by Miller Automation.

Ms. Young, Vice President, is currently active in the firm's day to day operations in charge of finance.

III. REFERENCES:

Foreign Firms Represented:
MILLER AUTOMATION for industrial automation products.
WILDWORLD WARE for Ministry of Machinery's industrial software.
ZXC for low voltage electrical components.
CONTON for industrial computer.
TBP for analyzing instruments.
TINNER for power station meter & instruments.

Bank References: The firm maintains banking relationships with the Industrial & Commercial Bank of China Beijing Branch. However, Mr. Sam declined to provide the account number.

Local Chamber/Trade Association:
Under current investigation, the firm is not known to be a member of any local chambers or trade associations. However, President Sam is a member of China Harbor Association and China Material Handling Association.

Trade references:
PURCHASE TERRITORY:
International: 100%
Import from 90% from the U.S.A., 10% from Germany, Sweden and other countries

SALES TERRITORY:
Local and International
Local: 95%; International: 5%
Exporting to South Africa

CUSTOMER TYPE:
Manufacturers: 100%
Major customers include Glass Bulb Co., Ltd.

Other customers include Iron & Steel Corporation.

PURCHASING AND SELLING ITEMS:
Purchasing Terms: L/C at sight T/T
Selling Terms: T/T
IMPORT & EXPORT: YES

IV. FINANCIAL DATA/CREDIT WORTHINESS INFORMATION:

Financial Highlights of the firm for the period January 1 to December 31, 1995 is shown below:

AMOUNT IN RMB
Sales   100,000,000
Total Assets   30,000,000

The firm declined to provide its financial statement due to "tax concerns".

V. MARKET INFORMATION AND OUTLOOK:

According to Mr. Sam, the firm is the sole "Gold Partner" of Miller Automation

Note: to be a "Gold Partner," the firm's sales volume should be more than 50 percent in the China market.

VI. SPECIAL REQUEST INFORMATION: n/a

VII. REPUTATION: Unknown

VIII. POST COMMENTS/ EVALUATION:

As far as can be seen from the information supplied, the firm seems to be a satisfactory contact. EAJ Ink may, however, wish to contact USFCS Hong Kong to obtain more information of China Power's parent company, Can International Ltd.

IX. SOURCES OF INFORMATION: Dun & Bradstreet Report

NOTE: The information in this report has been supplied to the United States Government by commercial and government sources in the countries covered and its intended for the sole use of the purchaser. You are requested to honor the trust of these sources by not making secondary distribution of the data. While every effort is made to supply current and accurate information, the U.S. Government assumes no responsibility or liability for any decision based on the content of the ICP.

SOURCE: Example provided by Export Promotion Services, International Trade Administration, U.S. Department of Commerce.

FIGURE	**13.5**	Advertisement for an Intermediary

Requirement

**Established networks to export America's leading brands of
canned fruits and vegetables into South America's Mercosur markets.**

Are you a highly motivated exporter looking for a huge new opportunity?
If so, send a fax to Del Monte's Export Department (415-247-3574) or send
us an e-mail at **delmonte.export@delmonte.com.** Qualify and you could
help us export products from Del Monte and Contadina, the world's most
respected names in high-quality fruit, vegetable and tomato products.
The market is there — 2 million people hungry for something better.

SOURCE: Courtesy of Del Monte Foods (**http://www.delmonte.com**)

TABLE 13.5	Sources for Locating Foreign Intermediaries

1. Distributor inquiries
2. U.S. Department of Commerce
　　Trade Opportunities Program
　　Commercial Service International Contacts
　　Country Directories of International Contacts
　　Agent/Distributor Service
　　International Company Profile
3. Trade sources
　　Magazines, journals
　　Directories
　　Associations
　　Banks, advertising agencies, carriers
4. Field sales organizations
5. Customers
6. Direct-mail solicitation/contact of previous applicants
7. Trade fairs
8. Web sites
9. Independent consultants

information of interest to intermediaries.[33] The marketer may also deal directly with contacts from previous applications, launch new mail solicitations, use its own sales organization for the search, or communicate with existing customers to find prospective distributors. The latter may happen after a number of initial (unsolicited) sales to a market, causing the firm to want to enter the market on a more formal basis. If resources permit, the international marketer can use outside service agencies or consultants to generate a list of prospective representatives.

The purpose of using the sources summarized in Table 13.5 is to generate as many prospective representatives as possible for the next step, screening.

Screening Intermediaries

In most firms, the evaluation of candidates involves both what to look for and where to go for the information. At this stage, the international marketer knows the type of distributor that is needed. The potential candidates must now be compared and contrasted against determining criteria. Although the criteria to be used vary by industry and by product, a good summary list is provided in Table 13.6. Especially when various criteria are being weighed, these lists must be updated to reflect changes in the environment and the marketer's own situation. Some criteria can be characterized as determinant, in that they form the core dimensions along which candidates must perform well, whereas some criteria, although important, may be used only in preliminary screening. This list should correspond closely to the exporter's own determinants of success—all the things that have to be done better to beat out competition.

Before signing a contract with a particular agent or a distributor, international marketers should satisfy themselves on certain key criteria. A number of these key criteria can be easily quantified, thereby providing a solid base for comparisons between candidates, whereas others are qualitative and require careful interpretation and confidence in the data sources providing the information.

Performance　The financial standing of the candidate is one of the most important criteria, as well as a good starting point. This figure will show whether the distributor is making

---

[33]Nick Wreden, "Internet Opens Markets Abroad," *Information Week*, November 16, 1998, 46–48.

TABLE 13.6	Selection Criteria for Choosing an International Distributor

CHARACTERISTICS	WEIGHT	RATING
Goals and strategies	—	—
Size of the firm	—	—
Financial strength	—	—
Reputation	—	—
Trading areas covered	—	—
Compatibility	—	—
Experience	—	—
Sales organization	—	—
Physical facilities	—	—
Willingness to carry inventories	—	—
After-sales service capability	—	—
Use of promotion	—	—
Sales performance	—	—
Relations with local government	—	—
Communications	—	—
Overall attitude	—	—

SOURCE: Franklin R. Root, *Foreign Market Entry Strategies* (New York: American Management Association, 1983), 74–75.

money and is able to perform some of the necessary marketing functions such as extension of credit to customers and risk absorption. Financial reports are not always complete or reliable, or they may lend themselves to interpretation differences, pointing to a need for third-party opinion. Many Latin American intermediaries lack adequate capital, a situation that can lead to more time spent managing credit than managing marketing strategy. Therefore, at companies like Xerox, assessment focuses on cash flow and the intermediary's ability to support its operations without outside help.[34]

Sales are another excellent indicator. What the distributor is presently doing gives an indication of how he or she could perform if chosen to handle the international marketer's product. The distributor's sales strength can be determined by analyzing management ability and the adequacy and quality of the sales team.

The distributor's existing product lines should be analyzed along four dimensions: competitiveness, compatibility, complementary nature, and quality. Quite often, international marketers find that the most desirable distributors in a given market are already handling competitive products and are therefore unavailable. In that case, the marketer can look for an equally qualified distributor handling related products. The complementary nature of products may be of interest to both parties, especially in industrial markets, where ultimate customers may be in the market for complete systems or one-stop shopping. The quality match for products is important for product positioning reasons; a high-quality product may suffer unduly from a questionable distributor reputation. The number of product lines handled gives the marketer an indication of the level of effort to expect from the distributor. Some distributors are interested in carrying as many products and product lines as possible to enhance their own standing, but they have the time and the willingness to actively sell only those

[34]Joseph V. Barks, "Penetrating Latin America," *International Business*, February 1996, 78–80.

that bring the best compensation. At this time, it is also important to check the candidate's physical facilities for handling the product. This is essential particularly for products that may be subject to quality changes, such as food products. The assessment should also include the candidate's marketing materials, including a possible web site, for adequacy and appropriateness.

The distributor's market coverage must be determined. The analysis of coverage will include not only how much territory, or how many segments of the market, are covered, but also how well the markets are served. Again, the characteristics of the sales force and the number of sales offices are good quantitative indicators. To study the quality of the distributor's market coverage, the marketer can check whether the sales force visits executives, engineers, and operating people or concentrates mainly on purchasing agents. In some areas of the world, the marketer has to make sure that two distributors will not end up having territorial overlaps, which can lead to unnecessary conflict.

Professionalism   The distributor's reputation must be checked. This rather abstract measure takes its value from a number of variables that all should help the marketer forecast fit and effectiveness. The distributor's customers, suppliers, facilitating agencies, competitors, and other members of the local business community should be contacted for information on the business conduct of the distributor in such areas as buyer-seller relations and ethical behavior. This effort will shed light on variables that may be important only in certain parts of the world; for example, variables such as political clout, which is essential in certain developing countries.

The marketer must acknowledge the distributor as an independent entity with its own goals. The distributor's business strategy must therefore be determined, particularly what the distributor expects to get from the relationship and where the international marketer fits into those plans. Because a channel relationship is long term, the distributor's views on future expansion of the product line or its distribution should be clarified. This phase will also require a determination of the degree of help the distributor would need in terms of price, credit, delivery, sales training, communication, personal visits, product modification, warranty, advertising, warehousing, technical support, and after-sales service.[35] Leaving uncertainties in these areas will cause major problems later.

Finally, the marketer should determine the distributor's overall attitude in terms of cooperation and commitment to the marketer. An effective way of testing this, and weeding out the less interested candidates, is to ask the distributor to assist in developing a local marketing plan or to develop one. This endeavor will bring out potential problem areas and will spell out which party is to perform the various marketing functions.

A criteria list is valuable only when good data are available on each and every criterion. Although the initial screening can take place at the firm's offices, the three to five finalists should be visited. No better method of assessing distributors exists than visiting them, inspecting their facilities, and interviewing their various constituents in the market. A number of other critical data sources are important for firms without the resources for on-site inspection. The distributor's suppliers or firms not in direct competition can provide in-depth information. A bona fide candidate will also provide information through a local bank. Credit reports are available through the National Association of Credit Management, Dun & Bradstreet, and local credit-reporting agencies as discussed in Chapter 5.

The Distributor Agreement

When the international marketer has found a suitable intermediary, a foreign sales agreement is drawn up. The agreement can be relatively simple, but given the nu-

---

[35]"How to Evaluate Foreign Distributors," 145–149.

merous differences in the market environments, certain elements are essential. The checklist prepared by *Business International* (see Table 13.7) is the most comprehensive in stipulating the nature of the contract and the respective rights and responsibilities of the marketer and the distributor.

Contract duration is important, especially when an agreement is signed with a new distributor. In general, distribution agreements should be for a specified, relatively short period (one or two years). The initial contract with a new distributor should stipulate a trial period of either three or six months, possibly with minimum purchase requirements. Duration should be determined with an eye on the local laws and their stipulations on distributor agreements. These will be discussed later in conjunction with distributor termination.

Geographic boundaries for the distributor should be determined with care, especially by smaller firms. Future expansion of the product market might be complicated if a distributor claims rights to certain territories. The marketer should retain the right to distribute products independently, reserving the right to certain customers. For example, many marketers maintain a dual distribution system, dealing directly with certain large accounts. This type of arrangement should be explicitly stated in the agreement. Transshipments, sales to customers outside the agreed-upon territory or customer type, have to be explicitly prohibited to prevent the occurrence of parallel importation.

TABLE 13.7 Elements of a Distributor Agreement

A. Basic Components
1. Parties to the agreement
2. Statement that the contract supersedes all previous agreements
3. Duration of the agreement (perhaps a three- or six-month trial period)
4. Territory:
    a. Exclusive, nonexclusive, sole
    b. Manufacturer's right to sell direct at reduced or no commission to local government and old customers
5. Products covered
6. Expression of intent to comply with government regulations
7. Clauses limiting sales forbidden by U.S. Export Controls or practices forbidden by the Foreign Corrupt Practices Act

B. Manufacturer's Rights
1. Arbitration:
    a. If possible, in the manufacturer's country
    b. If not, before international Chamber of Commerce or American Arbitration Association, or using the London Court of Arbitration rules
    c. Definition of rules to be applied (e.g., in selecting the arbitration panel)
    d. Assurance that award will be binding in the distributor's country
2. Jurisdiction that of the manufacturer's country (the signing completed at home); if not possible, a neutral site such as Sweden or Switzerland
3. Termination conditions (e.g., no indemnification if due notice given)
4. Clarification of tax liabilities
5. Payment and discount terms
6. Conditions for delivery of goods
7. Nonliability for late delivery beyond manufacturer's reasonable control
8. Limitation on manufacturer's responsibility to provide information
9. Waiver of manufacturer's responsibility to keep lines manufactured outside the United States (e.g., licensees) outside of covered territory
10. Right to change prices, terms, and conditions at any time
11. Right of manufacturer or agent to visit territory and inspect books
12. Right to repurchase stock
13. Option to refuse or alter distributor's orders
14. Training of distributor personnel in the United States subject to:
    a. Practicality
    b. Costs to be paid by the distributor
    c. Waiver of manufacturer's responsibility for U.S. immigration approval

(continued)

TABLE 13.7	**Elements of a Distributor Agreement (*continued*)**

C. Distributor's Limitations and Duties
1. No disclosure of confidential information
2. Limitation of distributor's right to assign contract
3. Limitation of distributor's position as legal agent of manufacturer
4. Penalty clause for late payment
5. Limitation of right to handle competing lines
6. Placement of responsibility for obtaining customs clearance
7. Distributor to publicize designation as authorized representative in defined area
8. Requirement to move all signs or evidence identifying distributor with manufacturer if relationship ends
9. Acknowledgment by distributor of manufacturer's ownership of trademark, trade names, patents
10. Information to be supplied by the distributor:
    a. Sales reports
    b. Names of active prospects
    c. Government regulations dealing with imports
    d. Competitive products and competitors' activities
    e. Price at which goods are sold
    f. Complete data on other lines carried (on request)
11. Information to be supplied by distributor on purchasers
12. Accounting methods to be used by distributor
13. Requirement to display products appropriately
14. Duties concerning promotional efforts
15. Limitation of distributor's right to grant unapproved warranties, make excessive claims
16. Clarification of responsibility arising from claims and warranties
17. Responsibility of distributor to provide repair and other services
18. Responsibility to maintain suitable place of business
19. Responsibility to supply all prospective customers
20. Understanding that certain sales approaches and sales literature must be approved by manufacturer
21. Prohibition of manufacture or alteration of products
22. Requirement to maintain adequate stock, spare parts
23. Requirement that inventory be surrendered in event of a dispute that is pending in court
24. Prohibition of transshipments

SOURCE: "Elements of a Distributor Agreement," *Business International,* March 29, 1963, 23–24. Reprinted with permission from Business International. Some of the sections have been changed to reflect the present situation.

The payment section of the contract should stipulate the methods of payment as well as how the distributor or agent is to draw compensation. Distributors derive compensation from various discounts, such as the functional discount, whereas agents earn a specific commission percentage of net sales (such as 15 percent). Given the volatility of currency markets, the agreement should also state the currency to be used. The international marketer also needs to make sure that none of the compensation forwarded to the distributor is in violation of the Foreign Corrupt Practices Act or the OECD guidelines. A violation occurs if a payment is made to influence a foreign official in exchange for business favors, depending on the nature of the action sought. So-called grease or **facilitating payments,** such as a small fee to expedite paperwork through customs, are not considered violations.[36]

Product and conditions of sale need to be agreed on. The products or product lines included should be stipulated, as well as the functions and responsibilities of the intermediary in terms of carrying the goods in inventory, providing service in conjunction with them, and promoting them. Conditions of sale determine which party is to

[36]Michael G. Harvey and Ilkka A. Ronkainen, "The Three Faces of the Foreign Corrupt Practices Act: Retain, Reform, or Repeal," in *1984 AMA Educators' Proceedings* (Chicago: American Marketing Association, 1984), 290–294.

be responsible for some of the expenses involved, which will in turn have an effect on the price to the distributor. These conditions include credit and shipment terms.

Effective means of communication between the parties must be stipulated in the agreement if a marketer-distributor relationship is to succeed. The marketer should have access to all information concerning the marketing of his or her products in the distributor's territory, including past records, present situation assessments, and marketing research concerning the future. Communication channels should be formal for the distributor to voice formal grievances. The contract should state the confidentiality of the information provided by either party and protect the intellectual property rights (such as patents) involved.

Channel Management

A channel relationship can be likened to a marriage in that it brings together two independent entities that have shared goals. For the relationship to work, each party must be open about its expectations and openly communicate changes perceived in the other's behavior that might be contrary to the agreement. The closer the relationship is to a distribution partnership, the more likely marketing success will materialize. Conflict will arise, ranging from small grievances (such as billing errors) to major ones (rivalry over channel duties), but it can be managed to enhance the overall channel relationship. In some cases, conflict may be caused by an outside entity, such as gray markets, in which unauthorized intermediaries compete for market share with legitimate importers and exclusive distributors. Nevertheless, the international marketer must solve the problem.

The relationship has to be managed for the long term. An exporter may in some countries have a seller's market situation that allows it to exert pressure on its intermediaries for concessions, for example. However, if environmental conditions change, the exporter may find that the channel support it needs to succeed is not there because of the manner in which it managed channel relationships in the past.[37]

Factors in Channel Management

An excellent framework for managing channel relationships is shown in Figure 13.6. The complicating factors that separate the two parties fall into three categories: ownership; geographic, cultural, and economic distance; and different rules of law. Rather than lament their existence, both parties need to take strong action to remedy them. Often, the major step is acknowledgment that differences do indeed exist.

In international marketing, manufacturers and distributors are usually independent entities. Distributors typically carry the products of more than one manufacturer and judge products by their ability to generate revenue without added expense. The international marketer, in order to receive disproportionate attention for its concerns, may offer both monetary and psychological rewards.

Distance, whether it is geographic, psychological, economic, or a combination, can be bridged through effective two-way communication. This should go beyond normal routine business communication to include innovative ways of sharing pertinent information. The international marketer may place one person in charge of distributor-related communications or put into effect an interpenetration strategy—that is, an exchange of personnel so that both organizations gain further insight into the workings of the other.[38] The existence of cross-cultural differences in people's belief systems and

[37]Gary L. Frazier, James D. Gill, and Sudhir H. Kale, "Dealer Dependence Levels and Reciprocal Actions in a Channel of Distribution in a Developing Country," *Journal of Marketing* 53 (January 1989): 50–69.

[38]Bert Rosenbloom, *Marketing Channels: A Management View,* 6th ed. (Hinsdale, IL: The Dryden Press, 1998), 404.

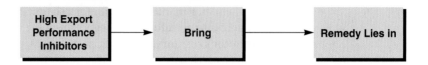

FIGURE 13.6 Performance Problems and Remedies When Using Overseas Distributors

High Export Performance Inhibitors	Bring	Remedy Lies in
Separate Ownership	• Divided Loyalties • Seller-Buyer Atmosphere • Unclear Future Intentions	Offering good incentives, helpful support schemes, discussing plan frankly, and interacting in a mutually beneficial way
Geographic, Economic, and Cultural Separation	• Communication Blocks • Negative Attitudes toward Foreigners • Physical Distribution Strains	Making judicious use of two-way visits, establishing a well-managed communication program
Different Rules of Law	• Vertical Trading Restrictions • Dismissal Difficulties	Full compliance with the law, drafting a strong distributor agreement

SOURCE: Adapted from Philip J. Rosson, "Success Factors in Manufacturer-Overseas Distributor Relationships in International Marketing," in *International Marketing Management,* ed. Erdener Kaynak, 1984 (New York: Praeger, 1984) 91–107.

behavior patterns have to be acknowledged and acted on for effective channel management. For example, in markets where individualism is stressed, local channel partners may seek arrangements that foster their own self-interest and may expect their counterparts to watch out for themselves. Conflict is seen as a natural phenomenon. In societies of low individualism, however, a common purpose is fostered between the partners.[39]

Economic distance manifests itself in exchange rates, for example. Instability of exchange rates can create serious difficulties for distributors in their trading activities, not only with their suppliers but also with their domestic customers. Manufacturers and distributors should develop and deploy mutually acceptable mechanisms that allow for some flexibility in interactions when unforeseen rate fluctuations occur.[40] For example, Harley Davidson has instituted a system of risk sharing in which it will maintain a single foreign currency price as long as the spot exchange rate does not move beyond a mutually agreed-upon rate. Should it happen, Harley Davidson and the distributor will share the costs or benefits of the change.

Laws and regulations in many markets may restrict the manufacturer in terms of control. For example, in the European Union, the international marketer cannot prevent a distributor from reexporting products to customers in another member country, even though the marketer has another distributor in that market. The only remedy is to include the necessary stipulations in the distributor agreement, for example, a clause prohibiting transshipments.

[39]Sudhir H. Kale and Roger P. McIntyre, "Distribution Channel Relationships in Diverse Cultures," *International Marketing Review* 8 (1991): 31–45.

[40]Constantine S. Katsikeas and Tevfik Dalgic, "Importing Problems Experienced by Distributors: The Importance of Level-of-Import Development," *Journal of International Marketing* 3 (Number 2, 1995): 51–70.

Most of the criteria used in selecting intermediaries can be used to evaluate existing intermediaries as well. If not conducted properly and fairly, however, evaluation can be a source of conflict. In addition to being given the evaluation results in order to take appropriate action, the distributor should be informed of the evaluative criteria and should be a part of the overall assessment process. Again, the approach should be as a partnership, not buyer-seller.

A part of the management process is channel adjustment. This can take the form of channel shift (eliminating a particular type of channel), channel modification (changing individual members while leaving channel structure intact), or role or relationship modification (changing functions performed or the reward structure) as a result of channel evaluation.[41] The need for channel change should be well established and not executed hastily because it will cause a major distraction in the operations of the firm. Some companies have instituted procedures that require executives to consider carefully all of the aspects and potential results of change before execution.

Gray Markets

Gray markets, or **parallel importation,** refer to authentic and legitimately manufactured trademark items that are produced and purchased abroad but imported or diverted to the United States by bypassing designated channels.[42] The value of gray markets in the United States has been estimated at $6 to $10 billion at retail. Gray marketed products vary from inexpensive consumer goods (such as chewing gum) to expensive capital goods (such as excavation equipment). The phenomenon is not restricted to the United States; Japan, for example, is witnessing gray markets because of the high value of the yen and the subsidization of cheaper exports through high taxes. Japanese marketers often find it cheaper to go to Los Angeles to buy export versions of Japanese-made products.[43]

An example of the phenomenon is provided in Figure 13.7, which shows the flow of Seiko watches through authorized and unauthorized channels. Seiko is a good example of a typical gray market product in that it carries a well-known trademark. Unauthorized importers, such as Progress Trading Company in New York, and retailers, such as Montgomery Ward, buy Seiko watches around the world at advantageous prices and then sell them to consumers at substantial discounts over authorized Seiko dealers. Seiko has fought back, for example, by advertising warnings to consumers against buying gray market watches on the grounds that these products may be obsolete or worn-out models and that consumers might have problems with their warranties. Many gray marketers, however, provide their own warranty-related service and guarantee watches sold through them.

Various conditions allow unauthorized resellers to exist. The most important are price segmentation and exchange rate fluctuations. Competitive conditions may require the international marketer to sell essentially the same product at different prices in different markets or to different customers.[44] Because many products are priced higher in, for example, the United States, a gray marketer can purchase them in Europe or the Far East and offer discounts between 10 and 40 percent below list price when reselling them in the U.S. market. Exchange rate fluctuations can cause price differentials and thus opportunities for gray marketers. For example, during the Asian

[41]J. Taylor Sims, J. Robert Foster, and Arch G. Woodside, *Marketing Channels: Systems and Strategies*, 3rd ed. (New York: Harper & Row, 1977).

[42]Ilkka A. Ronkainen and Linda van de Gucht, "Making a Case for Gray Markets," *Journal of Commerce*, January 6, 1987, 13A.

[43]Dan Koeppel, " 'Gyakuyunyu' Takes Hold in Japan," *Adweek's Marketing Week*, March 20, 1989, 22.

[44]Frank V. Cespedes, E. Raymond Corey, and V. Kasturi Rangan, "Gray Markets: Causes and Cures," *Harvard Business Review* 66 (July–August 1988): 75–82.

FIGURE 13.7   Seiko's Authorized and Unauthorized Channels of Distribution

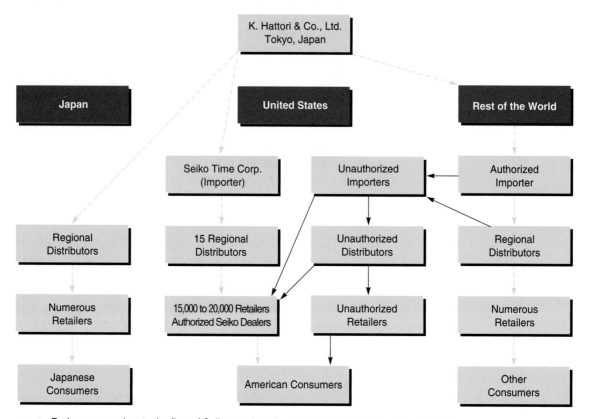

- - - -> Broken arrows denote the flow of Seiko watches through authorized channels of distribution.
——> Solid arrows denote the flow of Seiko watches through unauthorized channels of distribution.

SOURCE: Jack Kaikati, "Parallel Importation: A Growing Conflict in International Channels of Distribution," Symposium on Export-Import Interrelationships, Georgetown University, November 14–15, 1985.

financial crisis, gray marketers imported Caterpillar, Deere, and Komatsu construction and earth-moving equipment no longer needed for halted projects in markets such as Thailand and Indonesia—and usually never used—for as little as 60 percent of what U.S. dealers paid wholesale.[45] In some cases, gray markets emerge as a result of product shortages. For example, in 1988, many U.S. computer manufacturers had to turn to gray marketers to secure their supply of DRAMs or else watch their production lines grind to a halt.[46] However, in these cases, the gray market goods typically cost more than those usually available through authorized suppliers. In other cases, if there are multiple production sites for the same product, gray markets can emerge due to negative perceptions about the country of origin, as seen in the case highlighted in *The International Marketplace 13.4*.

Gray market flows have increased as current barriers to trade are being eliminated. The European Union has significant parallel importation due to significant price differentials in ethical drugs, which are in turn the result of differences in regulation,

[45]"The Earth is Shifting under Heavy Equipment," *Business Week*, April 6, 1998, 44.

[46]"How the Gray Marketeers Are Cashing In on DRAM Shortages," *Electronic Business*, June 1, 1988, 18–19.

insurance coverage, medical practice, and exchange rates. Of the fifteen member countries, only Denmark grants manufacturers the freedom to price their ethical drugs. The share of parallel trade is estimated at 15 percent and is expected to grow since the European Commission is supporting the practice.[47]

Opponents and supporters of the practice disagree on whether the central issue is price or trade rights. Detractors typically cite the following arguments: (1) the gray market unduly hurts the legitimate owners of trademarks; (2) without protection, trademark owners will have little incentive to invest in product development; (3) gray marketers will "free ride" or take unfair advantage of the trademark owners' marketing and promotional activities; and (4) parallel imports can deceive consumers by not meeting product standards or their normal expectations of after-sale service. The bottom line is that gray market goods can severely undercut local marketing plans, erode long-term brand images, eat up costly promotion funds, and sour manufacturer-intermediary relations.

Proponents of parallel importation approach the issue from an altogether different point of view. They argue for their right to "free trade" by pointing to manufacturers that are both overproducing and overpricing in some markets. The main beneficiaries are consumers, who benefit from lower prices and discount distributors, with whom some of the manufacturers do not want to deal and who have now, because of gray markets, found a profitable market niche.

In response to the challenge, manufacturers have chosen various approaches. Despite the Supreme Court ruling in May 1988 to legitimize gray markets in the United States,[48] foreign manufacturers, U.S. companies manufacturing abroad, and authorized retailers have continued to fight the practice. In January 1991, the U.S. Customs Service enacted a new rule whereby trademarked goods that have been authorized for manufacture and sale abroad by U.S. trademark holders will no longer be allowed into the United States through parallel channels.[49] Those parallel importing goods of overseas manufacturers will not be affected. Recently, courts have taken exception to cases that have shown evidence of deception. For example, Lever Brothers won a long case to stop discounters from selling Sunlight brand dishwashing detergent, produced for the British market, in the United States. Because tap water is generally harder in Britain, formulation of the product there is different from Lever's U.S. version, which produces more lather. Lever reported lost sales and complaints from customers who bought the British brand and were disappointed.[50]

The solution for the most part lies with the contractual relationships that tie businesses together. In almost all cases of gray marketing, someone in the authorized channel commits a diversion, thus violating the agreements signed. One of the standard responses is therefore disenfranchisement of such violators. This approach is a clear response to complaints from the authorized dealers who are being hurt by transshipments. Tracking down offenders is quite expensive and time-consuming, however. Some of the gray marketers can be added to the authorized dealer network if mutually acceptable terms can be reached, thereby increasing control of the channel of distribution.[51]

[47]Peggy E. Chaudry and Michael G. Walsh, "Managing the Gray Market in the European Union: The Case of the Pharmaceutical Industry," *Journal of International Marketing* 3 (Number 3, 1995): 11–33; and "Parallel Trade and Comparative Pricing of Medicines: Poor Choice for Patients," *Pfizer Forum,* 1996.

[48]"A Red-Letter Day for Gray Marketeers," *Business Week,* June 13, 1988, 30.

[49]Ellen Klein and J. D. Howard, "Strings Attached," *North American International Business* 6 (May 1991): 54–55.

[50]"Brand Battles," *International Business,* April 1993, 83.

[51]For a comprehensive discussion on remedies, see Robert E. Weigand, "Parallel Import Channel—Options for Preserving Territorial Integrity," *Columbia Journal of World Business* 26 (Spring 1991): 53–60, and S. Tamer Cavusgil and Ed Sikora, "How Multinationals Can Counter Gray Market Imports," *Columbia Journal of World Business* 23 (Winter 1988): 75–85.

THE INTERNATIONAL MARKETPLACE 13.4

Country of Origin and Gray Markets

IN THE MID-1990s, as part of a strategic initiative to relocate products and transfer technology, Canon moved the production of its basic model 1215 copier to China. One of the world's leading manufacturers of cameras, optical products, imaging equipment, and computer peripherals, Canon believes in being an organization that undertakes optimal production activities worldwide. It does so through its 120 subsidiaries around the globe.

The change of country of origin from Japan to China was not expected to affect buyers. However, in Russia, Canon found quite the opposite to be true. In many high-technology product categories, both Russian trade and retail customers divided products into three categories: "white" ones, made in Europe or the United States, the best made and subsequently premium priced; "red" ones, assembled in Russia and considered with suspicion; and "yellow" ones, from Asia and rated somewhere in between red and white. However, in China's case, the perception among Russians has traditionally been that technology flows there from Russia but not vice versa, and that nothing interesting in terms of technology can originate from China.

The problem was identified relatively quickly—within three months of the change in source of supply—and the sourcing was redirected back to Japan. However, in the meantime, many intermediaries in Dubai, Hong Kong, and Singapore identified an opportunity and offered Russian customers "made-in-Japan" versions of the same product while the official channel was stuck with the "made in China" counterparts.

In a worst-case scenario, Canon would have been forced to sell the copiers at any price. However, it undertook the following campaign, which resulted in the swift sale of all the Chinese-made copiers:

1. It developed an "officially imported" hologram, which was attached to every Canon product acquired through official channels in Russia
2. It offered to profile dealers as authorized resellers through a dealer-participatory campaign in which their names were included in the advertisements
3. It offered final customers a premium, a Canon BP-7 camera.

The accompanying advertisement appeared in Russian trade magazines to deliver this message. It portrays the hologram and states the following benefits of buying from official dealers (while implicitly warning readers not to buy from other sources): technical support and training, Russian-language instructions and manuals, product support, and local service.

SOURCE: Example courtesy of Jouko Tuominen, Oy Canon Ab; "Laptops from Lapland," *The Economist,* September 6, 1997, 67–68.

http://www.canon.com

Техническая
поддержка

Инструкция
для пользования
на русском языке

Запасные части

Сервисное
обслуживание

OFFICIALLY
IMPORTED
Canon

**Действуйте наверняка! Покупайте официально
импортированную копировальную машину**

Имейте в виду, что профессиональные услуги **Canon** по техобслуживанию и обеспечению запасными частями касаются только официально импортированных и проверенных машин.

Четкие инструкции на русском языке, техническая поддержка и приспособленные к местным условиям машины – все это является для официального импортера само собой разумеющимся. Машины, пришедшие в страну другими путями, слишком часто бывают в этом отношении далеко не безупречными.

Если на Вашей новой копировальной машине есть голограмма Canon «Официально импортировано» – можете быть уверены в том, что Вы приобрели первоклассную машину, которая Вас не подведет.

eüro96
England
Canon

Приобретая официально импортированную копировальную машину CANON, Вы получаете в подарок не только фотоаппарат.

Купите официально импортированную копировальную машину Canon NP 1215, и Вы получите в подарок высококачественный портативный фотоаппарат Canon Prima BF-7 (стоимостью долларов США).

- Скорость 15 копий в минуту
- Масштабирование от 50 до 200%
- Неподвижное стекло экспонирования
- Формат копий от A3 до A6
- Наибольший формат оригинала A3
- Автоматическое регулирование экспонирования
- Кассета на 250 листов

Canon

Представительство в Москве
Никольская ул. 54, 109004 Москва, Россия
Тел. (095) 258 5600, Факс. (095) 258 5601

A one-price policy can eliminate one of the main reasons for gray markets. This means choosing the most efficient of the distribution channels through which to market the product, but it may also mean selling at the lowest price to all customers regardless of location and size. A meaningful one-price strategy must also include a way to reward the providers of other services, such as warranty repair, in the channel.

Other strategies have included producing different versions of products for different markets. For example, Minolta Camera Company markets an identical camera in the United States and Japan but gives it different names and warranties.[52] Some companies have introduced price incentives to consumers. Hasselblad, the Swedish camera manufacturer, offers rebates to purchasers of legally imported, serial-numbered camera bodies, lenses, and roll-fill magazines.[53] Many manufacturers promote the benefits of dealing with authorized dealers (and, thereby, the dangers of dealing with gray market dealers). For example, Rolex's message states that authorized dealers are the only ones who are capable of providing genuine accessories and can ensure that the customer gets an authentic product and the appropriate warranty.

Termination of the Channel Relationship

Many reasons exist for the termination of a channel relationship, but the most typical are changes in the international marketer's distribution approach (for example, establishing a sales office) or a (perceived) lack of performance by the intermediary.

Channel relationships go through a life cycle. The concept of an international distribution life cycle is presented in Figure 13.8. Over time, the manufacturer's marketing capabilities increase while a distributor's ability and willingness to grow the manufacturer's business in that market decreases. When a producer expands its market presence, it may expect more of a distributor's effort than the distributor is willing to make available. Furthermore, with expansion, the manufacturer may want to expand its product line to items that the distributor is neither interested in nor able to support. In some cases, intermediaries may not be interested in growing the business beyond a certain point (e.g., due to progressive taxation in the country) or as aggressively as the principal may expect (i.e., being more of an order-taker than an order-getter). As a marketer's operations expand, it may want to start to coordinate operations across markets for efficiency and customer-service reasons or to cater to global accounts—thereby needing to control distribution to a degree that independent intermediaries are not willing to accept, or requiring a level of service that they may not be able to deliver. If termination is a result of such a structural change, the situation has to be handled carefully. The effect of termination on the intermediary has to be understood, and open communication is needed to make the transition smooth. For example, the intermediary can be compensated for investments made, and major customers can be visited jointly to assure them that service will be uninterrupted. The experience of the semiconductor maker Novellus is highlighted in *The International Marketplace 13.5.*

Termination conditions are one of the most important considerations in the distributor agreement, because the just causes for termination vary and the penalties for the international marketer may be substantial. Just causes include fraud or deceit, damage to the other party's interest, or failure to comply with contract obligations concerning minimum inventory requirements or minimum sales levels. These must be spelled out carefully because local courts are often favorably disposed toward local businesses. In some countries, termination may not even be possible.[54] In the EU and

---

[52]"Now, Japan Is Feeling the Heat from the Gray Market," *Business Week,* March 14, 1988, 50–51.

[53]Gay Jervey, "Gray Markets Hit Camera, Watch Sales," *Advertising Age,* August 15, 1983, 3, 62.

[54]Jack Kaikati, "The Marketing Environment in Saudi Arabia," *Akron Business and Economic Review* 7 (Summer 1976): 5–13.

FIGURE 13.8 | **International Distribution Life Cycle**

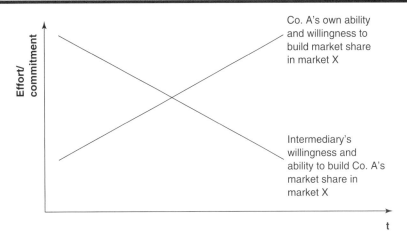

SOURCE: Framework courtesy of Professor David Arnold, Harvard Business School, and Professor John Quelch, London Business School.

Latin America, terminating an ineffective intermediary is time-consuming and expensive. One year's average commissions are typical for termination without justification. A notice of termination has to be given three to six months in advance. In Austria, termination without just cause and/or failure to give notice of termination may result in damages amounting to average commissions for between 1 and 15 years.[55]

The time to think about such issues is before the overseas distribution agreement is signed. It is especially prudent to find out what local laws say about termination and to check what type of experience other firms have had in the particular country. Careful preparation can allow the exporter to negotiate a termination without litigation.[56] If the distributor's performance is unsatisfactory, careful documentation and clearly defined performance measures may help show that the distributor has more to gain by going quietly than by fighting.

E-Commerce

At the beginning of a new century, the majority of firms still see a web site as a marketing and advertising tool without expanding it to order-taking capabilities.[57] That is changing rapidly. As shown in Table 13.8, e-commerce, the ability to offer goods and services over the Web, is expected to grow at a compound annual growth rate of 100 percent in the next five years around the world. While the United States accounts for the

[55]Ovidio M. Giberga, "Laws Restrain Agency Agreement Termination," in *Foreign Business Practices* (Washington, DC: Department of Commerce, 1981), 86–95.

[56]"Foreign Distributors: How MNCs Can Avoid the Termination Minefield," *Business International*, July 12, 1985, 217–218.

[57]Erika Morphy, "Making Cash Flow," *Export Today* (July 1998): 22–29.

THE INTERNATIONAL MARKETPLACE 13.5

Mastering the Japanese Distribution Maze

PART OF THE BLAME for many countries' trade deficits with Japan has been put on Japan's seemingly impenetrable distribution system. Increasingly, however, in addition to the strong yen and falling trade barriers, more marketing managers are mastering the skills required to penetrate the Japanese market. Despite these gains, many attempts still turn sour after the initial phase. The fault often lies with Western impatience for quick profits and failure to recognize the importance of creating personal relationships with Japanese partners.

Robert F. Graham, CEO of Novellus Systems Inc. (**www. novellus.com**), a San Jose–based semiconductor maker, took the company to Japan, from where it now derives more than $20 million in annual sales. Knowing that divorces with distributors give foreign entities a bad name, Mr. Graham took much time—including six one-week scouting trips to Japan—before deciding on a suitable partner. After ruling out seven options, including large trading firms, he settled on a small intermediary, Seki Technotron of Tokyo, with the main decision criterion being control. Sealing the relationship involved considerable personal interaction, well beyond what the company would do elsewhere. The resulting distributor agreement led to detailed, comprehensive customer support and bimonthly visits by Mr. Graham to Japan.

After three years Novellus was ready to strike out on its own. Mr. Graham strongly believed that U.S. companies really succeed in Japan only by going it alone as soon as possible and selling directly to customers. Unlike their counterparts in the United States and Europe, Japanese distributors keep their clients well away from the customers, a fact resented by the Novellus staff.

Novellus built a $7 million sales-support facility near Tokyo. Even so, Seki Technotron was not bid an abrupt *arigato* and *sayonara*. Novellus devised a plan under which the distributor would gradually hand over the big accounts during a three-year period. To ease the financial sting to Seki, Novellus fattened the commissions paid to the distributor during the transition period and let it keep Novellus's smaller accounts. Made to feel a continuing part of the new arrangement, Seki agreed to it. "It is important to keep up the relationship and not kill it," says Mr. Graham, who adds that "it is also important to customers that you do not completely cut off a distributor and cause him to lose face." Drop a distributor anywhere, but especially in Japan, and the word gets around that you are a calculating foreigner and not to be trusted.

SOURCE: Gregory L. Miles, "Unmasking Japan's Distributors," *International Business*, April 1994, 38–42.

majority of e-commerce activity, the non-U.S. portion is expected to double in the next five years, with Western Europe providing the most significant growth. A survey by KPMG Management Consulting in Europe shows that more than one-third of the 500 European-based large and medium-sized companies reported Internet sales in 1998. The same group states that those sales represent about 2 percent of their total sales, a figure they expect will jump to 12 percent in three years and 20 percent in five years.[58]

Many companies willing to enter e-commerce will not have to do it on their own. Hub sites (also known as virtual malls or digital intermediaries) will bring together buyers, sellers, distributors, and transaction payment processors in one single marketplace, making convenience the key attraction. The share of such hubs in retail e-commerce increased from 15 percent in 1998 to 26 percent in 1999, with entities such as Compare.net (**www.compare.net**), Priceline.com (**www.priceline.com**), eBay (**www.ebay.com**), and VerticalNet (**www.verticalnet.com**) leading the way.[59]

As soon as customers have the ability to access a company through the Internet, the company itself has to be prepared to provide 24-hour order taking and customer service, to acquire the regulatory and customs-handling expertise to deliver internationally, and to develop an in-depth understanding of marketing environments for the

[58]Miles Maguire, "Spinning the Web," *Export Today* (January 1998): 28–32.

[59]Rolf Rykken, "Opening the Gate," *Export Today* (February 1999): 35–42.

TABLE 13.8	Worldwide E-Commerce Revenue by Region (in $billions)

REGION	1998	2003	COMPOUND ANNUAL GROWTH
United States	37.25	707.92	80%
Western Europe	5.61	430.37	138
Japan	1.98	44.94	87
Asia/Pacific	0.69	27.51	109
Rest of world	1.41	53.02	107

SOURCE: International Data Corporation, "The Globalization of eCommerce," August 1999, www.idc.com.

further development of the business relationship.[60] The instantaneous interactivity users experience will also be translated into an expectation of expedient delivery of answers and products ordered. Many people living outside the United States who want to purchase on-line expect U.S.-style service. However, in many cases, they may find that shipping is not even available outside the United States.

The challenges faced in terms of response and delivery capabilities can be overcome by outsourcing services or by building international distribution networks. Air express carriers such as DHL, FedEx, and UPS offer full-service packages that leverage their own Internet infrastructure with customs clearance and e-mail shipment notification. If a company needs help in order fulfilment and customer support, logistics centers offer warehousing and inventory management services as well as same-day delivery from in-country stocks. DHL, for example, has seven express logistics centers and 45 strategic parts centers worldwide, with key centers in Bahrain for the Middle East, Brussels for Europe, and Singapore for Asia-Pacific. Some companies elect to build their own international distribution networks. Both QVC, a televised shopping service, and Amazon.com, an on-line retailer of books and consumer goods, have distribution centers in Britain and Germany to take advantage of the European Internet audience and to fulfill more quickly and cheaply the orders generated by their web sites.

Transactions and the information they provide about the buyer allow for greater customization and for service by region, by market, or even by individual customer. One of the largest on-line sellers, Dell Computer, builds a Premier Page for its corporate customers with more than 400 employees, which is linked to the customer's intranet and thus allows approved employees to configure PCs, pay for them, and track their delivery status. Premier Pages also provide access to instant technical support and Dell sales representatives. Presently there are 5,000 companies with such service, and $5 million worth of Dell PCs are ordered every day.[61]

Although English has long been perceived as the lingua franca of the Web, the share of non-English speakers worldwide increased to 60 percent in 1999. It has also been shown that Web users are three times more likely to buy when the offering is made in their own language.[62] However, not even the largest of firms can serve all markets with a full line of their products. Getting a web site translated and running is an expensive proposition, and, if done correctly, time-consuming as well. If the site is well developed, it will naturally lead to expectations that order fulfillment will be of equal caliber. Therefore, any worldwide Web strategy has to be tied closely with the company's overall growth strategy in world markets.

A number of hurdles and uncertainties are keeping some companies out of global markets or preventing them from exploiting these markets to their full potential. Some argue that the World Wide Web does not live up to its name, since it is mostly

[60]"Internet Opens Market Abroad," 46–48.

[61]Eryn Brown, "Nine Ways to Win on the Web," *Fortune,* May 24, 1999, 112–125.

[62]Hope Katz Gibbs, "Taking Global Local," *Global Business,* December 1999, 44–50.

THE INTERNATIONAL MARKETPLACE 13.6

E-Commerce in Emerging Markets

GENERAL MOTORS IS TESTING electronic commerce strategies in overseas markets such as Taiwan, where it already sells 10 percent of its vehicles through the Internet and plans to build cars to order starting in 2000. "Emerging markets are a lab for us," said Mark Hogan, who heads the new E-GM unit. "We do not have a lot of bricks and mortar in these markets, so they provide perfect conditions for us to learn from." The company hopes to sell about 30 percent of units on-line in upcoming years.

Although the United States has the greatest potential for on-line buying due to its large customer base, channel culture prevents the company from realizing it. The U.S. retail system consists of 20,000 dealers protected in many cases by state franchise laws that stand in the way of Internet sales. Additionally, automakers' production facilities cannot accommodate real-time Internet orders.

However, in many of the emerging markets, especially Asia and Latin America, both GM and Ford have factories that are more flexible and will allow for build-to-order programs to operate at a much faster pace. Furthermore, and more importantly, automakers do not have existing retail systems that need to be overhauled. In some cases, such as GM in Taiwan, the firms own a significant share of the retail operations. Ford is experimenting with Internet sales in markets such as the Philippines, where it has set up an e-commerce system that links consumers, dealers, the manufacturer, and suppliers to create a seamless e-business.

In addition to buying cars online, Taiwanese customers can make service appointments through the GM web site. The company will come to the owner's house or office, pick up the car, and return it within hours or overnight after completing the service.

SOURCE: "GM Tests E-Commerce Plans in Emerging Markets," *The Wall Street Journal,* October 25, 1999, B6.

http://www.gm.com

http://www.GMBuyPower.com

http://www.gmautoworld.com.tw

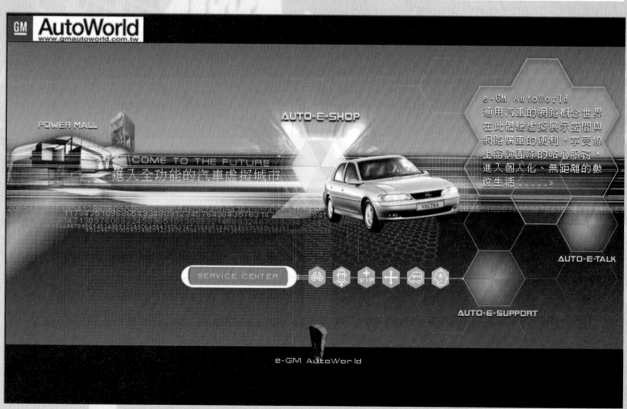

a tool for the United States and Europe. Yet, as Internet penetration levels increase in the near future, due to technological advances, improvements in many countries' Web infrastructures, and customer acceptance, e-business will become truly global. As a matter of fact, in some cases emerging markets may provide a chance to try out new approaches, because the markets and the marketers in them are not burdened by history, as seen in *The International Marketplace 13.6.*

The marketer has to be sensitive to the governmental role in e-commerce. No real consensus exists on the taxation of e-commerce, especially in the case of cross-border transactions. While the United States and the EU have agreed not to impose new taxes on sales through the Internet, there is no uniformity in the international taxation of transactions.[63] Other governments believe, however, that they have something to gain by levying new e-taxes. Until more firm legal precedents are established, international marketers should be aware of their potential tax liabilities and prepare for them, especially if they are considering substantial e-commerce investments. One likely scenario is an e-commerce tax system that closely resembles sales taxes at physical retail outlets. Vendors will be made responsible for collecting sales taxes and forwarding them to the governments concerned, most likely digitally. Another proposal involves the bit-tax, a variation of the Internet access tax.[64]

In addition, any product traded will still be subject to government regulations. For example, Virtual Vineyards has to worry about country-specific alcohol regulations, while software makers such as Softwareland.com Inc. have to comply with U.S. software export regulations. Dell Computer was fined $50,000 by the U.S. Department of Commerce for shipping computers on-line to Iran, a country on the sanctions list due to its sponsorship of terrorism.[65]

Governments will also have to come to terms with issues related to security, privacy, and access to the Internet.[66] The private sector argues for the highest possible ability to safeguard its databases, to protect cross-border transmission of confidential information, and to conduct secure financial transactions using global networks. This requires an unrestricted market for encryption products that operate globally. However, some governments, especially the United States, fear that encryption will enable criminals and terrorist organizations to avoid detection and tracking. Therefore, a strong argument is made in favor of limiting the extent of encryption.

Privacy issues have grown exponentially as a result of e-business. In 1998, the European Union passed a directive that introduced high standards of data privacy to ensure the free flow of data throughout its 15 member states. Each individual has the right to review personal data, correct them, and limit their use. But more importantly, the directive also requires member states to block transmission of data to countries, including the United States, if those countries' domestic legislation does not provide an adequate level of protection. The issue between the United States and the EU will most likely be settled by companies, such as IBM, adopting global privacy policies for managing information online and getting certified by groups, such as Better Business Bureaus or Trust-E, that are implementing privacy labeling systems to tell users when a site adheres to their privacy guidelines.[67] A register of such companies will also then have to be developed.

For industries such as music and motion pictures, the Internet is both an opportunity and a threat.[68] It provides a new and efficient method of distribution and customization of products. At the same time, it can be a channel for intellectual property

[63]Richard Prem, "Plan Your e-Commerce Tax Strategy," *e-Business Advisor,* April 1999, 36.

[64]Erika Morphy, "The Geography of e-Commerce," *Global Business,* November 1999, 26–33.

[65]"Internet Opens Markets Abroad," 46–48.

[66]Lou Gestner, "A Policy of Restraint," *Think Leadership,* March 1999, 1–3.

[67]Elizabeth De Bony, "EU, U.S. Plug Away at Data Privacy Abroad," *Industry Standard,* December 10, 1998, 45–46.

[68]Jodi Mardesich, "How the Internet Hits Big Music," *Fortune,* May 10, 1999, 96–102.

violations, through unauthorized postings on web sites from which protected material can be downloaded. In addition, the music industry is concerned about a shift in the balance of economic power: if artists can deliver their works directly to customers via technologies such as MP3, what will be the role of labels and distributors?

SUMMARY

Channels of distribution consist of the marketing efforts and intermediaries that facilitate the movement of goods and services. Decisions that must be made to establish an international channel of distribution focus on channel design and the selection of intermediaries for the roles that the international marketer will not perform. The channel must be designed to meet the requirements of the intended customer base, coverage, long-term continuity of the channel once it is established, and the quality of coverage to be achieved. Having determined the basic design of the channel, the international marketer will then decide on the number of different types of intermediaries to use and how many of each type, or whether to use intermediaries at all, which would be the case in direct distribution using, for example, sales offices or e-commerce. The process is important because the majority of international sales involve distributors, and channel decisions are the most long-term of all marketing decisions. The more the channel operation resembles a team, rather than a collection of independent businesses, the more effective the overall marketing effort will be.

QUESTIONS FOR DISCUSSION

1. Relate these two statements: "A channel of distribution can be compared to a marriage." "The number one reason given for divorce is lack of communication."
2. Channels of distribution tend to vary according to the level of economic development of a market. The more developed the economy, the shorter the channels tend to be. Why?
3. Using the web site of the U.S. Department of Commerce at **http://www.usatrade.com**, evaluate the type of help available to an exporter in establishing distribution channels, and its cost.
4. If a small exporter lacks the resources for an on-site inspection, what measures would you propose for screening potential distributors?

5. The international marketer and the distributor will have different expectations concerning the relationship. Why should these expectations be spelled out and clarified in the contract?
6. One method of screening candidates is to ask distributors for a simple marketing plan. What items would you want included in this plan?
7. Is gray marketing a trademark issue, a pricing issue, or a distribution issue?
8. Search for gray marketer's web site's on the Internet. What type of products are being made available? Why these particular ones?

RECOMMENDED READINGS

Czinkota, Michael R., and Jon Woronoff. *Unlocking Japan's Market.* Rutland, VT: Tuttle Co., 1993.

Hutt, Michael D., and Thomas W. Speh. *Business Marketing Management,* 6th ed. Fort Worth, TX: The Dryden Press, 1998.

International Chamber of Commerce. *The ICC Agency Model Contract.* New York: ICC Publishing Corp., 1999.

International Chamber of Commerce. *Incoterms 2000.* New York: ICC Publishing Corp., 2000.

Rosenbloom, Bert. *Marketing Channels: A Management View,* 6th ed. Hinsdale, IL: The Dryden Press, 1998.

U.S. Customs Service, *A Basic Guide to Importing,* 3rd ed. Washington, DC: U.S. Government Printing Office, 1996.

U.S. Department of Commerce. *A Basic Guide to Exporting.* Washington, DC: U.S. Government Printing Office, 1996.

Water from Iceland

tan Otis was in a contemplative mood. He had just hung up the phone after talking with Roger Morey, vice president of Citicorp. Morey had made him a job offer in the investment banking sector of the firm. The interviews had gone well, and Citicorp management was impressed with Stan's credentials from a major northeastern private university. "I think you can do well here, Stan. Let us know within a week whether you accept the job," Morey had said.

The three-month search had paid off well, Stan thought. However, an alternative plan complicated the decision to accept the position. Stan had returned several months before from an extended trip throughout Europe, a delayed graduation present from his parents. Among other places, he had visited Reykjavik, Iceland. Even though he could not communicate well, he found the island enchanting. What particularly fascinated him were the lack of industry and the purity of the natural landscape. In particular, he felt the water tasted extremely good. Returning home, he began to consider making this water available in the United States.

The Water Market in the United States

In order to consider the possibilities of importing Icelandic water, Stan knew that he first had to learn more about the general water market in the United States. Fortunately, some former college friends were working in a market research firm. Owing Stan some favors, these friends furnished him with a consulting report on the water market.

The Consulting Report

Bottled water has an 11 percent market share of total beverage consumption in the United States. The overall distribution of market share is shown in Exhibit 1.

Water is classified into two broad groups: surface water and ground water. Surface water is typically found in a river or lake. Ground water is trapped underneath the ground. Primary types of water available for human consumption in the United States are treated or processed water, mineral water, sparkling or effervescent water, spring well water, club soda, and tonic water.

Treated or processed water originates from a central reservoir supply or a well stream. This water usually flows as tap water and has been purified and fluoridated. Mineral water is spring water that contains a substantial amount of minerals, which may be injected or occur naturally. Natural mineral water is obtained from a natural spring or underground aquifers. The composition of the water at its source is constant, and the source discharge and temperature remain stable. Mineral water is distinguished from other types of water by its constant level and relatively high proportions of mineral and trace elements at the point of emergence from the source. An artificial process does not modify the natural content of the water at the source.

Sparkling or effervescent water contains natural or artificial carbonation. Some mineral waters come to the surface naturally carbonated through underground gases but lose their fizz on the surface with normal pressure. Many of these waters are injected with carbon dioxide later on. After treatment with carbon dioxide, such water contains the same amount of carbon dioxide that it had originally at emergence from the source.

Club soda is obtained by adding artificial carbonation to distilled or regular tap water. Mineral content in this water depends on the water supply used and the purification process the water has undergone. Tonic water is

This case study was prepared by Professor Michael R. Czinkota © with assistance from George Garcia.

| EXHIBIT | 1 | U.S. Retail Market Shares of Beverage Products, 1998 |

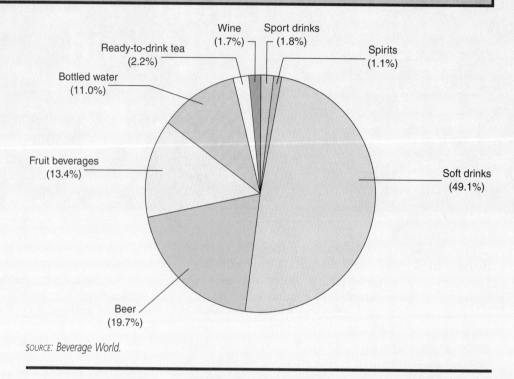

SOURCE: *Beverage World.*

derived from the same process as club soda, but has bitters added to it.

Minerals are important to the taste and quality of water. The type and variety of minerals present in the water can make it a very healthy and enjoyable drink. The combination of minerals present in the water determines its relative degree of acidity. The level of acidity is measured by the pH factor. The pH scale runs from 0 to 14; the neutral point is 7. A higher rating indicates that the water contains more solids, such as magnesium, and is said to be "hard." Conversely, water with a lower rating is classified as "soft." Most tap water is soft, whereas the majority of commercially sold waters tend to be hard.

Water Consumption in the United States

Tap water has generally been inexpensive, relatively pure, and plentiful in the United States. Traditionally, bottled water has been consumed in the United States by the wealthy. In the past decade, however, bottled water has begun to appeal to a wider market. The four main reasons for this change are:

1. An increasing awareness among consumers of the impurity of city water supplies (see Exhibit 2).
2. Increasing dissatisfaction with the taste, odor, and quality of tap water.
3. Rising affluence in society as well as lower prices for bottled water.

| EXHIBIT | 2 | Consumer Awareness of City Water Quality |

How would you rate the job being done by the state and federal governments in protecting the safety of public drinking water?	Very good—20% Somewhat good—49% Somewhat poor—18% Very poor—11%
What kind of water do you normally drink at home—straight tap water, tap water which has been filtered, or bottled water?	Tap water—53% Filtered tap water—24% Bottled water—22%
Have you ever received a notice or heard a community alert concerning safety problems with your drinking water supply?	Yes—21% No—79%

SOURCE: *Gallup Poll Monthly,* June 1998.

4. An increasing desire to maintain one's health and to avoid the excess consumption of caffeine, sugar, and other substances present in coffee and soft drinks.

Bottled water consumers are found chiefly in the states of California, Florida, Texas, New York, and Arkansas. These states combined represent 53.7 percent of nationwide bottled water sales in 1998, with California alone accounting for 26 percent of industry sales. Nationwide,

| EXHIBIT | 3 | U.S. Beverage Consumption in 1998 |

	RETAIL RECEIPTS ($BILLIONS)	PER CAPITA CONSUMPTION (GALLONS)
Soft Drinks	$53.7	54.6
Beer	53.3	21.9
Spirits	34.1	1.3
Fruit Beverages	15.2	15.0
Wine	13.0	2.5
Bottled Water	5.1	13.3
RTD Tea	3.2	2.7
Sports Drinks	2.2	2.2

SOURCE: Beverage Marketing Corporation, *Bottled Water in the U.S.*, 1999 Edition.

bottled water is drunk by 1 out of every 13 households. The average national per capita consumption was estimated to be 13.3 gallons. For a comparison of per capita consumption of bottled water and other beverages, see Exhibit 3.

Before 1976, bottled water was considered primarily a gourmet specialty, a luxury item consumed by the rich. Today, there are over 750 brands of bottled water available on the U.S. market. The volume of bottled water sold rose from 255 million gallons in 1976 to 3.6 billion gallons in 1998. From 1988 to 1998, U.S. consumption of bottled water increased by over 200 percent, taking market share from beverages such as coffee, tea, milk, juice, and alcoholic drinks (see Exhibit 4).

In 1998, the water industry's receipts totaled just under $4.0 billion at the wholesale level and $5.1 billion at the retail level. Bottled water gallonage increased by almost 9 percent between 1997 and 1998. For more information on the sales of bottled water consumption in the United States, see Exhibit 5. Nonsparkling water accounts for around 91 percent of total bottled water gallonage and increased by 11.9 percent in 1998. Sparkling water, on the other hand, decreased by 3.6 percent.

In 1998, imported water held a 4.5 percent share of the U.S. domestic market in terms of volume, but an 18.5 percent share in terms of wholesale dollars (see Exhibit 6). The leading country importing water to the United States is France, home of Perrier, with a 61.2 percent share of total bottled water import volume. Canada, home of Naya Water, is second with 25.3 percent, and Italy is third with 7.2 percent of the imported gallonage (see Exhibit 7).

Among domestic producers, Perrier Group of America is a strong leader with a 29.4 percent market share. Perrier Group's three top-selling brands are Poland Spring, Arrowhead, and Zephyrhills. With the top two brands and five of the biggest eight, Perrier Group is approaching the ownership of one-quarter of the market (see Exhibit 8).

| EXHIBIT | 4 | U.S. Beverage Consumption Growth, 1988–1998 |

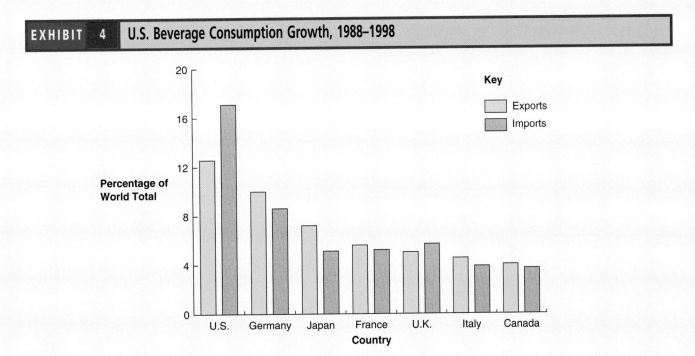

SOURCE: Norland International.

EXHIBIT 5 | U.S. Bottled Water Sales in Billions of Wholesale Dollars, 1998

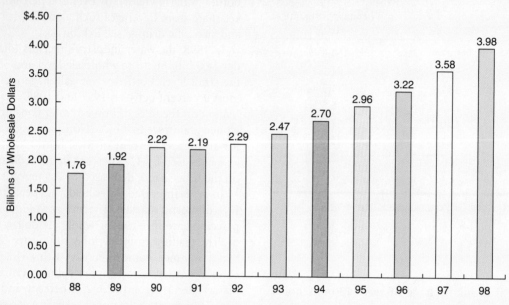

SOURCE: Beverage Marketing Corporation.

EXHIBIT 6 | Shares of Imports in the U.S. Bottled Water Market

	ESTIMATED WHOLESALE DOLLARS	GALLONAGE
1984	8.0%	1.8%
1985	11.7	2.8
1986	10.0	2.6
1987	11.0	2.7
1988	12.1	3.1
1989	11.9	3.1
1990	13.0	3.7
1991	11.2	3.5
1992	12.6	4.1
1993	15.0	4.1
1994	16.2	4.2
1995	14.4	3.6
1996	15.3	3.8
1997	17.9	4.6
1998	18.5	4.5

SOURCE: International Bottled Water Association, **http://www.bottledwater.org**.

EXHIBIT 7 | Bottled Water Imports by Country, 1998

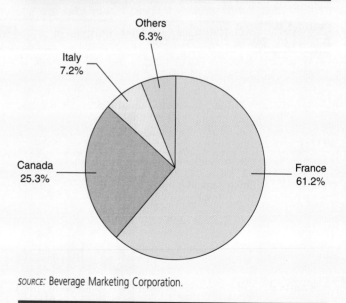

SOURCE: Beverage Marketing Corporation.

| | EXHIBIT | 8 | Top 10 Bottled Waters of 1998 |

RANK	BRAND	SALES ($ MILLIONS)
1	Poland Spring (Perrier)	350.90
2	Arrowhead (Perrier)	283.20
3	Sparkletts (McKesson)	205.00
4	Evian (Danone International)	200.70
5	Aquafina (Pepsi-Cola)	165.00
6	Zephyrhills (Perrier)	134.40
7	Hinckley & Schmitt (Suntory)	128.60
8	Deer Park (Perrier)	123.60
9	Ozarka (Perrier)	122.80
10	Crystal Geyser (Suntory)	113.10

SOURCE: *Beverage World*, April 1999.

 ## Additional Research

Segments

Within the bottled water business there are two distinct industries and segments. The biggest by volume is the five-gallon or returnable container water business. Companies like Arrowhead, Sparkletts, and Hinckley & Schmitt are leaders in this field. Often associated with the office cooler, bottlers also use two-and-one-half-gallon as well as one-gallon containers for supermarket distribution. This type of bottled water is sold as an alternative to tap water.

Premium bottled waters, such as Evian, Vittel, and Perrier, are sold as soft drink and alcohol alternatives. Packaging ranges from six-ounce to two-liter containers and from custom glass and polyethylene terephthalate (PET) plastic to aluminum cans. More and more bottled water producers have switched from glass to plastic because of the increased acceptance of this kind of packaging. PET bottles were a breakthrough in the bottled water industry. They protect nutritive properties without transfer of taste, and they are recyclable and reused by a number of industries. PET bottles come in different sizes and are the most widely used form of water bottle on the market today.

The bottled water market is getting more competitive as major beverage companies such as Coca-Cola introduce new brands of bottled water. Prices of bottled water continue to decrease. Image is also very important—a lot of bottled water containers show pictures of mountains and springs to capture the consumer's attention and make them feel that they are drinking the purest water available.

Bottled Water Regulation in the United States

The bottled water industry in the United States is regulated and controlled at three levels—by the federal government, state government, and trade association. The U.S. Food and Drug Administration (FDA) under the Federal Food, Drug and Cosmetic Act (FFDCA) regulates bottled water as a food product, including packaged water sold in smaller containers at retail outlets as well as larger five-gallon containers distributed to the home and office market. Like all food products except meat and poultry (which are regulated by the U.S. Department of Agriculture), bottled water is subject to the FDA's extensive food safety and labeling requirements. In addition, all bottled water products imported from countries outside the United States must meet the standards established by their own country as well as comply with all the U.S. regulations. Producers engaged in interstate commerce are subject to periodic, unannounced FDA inspections.

The Icelandic Scenario

Iceland's economy is basically market oriented, with an extensive welfare system, low unemployment, and a remarkably even distribution of income. In terms of products exported, the economy depends heavily on the fishing industry, which provides 75 percent of export earnings and employs 12 percent of the work force. The economy remains sensitive to declining fish stocks as well as to drops in world prices for its main exports: fish and fish products, aluminum, and ferrosilicon.

The government has the diversification of its export base as one of its key goals. It also plans to continue its policies of reducing the budget and current account deficits, limiting foreign borrowing, containing inflation, revising agricultural and fishing policies, and privatizing state-owned industries. The government remains opposed to EU membership, primarily because of Icelanders' concern about losing control over their fishing resources.

In recent years, economic growth has been high, inflation has been low, unemployment has declined, and living standards have risen. On these measures, Iceland is among the best performers in the OECD. Economic growth has averaged over 3.4 percent per year over 1994 through 1997 and reached a respectable 3.9 percent in 1998. Unemployment has fallen from 5 percent of the labor force in 1995 to 4 percent in 1996 and has fallen even lower in 1998 to 3.8 percent. For comparison, unemployment in 1998 averaged 11.1 percent in the European Union. Inflation, which has often been a problem in the economy, has declined from 2.3 percent in 1996 to 1.8 percent in 1998.

The Ministry of Commerce, after consulting the Central Bank, has the ultimate responsibility in matters concerning import and export licensing. The Central Bank is responsible for the regulation of foreign exchange transactions and exchange controls, including capital controls. It is also responsible for ensuring that all foreign exchange due to residents is surrendered to authorized banks. All commercial exports require licenses. The shipping documents must be lodged with an authorized bank. Receipts exchanged for exports must be surrendered to the Central Bank.

In general, the business climate in Iceland is favorable to foreign investments. All investments by nonresidents in Iceland are subject to individual approval. The participation of nonresidents in Icelandic joint venture companies may not exceed 49 percent. However, the government has started abolishing restrictions in order to create a more favorable investment climate. One restriction being analyzed is the fact that nonresident-owned foreign capital entering in the form of exchange must be surrendered.

Iceland is a member of the European Economic Area (EEA), which opens up the possibility of a duty-free access to European Union member states for U.S. and Canadian firms. It is also part of the United Nations, the European Free Trade Association, and the World Trade Organization. Iceland enjoys normal trade relations (formerly Most Favored Nation) status with the United States. Under this designation, mineral and carbonated water from Iceland is subject to a tariff of 0.33 cents per liter. Natural (still) water is tariff-free.

QUESTIONS FOR DISCUSSION

1. Is there sufficient information to determine whether importing water from Iceland would be a profitable business in the U.S. market? If not, what additional information is needed to make a determination?

2. Is the market climate in the United States conducive to water imports from Iceland?

3. What are some possible reasons for the fluctuation in the market share held by imports over the past 10 years?

Joemarin Oy

Finland's first customers in the sailboat business are generally believed to have been the Vikings. More recently, ships and boats were exported as partial payment for World War II reparations. This long tradition in building sailboats is due, no doubt, to Finland's proximity to the sea, long coastline, and 60,000 lakes. Among luxury sailing yachts, the Swan boats of Nautor Oy and the Finnsailers of Fiskars Oy are internationally known and admired. There are, however, over 100 other boat builders in Finland that turn out 10,000 sailing yachts yearly.

Although most of the Finnish sailboat companies are situated on the coast, for obvious reasons, Joemarin Oy is located in the town of Joensuu, roughly 450 kilometers northeast of Helsinki. Joemarin was founded in the town that lends part of its name to the company because of the efforts of Kehitysaluerahasto, which is the Development Area Foundation of the Finnish government. Kehitysaluerahasto provided a loan of four million Finnish marks to Joemarin, a privately owned company, to start its operations in the Joensuu area because of the town's high rate of unemployment.

The present product line consists of three types of fiberglass sailboats. The Joemarin 17 is a coastal sailing yacht with a new design approach. (See Figure 1.) This approach is to provide a craft that enables a family to make weekend and holiday cruises in coastal waters and also offers exciting sailing. The sailboat is very fast. The Finnish Yacht Racing Association stated in its test in which the Joemarin 17 was judged to be the best in her class: "She is delicate, lively, spacious, and easy to steer. She is well balanced and has a high-quality interior. She is especially fast on the beat and lively to handle in a free wind."

SOURCE: This case was prepared by James H. Sood of the American University. Reprinted with permission.

The Joemarin 17, a small day cruiser with berths for two adults and two children, has a sail area of 130 square feet, weighs one-half ton, and has an overall length of a little over 17 feet. The hull is made of glass-reinforced plastic (GRP), and the mast and boom are made of aluminum. The boat has a drop keel that is useful when negotiating shallow anchorages or when lifting the boat on a trailer for transportation. The layout of the boat is shown in Figure 2.

The Joemarin 34 is a relatively large motor sailer that sleeps seven people in three separate compartments. The main saloon contains an adjustable dining table, a complete galley, and a navigator's compartment. The main saloon is separated from the fore cabin by a folding door. The aft cabin, which is entered by a separate companionway, contains a double berth, wardrobe, wash basin, and lockers. The toilet and shower are situated between the fore cabin and the main saloon. The boat has a sail area of 530 square feet, weighs about five tons, and has an overall length of 33 feet 9 inches. A significant feature of the craft is that she is equipped with a 47 horsepower diesel engine.

The Joemarin 34 has the same design approach as the 17. She is well appointed, with sufficient space for seven people to live comfortably. An important feature is that the three separate living compartments allow for considerable privacy. In addition, however, the modern hull is quite sleek, making her an excellent sailing yacht.

The Joemarin 36 was designed for a different purpose. Whereas the 17 and 34 are oriented toward a family approach to sailing—combining the features of safety and comfortable accommodations with good sailing ability—the 36 is first and foremost a sailing craft. It does have two berths, a small galley, and toilet facilities, but the emphasis is on sailing and racing rather than comfort. The boat has a sail area of 420 square feet, weighs a little less than four tons, and has an overall length of 35 feet 10 inches. The boat is also equipped with a small (7 horsepower) diesel engine for emergency power situations.

| FIGURE | 1 | Joemarin 17: Ideal for Family Cruising as Well as Exciting Racing |

The Joemarin 36 is a traditional Swedish design and, therefore, is directed almost solely to the Swedish market.

The company was established in order to manufacture sailboats for export. The Finnish sailboat market is small because of the short sailing season. Nevertheless, the com-

pany has been successful in marketing the 17 in Finland, although this was difficult in the beginning because of the lack of boat dealers. To circumvent this problem, Joemarin persuaded a number of new car dealers throughout the country to handle the Joemarin 17 on an

| FIGURE | 2 | The Layout of the Joemarin 17 |

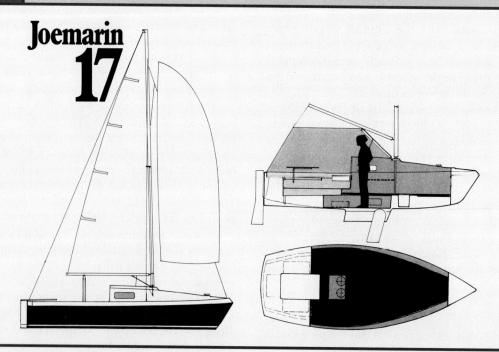

agency basis. This involved the company's providing one boat to each car dealer, who placed it in the showroom. The dealer then marketed the sailboats for a 15 percent sales commission.

Although many people scoffed at this idea, the system produced reasonable sales and also made the company known throughout Finland. This contributed to an arrangement with one of the largest cooperative wholesale-retail operations in Finland. Like most cooperatives, this organization began with agricultural products; however, the product range of the company now includes virtually every conceivable consumer product. The present contract states that the cooperative will purchase 80 Joemarin 17 boats per year for the next three years.

The Swedish market is served by a selling agent, although this representative has not been particularly effective. Because Sweden is also the home of many sailboat builders, the company has tried to market only the 36 in that country. In Denmark, France, Holland, Germany, and the United Kingdom, Joemarin has marketed the 34 through importers. These importers operate marinas in addition to new sailboat dealerships. They purchase the boats from Joemarin for their own accounts and mark up the price by about 20 percent. In return for exclusive marketing rights in their respective countries, they agree to purchase a minimum number (usually three or four) of the 34 design per year. None of these importers is interested in marketing the 17 or the 36; the shipping cost for the 17 is too high compared with the value of the boat, and there is little customer interest in the 36.

Joemarin is planning to introduce a new sailboat. Whereas the present products were designed by people in the company who were relatively unknown (to the customers), the hull of the new sailboat has been designed by an internationally known boat designer. The cost of these design services was a $10,000 initial fee plus a $1,200 royalty fee to be paid for each boat produced. The new sailboat, the Joemarin 29, has an interior quite similar to that of the Joemarin 34. This is not unexpected because the same Joemarin people designed the interiors and decks of both sailboats.

The new boat is a motor sailer that sleeps six people in three separate compartments, is 28 feet 9 inches long, weighs 4 tons, and has a joined cabin space and a separate aft cabin, small galley, toilet and shower facilities, and a 12 horsepower diesel engine. Because of a new construction technique that greatly reduces the amount of fiberglass required, the variable costs to construct the boat are only 60 percent of the costs for the 34. With a preliminary selling price of 195,000 Finnish marks, the Joemarin 29 is receiving favorable attention, and the company is concerned that sales may have an adverse effect on sales of the 34.

The company categorizes the marketing expenses as fixed costs because allocating these expenses to specific products is difficult. The major element of the program is participation in international boat shows in London, Paris, Hamburg, Amsterdam, Copenhagen, and Helsinki. The initial purpose of participating in these shows was to locate suitable importers in the target markets; however, this effort is maintained in order to support the marketing programs of the importers. The importers are also supported by advertising in the leading yachting magazines in the national markets. Joemarin's personal selling effort consists primarily of servicing the importers and agents and staffing the exhibitions at the boat shows. Most of the sales promotion costs are the result of the elaborate sales brochures that the company has developed for each boat. These brochures are printed in four colors on three folded pages of high-quality paper. The costs are greatly increased, however, by having to print a relatively small number of each brochure in Finnish, French, English, German, and Swedish. The brochures are provided to the agents and importers and are used at the boat shows.

The company is in the process of preparing its production and marketing plan for the coming year in order to arrange financing. The president is strongly committed to the continued growth of the company, and the market indications suggest that there is a reasonably strong demand for the 17 in Finland and for the 34 in most of the other national markets. The sales results of the previous and present years are shown in Table 1; the profit statement for the present year is shown in Table 2.

The main problem in developing the plan for next year is determining the price for each sailboat in each market. In previous years, Joemarin had established its prices in Finnish marks, on an ex-factory basis. Management has become convinced, however, that it must change the terms of its prices in order to meet competition in the foreign markets. Thus, the company has decided to offer CIF prices to its foreign customers in the currency of the foreign country. The use of truck ferries between Finland and Sweden, Denmark, and Germany is expected to make this pricing approach more competitive.

Joemarin would also like to assure its agents and importers that the prices will remain in effect for the entire year, but the financial manager is concerned about the possible volatility of exchange rates because of the varying rates of inflation in the market countries. The present exchange rates, the expected inflation rates in the market countries, and the estimated costs to ship the Joemarin 36 to Stockholm and the Joemarin 29 and 34 to the other foreign marinas are shown in Table 3.

A second difficulty in pricing the product line in Joemarin is to establish a price for the 29 that will reflect the value of the boat but will not reduce the sales of the 34. There are three schools of thought concerning the pricing of motor sailers. The predominant theory is that price is a function of the overall length of the sailboat. A number of people, however, believe that the overall weight

TABLE 1   Joemarin Sales

	LAST YEAR			PRESENT YEAR		
	NO.	AVERAGE PRICE[a]	REVENUE	NO.	AVERAGE PRICE[a]	REVENUE
J/M-17	200	27,000	5,400,000	240	29,700	7,128,000
J/M-29	—	—	—	—	—	—
J/M-34	30	324,000	9,720,000	36	356,000	12,830,000
J/M-36	4	189,000	756,000	5	207,900	1,039,500
			15,876,000			20,997,900

[a]All prices are manufacturer's prices; prices and revenues are in Finnish marks: 1.00 Finnmark = U.S. $0.185.

TABLE 2   Joemarin Profit Statement for Present Year

	IN FINNMARKS	AS A PERCENTAGE OF SALES
Sales revenue	20,790,000[a]	
Variable costs (direct labor and materials)	13,510,000	65.0%
Fixed costs:		
Production (building expenses, production management salaries)	945,000	4.5
Product design costs (salaries, prototypes, testing, consultants)	1,323,000	6.4
Administration costs (salaries, insurance, office expenses)	648,000	3.1
Marketing costs (salaries, advertising, boat shows, sales promotion, travel expenses)	2,284,000	11.0
Total fixed costs	5,200,000	25.0%
Profit before taxes	2,080,000	10.0

[a]All prices are manufacturer's prices; prices and revenues are in Finnish marks; 1.00 Finnmark = U.S. $0.185.

TABLE 3   Shipping Costs for Joemarin 36 to Sweden, and for Joemarin 29 and 34 to Other Countries

COUNTRY	PRESENT EXCHANGE RATES IN FINNISH MARKS	EXPECTED INFLATION RATES	ESTIMATED FREIGHT AND INSURANCE COSTS PER BOAT
Denmark	Danish Kroner = 0.628	12%	13,500 Fmks.
France	French Franc = 0.778	10	19,000 Fmks.
Holland	Dutch Guilder = 2.015	9	17,000 Fmks.
Sweden	Swedish Kroner = 0.725	12	10,000 Fmks.
United Kingdom	English Pound = 8.308	14	22,000 Fmks.
Germany	German Mark = 2.204	7	17,000 Fmks.
Finland	—	12	—

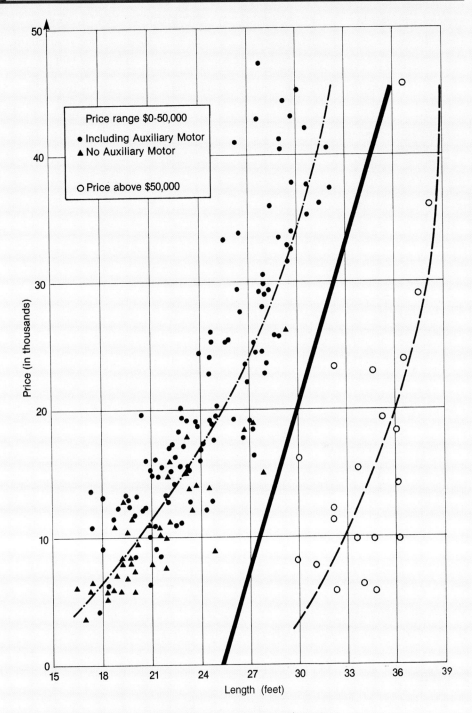

FIGURE 3 Retail Price in the European Market of Sailing Yachts as a Function of Overall Length

Price range $0-50,000
• Including Auxiliary Motor
▲ No Auxiliary Motor

○ Price above $50,000

Price (in thousands)

Length (feet)

Note: All yachts to the right of the bold dividing line are priced above $50,000.

of the craft is a much more accurate basis. The third opinion argues that price is a function of the special features and equipment. Figure 3, which was prepared by a Swiss market research firm, shows the relationship between present retail prices and the length of new motor sailers in the West European market.

QUESTIONS FOR DISCUSSION

1. Determine the optimal manufacturer's selling price in the Finnish market for the four Joemarin sailboats for the coming year.
2. Determine the CIF prices for the Joemarin 36 to the final customer in Sweden for the coming year. The agent's commission is 15 percent of the final selling price, and the final selling price should be in Swedish kroner.
3. Recommend a course of action for the company to take in regard to the Joemarin 36.
4. Determine the CIF prices, in the foreign currencies, for the Joemarin 29 and 34 to the importers in Denmark, France, Holland, the United Kingdom, and Germany for the coming year.
5. Develop a production and marketing plan for Joemarin for the coming year. What steps can the company take to ensure that the plan is in line with the demand for its products in its foreign markets?

Sperry/MacLennan Architects and Planners

In August 1988, Mitch Brooks, a junior partner and director of Sperry/MacLennan (S/M), a Dartmouth, Nova Scotia, architectural practice specializing in recreational facilities, is in the process of developing a plan to export his company's services. He intends to present the plan to the other directors at their meeting the first week of October. The regional market for architectural services is showing some signs of slowing, and S/M realizes that it must seek new markets. As Sheila Sperry, the office manager and one of the directors, said at their last meeting: "You have to go wider than your own backyard. After all, you can only build so many pools in your own backyard."

About the Company

Drew Sperry, one of the two senior partners in Sperry/MacLennan, founded the company in 1972 as a one-man architectural practice. After graduating from Nova Scotia Technical College (now the Technical University of Nova Scotia) in 1966, Sperry worked for six years for Robert J. Flinn before deciding that it was time to start his own company. By then he had cultivated a loyal clientele and a reputation as a good design architect and planner. In the first year, the business was supported part-time by a contract with the Province of Prince Edward Island Department of Tourism to undertake parks planning and the design of parks facilities, from park furniture to interpretive centers. At the end of its first year, the company was incorporated as H. Drew Sperry and Associates; by then Sperry had added three junior architects, a draftsman, and a secretary. One of those architects was John MacLennan, who would later become a senior partner in Sperry/MacLennan.

Throughout the 1970s, the practice grew rapidly as the local economy expanded, even though the market for architectural services was competitive. The architectural program at the Nova Scotia Technical College (TUNS) was graduating more architects wishing to stay in the Maritimes than could be readily absorbed. But that was not the only reason why competition was stiff; there was a perception among businesspeople and local government personnel that if you wanted the best, you had to get it from Toronto or New York. The company's greatest challenge throughout this period was persuading the local authorities that they did not have to go to Central Canada for first-class architectural expertise.

With the baby boom generation entering the housing market, more than enough business came its way to enable Sperry to develop a thriving architectural practice, and by 1979 the company had grown to fifteen employees and had established branch offices in Charlottetown and Fredericton. These branch offices had been established to provide a local market presence and meet licensing requirements during an aggressive growth period. The one in Charlottetown operated under the name of Allison & Sperry Associates, with Jim Allison as the partner, whereas in Fredericton, partner Peter Fellows was in charge.

But the growth could not last. The early 1980s was not an easy time for the industry, and many architectural firms found themselves unable to stay in business through a very slow period in 1981–1982. For Sperry/MacLennan, it meant a severe reduction in staff, and it also marked the end of the branch offices. Financially stretched and with work winding down on a multipurpose civic sports facility, the Dartmouth Sportsplex, the company was asked to enter a design competition for an aquatics center in Saint John, New Brunswick. They had to win or

SOURCE: This case has been prepared by Dr. Mary R. Brooks, of Dalhousie University, as a basis for classroom discussion rather than to illustrate effective or ineffective handling of an administrative situation. The assistance of the Secretary of State, Canadian Studies Program, in developing the case is gratefully acknowledged. Copyright © 1990 Mary R. Brooks. Reprinted with permission.

439

close their doors. The company laid off all but the three remaining partners—Drew, Sheila Sperry, and John MacLennan. However, one draftsman and the secretary refused to leave, working without pay for several months in the belief that the company would win; their faith in the firm is still appreciated today.

Their persistence and faith were rewarded. In 1983, Sperry won the competition for the aquatics facility for the Canada Games to be held in Saint John. The clients in Saint John wanted to build a new aquatic center that would house the Canada Games competition and provide a community facility that was self-supporting after the games were over. The facility needed to reflect a forward-thinking image to the world and act as a linchpin in the downtown revitalization plan. Therefore, it was paramount that the facility adhere to all technical competition requirements and that the design include renovation details for its conversion to a community facility sporting a new Sperry design element, the "indoor beach." The Saint John Canada Games Society decided to use Sperry for the contract and was very pleased with the building, the more so since the building won two design awards in 1985: the Facility of Merit Award for its "outstanding design" from *Athletics Business* and the Canadian Parks and Recreation Facility of Excellence Award. Sperry had gained national recognition for its sports facility expertise, and its reputation as a good design firm specializing in sports facilities was secured.

From the beginning, the company found recreational facilities work to be fun and exciting. To quote Sheila Sperry, this type of client "wants you to be innovative and new. It's a dream for an architect because it gives him an opportunity to use all the shapes and colors and natural light. It's a very exciting medium to work in." So they decided to focus their promotional efforts to get more of this type of work and consolidate their "pool designer" image by associating with Creative Aquatics on an exclusive basis in 1984. Creative Aquatics provided aquatics programming and technical operations expertise (materials, systems, water treatment, safety, and so on) to complement the design and planning skills at Sperry.

The construction industry rebounded in 1984; declining interest rates ushered in a mini building boom, which kept everyone busy for the 1984–1987 period. Jim Reardon joined the company in 1983 and quickly acquired the experience and knowledge that would ease the company through its inevitable expansion. John MacLennan, by then a senior shareholder in the firm, wanted to develop a base in the large Ontario market and establish an office in Toronto. Jim Reardon was able to take over John's activities with very little difficulty, since he had been working very closely with John in the recreational facilities aspect of the business. Reardon became a junior partner in 1986.

With John MacLennan's move to Toronto in 1985, the company changed its name to Sperry/MacLennan in hopes that the name could be used for both offices. But the Ontario Association of Architects ruled that the name could not include "Sperry" because Drew Sperry was not an Ontario resident, and the Toronto office was required to operate under the name of MacLennan Architects. The Ontario office gradually became self-supporting, and the company successfully entered a new growth phase.

Mitch Brooks joined the practice in 1987. He had graduated from TUNS in 1975 and had been one of the small number of his class to try to make a go of it in Halifax. The decision to add Brooks as a partner, albeit a junior one, stemmed from their compatibility. Brooks was a good production architect, and work under his supervision came in on budget and on time, a factor compatible with the Sperry/MacLennan emphasis on customer service. The company's fee revenue amounted to approximately $1.2 million in the 1987 fiscal year; however, salaries are a major business expense, and profits after taxes (but before employee bonuses) accounted for only 4.5 percent of revenue.

Now it is late August, and with the weather cooling, Mitch Brooks reflects on his newest task, planning for the coming winter's activities. The company's reputation in the Canadian sports facility market is secure. The company has completed or has in construction five sports complexes in the Maritimes and five in Ontario, and three more facilities are in design. The awards have followed, and just this morning, Drew was notified of their latest achievement—the company has won the $10,000 *Canadian Architect* Grand Award for the Grand River Aquatics and Community Center near Kitchener, Ontario. This award is a particularly prestigious one because it is given by fellow architects in recognition of design excellence. Last week, Sheila Sperry received word that the Amherst, N.S., YM-YWCA won the American National Swimming Pool and Spa Gold Medal for pool design against French and Mexican finalists, giving them international recognition. Mitch Brooks is looking forward to his task. With nineteen employees to keep busy and a competitor on the West Coast, they decided this morning that it is time to consider exporting their hard-won expertise.

The Architecture Industry

In order to practice architecture in Canada, an architect must graduate from an accredited school and serve a period of apprenticeship with a licensed architect, during which time he or she must experience all facets of the practice. At the end of this period, the would-be architect must pass an examination similar to that required of U.S. architects.

Architects are licensed provincially, and these licenses are not readily transferable from province to province. Various levels of reciprocity are in existence. For this reason, joint ventures are not that uncommon in the business. In order to "cross" provincial boundaries, architecture firms in one province often enter into a joint venture arrangement with a local company. For example, the well-known design firm of Arthur Erickson of Vancouver/ Toronto often engages in joint ventures with local production architects, as was the case for its design of the new Sir James Dunn Law Library on the campus of Dalhousie University in Halifax.

In the United States, Canadian architects are well respected. The primary difficulty in working in the United States has been in immigration policies, which limit the movement of staff and provide difficulties in securing contracts. These policies would be eliminated with the Free Trade Agreement and the reciprocity accord signed between the American Institute of Architects and the Royal Architectural Institute of Canada, a voluntary group representing the provincial associations.

Because architects in Nova Scotia are ethically prohibited from advertising their services, an architect's best advertisement is a good project, well done and well received. The provincial association (Nova Scotia Association of Architects—NSAA) will supply potential clients with basic information about licensed firms, their area of specialization, and so on. NSAA guidelines limit marketing to announcements of new partners, presentations to targeted potential clients, advertisements of a business card size with "business card" information, and participation in media events.

The provincial association also provides a minimum schedule of fees, although many clients view this as the maximum they should pay. Although architects would like to think that the client chooses to do business with them because they like their past work, the price of the service is often the decision point. Some developers prefer to buy services on a basis other than the published fee schedule, such as a lump-sum amount or a per-square-foot price. Although fee cutting is not encouraged by the professional organization, it is a factor in winning business, particularly when interest rates are high and construction slow.

Because the "product" of an architecture firm is the service of designing a building, the marketing of the "product" centers on the architect's experience with a particular building type. Therefore, it is imperative that the architect convince the client that he or she has the necessary experience and capability to undertake the project and to complete it satisfactorily. S/M has found with its large projects that the amount of time spent meeting

with the client requires some local presence, although the design need not be done locally.

The process of marketing architectural services is one of marketing ideas. Therefore, it is imperative that the architect and the client have the same objectives and ultimately the same vision. Although that vision may be constrained by the client's budget, part of the marketing process is one of communicating with the client to ensure these common objectives exist.

Architects get business in a number of ways. "Walk-in" business is negligible, and most of S/M's contracts are a result of one of the following five processes:

1. A satisfied client gives a referral.
2. A juried design competition is announced (S/M has found that these prestigious jobs, even though they offer "runners-up" partial compensation, are not worth entering except to win, since costs are too high and the compensation offered other entrants too low. Second place is the same as last place. The Dartmouth Sportsplex and the Saint John Aquatic Center were both design competition wins).
3. A client publishes a "Call for Proposals" or a "Call for Expressions of Interest" as the start of a formal selection process. (S/M rates these opportunities; unless it has a 75 percent chance of winning the contract, it views the effort as not worth the risk.)
4. A potential client invites a limited number of architectural firms to submit their qualifications as the start of a formal selection process. (S/M has prepared a qualification package that it can customize for a particular client.)
5. S/M hears of a potential building and contacts the client, presenting its qualifications.

The fourth and fifth processes are most common in buildings done for institutions and large corporations. Since the primary buyers of sports facilities tend to be municipalities or educational institutions, this is the way S/M acquires a substantial share of its work. Although juried competitions are not that common, the publicity possible from success in landing this work is important to S/M. The company has found that its success in securing a contract is often dependent on the client's criteria and the current state of the local market, with no particular pattern evident for a specific building type.

After the architect signs the contract, there will be a number of meetings with the client as the concept evolves and the drawings and specifications develop. On a large sports facility project, the hours of contact can run into the hundreds. Depending on the type of project, client meetings may be held weekly or every two weeks; during the development of working drawings and specifications for a complex building, meetings may be as often as once a day. Therefore, continuing client contact is as much a part of the service sold as the drawings, specifications, and site supervision and, in fact, may be the key factor in repeat business.

Developers in Nova Scotia are often not loyal buyers, changing architects with every major project or two. Despite this, architects are inclined to think the buyer's loyalty is greater than it really is. Therefore, S/M scrutinizes buyers carefully, interested in those that can pay for a premium product. S/M's philosophy is to provide "quality products with quality service for quality clients" and thus produce facilities that will reflect well on the company.

 The Opportunity

In 1987, External Affairs and the Royal Architectural Institute of Canada commissioned a study of exporting opportunities for architects on the assumption that free trade in architectural services would be possible under the Free Trade Agreement. The report, entitled *Precision, Planning, and Perseverance: Exporting Architectural Services to the United States,* identified eight market niches for Canadian architects in the United States, one of which was educational facilities, in particular postsecondary institutions.

This niche, identified by Brooks as most likely to match S/M's capabilities, is controlled by state governments and private organizations. Universities are known not to be particularly loyal to local firms and so present a potential market to be developed. The study reported that "post-secondary institutions require design and management competence, whatever the source." Athletic facilities were identified as a possible niche for architects with mixed-use facility experience. Finally, the study concluded that "there is an enormous backlog of capital maintenance and new building requirements facing most higher education institutions."

In addition to the above factors, the study indicated other factors that Brooks felt were of importance:

1. The United States has 30 percent fewer architectural firms per capita than Canada.
2. The market shares many Canadian values and work practices.
3. The population shift away from the Northeast to the sunbelt is beginning to reverse.
4. Americans are demanding better buildings.

Although Brooks knows that Canadian firms have always had a good reputation internationally for the quality of their buildings, he is concerned that American firms are well ahead of Canadian ones in their use of CADD (computer-assisted design and drafting) for everything from conceptual design to facility management. S/M, in-spite of best intentions, has been unable to get CADD off the ground but is in the process of applying to the Atlantic

Canada Opportunities Agency for financial assistance in switching over to CADD.

Finally, the study cautions that "joint ventures with a U.S. architectural firm may be required but the facility managers network of the APPA [Association of Physical Plant Administrators of Universities and Colleges] should also be actively pursued".

Under free trade, architects will be able to freely engage in trade in services. Architects will be able to travel to the United States and set up an architectural practice without having to become qualified under the American Institute of Architects; as long as they are members of their respective provincial associations and have passed provincial licensing exams and apprenticeship requirements, they will be able to travel and work in the United States and import staff as required.

 Where to Start?

In a meeting in Halifax in January 1988, the Department of External Affairs had indicated that trade to the United States in architectural services was going to be one positive benefit of the Free Trade Agreement to come into force in January 1989. As a response, S/M has targeted New England for its expansion because of its geographical proximity to S/M's home base in the Halifax/Dartmouth area and also because of its population density and similar climatic conditions. However, with all the hype about free trade and the current focus on the United States, Brooks is quite concerned that the company might be overlooking some other very lucrative markets for his company's expertise. As part of his October presentation to the board, he wants to identify and evaluate other possible markets for S/M's services. Other parts of the United States, or the affluent countries of Europe where recreational facilities are regularly patronized and design is taken seriously, might provide a better export market, given S/M's string of design successes at home and the international recognition afforded by the Amherst facility design award. Brooks feels that designing two sports facilities a year in a new market would be an acceptable goal.

As part of searching for leads, Brooks notes that the APPA charges $575 for a membership, which provides access to its membership list once a year. But this is only one source of leads. And, of course, there is the U.S. Department of Commerce, Bureau of the Census, as another source of information for him to tap. He wonders what other sources are possible.

S/M looks to have a very good opportunity in the New England market with all of its small universities and colleges. After a decade of cutbacks on spending, corporate donations and alumni support for U.S. universities has never been so strong, and many campuses have sports facilities that are outdated and have been poorly maintained. But Mitch Brooks is not sure that the New England market is the best. After all, a seminar on exporting that he attended last week indicated that the most geographically close market, or even the most psychically close one, may not be the best choice for long-run profit maximization and/or market share.

QUESTIONS FOR DISCUSSION

1. What types of information will Brooks need to collect before he can even begin to assess the New England market? Develop a series of questions you feel are critical to this assessment.
2. What selection criteria do you believe will be relevant to the assessment of any alternative markets? What preliminary market parameters are relevant to the evaluation of S/M's *global* options?
3. Assuming that S/M decides on the New England market, what information will be needed to implement an entry strategy?

Spectrum Color Systems, Inc.

Anthony Cordera, executive vice president of Spectrum Color Systems, sighed as he hung up the phone. The conversation still raced through his mind as he surveyed the fall foliage outside his office window. Cordera went over every nuance of the telephone conversation he had just completed with Roberto Cortez, vice president of European operations at BASF International. BASF had been a good customer for Spectrum, but today Cortez spoke with disdain, accusing Spectrum of questionable practices in its dealings with BASF. Cordera hated to see such a profitable relationship sour, but he saw no solution. As he turned back toward his desk, he wondered whether Spectrum might soon face similar sentiment from other large multinational clients. At the same time, he wondered how to address this issue at the upcoming board meeting without alarming the company president and the board of directors.

 ## History

Spectrum Color Systems is a medium-sized industrial firm with headquarters in the eastern United States. The firm was founded in 1952 when Daniel Clark, a government scientist working on techniques to measure aspects of color and appearance, was approached by Procter & Gamble (P&G).

Procter & Gamble recognized that customers held a perception of quality related to the color of its products. In order to offer consistency to its customers, and as part of its quality control program, P&G sought a process to help it standardize the color and appearance of the products it manufactured. Clark balked at the request to work for P&G, building a machine that could quantify aspects

of color, but as he recognized widespread commercial applications of such a machine, Clark went into business for himself. Spectrum Color Systems started with the simple philosophy of providing solutions to customers' problems relating to measurement and control of color and appearance attributes. The first machines were developed under contract with P&G. As the quality control movement developed throughout the industrialized world, the demand for Spectrum's products grew.

Spectrum Color Systems remains privately held; majority ownership and controlling voting rights remain in the Clark family. In 1990, Daniel Clark passed away. His son, Paul, is CEO and president; he runs domestic sales, finance, and human resources. Anthony Cordera joined Spectrum in 1985. As executive vice president, he is responsible for manufacturing, engineering, international sales, shipping, and receiving. He reports directly to Paul Clark.

The Clark family retains approximately 55 percent of company stock, including all voting stock. The executive and associate staff participate in an employee stock ownership plan and together own the remaining 45 percent of shares.

 ## Product Line

Spectrum Color Systems manufactures and sells an extensive array of colorimeters and spectrophotometers. These machines quantify aspects of color and appearance. Such measurements are important, but taking them is no easy task. A colorimeter is the most basic instrument, with some models starting at $2,000. Most large manufacturers choose spectrophotometers, which are more exacting in their measurement ability, providing better performance and more options. These are generally integrated systems that can cost as much as $150,000.

SOURCE: This case study was developed by Professor Michael R. Czinkota and MBA candidate Marc S. Gross. Funding support by the U.S. Department of Education is gratefully acknowledged. Some names have been disguised to protect proprietary interests. ©Michael R. Czinkota.

444

Spectrum offers both on-line products and lab products. On-line products are designed for use on a production line, where products run under the instrument, which continuously monitors the product's appearance. These systems are manufactured in batch operations and customized to meet customer specifications. Typically, custom features are oriented to specific user applications and include hardware components such as moving optical scanners that measure lateral color variance as well as software components designed to meet the needs of specific industries. The first instruments built in the 1950s provided users with numerical values via a primitive screen and tape printer system with a 15- to 30-second lag between measurement and numerical output. Today, all of Spectrum's products are driven by user-friendly software that monitors color trends throughout a production run with real-time output. Lab products are used when a customer takes a sample from a production line and brings it to the instrument for measurement.

Spectrum instruments are used in a wide variety of industries. Large food product companies measure the color of their products as well as packaging to ensure consistency. Paint companies purchase instruments to match colors and lease the machinery to paint stores. Automobile companies use Spectrum products to ensure that the color of interior cloth material, plastic molding, and exterior paint match. Some companies have forced suppliers to provide color-variance data sheets with all shipments. Spectrum recently supplied several instruments to a large bakery that produces buns for McDonald's. McDonald's had stipulated in its contract that buns be produced not only on time, but within certain color specifications. The bakery approached Spectrum to help meet these color standards.

A major manufacturer and supplier of denim uses Spectrum's "Color-Probe" spectrophotometer in its dye house to measure and grade the color of every strand of denim it produces. Color determines the value of the denim; it has tremendous impact when millions of yards of denim are produced and the price fluctuates significantly depending on color.

The Competition

The color- and appearance-measurement market is considered a niche market with approximately $130 million to $140 million in annual sales worldwide. Spectrum has averaged $20 million annually in both retail and wholesale sales revenue over the last three years, placing it second in terms of market share. The industry became concentrated in 1990 when Color Value, a Swiss company with $5 million to $10 million in annual sales revenue, decided to dominate the color business. Color Value International, owned by a large Swiss brewery, purchased two competitors: Color Systems (CS), based in the United

States and representing $35 million in annual sales, and International Color, based in the United Kingdom and representing $20 million in annual sales. Two smaller companies occupy third and fourth market share position; Speare accounts for approximately $12 million a year in sales, and Scientific Color generates about $9 million a year in sales (see Figure 1).

Although Color Value International holds almost 50 percent of world market share, Cordera believes that Spectrum now has a unique window of opportunity. The confusion associated with integrating three companies and the loss of goodwill caused by changing CS's company name, a well-established and respected brand, to Color Value International gave Spectrum a sales advantage. In addition, Spectrum entered the color matching and formulation market, one of Color Value's most profitable product lines. To gain market share in the United States, Spectrum's management decided to become the low-cost vendor and offered its new machines and color-matching software at prices of about one-half of the competition. Whereas the typical color-matching spectrophotometer by Color Value International was priced at $50,000, Spectrum offered a simpler $25,000 machine. In order to compete, Color Value International was forced to drastically reduce its prices to meet those of Spectrum, thus cutting deeply into profits.

International Expansion

In the 1950s and 1960s, Spectrum's management spent most of its time building the instruments and getting them out the door to meet the demand rather than developing a strategy to expand the company domestically and internationally. Spectrum's expansion into international markets succeeded despite its lack of strategic planning.

In the early days, Spectrum simply responded to requests from large companies such as Procter & Gamble to provide instruments to overseas subsidiaries. As the Clarks became more comfortable with this process, they decided to begin selling actively in Europe. By 1984 international sales comprised about one-fourth of total corporate sales. By 1992, the share had grown to more than one-third.

Sales Force

Spectrum Color Systems utilized independent sales agents domestically from its inception until 1986, when it developed an internal sales force. Cordera, drawing on his experience in marketing, set up the domestic sales force to provide more direct control over the marketing and sales strategies. After touring a number of agent offices, Cordera began to calculate the real cost of such a sales relationship. Working closely with Bob Holland, Spectrum's

FIGURE   1   Color Industry Concentration

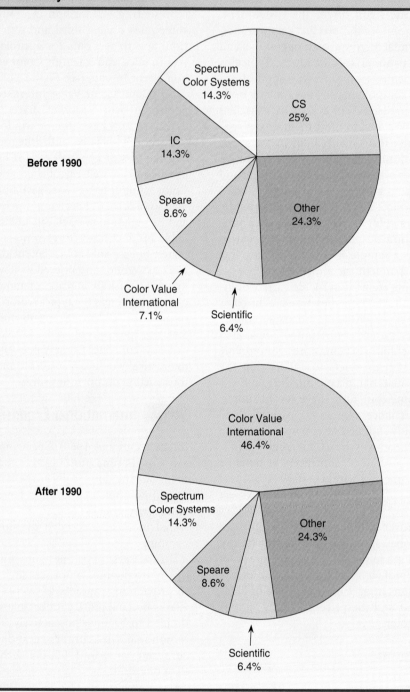

Before 1990

Spectrum
Color Systems
14.3%

CS
25%

IC
14.3%

Speare
8.6%

Other
24.3%

Color Value
International
7.1%

Scientific
6.4%

After 1990

Color Value
International
46.4%

Spectrum
Color Systems
14.3%

Other
24.3%

Speare
8.6%

Scientific
6.4%

chief financial officer, Cordera tried to quantify some of the intangible and hidden costs of the agent relationship. Spectrum spent significant resources lobbying for agents' time and attention to sales of Spectrum products and provided all the technical support since few of the agents had technical expertise. Additionally, although Spectrum was responsible for billing customers and paid 15 percent

of the sales price to the agent as commission, it had no access to lists of end users and decision makers within the client's organization. Spectrum is an application-oriented company; thus access to decision makers and end users within client organizations provides valuable information for product development and sales of transferable applications to current and future clients. A detailed financial analysis compared the true cost of using sales agents to the anticipated cost of an internal sales force. The analysis indicated that Spectrum could increase sales, reduce cost, and increase its control by developing its own sales force.

Internationally, Spectrum still relied mainly on independent distributors for its sales. Spectrum sold instruments outright to distributors at wholesale price. Spectrum billed the distributors on 30-day net terms. Spectrum provided its distributors sales brochures and manuals in English. Distributors then translated these brochures as needed.

In the early days, distributors were selected largely through happenstance. Distributors of other products would hear about Spectrum and write a letter to the Clarks expressing interest in the distribution of their instruments. The Clarks would invite the distributor to the United States to see the products and get trained in their operation and thus become a Spectrum distributor. Spectrum now has distributors all over the world with extensive market penetration in Europe and the Far East. Although the company has encountered a steady international demand for its products, it continues to encounter problems with international distributors.

In 1984, Spectrum's sole French distributor, Gerard Bieux, abruptly closed his operation for medical reasons. Bieux had kept his sales operation close to his vest and thus maintained no customer lists or sales records. There was no one who could fill the void Bieux left, and Spectrum's management was forced to start over again building up its French distribution.

Cordera spent a great deal of time locating another French distributor and developing a profitable relationship. The relationship served Spectrum well until 1990, when a major competitor purchased the distributor. Again Cordera was left without a French representative for Spectrum instruments.

Cordera realized that the distributor selection process was critical to Spectrum's international expansion and decided to become more proactive in selecting distributors. He worked closely with Holland to establish selection criteria for distributors based on financial stability, formal training programs, and financial goals. Additionally, Spectrum insisted that all distributors have service technicians trained at its U.S. facility. The distributor was responsible for paying the airfare for the technician, and Spectrum supplied food, lodging, and training. This strategy was not pursued so much for financial reasons, but to force the distributor to make both a financial and emotional investment in selling Spectrum products.

With the domestic direct sales force up and running, Cordera decided that if he was going to put the effort into forging an international presence, Spectrum should move toward an international direct sales force. In 1991, Spectrum opened its first European sales office in Paris. It opened an office in Germany in 1992.

Development of an International Direct Sales Force

In spite of the detailed planning, financial budgeting, and strategy analysis that preceded the opening of both European offices, each showed a net loss in its first year of operation. Cordera consulted with large accounting firms in both France and Germany to gain insight into European business law and to develop first-year budget projections. In addition, Spectrum management solicited information from its state Department of Economic Development on issues of taxation, international shipping, work permits, and visa restrictions for U.S. nationals working abroad. Despite such efforts, the combination of operating costs, which exceeded Spectrum's estimates, and slow sales associated with the European recession resulted in first-year losses in both France and Germany.

Cultural differences contributed to rising costs. Unlike the U.S. sales force, where the majority of a sales representative's compensation consists of commission, European sales representatives are traditionally paid high salaries and relatively low commissions. In addition, employees are paid an annual salary bonus equivalent to one month's salary regardless of performance. Terminated employees can receive up to one year of severance pay based on the longevity of their relationship and position with the company. Middle managers and above expect to be provided with company cars, which was particularly difficult for Spectrum management to swallow since neither Cordera nor Clark was provided with a company car. Despite his uneasiness, Cordera agreed to provide these benefits since he felt it important to attract high-quality employees for the new offices. All of these benefits were stipulated in the long-term employment contracts required in Europe.

Difficulties soon became apparent with Spectrum's sales representative in Paris. In staffing the Paris office, Cordera, largely out of a desire to get someone out on the road in France, settled for an individual who, although the most qualified of the candidates, lacked the aggressiveness, sales orientation, and technical competence for the position. Cordera was disappointed by the sales representative's performance but found the process of terminating the employee a long and arduous one. Spectrum began working with an attorney in Paris, providing the employee with written documentation detailing the reasons for dissatisfaction, as well as sales goals that were to be met in order to retain the position. In the end, Spectrum was forced to negotiate an expensive severance package.

But now, the international activities seemed to be on track. Spectrum had two international offices abroad. The Paris office consists of the international sales director, one sales representative, one service technician, and two secretaries. From that office, Spectrum conducts marketing activities, sales, installation, and service for France. The German office employs two sales representatives, one secretary, and one service technician covering the German market.

To avoid future hiring difficulties, Cordera instituted a program that brings key individuals from European operations to its headquarters facility. The mission of this program is to integrate those individuals into Spectrum's corporate culture and create a team environment. On this point Cordera remarked, "The fax machine and telephone are great pieces of equipment, but nothing beats a face-to-face dinner or lunch where we can sit down and talk to each other."

Commitment to European Customers

Spectrum management had historically marketed the same products throughout the world. Over time, Spectrum recognized that the European market and the U.S. market had different needs and preferences in both hardware and software. For example, Spectrum sales representatives frequently found their sales efforts focusing on the software that accompanies the instruments, since that is the part the customer sees, feels, and touches.

To achieve market success, Spectrum management felt it had to design products to meet the needs of European customers. There were two choices. The first was to translate existing software and then add the nuances the Europeans wanted. This proposition promised to be time consuming and very costly. The second option was to acquire a software company abroad.

In 1991, Cordera located a small software company in Switzerland that already had software written in Germany, French, Italian, and Spanish that was very applicable to the Spectrum system. Spectrum purchased the company for $275,000. Along with the company's assets and software copyrights, Spectrum also acquired the services of the company's founder. This proved invaluable as he speaks five languages and can adapt Spectrum's software products to meet the needs of the European market.

Spectrum Color Systems paid for its acquisition out of the cash it had generated from operations. Spectrum management has historically taken a conservative view of financing. The focus is on cash management, trying to generate enough cash to finance any expansion. In fact, Spectrum would not have made the purchase unless it had the cash.

Spectrum does maintain a line of credit, but as yet it has not used loans to finance expansion. Occasionally, management borrows $500,000 on its credit line, invests in short-term CDs, and repays the loan early just to show activity on its account.

Decision Situation

In all remaining international markets, Spectrum still uses distributors. Recently, this has resulted in significant problems. When BASF International in Germany purchased an instrument from Spectrum's German operation, it recommended that the BASF subsidiary in Spain buy the same instrument. When BASF received the invoice from Spectrum's Spanish distributor, the price was more than 50 percent higher than that paid in Germany. Cortez naturally felt that BASF was somehow being taken advantage of in Spain. However, there is little Spectrum can do about such disparities, since, pursuant to the distributor agreements, distributors purchase Spectrum products outright and determine the markup themselves. In addition, European Union antitrust regulations prevent Spectrum from setting a standardized price for its distributors.

This distributor arrangement is particularly advantageous in Italy and Spain. Given Spectrum's focus on cash management, the firm is leery about setting up direct operations in these countries. Cordera believes it is difficult to manage cash effectively in Italy and Spain, where vendors can wait six months to a year to receive payment from customers. There is an advantage to selling through distributors because Spectrum can collect cash on the sale in 30 or 45 days and the distributor has to wait for payment.

Future Strategies

By 1993, both European sales offices had become profitable. The emergence of the European Common Market could allow Spectrum to use its French and German operations as a base to expand into other countries without duplicating tasks. For example, the firm could place direct sales representatives throughout Europe with support provided by central office service technicians who would cross borders to perform installations and service. Yet Cordera still considered direct offices to be an expensive and somewhat risky proposition. His experience indicated that direct sales offices would not become self-sufficient for at least a year, and these types of financial losses caused friction with Spectrum's president and board of directors. Therefore, Cordera was not prepared for direct confrontation with distributors over markup. He dreaded the thought of being prematurely forced into opening other direct sales offices and repeating or even compounding the problems Spectrum had already endured.

In addition, recent changes in the exchange rates between the U.S. dollar and European currencies had tightened margins on export sales and decreased available cash. This pinch threatened to delay Cordera's planned expansion in the Far East.

Currently, Spectrum sells through distributors in the Pacific Rim and China, but Cordera was in the process of negotiating a joint venture in China. Cordera thought that in order for Spectrum to continue its growth throughout the world and especially in the Pacific Rim, it should es-tablish a joint operation. The cultural differences in the Pacific Rim seemed too great for Spectrum to overcome alone, so Cordera sought to marry Spectrum's technology and sales distribution with a company that has manufac-turing capabilities similar to Spectrum's.

QUESTIONS FOR DISCUSSION

1. Are current EU regulations beneficial or detrimental to Spectrum Color Systems' European operations in terms of distributor pricing and direct company sales?
2. How do fluctuations in the currency exchange rates affect Spectrum's revenues? Do you think Spectrum manage-ment would prefer to see a strong or weak dollar? Why?
3. How should Spectrum management respond to the BASF situation?
4. What has Spectrum done to meet the different needs of international customers? What more could be done to ac-commodate them?

Lakewood Chopsticks Exports

Since the 1970s, the United States has had a merchandise trade deficit with the rest of the world. Up to 1982, this deficit mattered little because it was relatively small. As of 1983, however, the trade deficit increased rapidly and became, due to its size and future implications, an issue of major national concern. Suddenly, trade moved to the forefront of national debate. Concurrently, a debate ensued on the issue of the international competitiveness of U.S. firms. The onerous question here was whether U.S. firms could and would achieve sufficient improvements in areas such as productivity, quality, and price to remain successful international marketing players in the long term.

The U.S.–Japanese trade relation took on particular significance because it was between those two countries that the largest bilateral trade deficit existed. In spite of trade negotiations, market-opening measures, trade legislation, and other governmental efforts, it was clear that the impetus for a reversal of the deficit through more U.S. exports to Japan had to come from the private sector. Therefore, the activities of any U.S. firm that appeared successful in penetrating the Japanese market were widely hailed. One company whose effort to market in Japan aroused particular interest was Lakewood Forest Products in Hibbing, Minnesota.

 ## Company Background

In 1983, Ian J. Ward was an export merchant in difficulty. Throughout the 1970s his company, Ward, Bedas Canadian Ltd., had successfully sold Canadian lumber and salmon to countries in the Persian Gulf. Over time, the company had opened four offices worldwide. However, when the Iran-Iraq war erupted, most of Ward's long-term trading relationships disappeared within a matter of months. In addition, the international lumber market began to collapse. As a result, Ward, Bedas Canadian Ltd. when into a survivalist mode and sent employees all over the world to look for new markets and business opportunities. Late that year, the company received an interesting order. A firm in Korea urgently needed to purchase lumber for the production of chopsticks.

Learning about the Chopstick Market

In discussing the wood deal with the Koreans, Ward learned that in the production of good chopsticks, more than 60 percent of the wood fiber is wasted. Given the high transportation cost involved, the large degree of wasted materials, and his need for new business, Ward decided to explore the Korean and Japanese chopstick industry in more detail.

He quickly determined that chopstick making in the Far East is a fragmented industry, working with old technology and suffering from a lack of natural resources. In Asia, chopsticks are produced in very small quantities, often by family organizations. Even the largest of the 450 chopstick factories in Japan turns out only 5 million chopsticks a month. This compares with an overall market size of 130 million pairs of disposable chopsticks a day. In addition, chopsticks represent a growing market. With increased wealth in Asia, people eat out more often and therefore have a greater demand for disposable chopsticks.

SOURCE: This case was written by Michael R. Czinkota based on the following sources: Mark Clayton, "Minnesota Chopstick Maker Finds Japanese Eager to Import His Quality Waribashi," *The Christian Science Monitor*, October 16, 1987, 11; Roger Worthington, "Improbable Chopstick Capitol of the World," *Chicago Tribune*, June 5, 1988, 39; Mark Gill, "The Great American Chopstick Master," *American Way*, August 1, 1987, 34, 78–79; "Perpich of Croatia," *The Economist*, April 20, 1991, 27; and personal interview with Ian J. Ward, president, Lakewood Forest Products.

The fear of communicable diseases has greatly reduced the utilization of reusable chopsticks. Renewable plastic chopsticks have been attacked by many groups as too new-fangled and as causing future ecological problems.

From his research, Ward concluded that a competitive niche existed in the world chopstick market. He believed that if he could use low-cost raw materials and ensure that the labor-cost component would remain small, he could successfully compete in the world market.

The Founding of Lakewood Forest Products

In exploring opportunities afforded by the newly identified international marketing niche for chopsticks, Ward set four criteria for plant location:

1. Access to suitable raw materials.
2. Proximity of other wood product users who could make use of the 60 percent waste for their production purposes.
3. Proximity to a port that would facilitate shipment to the Far East.
4. Availability of labor.

In addition, Ward was aware of the importance of product quality. Because people use chopsticks on a daily basis and are accustomed to products that are visually inspected one by one, he would have to live up to high quality expectations in order to compete successfully. Chopsticks could not be bowed or misshapen, have blemishes in the wood, or splinter.

To implement his plan, Ward needed financing. Private lenders were skeptical and slow to provide funds. This skepticism resulted from the unusual direction of Ward's proposal. Far Eastern companies have generally held the cost advantage in a variety of industries, especially those as labor-intensive as chopstick manufacturing. U.S. companies rarely have an advantage in producing low-cost items. Further, only a very small domestic market exists for chopsticks.

However, Ward found that the state of Minnesota was willing to participate in this new venture. Since the decline of the mining industry, regional unemployment had been rising rapidly in the state. In 1983, unemployment in Minnesota's Iron Range peaked at 22 percent. Therefore, state and local officials were eager to attract new industries that would be independent of mining activities. Of particular help was the enthusiasm of Governor Rudy Perpich. The governor had been boosting Minnesota business on the international scene by traveling abroad and receiving many foreign visitors. He was excited about Ward's plans, which called for the creation of over 100 new jobs within a year.

Hibbing, Minnesota, turned out to be an ideal location for Ward's project. The area had an abundance of aspen wood, which, because it grows in clay soil, tends to be unmarred. The fact that Hibbing was the hometown of the governor also did not hurt. In addition, Hibbing boasted an excellent labor pool, and both the city and the state were willing to make loans totaling $500,000. Further, the Iron Range Resources Rehabilitation Board was willing to sell $3.4 million in industrial revenue bonds for the project. Together with jobs and training wage subsidies, enterprise zone credits, and tax increment financing benefits, the initial public support of the project added up to about 30 percent of its start-up costs. The potential benefit of the new venture to the region was quite clear. When Lakewood Forest Products advertised its first 30 jobs, more than 3,000 people showed up to apply.

The Production and Sale of Chopsticks

Ward insisted that in order to truly penetrate the international market, he would need to keep his labor cost low. As a result, he decided to automate as much of the production as possible. However, no equipment was readily available to produce chopsticks because no one had automated the process before.

After much searching, Ward identified a European equipment manufacturer that produced machinery for making popsicle sticks. He purchased equipment from this Danish firm in order to better carry out the sorting and finishing processes. However, because aspen wood was quite different from the wood the machine was designed for, as was the final product, substantial design adjustments had to be made. Sophisticated equipment was also purchased to strip the bark from the wood and peel it into long, thin sheets. Finally, a computer vision system was acquired to detect defects in the chopsticks. This system rejected over 20 percent of the production, and yet some of the chopsticks that passed inspection were splintering. However, Ward firmly believed that further fine-tuning of the equipment and training of the new workforce would gradually take care of the problem.

Given this fully automated process, Lakewood Forest Products was able to develop capacity for up to 7 million pairs of chopsticks a day. With a unit manufacturing cost of $0.03 per pair and an anticipated unit selling price of $0.057, Ward expected to earn a pretax profit of $4.7 million in 1988.

Due to intense marketing efforts in Japan and the fact that Japanese customers were struggling to obtain sufficient supplies of disposable chopsticks, Ward was able to presell the first five years of production quite quickly. By late 1987, Lakewood Forest Products was ready to enter the international market. With an ample supply of raw materials and an almost totally automated plant, Lakewood was positioned as the world's largest and least labor-intensive manufacturer of chopsticks. The first shipment of 6 containers with a load of 12 million pairs of chopsticks was sent to Japan in October 1987.

QUESTIONS FOR DISCUSSION

1. Is Lakewood Forest Products ready for exports? Using the export-readiness framework developed by the U.S. Department of Commerce and available through various sites such as **www.tradeport.org** (from "Trade Expert" go to "Getting Started" and finally to "Assess Your Export Readiness"), determine whether Lakewood's commitment, resources, and product warrant the action they have undertaken.

2. What are the environmental factors that are working for and against Lakewood Forest Products both at home in the United States and in the target market, Japan?

3. New-product success is a function of trial and repurchase. How do Lakewood's chances look along these two dimensions?

Otjiwarongo Crocodile Ranch

In the hot and humid hatchery of his crocodile ranch in the small Namibian town of Otjiwarongo, Mr. van Dyk was worriedly stacking the plastic crates containing 1,350 newly laid crocodile eggs into the limited space. It was December 10, 1993, and he knew that he had to expand the hatching and nursing facilities of this crocodile ranch before January 1996 in order to provide the necessary space to accommodate twice the present production of eggs expected in the 1996 breeding season.

To finance this expansion, Mr. van Dyk hoped to enter a stable and regular market for his supply of crocodile skins. With his limited experience in marketing, he was not sure as to how and where to start exporting.

Mr. van Dyk was also considering the option of exporting processed crocodile skin products, like handbags, shoes, and belts. Without the resources to construct his own tannery, he would have to find processing and manufacturing facilities. There was the possibility to send the skins to South Africa for processing into finished products before exporting them. Thinking about options to finance the expansion, Mr. van Dyk also remembered the proposal for a partnership he had received from an investor in Europe who could process the skins into quality products: during a visit in September 1993, a German tourist had expressed interest in investing in Mr. van Dyk's crocodile ranch.

This case was written by Daan Strauss, Coordinator, Small Enterprise Development, Institute for Management and Leadership Training (IMLT), Namibia, under the ITC/PRODEC Project for Improving International Business Training at selected African institutions. The case is intended for use in training programs and is not meant to illustrate correct or incorrect handling of business situations.

SOURCE: *African Cases in International Business,* International Trade Centre and PRODEC, Geneva, 1995.

Stepping out of the hatchery into the equally hot, but less humid, nursery where he raised the young crocodiles, Mr. van Dyk knew he had to take some action well before the 1996 breeding season.

Background

Mr. van Dyk started the Otjiwarongo Crocodile Ranch in 1986. Prior to this, he had his own motor service station and a bakery in Khorixas, a town in the far north of Namibia. He has also farmed with cattle and sheep, but due to droughts and a high theft rate, he abandoned his farming operations. He sold his business and made the decision to start up a crocodile ranch because he considered himself to be a farmer at heart and also because he was very interested in tourism. He visited various crocodile farms in South Africa and Botswana, where he made a thorough study of crocodile farming during 1985.

Mr. van Dyk chose Otjiwarongo as the ideal location for his business. The climate of Otjiwarongo—hot during summer months and warm in winter—was favorable for crocodile farming. It was on the main tourism route of Namibia, and he could find a regular supply of meat to feed the crocodiles as the Otjiwarongo abattoir was prepared to supply him with unborn calves.

Breeding crocodiles was a capital intensive venture. A hatchery and nursery were built next to the breeding yard to ensure that the eggs could be hatched and the crocodiles raised in ideal conditions. The buildings on Mr. van Dyk's property were valued at N$800,000 in 1988. The planned expansion was expected to cost about N$600,000 (US$1.00 = N$3.60).

Mr. van Dyk had also built a curio shop which served as entrance to the ranch. In the curio shop, he kept various crocodile products like eggshells, skulls, and skeletons, along with a few crocodile skin products made from skins he had sent to South Africa to be manufactured into shoes and belts. Mr. van Dyk and his wife regretted the fact that they could not stock the shop with more products, but supplies had to be kept at a minimum due to the lack of funds.

Ever since they started the crocodile ranch, Mr. van Dyk and his wife had been inviting tourists to visit the ranch in Otjiwarongo, in the northern highlands of central Namibia. The crocodile ranch received an average of 1,000 tourists per month. The visitors' entry fees represented a substantial means of income before exports of crocodile skins started in 1991. In 1993, tourists still contributed N$6,000 per month to Mr. van Dyk's income, although exporting crocodile skins had become the main source of income.

Additional income for the crocodile ranch was earned by selling crocodile meat to interested restaurants in Namibian towns. During 1993, Mr. van Dyk sold 1,100 kg of crocodile meat. He planned to slaughter 600 crocodiles in 1994, which would mean that he could sell 15,000 kg of meat. There was a possibility for exporting crocodile meat to Singapore, but the dealer he spoke to in Singapore wanted at least four tons of meat at a time. This meant that Mr. van Dyk would have to slaughter at least 1,500 crocodiles at a time to be able to fill up a container for exporting purposes, which was not possible for him in 1993. He planned to start exporting meat by 1998.

Mr. van Dyk was a member of the Transvaal Crocodile Breeders' Association in Pretoria, South Africa. In 1991, he obtained his license to trade in endangered species from CITES (Convention on International Trade in Endangered Species of Wild Fauna and Flora) in Lausanne, Switzerland, which had a membership of 112 countries worldwide. Membership in CITES was a condition for exporting crocodile skins, as most crocodilians were on the endangered species list of the CITES.

According to an article published in the *Industrie du cuir* in Paris in February 1992, raising was considered a good method of preserving those species which had become rare while continuing trading in their skins. Two types of "farming" crocodilians had been developed:

- "Ranches," particularly in Southern Africa (notably Zimbabwe), which tended to concentrate on Nile crocodiles. Eggs were taken from the wild and the young were raised in captivity until the commercial length of 1.5 m to 2 m was attained, when they were slaughtered.
- "Farms," which, in general, handled the whole reproduction cycle. There were numerous "farms" in Thailand and the United States.

The article assumed that 80 percent of the current world supply of crocodile skins, estimated at around 400,000 per annum, were sourced from farms. Ten years earlier, before legislation on the protection of endangered species had been passed in many countries, the figure of world supply had been around 2 million skins per year.

Crocodile Breeding

Mr. van Dyk bought his original breeding stock of 49 adult Nile crocodiles from a farmer in Botswana in 1986 for N$220,000. The hatchlings from the first eggs were kept and after spending four years in the nursery, these 58 female crocodiles were housed in a second breeding yard that Mr. van Dyk had been developing since 1987. These females were expected to start producing in the 1996 breeding season.

Having adapted to their new environment, the adult crocodiles steadily increased production of eggs. Mr. van Dyk managed to successfully hatch crocodile eggs as follows:

1986	58 hatchlings out of	71 eggs
1987	364 hatchlings out of	408 eggs
1988	488 hatchlings out of	530 eggs
1989	540 hatchlings out of	630 eggs
1990	630 hatchlings out of	714 eggs
1991	705 hatchlings out of	838 eggs
1992	936 hatchlings out of	1,273 eggs
1993	1,050 hatchlings out of	1,356 eggs

During the mating season, outside temperatures influenced the fertility rate of the eggs. In 1993, 12 percent of the eggs were unfertilized, while the figure for 1992 was 23 percent.

The amount of eggs laid by a female crocodile depended on her age. The younger ones laid an average 21 per breeding season and the mature ones could lay up to 75. This gave an average of 48 eggs per female. As soon as the female crocodiles laid their eggs, they were packed into crates and taken to the hatchery. To further ensure successful hatching of the eggs, they had to be stacked into the crates in exactly the same position as they had been laid.

To maximize profits, Mr. van Dyk had to ensure that he produced first-grade skins. The newly hatched crocodiles were kept in a nursery for two and a half years, at which age they were about 1.4 m long and provided skins of 35 cm wide, fetching the best price. The nursery was free of stones to avoid scratches on the crocodile's skins. Maintenance of high humidity and ideal temperatures, a regular supply of vitamins to the young crocodiles, and clean and hygienic conditions were necessary to keep the young crocodiles healthy, which in turn meant a more favorable environment to ensure first-grade skins.

At the slaughter age of two and a half years, the crocodiles would normally start to fight among each other, resulting in skins being scratched or damaged, and thus reducing their value. This was also the age at which they became dangerous and would attack workers cleaning the nursery.

Being extremely sensitive creatures, the young crocodiles could easily be upset by loud noise, sudden movements, light, and vibrations. Because of the influence tourists had on the crocodiles, Mr. van Dyk kept only 10 percent of the young crocodiles on view for visiting purposes, and the tourists were always requested to keep their voices low and move slowly.

Costs and Revenues

Mr. van Dyk raised start-up capital for the crocodile ranch through a commercial bank and through a development corporation in Namibia. In 1993, he was still indebted to both institutions for loans taken in 1988, payable over a five- and thirteen-year period respectively.

Mr. van Dyk's monthly expenses in the last quarter of 1993 were as follows:

Water and electricity:	N$2,200
Crocodile feeding:	N$4,000
Wages:	N$2,000
Veterinarian costs:	N$150
Administrative costs:	N$100
Other (including his salary):	N$5,000
Installments and interest:	N$5,000

For December 1993, Mr. van Dyk expected the following revenues:

Export of 150 skins:	N$30,000
Sales of meat:	N$8,000
Tourists' entry fees:	N$6,000

December 1993 was, however, an exceptional month because of a planned initial export of 150 skins to Germany, an order that had not yet been confirmed. The average monthly income was N$20,000.

Marketing

The constitution of the Transvaal Crocodile Breeders' Association stipulated that each individual breeder was responsible for the marketing of his own products. This left the responsibility for marketing and selling with Mr. van Dyk, who did not have much experience in this field.

Although the Otjiwarongo Crocodile Ranch was the only one of its kind in Namibia, it faced worldwide competition for exports of crocodile skins. Crocodilians, including caimans and gharials, alligators and crocodiles,

were to be found all around the world: caimans in Central and South America, alligators in the southeast of the United States and in China. The more than 20 different species of crocodiles were scattered far more widely: north of Australia, Africa, Southeast Asia, India, Central and South America, and the West Indies. Size of the crocodilians varied with the species, from 1.5 m to 2 m in dwarf species, such as the dwarf crocodile and Schneider's caiman, up to 5 m to 7 m for the Nile and Indopacific crocodiles. In Southern Africa alone there were 23 competitors breeding crocodiles, most of them in the province of Natal, South Africa, but also in Zimbabwe, Zambia, Botswana, Malawi, and Mozambique. Zimbabwe was the leading exporter of Nile crocodile skins in southern Africa and was the second largest producer after the United States of America.

Other exotic hides, like ostrich and buffalo skins, formed part of the competition Mr. van Dyk faced. The trade in exotic skins was subject to fashion trends. Mr. van Dyk considered this to be one reason for fluctuating prices, which ranged from US$9.00 per centimeter in 1991 to US$3.00 in 1993 for first-grade skins of 30 cm wide.

Because of his limited funds, Mr. van Dyk did not advertise. "I have to first look after my crocodiles before I can find the money to advertise," he stated.

Mr. van Dyk had started exporting crocodile skins in December 1991. Quantities and destinations of exports were as follows:

1991	163 skins to Spain	(Direct transaction)
1992	250 skins to Spain	(Direct transaction)
1993	100 skins to Singapore	(Direct transaction)
1993	150 skins to Singapore	(Through a South African agent)

In November 1993, he managed to secure an order from a German buyer for an initial 150 skins followed by 50 skins per month through an agent in South Africa. The German buyer indicated that he would be in South Africa by the beginning of December 1993, but failed to show up. This left Mr. van Dyk quite unsure as to whether the deal would go through.

The few times that he had exported skins, he contacted embassies in Windhoek for addresses of potential buyers, or alternatively was contacted by buyers who had come to know about him.

The most recent order from Germany in November 1993 quoted the following prices per centimeter for first-grade skins:

20–24 cm:	US$1.80
25–29 cm:	US$2.80
30–34 cm:	US$3.50
35 cm + 1:	US$5.00

Prices for second-grade skins were 25 percent less, while third-grade skins were not accepted on the market.

For international business, Mr. van Dyk preferred to deal with German buyers. As Namibia had historical links with Germany, most of the tourists visiting the crocodile ranch were German speaking. Mr. van Dyk also communicated well in German and found direct communication with other countries difficult. If he were to enter into a partnership, he would prefer a German or Swiss partner. This preference, however, did not prevent him from selling to non-German buyers.

To do business with buyers abroad, Mr. van Dyk would deal with them either directly, through an agent, or eventually through a prospective foreign partner. However, both Mr. van Dyk and his wife were very reluctant to enter into a partnership because of a previous unpleasant incident with a partner abroad, who became disinterested when revenues were not as quickly forthcoming as he thought they would be. While still considering this as an alternative, the van Dyks were not sure whether the advantages outweighed the disadvantages. The potential German investor had indicated that he would visit them in January 1994 to take up further discussions, and Mr. and Mrs. van Dyk were thinking about the terms and conditions they should propose for an eventual partnership. Mr. van Dyk hoped to enter into an agreement where the partner would be responsible for all marketing activities, while he himself would see to the smooth running of the ranch and the visiting tourists.

Because of the pressing need for funds to finance expansion, Mr. van Dyk also thought about the possibility of exporting processed crocodile skin products. This could be done through a tannery in South Africa, but he knew that this would be expensive because of the time span between sending of the skins for processing and eventual sales of the finished products. He would have to carry the costs for the tanning and manufacturing of the products in the meantime. In 1993, the cost of tanning alone was N\$2.50 per centimeter, amounting to approximately N\$75.00 per skin. He also considered selling the products in his curio shop at the ranch, but these up-market products did not sell fast enough in Otjiwarongo. It was only the occasional well-off tourist that would buy some of the products, but it was a possible source of income nonetheless. The other option was to have the skins processed through the intended partner in Europe, so that the finished products would be nearer to the user.

There was another possibility—to do business with an Italian buyer who had announced his visit to the ranch for January 1994. This was not definite as yet and Mr. van Dyk was worried about dealings with buyers who did not seem to be reliable. However, he had got some information on the Italian market (see appendix) and was ready to explore any business opportunities.

In December 1993, Mr. van Dyk had 600 crocodiles ready for the market out of the 2,100 growing young crocodiles in the nursery. He forecasted a production of 2,000 hatchlings for 1994 and 3,000 hatchlings for 1995. As from 1996 he could double this production, when the females in the second breeding yard started producing. This implied that he would have to find a way to build the second hatchery and nursery before 1996. His average monthly income was only adequate to ensure the smooth running of the ranch. His forecasts for 1996 onwards promised enough income for expansion, but if the necessary facilities were not ready before 1996, he would not be in a position to cater to the increased production.

As the only crocodile farmer in Namibia and responsible for his own marketing, Mr. van Dyk wondered what action he should take to ensure the necessary expansion of his operations before 1996.

QUESTIONS FOR DISCUSSION

1. What are the advantages and disadvantages of options open to Mr. van Dyk?
2. Which criteria should Mr. van Dyk use in selecting his market(s)?
3. Depending on the suggested selection criteria, what additional information would Mr. van Dyk need to formulate his marketing strategy?
4. What should be the most urgent steps in Mr. van Dyk's export marketing action plan?

Appendix: International Trade in Nile Crocodile Skins

The Crocodile Skin Markets in Italy and France*

Overview World prices for Nile crocodile skins dropped tremendously since the late 1980s and demand was steeply going down. Changes in fashion trends and consumer tastes as well as the world recession had greatly contributed to this decline in demand for farmed skins of the crocodylus niloticus (the Nile crocodile from Africa).

Competition in the supply of wet-salted Nile crocodile skin was reported to come from Zimbabwe, Zambia, Malawi, Botswana, and Mozambique and also from Ethiopia, Kenya, Madagascar, and Tanzania, who had a reservation on the species and therefore traded under a specified annual export quota system. As indicated in the table below, Zimbabwe was the leading exporter of Nile crocodile skins and the second largest producer of crocodile or alligator skins after the United States.

Exports of African Countries (in number of skins)

COUNTRY	1986	1987	1988	1989
Zimbabwe	7,216	7,924	11,609	10,647
Malawi	684	1,173	1,329	2,104
Tanzania	763	1,724	2,311	1,715
South Africa	87	758	1,905	4,326
Madagascar	673	4,338	3,177	4,543
Kenya	—	150	1,400	2,499
Mozambique	—	529	795	1,554
Botswana	10	65	69	204
Zambia	3,117	3,235	3,738	2,389

SOURCE: CITES Annual Returns.

Since the 1990s, competition from the United States was increasing, flooding the market with cheaper skins from its farms. South America was also providing large quantities of wild skins of the caiman crocodiles.

Skins from the United States were cheaper than African skins, with an average price of about US$3.00/cm in the early 1990s, while skins from South America were larger and therefore preferred for the production of handbags, which required skins of more than 35 cm across the belly.

*Excerpts from the PRODEC Market Research Report No. 12/91 by Ms. Queen Sachile, "The Markets for Zambian Wet-Salted Crocodile Skins in Italy and France," Helsinki, 1991. Published by the Programme for Development Cooperation at the Helsinki School of Economics (PRODEC), Töölönkatu 11A, 00100 Helsinki, Finland.

World Imports of Nile Crocodile Skins (in number of skins)

YEAR	WORLD IMPORTS
1986	18,753
1987	24,147
1988	29,524
1989	35,515

SOURCE: CITES Annual Returns.

The Italian Market The report stated that Italy imported crocodile skins from various sources around the globe, and indicated the origin of imports as shown in the following table.

According to the views of the tanners interviewed for the report, the erratic import figures were a reflection of limited availability from the supplying countries, which forced the tanners to buy the maximum of available quantities from whatever source as the demand for the commodity was very high at the time.

All the interviewed tanners said they were currently operating about 50 percent below capacity due to declining demand, and were getting most of their raw skins from South America and the United States, which were cheaper sources. In addition, skins from South America were also larger. None of the interviewed processors was interested in a joint venture for the production of crocodylus niloticus skins.

Most crocodile skins were imported into Italy by tanneries who processed the skins and treated them into different colors as specified by manufacturers of crocodile items. Items included belts, handbags, wallets, and shoes for sale either in the local market or for export.

The majority of Italian tanners imported directly from farmers in the export countries. The import of raw skins did not attract any duty regardless of source of supply. Skins were air-freighted into Italy packed in double jute bags with labels indicating the number of skins and the weight.

The average CIF price indicated by CITES in 1990 for different types of skins were:

Nile crocodile	US$12–14/cm
Porosus	US$12–14/cm
Caiman crocodile	US$45–48/sq. ft.
Mississippi alligator	US$6–8/cm

CITES estimated that these prices had fallen by 50 percent in 1991.

Crocodylus Niloticus Imports in Italy (in number of skins)

COUNTRY OF ORIGIN	1985	1986	1987	1988	1989
Kenya	—	—	2	600	—
Madagascar	—	92	100	100	—
Malawi	—	191	—	766	700
South Africa	—	—	—	570	—
Sudan	108	289	1,251	—	—
Tanzania	—	3	—	1	—
Zambia	3	4	256	566	—
Zimbabwe	1	—	—	1,937	—
Total	112	569	1,609	4,540	700

SOURCE: CITES Annual Returns.

The French Market   Due to the oversupply of the French market with farmed skins from the United States at a lower price than that offered by African farmers, a competitive factor had been introduced which hitherto had been totally absent. African farmers faced a steadily increasing price competition among different African countries producing crocodylus niloticus skins, as well as the strong price competition from the United States.

Most French tanners were buying from the United States not only for the lower prices but also because of the assured United States market for the processed skins and items. French importers sourced their skins directly from farmers by air. Companies interviewed for the report were interested in importing farmed skins from Africa in the future, but at a price lower than US$5.00/cm. In 1991, skins from the United States were sourced in France at US$2.50/cm for skin sizes 18–24 cm, US$4.50/cm for skin sizes 25–35 cm and US$10.00/cm for skins above 35 cm.

With respect to joint ventures in Africa, French companies felt that market requirements with respect to delivery time, quality, and color specifications of crocodile items would make a tanning operation located in Africa difficult to manage. Their position was that they would get in touch with African farmers when the demand situation in Europe improved.

Crocodylus Niloticus Imports in France (in number of skins)

COUNTRY OF ORIGIN	1986	1987	1988	1989
Botswana	—	60	66	193
Kenya	—	150	551	2,184
Madagascar	418	4,231	3,074	4,525
Malawi	403	572	507	741
Congo	332	649	150	150
Mozambique	—	529	795	1,554
South Africa	40	757	633	3,612
Sudan	2,650	2,499	1,500	54
Zambia	2,082	1,552	2,692	2,385
Zimbabwe	4,714	7,159	6,042	10,237
Total	10,639	18,158	16,010	25,635

SOURCE: CITES Annual Returns.

Crocodylus Niloticus Imports in Other Major Importing Countries

COUNTRY	1990	1991	1992	TOTAL
Belgium	3,945	3	4	3,951
Egypt	900	—	7,900	8,800
Japan	12,979	7,075	11,693	31,747
Singapore	1	7,010	32,946	39,958
Switzerland	342	1,401	407	2,150

SOURCE: World Conservation Monitoring Centre, Cambridge, United Kingdom.

Damar International

Damar International, a fledgling firm importing handicrafts of chiefly Indonesian origin, was established in Burke, Virginia, a suburb of Washington, D.C. Organized as a general partnership, the firm is owned entirely by Dewi Soemantoro, its president, and Ronald I. Asche, its vice president. Their part-time, unsalaried efforts and those of Soemantoro's relatives in Indonesia constitute the entire labor base of the firm. Outside financing has been limited to borrowing from friends and relatives of the partners in Indonesia and the United States.

Damar International estimates that its current annual sales revenues are between $20,000 and $30,000. Although the firm has yet to reach the break-even point, its sales revenues and customer base have expanded more rapidly than anticipated in Damar's original business plan. The partners are generally satisfied with results to date and plan to continue to broaden their operations.

Damar International was established to capitalize on Soemantoro's international experience and contacts. The daughter of an Indonesian Foreign Service officer, Soemantoro spent most of her youth and early adulthood in western Europe and has for the past 18 years resided in the United States. Her immediate family, including her mother, now resides in Indonesia. In addition to English and Malay, Soemantoro speaks French, German, and Italian. Although she has spent the past four years working in information management in the Washington area, first for MCI and currently for Records Management Inc., her interest in importing derives from about six years she previously spent as a management consultant. In this capacity, she was frequently called on to advise clients about importing clothing, furniture, and decorative items from Indonesia. At the urging of family and friends, she decided to start her own business. While Soemantoro handles the purchasing and administrative aspects of the business, Asche is responsible for marketing and sales.

Damar International currently imports clothing, high-quality brassware, batik accessories, wood carvings, and furnishings from Indonesia. All of these items are handcrafted by village artisans working on a cottage-industry basis. Damar International estimates that 30 percent of its revenues from the sale of Indonesian imports are derived from clothing, 30 percent from batik accessories, and 30 percent from wood carvings, with the remainder divided equally between brassware and furnishings. In addition, Damar markets in the eastern United States comparable Thai and Philippine handcrafted items imported by a small California firm. This firm in turn markets some of Damar's Indonesian imports on the West Coast.

Most of Damar's buyers are small shops and boutiques. Damar does not supply large department stores or retail chain outlets. By participating in gift shows, trade fairs, and handicraft exhibitions, the firm has expanded its customer base from the Washington area to many locations in the eastern United States.

In supplying small retail outlets with handcrafted Indonesian artifacts, Damar is pursuing a niche strategy. Although numerous importers market similar mass-produced, manufactured Indonesian items chiefly to department stores and chain retailers, Damar knows of no competitors that supply handcrafted artifacts to boutiques. Small retailers find it difficult to purchase in sufficient volume to order directly from large-scale importers of mass-produced items. More important, it is difficult to organize Indonesian artisans to produce handcrafted goods in sufficient quantity to supply the needs of large retailers.

SOURCE: This case was prepared by Michael R. Czinkota and Laura M. Gould.

Damar's policy is to carry little if any inventory. Orders from buyers are transmitted by Soemantoro to her family in Indonesia, who contract production to artisans in the rural villages of Java and Bali. Within broad parameters, buyers can specify modifications of traditional Indonesian wares. Frequently, Soemantoro cooperates with her mother in creating designs that adapt traditional products to American tastes and to the specifications of U.S. buyers. Soemantoro is in contact with her family in Indonesia at least once a week by telex or phone to report new orders and check on the progress of previous orders. In addition, Soemantoro makes an annual visit to Indonesia to coordinate policy with her family and maintain contacts with artisans.

Damar also fills orders placed by Soemantoro's family in Indonesia. The firm therefore in essence acts as both an importer and an exporter despite its extremely limited personnel base. In this, as well as in its source of financing, Damar is highly atypical. The firm's great strength, which allows it to fill a virtually vacant market niche with extremely limited capital and labor resources, is clearly the Soemantoro family's nexus of personal connections. Without the use of middlemen, this single bicultural family is capable of linking U.S. retailers and Indonesian village artisans and supplying products that, while unique and nonstandardized, are specifically oriented to the U.S. market.

Damar's principal weakness is its financing structure. There are obvious limits to the amount of money that can be borrowed from family and friends for such an enterprise. Working capital is necessary because the Indonesian artisans must be paid before full payment is received from U.S. buyers. Although a 10 percent deposit is required from buyers when an order is placed, the remaining 90 percent is not due until 30 days from the date of shipment F.O.B. Washington, D.C. However, the simplicity of Damar's financing structure has advantages: To date, it has been able to operate without letters of credit and their concomitant paperwork burdens.

One major importing problem to date has been the paperwork and red tape involved in U.S. customers and quota regulations. Satisfying these regulations has occasionally delayed fulfillment of orders. Furthermore, because the Indonesian trade office in the United States is located in New York rather than Washington, assistance from the Indonesian government in expediting such problems has at times been difficult to obtain with Damar's limited personnel. For example, an order was once delayed in U.S. customs because of confusion between the U.S. Department of Commerce and Indonesian export authorities concerning import stamping and labeling. Several weeks were required to resolve the difficulty.

Although Damar received regulatory information directly from the U.S. Department of Commerce when it began importing, its routine contact with the government is minimal because regulatory paperwork is contracted to customs brokers.

One of the most important lessons that the firm has learned is the critical role of participating in gift shows, trade fairs, and craft exhibitions. Soemantoro believes that the firm's greatest mistake to date was not attending a trade show in New York. In connecting with potential buyers, both through trade shows and "walk-in scouting" of boutiques, Damar has benefited greatly from helpful references from existing customers. Buyers have been particularly helpful in identifying trade fairs that would be useful for Damar to attend. Here too, the importance of Damar's cultivation of personal contacts is apparent.

Similarly, personal contacts offer Damar the possibility of diversifying into new import lines. Through a contact established by a friend in France, Soemantoro is currently planning to import handmade French porcelain and silk blouses.

Damar is worried about sustained expansion of its Indonesian handicraft import business because the firm does not currently have the resources to organize large-scale cottage-industry production in Indonesia. Other major concerns are potential shipping delays and exchange rate fluctuations.

QUESTIONS FOR DISCUSSION

1. Evaluate alternative expansion strategies for Damar International in the United States.

2. Discuss Damar's expansion alternatives in Indonesia and France and their implications for the U.S. market.

3. How can Damar protect itself against exchange rate fluctuations?

4. What are the likely effects of shipment delays on Damar? How can these effects be overcome?

Part Three

International

Global Marketing Management

Part Three deals with advanced international marketing activities. The core marketing concerns of the beginning internationalist and the multinational corporation are the same. Yet multinational firms face challenges and opportunities that are different from those encountered by smaller firms. They are able to expend more resources on international marketing efforts than are small and medium-sized firms. In addition, their perspective can be more globally oriented. Multinational corporations also have more impact on individuals, economies, and governments. Therefore, they are much more subject to public scrutiny and need to be more concerned about repercussions of their activities. Yet their very size often enables them to be more influential in setting international marketing rules.

Chapter 14

Global Strategic Planning

THE INTERNATIONAL MARKETPLACE 14.1

Appliance Makers on a Global Quest

THE $11 BILLION HOME appliance market is undergoing major consolidation and globalization. Many U.S.-based manufacturers are faced in their home markets with increased competition from foreign companies, such as the world's largest appliance maker, Electrolux, and newcomers such as China's Haier and Kelon. In addition, industry fundamentals in the United States are rather gloomy: stagnating sales, rising raw material prices, and price wars. On the other hand, markets abroad are full of opportunities. The European market, for example, is growing quite fast, and the breakdown of barriers within the European Union has made establishing business there even more attractive. Market potential is significant as well: While 65 percent of U.S. homes have dryers, only 18 percent of Europeans have them. Markets in Latin America and Asia are showing similar trends as well; for example, only 15 percent of Brazil's households own microwave ovens compared with 91 percent in the United States. However, expansion was slowed down considerably by the crises of 1997–1999.

To take advantage of this growth, appliance makers have formed strategic alliances and made acquisitions. General Electric entered into a joint venture with Britain's General Electric PLC, and in its strategic shift to move the company's "center of gravity" from the industrialized world to Asia and Latin America, joint ventures were established in India with Godrej and in Mexico with Mabe. A strictly North American manufacturer before 1989, Whirlpool purchased the appliance business of Dutch giant N. V. Phillips. Whirlpool's move gave it ten plants on the European continent and some popular appliance lines, which is a major asset in a region characterized by loyalty to domestic brands. Today, Whirlpool is third in European market share after Electrolux and Bosch-

Siemens. The company ranks first in the Americas, and while it only has a 1 percent market share in Asia, it is the region's largest Western appliance maker. Whirlpool's advantage in Brazil, for example, is the strong loyalty it has earned in 40 years of operations (which it lacks in Asia). In the last five years, Whirlpool has expanded its operations in Eastern and Central Europe as well as South Africa, thus extending its total reach to 170 countries worldwide.

Product differences present global marketers with a considerable challenge. The British favor front-loading washing machines, while the French swear by top-loaders. The French prefer to cook their food at high temperatures, causing grease to splatter onto oven walls, which calls for self-cleaning ovens. This feature is in less demand in Germany, where lower temperatures are traditionally used. Manufacturers are hoping that European integration will bring about cost savings and product standardization. The danger to be avoided is the development of compromise products that in the end appeal to no one. Joint ventures present their share of challenges to the global marketers. For example, in Whirlpool's Shanghai facility, teams of American, Italian, and Chinese technicians must work through three interpreters to set up production.

Although opportunities do exist, competition is keen. Margins have suffered as manufacturers (more than 300 in Europe alone) scrape for business. The major players have decided to compete in all the major markets of the world. "Becoming a global appliance player is clearly the best use of our management expertise and well-established brand line-up," Whirlpool executives have said. Whirlpool's long-term goal is to leverage its global manufacturing and brand assets strategically across the world.

464

Not everyone has succeeded, however. In its move toward globalization, Maytag acquired Chicago Pacific Corporation, best known for its Hoover appliances. The products have a strong presence in the United Kingdom and Australia but not on the European continent, where Maytag ended up essentially trying to introduce new products to new markets. After six years, Maytag sold its European operations to an Italian manufacturer at a loss of $135 million in 1995. In early 2000, Maytag entered into an alliance with Sanyo Electric Co. to develop and market home appliances for the Japanese and Pacific Rim markets.

The most recent entrants into the global home appliance market are China's Haier and Kelon, both mainly in refrigerators and air conditioners, industries in which China's technology is up to world standards. Their biggest challenge is to establish their brand names as household words and to penetrate mass merchandising channels.

SOURCES: "Maytag's Share Price Falls on Earnings Warning," *The Wall Street Journal*, February 15, 2000, B8; "Chinese Brands out of the Shadows," *The Economist*, August 28, 1999, 78–81; "Whirlpool in the Wringer," *Business*

Week, December 14, 1998, 83–84; "Did Whirlpool Spin Too Far Too Fast?," *Business Week*, June 24, 1996, 134–136; Regina Fazio Maruca, "The Right Way to Go Global: An Interview with Whirlpool CEO David Whitwam," *Harvard Business Review* 72 (March–April 1994): 134–145; "Whirlpool Hangs Its Rivals out to Dry," *USA Today*, December 10, 1993, 3B; "GE's Brave New World," *Business Week*, November 8, 1993, 64–69; and "Can Maytag Clean Up around the World?" *Business Week*, January 30, 1989, 86–87.

http://www.whirlpool.com
http://www.ge.com
http://www.maytag.com
http://www.haieramerica.com

Global Marketing

Many marketing managers have to face the increasing globalization of markets and competition described in *The International Marketplace 14.1*. The rules of survival have changed since the beginning of the 1980s when Theodore Levitt first coined the phrase *global marketing*.[1] Even the biggest companies in the biggest home markets cannot survive on domestic sales alone if they are in global industries such as cars, banking, consumer electronics, entertainment, pharmaceuticals, publishing, travel services, or home appliances.[2] They have to be in all major markets to survive the shakeouts expected to leave three to five players per industry at the beginning of the 21st century.

Globalization reflects a business orientation based on the belief that the world is becoming more homogeneous and that distinctions between national markets are not only fading but, for some products, will eventually disappear. As a result, companies need to globalize their international strategy by formulating it across markets to take advantage of underlying market, cost, environmental, and competitive factors.

As shown in Figure 14.1, globalization can be seen as a result of a process that culminates a process of international market entry and expansion. Before globalization, marketers utilize a country-by-country multidomestic strategy to a great extent, with each country organization operated as a profit center. Each national entity markets a range of different products and services targeted to different customer segments, utilizing different marketing strategies with little or no coordination of operations between countries.

However, as national markets become increasingly similar and scale economies become increasingly important, the inefficiencies of duplicating product development and manufacture in each country become more apparent and the pressure to leverage resources and coordinate activities across borders gains urgency.

[1]Theodore Levitt, *The Marketing Imagination* (New York: Free Press, 1983), 20–49.

[2]Jeremey Main, "How to Go Global—and Why," *Fortune*, August 28, 1989, 70–76.

FIGURE 14.1   Global Marketing Evolution

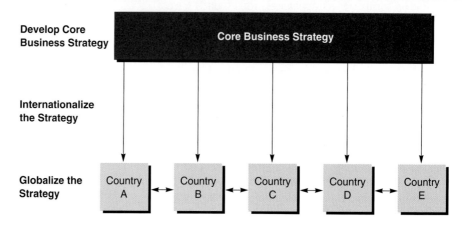

Globalization Drivers[3]

Both external and internal factors will create the favorable conditions for development of strategy and resource allocation on a global basis. These factors can be divided into market, cost, environmental, and competitive factors.

Market Factors   The world customer identified by Ernst Dichter more than 30 years ago has gained new meaning today.[4] For example, Kenichi Ohmae has identified a new group of consumers emerging in the **triad** of North America, Europe, and the Far East, whom marketers can treat as a single market with the same spending habits.[5] Approximately 600 million in number, these consumers have similar educational backgrounds, income levels, lifestyles, use of leisure time, and aspirations. One reason given for the similarities in their demand is a level of purchasing power (ten times greater than that of LDCs or NICs) that translates into higher diffusion rates for certain products. Another reason is that developed infrastructures—diffusion of telecommunication and an abundance of paved roads—lead to attractive markets for other products. Products can be designed to meet similar demand conditions throughout the triad. These similarities also enhance the transferability of other marketing elements.

At the same time, channels of distribution are becoming more global; that is, a growing number of retailers are now showing great flexibility in their strategies for entering new geographic markets.[6] Some are already world powers (e.g., Benetton and

---

[3]This section draws heavily from George S. Yip, "Global Strategy . . . In a World of Nations?" *Sloan Management Review* 31 (Fall 1989): 29–41; Susan P. Douglas and C. Samuel Craig, "Evolution of Global Marketing Strategy: Scale, Scope, and Synergy," *Columbia Journal of World Business* 24 (Fall 1989): 47–58; and George S. Yip, Pierre M. Loewe, and Michael Y. Yoshino, "How to Take Your Company to the Global Market," *Columbia Journal of World Business* 23 (Winter 1988): 28–40.

[4]Ernst Dichter, "The World Customer," *Harvard Business Review* 40 (July–August 1962): 113–122.

[5]Kenichi Ohmae, *Triad Power—The Coming Shape of Global Competition* (New York: Free Press, 1985), 22–27.

[6]Denise Incandela, Kathleen McLaughlin, and Christiana Smith Shi, "Retailers to the World," *The McKinsey Quarterly* 35 (Number 3, 1999): 84–97.

| **TABLE 14.1** | **Consolidation in the Paper Industry, 1998–2000** | | |

ACQUIRER	TARGET	VALUE	DATE ANNOUNCED
Norske Skogindustrier (Norway)	Fletcher Challenge Paper (New Zealand)	$2.5 billion	4/3/00
Smurfit-Stone (Chicago)	St. Laurent Paperboard (Montreal)	$1.0 billion	2/23/00
Stora Enso (Finland)	Consolidated Papers (U.S.)	$3.9 billion	2/22/00
UPM-Kymmene (Finland)	Champion Int'l (U.S.)	$5.7 billion	2/17/00
Abitibi-Consol. (Canada)	Donohue (Canada)	$4.0 billion	2/11/00
Weyerhaeuser (U.S.)	MacMillan Bloedel (Canada)	$2.3 billion	6/21/99
Int'l Paper (U.S.)	Union Camp (U.S.)	$5.9 billion	11/24/98
Stora (Sweden)*	Enso Oyj (Finland)*	Undisclosed	6/2/98

*Merger of equals

SOURCE: "Stora Enso to Buy Consolidated Papers," *The Wall Street Journal*, February 23, 2000, A3, A8. See also **http://www.storaenso.com**; Robert Frank, "The Emerging Global Paper Industry," www.worldleadersinprint.com, accessed April 25, 2001.

McDonald's), whereas others are pursuing aggressive growth (e.g., Toys 'Я' Us and IKEA). Also noteworthy are cross-border retail alliances, which expand the presence of retailers to new markets quite rapidly. The presence of global and regional channels makes it more necessary for the marketer to rationalize marketing efforts.

Cost Factors Avoiding cost inefficiencies and duplication of effort are two of the most powerful globalization drivers. A single-country approach may not be large enough for the local business to achieve all possible economies of scale and scope as well as synergies, especially given the dramatic changes in the marketplace. Take, for example, pharmaceuticals. In the 1970s, developing a new drug cost about $16 million and took four years. The drug could be produced in Britain or the United States and eventually exported. Now, developing a drug costs from $250 to $500 million and takes as long as 12 years, with competitive efforts close behind. Only a global product for a global market can support that much risk.[7] Size has become a major asset, which partly explains the many mergers and acquisitions in industries such as aerospace, pharmaceuticals, and telecommunications. The paper industry underwent major regional consolidation between 1998 and 2000, as shown in Table 14.1. Champion International, which was created when UPM bought Champion, is the most global of paper companies, with significant operations throughout the Americas, Asia, and Europe.[8] In the heavily contested consumer goods sectors, launching a new brand may cost as much as $100 million, meaning that companies such as Unilever and Procter & Gamble are not going to necessarily spend precious resources on one-country projects.

In many cases, expanded market participation and activity concentration can accelerate the accumulation of learning and experience. General Electric's philosophy is to be first or second in the world in a business or to get out. This can be seen, for example, in its global effort to develop premium computed tomography (CT), a diagnostic scanning system. GE swapped its consumer electronics business with the French Thomson for Thomson's diagnostic imaging business. At the same time, GE established GE Medical Systems Asia in Tokyo, anchored on Yokogawa Medical Systems, which is 75 percent owned by GE.

Environmental Factors As shown earlier in this text, government barriers have fallen dramatically in the last years to further facilitate the globalization of markets and the activities of marketers within them. For example, the forces pushing toward a pan-European

[7]"Vital Statistic: Disputed Cost of Creating a Drug," *The Wall Street Journal*, November 9, 1993, B1.

[8]"Finnish Paper Concern to Buy Champion," *The Wall Street Journal*, February 18, 2000, A3, A6.

market are very powerful: The increasing wealth and mobility of European consumers (favored by the relaxed immigration controls), the accelerating flow of information across borders, the introduction of new products where local preferences are not well established, and the publicity surrounding the integration process itself all promote globalization.[9] Also, the resulting removal of physical, fiscal, and technical barriers is indicative of the changes that are taking place around the world on a greater scale.

At the same time, rapid technological evolution is contributing to the process. For example, Ford Motor Company is able to accomplish its globalization efforts by using new communications methods, such as teleconferencing, intranet, and CAD/CAM links, as well as travel, to manage the complex task of meshing car companies on different continents.[10] Newly emerging markets will benefit from advanced communications by being able to leapfrog stages of economic development. Places that until recently were incommunicado in China, Vietnam, Hungary, or Brazil are rapidly acquiring state-of-the-art telecommunications that will let them foster both internal and external development.[11]

A new group of global players is taking advantage of today's more open trading regions and newer technologies. "Mininationals," or newer companies with sales between $200 million and $1 billion, are able to serve the world from a handful of manufacturing bases, compared with having to build a plant in every country as the established multinational corporations once had to do. Their smaller bureaucracies have also allowed these mininationals to move swiftly to seize new markets and develop new products—a key to global success.[12] This phenomenon is highlighted in *The International Marketplace 14.2.*

Competitive Factors Many industries are already dominated by global competitors that are trying to take advantage of the three sets of factors mentioned earlier. To remain competitive, the marketer may have to be the first to do something or to be able to match or preempt competitors' moves. Products are now introduced, upgraded, and distributed at rates unimaginable a decade ago. Without a global network, a marketer may run the risk of seeing carefully researched ideas picked off by other global players. This is what Procter & Gamble and Unilever did to Kao's Attack concentrated detergent, which they mimicked and introduced into the United States and Europe before Kao could react.

With the triad markets often both flat in terms of growth and fiercely competitive, many global marketers are looking for new markets and for new product categories for growth. Nestlé, for example, is setting its sights on consumer markets in fast-growing Asia, especially China, and has diversified into pharmaceuticals by acquiring Alcon and by becoming a major shareholder in the world's number-one cosmetics company, the French L'Oreal.[13]

Market presence may be necessary to execute global strategies and to prevent others from having undue advantage in unchallenged markets. Caterpillar faced mounting global competition from Komatsu but found out that strengthening its products and operations was not enough to meet the challenge. Although Japan was a small part of the world market, as a secure home base (no serious competitors), it generated 80 percent of Komatsu's cash flow. To put a check on its major global competitor's market share and cash flow, Caterpillar formed a heavy-equipment joint venture

[9]Gianluigi Guido, "Implementing a Pan-European Marketing Strategy," *Long Range Planning* 24 (1991): 23–33.

[10]Suzy Wetlaufer, "Driving Change: An Interview with Ford Motor Company's Jacques Nasser," *Harvard Business Review* 77 (March–April 1999): 76–88.

[11]Pete Engardio, "Third World Leapfrog," *Business Week/The Information Leapfrog 1994*, 47–49.

[12]"Mininationals Are Making Maximum Impact," *Business Week,* September 1993, 66–69.

[13]"Nestlé: A Giant in a Hurry," *Business Week*, March 22, 1993, 50–54; and **http://www.nestle.com**.

THE INTERNATIONAL MARKETPLACE 14.2

Born Global

EXPORTS ACCOUNT FOR 95 PERCENT of Cochlear's $40 million sales after a real annual compounded rate of 25 percent throughout the 1990s. Cochlear is a company specializing in the production of implants for the profoundly deaf. Based in Australia, it maintains a global technological lead through its strong links with hospitals and research units around the world and through its collaborative research with a network of institutions around the world.

Cochlear is a prime example of small to medium-sized firms that are remaking the global corporation of the 1990s. The term "mininational" has been coined to reflect their smaller size compared to the traditional multinationals. Sheer size is no longer a buffer against competition in markets where customers are demanding specialized and customized products. With the advent of electronic process technology, mininationals are able to compete on price and quality—often with greater flexibility. By taking advantage of today's more open trading regions, they can serve the world from a handful of manufacturing bases, sparing them from the necessity of building a plant in every country. Developments in information technology have enabled mininationals to both access data throughout most of the world and to run inexpensive and responsive sales and service operations across languages and time zones.

The smaller bureaucracies of the mininationals allow them to move swiftly in seizing new markets and developing new products, typically in focused markets. In many cases, these new markets have been developed by the mininationals themselves. For example, Symbol Technologies, Inc. of Bohemia, New York, invented the field of handheld laser scanners and now dominates this field. In a field that did not even exist in 1988, Cisco Systems, Inc. of Menlo Park, California, grew from a mininational to an entity that has over 14,500 employees in more than 200 offices in 55 countries. Other mininationals continue to focus on their core products and services, growing and excelling at what they do best.

The lessons from these new generation global players are to (1) keep focused and concentrate on being number one or number two in a technology niche; (2) stay lean by having small headquarters to save on costs and to accelerate decision making; (3) take ideas and technologies to and from wherever they can be found; (4) take advantage of employees regardless of nationality to globalize thinking; and (5) solve customers' problems by involving them rather than pushing on them standardized solutions. As a result of being flexible, they are better able to weather storms such as the Asian crisis by changing emphases in the geographical operations.

SOURCES: "Corporate Profile," available at **http://www.cisco.com**; "Turning Small into an Advantage," *Business Week*, July 13, 1998, 42–44; Michael W. Rennie, "Born Global," *The McKinsey Quarterly* (Number 4, 1993): 45–52; and "Mininationals Are Making Maximum Impact," *Business Week*, September 6, 1993, 66–69.

http://www.cochlear.com

http://www.cisco.com

with Matsushita to serve the Japanese market.[14] Similarly, when Unilever tried to acquire Richardson-Vicks in the United States, Procter & Gamble saw this as a threat to its home market position and outbid its archrival for the company.

The Outcome   The four globalization drivers have affected countries and industrial sectors differently. While some industries are truly globally contested, such as paper and soft drinks, some others, such as government procurement, are still quite closed and will open up as a decades-long evolution. Commodities and manufactured goods are already in a globalized state, while many consumer goods are accelerating toward more globalization. Similarly, the leading trading nations of the world display far more openness than low-income countries, thus advancing the state of globalization in general. The expansion of the global trade arena is summarized in Figure 14.2. The size

[14]Jordan D. Lewis, *Partnerships for Profit* (New York: Free Press, 1990): 86.

FIGURE 14.2 The Global Landscape by Industry and Market

Global GDP, US$ trillion

Country		Commodities and scale-driven goods	Consumer goods and locally delivered goods and services	Government services
Triad*		Old arena $4 Globalized in 1980s		
Developing countries†		Emerging arena $17 Globally contestable today		
Low-income countries ‡		Closed arena $3 Still blocked or lacking significant opportunity		

Industry

More globalized / Less globalized

Global ← → Local

* 19 OECD countries from North America, Western Europe, and Asia; Japan and Australia included

† 68 countries with middle income per capita, plus China and India

‡ Countries of small absolute size and low income per capita

SOURCE: Jane Fraser and Jeremy Oppenheim, "What's New about Globalization," *The McKinsey Quarterly* 33 (Number 2, 1997): 173.

of the market estimated to be global by the turn of the century is well over $21 billion, boosted by new sectors and markets that will become available.

Leading companies by their very actions drive the globalization process. There is no structural reason why soft drinks should be at a more advanced stage of globalization than beer and spirits, which remain more local, except for the opportunistic behavior of Coca-Cola. Similarly, Nike and Reebok have driven their businesses in a global direction by creating global brands, a global customer segment, and a global supply chain. By creating a single on-line trading exchange for all their parts and suppliers, General Motors, Ford, and DaimlerChrysler created a worldwide market of $240 billion in automotive components.[15]

The Strategic Planning Process

Given the opportunities and challenges provided by the new realities of the marketplace, decision makers have to engage in strategic planning to match markets with products and other corporate resources more effectively and efficiently to strengthen the company's long-term competitive advantage. While the process has been summarized as a sequence of steps in Figure 14.3, many of the stages can occur simultaneously. Furthermore, feedback as a result of evaluation and control may restart the process at any stage.

Understanding and Adjusting the Core Strategy

The planning process has to start with a clear definition of the business for which strategy is to be developed. Generally, the strategic business unit (SBU) is the unit around which decisions are based. In practice, SBUs represent groupings based on product-market similarities based on (1) needs or wants to be met, (2) end user customers to be targeted, or (3) the product or service used to meet the needs of specific

---

[15]"3 Big Carmakers to Create Net Site for Buying Parts," *The Washington Post*, February 26, 2000, E1, E8.

FIGURE 14.3 | **Global Strategy Formulation**

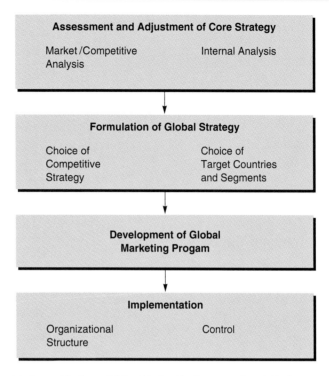

The authors appreciate the contributions of Robert M. Grant in the preparation of this figure.

customers. For a global marketer such as Black & Decker, the options may be to define the business to be analyzed as the home improvement business, the do-it-yourself business, or the power tool business. Ideally, these SBUs should have primary responsibility and authority in managing their basic business functions.

This phase of the planning process requires the participation of executives from different functions, especially marketing, production, finance, distribution, and procurement. Geographic representation should be from the major markets or regions as well as from the smaller, yet emerging, markets. With appropriate members, the committee can focus on product and markets as well as competitors whom they face in different markets, whether they are global, regional, or purely local. Heading this effort should be an executive with highest-level experience in regional or global markets; for example, one global firm called on the president of its European operations to come back to headquarters to head the global planning effort. This effort calls for commitment by the company itself both in calling on the best talent to participate in the planning effort and later in implementing their proposals.

Market and Competitive Analysis   For global marketers, planning on a country-by-country basis can result in spotty worldwide market performance. The starting point for global strategic planning is to understand that the underlying forces that determine business success are common to the different countries that the firm competes in. Planning processes that focus simultaneously across a broad range of markets provide global marketers with tools to help balance risks, resource requirements, competitive economies of scale, and profitability to gain stronger long-term positions.[16] On the

---

[16]Gilbert D. Harrell and Richard O. Kiefer, "Multinational Market Portfolios in Global Strategy Development," *International Marketing Review* 10 (Number 1, 1993): 60–72.

demand side this requires an understanding of the common features of customer requirements and choice factors. In terms of competition, the key is to understand the structure of the global industry in order to identify the forces that will drive competition and determine profitability.[17]

For Ford Motor Company, strategy begins not with individual national markets, but with understanding trends and sources of profit in the global automobile market. What are the trends in world demand? What are the underlying trends in lifestyles and transportation patterns that will shape customer expectations and preferences with respect to safety, economy, design, and performance? What is the emerging structure of the industry, especially with regard to consolidation among both automakers and their suppliers? What will determine the intensity of competition between the different automakers? The level of excess capacity (currently about 40 percent in the worldwide auto industry) is likely to be a key influence.[18] If competition is likely to intensify, which companies will emerge as winners? An understanding of scale economies, the state of technology, and the other factors that determine cost efficiency is likely to be critically important.

Internal Analysis Organizational resources have to be used as a reality check for any strategic choice in that they determine a company's capacity for establishing and sustaining competitive advantage within global markets. Industrial giants with deep pockets may be able to establish a presence in any market they wish, while more thinly capitalized companies may have to move cautiously. Human resources may also present a challenge for market expansion. A survey of multinational corporations revealed that good marketing managers, skilled technicians, and production managers were especially difficult to find. This difficulty is further compounded when the search is for people with cross-cultural experience to run future regional operations.[19]

At this stage it is imperative that the company assess its own readiness for the moves necessary. This means a rigorous assessment of organizational commitment to global or regional expansion, as well as an assessment of the product's readiness to face the competitive environment. In many cases this has meant painful decisions of focusing on certain industries and leaving others. For example, Nokia, the world's second largest manufacturer of cellular phones, started its rise in the industry when a decision was made at the company in 1992 to focus on digital cellular phones and to sell off dozens of other product lines. By focusing its efforts on this line, the company was able to bring to market new products quickly, build scale economies into its manufacturing, and concentrate on its customers, thereby communicating a commitment to their needs.[20]

Formulating Global Marketing Strategy

The first step in the formulation of global strategy is the choice of competitive strategy to be employed, followed by the choice of country markets to be entered or to be penetrated further.

Choice of Competitive Strategy In dealing with the global markets, the marketing manager has three general choices of strategies, as shown in Figure 14.4: (1) cost leadership, (2) differentiation, or (3) focus.[21] A focus strategy is defined by its emphasis on a single in-

[17]Michael E. Porter, *Competitive Strategy* (New York: Free Press, 1990), chapter 1.

[18]"Europe's Car Makers Expect Tidy Profits," *The Wall Street Journal*, January 27, 2000, A16.

[19]Lori Ioannou, "It's a Small World After All," *International Business*, February 1994, 82–88.

[20]"Grabbing Markets from the Giants," *Business Week/21st Century Capitalism*, 1994, 156.

[21]Michael Porter, *Competitive Advantage* (New York: Free Press, 1987), chapter 1.

FIGURE 14.4 Competitive Strategies

Source of Competitive Advantage

Low Cost | Differentiation

Competitive Scope

Industry-wide: Cost Leadership | Differentiation

Single Segment: Focus

SOURCE: Michael Porter, *Competitive Advantage* (New York: Free Press, 1987), chapter 1.

dustry segment within which the orientation may be toward either low cost or differentiation. Any one of these strategies can be pursued on a global or regional basis, or the marketer may decide to mix and match strategies as a function of market or product dimensions.

In pursuing cost leadership, the global marketer offers an identical product or service at a lower cost than competition. This often means investment in scale economies and strict control of costs, such as overhead, research and development, and logistics. Differentiation, whether it is industry-wide or focused on a single segment, takes advantage of the marketer's real or perceived uniqueness on elements such as design or after-sales service. It should be noted, however, that a low-price, low-cost strategy does not imply a commodity situation.[22] Although Japanese, U.S., and European technical standards differ, mobile phone manufacturers like Motorola and Nokia design their phones to be as similar as possible to hold down manufacturing costs. As a result, they can all be made on the same production line, allowing the manufacturers to shift rapidly from one model to another to meet changes in demand and customer requirements. In the case of IKEA, the low-price approach is associated with clear positioning and a unique brand image focused on a clearly defined target audience of "young people of all ages." Similarly, marketers who opt for high differentiation cannot forget the monitoring of costs. One common denominator of consumers around the world is their quest for value for their money. With the availability of information increasing and levels of education improving, customers are poised to demand even more of their suppliers.

Most global marketers combine high differentiation with cost containment to enter markets and to expand their market shares. Flexible manufacturing systems using mostly standard components and total quality management measures that reduce the occurrence of defects are allowing marketers to customize an increasing amount of their production while at the same time saving on costs. Global activities will in themselves permit the exploitation of scale economies not only in production but also in marketing activities, such as advertising.

Country-Market Choice A global strategy does not imply that a company should serve the entire globe. Critical choices relate to the allocation of a company's resources between different countries and segments.

The usual approach is first to start with regions and further split the analysis by country. Many marketers use multiple levels of regional groupings to follow the

[22]Robert M. Grant, *Contemporary Strategy Analysis: Concepts, Techniques, Applications* (Oxford, England: Blackwell, 1998), 203–205.

| FIGURE | 14.5 | Example of a Market-Portfolio Matrix |

Country Attractiveness

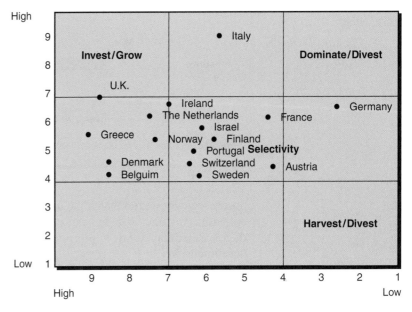

SOURCE: Gilbert D. Harrell and Richard O. Kiefer, "Multinational Market Portfolios in Global Strategy Development," *International Marketing Review* 10 (Number 1,1993): 60–72.

organizational structure of the company, e.g., splitting Europe into northern, central, and southern regions that display similarities in demographic and behavioral traits. An important consideration is that data may be more readily available if existing structures and frameworks are used.[23]

Various portfolio models have been proposed as tools for this analysis. They typically involve two measures—internal strength and external attractiveness.[24] As indicators of internal strength, the following variables have been used: relative market share, product fit, contribution margin, and market presence, which would incorporate the level of support by constituents as well as resources allocated by the company itself. Country attractiveness has been measured using market size, market growth rate, number and type of competitors, and governmental regulation, as well as economic and political stability. An example of such a matrix is provided in Figure 14.5.

The 3 × 3 matrix on country attractiveness and company strength is applied to the European markets. Markets in the invest/grow position will require continued commitment by management in research and development, investment in facilities, and the training of personnel and the country level. In cases of relative weakness in growing markets, the company's position may have to be strengthened (through acquisitions or strategic alliances) or a decision to divest may be necessary.[25] For example, Procter & Gamble decided to pull out of the disposable diaper markets in Australia and New Zealand due to well-entrenched competition, international currency fluctuations, and importation of products from distant production facilities into the mar-

[23]George S. Yip, *Total Global Strategy: Managing for Worldwide Competitive Advantage* (Englewood Cliffs, NJ: Prentice-Hall, 1992), 242–246.

[24]The models referred to are GE/McKinsey, Shell International, and A. D. Little portfolio models.

[25]"P&G Puts Nappies to Rest in Australia," *Advertising Age*, September 19, 1994, I-31.

TABLE 14.2 Factors Affecting the Choice between Concentration and Diversification Strategies

FACTOR	DIVERSIFICATION	CONCENTRATION
Market growth rate	Low	High
Sales stability	Low	High
Sales response function	Decreasing	Increasing
Competitive lead time	Short	Long
Spillover effects	High	Low
Need for product adaptation	Low	High
Need for communication adaptation	Low	High
Economies of scale in distribution	Low	High
Extent of constraints	Low	High
Program control requirements	Low	High

SOURCE: Igal Ayal and Jehiel Zif, "Marketing Expansion Strategies in Multinational Marketing," *Journal of Marketing* 43 (Spring 1979): 89. Reprinted from *Journal of Marketing*, published by the American Marketing Association.

kets.[26] General Mills, on the other hand, signed a complementary marketing arrangement with Nestlé to enter the European market dominated by its main global rival, Kellogg's. This arrangement allows General Mills effective market entry and Nestlé is able to utilize its distribution channels in Europe more efficiently, as well as enter a new product market.[27] Furthermore, it is critical that those involved in the planning process consider potential competitors and their impact on the markets should they enter. In Europe, many industrial giants are entering the telecommunications market, most of them without any previous experience in the industry. Some of these newcomers are joining forces with foreign telecommunications entities, thereby facilitating their new market development. For example, German steel maker Thyssen teamed up with energy conglomerate Veba and U.S. BellSouth to exploit Germany's need for digital cellular networks.[28]

In choosing country markets, a company must make decisions beyond those relating to market attractiveness and company position. A market expansion policy will determine the allocation of resources among various markets. The basic alternatives are **concentration** on a small number of markets and **diversification,** which is characterized by growth in a relatively large number of markets. Expansion strategy is determined by market-, mix-, and company-related factors, listed in Table 14.2. Market-related factors determine the attractiveness of the market in the first place. With high and stable growth rates only in certain markets, the firm will likely opt for a concentration strategy, which is often the case for innovative products early in their life cycle. If demand is strong worldwide, as the case may be for consumer goods, diversification may be attractive. If markets respond to marketing efforts at increasing rates, concentration will occur; however, when the cost of market share points becomes too high, marketers tend to begin looking for diversification opportunities.

The uniqueness of the product offering with respect to competition is also a factor in expansion strategy. If lead time over competition is considerable, the decision to diversify may not seem urgent. Very few products, however, afford such a luxury. In many product categories, marketers will be affected by spillover effects. Consider, for

[26]"P&G Puts Nappies to Rest in Australia," I-31.

[27]Richard Gibson, "Cereal Venture Is Planning Honey of a Battle in Europe," *The Wall Street Journal*, November 14, 1990, B1, B8.

[28]"A Feeding Frenzy in European Telecom," *Business Week*, November 21, 1994, 119–122.

example, the impact of satellite channels on advertising in Europe, where ads for a product now reach most of the West European market. The greater the degree to which marketing mix elements can be standardized, the more diversification is probable. Overall savings through economies of scale can then be utilized in marketing efforts. Finally, the objectives and policies of the company itself will guide the decision making on expansion. If extensive interaction is called for with intermediaries and clients, efforts are most likely to be concentrated because of resource constraints.

The conventional wisdom of globalization requires a presence in all of the major triad markets of the world. In some cases, markets may not be attractive in their own right but may have some other significance, such as being the home market of the most demanding customers, thereby aiding in product development, or being the home market of a significant competitor (a preemptive rationale). For example, Procter & Gamble rolled its Charmin bath tissue into European markets in 2000 to counter an upsurge in European paper products sales by its global rival Kimberly-Clark.[29] European PC makers, such as Germany's Maxdata and Britain's Tiny, are taking aim at the U.S. market based on the premise that if they can compete with the big multinationals (Dell, Compaq, Hewlett-Packard, and Gateway) at home, there is no reason why they cannot be competitive in North America as well.[30]

Therefore, for global marketers three factors should determine country selection: (1) the stand-alone attractiveness of a market (e.g., China in consumer products due to its size), (2) global strategic importance (e.g., Finland in shipbuilding due to its lead in technological development in vessel design), and (3) possible synergies (e.g., entry into Latvia and Lithuania after success in the Estonian market given the market similarities).

Segmentation

Effective use of segmentation, that is, the recognition that groups within markets differ sufficiently to warrant individual marketing mixes, allows global marketers to take advantage of the benefits of standardization (such as economies of scale and consistency in positioning) while addressing the unique needs and expectations of a specific target group. This approach means looking at markets on a global or regional basis, thereby ignoring the political boundaries that define markets in many cases. The identification and cultivation of such intermarket segments is necessary for any standardization of marketing programs to work.[31]

The emergence of segments that span markets is already evident in the world marketplace. Global marketers have successfully targeted the teenage segment, which is converging as a result of common tastes in sports and music fueled by their computer literacy, travels abroad, and, in many countries, financial independence.[32] Furthermore, a media revolution is creating a common fabric of attitudes and tastes among teenagers. Today satellite TV and global network concepts such as MTV are both helping create this segment and provide global marketers access to the teen audience around the world. For example, Reebok used a global ad campaign to launch its Instapump line of sneakers in the United States, Germany, Japan, and 137 other countries. Given that teenagers around the world are concerned with social issues, particularly environmentalism, Reebok has introduced a new ecological climbing shoe made from recycled and environmentally sensitive materials.

Despite convergence, global marketers still have to make adjustments in some of the marketing mix elements for maximum impact. For example, while Levi's jeans are globally accepted by the teenage segment, European teens reacted negatively to the ur-

[29]"Tissue Titans Target Globally with Key Brands," *Advertising Age*, December 20, 1999, 4.

[30]Richard Tomlinson, "Europe's New Computer Game," *Fortune*, February 21, 2000, 219–224.

[31]Saeed Samiee and Kendall Roth, "The Influence of Global Marketing Standardization on Performance," *Journal of Marketing* 56 (April 1992): 1–17.

[32]Shawn Tully, "Teens: The Most Global Market of All," *Fortune*, May 16, 1994, 90–97.

FIGURE 14.6 | **Bases for Global Market Segmentation**

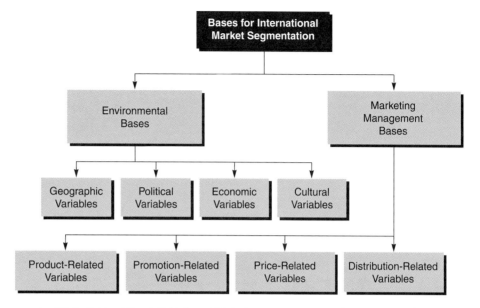

SOURCE: Imad B. Baalbaki and Naresh K. Malhotra, "Marketing Management Bases for International Market Segmentation: An Alternate Look at the Standardization/Customization Debate," *International Marketing Review* 10 (Number 1, 1993): 19–44.

ban realism of Levi's U.S. ads. Levi's converted its ads in Europe, drawing on a mythical America.[33] Similarly, two other distinct segments have been detected to be ready for a panregional approach, especially in Europe.[34] These include trendsetters who are wealthier and better educated and tend to value independence, refuse consumer stereotypes, and appreciate exclusive products. The second one includes Europe's businesspeople who are well-to-do, regularly travel abroad, and have a taste for luxury goods.

The greatest challenge for the global marketer is the choice of an appropriate base for the segmentation effort. The objective is to arrive at a grouping or groupings that are substantial enough to merit the segmentation effort (for example, there are nearly 230 million teenagers in the Americas, Europe, and the Asia-Pacific with the teenagers of the Americas spending nearly $60 billion of their own money yearly) and are reachable as well by the marketing effort (for example, the majority of MTV's audience consists of teenagers).

The possible bases for segmentation are summarized in Figure 14.6. Marketers have traditionally used environmental bases for segmentation. However, using geographic proximity, political system characteristics, economic standing, or cultural traits as stand-alone bases may not provide relevant data for decision making. Using a combination of them, however, may produce more meaningful results. One of the segments pursued by global marketers around the world is the middle-class family. Defining the composition of this global middle class is tricky, given the varying levels of development among nations in Latin America and Asia. However, some experts estimate that 23 percent of the world population enjoy middle-class lives.[35] Using household

[33]"The Euroteens (and How Not to Sell to Them)," *Business Week*, April 11, 1994, 84.

[34]S. Vandermerwe and M. L'Huillier, "Euro-Consumers in 1992," *Business Horizons* 32 (January–February 1989): 34–40.

[35]"Getting and Spending," *Business Week/21st Century Capitalism*, 1994, 178–185.

THE INTERNATIONAL MARKETPLACE 14.3

Global Segments Based on Values

THE 1997 ROPER REPORTS Worldwide Global Consumer Survey provided interview results of 1,000 people in 35 countries. As part of their responses, interviewers ranked 56 values by the importance they hold as guiding principles in their lives. Among adults, six global values segments were identified.

Strivers The largest group, Strivers, are slightly more likely to be men than women, and they place more emphasis on material and professional goals than do other groups. One-third of people in developing Asia are Strivers, as is about one-fourth of the population in Russia and developed Asia.

Devouts This group is 22 percent of adults. For Devouts, which includes more women than men, tradition and duty are very important. Devouts are most common in Asia and in Middle Eastern and African countries. They are least common in developed Asia and Europe.

Altruists This group is 18 percent of adults, with a slightly larger portion of females. Altruists are interested in social issues and the welfare of society. With a median age of 44, this group is older. More Altruists live in Latin America and Russia than in other countries.

Intimates Intimates, 15 percent of the population, value close personal relationships and family above all else. They are almost as likely to be men or women. One in four Europeans and North Americans qualify, compared with just 7 percent of developing Asia.

Fun Seekers Although found in disproportionate numbers in developed Asia, this group accounts for 12 percent of the global population. Not surprisingly, Fun Seekers are the youngest group, with a female-male ratio of 54–46.

Creatives This group is the smallest at 10 percent worldwide. Its hallmark trait is a strong interest in education, knowledge, and technology. Creatives are more common in Latin America and Europe. Along with Intimates, this group has the most balanced gender mix.

A country-by-country analysis revealed that Great Britain led the world in wanting to protect the family, Brazil had the most Fun Seekers, Saudi Arabia ranked first in faith, the Netherlands had the highest percentage worldwide in esteeming honesty, and Korea was the front-runner in valuing health and fitness.

SOURCE: Tom Miller, "Global Segments from 'Strivers' to 'Creatives,'" *Marketing News*, July 20, 1998, 11. **www.roper.com**

income alone may be quite a poor gauge of class. Income figures ignore vast differences in international purchasing power. Chinese consumers, for example, spend less than 5 percent of their total outlays on rent, transportation, and health, while a typical U.S. household spends 45 to 50 percent. Additionally, income distinctions do not reflect education or values—two increasingly important barometers of middle-class status. A global segmentation effort using cultural values is provided in *The International Marketplace 14.3*.

It has also been proposed that markets that reflect a high degree of homogeneity with respect to marketing mix variables could be grouped into segments and thereby targeted with a largely standardized marketing strategy.[36] Whether bases related to product, promotion, pricing, or distribution are used, their influence should be related to environmentally based variables. Product-related bases include the degree to which products are culture-based, which stage of the life cycle they occupy, consumption patterns, and attitudes toward product attributes (such as country of origin), as well as consumption infrastructure (for example, telephone lines for modems). The growth of microwave sales, for example, has been surprising in low-income coun-

[36]Imad B. Baalbaki and Naresh K. Malhotra, "Marketing Management Bases for International Market Segmentation: An Alternate Look at the Standardization/Customization Debate," *International Marketing Review* 10 (Number 1, 1993): 19–44.

tries; however, microwaves have become status symbols and buying them more of an emotional issue. Many consumers in these markets also want to make sure they get the same product as available in developed markets, thereby eliminating the need in many cases to develop market-specific products. Adjustments will have to made, however. Noticing that for reasons of status and space, many Asian consumers put their refrigerators in their living rooms, Whirlpool makes refrigerators available in striking colors such as red and blue.

With promotional variables, the consumers' values and norms may necessitate local solutions rather than opting for a regional approach. Similar influences may be exerted by the availability, or lack, of media vehicles or government regulations affecting promotional campaigns. On the pricing side, dimensions such as customers' price sensitivity may lead the marketer to go after segments that insist on high quality despite high price in markets where overall purchasing power may be low to ensure global or regional uniformity in the marketing approach. Affordability is a major issue for customers whose buying power may fall short for at least the time being. Offering only one option may exclude potential customers of the future who are not yet part of a targeted segment. Companies like Procter & Gamble and Gillette offer an array of products at different price points to attract them and to keep them as they move up the income scale.[37] As distribution systems converge, for example, with the increase of global chains, markets can also be segmented by outlet types that reach environmentally defined groups. For example, toy manufacturers may look at markets not only in terms of numbers of children but by how effectively and efficiently they can be reached by global chains such as Toys 'Я' Us, as opposed to purely local outlets.

Global Marketing Program Development

Decisions need to be made regarding how best to utilize the conditions set by globalization drivers within the framework of competitive challenges and the resources of the firm. Marketing-related decisions will have to be made in four areas: (1) the degree of standardization in the product offering, (2) the marketing program beyond the product variable, (3) location and extent of value-adding activities, (4) and competitive moves to be made.

Product Offering   Globalization is not equal to standardization except in the case of the core product or the technology used to produce the product. The components used in a personal computer may to a large extent be standard, with the localization needed only in terms of the peripherals; for example, IBM produces 20 different keyboards for Europe alone. Product standardization may result in significant cost savings upstream. For example, Stanley Works' compromise between French preferences for handsaws with plastic handles and "soft teeth" and British preferences for wooden handles and "hard teeth"—to produce a plastic-handled saw with "hard teeth"—allowed consolidation for production and results in substantial economies of scale. At Whirlpool, use of common platforms allow European and American appliances to share technology and suppliers to lower cost and to streamline production. Many of the same components are procedures used for products that eventually are marketed to segments looking for top-of-the-line or no-frills versions.[38] Similar differences in customer expectations have Bestfoods selling 15 versions of minestrone soup in Europe.

Marketing Approach   Nowhere is the need for the local touch as critical as in the execution of the marketing program. Uniformity is sought especially in elements that are strategic

[37]Rahul Jacob, "The Big Rise," *Fortune*, May 30, 1994, 74–90.

[38]"Call It Worldpool," *Business Week,* November 28, 1994, 98–99.

TABLE 14.3 Globalization of the Marketing Mix

MARKETING MIX ELEMENTS	ADAPTATION		STANDARDIZATION	
	FULL	PARTIAL	PARTIAL	FULL
Product design			N	C
Brand name			N	C
Product positioning		N		C
Packaging			C/N	
Advertising theme		N		C
Pricing		N	C	
Advertising copy	N		C	C
Distribution	N	C		
Sales promotion	N	C		
Customer service	N	C		

Key: C = Coca-Cola; N = Nestlé.

SOURCE: John A. Quelch and Edward J. Hoff, "Customizing Global Marketing," *Harvard Business Review*, May–June 1986 (Boston: Harvard Business School Publishing Division), 61. Reprinted by permission of Harvard Business Review. Copyright ® 1986 by the President and Fellows of Harvard College; all rights reserved.

(e.g., positioning) in nature, whereas care is taken to localize necessary tactical elements (e.g., distribution). This approach has been called **glocalization.** For example, Unilever achieved great success with a fabric softener that used a common positioning, advertising theme, and symbol (a teddy bear) but differing brand names (e.g., Snuggle, Cajoline, Kuschelweich, Mimosin, and Yumos) and bottle sizes. Gillette Co. scored a huge success with its Sensor shaver when it was rolled out in the United States, Europe, and Japan with a common approach based on the premise that men everywhere want the same thing in a shave. Although the language of its TV commercials varied, the theme ("the best a man can get") and most of the footage were the same. A comparison of the marketing mix elements of two global marketers is given in Table 14.3. Notice that adaptation is present even at Coca-Cola, which is acknowledged to be one of the world's most global marketers.

Location of Value-Added Activities Globalization strives to reduce costs by pooling production or other activities or exploiting factor costs or capabilities within a system. Rather than duplicating activities in multiple, or even all, country organizations, a firm concentrates its activities. For example, Texas Instruments has designated a single design center and manufacturing organization for each type of memory chip. To reduce high costs and to be close to markets, it placed two of its four new $250-million memory chip plants in Taiwan and Japan. To reduce high R&D costs, it has entered into a strategic alliance with Hitachi. Many global marketers have established R&D centers next to key production facilities so that concurrent engineering can take place every day on the factory floor. To enhance the global exchange of ideas, the centers have joint projects and are in real-time contact with each other.

The quest for cost savings and improved transportation methods has allowed some marketers to concentrate customer service activities rather than having them present in all country markets. For example, Sony used to have repair centers in all the Scandinavian countries and Finland; today, all service and maintenance activities are actually performed in a regional center in Stockholm, Sweden.

Competitive Moves A company with regional or global presence will not have to respond to competitive moves only in the market where it is being attacked. A competitor may be attacked in its profit sanctuary to drain its resources, or its position in its home market may be challenged.[39] When Fuji began cutting into Kodak's market share in the United States, Kodak responded by drastically increasing its advertising in Japan and created a new subsidiary to deal strictly with that market.

Cross-subsidization, or the use of resources accumulated in one part of the world to fight a competitive battle in another, may be the competitive advantage needed for the long term.[40] One major market lost may mean losses in others, resulting in a domino effect. Jockeying for overall global leadership may result in competitive action in any part of the world. This has manifested itself in the form of "wars" between major global players in industries such as soft drinks, automotive tires, computers, and cellular phones. The opening of new markets often signals a new battle, as has happened in the 1990s in Russia, in Mexico after the signing of the North American Free Trade Agreement, and in Vietnam after the normalization of relations with the United States. Given their multiple bases of operation, global marketers may defend against a competitive attack in one country by countering in another country or, if the competitors operate in multiple businesses, countering in a different product category altogether. In the cellular phone category, the winners in the future will be those who can better attack less mature markets with cheaper phones, while providing Internet-based devices elsewhere.[41]

The example of Nokia Corp., the leading manufacturer of cellular phones in the world (with a market share of 26.9 percent, followed by Motorola's 16.9 percent) highlights globalization as a strategy. The company's focus is on cellular phones (manufactured in Finland, Germany, and South Korea). The objective is to be a volume manufacturer, that is, to provide products for all major systems through a presence in all major markets. A global product range with customized variation for different distribution channels assures local acceptance.[42]

Implementing Global Marketing

The successful global marketers of the future will be those who can achieve a balance between the local and the regional/global concerns. Marketers who have tried the global concept have often run into problems with local differences. Especially early on, global marketing was seen as a standardized marketing effort dictated to the country organizations by headquarters. For example, when Coca-Cola re-entered the Indian market in 1993, it invested most heavily in its Coke brand, using its typical global positioning, and saw its market leadership slip to Pepsi. Recognizing the mistake, Coke re-emphasized a popular local cola brand (Thums Up) and refocused the Coke brand advertising to be more relevant to the local Indian consumer.[43]

Challenges of Global Marketing

Pitfalls that handicap global marketing programs and contribute to their suboptimal performance include market-related reasons, such as insufficient research and a tendency to overstandardize, as well as internal reasons, such as inflexibility in planning and implementation.

[39]W. Chan Kim and R. A. Mauborgne, "Becoming an Effective Global Competitor," *Journal of Business Strategy* 8 (January–February 1988): 33–37.

[40]Gary Hamel and C. K. Prahalad, "Do You Really Have a Global Strategy?" *Harvard Business Review* 63 (July–August 1985): 75–82.

[41]"Nokia Widens Lead in Wireless Market While Motorola, Ericsson Fall Back," *The Wall Street Journal*, February 8, 2000, B8.

[42]This example is courtesy of Jouko Hayrynen, vice president, exports, Nokia Corp.

[43]James A. Gingrich, "Five Rules for Winning Emerging Market Consumers," *Strategy and Business* (Second Quarter 1999): 19–33.

If a product is to be launched on a broader scale without formal research as to regional or local differences, the result may be failure. An example of this is Lego A/S, the Danish toy manufacturer, which decided to transfer sales promotional tactics successful in the U.S. market unaltered to other markets, such as Japan. This promotion included approaches such as "bonus packs" and gift promotions. However, Japanese consumers considered these promotions wasteful, expensive, and not very appealing.[44] Similarly, AT&T has had its problems abroad because its models are largely reworked U.S. models. Even after spending $100 million in adapting its most powerful switch for European markets, its success was limited because phone companies there prefer smaller switches.[45] Often, the necessary research is conducted only after a product or a program has failed.

Globalization by design requires a balance between sensitivity to local needs and deployment of technologies and concepts globally. This means that neither headquarters nor independent country managers can alone call the shots. If country organizations are not part of the planning process, or if adoption is forced on them by headquarters, local resistance in the form of the **not-invented-here syndrome (NIH)** may lead to the demise of the global program or, worse still, to an overall decline in morale. Subsidiary resistance may stem from resistance to any idea originating from the outside or from valid concerns about the applicability of a concept to that particular market. Without local commitment, no global program will survive.

Localizing Global Marketing

The successful global marketers of the new century will be those who can achieve a balance between country managers and global product managers at headquarters. This balance may be achieved by a series of actions to improve a company's ability to develop and implement global strategy. These actions relate to management processes, organization structures, and overall corporate culture, all of which should ensure cross-fertilization within the firm.[46]

Management Processes In the multidomestic approach, country organizations had very little need to exchange ideas. Globalization, however, requires transfer of information between not only headquarters and country organizations but also between the country organizations themselves. By facilitating the flow of information, ideas are exchanged and organizational values strengthened. Information exchange can be achieved through periodic meetings of marketing managers or through worldwide conferences to allow employees to discuss their issues and local approaches to solving them. IBM, for example, has a Worldwide Opportunity Council, which sponsors fellowships for employees to listen to business cases from around the world and develop global platforms or solutions. IBM has found that some country organizations find it easier to accept input of other country organizations than that coming directly from headquarters. The approach used at Levi Strauss & Co. is described in *The International Marketplace 14.4.*

Part of the preparation for becoming global has to be personnel interchange. Many companies encourage (or even require) midlevel managers to gain experience abroad during the early or middle stages of their careers. The more experience people have in working with others from different nationalities—getting to know other markets and surroundings—the better a company's global philosophy, strategy, and actions will be integrated locally.

---

[44]Kamran Kashani, "Beware the Pitfalls of Global Marketing," *Harvard Business Review* 67 (September–October 1989): 91–98.

[45]"AT&T Slowly Gets Its Global Wires Uncrossed," *Business Week*, February 11, 1991, 82–83.

[46]Quelch and Hoff, "Customizing Global Marketing"; and Yip, Loewe, and Yoshino, "Take Your Company to the Global Market."

THE INTERNATIONAL MARKETPLACE 14.4

Finding the Fit Overseas

TWICE A YEAR, LEVI STRAUSS & CO. calls together managers from its worldwide operations for a meeting of the minds. In sessions that could be described as a cross between the United Nations general assembly and MTV, the participants brainstorm and exchange ideas on what seems to work in their respective markets, regionally or globally. If a marketing manager finds an advertising campaign appealing, he or she is encouraged to take it back home to sell more Levi's blue jeans.

All told, Levi's marketing approach epitomizes a slogan that is becoming popular among companies around the world: Think globally, act locally. Levi's has deftly capitalized on the Levi's name abroad by marketing it as an enshrined piece of Americana, and foreign consumers have responded by paying top dollar for the product. An Indonesian commercial shows Levi's-clad teenagers cruising around Dubuque, Iowa, in 1960s convertibles. In Japan, James Dean serves as a centerpiece in virtually all Levi's advertising. Overseas, Levi's products have been positioned as an upscale product, which has meant highly satisfactory profit margins. To protect the image, Levi's has avoided the use of mass merchants and discounters in its distribution efforts.

Levi's success turns on its ability to fashion a global strategy that does not stifle local initiative. It is a delicate balancing act, one that often means giving foreign managers the freedom needed to adjust their tactics to meet the changing tastes of their home markets. In Brazil, Levi's prospers by letting local managers call the shots on distribution. For instance, Levi's penetrated the huge, fragmented Brazilian market by launching a chain of 400 Levi's Only stores, some of them in tiny rural towns. Levi's is also sensitive to local tastes in Brazil, where it developed the Feminina line of jeans exclusively for women, who prefer ultratight jeans. What Levi's learns in one market can often be adopted in another. The Dockers line of chino pants and casual wear originated in the

company's Argentine unit and was applied to loosely cut pants by Levi's Japanese subsidiary. The company's U.S. operation adopted both in 1986, and the line now generates $550 million in North American revenues.

Headquarters managers exercise control where necessary. To protect Levi's cherished brand identity and image of quality, the company has organized its foreign operations as subsidiaries rather than relying on a patchwork of licensees. "It is important for a brand like ours to have a single face," says Lee C. Smith, president of Levi Strauss International. "You cannot control that if you have 20 to 25 licensees around the world interpreting it in different ways." The company also keeps ahead of its competition by exporting its pioneering use of computers to track sales and manufacturing.

The company has also launched a reorganization to focus more on consumer needs. Levi's web site has been redesigned to feature a virtual dressing room, custom-tailored jeans ordering, and virtual salespeople who offer tips on matching outfits.

Levi's continues to focus on global sales with its three divisions: the Americas (NAFTA plus Latin America); Europe, Middle East, Africa; and Asia Pacific. In 1998, the Americas contributed 65 percent of its sales; Europe, the Middle East, and Africa 29 percent; and Asia Pacific 6 percent of $6 billion total sales.

SOURCES: Alice Z. Cuneo, "Levi Strauss Begins 1st Online Sales Effort," *Advertising Age*, November 23, 1998, 18; and "For Levi's, a Flattering Fit Overseas," *Business Week*, November 5, 1990, 76–77.

http://www.levistrauss.com

The role of headquarters staff should be that of coordination and leveraging the resources of the corporation. For example, this may mean activities focused on combining good ideas that come from different parts of the company to be fed into global planning. Many global companies also employ world-class advertising and market research staffs whose role should be to consult subsidiaries by upgrading their technical skills and to focus their attention not only on local issues but also on those with global impact.

Globalization calls for the centralization of decision-making authority far beyond that of the multidomestic approach. Once a strategy has been jointly developed, headquarters may want to permit local managers to develop their own programs within specified parameters and subject to approval rather than forcing them to adhere strictly to the formulated strategy. For example, Colgate Palmolive allows local units to use their own ads, but only if they can prove they beat the global "benchmark" version. With a properly managed approval process, effective control can be exerted without unduly dampening a country manager's creativity.

Overall, the best approach against the emergence of the NIH syndrome is utilizing various motivational policies such as (1) ensuring that local managers participate in the development of marketing strategies and programs for global brands, (2) encouraging local managers to generate ideas for possible regional or global use, (3) maintaining a product portfolio that includes local as well as regional and global brands, and (4) allowing local managers control over their marketing budgets so that they can respond to local customer needs and counter global competition (rather than depleting budgets by forcing them to participate only in uniform campaigns).[47] Acknowledging this local potential, global marketers can pick up successful brands in one country and make them cross-border stars. Since Nestlé acquired British candy maker Rowntree Mackintosh, it has increased its exports by 60 percent and made formerly local brands, into such as After Eight dinner mints, into pan-European hits. When global marketers get their hands on an innovation or a product with global potential, rolling it out in other regions or worldwide is important.

Organization Structures

Various organization structures have emerged to support the globalization effort. Some companies have established global or regional product managers and their support groups at headquarters. Their task is to develop long-term strategies for product categories on a worldwide basis and to act as the support system for the country organizations. This matrix structure focused on customers, which has replaced the traditional country-by-country approach, is considered more effective in today's global marketplace according to companies that have adopted it.

Whenever a product group has global potential, firms such as Procter & Gamble, 3M, and Henkel create strategic-planning units to work on the programs. These units, such as 3M's EMATs (European Marketing Action Teams) consist of members from the country organizations that market the products, managers from both global and regional headquarters, and technical specialists.

To deal with the globalization of customers, marketers are extending national account management programs across countries typically for the most important customers.[48] AT&T, for example, distinguishes between international and global customers and provides the global customers with special services including a single point of contact for domestic and international operations and consistent worldwide service. Executing **global account management** programs builds relationships not only with important customers but also allows for the development of internal systems and interaction.

Corporate Culture

Whirlpool's corporate profile states the following: "Beyond selling products around the world, being a global home-appliance company means identifying and respecting genuine national and regional differences in customer expectations, but also recognizing and responding to similarities in product development, engineering, purchasing, manufacturing, marketing and sales, distribution, and other areas. Companies which exploit the efficiencies from these similarities will outperform others in terms of market share, cost, quality, productivity, innovation, and return to shareholders.

---

[47]Quelch and Hoff, "Customizing Global Marketing."

[48]George S. Yip and Tammy L. Madsen, "Global Account Management: The New Frontier in Relationship Marketing," *International Marketing Review* 13 (Number 3, 1996): 24–42.

In truly global companies, very little decision making occurs that does not support the goal of treating the world as a single market. Planning for and execution of programs take place on a worldwide basis.

Examples of manifestations of the global commitment are a global identity that favors no specific country (especially the "home country" of the company). The management features several nationalities, and whenever terms are assembled, people from various country organizations get represented. The management development system has to be transparent, allowing nonnational executives an equal chance for the fast track to top management.[49]

In determining the optimal combination of products and product lines to be marketed, a firm should consider choices for individual markets as well as transfer of products and brands from one region or market to another. This will often result in a particular country organization marketing product lines and products that are a combination of global, regional, and national brands.

Decisions on specific targeting may result in the choice of a narrowly defined segment in the countries chosen. This is a likely strategy for marketers of specialized products to clearly definable markets, for example, ocean-capable sailing boats. Catering to multiple segments in various markets is typical of consumer-oriented companies that have sufficient resources for broad coverage.

SUMMARY

Globalization has become one of the most important strategy issues for marketing managers in the last ten years. Many forces, both external and internal, are driving companies to globalize by expanding and coordinating their participation in foreign markets. The approach is not standardization, however. Marketers may indeed occasionally be able to take identical technical and marketing concepts around the world, but most often, concepts must be customized to local tastes. Internally, companies must make sure that country organizations around the world are ready to launch global products and programs as if they had been developed only for their markets.

Marketing managers need to engage in strategic planning to better adjust to the realities of the new marketplace. Understanding the firm's core strategy (i.e., what business they are really in) starts the process and this assessment may lead to adjustments in what business the company may want to be in. In formulating global strategy for the chosen business, the decision makers have to assess and make choices about markets and competitive strategy to be used in penetrating them. This may result in the choice of one particular segment across markets or the exploitation of multiple segments in which the company has a competitive advantage. In manipulating and implementing the marketing mix for maximum effect in the chosen markets, the old adage, "think globally, act locally," becomes a critical guiding principle both as far as customers are concerned and in terms of country organization motivation.

QUESTIONS FOR DISCUSSION

1. What is the danger in oversimplifying the globalization approach? Would you agree with the statement that "if something is working in a big way in one market, you better assume it will work in all markets"?

2. In addition to teenagers as a global segment, are there possibly other such groups with similar traits and behaviors that have emerged worldwide?

---

[49]"Globalization Starts with Company's Own View of Itself," *Business International*, June 10, 1991, 197–198.

3. Suggest ways in which a global marketer is better equipped to initiate and respond to competitive moves.

4. Why is the assessment of internal resources critical as early as possible in developing a global strategic plan?

5. What are the critical ways in which the multidomestic and global approaches differ in country-market selection?

6. Outline the basic reasons why a company does not necessarily have to be large and have years of experience to succeed in the global marketplace.

7. Using the material available at Unilever's web site (**www.unilever.com**), suggest ways in which Unilever's business groups can take advantage of global and regional strategies due to interconnections in production and marketing.

8. Bestfoods is one of the largest food companies in the world, with operations in more than 60 countries and products sold in 110 countries in the world. Based on the brand information given at its web site (**www.bestfoods.com**), what benefits does a company derive from having a global presence?

RECOMMENDED READINGS

Bartos, Rena. *Marketing to Women around the World.* Cambridge, MA: Harvard Business Press, 1989.

Davidson, William H. *Global Strategic Management.* New York: Wiley, 1982.

The Economist Intelligence Unit. *151 Checklists for Global Management.* New York: The Economist Intelligence Unit, 1993.

Feist, William R., James A. Heely, Min H. Lau, and Roy L. Nersesian. *Managing a Global Enterprise.* Westport, CT: Quorum, 1999.

Foster, Richard. *Innovation: The Attacker's Advantage,* New York: Summit Books, 1986.

Grant, Robert M. and Kent E. Neupert. *Cases in Contemporary Strategy Analysis.* Oxford, England: Blackwell, 1999.

Humes, Samuel. *Managing the Multinational: Confronting the Global-Local Dilemma.* London: Prentice-Hall International (U.K.) Ltd, 1993.

Kanter, Rosabeth Moss. *World Class.* New York: Simon & Schuster, 1995.

Kaynak, Erdener, ed. *The Global Business.* Binghamton, NY: Haworth Press, 1992.

Kotabe, Masaaki. *Global Sourcing Strategy: R&D, Manufacturing, and Marketing Interfaces.* Greenwich, CT: Greenwood Publishing Group, 1992.

Makridakis, Spyros G. *Forecasting, Planning, and Strategy for the 21st Century.* New York: Free Press, 1990.

Prahalad, C. K., and Yves L. Doz. *The Multinational Mission: Balancing Local and Global Vision.* New York: Free Press, 1987.

Rosensweig, Jeffrey. *Winning the Global Game: A Strategy for Linking People and Profits.* New York: Free Press, 1998.

Global Market Expansion

Chapter 15

THE INTERNATIONAL MARKETPLACE 15.1

Nike Investments: Global Production and Working Conditions

NIKE, THE FOOTWEAR COMPANY, is based in Beaverton, Oregon. One hundred percent of its footwear is produced by subcontractors, most of them outside the United States. Nike's own people focus on the services part of the production process, including design, product development, marketing, and distribution. For example, through its "Futures" inventory control system, Nike knows exactly what it needs to order early enough to plan production accordingly. This avoids excess inventory and assures better prices from its subcontractors.

To achieve both stability and flexibility in its supplier relationships, Nike has three distinct groups of subcontractors in its network:

- Developed partners, the most important group, participate in joint product development and concentrate on the production of the newest designs. Traditionally, they have been located in the People's Republic of China and Republic of China but, given rising labor costs, some of the more labor-intensive activities have been moved out. The developed partners typically have worked exclusively for Nike on a minimum monthly order basis.
- The second group of Nike's suppliers are called developing sources and offer low labor costs and the opportunity for Nike to diversify assembly sites. Currently, they are located in the People's Republic of China, Indonesia, and Thailand. Nearly all are exclusive suppliers to Nike and receive considerable assistance from the company with a view of upgrading their production. They will be the next generation of developed partners for Nike.

- The third group, volume producers, are large-scale factories serving a number of other independent buyers. They generally manufacture a specific product for Nike, but they are not involved in any new product because of fears they could leak proprietary information to competitors. Orders from Nike for suppliers in this group fluctuate, with variations of 50 percent between monthly orders.

Nike's outsourcing activity over time follows a geographic pattern, as does its overall market participation. A "Nike index" has been developed by Jardine Fleming to track a country's economic development. Development starts when Nike products' manufacturing starts there (e.g., Indonesia in 1989, Vietnam in 1996). Second stage is reached when labor starts flowing from basic industries, such as footwear, to more advanced ones, such as automobiles and electronics (Hong Kong in 1985, South Korea in 1990). An economy is fully developed when a country is developed as a major market (Japan in 1984, Singapore in 1991, and South Korea in 1994).

Nike's outsourcing has been of concern. In Indonesia, for example, where Nike has 70 million shoes produced annually by contract manufacturers in 12 factories, there have been complaints about low wages and inhumane working conditions. These complaints have led to major debates about Nike's contribution to and exploitation of developing countries.

In response, Nike developed a code of conduct and its enforcement in countries where it has outsourcing activities. For example, apparel workers now need to be at least 16 years old. Factory indoor air quality is now being measured and improved. Meal and transportation allowances, education subsidies, and health care services are provided. Yet criticism of its outsourcing practices has not died down, much to Nike's frustration. When his alma mater, the University of Oregon, aligned itself with an anti-sweatshop group, Worker's Rights Consortium, Nike Chairman Phil Knight withdrew a planned $30 million contribution to the University's athletic fund.

SOURCES: "Pangs of Conscience," *Business Week*, July 29, 1996, 46–47;

United Nations, *World Investment Report 1994: An Executive Summary* (New York: United Nations, 1994), 15; and "Nike Contract Factory Owners Increase Minimum Wage in Indonesia," **http://www.nikebiz.com**, April 14, 2000; Stephen Greenhouse, *The New York Times*, April 25, 2000, www.corpwatch.org, April 17, 2001.

http://www.nike.com

www.nikebiz.com

ALL TYPES OF FIRMS, large and small, can carry out global market expansion through foreign direct investment or management contracts, and they are doing so at an increasing pace. Key to the decision to invest abroad is the existence of specific advantages that outweigh the disadvantages and risk of operating so far from home. Since foreign direct investment often requires substantial capital and a firm's ability to absorb risk, the most visible players in the area are large multinational corporations. These firms invest to enter markets or to assure themselves of sources of supply. *The International Marketplace 15.1* shows how Nike has based its outsourcing of products almost entirely on the international market. In this chapter, the section on foreign direct investment strategies focuses on the rationale for such investment and on investment alternatives such as full ownership, joint ventures, and strategic alliances. The section on contractual arrangements then focuses on the potential and the benefits and drawbacks of such arrangements.

Foreign Direct Investment

Foreign direct investment represents one component of the international investment flow. The other component is portfolio investment, which is the purchase of stocks and bonds internationally. Portfolio investment is a primary concern to the international financial community. The international marketer, on the other hand, makes foreign direct investments to create or expand a permanent interest in an enterprise. They imply a degree of control over the enterprise.[1]

Foreign direct investments have grown tremendously. The total global value of such investment, which in 1967 was estimated to be $105 billion, had climbed to an estimated $3.2 trillion by the end of 1998.[2] Among global investors, U.S. firms are major players due to significant investments in the developed world and in some developing countries. In 1998, the stock of foreign direct investment abroad by U.S. firms amounted to $5.95 trillion at market value. Major foreign direct investment activity has also been carried out by firms from other countries, many of which decided to invest in the United States. In 1998, the stock of direct investment by foreign firms in the United States totaled approximately $7.49 trillion, up from $6.9 billion in 1960.[3] Foreign direct investment has clearly become a major avenue for foreign market entry and expansion.

[1]Frank G. Vukmanic, Michael R. Czinkota, and David A. Ricks, "National and International Data Problems and Solutions in the Empirical Analysis of Intraindustry Direct Foreign Investment," in *Multinationals as Mutual Invaders: Intraindustry Direct Foreign Investment*, ed. A. Erdilek (Beckenham, Kent, England: Croom Helm Ltd., 1985), 160–184.

[2]United Nations, World Investment Report 1998, New York, United Nations, 1998, XV. **www.un.org**

[3]*Survey of Current Business*, U.S. Department of Commerce, Bureau of Economic Analysis, March 2000. **www.doc.gov**

Major Foreign Investors

Multinational corporations are defined by the United Nations as "enterprises which own or control production or service facilities outside the country in which they are based."[4] As a result of this definition, all foreign direct investors are multinational corporations. Today, there are more than 45,000 such corporations with 280,000 affiliates around the world and their global sales far exceed the value of global trade.[5] Yet large corporations are the key players. Table 15.1 lists the 50 largest corporations around

TABLE 15.1 The World's 50 Largest Corporations, 2001 (Ranked by Revenues)

		COUNTRY OF ORIGIN	REVENUES $ MILLIONS
1	General Motors	US	176,558.0
2	Wal-Mart Stores	US	166,809.0
3	Exxon Mobil	US	163,881.0
4	Ford Motor	US	162,558.0
5	DaimlerChrysler	Germany	159,985.7
6	Mitsui	Japan	118,555.2
7	Mitsubishi	Japan	117,765.6
8	Toyota Motor	Japan	115,670.9
9	General Electric	US	111,630.0
10	Itochu	Japan	109,068.9
11	Royal Dutch/Shell Group	Britain/Netherlands	105,366.0
12	Sumitomo	Japan	95,701.6
13	Nippon Telegraph & Telephone	Japan	93,591.7
14	Marubeni	Japan	91,807.4
15	AXA	France	87,645.7
16	Intl. Business Machines	US	87,548.0
17	BP Amoco	Britain	83,566.0
18	Citigroup	US	82,005.0
19	Volkswagen	Germany	80,072.7
20	Nippon Life Insurance	Japan	78,515.1
21	Siemens	Germany	75,337.0
22	Allianz	Germany	74,178.2
23	Hitachi	Japan	71,858.5
24	Matsushita Electric Industrial	Japan	65,555.6
25	Nissho Iwai	Japan	65,393.2
26	U.S. Postal Service	US	62,726.0
27	ING Group	Netherlands	62,492.4
28	AT&T	US	62,391.0
29	Philip Morris	US	61,751.0
30	Sony	Japan	60,052.7
31	Deutsche Bank	Germany	58,585.1
32	Boeing	US	57,993.0
33	Dai-ichi Mutual Life Insurance	Japan	55,104.7
34	Honda Motor	Japan	54,773.5
35	Assicurazioni Generali	Italy	53,723.2
36	Nissan Motor	Japan	53,679.9
37	E. ON	Germany	52,227.7
38	Toshiba	Japan	51,634.9
39	Bank of America Corp.	US	51,392.0

(continued)

[4]*Multinational Corporations in World Development* (New York: United Nations, 1973), 23.

[5]*World Investment Report: An Executive Summary* (New York: United Nations, 1998), xv.

TABLE 15.1	The World's 50 Largest Corporations, 2001 (Ranked by Revenues) *(continued)*		
		COUNTRY OF ORIGIN	REVENUES $ MILLIONS
40	Fiat	Italy	51,331.7
41	Nestlé	Switzerland	49,694.1
42	SBC Communications	US	49,489.0
43	Credit Suisse	Switzerland	49,362.0
44	Hewlett-Packard	US	48,253.0
45	Fujitsu	Japan	47,159.9
46	Metro	Germany	46,663.6
47	Sumitomo Life Insurance	Japan	46,445.1
48	Tokyo Electric Power	Japan	45,727.7
49	Kroger	US	45,351.6
50	Total Fina Elf	France	44,990.3

SOURCE: **http://www.fortune.com/fortune/global500**. Copyright ©2000 Time Inc.

the world. They come from a wide variety of countries, depend heavily on their international sales, and in terms of sales are larger than many countries. As these firms keep growing, they appear to benefit from greater abilities to cope with new, unfamiliar situations.[6] However, it also appears that there is an optimal size that, when exceeded, increases the costs of operations.[7]

Many of the large multinationals operate in well over 100 countries. For some, their original home market accounts for only a fraction of their sales. For example, Philips' sales in Holland are only 4 percent, SKF's sales in Sweden are less than 4 percent, and Nestlé's sales in Switzerland are only 2 percent of total sales. In some firms, even the terms *domestic* and *foreign* have fallen into disuse. Others are working to consider issues only from a global perspective. For example, in management meetings of ABB (Asea Brown Boveri), individuals get fined $100 every time the words *foreign* and *domestic* are used.

Through their investment, multinational corporations bring economic vitality and jobs to their host countries and often pay higher wages than the average domestically owned firms. Since such contributions to employment are sometimes forgotten in the heat of political discussions, some investors take pains to point them out to the public. Figure 15.1 shows an advertisement by a Japanese investor in the United States that highlights the contribution made by the firm to the U.S. economy.

At the same time, however, trade follows investment. This means that foreign direct investors often bring with them imports on an ongoing basis. The flow of imports in turn may contribute to the weakening of a nation's international trade position.

Reasons for Foreign Direct Investment

Firms expand internationally for a wide variety of reasons. Table 15.2 provides an overview of the major determinants of foreign direct investment.

Marketing Factors   Marketing considerations and the corporate desire for growth are major causes for the increase in foreign direct investment. This is understandable in view of John Kenneth Galbraith's postulation that "growth means greater responsibilities and

---

[6]Bernard L. Simonin, "Transfer of Marketing Know-How in International Strategic Alliances: An Empirical Investigation of the Role and Antecedents of Knowledge Ambiguity," *Journal of International Business Studies* 30 (Number 3, 1999): 463–490.

[7]Lenn Gomes and Kannan Ramaswamy, "An Empirical Examination of the Form of the Relationship between Multinationality and Performance," *Journal of International Business Studies* 30 (Number 1, 1999): 173–188.

FIGURE 15.1 Highlighting the Foreign Investment Contribution

AT TOYOTA we believe in the importance of investing in the economies where we do business. That's why we've invested over $5 billion in our operations here in America. That's why since 1988 we've increased our purchasing of U.S. made parts by 357% to over $4 billion per year. And that's why almost half the Toyota passenger cars sold in America are manufactured right here in Kentucky and California. *INVESTING IN THE THINGS WE ALL CARE ABOUT.* **TOYOTA**

For information on Toyota in America write Toyota Motor Corporate Services, 9 West 57th Street, Suite 4900, New York, NY 10019.

http://www.toyota.com

TABLE 15.2	**Major Determinants of Direct Foreign Investment**

A. Marketing Factors
  1. Size of market
  2. Market growth
  3. Desire to maintain share of market
  4. Desire to advance exports of parent company
  5. Need to maintain close customer contact
  6. Dissatisfaction with existing market arrangements
  7. Export base
B. Trade Restrictions
  1. Barriers to trade
  2. Preference of local customers for local products
C. Cost Factors
  1. Desire to be near source of supply
  2. Availability of labor
  3. Availability of raw materials
  4. Availability of capital/technology
  5. Lower labor costs
  6. Lower production costs other than labor
  7. Lower transport costs
  8. Financial (and other) inducements by government
  9. More favorable cost levels
D. Investment Climate
  1. General attitude toward foreign investment
  2. Political stability
  3. Limitation on ownership
  4. Currency exchange regulations
  5. Stability of foreign exchange
  6. Tax structure
  7. Familiarity with country
E. General
  1. Expected higher profits

SOURCE: *International Investment and Multinational Enterprises* (Paris: Organization for Economic Cooperation and Development, 1983), 41.

http://www.oecd.org

more pay for those who contribute to it."[8] Even large domestic markets present limitations to growth. Today's competitive demands require firms to operate simultaneously in the "triad" of the United States, Western Europe, and Japan and most other markets of the world as well. Corporations therefore need to seek wider market access in order to maintain and increase their sales. This objective can be achieved most quickly through the acquisition of foreign firms. Through such expansion, the corporation also gains ownership advantages consisting of political know-how and expertise. Examples are better intelligence about political actors and opportunities, readier access to political opinion makers and decision makers, and superior skills for influencing the latter.[9]

Another incentive is that foreign direct investment permits corporations to circumvent current barriers to trade and operate abroad as a domestic firm, unaffected by duties, tariffs, or other import restrictions. For example, research on Japanese for-

[8]John Kenneth Galbraith, *A Life in Our Times* (Boston: Houghton Mifflin, 1981), 518.

[9]Jean J. Boddewyn, "Political Aspects of MNE Theory," *Journal of International Business Studies* 19 (Fall 1988): 341–363.

eign direct investment in Europe has found that a substantial number of firms invested there in order to counteract future trade friction.[10]

In addition to government-erected barriers, restrictions may be imposed by customers through their insistence on domestic goods and services, either as a result of nationalistic tendencies or as a function of cultural differences. Further, local buyers may wish to buy from sources that they perceive to be reliable in their supply, which means buying from local producers. For some products, country-of-origin effects may force a firm to establish a plant in a country that has a built-in positive stereotype for production location and product quality.[11]

Still another incentive is the cost factor, with corporations attempting to obtain low-cost resources and ensure their sources of supply. Finally, once the decision is made to invest internationally, the investment climate plays a major role. Corporations will seek to invest in those geographic areas where their investment is most protected and has the best chance to flourish.

These determinants will have varying impact on the foreign direct investment decision, depending on the characteristics of the firm and its management, on its objectives, and on external conditions. Firms have been categorized as resource seekers, market seekers, and efficiency seekers.[12] **Resource seekers** search for either natural resources or human resources. Natural resources typically are based on mineral, agricultural, or oceanographic advantages and result in firms locating in areas where these resources are available. The alternatives open to firms therefore depend on the availability of the natural resources sought. Companies seeking human resources are likely to base their location decision on the availability of low-cost labor that matches their needs in terms of output quality. Alternatively, companies may select an area because of the availability of highly skilled labor. If natural resources are not involved, the location decision can be altered over time if the labor advantage changes. When the differential between labor costs in different locales becomes substantial, a corporation, in continuing to improve its human resource access, may relocate to take advantage of the "better" resources. A good example of such shifts was observed in Europe. In the 1980s, many non-European firms decided to gain their foothold in Europe by investing in the low-wage countries of Portugal, Spain, and Greece. In light of the major political changes of the 1990s, however, the investment interest shifted and began to focus on Hungary, the former East Germany, and the Czech Republic. Similarly, the implementation of the North American Free Trade Agreement (NAFTA) precipitated major investment flows from the United States into Mexico, led by firms seeking to obtain a key, low-cost Mexican factor endowment—labor.

Corporations primarily in search of better opportunities to enter and expand within markets are **market seekers.** Particularly when markets are closed or access is restricted, corporations have a major incentive to locate in them. **Efficiency seekers** attempt to obtain the most economic sources of production. They frequently have affiliates in multiple markets with highly specialized product lines or components and exchange their production in order to maximize the benefits to the corporation.

Derived Demand   A second major cause for the increase in foreign direct investment is the result of **derived demand,** where demand abroad is the result of the move abroad by established customers. As large multinational firms move abroad, they are quite interested in maintaining their established business relationships with other firms. Therefore,

[10]Detlev Nitsch, Paul Beamish, and Shige Makino, "Characteristics and Performance of Japanese Foreign Direct Investment in Europe," *European Management Journal* 13 (Number 3, 1995): 276–285.

[11]Phillip D. White and Edward W. Cundiff, "Assessing the Quality of Industrial Products," *Journal of Marketing* 42 (January 1978): 80–86.

[12]Jack N. Behrman, "Transnational Corporations in the New International Economic Order," *Journal of International Business Studies* 12 (Spring–Summer 1981): 29–42.

they frequently encourage their suppliers to follow them and continue to supply them from a foreign location. Many Japanese automakers have urged their suppliers in Japan to begin production in the United States in order for the new U.S. plants to have access to their products. As a result, a few direct investments can gradually form an important investment preference for subsequent investment flows. The same phenomenon holds true for service firms. Advertising agencies often move abroad to service foreign affiliates of their domestic clients. Similarly, engineering firms, insurance companies, and law firms are often invited to provide their services abroad. Yet not all of these developments are the result of co-optation by client firms. Often, suppliers invest abroad out of fear that their clients might find good sources abroad and therefore begin to import the products of services they currently supply. Many firms therefore invest abroad in order to forestall such a potentially dangerous development.

Government Incentives   A third major cause for the increase in foreign direct investment is government incentives. Governments are increasingly under pressure to provide jobs for their citizens. Over time, many have come to recognize that foreign direct investment can serve as a major means to increase employment and income. Countries such as Ireland have been promoting government incentive schemes for foreign direct investment for decades. Increasingly, state and local governments are also participating in investment promotion activities. Some states are sending out investment missions on a regular basis, and others have opened offices abroad in order to inform local businesses about the beneficial investment climate at home.

Government incentives are mainly of three types: fiscal, financial, and nonfinancial. **Fiscal incentives** are specific tax measures designed to serve as an attraction to the foreign investor. They typically consist of special depreciation allowances, tax credits or rebates, special deductions for capital expenditures, tax holidays, and other reductions of the tax burden on the investor. **Financial incentives** offer special funding for the investor by providing land or buildings, loans, loan guarantees, or wage subsidies. Finally, **nonfinancial incentives** can consist of guaranteed government purchases; special protection from competition through tariffs, import quotas, and local content requirements; and investments in infrastructure facilities. Figure 15.2 provides an example of such investment promotion that points out the benefits of a specific investment locale offering several financial and fiscal incentives.

Incentives are designed primarily to attract more industry and therefore create more jobs. They may slightly alter the advantage of a region and therefore make it more palatable for the investor to choose to invest in that region. By themselves, they are unlikely to spur an investment decision if proper market conditions do not exist. Consequently, when individual states or regions within a country offer special incentives to foreign direct investors, they may be competing against each other for a limited pie rather than increasing the size of the pie. Further, a question exists about the extent to which new jobs are actually created by foreign direct investment. Because many foreign investors import equipment, parts, and even personnel, the expected benefits in terms of job creation may often be either less than initially envisioned or only temporary. One additional concern arises from the competitive position of domestic firms already in existence. Since their "old" investment typically does not benefit from incentives designed to attract new investment, established firms may encounter problems when competing against the newcomer.

A Perspective on Foreign Direct Investors

All foreign direct investors, and particularly multinational corporations, are viewed with a mixture of awe and dismay. Governments and individuals praise them for bringing capital, economic activity, and employment, and investors are seen as key transferers of technology and managerial skills. Through these transfers, competition, market choice, and competitiveness are enhanced.

FIGURE 15.2	An Advertisement for Foreign Direct Investment

www.pridco.com

At the same time, the dependence on multinational corporations is seen negatively by many. Just as the establishment of a corporation can create all sorts of benefits, its disappearance can also take them away again. Very often, international direct investors are accused of actually draining resources from their host countries. By employing the best and the brightest, they are said to deprive domestic firms of talent, thus causing a **brain drain.** Once they have hired locals, multinational firms are often accused of not promoting them high enough, and of imposing many new rules on their employees abroad. *The International Marketplace 15.2* provides an example of the new environment that employees of foreign-owned firms have to get used to.

By raising money locally, multinationals are seen to starve smaller capital markets. By bringing in foreign technology, they are viewed either as discouraging local

THE INTERNATIONAL MARKETPLACE 15.2

Working for a Foreign-Owned Firm

INCREASING NUMBERS of U.S. managers are joining foreign-owned companies that are doing business in the U.S. market, but many of them don't know what they are getting into. Career success often hinges on a keen understanding of the differences in culture and management style. There are advantages to working for foreign employers, including job security. While times are changing, the Japanese still try to build loyalty with job security. "The Germans," says Dwight Foster of Foster Partners, an executive search firm, "go through agony when they have to let someone go." Many foreign owners also seem more willing to take a longer-term view than their American counterparts, who often make decisions based on quarterly performance. "I typically don't receive a phone call at the end of the quarter to discuss results," says George Gelfer, president of the U.S. unit of Francotyp-Postalia, a German postal equipment maker. "You don't need to remake the world in 120 days," he adds. Or, as John Bollock, vice president of human resources for Canon USA, puts it, "Americans view things in minutes; the Japanese think in centuries."

What are the disadvantages of working for foreign-owned companies? Top corporate management posts may be beyond your grasp. "There are very few Americans who work for Hitachi in Japan and usually at very low levels," says Bill Gsand, executive vice president of Hitachi America, and group president for converging technologies. Also, the devotion of foreign firms to careful strategic planning and consensus building may seem a bit slow for action-oriented U.S. managers. "The John Wayne management approach—ready, shoot, aim—doesn't work here," Mr. Bullock of Canon says.

Another problem for some U.S. managers: Career paths are often ill-defined and slow moving. The Japanese, in particular, like to hire people and expose them to all departments early in their careers. Career advancement might not come for years. That's great training for budding senior general managers, but not so great for those who want to specialize.

What kind of people do well in this environment? Patient people, obviously. Also foreign employers are "very concerned with personal integrity, reliability, and the ability to fit into the organization," Mr. Foster says. So just producing good results won't necessarily keep you in good standing. Of particular importance is punctuality, meeting commitments, and being a dependable team player. Stamina can also be a valuable asset. Besides the long hours most Japanese executives put in, managers visiting Japan must get used to frequent nights spent socializing into the wee hours.

Here are some additional points to ponder: Learn to interpret the subtleties of the company culture. The Japanese, for example, "don't like to say no," explains Gerry Shanholt, president and CEO of SRX. "So you have to look for key phrases. If you hear the phrase 'very difficult,' that probably means no."

Mr. Gelfer quickly learned that his German bosses at Francotyp-Postalia were far more fiscally conservative than he was used to. "I've got to carry a larger reserve for obsolescence and spare parts than I would if the same business was American owned," he says. Other executives notice a greater attention to detail and a greater insistence on documenting everything. Also, documentation can present misunderstandings caused by language differences. In any case, Mr. Gsand says, you should double-check to make sure your informal messages are being translated to others accurately. "Things often aren't heard the way they're spoken," he says.

SOURCE: Hal Lancaster, "How You Can Learn to Feel at Home in a Foreign-Based Firm," *The Wall Street Journal*, June 4, 1996, B1.

technology development or as perhaps transferring only outmoded knowledge. By increasing competition, they are declared the enemy of domestic firms. There are concerns about foreign investors' economic and political loyalty toward their host government and a fear that such investors will always protect only their own interests and those of their home governments. And, of course, their sheer size, which sometimes exceeds the financial assets that the government controls, makes foreign investors suspect.

Clearly, a love-hate relationship frequently exists between governments and the foreign direct investor. As the firm's size and investment volume grow, the benefits it brings to the economy increase. At the same time, the dependence of the economy on the firm increases as well. Given the many highly specialized activities of firms, their experts are often more knowledgeable than government employees and are therefore able to circumvent government rules. Particularly in developing countries, the knowledge advantage of foreign investors may offer opportunities for exploitation.

In light of the desire for foreign investment and the accompanying fear of it, a substantial array of guidelines for corporate behavior abroad has been publicized. Today, no set of normative corporate guidelines exists that is universally or globally accepted and observed.[13] Yet some organizations, such as the United Nations, the Organization for Economic Cooperation and Development, and the International Labor Organization, have recommended or proposed guidelines. Typically, these recommendations address the behavior of foreign investors in areas such as employment practices, consumer and environmental protection, political activity, and human rights. Corporations may not be legally bound by the guidelines but they should consider their implications for corporate activities. While the social acceptability of certain practices may vary among nations, the foreign investor can be expected to transfer, along with the best business practices, also such best acceptability across nations, therefore gradually increasing and improving the acceptability threshold in the world. The multinational firm can and should be a leader in improving economic and business practices and standards of living around the world. The true leaders will do so. Firms that do not accept national sovereignty or do not respect individuals will encounter growing hostility, resistance to their operations, and declining international success.

Types of Ownership

In carrying out its foreign direct investment, a corporation has a wide variety of ownership choices, ranging from 100 percent ownership to a minority interest. The different levels of ownership will result in varying degrees of flexibility for the corporation, a changing ability to control business plans and strategy, and differences in the level of risk assumed. In some instances, firms appear to select specific foreign ownership structures based on their experience with similar structures in the past.[14] In other words, these firms tend to keep using the same ownership model. However, it may be better to have the ownership decision be either a strategic response to corporate capabilities and needs, or a necessary consequence of government regulation. *The International Marketplace 15.3* explains how one firm used three different ownership approaches to its expansion in Asia.

Full Ownership   For many firms, the foreign direct investment decision is, initially at least, considered in the context of 100 percent ownership. Sometimes, this is the result of ethnocentric considerations, based on the belief that no outside entity should have an impact on corporation management. At other times, the issue is one of principle.

To make a rational decision about the extent of ownership, management must evaluate the extent to which total control is important for the success of its international marketing activities. Often, full ownership may be a desirable, but not a necessary, prerequisite for international success. At other times, it may be necessary, particularly when strong linkages exist within the corporation. Interdependencies between and among local operations and headquarters may be so strong that anything short of total coordination will result in a benefit to the firm as a whole that is less than

---

[13]William C. Frederick, "The Moral Authority of Transnational Corporate Codes," *Journal of Business Ethics* 10 (Number 3, 1991): 165–177.

[14]Prasad Padmanabhan and Kang Rae Cho, "Decision Specific Experience in Foreign Ownership and Establishment Strategies: Evidence from Japanese Firms," *Journal of International Business Studies* 30 (Number 1, 1999): 25–44.

THE INTERNATIONAL MARKETPLACE 15.3

One Company Chooses Three Modes of International Investment

IN THE EARLY 1990s, Fedders International, the largest U.S. manufacturer of room air conditioners, decided that the best way to grow was to venture abroad. The company concluded that China was the best option for investment.

The initial entrance of Fedders into the Chinese market in 1995 was organized through a joint venture with a struggling Chinese air conditioning company, Ningbo General Air Conditioning Factory. The agreement was that Ningbo General would increase production to 500,000 units in three years, and Fedders would handle all exporting. In March 2001, Fedders announced plans by its subsidiary, Envirco Corporation, to establish a 100 percent owned factory in China, as well as a new R & D facility to service Fedders' worldwide operations.

While stepping up production in China, Fedders has applied two other strategies to entering the foreign market. One consisted of a greenfield investment in June 1999, when the Indian Foreign Investment Promotion Board granted Fedders approval to set up a wholly owned facility for manufacturing of air conditioners in India. In the second most populous country in the world, air conditioners are the fastest growing category of consumer durables. Due to the hot climate of India, Fedders officials are highly optimistic about their new manufacturing site in Asia.

ABB Koppel Inc., in the Philippines, marks Fedders' third approach to expanding its product line and establishing a manufacturing base in Asia, this time through acquisition. The president of Fedders International, Mr. Gary Nahai, predicts that this January 2000 acquisition will greatly boost the firm's share in the Asian market. Fedders reported record sales in 2000 of $409.8 million, an increase of 15 percent over the previous year. Not bad for a company that just ten years ago had virtually no global reach.

www.fedders.com

SOURCES: "Fedders Obtains Indian Government Approval for Wholly Owned Manufacturing Facility in India," Fedders press release, June 8, 1999; "Fedders Acquires Air Conditioning Company," Fedders press release, January 18, 2000; "Fedders Second Quarter Sales Up 20 Percent; Net Income Rises 58 Percent," Fedders press release, March 16, 2000; and "Keeping Cool in China," *The Economist*, April 6, 1996, 73; "Fedders Announces Fiscal 2000 Results," Fedders press release, October 4, 2000; "Fedders to Step Up China Investments," March 20, 2001.

---

acceptable. This may be the case if central product design, pricing, or advertising is needed, as the following example illustrates:

> The Crane Company manufactures plumbing fixtures, pumps, and valves, and similar equipment which is used in oil refineries, paper mills, and many other types of installations. The firm sells to design engineers throughout the world; these engineers may not be actual buyers, but they design equipment into the plants they build, and so they at least recommend the equipment to be used. In advertising to this important segment of the international market, Crane recognizes that the design engineer in São Paolo reads engineering journals published in the United States, Great Britain, and perhaps Germany or France, as well as Latin America. So Crane wants its advertising in these journals to be consistent. Therefore, it does not let its foreign subsidiaries conduct their own advertising without advice and clearance from the New York headquarters. If Crane were to use joint ventures abroad, the partner would have to yield advertising authority to New York. This could conceivably lead to discontent on the part of the local partner. To avoid arguments on advertising policies, Crane insists on full ownership.[15]

As this example shows, corporations sometimes insist on full ownership for major strategic reasons. Even in such instances, however, it is important to determine whether these reasons are important enough to warrant such a policy or whether the needs of

---

[15]Richard H. Holton, "Making International Joint Ventures Work," presented at the seminar on the Management of Headquarters/Subsidiary Relationships in Transnational Corporations, Stockholm School of Economics, June 2–4, 1980, 4.

the firm can be accommodated with other ownership arrangements. Increasingly, the international environment is growing hostile to full ownership by multinational firms.

Many governments exert political pressure to obtain national control of foreign operations. Commercial activities under the control of foreigners are frequently believed to reflect the wishes, desires, and needs of headquarters abroad much more than those of the domestic economy. Governments fear that domestic economic policies may be counteracted by such firms, and employees are afraid that little local responsibility and empathy exist at headquarters. A major concern is the "fairness" of **profit repatriation,** or transfer of profits, and the extent to which firms operating abroad need to reinvest in their foreign operations. Governments often believe that transfer pricing mechanisms are used to amass profits in a place most advantageous for the firm and that, as a consequence, local operations often show very low levels of performance. By reducing the foreign control of firms, they hope to put an end to such practices.

Ownership options are limited either through outright legal restrictions or through measures designed to make foreign ownership less attractive—such as profit repatriation limitations. The international marketer is therefore frequently faced with the choice either of abiding by existing restraints and accepting a reduction in control or of losing the opportunity to operate in the country.

In addition to the pressure from host governments, general market instability can also serve as a major deterrent to full ownership of foreign direct investment. Instability may result from political upheavals or changes in regimes. More often, it results from threats of political action, complex and drawn-out bureaucratic procedures, and the prospect of arbitrary and unpredictable alterations in regulations after the investment decision has been made.[16]

Joint Ventures

Joint ventures are a collaboration of two or more organizations for more than a transitory period.[17] In this collaboration, the participating partners share assets, risks, and profits. Equality of partners is not necessary. In some joint ventures, each partner holds an equal share; in others, one partner has the majority of shares. The partners' contributions to the joint venture can also vary widely. Contributions may consist of funds, technology, know-how, sales organizations, or plant and equipment.

Advantages of Joint Ventures The two major reasons for carrying out foreign direct investments in the form of joint ventures are governmental and commercial. Governments often pressure firms either to form or accept joint ventures or to forgo participation in the local market. Such restrictions are designed to reduce the extent of control that foreign firms can exercise over local operations. As a basis for defining control, most countries have employed percentage levels of ownership. Over time, countries have shown an increasing tendency to reduce the thresholds of ownerships that define control. This tendency developed as it became apparent that even small, organized groups of stockholders may influence control of an enterprise, particularly if overall ownership is widely distributed. At the same time, however, many countries are also recognizing the beneficial effects of foreign direct investment in terms of technological progress and international competitiveness and are permitting more control of local firms by foreign entities.

Another reason may be the economic orientation of governments and a resulting requirement for joint venture collaboration. Joint ventures can help overcome existing market access restrictions and open up or maintain market opportunities that otherwise would not be available.

[16]Isaiah Frank, *Foreign Enterprise in Developing Countries* (Baltimore: Johns Hopkins University, 1980).

[17]W. G. Friedman and G. Kalmanoff, *Joint International Business Ventures* (New York: Columbia University Press, 1961).

Equally important to the formation of joint ventures are commercial considerations. If a corporation can identify a partner with a common goal, and if the international activities are sufficiently independent from each other not to infringe on the autonomy of the individual partner, joint ventures may represent the most viable vehicle for international expansion. The following is an example of a nearly ideal joint venture:

> The Trailmobile Company of Cincinnati, Ohio, produces truck trailers. It now participates in 27 joint ventures abroad. Truck trailers do not move in international markets in significant numbers because transportation costs are high and, more importantly, because tariffs typically serve to insulate the markets from each other. Therefore, pricing can be decided at the level of the joint venture, because one joint venture cannot invade the market of another. Each joint venture serves its own local market, and these differ from each other in significant ways; hence, the marketing policy decisions are made at the local level. Only a modest part of the total cost of manufacturing the trailer is represented by components bought from Trailmobile. Thus, the interdependencies are limited, decision making can be delegated to the level of the joint venture, and conflicts can be minimized.[18]

Joint ventures are valuable when the pooling of resources results in a better outcome for each partner than if each attempted to carry out its activities individually. This is particularly the case when each partner has a specialized advantage in areas that benefit the joint venture. For example, a firm may have new technology available, yet lack sufficient capital to carry out foreign direct investment on its own. By joining forces with a partner, the technology can be used more quickly, and market penetration is easier. Similarly, one of the partners may have a distribution system already established or have better access to local suppliers, either of which permits a greater volume of sales in a shorter period of time.

Joint ventures also permit better relationships with local organizations—government, local authorities, or labor unions. Government-related reasons are the major rationale for joint ventures in developing countries, making them four times more frequent there than in industrialized nations.[19] The most important attributes of the local partner are its reputation in the local market and its financial standing.[20] If the local partner can bring political influence to the undertaking, the new venture may be eligible for tax incentives, grants, and government support and may be less vulnerable to political risk. Negotiations for certifications or licenses may be easier because authorities may not perceive themselves as dealing with a foreign firm. Relationships between the local partner and the local financial establishment may enable the joint venture to tap local capital markets. The greater experience—and therefore greater familiarity—with the culture and environment of the local partner may enable the joint venture to be more aware of cultural sensitivities and to benefit from greater insights into changing market conditions and needs.

A final major commercial reason to participate in joint ventures is the desire to minimize the risk of exposing long-term investment capital while at the same time maximizing the leverage on the capital that is invested.[21] Economic and political conditions in many countries are volatile. At the same time, corporations increasingly tend to shorten their investment planning time span. This financial rationale therefore takes on growing importance.

[18]Holton, "Making International Joint Ventures Work," 5.

[19]Paul W. Beamish, "The Characteristics of Joint Ventures in Developed and Developing Countries," *Columbia Journal of World Business* 20 (Fall 1985): 13–19.

[20]Ali K. Al-Khalifa and S. Eggert Peterson, "The Partner Selection Process in International Joint Ventures," *European Journal of Marketing* 33 (Number 11/12, 1999).

[21]Charles Oman, *New Forms of International Investment in Developing Countries* (Paris: Organization for Economic Cooperation and Development, 1984), 79.

Disadvantages of Joint Ventures   Problem areas in joint ventures, as in all partnerships, involve implementing the concept and maintaining the relationship.

Many governments that require a joint venture formation are inexperienced in foreign direct investment. Therefore, joint venture legislation and the ensuing regulations are often subject to substantial interpretation and arbitrariness. Frequently, different levels of control are permitted depending on the type of product and the shipment destination. In some instances, only portions of joint venture legislation are made public. Other internal regulations are communicated only when necessary. Such situations create uncertainty, which increases the risk for the joint venture participants.

Major problems can also arise in assuring the maintenance of the joint venture relationship. Seven out of ten joint ventures have been found to fall short of expectations and/or are disbanded.[22] The reasons typically relate to conflicts of interest, problems with disclosure of sensitive information, and disagreement over how profits are to be shared; in general, a lack of communication before, during, and after the formation of the venture. In some cases, managers are interested in launching the venture but are concerned too little about actually running the enterprise. In other instances, managers dispatched to the joint venture by the partners may feel differing degrees of loyalty to the venture and its partners. Reconciling such conflicts of loyalty is one of the greatest human resource challenges for joint ventures.[23] Many of the problems encountered by joint ventures stem from a lack of careful, advance consideration of how to manage the new endeavor. A partnership works on the basis of trust and commitment, or not at all.

Areas of possible disagreement include the whole range of business decisions covering strategy, management style, accounting and control, marketing policies and practices, production, research and development, and personnel.[24] The joint venture may, for example, identify a particular market as a profitable target, yet the headquarters of one of the partners may already have plans for serving this market, plans that would require competing against its own joint venture.

Similarly, the issue of profit accumulation and distribution may cause discontent. If one partner supplies the joint venture with a product, that partner will prefer that any profits accumulate at headquarters and accrue 100 percent to one firm rather than at the joint venture, where profits are partitioned according to equity participation. Such a decision may not be greeted with enthusiasm by the other partner. Further, once profits are accumulated, their distribution may lead to dispute. For example, one partner may insist on a high payout of dividends because of financial needs, whereas the other may prefer the reinvestment of profits into a growing operation.

Strategic Alliances   One special form of joint ventures consists of strategic alliances, or partnerships. The result of growing global competition, rapid increases in the investment required for technological progress, and growing risk of failure, strategic alliances are informal or formal arrangements between two or more companies with a common business objective. They are more than the traditional customer-vendor relationship, but less than an outright acquisition. The great advantage of such alliances is their ongoing flexibility, since their formation, although stable at any given point in time, is subject to adjustment and change in response to environmental shifts.[25] In

[22]Yankelovich, Skelly and White, Inc., *Collaborative Ventures: A Pragmatic Approach to Business Expansion in the Eighties* (New York: Coopers and Lybrand, 1984), 10.

[23]Oded Shenkar and Shmuel Ellis, "Death of the 'Organization Man': Temporal Relations in Strategic Alliances," *The International Executive* 37 (Number 6, November/December 1995): 537–553.

[24]Holton, "Making International Joint Ventures Work," 7.

[25]John Hagedoorn, "A Note on International Market Leaders and Networks of Strategic Technology Partnering," *Strategic Management Journal* 16 (1995): 241–250.

essence, strategic alliances are networks of companies, which collaborate in the achievement of a given project or objective. However, partners for one project may well be fierce competitors for another.

Alliances can take forms ranging from information cooperation in the market development area to joint ownership of worldwide operations. For example, Texas Instruments has reported agreements with companies such as IBM, Hyundai, Fujitsu, Alcatel, and L. M. Ericsson using such terms as "joint development agreement," "cooperative technical effort," "joint program for development," "alternative sourcing agreement," and "design/exchange agreement for cooperative product development and exchange of technical data."

There are many reasons for the growth in such alliances. Market development is one common focus. Penetrating foreign markets is a primary objective of many companies. In Japan, Motorola is sharing chip designs and manufacturing facilities with Toshiba to gain greater access to the Japanese market. Some alliances are aimed at defending home markets. With no orders coming in for nuclear power plants, Bechtel Group has teamed up with Germany's Siemens to service existing U.S. plants.[26] Another focus is spreading the cost and risk inherent in production and development efforts. Texas Instruments and Hitachi have teamed up to develop the next generation of memory chips. The costs of developing new jet engines are so vast that they force aerospace companies into collaboration; one such consortium was formed by United Technologies' Pratt & Whitney division, Britain's Rolls Royce, Motoren-und-Turbinen Union from Germany, Flat of Italy, and Japanese Aero Engines (made up of Ishikawajima Heavy Industries and Kawasaki Heavy Industries). Some alliances are also formed to block and co-opt competitors.[27] For example, Caterpillar formed a heavy equipment joint venture with Mitsubishi in Japan to strike back at its main global rival, Komatsu, in its home market.

Even though many strategic alliances are formed to enable large firms to compete for very large projects, such alliances are by no means confined to large multinational firms. As *The International Marketplace 15.4* shows, small firms are taking advantage of the opportunities as well in order to expand and grow.

Of course, companies must carefully evaluate the effects of entering such a coalition. Depending on the objectives of the other partners, companies may wind up having their strategy partially driven by their competitors. Competitors may also gain strength through coalitions, unplanned transfers of technology might take place, and unexpected competitors might appear as a result.[28] The most successful alliances are those that match the complementary strengths of partners to satisfy a joint objective. Often the partners have different product, geographic, or functional strengths, which the alliance can build on in order to achieve success with a new strategy or in a new market. Table 15.3 shows how some firms have combined their individual strengths to achieve their joint objective. In light of growing international competition and the rising cost of innovation in technology, strategic alliances are likely to continue their growth in the future.

Recommendations   The first requirement when forming a joint venture is to find the right partner. Partners should have a commonality of orientation and goals and should bring complementary and relevant benefits to the joint venture. The venture makes little sense if the expertise of both partners is in the same area—for example, if both have production experience but neither has distribution know-how. Similarly, bringing a good distribution system to the joint venture may be of little use if the es-

[26]Louis Kraar, "Your Rivals Can Be Your Allies," *Fortune*, March 27, 1989, 66–76.

[27]Jordan D. Lewis, *Partnerships for Profit: Structuring and Managing Strategic Alliances* (New York: Free Press, 1990), 85–87.

[28]Pedro Nueno and Jan Oosterveld, "Managing Technology Alliances," *Long Range Planning* (June 1988): 11–17.

THE INTERNATIONAL MARKETPLACE 15.4

Small Firms Use Alliances Too

WHEN MICHAEL THIEMANN, vice present for new product development at San Diego–based HNC, Inc., went shopping in Japan, he was not looking for electronics or samurai swords. He wanted Japanese partners for his $14 million firm who could help in extending HNC's neural network technology into new markets. After nine months, he had secured three agreements. One of them was with Sumitomo Heavy Industries, a major steelmaker, to apply HNC's image-processing system to apple sorting; a production agreement with another steelmaker served to develop a sophisticated chip; and a venture with a large Japanese leasing firm was designed to create a new credit analysis program based on HNC's artificial intelligence capabilities.

Today, HNC is a $195 million company, with 1,100 employees worldwide. It is one example of U.S. firms, mostly high-tech start-ups, seeking partnerships with Japanese companies. Such alliances can secure new markets, profits, and applications without loss of equity. To avoid the risks of investment, many firms are creating nonequity strategic alliances. These can include nonexclusive distribution or licensing deals. For example, Boston-based Avid Technology, a maker of video-editing systems, established a distribution agreement in 1990. One year later, sales in Japan accounted for almost one-fifth of total sales. PeerLogic, a San Francisco–based firm specializing in advanced communications software, signed a licensing agreement with Chori Joho System Co. Says PeerLogic's Bob Scher of the match: "This is not just a licensing agreement, it's a relationship between our two companies. The better they do with our technology, the better we do."

SOURCE: Peter Fuchs, "Strategic Alliances," *Business Tokyo*, April 1991, 22–27; www.hnc.com.

tablished system is in the field of consumer products and the joint venture will produce industrial products.

Second, great care needs to be taken in negotiating the joint venture agreement. In these negotiations, extensive provisions must be made for contingencies. Questions such as profit accumulation and distribution and market orientation must be addressed in the initial agreement; otherwise, they may surface as points of contention over time. A joint venture agreement, although comparable to a marriage contract, should contain the elements of a divorce contract. Changing business conditions and priorities may make a dissolution necessary. Agreements should therefore cover issues

TABLE 15.3 Complementary Strengths Create Value

PARTNER STRENGTH . . .	+	PARTNER STRENGTH . . .	=	JOINT OBJECTIVE
Pepsico marketing clout for canned beverages		Lipton recognized tea brand and customer franchise		To sell canned iced tea beverages jointly
Coca-Cola marketing clout for canned beverages		Nestlé recognized tea brand and customer franchise		To sell canned iced tea beverages jointly
KFC established brand and store format, and operations skills		Mitsubishi real estate and site-selection skills in Japan		To establish a KFC chain in Japan
Siemens presence in range of telecommunications markets worldwide and cable-manufacturing technology		Corning technological strength in optical fibers and glass		To create a fiber-optic cable business
Ericsson technological strength in public telecommunications networks		Hewlett-Packard computers, software, and access to electronics channels		To create and market network management systems

SOURCES: Joel Bleeke and David Ernst, "Is Your Strategic Alliance Really a Sale?" *Harvard Business Review* 73 (January–February 1995): 97–105; and Melanie Wills, "Coca-Cola Proclaims Nestea Time for CAA," *Advertising Age*, January 30, 1995, 2.

such as conditions of termination, disposition of assets and liabilities, protection of proprietary information and property, rights over sales territories, and obligations to customers. In addition, it is important to plan for the continued employment or termination of the people working in a dissolved joint venture.[29]

Finally, joint ventures operate in dynamic business environments and therefore must be able to adjust to changing market conditions. The agreement therefore should provide for changes in the original concept so that the venture can grow and flourish.

Government Consortia   One form of cooperation takes place at the industry level and is typically characterized by government support or even subsidization. Usually, it is the reflection of escalating cost and a governmental goal of developing or maintaining global leadership in a particular sector. A new drug can cost $200 million to develop and bring to market; a new mainframe computer or a telecommunications switch can require $1 billion. To combat the high costs and risks of research and development, **research consortia** have emerged in the United States, Japan, and Europe. Since the passage of the **Joint Research and Development Act** of 1984 (which allows both domestic and foreign firms to participate in joint basic research efforts without the fear of antitrust action), well over 100 consortia have been registered in the United States. These consortia pool their resources for research into technologies ranging from artificial intelligence and electric car batteries to those needed to overtake the Japanese lead in semiconductor manufacturing. (The major consortia in the United States are the Car Battery Consortium and Sematech.) The Europeans have several megaprojects to develop new technologies registered under the names BRITE, COMET, ESPRIT, EUREKA, RACE, and SOKRATES. Japanese consortia have worked on producing the world's highest-capacity memory chip and advanced computer technologies. On the manufacturing side, the formation of Airbus Industries secured European production of commercial jets. The consortium, backed by France's Aerospatiale, Germany's DASA, British Aerospace, and Spain's Construciones Aeronauticas, has become a prime global competitor.

Contractual Arrangements

One final major form international market participation is contractual arrangements. Firms have found this method to be a useful alternative or complement to other international options, since it permits the international use of corporate resources and can also be an acceptable response to government ownership restrictions.

Such an arrangement may focus on cross-marketing, where the contracting parties carry out complementary activities. For example, Nestlé and General Mills have an agreement whereby Honey Nut Cheerios and Golden Grahams are made in General Mills's U.S. plants, shipped in bulk to Europe for packaging at a Nestlé plant, and then marketed in France, Spain, and Portugal by Nestlé.[30] Other contractual arrangements exist for outsourcing. For example, General Motors buys cars and components from South Korea's Daewoo, and Siemens buys computers from Fujitsu. As corporations look for ways to grow simultaneously and focus on their competitive advantage, outsourcing has become a powerful new tool for achieving these goals. Firms increasingly also develop arrangements for contract manufacturing, which allows the corporation to separate the physical production of goods from the research, development, and marketing stages, especially if the latter are the core competencies of the

[29]Manuel G. Serapio, Jr., and Wayne F. Cascio, "End-Games in International Alliances," *Academy of Management Executive* 10 (Number 1, 1996): 62–73.

[30]Richard Gibson, "Cereal Venture Is Planning Honey of a Battle in Europe," *The Wall Street Journal*, November 14, 1990, B1, B8.

firm. Such contracting has become particularly popular in the footwear and garment industries.

In a **management contract,** the supplier brings together a package of skills that will provide an integrated service to the client without incurring the risk and benefit of ownership. The activity is quite different from other contractual arrangements because people actually move and directly implement the relevant skills and knowledge in the client organization.[31] Management contracts can be used by the international marketer in various ways. When equity participation, in the form of either full ownership or a joint venture, is not possible or must be relinquished, a management contract can serve to maintain participation in a venture. Depending on the extensiveness of the contract, it may even permit some measure of control. As an example, the manufacturing process might have to be relinquished to foreign firms, yet international distribution is needed for the product. A management contract could serve to maintain a strong hold on the operation by ensuring that all the distribution channels remain firmly controlled.

Yet management contracts should not be seen as a last line of defense. Whenever lack of expertise exists in a particular venture, management contracts can be a most useful tool to help overcome barriers to international marketing activities. This is particularly useful if an outside party has specialized knowledge that is crucial to international marketing success, whether in the area of distribution technology, marketing know-how, or worldwide contacts. Some companies in the service sector have independent entities that specialize in delivering management services. For example, the German airline Lufthansa manages the operations of various airlines by handling the accounting system, setting salary and customer-service levels, and providing training programs.

A management contract can also be the critical element in the success of a project. A financial institution may gain confidence in a project because of the existence of a management contract and sometimes may even make it a condition of providing the funding.[32]

One specialized form of management contract is the **turnkey operation.** Here, the arrangement permits a client to acquire a complete operational system, together with the skills investment sufficient to allow unassisted maintenance and operation of the system following its completion.[33] The client need not search for individual contractors and subcontractors or deal with scheduling conflicts and difficulties in assigning responsibilities and blame. Instead, a package arrangement permits the accumulation of responsibility in one hand and greatly eases the negotiation and supervision requirements and subsequent accountability issues for the client.

Management contracts have clear benefits for the client. They can provide organizational skills that are not available locally, expertise that is immediately available rather than built up, and management assistance in the form of support services that would be difficult and costly to replicate locally. In addition, the outside involvement is clearly limited. When a turnkey project is on-line, the system will be totally owned, controlled, and operated by the customer. As a result, management contracts are seen by many governments as a useful alternative to foreign direct investment and the resulting control by nondomestic entities.

Similar advantages exist for the supplier. The risk of participating in an international venture is substantially lowered because no equity capital is at stake. At the same

[31]Lawrence S. Welch and Anubis Pacifico, "Management Contracts: A Role in Internationalization?," *International Marketing Review* 7 (1990): 64–74.

[32]Michael Z. Brooke, *Selling Management Services Contracts in International Business* (London: Holt, Rinehart & Winston, 1985), 7.

[33]Richard W. Wright and Colin Russel, "Joint Ventures in Developing Countries: Realities and Responses," *Columbia Journal of World Business* 10 (Spring 1975): 74–80.

time, a significant amount of operational control can be exercised. Clearly, being on the inside represents a strategic advantage in influencing decisions in a number of areas that may be of long-term interest, such as design specifications or sourcing.[34] In addition, existing know-how that has been built up with significant investment can be commercialized. Frequently, the impact of fluctuations in business volume can be reduced by making use of experienced personnel who otherwise would have to be laid off. In industrialized countries like the United States, with economies that are increasingly service based, accumulated service knowledge and comparative advantage should be used internationally. Management contracts permit a firm to do so.

From the client's perspective, the main drawbacks to consider are the risks of overdependence and loss of control. For example, if the management contractor maintains all international relationships, little if any expertise may be passed on to the local operation. Instead of a gradual transfer of skills leading to increasing independence, the client may have to rely more and more on the performance of the contractor.

On the contractor's side, the major risks to consider are (1) the effects of the loss or termination of a contract and the resulting personnel problems, and (2) a bid made without fully detailed insight into actual expenses. Winning a management contract could result in Pyrrhic victories, with the income not worth the expense.

SUMMARY

Foreign direct investment represents a major market-expansion alternative. Although such investment can be carried out by any type of firm, large or small, it typically occurs after some experience has been gathered with alternative forms of internationalization, such as exporting. The most visible and powerful players in the foreign direct investment field are larger-sized firms and multinational corporations. Market factors, barriers to trade, cost factors, and investment climate are the major causes of foreign direct investment, with market factors usually playing the major role.

Different ownership levels of foreign investments are possible, ranging from wholly owned subsidiaries to joint ventures. Although many firms prefer full ownership in order to retain full control, such a posture is often not possible because of governmental regulations. It may not even be desirable. Depending on the global organization and strategic needs of the firm, joint ventures with only partial ownership may be a profitable alternative.

In a joint venture, the partners can complement each other by contributing the strengths and resources that each is best equipped to supply. Joint ventures offer significant benefits in terms of closeness to markets, better acceptance by the foreign environment, and a lessening of the risks involved, but they also pose new problems due to potential clashes of corporate cultures, business orientations, and marketing policies. It is therefore important to select the appropriate joint venture partner and to design an agreement that ensures the long-term approval of all participants.

Strategic alliances, or partnerships, are a special form of joint venture in which the participants, at either the industry or the corporate level, join forces in order to make major strategic progress toward technology development and competitiveness. Given the complexities and cost of technological progress, the number of these alliances, sometimes encouraged through government-sponsored consortia, is rapidly growing.

As countries increasingly develop a service-based economy, the usefulness of contractual arrangements grows. Such contracts can enable the involvement of the international

---

[34]Lawrence S. Welch, "The International Marketing of Technology: An Interaction Perspective," *International Marketing Review* 2 (1985): 41–53.

marketer in a project when equity participation is not possible or desirable. They also permit a client to acquire operational skills and turnkey systems without relinquishing ownership of a project. Because management assistance, service delivery, and project planning are increasingly important, international marketers can use management contracting to carve out a profitable market niche.

QUESTIONS FOR DISCUSSION

1. Will the ongoing improvements in communications technology encourage or discourage foreign direct investments?
2. As a government official, would you prefer the foreign direct investment of a resource seeker, efficiency seeker, or market seeker?
3. Give some reasons why a multinational corporation might insist on 100 percent ownership abroad.
4. At what level of ownership would you consider a firm to be foreign controlled?
5. Do investment-promotion programs of state governments make sense from a national perspective?
6. How can a management contractor have more control than the client? What can the client do under such circumstances?

7. Discuss the benefits and drawbacks of strategic partnerings at the corporate level.
8. The Bureau of Economic Analysis (**www.bea.doc.gov**) and Stat-USA (**www.statusa.gov**) provides a multitude of information about the current state of the U.S. economy. Using the International Investment Tables (D-57), find the current market value of direct investment abroad as well as the value of direct investment in the United States.
9. Find the Fortune Global 500 listing of the world's largest corporations on the *Fortune* web site (**www.fortune.com**). What are the largest corporations in your region? Compare their sales to the GDP of some nations of your choice.

RECOMMENDED READINGS

Belanger, Jacques, Christian Berggren, Torsten Bjorkman, Jacque Belanger, and Christoph Kohler. *Being Local Worldwide: ABB and the Challenge of Global Management.* Ithaca, NY: Cornell University Press, 1999.

Buckley, Peter J., and Pervez N. Ghauri. *The Global Challenge for Multinational Enterprises.* New York: Pergamon Press, 2000.

Doz, Yves L., and Gary Hamel. *Alliance Advantage: The Art of Creating Value through Partnering.* Boston: Harvard Business School Press, 1998.

Dunning, Hohn H., and Rajneesh Narula, eds. *Foreign Direct Investment and Governments: Catalysts for Economic Restructuring.* New York: Routledge, 1998.

Ford, David, Lars-Erik Gadde, Hakan Hakansson, and Anders Lundgren. *Managing Business Relationships.* New York: Wiley, 1998.

Hood, Neil, and Stephen Young. *The Globalization of Multinational Enterprise Activity and Economic Development.* New York: Macmillan, 2000.

International Direct Investment Statistics Yearbook. Paris: Organization for Economic Cooperation and Development, 2000.

Mockler, Robert J. *Multinational Strategic Alliances.* New York: Wiley, 1999.

Moran, Theodore. *Foreign Direct Investment and Development.* Washington, DC: Institute for International Economics, 1998.

Spekman, Robert E., Lynn A. Isabella, and Thomas C. MacAvoy. *Alliance Competence: Maximizing the Value of Your Partnerships.* New York: Wiley, 2000.

Triantis, John E., *Creating Successful Acquisition and Joint Venture Projects: A Process and Team Approach.* New York: Quorum Books, 1999.

Chapter 16

Product and Brand Management

Anatomy of a Global Product Launch

BY THE END OF THE 1980s, with disposable razors taking up 50 percent of the market, executives at Gillette, the $9.3 billion Boston-based consumer products marketer, decided to break out of what they saw as a dead-end strategy. With disposables, the razor had become a commodity, and the buying decision was based solely on price and convenience. Gillette needed a differentiator, a product upon which the brand could be elevated and market share substantially increased. Rather than compete on the existing playing field, management decided to create a new category, the shaving system, and take control of it.

In 1990, after 10 years of research and development, Gillette introduced its Sensor twin-bladed shaving system. The design not only produced a markedly better shave but also brought the company back into an indisputable leadership position. The next step was to see whether three blades could do a better job than two. In order to ensure that consumers did not simply scoff at three blades as a marketing gimmick, the result—and the communication about it—had to be demonstrably better.

A group, code-named the 225 Task Force, worked for five full years in concert with R&D to produce and orchestrate the introduction of a new product, Mach 3. They concentrated as much on developing a great new brand as on developing a great new product. The five years were characterized by ceaseless product improvement, constant product testing around the world, and, eventually, creation of a marketing strategy not only to press the new value propositions but also to substantiate the claims. The marketing strategy was to look at the world as one market and rely on the following premises:

- Because the product would probably take off immediately, manufacturing had to ensure that it had enough capacity to avoid shortages at the outset.
- To facilitate smooth global introduction, all packaging, point-of-sale, and other promotional material had to be the same, simply translated into 30 languages. The company purposefully keeps the number of words on the front of the package to a minimum to avoid the need for design alterations.
- All marketing and advertising was based on a single campaign that was released in every market, again with minor local adjustments and translations. The European introduction was delayed by two months to September 1st to accommodate Europeans on their traditional summer holiday.
- Pricing needed built-in elasticity, but by carefully testing the concept with consumers, Gillette fixed a profitable price point based on the expected number of blades per user per year.

By 2000, Mach 3 had become the success its developers and marketers had planned for. It had captured more than 20 percent of the global blade and razor market. Moreover, market share varied from 13 to 16 percent in all the markets in which it had been launched. Its success is underscored by the introduction of copycats, especially British retailer Asda's Tri-Flex, retailing on the average for $1.00 less than Mach 3.

Product Development Summary for Mach 3

Patents	35 patent protections on Mach 3 and manufacturing processes
Development time	10 years
R&D costs	$200 million
Capital investments	$550 million
Advertising and marketing	$300 million
Launch dates	North America and Israel—July 1, 1998
	Europe—September 1998
	Worldwide—1999
Retail price	Razor, 2 cartridges and organizer: $6.49–$6.99
	Four-pack cartridges: $6.29–$6.79

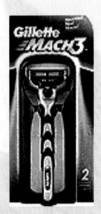

http://www.gillette.com

http://www.mach3.com

SOURCES: Glenn Rifkin, "Mach 3: Anatomy of Gillette's Latest Global Launch," *Strategy & Business* (Number 2, 1999): 34–41;" Gillette Flays Asda over 'Inferior' Tri-Flex Razor," *Marketing Week*, June 10, 1999, 9; and Hamantha S. B. Herath and Chan S. Park, "Economic Analysis of R&D Projects: An Options Approach," *The Engineering Economist* 44 (number 1, 1999): 1–35.

D EVELOPING AND MANAGING a product portfolio in the global marketplace is both a great challenge and an attractive opportunity, as shown in *The International Marketplace 16.1*. While market conditions may warrant changes in individual product features, products and product lines should be managed for the greatest possible effect globally, regionally, and locally. Global and regional products have to exploit to utilize best practice across borders, while local products should be monitored for possible use in other markets.

This chapter is divided into two parts to highlight these issues. The first part will focus on how the product development process can take into account the globalization of markets without compromising dimensions considered essential by local markets. To a large extent this means that the process is market-driven rather than determined by cost or convenience of manufacture. For example, Germany's Volkswagen operated for years under the philosophy that one car was good enough for the whole world, while U.S. marketing executives tried in vain to secure items such as cup holders or seatback release levers in cars destined for the U.S. market.[1]

The second half of the chapter features a discussion of product management, especially how marketers can utilize resources on a worldwide basis to exploit opportunities in product markets. Unilever, one of the world's largest food companies, often has to take a local view, given differences in the daily diet. Similarly, detergent formulas may have to differ between markets because washing habits, machines, clothes, and water quality vary. However, many strategic product decisions, such as branding,

[1]"Auto Marketers Gas Up for World Car Drive," *Advertising Age*, January 16, 1995, 1–16.

will benefit from worldwide experience and exposure applied to the local context. Some categories cross national borders quite well, such as ice cream, tea, and personal wash products, and translate to opportunities with a standard approach.[2]

Global Product Development

Product development is at the heart of the global marketing process. New products should be developed, or old ones modified, to cater to new or changing customer needs on a global or regional basis. At the same time, corporate objectives of technical feasibility and financial profitability must be satisfied.

To illustrate, Black & Decker, manufacturer of power tools for do-it-yourself household repairs, had done some remodeling of its own. With total sales of $1.17 billion, the company in the 1980s was the consummate customizer: the Italian subsidiary made tools for Italians, the British subsidiary for the British. At the same time, Japanese power tool makers, such as Makita Electric Works Ltd., saw the world differently. Makita was Black & Decker's first competitor with a global strategy. Makita management did not care that Germans prefer high-powered, heavy-duty drills and that U.S. consumers want everything lighter. They reasoned that a good drill at a low price will sell from Baden-Baden to Brooklyn. Using this strategy, Makita effectively cut into Black & Decker's market share. As a result, Black & Decker unveiled 50 new models—each standardized for world production.[3]

With competition increasingly able to react quickly when new products are introduced, worldwide planning at the product level provides a number of tangible benefits. A firm that adopts a worldwide approach is better able to develop products with specifications compatible on a worldwide scale. A firm that leaves product development to independent units will incur greater difficulties in transferring its experience and technology.

In many multinational corporations, each product is developed for potential worldwide usage, and unique multinational market requirements are incorporated whenever technically feasible. Some design their products to meet the regulations and other key requirements in their major markets and then, if necessary, smaller markets' requirements are met on a country-by-country basis. For example, Nissan develops lead-country models that can, with minor changes, be made suitable for local sales in the majority of markets. For the remaining situations, the company also provides a range of additional models that can be adapted to the needs of local segments. Using this approach, Nissan has been able to reduce the number of basic models from 48 to 18.[4] This approach also means that the new product can be introduced concurrently into all the firm's markets. Companies like 3M and Xerox develop most of their products with this objective in mind.

Some markets may require unique approaches to developing global products. At Gillette, timing is the only concession to local taste. Developing markets, such as Eastern Europe and China, are first weaned on older, cheaper products before they are sold up-to-date versions.[5] In a world economy where most of the growth is occurring in developing markets, the traditional approach of introducing a global product may keep new products out of the hands of consumers due to their premium price. As a result, Procter & Gamble figures out what consumers in various countries can afford and then develops products they can pay for. For example, in Brazil, the company in-

[2]*Introducing Unilever*, available at **http://www.unilever.com**.

[3]"Black & Decker's Gamble on 'Globalization,'" *Fortune*, May 14, 1984, 40–48.

[4]Kenichi Ohmae, "Managing in a Borderless World," *Harvard Business Review* 67 (May–June 1989): 152–161.

[5]"Blade-runner," *The Economist*, April 10, 1993, 68.

troduced a diaper called Pampers Uni, a less-expensive version of its mainstream product. The strategy is to create price tiers, hooking customers early and then encouraging them to trade up as their incomes and desire for better products grow.[6] For example, Unilever had little deodorant business in Mexico five years ago; now it leads the market.

The main goal of the product development process, therefore, is not to develop a standard product or product line but to build adaptability into products and product lines that are being developed to achieve worldwide appeal.

The Product Development Process

The product development process begins with idea generation. Ideas may come from within the company—from the research and development staff, sales personnel, or almost anyone who becomes involved in the company's efforts. Intermediaries may suggest ideas because they are closer to the changing, and often different, needs of international customers. In franchising operations, franchisees are a source of many new products. For example, the McFlurry, McDonald's ice-cream dessert, was the brainchild of a Canadian operator.[7] Competitors are a major outside source of ideas. A competitive idea from abroad may be modified and improved to suit another market's characteristics. As an example, when the president of d-Con returned from a trip to Europe, he brought with him what would seem in the United States to be an unusual idea for packaging insecticides. In a market dominated by aerosols, the new idea called for offering consumers insect repellent in a "felt-tip pen." d-Con obtained U.S. rights for the product, which in Europe is marketed by Tamana, a subsidiary of Shell Oil.[8]

For a number of companies, especially those producing industrial goods, customers provide the best source of ideas for new products.[9] Many new commercially important products are initially thought of and even prototyped by users rather than manufacturers. They tend to be developed by **lead users**—companies, organizations, or individuals who are ahead of trends or have needs that go beyond what is available at present. For example, a car company in need of a new braking system may look for ideas at racing teams or even at the aerospace industry, which has a strong incentive to stop their vehicles before they run out of runway.[10] Of the 30 products with the highest world sales in the 1990s, 70 percent trace their origins to manufacturing and marketing (rather than laboratories), via customer input.[11] Many companies work together with complementary-goods producers in developing new solutions; Whirlpool and Procter & Gamble developed new solutions for keeping people's clothes clean. With the increased diffusion of the Internet, chat rooms about products and features will become an important source of information pertinent to product development and adjustment. For example, Sony set up a web site to support hackers who are interested in exploring and developing new types of games that could be played on the Sony PlayStation.

For some companies, procurement requisitions from governments and supranational organizations (for example, the United Nations) are a good source of new

[6]Bill Saporito, "Behind the Tumult at P&G," *Fortune*, March 7, 1994, 74–82.

[7]Ben Van Houten, "Foreign Interpreter," *Restaurant Business*, November 1, 1999, 32.

[8]"D-Con Finds New Product Idea in Europe," *Advertising Age*, July 9, 1984, 58.

[9]Eric von Hippel, "Successful Industrial Products from Customer Ideas," *Journal of Marketing* 42 (January 1978): 39–49.

[10]Eric von Hippel, Stefan Thomke, and Mary Sonnack, "Creating Breakthroughs at 3M," *Harvard Business Review* 77 (September–October 1999): 47–57.

[11]"Could America Afford the Transistor Today?" *Business Week*, March 7, 1994, 80–84.

product ideas. When the United Nations Children's Fund (UNICEF) was looking for containers to transport temperature-sensitive vaccines in tropical climates, Igloo Corporation noticed that the technology from its picnic coolers could be used and adapted for UNICEF's use.[12] Facilitating agents, such as advertising agencies or market research organizations, can be instrumental in scanning the globe for new ideas. For example, DDB Needham Worldwide uses U.S. research company Market Access for "search-and-reapply" operations to keep clients informed about new ideas around the world, ranging from half-frozen mineral water in Korea to Argentine yogurt drinks containing cereal and fruit chunks.[13]

Most companies develop hundreds of ideas every year; for example, 3M may have 1,000 new product ideas competing for scarce development funds annually. Product ideas are screened on market, technical, and financial criteria: Is the market substantial and penetrable, can the product be mass produced, and if the answer to both of these questions is affirmative, can the company produce and market it profitably? Too often, companies focus on understanding only the current demand of the consumer. A repositioning of the concept may overcome an initial negative assessment; for example, in countries with no significant breakfast habit, cereal marketers present their products as snacks. Procter & Gamble created the perception that dandruff—traditionally a non-issue for the Chinese—is a social stigma and offered a product (Head & Shoulders anti-dandruff shampoo) to solve the problem. Today, P&G controls more than half the shampoo market in China.[14]

A product idea that at some stage fails to earn a go-ahead is not necessarily scrapped. Most progressive companies maintain data banks of "miscellaneous opportunities." Often, data from these banks are used in the development of other products. One of the most famous examples concerns 3M. After developing a new woven fabric some fifty years ago, 3M's Commercial Office Supply Company did not know what to do with the technology. Among the applications rejected were seamless brassiere cups (too expensive) and disposable diapers. The fabric was finally used to make surgical and industrial masks.[15]

When a new product idea earns a go-ahead, the first pilot models are built. This means a major commitment of funds, especially if the product requires separate facilities and special personnel. In the scale-up phase, which precedes full-scale commercialization, preliminary production units are tested on-site or in limited mini-launches.

All the development phases—idea generation, screening, product and process development, scale-up, and commercialization—should be global in nature with inputs into the process from all affected markets. If this is possible, original product designs can be adapted easily and inexpensively later on. The process has been greatly facilitated through the use of **computer-aided design (CAD)**. Some companies are able to design their products so that they meet most standards and requirements around the world, with minor modifications on a country-by-country basis. The product development process can be initiated by any unit of the organization, in the parent country or abroad. If the initiating entity is a subsidiary that lacks technical and financial resources for implementation, another entity of the firm is assigned the responsibility. Most often this is the parent and its central R&D department.

Larger multinational corporations naturally have development laboratories in multiple locations that can assume the task. Gillette, for example, maintains two toiletries

[12]David DeVoss, "The $3 Billion Question," *World Trade*, September 1998, 34–39.

[13]Laurel Wentz, "World Brands," *Advertising Age International*, September 1996, i–21.

[14]Edward Tse, "The Right Way to Achieve Profitable Growth in the Chinese Market," *Strategy & Business* (Second Quarter 1998): 10–21.

[15]"Herzog: New Products Mean New Opportunities," *International Ambassador*, March 23, 1979, 3.

laboratories, one in the United States and the other in the United Kingdom. In these cases, coordination and information flow between the units are especially critical.

Global companies may have an advantage in being able to utilize the resources from around the world. Otis Elevator Inc.'s latest product, the Elevonic, is a good example of this. The elevator was developed by six research centers in five countries. Otis' group in Farmington, Connecticut, handled the systems integration, Japan designed the special motor drives that make the elevators ride smoothly, France perfected the door systems, Germany handled the electronics, and Spain took care of the small-geared components. The international effort saved more than $10 million in design costs and cut the development cycle from four years to two.[16]

In some cases, the assignment of product development responsibility may be based on a combination of special market and technical knowledge. When a major U.S. copier manufacturer was facing erosion of market share in the smaller copier segment in Europe because of Japanese incursions, its Japanese subsidiary was charged with developing an addition to the company's product line. This product, developed and produced outside the United States, has subsequently been marketed in the United States.

Even though the product development activity may take place in the parent country, all the affected units actively participate in development and market planning for a new product. For example, a subsidiary would communicate directly with the product division at the headquarters level and also with the international staff, who could support the subsidiary on the scene of the actual development activity. This often also involves the transfer of people from one location to another for such projects. For example, when Fiat wanted to build a car specifically for the emerging markets, the task to develop the Palio was given to a 300-strong team which assembled in Turin, Italy. Among them were 120 Brazilians, ranging from engineers to shop-floor workers, as well as Argentines, Turks, and Poles.[17]

The activities of a typical global program are summarized in Figure 16.1. The managing unit has prime responsibility for accomplishing: (1) single-point worldwide technical development and design of a new product that conforms to the global design standard and global manufacturing and procurement standards as well as transmittal of the completed design to each affected unit; (2) all other activities necessary to plan, develop, manufacture, introduce, and support the product in the managing unit as well as direction and support to affected units to ensure that concurrent introductions are achieved; and (3) integration and coordination of all global program activities.

The affected units, on the other hand, have prime responsibility for achieving: (1) identification of unique requirements to be incorporated in the product goals and specifications as well as in the managing unit's technical effort; (2) all other activities necessary to plan, manufacture, introduce, and support products in affected units; and (3) identification of any nonconcurrence with the managing unit's plans and activities.

During the early stages of the product development process, the global emphasis is on identifying and evaluating the requirements of both the managing unit and the affected units and incorporating them into the plan. During the later stages, the emphasis is on the efficient development and design of a global product with a minimum of configuration differences and on the development of supporting systems capabilities in each of the participating units. The result of the interaction and communication is product development activity on a global basis, as well as products developed primarily to serve world markets. For example, Fiat's Palio is designed for the rough roads of the Brazilian interior rather than the smooth motorways of Italy. The car was

Following its instant success with Brazilian customers with sales of over 100,000 units in just six months, the Fiat Palio is now making conquests in the fleet market. The Betim plant is preparing 437 cars for delivery to companies in the São Paolo, Minas Gerais, Goiás, Paraná, Pernambuca, and Mato Grosso areas, among others.

---

[16]"The Stateless Corporation," *Business Week*, May 14, 1990, 98–106.

[17]"A Car Is Born," *Economist*, September 13, 1997, 68–69.

FIGURE 16.1 **Global Program Management**

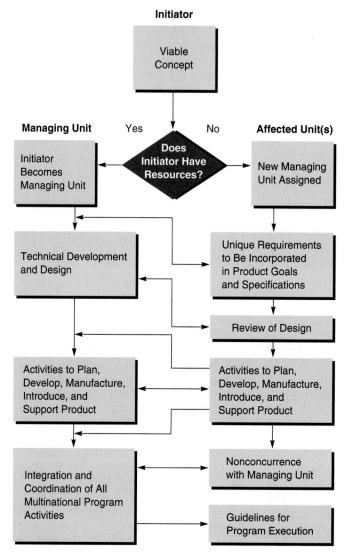

SOURCE: Ilkka A. Ronkainen, "Product Development in the Multinational Firm," *International Marketing Review* 1 (Winter 1983): 24–30.

also deliberately over-engineered, because market research revealed that customers' future preferences were developing that way.

This approach effectively cuts through the standardized-versus-localized debate and offers a clear-cut way of determining and implementing effective programs in several markets simultaneously. It offers headquarters the opportunity to standardize certain aspects of the product while permitting maximum flexibility, whenever technically feasible, to differing market conditions. For instance, in terms of technical development, members of subsidiaries' staffs take an active part in the development processes to make sure that global specifications are built into the initial design of the product.[18]

[18]Ilkka A. Ronkainen, "Product Development in the Multinational Firm," *International Marketing Review* 1 (Winter 1983): 24–30.

The process has to be streamlined in terms of duration as well. In industries characterized by technological change, coming to market nine to twelve months late can cost a new product half its potential revenues. To cut down on development time, companies like NEC and Canon use multidisciplinary teams that stay with the project from start to finish, using a parallel approach toward product launch. Designers start to work before feasibility testing is over; manufacturing and marketing begin gearing up well before the design is finished. Such teams depend on computer systems for designing, simulating, and analyzing products. Toyota Motor Company estimates that it will, sometime in the future, develop a new automobile in one year (its RAV4 mini-sport-utility vehicle was brought to market in 24 months), whereas some of its competitors may spend as much as five years on the process.[19] However, with new uncertain technologies for which market response is not clear, longer development cycles are still common and advisable.[20]

Firms using worldwide product management are better able to develop products that can be quickly introduced into any market.[21] Foreign market introduction can take the form of either production or marketing abroad. In general, the length of the lag will depend on (1) the product involved, with industrial products having shorter lags because of their more standardized general nature; (2) degree of newness; (3) customer characteristics—both demographics and psychographics; (4) geographic proximity; (5) firm-related variables—the number and type of foreign affiliations as well as overall experience in global marketing; and (6) degree of commitments of resources.

While research and development is a highly centralized function in a firm, many allow their research centers to devote part of their time purely to their own endeavors. These initiatives are both effective for the motivation of the local personnel and incubators for future regional and global products. For example, the current research and development activities of consumer-product companies, which tend to be centralized near world headquarters, will have to shift to take into account the increasing numbers of customers who live in emerging markets.

The Location of R&D Activities

Most multinational corporations have located most of their product development operations within the parent corporation. Recently, however, a number of experts have called for companies to start using foreign-based resources to improve their ability to compete internationally. At Asea Brown Boveri, for example, 90 percent of R&D is done in worldwide business units rather than in an isolated business laboratory.[22] Dutch electronics giant Philips once funded all its R&D centrally, but now 70 percent of its funding comes from business units.[23] The benefits are accrued from acquiring international contacts and having R&D investments abroad as ways to add new items to the company's existing product line, thus increasing chances for global success.[24]

[19]Durward K. Sobek, Jeffrey K. Liker, and Allen C. Ward, "Another Look at How Toyota Integrates Product Development," *Harvard Business Review* 76 (July–August 1998): 36–49; "Advantage for Toyota," *The Wall Street Journal*, August 5, 1989, 35.

[20]Edward G. Krubasik, "Customize Your Product Development," *Harvard Business Review* 66 (November–December 1988): 46–52.

[21]Georges LeRoy, *Multinational Product Strategies: A Typology for Analysis of Worldwide Product Innovation Diffusion* (New York: Praeger, 1976), 1–3.

[22]"In the Labs, the Fight to Spend Less, Get More," *Business Week*, June 28, 1993, 102–104.

[23]"For Best Results, Decentralize R&D," *Business Week*, June 28, 1993, 134.

[24]Alphonso O. Ogbuehi and Ralph A. Bellas, Jr., "Decentralized R&D for Global Product Development: Strategic Implications for the Multinational Corporation," *International Marketing Review* 9 (Number 5, 1992): 60–70.

Although the costs are high and recruitment difficult, W. R. Grace opened an $8 million R&D center in Japan. Japan provides the company heightened awareness of and access to technological developments that can be used to be more responsive not only to local markets but to global markets as well. The R&D center is part of Grace's triad approach involving the three leading areas for diffusion of technology: the United States, Europe, and Japan.[25] A dozen other companies, including DuPont, Upjohn, Campbell, and Eastman Kodak, have launched similar centers.[26] For example, Campbell's R&D center in Hong Kong was initially set up to adjust the company's product offering to the Chinese market. It has since acquired a new role of transferring product concepts developed for the Asian market to the Americas and Europe, due to an increasing interest in ethnic foods.

Investments for R&D abroad are made for four general reasons: (1) to aid technology transfer from parent to subsidiary, (2) to develop new and improved products expressly for foreign markets, (3) to develop new products and processes for simultaneous application in world markets of the firm, and (4) to generate new technology of a long-term exploratory nature. The commitment of the firm to international operations increases from the first type of investment to the third and fourth, in which there is no or little bias toward headquarters performing the job.[27]

A sample of 35 U.S.-based and 18 Europe-based multinational corporations was used in an attempt to determine the type of R&D being performed abroad, how the sites were selected how they are managed, and relations with local entities as well as collaborative efforts.[28] In many cases, companies must be close to their markets to satisfy local styles and needs. This strategy or requirement is not limited to consumer-goods companies. Regulations in the pharmaceutical industry often require U.S. companies to have European formulation laboratories.

In truly global companies, the location of R&D is determined by the existence of specific skills. At Ford Motor Company, development of a specific car or component will be allotted to whichever technical center has the greatest expertise, as seen in *The International Marketplace 16.2.* Placing R&D operations abroad may also ensure access to foreign scientific and technical personnel and information, either in industry or at leading universities. Investment in R&D facilities in the United States by non-U.S. companies is heavily concentrated in California's Silicon Valley, New Jersey, and North Carolina's Research Triangle Park.[29] The location decision may also be driven by the unique features of the market. For example, most of the major car makers have design centers in California to allow for the monitoring of technical, social, and aesthetic values of the fifth-largest car market in the world. Furthermore, the many technological innovations and design trends that have originated there give it a trendsetting image.

Given the increasing importance of emerging markets, many marketers believe that an intimate understanding of these new consumers can be achieved only through proximity. Consequently, Unilever has installed a network of innovation centers in 19 countries, many of which are emerging markets (such as Brazil, China, and Thailand).[30]

[25]"W. R. Grace Extends Global R&D to Japan," *Business International*, December 5, 1988, 377, 382.

[26]Susan Moffat, "Picking Japan's Research Brain," *Fortune*, March 25, 1991, 84–96.

[27]Robert Ronstadt, "International R&D: The Establishment and Evolution of Research and Development Abroad by U.S. Multinationals," *Journal of International Business Studies* 9 (Spring–Summer 1978): 7–24.

[28]Jack N. Behrman and William A. Fischer, "Transnational Corporations: Market Orientations and R&D Abroad," in *The Multinational Enterprise in Transition*, ed. Philip D. Grub, et al. (Princeton, NJ: Darwin Press, 1984), 378–389.

[29]Manuel G. Serapio and Donald H. Dalton, "Foreign R&D Facilities in the United States," *Research and Technology Management* (November–December 1993): 33–39.

[30]James A. Gingrich, "Five Rules for Winning Emerging Market Consumers," *Strategy & Business* (Second Quarter 1999): 68–76.

THE INTERNATIONAL MARKETPLACE 16.2

Centers of Excellence

LOCAL MARKETS are absorbing bigger roles as marketers scan the world for ideas that will cross borders. The consensus among marketers is that many more countries are now capable of developing products and product solutions that can be applied on a worldwide basis. This realization has given birth to centers of excellence.

Colgate-Palmolive has set up centers of excellence around the world, clustering countries with geographic, linguistic, or cultural similarities to exploit the same marketing plans. Unilever is extending the innovation centers it opened for personal care products to its food businesses, starting with ice cream. In addition to innovation centers for oral care in Milan and hair care in Paris, there are now similar centers for developing product ideas, research, technology, and marketing expertise for ice cream products in Rome; Hamburg; London; Paris; and Green Bay, Wisconsin; and Bangkok for the Asian market.

Countries have an edge if there is strong local development in a particular product category, such as hair care in France and Thailand, creating an abundance of research and development talent. Local management or existing products with a history of sensitivity to the core competence also helps win a worldwide role for a country unit. For example, ABB Strömberg in Finland was assigned as a worldwide center of excellence for electric drivers, a category for which it is a recognized world leader.

Ford's centers of excellence have been established with two key goals in mind: to avoid duplicating efforts, and to capitalize on the expertise of specialists on a worldwide basis. Located in several countries, the centers will work on key components for cars. One will, for example, work on certain kinds of engines. Another will engineer and develop common platforms—the suspension and other undercarriage components—for similar-sized cars. Designers in each market will then style exteriors and passenger compartments to appeal to local tastes. Each car will usually be built on the continent where it is sold. Ford of Europe introduced the Focus, originally intended to replace the Escort. The one-year time lag between the two continents was to allow the same team of engineers to direct factory launches in both in Europe and North America. Five Ford design studios had to compromise

on design proposals that ranged from a soft, rounded body to a sharply angular one. Although European operations maintained a leadership role, key responsibilities were divided. The U.S. side took over automatic transmissions, with Europe handling the manual version. "If we didn't do it this way, the Americans and the Europeans would have done their own vehicles," says Jacques Nasser, CEO of Ford. "What we have is a shortage of product-development resources, mainly engineering people, and this uses them more efficiently."

Centers of excellence do not necessarily have to be focused products or technologies. For example, Corning has established a Center for Marketing Excellence where sales and marketing staff from all Corning's businesses from glass to television components to electronic communications displays will be able to find help with marketing intelligence, strategies, new product lines, and e-business.

Whatever the format, centers of excellence have as the most important task to leverage and/or to transfer their current leading-edge capabilities, and to continually fine-tune and enhance those capabilities so that they remain state-of-the-art.

SOURCES: Erin Strout, "Reinventing a Company," *Sales and Marketing Management* 152 (February 2000): 86–92; Karl Moore and Julian Birkinshaw, "Managing Knowledge in Global Service Firms: Centers of Excellence," *Academy of Management Executive* 12 (November 1998): 81–92; Laurel Wentz, "World Brands," *Advertising Age International*, September 1996, i–21; "Ford to Merge European, North American Car Units," *The Washington Post*, April 22, 1994, G1–2; and "Percy Barnevik's Global Crusade," *Business Week Enterprise 1993*, 204–211.

http://www.colgate.com

http://www.abb.com

http://www.ford.com

http://www.corning.com

Many companies regionalize their R&D efforts; for example, U.S.-based multinational corporations often base their European R&D facilities in Belgium because of its central location and desirable market characteristics, which include serving as headquarters for the European Union and providing well-trained personnel. Regional centers may also be needed to adequately monitor customer trends around the world.

Sharp, one of Japan's leading electronics companies, has set up centers in Hamburg, Germany, and Mahwah, New Jersey, in addition to its two centers at home.[31]

R&D centers are seen as highly desirable investments by host governments. Developing countries are increasingly demanding R&D facilities as a condition of investment or continued operation, to the extent that some companies have left countries where they saw no need for the added expense. Countries that have been known to have attempted to influence multinational corporations are Japan, India, Brazil, and France. The Chinese government has maintained a preference for foreign investors who have promised a commitment to technology transfer, especially in the form of R&D centers. Volkswagen's ability to develop its business in China is largely due to its willingness to do so. Some governments, such as Canada, have offered financial rewards to multinational corporations to start or expand R&D efforts in the host markets. In addition to compliance with governmental regulation, local R&D efforts can provide positive publicity for the company involved. Internally, having local R&D may boost morale and elevate a subsidiary above the status of merely a manufacturing operation.[32]

In many multinational corporations that still employ multidomestic strategies, product development efforts amount to product modifications—for example, making sure that a product satisfies local regulations. Local content requirements may necessitate major development input from the affected markets. In these cases, local technical people identify alternate, domestically available ingredients and prepare initial tests. More involved testing usually takes place at a regional laboratory or at headquarters.

The Organization of Global Product Development

The product development activity is undertaken by specific teams, whose task is to subject new products to tough scrutiny at specified points in the development cycle to eliminate weak ones before too much is invested in them and to guide promising prototypes from labs to the market.[33] Representatives of all the affected functional areas serve on each team to ensure the integrity of the project. A marketing team member is needed to assess the customer base for the new product, engineering to make sure that the product can be produced in the intended format, and finance to keep costs in control. An international team member should be assigned a permanent role in the product development process and not simply called in when a need arises.

In addition to having international representation on each product development team, some multinational corporations hold periodic meetings of purely international teams. A typical international team may consist of five members, each of whom also has a product responsibility (such as cable accessories) as well as a geographical responsibility (such as the Far East). Others may be from central R&D and domestic marketing planning. The function of international teams is to provide both support to subsidiaries and international input to overall planning efforts. A critical part of this effort is customer input before a new product design is finalized. This is achieved by requiring team members to visit key customers throughout the process. A key input of international team members is the potential for universal features that can be used worldwide as well as unique features that may be required for individual markets.

[31]"Sharp Puts the Consumer on Its New-Product Team," *Business International*, December 14, 1992, 401–402.

[32]Lester C. Krogh, "Managing R&D Globally: People and Financial Considerations," *Research & Technology Management* 14 (July–August 1994): 25–28.

[33]"A Warm Feeling Inside," *Business Week*, December 2, 1991, 70; John Narver and Stanley Slater, "The Effect of Marketing Orientation on Business Profitability," *Journal of Marketing* 54 (October 1990): 20–35.

Such multidisciplinary teams maximize the payoff from R&D by streamlining decision making; that is, they reduce the need for elaborate reporting mechanisms and layers of committee approvals.[34] With the need to slash development time, these teams can be useful. For example, in response to competition, Honeywell set up a multidisciplinary "tiger team" to build a thermostat in twelve months rather than the usual four years.[35]

Challenges to using teams or approaches that require cooperation between R&D centers are often language and cultural barriers. For example, pragmatic engineers in the United States may distrust their more theoretically thinking European counterparts. National rivalries may also inhibit the acceptance by others of solutions developed by one entity of the organization. Many companies have solved these problems with increased communication and exchange of personnel.

With the costs of basic research rising and product life cycles shortening, many companies have joined forces in R&D. The U.S. government and many U.S.-based multinational corporations have seen this approach as necessary to restore technological competitiveness. In 1984, the United States passed the National Cooperative Research Act, which allows companies to collaborate in long-term R&D projects without the threat of antitrust suits. Since then, more than seventy **R&D consortia** have been established to develop technologies ranging from artificial intelligence to those needed to overtake the Japanese lead in semiconductor manufacturing.[36] The major consortia in those fields are *Microelectronics* and *Computer Technology Corporation* and *Sematech*, both founded to match similar Japanese alliances. *The Consortium for Automotive Research* was set up by GM, Ford, and DaimlerChrysler to work on new concepts for use in the automotive sector, such as new battery technology and safety features. Consortia exist in Europe as well, for example, the Joint European Submicron Silicon, which spends $1 billion a year on research.

These consortia can provide the benefits and face the challenges of any strategic alliance. Countering the benefits of sharing costs and risks are management woes from mixing corporate cultures as well as varying levels of enthusiasm by the participants.

The Testing of New Product Concepts

The final stages of the product development process will involve testing the product in terms of both its performance and its projected market acceptance. Depending on the product, testing procedures range from reliability tests in the pilot plant to minilaunches, from which the product's performance in world markets will be estimated. Any testing will prolong full-scale commercialization and increase the possibility of competitive reaction. Further, the cost of test marketing is substantial—on the average, $1 to $1.5 million per market.

Because of the high rate of new product failure estimated at 67–75 percent[37] and usually attributed to market or marketing reasons, most companies want to be assured that their product will gain customer acceptance. They therefore engage in testing or a limited launch of the product. This may involve introducing the product in one country—for instance, Belgium or Ireland—and basing the go-ahead decision for the rest of Europe on the performance of the product in that test market. Some countries

---

[34]"Companies Try New Approaches to Maximize Payoff from R&D," *Business International*, January 25, 1988, 17–21.

[35]"Manufacturers Strive to Slice Time Needed to Develop Products," *The Wall Street Journal*, February 23, 1988, 1, 24.

[36]"Why High-Tech Teams Just Aren't Enough," *Business Week*, January 30, 1989, 63.

[37]Robert G. Cooper and Elko J. Kleinschmidt, "New Product Processes at Leading Industrial Firms," *Industrial Marketing Management* 14 (May 1991): 137–147; David S. Hopkins, "Survey Finds 67% of New Products Fail," *Marketing News*, February 8, 1986, 1.

are emerging as test markets for global products. Brazil is a test market used by Procter & Gamble and Colgate before rollout into the Latin American market. Unilever uses Thailand for a test market for the Asian market.

In many cases, companies rely too much on instinct and hunch in their marketing abroad, although in domestic markets they make extensive use of testing and research. Lack of testing has led to a number of major product disasters over the years. The most serious blunder is to assume that other markets have the same priorities and lifestyles as the domestic market. After a failure in introducing canned soups in Italy in the 1960s, Campbell Soup Company repeated the experience by introducing them in Brazil in 1979. Research conducted in Brazil after the failure revealed that women fulfill their roles as homemakers in part by such tasks as making soups from scratch. A similar finding had emerged in Italy more than twenty years earlier. However, when Campbell was ready to enter the Eastern and Central European markets in the 1990s, it was prepared for this and was careful to position the product initially as a starter or to be kept for emergencies.

Other reasons for product failure are a lack of product distinctiveness, unexpected technical problems, and mismatches between functions.[38] Mismatches between functions may occur not only between, for example, engineering and marketing, but within the marketing function as well. Engineering may design features in the product that established distribution channels or selling approaches cannot exploit. Advertising may promise the customer something that the other functions within marketing cannot deliver.

The trend is toward a complete testing of the marketing mix. All the components of the brand are tested, including formulation, packaging, advertising, and pricing. Test marketing is indispensable because prelaunch testing is an artificial situation; it tells the researcher what people say they will do, not what they will actually do. Test marketing carries major financial risks, which can be limited only if the testing can be conducted in a limited area. Ideally, this would utilize localized advertising media— that is, broadcast and print media to which only a limited region would be exposed. However, localized media are lacking even in developed markets such as Western Europe.

Because test marketing in Europe and elsewhere is risky or even impossible, researchers have developed three research methods to cope with the difficulty. **Laboratory test markets** are the least realistic in terms of consumer behavior over time, but this method allows the participants to be exposed to television advertisements, and their reactions can be measured in a controlled environment. **Microtest marketing** involves a continuous panel of consumers serviced by a retail grocery operated by the research agency. The panelists are exposed to new products through high-quality color print ads, coupons, and free samples. Initial willingness to buy and repeat buying are monitored. **Forced distribution tests** are based on a continuously reporting panel of consumers, but they encounter new products in normal retail outlets. This is realistic, but competitors are immediately aware of the new product. An important criterion for successful testing is to gain the cooperation of key retailing organizations in the market. Mars Confectionery, which was testing a new chocolate malted-milk drink in England, could not get distribution in major supermarkets for test products. As a result, Mars changed its approach and focused its marketing on the home delivery market.[39]

---

[38]Steven C. Wheelwright and W. Earl Sasser, Jr., "The New Product Development Map," *Harvard Business Review* 67 (May–June 1989): 112–125.

[39]Laurel Wentz, "Mars Widens Its Line in U.K.," *Advertising Age*, May 16, 1988, 37.

The Global Product Launch[40]

The impact of an effective global product launch can be great, but so can the cost of one that is poorly executed. High development costs as well as competitive pressures are forcing companies to rush products into as many markets as possible. But at the same time, a company can ill afford new products that are not effectively introduced, marketed, and supported in each market the company competes in.

A global product launch means introducing a product into countries in three or more regions within a narrow time frame. To achieve this, a company must undertake a number of measures. The country managers should be involved in the first stage of product strategy formulation to ensure that local and regional considerations are part of the overall corporate and product messages. A product launch team (consisting of product, marketing, manufacturing, sales, service, engineering, and communication representatives) can also approach problems from an industry standpoint, as opposed to a home country perspective, enhancing product competitiveness in all markets.

Adequate consideration should be given to localization and translation requirements before the launch. This means that right messages are formulated and transmitted to key internal and external audiences. Support materials have to take into account both cultural and technical differences. The advantage of a simultaneous launch is that it boosts the overall momentum and attractiveness of the product by making it immediately available in key geographic markets.

Global product launches typically require more education and support of the sales channel than do domestic efforts or drawn-out efforts. This is due to the diversity of the distribution channels in terms of the support and education they may require before the launch.

A successfully executed global launch offers several benefits. First, it permits the company to showcase its technology in all major markets at the same time. Setting a single date for the launch functions as a strict discipline to force the entire organization to gear up quickly for a successful worldwide effort. A simultaneous worldwide introduction also solves the "lame duck" dilemma of having old models available in some markets while customers know of the existence of the new product. If margins are most lucrative at the early stages of the new product's life cycle, they should be exploited by getting the product to as many markets as possible from the outset. With product development costs increasing and product life cycles shortening, marketers have to consider this approach seriously. An additional benefit of a worldwide launch may be added publicity to benefit the marketer's efforts, as happened with the introductions worldwide of Microsoft's Windows 95, 98, and 2000 versions.

Management of the Product and Brand Portfolio

Most marketers have a considerable number of individual items in their product portfolios, consisting of different product lines, that is, grouping of products managed and marketed as a unit. The options for a particular portfolio (or multiple portfolios) are to expand geographically to new markets or new segments or add to existing market operations through new product lines or new product business. The marketer will need to have a balanced product and market portfolio—a proper mix of new, growing, and mature products to provide a sustainable competitive advantage.[41]

[40]Glenn Rifkin, "Mach 3: Anatomy of Gillette's Latest Global Launch," *Strategy & Business* (Number 2, 1999): 34–41; Robert Michelet and Laura Elmore, "Launching Your Product Globally," *Export Today* 6 (September 1990): 13–15; Laura Elmore and Robert Michelet, "The Global Product Launch," *Export Today* 6 (November–December 1990): 49–52.

[41]George S. Day, "Diagnosing the Product Portfolio," *Journal of Marketing* 41 (April 1977): 9–19.

The assessment of the product portfolio will have to take into account various interlinkages both external and internal to the firm. Geographic interlinkages call attention to market similarities, especially to possibilities of extending operations across borders. Product-market interlinkages are manifested in common customers and competitors. Finally, the similarities in present-day operations should be assessed in terms of product lines, brands, and brand positionings. As a result of such an analysis, Mars has stayed out of the U.S. chocolate milk market, despite a product-company fit, because the market is dominated by Hershey and Nestlé. However, it has entered this particular market elsewhere, such as Europe.

Analyzing the Product Portfolio

The specific approach chosen and variables included will vary by company according to corporate objectives and characteristics as well as the nature of the product market. A product portfolio approach based on growth rates and market share positions allows the analysis of business entities, product lines, or individual products. Figure 16.2 represents the product-market portfolio of Company *A*, which markets the same product line in several countries. The company is a leader in most of the markets in which it has operations, as indicated by its relative market shares. It has two cash cows (United States and Canada), four stars (Germany, Great Britain, France, and Spain), and one "problem child" (Brazil). In the mature U.S. market, Company *A* has its largest volume but only a small market share advantage compared with competition. Company *A*'s dominance is more pronounced in Canada and in the EU countries.

At the same time, Company *B*, its main competitor, although not a threat in Company *A*'s major markets, does have a commanding lead in two fast-growing markets: Japan and Brazil. As this illustration indicates, an analysis should be conducted not only of the firm's own portfolio but also of competitors' portfolios, along with a projection of the firm's and the competitors' future international products—market portfolios.[42] Building future scenarios based on industry estimates will allow Company

| FIGURE | 16.2 | Example of a Product-Market Portfolio |

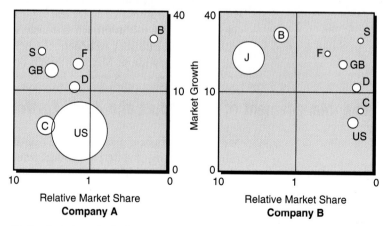

(B=Brazil, C=Canada, D=Germany, F=France, GB=Great Britain, J=Japan, S=Spain, US=United States)

SOURCE: Jean-Claude Larréché, "The International Product-Market Portfolio," in *1978 AMA Educators' Proceedings* (Chicago: American Marketing Association, 1978), 276.

---

[42]Jean-Claude Larréché, "The International Product-Market Portfolio," in *1978 AMA Educators' Proceedings* (Chicago: American Marketing Association, 1978), 276–281.

A to take remedial long-term action to counter Company *B's* advances. In this case, Company A should direct resources to build market share in fast-growing markets such as Japan and Brazil.

In expanding markets, any company not growing rapidly risks falling behind for good. Growth may mean bringing out new items or lines or having to adjust existing products. Between 1996 and 2000, General Motors invested a total of $4 billion in the Brazilian car market, which is the eighth largest in the world. While production capacity of the world's two dozen car makers is more than double the expected demand of 1.1 million cars and all makers were losing money in 1998–1999, GM, with its investments and new models, has positioned itself to take advantage of significant growth rates projected for the future. Volkswagen and Fiat have seen their market shares fall, mainly because they have been milking the market with old models: Volkswagen with the 18-year-old Golf and Fiat with the Uno, which dates back to 1984.[43] GM is not going to be left unchallenged, however. Fiat, for example, is hoping to regain lost ground with the Palio.

Portfolios should also be used to assess market, product, and business interlinkages.[44] This effort will allow the exploitation of increasing market similarities through corporate adjustments in setting up appropriate strategic business units (SBUs) and the standardization of product lines, products, and marketing programs.

The presentation in Figure 16.3 shows a market-product-business portfolio for a food company, such as Nestlé or Unilever. The interconnections are formed by common target markets served, sharing of research and development objectives, use of similar technologies, and the benefits that can be drawn from sharing common marketing experience. The example indicates possibilities within regions and between regions; frozen foods both in Europe and the United States, and ice cream throughout the three mega-markets.

Such assessments are integral in preparing future strategic outlines for different groups or units. For example, at Nestlé, ice cream was identified as an area of global development since the company already had a presence in a number of market areas and had identified others for their opportunity. The U.S. operations had to be persuaded to get more involved; they classified ice cream as a dairy product, whereas corporate planners saw it more as a frozen confectionery. U.S. operations produced machines and cones, and licensed brands to dairies, while corporate planners wanted to move over to self-manufacture and direct store delivery. Currently, Nestlé in the United States ranks second in the impulse-ice segment, and the machinery and cone businesses have been sold.[45]

Advantages of the Product Portfolio Approach

The major advantages provided by the product portfolio approach are as follows:

1. A global view of the competitive structure, especially when longer-term considerations are included
2. A guide for the formulation of a global marketing strategy based on the suggested allocation of scarce resources between product lines
3. A guide for the formulation of marketing objectives for specific markets based on an outline of the role of each product line in each of the markets served—for example, to generate cash or to block the expansion of competition

---

[43]"Even Rivals Concede GM Has Deftly Steered Road to Success in Brazil," *The Wall Street Journal*, February 25, 1999, A1, A8.

[44]Susan P. Douglas and C. Samuel Craig, "Global Portfolio Planning and Market Interconnectedness," *Journal of International Marketing* 4 (Number 1, 1996): 93–110.

[45]Andrew J. Parsons, "Nestlé: The Visions of Local Managers," *The McKinsey Quarterly* 36 (Number 2, 1996): 5–29.

FIGURE 16.3 **Example of Market-Product-Business Portfolio**

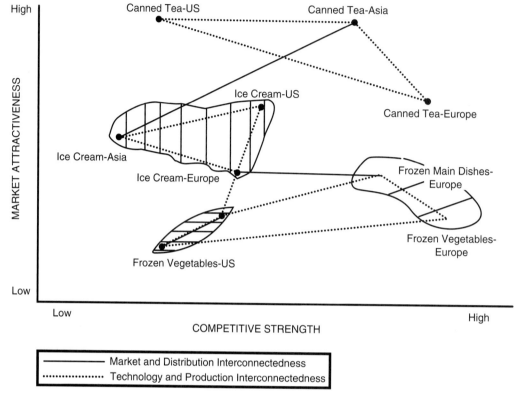

SOURCE: Adapted from Susan P. Douglas and C. Samuel Craig, "Global Portfolio Planning and Market Interconnectedness," *Journal of International Marketing* 4 (Number 1, 1996): 93–110.

---

4. A convenient visual communication goal, achieved by integrating a substantial amount of information in an appealingly simple format including assessment of interlinkages between units and products.

Before making strategic choices based on such a portfolio, the global marketer should consider the risks related to variables such as entry mode and exchange rates; management preferences for idiosyncratic objectives, such as concentrating on countries with similar market characteristics; and marketing costs. For example, the cost of entry into one market may be less because the company already has a presence there and the possibility exists that distribution networks may be shared.[46]

The portfolio assessment also needs to be put into a larger context. The Korean market and Korean automakers may not independently warrant urgent action on the part of the leading companies. However, as part of the global strategic setting in the auto industry, both the market and its companies become critically important. Asia is expected to account for 70 percent of the growth in the world auto market between 2000 and 2004. Korea, along with China and Japan, is one of the three most important vehicle markets in Asia and can be considered an ideal platform for exporting to other parts of the continent. While Korean automakers, such as Daewoo Motor Co. and Samsung Motors, are heavily in debt, acquiring them would carry some benefits.

[46]Yoram Wind and Susan P. Douglas, "International Portfolio Analysis and Strategy, Challenge of the '80s," *Journal of International Business Studies* 12 (Fall 1981): 69–82.

Both Ford and GM want to acquire Daewoo to attain the top-producer position in the world. Renault, which wants to acquire Samsung, sees synergistic benefits in that Samsung relies heavily on technology from Nissan, acquired by Renault earlier. There are also other indirect benefits; whoever acquires Daewoo will gain the number-one spot in Poland, long deemed crucial for tapping growth in Eastern Europe.[47]

Disadvantages of the Product Portfolio Approach   The application of the product portfolio approach has a number of limitations. International competitive behavior does not always follow the same rules as in the firm's domestic market; for example, the major local competitor may be a government-owned firm whose main objective is to maintain employment. With European integration, many believed that the continent's $20 billion appliance business would consolidate into a handful of companies. Whirlpool was the major non-EU company that wanted to take advantage of the emerging opportunity and was expected to gain 20 percent of the market. However, its 12 percent share is testimony that local companies are not standing still while foreigners invade their turf. They have shifted their orientation from local and regional to global by laying off workers, building up core businesses, and focusing on profits.[48]

The relationship between market share and profitability may be blurred by a number of factors in the marketing environment. Government regulations in every market will have an impact on the products a company can market. For instance, major U.S. tobacco manufacturers estimate they could capture 30 percent of Japan's cigarette market of $10 billion a year if it were not for restrictions that apply only to non-Japanese producers.

Product lines offered will also be affected by various local content laws—those stipulating that a prescribed percentage of the value of the final product must be manufactured locally. Market tastes have an important impact on product lines. These not only may alter the content of a product but also may require an addition in a given market that is not available elsewhere. The Coca-Cola Company has market leadership in a product category unique to Japan: coffee-flavored soft drinks. The market came into existence some 20 years ago and grew rapidly, eventually accounting for 10 percent of soft drink sales. The beverage is packaged like any other soft drink and is available through vending machines, which dispense hot cans in the winter and cold servings during warm weather. Although Coca-Cola executives have considered introducing "Georgia" in the United States, they are skeptical about whether the product would succeed, mainly because of declining coffee consumption and the lack of a vending machine network. Also, adoption of the concept by U.S. consumers is doubtful.

The fact that multinational firms produce the same products in different locations may have an impact on consumer perceptions of product risk and quality. If the product is produced in a developing country, for example, the global marketer has to determine whether a well-known brand name can compensate for the concern a customer might feel. The situation may be more complicated for retailers importing from independent producers in developing nations under the retailer's private labels. In general, country-of-origin effects on product perceptions are more difficult to determine since the introduction of hybrid products.

Managing the Brand Portfolio

Branding is one of the major beneficiaries of a well-conducted portfolio analysis. Brands are important because they shape customer decisions and, ultimately, create

---

[47]"Will Renault Go for Broke in Asia?" *Business Week*, February 28, 2000; and "Ford, GM Square Off over Daewoo Motor: The Question Is Why?" *The Wall Street Journal*, February 14, 2000, A1, A13.

[48]"Whirlpool Expected Easy Going in Europe, And It Got a Big Shock," *The Wall Street Journal*, April 10, 1998, A1, A6.

| FIGURE 16.4 | Importance of Brand in Decision Making |

Relative importance of brand

☐ Consumer market ☐ Business market

Type	Brand importance	Location of study
Electronics–computer	39	Europe
Electronics–computer	36	Europe
Electronics–computer	35	Europe
Electrical utilities	25	US
Electronics–computer	26	US
Telecom–international calls	21	US
Airline	21	US
Telecom–inbound calls	20	US
Food beverage	20	US
Telecom–outbound calls	19	US
PFS–retail banking	18	Europe
Telecom–fixed lines	17	Asia
Telecom–mobile	16	US
PFS–retail banking	15	US
Telecom–fixed lines	15	US
Telecom–mobile	15	US
Telecom–fixed line	14	Asia
HMO	14	US
PFS–mortgages	15	Europe
PFS–direct insurance	13	Europe
Car	12	Europe
Electronics–computer	12	US
Electronics–computer	12	US
PFS–mortgages	7	Europe
Telecom–mobile	7	Europe
Telecom–mobile	7	Europe
Electronics–computer	3	US

SOURCE: David Court, Anthony Freeling, Mark Leiter, and Andre J. Parsons, "Uncovering the Value of Brands," *The McKinsey Quarterly* 32 (Number 4, 1996): 176.

economic value. Brand is a key factor behind the decision to purchase in both consumer and business-to-business situations, as shown in the results of a worldwide study summarized in Figure 16.4. On the average, brand was responsible for 18 percent of total purchase decisions, and the majority of the studies revealed a brand-loyal segment of individuals for whom the brand was the major influencing factor. In addition, strong brands are able to charge a price premium of 19 percent.[49] Gillette's Mach 3, although priced more than 50 percent above its predecessor (Sensor Excel), has been able to increase sales by 30 percent since rollout.[50] Research into the connection of brand strength and corporate performance at 130 multinational companies revealed that strong brands generate total returns to shareholders that are 1.9 percent above the industry average, while weaker brands lag behind the average by 3.1 percent.[51]

[49]David C. Court, Anthony Freeling, Mark G. Leiter, and Andrew J. Parsons, "Uncovering the Value of Brands," *The McKinsey Quarterly* 32 (Number 4, 1996): 176–178.

[50]"Everything's at a Premium," *Advertising Age*, August 2, 1999, 12, 15.

[51]David C. Court, Mark G. Leiter, and Mark A. Loch, "Brand Leverage," *The McKinsey Quarterly* 35 (Number 2, 1999): 100–110.

Brands are a major benefit to the customer as well. They simplify everyday choices, reduce the risk of complicated buying decisions, provide emotional benefits, and offer a sense of community. In technology (e.g., computer chips), where products change at an ever-increasing pace, branding is critical—far more so than in packaged goods, where a product may be more understandable because it stays the same or very similar over time. "Intel Inside," which derived from Intel's ad agency recommending "Intel, the Computer Inside" and the Japanese operation's "Intel In It," increased the company's brand awareness from 22 percent to 80 percent within two years of its introduction.[52]

The benefit of a strong brand name is, in addition to the price premium that awareness and loyalty allow, the ability to exploit the brand in a new market or a new product category. In a global marketplace, customers are aware of brands even though the products themselves may not be available. This was the case, for example, in many of the former Soviet Republics, before their markets opened up.

Market power is usually in the hands of brand-name companies who have to determine the most effective use of this asset across markets. The value of brands can be seen in recent acquisitions where prices have been many times over the book value of the company purchased. Nestlé, for example, paid five times the book value for the British Rowntree, the owner of such brands as Kit Kat and After Eight. Many of the world's leading brands command high brand equity values, in other words, the price premium the brand commands times the extra volume it moves over what an average brand commands.[53]

An example of global rankings of brands in provided in Table 16.1. This Interbrand-sponsored study rates brands on their value and their strength. The brand value has been determined using publicly available financial information and market analysis. Brand strength is scored using seven attributes: market, stability, leadership, support, trend, geography, and protection. GE has introduced the tagline "We bring good things to life," across all its marketing communications, and it has set up a number of co-branding and co-marketing agreements with other known brands as a means of leveraging its brand value and ensuring that the GE umbrella covers more. The dot. coms have also appreared on the list: AOL is at 35 ($4.3 billion), Yahoo! at 53 ($1.7 billion), and Amazon.com at 57 ($1.3 billion). This analysis looks at brands, not companies, which means that companies that are all one brand have a better chance of being featured. An assessment has also been made of the portfolio brands; the top five are Procter & Gamble ($49 billion), Johnson & Johnson ($47 billion), Nestlé ($38 billion), Unilever ($34 billion), and L'Oreal ($15 billion).[54]

Brand Strategy Decisions   Global marketers have three choices of branding within the global, regional, and local dimensions: brands can feature the corporate name, have family brands for a wide range of products or product variations, or have individual brands for each item in the product line. With the increase in strategic alliances, cobranding, in which two or more well-known brands are combined in an offer, has also become popular. Examples of these approaches include Heinz, which has a policy of using its corporate name in all its products, Procter & Gamble, which has a policy of stand-alone products or product lines, and Nestlé, which uses a mixture of Nestlé and Nes-designated brands and stand-alones. In the case of marketing alliances, the brand portfolio may be a combination of both partners' brands. General Foods' alliance with Nestlé in cereals, Cereal Partners Worldwide, features General Mills brands such as

[52]Betsy Morris, "The Brand's the Thing," *Fortune*, March 4, 1996, 72–86.

[53]David A. Aaker, *Managing Brand Equity: Capitalizing on the Value of a Brand Name* (New York: Free Press, 1995), 21–33.

[54]Jane Bainbridge, "The World's Biggest Brands," *Marketing*, June 24, 1999, 22–23.

TABLE 16.1	World's Leading Brands			
	BRAND NAME	INDUSTRY	BRAND VALUE ($US M)	BRAND STRENGTH SCORE
1	Coca-Cola	beverages	83,845	82
2	Microsoft	software	56,654	80
3	IBM	computers	43,781	75
4	General Electric	diversified	33,502	71
5	Ford	automobiles	33,197	72
6	Disney	entertainment	32,275	79
7	Intel	computers	30,021	74
8	McDonald's	food	26,231	78
9	AT&T	telecoms	24,181	70
10	Marlboro	tobacco	21,048	74
11	Nokia	telecoms	20,694	64
12	Mercedes	automobiles	17,781	78
13	Nescafé	beverages	17,595	79
14	Hewlett-Packard	computers	17,132	65
15	Gillette	personal care	15,894	80
16	Kodak	imaging	14,830	71
17	Ericsson	telecoms	14,766	63
18	Sony	electronics	14,231	75
19	Amex	financial services	12,550	71
20	Toyota	automobiles	12,310	68
21	Heinz	food	11,806	75
22	BMW	automobiles	11,281	74
23	Xerox	office equipment	11,225	68
24	Honda	automobiles	11,101	64
25	Citibank	financial services	9,147	67

SOURCE: **http://www.marketing.haynet.com/leagues/brand99/tables.htm**

Trix and Nestlé brands such as Chocapic. The alliance between General Mills and Bestfoods, International Dessert Partners, features products with both the Betty Crocker trademark red spoon and and Bestfoods' Maizena brand.[55]

Branding is an integral part of the overall identity management of the firm.[56] Therefore, it is typically a centralized function to exploit to the fullest the brand's assets as well as to protect the asset from dilution by, for example, extending the brand to inappropriate new lines. The role of headquarters, strategic business unit management, global teams, or global managers charged with a product is to provide guidelines for the effort without hampering local initiative at the same time.[57] An example of this effort is provided in *The International Marketplace 16.3*. In addition to the use of a global brand name from the very beginning, many marketers are consolidating their previously different brand names (often for the same or similar products) with

[55]**http://www.generalmills.com/explore/overview**

[56]Bernd Schmitt and Alexander Simonson, *Marketing Aesthetics: The Strategic Management of Brands, Identity, and Image* (New York: Free Press, 1997), Chapter 1.

[57]David Aaker and Erich Joachimsthaler, "The Lure of Global Branding," *Harvard Business Review* 77 (November/December 1999): 137–144.

THE INTERNATIONAL MARKETPLACE 16.3

Development and Management of a Global Brand

IN 1992, BLACK & DECKER launched a new range of professional portable power tools under the DeWalt brand, in response to a global competitive threat from the Japanese Makita that had increased its market share in the fast-growing professional tool market. The company had determined that the quality of Black & Decker professional tools was not what was causing them to lose share to Makita. Instead, the reason was the brand-name perception of Black & Decker among professional contractors. Contractors did not believe in the performance of tools made by the same company that made toaster ovens, popcorn makers, and consumer-grade power tools.

After the successful launch of DeWalt in the United States, the same approach has been used in Australia, Canada, Europe, Latin America, and Asia. A set of guidelines govern the marketing of the brand, which is approaching $1 billion in worldwide sales. Some of the areas covered in the guidelines include the brand's position, logo/color, industrial design, brand

with Black & Decker products in marketing communication programs. All of this allows DeWalt to charge a premium price for their products.

The visual identity program for DeWalt is used to project clearly the image the company wants to project worldwide. The DeWalt logo (shown below) uses bold, capital letters and a solid color (yellow) to project strength. The purpose of this guideline is not only to ensure consistency but also to ensure appropriate legal protection for the brand.

Part of the consistency dimension relates to controlling the industrial design of the tools. The four design centers located in Singapore, Frankfurt, Civate (Italy), and Towson, Maryland, have to adhere to agreed-upon rules with any deviation requiring approval from the global team. Similarly, extending the brand to new products or categories needs approval to avoid dilution of the brand.

As both customers (such as large contractors) and intermediaries (such as Home Depot or Hagebau) are becoming

High Performance Industrial Tools

extensions, and packaging and cataog numbering. In addition to ensuring consistencies, these guidelines also enable country managers to share their best-practice ideals with others in the system. A global team has been set up to monitor these policies as well as to ensure exchange of ideas on the brand.

The DeWalt brand is positioned as the premier brand of tools and accessories for people who make their living using professional grade power tools. This adroit positioning allows efficient target marketing. Although do-it-yourselfers are not part of the targeted effort, they very often choose products used by professionals, thereby broadening the market. As part of this positioning, DeWalt is never combined

more global, packaging standards will have to change. This means one global packaging execution per tool using icon packaging with a country-specific sticker attached. DeWalt is also using one catalog number for each product for all geographic regions.

SOURCE: Courtesy of David Klatt, Black & Decker, March 2000.

http://www.dewalt.com

http://www.blackanddecker.com

global or regional brand names. For example, Mars replaced its Treets and Bonitas names with M&M worldwide and renamed its British best-seller, Marathon, with the Snickers name it uses in North and South America. The benefits in global branding are in marketing economies and higher acceptance of products by consumers and intermediaries. The drawbacks are in the loss of local flavor, especially when a local brand is replaced by a regional or global brand name.

An example of a brand portfolio is provided in Figure 16.5. It indicates four levels of brands at Nestlé: worldwide corporate and strategic brands, regional strategic brands, and local brands. The worldwide brands are under the responsibility of SBU and general management, which establish a framework for each in the form of a planning policy document. These policies lay out the brand's positioning, labeling standards, packaging features, and other related marketing mix issues, such as a communications platform. The same principle applies to regional brands where guidelines are issued and decisions made by SBU and regional management. Among the 7,500 local brands are 700 local strategic brands, such as Brigadeiro in Brazil, which are monitored by the SBUs for positioning and labeling standards. Nestlé is consolidating its efforts behind its corporate and strategic brands. This is taking place in various ways. When Nestlé acquired Rowntree, which had had a one-product one-brand policy, it added its corporate name to some of the products, such as Nestlé Kit Kat. Its refrigerated products line under the Chambourcy brand is undergoing a name change to Nestlé. Some of the products that do not carry the corporate name feature a Nestlé Seal of Guarantee on the back. About 40 percent of the company's sales come from products covered by the corporate brand.[58]

Carefully crafted brand portfolios allow marketers to serve defined parts of specific markets. At Whirlpool, the Whirlpool brand name will be used as the global brand to serve the broad middle market segment, while regional and local brands will cover the others. For example, throughout Europe, the Bauknecht brand is targeted at the upper end of the market seeking a reputable German brand. Ignis and Laden are positioned as price value brands, Ignis Europe-wide, Laden in France. This approach applies to Whirlpool's other markets as well: in Latin America, Consul is the major regional brand.[59]

The brand portfolio needs to periodically and regularly assessed. A number of global marketers are focusing their attention on A-brands with the greatest growth potential. By continuing to dispose of non-core brands, the marketer can concentrate on the global ones and reduce production, marketing, storage, and distribution costs. It is increasingly difficult for the global company to manage purely local brands. The surge of private label products has also put additional pressure on B brands.[60]

However, before disposing of a brand, managers need to assess it in terms of current sales, loyalty, potential, and trends. For example, eliminating a local brand that may have a strong following, has been created by local management, and shows potential to be extended to nearby markets is not necessarily in the best interests of the company.

Private Brand Policies   The emergence of strong intermediaries has led to the significant increase in private brand goods; that is, the intermediaries' own branded products or "store brands." Two general approaches have been used: umbrella branding, where a number of products are covered using the same brand (often the intermediary's name), and separate brand names for individual products or product lines.

With price sensitivity increasing and brand loyalty decreasing, private brand goods have achieved a significant penetration in many countries, as seen in *The International Marketplace 16.4*. The overall penetration of private brand goods in the United

[58]Andrew J. Parsons, "Nestlé: The Visions of Local Managers," *The McKinsey Quarterly* 36 (Number 2, 1996): 5–29.

[59]Ilkka A. Ronkainen and Ivan Menezes, "Implementing Global Marketing Strategy: An Interview with Whirlpool Corporation," *International Marketing Review* 13 (Number 3, 1996): 56–63.

[60]"Unilever's Goal: Power Brands," *Advertising* Age, January 3, 2000, 1, 12; "Why Unilever B-Brands Must Be Cast Aside," *Marketing*, June 10, 1999, 13.

FIGURE 16.5 **Nestlé's Branding Tree**

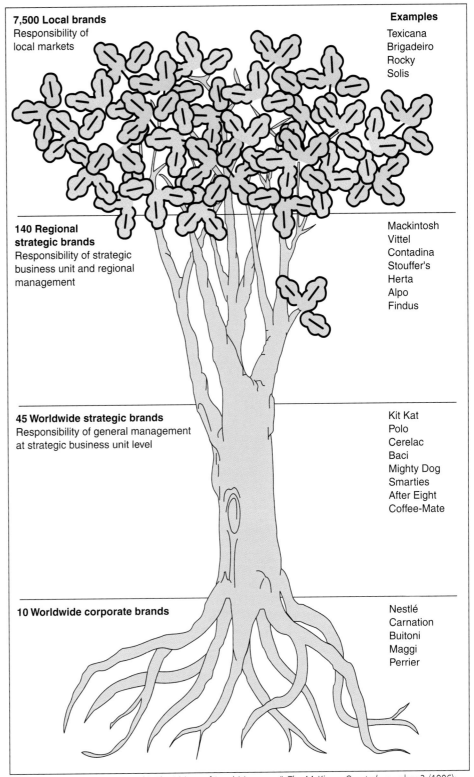

7,500 Local brands
Responsibility of
local markets

Examples
Texicana
Brigadeiro
Rocky
Solis

**140 Regional
strategic brands**
Responsibility of strategic
business unit and regional
management

Mackintosh
Vittel
Contadina
Stouffer's
Herta
Alpo
Findus

45 Worldwide strategic brands
Responsibility of general management
at strategic business unit level

Kit Kat
Polo
Cerelac
Baci
Mighty Dog
Smarties
After Eight
Coffee-Mate

10 Worldwide corporate brands

Nestlé
Carnation
Buitoni
Maggi
Perrier

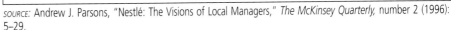

SOURCE: Andrew J. Parsons, "Nestlé: The Visions of Local Managers," *The McKinsey Quarterly,* number 2 (1996): 5–29.
See also **http://www.nestlefaq.com**.

THE INTERNATIONAL MARKETPLACE 16.4

Here Come the Private Brands

CLASSIC COLA, a private brand made by Cott Corporation for J. Sainsbury supermarkets in the United Kingdom, was launched in April 1994 at a price 28 percent lower than that of Coca-Cola. In 1996, the private brand accounted for 65 percent of total cola sales through Sainsbury's and 15 percent of the cola market in the United Kingdom. All across Europe, private brand goods are increasing sales and increasing their presence in more categories.

There has been a significant shift in the way retailers are perceived by consumers. Before 2000, the consumer's prime relationship was with the product manufacturer brand, with retailers being just the intermediary. Now, consumers see themselves as a Safeway or Tesco person, not as a Heinz or BirdsEye person.

Retailers are rearranging their shelves with the result that third-ranking, and even second-ranking, brand names come under pressure. While BSN's Dannon dominates the French yogurt market with 33 percent, second place is held by private brands—ahead of both Yoplait and Nestlé.

Among the pioneers of private brand products were such British stores as J. Sainsbury (in 1869) and Marks & Spencer. Marks & Spencer is considered Britain's most successful private brand purveyor, selling not only chocolate, snacks, and smoked salmon under its St. Michael brand, but also shirts and underwear. Private brands are also popular in the Netherlands and Switzerland and are growing in Spain, through the expansion of French chains. In Italy, laws restricting the development of chain stores have slowed down the growth.

Some stores, such as the German Aldi, sell only their own brand. Being the twentieth-largest retailer in the world, Aldi is now reaching beyond its borders. Already the market leader in Germany and Belgium, it is ranked the seventh largest European grocery retailer, with operations expanding throughout the United Kingdom and the continent. Aldi has one-quarter of the German food market for the goods it sells, largely basic goods. In 2000, Aldi began plans to penetrate Australia. Aldi "engineers" food, say industry analysts, cutting costs rather than quality, permitting it to drive out low-quality brands that trade only on price.

Other chains, such as French Carrefour, have tried to block Aldi by launching their own private brand products as bottom-of-the-line, low-priced goods, only to discover that profit margins were unacceptable. Today, they position them against the better brands on quality—but at a price of lower-quality goods. At the same time, manufacturers are defending their brands by increasing research and development budgets and focusing on product innovations.

SOURCES: "Michael Evamy, "Own-Label Ranges Enjoy a Makeover," *Marketing*, August 5, 1999, 25–26; John A. Quelch and David Harding, "Brands Versus Private Label: Fighting to Win," *Harvard Business Review* 74 (January–February 1996): 99–109; *Global Retailing 2000* (Columbus, OH: Management Horizons, 1993); "Retailers Hungry for Store Brands," *Advertising Age*, January 11, 1993, 20; and "Europeans Witness Proliferation of Private Labels," *The Wall Street Journal*, October 20, 1992, B1, B5; "The Billionaire Brothers Grim," *The Australian*, March 24, 2000, p. 34, Marins Benson.

Kingdom is 30 percent, in Germany 23 percent, in Switzerland 23 percent, and in France 20 percent. Over the past 20 years, private brand sales in the United States have averaged 14 percent of supermarket sales. As both the trade and consumers become more sophisticated, private brands' market share is expected to reach U.K. levels in many parts of Europe and the world.

While private brand success can be shown to be affected strongly by economic conditions and the self-interest of retailers who want to improve their bottom lines through the contribution of private label goods, new factors have emerged to make the phenomenon more long-lived and significant in changing the product choices worldwide. The level of private brand share will vary by country and by product category reflecting variations in customer perceptions, intermediary strength, and behavior of leading branders.[61]

[61]David Dunne and Chakravarthi Narasimhan, "The New Appeal of Private Labels," *Harvard Business Review* 77 (May–June 1999): 41–52; John A. Quelch and David Harding, "Brands Versus Private Labels," *Harvard Business Review* 74 (January–February 1996): 99–109.

TABLE 16.2 Private Brand Strategies

STRATEGY	RATIONALE	CIRCUMSTANCE
No participation	Refusal to produce private label	Heavily branded markets; high distinctiveness; technological advantage
Capacity filling	Opportunistic	
Market control	Influence category sales	High brand shares where distinctiveness is less; more switching by consumers
Competitive leverage	Stake in both markets	
Chief source of business	Major focus	Little or no differentiation by consumers
Dedicated producer	Leading cost position	

SOURCE: Adapted from François Glémet and Rafael Mira, "The Brand Leader's Dilemma," *The McKinsey Quarterly* 33 (Number 2, 1993): 4.

The improved quality of private brand products and the development of segmented private brand products have been major changes in the last ten years. While 60 percent of consumers still state that they prefer the comfort, security, and value of a manufacturer's brand over a private brand, as found in a DDB Needham survey,[62] a McKinsey survey found most consumers preferring such products also had no hesitation in buying the private brand.[63] Encouraged by this, private brands have been expanding to new product categories with the hope of increased acceptance by consumers.[64] Beyond just offering products, many retailers are focusing on a broader approach. For example, Tesco in the United Kingdom has focused on the design of its own-label products with the goal of projecting a more uniform image across product categories. Some premium private brand products have been developed to reposition manufacturer's brands. In Canada, for example, Loblaw's President's Choice brand and its regular private brand line squeeze national brands in between the two. Some U.S. chains have also started carrying this line of premium products.

European supermarket chains have had enormous success with private brands mainly due to their power over manufacturers. While the five largest operators in the United States command only 21 percent of supermarket sales, the figure in the United Kingdom is 62 percent, and in Finland the four leading wholesaler-led chains control over 90 percent. With the emergence of new types of intermediaries, such as mass merchandisers and warehouse clubs, this phenomenon will expand as these players exercise their procurement clout over manufacturers. Furthermore, many retailers believe that strong private brand programs can successfully differentiate their outlets and solidify shoppers' loyalty, thereby strengthening their position vis-à-vis manufacturers, and resulting in increasing profitability.

With the increasing opportunities in the private brand categories, the marketing manager will have to make critical strategic choices, which are summarized in Table 16.2. If the marketer operates in an environment where consumers have an absolute preference for manufacturers' brands and where product innovation is a critical factor of success, the marketer can refuse to participate. Brand leaders can attack private

[62]"Shoot Out at the Check-Out," *The Economist*, June 5, 1993, 69–72.

[63]François Glémet and Rafael Mira, "The Brand Leader's Dilemma," *The McKinsey Quarterly* 33 (Number 2, 1993): 3–15.

[64]"Retailers Hungry for Store Brands," *Advertising Age*, January 11, 1993, 20.

brands and thereby direct their ambitions on smaller competitors, which often may be local-only players. The argument for strategic participation is that since the phenomenon cannot be eliminated, it is best to be involved. Reasons include capacity filling, economies of scale, improved relationships with trade, and valuable information about consumer behavior and costs. The argument that profits from private brand manufacture can be used for promotion of the manufacturer's own brands may be eliminated by the relatively thin margins and the costs of having to set up a separate private brand manufacturing and marketing organization. Participation in the private brand category may, however, be inconsistent with the marketer's global brand and product strategy by raising questions about quality standards, by diluting management attention, and by affecting consumers' perception of the main branded business. Many marketers pursue a mixture of these strategies as a function of marketing and market conditions. Wilkinson Sword, for example, produces private brand disposable razors for the most dominant chain in Finland, the K-Group, thereby enabling it to compete on price against other branded products (especially the French Bic) and increasing its share of shelf space. While H.J. Heinz produces insignificant amounts for private brand distributors in the United States, most of its U.K. production is for private brand.

SUMMARY

The global product planning effort must determine two critical decisions: (1) how and where the company's products should be developed, and (2) how and where the present and future product lines should be marketed.

In product development, multinational corporations are increasingly striving toward finding common denominators to rationalize worldwide production. This is achieved through careful coordination of the product development process by worldwide or regional development teams. No longer is the parent company the only source of new products. New product ideas emerge throughout the system and are developed by the entity most qualified to do so.

The global marketer's product line is not the same worldwide. The standard line items are augmented by local items or localized variations of products to better cater to the unique needs of individual markets. External variables such as competition and regulations often determine the final composition of the line and how broadly it is marketed.

Global marketers will also have to determine the extent to which they will use one of their greatest asset, brands, across national markets. Marketers will have to choose between global brands, regional brands, and purely local approaches as well as forgoing their own branding in favor of becoming a supplier for private brand efforts of retailers.

QUESTIONS FOR DISCUSSION

1. How can a company's product line reflect the maxim "think globally, act locally"?
2. Will a globally oriented company have an advantage over a multidomestic, or even a domestic, company in the next generation of new product ideas?
3. What factors should be considered when deciding on the location of research and development facilities?
4. What factors make product testing more complicated in the international marketplace?
5. What are the benefits of a coordinated global product launch? What factors will have to be taken into consideration before the actual launch?
6. Argue for and against the use of the corporate name in global branding.

Using the list of the world's leading brands (available at **www.marketing.haynet.com/leagues/brand99/index.htm**), evaluate why certain brands place high, some lower. Speculate on the future of, for example, the dot.coms.

8. Using the Mach 3 as an example, evaluate how the different country Web sites of Gillette (accessible through **www.gillette.com**) support its worldwide brand effort.

RECOMMENDED READINGS

Aaker, David A. *Building Strong Brands.* New York: The Free Press, 1996.

Cooper, Robert G. *Product Leadership: Creating and Launching Superior New Products.* New York: Perseus Books, 1998.

Deschamps, Jean-Philippe, and P. Raganath Nayak. *Product Juggernauts: How Companies Mobilize to Generate a Stream of Market Winners.* Boston: Harvard Business School Press, 1995.

Kapferer, Jean-Noël. *Strategic Brand Management.* New York: The Free Press, 1992.

Keller, Kevin L. *Strategic Brand Management: Building, Measuring, and Managing Brand Equity.* New York: Prentice Hall, 1997.

Kitcho, Catherine. *High Tech Product Launch.* Mountain View, CA: Pele Publications, 1999.

Kotabe, Masaaki. *Global Sourcing Strategy: R&D, Manufacturing, and Marketing Interfaces.* Greenwich, CT: Greenwood Publishing Group, 1992.

Macrae, Chris. *The Brand Chartering Handbook.* Harlow, England: Addison-Wesley, 1996.

Ries, Laura, and Al Ries. *The 22 Immutable Laws of Branding: How to Build a Product or Service into a World-Class Brand.* New York: Harper Collins, 1998.

Schmitt, Bernd, and Alexander Simonson. *Marketing Aesthetics: The Strategic Management of Brands, Identity and Image.* New York, The Free Press, 1997.

Services Marketing

Chapter 17

THE INTERNATIONAL MARKETPLACE 17.1

The Global Temp

THE TEMPORARY HELP business is going global. Once a business that consisted almost exclusively of local orders for secretaries and assembly line workers, big temp help companies now routinely scramble for huge national contracts to supply all the temporary help needs of big corporations. Now, some of those same employment services companies are gearing up for the next big battle—a fight over international business, as the demand for "flexible staffing" crosses borders.

The information and telecommunications industries are particularly short-handed in industrialized nations. As a result, many efforts are underway to procure highly trained temporary labor. In each year from 2001 to 2003, the United States will issue 195,000 temporary visas to skilled IT workers from overseas, 80,000 more than in 2000. In Germany, Chancellor Schroeder sketched plans to issue work permits for engineers, programmers and other information technology specialists from outside the European Union.

Temporary help companies are finding that farflung networks outside their home countries are big assets as their customers expand internationally. "We like to be a preferred supplier, and if it's on a global scale, we have the horses out there," says Manpower chairman Mitchell Fromstein.

Increasingly, that means taking staffing services to the doorsteps of international clients. In an office opposite Northern Telecom Ltd.'s headquarters in Toronto, Manpower fields toll-free calls for temporary workers from Northern Telecom managers in the United States, Canada, and Mexico. Manpower also stations managers at five other Northern Telecom locations in the United States and Canada to coordinate the hiring of temps.

Manpower enabled Northern Telecom to shrink its list of North American temporary help suppliers from 125 in the early 1990s to one. On any given day, Manpower might supply Northern Telecom with some 2,000 temporaries, ranging from office workers to telecommunications equipment installers. Instead of hundreds of invoices each month, Northern Telecom now deals with "one bill, one company and one point of contact," says Joe Simeone, the company's director of supply and services. Now, Manpower and Northern Telecom are talking about extending their relationship overseas—something Manpower has already done with computer giant Hewlett-Packard Co.

Industry giants aren't the only ones finding a need to cross borders with their temporary help and other staffing needs. W.H. Brady Co., a Milwaukee-based maker of identification and specialty tape products, recently hired Manpower to supply temporary workers and help recruit new full-time workers in about a dozen countries in which the company does business. Turning the work over to Manpower allowed Brady to redeploy some human resource workers to other jobs. "For the first time, we know what it costs to do recruiting, because we pay Manpower," says Katherine Hudson, Brady's chief executive officer. It also fits a goal of Hudson and a growing number of executives, in the United States and Europe, to create a "buffer" of temporary workers to help shield full-time workers from dismissal should times get tough or markets change.

In Europe, rigid rules on hiring and firing full-time workers make temporary help an attractive alternative. From Madrid to Manchester, England, temporary help offices are sprouting up as the leading players rush to build market share. Industry experts in Europe expect annual revenue growth of 10 to 15 percent over the next decade.

For the most part, temporary help companies export their expertise, not their workers. But even that is changing. Randstad says it recently signed a contract to send about 20 aircraft engineers from the Netherlands to temporary jobs with Boeing Co. in Seattle. And when phone calls flood a customer service center that Manpower staffs for a big computer company in Britain, Manpower sends the overflow to the United States. For callers, the only thing that changes is the accent at the other end of the line.

SOURCES: "Schroeder Outlines 'Green Card' Plan to Address High Tech Labor Shortage," *The Week in Germany*, March 17, 2000: 1; and Robert Rose, "Temporary-Help Firms Start New Game: Going Global," *The Wall Street Journal*, May 16, 1996, B4; Jennifer Schu "Extra Visas Offer Relief to Companies Hungry for IT Workers," February 16, 2001, www.workforce.com, accessed April 17, 2001.

www.oecd.org

INTERNATIONAL SERVICES MARKETING is a major component of world business. As *The International Marketplace 17.1* shows, a wide variety of services can be marketed globally. This chapter will highlight marketing dimensions that are specific to services, with particular attention to their international aspects. A discussion of the differences between the marketing of services and of goods will be followed by insights on the role of services in the United States and in the world economy. The chapter will explore the opportunities and new problems that have arisen from the increase in international services marketing, focusing particularly on the worldwide transformations of industries as a result of profound changes in the environment and in technology. The strategic responses to these transformations by both governments and firms will be described. Finally, the chapter will outline the initial steps that firms need to undertake in order to offer services internationally—and will look at the future of international services marketing.

Differences between Services and Goods

We rarely contemplate or analyze the precise role of services in our lives. Services often accompany goods, but they are also, by themselves, an increasingly important part of our economy, domestically and internationally. One writer has contrasted services and products by stating that "a good is an object, a device, a thing; a service is a deed, a performance, an effort."[1] This definition, although quite general, captures the essence of the difference between goods and services. Services tend to be more intangible, personalized, and custom-made than goods. Services are also often marketed differently from goods. While goods are typically distributed to the customer, services can be transferred across borders or originated abroad, and the service provider can be transferred to the customer or the customer can be transferred to the service territory. Services also are typically using a different approach to customer satisfaction. It has been stated that "service firms do not have products in the form of preproduced solutions to customers' problems; they have processes as solutions to such problems."[2]

Services are the fastest-growing sector of world trade, and U.S. service firms in particular have been consistently able to increase their world market share.[3] These major

[1] Leonard L. Berry, "Services Marketing Is Different," in *Services Marketing*, ed. Christopher H. Lovelock (Englewood Cliffs, NJ: Prentice-Hall, 1984), 30.

[2] Christian Grönroos, "Marketing Services: The Case of a Missing Product," *Journal of Business & Industrial Marketing* 13 (Number 4/5, 1998): 322–338.

[3] *Services: Statistics on International Transactions 1970–1989* (Paris: Organization for Economic Cooperation and Development, 1992).

Services as a Portion of Gross Domestic Product

Services as a percent of GDP

- 61% to 85%
- 41% to 60%
- 21% to 40%
- 0% to 20%
- No current data available

Source: *2001 World Development Indicators*, The World Bank.

differences add dimensions to services that are not present in goods and thus call for a major differentiation.

Linkage between Services and Goods

Services may complement goods; at other times, goods may complement services. Offering goods that are in need of substantial technological support and maintenance may be useless if no proper assurance for service can be provided. For this reason, the initial contract of sale often includes the service dimension. This practice is frequent in aircraft sales. When an aircraft is purchased, the buyer often contracts not only for the physical good—namely, the plane—but also for training of personnel, maintenance service, and the promise of continuous technological updates. Similarly, the sale of computer hardware is critically linked to the availability of proper servicing and software.

This linkage between goods and services can make international marketing efforts quite difficult. A foreign buyer, for example, may wish to purchase helicopters and contract for service support over a period of ten years. If the sale involves a U.S. firm, both the helicopter and the service sale will require an export license. Such licenses, however, are issued only for an immediate sale. Therefore, over the ten years, the seller will have to apply for an export license each time service is to be provided. Because the issuance of a license is often dependent on the political climate, the buyer and seller are haunted by uncertainty. As a result, sales may be lost to firms in countries that can unconditionally guarantee the long-term supply of support services.

Services can be just as dependent on goods. For example, an airline that prides itself on providing an efficient reservation system and excellent linkups with rental cars and hotel reservations could not survive without its airplanes. As a result, many offerings in the marketplace consist of a combination of goods and services. A graphic illustration of the tangible and intangible elements in the market offering of an airline is provided in Figure 17.1.

The simple knowledge that services and goods interact, however, is not enough. Successful managers must recognize that different customer groups will frequently view the service/good combination differently. The type of use and usage conditions will also affect evaluations of the market offering. For example, the intangible dimension of "on-time arrival" by airlines may be valued differently by college students than by business executives. Similarly, a 20-minute delay will be judged differently by a passenger arriving at her final destination than by one who has just missed an overseas connection. As a result, adjustment possibilities in both the service and the goods area can be used as strategic tools to stimulate demand and increase profitability. As Figure 17.2 shows, service and goods elements may vary substantially. The marketer must identify the role of each and adjust all of them to meet the desires of the target customer group. By rating the offerings on a scale ranging from dominant tangibility to dominant intangibility, the marketer can obtain a mechanism for comparison between offerings and also information for subsequent market positioning strategies.

Stand-Alone Services

Services do not always come in unison with goods. Increasingly, they compete against goods and become an alternative offering. For example, rather than buy an in-house computer, the business executive can contract computing work to a local or foreign service firm. Similarly, the purchase of a car (a good) can be converted into the purchase of a service by leasing the car from an agency.

Services may also compete against each other. As an example, a store may have the option of offering full service to consumers who purchase there or of converting to the self-service format. Only checkout services may be provided by the store, with

FIGURE 17.1   Tangible and Intangible Offerings of Airlines

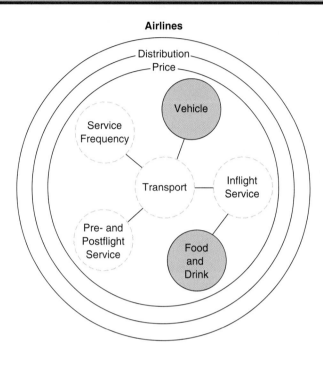

SOURCE: G. Lynn Shostack, "Breaking Free from Product Marketing," in *Services Marketing*, ed. Christopher H. Lovelock (Englewood Cliffs, NJ: Prentice-Hall, 1984), 40.

consumers engaging in other activities such as selection, transportation, and sometimes even packaging and pricing.

Services differ from goods most strongly in their **intangibility:** They are frequently consumed rather than possessed. Even though the intangibility of services is a primary differentiating criterion, it is not always present. For example, publishing services ultimately result in a tangible good, namely, a book or an article. Similarly, construction services eventually result in a building, a subway, or a bridge. Even in those instances, however, the intangible component that leads to the final product is of major concern to both the producer of the service and the recipient of the ultimate output because it brings with it major considerations that are nontraditional to goods.

One major difference concerns the storing of services. Because of their nature, services are difficult to inventory. If they are not used, the "brown around the edges" syndrome tends to result in high services **perishability.** Unused capacity in the form of an empty seat on an airplane, for example, becomes nonsaleable quickly. Once the plane has taken off, selling an empty seat is virtually impossible—except for an inflight upgrade from coach to first class—and the capacity cannot be stored for future usage. Similarly, the difficulty of inventorying services makes it troublesome to provide service backup for peak demand. To maintain **service capacity** constantly at levels necessary to satisfy peak demand would be very expensive. The marketer must therefore attempt to smooth out demand levels in order to optimize the use of capacity.

FIGURE 17.2 **Scale of Elemental Dominance**

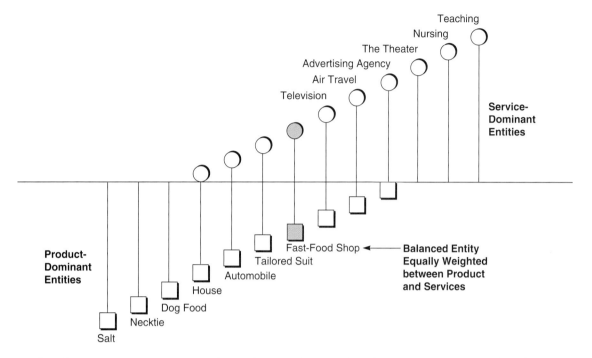

SOURCE: G. Lynn Shostack, "How to Design a Service," in *Marketing of Services*, eds. J. Donnelly and W. George, 1981, p. 222, published by the American Marketing Association.

For many service offerings, the time of production is very close to or even simultaneous with the time of consumption. This fact points toward close **customer involvement** in the production of services. Customers frequently either service them-

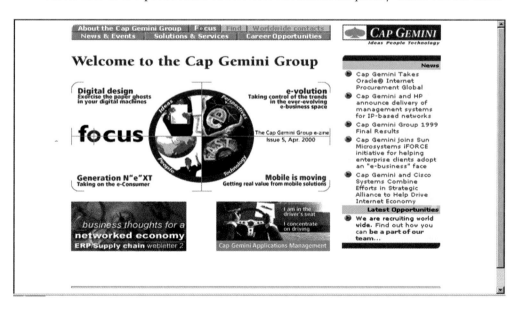

Firms such as Cap Gemini, based in France, market IT Consulting Services worldwide.
www.capgemini.com

selves or cooperate in the delivery of services. As a result, the service provider often needs to be physically present when the service is delivered. This physical presence creates both problems and opportunities, and it introduces a new constraint that is seldom present in the marketing of goods. For example, close interaction with the customer requires a much greater understanding of and emphasis on the cultural dimension. A good service delivered in a culturally unacceptable fashion is doomed to failure. Sensitivity to culture, beliefs, and preferences is imperative in the services industry. In some instances, the need to be sensitive to diverse customer groups in domestic markets can assist a company greatly in preparing for international market expansion. Figure 17.3 provides an example of such a situation. A common pattern of internationalization for service businesses is therefore to develop stand-alone business systems in each country. At the same time, however, some services have become "de-localized" as advances in modern technology have made it possible for firms to delink production and service processes and switch labor-intensive service performance to countries where qualified, low-cost labor is plentiful.

The close interaction with customers also points toward the fact that services often are custom-made. This contradicts the desire of a firm to standardize its offering; yet at the same time, it offers the service provider an opportunity to differentiate the service from the competition. The concomitant problem is that in order to fulfill customer expectations, **service consistency** is required. As with anything offered on-line, however, consistency is difficult to maintain over the long run. The human element in the service offering therefore takes on a much greater role than in the offering of goods. Errors can enter the system, and nonpredictable individual influences can affect the outcome of the service delivery. The issue of quality control affects the provider as well as the recipient of services. In fact, efforts to increase such control

FIGURE 17.3   A Culturally Sensitive Telephone Number

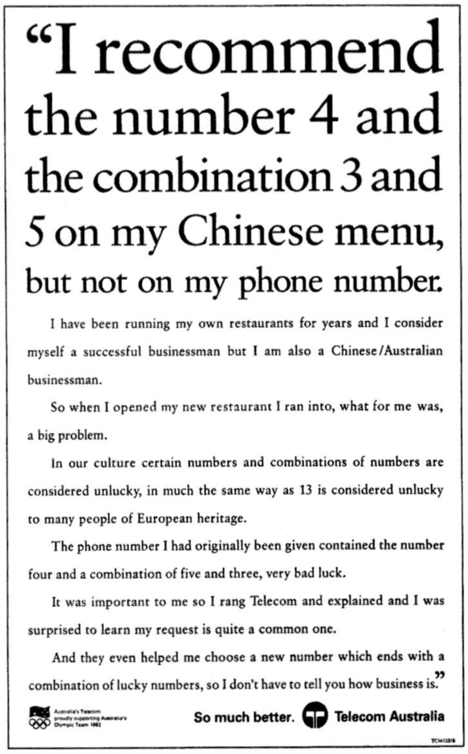

"I recommend the number 4 and the combination 3 and 5 on my Chinese menu, but not on my phone number.

I have been running my own restaurants for years and I consider myself a successful businessman but I am also a Chinese/Australian businessman.

So when I opened my new restaurant I ran into, what for me was, a big problem.

In our culture certain numbers and combinations of numbers are considered unlucky, in much the same way as 13 is considered unlucky to many people of European heritage.

The phone number I had originally been given contained the number four and a combination of five and three, very bad luck.

It was important to me so I rang Telecom and explained and I was surprised to learn my request is quite a common one.

And they even helped me choose a new number which ends with a combination of lucky numbers, so I don't have to tell you how business is."

So much better.   Telecom Australia

through uniform service may sometimes be perceived by customers as a limiting of options. It may therefore have a negative market effect.[4]

Buyers have more problems in observing and evaluating services than goods. This is particularly true when a shopper tries to choose intelligently among service providers. Even when sellers of services are willing and able to provide more **market transparency** where the details of the service are clear, comparable, and available to all interested parties, the buyer's problem is complicated: Customers receiving the same service may use it differently and service quality may vary for each delivery. Since production lines cannot be established to deliver an identical service each time, and the quality of a service cannot be tightly controlled, the problem of service heterogeneity emerges,[5] meaning that services may never be the same from one delivery to another. For example, a teacher's counsel, even if it is provided on the same day by the same person, may vary substantially depending on the student. Over time, even for the same student, the counseling may change. As a result, service offerings are not directly comparable, which makes quality measurements quite challenging. Therefore, the reputation of the service provider plays an overwhelming role in the customer choice process.

Services often require entirely new forms of distribution. Traditional channels are often multitiered and long and therefore slow. They often cannot be used because of the perishability of services. A weather news service, for example, either reaches its audience quickly or rapidly loses its value. As a result, direct delivery and short distribution channels are often required. When they do not exist—which is often the case domestically and even more so internationally—service providers need to be distribution innovators in order to reach their market.

All these aspects of services exist in both international and domestic settings. However, their impact takes on greater importance for the international marketer. For example, because of the longer distances involved, service perishability that may be an obstacle in domestic business becomes a barrier internationally. Similarly, the issue of quality control for international services may be much more difficult to deal with due to different service uses, changing expectations, and varying national regulations.

Because services are delivered directly to the user, they are frequently much more sensitive to cultural factors than are products. Sometimes their influence on the individual may even be considered with hostility abroad. For example, the showing of U.S. films in cinemas or television abroad is often attacked as an imposition of U.S. culture. National leaders who place strong emphasis on national cultural identity frequently denounce foreign services and attempt to hinder their market penetration. Similarly, services are subject to many political vagaries occurring almost daily. Yet coping with these changes can become the competitive advantage of the service provider.

The Role of Services in the U.S. Economy

Since the industrial revolution, the United States has seen itself as a primary international competitor in the area of production of goods. In the past few decades, however, the U.S. economy has increasingly become a service economy, as Figure 17.4 shows. The service sector now produces 77 percent of the U.S. GNP[6] and employs 80 percent of the workforce.[7] The service sector accounts for most of the growth in total nonfarm employment. In excess of 58 percent of the average U.S. family's budget is spent on services.[8]

[4]G. Lynn Shostack, "Service Positioning through Structural Change," *Journal of Marketing* 51 (January 1987): 38.

[5]Pierre Berthon, Leyland Pitt, Constantine S. Katsikeas, and Jean Paul Berthon, "Virtual Services Go International: International Services in the Marketspace," *Journal of International Marketing* 7 (Number 3, 1999): 84–106.

[6]Coalition of Service Industries, **http://www.uscsi.org**, March 23, 2000.

[7]U.S. Department of Commerce, *Services 2000* (Washington DC: Office of Service Industries, 1999), 47.

[8]U.S. Dept. of Commerce, Bureau of Economic Analysis, *Survey of Current Business,* March 2000. **www.bea.doc.gov**

| FIGURE | 17.4 | Employment in Industrial Sectors as a Percentage of the Total Labor Force |

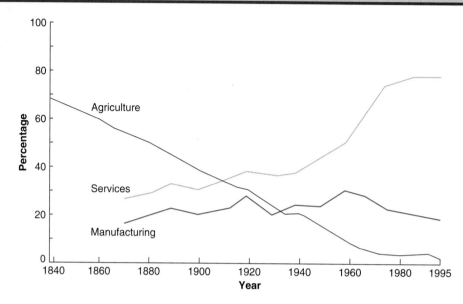

SOURCES: Quarterly Labor Force Statistics, Paris, Organization for Economic Cooperation and Development, 1996, no. 2; and J. B. Quinn, "The Impacts of Technology on the Services Sector," *Technology and Global Industry: Companies and Nations in the World Economy*, © 1987 by the National Academy of Sciences, Washington, DC. Reprinted with permission.

Of course, only a limited segment of the total range of services is sold internationally. Federal, state, and local government employees, for example, sell few of their services to foreigners. U.S. laundries and restaurants only occasionally service foreign tourists. However, many service industries that do market abroad often have at their disposal large organizations, specialized technology, or advanced professional expertise. Strength in these characteristics has enabled the United States to become the world's largest exporter of services. Total U.S. services exported grew from $6 billion in 1958 to $275 billion in 1999.[9] The contribution of services to the U.S. balance of payments is highlighted in Table 17.1. It shows that the U.S. services trade balance is producing a substantial surplus and makes up for a large part of the huge deficits in merchandise trade.

International service trade has had very beneficial results for many firms and industries. Most of the large management consulting firms derive more than half their revenue from international sources. The largest advertising agencies serve customers around the globe, some of them in 107 countries. Table 17.2 shows how many countries are served by these agencies and how many accounts they service in ten or more countries. Interesting is also the fact that six of the firms have the term "worldwide" in their name. Bechtel, one of the largest U.S. engineering and construction firms, had more than 45 percent of its workforce outside North America.[10]

Large international growth, however, is not confined to U.S. service exports only. The import of services into the United States is also increasing dramatically. In 1999, the United States imported about $200 billion worth of services.[11] Competition in in-

[9]U.S. Department of Commerce, Bureau of Economic Analysis, *Survey of Current Business* (Washington, DC: February 18, 2000). **www.bea.doc.gov**

[10]1999 Bechtel Global Report, Bechtel Group, Inc. **www.bechtel.com**

[11]U.S. Department of Commerce, *Survey of Current Business*, February 2000.

TABLE 17.1	U.S. Balances of Trade in Goods and Services, 2000 (in billions)

Exports of Goods and Services		$1,068.40
Goods		773.3
As a percentage of total exports	72.40%	
Services		295.1
As a percentage of total exports	27.60%	
Imports of Goods and Services		$1,438.10
Goods		1,222.80
As a percentage of total imports	85.00%	
Services		215.3
As a percentage of total imports	15.00%	
Balance on Goods Trade		−449.5
Balance on Services		79.8
Balance on Goods and Services		−369.7

SOURCE: U.S. Department of Commerce, Bureau of Economic Analysis, *Annual Summary for 1999*, June 29, 2001.

www.bea.doc.gov

ternational services is rising rapidly at all levels. Hong Kong, Singapore, and Western Europe are increasingly active in service industries such as banking, insurance, and advertising. Although the United States has long been recognized as the leader in software development, U.S. businesses are increasingly routing their software projects to India, China, and Central Europe.

TABLE 17.2	Top Ten Global Advertising Agencies 2000

AGENCY	CLIENTS	MARKETS
McCann–Erickson Worldwide	1,495	65
DDB Worldwide	782	41
Grey Worldwide	693	48
Ogilvy & Mather Worldwide	689	39
J. Walter Thompson Co.	669	30
EURO RSCG Worldwide	668	43
BBDO Worldwide	624	42
Y&R Advertising	586	34
Publicis Worldwide	559	29
Lowe Lintas & Partners Worldwide	501	27

SOURCE: *AdAge Global* Web site, www.adageglobal.com/cgi-bin/worldAdvSearch.pl., accessed April 25, 2001.

The Role of International Services in the World Economy

The rise of the service sector is a global phenomenon. Services contribute an average of more than 60 percent to the gross national product of industrial nations. Services are also rapidly moving to the forefront in many other nations as well, accounting for 65 percent of GDP in Argentina, 64 percent in Mexico, 65 percent in South Africa, and over 50 percent in Thailand.[12] Even in the least developed countries, services typically contribute at least 45 percent of GDP. With growth rates higher than other sectors such as agriculture and manufacturing, services are instrumental in job creation in these countries.[13] Table 17.3 lists some of the service industries most actively participating in world trade. In addition, world trade in services has grown much more rapidly than trade in merchandise. As a result, trade in services constitutes about 25 percent of overall world trade and, in some regions, accounts for well above 40 percent of merchandise trade. At the current time, services trade is taking place mainly between the developed countries, with the 29 member nations of the Organization for Economic Cooperation and Development (OECD) alone accounting for the largest portion of total trade. Within these countries, the names of such firms as American Express, McDonald's, Club Med, Thomas Cook, Mitsubishi, and Hilton have become widely familiar.

Global Transformation of Services

The rapid rise in international services marketing has been the result of major shifts in the business environment and innovations in technology. One primary change in the past decade has been the reduction of governmental regulation of services. This **deregulation** is clearly seen within the United States. In the mid-1970s, a philosophical decision was made to reduce government interference in the marketplace, in the hope that this would enhance competitive activity. As a consequence, some service sectors have benefited, and others have suffered, from the withdrawal of government intervention. The primary deregulated industries in the United States have been transportation, banking, and telecommunications. As a result, new competitors participate in the marketplace. Regulatory changes were initially thought to have primarily do-

TABLE 17.3 Major Exporters of Services, by Industry	
Accounting	Health care
Advertising	Hospital management
Architecture	Insurance
Banking and other financial services	Leasing
Communications	Legal
Computers	Lodging
Construction and engineering	Management and catering
Education and training	Management consulting
Equipment maintenance and repair	Publishing
Franchising	Software development

[12]Joseph P. Quinlan, "International Economics Trade in Global Services," **www.uscsi.org**, March 22, 2000.

[13]International Trade Centre, Geneva, **www.intracen.org/serviceexport**, September 1999.

THE INTERNATIONAL MARKETPLACE 17.2

The Effects of Global Telecom Deregulation

SOME OF THE MOST IMPORTANT future trade talks will focus on talking—on the phone, via the fax, over the Internet, through satellite linkups, and through other revolutionary technologies—and the services that make it possible. Such talks have been taking place since the signing of GATT's Uruguay Round. There is, unfortunately, much static on the line. As a result, trade negotiators may hang up on more than $1 trillion in benefits that users stand to gain from open markets between now and 2010.

The stakes are extremely high. The technological revolution is sweeping telecommunications. But only a tiny fraction of the world's homes and firms have access to the technology at affordable prices, if at all. Most users in the developing parts of Asia, Latin America, and Europe are fast becoming second- or even third-class telecom citizens. There are fewer than 15 telephones per 100 households in most developing countries, compared to more than 100 phones per 100 households in the United States Data transmission, which drives the Internet, is poor or nonexistent. Rates for long distance and international service are astronomical, often five to ten times higher than U.S. rates.

Telecom reform also means big business for the United States. With domestic liberalization, U.S. firms are able to meet the telecom needs of new export markets. Competition in those markets would mean both cutting-edge products for foreign buyers and high-skill, high-wage jobs at home. And commercial interests in the telecom sector support broader U.S. foreign policy goals: phones, fax, and other value-added telecom products promote democratization by improving communications and access to information around the world.

Expensive, substandard telecom systems in most countries are the result of a reliance on monopoly public telecom operators (PTOs). Monopoly PTOs charge high prices, especially for international calls, and are slow to innovate—why create a cellular service that will threaten your copper lines? They usually offer poor quality, taking months to install phones and days to clear faults. They are enormously overstaffed and therefore tough to slim down.

A conservative computation of the benefits of phasing in competitive markets suggests that between 1997 and 2010, users could save more than $1 trillion from lower rates, better service, and improved technology. With liberalization, the cost of a long distance call in Argentina could easily fall by $1 a minute or more. Developing countries, which are least able to afford the current waste, could save $500 billion between 1997 and 2010.

Opposition to opening the world's telecom markets to real competition comes primarily from, ironically, Asian and Latin American nations—which are most likely to gain from telecom liberalization. PTOs in these countries, which would suddenly have to compete, are blocking the trillion-dollar trade deal. They raise familiar arguments to defend the status quo: Universal service, a phone for every household, will be denied without benevolent PTOs that subsidize home telephones on the backs of international callers; jobs will be threatened.

Yet telecoms in South Korea have managed to find a way forward. While European telecoms battle escalating costs of buying licenses for next-generation cell-phone networks, the Seoul government charges Korea Telecom and SK Telecom Co. modest fees of under $1 billion for the right to build state-of-the-art 3G networks. Better still, only 50 percent is payable up front. In 2000, SK posted record profits of $750 million. In China, too, where 7 percent of the population own mobile phones, the number of subscribers more than doubled to 85.5 million in 2000 and is expected to reach 132 million by the end of 2001.

SOURCE: Gary Hufbauer and Daniel Rosen, "Dialing Up a Trillion Dollar Telecom Deal," *The Wall Street Journal*, April 22, 1996, A22; Frederik Balfour, Moon Ihlwan, and Dan Nystedt, "What They're Doing Right in Asia," April 23, 2001, *Business Week* www.businessweek.com.

mestic effects, but they have rapidly spread internationally. For example, the 1984 deregulation of AT&T has given rise to competition not only in the United States. Japan's telecommunications monopoly, NT&T, was deregulated shortly afterward and European deregulation followed in the mid-1990s. *The International Marketplace 17.2* shows the economic potential that has been and will be unleashed due to deregulation of the telecommunications sector.

Similarly, deregulatory efforts in the transportation sector have had international repercussions. New air carriers have entered the market to compete against established trunk carriers and have done so successfully by pricing their services lower both nationally and internationally. In doing so, these airlines also affected the regulatory climate abroad. Obviously, a British airline can count only to a limited extent on government support to remain competitive with new low-priced fares offered by other carriers also serving the British market. As a result, the deregulatory movement has spread internationally, and fostered the emergence of new competition and new competitive practices. Because many of these changes resulted in lower prices, demand has been stimulated, leading to a rise in the volume of international services trade.

Another major change has been the decreased regulation of service industries by their industry groups. For example, business practices in fields such as health care, law, and accounting are increasingly becoming more competitive and aggressive. New economic realities require firms in these industries to search for new ways to attract market share. International markets are one frequently untapped possibility for market expansion and have therefore become a prime target for such service firms.

Technological advancement is another major factor in increasing service trade. Progress in technology offers new ways of doing business and permits businesses to expand their horizons internationally. For example, Ford Motor Company uses one major computer system to carry out its new car designs in both the United States and Europe. This practice not only lowers expenditures on hardware but also permits better utilization of existing equipment and international design collaboration by allowing design groups in different time zones to use the equipment around the clock. However, this development could take place only after advances in data transmission procedures.

In a similar fashion, more rapid transmission of data has permitted financial institutions to expand their service delivery through a worldwide network. Again, were it not for advances in technology, such expansion would rarely have been possible or cost-effective.

Another result of these developments is that service industry expansion has not been confined to the traditional services that are labor-intensive and could therefore have been performed better in areas of the world where labor possesses a comparative advantage because of lower prices. Rather, technology-intensive services are the sunrise industries of the new century. Increasingly, firms can reconfigure their service delivery in order to escape the location-bound dimension. Banks, for example, can offer their services through automatic teller machines or telephone banking. Consultants can advise via video conferences, and teachers can teach the world through multimedia classrooms. Physicians can perform operations in a distant country if proper computer linkages can drive roboticized medical equipment.

As a result, many service providers have the opportunity to become truly global marketers. To them, the traditional international market barrier of distance no longer matters. Knowledge, the core of many service activities, can offer a global reach without requiring a local presence. Service providers therefore may have only a minor need for local establishment, since they can operate without premises. You don't have to be there to do business! The effect of such a shift in service activities is major. Insurance and bank buildings in the downtowns of the world may soon become obsolete. Talented service providers see the demand for their performance increase, while less capable ones will suffer from increased competition. Most importantly, consumers and society have a much broader range and quality of service choices available, often at a lower cost.

International Trade Problems in Services

Together with the increasing importance of service marketing, new problems have beset the service sector. Even though many of these problems have been characterized as affecting mainly the negotiations between nations, they are of sufficient importance to the firm in its international activities to merit a brief review.

Software firms such as SAP, headquartered in Germany, have created many options for the organization of worldwide data in order to assist enterprises in the running of their businesses. **www.mysap.com**

Data Collection Problems

The data collected on service trade are quite poor. Service transactions are often "invisible" statistically as well as physically. The fact that governments have precise data on the number of trucks exported, down to the last bolt, but little information on reinsurance flows reflects past governmental inattention to services.

Only recently has it been recognized that the income generated and the jobs created through the sale of services abroad are just as important as income and jobs resulting from the production and exportation of goods. As a result, many governments are beginning to develop improved measuring techniques for the services sector. For example, the U.S. government has improved its estimates of services by covering more business, professional, and technical services and incorporating improved measurement of telecommunications services and insurance services. New data are also developed on travel and passenger fares, foreign students' expenditures in the United States, repairs and alterations of equipment, and noninterest income of banks.

It is easy to imagine how many data collection problems are encountered in countries lacking elaborate systems and unwilling to allocate funds for such efforts. The gathering of information is, of course, made substantially more difficult because services are intangible and therefore more difficult to measure and to trace than goods. The lack of service homogeneity does not make the task any easier. In an international setting, of course, an additional major headache is the lack of comparability between services categories as used by different national statistical systems. For example, while gas and electricity production and distribution are classified as goods by most governments, they are classified as services in the United States.[14]

Insufficient knowledge and information have led to a lack of transparency. As a result, governments have great difficulty gauging the effect of service transactions internationally or influencing service trade. Consequently, international services negotiations progress only slowly, and governmental regulations are often put into place without precise information as to their repercussions on actual trade performance.

[14]Terry Clark, Daniel Rajaratnam, and Timothy Smith, "Toward a Theory of International Services: Marketing Intangibles in a World of Nations," *Journal of International Marketing* 4 (Number 2, 1995): 9–28.

Regulation of Services Trade

Typical obstacles to services trade can be categorized into two major types: barriers to entry and problems in performing services. Governments often justify **barriers to entry** by referring to **national security** and economic security. For example, the impact of banking on domestic economic activity is given as a reason why banking should be carried out only by nationals or indeed be operated entirely under government control. Sometimes, the protection of service users is cited, particularly of bank depositors and insurance policyholders. Some countries claim that competition in societally important services is unnecessary and wasteful and should be avoided. Another justification for barriers is the frequently used **infant industry** argument: "With sufficient time to develop on our own, we can compete in world markets." Often, however, this argument is used simply to prolong the ample licensing profits generated by restricted entry. Impediments to services consist of either tariff or nontariff barriers. Tariff barriers typically restrict or inhibit market entry for the service provider or consumer, while nontariff barriers tend to impede service performance. Table 17.4 shows selected tariff and nontariff barriers. Yet, defining a barrier to service marketing is not always easy. For example, Taiwan gives an extensive written examination to prospective accountants (as do most countries) to ensure that licensed accountants are qualified to practice. Naturally, the examination is given in Chinese. The fact that few U.S. accountants read and write Chinese, and hence are unable to pass the examination, does not necessarily constitute a barrier to trade in accountancy services.[15]

Even if barriers to entry are nonexistent or can be overcome, service companies have difficulty in performing effectively abroad once they have achieved access to the

TABLE 17.4	Selected Barriers to the International Marketing of Services	
TYPE	**EXAMPLE**	**IMPACT**
Tariff	Tax on imported advertising	Discriminates against foreign agencies
	Tax on computer service contracts	Prices international service providers higher than domestic providers that stand alone
	Higher fees for university students from outside the country	Decreases foreign student enrollment
Nontariff		
Buy national policies	U.S. government buying training services from only U.S. companies	Discriminates against foreign suppliers
Prohibit employment of foreigners	Canadian priority to citizens for available jobs	May prevent suppliers from going to buyers
Distance	International business education	May raise cost of bringing supplier to buyer, buyer to supplier
Direct government competition	Indonesian monopoly on telecommunications	Must market services to government
Scarce factors of production	Lack of trained medical workers in Biafra	Limits production of services
Restrictions on service buyers or sellers	North Korea limiting the number of tourists allowed to enter and exit the country	Limits the restricted industry

SOURCE: Adapted from Lee D. Dahringer, "Marketing Services Internationally: Barriers and Management Strategies," *Journal of Services Marketing* 5 (Number 3, 1991): 5–17.

[15]Dorothy I. Riddle, *Key LDC's: Trade in Services* (Glendale, AZ: American Graduate School of International Studies, March 1987), 346–347.

local market. One reason is that rules and regulations based on tradition may inhibit innovation. A more important reason is that governments aim to pursue social or cultural objectives through national regulations. Of primary importance here is the distinction between **discriminatory** and **nondiscriminatory regulations.** Regulations that impose larger operating costs on foreign service providers than on the local competitors, that provide subsidies to local firms only, or that deny competitive opportunities to foreign suppliers are a proper cause for international concern. The discrimination problem becomes even more acute when foreign firms face competition from government-owned or government-controlled enterprises, which are discussed in more detail in a later chapter. On the other hand, nondiscriminatory regulations may be inconvenient and may hamper business operations, but they offer less opportunity for international criticism.

For example, barriers to services destined for the U.S. market result mainly from regulatory practices. The fields of banking, insurance, and accounting provide some examples. These industries are regulated at both federal and state levels, and the regulations often pose formidable barriers to potential entrants from abroad. The chief complaint of foreign countries is not that the United States discriminates against foreign service providers but rather that the United States places more severe restrictions on them than do other countries. In addition, the entire U.S. regulatory process gives little weight to international policy issues and often operates in isolation from executive branch direction.[16] These barriers are, of course, a reflection of the decision-making process within the U.S. domestic economy and are unlikely to change in the near future. A coherent approach toward international commerce in services is hardly likely to emerge from the disparate decisions of agencies such as the Interstate Commerce Commission (ICC), the Federal Communications Commission (FCC), the Securities and Exchange Commission (SEC), and the many licensing agencies at the state level.

All these regulations make it difficult for the international service marketer to penetrate world markets. At the governmental level, services frequently are not recognized as a major facet of world trade or are viewed with suspicion because of a lack of understanding, and barriers to entry often result. To make progress in tearing them down, much educational work needs to be done.

Government Responses to Problems in International Services Marketing

One of the early postwar multilateral efforts to liberalize international trade in services was the OECD code on invisible transactions, which in the 1950s removed some barriers to service trade. Within the GATT, the United States attempted in the late 1970s, near the end of the **Tokyo Round** of trade negotiations, to add service issues to the agenda. However, this move was greeted with international suspicion. Because the United States has the largest service economy and the most service exports, other nations suspected that any liberalization would principally benefit the United States. Moreover, some of the negotiating partners had the same lack of knowledge about services trade that U.S. negotiators had had a few years before.

As a result, services were addressed only to a very limited extent in the Tokyo Round. Until recently, services therefore were covered only in the international trade framework by the **Government Procurement Code** and the **Subsidies and Countervailing Measures Code.** The former covers services only to the extent that they are ancillary to purchases of goods and do not exceed the goods in value. The latter is restricted to services that are ancillary to trade in goods.

---

[16]Gary C. Hufbauer, remarks, Seminar on Services in the World Economy, organized by the United States Council of the International Chamber of Commerce, New York, May 5, 1980, 3.

In a major breakthrough in the Uruguay Round, the major GATT participants agreed to conduct services trade negotiations parallel with product negotiations. These negotiations resulted in 1995 in the forging of a **General Agreement on Trade in Services (GATS)** as part of the World Trade Organization, the first multilateral, legally enforceable agreement covering trade and investment in the services sector. Similar to earlier agreements in the product sector, GATS provides for most-favored-nation treatment, national treatment, transparency in rule making, and the free flow of payments and transfers. Market-access provisions restrict the ability of governments to limit competition and new-market entry. In addition, sectoral agreements were made for the movement of personnel, telecommunications, and aviation. However, in several sectors, such as financial services and entertainment, no agreement was obtained. In addition, many provisions, due to their newness, are very narrow. Therefore, future negotiations have been agreed upon, which, at five-year intervals, will attempt to improve free trade in services.[17]

Corporate Involvement in International Services Marketing

Services and E-Commerce

Electronic commerce has opened up new horizons for global services reach and has drastically reduced the meaning of distance. For example, when geographic obstacles make the establishment of retail outlets cumbersome and expensive, firms can approach their customers via the World Wide Web. Government regulations that might be prohibitive to a transfer of goods may not have any effect on the international marketing of services. Also, regardless of size, companies are finding it increasingly easy to appeal to a global marketplace. The Internet can help service firms in developing and transitional economies overcome two of the biggest tasks they face: gaining credibility in international markets and saving on travel costs. Little-known firms can become instantly "visible" on the Internet. Even a small firm can develop a polished and sophisticated Web presence and promotion strategy. Customers are less concerned about geographic location if they feel the firm is electronically accessible. An increasing number of service providers have never met their foreign customers except "virtually," on-line.[18]

Nonetheless, several notes of caution must be kept in mind. First, the penetration of the Internet has occurred at different rates in different countries. There are still many businesses and consumers who do not have access to electronic business media. Unless they are to be excluded from a company's focus, more traditional ways of reaching them must be considered. Also, firms need to prepare their Internet presence for global visitors. For example, the language of the Internet is English—at least as far as large corporations are concerned. Yet, many of the visitors coming to web sites either may not have English as their first language or may not speak English at all.

Companies respond differently to such visitor language capabilities. For example, one study determined that 70 percent of non-U.S. companies with a web site offered more than their local language on their sites, while only 14 percent of U.S. companies offered non-English language content.[19] Many companies also do not permit any interaction on their web sites, thus missing out on feedback from visitors. Some web sites are so culture-bound that they often leave their visitors bewildered and disappointed. However, over time, increasing understanding about doing business in the

---

[17]Letter from President Clinton to Speaker of the House Tom Foley, Washington, DC, December 15, 1993.

[18]Dorothy Riddle, "Using the Internet for Service Exporting: Tips for Service Firms," *International Trade Forum*, 1 (1999): 19–23.

[19]Michael R. Czinkota, "Global Giants Slow to Join Net Revolution," *Journal of Commerce* (November 5, 1999): 9.

global market place will enable companies to be more refined in their approach to their customers.

Typical International Services

Although many firms are already active in the international service arena, others often do not perceive their existing competitive advantage. Numerous services have great potential for internationalization.

Financial institutions can offer some functions very competitively in the international field of banking services. Increased mergers and acquisitions on a global basis have led to the emergence of financial giants in Europe, Japan, and the United States. Table 17.5 shows the diversity of countries in which the largest banks are now headquartered. These firms are likely to continue increasing in size and international orientation. With the increased reach made possible by electronic commerce, they can develop direct linkages to clients around the world, offering tailor-made financial services and reduction in intermediation cost. Figure 17.5 provides an example of the international positioning of a bank.

Another area with great international potential is construction, design, and engineering services. Economies of scale work not only for machinery and material but also for areas such as personnel management and the overall management of projects. Particularly for international projects that are large scale and long term, the experience advantage could weigh heavily in favor of seasoned firms. The economic significance of these services far exceeds their direct turnover because they encourage subsequent demand for capital goods. For example, having an engineering consultant of a certain nationality increases the chances that contracts for the supply of equipment, technology, and know-how will be won by an enterprise of the same nationality, given the advantages enjoyed in terms of information, language, and technical specification.[20]

Firms in the fields of legal and accounting services can aid their domestic clients abroad through support activities; they can also aid foreign firms and countries in improving business and governmental operations. In computer and data services, international potential is rapidly growing, as shown by the advertisement in Figure 17.6. Knowledge of computer operations, data manipulations, data transmission, and data analysis are insufficiently exploited internationally by many small and medium-sized firms. For example, India is increasingly participating in the provision of international data services. Although some aspects of the data field are high-technology intensive, many operations still require skilled human service input. The coding and entering of data often has to be performed manually because appropriate machine-readable forms may be unavailable or not usable. Because of lower wages, Indian companies can offer data entry services at a rate much lower than in more industrialized countries. As a result, data are transmitted in raw form to India, encoded on a proper medium there, and returned to the ultimate user. To some extent, this transformation can be equated to the value-added steps that take place in the transformation of a raw commodity into a finished product. Obviously, using its comparative advantage for this labor-intensive task, India can compete in the field of international services. With an ongoing annual growth rate of over 50 percent, India is expected to reach $10 billion in software exports by the year 2002.[21] However, many countries are also becoming providers of software for computer operations, thus moving up on the scale of value-added services.

Many opportunities exist in the field of teaching services. Both the academic and the corporate educational sector largely have concentrated their work in the

[20]"Engineering, Technical, and Other Services to Industry," Synthesis Report, Organization for Economic Cooperation and Development, Paris, 1988.

[21]"Software Industry in India," *India Times*, **www.india-times.com**, March 14, 1999.

TABLE | 17.5 | World's 40 Largest Banks

	COMPANY NAME	COUNTRY	TOTAL ASSETS ($MILLIONS)	MARKET CAPITAL ($MILLIONS)	NET INCOME ($MILLIONS)
1	DEUTSCHE BANK AG	GERMANY	$727,890	$31,312	$1,981
2	CITIGROUP INC.	UNITED STATES	668,641	112,194	5,807
3	UBS AG	SWITZERLAND	667,308	62,964	2,144
4	BANK OF TOKYO-MITSUBISHI, LTD.	JAPAN	638,927	63,484	−723
5	BANK OF AMERICA CORPORATION	UNITED STATES	632,574	84,179	7,882
6	BAYERISCHE HYPO- UND VEREINSBANK	GERMANY	523,740	32,500	2,242
7	ABN AMRO HOLDING N.V.	NETHERLANDS	504,874	30,200	2,141
8	HSBC HOLDINGS PLC	UNITED KINGDOM	482,932	73,273	4,318
9	HSBC HOLDINGS PLC (HK)	HONG KONG	482,862	67,240	4,317
10	FUJI BANK, LIMITED	JAPAN	467,410	20,073	−3,511
11	ING GROEP N.V.	NETHERLANDS	462,678	57,594	3,127
12	CREDIT SUISSE GROUP	SWITZERLAND	459,799	40,879	2,171
13	CREDIT AGRICOLE SA	FRANCE	456,770	N/A	2,202
14	SOCIETE GENERALE DE FRANCE SA	FRANCE	449,425	16,157	855
15	DAI-ICHI KANGYO BANK, LTD.	JAPAN	442,555	20,512	−3,705
16	SUMITOMO BANK, LIMITED	JAPAN	440,137	41,892	−4,733
17	DRESDNER BANK AG	GERMANY	426,891	21,686	1,090
18	WESTDEUTSCHE LANDESBANK	GERMANY	411,104	N/A	398
19	SANWA BANK, LIMITED	JAPAN	403,124	31,027	−3,915
20	SAKURA BANK, LIMITED	JAPAN	396,525	12,196	−3,988
21	NORINCHUKIN BANK	JAPAN	390,119	N/A	1,007
22	BANQUE NATIONALE DE PARIS SA	FRANCE	380,124	17,950	1,306
23	COMMERZBANK AG	GERMANY	376,008	15,649	1,045
24	INDUSTRIAL BANK OF JAPAN, LTD.	JAPAN	371,900	17,569	−1,508
25	CHASE MANHATTAN CORPORATION	UNITED STATES	365,875	60,207	3,782
26	BARCLAYS PLC	UNITED KINGDOM	363,931	32,379	2,214
27	PARIBAS	FRANCE	310,103	13,333	1,170
28	NATIONAL WESTMINSTER BANK PLC	UNITED KINGDOM	308,445	32,740	2,682
29	SCHWEIZERISCHER BANKVEREIN	SWITZERLAND	300,329	23,480	−170
30	ABBEY NATIONAL PLC	UNITED KINGDOM	294,823	30,252	1,755
31	RABOBANK	NETHERLANDS	290,724	N/A	1,096
32	LLOYDS/TSB PLC	UNITED KINGDOM	278,566	78,029	3,516
33	BAYERISCHE LANDESBANK	GERMANY	277,309	N/A	357
34	BANK ONE CORP.	UNITED STATES	261,496	60,117	3,108
35	MORGAN (J.P.) & CO. INCORPORATED	UNITED STATES	261,067	18,387	963
36	TOKAI BANK, LIMITED	JAPAN	259,113	14,313	−2,386
37	CREDIT LYONNAIS SA	FRANCE	244,739	10,467	193
38	HALIFAX GROUP PLC	UNITED KINGDOM	239,749	34,432	1,942
39	ASAHI BANK, LTD.	JAPAN	237,386	14,591	−2,114
40	FIRST UNION CORPORATION	UNITED STATES	237,363	59,718	2,891

SOURCE: Primark, Worldscope Database, March 2000.

Note: Ranked by assets as determined by Worldscope, March 16, 2000.

| FIGURE | 17.5 | Financial Services Firm Positions Itself |

En España somos Españoles.

In Deutschland sind wir Deutsche.

In Australia, we are Australian.

日本では、日本人。

In Canada, we are Canadian.

In Nederland zijn we Nederlands.

In England, we are English.

In der Schweiz sind wir Schweizer.

在香港我們是中國人。

In America, we are American.

Di Singapura kami ialah orang Singapura.

En France, nous sommes Français.

Around the world we are the

CS First Boston Group.

Announcing a worldwide investment banking firm that draws its strength from established investment banks in the world's financial capitals.

Operating as First Boston in the Americas, Credit Suisse First Boston in Europe and the Middle East, and CS First Boston Pacific in the Far East and Asia, the CS First Boston Group – together with Credit Suisse – offers unparalleled expertise in capital raising, mergers and acquisitions, securities sales, trading and research, asset management, and merchant banking.

So regardless of what language you speak, the words for powerful investment banking are the same all over the world – CS First Boston Group.

| **CS First Boston Group** | First Boston | Credit Suisse First Boston | CS First Boston Pacific |

SOURCE: Courtesy First Boston Corporation.

http://www.csfb.com

domestic market. Yet the teaching of knowledge is in high global demand and offers new opportunities for growth. Technology allows teachers to go global via video conferences, e-mail office hours, and Internet-relayed teaching materials. Removing the confinement of the classroom may well trigger the largest surge in learning that humankind has ever known.

Management consulting services can be provided by firms to institutions and corporations around the globe. Of particular value is management expertise in areas where firms possess global leadership, be it in manufacturing or process activities. For example, companies with highly refined transportation or logistics activities can sell their management experience abroad. Yet consulting services are particularly sensitive to the cultural environment, and their use varies significantly by country and field of expertise. *The International Marketplace 17.3* provides an example of how international service providers help in locating and providing basketball talent from around the world.

THE INTERNATIONAL MARKETPLACE 17.3

A New Services Industry: Finding Basketball Players

TALL KIDS IN COUNTRIES around the world are finding golden opportunities on American basketball courts. The number of foreign players on U.S. college and professional basketball teams has recently jumped from 144 to 243 in a four-year period, and American recruiters can't seem to get enough of the foreign imports. Hakeem Olajuwon, an NBA star from Nigeria, has achieved the status of folk hero among many fans around the globe. Many credit his success with the current rush to recruit players from abroad.

Stiff competition for the tallest players has even led to recruiting foreign players at younger levels of the sport; high schools commonly use foreign exchange programs to fortify their teams with international talent. High school coaches are linked with foreign players through middlemen, like the Nigerian lawyer, Toyin Sonoiki, who spent $500,000 to send nine players to U.S. schools.

The role of middlemen is crucial in obtaining visas for the students. Another Nigerian lawyer, Lloyd Ukwu, lives in Washington, D.C., and recruits on business trips back home. He started helping young Nigerians obtain U.S. visas in 1988. After meeting some players on a trip to Nigeria, he asked an assistant basketball coach at American University to write invitations for eight Nigerian players to visit the United States,

and these letters were influential in helping them win visas. Word spread about Ukwu's recruiting efforts, and soon other universities were using his services.

The internationalization of the sport has changed the jobs of many American coaches and recruiters. For years, college recruiting has used tip sheets to describe U.S. high school players, but now there is one recruiting service that gives the scoop on foreign players as well. Dale Mock, a Georgia elementary-school physical-education teacher, runs International Scouting Service, begun in 1993. His tip sheets give subscribers the details about foreign players and contact information for $250–$350 a year. Mock's subscriber list is up to 100, from a start of only 20 his first year. Dale Brown, Louisiana State's former coach, described the internationalization of the recruiting scene: "In the 1960s, I would go to the European championships, to the Asian games and all the rest—and I was the only American. Now, so many Americans are there it's like being in Grand Central Station."

SOURCES: International Scouting Service web site, accessed June 17, 1999, **www.inthoops.com;** and Marc Fisher and Ken Denlinger, "The Market for Imports Is Booming," *The Washington Post*, March 28, 1997, C1.

All domestic service expenditures funded from abroad by foreign citizens also represent a service export. This makes tourism an increasingly important area of services trade. For example, every foreign visitor who spends foreign currency in the United States contributes to an improvement in the current account. The natural resources and beauty offered by so many countries have already made tourism one of the most important services trade components. Table 17.6 shows the extent of tourism arrivals and receipts around the world.

TABLE 17.6 Tourism Arrivals and Receipts Around the World*

	TOURIST ARRIVALS (MILLIONS), 1999	% CHANGE, 99/98	TOURISM RECEIPTS (US$ MILLION), 1998	% CHANGE, 98/97
WORLD	662.9	4.1	439,393	0.3
AFRICA	27.3	9.1	9,612	6.6
AMERICAS	123.0	2.5	119,965	0.9
EAST ASIA/PACIFIC	96.6	10.5	68,598	−10.2
EUROPE	392.5	2.3	228,856	3.8
MIDDLE EAST	17.9	17.4	8,022	−12.2
SOUTH ASIA	5.7	8.3	4,340	1.5

SOURCE: World Tourism Organization, *Tourism Highlights 2000,* **www.world-tourism.org**.

*Arrivals are 1999 data, Receipts are 1998 data

| FIGURE 17.6 | More International Marketing Requires More International Communication |

The difference between international lines and international service.

If your business is crossing into foreign markets without AT&T, you might be working without a net. The fact is, nobody has more ways to help an international business.

We have the Export Hotline, which can help you discover and explore new markets for your products by providing you—free of charge—with insightful information on more than 50 industries throughout more than 75 countries. You pay only the transmission cost to your fax machine.

**For more information call
1 800 222-0900**

We have AT&T **Favorite Nation Option,** a discount program that gives you savings on calls to the two countries you call the most each month—automatically.

We have AT&T **CustomNet** FAX Option which offers some of the lowest prices in the industry for direct-dial international faxes under three minutes.

And if you're calling Japan, Hong Kong or the Philippines, there's AT&T **International Advanced FAX** Service, which offers access to special international digital phone lines which are constantly monitored to ensure higher quality and speed.

So if you want high-quality international phone service, call AT&T. Because your business is too important to leave hanging by a thread.

AT&T. Far and Away. The Best in the Business.

AT&T

SOURCE: **http://www.att.com**

A proper mix in international services might also be achieved by pairing the strengths of different partners. For example, information technology expertise from one country could be combined with financial resources from another. The strengths of both partners can then be used to obtain maximum benefits.

Combining international advantages in services may ultimately result in the development of an even newer and more drastic comparative lead. For example, if a firm has an international head start in such areas as high technology, information gathering, information processing, and information analysis, the major thrust of its international service might not rely on providing these service components individually but rather on enabling clients, based on all resources, to make better decisions. If better decision making is transferable to a wide variety of international situations, that in itself might become the overriding future competitive advantage of the firm in the international market.

Starting to Market Services Internationally

For many firms, participation in the Internet will offer the most attractive starting point in marketing services internationally. The setup of a web site will allow visitors from any place on the globe to come see the offering. Of course, the most important problem will be communicating the existence of the site and enticing visitors to come. For that, very traditional advertising and communication approaches often need to be used. In some countries, for example, rolling billboards announce web sites and their benefits. Overall, however, we need to keep in mind that not everywhere do firms and individuals have access to or make use of the new e-commerce opportunities.

For services that are delivered mainly in the support of or in conjunction with goods, the most sensible approach for the international novice is to follow the path of the good. For years, many large accounting and banking firms have done so by determining where their major multinational clients have set up new operations and then following them. Smaller service marketers who cooperate closely with manufacturing firms can determine where the manufacturing firms are operating internationally. Ideally, of course, it would be possible to follow clusters of manufacturers in order to obtain economies of scale internationally while, at the same time, looking for entirely new client groups abroad.

For service providers whose activities are independent from goods, a different strategy is needed. These individuals and firms must search for market situations abroad that are similar to the domestic market. Such a search should concentrate in their area of expertise. For example, a design firm learning about construction projects abroad can investigate the possibility of rendering its design services. Similarly, a management consultant learning about the plans of a foreign country or firm to computerize operations can explore the possibility of overseeing a smooth transition from manual to computerized activities. What is required is the understanding that similar problems are likely to occur in similar situations.

Another opportunity consists of identifying and understanding points of transition abroad. Just as U.S. society has undergone change, foreign societies are subject to a changing domestic environment. If, for example, new transportation services are introduced, an expert in containerization may wish to consider whether to offer service to improve the efficiency of the new system.

Leads for international service opportunities can also be gained by staying informed about international projects sponsored by domestic organizations such as the U.S. Agency for International Development, as well as international organizations such as the United Nations, the International Finance Corporation, or the World Bank. Very frequently, such projects are in need of support through services. Overall, the international service marketer needs to search for familiar situations or similar problems requiring similar solutions in order to formulate an effective international expansion strategy.

Strategic Implications of International Services Marketing

To be successful, the international service marketer must first determine the nature and the aim of the service offering—that is, whether the service will be aimed at people or at things, and whether the service act in itself will result in tangible or intangible actions. Table 17.7 provides examples of such a classification that will help the marketer to better determine the position of the services effort.

TABLE 17.7 Understanding the Nature of the Service Act

NATURE OF THE SERVICE ACT	DIRECT RECIPIENT OF THE SERVICE	
	PEOPLE	THINGS
Tangible Actions	*Services directed at people's bodies:*	*Services directed at goods and other physical possessions:*
	Health care	Freight transportation
	Passenger transportation	Industrial equipment repair and maintenance
	Beauty salons	Janitorial services
	Exercise clinics	Laundry and dry cleaning
	Restaurants	Landscaping/lawn care
	Haircutting	Veterinary care
Intangible Actions	*Services directed at people's minds:*	*Services directed at intangible assets:*
	Education	Banking
	Broadcasting	Legal services
	Information services	Accounting
	Theaters	Securities
	Museums	Insurance

SOURCE: Adapted from Christopher H. Lovelock, *Services Marketing*, 3rd ed. (Upper Saddle River, NJ: Prentice-Hall, 1996), 29.

During this determination, the marketer must consider other tactical variables that have an impact on the preparation of the service offering. The measurement of services capacity and delivery efficiency often remains highly qualitative rather than quantitative. In the field of communications, the intangibility of the service reduces the marketer's ability to provide samples. This makes communicating the service offer much more difficult than communicating an offer for a good. Brochures or catalogs explaining services often must show a "proxy" for the service in order to provide the prospective customer with tangible clues. A cleaning service, for instance, can show a picture of an individual removing trash or cleaning a window. However, the picture will not fully communicate the performance of the service. Because of the different needs and requirements of individual consumers, the marketer must pay very close attention to the two-way flow of communication. Mass communication must often be supported by intimate one-on-one follow-up.

The role of personnel deserves special consideration in the international marketing of services. Because the customer interface is intense, proper provisions need to be made for training personnel both domestically and internationally. Major emphasis must be placed on appearance. Most of the time, the person delivering the service—rather than the service itself—will communicate the spirit, value, and attitudes of the service corporation. Since the service person is both the producer as well as the marketer of the service, recruitment and training techniques must focus on dimensions such as customer relationship management and image projection as well as competence in the design and delivery of the service.[22]

This close interaction with the consumer will also have organizational implications. Whereas tight control over personnel may be desired, the individual interaction that

[22]Paul G. Patterson and Muris Cicic, "A Typology of Service Firms in International Markets: An Empirical Investigation," *Journal of International Marketing* 3 (Number 4, 1995): 57–83.

is required points toward the need for an international decentralization of service delivery. This, in turn, requires delegation of large amounts of responsibility to individuals and service "subsidiaries" and requires a great deal of trust in all organizational units. This trust, of course, can be greatly enhanced through proper methods of training and supervision. Sole ownership also helps strengthen this trust. Research has shown that service firms, in their international expansion, tend greatly to prefer the establishment of full-control ventures. Only when costs escalate and the company-specific advantage diminishes will service firms seek out shared-control ventures.[23]

The areas of pricing and financing require special attention. Because services cannot be stored, much greater responsiveness to demand fluctuation must exist, and therefore, much greater pricing flexibility must be maintained. At the same time, flexibility is countered by the desire to provide transparency for both the seller and the buyer of services in order to foster an ongoing relationship. The intangibility of services also makes financing more difficult. Frequently, even financial institutions with large amounts of international experience are less willing to provide financial support for international services than for products. The reasons are that the value of services is more difficult to assess, service performance is more difficult to monitor, and services are difficult to repossess. Therefore, customer complaints and difficulties in receiving payments are much more troublesome for a lender to evaluate for services than for products.

Finally, the distribution implications of international services must be considered. Usually, short and direct channels are required. Within these channels, closeness to the customer is of overriding importance in order to understand what the customer really wants, to trace the use of the service, and to aid the consumer in obtaining a truly tailor-made service.

SUMMARY

Services are taking on an increasing importance in international marketing. They need to be considered separately from the marketing of goods because they no longer simply complement goods. Increasingly, goods complement services or are in competition with them. Because of service attributes such as intangibility, perishability, customization, and cultural sensitivity, the international marketing of services is frequently more complex than that of goods.

Services play an increasing role in the global economy. As a result, international growth and competition in this sector outstrips that of merchandise trade and is likely to intensify in the future. Even though services are unlikely to replace production, the sector will account for the shaping of new comparative advantages internationally, particularly in light of new facilitating technologies that encourage electronic commerce.

The many service firms now operating domestically need to investigate the possibility of going global. The historical patterns in which service providers followed manufacturers abroad have become obsolete as stand-alone services have become more important to world trade. Management must therefore assess its vulnerability to service competition from abroad and explore opportunities to provide its services internationally.

---

[23]M. Krishna Erramilli and C. P. Rao, "Service Firms' International Entry-Mode Choice: A Modified Transaction–Cost Analysis Approach," *Journal of Marketing* 57 (July 1993): 19–38.

QUESTIONS FOR DISCUSSION

1. How has the Internet affected your services purchases?
2. Discuss the major reasons for the growth of international services.
3. How does the international sale of services differ from the sale of goods?
4. What are some of the international marketing implications of service intangibility?
5. Discuss the effects of cultural sensitivity on international services.
6. What are some ways for a firm to expand its services internationally?

7. How can a firm in a developing country participate in the international services boom?
8. Which services would be expected to migrate globally in the next decade? Why?
9. Find the most current data on the five leading export and import countries for commercial services. The information is available on the World Trade Organization site, **www.wto.org.** Click the resources button.
10. What are the key U.S. services exports and imports? What is the current services trade balance? (**www.bea.doc.gov**)

RECOMMENDED READINGS

Aharoni, Yair. *Coalitions and Competition: The Globalization of Professional Business Services.* New York: Routledge, 1993.

Bateson, John E.G., *Managing Services Marketing*, 4th ed., Fort Worth: The Dryden Press, 1999.

Business Guide to the World Trading System. Geneva: International Trade Centre UNCTAD/WTO and London, Commonwealth Secretariat, 1999.

Hoekman, Bernard M. *Liberalizing Trade in Services.* Washington, DC: The World Bank, 1994.

Kurtz, David L. and Kenneth Clow. *Services Marketing*, New York: John Wiley & Sons, 1998.

Lovelock, Christopher H. *Principles of Services Marketing and Management.* Upper Saddle River, N.J.: Prentice-Hall, 1999.

Meyer, Anton and Frank Dornach, *The German Customer Barometer*, Annual, Munich, FMG–Verlag, 2000.

Primo Braga, Carlos. "The Impact of the Internationalization of Services on Developing Countries," *Finance and Development* 33 (Number 1, 1996): 34–37.

Global Pricing Strategies

Chapter 18

THE INTERNATIONAL MARKETPLACE 18.1

A Global Tax War?

THE U.S. INTERNAL REVENUE SERVICE has begun to look more closely at transfer pricing on sales of goods and services among subsidiaries or between subsidiaries and the parent company. It has filed claims against hundreds of companies in recent years, claiming that multinational companies too often manipulate intracompany pricing to minimize their worldwide tax bills. Experts calculate that foreign-based multinationals evade at least $20 billion in U.S. taxes. Other countries have also strengthened their review systems. Japan has created specific transfer pricing legislation that penalizes marketers for not providing information in time to meet deadlines set by the government. German tax authorities are carefully checking intracompany charges to deem their appropriateness.

In its biggest known victory, the IRS made its case that Japan's Toyota had been systematically overcharging its U.S. subsidiary for years on most of the cars, trucks, and parts sold in the United States. What would have been profits in the United States were now accrued in Japan. Toyota denied improprieties but agreed to a reported $1 billion settlement, paid in part with tax rebates from the government of Japan.

And now Japan is striking back. The Japanese National Tax Administration Agency (NTAA) has charged the Coca-Cola Co. with a $145 million tax deficiency for 1990–92. They also hit AIU Insurance Co., the Japanese subsidiary of giant American International Group Inc., with an $87 million bill that was later reduced to $37 million in a settlement. "There is clearly a war going on," says a Tokyo lawyer who advises foreign companies on Japanese tax laws. Some fear that the agency will target sectors in which U.S. firms are doing well,

such as pharmaceuticals, computers, and chemicals, for retaliatory tax investigations. Companies would also be questioned over intangibles, such as R&D and marketing costs, which are typically higher for U.S. firms.

Other countries are also trying to tap into what they see as a potentially lucrative revenue stream. The German tax agency is heightening audit activity beyond what they ordinarily do. Fear is widespread, therefore, that an all-out tax war is about to erupt. To avoid that, the Organization for Economic Cooperation and Development (OECD) published its transfer-pricing guidelines in mid-1995, with periodic revisions since then. Experts also speculate that the European Court may move to standardize corporate tax rates within the EU, which would please high-taxing Germany and France but concern lower-taxing Britian and Ireland.

Until recently, countries such as Argentina, Brazil, and Mexico relied on other mechanisms, such as exchange controls, high import duties, and other non-tariff barriers, to protect their tax bases. However, as those regimes are being abolished as part of multilateral and regional agreements, transfer pricing rules are being enacted to do the same job.

Increasing communication among tax authorities is having a dramatic effect and will continue to accelerate, especially with the trend toward shifting profits. Historically, transfer pricing from the point of view of a U.S. company meant the shifting of income out of the United States, but with the corporate tax rate at 34 percent, many U.S. companies are now trying to use transfer pricing to shift profits into the country. Thus, U.S. multinationals must be prepared to justify transfer pricing policies on two or more fronts.

The entire tax equation has become more complicated because of changes in customs duties. In many countries, revenues from customs and indirect taxes are greater than revenue from corporate taxes. Authorities will jealously guard the income stream from customs taxes, and marketers could find gains on income taxes erased by losses on customs taxes.

Most multinationals are moving cautiously. Glen White, director of taxes at Dow Chemical, stresses this point. "I don't think anybody can afford to have a transfer-pricing system that cannot be revealed to all the relevant governments."

sources: Erika Morphy, "Global Reaching," *Export Today*, May 1999, 60–76; "Transfer Pricing Problem," *Journal of Commerce*, November 14, 1997, 3A; "Here Comes the Great Global Tax War," *Business Week*, May 30, 1994,

55–56; "Pricing Yourself into a Market," *Business Asia*, December 21, 1992, 1; "The Corporate Shell Game," *Newsweek*, April 15, 1991, 48–49; and "Worldwide Tax Authorities Promise Increased Scrutiny of Transfer Pricing," *Business International Money Report*, February 22, 1988, 72, "Gimme Shelter: Is Tax Competition Among Countries a Good or Bad Thing?, *The Economist*, vol. 354, January 29, 2000.

See http://www.oecd.org for *The OECD Transfer Pricing Guidelines*, 1998. See also http://www.irs. ustreas.gov for *Development of IRC 482 Cases.*

SUCCESSFUL PRICING IS A KEY ELEMENT in the marketing mix. A study of 202 U.S. and non-U.S. multinational corporations found pricing to rank second only to the product variable in importance among the concerns of marketing managers.[1] This chapter will focus on price setting by multinational corporations that have direct inventories in other countries. This involves the pricing of sales to members of the corporate family as well as pricing within the individual markets in which the company operates. With increased economic integration and globalization of markets, the coordination of pricing strategies between markets becomes more important.

Transfer Pricing

Transfer pricing, or intracorporate pricing, is the pricing of sales to members of the extended corporate family. With rapid globalization and consolidation across borders, estimates have up to two-thirds of world trade taking place between related parties, including shipments and transfers from parent company to affiliates as well as trade between alliance partners.[2] This means that transfer pricing has to be managed in a world characterized by different tax rates, different foreign exchange rates, varying governmental regulations, and other economic and social challenges, as seen in *The International Marketplace 18.1.* Allocation of resources among the various units of the multinational corporation requires the central management of the corporation to establish the appropriate transfer price to achieve these objectives:

1. Competitiveness in the international marketplace
2. Reduction of taxes and tariffs
3. Management of cash flows
4. Minimization of foreign exchange risks
5. Avoidance of conflicts with home and host governments
6. Internal concerns such as goal congruence and motivation of subsidiary managers[3]

[1]Saeed Samiee, "Elements of Marketing Strategy: A Comparative Study of U.S. and Non-U.S. Based Companies," *International Marketing Review* 1 (Summer 1982): 119–126.

[2]"Transfer Pricing Moves to the Forefront," *Journal of Commerce*, November 14, 1997, 3A.

[3]Wagdy M. Abdallah, "How to Motivate and Evaluate Managers with International Transfer Pricing Systems," *Management International Review* 29 (1989): 65–71.

TABLE 18.1	**Influences on Transfer Pricing Decisions**

1. Market conditions in the foreign country
2. Competition in the foreign country
3. Reasonable profit for the foreign affiliate
4. U.S. federal income taxes
5. Economic conditions in the foreign country
6. Import restrictions
7. Customs duties
8. Price controls
9. Taxation in the foreign country
10. Exchange controls

SOURCE: Jane O. Burns, "Transfer Pricing Decisions in U.S. Multinational Corporations," *Journal of International Business Studies* 11 (Fall 1980): 23–39.

Intracorporate sales can so easily change the consolidated global results that they compose one of the most important ongoing decision areas in the company. Transfer prices are usually set by the major financial officer—normally the financial vice president or comptroller—and parent company executives are uniformly unwilling to allow much participation by other department or subsidiary executives.[4] However, even among the largest companies, only 28 percent have made transfer pricing a part of their overall corporate policies, while a full 30 percent still view transfer pricing only as a compliance matter.[5]

Transfer prices can be based on costs or on market prices. The cost approach uses an internally calculated cost with a percentage markup added. The market price approach is based on an established market selling price, and the products are usually sold at that price minus a discount to allow some margin of profit for the buying division. In general, cost-based prices are easier to manipulate[6] because the cost base itself may be any one of these three: full cost, variable cost, or marginal cost.

Factors that have a major influence on intracompany prices are listed in Table 18.1. Market conditions in general, and those relating to the competitive situation in particular, were mentioned as key variables by 210 senior financial officers of multinational corporations.[7] In some markets, especially in the Far East, competition may prevent the international marketer from pricing at will. Prices may have to be adjusted to meet local competition with lower labor costs. This practice may provide entry to the market and a reasonable profit to the affiliate. However, in the long term, it may also become a subsidy to an inefficient business. Further, tax and customs authorities may object because underpricing means that the seller is earning less income than it would otherwise receive in the country of origin and is paying duties on a lower base price on entry to the destination country.

Economic conditions in a market, especially the imposition of controls on movements of funds, may require the use of transfer pricing to allow the company to repatriate revenues. As an example, a U.S.-based multinational corporation with central procurement facilities required its subsidiaries to buy all raw materials from the parent; it began charging a standard 7 percent for its services, which include guarantee-

[4]J. Fremgen, "Measuring Profit of Part of a Firm," *Management Accounting* 47 (January 1966): 7–18; Jeffrey Arpan, "Multinational Firm Pricing in International Markets," *Sloan Management Review* 15 (Winter 1973): 1–9.

[5]Ernst & Young, *Strategic Transfer Pricing*, available at **http://www.ey.com**.

[6]Paul Cook, "New Techniques for Intracompany Pricing," *Harvard Business Review* 35 (July–August 1957): 37–44.

[7]Jane O. Burns, "Transfer Pricing Decisions in U.S. Multinational Corporations," *Journal of International Business Studies* 11 (Fall 1980): 23–39.

ing on-time delivery and appropriate quality. The company estimates that its revenue remittances from a single Latin American country, which had placed restrictions on remittances from subsidiaries to parent companies, increased by $900,000 after the surcharge was put into effect.[8]

International transfer pricing objectives may lead to conflicting objectives, especially if the influencing factors vary dramatically from one market to another. For example, it may be quite difficult to perfectly match subsidiary goals with the global goals of the multinational corporation. Specific policies should therefore exist that would motivate subsidiary managers to avoid making decisions that would be in conflict with overall corporate goals. If transfer pricing policies lead to an inaccurate financial measure of the subsidiary's performance, this should be taken into account when a performance evaluation is made.

Use of Transfer Prices to Achieve Corporate Objectives

Three philosophies of transfer pricing have emerged over time: (1) cost-based (direct cost or cost-plus), (2) market-based (discounted "dealer" price derived from end market prices), and (3) **arm's-length price,** or the price that unrelated parties would have reached on the same transaction. The rationale for transferring at cost is that it increases the profits of affiliates, and their profitability will eventually benefit the entire corporation. In most cases, cost-plus is used, requiring every affiliate to be a profit center. Deriving transfer prices from the market is the most marketing-oriented method because it takes local conditions into account. Arm's-length pricing is favored by many constituents, such as governments, to ensure proper intracompany pricing. However, the method becomes difficult when sales to outside parties do not occur in a product category. Additionally, it is often difficult to convince external authorities that true negotiation occurs between two entities controlled by the same parent. In a study of 32 U.S.-based multinational corporations operating in Latin America, a total of 57 percent stated that they use a strategy of arm's-length pricing for their shipments, while the others used negotiated prices, cost-plus, or some other method.[9] Generally tax authorities will honor agreements among companies provided those agreements are commercially reasonable, and the companies abide by the agreements consistently.[10]

The effect of environmental influences in overseas markets can be alleviated by manipulating transfer prices.[11] High transfer prices on goods shipped to a subsidiary and low ones on goods imported from it will result in minimizing the tax liability of a subsidiary operating in a country with a high income tax. For example, with the lowering in 1986 of the corporate tax rate in the United States to 34 percent, which is one of the lowest rates among industrialized nations, many multinational corporations now have an incentive to report higher profits in the United States and lower profits in other countries. On the other hand, a higher transfer price may have an effect on the import duty, especially if it is assessed on an ad valorem basis. Exceeding a certain threshold may boost the duty substantially when the product is considered a luxury and will have a negative impact on the subsidiary's competitive posture. Adjusting transfer prices for the opposite effects of taxes and duties is, therefore, a delicate balancing act.

Transfer prices may be adjusted to balance the effects of fluctuating currencies when one partner is operating in a low-inflation environment and the other in one of

---

[8]"How to Free Blocked Funds via Supplier Surcharges," *Business International*, December 7, 1984, 387.

[9]Robert Grosse, "Financial Transfers in the MNE: The Latin American Case," *Management International Review* 26 (1986): 33–44.

[10]Erika Morphy, "Spend and Tax Politics," *Export Today*, April 1999, 50–56.

[11]James Shulman, "When the Price Is Wrong—By Design," *Columbia Journal of World Business* 4 (May–June 1967): 69–76.

rampant inflation. Economic restrictions such as controls on dividend remittances and allowable deductions for expenses incurred can also be blunted. For example, if certain services performed by corporate headquarters (such as product development or strategic planning assistance) cannot be charged to the subsidiaries, costs for these services can be recouped by increases in the transfer prices of other product components. A subsidiary's financial and competitive position can be manipulated by the use of lower transfer prices. Start-up costs can be lowered, a market niche carved more quickly, and long-term survival guaranteed. Ultimately, the entire transfer price and taxation question is best dealt with at a time when the company is considering a major expansion or restructuring of operations. For example, if it fits the overall plan, a portion of a unit's R&D and marketing activities could be funded in a relatively low tax jurisdiction.

With the increase of government regulation on foreign participation, transfer pricing becomes an important tool for recouping expenses from joint ventures, especially if there are restrictions on profit repatriation. A study of transfer price setting in Canada found that the impetus toward a high or low transfer price depends on the level of ownership in the subsidiary, the dividend payout ratios, the effective marginal tax rates in both parent and subsidiary countries, and the tariff on goods transferred.[12] A study of national differences in the use of transfer prices found that British companies set transfer prices at their best estimate of market prices, whereas the dominant feature of French companies is the use of transfer prices that are roughly equivalent to marginal cost.[13] Of two U.S. companies studied, one used a system of market prices, and the second used a system of marginal cost prices. Top management in the U.S. companies, however, were found to be more conscious than the British or the French of the importance and the difficulty of establishing transfer prices, and corporate headquarters played a far more active role in price setting.

Transfer pricing problems grow geometrically as all of the subsidiaries with differing environmental concerns are added to the planning exercise, calling for more detailed intracompany data for decision making. Further, fluctuating exchange rates make the planning even more challenging. However, to prevent double taxation and meet arm's-length requirements, it is essential that the corporation's pricing practices be uniform. Many have adopted a philosophy that calls for an obligation to maintain a good-citizen fiscal approach (that is, recognizing the liability to pay taxes and duties in every country of operation and to avoid artificial tax-avoidance schemes) and a belief that the primary goal of transfer pricing is to support and develop commercial activities.[14]

Transfer Pricing Challenges

Transfer pricing policies face two general types of challenges. The first is internal to the multinational corporation and concerns the motivation of those affected by the pricing policies of the corporation. The second, an external one, deals with relations between the corporation and tax authorities in both the home country and the host countries.

Performance Measurement   Manipulating intracorporate prices complicates internal control measures and, without proper documentation, will cause major problems. If the firm operates on a profit center basis, some consideration must be given to the effect of

[12]D. J. Fowler, "Transfer Prices and Profit Maximization in Multinational Enterprise Operations." *Journal of International Business Studies* (Winter 1975): 9–26.

[13]David Granick, "National Differences in the Use of Internal Transfer Prices," *California Management Review* 17 (Summer 1975): 28–40.

[14]Michael P. Casey, "International Transfer Pricing," *Management Accounting* 66 (October 1985): 31–35.

transfer pricing on the subsidiary's apparent profit performance and its actual performance. To judge a subsidiary's profit performance as not satisfactory when it was targeted to be a net source of funds can easily create morale problems. The situation may be further complicated by cultural differences in the subsidiary's management, especially if the need to subsidize less-efficient members of the corporate family is not made clear. An adjustment in the control mechanism is called for to give appropriate credit to divisions for their actual contributions. The method may range from dual bookkeeping to compensation in budgets and profit plans. Regardless of the method, proper organizational communication is necessary to avoid conflict between subsidiaries and headquarters.

Taxation

Transfer prices will by definition involve the tax and regulatory jurisdictions of the countries in which the company does business, as is pointed out in *The International Marketplace 18.1.* Sales and transfers of tangible properties and transfers of intangibles such as patent rights and manufacturing know-how are subject to close review and to determinations about the adequacy of compensation received. This quite often puts the multinational corporation in a difficult position. U.S. authorities may think the transfer price is too low, whereas it may be perceived as too high by the foreign entity, especially if a less-developed country is involved. Section 482 of the Internal Revenue Code gives the Commissioner of the IRS vast authority to reallocate income between controlled foreign operations and U.S. parents and between U.S. operations of foreign corporations.

Before the early 1960s, the enforcement efforts under Section 482 were mostly domestic. However, since 1962, the U.S. government has attempted to stop U.S. companies from shifting U.S. income to their foreign subsidiaries in low- or no-tax jurisdictions and has affirmed the arm's-length standard as the principal basis for transfer pricing. Because unrelated parties normally sell products and services at a profit, an arm's-length price normally involves a profit to the seller.

A significant portion of Section 482 adjustments, including those resulting from the 1986 Tax Reform Act, have focused on licensing and other transfer of intangibles such as patents and trademarks. Historically, transfer pricing from a U.S. company's point of view has meant the shifting of income out of the United States. But with the lower corporate tax rate, the question now is how to use transfer pricing to shift profits into the United States.

According to Section 482, there are four methods of determining an arm's-length price, and they are to be used in the following order:

1. The comparable uncontrolled price method
2. The resale price method
3. The cost-plus method
4. Any other reasonable method

Beginning with the 1994 tax return, U.S. firms have had to disclose the pricing method they use so that the IRS can ascertain that the price was established using the arm's-length principle.[15] Guidelines of the Organization for Economic Cooperation and Development (OECD) to transfer pricing are similar to those used by U.S. authorities.[16] Some experts who argue that the arm's-length standard is only applicable for commodities businesses have proposed a simpler system that allocates profits by a formula such as that of the state of California that factors in percentages of world sales, assets, and other indicators. The rapid changes in international marketing caused by e-business will also have an impact on transfer pricing. Although transactions

---

[15]Weston Anson, "An Arm's Length View of Transfer Pricing," *International Tax Review* (December 1999): 7–9; "Pricing Foreign Transactions," *Small Business Reports* (April 1993): 65–66.

[16]Organization for Economic Cooperation and Development, Paris, *1979 Report on Transfer Pricing*, 1979, para. 45.

involving e-commerce represent new ways of conducting business, the fundamental economic relationships will remain the same. As a result, the existing principle of arm's length will probably be retained and adapted to address cross-border activities in a virtual economy.[17]

The starting point for testing the appropriateness of transfer prices is a comparison with *comparable uncontrolled* transactions, involving unrelated parties. Uncontrolled prices exist when (1) sales are made by members of the multinational corporation to unrelated parties, (2) purchases are made by members of the multinational corporation from unrelated parties, and (3) sales are made between two unrelated parties, neither of which is a member of the multinational corporation. In some cases, marketers have created third-party trading where none existed before. Instead of selling 100 percent of the product in a market to a related party, the seller can arrange a small number of direct transactions with unrelated parties to create a benchmark against which to measure related-party transactions.

If this method does not apply, the *resale* method can be used. This usually applies best to transfers to sales subsidiaries for ultimate distribution. The arm's-length approximation is arrived at by subtracting the subsidiary's profit from an uncontrolled selling price. The appropriateness of the amount is determined by comparison with a similar product being marketed by the multinational corporation.

The *cost-plus* approach is most applicable for transfers of components or unfinished goods to overseas subsidiaries. The arm's-length approximation is achieved by adding an appropriate markup for profit to the seller's total cost of the product.[18] The key is to apply such markups consistently over time and across markets.

Such comparisons, however, are not always possible even under the most favorable circumstances and may remain burdened with arbitrariness. Comparisons are impossible for products that are unique or when goods are traded only with related parties. Adjusting price comparisons for differences in the product mix, or for the inherently different facts and circumstances surrounding specific transactions between unrelated parties, undermines the reliance that can be placed on any such comparisons. The most accepted of the other reasonable methods is the *functional analysis approach.*[19] The functional analysis measures the profits of each of the related companies and compares it with the proportionate contribution to total income of the corporate group. It addresses the question of what profit would have been reported if the intercorporate transactions had involved unrelated parties. Understanding the functional interrelationships of the various parties (that is, which entity does what) is basic to determining each entity's economic contribution via-à-vis total income of the corporate group.

Since 1991, the Internal Revenue Service has been signing "advance pricing" agreements (APAs) with multinational corporations to stem the tide of unpaid U.S. income taxes. By December 31, 1999, a total of 231 such agreements were completed and 187 were under negotiation.[20] Since 1998, special provisions have been made for small and medium-sized companies to negotiate such arrangements. Agreement on transfer pricing is set ahead of time, thus eliminating court challenges and costly audits. The harsh penalties have also caused companies to consider APAs. In the United States, a transfer pricing violation can result in a 40 percent penalty on the amount of underpayment, whereas in Mexico the penalty can reach 100 percent. The main

[17]Brad Rolph and Jay Niederhoffer, "Transfer Pricing and E-Commerce," *International Tax Review* (September 1999): 34–39.

[18]David P. Donnelly, "Eliminating Uncertainty in Dealing with Section 482," *International Tax Journal* 12 (Summer 1986): 213–227.

[19]Gunther Schindler, "Income Allocation under Revenue Code Section 482," *Trade Trends* 2 (September 1984): 3.

[20]Data provided by the Internal Revenue Service by interview, March 2, 2000.

THE INTERNATIONAL MARKETPLACE 18.2

Advance Pricing Agreements: Knocking on the IRS's Door

HALFWAY THROUGH FORD MOTOR COMPANY'S negotiations to set up an advance pricing agreement to govern transfer prices between its U.S. and German operations, Ford executives began wondering whether they should have started the process at all. The German tax authorities were advancing some theories the company could never have imagined. However, after the 30-month-long process, Ford negotiators believe they are better off with the agreement than without one. Had the company been audited instead, the level of double taxation that could have been assessed would have made for an even longer ordeal.

In cases where a company is doing business in a country that has a bilateral tax treaty with the United States, the company can seek a bilateral APA that is negotiated simultaneously with the tax authorities of both countries. In the case of Ford, for example, most of the negotiations actually took place between the IRS and the German tax authorities, while Ford sat by and watched them divide up the company's taxable earnings.

Ford is somewhat unusual in that it has negotiated three bilateral APAs; the other two cover U.S.-Canada and U.S.-U.K. operations. Most other large multinationals, however, are still debating whether these proactive tax negotiations are worth the cost and effort. They are rare, despite intense IRS marketing efforts on their behalf. Only 10 percent of U.S. multinationals have or plan to pursue an APA with the IRS, while 4 percent are considering an APA with a host country tax authority.

Many countries, especially emerging economies, do not have bilateral tax agreements with the United States. In such cases, a company can negotiate a unilateral APA with the IRS on its cross-border operations with that country.

As the Ford example showed, APAs involve a great deal of analysis. Some companies are concerned about sitting down with tax authorities, for fear of other issues emerging. However, the cost of transfer pricing accounting services has declined since 1994, when it was still a new field. Now more of the needed data are online, and software has been developed to address the issue. A study can be had for $15,000, and many of the big accounting firms include these studies as part of their global tax strategy services.

SOURCE: "Knocking on the IRS's Door," *Export Today*, April 1999, 52–73.

See also http://www.irs.ustreas.gov.

criticism of this approach is the exorbitant amounts of staff time that each agreement requires.[21] Some also argue that such agreements may result in worse transfer pricing systems, from the corporate point of view, because companies with effective intracompany bargaining processes may have to replace them with poorly designed ones to satisfy the tax authorities.[22] APAs are discussed further in *The International Marketplace 18.2*.

The most difficult of cases are those involving intangibles, because comparables are absent in most cases. The IRS requires that the price or royalty rate for any cross-border transfer be commensurate with income; that is, it must result in a fair distribution of income between the units. This requires marketers to analyze and attach a value to each business function (R&D, manufacturing, assembly, marketing services, and distribution). Comparable transactions, when available—or, if absent, industry norms—should be used to calculate the rates of return for each function. Take, for example, a subsidiary that makes a $100 profit on the sale of a product manufactured with technology developed and licensed by the U.S. parent. If the firm identifies rates of return for manufacturing and distribution of 30 percent and 10 percent, then $40 of the profit must be allocated to the subsidiary. The remaining $60 would be taxable

[21]Stephen Barlas, "Taxation of Foreign Companies," *Management Accounting* 74 (June 1993): 10.

[22]"Pricing Yourself into a Market," *Business Asia*, December 21, 1992, 1.

income to the parent.[23] Needless to say, many of the analyses have to be quite subjective, especially in cases that involve the transfer of intellectual property, and may lead to controversies and disputes with tax authorities.

In the host environments, the concern of multinational corporations is to maintain the status of good corporate citizenship. Many corporations, in drafting multinational codes of conduct, have specified that their intracorporate pricing will follow arm's-length pricing.

Pricing within Individual Markets

Pricing within the individual markets in which the company operates is determined by (1) corporate objectives, (2) costs, (3) customer behavior and market conditions, (4) market structure, and (5) environmental constraints.[24] Because all these factors vary among the countries in which the multinational corporation might have a presence, the pricing policy is under pressure to vary as well. At the same time, convergence of markets is requiring companies to increase the coordination of prices across markets. In a study of the price decision making for nondomestic markets of 42 U.S.-based multinational corporations, the major problem areas in international pricing were meeting competition, cost, lack of competitive information, distribution and channel factors, and government barriers.[25]

Although many global marketers, both U.S.-based[26] and foreign-based,[27] emphasize nonprice methods of competition, they rank pricing high as a marketing tool overseas, even though the nondomestic pricing decisions are made at middle management level in a majority of firms. Pricing decisions also tend to be made more at the local level, with coordination from headquarters in more strategic decision situations.[28]

Corporate Objectives

Global marketers must set and adjust their objectives, both financial (such as return on investment) and marketing-related (such as maintaining or increasing market share), based on the prevailing conditions in each of their markets. Pricing may well influence the overall strategic moves of the company as a whole. This is well illustrated by the decision of many foreign-based companies, automakers for example, to begin production in the United States rather than to continue exporting. To remain competitive in the market, many have had to increase the dollar component of their output. Apart from trade barriers, many have had their market shares erode because of higher wages in their home markets, increasing shipping costs, and unfavorable exchange rates. Market share very often plays a major role in pricing decisions in that marketers may be willing to sacrifice immediate earnings for market share gain or

[23]"MNCs Face Tighter Net over Transfer Pricing Rules," *Business International*, October 31, 1988, 337–338.

[24]Helmut Becker, "Pricing: An International Marketing Challenge," in *International Marketing Strategy*, eds. Hans Thorelli and Helmut Becker (New York: Pergamon Press, 1980), 206–217.

[25]James C. Baker and John K. Ryans, "Some Aspects of International Pricing: A Neglected Area of Management Policy," *Management Decisions* (Summer 1973): 177–182.

[26]J. J. Boddewyn, Robin Soehl, and Jacques Picard, "Standardization in International Marketing: Is Ted Levitt in Fact Right?" *Business Horizons* 29 (November–December 1986): 69–75.

[27]Saeed Samiee, "Pricing in Marketing Strategies of U.S.- and Foreign-Based Companies," *Journal of Business Research* 15 (March 1987): 17–30.

[28]For an example of pricing processes by multinational marketers, see John U. Farley, James M. Hulbert, and David Weinstein, "Price Setting and Volume Planning by Two European Industrial Companies: A Study and Comparison of Decision Processes," *Journal of Marketing* 44 (Winter 1980): 46–54.

TABLE 18.2	South Korea's Price Edge over Japan							
	KOREAN BRAND				JAPANESE BRAND			
PRODUCT	1985	1989	1996	2000	1985	1989	1996	2000
Subcompact autos	Excel/Accent (Hyundai) $5,500	$5,999	$9,079	$9,699	Sentra (Nissan) $7,600	$7,299	$11,499	$11,649
Videocassette recorders	Samsung $270	$189	$260	$120	Toshiba $350	$299	$430	$199
Compact refrigerators	Goldstar $149	$88	$150	N/A	Sanyo $265	$99	$180	$99
13-inch color televisions	Samsung $148	$159	$179	$170	Hitachi $189	$199	$229	$180
Microwave ovens	Goldstar $149	$79	$120	$130	Toshiba $180	$99	$140	$130

SOURCE: Originally published in L. Helm, "The Koreans Are Coming," *Business Week*, December 23, 1985, 46–52; direct manufacturer/retailer inquiries, June 1989, December 1996, and March 2000; In the absence of information/availability, a similar make/model has been used based on *Consumer Reports* data.

maintenance. This is especially true in highly competitive situations; for example, during a period of extremely high competitive activity in Japan in the computer sector, the local Fujitsu's one-year net income was only 5 percent of sales, compared with IBM's 12.7 percent worldwide and 7.6 percent in Japan.

Pricing decisions will also vary depending on the pricing situation. The basics of first-time pricing, price adjustment, and product line pricing as discussed earlier apply to pricing within nondomestic situations as well. For example, companies such as Kodak and Xerox, which introduce all of their new products worldwide within a very short time period, have an option of either skimming or penetration pricing. If the product is an innovation, the marketer may decide to charge a premium for the product. If, however, competition is keen or expected to increase in the near future, lower prices may be used to make the product more attractive to buyers and the market less attractive to competition. The Korean general trading companies (such as Daewoo, Goldstar, Hyundai, and Samsung) were able to penetrate and capture the low end of many consumer goods markets in both the United States and Europe based on price competitiveness over the past ten years (as shown in Table 18.2).

For the most part, the Korean general trading companies have competed in the world marketplace, especially against the Japanese, on price rather than product traits, with the major objective of capturing a foothold in various markets. For example, Samsung was able to gain access to U.S. markets when J. C. Penney was looking for lower-priced microwave ovens in the early 1980s. Samsung's ovens retailed for $299, whereas most models averaged between $350 and $400 at the time.[29] However, substantial strides in production technology and relentless marketing have started to make Korean products serious competitors in the medium to high price brackets as well.[30]

Price changes may be frequent if the company's objective is to undersell a major competitor. A marketer may, for example, decide to maintain a price level 10 to 20 percent below that of a major competitor; price changes would be necessary

[29]Ira C. Magaziner and Mark Patinkin, "Fast Heat: How Korea Won the Microwave War," *Harvard Business Review* 67 (January–February 1989): 83–92.

[30]"Ford, GM Square Off over Daewoo Motor; The Question Is: Why?" *The Wall Street Journal*, February 14, 2000, A1, A13.

whenever the competitor made significant changes in its prices. Price changes may also be required because of changes in foreign exchange rates. Many marketers were forced to increase prices in the United States on goods of non-U.S. origin when the dollar weakened during the late 1980s and early to mid-1990s. With longer-term unfavorable currency changes, marketers have to improve their efficiency and/or shift production bases. For example, Japanese car manufacturers have transplanted more manufacturing into the United States to ensure that yen-dollar changes do not have as sharp an impact as they once did. Furthermore, design and production was improved so that profitability could be maintained even at 80 or 85 yen to the dollar. When 1996 yen values were over 110 to the dollar, Japanese companies were able to cut prices 1.1 percent for the 1997 model year, while their U.S. competitors increased them by 2.8 percent on the average.[31]

Product line pricing occurs typically in conjunction with positioning decisions. The global marketer may have a premium line as well as a standard line and, in some cases, may sell directly to retailers for their private label sales. Products facing mass markets have keener competition and smaller profit margins than premium products, which may well be priced more liberally because there is less competition. For example, for decades, Caterpillar's big ticket items virtually sold themselves. But environmental factors, such as the U.S. budget deficit, the Gulf states oil crunch, and the Asian crisis, resulted in fewer large-scale highway and construction projects. The company then focused on smaller equipment to remain competitive globally.[32]

Costs

Costs are frequently used as a basis for price determination largely because they are easily measured and provide a floor under which prices cannot go in the long term. These include procurement, manufacturing, logistics, and marketing costs, as well as overhead. Quality at an affordable price drives most procurement systems. The decision to turn to offshore suppliers may often be influenced by their lower prices, which enable the marketer to remain competitive.[33] Locating manufacturing facilities in different parts of the world may lower various costs, such as labor or distribution costs, although this may create new challenges. While a market may be attractive as far as labor costs are concerned, issues such as productivity, additional costs (such as logistics), and political risk will have to be factored in. Furthermore, a country may lose its attraction due to increasing costs (for example, the average industrial wage rose 110 percent in Korea in the 1990s), and the marketer may have to start the cycle anew by going to new markets (such as Indonesia or Vietnam).

Varying inflation rates will have a major impact on the administration of prices, especially because they are usually accompanied by government controls. The task of the parent company is to aid subsidiaries in their planning to ensure reaching margin targets despite unfavorable market conditions. Most experienced companies in the emerging markets generally have strong country managers who create significant value through their understanding of the local environment. Their ability to be more agile in a turbulent environment is a significant competitive advantage. Inflationary environments call for constant price adjustments; in markets with hyperinflation, pricing may be in a stable currency such as the U.S. dollar or the euro with daily translation into the local currency. In such volatile environments, the marketer may want to shift supply arrangements to cost-effective alternatives, pursue rapid inventory turnovers, shorten credit terms, and make sure contracts have appropriate safety mechanisms against inflation (e.g., choice of currency or escalator clause).

[31]"Detroit Is Getting Sideswiped by the Yen," *Business Week*, November 11, 1996, 54.

[32]Ronald Henkoff, "This Cat Is Acting Like a Tiger," *Fortune*, December 19, 1988, 69–76.

[33]"The Why, How, and What of Overseas Purchasing," *Purchasing*, June 25, 1987, 54–55.

THE INTERNATIONAL MARKETPLACE 18.3

Just Do It in a Recession!

W ITH THE ASIAN RECESSION having sapped purchasing power in Southeast Asia, Nike is targeting teens living in the region's rural and suburban areas with a range of "entry-level" footwear. The Nike Play Series line, launched in September 1999 in India, Indonesia, Singapore, and Thailand, retails for about $25, roughly half the price of most Nike shoes and far less than the $150 charged for its top-range products.

Asian kids in rural areas might be playing sports with no shoes at all, so they cannot relate to Nike's high-end products. Nike Play Series was created to introduce them to the concept of different shoes for different sports. Even among those who purchase luxury products, sales have fallen 30 percent in the Asian markets hardest hit by the 1997-1998 Asian currency crisis.

Ads for the new product line use the slogan "It's My Turn" and depict young Asian athletes (such as Singaporean soccer sensation Aliff Shafaein and Philippine basketball star Alvin Patrimonio) alongside images of major sports stars. Nike also built branded Play Zones in new or refurbished urban centers such as Singapore, Kuala Lumpur, Bangkok, Manila, and Johor Bahru. Each includes a multi-court facility where kids play everything from badminton to basketball, highlighted by "event days" with tournaments. In rural areas, Nike donated equipment such as basketball hoops and football goal posts to raise the profile of the Nike Play Series.

SOURCE: Normandy Madden, "Nike Sells $25 Shoe Line in Recession-Hit Region," *Advertising Age*, November 1999, 17.

http://nikebiz.com/story/stry_wdshoe.shtml
http://nikebiz.com/community/gcastry.shtml

Nike's World Shoe Project featuring Play Series line

Kickster   Hoopster

Sportster   Trainster

Shoes from Nike Play Series line.

The opposite scenario may also be encountered; that is, prices cannot be increased due to economic conditions. Strategies for thriving in disinflationary times may include (1) target pricing, in which efficiencies are sought in production and marketing to meet price-driven costing; (2) value pricing, to move away from coupons, discounts, and promotions to everyday low prices; (3) stripping down products, to offer quality without all the frills; (4) adding value by introducing innovative products sold at a modest premium (accompanied by strong merchandising and promotion) but perceived by customers to be worth it; and (5) getting close to customers by using new technologies (such as the Internet and EDI) to track their needs and your costs more closely.[34] An example of Nike's adjustment to the new realities in Asia appears in *The International Marketplace 18.3.*

[34]"Stuck!" *Business Week*, November 15, 1993, 146–155.

Internally, controversy may arise in determining which manufacturing and marketing costs to include. For example, controversy may arise over the amounts of research and development to charge to subsidiaries or over how to divide the costs of a pan-regional advertising campaign when costs are incurred primarily on satellite channels and viewership varies dramatically from one market to the next.

Demand and Market Factors

Demand will set a price ceiling in a given market. Despite the difficulties in obtaining data on foreign markets and forecasting potential demand, the global marketer must make judgments concerning the quantities that can be sold at different prices in each foreign market. The global marketer must understand the **price elasticity of consumer demand** to determine appropriate price levels, especially if cost structures change. A status-conscious market that insists on products with established reputations will be inelastic, allowing for far more pricing freedom than a market where price-consciousness drives demand. Many U.S. and European companies have regarded Japan as a place to sell premium products at premium prices. With the increased information and travel that globalization has brought about, status-consciousness is being replaced by a more practical consumerist sensibility: top quality at competitive prices.[35]

The marketer's freedom in making pricing decisions is closely tied to customer perceptions of the product offering and the marketing communication tied to it. *The International Marketplace 18.4* highlights the critical nature of quality perceptions on demand and the marketer's ability to shape that demand by price. Toyota is able to outsell Chevys, which are identical and both produced by NUMMI Inc., which is a joint venture between Toyota and GM, even though its version (the Corolla) is priced $2,000 higher on the average.

Prices have to be set keeping in mind not only the ultimate consumers but also the intermediaries involved. The success of a particular pricing strategy will depend on the willingness of both the manufacturer and the intermediary to cooperate. For example, if the marketer wants to undercut its competition, it has to make sure that retailers' margins remain adequate and competitive to ensure appropriate implementation. At the same time, there is enormous pressure on manufacturers' margins from the side of intermediaries who are growing in both size and global presence. These intermediaries, such as the French Carrefour and the British Marks & Spencer, demand low-cost, direct-supply contracts, which many manufacturers may not be willing or able to furnish.[36] The only other option may be to resort to alternate distribution modes, which may be impossible.

Market Structure and Competition

Competition helps set the price within the parameters of cost and demand. Depending on the marketer's objectives and competitive position, it may choose to compete directly on price or elect for nonprice measures. If a pricing response is sought, the marketer can offer bundled prices (e.g., value deals on a combination of products) or loyalty programs to insulate the firm from a price war. Price cuts can also be executed selectively rather than across the board. New products can be introduced to counter price challenges. For example, when Japanese Kao introduced a low-priced diskette to compete against 3M, rather than drop its prices 3M introduced a new brand, Highland,

---

[35]"The New Affluent Japanese Consumer: Affluent and Ready to Shop for the Right Products," *Business International*, January 27, 1992, and Mike Van Horn, "Consumer Revolution in the Japanese Market," *Export Today* 7 (May 1991): 54–56.

[36]Alan D. Treadgold, "The Developing Internationalisation of Retailing," *International Journal of Retail and Distribution Management* 18 (1990): 4–11.

THE INTERNATIONAL MARKETPLACE 18.4

When a Rose Is Not a Rose

A SURVEY BY *POPULAR MECHANICS* found that many U.S. car buyers would rather buy American than Japanese if the cars were similar. In many commercial compaigns, U.S. manufacturers have promoted the fact that their cars were every bit as good as those of the Japanese, and in most cases priced lower. What if they were indeed not only similar, but for the most part the same?

Diamondstar Motors was a 50-50 partnership between Chrysler and Mitsubishi set up in 1990 in Illinois. Although the venture ended in 1991, it launched the concept of producing identical models under different names—the Plymouth Laser, the Mitsubishi Eclipse, and the Eagle Talon—that continued in the companies' alliance. In 1991, the Plymouth Laser and Mitsubishi Eclipse sold for $11,000 for a basic model and $17,500 for a souped-up version. Sales were different, however, and could not be explained, for example, using dealer network size. In fact, 100 cars were sold per Mitsubishi dealer compared to 13 per Chrysler dealer, indicating an image problem of U.S. nameplates. "People perceive the Japanese car to be of better quality. It is a lot easier to sell than the Laser," says Ira Rosenberg, the owner of adjoining Plymouth and Mitsubishi dealerships in Crystal Lake, Illinois. In 1995, the Plymouth brand name was dropped. In 1996, Eagle Talon prices were $1,000 to $5,000 lower than those of the Mitsubishi Eclipse.

Like the U.S. car manufacturers, Korea's Hyundai, despite marketing efforts, has not been able shed its image as a high-risk purchase. Hyundai's focus group research on its Elantra model shows good marks on styling and features, but when buyers were asked whether they would give the car any consideration, the answers were often negative. The overall perception is that Hyundai builds an inexpensive car that is of very poor quality. Given that the United States accounts for more than 50 percent of the company's worldwide sales outside of its home base, it is necessary for the company to get U.S. buyers to at least consider the product. By expanding to markets around the world, the company is hoping its status as a global company will help it achieve brand recognition and thereby more freedom in pricing.

SOURCES: "Ford, GM Square Off over Daewoo Motor; The Question Is: Why?" *The Wall Street Journal*, February 14, 2000, A1, A13; Louis Kraar, "The Korean Invasion of Europe," *Fortune*, May 13, 1996, 150; "When There's No Wheel Distinction," *The Washington Post*, May 6, 1995, C1–2; John Harris, "Advantage Mitsubishi," *Forbes*, March 18, 1991, 100–104; and "Hyundai May Be Running Out of American Road," *Business Week*, October 14, 1991, 25; "Fall of a Keiretsu," *Business Week International*, March 15, 1999, Brain Bremner and Emily Thornton, p. 34.

www.chrysler.com

www.mitsubishi-motors.co.jp

www.dsm.org

www.hmc.co.kr

that effectively flanked Kao's competitive incursion. Simply dropping the price on the 3M brand could have badly diluted its image. On the nonprice front, the company can opt to fight back on quality by adding and promoting value-adding features.[37]

If a company's position is being eroded by competitors who focus on price, the marketer may have no choice but to respond. For example, IBM's operation in Japan lost market share in mainframes largely because competitors undersold the company. A Japanese mainframe was typically listed at 10 percent less than its IBM counterpart, and it frequently carried an additional 10 to 20 percent discount beyond that. This created an extremely competitive market. IBM's reaction was to respond in kind with aggressive promotion of its own, with the result that it began regaining its lost share. Motorola and Nokia, the leading cellular phone makers, are facing tough conditions in the Korean market. In addition to being competitive in price and quality, local companies such as Samsung and Goldstar are quick to come up with new models to

[37]Akshay R. Rao, Mark E. Bergen, and Scott Davis, "How to Fight a Price War," *Harvard Business Review* 78 (March–April 2000): 107–116.

satisfy the fast-changing needs of consumers while providing better after-sales service, free of charge or at a marginal price, than the two global players.[38]

In some cases, strategic realignment may be needed. To hold on to its eroding worldwide market share, Caterpillar has strived to shrink costs and move away from its old practice of competing only by building advanced, enduring machines and selling them at premium prices. Instead, the company has cut prices and has used strategic alliances overseas to produce competitive equipment to better suit local and regional needs.

Some marketers can fend off price competition by emphasizing other elements of the marketing mix, even if they are at an absolute disadvantage in price. Singer Sewing Machine Co., which gains nearly half its $500 million in non-U.S. sales from developing countries, emphasizes its established reputation, product quality, and liberal credit terms, as well as other services (such as sewing classes), rather than compete head-on with lower-cost producers.[39]

The pricing behavior of a global marketer may come under scrutiny in important market sectors, such as automobiles. If local companies lose significant market share to outsiders as a result of lower prices, they may ask for government interference against alleged dumping.

Environmental Constraints

Governments influence prices and pricing directly as well. In addition to the policy measures, such as tariffs and taxes, governments may also elect to directly control price levels. Once under **price controls,** the global marketer has to operate as it would in a regulated industry. Setting maximum prices has been defended primarily on political grounds: It stops inflation and an accelerating wage-price spiral, and consumers want it. Supporters also maintain that price controls raise the income of the poor. Operating in such circumstances is difficult. Achieving change in prices can be frustrating; for example, a company may wait 30 to 45 days for an acknowledgment of a price-increase petition.

To fight price controls, multinational corporations can demonstrate that they are getting an unacceptable return on investment and that, without an acceptable profit opportunity, future investments will not be made and production perhaps will be stopped.[40] Cadbury Schweppes sold its plant in Kenya because price control made its operation unprofitable. At one time, Coca-Cola and PepsiCo withdrew their products from the shelves in Mexico until they received a price increase. Pakistani milk producers terminated their business when they could not raise prices, and Glaxo Wellcome, a pharmaceutical manufacturer, canceled its expansion plans in Pakistan because of price controls.

In general, company representatives can cite these consequences in arguing against price controls: (1) the maximum price often becomes the minimum price if a sector is allowed a price increase, because all businesses in the sector will take it regardless of cost justification; (2) the wage-price spiral advances vigorously in anticipation of controls; (3) labor often turns against restrictions because they are usually accompanied by an income policy or wage restrictions; (4) noninflationary wage increases are forestalled; (5) government control not only creates a costly regulatory body but also is difficult to enforce; (6) authorities raise less in taxes because less money is made; and (7) a government may have to bail out many companies with cheap loans or make grants to prevent bankruptcies and unemployment. Once price controls are invoked, management will have to devote much time to resolving the many difficulties that controls present. The best interest of multinational corporations is therefore served by

---

[38]"Domestic Electronic Products Overtaking Foreign Goods," *Korea Times*, May 12, 1996, 8.

[39]Louis Kraar, "How to Sell to Cashless Buyers," *Fortune*, November 7, 1988, 147–154.

[40]Victor H. Frank, "Living with Price Control Abroad," *Harvard Business Review* 63 (March–April 1984): 137–142.

working with governments, especially in the developing countries, to establish an economic policy centered on a relatively free market in order to ameliorate the problem of rapidly escalating prices without price controls.

Pricing Coordination

The issue of standard worldwide pricing is mostly a theoretical one because of the influence of the factors already discussed. However, coordination of the pricing function is necessary, especially in larger, regional markets such as the European Union, especially after the introduction of the euro. With the increasing level of integration efforts around the world, and even discussion of common currency elsewhere such as in MERCOSUR, control and coordination of global and regional pricing takes on a new meaning.

With more global and regional brands in the global marketer's offering, control in pricing is increasingly important. Of course, this has to be balanced against the need for allowing subsidiaries latitude in pricing so that they may quickly react to specific market conditions.

Studies have shown that foreign-based multinational corporations allow their U.S. subsidiaries considerable freedom in pricing. This has been explained by the size and unique features of the market. Further, it has been argued that these subsidiaries often control the North American market (that is, a Canadian customer cannot get a better deal in the United States, and vice versa), and that distances create a natural barrier against arbitrage practices that would be more likely to emerge in Europe.[41] However, recent experience has shown that pricing coordination has to be worldwide because parallel imports will surface in any markets in which price discrepancies exist, regardless of distances.

The Euro and Marketing Strategy

On January 1, 1999, the euro (€) was officially launched by the European Union to become the one and only currency of the 12 nations in the eurozone, or Euroland, by July 1, 2002. Retooling for the euro is expected to cost European businesses $65 billion during that time.[42] Although the early focus was largely on managing the operational aspects of converting to the use of the euro for all business activities (such as preparing to account for sales and purchasing in euros as well as transforming internal accounting for areas such as R&D budgeting), the strategic issues are the most significant for the future.

In the longer term all firms will need to reexamine the positioning of their businesses. The potential advantages of a single-currency Europe (such as a more competitive market, both internally and externally) have been widely expounded, but the threats to businesses of all nationalities, sizes, and forms have not been so widely discussed. The threats are many. As barriers to the creation of a single domestic market are eliminated, more production and operating strategy decisions will be made on the basis of true-cost differentials (proximity to specific inputs, materials, immobile skills, or niche customers, for example). Consolidation will be the norm for many business units whose existence was in some way perpetuated by the uses of different currencies. This restructuring will have lasting effects on the European business landscape. For example, many marketers are streamlining their operations throughout Euroland and eliminating overlapping entities, such as distribution facilities.[43]

[41]Samiee, "Pricing in Marketing Strategies of U.S.- and Foreign-Based Companies," 17–30.

[42]"Ready, Set—Retool," *Business Week*, December 14, 1998, 68–70.

[43]"Faster Forward," *The Economist*, November 28, 1998, 84; "The Euro," *Business Week*, April 27, 1998, 38.

The euro will push national markets closer together. First and foremost in this area is the transparency to consumers of a single currency and a single cross-border price. The euro combined with the growing use of e-business, for example, will allow consumers in Barcelona to surf the Web for the cheapest source of fresh seafood delivered from anywhere within the EU12. Although theoretically possible before, the quotation of prices by individual currency and complexity of payment often posed a barrier—somewhat real, somewhat imagined—to cross-border purchasing. This barrier no longer exists, as consumers are now able to demand the highest quality product and service at the lowest price from businesses throughout the European community.

A more troublesome result is pricing, both within the firm and to the marketplace. Within the firm, the transfer prices between business units of the firm, whether in-country or cross-border, will now be held to an even more rigorous standard of no differentiation. Transfer prices internationally, however, are one of the key factors in how firms re-position profits in order to reduce their global tax burdens. Without this veil of differences in currency of denomination, any differences in transfer prices across multinational units will be even more apparent (and will not be allowed).

The pricing to the market and to the consumer is a more strategic concern. A price set for a particular demand segment, a pricing-point, in one currency such as the French franc, will now need to be reset in euro. For example, imagine a French boutique's pricing of a Parisian cologne that has a long-established price of FF99. The euro price, which will now be posted on the boutique's shelf side by side with the franc price, will be:

$$\frac{FF99.00}{(FF6.55957/€)} = €15.09.$$

But at €15.09, the consumer is faced with a qualitatively different price.[44] Should the Parisian boutique cut the franc price to FF98.33 (reducing the profit margin) so that the euro price is €14.99, or keep the price the same believing the consumer will continue to focus on the franc price first, the euro second? If the price is kept the same in francs, will this pricing in euro remain second in the minds of the consumer? Almost every pricing strategy both within and without the EU11 (U.S. or Japanese exporters who price product in local currency—now the euro—will have to likewise worry), will now have to be reevaluated.

Firms must plan strong promotional and educational materials for their products and services to allow consumers to adequately assess comparable qualities and characteristics given the transparency in pricing. Retailers are not generally required to always display national currency and euro prices. Some member states, however, have instituted their own requirements in order to protect consumers against pricing or conversion inconsistencies. Small firms and shopkeepers are expected to maintain national currency pricing in the interim, with a posted price conversion chart readily available to shoppers.

The single currency will make prices completely transparent for all buyers. If discrepancies are not justifiable due to market differences such as consumption preferences, competition, or government interference, parallel importation may occur. The simplest solution would be to have one euro throughout the market. However, given the huge differences of up to 500 percent at the present (as shown in Table 18.3), that solution would lead to significant losses in sales and profits, as a single price would likely be closer to the lower-priced countries' level. The recommended approach is a

[44]Apart from the strategic pricing decision, there are also simple rounding decisions to be made to report two different currency values or prices side-by-side. The EU has an official rounding practice that requires rounding up to the nearest cent; with EUR 1.455, it is rounded up to EUR 1.46; with 1.454 to 1.45. See **http://europa.eu.int/euro/quest**.

THE INTERNATIONAL MARKETPLACE 18.5

Coordinating Prices in Integrating Markets

PRICE DIFFERENTIALS CAN SURVIVE across individual European Union markets only if marketers act decidedly. This calls for centralizing pricing authority and establishing "pricing corridors." Some marketers may have to pull out of low-margin markets where price increases cannot be sustained.

Future European price levels will be markedly lower than current ones, and firms must take quick action to avoid seeing prices fall to the lowest level prevailing in marginal markets. This is due to the large differentials that existed and continue to exist among EU member states. Prices in markets such as Portugal and Spain are often significantly lower than those in northern Europe markets, where consumers can afford much larger margins and where costs are higher. The differentials can range from 30 percent for natural yogurt to as much as 200 percent for pharmaceuticals. Even among northern nations, a 2001 European Commission study found that consumers in the United Kingdom were paying 66 percent more for the exact same car model as their counterparts in the Netherlands.

Parallel imports into affluent markets will force prices down as buyers simply go to the cheapest available source for their goods. If manufacturers leave it to market forces, prices may go down to the lowest level. For example, Portugal may influence prices in Germany through parallel imports and the centralization of buying power.

In order to avoid this, manufacturers must compromise now between the current policy of individually optimized prices and a uniform European price. Such a compromise will be possible because, even after the 1992 phenomenon and the introduction of the euro, Europe has not become a homogeneous market. Consumer habits will adjust gradually, allowing certain price differentials to be retained and defended.

Some experts recommend that manufacturers set up a European pricing corridor dropping high prices somewhat and raising low ones, creating a sustainable differential among markets in member states. The corridor would be much narrower for easily transportable items like photographic film than for heavy ones such as industrial machinery.

These changing market conditions imply a new focus on centralized price setting for Europe. The price corridor will be set by the head office, with local subsidiaries free to set prices within it. This approach runs contrary to the prevailing corporate culture, which is based on decentralization.

Manufacturers ought to consider pulling out of poorer markets where price hikes cannot be sustained. It is better to lose a small percentage of sales rather than see turnover, margins, and profits plummet. So far, however, there appears to be little movement toward more centralized pricing. Some experts are concerned by the lack of urgency apparently felt by many European executives, who seem content to wait and see what happens.

Indeed, a number of European industrialists argue that large price differences can be maintained in Europe through product differentiation. Simpler products could be sold into less-prosperous markets, whereas more elaborate items might go to those markets that are able to afford them.

In at least one industry—pharmaceuticals—executives fear that neither pricing corridors nor product differences will prevent prices from falling to the lowest level. In markets such as France, Spain, and Portugal, prices for drugs are already very low because of national reimbursement schemes.

"We are sandwiched between the European Commission, which is determined to eliminate all trade barriers at whatever cost, and some national governments that are keeping pharmaceutical products artificially low," comments an executive at a major European drug maker. "In practice, the Commission has absolutely no control over the prices set by national governments." Pharmaceutical firms, which have heavy research and development costs, say they need high margins if they are to continue investing and competing with Japanese and U.S. companies. But if countries such as France, which accounts for a substantial part of the European drug market, continue to keep prices low, customers from other countries will simply buy their supplies in those markets. Manufacturers may well find themselves locked in an untenable position in an industry in which specifications are standardized, products cannot be differentiated, and suppliers cannot withdraw from the market for ethical reasons.

SOURCES: Stephen A. Butscher, "Maximizing Profits in Euroland," *Journal of Commerce*, May 5, 1999, 5; "Pricing in Post 1992 EC: Expert Urges Fast Action to Protect Margins," *Business International*, August 24, 1992, 267; "Car Prices in Britain Are Still the Highest in Europe," *Independent*, February 20, 2001, Stephen Castle, p.11.

http.//europa.eu.int/euro/quest

TABLE 18.3 Prices of Selected Goods and Services in Euroland

	BELGIUM	FRANCE	GERMANY	ITALY	SPAIN
1.5 liter bottle of Coca-Cola	2.05	1.05	1.89	1.65	1.14
Big Mac	2.86	3.08	2.67	2.48	2.38
Liter of unleaded gasoline	0.93	1.03	0.87	0.94	0.73
Dry-cleaned men's shirt	3.68	4.57	2.43	3.75	2.92
Pair of Levi's 501 jeans	71.00	83.00	81.00	69.00	70.00
Compaq Presario 2240	1,316.00	1,348.00	917.00	1,208.00	1,267.00
One day rental car, Mercedes C	154.00	110.00	103.00	253.00	113.00
One hour translation	89.00	104.00	78.00	55.00	39.00

SOURCE: "Gaps the Euro May Close," *Business Week*, April 27, 1998, 40.

pricing corridor that considers existing country-specific prices while optimizing the profits at a pan-European level.[45] As described in *The International Marketplace 18.5*, such a corridor defines the maximum and minimum prices that country organizations can charge—enough to allow flexibility as a result of differences in price elasticities, competition, and positioning, but not enough to attract parallel imports that may start at price differences of 20 percent and higher.[46] This approach moves pricing authority away from country managers to regional management and requires changes in management systems and incentive structures.

As if the systems people in the firms hadn't had enough trouble with the Y2K issue, the operating systems in the firm may suffer varying problems in conversion. All monetary systems that carry local currency and now euro-denominated amounts will have to be checked for integration with non-monetary operating systems (for example, with inventory systems that track volumes and quantities).

During the transition period, monetary systems will need to support both local currency and euro-denominated values. Conversion of local currency to euro, standardized by the EU12 to six significant figures (three decimal places), will be tricky. Firms using electronic data interchange systems (EDI) will need to adjust not only for intra-EU12 commerce, but also for the extended EU15 and external European suppliers and customers.

SUMMARY

In a world of increasing competition, government regulation, accelerating inflation, and widely fluctuating exchange rates, global marketers must spend increasing amounts of time planning pricing strategy. Because pricing is the only revenue-generating element of the marketing mix, its role in meeting corporate objectives is enhanced. However, it comes under increasing governmental scrutiny as well, as evidenced by intracompany transfer pricing.

The three philosophies of transfer pricing that have emerged over time are cost-based, market-based, and arm's-length. Transfer pricing concerns are both internal and external to the company. Internally, manipulating transfer prices may complicate control procedures and documentation. Externally, problems arise from the tax and regulatory entities of the countries involved.

[45]"Even After Shift to Euro, One Price Won't Fit All," *The Wall Street Journal Europe*, December 28, 1998, 1.

[46]Stephen A. Butscher, "Maximizing Profits in Euroland," *Journal of Commerce*, May 5, 1999, 5.

Pricing decisions are typically left to the local managers; however, planning assistance is provided by the parent company. Pricing in individual markets comes under the influence of environmental variables, each market with its own unique set. This set consists of corporate objectives, costs, customer behavior and market conditions, market structure, and environmental constraints.

The individual impact of these variables and the result of their interaction must be thoroughly understood by the global marketer, especially if regional, or even worldwide, coordination is attempted. This control and coordination is becoming more important with increasing economic integration.

QUESTIONS FOR DISCUSSION

1. Comment on the pricing philosophy "Sometimes price should be wrong by design."
2. The standard worldwide base price is most likely looked on by management as full-cost pricing, including an allowance for manufacturing overhead, general overhead, and selling expenses. What factors are overlooked?
3. In combating price controls, multinational corporations will deal with agency administrators rather than policymakers. How can they convince administrators that price relief is fair to the company and also in the best interest of the host country?
4. Should there be governmental action against gray markets? Are gray markets not an expression of free trade?
5. Which elements of pricing can be standardized?
6. Using the price differences presented in Table 18.3 as a base, argue why such price differences will stay in place even with the euro.
7. What is behind the euro as a common currency? Utilizing the discussion prepared by the European Commission at **www.europa.eu.int/euro/quest/**, determine what made the euro a possibility. See also **www.captaineuro.com**.
8. The euro will be either a source of competitive advantage or a disadvantage for marketers. Using "Euro case study: Siemens," available at **news.bbc.co.uk/hi/english/events/ the_launch_of_emu**, assess the validity of the two points of view.

RECOMMENDED READINGS

Carrero Caldreon, Jose Manuel. *Advance Pricing Agreements: A Global Analysis.* Cambridge, MA: Kluwer Law International, 1998.

Chabot, Christian N. *Understanding the Euro: The Clear and Concise Guide to the New Trans-European Currency.* New York: McGraw-Hill, 1998.

Dolan, Robert J. and Hermann Simon. *Power Pricing: How Managing Price Transforms the Bottom Line.* New York: Free Press, 1997.

Engelson, Morris. *Pricing Strategy: An Interdisciplinary Approach.* New York: Joint Management Strategy, 1995.

Feinschreiber, Robert. *Transfer Pricing Handbook.* New York: John Wiley & Sons, 1998.

Nagle, Thomas T. and Reed K. Holden. *The Strategy and Tactics of Pricing: A Guide to Profitable Decision Making.* New York: Pearson, 1994.

Tang, Roger Y. W. *Intrafirm Trade and Global Transfer Pricing Regulations.* Westport, CT: Quorum Books, 1997.

Chapter 19

Logistics and Supply Chain Management

THE INTERNATIONAL MARKETPLACE 19.1

Global Supply Chain Management at McDonald's

EXCEPT FOR SAUDI WHEAT, Big Macs sold in Saudi Arabia are made entirely from foreign ingredients: beef patties from Spain, sauce from the United States, Mexican onions and sesame seeds, Brazilian oil and sugar, and packaging from Germany. The world's giant fast-food chain consolidates global warehousing and distribution so that all the materials of the uniform Big Mac can come together, however far-flung producers and distributors may be.

McDonald's "cracks the global supply chain to create a borderless environment," said its global logistics manager, Raymond Cesca. In order to keep McDonald's restaurants—in 120 countries worldwide with an estimate of 40 million customers per day—in continuous supply, the company has become one of the world's largest buyers of beef and other ingredients for its products. In large markets the company sources its ingredients locally, while in small markets like Saudi Arabia, McDonald's uses its distribution system so that items like beef patties can be supplied almost anywhere in the world. The benefits of this type of supply chain management for global retailers like McDonald's are assurance of a stable source of supply and protection against fluctuations in the value of local currencies.

In new markets, McDonald's slashes costs by switching from importing to local manufacturing. Local production is not just cheap but also helps the company protect its position. In Russia, for example, McDonald's has set up local companies to supply everything from pickles to construction materials for its restaurants. Because of local sourcing, McDonald's says, its Russian operations remain profitable in spite of slackening sales due to economic slowdown.

SOURCES: Aviva Freudmann, "Supplying Big Macs: A Lesson in Logistics," *Journal of Commerce*, May 19, 1999, 3A; and Carol Matlack, "Betting on a New Label: Made in Russia," *Business Week*, April 12, 1999, 122E6.

http://www.mcdonalds.com

FOR THE INTERNATIONAL FIRM, customer locations and sourcing opportunities are widely dispersed. The physical distribution and logistics aspects of international marketing therefore have great importance, as shown in *The International Marketplace 19.1.* To obtain and maintain favorable results from the complex international environment, the international logistics manager must coordinate activities globally, both within and outside of the firm. Neglect of logistics issues brings not only higher costs but also the risk of eventual noncompetitiveness due to diminished market share, more expensive supplies, or lower profits. In an era of new trade opportunities in regions such as Central Europe, which are suffering from major shortcomings in logistical infrastructure, competent logistics management is more important than ever before.

This chapter will focus on international logistics and supply-chain management. Primary areas of concentration will be the linkages between the firm, its suppliers, and its customers, as well as transportation, inventory, packaging, and storage issues. The logistics management problems and opportunities that are peculiar to international marketing will also be highlighted.

A Definition of International Logistics

International logistics is the design and management of a system that controls the flow of materials into, through, and out of the international corporation. It encompasses the total movement concept by covering the entire range of operations concerned with goods movement, including therefore both exports and imports simultaneously. By taking a systems approach, the firm explicitly recognizes the linkages among the traditionally separate logistics components within and outside of the corporation. By incorporating the interaction with outside organizations and individuals such as suppliers and customers, the firm is enabled to build on jointness of purpose by all partners in the areas of performance, quality, and timing. As a result of implementing these systems considerations successfully, the firm can develop just-in-time (JIT) delivery for lower inventory cost, electronic data interchange (EDI) for more efficient order processing, and early supplier involvement (ESI) for better planning of goods development and movement. In addition, the use of such a systems approach allows a firm to concentrate on its core competencies and to form outsourcing alliances with other companies. For example, a firm can choose to focus on manufacturing and leave all aspects of order filling and delivery to an outside provider. By working closely with customers such as retailers, firms can also develop efficient customer response (ECR) systems, which can track sales activity on the retail level. As a result, manufacturers can precisely coordinate production in response to actual shelf replenishment needs, rather than based on forecasts.

Two major phases in the movement of materials are of logistical importance. The first phase is **materials management,** or the timely movement of raw materials, parts, and supplies into and through the firm. The second phase is **physical distribution,** which involves the movement of the firm's finished product to its customers. In both phases, movement is seen within the context of the entire process. Stationary periods (storage and inventory) are therefore included. The basic goal of logistics management is the effective coordination of both phases and their various components to result in maximum cost effectiveness while maintaining service goals and requirements.

The growth of logistics as a field has brought to the forefront three major concepts: the systems concept, the total cost concept, and the trade-off concept. The **systems concept** is based on the notion that materials-flow activities within and outside of the firm are so extensive and complex that they can be considered only in the context of

FOS DISTRIPORT
EURO-MEDITERRANEAN LOGISTICS CENTRE

160 ha linked directly to the Fos container terminal

Could there be a better location from where you can distribute to the whole of South Europe and to the Mediterranean ?

Please feel free to contact :
PORT OF MARSEILLES AUTHORITY
Fos Distriport commercial department
USA Rep: Bernard A.Friedrich
Tel: 805.379.3994
Fax: 805.495.9568

their interaction. Instead of each corporate function, supplier, and customer operating with the goal of individual optimization, the systems concept stipulates that some components may have to work suboptimally to maximize the benefits of the system as a whole. The systems concept intends to provide the firm, its suppliers, and its customers, both domestic and foreign, with the benefits of synergism expected from the coordinated application of size.

In order for the systems concept to work, information flows and partnership trust are instrumental. Logistics capability is highly information dependent, since information availability influences not only the network planning process but also the day-to-day decisions that affect performance.[1] Long-term partnership and trust are required in order to forge closer links between firms and managers. An abuse of power is the fastest way to build barriers to such linkages.[2]

A logical outgrowth of the systems concept is the development of the **total cost concept.** To evaluate and optimize logistical activities, cost is used as a basis for measurement. The purpose of the total cost concept is to minimize the firm's overall logistics cost by implementing the systems concept appropriately.

Implementation of the total cost concept requires that the members of the system understand the sources of costs. To develop such understanding, a system of activity-based costing has been developed, which is a technique designed to more accurately assign the indirect and direct resources of an organization to the activities performed based on consumption.[3] In the international arena, the total cost concept must also incorporate the consideration of total after-tax profit, by taking the impact of national tax policies on the logistics function into account. The objective is to maximize after-tax profits rather than minimizing total cost. Tax variations in the international arena often have major consequences, therefore, the focus can be quite important.[4]

The **trade-off concept,** finally, recognizes the linkages within logistics systems that result from the interaction of their components. For example, locating a warehouse near the customer may reduce the cost of transportation. However, additional costs are associated with new warehouses. Similarly, a reduction of inventories will save money but may increase the need for costly emergency shipments. Managers can maximize performance of logistics systems only by formulating decisions based on the recognition and analysis of such trade-offs. A trade-off of costs may go against one's immediate interests. Consider a manufacturer building several different goods. The goods all use one or both of two parts. A and B, which the manufacturer buys in roughly equal amounts. Most of the goods produced use both parts. The unit cost of part A is $7, of part B, $10. Part B has more capabilities than part A; in fact, B can replace A. If the manufacturer doubles its purchases of part B, it qualifies for a discounted $8 unit price. For products that incorporate both parts, substituting B for A makes sense to qualify for the discount, since the total parts cost is $17 using A and B, but only $16 using Bs only. Part B should therefore become a standard part for the manufacturer. But departments building products that only use part A may be reluctant to accept the substitute part B because, even discounted, the cost of B exceeds that of A. Use of the trade-off concept will solve the problem.[5]

[1]Stanley E. Fawcett, Linda L. Stanley, and Sheldon R. Smith, "Developing a Logistics Capability to Improve the Performance of International Operations," *Journal of Business Logistics* 18 (Number 2, 1997): 101–127.

[2]Patrick M. Byrne and Stephen V. Young, "UK Companies Look at Supply Chain Issues," *Transportation and Distribution* (February 1995): 50–56.

[3]Bernard LaLonde and James Ginter, "Activity-Based Costing: Best Practices," *Paper #606*, The Supply Chain Management Research Group, The Ohio State University, September 1996.

[4]Paul T. Nelson and Gadi Toledano, "Challenges for International Logistics Management," *Journal of Business Logistics* 1 (Number 2, 1979): 7.

[5]Toshiro Hiromoto, "Another Hidden Edge: Japanese Management Accounting," in *Trends in International Business: Critical Perspectives,* ed. M. Czinkota and M. Kotabe (Oxford, England: Blackwell Publishers, 1998), 217–222.

Supply-Chain Management

The integration of these three concepts has resulted in the new paradigm of **supply-chain management,** where a series of value-adding activities connect a company's supply side with its demand side. This approach views the supply chain of the entire extended enterprise, beginning with the supplier's suppliers and ending with consumers or end users. The perspective encompasses the entire product and information and funds flow that form one cohesive link to acquire, purchase, convert/manufacture, assemble, and distribute goods and services to the ultimate consumers. The implementation effects of such supply-chain management systems can be major. Efficient supply-chain design can increase customer satisfaction and save money at the same time.[6] For example, it has permitted Wal-Mart, the largest U.S. retailer, to reduce inventories by 90 percent, has saved the company hundreds of millions of dollars in inventory holding costs, and allows it to offer low prices to its customers.[7] On an industry-wide basis, research by Coopers and Lybrand has indicated that the use of such tools in the structuring of supplier relations could reduce operating costs of the European grocery industry by $27 billion per year, with savings equivalent to a 5.7 percent reduction in price.[8]

Companies such as GE and Pitney Bowes have implemented Web-based sourcing and payables systems. GE's Trading Process Network (**www.tpnregister.com**) allows GE Lighting's 25 production facilities and other buying facilities around the world to quickly find and purchase products from approved suppliers electronically. The electronic catalog information reflects the pricing and contract terms GE has negotiated with each of the suppliers and also ties in with GE's inventory and accounts payable systems. The result has been the virtual elimination of paper and mailing costs, a reduction in cycle time from 14 days to 1 day, 50 percent staff reduction, and 20 percent overall savings in the procurement process. Pitney Bowes' suppliers need only Internet access and a standard Web browser to be electronically linked to the manufacturer's supply system to see how many of their products are on hand and to indicate how many will be needed in the future. The site, VendorSite, even includes data that small suppliers can use for production planning.

These developments open up supplier relationships for smaller companies and those outside of the buyer's domestic market; however, the supplier's capability of providing satisfying goods and services will play the most critical role in securing long-term contracts. In addition, the physical delivery of goods often can be old-fashioned and slow. Nevertheless, the use of such strategic tools will be crucial for international managers to develop and maintain key competitive advantages. An overview of the international supply chain is shown in Figure 19.1.

The Impact of International Logistics

Logistics costs comprise between 10 and 30 percent of the total landed cost of an international order.[9] International firms have already achieved many of the cost reductions that are possible in financing and production, and they are now beginning to look at international logistics as a competitive tool. Research shows that the

---

[6]Tom Davis, "Effective Supply Chain Management," *Sloan Management Review* (Summer 1993): 35–45.

[7]Perry A. Trunick, "CLM: Breakthrough of Champions, Council of Logistics Management's 1994 Conference," *Transportation and Distribution* (December 1994).

[8]Coopers and Lybrand, "The Value Chain Analysis," *Efficient Consumer Response Europe* (London, 1995).

[9]Richard T. Hise, "The Implications of Time-Based Competition on International Logistics Strategies," *Business Horizons* (September/October 1995): 39–45.

FIGURE	19.1	The International Supply Chain

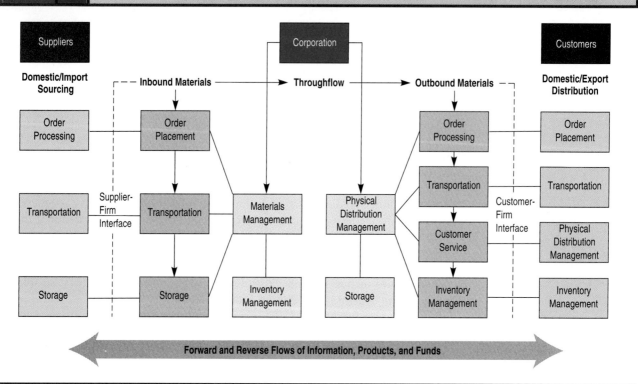

environment facing logistics managers in the next ten years will be dynamic and explosive. Technological advances and progress in communication systems and information-processing capabilities will be particularly significant in designing and managing logistics systems.

For example, close collaboration with suppliers is required in order to develop a just-in-time inventory system, which in turn may be crucial to maintain manufacturing costs at a globally competitive level. Yet without electronic data interchange, such collaborations or alliances are severely handicapped. While most industrialized countries can offer the technological infrastructure for such computer-to-computer exchange of business information, the application of such a system in the global environment may be severely restricted. Often, it is not just the lack of technology that forms the key obstacle to modern logistics management, but rather the entire business infrastructure, ranging from ways of doing business in fields such as accounting and inventory tracking, to the willingness of businesses to collaborate with one another. A contrast between the United States and Russia is useful here.

In the United States 40 percent of shipments are made under a just-in-time/quick response regime. For the U.S. economy, the total cost of distribution is close to 11 percent of GNP. By contrast, Russia is only now beginning to learn about the rhythm of demand and the need to bring supply in line. The country is battling space constraints, poor lines of supply, nonexistent distribution and service centers, limited rolling stock, and insufficient transportation systems. Producers are uninformed about issues such as inventory carrying cost, store assortment efficiencies, and replenishment techniques. The need for information development and exchange systems for integrated supplier-distributor alliances and for efficient communication sys-

FIGURE | 19.2 | International Airfreight, 1960–2000

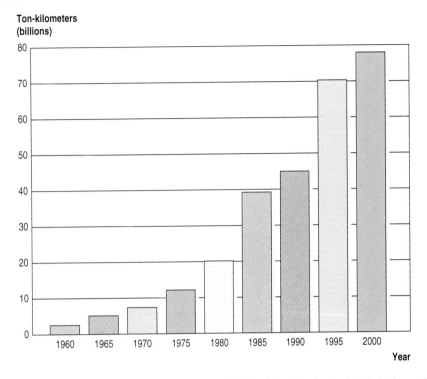

Ton-kilometers
(billions)

Based on data supplied by member states of the International Civil Aviation Organization (ICAO). As the number of member states increased from 116 in 1970 to 150 in 1983, there is some upward bias in the data, particularly from 1970 on, when data for the USSR were included for the first time.

SOURCES: *Civil Aviation Statistics of the World* (Montreal: ICAO, 1996); **http://www.icao.org**; and Michael Kayal, "World Air Cargo Seen Growing 7.5% a Year to 2001," *Journal of Commerce*, December 30, 1997, 10A.

FIGURE | 19.3 | Loading a Train on a Plane

Shipping by air freight has really taken off in the past 20 years. Even large and heavy items, such as this locomotive, are shipped to their destination by air.

SOURCE: Printed in the *Journal of Commerce*.

needs of the firm and its customers. The manager must consider the performance of each mode on four dimensions: transit time, predictability, cost, and noneconomic factors.

Transit Time   The period between departure and arrival of the carrier varies significantly between ocean freight and airfreight. For example, the 45-day transit time of an ocean shipment can be reduced to 24 hours if the firm chooses airfreight. The length of transit time will have a major impact on the overall logistical operations of the firm. As an example, a short transit time may reduce or even eliminate the need for an overseas depot. Also, inventories can be significantly reduced if they are replenished frequently. As a result, capital can be freed up and used to finance other corporate opportunities. Transit time can also play a major role in emergency situations. For example, if the shipper is about to miss an important delivery date because of production delays, a shipment normally made by ocean freight can be made by air.

Perishable products require shorter transit times. Rapid transportation prolongs the shelf life in the foreign market. For products with a short life span, air delivery may be the only way to enter foreign markets successfully. For example, international sales of cut flowers have reached their current volume only as a result of airfreight, as Figure 19.4 shows. UPS Aviation Technologies, a subsidiary of United Parcel Service, reduced, with the help of EDI, the administrative time necessary for creating and sending purchase orders by 67 percent and order processing time by 30 percent.[17] With the Internet offering a lower-cost alternative to the development of private value-added networks, such collaboration is expected to increase markedly.

Predictability   Providers of both ocean and airfreight service wrestle with the issue of **reliability.** Both modes are subject to the vagaries of nature, which may impose delays. Yet because reliability is a relative measure, the delay of one day for airfreight tends to be seen as much more severe and "unreliable" than the same delay for ocean freight. However, delays tend to be shorter in absolute time for air shipments. As a result, arrival time via air is more predictable. This attribute has a major influence on corporate strategy. For example, because of the higher predictability of airfreight, inventory safety stock can be kept at lower levels. Greater predictability can also serve as a useful sales tool for foreign distributors, who are able to make more precise delivery promises to their customers. If inadequate port facilities exist, airfreight may again be the better alternative. Unloading operations from oceangoing vessels are more cumbersome and time-consuming than for planes. Finally, merchandise shipped via air is likely to suffer less loss and damage from exposure of the cargo to movement. Therefore, once the merchandise arrives, it is more likely to be ready for immediate delivery—a facet that also enhances predictability.

Cost   A major consideration in choosing international transportation modes is the cost factor. International transportation services are usually priced on the basis of both cost of the service provided and value of the service to the shipper. Because of the high value of the products shipped by air, airfreight is often priced according to the value of the service. In this instance, of course, price becomes a function of market demand and the monopolistic power of the carrier.

The international marketer must decide whether the clearly higher cost of airfreight can be justified. In part, this will depend on the cargo's properties. For example, the physical density and the value of the cargo will affect the decision. Bulky products may be too expensive to ship by air, whereas very compact products may be more amenable to airfreight transportation. High-priced items can absorb transportation cost more easily than low-priced goods because the cost of transportation as a percentage of total product cost will be lower. As a result, sending diamonds by airfreight

[17]Philip Wintermyer, "EDI Saves Partners Cost and Time," *Electronic Buyer's News*, July 19, 1999, 46.

FIGURE 19.4 **Advertisement for Cut Flowers**

is easier to justify than sending coal by air. To keep cost down, a shipper can join groups such as shippers associations, which give the shipper more leverage in negotiations. Alternatively, a shipper can decide to mix modes of transportation in order to reduce overall cost and time delays. For example, part of the shipment route can be covered by air, while another portion can be covered by truck or ship.

Most important, however, are the overall logistical considerations of the firm. The manager must determine how important it is for merchandise to arrive on time, which will be different for regular garments than for high-fashion dresses. The effect of transportation cost on price and the need for product availability abroad must also

TABLE 19.1 **Evaluating Transportation Choices**

CHARACTERISTICS OF MODE	MODE OF TRANSPORTATION				
	AIR	PIPELINE	HIGHWAY	RAIL	WATER
Speed (1 = fastest)	1	4	2	3	5
Cost (1 = highest)	1	4	2	3	5
Loss and Damage (1 = least)	3	1	4	5	2
Frequency* (1 = best)	3	1	2	4	5
Dependability (1 = best)	5	1	2	3	4
Capacity† (1 = best)	4	5	3	2	1
Availability (1 = best)	3	5	1	2	4

SOURCE: Ronald H. Ballou, *Business Logistics Management*, 4th ed., (Upper Saddle River, NJ: Prentice Hall, 1998), p. 146.

*Frequency: number of times mode is available during a given time period
†Capacity: ability of mode to handle large or heavy goods

be considered. For example, some firms may wish to use airfreight as a new tool for aggressive market expansion. Airfreight may also be considered a good way to begin operations in new markets without making sizable investments for warehouses and distribution centers.

Although costs are the major consideration in modal choice, an overall perspective must be employed. Simply comparing transportation modes on the basis of price alone is insufficient. The manager must factor in all corporate activities that are affected by modal choice and explore the total cost effects of each alternative. The final selection of a mode will depend on the importance of different modal dimensions to the markets under consideration. A useful overall comparison between different modes of transportation is provided in Table 19.1.

Noneconomic Factors Often, noneconomic dimensions will enter into the selection process for a proper form of transportation. The transportation sector, nationally and internationally, both benefits and suffers from heavy government involvement. Carriers may be owned or heavily subsidized by governments. As a result, governmental pressure is exerted on shippers to use national carriers, even if more economical alternatives exist. Such preferential policies are most often enforced when government cargo is being transported. Restrictions are not limited to developing countries. For example, in the United States, all government cargo and all official government travelers must use national flag carriers when available.

For balance-of-payments reasons, international quota systems of transportation have been proposed. The United Nations Commission on International Trade and Development (UNCTAD), for example, has recommended a 40/40/20 treaty whereby 40 percent of the traffic between two nations is allocated to vessels of the exporting country, 40 percent to vessels of the importing country, and 20 percent to third-country vessels (40/40/20). However, stiff international competition among carriers and the price sensitivity of customers frequently render such proposals ineffective, particularly for trade between industrialized countries.

Although many justifications are possible for such national policies, ranging from prestige to national security, they may distort the economic choices of the international corporation. These policies are a reflection of the international environment within which the firm must operate.

The International Shipment

Air France Cargo provides special international handling for animals, hazardous materials, valuables, diplomatic bags, oversize shipments, and much more.

With a channel system in place, the next concern of the international marketer is getting the product to the distributor. In domestic operations, this typically involves only (1) the shipper, a carrier, and the receiver and (2) relatively simple paperwork. International shipments are more complicated on both dimensions.

International shipments usually involve not just one carrier but multiple types of carriers. The shipment must be routed to the port of export, where it is transferred to another mode of transportation—for example, from truck or rail to vessel. Documentation for international shipments is universally perceived as so complicated, especially by smaller firms, that it becomes a trade barrier. A Canadian study found that 46 person-hours were needed for the processing of one export shipment;[18] the U.S. Department of Transportation pegged the required time at 36 hours.[19] As the result of recent efforts toward standardization, most of the documents needed are now aligned through a system called the U.S. Standard Master for International Trade. Certain standard entries, such as export carrier and document number, are in the same position on all of the forms. As part of the 1992 program, the EU simplified its required documentation for shipments. Whereas drivers earlier needed two pounds of documents on a route, for example, from Amsterdam to Lisbon, they now need only a single piece of paper. The savings on the elimination of this red tape are significant. Increasingly, electronic data transfer will be replacing paperwork and best practices used by customs services around the world are being adopted by other countries to achieve eventual international standards.[20]

Few international marketers, especially small or medium-sized firms and those new to exporting, are familiar with the many and varied details involved in transportation. These may include arranging for shipment from the factory, transfer from train to vessel, securing of rates and space on vessels, clearing customs, stowing, delivery at the port of destination to docks, clearance through local customs, and finally, delivery to the buyer. Larger exporters have a separate department or staff to secure transportation services and proper documentation, whereas smaller firms rely on support agencies for this work.

Documentation

In the most simple form of exporting, the only documents needed are a **bill of lading** and an export declaration. Most exports fit under a general license, which is a generalized authorization consisting simply of a number to be shown on the documents. Certain goods and data require a special validated license for export, as discussed in a previous chapter. For importation, the basic documents are a bill of lading and an invoice. Table 19.2 provides a summary of the main documents used in international shipments.

The **bill of lading** (see Figure 19.5) is the most important document to the shipper, the carrier, and the buyer. It acknowledges receipt of the goods, represents the basic contract between the shipper and the carrier, and serves as evidence of title to the goods for collection by the purchaser. Various types of bills of lading exist. The inland bill of lading is a contract between the inland carrier and the shipper. Bills of lading may be negotiable instruments in that they may be endorsed to other parties (order

[18]Wayne D. Mays, "Documentary Problems of International Transportation," *Journal of World Trade Law* 12 (November–December 1978): 506–518.

[19]Roy J. Sampson, Martin Farris, and David L. Shrock, *Domestic Transportation: Practice, Theory, and Policy* (Boston: Houghton Mifflin, 1985), 106.

[20]Daniel B. Maskowitz, "Changing Customs," *International Business*, October 1996, 38–39.

TABLE 19.2	**Documentation for an International Shipment**

A. Documents Required by the U.S. Government
    1. Shipper's export declaration
    2. Export license
B. Commercial Documents
    1. Commercial invoice
    2. Packing list
    3. Inland bill of lading
    4. Dock receipt
    5. Bill of lading or airway bill
    6. Insurance policies or certificates
    7. Shipper's declaration for dangerous goods
C. Import Documents
    1. Import license
    2. Foreign exchange license
    3. Certificate of origin
    4. Consular invoice
    5. Customs invoice

SOURCES: Dun & Bradstreet, *Exporter's Encyclopedia* (New York: Dun & Bradstreet, 1985); and Marta Ortiz-Buonafina, *Profitable Export Marketing* (Englewood Cliffs, NJ: Prentice-Hall, 1984), 218–246; www.ams.usda.gov/tmd/export/documentation.

bill) or may be non-negotiable (straight). The **shipper's export declaration** (see Figure 19.6) states proper authorization for export and serves as a means for governmental data collection efforts.

The packing list, if used, lists in some detail the contents, the gross and net weights, and the dimensions of each package. Some shipments, such as corrosives, flammables, and poisons, require a **shipper's declaration for dangerous goods.** When the international marketer is responsible for moving the goods to the U.S. port of export, a dock receipt (for ocean freight) or a warehouse receipt (if the goods are stored) is issued before the issuance of the bill of lading. Collection documents must also be produced and always include a commercial invoice (a detailed description of the transaction), often a **consular invoice** (required by certain countries for data collection purposes), and a **certificate of origin** (required by certain countries to ensure correct tariffs). Insurance documents are produced when stipulated by the transaction. In certain countries, especially in Latin America, two additional documents are needed. An **import license** may be required for certain types or amounts of particular goods, while a **foreign exchange license** allows the importer to secure the needed hard currency to pay for the shipment. The exporter has to provide the importer with the data needed to obtain these licenses from governmental authorities and should make sure, before the actual shipment, that the importer has indeed secured the documents. All commercial shipments to Germany, regardless of value or mode of transport, require a commercial invoice, bill of lading (or airway bill), certificate of origin, and any special documents required due to the type of goods being forwarded.

Two guidelines are critical in dealing with customs anywhere in the world: sufficient knowledge or experience in dealing with the customs service in question and sufficient preparation for the process.[21] Whatever the required documents, their proper preparation is of utmost importance. Improper or missing documents can easily lead to difficulties that will delay payment or even prevent it. Furthermore, improper documentation may cause problems with customs. If a customs service seizes the merchandise, delays can be measured in weeks and may end up in a total financial loss for the particular shipment. However, with adherence to release procedures,

[21]Philippe Bruno, "Getting Your Goods Through EC Customs," *Export Today* 9 (January–February 1993): 17–23.

FIGURE 19.5 **Bill of Lading**

ACL **BILL OF LADING** ACL

SHIPPER/EXPORTER	DOCUMENT NO.	BOOKING NO.
	EXPORT REFERENCES FORWARDER REF. NO. SHIPPER'S REF. NO.	
CONSIGNEE	FORWARDING AGENT. F.M.C. NO.	
	POINT AND COUNTRY OF ORIGIN	PLACE OF RECEIPT *
NOTIFY PARTY	DOMESTIC ROUTING/EXPORT INSTRUCTIONS	
PIER		

EXPORTING CARRIER	PORT OF LOADING	PLACE OF DELIVERY *
PORT OF DISCHARGE	FOR TRANSSHIPMENT TO	

PARTICULARS FURNISHED BY SHIPPER

MARKS AND NUMBERS	NO. OF PKGS.	DESCRIPTION OF PACKAGES AND GOODS	GROSS WEIGHT	MEASUREMENT
		*APPLICABLE ONLY WHEN USED AS THROUGH BILL OF LADING AS PER CLAUSE 3 (III) ON REVERSE HEREOF.		

PREPAID	COLLECT	FREIGHT AND CHARGES PAYABLE AT________	ALL CHARGES EX SHIPS TACKLE FOR ACCOUNT OF CARGO

ACL
an affiliate of:
Cie Generale Maritime
The Cunard Steam-Ship Company Ltd.
Intercontinental Transport (ICT) BV
Swedish American Line
Swedish Transatlantic Line
Wallenius Line

B/L NUMBER DATE

RECEIVED by ACL for shipment by ocean vessel, between port of loading and port of discharge, and for arrangement or procurement of precarriage from place of receipt and on-carriage to place of delivery where stated above, the goods as specified above in appraent good order and condition unless otherwise stated. The goods to be delivered at the above mentioned port of discharge or place of delivery, whichever applicable. Subject always to the exceptions, limitations, conditions and liberties set out on the reverse side hereof, to which the Merchant agrees by accepting this B/L.

In Witness whereof three (3) original Bs/L have been signed, if not otherwise stated above, one of which being accomplished the other(s) to be void.

For **ACL**

SOURCE: Seaschott.

a seizure can usually be guided through without major loss to the international marketer.[22]

Support Agencies for International Shipments

Several types of support agencies provide services in the physical movement of goods. Since any delays in product delivery are likely to have an immediate adverse effect on future sales, one of the most crucial distribution decisions an exporter makes involves

[22]David Serko and Barry Kaplan, "What to Do When Customs Seizes Your Merchandise," *Global Trade* 3 (October 1988): 15–16.

| FIGURE | 19.6 | Shipper's Export Declaration |

SOURCE: Seaschott.

the selection of an international freight forwarder.[23] An **international freight forwarder** acts as an agent for the international marketer in moving cargo to the overseas destination. Independent freight forwarders are regulated and should be certified by the Federal Maritime Commission. The forwarder advises the marketer on shipping documentation and packing costs and will prepare and review the documents to ensure that they are in order. Forwarders will also book the necessary space aboard a carrier. They will make necessary arrangements to clear outbound goods with customs and, after clearance, forward the documents either to the customer or to the pay-

[23]Ken Yokeum, "How to Select a Freight Forwarder," *Export Today* 6 (October 1990): 35–37.

ing bank. A **customs broker** serves as an agent for an importer with authority to clear inbound goods through customs and ship them on to their destination. These functions are performed for a fee. Customs brokers are often regulated by their national Customs Service.

International Inventory Issues

Inventories tie up a major portion of corporate funds. As a result, capital used for inventory is not available for other corporate opportunities. Because annual **inventory carrying costs** (the expense of maintaining inventories) can easily comprise up to 25 percent or more of the value of the inventories themselves,[24] proper inventory policies should be of major concern to the international marketing manager. Just-in-time inventory policies are increasingly adopted by multinational manufacturers. These policies minimize the volume of inventory by making it available only when it is needed for the production process. Firms using such a policy will choose suppliers on the basis of their delivery and inventory performance. Proper inventory management may therefore become a determinant variable in obtaining a sale.

In its international inventory management, the multinational corporation is faced not only with new situations that affect inventories negatively but also with new opportunities and alternatives. The purpose of establishing inventory—to maintain product movement in the delivery pipeline in order to satisfy demand—is the same for domestic and international inventory systems. The international environment, however, includes unique factors such as currency exchange rates, greater distances, and duties. At the same time, international operations provide the corporation with an opportunity to explore alternatives not available in a domestic setting, such as new sourcing or location alternatives. In international operations, the firm can make use of currency fluctuations by placing varying degrees of emphasis on inventory operations, depending on the stability of the currency of a specific country. Entire operations can be shifted to different nations to take advantage of newly emerging opportunities. International inventory management can therefore be much more flexible in its response to environmental changes.

In deciding the level of inventory to be maintained, the international marketer must consider three factors: the order cycle time, desired customer service levels, and use of inventories as a strategic tool.

Order Cycle Time   The total time that passes between the placement of an order and the receipt of the merchandise is referred to as order cycle time. Two dimensions are of major importance to inventory management: the length of the total order cycle and its consistency. In international marketing, the order cycle is frequently longer than in domestic business. It comprises the time involved in order transmission, order filling, packing and preparation for shipment, and transportation. Order transmission time varies greatly internationally depending on whether telephone, fax, mail, or electronic order placement is used in communicating. The order filling time may also be increased because lack of familiarity with a foreign market makes the anticipation of new orders more difficult. Packing and shipment preparation require more detailed attention. Finally, of course, transportation time increases with the distances involved. As a result, total order cycle time can frequently approach a hundred days or more. Larger inventories may have to be maintained both domestically and internationally to bridge these time gaps.

Consistency, the second dimension of order cycle time, is also more difficult to maintain in international marketing. Depending on the choice of transportation

---

[24]Bernard J. LaLonde and Paul H. Zinszer, *Customer Service: Meaning and Measurement* (Chicago: National Council of Physical Distribution Management, 1976).

THE INTERNATIONAL MARKETPLACE 19.3

Switching to Global Electronic Orders

ELECTRONIC COMMERCE is growing rapidly and is expected to grow into an inevitable international trend as businesses are trying to push overseas vendors into electronic communication. Although presently three-fourths of the purchase orders sent to international vendors are still sent in paper form, electronic order filing and processing are poised for takeoff.

The benefits are potentially huge: Electronic commerce eliminates paperwork, which is costly and error-prone, and can speed up the whole order-filing and processing process. Electronic filing also allows management an effective information system to plan business better. With electronic communication, importers can take various measures to force foreign vendors to provide accurate and timely information on shipments. For example, importers will impose a "charge-back" to the foreign wholesaler if they have to relabel or re-

count the contents of a shipment because the documentation contained inaccurate information about the quantity, size, or color of the merchandise. These charge-backs can be high enough to wipe out the entire profit of a shipment.

However, the switch can be a Herculean task. Large U.S. retailers had to struggle for five years before they could achieve electronic compliance from their domestic vendors. This e-commerce strategy is likely to meet with even fiercer resistance from overseas vendors, especially those in developing countries, given the poor state of electronic infrastructure there and vendors' unwillingness to invest even a modest amount in electronic facilities.

SOURCE: "Importers Push Overseas Vendors to Communicate Electronically," *Journal of Commerce*, January 27, 1999, 17A.

mode, delivery times may vary considerably from shipment to shipment. This variation requires the maintenance of larger safety stocks in order to be able to fill demand in periods when delays occur.

The international marketer should attempt to reduce order cycle time and increase its consistency without an increase in total costs. This objective can be accomplished by altering methods of transportation, changing inventory locations, or improving any of the other components of the order cycle time, such as the way orders are transmitted. By shifting order placement from mail to telephone or to direct computer-order entry, for example, a firm can reduce the order cycle time substantially. The shift to such a new system can be very expensive. *The International Marketplace 19.3* explains how technology affects the electronic ordering activities of firms.

Customer Service Levels The level of customer service denotes the responsiveness that inventory policies permit for any given situation. Customer service is therefore a management-determined constraint within the logistics system. A customer service level of 100 percent could be defined as the ability to fill all orders within a set time—for example, three days. If within these three days only 70 percent of the orders can be filled, the customer service level is 70 percent. The choice of customer service level for the firm has a major impact on the inventories needed. In their domestic operations, U.S. companies frequently aim to achieve customer service levels of 90 to 95 percent. Often, such "homegrown" rules of thumb are then used in international inventory operations as well.

Many managers do not realize that standards determined heuristically and based on competitive activity in the home market are often inappropriate abroad. Different locales have country-specific customer service needs and requirements. Service levels should not be oriented primarily around cost or customary domestic standards. Rather, the level chosen for use internationally should be based on customer expectations encountered in each market. These expectations are dependent on past performance, product desirability, customer sophistication, the competitive status of the firm, and whether a buyers' or sellers' market exists.

Because high customer service levels are costly, the goal should not be the highest customer service level possible but rather an acceptable level. Different customers have different priorities. Some will be prepared to pay a premium for speed. In industrial marketing, for example, even an eight-hour delay may be unacceptable for the delivery of a crucial product component, since it may mean a shutdown of the production process. Other firms may put a higher value on flexibility, and another group may see low cost as the most important issue. Flexibility and speed are expensive, so it is wasteful to supply them to customers who do not value them highly.[25] If, for example, foreign customers expect to receive their merchandise within 30 days, for the international corporation to promise delivery within 10 or 15 days does not make sense. Indeed, such delivery may result in storage problems. In addition, the higher prices associated with higher customer service levels may reduce the competitiveness of a firm's product.

Inventory as a Strategic Tool International inventories can be used by the international corporation as a strategic tool in dealing with currency valuation changes or hedging against inflation. By increasing inventories before an imminent devaluation of a currency, instead of holding cash, the corporation may reduce its exposure to devaluation losses. Similarly, in the case of high inflation, large inventories can provide an important inflation hedge. In such circumstances, the international inventory manager must balance the cost of maintaining high levels of inventories with the benefits accruing to the firm from hedging against inflation or devaluation. Many countries, for example, charge a property tax on stored goods. If the increase in tax payments outweighs the hedging benefits to the corporation, it would be unwise to increase inventories before a devaluation.

Despite the benefits of reducing the firm's financial risk, inventory management must still fall in line with the overall corporate market strategy. Only by recognizing the trade-offs, which may result in less than optimal inventory policies, can the corporation maximize the overall benefit.

International Storage Issues

Although international logistics is discussed as a movement or flow of goods, a stationary period is involved when merchandise becomes inventory stored in warehouses. Heated arguments can arise within a firm over the need for and utility of warehousing internationally. On the one hand, customers expect quick responses to orders and rapid delivery. Accommodating the customer's expectation may require locating many distribution centers around the world. On the other hand, warehousing space is expensive. In addition, the larger volume of inventory increases the inventory carrying cost. The international marketer must consider the trade-offs between service and cost to determine the appropriate levels of warehousing. Other trade-offs also exist within the logistics function. As an example, fewer warehouses will allow for consolidation of transportation and therefore lower transportation rates to the warehouse. However, if the warehouses are located far from customers, the cost of outgoing transportation from the warehouse will increase.

Storage Facilities

One important location decision is how many distribution centers to have and where to locate them. The availability of facilities abroad will differ from the domestic situ-

[25]Bernard LaLonde, Kee-Hian Tan, and Michael Standing, "Forget Supply Chains, Think of Value Flows," *Transformation*, Gemini Consulting, 3 (Summer 1994): 24–31.

ation. For example, whereas public storage is widely available in some countries, such facilities may be scarce or entirely lacking in others. Also, the standards and quality of facilities abroad may often not be comparable to those offered at home. As a result, the storage decision of the firm is often accompanied by the need for large-scale, long-term investments. Despite the high cost, international storage facilities should be established if they support the overall marketing effort. In many markets, adequate storage facilities are imperative in order to satisfy customer demands and to compete successfully.

Once the decision is made to utilize storage facilities abroad, the warehouse conditions must be carefully analyzed. As an example, in some countries, warehouses have low ceilings. Packaging developed for the high stacking of products is therefore unnecessary. In other countries, automated warehousing is available. Proper bar coding of products and the use of package dimensions acceptable to the warehousing system are basic requirements. In contrast, in warehouses still stocked manually, weight limitations will be of major concern.

To optimize the logistics system, the marketer should analyze international product sales and then rank products according to warehousing needs. Products that are most sensitive to delivery time may be classified as "A" products. "A" products would be stocked in all distribution centers, and safety stock levels would be kept high. Products for which immediate delivery is not urgent may be classified as "B" products. They would be stored only at selected distribution centers around the world. Finally, products for which short delivery time is not important, or for which there is little demand, would be stocked only at headquarters. Should an urgent need for delivery arise, airfreight could be considered for rapid shipment. Classifying products enables the international marketer to substantially reduce total international warehousing requirements and still maintain acceptable service levels.

Foreign Trade Zones

The existence of foreign trade zones can have a major effect on the international logistician, since production cost advantages may require a reconfiguration of storage, processing, and distribution strategies. Trade zones are considered, for purposes of tariff treatment, to be outside the customs territory of the country within which they are located. They are special areas and can be used for warehousing, packaging, inspection, labeling, exhibition, assembly, fabrication, or transshipment of imports without burdening the firm with duties.[26] Trade zones can be found at major ports of entry and also at inland locations near major production facilities. For example, Kansas City, Missouri, has one of the largest foreign trade zones in the United States.

Trade zones can be quite useful to the international firm. In some countries, the benefits derived from lower factor costs, such as labor, may be offset by high duties and tariffs. As a result, location of manufacturing and storage facilities in these countries may prove uneconomical. Foreign trade zones are designed to exclude the impact of duties from the location decision. This is done by exempting merchandise in the foreign trade zone from duty payment. The international firm can therefore import merchandise; store it in the foreign trade zone; and process, alter, test, or demonstrate it—all without paying duties. If the merchandise is subsequently shipped abroad (that is, reexported), no duty payments are ever due. Duty payments become due only if and when the merchandise is shipped into the country from the foreign trade zone.

Firms can also make use of sharp differentials in factor endowments, such as labor costs, between adjoining countries by locating close to their border. For instance, the **maquiladora program** between the United States and Mexico permits firms to carry out their labor-intensive operations in Mexico while sourcing raw materials or com-

[26]Patriya S. Tansuhaj and George C. Jackson, "Foreign Trade Zones: A Comparative Analysis of Users and Non-Users," *Journal of Business Logistics* 10 (1989): 15–30.

ponent parts from the United States, free of Mexican tariffs. Subsequently, the semi-finished or assembled products are shipped to the U.S. market and are assessed duties only for the foreign labor component. The benefits of the maquiladora program are available for any firm that chooses to locate close to the border. For example, many Japanese firms have made use of this program.

One country that has used trade zones very successfully for its own economic development is China. Through the creation of *special economic zones* in which there are no tariffs, substantial tax incentives, and low prices for land and labor, the government has attracted many foreign investors bringing in billions of dollars. These investors have brought new equipment, technology, and managerial know-how and have therefore substantially increased the local economic prosperity. The job-generation effect has been so strong that the central Chinese government has expressed concern about the overheating of the economy and the inequities between regions with and without trade zones.[27]

Both parties to the arrangement benefit from foreign trade zones. The government maintaining the trade zone achieves increased employment. The firm using the trade zone obtains a spearhead in or close to the foreign market without incurring all of the costs customarily associated with such an activity. As a result, goods can be reassembled and large shipments can be broken down into smaller units. Also, goods can be repackaged when packaging weight becomes part of the duty assessment. Finally, goods can be given domestic "made-in" status if assembled in the foreign trade zone. Thus, duties may be payable only on the imported materials and component parts rather than on the labor that is used to finish the product. Whenever use of a trade zone is examined, however, the marketer must keep the additional cost of storage, handling, and transportation in mind before making a decision.

International Packaging Issues

Packaging is instrumental in getting the merchandise to the ultimate destination in a safe, maintainable, and presentable condition. Packaging that is adequate for domestic shipping may be inadequate for international transportation because the shipment will be subject to the motions of the vessel on which it is carried. Added stress in international shipping also arises from the transfer of goods among different modes of transportation. Figure 19.7 provides examples of some sources of stress that are most frequently found in international transportation.

The responsibility for appropriate packaging rests with the shipper of goods. The U.S. Carriage of Goods by Sea Act of 1936 states: "Neither the carrier nor the ship shall be responsible for loss or damage arising or resulting from insufficiency of packing." The shipper must therefore ensure that the goods are prepared appropriately for international shipping. This is important because it has been found that "the losses that occur as a result of breakage, pilferage, and theft exceed the losses caused by major maritime casualties, which include fires, sinkings, and collision of vessels. Thus, the largest of these losses is a preventable loss."[28]

Packaging decisions must also take into account differences in environmental conditions—for example, climate. When the ultimate destination is very humid or particularly cold, special provisions must be made to prevent damage to the product. The task becomes even more challenging when one considers that, in the course of long-distance transportation, dramatic changes in climate can take place. An example of a major packaging blunder was provided by a firm in Taiwan that shipped drinking

---

[27]Li Rongxia, "Free Trade Zones in China," *Beijing Review*, August 2–8, 1993, 14–21.

[28]Charles A. Taft, *Management of Physical Distribution and Transportation*, 7th ed. (Homewood, IL: Irwin, 1984), 324.

FIGURE 19.7 Stresses in Intermodal Movement

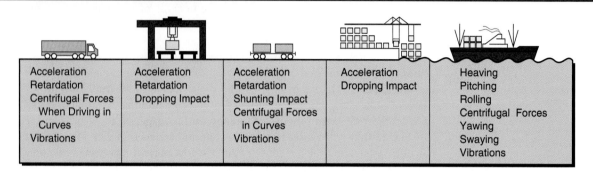

Acceleration Retardation Centrifugal Forces When Driving in Curves Vibrations	Acceleration Retardation Dropping Impact	Acceleration Retardation Shunting Impact Centrifugal Forces in Curves Vibrations	Acceleration Dropping Impact	Heaving Pitching Rolling Centrifugal Forces Yawing Swaying Vibrations

Note: Each transportation mode exerts a different set of stresses and strains on containerized cargoes. The most commonly overloaded are those associated with ocean transport.

SOURCE: Reprinted with permission from *Handling and Shipping Management*, September 1980 issue, p. 47; and David Greenfield, "Perfect Packing for Export." Copyright © 1980, Penton Publishing, Cleveland, OH.

glasses to the Middle East. The company used wooden crates and padded the glasses with hay. Most of the glasses, however, were broken by the time they reached their destination. As the crates traveled into the drier Middle East, the moisture content of the hay had dropped. By the time the crates were delivered, the thin straw offered almost no protection.[29]

Packaging issues also need to be closely linked to overall strategic plans. The individual responsible for international packaging should utilize transportation modes as efficiently as possible. This requires appropriate package design, which takes into account the storage properties of the product. For example, John Deere was shipping its combines from the United States to Australia for years, at a shipping cost of $2,500 each. Each combine took up much more space than its footprint, since the harvesting arm stuck out on its side. Once the company decided to ship the harvesting arm unmounted, shipping costs were reduced by $1,000 per combine.

The weight of packaging must also be considered, particularly when airfreight is used, since the cost of shipping is often based on weight. At the same time, packaging material must be sufficiently strong to permit stacking in international transportation. Another consideration is that, in some countries, duties are assessed according to the gross weight of shipments, which includes the weight of packaging. Obviously, the heavier the packaging, the higher the duties will be.

The shipper must pay sufficient attention to instructions provided by the customer for packaging. For example, requests by the customer that the weight of any one package should not exceed a certain limit, or that specific package dimensions should be adhered to, usually are made for a reason. Often they reflect limitations in transportation or handling facilities at the point of destination.

Although the packaging of a product is often used as a form of display abroad, international packaging can rarely serve the dual purpose of protection and display. Therefore, double packaging may be necessary. The display package is for future use at the point of destination; another package surrounds it for protective purposes.

One solution to the packaging problem in international logistics has been the development of intermodal containers—large metal boxes that fit on trucks, ships, railroad cars, and airplanes and ease the frequent transfer of goods in international shipments. In addition, containers offer greater safety from pilferage and damage. Of course, if merchandise from a containerized shipment is lost, frequently the entire

[29]David A. Ricks, *Blunders in International Business* (Oxford, England: Blackwell Publishers, 1997), 27.

container has been removed. Developed in different forms for both sea and air transportation, containers also offer better utilization of carrier space because of standardization of size. The shipper therefore may benefit from lower transportation rates.

Container traffic is heavily dependent on the existence of appropriate handling facilities, both domestically and internationally. In addition, the quality of inland transportation must be considered. If transportation for containers is not available and the merchandise must be removed and reloaded, the expected cost reductions may not materialize.

In some countries, rules for the handling of containers may be designed to maintain employment. For example, U.S. union rules obligate shippers to withhold containers from firms that do not employ members of the International Longshoreman Association for loading and unloading containers within a 50-mile radius of Atlantic or Gulf ports. Such restrictions can result in an onerous cost burden.

Overall, close attention must be paid to international packaging. The customer who ordered and paid for the merchandise expects it to arrive on time and in good condition. Even with replacements and insurance, the customer will not be satisfied if there are delays. This dissatisfaction will usually translate directly into lost sales.

Management of International Logistics

Because the very purpose of a multinational firm is to benefit from system synergism, a persuasive argument can be made for the coordination of international logistics at corporate headquarters. Without coordination, subsidiaries will tend to optimize their individual efficiency but jeopardize the overall performance of the firm.

Centralized Logistics Management

A significant characteristic of the centralized approach to international logistics is the existence of headquarters staff that retains decision-making power over logistics activities affecting international subsidiaries. Such an approach is particularly valuable in instances where corporations have become international by rapid growth and have lost the benefit of a cohesive strategy.

If headquarters exerts control, it must also take the primary responsibility for its decisions. Clearly, ill will may arise if local managers are appraised and rewarded on the basis of performance they do not control. This may be particularly problematic if headquarters staff suffers from a lack of information or expertise.

To avoid internal problems both headquarters staff and local logistics management should report to one person. This person, whether the vice president for international logistics or the president of the firm, can then become the final arbiter to decide the firm's priorities. Of course, this individual should also be in charge of determining appropriate rewards for managers, both at headquarters and abroad, so that corporate decisions that alter a manager's performance level will not affect the manager's appraisal and evaluation. Further, this individual can contribute an objective view when inevitable conflicts arise in international logistics coordination. The internationally centralized decision-making process leads to an overall logistics management perspective that can dramatically improve profitability.

Decentralized Logistics Management

An alternative to the centralized international logistics system is the "decentralized full profit center model."[30] The main rationale for such decentralization is the fact that "when an organization attempts to deal with markets on a global scale, there are

[30]Jacques Picard, "Physical Distribution Organization in Multinationals: The Position of Authority," *International Journal of Physical Distribution and Materials Management* 13 (1983): 24.

problems of coordination."[31] Particularly when the firm serves many international markets that are diverse in nature, total centralization would leave the firm unresponsive to local adaptation needs.

If each subsidiary is made a profit center in itself, each one carries the full responsibility for its performance, which can lead to greater local management satisfaction and to better adaptation to local market conditions. Yet often such decentralization deprives the logistics function of the benefits of coordination. For example, whereas headquarters, referring to its large volume of total international shipments, may be able to extract bottom rates from transportation firms, individual subsidiaries by themselves may not have similar bargaining power. The same argument applies also to the sourcing situation, where the coordination of shipments by the purchasing firm may be much more cost-effective than individual shipments from many small suppliers around the world.

Once products are within a specific market, however, increased input from local logistics operations should be expected and encouraged. At the very least, local managers should be able to provide input into the logistics decisions generated by headquarters. Ideally, within a frequent planning cycle, local managers can identify the logistics benefits and constraints existing in their particular market and communicate them to headquarters. Headquarters can then either adjust its international logistics strategy accordingly or can explain to the manager why system optimization requires actions different from the ones recommended. Such a justification process will greatly help in reducing the potential for animosity between local and headquarters operations.

Contract Logistics

While the choice is open to maintain either centralized or decentralized in-house logistical management, a growing preference among international firms is to outsource, which means to employ outside logistical expertise. Often referred to as contract, or "third-party," logistics, it is a rapidly expanding industry with a third of the Fortune 500 companies as clientele. The main thrust behind the idea is that individual firms are experts in their industry and should therefore concentrate only on their operations. Third-party logistics providers, on the other hand, are experts solely at logistics, with the knowledge and means to perform efficient and innovative services for those companies in need. The goal is improved service at equal or lower cost. *The International Marketplace 19.4* provides an example.

Logistics providers' services vary in scope. For instance, some may use their own assets in physical transportation, while others subcontract out portions of the job. Certain other providers are not involved as much with the actual transportation as they are with developing systems and databases or consulting on administrative management services. In many instances, the partnership consists of working closely with established transport providers such as Federal Express or UPS. These firms happily provide their self-service parcel boxes by the entrances for stores and firms. This way, a customer desiring overnight delivery does not have to expend energy trying to find a carrier willing to perform the service.[32] The concept of improving service, cutting costs, and unloading the daily management onto willing experts is driving the momentum of contract logistics. Figure 19.8 shows an advertisement for outside logistics services.

[31]Philip B. Schary, *Logistics Decisions* (Hinsdale, IL: The Dryden Press, 1984), 407.

[32]Joseph C. Andraski and Robert A. Novack, "Marketing Logistics Value: Managing the 5 P's," *Journal of Business Logistics* 17 (Number 1): 23–34.

THE INTERNATIONAL MARKETPLACE 19.4

Outsourcing the Logistics Function

CONTRACT LOGISTICS (or "third-party logistics") is the process undertaken by an outside company of strategically managing the movement of another company's products and related information from any point in the manufacturing process to the consumer market. This relatively new industry had revenues of $56.4 billion in 2000.

A growing number of companies across the nation turn to third-party contractors for their international logistics needs. The principal reasons include cost, convenience, and the superior technology many "third parties" now offer, including such services as electronic cargo tracking and bar coding. If that isn't enough, many companies have also decided in recent years to focus intently on their core business, deploying outside sources for such matters as logistics. Logistics providers can offer some unique skills, including inventory and returns management, contract warehousing, manufacturing support, dedicated contract carriage, custom packaging, distribution real estate, and technical support.

National Semiconductor wanted to change its five- to eighteen-day delivery time and offer a two-day delivery guarantee. BLS was able to provide NSC with a formidable logistics network by granting access to 420 aircraft, 1,869 worldwide facilities, more than 100,000 computer terminals, 31,211 surface vehicles, and an infrastructure with more than 90,000 employees. NSC views the partnership as "using the experts who spend billions on logistics."

The need to meet customer deliverables led Compaq, the world's largest maker of personal computers, to outsource its international logistics function to FedEx. By integrating its tech-

nology with compaq systems in Asia and by applying its expertise in global supply-chain management, FedEx was able to shorten dramatically the delivery cycle of portable computers manufactured in Taipei, Taiwan, and shipped to the United States. Point-to-point delivery and consolidated customs entry eliminated the need for costly warehousing.

There are common-sense rules to remember to ensure smooth relations with a third-party provider. Communications must be clear and concise from the outset. Expectations, especially regarding data availability and accuracy, should be put in writing and closely monitored. Any agreement should contain alternative plans, preferably pretested, and a comprehensive contingency plan in case a dispute arises and both parties go separate ways. Make sure your third-party provider understands the unique needs of your business. Lastly, don't abdicate the entire process, assuming that they'll take care of everything. Monitor their operations, ask for an accounting, and make sure they're following through on their end of the deal.

SOURCES: Jim Shaw, "The Third Wave," *World Trade*, August 1996, 66; "Macro Logistics for Microprocessors," *Distribution*, April 1993, 66–72; Armstrong & Associates, Inc., web site, armstrong@3plogistics.com, accessed April 18, 2001; FedEx Corporation press release, www.fedex.com, accessed April 18, 2001.

http://www.fedex.com

One of the greatest benefits of contracting out the logistics function in a foreign market is the ability to take advantage of an in-place network complete with resources and experience. The local expertise and image are crucial when a business is just starting up. The prospect of newly entering a region such as Europe with different regions, business formats, and languages can be frightening without access to a seasoned and familiar logistics provider.

One of the main arguments leveled against contract logistics is the loss of the firm's control in the supply chain. Yet contract logistics does not and should not require the handing over of control. Rather, it offers concentration on one's specialization—a division of labor. The control and responsibility toward the customer remain with the firm, even though operations may move to a highly trained outside organization.

The Supply Chain and the Internet

At the turn of the century, the majority of firms still used their Web sites as a marketing and advertising tool without expanding them to order-taking capabilities.[33] That is changing rapidly. A survey by KPMG Management Consulting in Europe shows that more than one-third of the 500 European-based large and medium-sized companies reported Internet sales in 1998. The group stated that those sales represented about 2 percent of their total sales, a figure they expect to jump to 12 percent in three years and 20 percent in five years.[34]

Companies wishing to enter e-commerce will not have to do so on their own. Hub sites (also known as virtual malls or digital intermediaries) bring together buyers, sellers, distributors, and transaction payment processors in a single marketplace, making convenience the key attraction. The share of such hubs in retail e-commerce increased from 15 percent in 1998 to 26 percent in 1999, with entities such as Compare.net (**www.compare.net**), Priceline.com (**www.priceline.com**), eBay (**www.ebay.com**), and VerticalNet (**www.verticalnet.com**) leading the way.[35]

[33]Erika Morphy, "Making Cash Flow," *Export Today*, July 1998, 22–29.

[34]Miles Maguire, "Spinning the Web," *Export Today*, January 1998, 28–32.

[35]Rolf Rykken, "Opening the Gate," *Export Today*, February 1999, 35–42.

THE INTERNATIONAL MARKETPLACE 19.5

Internet to Lead to Delivery Changes

ANYONE WHO HAS ORDERED a product from a catalog or online retailer knows the routine. The goods are shipped with a package-express company, which delivers the product while the buyer is away. When the buyer returns, all that's there is a yellow receipt in the mailbox. That may no longer be true in the near future. Express delivery giants including FedEx, UPS, and DHL Worldwide Express are all planning to provide new services that will make off-hour and weekend deliveries at scheduled times.

"There will be a re-engineering of the process toward same day rather than next day delivery," said a consultant for the Boston Consulting Group (BCG). Due to the unique demands of e-commerce, expectations of performance will be much higher than they are today, BCG said.

In Brazil, for example, Federal Express has begun an experimental 24-hour delivery service in an area around the cargo airport in Viracopos, some 70 miles from Sao Paulo.

DHL Express Worldwide, which has a partnership with one of the largest e-commerce companies, Amazon.com, is currently working with Internet service providers in order to identify value-added products that can be traded on the Web in Brazil.

Doug Aldrich, vice president of the Global Strategic Information Technology Practice for consultant AT Kearney, predicts growth in less-than-truckload (LTL) services as e-commerce flourishes. As book, music, clothing, and other retailers race to find warehouse space and distribution services to meet their growing sales, LTL trucking will be in greater demand, he said.

SOURCES: Thierry Orgier, "Internet Could Spur Air Cargo Changes," *Journal of Commerce*, August 4, 1999, 3; and Kevin Hall, "Internet to Spur Delivery Changes," *Journal of Commerce*, September 14, 1999, 16.

As soon as customers have the ability to access a company through the Internet, the company itself has to be prepared to provide 24-hour order-taking and customer service, to have the regulatory and customs-handling expertise for international delivery, and to understand marketing environments for the further development of the business relationship.[36] The instantaneous interactivity that users experience will also be translated into an expectation of expedient delivery of answers and products ordered.

The challenges of response and delivery capabilities can be overcome through outsourcing services or by building international distribution networks. Air express carriers such as DHL, FedEx, and UPS offer full-service packages that leverage their own Internet infrastructure with customs clearance and e-mail shipment notification. If a company needs help in order fulfillment and customer support, logistics centers offer warehousing and inventory management services as well as same-day delivery from in-country stocks. DHL, for example, has seven express logistics centers and 45 strategic parts centers worldwide with key centers in Bahrain for the Middle East, Brussels for Europe, and Singapore for Asia-Pacific. A study by DHL indicated that in spite of rapidly growing use of the Internet, many firms are still weak in the areas of delivery and customer service.[37] Some even believe that if fulfillment aspects remain unaddressed, the ensuing "logistics chaos" might threaten to derail the e-commerce boom.[38] *The International Marketplace 19.5* explains some of the different kinds of services available from such intermediaries.

Some companies elect to build their own international distribution networks. Both QVC, a televised shopping service, and Amazon.com, an online retailer of books, have distribution centers in Britain and Germany to take advantage of the European

[36]Nick Wreden, "Internet Opens Markets Abroad," *Information Week*, November 16, 1998, 46–48.

[37]DHL, *Global E-Commerce Report 2000*, Geneva, January 2000.

[38]John Zarocostas, "Internet Firms Neglect Logistics, Study Concludes," *Journal of Commerce*, February 15, 2000, 3.

Internet audience and to fulfill more quickly and cheaply the orders generated by their web sites. Transactions and the information they provide about the buyers also allow for more customization and service by region, market, or even individual customer.

For industries such as music and motion pictures, the Internet is both an opportunity and a threat. The Web provides a new efficient method of distribution and customization of products. At the same time, it can be a channel for intellectual property violation through unauthorized posting on other web sites where these products can be downloaded.[39] In addition, the music industry is concerned about a shift in the balance of economic power: if artists can deliver their works directly to customers via technologies such as MP3, what will be the role of labels and distributors?

A number of hurdles and uncertainties may keep companies out of global markets or from exploiting them to their full potential. Some argue that the World Wide Web does not live up to its name, since it is mostly a tool for the United States and Europe. For all countries, but particularly developing nations, the issue of universal access to the Internet is crucial. Such access depends on the speed with which governments end their monopolistic structures in telecommunication and open their markets to competition. The 1997 World Trade Organization agreement on telecommunication accelerated the process of liberalization, while access to the Internet is undergoing major expansion through new technologies such as NetTV and Web phones. As Internet penetration levels increase in the near future due to technological advances, improvements in many countries' Web infrastructures, and customer acceptance, e-business will become truly global.

Logistics and the Environment

The logistician plays an increasingly important role in allowing the firm to operate in an environmentally conscious way. Environmental laws, expectations, and self-imposed goals set by firms are difficult to adhere to without a logistics orientation that systematically takes these concerns into account. Since laws and regulations differ across the world, the firm's efforts need to be responsive to a wide variety of requirements. One logistics orientation that has grown in importance due to environmental concerns is the development of **reverse distribution systems.** Such systems are instrumental in ensuring that the firm not only delivers the product to the market, but also can retrieve it from the market for subsequent use, recycling, or disposal. To a growing degree, the ability to develop such reverse logistics is a key determinant for market acceptance and profitability.

Society is beginning to recognize that retrieval should not be restricted to short-term consumer goods, such as bottles. Rather, it may be even more important to devise systems that enable the retrieval and disposal of long-term capital goods, such as cars, refrigerators, air conditioners, and industrial goods, with the least possible burden on the environment. Increasingly, governments establish rules that hold the manufacturer responsible for the ultimate disposal of the product at the end of its economic life. In Germany, for example, car manufacturers are required, since January 1995, to take back their used vehicles for dismantling and recycling. The design of such long-term systems across the world may well be one of the key challenges and opportunities for the logistician and will require close collaboration with all other functions in the firm, such as design, production, and marketing. *The International Marketplace 19.6* presents some of the major issues connected to the design of a reverse logistics system.

On the transportation side, logistics managers will need to expand their involvement in carrier and routing selection. Shippers of oil or other potentially hazardous materials are increasingly expected to ensure that the carriers used have excellent

[39]Jodi Mardesich, "How the Internet Hits Big Music," *Fortune*, May 10, 1999, 96–102.

THE INTERNATIONAL MARKETPLACE 19.6

Reverse Logistics Management Is Crucial

REVERSE LOGISTICS—the handling and disposition of returned products and use of related materials and information—is a new way for firms in a wide array of industries to improve customer service and increase revenue.

According to the Reverse Logistics Executive Council, U.S. firms pay more than an estimated $35 billion annually for handling, transportation, and processing of returned products. That does not include disposition management, administration time, and the cost of converting unproductive returns into productive assets. Monitoring this operation can help firms increase efficiency significantly.

Reverse logistics planning involves better gatekeeping of returns, quick disposition of returned products, and sound financial warehouse and transportation management. It also includes well-defined recycling, product refurbishment, and other return reuse features. It combines relevant software, policies, practices, systems, and training with commitment and dedication. Further complicating matters is the fact that each product has its own life cycle, and each return may require different treatment, depending on whether the product is defective, damaged, recyclable, or repackageable.

Despite the challenges, some firms are managing reverse logistics admirably. Even though returns can be as high as 50 percent for goods sold online, Office Depot Online, a division of the large office-supply retailer, is recording returns of under 10 percent. To reduce the number of returns, Office Depot tries to ensure that customers don't order the wrong thing by mistake. When customers order laser printer toner cartridges, for example, they're automatically asked their printer's brand name to prevent mix-ups. Online shoppers are also allowed to review the list of products they purchased earlier, which reduces unnecessary duplication.

New York–based cosmetics company Estee Lauder is a champion of return management. At the heart of Lauder's reverse logistics operation is its proprietary software system. Since the system has been up and running, the company has been able to reduce production and inventory levels, shave $500,000 from annual labor costs, and write off far fewer destroyed products. The system automates the previously time-intensive process of sorting through returns. When Lauder receives returns, it scans package bar codes to determine the products' expiration date and condition. Based on this information, it can consolidate the items and immediately scrap damaged or expired ones.

Reverse logistics goes beyond keeping track of returns. It also encompasses disposing of them. Many firms are taking innovative approaches to reduce scrap and even produce surprising revenues. While all these reverse logistics activities are impressive, contributing to trimmed costs and enhanced revenues, the ultimate benefit of effectively managing reverse logistics is the information generated about product returns and related materials that can be shared within the company.

SOURCE: Harvey Meyer, "Many Happy Returns," *Journal of Business Strategy* 20 (July–August 1999): 27–31.

http://www.officedepot.com
http://www.esteelauder.com

safety records and use only double-hulled ships. Society may even expect corporate involvement in choosing the route that the shipment will travel, preferring routes that are far from ecologically important and sensitive zones.

In the packaging field, environmental concerns are also growing on the part of individuals and governments. Increasingly, it is expected that the amount of packaging materials used is minimized and that the materials used are more environmentally friendly.

Companies need to learn how to simultaneously achieve environmental and economic goals. Esprit, the apparel maker, and The Body Shop, a British cosmetics producer, screen all their suppliers for environmental and socially responsible practices. ISO 14000 is a standard specifically targeted at encouraging international environmental practices by evaluating companies both at the organization level (management systems, environmental performance, and environmental auditing) and at the product level (life-cycle assessment, labeling, and product standards). [40] From the environmental perspective, those practices are desirable that bring about fewer shipments, less handling, and more direct movement. Such practices are to be weighted against optimal efficiency routings, including just-in-time inventory and quantity discount purchasing. For example, even though a just-in-time inventory system may connote highly desirable inventory savings, the resulting cost of frequent delivery, additional highway congestion, and incremental air pollution also need to be factored into the planning horizon. Despite the difficulty, firms will need to assert leadership in such trade-off considerations in order to provide society with a better quality of life.

SUMMARY

The relevance of international logistics and supply chain management was not widely recognized in the past. As competitiveness is becoming increasingly dependent on cost efficiency, however, the field is emerging as one of major importance because international distribution comprises between 10 and 30 percent of the total landed cost of an international order.

International logistics is concerned with the flow of materials into, through, and out of the international corporation and therefore includes materials management as well as physical distribution. The logistician must recognize the total systems demands of the firm in order to develop trade-offs between various logistics components. By taking a supply chain perspective, the marketing manager can develop logistics systems that are highly customer focused and very cost efficient. Implementation of such a system requires close collaboration between all members of the supply chain.

International logistics differs from domestic activities in that it deals with greater distances, new variables, and greater complexity because of country-specific differences. One major factor to consider is transportation. The international marketer needs to understand transportation infrastructures in other countries and modes of transportation such as ocean shipping and airfreight. The choice among these modes will depend on the customer's demands and the firm's transit time, predictability, and cost requirements. In addition, noneconomic factors such as government regulations weigh heavily in this decision.

Inventory management is another major consideration. Inventories abroad are expensive to maintain yet often crucial for international success. The marketer must evaluate requirements for order cycle times and customer service levels in order to develop an international inventory policy that can also serve as a strategic management tool.

The marketer must also deal with international storage issues and determine where to locate inventories. International warehouse space will have to be leased or purchased and decisions made about utilizing foreign trade zones.

International packaging is important because it ensures arrival of the merchandise at the ultimate destination in safe condition. In developing packaging requirements, the marketer must consider environmental concerns as well as climate, freight, and handling conditions.

International logistics management is increasing in Importance. Connecting the logistics function with overall corporate strategic concerns and with customers and suppliers alike will increasingly be a requirement for successful global competitiveness.

[40]Haw-Jan Wu and Steven C. Dunn, "Environmentally Responsible Logistics Systems," *International Journal of Physical Distribution and Logistics Management* 2 (1995): 20–38.

QUESTIONS FOR DISCUSSION

1. Why do international firms pay so little attention to international logistics issues?
2. Contrast the use of ocean shipping to airfreight.
3. Explain the meaning of supply chain management.
4. What are the prerequisites for effective supply chain management?
5. What is the impact of transit time on international logistics and how can a firm improve its performance?
6. How can an international firm reduce its order cycle time?
7. Why should customer service levels differ internationally? Is it, for example, ethical to offer a lower customer service level in developing countries than in industrialized countries?
8. How can an improved logistics infrastructure contribute to the economic development of Eastern Europe?

9. In which areas can contract logistics be most effective for the international marketer?
10. What steps can logisticians take to make their effort more environmentally friendly?
11. What is your view of the 40/40/20 freight allocation rule of the United Nations Commission on International Trade and Development?
12. What types of information are available to exporters on the Transport web? Go to the site, **www.transportweb.com** and give examples of transportation links that an exporter would find helpful and explain why.
13. Determine the length of transit time a shipment takes between two international destinations. What is the business purpose of a "To Order Bill of Lading"? Go to **http:// www.apl.com/content/ship/ship.html** and check "schedules."

RECOMMENDED READINGS

Ballou, Ronald H. *Business Logistics Management*, 4th ed. Upper Saddle River, NJ: Prentice-Hall, 1998.

Boyson, Sandor, Martin E. Dresner, and H. James Harrington, *Logistics and the Extended Enterprise: Benchmarks and Best Practices for the Manufacturing Professional.* New York: John Wiley & Sons, 1999.

Ernst, Ricardo, Panos Kouvelis, Phillippe-Pierre Dornier, and Michel Fender. *Global Operations and Logistics: Text and Cases.* New York: John Wiley & Sons, 1998.

Martin, Christopher. *Logistics and Supply Chain Management*, 2nd ed. London: Financial Times Management, 1999.

Monczka, Robert M., Robert J. Trent, and Robert B. Handfield. *Purchasing and Supply Chain Management.* Cincinnati: South-Western Publishing, 1998.

Stock, James R., and Douglas M. Lambert. *Strategic Logistics Management*, 4th ed. Burr Ridge, IL: McGraw Hill, 2001.

Wood, Donald F., Daniel L. Wardlow, Paul R. Murphy, Mae Johnson, and James C. Johnson. *Contemporary Logistics*, 7th ed. Upper Saddle River, NJ: Prentice-Hall, 1999.

Chapter 20

Global Promotional Strategies

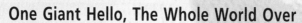

One Giant Hello, The Whole World Over

FORD MOTOR COMPANY made history on November 1, 1999, with a television commercial shown in virtually every country around the world. The commercial showcased the company's seven product brands—Ford, Lincoln, Mercury, Mazda, Jaguar, Aston Martin, and Volvo—the first time all of them were shown together in a broadcast commercial, and the first time any corporation has run simultaneous advertising campaigns around the world. Viewers in New Zealand saw the ad first; Ford had bought the 9 P.M. spot based on local time in each market. In Europe, one of the placements was on CNN International's World News and was shown in London at 6 P.M., Paris at 7 P.M., Helsinki at 8 P.M., and Moscow at 9 P.M. In the United States, the ad was carried at 9 P.M. on 38 different television networks.

The two-minute ad highlights the cultural diversity of the company's customers around the world. It is a montage of nearly 60 scenes that jump from Australia to China to Brazil to the United States—nine countries in all. Interspersed at various points are the logos of the company's car marques. There is no voice-over. The images are supposed to convey the message that "it's time to wave goodbye to the old millennium and hello to the new one, in a passionate and compassionate way." The ad is built on emotional images: a hand waving goodbye in Australia; a homecoming parade using a Ford Mustang; a young man's farewell to his dying mother; a reunion in Australia between a girl and her father (with a Ford pickup in the background). The final rush of scenes depicts joyous greetings—Carnival dancers in Brazil, Chinese

New Year celebrations in Beijing, and 13-year-old Welsh soprano Charlotte Church singing "Just Wave Hello," the theme song of the ad, as the sun rises over an outdoor theater in Cornwall.

"It shows how Ford vehicles relate to people around the world on many different levels in many different cultures," said Ted Powell, J. Walter Thompson international creative director on the Ford account, who created the idea and sold it to Ford. Ford itself says that part of the objective is to link Ford's seven brands in people's minds and add to people's regard for the company.

Ford has called the campaign its "global anthem." The ad has been broken into one-minute versions for future show-

ings. For example, it was shown globally again January 4–6, 2000.

SOURCES: "Ford Motor Company Airs First Ever Global Advertising Campaign," *Ford Motor Company News*, November 1, 1999; "Ford to Debut Ad at the Same Time Globally," *The Wall Street Journal*, October 27, 1999, B10.

http://www.ford.com

THE GENERAL REQUIREMENTS of effective marketing communications apply to the multinational corporation as well; however, the environments and the situations usually are more numerous and call for coordination of the promotional effort. Increasingly, marketers opt for varying degrees of panregional approaches to take advantage of similarities in markets they serve, as seen in *The International Marketplace 20.1*.

The technology is in place for global communication efforts, but difficult challenges still remain in the form of cultural, economic, ethnic, regulatory, and demographic differences in the various countries and regions. Standardization of any magnitude requires sound management systems and excellent communication to ensure uniform strategic and tactical thinking of all the professionals in the overseas marketing chain. One marketer has suggested the development of a worldwide visual language that would be understandable and that would not offend cultural sensitivities.[1]

This chapter will analyze the elements to be managed in promotional efforts in terms of environmental opportunities and constraints. A framework is provided for the planning of promotional campaigns. Although the discussion focuses mostly on advertising, other elements of the promotion mix, especially sales promotion and publicity, fit integrally into the planning model. Naturally, all of the mass selling methods have to be planned in conjunction with personal selling efforts. For example, personal selling often relies on updated direct mailing lists and promotional materials sent to prospects before the first sales call.

Planning Promotional Campaigns

The planning for promotional campaigns consists of the following seven stages, which usually overlap or take place concurrently, especially after the basics of the campaign have been agreed on:

1. Determine the target audience
2. Determine specific campaign objectives
3. Determine the budget

[1]John Eger, "Globalancing Act Is Real," *Advertising Age*, January 30, 1984, 20, 24.

4. Determine media strategy
5. Determine the message
6. Determine the campaign approach
7. Determine campaign effectiveness[2]

The actual content of these stages will change by type of campaign situation; compare, for example, a local campaign for which headquarters provides support versus a global corporate image campaign.

The Target Audience

Global marketers face multiple audiences beyond customers. The expectations of these audiences have to be researched to ensure the appropriateness of the campaign decision making. Consider the following publics with whom communication is necessary: suppliers, intermediaries, government, the local community, bankers and creditors, media organizations, shareholders, and employees. Each can be reached with an appropriate mix of tools. A multinational corporation that wants to boost its image with the government and the local community may sponsor events. One of the approaches available is **cause-related marketing,** in which the company, or one of its brands, is linked with a cause such as environmental protection or children's health. For example, Unilever's Funfit Program for its Persil washing powder brand in Europe creates resource packs for teachers to help boost children's fitness through physical education lessons. Microsoft launched a site in Singapore (**www.you-can-do-more.com.sg**) to further the use of information technology. For every page hit within the site, Microsoft will donate one cent to three local charities. This type of activity can benefit a brand but will have to be backed by a genuine effort within the company to behave responsibly.[3]

Some campaigns may be targeted at multiple audiences. For example, British Airways' "Manhattan Landing" campaign (in which Manhattan Island takes to the air and lands in London) was directed not only at international business travelers but also at employees, the travel industry, and potential stockholders (the campaign coincided with the privatization of the airline).[4] As companies such as airlines become more internationally involved, target audience characteristics change. American Airlines, which enjoys a huge domestic market, had foreign routes generate 32 percent of passenger miles in 1999 compared with virtually none in 1980.[5]

An important aspect of research is to determine multimarket target audience similarities. If such exist, panregional or global campaigns can be attempted. Grey Advertising checks for commonalities in variables such as economic expectations, demographics, income, and education. Consumer needs and wants are assessed for common features. An increasing number of companies are engaging in **corporate image advertising** in support of their more traditional tactical product-specific and local advertising efforts. Especially for multidivisional companies, an umbrella campaign may help either to boost the image of lesser-known product lines or make the company itself be understood correctly or perceived more positively. ABB, the global engineering and technology company, wants to be better known among its constituents and in 1999 launched a major global campaign to ensure that (an example of which is provided in Figure 20.1). Canon, for example, is using the approach to reposition itself

[2]Framework adapted from Dean M. Peebles and John K. Ryans, *Management of International Advertising: A Marketing Approach* (Boston: Allyn & Bacon, 1984), 72–73.

[3]"Why P&G is Linking Brands to Good Causes," *Marketing*, August 26, 1999, 11; "Microsoft's Singapore Site Ties Page Views to Charity," *Advertising Age International*, October 1999, 4.

[4]"Berkeley Square Takes on Madison Avenue," *The Economist*, September 17, 1988, 25–28.

[5]**http://www.amrcorp.com/news/jan0300.htm**

| FIGURE 20.1 | An Example of a Corporate Image Campaign |

SOURCE: **http://www.abb.com**.

as an information technology specialist instead of just a manufacturer of office automation machines.[6] Costs may also be saved in engaging in global image campaigning, especially if the same campaign or core concepts can be used across borders. Corporate advertising as a strategic tool is highlighted in *The International Marketplace 20.2*.

Often, however, problems may emerge. For example, Tang was marketed in the United States as an orange juice substitute, which did not succeed in testing abroad. In France, for example, Tang was repositioned as a refreshment because the French rarely drink orange juice at breakfast. In countries like the Philippines, Tang could be marketed as a premium drink, whereas in Brazil, it was a low-priced item.[7] Audience similarities are more easily found in business markets.[8]

Campaign Objectives

Nothing is more essential to the planning of international promotional campaigns than the establishment of clearly defined, measurable objectives. These objectives can be divided into overall global and regional objectives as well as local objectives. Compaq, for example, declared that it intended to be number one in PC and workstation market share.[9] For Compaq to reach this goal, international sales had to represent 50 percent of total sales. In 1998, sales outside of North America reached 51 percent of total.[10] Such objectives offer the general guidelines and control needed for broad-based campaigns.

The objectives that are set at the local level are more specific and set measurable targets for individual markets. These objectives may be product- or service-related or related to the corporation itself. Typical goals are to increase awareness, enhance image, or improve market share in a particular market. Whatever the objective, it has to be measurable for control purposes.

[6]"Corporate Campaigns Attract Bigger Slices of Advertising Pie," *Advertising Age International*, March 8, 1999, 2.

[7]"Global Marketing Campaigns with a Local Touch," *Business International*, July 4, 1988, 205–210.

[8]Robert E. Hite and Cynthia Fraser, "International Advertising Strategies of Multinational Corporations," *Journal of Advertising Research* 28 (August–September 1988): 9–17.

[9]Stephanie Losee, "How Compaq Keeps the Magic Going," *Fortune*, February 21, 1994, 90–92.

[10]http://www.compaq.com

THE INTERNATIONAL MARKETPLACE 20.2

Nurturing a Global Image

CORPORATE ADVERTISING CAN PLAY a vital role in providing constituents with reassurances of quality and promises of trusted service. It is typically focused to support the company in several areas such as product support, employment recommendation, crisis support, joint venture consideration, and stock purchase.

Several global marketers have used global image advertising to achieve particular objectives. Nokia is the world's largest company in the cellular phone business. However, many customers are not aware of Nokia to the extent that they know its competitors such as Motorola. Nokia has, therefore, engaged in a number of corporate efforts, one of which is the title sponsorship of the Sugar Bowl in the United States. The sponsorship costs Nokia approximately $2.5 million annually. Worldwide, it sponsors the FIS Snowboard World Cup. Similarly, the German chemical company BASF has wanted to increase constituent awareness of its far-flung operations: it has 164 subsidiaries under its umbrella producing in 38 countries and markets them in over 170. Its campaign theme, "We do not make many of the products you use, but we make many of the products you use better," is intended to increase its brand equity and subsequently the behavior of important stakeholders.

In some cases corporations may look to reposition themselves. As a bloated, government-owned company, British Airways had to, upon privatization, quickly change its image among stakeholders from "Bloody Awful" to a more positive perception. A series of corporate image campaigns since 1983 have helped change the airline into one of the most positively regarded in the industry.

Some consider crises to be as sure as death and taxes. A solid corporate image and the ability to get the company's point of view are tasks for image campaigns. Companies such as Exxon Mobil have regularly engaged in extending the corporate view to dispel myths or misconceptions. In 2000, for example, the ads have focused on climate change, unilateral trade sanctions, and international anti-corruption efforts. The firm has also focused on its investments in developing countries, especially those in the public eye (e.g., Indonesia). The message argues that rather than cut and run from these country markets, the company can do more good by working in them. Microsoft has engaged in a similar program of "essays on technology and its impact on society." Its campaign of April 25, 2001 discussed how information technology and online solutions can be used by governments worldwide to improve their efficiency.

Some marketers have elected to engage in promoting social causes as part of their image advertising. Probably the most controversial in this category are advertisements from Benetton (see case on page 683), which have focused on promoting harmony and understanding among peoples but have created discussion about the appropriateness of the message delivery.

SOURCES: "China, Trade and Technology," *The Washington Post*, March 6, 2000, A17; "Corporate Campaigns Attract Bigger Slices of Advertising Pie," *Advertising Age International*, March 8, 1999, 2; "Growing from the Top," *Marketing Management*, Winter/Spring 1996, 10–19; and Rahul Jacob, "Nokia Fumbles, But Don't Count It Out," *Fortune*, February 19, 1996, 86–88.

http://www.nokia.com

http://www.basf.com

http://www.british-airways.com

http://www.mobil.com

http://www.benetton.com

http://www.microsoft.com

TABLE 20.1	Budgeting Methods for Promotional Programs		

BUDGETING METHOD	PERCENTAGE OF RESPONDENTS USING THIS METHOD[*]	MAJOR DIFFERENCES	
		LOWEST PERCENTAGES	HIGHEST PERCENTAGES
Objective and task	64	Sweden (36%) Argentina (44%)	Canada (87%) Singapore (86%)
Percentage of sales	48	Germany (31%)	Brazil (73%) Hong Kong (70%)
Executive judgment	33	Finland (8%) Germany (8%)	USA (64%) Denmark (51%) Brazil (46%) Great Britain (46%)
All-you-can-afford	12	Argentina (0%) Israel (0%)	Sweden (30%) Germany (25%) Great Britain (24%)
Matched competitors	12	Denmark (0%) Israel (0%)	Germany (33%) Sweden (33%) Great Britain (22%)
Same as last year plus a little more	9	Israel (0%)	
Same as last year	3		
Other	10	Finland (0%) Germany (0%) Israel (0%)	Canada (24%) Mexico (21%)

[*]Total exceeds 100 percent because respondents checked all budgeting methods that they used.

SOURCE: Nicolaos E. Synodinos, Charles F. Keown, and Laurence W. Jacobs, "Transnational Advertising Practices," *Journal of Advertising Research* 29 (April–May 1989): 43–50.

Local objectives are typically developed as a combination of headquarters country organization involvement. Basic guidelines are initiated by headquarters, whereas local organizations set the actual country-specific goals. These goals are subject to headquarters approval, mainly to ensure consistency. Although some campaigns, especially global ones, may have more headquarters involvement than usual, local input is still quite important, especially to ensure appropriate implementation of the subsequent programs at the local level.

The Budget

The promotional budget links established objectives with media, message, and control decisions. Ideally, the budget would be set as a response to the objectives to be met, but resource constraints often preclude this approach. Many marketers use an objective task method, as a recent survey of 484 advertising managers for consumer goods in fifteen countries indicates (see Table 20.1); however, realities may force compromises between ideal choices and resources available.[11] As a matter of fact, available funds may dictate the basis from which the objective task method can start.

Budgets can also be used as a control mechanism if headquarters retains final budget approval. In these cases, headquarters decision makers must have a clear understanding of cost and market differences to be able to make rational decisions.

[11]Nicolaos E. Synodinos, Charles F. Keown, and Laurence W. Jacobs, "Transnational Advertising Practices: A Survey of Leading Brand Advertisers in Fifteen Countries," *Journal of Advertising Research* 29 (April–May 1989): 43–50.

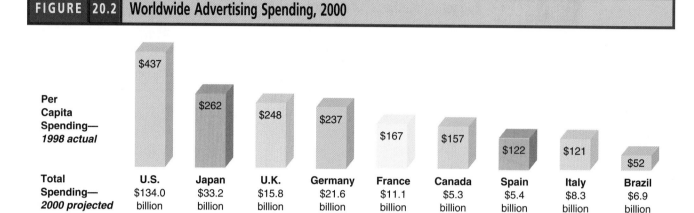

FIGURE 20.2 Worldwide Advertising Spending, 2000

Per Capita Spending— *1998 actual*

	U.S.	Japan	U.K.	Germany	France	Canada	Spain	Italy	Brazil
Per Capita	$437	$262	$248	$237	$167	$157	$122	$121	$52

Total Spending— *2000 projected*

	U.S.	Japan	U.K.	Germany	France	Canada	Spain	Italy	Brazil
Total	$134.0 billion	$33.2 billion	$15.8 billion	$21.6 billion	$11.1 billion	$5.3 billion	$5.4 billion	$8.3 billion	$6.9 billion

SOURCE: "Top Global Ad Markets," *AdAge Global* Web site, www.adagaglobal.com, accessed April 25, 2001.

In terms of worldwide ad spending, some of the leaders in 1998 were Procter & Gamble ($4.7 billion), Unilever ($3.4 billion), General Motors ($3.2 billion), Ford ($2.2 billion), DaimlerChrysler ($1.9 billion), Nestlé ($1.8 billion), and Toyota ($1.7 billion). Geographic differences exist in spending; for example, while Procter & Gamble spent 36 percent of its budget in the United States, Unilever's spending there was only 20 percent.[12]

Media Strategy

Target audience characteristics, campaign objectives, and the budget form the basis for the choice between media vehicles and the development of a media schedule. The major factors determining the choice of the media vehicles to be used are (1) the availability of the media in a given market, (2) the product or service itself, and (3) media habits of the intended audience.

Media Availability Media spending, which totaled $300 billion in 1999, varies dramatically around the world, as seen in Figure 20.2. In absolute terms, the United States spends more money on advertising than most of the other major advertising nations combined. Other major spenders are Japan, the United Kingdom, Germany, Canada, and France. The mature U.S. market anticipates continued growth in the future, but European integration and the development of the Pacific Rim's consumer markets are likely to fuel major growth.[13] Latin America's temporary decline of the late 1990s will start to change to strong growth in 2000.

Naturally, this spending varies by market. Countries devoting the highest percentage to television were Peru (84 percent), Mexico (73 percent), and Venezuela (67 percent). In some countries, the percentage devoted to print is still high: Kuwait (91 percent), Norway (77 percent), and Sweden (77 percent). Radio accounts for more than 20 percent of total measured media in only a few countries, such as Trinidad and Tobago, Nepal, and Honduras. Outdoor/transit advertising accounted for 48 percent of Bolivia's media spending but only 3 percent in Germany.[14] Cinema advertising is important in countries such as India and Nigeria. Until a few years ago, the prevail-

[12]"Top 100 Global Marketers 1999," *Advertising Age International*, November 8, 1999, 1–11.

[13]http://www.zenithmedia.com/praddc99.htm

[14]Compiled from Leo Burnett, *Worldwide Advertising and Media Fact Book* (Chicago: Triumph Books, 1994).

TABLE 20.2	Internet Advertising Spending by Region (in $ millions)				
REGION	1998	1999	2000	2001	2002
North America	$1,300	$2,805	$5,358	$8,680	$12,587
Europe	105	286	621	1,217	2,169
Asia-Pacific	80	166	346	691	1,235
Latin America	20	51	121	259	949
Rest of the world	1	2	4	8	14
TOTAL	$1,506	$3,310	$6,450	$10,855	$16,954

SOURCE: **http://www.forrester.com**

ing advertising technique used by the Chinese consisted of outdoor boards and posters found outside factories; today, more new TV and radio stations are coming on-air. The Internet is well on the way to establishing itself as a complementary advertising medium in Europe and the Americas. In other parts of the world it has yet to make its mark. The projection is that the Internet may have a 5 percent market share in world advertising by 2002, with Internet ad spending reaching $17 billion, as shown in Table 20.2.[15] The level is estimated to reach $33 billion by 2004 as other markets increase their volume as well. In addition to PCs, cellular phones and interactive TV will become delivery mechanisms.

The media available to the international marketer in major Latin American countries are summarized in Table 20.3. The breakdown by media points to the enormous diversity in how media are used in a given market. These figures do not tell the whole story, however, which emphasizes the need for careful homework on the part of the international manager charged with media strategy. As an example, Brazil has five television networks, but one of them—Rede Globo TV—corners 70 percent of all television advertising spending. Throughout Latin America, the tendency is to allocate half or more of total advertising budgets to television, with the most-coveted spots on prime-time soap operas that attract viewers from Mexico to Brazil. In general, advertising in Latin America requires flexibility and creativity. Inflation rates have caused advertising rates to increase dramatically in countries like Argentina. In Mexico, advertisers can use the "French Plan," which protects participating advertisers from price increases during the year and additionally gives the advertiser two spots for the price of one. For these concessions, the advertiser must pay for the year's entire advertising schedule by October of the year before.

The major problems affecting global promotional efforts involve conflicting national regulations. Even within the EU there is no uniform legal standard. Conditions do vary from country to country, and ads must comply with national regulation. Most European countries either observe the Code of Advertising Practice of the International Chamber of Commerce or have their guidelines based on it.[16] Some of the regulations include limits on the amount of time available for advertisements; for example, in Italy, the state channels allow a maximum of 12 percent advertising per hour and 4 percent per week, and commercial stations allow 18 percent per hour and 15 percent per week. Furthermore, the leading Italian stations do not guarantee audience delivery when spots are bought. Strict separation between programs and commercials is almost a universal requirement, preventing U.S.-style sponsored programs. Restrictions on items such as comparative claims and gender stereotypes are prevalent; for example, Germany prohibits the use of superlatives such as "best."

[15]http://www.forrester.com

[16]http://www.iccwbo.org/home/statements_rules/rules/1997/advercod.asp

TABLE 20.3   Latin American Media Breakdown

	ARGENTINA	BRAZIL	CHILE
Total Advertising Expenditure, 1997 ($ millions)	$2,704	$8,649	$814
Breakdown by Media			
Television	37%	59%	45%
Newspapers	34%	24%	35%
Radio	8%	5%	11%
Magazines	5%	9%	5%
Outdoor	6%	3%	4%
Cinema	2%	—	—
Media Facts			
Television	7 government, 5 private stations	Rede/Globo TV/and other private	Government and Chilean universities
Newspapers	384 national daily papers	Regional/local medium; no national newspapers	9 national and 43 regional dailies
Radio	247 AM and FM stations, all of which are commercial	1,519 AM and 1,127 FM stations, most of which are commercial	404 commercial stations
Media Buying	Handled by ad agencies. For TV, agencies combine clients' budgets for discounts	Done within the agency. Variation according to client, product, and ranking of media vehicle	Media and clients pay 15% commission
Internet Users	503,600	3,423,000	201,600

SOURCES: Compiled from "Web *Hot:* Net Marketing Surges in Latin America," *Advertising Age International*, March 8, 1999, 28; "Latin American Media Map," *Advertising Age International*, October 5, 1998, supplement; and Leo Burnett, *Worldwide Advertising and Media Fact Book* (Chicago: Triumph Books, 1994), 331–468.

Until now, with few exceptions, most nations have been very successful in controlling advertising that enters their borders. When commercials were not allowed on the state-run stations, advertisers in Belgium had been accustomed to placing their ads on the Luxembourg station. Radio Luxembourg has traditionally been used to beam messages to the United Kingdom. By the end of the 1990s, however, approximately half of the homes in Europe will have access to additional television broadcasts through either cable or direct satellite, and television will no longer be restricted by national boundaries. The implications of this to global marketers are significant. The viewer's choice will be expanded, leading to competition among government-run public channels, competing state channels from neighboring countries, private channels, and pan-European channels.

This means that marketers need to make sure that advertising works not only within markets but across countries as well.[17] As a consequence, media buying will become more challenging.

Product Influences   Marketers and advertising agencies are currently frustrated by wildly differing restrictions on how products can be advertised. Agencies often have to produce several separate versions to comply with various national regulations. Consumer protection in general has dominated the regulatory scene in the 1980s.[18] Changing and

[17]John Clemens, "Television Advertising in Europe," *Columbia Journal of World Business* 22 (Fall 1987): 35–41.

[18]Jean J. Boddewyn, "Advertising Regulation in the 1980s," *Journal of Marketing* 46 (Winter 1982): 22–28.

COLOMBIA	MEXICO	PERU	VENEZUELA
$2,854	$4,246	$1,081	$1,008
60%	73%	84%	67%
14%	8%	6%	25%
21%	11%	6%	2%
5%	4%	1%	3%
—	3%	1%	2%
—	1%	2%	1%
Government owned and operated	Televisia	One government, 6 private channels	Private (9) and government (2)
2 national dailies	6 national dailies	12 national, 15 regional	13 national dailies
545 commercial stations; 70% of inventory controlled by two large monopolies	923 commercial stations	Lima has 50 commercial stations; regional/local time are available	212 commercial stations
Agencies as well as clients negotiate with media; discounts prevalent	Payments in advance with bonuses up to 300%	Companies with large budgets negotiate directly. Intermediaries used in the interior of Peru	Only one media buying consortium exists for each group of agencies
576,000	795,400	N/A	357,000

standardizing these regulations, even in an area like the EU, is a "long and difficult road." For example, after years of debate within Europe to prohibit tobacco advertising everywhere (except point-of-purchase ads in tobacco specialty shops), the EU decided that the final ratification of the Maastricht Treaty completed the single European market, and the mandate to come up with community-wide directives ended. The issue will now be handled by each member country separately.[19] While some countries have banned tobacco advertising altogether (e.g., France), some have voluntary restriction systems in place. For example, in the United Kingdom, tobacco advertising is not allowed in magazines aimed at very young women, but it is permitted in other women's magazines. A summary of product-related regulations found in Western Europe is provided in Table 20.4. Tobacco products and alcoholic beverages are the most heavily regulated products in terms of promotion.

However, the manufacturers of these products have not abandoned their promotional efforts. Philip Morris engages in corporate image advertising using its cowboy spokesperson. John Player sponsors sports events, especially Formula One car racing. Some European cigarette manufacturers have diversified into the entertainment business (restaurants, lounges, movie theaters) and named them after their cigarette brands. Tobacco and alcohol advertisers have also welcomed an innovation in advertising: in-flight ads. Brown & Williamson Tobacco Corporation, marketer of Kool cigarettes, sponsors the Kool Jazz Network, a music channel on American Airlines.

[19]Amy Haight, "EC Ad Ban May Go up in Smoke," *Advertising Age*, January 17, 1994, I–8.

TABLE 20.4	Restrictions on Advertisements for Specific Products in Selected European Countries		
COUNTRY	CIGARETTES AND TOBACCO PRODUCTS	ALCOHOLIC BEVERAGES	PHARMACEUTICAL PRODUCTS
France	Banned as of 1993	Banned (for products over 1.2% alcohol)	Prior authorization from appropriate government health authority required
Republic of Ireland	Banned in all media except magazines	Banned in broadcast; print allowed but regulated	Advertisements for certain products or treatments prohibited, others regulated
Italy	Banned	Restricted	Restricted; some products banned from TV
Netherlands	Banned in broadcast; must carry health warning elsewhere	Permitted in all media but regulated	Allowed but with restrictions in all media
United Kingdom	Banned in broadcast; approval needed for print	Banned in broadcast; other media carry voluntary restrictions	Prior opinion sought from Medical Advisory Board; advertisements for certain products or treatments prohibited

sources: Euromonitor, *European Advertising, Marketing, and Media Factbook 1992* (London: Euromonitor, 1992), 751–767; and D. Pridgen, "Satellite Television Advertising and the Regulatory Conflict in Western Europe," *Journal of Advertising* 14 (Winter 1985): 23–29.

Certain products are subject to special rules. In the United Kingdom, for example, advertisers cannot show a real person applying an underarm deodorant; the way around this problem is to show an animated person applying the product. What is and is not allowable is very much a reflection of the country imposing the rules. Explicit advertisements of contraceptives are commonplace in Sweden, for example, but far less frequent in most parts of the world.

Beyond the traditional media, the international marketer may also consider **product placement** in movies, TV shows, games, or web sites. Although there is disagreement about the effectiveness of the method beyond creating brand awareness,[20] products from makers such as BMW, Omega, Nokia, and Heineken have been placed in movies to help both parties to the deal: to create a brand definition for the product and a dimension of reality for the film.[21] In some markets, product placement may be an effective method of attracting attention due to constraints on traditional media. In China, for example, most commercials on Chinese state-run television are played back-to-back in ten-minute segments, making it difficult for any 30-second ad to be singled out. Soap operas, such as "Love Talks," have been found to be an effective way to get to the burgeoning middle class in the world's most populous country.[22]

Audience Characteristics   A major objective of media strategy is to reach the intended target audience with a minimum of waste. As an example, Amoco Oil Company wanted to launch a corporate image campaign in China in the hope of receiving drilling contracts. Identifying the appropriate decision makers was not difficult because they all work for the government. The selection of appropriate media proved to be equally simple because most of the decision makers overseeing petroleum exploration were

[20]Pola B. Gupta and Kenneth R. Lord, "Product Placement in Movies: The Effect of Prominence and Mode on Audience Recall," *Journal of Current Issues and Research in Advertising* 20 (Spring 1998): 47–60.

[21]Allyson Stewart-Allen, "Product Placement Helps Sell Brand," *Marketing News*, February 15, 1999, 8.

[22]"Chinese TV Discovers Product Placement," *The Wall Street Journal*, January 26, 2000, B12.

found to read the vertical trade publications: *International Industrial Review, Petroleum Production,* and *Offshore Petroleum.*

If conditions are ideal, and they seldom are in international markets, the media strategist would need data on (1) media distribution, that is, the number of copies of the print medium or the number of sets for broadcast; (2) media audiences; and (3) advertising exposure. For instance, an advertiser interested in using television in Brazil would like to know that the music show "Cassino do Chacrinha" averages a 25 rating and a 50 percent share of audience for the 4:00 P.M. to 6:00 P.M. time slot. In markets where more sophisticated market research services are available, data on advertising perception and consumer response may be available. In many cases, advertisers have found circulation figures to be unreliable or even fabricated.

An issue related to audience characteristics is the move by some governments to protect their own national media from foreign ones. In Canada, for example, the government prevents foreign publishers from selling space to Canadian advertisers in so-called split-run editions that, in effect, have no local content. If U.S. publications, such as *Sports Illustrated,* were allowed to do it, Canadian publications would be threatened with insufficient amounts of advertising.[23]

Global Media

Media vehicles that have target audiences on at least three continents and for which the media buying takes place through a centralized office are considered to be **global media.**[24] Global media have traditionally been publications that, in addition to the worldwide edition, have provided advertisers the option of using regional editions. For example, *Time* provides 133 editions, enabling advertisers to reach a particular country, continent, or the world. In print media, global vehicles include dailies such as *International Herald Tribune*, weeklies such as *The Economist*, and monthlies such as *National Geographic.* Included on the broadcast side are BBC Worldwide TV, CNN, the Discovery Channel, and MTV. The Discovery Channel reaches more than 87 million subscribers in 90 countries through Discovery Channel–Europe, Discovery Channel–Latin America/Iberia, Discovery Channel–Asia, Discovery Canada, Discovery New Zealand, and several other language-tailored networks.[25] MTV as a global medium is profiled in *The International Marketplace 20.3.*

Advertising in global media is dominated by major consumer ad categories, particularly airlines, financial services, telecommunications, automobiles, and tobacco. The aircraft industry represents business market advertisers.[26] Companies spending in global media include AT&T, IBM, and General Motors. In choosing global media, media buyers consider the three most important media characteristics: targetability, client-compatible editorial, and editorial quality.[27] Some global publications have found that some parts of the globe are more appealing to advertisers than others; *International Management*, for example, had to eliminate its editions in Latin America, Africa, and Asia-Pacific because of lack of advertising.[28]

In broadcast media, panregional radio stations have been joined by television as a result of satellite technology. The pan-European satellite channels, such as Sky Channel and Super Channel, were conceived from the very beginning as advertising media. Many are skeptical about the potential of these channels, especially in the short term, because of the challenges of developing a cross-cultural following in Europe's still

[23]"Canada Moves toward New Laws on Magazines," *Advertising Age International*, January 11, 1999, 29.

[24]"Global Media," *Advertising Age International*, February 8, 1999, 23.

[25]Wayne Walley, "Programming Globally—With Care," *Advertising Age International*, September 18, 1995, I-14.

[26]"Marketers Take New Look at Trying Panregional TV," *Advertising Age International*, March 30, 1999, 2.

[27]David W. Stewart and Kevin J. McAuliffe, "Determinants of International Media Buying," *Journal of Advertising* 17 (Fall 1988): 22–26.

[28]Lawrence Wentz, "Why 'IM' Heads Away from Global," *Advertising Age*, December 2, 1985, 45, 58.

THE INTERNATIONAL MARKETPLACE 20.3

The World Wants Its MTV!

MTV HAS EMERGED as a significant global medium, with more than 340 million households in 140 countries subscribing to its services. The reason for its success is simple—MTV offers consistent, high-quality programming that reflects the tastes and lifestyle of young people.

Its balance of fashion, film, news, competitions, and comedy wrapped in the best music and strong visual identity has made it "the best bet to succeed as a pan-European thematic channel, with its aim to be in every household in Europe by the mid-1990s" according to *Music Week*, Britain's leading music trade paper. Given that 79 percent of the channel's viewers are in the elusive 16–34 age group, MTV is a force as an advertising medium for those who want to closely target their campaigns. MTV has proven to be the ultimate youth marketing vehicle for companies such as Wrangler, Wrigleys, Braun, Britvic, Levi Strauss, Pepsi, Pentax, and many others. Although many knockoffs have been started around the world, the enormous cost of building a worldwide music video channel will most likely protect MTV.

Digital compression allows the number of services offered on a satellite feed to be multiplied. The network will use the new capacity to complement panregional programming and playlists, customizing them to local tastes in key areas. For example , MTV Asia has launched MTV India to have five hours of India-specific programming during the 24-hour satellite feed to the subcontinent.

Owned by Viacom, MTV's global network consists of the following entities:

- **MTV USA** is seen 24 hours a day on cable television in over 76 million U.S. television homes. Presented in stereo, MTV's overall on-air environment is unpredictable and irreverent, reflecting the cutting-edge spirit of rock 'n' roll that is the heart of its programming. Through its graphic look, VJs, music news, promotions, interviews, concert tour information, specials, and documentaries, as well as its original strip programming, MTV has become an international institution of pop culture and the leading authority on rock music since it launched on August 1, 1981.
- **MTV Europe** reaches 43 territories (89 million households), 24 hours a day in stereo, via satellite, cable, and terrestrial distribution. The station acquires its own video clips, drawing from the domestic markets in individual European countries to discover bands making an international sound. It has its own team of VJs presenting shows specially tailored for the European market. The channel's programming mix reflects its diverse audience, with coverage of music, style, news, movie information, comedy, and more. MTV Europe has five local programming feeds and five local advertising windows—i.e., U.K./Ireland; MTV

Central (Austria, Germany, and Switzerland); MTV European (76 territories, including France and Israel); MTV Southern (Italy); and MTV Nordic (Sweden, Norway and others). It was launched August 1, 1987.
- **MTV Asia** was launched September 15, 1991. MTV reaches over 118 million households in 21 territories. Programming is tailored to the musical tastes, lifestyles, and sensibilities of Asian audiences in three regions: MTV Mandarin, MTV Southeast Asia, and MTV India.
- Although Japan was originally launched in October 1984 under a licensing agreement, it was reintroduced in 2001 as a wholly-owned entity of MTV Networks International. The 24-hour music television channel and web site features original Japanese-language programming and reaches 2.8 million households.
- **MTV Latin America** reaches 10 million households in 21 countries and territories. The network features a mix of U.S. and Latin music, regional production, music and entertainment news, artist interviews, concert coverage, and specials.
- **MTV Internacional** is a one-hour weekly Spanish language program. MTV Internacional is a mix of Spanish and English language videos, interviews, entertainment news, and on-location specials. The program is broadcast in the United States on the Telemundo Network and in various Latin American countries and is distributed by MTV Syndication Sales.
- **MTV Brazil** was launched in 1990 and is a joint venture of MTV Networks and Abril S.A., Brazil's leading magazine publisher. The Portuguese language network, viewed in 16 million households, is broadcast via UHF in São Paulo and via VHF in Rio de Janeiro.
- **MTV Russia**, launched in September 1998, is a free over-the-air service reaching more than 17 million homes in major cities. The entity was established with BIZ Enterprises in a multi-year licensing agreement. In 2000 MTV Networks International gained an equity position in MTV Russia. Programming includes music videos from Russian and international artists, as well as coverage of social issues relevant to Russian youth.

SOURCES: "Focus: Trends in TV," *Advertising Age International*, January 11, 1999, 33; "MTV Fights Back from Nadir to Hit High Notes in India," *Advertising Age International*, March 30, 1998, 10; "High Tech helps MTV Evolve," *World Trade*, June 1996, 10; "Will MTV Have to Share the Stage?" *Business Week*, February 21, 1994, 38; press releases from MTV, March 14, 1994; http://www.viacom.com.

http://www.mtv.com

| FIGURE | 20.3 | Example of a Pan-Regional Medium |

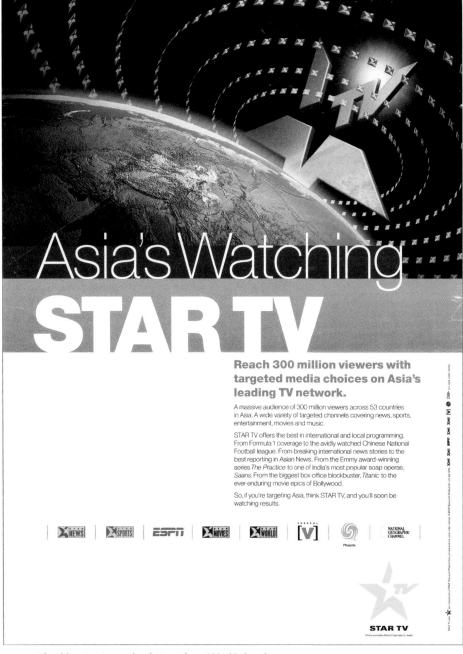

SOURCE: *Advertising Age International*, November 1999, 68. See also
http://www.startv.com.

highly nationalistic markets.[29] Pan-European channels have had to cut back, whereas native language satellite channels like Tele 5 in France and RTL Plus in Germany have increased their viewership. The launch of STAR TV (see Figure 20.3) has increased the use of regional advertising campaigns in Asia. While this medium is still regarded as

[29]"Eurosport Posts Big Victory: First Profit Since Rocky Start," *Advertising Age International*, March 30, 1998, 17.

FIGURE 20.4 Online Advertising

SOURCE: **http://womencentral.msn.com**

a corporate advertising vehicle, it has nonetheless attracted the interest of consumer goods manufacturers as well.[30] The alternative showing the most immediate promise is cable channels that cater to universal segments with converging tastes, such as MTV, Animal Planet, or the Cartoon Network.

The Internet provides the international marketer with a global medium. U.S. marketers have been slow to react to its potential because their domestic market is so dominant. They have also been reluctant to adapt their web sites but are willing to repeat what happened in the United States in these regions. One simple way of getting started is to choose a few key languages for the web site. For example, Gillette decided to add German and Japanese to its Mach 3 web site after studying the number of Internet users in those countries.[31] If the marketer elects to have a global site and region-specific sites (e.g., organized by country), they all should have a similar look, especially in terms of the level of sophistication. Another method is to join forces with Internet service providers. For example, Unilever has expanded its sponsorship of the Microsoft online network in the United States to France, Germany, and the United Kingdom.[32] Under the agreement, Unilever will provide banner ads, links, and sponsorship to MSN sites, particularly Women Central. Premier sponsorship on the MSN sites will include logo placement at the top right corner of the web pages, as shown in Figure 20.4 where a Unilever brand, Helene Curtis, is featured.

[30]"Remixing the Message," *Business Asia*, February 15, 1993, 4–5.

[31]"The Internet," *Advertising Age International*, June 1999, 42.

[32]"Unilever, Microsoft in European Net Deal," *The Wall Street Journal*, February 2, 2000, B8.

The Promotional Message

Owens Corning recently acquired the global rights to the Pink Panther to help the company build a unified marketing campaign around the world.

www.owenscorning.com

The creative people must have a clear idea of the characteristics of the audience expected to be exposed to the message. In this sense, the principles of creating effective advertising are the same as in the domestic marketplace. The marketer must determine what the consumer is really buying—that is, the customer's motivations. These will vary, depending on the following:

1. The diffusion of the product or service into the market. For example, to penetrate Third World markets with business computers is difficult when few potential customers know how to type or with Internet advertising when the infrastructure is lacking.
2. The criteria on which the customer will evaluate the product. For example, in traditional societies, advertising the time-saving qualities of a product may not be the best approach, as Campbell Soup Company learned in Italy, Brazil, and Poland where women felt inadequate as homemakers if they did not make soups from scratch.
3. The product's positioning. For example, Parker Pen's upscale market image around the world may not be profitable enough in a market that is more or less a commodity business. The solution is to create an image for a commodity product and make the public pay for it—for example, the positioning of Perrier in the United States as a premium mineral water.

The ideal situation in developing message strategy is to have a world brand—a product that is manufactured, packaged, and positioned the same around the world. Companies that have been successful with the global approach have shown flexibility in the execution of the campaigns. The idea may be global, but overseas subsidiaries then tailor the message to suit local market conditions and regulations. Executing an advertising campaign in multiple markets requires a balance between conveying the message and allowing for local nuances. The localization of global ideas can be achieved by various tactics, such as adopting a modular approach, localizing international symbols, and using international advertising agencies.[33]

Marketers may develop multiple broadcast and print ads from which country organizations can choose the most appropriate for their operations. This can provide local operations with cost savings and allow them to use their budgets on tactical campaigns (which may also be developed around the global idea). For example, the "Membership Has Its Privileges" campaign of American Express, which has run in 24 countries on TV and three more in print, was adjusted in some markets to make sure that "privileges" did not have a snob or elitist appeal, especially in countries with a strong caste or class system. An example of local adjustment in a global campaign for Marriott International is provided in Figure 20.5. While the ads share common graphic elements, two distinct approaches are evident. The top set of advertisements from the United States and Saudi Arabia are an example of a relatively standard approach, given the similarity in target audiences (i.e., the business traveler) and in the competitive conditions in the markets. The second set features ads for Latin American and German-speaking Europe. While the Latin advertisement stresses comfort, the German version focuses on results. While most of Marriott's ads translate the theme ("When you're comfortable you can do anything"), the German version keeps the original English-language theme.

Product-related regulations will affect advertising messages as well. When General Mills Toy Group's European subsidiary launched a product line related to G.I. Joe–type war toys and soldiers, it had to develop two television commercials, a general version for most European countries and another for countries that bar advertisements for

[33]"Global Marketing Campaigns with a Local Touch," *Business International*, July 4, 1988, 205–210.

FIGURE	20.5	Local Adjustments in a Global Campaign

We have just the right environment and services that allow your clients to conduct their business in peace. So whether they're working on that important speech, finishing a project, making a conference call or just relaxing, we'll help them do it with absolute ease and comfort. Because at Marriott, we believe:

When you're comfortable you can do anything.℠

Usted puede contar con los Hoteles Marriot, ya que le proveen los servicios más confiables y eficientes y el staff necesario para hacer el trabajo de manera que usted pueda llevarse todo el crédito.

Cuando usted está cómodo puede lograr lo que quiera.℠

Legen Sie ganz entspannt die Füße hoch. Schließlich haben Sie alles, was man für einen erfolgreichen Deal braucht: die nötige Ruhe, die richtige Umgebung – und den Business-Service. Wir stellen Ihnen unser gesamtes Equipment zur Verfügung. Und tun für Sie, was wir können. Damit Sie tun können, was Ihnen wirklich wichtig ist. Reservierungen in über 300 Marriott Hotels, Resorts & Suites weltweit unter 0130/85 44 22.

When you're comfortable you can do anything.

products with military or violent themes. As a result, in the version running in Germany, Holland, and Belgium, Jeeps replaced the toy tanks, and guns were removed from the hands of the toy soldiers. Other countries, such as the United Kingdom, do not allow children to appear in advertisements.

Marketers may also want to localize their international symbols. Some of the most effective global advertising campaigns have capitalized on the popularity of pop music worldwide and used well-known artists in the commercials, such as Pepsi's use of Tina Turner. In some versions, local stars have been included with the international stars to localize the campaign. Aesthetics play a role in localizing campaigns. The global marketer does not want to chance the censoring of the company's ads or risk offending customers. For example, even though importers of perfumes into Saudi Arabia want to use the same campaigns as are used in Europe, they occasionally have to make adjustments dictated by moral standards. In one case, the European version shows a man's hand clutching a perfume bottle and a woman's hand seizing his bare forearm. In the Saudi Arabian version, the man's arm is clothed in a dark suit sleeve, and the woman's hand is merely brushing his hand.

The use of one agency—or only a few agencies—ensures consistency. The use of one agency allows for coordination, especially when the global marketer's operations are decentralized. It also makes the exchange of ideas easier and may therefore lead, for example, to wider application of a modification or a new idea. In May 1994 IBM concentrated its $500 million account to Ogilvy & Mather, from 40 different agencies in 144 countries.

The environmental influences that call for these modifications, or in some cases totally unique approaches, are culture, economic development, and lifestyles. Of the cultural variables, language is most apparent in its influence on promotional campaigns. The European Union alone has eleven languages: English, Finnish, French, German, Dutch, Danish, Italian, Greek, Spanish, Swedish, and Portuguese. Advertisers in the Arab world have sometimes found that the voices in a TV commercial speak in the wrong Arabic dialect. The challenge of language is often most pronounced in translating themes. For example, Coca-Cola's worldwide theme "Can't Beat the Feeling" is the equivalent of "I Feel Coke" in Japan, "Unique Sensation" in Italy, and "The Feeling of Life" in Chile. In Germany, where no translation really worked, the original English language theme was used. One way of getting around this is to have no copy or very little copy and to use innovative approaches, such as pantomime. Using any type of symbolism will naturally require adequate copy testing to determine how the target market perceives the message.

The stage of economic development—and therefore the potential demand for and degree of awareness of the product—may vary and differentiate the message from one market to another. Whereas developed markets may require persuasive messages (to combat other alternatives), a developing market may require a purely informative campaign. Campaigns may also have to be dramatically adjusted to cater to lifestyle differences in regions that are demographically quite similar. For example, N. W. Ayer's Bahamas tourism campaign for the European market emphasizes clean water, beaches, and air. The exceptions are in Germany, where it focuses on sports activities, and in the United Kingdom, where it features humor.

Unique market conditions may require localized approaches. Although IBM has utilized global campaigns (the Little Tramp campaign, for example), it has also used major local campaigns in Japan and Europe for specific purposes. In Japan, it used a popular television star in poster and door-board ads to tell viewers, "Friends, the time is ripe" (for buying an IBM personal computer). The campaign was designed to bolster the idea that the machine represents a class act from America. At the same time, IBM was trying to overcome a problem in Europe of being perceived as "too American." Stressing that IBM is actually a "European company," an advertising campaign told of IBM's large factories, research facilities, and tax-paying subsidiaries within the EU.

The Campaign Approach

Many multinational corporations are staffed and equipped to perform the full range of promotional activities. In most cases, however, they will rely on the outside expertise of advertising agencies and other promotions-related companies such as media-buying companies and specialty marketing firms. In the organization of promotional efforts, a company has two basic decisions to make: (1) what type of outside services to use, and (2) how to establish decision-making authority for promotional efforts.

Outside Services   Of all the outside promotion-related services, advertising agencies are by far the most significant. A list of the world's top 50 agencies and agency groups is given in Table 20.5. Of the top 50 agencies, 30 are based in the United States, 9 in Japan, and the rest in the United Kingdom, France, Australia, and South Korea, Sweden, Canada, and Germany. Whereas the Japanese agencies tend to have few operations outside their home country, U.S. and European agencies are engaged in worldwide expansion. Size is measured in terms of gross income and billings. Billings are the cost of advertising time and space placed by the agency plus fees for certain extra services, which are converted by formula to correspond to media billings in terms of value of services performed. Agencies do not receive billings as income; in general, agency income is approximately 15 percent of billing.

Agencies form world groups for better coverage. One of the largest world "super" groups, WPP Group, includes such entities as Ogilvy & Mather, J. Walter Thompson, Brouillard Communications, and Hill and Knowlton. Smaller advertising agencies have affiliated local agencies in foreign markets.

The choice of an agency will largely depend on the quality of coverage the agency will be able to give the multinational company. Global marketing requires global advertising, according to proponents of the globalization trend. The reason is not that significant cost savings can be realized through a single worldwide ad campaign but that such a global campaign is inseparable from the idea of global marketing. Some predict that the whole industry will be concentrated into a few huge multinational agencies. Agencies with networks too small to compete have become prime takeover targets in the creation of worldwide mega-agencies. Many believe that local, midsized agencies can compete in the face of globalization by developing local solutions and/or joining international networks.[34]

Although the forecast that six large agencies will eventually place most international advertising may be exaggerated, global marketing is the new wave and is having a strong impact on advertising. Major realignments of client-agency relationships have occurred due to mergers and to clients' reassessment of their own strategies toward more global or regional approaches.

Advertising agencies have gone through major geographic expansion in the last five years. The leader is McCann-Erickson, with advertising running in 127 countries, compared with 72 in 1991. In 1999, it handled almost twice as many multinational client assignments as its nearest competitor.[35] Some agencies, such as DDB Needham, were domestically focused in the early 1990s but have been forced to rethink with the globalization of their clients. As a result, DDB Needham has doubled its country presence to 96 from five years ago.[36] New markets are also emerging, and agencies are establishing their presence in them. For example, DDB Needham, which has been servicing its clients in the Chinese market from Hong Kong, formed a joint venture with

[34]So What Was the Fuss About?" *The Economist*, June 22, 1996, 59–60.

[35]"Ranking the Ad Agencies," *Advertising Age International*, September 1999, 30. **http://www.mccann.com**.

[36]Laurel Wentz and Sasha Emmons, "AAI Charts Show Yearly Growth, Consolidation," *Advertising Age International*, September 1996, I-33. **http://www.ddbn.com**.

| TABLE 20.5 | Top 50 Advertising Organizations Worldwide |

RANK '00	'99	COMPANY	HEADQUARTERS	WORLDWIDE GROSS INCOME ($M) 2000	BILLINGS ($M) 2000
1	1	WPP Group	London	$7,971.0	$67,225.0
2	2	Omnicom Group	New York	6,986.2	55,651.6
3	3	Interpublic Group of Cos.	New York	6,595.9	54,828.2
4	5	Dentsu	Tokyo	3,089.0	21,689.1
5	4	Havas Advertising	Levallois-Perret, France	2,757.3	26,345.5
6	6	Publicis Groupe	Paris	2,479.1	29,302.7
7	7	Bcom3 Group	Chicago	2,215.9	17,932.6
8	8	Grey Global Group	New York	1,863.2	11,406.3
9	9	True North Communications	Chicago	1,539.1	13,171.7
10	10	Cordiant Communications Group	London	1,254.8	11,256.0
11	11	Hakuhodo	Tokyo	1,008.7	7,640.0
12	13	Asatsu-DK	Tokyo	431.4	3,740.1
13	12	Carlson Marketing Group	Minneapolis	390.2	2,977.3
14	14	TMP Worldwide	New York	332.1	3,386.5
15	19	Digitas	Boston	288.2	NA
16	16	Aspen Marketing Group	Los Angeles	256.2	1,709.1
17	17	Tokyu Agency	Tokyo	235.4	2,041.4
18	15	Ha-Lo Industries	Niles, Ill.	233.1	973.6
19	18	Daiko Advertising	Tokyo	226.0	1,719.0
20	20	Incepta Group	London	217.5	655.4
21	21	Maxxcom	Toronto	177.4	1,109.1
22	22	Cheil Communications	Seoul	150.4	949.3
23	25	I&S/BBDO	Tokyo	118.0	967.0
24	29	Panoramic Communications	New York	116.0	1,315.0
25	24	SPAR Group	Tarrytown, N.Y.	111.0	740.4
26	27	Yomiko Advertising	Tokyo	110.8	1,097.2
27	28	Doner	Southfield, Mich.	109.8	968.0
28	26	Clemenger Group	Melbourne, Australia	101.8	679.2
29	31	Asahi Advertising	Tokyo	98.0	642.0
30	30	Harte-Hanks	Langhorne, Pa.	97.2	417.1
31	44	Hawkeye Communications	New York	93.6	624.3
32	23	Simon Marketing	Gloucester, Mass.	92.0	NA
33	32	HMG Worldwide	New York	90.4	600.7
34	33	Rubin Postaer & Associates	Santa Monica, Calif.	87.1	826.2
35	34	Richards Group	Dallas	83.5	560.0
36	39	Nikkeisha	Tokyo	80.7	511.7
37	43	LG Ad	Seoul	78.2	597.5
38	42	Bartle Bogle Hegarty	London	77.8	608.4
39	37	Gage	Minneapolis	76.8	512.4
40	NA	AKQA	New York	76.0	NA
41	40	Cossette Communication Group	Quebec	74.3	496.6
42	35	Marketing Services Group	New York	73.4	194.7
43	38	Cramer-Krasselt	Chicago	70.6	466.2
44	41	Wolf Group Integrated Communications	Toronto	67.7	590.5
45	47	Armando Testa Group	Turin, Italy	67.0	731.0
46	51	M&C Saatchi Worldwide	London	64.4	615.7
47	46	Sogei	Tokyo	61.8	483.7
48	45	Wieden & Kennedy	Portland, Ore.	60.1	863.2
49	60	ChoicePoint Direct	Peoria, Ill.	59.2	392.7
50	85	Talent Communicacao	Sao Paulo	59.1	243.0

SOURCE: "World's Top 100 Advertising Organizations," Advertising Age Web site, adage.com/dataplace, accessed April 26, 2001.

TABLE 20.6   Worldwide Agency-Client Relationships

Agency	American Home Products	Bayer Corp.	Bristol-Meyers Squibb Co.	British American Tobacco Co.	Coca-Cola Co.	Danone	Diageo	Ford Motor Co.	General Motors Corp.	Gillette Co.	Henkel	Hewlett-Packard Co.	Johnson & Johnson Co.	Kellogg Co.	Kraft Foods	L'Oreal	Mars Inc.	Nestlé	Novartis	Philip Morris Cos.	Procter & Gamble Co.	Siemens	SmithKline Beecham Corp.	Sony Corp.	Unilever	Warner-Lambert Co.
Ammirati Puris Lintas					•				•				•					•							•	
Bartle Bogle Hegarty																									•	
Bates Worldwide			•	•								•								•	•				•	
Batey Ads																										
BBDO Worldwide	•								•	•						•								•		
Bozell Worldwide		•																								
D'Arcy Masius Benton & Bowles		•	•		•		•														•			•		•
DDB Worldwide		•			•																					
Dentsu																		•								
Dentsu Young & Rubicam																•								•		
EURO RSCG Worldwide	•	•	•		•		•																		•	
FCA! BMZ International													•													
FCB Worldwide				•																						
Grey Advertising					•													•	•		•		•		•	
Hakuhodo																										
Leagas Delaney																										
Leo Burnett Co.					•									•	•			•		•	•					
Lowe & Partners Worldwide					•				•	•	•															
McCann-Erickson Worldwide	•			•	•			•	•		•	•			•		•				•			•	•	
Ogilvy & Mather Worldwide		•	•				•		•							•	•				•		•	•		
Publicis Communication					•								•			•	•						•			
Saatchi & Saatchi							•						•	•				•	•		•		•	•	•	
Scholz & Friends																										
TBWA Worldwide												•							•					•		
J. Walter Thompson Co.				•	•					•	•			•	•		•				•			•	•	•
Wieden & Kennedy																										
Y&R Advertising					•			•									•				•			•		

SOURCE: "World Brands," *Advertising Age International*, September 1999, 29.

the Chinese government in 1989.[37] In September 1988, Young & Rubicam signed a letter of intent to form a joint venture with the largest ad agency in the then Soviet Union, Vneshtorgreklama.[38]

An example of an agency's client relationships is provided in Table 20.6. The J. Walter Thompson agency, which serves 92 countries worldwide, has 25 accounts that it serves in more than ten countries including Kraft, Nestlé, and Unilever. In a study of 40 multinational marketers, 32.5 percent are using a single agency worldwide, 20 percent are using two, 5 percent are using three, 10 percent are using four, and 32.5 percent are using more than four agencies. Of the marketers using only one or

---

[37]Nancy Giges, "DDB Needham to Enter China for Asian Growth," *Advertising Age*, May 1, 1989, 57–58.

[38]Charles Joseph, "Soviet Union," *Advertising Age*, November 9, 1988, 114.

two agencies, McCann-Erickson was the most popular with 17 percent of the companies.[39] Most large companies typically use more than one agency, with the division of labor usually along product lines. For example, Matsushita Electric Industrial Company, an innovator in the consumer electronics industry, uses two major agencies. Backer Spielvogel Bates Worldwide handles everything involving portables, audio, VHS, and television. Grey Advertising handles the hi-fi area, the Technics label, and telephone products. Panasonic, one of Matsushita's U.S. brands, has a small agency for primarily nonconsumer items. Marketers are choosing specialized interactive shops over full-service agencies for Internet advertising. However, a major weakness of interactive agencies is their lack of international experience.

The main concern arising from the use of mega-agencies is conflict. With only a few giant agencies to choose from, the global marketer may end up with the same agency as the main competitor. The mega-agencies believe they can meet any objections by structuring their companies as rigidly separate, watertight agency networks (such as the Interpublic Group) under the umbrella of a holding group. Following that logic, Procter & Gamble, a client of Saatchi & Saatchi Advertising Worldwide, and Colgate-Palmolive, a client of Ted Bates, should not worry about falling into the same network's client base. However, when the Saatchi & Saatchi network purchased Ted Bates, Colgate-Palmolive left the agency.

Despite the globalization trend, local agencies will survive as a result of governmental regulations. In Peru, for example, a law mandates that any commercial aired on Peruvian television must be 100 percent nationally produced. Local agencies also tend to forge ties with foreign agencies for better coverage and customer service and thus become part of the general globalization effort. A basic fear in the advertising industry is that accounts will be taken away from agencies that cannot handle world brands. An additional factor is contributing to the fear of losing accounts. In the past, many multinational corporations allowed local subsidiaries to make advertising decisions entirely on their own. Others gave subsidiaries an approved list of agencies and some guidance. Still others allowed local decisions subject only to headquarters' approval. Now the trend is toward centralization of all advertising decisions, including those concerning the creative product.

Decision-Making Authority   The alternatives for allocating decision-making authority range from complete centralization to decentralization. With complete centralization, the headquarters level is perceived to have all the right answers and has adequate power to impose its suggestions on all of its operating units. Decentralization involves relaxing most of the controls over foreign affiliates and allowing them to pursue their own promotional approaches.

Of 40 multinational marketers, 26 percent have centralized their advertising strategies, citing as their rationale the search for economies of scale, synergies, and brand consistency. Xerox's reason is that its technology is universal and opportunities abound for global messages. Centralization is also occurring at the regional level. GM's Opel division in Europe is seeking to unify its brand-building efforts with central direction. A total of 34 percent of the companies favor decentralization with regional input. This approach benefits from proximity to market, flexibility, cultural sensitivity, and faster response time. FedEx allows local teams to make advertising decisions as needed. The majority of marketers use central coordination with local input. While Ford Motor Company conceives brand strategy on a global level, ad execution is done at the regional level, and retail work is local.[40] However, multinational corporations are at various stages in their quest for centralization. Procter & Gamble and Gillette generally

[39]"U.S. Multinationals," *Advertising Age International*, June 1999, 39.

[40]"Centralization," *Advertising Age International*, June 1999, 40.

have an approved list of agencies, whereas Quaker Oats and Johnson & Johnson give autonomy to their local subsidiaries but will veto those decisions occasionally.

The important question is not who should make decisions but how advertising quality can be improved at the local level. Gaining approval in multinational corporations is an interactive approach using coordinated decentralization.[41] This eight-step program, which is summarized in Figure 20.6, strives for development of common strategy but flexible execution. The approach maintains strong central control but at the same time capitalizes on the greatest asset of the individual markets—market knowledge. Interaction between the central authority and the local levels takes place at every single stage of the planning process. The central authority is charged with finding the commonalities in the data provided by the individual market areas. This procedure will avoid one of the most common problems associated with acceptance of plans—the NIH syndrome (not invented here)—by allowing for local participation by the eventual implementers.

A good example of this approach was Eastman Kodak's launch of its Ektaprint copier-duplicator line in eleven separate markets in Europe. For economic and organizational reasons, Kodak did not want to deal with different campaigns or parameters. It wanted the same ad graphics in each country, accompanied by the theme "first name in photography, last word in copying." Translations varied slightly from country to country, but the campaign was identifiable from one country to another. A single agency directed the campaign, which was more economical than campaigns in each country would have been and was more unified and identifiable through Europe. The psychological benefit of association of the Kodak name with photography was not lost in the campaign.

Agencies are adjusting their operations to centrally run client operations. Many accounts are now handled by a lead agency, usually in the country where the client is based. More and more agencies are moving to a strong international supervisor for global accounts. This supervisor can overrule local agencies and make personnel changes. Specialty units have emerged as well. For example, Ogilvy & Mather established the Worldwide Client Service organization at headquarters in New York specializing in developing global campaigns for its clients.[42]

Measurement of Advertising Effectiveness

John Wanamaker reportedly said, "I know half the money I spend on advertising is wasted. Now, if I only knew which half." Whether or not advertising effectiveness can be measured, most companies engage in the attempt. Measures of advertising effectiveness should range from pretesting of copy appeal and recognition, to posttesting of recognition, all the way to sales effects. The measures most used are sales, awareness, recall, executive judgment, intention to buy, profitability, and coupon return, regardless of the medium used.[43]

The technical side of these measurement efforts does not differ from that in the domestic market, but the conditions are different. Very often, syndicated services, such as A.C. Nielsen, are not available to the global marketer. If available, their quality may not be at an acceptable level. Testing is also quite expensive and may not be undertaken for the smaller markets. Compared with costs in the U.S. market, the costs of research in the international market are higher in relation to the overall expenditure

[41]Dean M. Peebles, John K. Ryans, and Ivan R. Vernon, "Coordinating International Advertising," *Journal of Marketing* 42 (January 1978): 28–34.

[42]*Global Vision* (New York: Ogilvy & Mather, 1994), 8.

[43]Debra A. Williamson, "ARF to Spearhead Study on Measuring Web Ads," *Advertising Age*, February 10, 1997, 8; Nicolaos E. Synodinos, Charles F. Keown, and Laurence W. Jacobs, "Transnational Advertising Practices: A Survey of Leading Brand Advertisers in Fifteen Countries," *Journal of Advertising Research* 29 (April–May 1989): 43–50.

FIGURE 20.6   **Coordinated Approach to Pan-Regional Campaign Development**

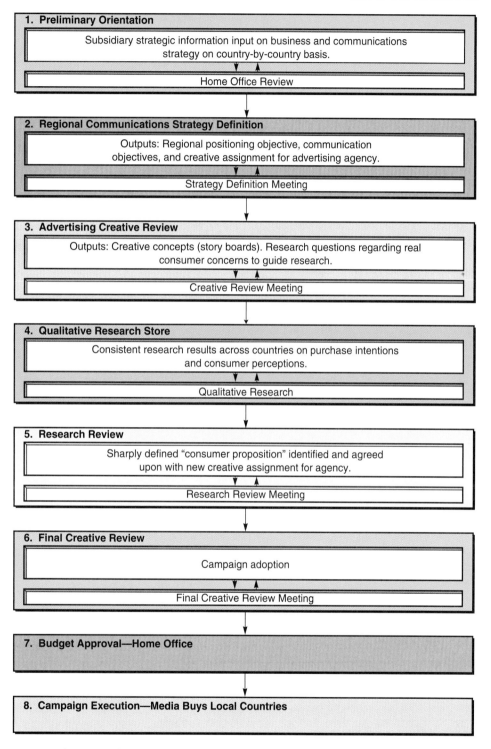

1. Preliminary Orientation

Subsidiary strategic information input on business and communications strategy on country-by-country basis.

Home Office Review

2. Regional Communications Strategy Definition

Outputs: Regional positioning objective, communication objectives, and creative assignment for advertising agency.

Strategy Definition Meeting

3. Advertising Creative Review

Outputs: Creative concepts (story boards). Research questions regarding real consumer concerns to guide research.

Creative Review Meeting

4. Qualitative Research Store

Consistent research results across countries on purchase intentions and consumer perceptions.

Qualitative Research

5. Research Review

Sharply defined "consumer proposition" identified and agreed upon with new creative assignment for agency.

Research Review Meeting

6. Final Creative Review

Campaign adoption

Final Creative Review Meeting

7. Budget Approval—Home Office

8. Campaign Execution—Media Buys Local Countries

SOURCE: David A. Hanni, John K. Ryans, Jr., and Ivan R. Vernon, "Coordinating International Advertising: The Goodyear Case Revisited for Latin America," *Journal of International Marketing* 3 (Number 2, 1995): 83–98.

on advertising.[44] The biggest challenge to advertising research will come from the increase of global and regional campaigns. Comprehensive and reliable measures of campaigns for a mass European market, for example, are difficult because audience measurement techniques and analysis differ for each country. Advertisers are pushing for universally accepted parameters to compare audiences in one country to those in another.

Other Promotional Elements

Personal Selling

Advertising is often equated with the promotional effort; however, a number of other efforts are used to support advertising. The marketing of industrial goods, especially of high-priced items, requires strong personal selling efforts. In some cases, personal selling may be truly international; for example, Boeing and Northrop-Grumman salespeople engage in sales efforts around the world from their domestic bases. However, most personal selling is done by the subsidiaries, with varying degrees of headquarters' involvement. In cases where personal selling constitutes the primary thrust of the corporate promotional effort and where global customer groups can be identified, unified and coordinated sales practices may be called for. When distribution is intensive, channels are long, or markets have tradition-oriented distribution, headquarters' role should be less pronounced and should concentrate mostly on offering help and guidance.[45]

Eastman Kodak has developed a line-of-business approach to allow for standardized strategy throughout a region.[46] In Europe, one person is placed in charge of the entire copier-duplicator program in each country. That person is responsible for all sales and service teams within the country. Typically, each customer is served by three representatives, each with a different responsibility. Sales representatives maintain ultimate responsibility for the account; they conduct demonstrations, analyze customer requirements, determine the right type of equipment for each installation, and obtain the orders. Service representatives install and maintain the equipment and retrofit new product improvements to existing equipment. Customer service representatives are the liaison between sales and service. They provide operator training on a continuing basis and handle routine questions and complaints. Each team is positioned to respond to any European customer within four hours.

The training of the sales force usually takes place in the national markets, but multinational corporations' headquarters will have a say in the techniques used. For instance, when Kodak introduced the Ektaprint line, sales team members were selected carefully. U.S. copier personnel could be recruited from other Kodak divisions, but most European marketing personnel had to be recruited from outside the company and given intensive training. Sales managers and a select group of sales trainers were sent to the Rochester, New York, headquarters for six weeks of training. They then returned to Europe to set up programs for individual countries so that future teams could be trained there. To ensure continuity, all the U.S. training materials were translated into the languages of the individual countries. To maintain a unified pro-

[44]Joseph T. Plummer, "The Role of Copy Research in Multinational Advertising," *Journal of Advertising Research* 26 (October–November 1986): 11–15.

[45]John S. Hill, Richard R. Still, and Unal O Boya, "Managing the Multinational Sales Force," *International Marketing Review* 8 (1991): 19–31.

[46]Joseph A. Lawton, "Kodak Penetrates the European Copier Market with Customized Marketing Strategy and Product Changes," *Marketing News*, August 3, 1984, 1, 6.

gram and overcome language barriers, Kodak created a service language consisting of 1,200 words commonly found in technical information.

Foreign companies entering the Japanese market face challenges in establishing a sales force. Recruitment poses the first major problem, since well-established, and usually local, entities have an advantage in attracting personnel. Many have, therefore, entered into joint ventures or distribution agreements to obtain a sales force. Companies can also expect to invest more in training and organizational culture-building activities than in the United States. These may bring long-term advantages in fostering loyalty to the company.[47]

Sales Promotion

Sales promotion has been used as the catchall term for promotion that does not fall under advertising, personal selling, or publicity. Sales promotion directed at consumers involves such activities as couponing, sampling, premiums, consumer education and demonstration activities, cents-off packs, point-of-purchase materials, and direct mail. The use of sales promotions as alternatives and as support for advertising is increasing worldwide.[48] The appeal is related to several factors: cost and clutter of media advertising, simpler targeting of customers compared with advertising, and easier tracking of promotional effectiveness (for example, coupon returns provide a clear measure of effectiveness).

The success in Latin America of Tang, General Foods' presweetened powder juice substitute, is for the most part traceable to successful sales promotion efforts. One promotion involved trading Tang pouches for free popsicles from Kibon, General Foods' Brazilian subsidiary. Kibon also placed coupons for free groceries in Tang pouches. In Puerto Rico, General Foods ran Tang sweepstakes. In Argentina, in-store sampling featured Tang pitchers and girls in orange Tang dresses. Decorative Tang pitchers were a hit throughout Latin America. Sales promotion directed at intermediaries, also known as trade promotion, includes activities such as trade shows and exhibits, trade discounts, and cooperative advertising.

For sales promotion to be effective, the campaign planned by manufacturers, or their agencies, must gain the support of the local retailer population. Coupons from consumers, for example, have to be redeemed and sent to the manufacturer or to the company handling the promotion. A.C. Nielsen tried to introduce cents-off coupons in Chile and ran into trouble with the nation's supermarket union, which notified its members that it opposed the project and recommended that coupons not be accepted. The main complaint was that an intermediary, like Nielsen, would unnecessarily raise costs and thus the prices to be charged to consumers. Also, some critics felt that coupons would limit individual negotiations because Chileans often bargain for their purchases.

Tools of sales promotion fall under varying regulations, as can be seen from Table 20.7. A particular level of incentive may be permissible in one market but illegal in another. The Scandinavian countries present the greatest difficulties in this respect because every promotion has to be approved by a government body. In France, a gift cannot be worth more than 4 percent of the retail value of the product being promoted (subject to a maximum of 10 francs), whereas the maximum prize value in the Netherlands is 250 guilders, making certain promotions virtually impossible. Although competitions are allowed in most of Western Europe, to insist on receiving proofs of purchase as a condition of entry is not permitted in Germany.

[47]John L. Graham, Shigeru Ichikawa, and Yao Apasu, "Managing Your Sales in Japan," *Euro-Asia Business Review* 6 (January 1987): 37–40.

[48]Jean J. Boddewyn, *Premiums, Gifts, and Competitions* (New York: International Advertising Association, 1986), Chapter 1.

TABLE 20.7	Regulations Regarding Premiums, Gifts, and Competitions in Selected Countries

COUNTRY	CATEGORY	NO RESTRICTIONS OR MINOR ONES	AUTHORIZED WITH MAJOR RESTRICTIONS	GENERAL BAN WITH IMPORTANT EXCEPTIONS	ALMOST TOTAL PROHIBITION
Australia	Premiums	x			
	Gifts	x			
	Competitions		x		
Austria	Premiums				x
	Gifts		x		
	Competitions		x		
Canada	Premiums	x			
	Gifts	x			
	Competitions		x		
Denmark	Premiums			x	
	Gifts		x		
	Competitions			x	
France	Premiums	x			
	Gifts	x			
	Competitions	x			
Germany	Premiums				x
	Gifts		x		
	Competitions		x		
Hong Kong	Premiums	x			
	Gifts	x			
	Competitions	x			
Japan	Premiums		x		
	Gifts		x		
	Competitions		x		
Korea	Premiums		x		
	Gifts		x		
	Competitions		x		
United Kingdom	Premiums	x			
	Gifts	x			
	Competitions		x		
United States	Premiums	x			
	Gifts	x			
	Competitions	x			
Venezuela	Premiums		x		
	Gifts		x		
	Competitions		x		

SOURCE: Jean J. Boddewyn, *Premiums, Gifts, and Competitions*, 1988, published by International Advertising Association, 342 Madison Avenue, Suite 2000, NYC, NY 10017. Reprinted with permission.

Regulations such as these make truly global sales promotions rare and difficult to launch.[49] Although only a few multinational brands have been promoted on a multiterritory basis, the approach can work. In general, such multicountry promotions may be suitable for products such as soft drinks, liquor, airlines, credit cards, and jeans, which span cultural divides. Naturally, local laws and cultural differences have to be taken into account at the planning stage. Although many of the promotions may be funded centrally, they will be implemented differently in each market so that they can

[49]"An English Plan Abroad," *Sales Promotion*, April 25, 1985, 2–6.

be tied with the local company's other promotional activities. For example, 7Up's multiterritory Music Machine promotion carries a common theme—youth-oriented rock music. The promotion involves sponsored radio shows, featuring specially recorded concerts by leading contemporary artists, and promotional gifts such as music videos and audiotapes.

In the province of Quebec in Canada, advertisers must pay a tax on the value of the prizes they offer in a contest, whether the prize is a trip, money, or a car. The amount of the tax depends on the geographical extent of the contest. If it is open only to residents of Quebec, the tax is 10 percent; if open to all of Canada, 3 percent; if worldwide, 1 percent. Subtle distinctions are drawn in the regulations between a premium and a prize. As an example, the Manic soccer team was involved with both McDonald's and Provigo Food stores. The team offered a dollar off the price of four tickets, and the stubs could be cashed for a special at McDonald's. Provigo was involved in a contest offering a year's supply of groceries. The Manic-McDonald's offer was a premium that involved no special tax; Provigo, however, was taxed because it was involved in a contest. According to the regulation, a premium is available to everyone, whereas a prize is available to a certain number of people among those who participate. In some cases, industries may self-regulate the use of promotional items.

Public Relations

Image—the way a multinational corporation relates to and is perceived by its key constituents—is a bottom-line issue for management. Public relations is the marketing communications function charged with executing programs to earn public understanding and acceptance, which means both internal and external communication. The function can further be divided into proactive and reactive forms.

Internal Public Relations
Especially in multinational corporations, internal communication is important to create an appropriate corporate culture. The Japanese have perfected this in achieving a *wa* (we) spirit. Everyone in an organization is, in one way or another, in marketing and will require additional targeted information on issues not necessarily related to his or her day-to-day functions. A basic part of most internal programs is the employee publication produced and edited typically by the company's public relations or advertising department and usually provided in both hard-copy and electronic format. Some, such as the example in Figure 20.7 from Deere & Company, have foreign language versions. More often, as at ExxonMobil, each affiliate publishes its own employee publication. The better this vehicle can satisfy the information needs of employees, the less they will have to rely on others, especially informal sources such as the grapevine. Audiovisual media in the form of e-mails, films, videotapes, slides, and videoconferencing are being used, especially for training and indoctrination purposes. Some of the materials that are used internally can be provided to other publics as well; for example, booklets, manuals, and handbooks are provided to employees, distributors, and visitors to the company.[50]

External Public Relations
External public relations (also known as marketing public relations) is focused on the interactions with customers. In the **proactive** context, marketers are concerned about establishing global identities to increase sales, differentiate products and services, and attract employees. Non-U.S. marketers have been found to be far more active than U.S. firms in trying to boost their global identities.[51] These activities have been seen as necessary to compete against companies with strong local identities. External campaigns can be achieved through the use of corporate symbols, corporate advertising, customer relations programs, and publicity. For example, Black &

[50]S. Watson Dunn, *Public Relations* (Homewood, IL: Irwin, 1986), 275–286.

[51]"Foreign Companies' Global Awareness Cited in Study," *Marketing News*, August 1, 1988, 14.

FIGURE	20.7	Internal Media: Deere & Company

   *SOURCE:* Deere & Company. **http://www.johndeere.com**

Decker's corporate logo, which is in the shape and color of an orange hexagon, is used for all B&D products.[52] Some material is produced to assist specifically in personal selling efforts.

Publicity, in particular, is of interest to the multinational corporation. Publicity is the securing of editorial space (as opposed to paid advertising) to further marketing objectives. Because it is editorial in content, the consuming public perceives it as more trustworthy than advertising. A good example of how publicity can be used to aid in advertising efforts was the introduction by Princess Lines (known from the television show *Love Boat*) of a new liner, the *Royal Princess*. Because of its innovative design and size, the *Royal Princess* was granted substantial press coverage, which was especially beneficial in the travel and leisure magazines. Such coverage does not come automatically but has to be coordinated and initiated by the public relations staff of the company.

Unanticipated developments in the marketplace can place the company in a position that requires **reactive** public relations, including anticipating and countering criticism. The criticisms range from general ones against all multinational corporations to more specific ones. They may be based on a market; for example, doing business with prison factories in China. They may concern a product; for example, Nestlé's practices of advertising and promoting infant formula in developing countries where infant mortality is unacceptably high. They may center on conduct in a given situation; for example, Union Carbide's perceived lack of response in the Bhopal dis-

[52]"How Black & Decker Forged a Winning Brand Transfer Strategy," *Business International*, July 20, 1987, 225–227.

aster. The key concern is that, if not addressed, these criticisms can lead to more significant problems, such as the internationally orchestrated boycott of Nestlé's products. The six-year boycott did not so much harm earnings as it harmed image and employee morale.

Crisis management is becoming more formalized in companies with specially assigned task forces ready to step in if problems arise. In general, companies must adopt policies that will allow them to effectively respond to pressure and criticism, which will continue to surface. Oliver Williams suggests that crisis management policies have the following traits: (1) openness about corporate activities, with a focus on how these activities enhance social and economic performance; (2) preparedness to utilize the tremendous power of the multinational corporation in a responsible manner and, in the case of pressure, to counter criticisms swiftly; (3) integrity, which often means that the marketer must avoid not only actual wrongdoing but the mere appearance of it; and (4) clarity, which will help ameliorate hostility if a common language is used with those pressuring the corporation.[53] He proposes that the marketer's role is one of enlightened self-interest; reasonable critics understand that the marketer cannot compromise the bottom line.

Complicating the situation often is the fact that groups in one market criticize what the marketer is doing in another market. For example, the Interfaith Center on Corporate Responsibility urged Colgate-Palmolive to stop marketing Darkie toothpaste under that brand name in Asia because of the term's offensiveness elsewhere in the world. Darkie toothpaste was sold in Thailand, Hong Kong, Singapore, Malaysia, and Taiwan and was packaged in a box that featured a likeness of Al Jolson in blackface.[54] Colgate-Palmolive redid the package and changed the brand name to Darlie. Levi Strauss decided to withdraw from $40 million worth of production contracts in China after consultations with a variety of sources, including human rights organizations, experts on China, and representatives of the U.S. government, led it to conclude that there was pervasive abuse of human rights.[55]

The public relations function can be handled in-house or with the assistance of an agency. The largest agencies and agency groups are presented in Table 20.8. The use and extent of public relations activity will vary by company and the type of activity needed. Product-marketing PR may work best with a strong component of control at the local level and a local PR firm, while crisis management—given the potential for worldwide adverse impact—will probably be controlled principally from a global center.[56] This has meant that global marketers funnel short-term projects to single offices for their local expertise while maintaining contact with the global agencies for their worldwide reach when a universal message is needed. Some multinational corporations maintain public relations staffs in their main offices around the world, while others use the services of firms such as Burson-Marsteller, Hill and Knowlton, and Grey & Company on specific projects.

Sponsorship Marketing

Sponsorship involves the marketer's investment in events or causes. Sponsorship funds worldwide are directed for the most part at sports events (both individual and team sports) and cultural events (both in the popular and high-culture categories). Examples range from Coca-Cola's sponsorship of the 2000 Olympic Games in Sydney

[53]Oliver Williams, "Who Cast the First Stone?" *Harvard Business Review* 62 (September–October 1984): 151–160.

[54]"Church Group Gnashes Colgate-Palmolive," *Advertising Age*, March 24, 1986, 46.

[55]"Levi to Sever Link with China; Critics Contend It's Just a PR Move," *Marketing News*, June 7, 1993, 10.

[56]Michael Carberry, "Global Public Relations," keynote speech at Public Relations Association of Puerto Rico's Annual Convention, San Juan, September 17, 1993.

TABLE 20.8	The Top Worldwide Public Relations Firms	
FIRM	2000 NET FEES	EMPLOYEES
1. Edelman PR Worldwide	233,415,105	2,319
2. Ruder Finn	84,125,000	627
3. Waggener Edstrom	57,905,000	435
4. Text 100	33,678,272	445
5. Schwartz Comms	33,185,571	239
6. FitzGerald Comms	21,400,000	180
7. CCo Communications	16,105,177	168
8. PR21	14,661,691	152
9. Chandler Chicco Agency	14,441,862	71
10. Neale-May & Partners	14,078,803	69
11. Noonan/Russo	13,980,000	81
12. Dan Klores Communc	13,747,263	95
13. Sterling Hager	13,648,800	104
14. Gibbs & Soell	12,637,000	94
15. Hoffman Agency	11,700,000	78
16. Rogers & Associates	11,068,252	88
17. Applied Communications	11,000,000	84
18. KCSA PR Worldwide	10,651,146	73
19. Padilla Speer Beardsley	10,077,722	89
20. Stoorza Communications	10,049,203	87
21. DeVries	10,024,393	48
22. Wilson McHenry Company	9,810,886	74
23. Makovsky & Co	9,610,000	70
24. PepperCom	9,275,456	58
25. The Horn Group	9,231,000	70

SOURCE: "2000 Worldwide Fees of Independent Firms with Major U.S. Operations," O'Dwyer's PR Daily Web Site, accessed April 26, 2001.

http://www.odwyerpr.com.

and MasterCard's sponsorship of World Cup Soccer in 2002 in Japan and South Korea to VISA's sponsoring of Eric Clapton's tour and Ford's sponsoring of the 1999 Montreux Detroit Jazz Festival. Sponsorship of events such as the Olympics is driven by the desire to be associated with a worldwide event that has a positive image, global reach, and a proven strategic positioning of excellence.

The challenge is that an event may become embroiled in controversy, thus hurting the sponsors' images as well. Furthermore, in light of the high expense of sponsorship, marketers worry about **ambush marketing** by competitors. During the Atlanta Olympic Games in 1996, some of the sponsors' competitors garnered a higher profile than the sponsors themselves. For example, Pepsi erected stands outside venues and plastered the town with signs. Nike secured substantial amounts of air time on radio and TV stations. Fuji bought billboards on the route from the airport into downtown Atlanta. None of the three contributed anything to the International Olympic Committee during this time.[57]

Cause-related marketing is a combination of public relations, sales promotion, and corporate philanthropy. This activity should not be developed merely as a response to a crisis, nor should it be a fuzzy, piecemeal effort; instead, marketers should have a social vision and a planned long-term social policy. For example, in Casanare, Colombia, where it is developing oil interests, British Petroleum invests in activities that support its business plan and contribute to the region's development. This has meant an investment of $10 million in setting up a loan fund for entrepreneurs, giving students

[57]"Olympic Torch Burns Sponsors' Fingers," *Financial Times*, December 13, 1999, 6.

THE INTERNATIONAL MARKETPLACE 20.4

Expanding the Social Vision: Global Community Relations

A RECENT ROPER SURVEY found that 92 percent of the respondents feel that it is important for marketers to seek out ways to become good corporate citizens, and they are most interested in those who get involved in environmental, educational, and health issues. Community relations is, as one chief executive put it, "food for the soul of the organization." It has become a strategic aspect of business and a fundamental ingredient for the long-term health of the enterprise. As a global company, IBM has a network of staff responsible for corporate responsibility throughout the 152 countries of operation. Major initiatives that address environmental concerns, support programs for the disabled, and support education reform have been pioneered by IBM around the world.

IBM's policy of good corporate citizenship means accepting responsibility as a participant in community and national affairs and striving to be among the most-admired companies in its host countries. In 1989, IBM introduced Worldwide Initiatives in Volunteerism, a $1 million–plus program to fund projects worldwide and promote employee volunteerism. In Thailand, for example, IBM provides equipment and personnel to universities and donates money to the nation's wildlife fund and environmental protection agency. In 1986, the firm became one of only two companies with a U.S.-based parent to win the Garuda Award, which recognizes significant contributions to Thailand's social and economic development.

As part of its long-term strategy for growth in Latin America, IBM is investing millions of dollars in an initiative that brings the latest technology to local schools. IBM does not donate the computers (they are bought by governments, institutions, and other private firms), but it does provide the needed instruction and technological support. By 1993, some 800,000 children and 10,000 teachers had benefited from the program in ten countries. IBM Latin America's technology-in-education initiative is a creative combination of marketing, social responsibility, and long-term relationship building that fits in with the company's goal of becoming a "national asset" in Latin American countries. In Venezuela, IBM teamed with the government to bring computers to the K–12 environment to enhance the learning process through technology.

Increased privatization and government cutbacks in social services in many countries offer numerous opportunities for companies to make substantive contributions to solving various global, regional, and local problems. Conservative governments in Europe are welcoming private-sector programs to provide job training for inner-city youth, to meet the needs of immigrants, and to solve massive pollution problems. And in Eastern and Central Europe, where the lines between the private and public sectors are just now being drawn, corporations have a unique opportunity to take a leadership role in shaping new societies. IBM Germany provided computer equipment and executive support to clean the heavily polluted River Elbe, which runs through the Czech Republic and Germany into the North Sea.

James Parkel, director of IBM's Office of Corporate Support Programs, summarizes the new expectations in the following way: "Employees don't want to work for companies that have no social conscience, customers don't want to do business with companies that pollute the environment or are notorious for shoddy products and practices, and communities don't welcome companies that are not good corporate citizens. Many shareholder issues are socially driven."

SOURCES: Bradley K. Googins, "Why Community Relations Is a Strategic Imperative," *Strategy and Business* (Third Quarter, 1997): 64–67; "Consumers Note Marketers' Good Causes: Roper," *Advertising Age*, November 11, 1996, 51; Paul N. Bloom, Pattie Yu Hussein, and Lisa R. Szykman, "Benefiting Society and the Bottom Line," *Marketing Management*, Winter 1995, 8–18; " IBM Promotes Education," *Business Latin America*, May 24, 1993, 6–7; "Corporate Generosity Is Greatly Appreciated," *Business Week*, November 2, 1992, 118–120; "Achieving Success in Asia: IBM Sees 'Localization' as a Critical Element," *Business International*, November 11, 1991, 379–383; "Global Community Relations: Expanding the Social Vision," *Business International*, September 16, 1991, 313–314; and "How Corporate Activism Can Spread Your Message," *Business International*, June 10, 1991, 199.

http://www.ibm.com

technical training, supporting a center for pregnant women and nursing mothers, working on reforestation, building aqueducts, and helping to create jobs outside the oil industry.[58] Examples of IBM's contributions to local communities are provided in *The International Marketplace 20.4.*

[58]Bradley K. Googins, "Why Community Relations Is a Strategic Imperative," *Strategy and Business* (Third Quarter 1997): 64–67.

SUMMARY

As multinational corporations manage the various elements of the promotions mix in differing environmental conditions, decisions must be made about channels to be used in the communication, the message, who is to execute or help execute the program, and how the success of the endeavor is to be measured. The trend is toward more harmonization of strategy, at the same time allowing for flexibility at the local level and early incorporation of local needs into the promotional plans.

The effective implementation of the promotional program is a key ingredient in the marketing success of the firm. The promotional tools must be used within the opportunities and constraints posed by the communications channels as well as by the laws and regulations governing marketing communications.

Advertising agencies are key facilitators in communicating with the firm's constituent groups. Many multinational corporations are realigning their accounts worldwide in an attempt to streamline their promotional efforts and achieve a global approach.

The use of other promotional tools, especially personal selling, tends to be more localized to fit the conditions of the individual markets. Decisions concerning recruitment, training, motivation, and evaluation must be made at the affiliate level, with general guidance from headquarters.

An area of increasing challenge to multinational corporations is public relations. Multinationals, by their very design, draw attention to their activities. The best interest of the marketer lies in anticipating problems with both internal and external constituencies and managing them, through communications, to the satisfaction of all parties.

QUESTIONS FOR DISCUSSION

1. Comment on the opinion that "practically speaking, neither an entirely standardized nor an entirely localized advertising approach is necessarily best."
2. What type of adjustments must advertising agencies make as more companies want "one sight, one sound, one sell" campaigns?
3. Assess the programmed management approach for coordinating international advertising efforts.
4. Discuss problems associated with measuring advertising effectiveness in foreign markets.
5. Is international personal selling a reality? Or is all personal selling national, regardless of who performs it?
6. Why is there a need for some degree of centralization in global advertising decision making?

7. Rumors are one of the most difficult problems faced by public relations personnel, especially if they spread worldwide or occur in multiple-country markets. Procter & Gamble faced a rumor that it was associated with "forces of the dark side," and that its corporate logo was proof of that. Using Procter & Gamble's web site (**www.pg.com**) and its "Trademark Facts," assess the company's efforts to eliminate the problem.
8. A company wishing to engage global markets through the Internet has to make sure that its regional/local web sites are of the same caliber as its global site. Using Kodak as an example (**www.kodak.com**), evaluate whether its sites abroad satisfy this criterion.

RECOMMENDED READINGS

Anholt, Simon. *Another One Bites the Grass: Making Sense of International Advertising.* New York: John Wiley & Sons, 2000.

Bly, Robert W. *Advertising Manager's Handbook.* Englewood Clliffs, NJ: Prentice-Hall, 1998.

Burnett, Leo. *Worldwide Advertising and Media Fact Book.* Chicago, IL: Triumph Books, 1994.

De Mooij, Marieke K. *Global Marketing and Advertising: Understanding Cultural Paradoxes.* San Francisco, CA: Sage Publications, 1997.

Grey, Anne-Marie, and Kim Skildum-Reid. *The Sponsorship Seeker's Toolkit.* New York: McGraw-Hill, 1999.

Jones, John Philip. *International Advertising: Realities and Myths.* San Francisco: Sage Publications, 1999.

Monye, Sylvester O., ed. *The Handbook of International Marketing Communications.* Cambridge, MA: Blackwell Publishers, 2000.

Niefeld, Jaye S. *The Making of an Advertising Campaign: The Silk of China.* Englewood Cliffs, NJ: Prentice-Hall, 1989.

Peebles, Dean M., and John K. Ryans. *Management of International Advertising: A Marketing Approach.* Boston: Allyn & Bacon, 1984.

Roberts, Mary-Lou, and Robert D. Berger. *Direct Marketing Management.* Englewood Cliffs, NJ: Prentice-Hall, 1999.

Shimp, Terence A. *Advertising, Promotion, and Supplemental Aspects of Integrated Marketing Communications.* Fort Worth, TX: The Dryden Press, 2000.

Zenith Media. *Advertising Expenditure Forecasts.* London: Zenith Media, 1999.

Marketing Organization, Implementation, and Control

Chapter 21

Procter & Gamble: Organization 2005

GLOBALIZATION IS AT THE HEART of Procter & Gamble's restructuring of its organization, code-named Organization 2005. Organization 2005 recognizes that there is a big difference between selling products in 140 countries around the world and truly planning and managing lines of business on a global basis.

There are five key elements to Organization 2005:

- Global Business Units (GBUs). P&G is moving from four business units based on geographic regions to seven GBUs based on product lines. This will drive greater innovation and speed by centering global strategy and profit responsibility on brands, rather than on geographics.
- Market Development Organizations (MDOs). The company is establishing eight MDO regions that will tailor global programs to local markets and develop market-

ing strategies to build P&G's entire business based on superior local consumer and customer knowledge.

- Global Business Services (GBS). GBS brings business activities such as accounting, human resource systems, order management, and information technology into a single global organization to provide these services to all P&G business units at best-in-class quality, cost, and speed. They will be in the following locations: Americas (Cincinnati, United States; and San Jose, Costa Rica); Europe, Middle East, Africa (Newcastle, United Kingdom; Brussels, Belgium; and Prague, the Czech Republic); and Asia (Kobe, Japan; Manila, Philippines; Guangzhou, China; and Singapore).
- Corporate Functions. P&G has redefined the role of corporate staff. Most have moved into new business units, with the remaining staff refocused on developing

The New Procter & Gamble

Global Business Units	Market Development Organizations	Global Business Services	Corporate Functions
• Baby Care	• North America	• Global Enabling Team	• Customer Business Development
• Beauty Care	• Latin America	• Regional Leadership Team	• Finance Resources
• Fabric & Home Care	• Western Europe	• Global Process Owners	• IT
• Feminine Protection	• Central & Eastern Europe		• Legal
• Food & Beverage	• ASEAN/India/Australia		• Market Research/ Gov't Relations
• Health Care & Corporate Ventures	• Northeast Asia		• Product Supply
• Tissue & Towel	• Greater China		• Public Affairs
	• Middle East/Africa General Export		• R&D

SOURCE: Procter & Gamble

cutting-edge new knowledge and serving corporate needs. For example, the company decentralized its 3,600-person information technology department so that 97 percent of its members now work in P&G's individual product, market, and business teams or are part of GBS, which provides shared services such as infrastructure to P&G units. The remaining 3 percent are still in corporate IT. In addition, 54 "change agents" have been assigned to work across the seven GBUs to lead cultural and business change by helping teams work together more effectively through greater use of IT, in particular, real-time collaboration tools.

■ Culture. Changes to P&G's culture should create an environment that produces bolder, mind-stretching goals and plans; bigger innovations; and greater speed. For example, the reward system has been redesigned to better link executive compensation with new business goals and results.

A good example of the increased use of collaborative technology is a product called Swiffer, a dust sweeper with disposal cloths electrostatically charged to attract dust and dirt. Swiffer, which was introduced to the market in August 1999, represents collaboration among multiple P&G product groups, including paper and chemicals. Swiffer took just 18 months to go from test market to global availability. In the past, when a product was introduced, it might have taken years for it to be available worldwide, since management in each region was responsible for the product's launch there, including everything from test marketing to getting products onto retailers' shelves. Collaborative technologies, including chat rooms on the company's intranet, are transforming the

Introducing Swiffer...

DIRT can't dodge it.

HAIR can't hide from it.

When Swiffer's the One,

Consider it Done.

company's conservative culture to one that encourages employees to be candid, test boundaries, and take chances.

SOURCES: P&G Jump-Starts Corporate Change," *Internetweek*, November 1, 1999, 30; "All around the World," *Traffic World*, October 11, 1999, 22–24; "Organization 2005 Drive for Accelerated Growth Enters Next Phase," P&G News Releases, June 9, 1999, 1–5; and "Procter & Gamble Moves Forward with Reorganization," *Chemical Market Reporter*, February 1, 1999, 12.

As COMPANIES EVOLVE from purely domestic entities to multinationals, their organizational structure and control systems must change to reflect new strategies. With growth comes diversity in terms of products and services, geographic markets, and personnel, leading to a set of challenges for the company. Two critical issues are basic to addressing these challenges: (1) the type of organization that provides the best framework for developing worldwide strategies while at the same time maintaining flexibility with respect to individual markets and operations, and (2) the type and degree of control to be exercised from headquarters to maximize total effort. Organizational structures and control systems have to be adjusted as market conditions change, as seen in *The International Marketplace 21.1*.

This chapter will focus on the advantages and disadvantages of the organizational structures available as well as their appropriateness at various stages of internationalization. A determining factor is where decision-making authority within the organizational structures will be placed. The roles of different entities of the organization need to be defined, including how to achieve collaboration among these units for the benefit of the entire global organization. The chapter will also outline the need for devising a control system to oversee the international operations of the company, emphasizing the control instruments needed in addition to those used in domestic business, as well as the control strategies of multinational corporations. The appropriateness and eventual cost of the various control approaches will vary as the firm expands its international operations. Overall, the objective of the chapter is to study intraorganizational relationships in the firm's attempt to optimize competitive response in areas most critical to its business.

Organizational Structure

The basic functions of an organization are to provide (1) a route and locus of decision making and coordination, and (2) a system for reporting and communications. Authority and communication networks are typically depicted in the organizational chart.

Organizational Designs

The basic configurations of international organizations correspond to those of purely domestic ones; the greater the degree of internationalization, the more complex the structures can become. The core building block is the individual company operating in its particular market. However, these individual companies need to work together for maximum effectiveness; thus, the need for organizational design. The types of structures that companies use to manage foreign activities can be divided into three categories based on the degree of internationalization:

1. Little or no formal organizational recognition of international activities of the firm. This category ranges from domestic operations handling an occasional international transaction on an ad hoc basis to separate export departments.
2. International division. Firms in this category recognize the ever-growing importance of international involvement.
3. Global organizations. These can be structured by product, area, function, process, or customer.

Hybrid structures may exist as well, in which one market may be structured by product, another by area. Matrix organizations have emerged in large multinational corporations to combine product, regional, and functional expertise. As worldwide competition has increased dramatically in many industries, the latest organizational response is networked global organizations in which heavy flows of technology, personnel, and communication take place between strategically interdependent units to establish greater global integration. The ability to identify and disseminate best practices throughout the organization is an important competitive advantage for global companies. For example, a U.S. automaker found that in the face of distinctive challenges presented by the local environment, Brazilian engineers developed superior seals, which the company then incorporated in all its models worldwide.[1]

Little or No Formal Organization
In the very early stages of international involvement, domestic operations assume responsibility for international marketing activities. The share of international operations in the sales and profits of the corporation is initially so minor that no organizational adjustment takes place. No consolidation of information or authority over international sales is undertaken or is necessary. Transactions

---

[1]Robert J. Flanagan, "Knowledge Management in Global Organizations in the 21st Century," *HR Magazine* 44 (Number 11, 1999): 54–55.

FIGURE 21.1 | **The Export Department Structure**

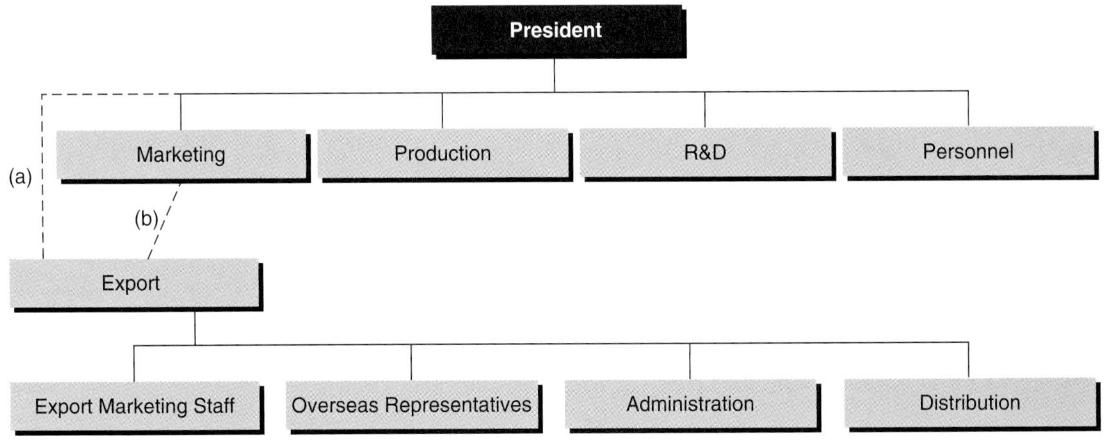

are conducted on a case-by-case basis either by the resident expert or quite often with the help of facilitating agents, such as freight forwarders.

As demand from the international marketplace grows and interest within the firm expands, the organizational structure will reflect it. An export department appears as a separate entity. This may be an outside export management company—that is, an independent company that becomes the de facto export department of the firm. This is an indirect approach to international involvement in that very little experience is accumulated within the firm itself. Alternatively, a firm may establish its own export department, hiring a few seasoned individuals to take full responsibility for international activities. Organizationally, the department may be a subdepartment of marketing (alternative b in Figure 21.1) or may have equal ranking with the various functional departments (alternative a). This choice will depend on the importance assigned to overseas activities by the firm. Because the export department is the first real step for internationalizing the organizational structure, it should be a full-fledged marketing organization and not merely a sales organization; i.e., it should have the resources for market research and market-development activities (such as trade show participation).

Licensing is the international entry mode for some firms. Responsibility for licensing may be assigned to the R&D function despite its importance to the overall international strategy of the firm. A formal liaison among the export, marketing, production, and R&D functions should be formed for the maximum utilization of licensing.[2] A separate manager should be appointed if licensing becomes a major activity for the firm.

As the firm becomes more involved in foreign markets, the export department structure will become obsolete. The firm may then undertake joint ventures or direct foreign investment, which require those involved to have functional experience. The firm therefore typically establishes an international division.

Some firms that acquire foreign production facilities pass through an additional stage in which foreign subsidiaries report directly to the president or to a manager specifically assigned this duty.[3] However, the amount of coordination and control that

[2]Michael Z. Brooke, *International Management: A Review of Strategies and Operations* (London: Hutchinson, 1986), 173–174; "Running a Licensing Deparment," *Business International*, June 13, 1988, 177–178.

[3]Stefan Robock and Kenneth Simmonds, *International Business and Multinational Enterprises* (Homewood, IL: Irwin, 1983), 414.

FIGURE 21.2 | **The International Division Structure**

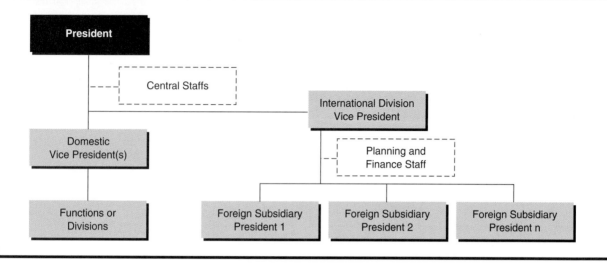

is required quickly establishes the need for a more formal international organization in the firm.

The International Division The international division centralizes in one entity, with or without separate incorporation, all of the responsibility for international activities, as illustrated in Figure 21.2. The approach aims to eliminate a possible bias against international operations that may exist if domestic divisions are allowed to independently serve international customers. In some cases, international markets have been found to be treated as secondary to domestic markets. The international division concentrates international expertise, information flows concerning foreign market opportunities, and authority over international activities. However, manufacturing and other related functions remain with the domestic divisions in order to take advantage of economies of scale.

To avoid situations in which the international division is at a disadvantage in competing for production, personnel, and corporate services, corporations need to coordinate between domestic and international operations. Coordination can be achieved through a joint staff or by requiring domestic and international divisions to interact in strategic planning and to submit the plans to headquarters. Further, many corporations require and encourage frequent interaction between domestic and international personnel to discuss common challenges in areas such as product planning. Coordination is also important because domestic operations may be organized along product or functional lines, whereas international divisions are geographically oriented.

International divisions best serve firms with few products that do not vary significantly in terms of their environmental sensitivity, and when international sales and profits are still quite insignificant compared with those of the domestic divisions.[4] Companies may outgrow their international divisions as their international sales grow in significance, diversity, and complexity. European companies used international divisions far less than their U.S. counterparts due to the relatively small size of their domestic markets. N.V. Philips, for example, would have never grown to its current prominence by relying on the Dutch market alone. While international divisions were popular among U.S. companies in the 1970s and 1980s, globalization of markets and

[4]Richard D. Robinson, *Internationalization of Business: An Introduction* (Hinsdale, IL: The Dryden Press, 1984), 84.

the increased share of overseas sales have made international divisions less suitable than global structures.[5] For example, Loctite, a leading marketer of sealants, adhesives, and coatings, moved from having an international division to being a global structure in which the company is managed by market channel (e.g., industrial automotive and electronics industry), to enable Loctite employees to synergize efforts and expertise worldwide.[6]

Global Organizational Structures

Global structures have grown out of competitive necessity. In many industries, competition is on a global basis, with the result that companies must have a high degree of reactive capability.

Five basic types of global structures are available:

1. Global product structure, in which product divisions are responsible for all manufacture and marketing worldwide
2. Global area structure, in which geographic divisions are responsible for all manufacture and marketing in their respective areas
3. Global functional structure, in which the functional areas (such as production, marketing, finance, and personnel) are responsible for the worldwide operations of their own functional areas
4. Global customer structure, in which operations are structured based on distinct worldwide customer groups
5. Mixed—or hybrid—structure, which may combine the other alternatives

Product Structure The **product structure** is the one that is most used by multinational corporations.[7] This approach gives worldwide responsibility to strategic business units for the marketing of their product lines, as shown in Figure 21.3. Most consumer product firms utilize some form of this approach, mainly because of the diversity of their products. One of the major benefits of the approach is improved cost efficiency through centralization of manufacturing facilities. This is crucial in industries in which competitive position is determined by world market share, which in turn is often determined by the degree to which manufacturing is rationalized.[8] Adaptation to this approach may cause problems because it is usually accompanied by consolidation of operations and plant closings. A good example is Black & Decker, which rationalized many of its operations in its worldwide competitive effort against Makita, the Japanese power tool manufacturer. Similarly, Goodyear reorganized itself into a single global organization with a complete business team approach for tires and general products. The move was largely prompted by tightening worldwide competition.[9] In a similar move, Ford merged its large and culturally distinct European and North American auto operations by vehicle platform type to make more efficient use of its engineering and product development resources against rapidly globalizing

[5]William H. Davidson, "Shaping a Global Product Organization," *Harvard Business Review* 59 (March–April 1982): 69–76.

[6]See **http://www.loctite.com/about/global_reach.html**, and "How Loctite Prospers with 3-Man Global HQ, Strong Country Managers," *Business International*, May 2, 1988, 129–130.

[7]See Joan P. Curhan, William H. Davidson, and Suri Rajan, *Tracing the Multinationals* (Cambridge, MA: Ballinger, 1977), 15; M. E. Wicks, *A Comparative Analysis of the Foreign Investment Evaluation Practices of U.S.-Based Multinational Corporations* (New York: McKinsey & Co., 1980), 3; and Lawrence G. Franko, "Organizational Structures and Multinational Strategies of Continental European Enterprise," in *European Research in International Business*, ed. Michel Ghertman and James Leontiades (Amsterdam, Holland: North Holland, 1977), 111–137.

[8]William H. Davidson and Philippe Haspeslagh, "Shaping a Global Product Organization," *Harvard Business Review* 59 (March–April 1982): 69–76.

[9]"How Goodyear Sharpened Organization and Production for a Tough World Market," *Business International*, January 16, 1989, 11–14.

FIGURE 21.3 **The Global Product Structure**

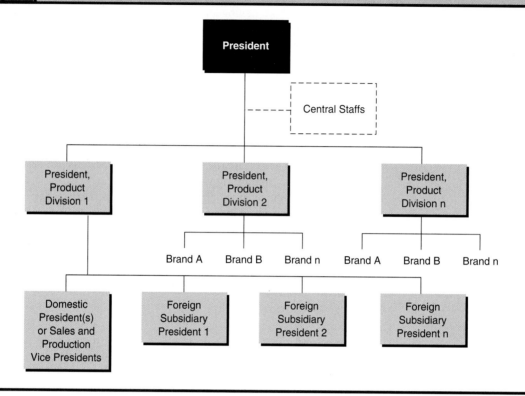

rivals.[10] The Ford Focus, Ford's compact car introduced in 1999, was designed by one team of engineers for worldwide markets.

Another benefit is the ability to balance the functional inputs needed by a product and to react quickly to product-specific problems in the marketplace. Even smaller brands receive individual attention. Product-specific attention is important because products vary in terms of the adaptation they need for different foreign markets. All in all, the product approach ideally brings about the development of a global strategic focus in response to global competition.

At the same time, this structure fragments international expertise within the firm because a central pool of international experience no longer exists. The structure assumes that managers will have adequate regional experience or advice to allow them to make balanced decisions. Coordination of activities among the various product groups operating in the same markets is crucial to avoid unnecessary duplication of basic tasks. For some of these tasks, such as market research, special staff functions may be created and then hired by the product divisions when needed. If product managers lack an appreciation for the international dimension, they may focus their attention on only the larger markets, often with emphasis on the domestic markets, and fail to take the long-term view.

Area Structure   The second most frequently adopted approach is the **area structure**, illustrated in Figure 21.4. The firm is organized on the basis of geographical areas; for example, operations may be divided into those dealing with North America, the Far East, Latin America, and Europe. Regional aggregation may play a major role in this structuring; for example, many multinational corporations have located their

[10]"Red Alert at Ford," *Business Week*, December 2, 1996, 38–39.

| FIGURE | 21.4 | The Global Area Structure |

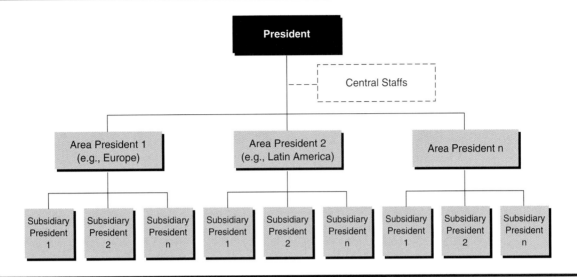

European headquarters in Brussels, where the EU has its headquarters. The inevitability of a North American trading bloc led to the creation of Campbell Soup Co.'s North American division, which replaced the U.S. operation as the power center of the company.[11] Organizational changes made at 3M Company as a result of NAFTA are recounted in *The International Marketplace 21.2*. The driver of the choice can also be cultural similarity, such as in the case of Asia, or historic connections between countries, such as in the case of combining Europe with the Middle East and Africa. Ideally, no special preference is given to the region in which the headquarters is located—for example, North America or Europe. Central staffs are responsible for providing coordination support for worldwide planning and control activities performed at headquarters.

The area approach follows the marketing concept most closely because individual areas and markets are given concentrated attention. If market conditions with respect to product acceptance and operating conditions vary dramatically, the area approach is the one to choose. Companies opting for this alternative typically have relatively narrow product lines with similar end uses and end users. However, expertise is most needed in adapting the product and its marketing to local market conditions. Once again, to avoid duplication of effort in product management and in functional areas, staff specialists—for product categories, for example—may be used.

Without appropriate coordination from the staff, essential information and experience may not be transferred from one regional entity to another. Also, if the company expands in terms of product lines, and if end markets begin to diversify, the area structure may become inappropriate.

Some marketers may feel that going into a global product structure may be too much too quickly and opt, therefore, to have a regional organization for planning and reporting purposes. The objective may also be to keep profit or sales centers of similar size at similar levels in the corporate hierarchy. If a group of countries has small sales compared with other country operations, they can be consolidated into a region. The benefits of a regional operation and regional headquarters are more efficient coordination of programs across the region (as opposed to globally), a management

[11]Bill Saporito, "Campbell Soup Gets Piping Hot," *Fortune*, September 9, 1991, 94–98.

THE INTERNATIONAL MARKETPLACE 21.2

Restructuring for Global Competitiveness

As REGIONS CONTINUE their drive toward single economic markets, companies are positioning themselves to capitalize on the resulting opportunities. 3M is responding in its European and American markets by bold organizational moves. In Europe, the formation of European Business Centers (EBCs) is focused on reaching the pan-European marketplace more efficiently. Each of the EBCs operates along product rather than geographic lines, and each is responsible for its business functions throughout Europe.

3M's North American Operational Plan centers on organizational restructuring based on three concepts: simplification, linkage, and empowerment. The plan was fully implemented in the United States and Canada in 1992, with Mexico added in 1994. Key goals of the operational plan are:

- Eliminate the role of 3M International Operations in cross-border activities within North America. All business units in Canada and Mexico deal directly with 3M's divisions in the United States.
- Redefine management functions. General sales and marketing managers in Canada and Mexico have a new title—business manager—and serve as the key link between local customers and the corresponding U.S. general managers. The business managers are also members of 3M U.S.'s planning, pricing, and operating committees; participate in the early stages of the global business planning; and execute the global strategy in Canada and Mexico.
- Coordinate functions and share resources among the three countries, especially in marketing, advertising, and sales. New product launches are synchronized throughout North America, with standardized sizing and part numbers wherever possible. Distribution strategies and agreements are coordinated. Sales literature, packaging, and labeling are uniform, written in the appropriate local language.
- Establish North American tactical teams. Members from these groups, drawn from all three countries, work on projects such as market research, new product development, and competitor monitoring.
- Set up centers of excellence. To maximize efficiency and

to avoid duplication of effort, each country specializes in the function or process that it does best and eliminates those that can be performed elsewhere. These centers are built around manufacturing of a product or product line, market niches, customer service, or technical skills.
- Modify performance measurement criteria. North American performance is gauged by North American—not U.S., Canadian, or Mexican—market share, earnings growth, and income.

At 3M Canada, major changes have taken place. Layers of management have been trimmed, communication and coordination greatly enhanced, and the requirement to go through the international division removed. Incorporating Mexico into the plan presents some unique challenges, however. For 3M U.S. headquarters, meeting or communicating electronically with Canadian counterparts is far easier than doing the same with Mexico. Language and cultural barriers also present potential challenges.

In April 2001, 3M's new CEO announced a further worldwide restructuring that would eliminate 5,000 jobs—half of them overseas—yet retain the existing international organization. The company continues to expand in emerging markets; Latin America, Asia-Pacific, and Africa.

SOURCES: 3M 1998 Annual Report, 1–3; and "3M Restructuring for NAFTA," *Business Latin America*, July 19, 1993, 6–7; "3M CEO Sees Benefits in Some Centralization," *Saint Paul Pioneer Press*, May 3, 2001, Kevin Maler.

http://www.mmm.com

more sensitized to country-market operations in the region, and the ability for the region's voice to be heard more clearly at global headquarters (as compared to what an individual, especially smaller, country operation could achieve).[12]

[12]John D. Daniels, "Bridging National and Global Marketing Strategies through Regional Operations," *International Marketing Review* 4 (Autumn 1987): 29–44; Philippe Lasserre, "Regional Headquarters: The Spearhead for Asia Pacific Markets," *Long Range Planning* 29 (February 1996): 30–37.

FIGURE 21.5 **The Global Functional Structure**

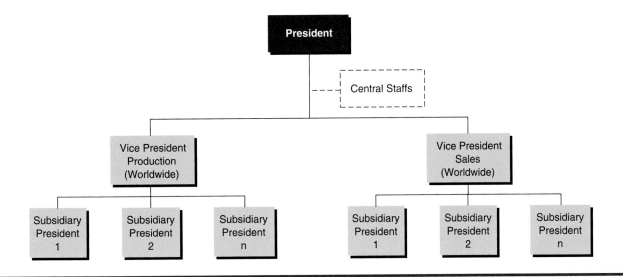

Functional Structure   Of all the approaches, the **functional structure** is the most simple from the administrative viewpoint because it emphasizes the basic tasks of the firm—for example, manufacturing, sales, and research and development. This approach, illustrated in Figure 21.5, works best when both products and customers are relatively few and similar in nature. Because coordination is typically the key problem, staff functions have been created to interact between the functional areas. Otherwise, the company's marketing and regional expertise may not be exploited to the fullest extent.

A variation of this approach is one that uses processes as a basis for structure. The **process structure** is common in the energy and mining industries, where one corporate entity may be in charge of exploration worldwide and another may be responsible for the actual mining operation.

Customer Structure   Firms may also organize their operations using the **customer structure,** especially if the customer groups they serve are dramatically different—for example, consumers versus businesses versus governments. Catering to these diverse groups may require the concentrating of specialists in particular divisions. The product may be the same, but the buying processes of the various customer groups may differ. Governmental buying is characterized by bidding, in which price plays a larger role than when businesses are the buyers.

Mixed Structure   Mixed, or hybrid, organizations also exist. A **mixed structure,** such as the one in Figure 21.6, combines two or more organizational dimensions simultaneously. It permits attention to be focused on products, areas, or functions, as needed. This approach may occur in a transitionary period after a merger or an acquisition, or it may come about because of a unique customer group or product line (such as military hardware). It may also provide a useful structure before the implementation of the matrix structure.[13]

Organization structures are, of course, never as clear-cut and simple as they have been presented here. Whatever the basic format, inputs are needed for product, area, and function. One alternative, for example, might be an initial product structure that would eventually have regional groupings. Another alternative might be an initial area

[13]Daniel Robey, *Designing Organizations: A Macro Perspective* (Homewood, IL: Irwin, 1982), 327.

FIGURE 21.6   The Global Mixed Structure

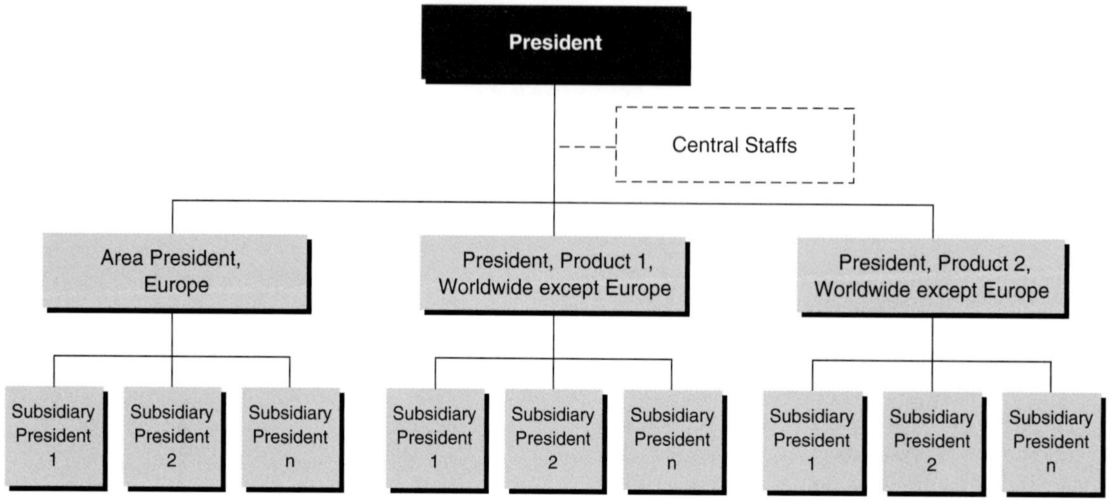

structure with eventual product groupings. However, in the long term, coordination and control across such structures become tedious.

Matrix Structure   Many multinational corporations—in an attempt to facilitate planning, organizing, and controlling interdependent businesses, critical resources, strategies, and geographic regions—have adopted the **matrix structure**.[14] Eastman Kodak shifted from a functional organization to a matrix system based on business units. Business is driven by a worldwide business unit (for example, photographic products or commercial and information systems) and implemented by a geographic unit (for example, Europe or Latin America). The geographical units, as well as their country subsidiaries, serve as the "glue" between autonomous product operations.[15]

Organizational matrices integrate the various approaches already discussed, as the Philips example in Figure 21.7 illustrates. The seven product divisions (which are then divided into 60 product groups) have rationalized manufacturing to provide products for continent-wide markets rather than lines of products for individual markets. Philips has three general types of country organizations: In "key" markets, such as the United States, France, and Japan, product divisions manage their own marketing as well as manufacturing. In "local business" countries, such as Nigeria and Peru, the organizations function as importers from product divisions, and if manufacturing occurs, it is purely for the local market. In "large" markets, such as Brazil, Spain, and Taiwan, a hybrid arrangement is used depending on the size and situation. The product divisions and the national subsidiaries interact together in a matrix-like configuration with the product divisions responsible for the globalization dimension and the national subsidiaries responsible for local representation and coordination of common areas of interest, such as recruiting. The matrix structure manager has functional, product, and resource managers reporting to him or her. The approach is based on team building and multiple command, each team specializing in its own area of expertise. It provides a mechanism for cooperation between country managers, busi-

[14]Thomas H. Naylor, "International Strategy Matrix," *Columbia Journal of World Business* 20 (Summer 1985): 11–19.

[15]"Kodak's Matrix System Focuses on Product Business Units," *Business International*, July 18, 1988, 221–223.

FIGURE 21.7 **The Global Matrix Structure at Philips**

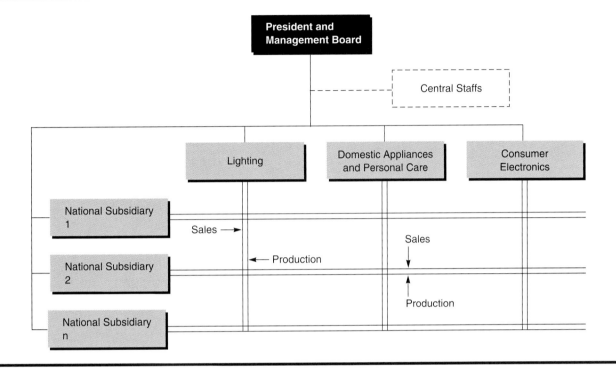

ness managers, and functional managers on a worldwide basis through increased communication, control, and attention to balance in the organization.

The matrices used vary according to the number of dimensions needed. For example, Dow Chemical's matrix is three-dimensional, consisting of six geographic areas, three major functions (marketing, manufacturing, and research), and more than 70 products. The matrix approach helps cut through enormous organizational complexities by building in a provision for cooperation among business managers, functional managers, and strategy managers. However, the matrix requires sensitive, well-trained middle managers who can cope with problems that arise from reporting to two bosses—for example, a product line manager and an area manager. For example, every management unit may have some sort of multidimensional reporting relationship, which may cross functional, regional, or operational lines. On a regional basis, group managers in Europe, for example, report administratively to a vice president of operations for Europe. But functionally, they report to group vice presidents at global headquarters.

Many companies have found the matrix structure problematic.[16] The dual reporting channel easily causes conflict; complex issues are forced into a two-dimensional decision framework; and even minor issues may have to be resolved through committee discussion. Ideally, managers should solve problems themselves through formal and informal communication; however, physical and psychic distance often make that impossible. Especially when competitive conditions require quick reaction, the matrix, with its inherent complexity, may actually lower the reaction speed of the company. As a result, the authority has started to shift in many organizations from area to product although the matrix may still officially be used.

[16]Thomas J. Peters, "Beyond the Matrix Organization," *Business Horizons* 22 (October 1979): 15–27.

FIGURE 21.8 **Evolution of International Structures**

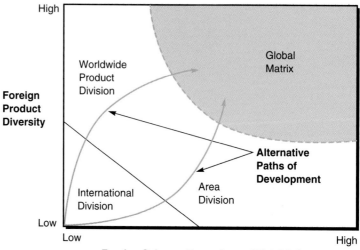

SOURCE: From Christopher A. Bartlett, "Building and Managing the Transnational: The New Organizational Challenge," in Michael E. Porter, ed., *Competition in Global Industries*. Boston: Harvard Business School Press, 1986, p. 368. Reprinted by permission of Harvard Business School from *Competition in Global Industries*, Michael E. Porter, ed. Boston: 1986, p. 368. Copyright © by the President and Fellows of Harvard College.

Evolution of Organizational Structures   Companies develop new structures in stages as their product diversity develops and the share of foreign sales increases.[17] At the first stage are autonomous subsidiaries reporting directly to top management, followed by the establishment of an international division. With increases in product diversity and in the importance of the foreign marketplace, companies develop global structures to coordinate subsidiary operations and rationalize worldwide production. As multinational corporations have faced pressures to adapt to local market conditions while trying to rationalize production and globalize competitive reaction, many have opted for the matrix structure.[18] The matrix structure probably allows a corporation to best meet the challenges of global markets: to be global and local, big and small, decentralized with centralized reporting by allowing the optimizing of businesses globally and maximizing performance in every country of operation.[19] The evolutionary process is summarized in Figure 21.8.

Implementation

Organizational structures provide the frameworks for carrying out marketing decision making. However, for marketing to be effective, a series of organizational initiatives are needed to develop marketing strategy to its full potential; that is, secure implementation of such strategies at the national level and across markets.[20]

[17]See John N. Stopford and Louis T. Wells, *Managing the Multinational Enterprise: Organization of the Firm and Ownership of the Subsidiary* (New York: Basic Books, 1972), 25; also A. D. Chandler, *Strategy and Structure* (Cambridge, MA: MIT Press, 1962), 3, and B. R. Scott, *Stages of Corporate Development* (Boston: ICCH, 1971), 2.

[18]Stanley M. Davis, "Trends in the Organization of Multinational Corporations," *Columbia Journal of World Business* 11 (Summer 1976): 59–71.

[19]William Taylor, "The Logic of Global Business," *Harvard Business Review* 68 (March–April 1990): 91–105.

[20]Ilkka A. Ronkainen, "Thinking Globally, Implementing Successfully," *International Marketing Review* 13 (Number 3, 1996): 4–6.

| **TABLE 21.1** | Levels of Coordination |

LEVEL	DESCRIPTION
5. Central control	No national structures
4. Central direction	Central functional heads have line authority over national functions
3. Central coordination	Central staff functions in coordinating role
2. Coordinating mechanisms	Formal committees and systems
1. Informal cooperation	Functional meetings: exchange of information
0. National autonomy	No coordination between decentralized units, which may even compete in export markets

Level 5 = highest; Level 0 = lowest. Most commonly found levels are 1–4.

SOURCE: Norman Blackwell, Jean-Pierre Bizet, Peter Child, and David Hensley, "Creating European Organizations That Work," *The McKinsey Quarterly* 27 (Number 2, 1991): 376.

Locus of Decision Making

Organizational structures themselves do not indicate where the authority for decision making and control rests within the organization nor will they reveal the level of co-ordination between units. The different levels of coordination between country units are summarized in Table 21.1. Once a suitable form of structure has been found, it has to be made to work.

If subsidiaries are granted a high degree of autonomy, the result is termed **decentralization.** In decentralized systems, controls are relatively loose and simple, and the flows between headquarters and subsidiaries are mainly financial; that is, each subsidiary operates as a profit center. On the other hand, if controls are tight and if strategic decision making is concentrated at headquarters, the result is termed **centralization.** Firms are typically neither totally centralized nor totally decentralized. Some functions, such as finance, lend themselves to more centralized decision making, whereas other functions, such as promotional decisions, lend themselves to far less. Research and development is typically centralized in terms of both decision making and location, especially when basic research work is involved. Partly because of governmental pressures, some companies have added R&D functions on a regional or local basis. In many cases, however, variations in decision making are product- and market-based; for example, Corning Glass Works' television tube marketing strategy requires global decision making for pricing and local decisions for service and delivery.

Allowing maximum flexibility at the country-market level takes advantage of the fact that subsidiary management knows its market and can react to changes quickly. Problems of motivation and acceptance are avoided when decision makers are also the implementors of the strategy. On the other hand, many multinational companies faced with global competitive threats and opportunities have adopted global strategy formulation, which by definition requires some degree of centralization. What has emerged as a result can be called **coordinated decentralization.** This means that over-all corporate strategy is provided from headquarters, but subsidiaries are free to implement it within the range established in consultation between headquarters and the subsidiaries.

However, moving into this new mode may raise significant challenges. Among these systemic difficulties are a lack of widespread commitment to dismantling traditional national structures, driven by an inadequate understanding of the larger, global forces at work. Power barriers—especially if the personal roles of national managers are under threat of being consolidated into regional organizations—can lead to proposals being challenged without valid reason. Finally, some organizational initiatives (such as multicultural teams or corporate chat rooms) may be jeopardized by the fact that people do not have the necessary skills (e.g., language ability) or that an infrastructure (e.g., intranet) may not exist in an appropriate format.[21]

One particular case is of special interest. Organizationally, the forces of globalization are changing the country manager's role significantly. With profit-and-loss responsibility, oversight of multiple functions, and the benefit of distance from headquarters, country managers enjoyed considerable decision-making autonomy as well as entrepreneurial initiative. Today, however, many companies have to emphasize the product dimension of the product-geography matrix, which means that the power has to shift at least to some extent from country managers to worldwide strategic business unit and product line managers. Many of the previously local decisions are now subordinated to global strategic moves. Therefore, the future country manager will have to have diverse skills (such as government relations and managing entrepreneurial teamwork) and wear many hats in balancing the needs of the operation for which the manager is directly responsible with those of the entire region or strategic business unit.[22] To emphasize the importance of the global/regional dimension in the country manager's portfolio, many companies have tied the country manager's compensation to the way the company performs globally or regionally, not just in the market for which the manager is responsible.

Factors Affecting Structure and Decision Making

The organizational structure and locus of decision making in multinational corporations are determined by a number of factors. They include (1) the degree of involvement in international operations, (2) the business(es) in which the firm is engaged (in terms, for example, of products marketed), (3) the size and importance of the markets, and (4) the human resource capability of the firm.[23]

The effect of the degree of involvement on structure and decision making was discussed earlier in the chapter. With low degrees of involvement by the parent company, subsidiaries can enjoy high degrees of autonomy as long as they meet their profit targets. The same situation can occur in even the most globally involved companies, but within a different framework. As an example, consider Philips USA, which generates 20 percent of the company's worldwide sales. Even more important, it serves a market that is on the leading edge of digital media development. Therefore, it enjoys an independent status in terms of local policy setting and managerial practices but is nevertheless within the parent company's planning and control system.

The firm's country of origin and the political history of the area can also affect organizational structure and decision making. For example, Swiss-based Nestlé, with only 3 to 4 percent of its sales in the small domestic market, has traditionally had a highly decentralized organization. Moreover, events of the past 90 years, particularly during the two world wars, have often forced subsidiaries of European-based companies to act independently in order to survive.

The type and variety of products marketed will have an effect on organizational decisions. Companies that market consumer products typically have product organizations with high degrees of decentralization, allowing for maximum local flexibility. On the other hand, companies that market technologically sophisticated products, such as General Electric's turbines, display centralized organizations with worldwide product responsibilities. Even in matrix organizations, one of the dimensions may be granted more say in decisions; for example, at Dow Chemical, geographical managers have the strongest voice.

[21]Norman Blackwell, Jean-Pierre Bizet, Peter Child, and David Hensley, "Creating European Organizations That Work," *The McKinsey Quarterly* 27 (Number 2, 1991): 376–385.

[22]John A. Quelch and Helen Bloom, "The Return of the Country Manager," *McKinsey Quarterly* 33 (Number 2, 1996): 31–43; Jon I. Martinez and John A. Quelch, "Country Managers: The Next Generation," *International Marketing Review* 13 (Number 3, 1996): 43–55.

[23]Rodman Drake and Lee M. Caudill, "Management of the Large Multinational: Trends and Future Challenges," *Business Horizons* 24 (May–June 1981): 83–91.

FIGURE 21.9 | The Networked Global Organization

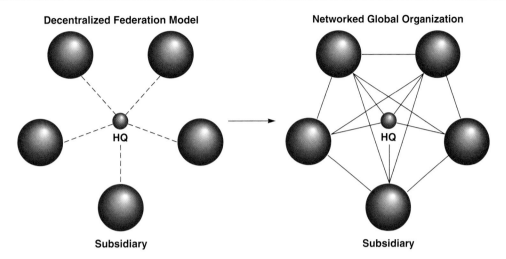

SOURCE: Thomas Gross, Ernie Turner, and Lars Cederholm, "Building Teams for Global Operations," *Management Review*, June 1987, 34.

Going global has recently meant transferring world headquarters of important business units abroad. For example, Philips has moved headquarters of several of its global business units to the United States, including taking its Digital Video Group, Optimal Storage, and Flat Panel Display activities to Silicon Valley.

Apart from situations that require the development of an area structure, the characteristics of certain markets or regions may require separate arrangements for the firm. For many Japanese and European companies, the North American market has been granted such attention with, for example, direct organizational links to top management at headquarters.

The human factor in any organization is critical. Managers both at headquarters and in the subsidiaries must bridge the physical and psychic distances separating them. If subsidiaries have competent managers who rarely need to consult headquarters about their problems, they may be granted high degrees of autonomy. In the case of global organizations, subsidiary management must understand the corporate culture because subsidiaries must sometimes make decisions that meet the long-term objectives of the firm as a whole but that are not optimal for the local market.

The Networked Global Organization

No international structure is ideal, and some have challenged the wisdom of even looking for an ideal one. They have called attention to new processes that would, in a given structure, develop new perspectives and attitudes to reflect and respond to complex demands of the opposite forces of global integration and local responsiveness.[24] Rather than a question of which structural alternative is best, the question is thus one of how best to take into account the different perspectives of various corporate entities when making decisions. In structural terms, nothing may change. As a matter of fact, Philips still has its basic matrix structure, yet major changes have occurred in internal relations. The basic change was from a decentralized federation model to a networked global organization; the effects are depicted in Figure 21.9. The term **glocal** has been coined to describe the approach.[25]

[24]Christopher Bartlett, "MNCs: Get off the Reorganization Merry-Go-Round," *Harvard Business Review* 60 (March–April 1983): 138–146.

[25]Thomas Gross, Ernie Turner, and Lars Cederholm, "Building Teams for Global Operations," *Management Review*, June 1987, 32–36.

Companies that have adopted the approach have incorporated the following three dimensions into their organizations: (1) the development and communication of a clear corporate vision, (2) the effective management of human resource tools to broaden individual perspectives and develop identification with corporate goals, and (3) the integration of individual thinking and activities into the broad corporate agenda.[26] The first dimension relates to a clear and consistent long-term corporate mission that guides individuals wherever they may work in the organization. Examples of this are Johnson & Johnson's corporate credo of customer focus and NEC's C&C (computers and communication). The second relates both to developing global managers who can find opportunities in spite of environmental challenges and to creating a global perspective among country managers. The last dimension refers to tackling the "not-invented-here" syndrome to co-opt possibly isolated, even adversarial managers into the corporate agenda.

The network avoids the problems of duplication of effort, inefficiency, and resistance to ideas developed elsewhere by giving subsidiaries the latitude, encouragement, and tools to pursue local business development within the framework of the global strategy. Headquarters considers each unit as a source of ideas, skills, capabilities, and knowledge that can be utilized for the benefit of the entire organization. This means that the subsidiaries must be upgraded from the role of implementation and adaptation to that of contribution and partnership in the development and execution of worldwide strategies. Efficient plants may be converted into international production centers, innovative R&D units may become centers of excellence (and thus role models), and leading subsidiary groups may be given a leadership role in developing new strategy for the entire corporation.

Promoting Internal Cooperation

The global marketing entity in today's environment can be successful only if it is able to move intellectual capital within the organization; i.e., take ideas and move them around faster and faster.[27]

One of the tools for moving ideas is teaching. For example, at Ford Motor Company, teaching takes three distinct forms, as shown in Table 21.2. Ford's approach is similar to those undertaken at many leading global marketing companies. The focus is on teachable points of view, i.e., an explanation of what a person knows and believes about what it takes to succeed in his or her business.[28] For example, GE's Jack Welch coined the term "boundarylessness" to describe the way people can act without regard to status or functional loyalty and look for better ideas from anywhere. Top leadership of GE spends considerable time at training centers interacting with up-and-comers from all over the company. Each training class is given a real, current company problem to solve, and the reports can be career makers (or breakers).

A number of benefits arise from this approach. A powerful teachable point of view can reach the entire company within a reasonable period by having students become teachers themselves. At PepsiCo, the CEO passed his teachable point on to 110 executives, who then passed it on to 20,000 people within 18 months. Secondly, participants in teaching situations are encouraged to maintain the international networks they develop during the sessions.

Teachers do not necessarily need to be top managers. When General Electric launched a massive effort to embrace e-commerce, many managers found that they knew little about the Internet. Following a London-based manager's idea to have an

[26]Christopher A. Bartlett and Sumantra Ghoshal, "Matrix Management: Not a Structure, a Frame of Mind," *Harvard Business Review* 68 (July–August 1990): 138–145.

[27]"See Jack. See Jack Run Europe," *Fortune*, September 27, 1999, 127–136.

[28]Noel Tichy, "The Teachable Point of View: A Primer," *Harvard Business Review* 77 (March–April 1999): 82–83.

TABLE 21.2	Teaching Programs at Ford Motor Co.		
PROGRAM	PARTICIPANTS	TEACHERS	COMPONENTS
Capstone	24 senior executives at a time	Jacques Nasser and his leadership team	■ Conducted once a year ■ About 20 days of teaching and discussion ■ Teams given six months to solve major strategic challenges ■ 360-degree feedback ■ Community service
Business Leadership Initiative	All Ford salaried employees—55,000 to date	The participants' managers	■ Three days of teaching and discussion ■ Teams assigned to 100-day projects ■ Community service ■ 360-degree feedback ■ Participants make videos that contrast the old with the new Ford
Executive Partnering	Promising young managers—12 so far	Nasser and his leadership team	■ Participants spend eight weeks shadowing seven senior executives
Let's Chat about the Business	Everyone who receives e-mail at Ford—about 100,000 employees	Nasser	■ Weekly e-mails describing Ford's new approach to business

SOURCE: Suzy Wetlaufer, "Driving Change: An Interview with Ford Motor Company's Jacques Nasser," *Harvard Business Review* 77 (March–April 1999): 76–88.

Internet mentor, GE encourages all managers to have one for a period of training each week.[29]

Another method to promote internal cooperation for global marketing implementation is the use of international teams or councils. In the case of a new product or program an international team of managers may be assembled to develop strategy. Although final direction may come from headquarters, the input has included information on local conditions, and implementation of the strategy is enhanced because local managers were involved from the beginning. This approach has worked even in cases that, offhand, would seem impossible because of market differences. Both Procter & Gamble and Henkel have successfully introduced pan-European brands for which strategy was developed by European strategy teams. These teams consisted of local managers and staff personnel to smooth eventual implementation and to avoid unnecessarily long and disruptive discussion about the fit of a new product to individual markets.

On a broader and longer-term basis, companies use councils to share **best practice,** an idea that may have saved money or time, or a process that is more efficient than existing ones. Most professionals at the leading global marketing companies are members of multiple councils.

While technology has made teamwork of this kind possible wherever the individual participants may be, technology alone may not bring about the desired results; "high-tech" approaches inherently mean "low touch," sometimes at the expense of results. Human relationships are still paramount.[30] A common purpose is what binds team members to a particular task and can only be achieved through trust, achievable through face-to-face meetings. At the start of its 777 project, Boeing brought

[29]"GE Mentoring Program Turns Underlings into Teachers of the Web," *The Wall Street Journal*, February 15, 2000, B1, B16.

[30]Richard Benson-Armer and Tsun-Yan Hsieh, "Teamwork across Time and Space," *The McKinsey Quarterly* 33 (Number 4, 1997): 18–27.

members of the design team from a dozen different countries to Everett, Washington, giving them the opportunity to work together for up to 18 months. Beyond learning to function effectively within the company's project management system, they also shared experiences that, in turn, engendered a level of trust between individuals that later enabled them to overcome obstacles raised by physical separation. The result was a design and launch in 40 percent less time than for comparable projects.

The term *network* also implies two-way communications between headquarters and subsidiaries and between subsidiaries themselves. While this communication can take the form of newsletters or regular and periodic meetings of appropriate personnel, new technologies are allowing marketers to link far-flung entities and eliminate traditional barriers of time and distance. **Intranets** integrate a company's information assets into a single and accessible system using Internet-based technologies such as e-mail, newsgroups, and the World Wide Web. For example, employees at Levi Strauss & Co. can join an electronic discussion group with colleagues around the world, watch the latest Levi's commercials, or comment on the latest marketing program or plan.[31] "Let's Chat about the Business" e-mails go out at Ford every Friday at 5 P.M. to about 100,000 employees to share as much information as possible throughout the company and encourage dialogue. In many companies, the annual videotaped greeting from management has been replaced by regular and frequent e-mails (called e-briefs at GE). The benefits of intranets are (1) increased productivity in that there is no longer lag time between an idea and the information needed to implement it; (2) enhanced knowledge capital that is constantly updated and upgraded; (3) facilitated teamwork enabling online communication at insignificant expense; and (4) incorporation of best practice at a moment's notice by allowing marketing managers and sales personnel to make to-the-minute decisions anywhere in the world.

As the discussion indicates, the networked approach is not a structural adaptation but a procedural one that requires a change in management mentality. Adjustment is primarily in the coordination and control functions of the firm. While there is still considerable disagreement as to which of the approaches works, some measures have been shown to correlate with success, as seen in *The International Marketplace 21.3*.

The Role of Country Organizations

Country organizations should be treated as a source of supply as much as they are considered a source of demand. Quite often, however, headquarters managers see their role as the coordinators of key decisions and controllers of resources and perceive subsidiaries as implementors and adapters of global strategy in their respective local markets. Furthermore, all country organizations may be seen as the same. This view severely limits the utilization of the firm's resources by not using country organizations as resources and by depriving country managers of possibilities of exercising their creativity.[32]

The role that a particular country organization can play depends naturally on that market's overall strategic importance as well as the competencies of its organization. From these criteria, four different roles emerge (see Figure 21.10).

The role of **strategic leader** can be played by a highly competent national subsidiary located in a strategically critical market. The country organization serves as a partner of headquarters in developing and implementing strategy. Procter & Gamble's Eurobrand teams, which analyze opportunities for greater product and marketing program standardization, are chaired by a brand manager from a "lead country."[33]

[31]"Internet Software Poses Big Threat to Notes, IBM's Stake in Lotus," *The Wall Street Journal*, November 7, 1995, A1–5.

[32]Christopher A. Bartlett and Sumantra Ghoshal, "Tap Your Subsidiaries for Global Reach," *Harvard Business Review* 64 (November–December 1986): 87–94.

[33]John A. Quelch and Edward J. Hoff, "Customizing Global Marketing," *Harvard Business Review* 64 (May–June 1986): 59–68.

THE INTERNATIONAL MARKETPLACE 21.3

Characteristics of Success

A SURVEY OF CHIEF EXECUTIVE OFFICERS of 43 leading U.S. consumer companies, made by McKinsey & Co., sheds light on organizational features that distinguish internationally successful companies. Companies were classified as more or less successful compared to their specific industry average, using international sales and profit growth over the 1986–1991 period as the most important indicators of success.

The survey results indicate 11 distinctive traits that are correlated with high performance in international markets. The following are moves that companies can make to enhance prospects for international success:

- Take a different approach to international decision making
- Differentiate treatment of international subsidiaries
- Let product managers in subsidiaries report to the country general manager

- Have a worldwide management development program
- Make international experience a condition for promotion to top management
- Have a more multinational management group
- Support international managers with global electronic networking capabilities
- Manage cross-border acquisitions particularly well
- Have overseas R&D centers
- Remain open to organizational change and continuous self-renewal

In general, successful companies coordinate their international decision making globally, with more central direction than less successful competitors, as seen in the following exhibit. This difference is most marked in brand positioning, package design, and price setting. The one notable exception is an increasing tendency to decentralize product development.

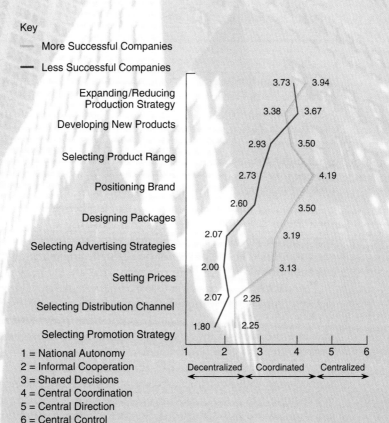

Key

— More Successful Companies

— Less Successful Companies

Expanding/Reducing Production Strategy	3.73 / 3.94
Developing New Products	3.38 / 3.67
Selecting Product Range	2.93 / 3.50
Positioning Brand	2.73 / 4.19
Designing Packages	2.60 / 3.50
Selecting Advertising Strategies	2.07 / 3.19
Setting Prices	2.00 / 3.13
Selecting Distribution Channel	2.07 / 2.25
Selecting Promotion Strategy	1.80 / 2.25

1 = National Autonomy
2 = Informal Cooperation
3 = Shared Decisions
4 = Central Coordination
5 = Central Direction
6 = Central Control

1   2   3   4   5   6
Decentralized   Coordinated   Centralized

SOURCE: Adapted from Ingo Theuerkauf, David Ernst, and Amir Mahini, "Think Local, Organize . . . ?" *International Marketing Review* 13 (Number 3, 1996): 7–12.

FIGURE	21.10	Roles for Country Organizations

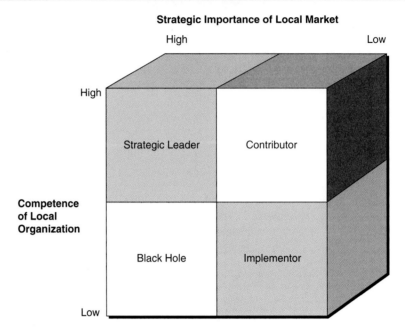

A **contributor** is a country organization with a distinctive competence, such as product development. Increasingly, country organizations are the source of new products. These range from IBM's recent breakthrough in superconductivity research, generated in its Zurich lab, to low-end innovations like Procter & Gamble's liquid Tide, made with a fabric-softening compound developed in Europe.[34] Similarly, country organizations may be assigned as worldwide centers of excellence for a particular product category, for example, ABB Strömberg in Finland for electric drives, a category for which it is a recognized world leader.[35]

The critical mass for the international marketing effort is provided by **implementors.** These country organizations may exist in smaller, less-developed countries in which corporate commitment to market development is less. Although most entities are given this role, it should not be slighted: Implementors provide the opportunity to capture economies of scale and scope that are the basis of a global strategy.

The **black hole** is a situation that the international marketer has to work out of. As an example, in strategically important markets, such as the European Union, local presence is considered necessary for maintaining the company's overall global competitiveness and, in some cases, to anticipate competitive moves in other markets. One of the major ways of exiting this position is to enter into strategic alliances. AT&T, which had long restricted itself to its domestic market, needed to go global fast. Some of the alliances it formed were with Philips in telecommunications and Olivetti in computers and office automation.[36] In some cases, firms may use their presence in a major market as an observation post to keep up with developments before a major thrust for entry is executed.

[34]Richard I. Kirkland, "Entering a New Age of Boundless Competition," *Fortune*, March 14, 1988, 18–22.

[35]"Percy Barnevik's Global Crusade," *Business Week Enterprise 1993*, 204–211.

[36]Louis Kraar, "Your Rivals Can Be Your Allies," *Fortune*, March 27, 1989, 66–76.

Depending on the role, the relationship between headquarters and the country organization will vary from loose control based mostly on support to tighter control in making sure strategies are implemented appropriately. Yet in each of these cases, it is imperative that country organizations have enough operating independence to cater to local needs and to provide motivation to the country managers. For example, an implementor should provide input in the development of a regional or a global strategy or program. Strategy formulation should ensure that appropriate implementation can be achieved at the country level.

Control

The function of the organizational structure is to provide a framework in which objectives can be met. A set of instruments and processes is needed, however, to influence the behavior and performance of organization members to meet the goals. Controls focus on actions to verify and correct actions that differ from established plans. Compliance needs to be secured from subordinates through various means of coordinating specialized and interdependent parts of the organization.[37] Within an organization, control serves as an integrating mechanism. Controls are designed to reduce uncertainty, increase predictability, and ensure that behaviors originating in separate parts of the organization are compatible and in support of common organizational goals despite physical, psychic, and temporal distances.[38]

The critical issue is the same as with organizational structure: What is the ideal amount of control? On the one hand, headquarters needs information to ensure that international activities contribute maximum benefit to the overall organization. On the other hand, controls should not be construed as a code of law and allowed to stifle local initiative.

This section will focus on the design and functions of control instruments available for the international marketer, along with an assessment of their appropriateness. Emphasis will be placed on the degree of formality of controls used.

Types of Controls

Most organizations display some administrative flexibility, as demonstrated by variations in the application of management directives, corporate objectives, or measurement systems. A distinction should be made, however, between variations that have emerged by design and those that are the result of autonomy. The one is the result of management decision, whereas the other has typically grown without central direction and is based on emerging practices. In both instances, some type of control will be exercised. Here, we are concerned only with controls that are the result of headquarters initiative rather than consequences of tolerated practices. Firms that wait for self-emerging controls often find that such an orientation may lead to rapid international growth but may eventually result in problems in areas of product-line performance, program coordination, and strategic planning.[39]

Whatever the system, it is important in today's competitive environment to have internal benchmarking. Benchmarking relays organizational learning and sharing of best practices throughout the corporate system to avoid the costs of reinventing solutions that have already been discovered. A description of the knowledge transfer process by which this occurs is provided in *The International Marketplace 21.4.*

[37]Amitai Etzioni, *A Comparative Analysis of Complex Organizations* (Glencoe, England: The Free Press, 1961), 8.

[38]William G. Egelhoff, "Patterns of Control in U.S., U.K., and European Multinational Corporations," *Journal of International Business Studies* 15 (Fall 1984): 73–83.

[39]William H. Davidson, "Administrative Orientation and International Performance," *Journal of International Business Studies* 15 (Fall 1984): 11–23.

THE INTERNATIONAL MARKETPLACE 21.4

International Best Practice Exchange

As GROWING COMPETITIVE PRESSURES challenge many global firms, strategies to improve the transfer of best practice across geographically dispersed units and time zones becomes critical. The premise is that a company with the same product range targeting the same markets pan-regionally should be able to use knowledge gained in one market throughout the organization. The fact is, however, that companies use only 20 percent of their most precious resources—knowledge, in the form of technical information, market data, internal know-how, and processes and procedures. Trying to transfer best practices internationally amplifies the problem even more.

U.K.-based copier maker Xerox (formerly Rank Xerox), with over 60 subsidiaries, is working hard to make better use of the knowledge, corporatewide. A 35-person group identified nine practices that could be applicable throughout the group. These ranged from the way the Australian subsidiary retains customers to Italy's method of gathering competitive intelligence to a procedure for handling new major accounts in Spain. These practices were thought to be easier to "sell" to other operating companies, were considered easy to implement, and would provide a good return on investment.

Three countries were much quicker in introducing new products successfully than others. In the case of France, this was related to the training given to employees. The subsidiary gave its sales staff three days of hands-on practice, including competitive benchmarking. Before they attended the course, salespeople were given reading materials and were tested when they arrived. Those remaining were evaluated again at the end of the course, and performance reports were sent to their managers.

The difficult task is to achieve buy-in from the other country organizations. Six months might be spent in making detailed presentations of the best practices to all the companies and an additional three years helping them implement the needed changes. It is imperative that the country manager is behind the proposal in each subsidiary's case. However, implementation cannot be left to the country organizations after the concept has been presented. This may result in the dilution of both time and urgency and with possible country-specific customization that negate comparisons and jeopardize the success of the change.

When half the recommendations had been adopted by half of the organization, Xerox executives were pleased with the $400 million savings. However, the company continues to face challenges, eliminating 9,000 jobs in the late '90s and another 5,200 in 2000.

SOURCE: Michael McGann, "Chase Harnesses Data with Lotus Notes," *Bank Systems and Technology* 34 (May 1997): 38; "Rank Xerox Aims at Sharing Knowledge," *Crossborder Monitor* (September 18, 1996): 8; and "World-Wise: Effective Networking Distinguishes These 25 Global Companies," *Computerworld* (August 26, 1996): 7.

http://www.rankxerox.co.uk

Three critical features are necessary in sharing best practice. First, there needs to be a device for organizational memory. For example, at Xerox, contributors to solutions can send their ideas to an electronic library where they are indexed and provided to potential adopters in the corporate family. Second, best practice must be updated and adjusted to new situations. For example, best practice adopted by the company's Chinese office will be modified and customized, and this learning should then become part of the database. Finally, best practice must be legitimized. This calls for a shared understanding that exchanging knowledge across units is valued in the organization and that these systems are important mechanisms for knowledge exchange. An assessment of how effectively employees share information with colleagues and utilize the databases can also be included in employee performance evaluations.

In the design of the control system, a major decision concerns the object of control. Two major objects are typically identified: output and behavior.[40] Output con-

---

[40]William G. Ouchi, "The Relationship between Organizational Structure and Organizational Control," *Administrative Science Quarterly* 22 (March 1977): 95–112.

TABLE 21.3	Comparison of Bureaucratic and Cultural Control Mechanisms	

| | TYPE OF CONTROL | |
OBJECT OF CONTROL	PURE BUREAUCRATIC/ FORMALIZED CONTROL	PURE CULTURAL CONTROL
Output	Formal performance reports	Shared norms of performance
Behavior	Company policies, manuals	Shared philosophy of management

SOURCE: B. R. Baliga and Alfred M. Jaeger, "Multinational Corporations: Control Systems and Delegation Issues," *Journal of International Business Studies* 15 (Fall 1984): 28.

trols consist of balance sheets, sales data, production data, product line growth, or a performance review of personnel. Measures of output are accumulated at regular intervals and forwarded from the foreign operation to headquarters, where they are evaluated and critiqued based on comparisons to the plan or budget. Behavioral controls require the exertion of influence over behavior after, or ideally before, it leads to action. This influence can be achieved, for example, by providing sales manuals to subsidiary personnel or by fitting new employees into the corporate culture.

To institute either of these measures, corporate officials must decide on instruments of control. The general alternatives are bureaucratic/formalized control or cultural control.[41] **Bureaucratic controls** consist of a limited and explicit set of regulations and rules that outline desired levels of performance. **Cultural controls,** on the other hand, are much less formal and are the result of shared beliefs and expectations among the members of an organization. A comparison of the two types of controls and their objectives is provided in Table 21.3.

Bureaucratic/Formalized Control

The elements of bureaucratic/formalized controls are (1) an international budget and planning system, (2) the functional reporting system, and (3) policy manuals used to direct functional performance. **Budgets** are short-term guidelines in such areas as investment, cash, and personnel, whereas **plans** refer to formalized long-range programs with more than a one-year horizon. The budget and planning process is the major control instrument in headquarters-subsidiary relationships. Although systems and their execution vary, the objective is to achieve the best fit possible with the objectives and characteristics of the firm and its environment.

The budgetary period is typically one year because budgets are tied to the accounting systems of the company. The budget system is used for four main purposes: (1) allocation of funds among subsidiaries; (2) planning and coordination of global production capacity and supplies; (3) evaluation of subsidiary performance; and (4) communication and information exchange between subsidiaries, product organizations, and corporate headquarters.[42] Long-range plans, on the other hand, extend over periods of two to ten years, and their content is more qualitative and judgmental in nature than that of budgets. Shorter periods, such as two years, are the norm because of the uncertainty of diverse foreign environments.

Although firms strive for uniformity, this may be comparable to trying to design a suit to fit the average person. The budget and planning processes themselves are formalized in terms of the schedules to be followed.

Functional reports are another control instrument used by multinational corporations. The reports required by headquarters from subsidiaries vary in number, amount

[41]B. R. Baliga and Alfred M. Jaeger, "Multinational Corporations: Control Systems and Delegation Issues," *Journal of International Business Studies* 15 (Fall 1984): 25–40.

[42]Laurent Leksell, *Headquarters-Subsidiary Relationships in Multinational Corporations* (Stockholm, Sweden: Stockholm School of Economics, 1981), Chapter 5.

5. One of the most efficient means of control is self-control. What type of program would you prepare for an incoming employee?

6. "Implementors are the most important country organizations in terms of buy-in for effective global marketing strategy implementation." Comment.

7. Improving internal communications is an objective for networked global organizations. Using the web site of the Lotus Development Corporation (**www.lotus.com**) and its section on solutions and success stories, outline how marketers have used Lotus Notes to interactively share information.

8. Using company and product information available on their web sites, determine why Dow (**www.dow.com**) and Siemens (**www.siemens.com**) have opted for global product/business structures for their organizations.

RECOMMENDED READINGS

Bartlett, Christopher, and Sumantra Ghoshal. *Managing across Borders*. Cambridge, MA: Harvard Business School Press, 1998.

Bartlett, Christopher, and Sumantra Ghoshal. *Transnational Management: Text, Cases, and Readings in Cross-Border Management*. New York: McGraw-Hill, 1995.

Chisholm, Rupert F. *Developing Network Organizations: Learning from Practice and Theory*. Boston: Addison-Wesley, 1997.

Davidson, William H., and Jose de la Torre. *Managing the Global Corporation*. New York: McGraw-Hill, 1989.

Ghoshal, Sumantra, and Christopher Bartlett. *The Individualized Corporation: A Fundamentally New Approach to Management*. New York: Harper Business, 1999.

Goehle, Donna D. *Decision-Making in Multinational Corporations*. Ann Arbor, MI: UMI Research Press, 1980.

Hedlund, Gunar, and Per Aman. *Managing Relationships with Foreign Subsidiaries*. Stockholm, Sweden: Mekan, 1984.

Humes, Samuel. *Managing the Multinational: Confronting the Global-Local Dilemma*. London: Prentice-Hall, 1993.

Moran, Robert T., Philip R. Harris, and William G. Stripp. *Developing the Global Organization*. Houston, TX: Gulf Publishing Co., 1993.

Negandhi, Anant R., and Martin Welge. *Beyond Theory Z*. Greenwich, CT: JAI Press, 1984.

Otterbeck, Lars, ed. *The Management of Headquarters-Subsidiary Relationships in Multinational Corporations*. Aldershot, England: Gower Publishing Company, 1981.

Pasternak, Bruce A., and Albert J. Viscio. *The Centerless Corporation: A New Model for Transforming our Organization for Growth and Prosperity*. New York: Simon and Schuster, 1998.

Pfeffer, Jeffrey, and Robert I. Sutton. *The Knowing-Doing Gap: How Smart Companies Turn Knowledge into Action*. Cambridge, MA: Harvard Business School Press, 1999.

Transforming the Global Corporation. New York: The Economist Intelligence Unit, 1994.

Amazon.com

Amazon.com opened its virtual doors in July 1995 with a mission "to use the Internet to offer products that educate, inform, and inspire." In early 1999, Amazon.com was the largest Internet-based seller of books and music and operated one of the most frequently used web sites on the Internet, offering over 4.7 million discounted books as well as CDs, DVDs, computer games, audio books, and videotapes. The company had an 85 percent share of online book sales, with over 6 million customers in more than 160 countries.

Customers use Amazon.com's interactive web site both to select and to purchase products. Specifically, customers are able to use the site to search for titles, browse selections, read and post reviews, register for personalized services, make a credit card purchase, and check order status. Most orders are shipped to customers directly from Amazon.com's warehouses, usually within 24 to 72 hours. If a customer needs to return a product, complimentary return postage is provided to the customer.

Amazon.com communicates with its customers electronically throughout the order process. A confirmation e-mail is sent to the customer when the order is received, and another when the order has been processed. Customers can then track the delivery status of orders online by using a key code number. Customers who prefer not to use a credit card on the Internet may fax or telephone in the credit card number using Amazon.com's toll-free numbers.

Amazon.com's headquarters are located in Seattle, Washington, with distribution facilities in Seattle, Delaware, Nevada, the United Kingdom, and Germany. In 1999, the firm had over 2,100 employees and was ex-

NOTE: Georgetown MBA candidates Sarah Knight, Harry Kobrak, and Paul Lewis prepared this case study under the direction of Professor Michael R. Czinkota; © Michael R. Czinkota. In addition to interviews with Amazon.com personnel, use was made of company reports and media coverage of Amazon.com.

panding rapidly. Since May 1997, Amazon.com has been publicly owned, with common stock shares traded on the NASDAQ National Market exchange in the United States. Despite persistent operating losses, Amazon.com's stock was trading at $209 a share, or 23 times its initial public offering price of $9 in December of 1998.

Major Events and Players in Its Development

The most significant player in Amazon.com's short history is its founder and chief executive officer, Jeff Bezos. With a background in computer science and finance, including fund management at Bankers Trust, Bezos decided in 1994 that the Internet could provide customers with services unavailable through traditional retailers, including discounted prices, wider selection, and greater product information.

In a November 1998 interview with *The Washington Post*, Bezos explained that he sees the success of electronic retailers as depending on their ability to analyze each customer's tastes. "If we have 4.5 million customers, we shouldn't have one store," he said. "We should have 4.5 million stores." Using its proprietary personalization technology, the Amazon.com web page greets customers by name and, through mathematical formulas that analyze a customer's purchase history, provides instant recommendations for other products to consider for purchase.

Bezos oversees seven vice presidents, a chief financial officer, chief information officer, and chief logistics officer. The CLO, Jimmy Wright, was hired in July 1998 after retiring from Wal-Mart. Wright is responsible for all global supply-chain activities, including management of distribution centers, product purchasing, distribution, and shipping.

Since its founding, Amazon.com has undergone frequent and significant changes to maintain its leadership position as an Internet firm. Among the most notable developments are:

- *May 1997* **Initial public offering** of 3 million shares of common stock. The capital generated from going public was used to pay existing debts and make future systems investments.

- *July 1997* **Multimillion-dollar advertising and promotional agreements** finalized with America Online and Excite. Similar agreements have been made with Yahoo!, Netscape, @Home, GeoCities, and AltaVista.

- *June 1998* **Expanded product line** to include music. Amazon.com now offers more than 125,000 CD titles. Through its web site, Amazon.com's customers can listen to song samples before purchasing. As of December 1998, Amazon.com stood as the Internet's largest music retailer.

- *August 1998* Purchase of **Junglee Corporation** for its comparison-shopping technology and **PlanetAll,** an address book and scheduler program for customers, for $270 million.

- *September 1998* Amazon.com **established local Internet presence in Germany and the United Kingdom** by purchasing two existing online book companies. In just three months, Amazon.com became the leading online bookseller in these markets.

Sales and Profit Record

In its four-year existence, Amazon.com has experienced explosive sales. In 1998, sales jumped to just under $610 million, a 312 percent increase from 1997 sales of $147.8 million (see Table 1 for details). Amazon.com's customer base has been building at a similar rate. In 1998 customer accounts stood at 6,700,000, a 343 percent increase from 1,510,000 in 1997.

Despite rapidly growing sales, Amazon.com continues to generate multimillion-dollar operating losses ($111.9 million in 1998, compared with $32.6 million in 1997). According to the company's 1998 10-K: "the company will continue to incur substantial operating losses for the foreseeable future and these losses may be significantly higher than our current losses." These persistent losses are due primarily to low product gross margins. The company is also making significant investments in its technological and distribution infrastructure, as well as on building brand recognition.

The Amazon.com Business Model

The Amazon.com business model creates value for customers by offering:

1. Shopping convenience (from home or office)
2. Decision-enabling information
3. Discounted pricing
4. Ease of purchase
5. A wide selection

TABLE 1   Amazon.com Financial History

	1998	1997	1996
Net Sales	$609,996	$147,787	$15,746
Cost of Sales	476,155	118,969	12,287
Gross Profit	**133,841**	**28,818**	**3,459**
Operating Expenses:			
Marketing & Sales	133,023	40,486	6,090
Product Development	46,807	13,916	2,401
General & Administrative	15,799	7,011	1,411
Merger & Acquisition-Related Costs	50,172		
Total Operating Expenses	**245,801**	**61,413**	**9,902**
Loss from Operations	**(111,960)**	**(32,595)**	**(6,443)**
Interest Income	14,053	1,901	202
Interest Expense	(26,639)	(326)	(5)
Net Interest Income	(12,586)	1,575	197
Net Loss	**$(124,546)**	**$(31,020)**	**$(6,246)**

Figures in Thousands of U.S. Dollars.

SOURCE: Amazon.com 1998 10-K report.

6. Speed, and

7. Reliability of order fulfillment

No single aspect of Amazon.com's business model is sufficient to create a competitive advantage. Locational shopping convenience, ease of purchase, and wide selection are clearly not sources of sustainable competitive advantage. Customers have long been able to order books from wide selections through catalogs or by telephone. Furthermore, decision-enabling information is available at a plethora of online sites and most public libraries. Finally, speed and reliability are clearly superior at a "real" bookstore, where one can receive the product immediately (as long as it is in stock). Thus, it is the combination of some or all of these characteristics that comprise Amazon.com's competitive advantage. As a pure retailer, which does not engage in the physical customization of the products it sells, Amazon.com creates value for customers through a series of information services and logistical processes.

Logistical Processes as a Source of Competitive Advantage

Maintaining and improving operational efficiencies is absolutely essential for Amazon.com. The ability to offer a wide selection, discounted prices, speed and reliability are all tied directly to the company's logistical competencies.

In a bid to simultaneously improve its margins and increase price discounts, Amazon.com is attempting to purchase more product directly from publishers. The firm hopes to increase the mid-40 percent discounts received from wholesalers to the mid-50 percent rates available from publishers. Circumventing wholesalers would also enable the company to shorten shipping times.

Between 1996 and 1998, Amazon.com increased its Seattle warehouse space by 70 percent and built a new warehouse in Delaware. It also began leasing a highly mechanized distribution facility in Fernley, Nevada. These recent investments in material handling systems, together with the increases in warehouse capacity, are expected to result in a six- to eightfold improvement in throughput within one year. Currently, Amazon.com ships 20 percent of books on the day they are ordered and aims to raise that rate to 95 percent. This is a staggering logistical challenge as the company stocks over 700,000 copies of approximately 200,000 titles.

Despite Amazon.com's focus on improving operational efficiencies, industry analysts are sharply divided on whether the company's logistical processes are truly competitive. J. Cohen at Merrill Lynch Capital Markets observed that:

> [Amazon.com] is not large enough (in terms of order volumes and distribution infrastructure) to generate the economies of scale necessary to compete effectively with large physical-world retail chains. At the same time, Amazon.com is far too large in terms of the cost structure (associated with its proprietary inventory and distribution systems) to compete effectively with companies that forego that structure and provide a linkage with existing distributors.

Amazon.com's disadvantages in scale relative to traditional booksellers, such as Barnes and Noble, are apparent. It is important to note that in 1998, Internet book sales accounted for approximately $300 million, slightly less than 1 percent of the U.S. market. Despite the expectation that Internet book sales will double in 1999, national retailers will retain massive scale economies. Furthermore, both Borders and Barnes and Noble have web sites, which are expected to grow with the market (or faster). Barnes and Noble, which formed a strategic alliance with the German media conglomerate Bertelsmann, has direct relationships with some 20,000 publishers and distributors. In addition, Barnes and Noble's state-of-the-art distribution center has roughly 750,000 titles available for same-day shipping.

Building Brand Equity

Amazon.com has steadily increased its spending on advertising and promotion both in absolute terms and as a percentage of revenue. Between 1996 and 1998, Amazon.com spent roughly one-quarter of its sales on advertising and promotion. The company invested in promotional relationships with both the domestic and international sites of America Online, Excite, and Yahoo!.

Amazon.com's efforts to build brand equity through its extensive advertising and promotion have received mixed reviews from industry analysts. One Merrill Lynch analyst criticized Amazon.com's attempt to develop brand equity, questioning its value for the distributor of commodity products, such as books:

> We do not believe that online commodity product sales produce the sort of brand equity generated by the distribution of proprietary information or media products. The implication here is that while it may make economic sense for Yahoo! to lose money while building a user population, it probably does not make sense for Amazon.com to follow the same path.

Although advertising and promotion are extremely important to a growing business, it is doubtful brand equity alone will be enough to gain new customers and retain old ones if competitors with superior logistical systems and identical products enter the market. This increases the importance of Amazon.com's value-added information services to customers.

Value-Added Information Services

Amazon.com is strongly focused on achieving value-added differentiation through customer-oriented information services. Perhaps the most important information service Amazon.com provides is a comprehensive online catalog, which enables customers to search for books or CDs. Amazon.com's proprietary software will also track individual customer orders and subsequently recommend titles of a similar genre or related subject matter. Thus, Amazon.com's site provides automated customization for users. Jeff Bezos, the founder and CEO, has a vivid vision for how this technology will be used:

> Personalization is like retreating to the time when you have small-town merchants who got to know you, and they could help you get the right products. The right products can improve your life, and the wrong products detract from it. Before the era of mass merchandising, it used to be that most things were personalized. The promise of . . . customization is . . . you get the economies of mass merchandising and the individuality of 100-years-ago merchandising.

In addition to retaining customer preferences, the system retains customer purchase information, eliminating the need for repeat customers to reenter the same address and billing information. This is an extremely powerful tool and may represent a strong incumbency advantage. For example, in the fourth quarter of 1997, Amazon.com's automated system captured information for over 1.5 million customers, including e-mail address, mailing address, credit card number, and the products they purchased (including various classifications such as genre or topic). Unless a customer objects, Amazon.com reserves the right to utilize—or even possibly sell—this information.

Repeat customers account for approximately 60 percent of Amazon.com's orders and this proportion appears to be growing. This statistic *may* indicate a high level of customer satisfaction. However, it could merely indicate customers' lack of awareness of Amazon.com's new online competitors, such as barnesandnoble.com. In the Barnes and Noble and Bertelsmann joint venture announced in late 1998, both companies pledged to invest $100 million in expanding barnesandnoble.com's U.S. sales (compared to $20 million for the Barnes and Noble superstores). This will lessen the incumbency advantage of brand awareness. Amazon.com will be under pressure to provide a higher level of value-added differentiation in customer service. Ultimately, Amazon.com's market success depends on its ability to maintain and grow its customer base by knowing and serving its customers better than its competitors.

International Activities

Amazon.com began direct exporting almost immediately after its inception in 1995. Preliminary exports could be described as reactive, as the company's first international customers sought out Amazon.com rather than vice versa. Early on, international orders were more concentrated in nonfiction technological and computer-oriented publications, although that customer base soon diversified. Amazon.com's international orders now follow a similar pattern to domestic orders, with customer interest in a wide range of subject matter.

Amazon.com currently sells to over 160 countries and is aggressively pursuing international sales through direct exporting as well as local overseas presence. In 1998 Amazon.com established a local presence in the United Kingdom and Germany by purchasing two existing online book companies, Telebook and BookPages. Amazon.com is currently the largest online retailer in these markets. The European subsidiaries have been set up to serve the entire EU market and have currency and shipping procedures in place. These efforts, as part of Amazon.com's international strategy, appear to be paying off; in 1998, about 20 percent of Amazon.com's sales were from international customers.

Despite the fact that Amazon.com exports to such a high number of countries, the company is still in the process of establishing an international presence. Amazon.com is continually increasing its efforts to reach out to international customers. As the company explained in its 1997 annual report:

> [Amazon.com] has only limited experience in sourcing, marketing, and distributing products on an international basis and in developing localized versions of its Web site and other systems. The Company expects to incur significant costs in establishing international facilities and operations, in promoting its brand internationally, in developing localized versions of its Web site and other systems, and in sourcing, marketing, and distributing products in foreign markets.

Amazon.com's use of regional interfaces adds a third layer to its international business activities. The cornerstone of Amazon.com's approach to international business is to leverage its existing systems and routines to serve all of its customers, regardless of location. The regional interfaces allow most of Amazon.com's customers to use their own language. Standardized algorithms and routines provide the same automated personalized services to international customers.

Continuing to expand local overseas operations, according to CEO Jeff Bezos, is the only way Amazon.com can stay competitive in the face of growing international competition. As in the U.S. market, Amazon.com has strong, albeit relatively new, competitors in the international marketplace. This competition increased considerably when in the fall of 1998, Bertelsmann agreed to purchase half of the interest in barnesandnoble.com for $200 million. Both Bertelsmann and Barnes and Noble plan to invest heavily in expanding barnesandnoble.com's international business.

The partnership between Bertelsmann and Barnes and Noble thus far does not appear to be hurting Amazon.com's international or domestic sales. Nonetheless, Media Metrix, a company that measures traffic on the Internet, calculates that the number of people visiting barnesandnoble.com's site is skyrocketing. As research shows that online customers like to browse for six months or longer before buying, Barnes and Noble is hoping that its domestic and international sales will soon pick up.

Amazon.com uses global merchant agreements with other Internet-based companies to promote the company internationally. In September 1998, Yahoo! Inc. agreed to place Amazon.com merchant links on its international sites, including those in Asia, UK and Ireland, France, Germany, Denmark, Sweden, Norway, Canada, Australia and New Zealand, Japan, and Korea. According to David Risher, senior vice president at Amazon.com: "This agreement with Yahoo!, combined with our local presence in Germany and the United Kingdom, strengthens our position around the world as a leading global book merchant." Similar agreements have been established with other popular Internet web sites including Netscape, @Home, GeoCities, and AltaVista.

Like its domestic customers, Amazon.com's international customers select and purchase products through the company's U.S. or European web pages. There are several foreign language versions, including Japanese, Dutch, French, Italian, Portuguese, German, and Spanish. The majority of Amazon.com's international customers pay with a credit card, such as Visa, MasterCard, and JB. International customers are required to bear all customs and duty charges.

For shipping, Amazon.com gives its customers a choice of international mail (estimated time of 7–21 business days with a minimum shipping and handling charge of $12.95) or DHL Worldwide Express International (1–4 business days with a minimum charge of $35.95). Amazon.com has been actively working to reduce the delivery times and shipping costs for its international (as well as its domestic) customers. The establishment of local distribution centers in Germany and the UK significantly reduces both delivery lead times and shipping costs for customers, and thus brings Amazon.com closer to its customers, both physically and psychologically.

 ## Export Complaint Management

Amazon.com prides itself on superior service for both its international and domestic customers. The company has seen superior customer service and in particular complaint management as a key point of differentiation and therefore a source of competitive advantage. Amazon.com believes its international customers are "quite happy" with the level of service they have received.

One key to the quality of service is a high degree of responsiveness from Amazon.com's customer service department. Customer service representatives in the Seattle, Washington headquarters handle complaints from both domestic and international customers. These representatives are given a great deal of authority to resolve customer complaints. As Amazon.com's Customer Service Manager explained, complaints are rarely elevated to higher level managers:

> Most things are caught on the first shot. Escalations occur if a customer is not satisfied with a response, or if there is a complex issue such as large quantities or a complex billing issue like suspected fraud. Non-English phone or e-mail messages are escalated—e-mail is escalated mostly for tracking purposes since [it is usually] obvious what the customer needs from the e-mail message. Obviously, phone calls are more difficult if English is not spoken at all.

 ## Training for Customer Satisfaction

Training is vital to ensure Amazon.com can run a highly responsive customer service program. Founder and CEO Bezos emphasizes the importance of developing people with the term "people bandwidth." Bezos describes people bandwidth as "smart people, working hard, passionately and smartly." With huge numbers of investors eager to purchase a stake in Amazon.com, Bezos claims that the real constraint on the company's growth is not capital, but people. The CEO's comments provide insight into the strategic importance the company places on training. Amazon.com's Customer Service Manager described how the training process certifies representatives at different levels on an ongoing basis to respond quickly to customer needs:

> Classroom and on-the-job training and mentoring are all utilized. There is follow-up training to advance to the next skill/task level and review training on any new products or business processes. We also keep a pretty extensive intranet for reference.

Within the standard training curriculum, Amazon.com's customer service representatives also receive special training in how to correspond with international customers.

Communicating with Overseas Customers

As its business is based on the Internet, the majority of Amazon.com's international customers communicate via e-mail. Some customers choose to complain by telephone, although toll-free numbers are offered only domestically. The benchmark for answering e-mails is 100 percent within 24 hours or less. Customer service response routines are designed to be predictive, automated, and efficient.

Most international customers complain in English or Spanish, but customer service representatives are equipped to handle complaints in other languages. In fact, Amazon.com claims to have representatives conversant in 19 languages. These include all the major European languages, as well as Japanese, Chinese, Korean, Vietnamese, Thai, Hebrew, Zulu, Swazi, and Hausa.

Export Complaints and Resolution Policies

The most frequent complaints from international customers center on distribution problems. This is not surprising, given the long lead times and high shipping costs Amazon.com's international customers must endure. As a result, customers are dissatisfied if their purchases arrive later than expected, or if their order is never received. According to Amazon.com's customer service department, the quantity of complaints are similar for domestic and overseas customers.

There is no separate department at Amazon.com to deal with overseas complaints. Within this organizational structure, customer service representatives must rely largely on standardized routines and protocol for interacting with customers. As a heuristic, customer service representatives are taught to mirror the tone and formality of their e-mail to the complaint they receive. Amazon.com's standard methods for placating dissatisfied international customers include a range of remedies that are designed to cost-effectively maintain customer goodwill. These remedies include:

1. Upgraded or complimentary shipping
2. Free replacements for lost or damaged items
3. Allowing customers to donate to charity a book delivered late or incorrectly where return shipping is not cost effective

Amazon.com tracks customer complaints through regular internal management reports. Complaints are routinely used to make continuous improvements to the shipping, billing, and order taking processes. Also, other departments, including Website Software, Product Development, and Marketing use customer service reports to make continuous improvements to their operating processes.

QUESTIONS FOR DISCUSSION

1. Approximately a quarter of Amazon.com's sales are to overseas customers. How could Amazon.com structure its customer service department to better serve an increasingly international and culturally and linguistically diverse customer base? Should Amazon.com have "country specialists" for markets where it lacks an overseas presence?

2. How should Amazon.com address the two key areas of export complaints—long distribution times and high shipping costs? Although Amazon.com's existing international expansion strategy has emphasized in-house ownership of warehousing and inventory, potential arrangements with specialized third parties are an alternative model. Is the outsourcing of warehousing and inventory management consistent with their existing business model?

3. How could Amazon.com better measure customer service? How could the customer service manager implement a continuous improvement process? What companies would you benchmark and how?

Benetton

Benetton, the Italian manufacturer of sportswear, has been in the center of controversy ever since its "United Colors" campaigns were launched in 1985 to symbolize the marketer's "commitment to racial and multicultural harmony."

Benetton has 6,300 stores around the world and sales of $1.5 billion, with a total marketing budget of $78 million. It has been one of the most dynamic marketing entities of the last decade. But it has been the company's advertising that has cemented its reputation as an offbeat, socially conscious firm.

In the fall of 1991, Benetton launched a new series of ads, created in-house, which included a priest kissing a nun; a placenta-covered newborn baby with an umbilical cord still attached; and what the company calls an "angelic" white girl and a "dark and mysterious" black boy, replete with devilish horns. The campaign was intended for 92 countries to constitute the majority of countries' promotional efforts. For example, the $3.5 million U.S. magazine campaign represented half of Benetton's local budget. "It's fair to say that this is the most provocative campaign we have ever mounted," said Peter Fressola, director of communications for Benetton Services Corp., the company's U.S. marketing arm. "The images are more provocative, and there seem to be more of them."

Although previous campaigns showing black and white men handcuffed together and a black woman breast-feeding a white baby had generated publicity, the storm broke with the most recent series of ads.

After the effort was launched, various governmental and industry bodies in the United Kingdom, France, Germany, Italy, and Ireland asked Benetton to withdraw the campaign. For example, in the United Kingdom, the Advertising Standards Authority (ASA) formally asked Benetton to stop using outdoor boards showing the newborn.

In the United States, magazine publishers refused to run some or all of the campaign. *Self* and *YM* rejected the priest/nun combo; *Cosmopolitan*, *Elle*, and *Child* all passed on the newborn ad; and *Essence*, *YM*, and *Child* passed on the angel/devil ad. "We rejected the ads because being a book geared to the younger market, I think the spotlight is put on us a little more than the adult books," said Alex Mironovich, publisher of teen magazine *YM*. "I am Catholic and I was not offended by the priest kissing the nun, but I have to recognize that religion is very powerful in a lot of people's lives."

In the letter rejecting the newborn ad, Mary Anne Sommers, publisher of *Child*, wrote, "Birth is still an extremely private and personal subject for Americans . . . and there was a strong likelihood the ad would not be favorably received by a good portion of our readers." She also rejected the angel/devil ad, contending the image "will be perceived by our readers as reinforcing, rather than helping to eliminate, negative racial stereotypes." Benetton and its agency, J. Walter Thompson, offered two ads to each magazine but said if one or both were rejected, they would not be replaced by others.

At Benetton, the response was that of surprise. "We were very surprised by this general hysteria created by the new campaign," said Laura Pollini, Benetton's spokesperson in the United Kingdom. In the United States, Peter Fressola denied that there was any attempt to stir trouble. The creator of the ads, Oliviero Toscani, was astonished

SOURCE: This case was prepared by Ilkka A. Ronkainen. It is largely based on "Heart-to-Heart (to Heart)," *Advertising Age*, March 18, 1996, 4; "Benetton: The Next Era," *Economist*, April 23, 1994, 68; "Benetton on Bosnia," *The Washington Post*, February 16, 1994, C3; "Benettonin Shokkimainosta Paheksutaan," *Iltasanomat*, February 4, 1992, A14; Eleana Bowes, "Benetton Forges Ahead," *Advertising Age*, September 9, 1991, 14; and Gary Levin, "Benetton Gets the Kiss-Off," *Advertising Age*, July 22, 1991, 1, 40. *For a gallery of Benetton ads, see* http://www.benetton.com.

by the reaction to the campaign. The newborn ad is a documentary-style bit of "ultra-reality," he said, and there is "nothing sinful" about a priest and a nun kissing. "I take pictures, I don't sell clothes." Benetton expressed its confidence in Toscani and vowed not to interfere with his provocative style.

In 1992, Benetton used a picture of a man who had three minutes earlier died of AIDS in its newest worldwide campaign. The ASA recommended that publishers in the United Kingdom boycott the campaign. In early 1994, Benetton made waves throughout the world with its new ad featuring the blood-soaked clothes of a soldier killed in Bosnia. The photo, which shows a white T-shirt pierced by a bullet hole, as well as a pair of combat trousers, is part of a $15 million campaign in newspapers and on billboards in 110 countries. Immediately, five publications in France, including *Le Monde* and *Le Figaro*, and Germany's *Frankfurter Allgemeine Zeitung* refused to publish the ad. The Vatican newspaper *L'Osservatore Romano* denounced the ad, calling it "a horrendous poster that has managed to make a mockery even of death." In

the United States, many newspapers, such as *The Washington Post*, ran the ad. Benetton's reaction was as unique as expected. The company spokesperson was not optimistic about the campaign's ability to boost retail sales, saying, however, "if we were trying to sell T-shirts, there probably wouldn't be a worse way of doing it."

In 1996, Benetton launched a campaign created inhouse that featured three hearts. At the same time, the company launched its own web site (**www.benetton.com**), offering a review of its past campaigns and a sneak preview of its upcoming global campaign.[1] The campaign prompted the ASA to issue an immediate Ad Alert, urging newspapers and magazines to contact it for advice before accepting the ad. The advice would depend on the publication's target audience.

More controversy erupted with Benetton's 2000 advertising campaign, which featured prisoners on death row. The ASA received 144 complaints about the ads, and Sears, Roebuck banned sales of Benetton USA apparel in reaction to the advertisement.

QUESTIONS FOR DISCUSSION

1. Do shock and publicity value fit in with global advertising campaigns?
2. Is Benetton facing a crisis in various country markets, or will it benefit from the outcry?

3. Are there ways in which the social message of Benetton could be conveyed in a less-provocative manner?

---

[1]For additional information, see **http://www.benetton.com**.

Parker Pen Company

Parker Pen Company, the manufacturer of writing instruments based in Janesville, Wisconsin, is one of the world's best-known companies in its field. It sells its products in 154 countries and considers itself number one in "quality writing instruments," a market that consists of pens selling for $3 or more.

In early 1984, the company launched a global marketing campaign in which everything was to have "one look, one voice," and with all planning to take place at headquarters. Everything connected with the selling effort was to be standardized. This was a grand experiment of a widely debated concept. A number of international companies were eager to learn from Parker's experiences.

Results became evident quickly. In February 1985, the globalization experiment was ended, and most of the masterminds of the strategy either left the company or were fired. In January 1986, the writing division of Parker Pen was sold for $100 million to a group of Parker's international managers and a London venture-capital company. The U.S. division was given a year to fix its operation or close.

 ## Globalization

Globalization is a business initiative based on the conviction that the world is becoming more homogeneous and that distinctions between national markets are not only fading but, for some products, they will eventually disappear. Some products, such as Coca-Cola and Levi's, have already proven the existence of universal appeal. Coke's "one sight, one sound, one sell" approach is a legend in the world of global marketers. Other companies have some products that can be "world products," and some that cannot and

should not be. For example, if cultural and competitive differences are less important than their similarities, a single advertising approach can exploit these similarities to stimulate sales everywhere, and at far lower cost than if campaigns were developed for each individual market.

Compared with the multidomestic approach, globalization differs in these three basic ways:

1. The global approach looks for similarities between markets. The multidomestic approach ignores similarities.
2. The global approach actively seeks homogeneity in products, image, marketing, and advertising message. The multidomestic approach produces unnecessary differences from market to market.
3. The global approach asks, "Should this product or process be for world consumption?" The multidomestic approach, relying solely on local autonomy, never asks the question.

Globalization requires many internal modifications as well. Changes in philosophy concerning local autonomy, concern for local operating results rather than corporate performance, and local strategies designed for local—rather than global—competitors are all delicate issues to be solved. By design, globalization calls for centralized decision making; therefore, the "not-invented-here" syndrome becomes a problem. This can be solved by involving those having to implement the globalization strategy at every possible stage as well as keeping lines of communication open.[1]

 ## Globalization at Parker Pen Company

In January 1982, James R. Peterson became the president and CEO of Parker Pen. At that time, the company was struggling, and global marketing was one of the key

SOURCE: This case was prepared by Ilkka A. Ronkainen for discussion purposes and not to exemplify correct or incorrect decision making. The case draws facts from Joseph M. Winski and Laurel Wentz, "Parker Pen: What Went Wrong?" *Advertising Age*, June 2, 1986, 1, 60–61, 71; and Lori Kesler, "Parker Rebuilds a Quality Image," *Advertising Age*, March 21, 1988, 49.

[1]Laurence Farley, "Going Global: Choices and Challenges," presented at the American Management Association Conference, June 10, 1985, Chicago, Illinois.

measures to be used to revive the company. While at R. J. Reynolds, Peterson had been impressed with the industry's success with globalization. He wanted for Parker Pen nothing less than the writing instrument equivalent of the Marlboro man.

For most of the 1960s and 1970s, a weak dollar had lulled Parker Pen into a false sense of security. About 80 percent of the company's sales were abroad, which meant that when local currency profits were translated into dollars, big profits were recorded.

The market was changing, however. The Japanese had started marketing inexpensive disposable pens with considerable success through mass marketers. Brands such as Paper Mate, Bic, Pilot, and Pentel each had greater sales, causing Parker's overall market share to plummet to 6 percent. Parker Pen, meanwhile, stayed with its previous strategy and continued marketing its top-of-the-line pens through department stores and stationery stores. Even in this segment, Parker Pen's market share was eroding because of the efforts of A. T. Cross Company and Montblanc of Germany.

Subsidiaries enjoyed a high degree of autonomy in marketing operations, which resulted in broad and diverse product lines and 40 different advertising agencies handling the Parker Pen account worldwide.

When the dollar's value skyrocketed in the 1980s, Parker's profits plunged and the loss of market share became painfully evident.

Peterson moved quickly upon his arrival. He trimmed the payroll, chopped the product line to 100 (from 500), consolidated manufacturing operations, and ordered an overhaul of the main plant to make it a state-of-the-art facility. Ogilvy & Mather was hired to take sole control of Parker Pen advertising worldwide. The logic behind going with one agency instead of the 40 formerly employed was cost savings and the ability to coordinate strategies on a worldwide basis. Among the many agencies terminated was Lowe Howard-Spink in London, which had produced some of the best advertising for Parker Pen's most profitable subsidiary. The immediate impact was a noticeable decline in employee morale and some expressed bitterness at the subsidiary being dictated to by a subsidiary that had been cross-subsidizing the American operations over the years.

A decision was also made to go aggressively after the low end of the market. The company would sell an upscale line called Premier, mainly as a positioning device. The biggest profits were to come from a roller-ball pen called Vector, selling for $2.98. Plans were drawn to sell an even cheaper pen called Itala—a disposable pen never thought possible at Parker.

Three new managers, to be known as Group Marketing, were brought in. All three had extensive marketing experience, most of it in international markets. Richard Swart, who became marketing vice president for

writing instruments, had handled 3M's image advertising worldwide and taught company managers the ins and outs of marketing planning. Jack Marks became head of writing instruments advertising. At Gillette, he had orchestrated the worldwide marketing of Silkience hair care products. Carlos Del Nero, brought in to be Parker's manager of global marketing planning, had gained broad international experience at Fisher-Price. The concept of marketing by centralized direction was approved.

The idea of selling pens the same way everywhere did not sit well with many Parker subsidiaries and distributors. Pens were indeed the same, but markets, they believed, were different: France and Italy fancied expensive fountain pens; Scandinavia was a ballpoint market. In some markets, Parker could assume an above-the-fray stance; in others it had to get into the trenches and compete on price. Nonetheless, headquarters communicated to them all:

> Advertising for Parker Pens (no matter model or mode) will be based on a common creative strategy and positioning. The worldwide advertising theme, "Make Your Mark With Parker," has been adopted. It will utilize similar graphic layout and photography. It will utilize an agreed-upon typeface. It will utilize the approved Parker logo/design. It will be adapted from centrally supplied materials.

Swart insisted that the directives were to be used only as "starting points" and that they allowed for ample local flexibility. The subsidiaries perceived them differently. The U.K. subsidiary, especially, fought the scheme all the way. Ogilvy & Mather London strongly opposed the "one world, one brand, one advertisement" dictum. Conflict arose, with Swart allegedly shouting at one of the meetings: "Yours is not to reason why; yours is to implement." Local flexibility in advertising was out of the question (see Figure 1).

The London-created "Make Your Mark" campaign was launched in October 1984. Except for language, it was essentially the same: long copy, horizontal layout, illustrations in precisely the same place, the Parker logo at the bottom, and the tag line or local equivalent in the lower right-hand corner. Swart once went to the extreme of suggesting that Parker ads avoid long copy and use just one big picture.

Problems arose on the manufacturing side. The new $15 million plant broke down repeatedly. Costs soared, and the factory turned out defective products in unacceptable numbers. In addition, the new marketing approach started causing problems as well. Although Parker never abandoned its high-end position in foreign markets, its concentration on low-priced, mass distribution products in the United States caused dilution of its image and ultimately losses of $22 million in 1985. Conflict was evident internally, and the board of directors began to turn against the concept of globalization.

In January 1985, Peterson resigned. Del Nero left the company in April; Swart was fired in May, Marks in June.

FIGURE 1 Ads for Parker's Global Campaign

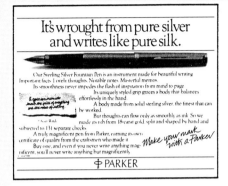

When Michael Fromstein became CEO of the company, he assembled the company's country managers in Janesville and announced: "Global marketing is dead. You are free again."

QUESTIONS FOR DISCUSSION

1. Should the merits of global marketing be judged by what happened at Parker Pen Company?
2. Was the globalization strategy sound for writing instruments? If yes, what was wrong in the implementation? If not, why not?
3. What marketing miscalculations were made by the advocates of the globalization effort at Parker Pen?
4. The task is to "fix it or close it." What should be done?

Nova Scotia

The U.S. Market for Canadian Travel Services

The more than 12 million Americans who travel to Canada annually constitute 42 percent of all departures from the United States. The U.S. market is of crucial importance to the Canadian tourism industry because 95 percent of all tourists are Americans, who spend approximately $2.7 billion a year on these trips.

The 1980s witnessed a major escalation in campaigns that try to lure tourists to a particular state or foreign country. Tourism areas spent over $100 million in U.S. media annually in the 1980s, and the level is expected to grow considerably in the 1990s. Tourism Canada, the government tourist organization, in 1986 launched a campaign with the theme "Come to the world next door" as an umbrella campaign for Canada as a whole. The provinces conduct their own independent campaigns to segments they deem most attractive and profitable. For example, ads for Manitoba are mostly written for the outdoor vacationer.

TABLE 1 Benefit Segments of U.S. Travelers to Canada

Segment I: Friends and relatives—nonactive visitor (29 percent). These vacationers seek familiar surroundings where they can visit friends and relatives. They are not very inclined to participate in any activity.

Segment II: Friends and relatives—active city visitor (12 percent). These vacationers also seek familiar surroundings where they can visit friends and relatives, but they are more inclined to participate in activities—especially sightseeing, shopping, and cultural and other entertainment.

Segment III: Family sightseers (6 percent). These vacationers are looking for a new vacation place that would be a treat for the children and an enriching experience.

Segment IV: Outdoor vacationer (19 percent). These vacationers seek clean air, rest and quiet, and beautiful scenery. Many are campers, and availability of recreation facilities is important. Children are also an important factor.

Segment V: Resort vacationer (19 percent). These vacationers are most interested in water sports (for example, swimming) and good weather. They prefer a popular place with a big-city atmosphere.

Segment VI: Foreign vacationer (26 percent). These vacationers look for a place they have never been before with a foreign atmosphere and beautiful scenery. Money is not of major concern but good accommodation and service are. They want an exciting, enriching experience.

SOURCE: Shirley Young, Leland Ott, and Barbara Feigin, "Some Practical Considerations in Market Segmentation," *Journal of Marketing Research* 15 (August 1978): 405–412.

SOURCE: This case was written by Arch G. Woodside and Ilkka A. Ronkainen for discussion purposes and not to exemplify correct or incorrect decision making. The case is largely based on Arch G. Woodside, "Positioning a Province Using Travel Research," *Journal of Travel Research* 20 (Winter 1982): 2–6. For additional information, please see http://www.gov.ns.ca.

The Canadian Government Office of Tourism (CGOT) sponsored a large-scale benefit-segmentation study of the American market for pleasure travel to Canada, the results of which are summarized in Table 1. Segmenting the market by benefits provides many advantages over other methods. Segmenting by attitude toward Canada or by geographic area would be feasible if substantial variation occurred. This is not the case, however. Segmenting by benefits reveals what consumers were and are seeking in their vacations. Knowing this is central to planning effective marketing programs.

A Benefit-Matching Model

Table 2 summarizes a strategic view for understanding tourism behavior and developing a marketing campaign. The model emphasizes the dominant need to define markets by benefits sought and the fact that separate markets seek unique benefits or activity packages. Membership in the segments will fluctuate from year to year; the same individuals may seek rest and relaxation one year and foreign adventure the next.

Identifying benefits is not enough, however. Competition (that is, other countries or areas) may present the same type of benefits to the consumers. Because travelers seriously consider only a few destinations, a sharp focus is needed for promoting a destination. This also means that a destination should avoid trying to be "everything to everybody" by promoting too many benefits. Combining all of these concerns calls for positioning, that is, generating a unique, differentiated image in the mind of the consumer.

Three destinations are shown in Table 2. Each destination provides unique as well as similar benefits for travelers. Marketers have the opportunity to select one or two specific benefits from a set of benefits when developing a marketing program to attract visitors. The benefits selected for promotion can match or mismatch the benefits sought by specific market segments. The letters S, M, and N in the table express the degree of fit between the benefits provided and those sought. For example, a mismatch is promoting the wrong benefit to the wrong market, such as promoting the scenic mountain beauty of North Carolina to Tennessee residents.

The Case of Nova Scotia

Nova Scotia is one of ten provinces and two territories that make up Canada. Given its location, it is known as Canada's Ocean Playground (see Figure 1). For many Nova Scotians the sea is their main source of livelihood and leisure. For 200 years the sea has played an integral role in the history and economy of the province (see Table 3). It was the abundant fisheries that drew settlers into the area. Today, many of their descendants work in a variety of professions related to the water, including tourism. The importance of tourism has increased with both the mining and fishing sectors having difficulties from their resources drying up. Total tourism receipts exceed $800 million and over 30,000 workers are employed directly and in spin-off jobs. More than a million people visit the province every year, with almost a quarter of these coming from outside of Canada, mainly the United States.

Canada as a whole has a rather vague and diffused image among Americans. This is particularly true of the Atlantic provinces. The majority of Nova Scotia's nonresident travelers reside in New England and the mid-Atlantic states of New York, Pennsylvania, and New Jersey. Most of these travelers include households with married couples having incomes substantially above the U.S. national average, that is, $50,000 and above. Such households represent a huge, accessible market—10 million households that are one to two and a half days' drive from Halifax, the capital. Most households in this market have not visited the Atlantic provinces and have no plans to do so. Thus, the market exhibits three of the four requirements necessary to be a very profitable customer base for the province: size, accessibility, and purchasing power. The market lacks the intention to visit for most of the households described. Nova Scotia is not one of the destinations considered when the next vacation or pleasure trip is being planned. Worse still, Nova Scotia does not exist in the minds of its largest potential market.

In the past, Nova Scotia had a number of diverse marketing themes, such as "Good times are here," "International gathering of the clans," "The 375th anniversary of Acadia," "Seaside spectacular," and the most recent, "There's so much to sea" (see Figure 2). These al-

TABLE	2	Benefit-Matching Model			

MARKETS	BENEFITS SOUGHT	BENEFIT MATCH	BENEFITS PROVIDED	DESTINATIONS
A ⟶	A_s, B_s ⟶	S ⟵	A_p, B_p ⟵	X
B ⟶	B_s, C_s ⟶	M ⟵	C_p, D_p ⟵	Y
C ⟶	C_s, D_s ⟶	N ⟵	E_p, F_p ⟵	Z

SOURCE: Arch G. Woodside, "Positioning a Province Using Travel Research," *Journal of Travel Research* 20 (Winter 1982): 3.

FIGURE 1   Nova Scotia and Its Main Travel Markets

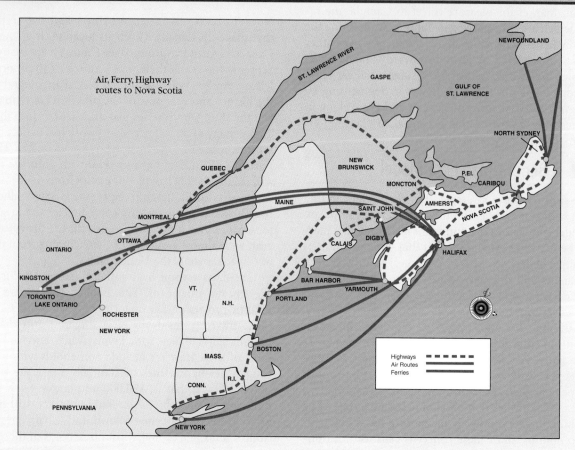

SOURCE: "Nova Scotia," *Travel Agent*, February 27, 1986, 14.

most annual changes in marketing strategy contributed to the present situation both by confusing the consumer as to what Nova Scotia is all about and by failing to create a focused image based on the relative strengths of the province. Some critics argue that Nova Scotia is not being promoted on its unique features but on benefits that other locations can provide as well or better.

Examples of Successful Positioning

Most North Atlantic passengers flying to Europe used to have a vague impression of Belgium. This presented a problem to the tourism authorities, who wanted travelers to stay for longer periods. Part of the problem was a former "Gateway to Europe" campaign that had positioned Belgium as a country to pass through on the way to somewhere else.

The idea for new positioning was found in the *Michelin Guides*, which rate cities as they do restaurants. The Benelux countries have six three-star cities (the highest ranking), of which five are in Belgium and only one

(Amsterdam) is in the Netherlands. The theme generated was "In Belgium, there are five Amsterdams." This strategy was correct in three different ways: (1) it related Belgium to a destination that was known to the traveler, Amsterdam; (2) the *Michelin Guides*, another entity already known to the traveler, gave the concept credibility; and (3) the "five cities to visit" made Belgium a bona fide destination.[1]

The state of Florida attracts far more eastern North American beach seekers than does South Carolina. Tourism officials in South Carolina had to find a way in which the state could be positioned against Florida.

The positioning theme generated was "You get two more days in the sun by coming to Myrtle Beach, South Carolina, instead of Florida." Florida's major beaches are a one-day drive beyond the Grand Strand of South Carolina—and one additional day back. Most travelers to Florida go in the May-to-October season when the

[1]Al Ries and Jack Trout, *Positioning: The Battle for Your Mind* (New York: McGraw-Hill, 1980), 171–178.

TABLE	**3**	Nova Scotia Facts

THE LAND

Nova Scotia is surrounded by four bodies of water—the Atlantic, the Bay of Fundy, the Northumberland Strait, and the Gulf of St. Lawrence. Its average width of 70 miles (128 kilometers) means that no part of the province is far from the sea. Nova Scotia lies in the northern temperate zone and although it is surrounded by water, the climate is continental rather than maritime. The temperature extremes are moderated, however, by the ocean.

THE HISTORY

The Micmac Indians inhabited Nova Scotia long before the first explorers arrived from Europe. The first visitors were Norsemen (in 1000), and, in 1497, Italian explorer John Cabot had noted the rich fishing grounds in the area. In the seventeenth century, all of Nova Scotia was settled by the French and formed a larger are a known as Acadia. Feuds between the British and the French resulted in all of Acadia being ceded to the British in 1713. The British perceived the Acadians as a security threat and expelled them to Virginia and Louisiana. In 1783, there was an influx of loyalists from the newly independent New England states. Nova Scotia and three other provinces joined a federation called the Dominion of Canada in 1867. At the time, the province was known for international shipbuilding and trade in fish and lumber. The first and second world wars emphasized the importance of Halifax, Nova Scotia's capital, as a staging point for convoys and confirmed it as one of the world's major ports.

THE PEOPLE

Over 80 percent of Nova Scotia's population of 937,800 trace their ancestry to the British Isles, while 18 percent of residents are of French ancestry. The next largest groups by ancestry are German and Dutch. Almost 22,000 residents have Indian roots, primarily belonging to the Micmac nation.

THE ECONOMY

Nova Scotia's economy is highly diversified, having evolved from resource-based employment to manufacturing as well as business and personal services. The breakdown is as follows: (1) manufacturing/fish $5.4 billion; (2) tourism $900 million; (3) forestry $870 million; (4) mining $610 million; (5) fishing $473 million; and (6) agriculture $311 million.

SOURCE: "Canadian Provinces and Territories," **http://www.canada.gc.ca**.

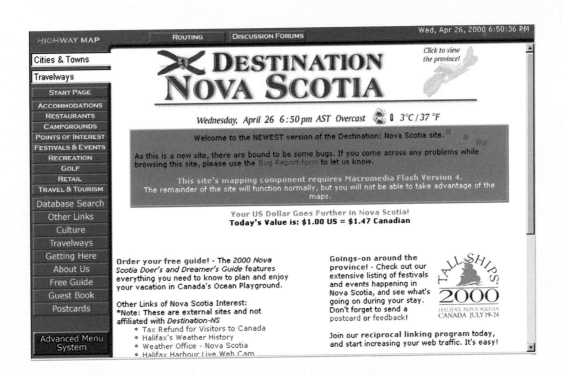

FIGURE 2 Example of "There's So Much to Sea" Campaign

weather is similar to that in South Carolina. Thus, more beach time and less driving time became the central benefit provided by the state.

Positioning Nova Scotia

The benefits of Nova Scotia as a Canadian travel destination cover segments III to VI of U.S. travelers (see Table 1). Those providing input to the planning process point out water activities, seaside activities, camping, or scenic activities. The segment interested in foreign adventure could be lured by festivals and other related activities.

The planners' argument centers not so much on which benefits to promote but on which should be emphasized if differentiation is desired. The decision is important because of (1) the importance of the industry to the province and (2) the overall rise in competition for the travelers in Nova Scotia's market, especially competition by U.S. states.

QUESTIONS FOR DISCUSSION

1. How would you position Nova Scotia to potential American travelers? Use the benefit-matching model to achieve your supermatch.

2. Constructively criticize past positioning attempts, such as "There's so much to sea."

3. What other variables, apart from positioning, will determine whether Americans will choose Nova Scotia as a destination?

AOL: International Expansion

On Thursday, September 16, 1999, Scott Geltz, director of New Market Operations for AOL International, sat in his hotel room in Hong Kong overlooking Victoria Harbor. Typhoon York was bearing down with 100 mph winds as Scott gazed into the distance thinking about the irony of the long, sometimes stormy voyage that had brought him to this moment. In just a few days AOL would launch AOL–Hong Kong. Scott, along with Greg Consiglio, managing director for AOL-Asia, had worked incredibly hard during the preceding 16 months. As a result of their persistence and creativity, and the timely assistance from senior AOL executives, the service would finally be launched on Monday, September 28. Scott's thoughts were interrupted by the buzz of the telephone and Scott was, once again, caught up in the flurry of prelaunch activity.

Typically AOL has expanded internationally through joint ventures. But, as demonstrated both in Europe and in Hong Kong, AOL has proved itself willing to take risks on new market entry methods and new business models. In Europe, AOL has launched Free ISP Netscape Online to compete with Freeserve and low-cost ISPs in the increasingly competitive European market. In Hong Kong, AOL selected a franchise model and, when the task proved more complicated than initially thought, AOL refocused its efforts, committed additional resources, and made the model work.

A New Business Model

AOL signed a licensing agreement with China Internet Corporation (CIC) in February 1998. The business plan called for a 1999 launch of AOL's Hong Kong service, a service operated by CIC but using the AOL brand. AOL saw the franchise arrangement as a chance to use a new business model for international expansion and, furthermore, as an opportunity to begin to learn to develop Chinese software to meet the needs of Chinese consumers.

In late 1998 and early 1999 Scott and Greg were focusing on the challenge of knowledge transfer—more specifically, how to make appropriate portions of AOL's expertise available to CIC. Greg and Scott flew to Hong Kong for several visits. In turn, CIC personnel made several visits to AOL offices in Virginia to learn about "the AOL way." Scott had previously assembled a three-inch-thick manual. He and Greg were also exploring the possibility of relocating to Hong Kong so that they would be more available to the CIC staff. Having these AOL experts on site would provide CIC access to an accurate and detailed understanding of the information they had collected over their combined years working at AOL and that Scott had documented in his manual, not to mention the tacit knowledge and network of contacts they had developed within the company.

Scott and Greg were attempting to assist CIC with several tasks. CIC needed to build (or adapt) the client software, localizing the forms and features. For example, the AOL e-mail form included an ad spot, but that spot had to be adapted to accept ads in Chinese rather than in English. Decisions had to be made about the number of channels, the color scheme for the various screens, and how much of the content would be in English and how much in Chinese. Technical and legal challenges included securing the proper font packs from Microsoft (so that the browser could render Chinese characters) and securing a PNETs license so that the local operator could func-

NOTE: Professors N. Lamar Reinsch, Jr. and Robert J. Bies prepared this case as a basis for class discussion rather than to illustrate either effective or ineffective handling of an administrative situation. Certain facts and figures have been disguised. Copyright 1999 by Robert Bies, Lamar Reinsch, and Georgetown University. Copyright 1999 McDonough School of Business, Georgetown University, Washington DC, 20057, USA.

tion as an ISP.[1] Direct mailing regulations had to be reviewed with the postal authority. Decisions had to be made about issues such as which credit cards to accept. And, as Scott and Greg well knew, a successful launch requires detailed preparation (project plans, Gantt charts, etc.[2]). Ideally, all of this needed to be done in time to allow a 60-to-90-day cushion, AOL's normal timing to have its software at the "Golden Master" stage prior to launch.

A Major Opportunity

Then came the decision to take the assets in CIC public under the name China.com Corporation (CCC). Both AOL and CIC came to see China.com's IPO as a chance to expand their relationship and, thereby, to strengthen the alignment of their interests. AOL also saw it as an opportunity to learn how Chinese companies deliver Internet products and services to Chinese customers. From the other perspective, CIC saw AOL's involvement as an opportunity to learn more from AOL, the world's most successful Internet company, and as an opportunity to enhance the credibility and the value of the IPO.

The launch date for the service was set when Scott and Greg noted that a *Fortune* CEO conference had been scheduled in Shanghai during the week of September 27. They secured an invitation for Steve Case, AOL's chairman and the world's leading Internet visionary, to speak at the conference and then scheduled the launch to fit around Case's schedule.

On September 12 both Greg and Scott flew, once again, to Hong Kong. Scott planned to remain through launch and Greg planned to take up residence.

 ## What Does It Mean?

On September 16, when Scott finished the telephone call, he turned away from the window and began to review the schedule for the coming days. Steve Case was flying to Hong Kong where he would conduct a "business round table" with local executives and give a speech at the American Chamber of Commerce. Then Case would officially launch AOL's Hong Kong service before flying on to Shanghai for the *Fortune* CEO Conference. Once Case was safely in the air, Scott, Greg, and the rest of the staff would attend a well-deserved launch party.

Both Scott and Greg viewed the launch party as an occasion to celebrate the successes of the past year and the launch, and also as an opportunity to recharge for the even more challenging year ahead.

QUESTIONS FOR DISCUSSION

1. Based on his experience in Hong Kong, what lessons (if any) should Scott Geltz have learned about international expansion?

2. Based on its experience in Hong Kong, what lessons (if any) should AOL have learned about international expansion? What modifications (if any) should AOL make in its business model?

3. What is the likely future of AOL–Hong Kong, especially given China's membership in the WTO?

4. In terms of AOL's global business strategy, what should AOL do next?

---

[1] A PNETs license is a specific type of Hong Kong telecommunications license.

[2] H. L. Gantt, a U.S. engineer, developed a chart that presents production data in graphic form.

NIKE in Southeast Asia

"Good shoes are made in good factories. Good factories have good labor relations." These are the words from Nike's chairman and CEO Phillip Knight responding to an attack on the company's labor relations. Over the past few years, Nike has had to answer a number of charges regarding its labor practices in its Southeast Asian plants.

Nike celebrated its 25th anniversary during the summer of 1997. Since its inception from the back of chairman and CEO Philip Knight's car, Nike has grown into one of the most successful companies in the sports apparel industry. In 1972, the company began with seven models of shoes and collected $3 million in sales that first year. Sales of Nike athletic shoes have continued to grow over the past 25 years. Shoe sales reached $2.2 billion in 1990 and $9.2 billion at the end of 1997.

Nike's amazing growth is the result of an effective international marketing and promotion strategy. The company's sponsorship of Michael Jordan, Tiger Woods, and other top athletes helped Nike become associated with high-performance athletics. In addition, the company's motto "Just Do It!"is one of the most recognizable in the world and has become a part of popular culture. These are just a few examples of the shrewd moves that helped fuel Nike's rapid growth. Another essential factor of Nike's success is its ability to limit labor expenses. Since its inception the company has attempted to find the least expensive labor to manufacture its shoes, often finding Southeast Asia to offer the most attractive labor setting. Nike subcontracts production to a number of independent facilities throughout Asia for manufacturing of its shoes and its sportswear and concentrates itself in the design, marketing, and technology of footwear and apparel.

Traditionally, the company located in markets where labor unions were not very strong or were illegal. With the support of the governments in these countries, Nike limits its exposure to labor problems and keeps costs low. These facilities allow Nike to assemble and ship shoes for a cost of $22.50, then sell them in the United States for $90 (see Figure 1). In some cases, such as South Korea and Taiwan, Nike even moved production facilities after workers gained significant individual rights and labor costs began to rise. While these moves may have helped Nike's profitability, it opened the company up to increased criticism for creating sweatshop conditions in these plants. Nike began to face increased allegations of worker mistreatment in the early 1990s, forcing the company to develop some guidelines for its subcontractors to follow.

In 1992, Nike introduced its first Code of Conduct document. The Code was designed to illustrate the company's commitment to improving workers' rights in all respects. (A summary of the code's provisions are provided in Table 1.) In addition, the Code requires that management respect individual workers' right to form a union and forbids management from harassing, abusing, or punishing employees. Although the guidelines are in place, many subcontractor plants still do not follow the code. Even after the Nike Code of Conduct was adopted, the company faced continued criticism concerning its labor relations. Nike defended itself by saying that employing 500,000 people worldwide in contract manufacturing makes it very difficult to enforce the code, especially when Nike does not own the factories. Many people, however, doubted Nike's desire to enforce its own Code of Conduct. Critics believed that strict enforcement of the Code would raise production costs for the company.

In September 1997, Nike terminated its contract with four subcontractors in Indonesia. The company stated

SOURCE: This case study was written by William H. Heuer and Ilkka A. Ronkainen. The contribution of André Gamrasni is appreciated. For more information, see http://www.nike.com/faq/ for the Nike point of view, and http://www.caa.org.au/campaigns/nike/index.html for an example of the criticism.

| FIGURE | 1 | Cost of a Pair of Nike Shoes |

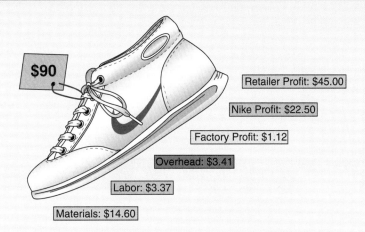

- Retailer Profit: $45.00
- Nike Profit: $22.50
- Factory Profit: $1.12
- Overhead: $3.41
- Labor: $3.37
- Materials: $14.60
- $90

| TABLE | 1 | Excerpts from the Nike Code of Conduct |

NIKE designs, manufactures and markets products for sports and fitness consumers. At every step in that process, we are driven to do not only what is required, but what is expected of a leader. We expect our business partners to do the same. Specifically, NIKE seeks partners that share our commitment to the promotion of best practices and continuous improvement in:

1) Occupational health and safety, compensation, hours of work and benefits.
2) Minimizing our impact on the environment.
3) Management practices that recognize the dignity of the individual, the rights of free association and collective bargaining, and the right to a workplace free of harassment, abuse or corporal punishment.
4) The principle that decisions on hiring, salary, benefits, advancement, termination or retirement are based solely on the ability of an individual to do the job.

Wherever NIKE operates around the globe, we are guided by this Code of Conduct. We bind our business partners to these principles. While these principles establish the spirit of our partnerships, we also bind these partners to specific standards of conduct. These are set forth below:

- **Forced Labor (Contractor)** certifies that it does not use any forced labor—prison, indentured, bonded or otherwise.
- **Child Labor (Contractor)** certifies it does not employ any person under the minimum age established by local law, or the age at which compulsory schooling has ended, whichever is greater, but in no case under the age of 14.
- **Compensation (Contractor)** certifies that it pays at least the minimum total compensation required by local law, including all mandated wages, allowances and benefits.
- **Benefits (Contractor)** certifies that it complies with all provisions for legally mandated benefits, including but not limited to housing; meals; transportation and other allowances; health care; child care; sick leave; emergency leave; pregnancy and menstrual leave; vacation, religious, bereavement and holiday leave; and contributions for social security, life, health, worker's compensation and other insurance.
- **Hours of Work/Overtime (Contractor)** certifies that it complies with legally mandated work hours; uses overtime only when employees are fully compensated according to local law; informs the employee at the time of hiring if mandatory overtime is a condition of employment; and, on a regularly scheduled basis, provides one day off in seven, and requires no more than 60 hours of work per week, or complies with local limits if they are lower.
- **Health and Safety (Contractor)** certifies that it has written health and safety guidelines, including those applying to employee residential facilities, where applicable; and that it has agreed in writing to comply with NIKE's factory/vendor health and safety standards.
- **Environment (Contractor)** certifies that it complies with applicable country environmental regulations; and that it has agreed in writing to comply with NIKE's specific vendor/factory environmental policies and procedures, which are based on the concept of continuous improvement in processes and programs to reduce the impact on the environment.

that the four factories did not comply with Nike standards in three important areas: overtime requirements, physical work environment, and meeting minimum wage requirements. According to the company, the move represented an effort by Nike to improve the labor conditions in the subcontracted facilities. Nike did not name the factories, although the company did state that they were not shoe manufacturers. By not mentioning the production facilities, Nike kept open the option that it would use the factories once they were able to meet Nike standards.

While Nike acknowledged the move in Indonesia as a positive move, many critics felt that the company was just attempting to counter recent criticism over its labor practices in Asia. In either case, Nike has become the most visible target for exploitation of labor by large multinational corporations. The company realizes the damage that these allegations cause to its reputation and its business; however, the company does not seem to have the answer to ending the problem.

QUESTIONS FOR DISCUSSION

1. What recommendations would you offer Nike for dealing with the allegations of labor exploitation in Asia?
2. What value does the Code of Conduct offer to Nike? How can the company ensure proper adherence to the Code?
3. Should Nike cancel contracts with these facilities if they do not meet Nike's requirements? What about the company's responsibility to the workers employed in these facilities? Does Nike have better options besides termination of the production contract?
4. Are there differences between Nike's responsibility to its shareholders and its responsibility to its stakeholders?
5. Do you think Nike should be responsible for the labor practices in subcontracted facilities? What should be its level of responsibility?

ESPN

Video Case

It began by mistake. Back in the late 1970s, Bill Rasmussen decided to launch a cable station to broadcast Connecticut-area sports. With the assistance of his partners, Rasmussen leased a building in Bristol from which to broadcast and then bought some satellite time. Only after signing the agreement did he learn that his satellite coverage was national—and his small-scale plan of New England sports coverage began to grow. Their early name for the channel—Entertainment and Sports Programming Network—proved too much of a tongue twister and, in 1985, they settled on the ESPN acronym as the corporate name. The letters now stand for nothing—except a sports phenomenon.

Since those early days during which the network scrambled to televise whatever it could—from a men's pro, slow-pitch softball game to its first NHL game in 1979—the organization has grown dramatically, filling what Will Burkhardt of ESPN says is now a saturated market for televised sports in the United States and rapidly moving overseas. "We reach 150 to 155 million households around the world [excluding the United States]; that encompasses about 180 markets and territories," says Burkhardt. ESPN reaches all seven continents, including one of the scientific stations located in Antarctica. The expansion has taken place over the last 15 years, beginning when ESPN provided groundbreaking coverage of the America's Cup international sailing race from Australia in 1987. That race seemed to be a turning point not only for ESPN, but for cable broadcasting itself. From there, ESPN purchased a majority interest in the European Sports Network (called Eurosport) and began service to 25 Middle Eastern and Northern

African nations. In addition to its Eurosport market, ESPN's largest international markets have become China, India, and Argentina.

Burkhardt notes that ESPN entered the international marketplace because of a "desire to grow outside of the U.S. borders and to take what we had learned in the United States in terms of people's passion for sport . . . and bring that to the international marketplace." This was around the same time that cable and satellite television were expanding around the world, so ESPN's timing seemed perfect.

However, marketing around the world isn't easy. For instance, although India has a huge middle class population, middle class in that country means that a family might earn about $1,800 per year, as opposed to an American middle class family's earnings of $35,000 per year. Thus, attracting viewers to pay for television is more difficult in India. In addition, the infrastructure for cable television is very different from that of the United States, which requires more effort for ESPN marketers. India has tens of thousands of cable entrepreneurs serving approximately 100 customers each, instead of a giant like AOL–Time Warner, which serves 13 million. Still, ESPN thinks that serving India is worth the effort and tailors its programming to the single most-watched sport in the nation: cricket.

In the burgeoning South American markets, where sports fanatics thrive, viewers can watch all kinds of programming—Argentine rugby, Argentine polo, Brazilian basketball, and Brazilian tennis, to name a few. But Burkhardt emphasizes that ESPN starts with a regional marketing strategy, "building a bed of programming from

SOURCES: Telephone interview with Will Burkhardt of ESPN, January 2000; "TV Listings," February 8, 2000, ESPN.com; "ESPN International Land Masters for Latin America," company press release, November 11, 1999, ESPN.com; Michael Hiestand, "Did You Know? ESPN Is 20 Today," *USA Today*, September 7, 1999, www.USAToday.com; "Looking Back, Back, Back . . .," company press release, September 6, 1999, ESPN.com; and Rudy Martzke, "ESPN at 20," *USA Today*, August 18, 1999, p. 2c.

699

which you then start to localize." Currently, most broadcasts are in English or the local language, but dealing with some countries' multiple local dialects is extremely difficult. In addition, consumers in smaller markets want to see broadcasters of their own nationality instead of ESPN's standard crew of broadcasters. "There is no question that people in Mexico would prefer all of our commentators to be Mexican instead of some which are Argentine," remarks Burkhardt. ESPN simply can't afford to provide this degree of customization yet.

Ultimately, ESPN's goal is to reach as many households worldwide as possible, despite any difficulties in penetrating new markets. For example, the company landed a huge deal that gave it distribution rights in Latin America for all four rounds of the Masters Golf Tournament. ESPN Latin America alone is now distributed in more than 11 million households in 41 countries and territories, broadcasting in English, Spanish, and Portuguese.

In spite of recent victories like the Masters, perhaps one of the greatest challenges to ESPN is that the company must, in large part, make its pitch to cable and satellite television operators before its programming ever reaches the consumers themselves. Those operators conduct business in different ways, they lack rating systems, and some even replace ESPN programming with homegrown shows. Then there are political challenges, such as when ESPN was thrown off Chinese cable after the United States mistakenly bombed its embassy in Eastern Europe. And there are legal tangles in each country that need to be dealt with, as well. But sports are an international language that tries to provide entertainment without political ramifications, and people everywhere love to watch. "We're obviously not trying to promote any kind of political message through the showing of an American baseball game," says Burkhardt. And perhaps that is the key to ESPN's success—its ability to bring sport to everyone, everywhere, anytime.

QUESTIONS FOR DISCUSSION

1. What questions might ESPN marketers ask themselves as they try to develop business in Asia or South America?
2. Why is it important for ESPN to be global? What might be some barriers to trade for ESPN?
3. How would you describe ESPN's global marketing strategy?
4. Search ESPN's web site at **www.espn.com** and summarize what it is currently doing in international markets.

Aftermath of an Environmental Disaster: Union Carbide in Bhopal

On Sunday, December 3, 1984, the peaceful life of a city in India was joltingly disrupted. The Union Carbide plant at Bhopal, a city less than 400 miles from New Delhi, India, had leaked poisonous gas into the air. Within one week, over 2,000 people died and more remained critically ill. Over 100,000 people were treated for nausea, blindness, and bronchial problems. It was one of history's worst industrial accidents, which continues to affect lives today. Through 1998, more than 8,000 people have died as a result of the accident and 500,000 have become ill. According to the International Medical Commission on Bhopal, some 50,000 survivors are permanently disabled. Families still live just outside the barbed wire fence of the abandoned Union Carbide facility, which is dismantled and waiting to be sold. Contamination of nearby water and soil has been detected. Potable water flows each morning for only 30 minutes. The ground water in the areas most affected continues to be polluted by the toxic waste that was dumped by the plant in the waste disposal area. Local farmlands have been abandoned due to sharp drops in crop yields in the years following the accident.

In 1984, Union Carbide was America's 37th largest industrial corporation, with more than 100,000 employees and an annual sales volume of over $9 billion. The firm was active in petrochemicals, industrial gases, metals and carbon products, consumer products, and technology transfers.

Union Carbide operated 14 plants in India. Total Indian operations accounted for less than 2 percent of corporate sales. In spite of a policy by the Indian government to restrict foreign majority ownership of plants, Union Carbide owned 50.9 percent of the Bhopal plant. The government granted this special arrangement because the plant served as a major technology transfer project. In order to achieve lasting technology transfer, management of the plant was mostly carried out by Indian nationals. General corporate safety guidelines applied to the plant, but local regulatory agencies were charged with enforcing Indian environmental laws. Only three weeks before the accident, the plant had received an "environmental clearance certificate" from the Indian State Pollution Board.

The accident resulted in wide public awareness in the United States. A poll afterwards showed that 47 percent of those questioned linked Union Carbide's name to the Bhopal disaster. The direct impact of this awareness on Union Carbide's business remains uncertain. Most U.S. consumers did not connect the Union Carbide name to its line of consumer products, which consisted of brands such as Energizer, Glad, and Presto. Industrial users, on the other hand, were highly aware of Union Carbide's products. One area that could be particularly affected was technology transfer, which in 1983 accounted for 24 percent of Union Carbide's revenues. The firm had concentrated increasingly on that sector, selling mainly its

SOURCES: This case was written by Michael Czinkota © with the assistance of George Garcia by adapting secondary source materials from Kenneth J. Cooper. "Slums Sprawl in Shadow of Bhopal Gas Leak," *The Washington Post*, June 27, 1996, A19; "Bhopal Legacy Still Being Felt," *Occupational Hazards* (February 1996): 28; Clemens P. Work, "Inside Story of Union Carbide's India Nightmare," *U.S. News & World Report* (January 21, 1985): 51–52; Armin Rosencranz, "Bhopal Transnational Corporations and Hazardous Technologies," *Ambio* 17 (1988): 336–341; Sanjoy Hazarika, "Carbide Plant Closed by India Unrest," *The New York Times*, Monday, May 13, 1991, D12; Scott McMurray, "India's High Court Upholds Settlement Paid by Carbide in Bhopal Gas Leak," *The Wall Street Journal*, October 4, 1991, B8; Eirmalasare Bani, "Kvaerner, Linde Groups Appointed Contractors," *Business Times* (Malaysia), November 10, 1998, Companies/Markets, 5; "Fires at Defunct Carbide Factory Worry Gas Victims," *The Statesman* (India), June 3, 1999: News; Mike Allen, "In Danbury, Employees Fear Cutbacks," *The New York Times*, August 5, 1999, C6; "Environmental Manager and Changing Business Perspectives," *The Hindu*, April 14, 1999; News; Martha M. Hamilton, "Chemical Giants Agree to Merger; Dow to Acquire Union Carbide," *The Washington Post*, August 5, 1999, E1.

know-how in the fields of engineering, manufacturing, and personnel training.

The Public Reaction

Internationally, the reaction was one of widespread consumer hostility. In India, demonstrations were held in New Delhi. The protesters demanded that the Indian government ensure steps would be taken for the extradition of the foreign accused, including Warren Anderson, former chairman of the Union Carbide Corporation. Environmentalists also demonstrated at Union Carbide plants in West Germany and Australia. Some facilities were firebombed; most were spray painted. Plans for plants in Scotland had to be frozen. The operation of a plant in France was called into question by the French government.

Major financial repercussions occurred as well. Within a week of the accident, Union Carbide stock dropped by $10, a loss in market value of nearly $900 million. A $1.2 billion line of credit was frozen. Profits of Union Carbide India Ltd., which in 1984 had been about 8.2 million rupees, or about $480,000, dropped by 1985 to 1.3 million rupees, or $78,000. In 1985, with its shares devastated by the disaster, Union Carbide became the target of a hostile takeover bid and was forced to sell valuable assets, including its consumer-products division. It raised $3 billion of debt to buy back 55 percent of its shares and managed to stay independent. The following year it sold its battery, agricultural, and home and auto product divisions.

In the ensuing debate of the Bhopal disaster, three basic issues were highlighted—responsible industrial planning, adequate industrial safety measures, and corporate accountability. In terms of industrial planning, both Union Carbide and the Indian government were said to have failed. The Indian subsidiary of Union Carbide did little to inform workers about the highly toxic methyl isocyanate (MIC) the plant was producing and the potential health threat to neighboring regions. When the accident occurred, the subsidiary's management team reportedly resisted the parent company's instructions to apply first aid to victims for fear of generating widespread panic within the corporation and the region. The Indian government, on the other hand, seemed to regard technology transfer as a higher priority than public safety. The local government approved construction of the plant with little medical and scientific investigation into its biological effects on the environment and on people.

The second issue was the absence of a "culture of safety" among Indian technicians, engineers, and management. From the very beginning, the project lacked a team of experienced maintenance personnel who would have recognized the need for higher safety measures and,

more important, a different choice of technology. When the entire Indian government wholeheartedly approved the import of the most advanced chemical production facility to a developing country without qualified personnel to handle the material and without insight into appropriate precautionary measures in case of an accident, the seeds were sown for potential disaster.

The third area of interest in the Bhopal incident is that of corporate accountability. There are three general norms of international law concerning the jurisprudence of the home government over the foreign subsidiary:

1. Both state and nonstate entities are liable to pay compensation to the victims of environmental pollution and accidents.
2. The corporation is responsible for notifying and consulting the involved officials of actual and potential harm involved in the production and transport of hazardous technologies and materials.
3. The causer or originator of environmental damage is liable to pay compensation to the victims.

These and other developing norms of international law serve to make transnational corporations more responsible for their operation.

Compensation to Victims: "The Second Tragedy"

Five days after the incident, the first damage suit, asking for $15 billion, was filed in U.S. Federal District Court. Since then, more than 150 suits have been filed in the United States and more than 2,700 in India. Union Carbide offered to pay $300 million over a period of 30 years to settle the cases before the courts in the United States and India. The Indian government rejected the offer, claiming that the amount was far below its original request of $615 million. By 1986, most U.S. lawsuits had been consolidated in the New York federal court. In May 1986, however, the judge presiding over the collective Bhopal cases ruled that all suits arising out of the accident should be heard in the Indian judicial system, claiming that "India is where the accident occurred, and where the victims, witnesses, and documents are located." Although this decision appeared to benefit Union Carbide because of lower damage awards in India, the judge explicitly stated that (1) Union Carbide (USA) and its Indian affiliate must submit to the jurisdiction of the Indian court system; (2) Union Carbide must turn over all relevant documents to the plaintiffs' lawyers in India, as they would if in the United States; and (3) Union Carbide must agree to whatever judgment is rendered in India. This decision had a major effect on Union Carbide (USA) because both Union Carbide and its Indian subsidiary now had to answer to the Indian court, and the entire company's assets had become involved.

In India, the class suit traveled from the Bhopal District court to the Madhya Pradesh High Court and finally to the Indian Supreme Court. Although a settlement agreement was reached between Union Carbide and the Indian government, the descendants of the 2,000 victims were not satisfied. Several victims' consumer groups and public interest lawyers filed petitions contesting the authority of the government to handle the lawsuit on behalf of the victims' descendants. The petitions claimed that the government had no right to represent the victims because governmental negligence had caused the accident in the first place and the government itself should be as much a target as Union Carbide in the suit. It was expected that if the Indian Supreme Court upheld this rationale, then the government would be unable to settle on the victims' behalf. In this case, the agreed-upon settlement amount would also be voided. As a result of the internal debate in India, the $421 million paid in settlement by Union Carbide was frozen. Instead the Indian government disbursed 200 rupees, about $10, a month to all persons who lived in the neighborhoods affected by the gas leak.

On October 3, 1991, almost seven years after the incident, the Supreme Court of India rendered its decision. The total amount of $470 million, which had already been paid by Union Carbide, was upheld as settlement. Criminal charges against the Union Carbide Corporation were reinstated, even though the court acknowledged that due to its lack of jurisdiction, it could not enforce any criminal fines in the United States.

Since the decision cannot be reviewed further, it freed up the frozen funds to be distributed to Bhopal victims and their families. Although many victims were delighted about that fact, Prashant Bhushan, a New Delhi attorney, had severe misgivings. He believed the upholding of the civil settlement to be a big blow to the development of law on the subject—particularly since he had argued that Carbide should be forced to pay "first-world" compensation rates to victims rather than "third-world" rates. He was not alone in his fight. A consortium of 25 human rights and environmental organizations demanded in 1996 that Union Carbide stand trial in India on the charge of culpable homicide. The group, which includes Greenpeace and Friends of the Earth, has urged the New York State Attorney General to begin charter revocation proceedings against Union Carbide based on a state law that provides for dissolving corporations that cause great harm.

The Union Carbide Corporation has taken private measures to aid the gas victims. It established an independent charitable trust in London that works closely with an Indian government committee and prominent Bhopal citizens. A new hospital and clinics have been built with $100 million from the trust. Union Carbide Corporation officials have also been carrying on a media campaign on the humanitarian initiative of the corporation through the trust.

Another Bhopal?

Were any lessons learned from the Bhopal disaster? As a result of Union Carbide's experience in Bhopal, several chemical companies have reduced the size of their storage tanks of toxic materials, while others have cut their inventories by as much as 50 percent. Many have provided information to the communities in which they manufacture. Some have even invested in risk assessment studies of their operations of hazardous materials.

The most significant regulatory changes have been the introduction of the Environmental Protection Act (EPA) in India, which makes environmental plans compulsory. The act empowers the Ministry of Environment and Forests (MOEF) to directly order closure of firms without going through the State Pollution Control Boards. Another result has been public interest legislation, together with a statutory right to information. The government of India has now made environmental clearance mandatory for every new project supported by the government or international agencies.

Union Carbide Corporation continues to be in the spotlight for environmental problems. Environmental groups attacked UCC following the discovery of 69 drums of highly toxic dioxin waste near the Olympics 2000 site in Australia. From March 13 to June 1, 1999, three fires on the premises of the defunct Union Carbide factory in Bhopal sparked panic among survivors of the Bhopal gas disaster.

In 1998, controversy erupted when Union Carbide Corporation and Petronas National Oil joined forces to build the Integrated Petrochemical Complex in Kereth, Terengganu, a territory under the Malaysian government. What guarantee did Malaysia have that there would not be a repeat of Bhopal? UCC corporate ventures director Charles Zeynel stated, "UCC will adhere to the strictest standards. . . . There will be no double standards and we won't allow another Bhopal to happen." The building of the new plant will cost $1.6 billion and is expected to be completed by 2001.

As to the standing of Union Carbide in the financial community, the firm had profits of $403 million in 1998 on sales of $5.7 billion. On November 1, 1999, the firm was replaced as a member of the 30 stocks that are used to compute the Dow Jones Industrial Average index. In October 1999, Union Carbide was acquired by Dow Chemical for $9.3 billion in stock, creating the world's second largest chemical company behind DuPont.

QUESTIONS FOR DISCUSSION

1. Why did Union Carbide invest in India?
2. How could Union Carbide have planned for an event such as the accident in Bhopal?
3. How would such planning have improved corporate response to the disaster?

4. What are the implications for Union Carbide being allowed to construct a new plant in Malaysia?
5. Do you feel that Union Carbide has learned from its experience in Bhopal?

Establishing an Overseas Law Office

tuffim & Bacom is a 20-year-old, 125-member law firm based in St. Paul, Minnesota. Aside from its home office, the firm maintains offices in Washington, D.C.; Denver, Colorado; and Paris, France. As in any major firm, there are many areas of practice, but the firm's fastest-growing section is its international business department. This department is headed by the firm's principal rainmaker and senior Washington partner, Harley Hambone, assisted by an aggressive junior partner, Sylvester Soupspoon, also based in Washington.

Stuffim & Bacom has just begun to acquire business on the African continent. Their biggest client, Safari Air Lines (SAL), is an international airfreight company with corporate headquarters in Abidjan, Ivory Coast. Last year, SAL was the major airfreight carrier for all of East, Central, and West Africa. Recently, Hambone, an international finance expert and master salesman, persuaded SAL to drop the law firm of Bend, Spindell & Mutilate, an old-line New York City firm, as the company's U.S. counsel and transfer all of SAL's business to the Stuffim firm. SAL is now almost a $1 million-per-year account for Stuffim & Bacom, which includes work with airline regulatory agencies in the United States, as well as general advice regarding international aviation matters.

In addition, Soupspoon, a transportation attorney, recently brought in Livingstone Tours, Inc., a small but burgeoning U.S.-based travel agency specializing in three-month African safaris, as a new client. Livingstone maintains its only overseas office in Nairobi, Kenya. Stuffim bills Livingstone less than $500,000 per year, mainly for preparing and negotiating agreements with international charter airlines and local tour operators serving East Africa.

Due to their already substantial client obligations, as well as the sudden, unexpected growth in their business on the African continent and the impracticality of handling this work out of their Washington, D.C., office, Hambone and Soupspoon have decided to propose that the firm open an office in Africa to cover its growing client needs in that part of the world. This would not only enable the firm to better serve SAL and Livingstone Tours, but it would also help the firm garner more African business.

SAL and Livingstone Tours are each pressing Stuffim & Bacom to set up an African office as soon as possible, preferably close to their respective African operations. This will require the firm to invest $250,000 to start up an office, as well as yearly expenditures (including related overhead) of $125,000 per U.S. attorney and $75,000 per local attorney to staff it with qualified lawyers.

Establishing a foreign office is nothing new to Stuffim & Bacom. For almost ten years the firm has maintained an office in Paris, France. As with many foreign branches of U.S. law firms, the Paris office generates very little profit and is regarded by the firm as something of a prestigious "foreign outpost." The firm continues to maintain the Paris office at a break-even level, mainly for the benefit of one major client, Ali Nord, an Arab- and French-owned freight forwarding company with extensive business in the United States, Central America, and the Middle East.

The Paris office's only attorney, Sylvia Souffle, a senior partner and member of the Colorado bar, is qualified under French law to advise clients, such as Ali Nord, on questions of foreign and international law but may not appear in French courts or advise clients regarding French

SOURCE: This case was written by William E. Casselman II of counsel to the firm of Stairs Dillenbeck Finley & Merrill, New York City. Reprinted with permission. It is intended only to describe fictional business situations, and any resemblance to real individuals or business organizations is purely co-incidental. The various economic, legal, political, and cultural conditions described in the case are for illustration only and do not necessarily reflect the actual conditions prevailing within the regions or countries mentioned.

law. After ten years of general corporate practice in France, she has recently indicated her desire to leave the Paris office and head the proposed office in the Ivory Coast, a former French colony in West Africa. Souffle has many contacts in the Ivory Coast, where French is the official language.

The firm has also opened two other offices abroad, neither of which succeeded. The first office was opened six years ago in Saudi Arabia to represent U.S. engineering and construction firms doing business there. This branch closed after one year due to a lack of business stemming from a decline in the price of oil and threats from Middle East terrorists, who were upset over Stuffim's representation of Ali Nord, which they wrongly believed to be a CIA front. More recently, a heretofore unknown terrorist group announced in the Middle East that it would "go to the ends of the earth" to wreak revenge upon Ali Nord and its "yellow running dog lackeys of Yankee imperialism," including the Stuffim firm.

The second office was opened three years ago in Bangkok, Thailand, to service Torch & Glow Industries, a Colorado corporation and major provider of fire-resistant tiling and roofing materials. Torch & Glow had experienced an unanticipated boom in business in Southeast Asia. Therefore, Stuffim & Bacom opened a regional office in Bangkok with special permission of the Thai government to represent Torch & Glow in Thailand, and then only on matters not requiring appearances in the courts of Thailand. Unfortunately, a massive class action suit was brought against Torch & Glow in both the United States and Thailand for damages caused by the unexplained flammability of the company's products when used in tropical climates. As a result, Torch & Glow recently went out of business; as did Stuffim's office in Bangkok. Both of these failures cost the firm a great deal of money in lost start-up expense and attorney and employee severance payments, and the firm's partners swore never again to open another overseas office.

Undaunted by these past failures, Hambone and Soupspoon wish to pursue the concept of a Stuffim & Bacom office in Africa. They have several options, which include but are not limited to the following: First, they could send a contingent of at least three Stuffim lawyers, possibly led by Souffle, to establish an Abidjan office. Unfortunately, none of the firm's current attorneys, other than Souffle, speaks adequate French. Second, they could recruit a group of SAL's in-house Ivory Coast lawyers from its headquarters in Abidjan, make them special partners in the Stuffim firm, and have them run Stuffim's office. Third, they could send one or more lawyers to open an office in Kenya, an English-speaking nation and former British colony, to work principally on the Livingstone account and secondarily on the SAL account. Fourth, they could form a joint venture with a Kenyan law firm to staff and run the Nairobi office.

Soupspoon, aware that Livingstone already employs a local law firm, Amen & Hadafly, to handle some of its legal needs in Kenya, approached that firm about its willingness to form a joint venture with Stuffim to run the Nairobi office. However, Amen & Hadafly, although personal friends of Soupspoon, would agree only on the condition that they receive full partnership status, not just a share of the local office profits to which special partners are entitled. In view of this demand, as well as Amen & Hadafly's somewhat questionable reputation in the Kenyan legal community, Hambone was reluctant to accept this offer. On the other hand, because Amen & Hadafly is well connected to the local legal establishment, it is unlikely that any other local firm would agree to such a joint venture. There are no joint venture possibilities in the Ivory Coast, owing to SAL's having its own in-house attorneys and preferring to work only with the Stuffim firm because of its expertise in international transportation law.

In addition to the differences in legal systems and languages, Kenya and the Ivory Coast also have different infrastructure conditions. For example, Nairobi has good telecommunications but a shortage of available office space. Abidjan is known for its modern office buildings but lacks the more up-to-date communications facilities found in Nairobi. Both countries enjoy roughly the same political and economic stability and have a generally favorable attitude toward foreign investment.

Further complicating matters, the laws of both the Ivory Coast and Kenya place serious restrictions on foreign law firms establishing local offices with foreign lawyers, requiring any foreign law firm to employ a majority of local lawyers or to ensure that their local office is managed by a local lawyer. Moreover, any foreign lawyer wishing to practice before the courts of either country has to be certified by the local bar association as being competent to do so (and no Stuffim lawyers are so certified in either the Ivory Coast or Kenya). There is one exception—any lawyer qualified in a comparable legal system can practice without satisfying the formal requirements. The United States common law system has not been recognized in the Ivory Coast, but, because of the Ivory Coast's close ties to France, the French code system has. Conversely, the Kenyan bar recognizes the English and U.S. systems, but not the French system. Of course, it might be possible to persuade either government to create an exception for a single Stuffim & Bacom client, as was done in Thailand for Torch & Glow.

Even if Hambone and Soupspoon could persuade the governments involved to permit them to practice locally without meeting local requirements, they would still have to persuade the rest of Stuffim & Bacom's partners that an African office is a good idea. In light of the two recent overseas office failures, the remaining partners, most of whom are in the St. Paul office, are not expected to enthusiastically embrace Hambone and Soupspoon's idea for an office in Africa.

The time has come for Hambone and Soupspoon to lay their idea on the line. Hambone has arranged meetings with government officials in the Ivory Coast and Kenya to negotiate an office in one of the two countries.

Soupspoon must convince the Stuffim & Bacom partners of the merits of establishing an African office in the country selected by Hambone. You have been asked by Hambone and Soupspoon to prepare them for these crucial meetings.

QUESTIONS FOR DISCUSSION

1. Advise Hambone of the various business, legal, political, and cultural obstacles standing in the way of opening an office in each country and how he can best overcome them. Also make a recommendation as to where you think the office should be located and how (and by whom) it should be staffed and operated.
2. Advise Soupspoon as to how he can convince his fellow partners that an African office will be profitable for the firm, if not in the short term, then in the long term. This would include the type of representation arrangements that the Stuffim firm should make with its clients in Africa to minimize its financial risk.
3. How do you believe Stuffim & Bacom, as a growing international law firm, should respond to terrorist threats?

Whirlpool and the Global Appliance Industry

Video Case

Within a few months after becoming CEO of Whirlpool Corp. in 1987, David Whitwam met with his senior managers to plot a strategy for securing future company growth. At the time, Whirlpool was the market leader among U.S. appliance makers, but it generated only weak sales outside North America. Operating in a mature market, it faced the same low profit margins as major competitors like General Electric and Maytag. In addition to price wars, especially in mature markets, the industry had started to consolidate, and consumers were demanding more environmentally friendly products.

Whirlpool and Its Options

Whitwam and his management team explored several growth options, including diversifying into other industries experiencing more rapid growth, such as furniture or garden products; restructuring the company financially; and expanding vertically and horizontally. The group sharpened its focus to consider opportunities for expanding the appliance business beyond North American markets. After all, the basics of managing the appliance business and the product technologies are similar in Europe, North America, Asia, and Latin America. As Whitwam put it, "We were very good at what we did. What we needed was to enter appliance markets in other parts of the world and learn how to satisfy different kinds of customers."

Whirlpool industry data predicted that, over time, appliance manufacturing would become a global industry. As Whitwam saw it, his company had three options: "We could ignore the inevitable—a decision that would have condemned Whirlpool to a slow death. We could wait for globalization to begin and then try to react, which would have put us in a catch-up mode, technologically and organizationally. Or we could control our own destiny and try to shape the very nature of globalization in our industry. In short, we could force our competitors to respond to us."

Whitwam and his team chose the third option and set out on a mission to make Whirlpool "one company worldwide." They aimed much higher than simply marketing products or operating around the globe. For decades, Whirlpool had sold some appliances in other countries to buyers who could afford them. Whitwam wanted to expand this reach by establishing a vision of a company that could leverage global resources to gain a long-term competitive advantage. In his words, this effort meant "having the best technologies and processes for designing, manufacturing, selling, and servicing your products at the lowest possible costs. Our vision at Whirlpool is to integrate our geographical businesses wherever possible, so that our most advanced expertise in any given area—whether it's refrigeration technology or distribution strategy—isn't confined to one location or one division. We want to be able to take the best capabilities we have and leverage them in all of our operations worldwide."

As its first step in transforming a largely domestic operation into a global powerhouse, Whirlpool purchased the European appliance business of Dutch consumer-goods giant, Philips Electronics. Philips had been losing market share for years, running its European operations as independent regional companies that made different

SOURCES: Portions of this case were researched from material available at **http://www.whirlpool.com**. The Global Success Factors section is derived from a report on the global appliance industry by John Bonds, German Estrada, Peter Jacobs, Jorge Harb-Kallab, Paul Kunzer, and Karin Toth at Georgetown University, March 2000. See also Ilkka A. Ronkainen and Ivan Menezes, "Implementing Global Marketing Strategy," *International Marketing Review* 13 (Number 3, 1996): 56–63; and "The Right Way to Go Global: An Interview with Whirlpool CEO David Whitwam," *Harvard Business Review* 72 (March–April 1994): 134–145.

appliances for individual markets. "When we bought this business," Whitwam recalls, "we had two automatic washer designs, one built in Italy and one built in Germany. If you as a consumer looked at them, they were basically the same machines. But there wasn't anything common about those two machines. There wasn't even a common screw."

The Whirlpool strategy called for reversing the decline in European market share and improving profitability by changing product designs and manufacturing processes and by switching to centralized purchasing. The change reorganized the national design and research staffs inherited from Philips into European product teams that worked closely with Whirlpool's U.S. designers. Redesigned models shared more parts, and inventory costs fell when Whirlpool consolidated warehouses from 36 to 8. The transformation trimmed Philips's list of 1,600 suppliers by 50 percent, and it converted the national operations to regional companies.

Whitwam believed that the drive to become one company worldwide required making Whirlpool a global brand—a formidable task in Europe, where the name was not well-known. The company rebranded the Philips product lines, supported by a $135 million pan-European advertising campaign that initially presented both the Philips and Whirlpool names and eventually converted to Whirlpool alone.

Another important component of the Whirlpool global strategy—product innovation—sought to develop superior products based on consumer needs and wants. "We have to provide a compelling reason other than price for consumers to buy Whirlpool-built products," says Whitwam. "We can do that only by understanding the consumer better than anyone else does and then translating our understanding into clearly superior product designs, features, and after-sales support. Our goal is for consumers to prefer the Whirlpool brand because it offers greater overall value than competing products."

One successful product innovation led to the Whirlpool Crispwave microwave oven. Extensive research with European consumers revealed a desire for a microwave that could brown and crisp food. In response, Whirlpool engineers designed the VIP Crispwave, which can fry crispy bacon and cook a pizza with a crisp crust. The new microwave proved successful in Europe, and Whirlpool later introduced it in the United States.

Whirlpool's global strategy includes a goal to become the market leader in Asia, which will be the world's largest appliance market in the 21st century. In 1988, it began setting up sales and distribution systems in Asia to help it serve Asian markets and to make the firm more familiar with those markets and potential customers. The company established three regional offices: one in Singapore to serve Southeast Asia, a second in Hong Kong to handle the Chinese market, and a Tokyo office for Japan.

Through careful analysis, Whirlpool marketers sought to match specific current products with Asian consumers. They studied existing and emerging trade channels and assessed the relative strengths and weaknesses of competitors in the Asian markets. The company set up joint ventures with five Asian manufacturers for four appliance lines with the highest market potential: refrigerators, washers, air conditioners, and microwave ovens. With a controlling interest in each of the joint ventures, the newly global company confidently expects to excel in the world's fastest-growing market.

Whirlpool has come a long way since embarking on its global strategy. By 2000, revenues had doubled to more than $10 billion. The company now reaches markets in more than 170 countries, leading the markets in both North America and Latin America. Whirlpool is number three in Europe and the largest Western appliance company in Asia. For building its integrated global network, "Whirlpool gets very high marks," says an industry analyst. "They are outpacing the industry dramatically."

Global Success Factors

From a global perspective, there are two success factors that affect all of the different geographic regions. The first key success factor on a global scale is successful branding. Each of the large global manufacturers has been very successful in developing a branding strategy. Most of these players sell a variety of brands, where each is targeted to certain quality and price levels. In addition, the strong brand reputation has been necessary for the major manufacturers either to expand operations into new regions or to launch new product lines. For example, Maytag did not have a line of products in the dishwasher category but had a large brand presence in the washer/dryer category. To expand its product line, Maytag decided to launch a new line of products in the dishwasher segment. Through a successful branding campaign, in less than two years Maytag captured the second largest market share in the segment. It leveraged its successful brand image in one segment to quickly steal share from less successful competitors.

The second key success factor on a global scale is price sensitivity. Given the large cost of these goods, large-scale manufacturers have been able to lower prices to meet the demand of customers. While there is little price elasticity, some manufacturers have been able to raise prices on their high-end goods, but for the most part, most manufacturers have lowered prices, and thus margins, to stay competitive with other brands. With razor-thin margins across each segment, only manufacturers that have the size to realize economies of scale have been able to remain competitive and lower prices to meet demands of their customers. This price sensitivity and the need to continually lower prices made up one of the major forces driving the consolidation within the industry. Many smaller brands were not able to compete and therefore were sold to the larger appliance brands.

China and Asia

Aside from the global key success factors, two key success factors within China and Asia are very important. First, appliance manufacturers must have access to distribution channels and therefore the ability to provide the products across several different Chinese regions. The access to Chinese distribution channels can be very limiting for international corporations whereas China-based companies, such as Kelon and Haier, have a definite competitive advantage.

Second, large appliance manufacturers must have a large scope of products for success. Specifically, it is the number of different segments in which a company sells products that will lead to success in China, not the scope of products within a given segment. Kelon manufactures 112 different types of air conditioners, but it is not a full-line supplier of appliances to its customers. Contrarily, Haier is a full-line supplier that manufactures products in each product segment and so provides its customers with a variety of appliances under one brand name.

The Japanese market has a different set of criteria for success than China and the rest of Asia. Instead, the Japanese market closely resembles certain aspects of the European and U.S. markets. Aside from the global success factors, success in the Japanese market is based on two key factors. First, due to the size of dwellings in Japan, innovation with regard to product size is very important. Japanese customers are looking for product innovations that will fit into smaller spaces while providing the most use of cabinet space. Second, to be successful in Japan, a manufacturer must sell a product that is very high in quality. Japanese customers are very demanding in regard to product quality, and they expect their products to last decades. Therefore, manufacturers selling products that are very high in quality will have a competitive advantage.

United States

Within the United States, two key success factors outside of the global factors are necessary for a company's success. First, a company must develop innovative products that incorporate new features while still operating efficiently. U.S. customers are very aware that energy consumption of a product will have a long-term effect on their utility bills, so they look for products that operate more efficiently. In addition, customers are willing to pay a premium for innovative features on a high-end product. Many manufacturers were surprised that Maytag was able to raise its prices for its front-loading washer not once, but twice. Customers were not as concerned with the price as they were concerned with the convenience of the product.

The second key success factor within the U.S. market is product quality, in respect to durability. U.S. consumers are willing to pay more for a product, but they expect it to operate for well over a decade with little to no maintenance. Therefore, for an appliance manufacturer to succeed in the United States, it must deliver products that are of high quality and of innovative design.

Europe

Outside of the two global success factors, the European market has two distinct factors that are required for success. First, to succeed in Europe, manufacturers must develop innovative products. In this context, innovative products are defined as products that are efficient and environmentally friendly. The "green" movement within Europe is very strong, and therefore a manufacturer that does not sell "eco-products" will not succeed when compared to a company that offers that type of product.

Second, quality is a key success factor for Europe. Similar to other markets, in this context quality refers to durability. European consumers are looking for products that are durable and will last over a long period of time. In this regard, the European market is very similar to the U.S., Japanese, and Latin American markets.

Latin America

Within Latin America, there are two additional success factors for a manufacturer to consider outside the global success factors. First, Latin American companies that provide excellent service to customers will have an advantage over the competition. The amount of time that the average consumer owns an appliance in Latin America is somewhat longer than in other global regions, so consumers are looking for excellent service. The economy in Latin America has had several challenges in recent history, and so consumers would much rather repair an existing product than buy a new appliance.

Second, quality is another success factor for Latin America. This key success factor ties directly into the service success factor. Initially, Latin Americans are looking for a durable product that will last for over a decade; then through customer service, the product will be repaired to extend its life for several more years.

QUESTIONS FOR DISCUSSION

1. Whirlpool's marketing goal is to leverage resources across borders. How is this evident in its marketing approach? Consult **www.whirlpool.com** for additional information.

2. The challenge facing Whirlpool is not only external in catering to local customers' needs worldwide, but also internal—all the regional and local units have to "buy in" to the global vision. What types of particular issues (such as product or technology transfers) may arise, and how should they be dealt with?

3. Visit the web site of the Association of Home Appliance Manufacturers, **www.aham.org**, and suggest some of the global trends among the major manufacturers of household appliances.

Attracting Foreign Direct Investment: German Luxury Cars in the U.S.

Two southern U.S. states, South Carolina and Alabama, received what many view as just rewards for their hospitality, generosity, and probusiness environment. These rewards came in the form of multimillion-dollar investments for new automobile plants. The German luxury car legends BMW and Mercedes-Benz both chose to invest in new production sites in the southern United States. For BMW, the search ended in the summer of 1992, when management decided to locate its plant in the Greenville-Spartanburg area of South Carolina. Mercedes concluded its closely watched search in the fall of 1993, choosing tiny Vance, Alabama, as home for its new plants.

The German investments represent two key facets of a very competitive industry: the need to cut costs and easy access to target markets. U.S. wages are, on average, 60 percent lower than in Germany. The U.S. market has also been the chief driver of Germany's export boom. To remain competitive, DaimlerChrysler and BMW have made it a priority to move to the United States in order to set up new plants to serve the fast-growing market more directly. Both German carmakers are now competing head to head with Japanese producers that are already well ensconced on the U.S. production scene.

South Carolina and Alabama fought hard battles that won them thousands of future jobs, billion-dollar financial returns, and the prestige of having landed such world-class companies. The success of these two southeastern states in landing these auto giants comes as no surprise. The U.S. southeast has become extremely aggressive in trying to attract foreign investment and has become the fastest growing region in the United States. South Carolina, Alabama, Georgia, and Florida have created their own regional development alliances that market their states to lure more projects and investments. State, local, and county governments work together as well on the preparation and research needed. This whole collective effort, coupled with the fact that the southeast has a strong reputation for hard-working, low-wage workers and that unions are stronger in the north, gives this region many critical incentives.

Each investment decision was based on different details; however, the underlying case of landing a world-class investor using any means possible is present in both examples. A closer look at the two foreign direct investments provides the opportunity to consider some of the different details and circumstances, as well as the similarities, that exist in luring a desirable investment.

The BMW Decision

Over three years, BMW looked at 250 locations in ten countries. In the meantime, its shrinking presence in the U.S. import car market, BMW's second largest market, added to the pressure of starting up a new factory. North American sales had plummeted from 90,000 in 1986 to

SOURCES: This case was written by Michael R. Czinkota © with the assistance of George Garcia, based on the following sources: "UAW Holds Talk with GM, Daimler, but All Sides Maintain Veil of Secrecy," *The Wall Street Journal,* September 13, 1999, A3; Karen Thuerner, "The Southeast Picks Up the Pace," *World Trade,* September 1998; Stephen Plumb, "What Merger?" *Ward's Auto World,* December 1998; Sam Gresock, "BMW to Mark Five-Year Anniversary of South Carolina Facilities," *The State,* September 5, 1999; Alex Johnson, "Chrysler Facility to Make Mercedes," *Atlanta Journal-Constitution,* October 30, 1998, Wheels 02S; Ken Gepfert, "Booming Car Sector Is Good for the Region—Isn't It?" *The Wall Street Journal,* May 26, 1999, S1; Jim Parker, "South Carolina Commerce Leaders Aim to Draw Big Companies to the State," *Charleston Post and Courier,* August 25, 1999; Edward Graves, "South Carolina Ads Tap BMW Credibility—Suppliers Quick to Point Out Automaker's Impact on Car Parts Manufacturers," *Atlanta Journal-Constitution,* September 9, 1999, F6; "Bayersiche Motoren Werke AG: Investment in US Plant to Increase by $200 Million," *The Wall Street Journal,* February 28, 1996, B6; and Bill McAllister, "BMW Plant Becomes Symbol of Free Trade," *The Washington Post,* March 1, 1996, A9. For more information, see **www.daimlerbenz.com, www.daimlerchrysler.com, www.bmw.com.**

55,000 in 1991. When it was clear that BMW planned on locating its facility in the United States, a race ensued among competing states to win the cherished investment. In the end, the choice came down to Nebraska and South Carolina.

South Carolina Governor Carroll Campbell put up a strong recruiting effort, visiting BMW in Germany and making offers that were hard to refuse. In order to obtain the $640 million plant and the expected 6,000 new state jobs, a bit of southern finesse was used. For instance, the site most desired by BMW had 134 separate landowners. In order to ease land acquisition problems, Governor Campbell secured a $25 million appropriation from the state legislature to buy the property. He personally telephoned reluctant sellers and within 14 weeks, the state and local governments had spent $36.6 million to buy every single property—including a home that one family had just finished building two weeks before they were approached. To sweeten the deal for BMW, new roads and site improvement were included, and the runway at the local airport was extended to accommodate BMW's cargo planes. The state also offered a $41 million property tax break to BMW. Furthermore, the local airport's free trade zone status was extended to include the 900-acre plant site, meaning BMW would not have to pay duties on parts imported from Germany or elsewhere until cars actually left the plant for sale in the United States.

One of the big determinants for BMW was South Carolina's excellent technical school system. Under the investment agreement, the state customized its training program for the company, even sending instructors to Munich, Germany, to study the equipment that would be used. In all, the state had promised to spend $3 million to train workers for BMW alone, a considerable sum when one takes into account that in 1992 South Carolina spent $5.8 million on technical training for the entire state. In addition, local businesses offered to pay up to $3 million for additional training.

The constant stream of amenities and special treatment that South Carolina extended to BMW was especially critical to completing this deal, according to industry analysts, given the fact that BMW is a conservative corporation not prone to bold moves. The firm does not just want to be accepted, it wants to be welcomed. Carl Flescher, a vice president with BMW North America, stated: "I've only been down there for about ten or fifteen days and I am very impressed. The embracing of this whole thing is incredible. You go to the Holiday Inn and there is a sign that says 'Welcome BMW.' You pulled up to the Hertz rental car and they know who you are. People are genuinely friendly, open, and elated." Governor Campbell summed up the whole mission best: "The name BMW is generally associated with excellence and quality and that by itself is a benefit. Other companies will say, 'Well, wait a minute, BMW is rated as one of the best, and

they chose South Carolina. So, they must be doing something right.'"

When BMW chose to locate in South Carolina, it joined a group of European firms (including BASF, Rieter, Marzoli International, and Michelin) that had already discovered the state's comparatively cheaper and skilled workforce as well as its hospitable, probusiness atmosphere. In fact, South Carolina's Spartanburg County, the home of BMW's plant, hosts over 100 foreign-affiliated companies, and about half of South Carolina's workers are employed by foreign-owned firms, one of the highest percentages in the country.

In 1995, BMW began U.S. production of a new, more affordable model (the 3-series sedans) aimed at the American market, specifically graying baby boomers. The plant was up and running ahead of schedule and producing 300 cars a day within several months of start-up. By 1996, suppliers had invested more than $70 million in the county and hired over 600 people. The plant's success resulted in some unexpected attention during South Carolina's 1996 Republican presidential primary. A few leading candidates chose the plant as a showcase of their free-trade stances in this highly internationalized state. Candidate Bob Dole, on site, commented: "This is one perfect example of what can happen when you trade."

The first three years, however, did not come without difficulties. BMW found itself at the center of several conflicts, including efforts by Greer City in Spartanburg County in 1993 to annex BMW into the city, and disagreements between Spartanburg and Greenville counties about spending $16.7 million in state funds for widening Interstate 101 near the plant site. Another controversy evolved when a car tax break available to BMW employees leasing cars from the company was revoked by the South Carolina Senate Finance Committee in 1997.

BMW's impact on South Carolina's economy has been quite tangible and continues growing as shown in Table 1. Since its startup in 1992, BMW's capital investment has grown to over $1.2 billion, and its plant capacity has

TABLE	1	BMW by the Numbers, 1998
Total employees at plant		2,500
Annual payroll		$127 million
Size of plant		2.1 million sq. feet on 1039 acres
Total capital investment at plant		$1.3 billion
Number of suppliers		38
Investment by suppliers in South Carolina		$335 million
Jobs created by suppliers since 1992		3,000

SOURCES: South Carolina Department of Commerce: Spartanburg Area Chamber of Commerce; BMW.

grown to over 62,000. One of the company's contributions has been through its payroll. In 1998, company employees maintained a payroll of $127 million, an average of $50,800 per employee. A total of 3,000 jobs with suppliers have also been created. When combined with its 38 suppliers in South Carolina, over 5,500 new jobs have been created with an investment of $1.6 billion in capital.

BMW spends $1 billion buying goods and services every year in North America. Half of that investment goes to 500 companies in South Carolina. BMW is also credited with expediting improvements to Interstate 85 and generating nearly $20 million in tax revenue over 1995 to 1998 that has improved the county's schools. Commerce Department spokeswoman Helen Munnerlyn said BMW's greatest contribution might be proving that a high-profile, international corporation could successfully do business in South Carolina. She stated, "BMW has made it possible for South Carolina to be a respected location. I'm not sure you can actually measure that."

The Daimler-Benz Investment

Daimler-Benz's Mercedes automobile division was searching for a U.S. location to construct a $300 million plant that would manufacture its new sport utility vehicle, the Mercedes M-Class, which has offered stiff competition to the Ford Explorer and the Jeep Grand Cherokee. Initially, Mercedes's search included 170 sites in 30 states. Alabama knew that to win the investment, its offer would have to be outstanding. One Alabama state official recalls the message from a Mercedes consulting firm representative: "Everyone knows what South Carolina gave BMW. My client feels they are better than BMW!"

The race was on. In the end, Alabama won the "industrial crown jewel," as Governor Jim Folsom, Jr., referred to it. Mercedes was impressed by the entrepreneurial, nonbureaucratic attitude of Alabama's state government. The firm also liked the access to interstate highways, railroads, and ports; adequate available labor; proximity to schools; quality of life; and of course, a lucrative package of financial incentives. A partial list of these incentives includes $92.2 million to buy and develop the site, create a foreign trade zone, and build an employee training center; $77.5 million to extend water, gas, and sewer lines along with other infrastructure elements; $75 million to purchase 2,500 of the new vehicles for use by state employees; $60 million in government funds to train Mercedes employees, suppliers, and workers in related industries, enriched by another $15 million from the private sector; and $8.7 million in tax breaks—in all, Alabama offered a package of more than $300 million. Along with the financial incentive package, the state's commitment to build this one-of-a-kind facility correctly

TABLE 2 DaimlerChrysler by the Numbers, 1998

Total employees at plant	1,600
Annual payroll	$78.5 million
Size of plant	1.7 million sq. feet on 1,002 acres
Total capital investment at plant	$420 million
Number of suppliers	16
Investment by suppliers in Alabama	$130 million
Jobs created by suppliers since 1997	1,300

SOURCES: Alabama Department of Commerce; Tuscaloosa Area Chamber of Commerce; Daimler-Benz.

and on time was cited as an important factor in the automaker's decision.

The plant began production in early 1997. Annual volume was an estimated 70,000 cars, half of which were sold in the United States. Direct employment generated by the plant stood at 1,600 by 1999. Additional employment has also come via suppliers. According to the Economic Development Partnership of Alabama, the plant has created over 1,300 jobs among eleven major suppliers. Further job growth is coming from additional areas. The overwhelming market demand for the award-winning Mercedes-Benz M class resulted in a $40 million expansion of the Alabama plant as well as a 20 percent increase in production for 1999. The plant's capacity has grown from 67,000 in 1997 to a projected 80,000 in 1999, as shown in Table 2.

Daimler-Benz's merger with Chrysler in 1998 has had a noticeable impact on the Alabama plant. The merger caused an increase in jobs at the plant, and its 80,000 M-Classes were sold primarily in the United States. Daimler will expand a Chrysler facility in Austria that produces Jeep Grand Cherokees and equip it to build the Mercedes vehicle. One problem after the merger is the status of the Alabama factory as a non-union plant. Chrysler Corporation has over 76,000 workers who belong to the United Auto Workers union. The UAW union is trying to insist that Daimler convert its non-union plant in Alabama to a union shop. Daimler has continuously pledged "neutrality" on the issue.

Alabama believes it invested wisely. One study found that the $300 million it spent to lure the German investment will yield shining returns of $365 million during the first year of operation and $7.3 billion over the next 20 years. But there are limits to the lure of state incentives. One state official commented, "Ultimately it comes down to the company's personal choice." Says Mercedes project leader Andreas Renschler, "Whether you get $10 million more or less in one state doesn't make any difference. We sensed a much higher dedication to our project."

Many experts contend that states are "buying" industry at too steep a price. The financial incentives necessary to land the BMW plant, including a $1 per year land lease, will cost South Carolina $130 million over 30 years. Then-governor Jim Hunt of North Carolina criticized much of Alabama's incentives package to Mercedes, saying "We do not need to risk the future of the franchise to recruit star players." In particular, Hunt pointed to what some refer to as the "Benz bill," which allows 5 percent of corporate income tax from the plant and 5 percent of the plant employees' taxes to be used to retire Mercedes debt. The cost of incentives for the Mercedes plant, on a per new job basis, is 18 times what Tennessee paid for a Nissan plant in 1980 and 4 times what Kentucky paid for a Toyota plant in 1985.

Some economists argue that rich incentives often fail to yield adequate returns for a city or state. Corporate welfare, they say, diverts money better spent attracting businesses through improved infrastructure and schools. "It's nothing but a zero-sum game," said former U.S. Labor Secretary Robert Reich. "Resources are moved around; Peter is robbed to pay Paul." Proposals to halt the growth in financial incentives offered to large corporations, often foreign, include a tax on all incentives received by a corporation to move facilities.

The attitude of "not giving away the franchise," however, is increasingly being seen by decision makers as detrimental, especially in days of corporate downsizing, where politicians are judged on how many jobs they create in the private sector. A report by an international site-selection consultant, commissioned by North Carolina after losing the chance to land BMW, found that the state "is increasingly seen as a nonparticipant in incentive practices at a time when incentive practices are growing in importance." So the question "How much is too much?" is complicated by the fact that growing expectations and necessities may seemingly warrant the types of grandiose offers that are portrayed in the Mercedes and BMW cases.

QUESTIONS FOR DISCUSSION

1. Do you believe that states should encourage foreign direct investment? Why or why not?
2. Do incentives determine whether or not a company will invest in a particular country?
3. How should a state government determine the upper limit of its investment support?
4. Do foreign direct investment (FDI) incentives place locally established firms at a disadvantage?

Comeback from a Near-Death Experience: Audi of America 1992–1997

In the mid-1980s, Audi was one of the American auto industry's most attractive franchises, selling more vehicles than BMW. Its cars were stylish and technologically sophisticated, especially the Quattro all-wheel-drive models. Negative media coverage suddenly reversed this trend. A report on CBS's newsmagazine *60 Minutes* claimed that Audi's hot-selling 5000 sedan could unexpectedly accelerate out of control. Ultimately, government safety agencies in the United States and Germany cleared the 5000, but Audi of America could not recover from the bad publicity and its own mishandling of the situation, and its sales fell precipitously.

The Bad Times Continue

In the beginning of the 1990s, most news coverage of Audi still started with the "unintended acceleration" story, although most writers acknowledged that the company was officially exonerated. However, the safety issue was not the only problem Audi faced. Audi's quality was seen as lower than the industry average, and repairs were costly. Some dealers lost interest in the slow-selling cars and dropped the Audi franchise. The public perception was that Audi's products were underpowered and overpriced. Some of Audi's troubles were self-inflicted. The company insisted on maintaining its high prices, even though the cars no longer carried a premium image. Audi's Quattro four-wheel-drive system, unique in the luxury passenger class, was available only in the top-of-the-line models. In addition, automotive analysts insisted that Audi of America lacked the marketing muscle it needed to revitalize its image in the United States.

In 1991–1992, Audi offered a new and simplified vehicle lineup, aimed at materializing the company's claim that it offered "German engineering at Japanese prices." What had been the 80/90 series in the smaller-car lineup was now simply the 90; the 100/200 series was now the 100 midsize sedan plus an S4 performance version; at the top was the V8 sedan. (The original 90 and 100 lines had replaced the 5000 series in 1988, offering better overall quality at lower prices.) The new 90CS carried a sticker price of about $25,000, or $2,000 less than the comparable BMW 325i. The all-wheel-drive 90CS Quattro Sport was only available with a five-speed manual transmission.

At the end of 1993, Audi again drew attention to the brand with the introduction of the new Cabriolet and a new station wagon. The Cabriolet was likely to attract new customers because of its stylish design; the wagon offered minivan customers a practical and well-designed alternative. To counter the image of low reliability and high maintenance costs, Audi of America started offering the most extensive warranty in the luxury class, featuring free routine maintenance on all new Audis for three years. The company pioneered the short-term lease, which was marketed as "Audi's three-year test-drive."

U.S. sales remained disappointing, however. In 1991, when Audi sold a record 448,000 vehicles world-wide, Audi of America sold only 12,283 cars, or 42 percent less than in 1990, and 83 percent less than the 1985 peak. In 1992, sales rebounded to 14,756 cars, but fell again the following year to 12,943. On the other hand, Volkswagen, the parent company, as a whole remained the country's top-selling European importer.

Audi of America appeared to be at a dead end, and the rumor that Volkswagen was going to pull the brand from the U.S. market seemed well-grounded. However, VW's new chairman, Ferdinand Piech, insisted that "if you lose

SOURCE: This case was prepared by Michael R. Czinkota and Vlado Loukanov based on public sources such as *Advertising Age, Los Angeles Times, Business Week, USA Today, The New York Times, Chicago Tribune, Adweek Southeast, Medical Economics, Ward's Auto World, Investor's Business Daily, Reuters Financial Service, PR Newswire,* and *Marketing and Media Decisions*.

See Audi Web sites at http:// www.audi.com and http://www.audiusa.com.

America, you lose the world." Gerd Klauss, the then-new vice president in charge of Audi of America at Volkswagen of America, enjoyed the full support of the parent's management during those hard times. Chairman Piech, whose previous job was CEO of Audi, was facing similar issues globally at Volkswagen. VW was still financially sound, but without a deep-cutting reorganization its plans to become a major global competitor could be jeopardized.

A New Approach

In 1993, Piech outlined a plan for sweeping reforms, including a "lean manufacturing program" borrowed from the Japanese and a speedup of new-car development. Compared to the Japanese, VW was estimated to take twice as much time to develop a car, and its assembly lines employed four times the amount of labor. Concurrently, Piech started, a multibillion-dollar spending program to finance corporate growth in Europe and North America. In the spring of 1993, a series of management changes were announced at both Volkwagen of America and Audi of America. Klauss, the new chief executive of Audi, came from Mercedes-Benz of North America where he had been responsible for developing and coordinating the overall corporate strategy as well as the strategic positioning within the parent company's worldwide business. Audi of America also saw new executives appointed to the positions of General Service Manager, Controller, and Director of Marketing and Product Planning. The latter, Ken Moriarty, had served as a senior marketing and promotions manager at Mercedes-Benz of North America.

Audi's new philosophy reflected what company officials called the three "Ps"—lower prices, an emphasis on higher performance, and a range of new products. Klauss realized two important facts about the Audi brand on the U.S. market: first, the company could not support a price positioning similar to BMW and Mercedes, and second, it was not putting sufficient marketing effort behind the benefits of the Quattro four-wheel-drive system.

Competitive Positioning

Audi began its new strategy by slashing the prices of its 1995 model year cars on the average by several thousand dollars. (At the same time, the stronger yen began driving up prices on Japanese luxury imports.) Audi also strengthened the performance of its automobiles by introducing a range of more powerful engines. Essential in the brand's repositioning, according to marketing director Moriarty, was the new emphasis on all-wheel drive. To make the Quattro more accessible to a wider range of customers, Audi dropped it as standard equipment on the high-end models and offered it as a $1,500 option on its entire product line. The move reduced the effective transaction price of an average Audi car with the system by $5,000. Within one year, the percentage of buyers ordering the Quattro jumped from 2 percent to 50 percent. This pricing strategy provided some momentum for Audi so it could add a third "P" to *performance* and *pricing* with the introduction of the all-new A line of *products* in 1995–1997.

The A4 was to take on such tough import competitors as the Mercedes C-Class, BMW's 3-series, and the Lexus ES300. Audi officials admitted they faced a challenge in attempting to seize share from the better-established nameplates. However, they hoped the new compact sedan would win over buyers with its radically new design and a blend of features, including a new five-speed automatic transmission and a revised four-wheel-drive system. The new 1.8-liter Turbo engine won several "ten best engines of the year" awards. With a base price at about $23,000, the A4 1.8T, introduced in 1996, became the lowest priced luxury sedan sold in the United States (see Table 1). The A4, with the more powerful 2.8-liter, six-cylinder engine, had been launched the previous year. Audi was luring a new generation of buyers, many of them unaware of the problems the car manufacturer faced ten years earlier. As one automotive analyst on Wall Street put it, "the passage of time has also helped. People have forgotten about the 'unintended acceleration' scare." The aggressive pricing and bold new design of the A4 made it a big hit throughout North America, especially in areas where the company had never been very strong, such as Southern California.

A Product Breakthrough

The true revolutionary newcomer, however, was the A8, the all-aluminum challenge to the BMW 7-series and the Mercedes S-Class. The A8 was about one-third lighter than comparable steel units and was the first car in the world to offer six airbags—two for each the driver and the front-seat passenger (front and side impact) and one for each rear-seat passenger. The lighter car offered better fuel economy, livelier engine power, and more responsiveness because there was less mass to shift. Audi had achieved lightness without sacrificing strength, rigidity, or crash performance. One automotive writer called the A8 a "rolling testbed for technology." The downside for customers was that aluminum frame repairs and insurance policies were more expensive. Audi's new flagship, which replaced the previous V8 saloon, was also priced significantly lower than its German competitors.

Audi kept surprising its customers and the industry with continuous innovation. When the redesigned A6 sedan came to market in the fall of 1997, industry experts predicted it would duplicate the success of the A4. The A6 featured striking design, a longer wheelbase, and sub-

TABLE 1	Manufacturer Suggested Retail Prices (MSRP) for the 1998 Model Year				
AUDI	MSRP	BMW	MSRP	MERCEDES	MSRP
A4 1.8T	$23,790	318ti Coupe	$21,960		
		318i Sedan	$26,720		
A4 2.8	$28,390	323is Coupe	$29,270	C230 Sedan	$30,450
		328i Sedan	$33,670	C280 Sedan	$35,400
		328is Coupe	$33,770		
A4 Avant	$30,465				
Cabriolet	$34,600	323i Convertible	$35,270	SLK230	$39,700
		328i Convertible	$42,070	CLK320	$39,850
A6	$33,750	528i Sedan	$39,470	E300 TD Sedan	$41,800
		540i (automatic)	$51,070	E320 Sedan	$45,500
A6 Wagon	$34,600			E320 Wagon	$46,500
A8 3.7	$57,400			S320 Sedan	$64,000
		740i Sedan	$62,070		
A8 4.2	$65,000	740iL Sedan	$66,070	S420 Sedan	$73,900
		750iL Sedan	$92,100	S500 Sedan	$87,500
				S600 Sedan	$132,250

NOTE: The table compares all Audi models to most BMW and Mercedes models in relevant classes. BMW's M-3 and the 800 series and Mercedes' SL and CL classes are not shown.

SOURCE: Audi, BMW, and Mercedes-Benz.

stantial improvements in technology, safety, and equipment levels, including a five-speed automatic transmission with Porsche's "Tiptronic" technology, which allowed the driver to choose between automatic and manual mode. The new luxury touring car introduced a new interior concept with three different environments called "atmospheres," which customers could choose from at no extra cost. The A6 was aggressively positioned in the $35,000 price range and compared very favorably to the BMW 528i, which started at around $40,000.

Customer Satisfaction

All cars in the A line came standard with the "Audi Advantage" warranty package, including the luxury market's customary three-year/50,000 mile limited warranty, ten-year limited warranty against corrosion perforation, and 24-hour roadside assistance for three years. The three-year/50,000 miles free scheduled maintenance, however, continued to distinguish Audi from other luxury imports. This feature significantly improved customer satisfaction with dealers, a longtime weak point for Audi. Customer satisfaction rates outranked those of BMW and Mercedes in 1995–1997.

In October 1997, the company established Audi Financial Services (AFS), a division of VW Credit, Inc., to serve Audi customers and the 270 dealers throughout the United States. By establishing the new division, corporate management was aiming at better customer satisfaction and higher customer retention rates. A 1997 Consumer Satisfaction Study by J.D. Power and Associates had found

that customer retention is 20 percent higher when financing is placed with a captive provider, compared to when financing is placed with a bank.

Marketing and Advertising

A 1993 corporate study showed that, while rising among Audi owners, Audi's image continued to worsen among U.S. consumers overall. The company fired its longtime advertising agency, DDB Needham, and hired McKinney & Silver to take over the $30 million account. One Audi dealer characterized DDB Needham's work as inconsistent, but added that the blame lay with both the agency and the marketer. Ending the relationship with DDB was a difficult decision for Gerd Klauss, the new chief executive of Audi of America, since the agency was handling VW's and Audi's global accounts. According to some accounts, McKinney & Silver won the account because it convinced company officials that it knew what the Audi should do to lure customers back—in essence, to position Audi as "the single most underrated car in the country."

McKinney launched its face makeover campaign with a four-page spread in many national publications titled, "What Is Audi." Rather than focusing on image, as previous advertising did (DDB's last campaign was carried under the slogan "Take Control"), new ads touted product attributes and value and claimed that Audi gives customers more—for less. An ad by DDB Needham, "Welcome to the '90s," featured a sophisticated-looking working mother. She takes her kids to school, goes to work, and has an exciting nightlife—all on jazzy background music. The new McKinney ad contained a simply laundry list of safety and performance features, including "the safety and traction of the Quattro all-wheel drive [and] child safety seat locks." Unusual for the luxury category, some ads even mentioned rivals BMW and Mercedes and pointed out that the Audi offered better value.

"We are positioning the A-6 midsize sedan as excellent German engineering for a more affordable price." said McKinney's Cameron McNaughton. The 1996 campaign for the A4 sedan, in the words of Ken Moriarty, the marketing director for Audi of America, used more of a human touch. With its A8 luxury sedan, Audi pioneered lending cars to Hollywood celebrities. The company gave free loaners to two dozen entertainment personalities "with active social lives," including Jay Leno, Jerry Seinfeld, and Quincy Jones. "They are extroverted movers and shakers who go out a lot," Moriarty said. "And when they do, they take the car with them." (Seinfeld did actually end up buying an A8.) Following a long sponsoring tradition in Europe, Audi began contributing to the arts in the United States in 1996, when it sponsored the Three Tenors Concert at Giant Stadium. The following year, the company contributed $100,000 to the San Diego opera.

As demand for luxury sport-utility vehicles soared in the mid-1990s, Audi's marketing strengthened its emphasis on the benefits of the Quattro four-wheel-drive system. In 1996, Audi launched a $10 million TV and print advertising campaign based on the "un-SUV" theme. One spot showed a woman struggling to climb down from a towering SUV as another woman drove up in an A6 Quattro wagon and easily got out. The announcer claimed that the Audi is also easy to get in, obviously referring to the price difference with luxury SUVs, such as Lexus and Lincoln-Mercury. The Quattro ad for the 1998 model year, dubbed "Tracks," features an elderly Inuit (native of Alaska) coaching his grandson in the ancient art of tracking caribou and bear. When he comes to a car track, he picks up a bit of snow, smells it and then exclaims, "Quattro." The A6 spot claimed that the model could not be compared to other cars like "apples to apples" because "the A6 is not an apple." The car then speeds up through a discord chorus of apples.

The Market's Response

Audi's U.S. sales went up by 44 percent in 1995, up again by 52 percent in 1996, and up by 33 percent in the first half of 1997. With these increases, Audi achieved the fastest growth of any brand in the luxury passenger-car market. Sales were so brisk that dealers had to ask customers to wait for weeks and sometimes months to fulfill orders. About half of new Audi buyers had previously owned Japanese brands. Still, the 27,400 vehicles sold in 1996 represented a little more than one-third of the 1985 peak level.

The company hoped that this level would be eclipsed by the year 2000. The A-line clearly identified what Audi represented to the consumer: a provider of boldly styled performance and cars that offer substantial value. With consumer tastes evolving in the direction of its renovated product portfolio, Audi appeared poised for success in the U.S. market. Audi growth reflected in part the gains achieved by European luxury imports in the mid-1990s, largely at the expense of the Japanese. The resurgence of the former came as they lowered costs and prices, improved customer service and introduced stylish products with more features that affluent Americans wanted. On the average, European luxury car sales grew about 50 percent faster in 1994–1997 than Japanese imports.

When in 1992–1993 both BMW and Mercedes-Benz announced they were going to open production lines in the United States, Gerd Klauss declared that Audi would follow suit. One of the Audi board members reasoned in the fall of 1995, after the German competitors had built their U.S. plants, that the company "needed to be involved in a dollar base" in order to offset the strong D-mark. Another senior executive noted in early 1996 that a dollar base did not necessarily mean producing in the United States. Gerd Klauss insisted that the company needed a U.S. plant to produce cars geared specifically to the American customers, more interested in safety and comfort than speed like the Germans. If the Audi board said "yes," such a huge investment—likely to top $500 million—had to be approved by Volkswagen. In the spring of 1997, the company leadership was considering possible plant locations in the Sunbelt region of the United States.

QUESTIONS FOR DISCUSSION

1. What were the problems in the beginning of the '90s that kept Audi of America from regaining its market position of the mid-1980s?
2. How did the new management reposition the company on the U.S. market after 1993 and why?
3. What are the major factors that contributed to Audi's increasing sales in the second half of the 1990s?
4. Will the prepaid maintenance affect the quality of services performed by Audi dealers?

Marketing and the Environment: Tuna versus Dolphins

In the eastern tropical areas of the Pacific Ocean (a major tuna-fishing area), schools of yellowfish, skipjack, and bigeye tuna often swim beneath schools of dolphins. To catch quantities of tuna, fishermen look for the leaping dolphins and cast purse seines (nets pulled into a baglike shape to enclose fish) around both tuna and dolphins. When tuna is harvested with the purse seine method, fishermen can efficiently and reliably catch a high number of good-sized tuna. Unfortunately, dolphins are also trapped in the nets. Because they are mammals, dolphins must surface to breathe oxygen. Entangled in the net, they can asphyxiate and die unless they are released.

In the late 1960s and early 1970s, the "incidental" catch of various species of dolphins by tuna fishers in the eastern tropical Pacific (ETP) was in the hundreds of thousands. Because of society's growing and vociferous concern for these senseless deaths, new fishing techniques were developed to reduce dolphin mortality.

Perhaps the most important new technique is the "backdown operation." After "setting on" dolphins to catch tuna—that is, encircling both tuna and dolphins with the purse seine—the ship backs away, elongates the net, submerges the corkline in the back, and pulls the net out from under the dolphins. If the operation works correctly, the tuna remain in the bottom of the net and the dolphins swim free. However, if the operation is flawed, dolphins are injured or killed and discarded from the catch as waste.

Rather than relying on this imperfect correction of the purse seine method, some environmental groups think that entirely different methods of fishing for tuna should be employed. Alternatives could include using a pole and line or setting on tuna not associated with dolphins. However, according to marine scientists and fishermen, the alternative methods have serious drawbacks as well.

Some catch many sexually immature tuna, which for some reason don't associate with dolphins. Juvenile tuna often are too small to be marketed. If too many are caught, the sustainability of the population could be jeopardized. In addition, alternative methods frequently catch high numbers of other incidental species, such as sharks, turtles, rays, mahimahi, and many kinds of noncommercial fish. Finally, all fishing methods expend energy. The practice of setting on dolphins uses the least amount of energy per volume of tuna caught.

According to many of the experts involved, including the Inter-American Tropical Tuna Commission, the U.S. National Marine Fisheries Service, and the scientific advisor to the American Tunaboat Association, the most efficient method for fishing tuna, in terms of operational cost yield and the conservation of tuna population, is to set on dolphins with a purse seine. From the canning industry's the point of view only purse seine fishing provides the volume of catch necessary for the growth of the industry.

Many experts also believe that with current technology, it is not possible to abandon the practice of setting on dolphins without falling into other, more grave problems. Although research to develop better techniques continues, positive results are not expected in the near future.

This case was written by Professor Michael Czinkota © with George Garcia and Kristen M. Mehlum using the following sources: John Alexander, "Meaning of Dolphin-Safe Tuna Label Changed," *Environment News Service*, May 5, 1999; Saul Alvarez-Borrego, "The Tuna Dolphin Controversy," UC Mexus News, University of California Institute for Mexico and the United States, 31 (Fall 1993): 8–13; CNIE Organization, "Dolphin Protection and Tuna Seining," March 14, 1999; Department of Commerce, "Tuna Purse Seine Vessels in the Eastern Tropical Pacific Ocean," *Federal Register* 64 (Number 113, June 14, 1999); Josef Herbert, "Tuna Restrictions Relaxed," The Associated Press, April 30, 1999; and Michael Simons, "Commerce Department Sued over Dolphin Ruling," *The San Francisco Examiner*, August 19, 1999, A12.

The Trade Aspects

This tuna-dolphin problem has been the source of serious friction on the international level. The United States and Mexico, two countries sensitive to marine mammal protection and with solid laws in place for many years, have come head-to-head over the issue. The conflict between environmental concerns and free trade for the United States and Mexico is further complicated by the existence of the North American Free Trade Agreement.

In 1988 the United States amended the U.S. Marine Mammal Act to prohibit the incidental killing of dolphins during commercial tuna fishing. The amendment required the banning of tuna imports from any country that did not implement several specific measures to reduce dolphin mortality and achieve a kill-per-set rate (the number of dolphins killed in each casting of the fishing net) of no more than 1.25 times the U.S. rate.

In February 1991, a U.S. trade embargo was imposed on tuna caught by foreign fishing fleets using the purse seine method in the ETP, with Mexico as a prime target. This harsh step was seen as necessary, because over the previous 15 years, an estimated seven million dolphins died in tuna nets. The embargo cost tuna-exporting countries such as Mexico, Costa Rica, and Ecuador hundreds of millions of dollars. To avoid future losses, the embargoed nations met with U.S. officials in 1992 to determine ways in which they could improve their fishing methods, end the embargo, and regain access to the lucrative U.S. market.

Several changes in fishing methods were introduced after these negotiations. Although foreign fishers did not abandon the purse seine method, they learned to dip their nets deeper to allow dolphins to escape. Dolphin safety panels were installed in many nets, serving as escape hatches for the dolphins. Divers are now deployed to assist dolphins unable to find their way out of the nets. A biologist is assigned to every ship to observe fishing methods and to record dolphin mortality. The participating governments also adopted a vessel quota system in which the overall yearly quota for dolphin mortality is equally divided among the boats fishing in the region. This way, each boat is individually held responsible for its dolphin kill. Otherwise, a few careless ships could destroy the entire fishery's attempts to meet lower mortality rates for the year.

The effect of these changes on dolphin survival were major. Figure 1 shows that in 1986 over 20,000 dolphin mortalities were caused by U.S. vessels in the ETP. By 1998, the estimated number was 738. The amount of dolphin mortalities caused by non-U.S. vessels also dropped drastically from 112,482 in 1986 to a preliminary estimate of 2,000 for 1998.

As of the mid-1990s, the total yearly mortality for each dolphin species was under 1 percent of its population, an amount that can be sustained without reducing the total number; in fact, the dolphin population was increasing. Thus, concern for dolphin conservation started to diminish. Most scientists started to view the mortality of dolphins incidental to tuna fishing not as an environmental problem, but as one of avoiding unnecessary killing. In fact, a National Marine Fisheries Service scientist stated

FIGURE	1	Incidental Dolphin Mortalities

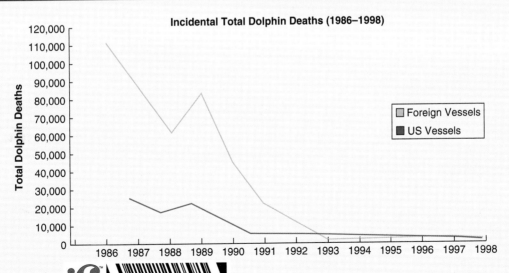

SOURCE: http://www.cnie.org.

that if Mexico had money for research, it would be better invested on behalf of the Vaquita, a species in real danger of extinction, than in the tuna-dolphin issue, because there is no danger to the dolphin population as a whole.

In November 1996, President Clinton promised that a revision of U.S. tuna-dolphin legislation would be a priority for the next convening Congress. A revision was necessary in order to appease Mexican discontent about restrictions on their tuna imports to the United States. The International Dolphin Conservation Program Act (IDCPA) was the result and became law in August 1997. This act served to weaken the U.S. Marine Mammal Act of 1988. The legislation called for the lifting of the U.S. embargo on tuna imports from countries that continued to use the purse seine during fishing operations. However, these nations had to be certified by the U.S. State Department as having joined a binding international program and having domestic legislation in place to enforce international dolphin protection efforts. The program consists of nations working together through having international observers on board when the purse seine nets are tossed, to see if any dolphins are killed.

The IDCPA also allowed "dolphin-deadly" tuna (or tuna caught by purse seine method) to be sold in the U.S. market. Eventually, such a catch would even be allowed to use a "dolphin-safe" label. However, until a study could be completed by the U.S. Department of Commerce concerning the positive or negative impact of purse seines on dolphin populations, "dolphin-safe" labels were still restricted to non–purse seine tuna. This was to ensure that consumers knew which brands of tuna use fishing methods that threaten dolphin conservation efforts.

In April 1999, the U.S. Secretary of Commerce decided that "catching tuna by chasing and ensnaring dolphins in large encircling nets does not cause a significant adverse impact on the dolphin population." This decision enables the enactment of new dolphin-safe standards under the IDCPA. Thus, "dolphin-safe" labels can now be used for purse seine tuna, provided that an international observer and a captain do not see dead or injured dolphins in the nets.

A number of environmental organizations, including the Center for Marine Conservation, Greenpeace, and the World Wildlife Fund, support the change. Greenpeace believes the U.S. Department of Commerce decision reflects the success of the IDCPA to reduce dolphin kills in the ETP. Gerald Leape of Greenpeace also states that it is "appropriate for the U.S. to now modify the definition of dolphin-safe . . . since 1992, the nations fishing for tuna in the ETP have reduced the number of dolphins killed from 27,000 to fewer than 2,100 annually . . . this is an undeniable improvement in the way we manage the marine ecosystem."

But other groups feel the dolphin-safe label will now become meaningless. Representatives from countless environmental groups and organizations such as Earth Island Institute, Humane Society of the United States, Dolphin Safe/Fair Trade Campaign, and Sierra Club say the decision was made contrary to all available scientific information. David Phillips of the Earth Island Institute states, "Scientists, U.S. tuna companies, and the public know that chasing and netting dolphins is not safe for dolphins . . . the decision is consumer fraud and a death warrant for thousands of dolphins." Patricia Forkan, executive vice president of the Humane Society, states, "The decision by the Secretary is an outrageous attack on environmental protection laws in order to allow Mexico and other dolphin-killing nations access to the lucrative U.S. tuna market. Once again, trade trumps science."

The Ongoing Debate

On August 19, 1999, a coalition of environmental groups including Earth Island Institute filed a lawsuit against Secretary of Commerce William Daley and the National Marine Fisheries Service (NMFS). They alleged that the federal government decision to relax dolphin-safe standards wrongly weakened the protections guaranteed by the dolphin-safe label on cans of tuna. Mark Palmer, a spokesman for Earth Island Institute, states that "the research done so far by the National Marine Fisheries Service (NMFS) staff scientists and the Inter-American Tropical Commission already shows that the [dolphin] populations are not rebounding and in some cases are still declining." Others also argue that "some dolphins that are not observed to die in the nets die later from stress." The suit, filed in the U.S. District Court in San Francisco, seeks to overturn the Marine Fisheries Service decision.

Despite the controversy surrounding labeling, the three major U.S. tuna processors—StarKist, Chicken of the Sea, and Bumble Bee—have said they will continue to use only tuna caught by methods other than encirclement. This decision does not seem to greatly affect the growth in the sales or volume of these three major processors, who share about 90 percent of the U.S. tuna market. StarKist Tuna, part of the H. J. Heinz Company, has stated in its fourth quarter fiscal 1999 report that seafood sales volume for the quarter increased by 6 percent.[1]

In the midst of the legal action and the continued debate, the NMFS will continue the second half of its scientific study. The finding of this study will be announced by December 31, 2002. At that point the secretary of commerce will make yet another decision regarding the dolphin-safe label.

[1]http://www.starkist.com/insideskt/corp/press/index.html